Access™ 2

Developer's Guide, Second Edition

Access™ 2

Developer's Guide, Second Edition

SAMS
PUBLISHING

A Division of Macmillan
Computer Publishing

201 West 103rd Street,
Indianapolis, Indiana 46290

Roger
Jennings

*This book is dedicated to
the memory of my father,
George H. Jennings,
Structural Engineer.*

Publisher

Richard K. Swadley

Associate Publisher

Jordan Gold

Acquisitions Manager

Stacy Hiquet

Managing Editor

Cindy Morrow

Acquisitions Editor

Gregory S. Croy

Development Editor

Phillip W. Paxton

Production Editor

James Grass

Copy Editors

Matthew Usher

Joe Williams

Editorial and Graphics Coordinator

Bill Whitmer

Editorial Assistants

Carol Ackerman

Sharon Cox

Lynette Quinn

Technical Reviewer

Karen Jaskolka

Marketing Manager

Gregg Bushyeager

Cover Designer

Karen Ruggles

Director of Production and Manufacturing

Jeff Valler

Imprint Manager

Kelli Widdifield

Manufacturing Coordinator

Barry Pruett

Book Designer

Michele Laseau

Production Analyst

Dennis C. Hager

Mary Beth Wakefield

Proofreading/Indexing Coordinator

Joelynn Gifford

Graphics Image Specialists

Teresa Forrester

Tim Montgomery

Dennis Sheehan

Sue VandeWalle

Production

Carol Bowers

Lisa Daugherty

Steph Davis

Terri Edwards

Rich Evers

Angela P. Judy

Debbie Kincaid

Stephanie McComb

Jamie Milazzo

Chad Poore

Casey Price

Ryan Rader

Bobbi Satterfield

Kim Scott

Susan Shepard

Tonya R. Simpson

Ann Sippel

SA Springer

Suzanne Tulley

Scott Tullis

Elaine Webb

Indexers

Charlotte Clapp

Michael Hughes

Overview

Contents

Part II   Using Access Basic

Part VI Networked and Client-Server Applications

Part VII Advanced Access Topics

Part VIII   Adding the Finishing Touches to Your Application

Appendixes

Preface to the Second Edition

Version 2.0 of Microsoft Access differs greatly from version 1.x. Substantial changes have been made to Access 2.0's user interface to make database design and application development simpler for beginning users. Another objective of the facelift to Access 1.x is to integrate Access 2.0 with other members of the Microsoft Office software suite, providing each member a similar look and feel. The most important new features of Access 2.0, however, are directed to the database developer community. Thus *Access 2 Developer's Guide*, the second edition of this book, has been reorganized and expanded in order to provide complete coverage of the enhancements Microsoft added to Access 2.0 and the Access Developer's Toolkit.

Access 2.0's data access object (DAO), implemented by version 2.0 of the Jet database engine, and OLE 2.0 compatibility are, without question, the two most important new features of Access 2.0 for database developers.

The data access object exposes the entire object hierarchy of Access databases. The **DBEngine** object, two levels above Access 1.x's topmost **Database** object, lets you use Access Basic code to open multiple database sessions and program database security parameters. In conjunction with Access 2.0's transition to the DAO, almost all of the design properties of Access objects are now read-write in run mode. Access 2.0 now lets you create new database objects with Access Basic code. This, together with many added events and the new event-handling code modules contained within **Form** and **Report** objects, makes Access 2.0 more compatible with the Visual Basic 3.0 and Visual Basic for Applications programming model. A new chapter has been added to this edition that explains the hierarchy of the DAO and supplies examples of its use.

OLE 2.0 is destined to change forever how Windows productivity applications interact and ultimately how database, spreadsheet and word processing applications are designed. Access is an OLE 2.0 container application, offering in-place activation of objects in unbound object frames. Access Basic also supports OLE Automation that lets you program objects "exposed" by OLE 2.0 servers, such as Microsoft Excel 5.0 and Graph 5.0. Access 2.0 is the first Windows productivity application to support OLE 2.0 Custom Controls (OCXs), which are destined to replace .VBX custom control in Visual Basic and add new capabilities to future versions of all mainstream Microsoft applications. The five new chapters of Part V, "Taking Advantage of OLE

2.0," describe this new building-block approach to application programming and include a wide range of examples of Access Basic code to implement OLE 2.0 and OLE Automation.

New sections have been added to the first edition's chapters to show you how to use other new features of Access 2.0, such as the Data Definition Language extensions to Access SQL, the add-in manager, custom toolbars for forms and reports, and Access 2.0's native SQL pass-through mode for client-server applications. The networking and client-server chapters now use Windows NT Advanced Server 3.1 and Microsoft SQL Server 4.2 for Windows NT in the examples.

Access 2.0 is an upgrade of major proportion over Access 1.1; so this book, of necessity, is a major revision of the first edition. More than 75 percent of the text of this edition has been added, rewritten, or extensively revised. All of the example code on the accompanying diskette has been modified to take advantage of the new features of Access 2.0.

As a member of the Professional Edition of Microsoft Office 4.0, the most successful of the Windows software suites, Access 2.0 and its successors are destined to usurp dBASE's position as the "standard" of the desktop database industry. Riding the crest of the Access 2.0 wave undoubtedly will pay handsome dividends to both independent and in-house database developers.

Oakland, California
May 1994

Acknowledgments

Special thanks are due to the authors of the chapters in Part IV of this book that describe the first commercial Access desktop database applications. They are as follows:

Gerry Novreske, the author of Chapter 11, "Examining an Access Accounting Application," is the founder, president, and chief executive officer of MTX International, Inc., of Englewood, CO. The MTX Accounting SDK for Access, based on the firm's successful character-based accounting package for DOS, is the first large-scale commercial database application to use Microsoft Access. The MTX Accounting SDK is designed for modification by Access developers, so source code is included with the product.

Michael Gilbert, who wrote Chapter 12, "Looking at an Access Training Database," is project manager for Meliora Systems, Inc., of Rochester, NY. Mike was instrumental in the development of Meliora's Ingenium for Windows, a commercial application that tracks employee job skills, training requirements, and the training courses that meet an employer's needs to upgrade employees' job skills. Meliora Systems also provides consulting and training services for Microsoft Access.

William J. Serrahn, the author of Chapter 13, "Analyzing an Access Time and Billing System," created WorkGroup Billing/EIS, a commercial Access application designed for invoicing professional services. Bill is the owner of WorkGroup Solutions, a Seattle-based firm that specializes in database-application development, training, and consulting. WorkGroup Billing/EIS is intended specifically for use by software-consulting and application-development firms, but the product can be customized by Access developers for a variety of other professions.

The address, telephone, and fax numbers of each of the contributing authors' firms appear in Appendix A, "Access Resources."

A particular note of appreciation is due to Karen Jaskolka, who was the technical editor for this book. Karen's sharp eye for my slip-ups and her suggestions for improvements and clarification made a major contribution to this book The responsibility for any errors or omissions that remain in this book, however, rests solely with the author.

Thanks to the Microsoft product-support specialists and the other contributors to the MSACCESS and MSBASIC forum on CompuServe. Many of the notes and tips in this book derive from bug reports in the beta forum for Access 2.0, and work-arounds and suggestions that appeared in the MSACCESS forum, one of the most active of the product-support forums on CompuServe.

Finally, thanks to Phil Paxton, development editor for this book (who is a database expert in his own right), and Greg Croy, acquisitions editor. Together, Phil and Greg made the writing of both editions of this book a truly enjoyable task.

About the Author

Roger Jennings is a consultant specializing in Windows database and multimedia applications. He was a member of the Microsoft beta-test team for Microsoft Access 1.0, 1.1, and 2.0; The Microsoft ODBC Desktop Database Drivers kit; Excel 4.0 and 5.0; Word for Windows 2.0 and 6.0; Windows 3.1, Windows for Workgroups 3.1 and 3.11; Video for Windows; Multimedia Viewer 2.0; Visual Basic for DOS; and Visual Basic 2.0 and 3.0. He is the author of Sams Publishing's *Database Developer's Guide with Visual Basic 3.0*, two other books on Access, and a book devoted to Windows 3.1 multimedia techniques. Roger is a Contributing Editor of Pinnacle Publishing's *Smart Access* newsletter, and his articles have appeared in the *Microsoft Developer Network News*, Fawcette Technical Publication's *Visual Basic Programmer's Journal*, and Advisor Communication's *Access Advisor* magazine.

Jennings has more than 25 years of computer-related experience and has presented technical papers on computer hardware and software to Visual Basic Insiders Technical Summit (VBITS), the Academy of Sciences of the former USSR, the Society of Automotive Engineers, the American Chemical Society, and a wide range of other scientific and technical organizations. He is a principal of OakLeaf Systems, a Northern California software development and consulting firm. You may contact him via CompuServe (ID 70233,2161), on the Internet (70233.2161@compuserve.com), or by fax at (510) 839-9422.

Introduction

Version 1.0 of Microsoft Access established a new record for the sales of a Windows application. Microsoft received orders for about 750,000 copies of Access between its formal introduction at the Fall Comdex exposition in Las Vegas in mid-November 1992 to January 31, 1993. A low introductory price, combined with pent-up demand for an "easy-to-use" Windows relational database application from a major software publisher, explains Access's initial success. Industry sources estimate that worldwide sales of desktop RDBMSs for the year 1992, excluding Access, totaled between 1.2 and 1.5 million units. This means that Access garnered 33 percent to 40 percent of the 1992 desktop RDBMS market segment in less than three months. At the time this edition was written, total sales of Access 1.x, not including upgrades, were well over 1 million copies.

Microsoft's promotional material for Access has been aimed at both end users and developers, but end users always have been the primary target. This is understandable, since there are many more potential end users than developers of database applications. Nonetheless, the long-term success of Microsoft Access hinges on its acceptance by database developers. There was much for developers to dislike in Access 1.x: frozen property values that were read-only in run mode; no table-level enforcement of domain integrity; no referential integrity enforcement with attached tables; a Byzantine security system with "leaks"; a lack of SQL Data Definition Language statements; the inability to execute SQL UNION queries and subqueries; and performance that was often slow with large attached tables. Microsoft Corp. has addressed and solved these problems with the introduction of Access 2.0 in Spring 1994.

A Developer's View of Access 2.0

Access 2.0's ease of usage is deceptive; Access 2.0 is a power product. Clients or in-house end users who have acquired Access may have been led to believe that they can create an industrial-strength database application just by reading the accompanying documentation, which has been expanded considerably for version 2.0, and by trying a few of the examples given for the Northwind Traders sample database. In most cases, this approach will not lead to the desired result. It takes time to learn the new application design concepts introduced by Access, as well as to avoid the few remaining traps and pitfalls inherent in Access 2.0's design. Thus, as a developer, you often may be called upon to complete applications that were initiated by users, a process that is likely to tax your skills as a diplomat.

Microsoft Access also may surprise developers who are accustomed to writing a thousand (or more) lines of code to create character-based RDBMS applications in xBase, PAL, C, or other programming languages. You can create a usable Access application with macros and only a few lines of Access Basic code. Simple applications may require no code at all (if you don't classify Access macros as an elementary form of program code). Access macros let you write sequences of "actions" that occur in response to events, such as clicking a command button. You can employ most of these actions in your Access Basic code. This book concentrates on using Access Basic code, rather than macros, for reasons that are explained later in this introduction.

If you have invested several years in developing xBase or PAL programming skills and now face the prospect of abandoning xBase, PAL, or Object PAL (OPAL) for the new language of Access Basic, welcome to the crowd. COBOL programmers have the same problem when their employers downsize from mainframe "legacy" databases to client-server systems running on PCs. Fortunately, Access Basic resembles xBase and PAL more closely than COBOL resembles C or any other programming language common to PCs. xBase, PAL, and Access Basic all have their roots in the original Dartmouth BASIC. One of the principal advantages of learning Access Basic is that you will learn Object Basic in the process. Object Basic, derived from Visual Basic, is now Microsoft's root language for Windows application programming. Access Basic, Visual Basic, and Visual Basic for Applications are dialects of Object Basic. Ultimately, all Microsoft mainstream Windows applications will incorporate Visual Basic for Applications to replace or supplement the application-specific macro languages of the present versions of Word 6.0's WordBasic and Access 2.0's Access Basic. Version 2.0 of Access Basic, by the way, is now very similar to Visual Basic for Applications, which in turn resembles Visual Basic 3.0.

Whether you decide to use macros or Access Basic code, you must adapt to Access's event-driven approach to application design, inherited from the Windows graphical user interface (GUI). You also need to face the fact that Access applications, at least those created with Access version 2.0, will not perform with the blazing speed of your Clipper or FoxPro applications running directly under DOS. (Access 2.0, in most instances, runs applications faster than Access 1.x.) Few, if any, Windows applications can match their DOS counterparts in a speed contest, but this situation is likely to change when Windows NT appears on RISC workstations and "Access 3.0" becomes a 32-bit (Win32) Windows product.

The fact that users of database applications will trade speed for a graphical user interface is supported by the success of Windows front-end applications for client-server database-management systems. PowerBuilder, Forest and Trees, SQLWindows, and a hundred or two other Windows front-ends for Microsoft and Sybase SQL Server, ORACLE, Informix, and other client-server RDBMSs compete in the rapidly downsizing marketplace. Character-based applications are giving way to new GUI replacements in all segments of the PC software market. Access is an ideal replacement for any of the current crop of Windows client-server front-end applications, especially those front-ends that require payment of a license fee for each workstation that uses them.

Who Should Read This Book

The *Access 2 Developer's Guide* is designed for developers, not end-users of database applications. This book makes the assumption that you have learned the fundamental methods of creating Access tables, queries, forms, reports, and macros. Information on these Access database objects, contained in the Access documentation or available in books designed for beginning-to-intermediate users, is not repeated in this book. Nor will this book attempt to teach you the principles of database design; there are many excellent texts that cover relational database theory in general and the rules of normalization of data in particular. Some familiarity with programming in a structured language is a prerequisite for using this book; you need a basic understanding of programming flow-control constructs, such as `If...Else...End If`, `For...Next`, and `Do While...Loop`, or their equivalents, to benefit fully from the chapters that deal with Access Basic code. No familiarity with programming in the Windows environment, however, is assumed.

This book is intended to aid independent developers in maximizing their income and to assist in-house developers in minimizing the time and cost of creating commercial-quality Access applications. Rather than reiterating introductory concepts, the *Access 2 Developer's Guide* leads you through the steps necessary to create fully integrated, commercial Access applications. Writing substantive, heavy-duty Access Basic code is covered in depth. Tips, warnings, "gotchas," and workarounds that have been collected by the author during two years of working with the beta and retail versions of Access 1.x and the beta versions of Access 2.0 are distributed liberally throughout the book. Several of the first commercial applications that use Access are analyzed in detail by their authors. Developers of these applications explain their approach to the design, how they implemented the product, and how the release of Access 2.0 contributed to their product. Many of the tricks and workarounds these developers learned while implementing their products in Access are included in the chapters comprising Part IV of this book.

The use of Object Linking and Embedding (OLE) 2.0 is given broad coverage in this book because of the importance of OLE 2.0 and OLE Automation in future versions of Windows, such as Chicago (Windows 4?), Daytona (Windows NT 3.11?), and Cairo (Windows NT 4?). Using both OLE 1.0 and 2.0 to handle graphic images with Access 2.0 is emphasized in this book because incorporating graphics in tables, forms, and reports is much more common in Windows than in DOS-based applications. Embedding and linking multimedia objects, such as sound and video, in Access databases is discussed in detail. OLE is a relatively new methodology, and the use of PCs, rather than Apple Macintosh computers, for multimedia is an even-newer trend. Many clients opt to use Windows database applications because of their graphics and multimedia capabilities.

The majority, if not all, of the Access applications you develop will employ the runtime version of Access, which is included in the Access Developer's Toolkit (ADT, replacing the Access 1.1 Distribution Kit, ADK). The examples in this book are designed for use with runtime Access 2.0; modifications that are necessary to optimize applications for use with MSARN200.EXE, the runtime version of MSACCESS.EXE, are discussed in detail. It is not necessary to possess the ADT to use the example databases included in this book and its accompanying diskette. You will gain the benefit of experience with the ADT, however, if you use MSARN200.EXE with the examples. The ADT also includes the Microsoft Help Compiler (HC31.EXE) and documentation for using HC31.EXE in creating .HLP files for your Access applications. The ADT also includes the documentation for using (and some examples of) simple OLE 2.0 Custom Controls. Access 2.0 is the first retail Microsoft product to provide OLE Custom Control compliance. *Access 2 Developer's Guide* explains how you use the components of the ADT to best advantage and how to sidestep some of the problems that using MSARN200.EXE creates.

An example of a modification necessary for runtime applications is the substitution of Access Basic **DoCmd** *MacroAction* statements for Access macros. You cannot trap errors that might occur when users execute macros included in runtime Access applications. Access Basic provides error-trapping capability through its **On Error GoTo** *LabelName* instruction. Any untrapped error that occurs during the runtime execution of a macro or Access Basic code causes an abrupt exit from your application. The user receives no warning when an error occurs; your application simply terminates. Examples of standard error-trapping routines for Access Basic procedures appear in most of the code listings in this book. Macros are used only for two purposes: for starting your application with the Autoexec macro (which executes the `RunCode` action) and for creating custom menus with the `AddMenu` action.

How This Book Is Organized

Access 2 Developer's Guide is written in a different sequence than tutorials that aid you in learning Access fundamentals. Tutorials follow the sequence of the buttons that appear in Access's Database Container (window): tables, queries, forms, reports, macros, and modules. This book discusses Access Basic code before dealing with form design because it is unlikely that you will ever create a form without associated Access Basic event-handling code that you now can store within **Form** and **Report** objects. Storing event-handling code in forms, called "code-behind-forms" or CBF by Microsoft, makes Access Basic 2.0 and Visual Basic 3.0 programming methodology almost identical. New database objects that are members of collections exposed by the data access object (DAO) let you create and manipulate any type of database object.

This book is divided into eight parts and contains a total of 29 chapters. Each chapter deals in depth with a particular subject of interest to developers of Access database applications. Together, the chapters cover the topics that are critical to the successful development of commercial database applications with Access.

Part I: An Overview of Application Design with Access

Part I, "Access as a Database-Development Platform," presents an overview of Access and its use in developing commercial database applications. The chapters in Part I emphasize the differences between developing database applications with Access and the methods used with traditional character-based DOS desktop RDBMSs. Part I stresses Access's object-oriented approach, and you're given a brief introduction to Access Basic code within Access libraries and wizards.

Chapter 1, "Viewing Access 2.0 from a Developer's Perspective," sets forth the pros and cons of using Access as a Windows database development tool. The chapter outlines what's new in Access 2.0, with emphasis on the features developers found missing in Access 1.x, plus OLE 2.0. It includes a brief analysis of Access as a client-server front-end environment and the use of the Open Database Connectivity (ODBC) application programming interface (API). Recommendations for hardware that you use to develop Access applications and run the applications on workstations with the Access Developer's Toolkit (ADT) are provided.

Chapter 2, "Developing a Design Strategy for Access Applications," explains how to reorient your thinking from the keyboard menu selections of DOS database applications to mouse clicks on command buttons of Access forms. Database-application design requires up-front analysis and design documentation; thus, using computer-aided software engineering (CASE) tools to diagram Access applications and create database schema is covered. Chapter 2 also discusses design principles for Access applications that are intended for distribution with the Access Developer's Toolkit.

Chapter 3, "Using Libraries, Wizards, Builders, and Add-Ins," shows you how to take advantage of libraries (now called add-ins), the many new Access 2.0 wizards, and other tools that speed development of Access applications. Using third-party add-ins to convert macros to Access Basic code and Microsoft's new Menu Builder add-in to create menu macros can save you many development hours.

Part II: Using Access Basic

Part II is devoted to the fundamentals of Access Basic as implemented by Access 2.0.

Chapter 4, "Writing Access Basic Code," introduces you to Access 2.0's particular dialect of Object Basic. The chapter begins with a description of Access Basic modules that contain your code and how to use Access's code-editing windows, in modules and behind forms and reports, to write and debug Access Basic code. A discussion of Object Basic variables, data types, and the scope of variables constitutes the primary content of this chapter. Examples of code that use the new **Variant** data type introduced by Object Basic are included. Error handling using the **On Error...** structures, a holdover from the original Dartmouth BASIC, is explained in detail. Access 2.0's new **Error** event also is discussed.

Chapter 5, "Understanding Access 2.0's Data Access Objects," describes the hierarchical structure that underlies the database objects you manipulate with Access Basic code. Access 2.0 objects are designed for compatibility with OLE Automation, although Access is not yet an OLE Automation server. (It is, however, an OLE Automation client or "container" application.) Unlike Access 1.x, Access 2.0 lets you create new database objects "programmatically," that is, with Access Basic code.

Chapter 6, "Creating and Using Object Variables," explains how you create and use the new object data types, such as **Workspace**, **Database**, **TableDef**, **Recordset**, and **QueryDef**. These object variables were introduced with Visual Basic 2.0 and 3.0, but Access is the first Microsoft product to bring database object variables into the programming mainstream.

Chapter 7, "Using Access Objects, Methods, and Events," concentrates on the differences between Access Basic event-handling code and conventional top-down programming associated with DOS RDBMSs. This chapter takes an object-oriented view of the properties and methods applicable to Access objects. Preferred methods of addressing Access database objects are explained in detail.

Part III: Creating Effective Forms and Reports

Part III deals with the integration of forms and reports with Access Basic code, emphasizing the use of CBF event-handling code.

Chapter 8, "Optimizing Transaction-Processing Forms," provides examples of data-entry forms, ranging from the elegant, colorful variety that are used to decorate magazine advertisements for Windows RDBMSs to the bland-but-fast types needed for heads-down data entry. This book considers transaction-processing and data-display forms to be two distinctly different species of the form object. Chapter 6 explains how to enforce referential and domain integrity using Access Basic code with attached databases, and how to use Access's transaction-processing methods to commit and roll back bulk updates to Access and client-server tables.

Chapter 9, "Designing Decision-Support Forms for Management," stresses the design of data-display forms that are used to summarize and analyze the information contained in your database. Designing graphs, using drill-down techniques to display detail underlying summaries, and creating full-scale executive information systems are the principal topics of this chapter.

Chapter 10, "Generating Meaningful Reports," shows you how to use Access's versatile report generator to print fully formatted detail and summary data. Tips on modifying report design for specific types of laser printers are included. Chapter 10 also describes how to take best advantage of the new Output To feature of Access 2.0 to "print" Access objects, including reports, to files.

Part IV: How Other Developers Approach Access Applications

Part IV, "Exploring Commercial Access Applications," dissects some examples of complete, commercial Access database applications. The advantage of exploring commercial Access applications, rather than small-scale applications that you duplicate while reading a book, is that the applications chosen for inclusion in this book typify the size and scope of applications that developers are called upon to create. Each chapter examines a different category of Access applications, ranging from complete accounting packages to specialty applications designed for resource management, both human and physical. Each chapter points out the unique features of the application and shows how these features were implemented by macros, Access Basic code, or both. The names and addresses of the firms that supply these applications are included in Appendix A, "Access Resources."

Chapter 11, "Examining an Access Accounting Application," is written by Gerry Novreske, president of MTX International, Inc., publishers of the MTX Accounting SDK for Access. The MTX SDK is a full-featured application for general ledgers, accounts payable and receivable, and payroll, all in the form of an .MDB that you can modify to suit your client's or firm's requirements.

Chapter 12, "Looking at an Access Training Database," was created by Meliora Systems, Inc., one of the independent software vendors (ISVs) selected to demonstrate its product in the Microsoft Comdex booth when Access was introduced. In the chapter, Mike Gilbert, a frequent contributor to the MSACCESS forum on CompuServe, explains the unique features of Meliora's Ingenium for Windows application and the strategy he used to develop Ingenium.

Chapter 13, "Analyzing an Access Time and Billing System," shows how Bill Serrahn of WorkGroup Solutions implemented a sophisticated time-tracking and invoicing system with Access. The WorkGroup Billing/EIS application demonstrates just how complex the forms you create with Access can be, while achieving intuitive data entry methodology. Bill's method of employing Access's security techniques to allow or limit modifications by licensees gives you insight into the power of the client-server security model employed by Access.

Part V: Taking Advantage of OLE 2.0

Chapter 14, "Understanding OLE 2.0," provides an overview of Object Linking and Embedding 2.0 and its use in Access applications. The chapter briefly describes how such OLE 2.0 functions as seamless in-place activation of embedded objects, OLE Automation, and OLE Custom Controls relate to Access 2.0 application design and to future Windows operating systems. Chapter 14 also includes details on how entries in the registration database, REG.DAT, control the associations for OLE servers and how to use the Registration Database Editor (REGEDIT.EXE) to make your OLE objects behave the way you want.

Chapter 15, "Embedding and Linking Objects with OLE," shows you how to make effective use of Microsoft and third-party OLE servers to create image databases or add logos and other decorative elements to forms and reports. Topics include using Object Packager and third-party OLE servers to control the size of presentations of linked images, trade-offs between bit-mapped and vector-based images, and handling complex image files such as those used to develop geographic information systems (GIS).

Chapter 16, "Using Access as an OLE Automation Client," shows you how to use OLE Automation (OA) to manipulate other applications' objects with Access Basic code. The chapter concentrates on creating programmable Excel 5.0 and Word 6.0 objects with Access 2.0's new **CreateObject**( ) and **GetObject**( ) functions. The OA principles you learn in this chapter, however, also apply to other newly-released OLE Automation servers, such as Visio 2.0.

Chapter 17, "Charting Data with Microsoft Graph 5.0," shows you how to take advantage of the programmable objects exposed by MSGraph5 by manipulating these objects with OLE Automation methodology.

Chapter 18, "Introducing OLE 2.0 Custom Controls," describes how to use the new OLE Custom Controls that you embed in unbound object frames. OLE Custom Controls (.OCX) are similar in concept to Visual Basic custom controls (.VBX). Access 2.0 is the first Windows application to use OLE Custom Controls, so only a few example controls were available when Access 2.0 was released. You can expect Microsoft and third-party publishers of Visual Basic .VBXs to release many useful .OCXs in 1994.

Part VI: Networked and Client-Server Applications

Part VI covers multiuser applications installed in a network environment. Windows for Workgroups 3.11 and Windows NT Advanced Server are used as peer-to-peer and client-server networks in the examples contained in this section's chapters. The networking principles explored in these chapters, however, apply equally to other network operating systems, such as Novell Netware and Banyan VINES. Microsoft SQL Server for Windows NT is used as the client-server database system.

Chapter 19, "Networking Secure Access Applications," explores the details of Access's labyrinthine (some say Byzantine) approach to securing shared databases, which is modeled on client-server security systems. Once you comprehend the concepts of database and object ownership, user accounts, workgroup SYSTEM.MDA files, personal identification numbers (PINs), and permissions assignment for objects in your database, you can confidently develop applications that take advantage of Access's advanced security and workgroup features. Chapter 19 also covers Access 2.0's new Groups and Users collections, which enable you to add new groups and users, and techniques for altering permissions with Access Basic code.

Chapter 20, "Front-Ending Client-Server Databases," delves into Microsoft's Open Database Connectivity API and explains how you use the ODBC Administrator to create Access data sources from client-server and ISAM RDBMSs. If you don't have a connection to a client-server database, you can use the new Microsoft ODBC Desktop Database Drivers kit to emulate client-server tables. Chapter 20 also discusses third-party ODBC drivers, such as those supplied by Pioneer Software in its

ODBC Driver Pack, and the proprietary ODBC drivers supplied by client-server RDBMS vendors.

Chapter 21, "Employing Access as a DDE Client and Server," shows you how to write Access Basic code to substitute for the very limited capability of Access's **DDE**() and **DDESend**() functions, which are employed by control objects of forms. You write Access Basic code that you can use to initiate DDE conversations with any server and with any topic you choose. Chapter 21 gives specific examples of using Access as a DDE client and server with Excel 4.0 and Word for Windows 2.0, but the techniques demonstrated are equally applicable to other DDE-compliant Windows applications. This chapter is included in Part VI, because DDE is likely to be relegated to second-class status as OLE Automation gains ground to become the primary Windows interprocess communication method.

Part VII: Advanced Access Topics

Part VII covers special techniques that you need to know to make effective use of Access libraries, to use graphics and multimedia objects in your applications, to create Access applications for a multiuser environment, and to take advantage of Access as a DDE client and server. The section also includes discussions on using the Microsoft ODBC API to create front-ends for a variety of client-server RDBMSs, writing Access Basic code that employs the Windows API and functions contained in third-party dynamic link libraries (DLLs), and taking advantage of some of the less-documented features of Access Basic.

Chapter 22, "Using the Windows API with Access Basic," gives you the background you need to declare Windows API and other DLL function prototypes in your module's declaration section, and then to call the functions in your code. Examples range from using Windows functions for creating private .INI files to using an Access library, WINAPI.MDA, to create the Windows API function prototypes and function calls for your Access applications.

Chapter 23, "Developing Access Libraries and Add-Ins," demonstrates the techniques you employ to create libraries containing reusable code that you attach to your Access applications. This chapter shows you how to create an advanced autodialer library that you can use with any Access application that includes telephone numbers. The library provides several important features that are not included in Access's built-in autodialer.

Chapter 24, "Using Access Wizard Functions," explains the syntax and usage of the Access **CreateForm**(), **CreateReport**() and **CreateControl**() functions you need to create form and report objects and the control objects they contain, using Access Basic code rather than form and report design windows.

Chapter 25, "Stretching the Limits of Access," explores topics such as SQL pass-through, using the Access Data-Definition Language, binary file input and output with `Get` and `Put`, using the OLE Object field to store other types of data with the **AppendChunk** and **GetChunk** methods, and other advanced Access Basic techniques that are either not included or not explained fully in the Access documentation. The chapter also explains how you can take advantage of much of the vast quantity of existing Visual Basic code by adapting it for use in your Access Basic modules.

Part VIII: Completing an Access Application

Part VIII, "Adding the Finishing Touches to Your Application," puts the techniques you've learned in Parts I through VII to use in creating applications that have a polished, professional look and feel.

Chapter 26, "Customizing Access Applications with Special Menus and Toolbars," shows you how to take full advantage of the Menu Builder Add-in, the new `MenuBar` property and the `AddMenu` macro action to expand or limit the user's menu choices. This chapter also explains the techniques you use to create custom toolbars for both the retail version of Access and applications distributed with the ADT.

Chapter 27, "Documenting Your Access Applications," shows you how to use Access 2.0's Database Documenter add-in to print detailed reports that describe each object in your Access application. The chapter gives an example of the Access Basic code needed to create data dictionaries for your applications.

Chapter 28, "Writing Help Files for Access Applications," gives you the details for writing the help files that are necessary for most commercial applications. This chapter explains how to use help file generators, such as WexTech Systems' Doc-To-Help application, to convert the manuals you write to context-sensitive WinHelp files and compile them for use with Access databases.

Chapter 29, "Distributing Runtime Versions of Your Databases," describes how to use the Access Developer's Toolkit (ADT) to create runtime Access applications that users execute with MSARN110.EXE. Detailed instructions for use of the Access SetupWizard to create distribution diskettes are included.

Appendixes and Reference Material

Appendix A, "Access Resources," includes the names and addresses of all the third-party suppliers whose products are described in this book, together with a list of other vendors that publish applications you can use to shorten the time you need to develop Access databases.

Appendix B, "Naming Conventions for Microsoft Access," provides a standardized method for assigning names to Access Basic objects and variables, according to their data type. These conventions have been proposed by Stan Leszynski and Greg Reddic, both well-know Access developers, and are used by many developers of commercial Access applications.

Appendix C, "Upgrading Access 1.1 Applications to Access 2.0," provides the information you need when you decide to upgrade your Access 1.1 applications to take advantage of the new features of Access 2.0.

Appendix D, "Using the Accompanying Diskette," lists the DLLs, libraries, wizards, example databases, and Access Basic code included on the 3 1/2-inch high-density diskette that accompanies this book.

Keeping Up-to-Date on Access

A variety of sources of up-to-date information are available to Access developers in print and electronic formats. Some magazines and newsletters provide articles directed to end-users, with a mix of topics directed at those with beginning- to intermediate-level skills. Other periodicals address management and development issues that are applicable to database development as a whole. Several forums on CompuServe Information Service offer product-support services for Access and Windows.

Periodicals

The following are a few of the magazines and newsletters that cover Access exclusively or in which articles on Microsoft Access appear on a regular basis:

- *Access Advisor*, published by Advisor Communications International, Inc., is a full-color, bimonthly magazine intended to serve Access users and developers alike. You can supplement your subscription with an accompanying diskette that includes sample databases, utilities, and other software tools for Access.

- *Visual Basic Programmer's Journal* is a bimonthly magazine from Fawcette Technical Publications that covers all the dialects of Object Basic with emphasis on Visual Basic, Visual Basic for Applications, and Access Basic.

- *Data Based Advisor* is published by Data Based Solutions, Inc., a firm related to the publishers of *Access Advisor*. John Hawkins, Editor-in-Chief of *Data Based Advisor*, holds the same position with *Access Advisor* and *FoxPro Advisor* magazines. *Data Based Advisor* covers the gamut of desktop databases, with emphasis on xBase products.

- *DBMS* magazine, published by M&T, a Miller-Freeman company, is devoted to database technology as a whole, with emphasis on the growing field of client-server RDBMSs. *DBMS* covers subjects (such as SQL and relational database design) that are of interest to all developers, not just those who use Access.

- *Smart Access* is a monthly newsletter from Pinnacle Publishing, Inc., which publishes several other database-related newsletters. *Smart Access* is directed primarily to developers and Access power users. This newsletter emphasizes advanced topics, such as creating libraries and using the Windows API with Access Basic. A diskette is included with each issue.

- *Windows Watcher,* Jesse Berst's monthly newsletter, analyzes the market for Windows applications, reviews new products for Windows, and provides valuable insight on Microsoft's future plans for Windows 3.x, Windows for Workgroups, and Windows NT.

The majority of the magazines are available from newsstands and bookstores. Names and addresses of the publishers are listed in Appendix A, "Access Resources."

The MSACCESS and Other Forums on CompuServe

Microsoft and other firms sponsor several product-support forums on CompuServe Information Service's online information utility. The following forums are a vital source of information for Access developers:

- Microsoft Product Support Specialists (PSSs) and an informal group of experienced Access users and developers provide answers to users' questions in the Microsoft Access Forum (GO MSACCESS). MSACCESS is one of the most active forums on CompuServe, and several authors of books about Access are participants. Useful example databases, Access utilities, and DLLs that enable you to unlock otherwise undocumented features of Access are available to download from the libraries of MSACCESS. One section is devoted to third-party toolkits and add-in applications. All developers are urged to monitor MSACCESS for messages and files that include tricks, tips, and workarounds for Access 1.x and 2.0.

- Support for the ODBC API is provided by the ODBC section (10) of Microsoft's Windows Extensions Forum (GO WINEXT). You can download the complete ODBC SDK from WINEXT for only the cost of connect time. If you want to create Access applications that interact with Microsoft's Schedule+, which is supplied with Windows for Workgroups, the Schedule+ Access Library (SAL, a library that lets you access Schedule+ functions) is available in Section 11. The Video for Windows section (2) has the runtime version of Microsoft Video for Windows available for downloading.

- Visual Basic for Windows' product support is handled in several sections of the Microsoft Basic forum (GO MSBASIC). The similarities of Visual Basic 2.0 and Access Basic code behind forms make many of the sample applications and utilities in the Visual Basic for Windows section equally useful to Access developers. For example, you can use the Windows API function prototypes and constant declarations for Visual Basic in the declarations section of your Access modules with no changes at all.

- Windows for Workgroups is the subject of the MSWRKGRPS forum. The Workgroups Forum provides product support for Windows for Workgroups 3.1x, Microsoft Mail 3.x, MAPI (Messaging API), and the Microsoft Workgroup Templates. You can download the Workgroup Templates, several of which use Access databases, from the MSWRKGRPS forum.

- The Microsoft Knowledge Base (GO MSKB) is a database of technical articles, as well as press releases, for Microsoft products. Technical articles specifically related to Access, however, are periodically collected by the Microsoft Access Product Support Services group and are added to the current version of a WinHelp file, PSS-KB.ZIP, that you can download from section 1 of the MSACCESS forum.

- Independent software vendors (ISVs) have their own sections of Windows Vendors forums, coordinated by Microsoft. At the time this book was written, there were four separate ISV forums. Pioneer Software, for example, supports its ODBC drivers in the WINVEN D forum. Enter GO WINVEN, and then select the number corresponding to the forum you want to explore.

- Data Based Solutions, Inc., publisher of *Data Based Advisor* magazine, maintains a forum on CompuServe (GO DBA), as does *DBMS* magazine (GO DBMS). These forums cover topics of general interest to database developers for a wide range of RDBMS platforms. The DBA forum has a section devoted to Microsoft Access.

If you don't have a CompuServe account, call (800) 848-8199 for information on how to obtain your CompuServe ID number.

Publishers of Database Standards

The syntax of SQL is the subject of a standard published by the American National Standards Institute (ANSI). When this book was written, the current standard, X3.135.1-1992 (commonly called SQL-92), was available from

American National Standards Institute
11 West 42nd Street
New York, NY 10036
(212) 642-4900 (Sales Department)

If you want to fully comprehend the implementation of the American National Standards Institute's X3.135.1-1992 standard for SQL-92, obtain a copy of Jim Melton and Alan R. Simpson's *Understanding the New SQL: A Complete Guide*, ISBN 1-55860-245-3 (San Mateo, CA, Morgan Kaufmann Publishers, 1993). Jim Melton of Digital Equipment Corp. was the editor of the ANSI SQL-92 standard, which consists of more than 500 pages of fine print.

The SQL Access Group (SAG) consists of users and vendors of SQL database-management systems. SAG publishes standards that supplement ANSI X3.135.1-1989 and ANSI X3.135.1-1992, such as the Call-Level Interface (CLI) standard. You can obtain SAG documents from

SQL Access Group
1010 El Camino Real, Suite 380
Menlo Park, CA 94025
(415) 323-7992 x221

I

Access as a Database Development Platform

P
I

1

Viewing Access 2.0 from a Developer's Perspective

Users acquire a *desktop relational database management system* (RDBMS) for a variety of reasons: to solve an immediate problem, to acquire database skills, or simply to satisfy their curiosity. Database developers, on the other hand, rely on desktop RDBMSs for all or a major part of their livelihood. Independent developers must invest the time required to become proficient with a new desktop RDBMS before receiving significant development revenue. For in-house developers, employers must underwrite the learning curve before receiving any benefit from the new RDBMS. In either case, the up-front capital investment involved in learning to use a new RDBMS is substantial; a rule of thumb is 10 to 20 times the amount of the manufacturer's suggested retail price (MSRP) of the software per developer.

Significant capital investments require careful cost-benefit analyses. This chapter summarizes the benefits of adopting Access as a database development platform and points out a few of the drawbacks of Access 1.x that have been rectified by Access 2.0. You can develop commercial-quality Windows database applications in Access in less time than required with competitive desktop RDBMSs or front-ends. When you make your initial development proposals, however, you need to take into consideration the problems associated with attaching certain types of database files to Access 2.0. You may find that your projected time savings are offset by the time spent writing creative workarounds. Thus, much of this chapter is devoted to the business aspects of database applications in general and of Access in particular.

This book classifies RDBMSs in three categories: desktop RDBMSs, client-server RDBMSs, and database front-ends. The definitions of each of these categories are as follows:

■ A desktop RDBMS development product is a shrink-wrapped software publication designed to create database applications that employ database files of a single structure, referred to collectively as ISAM (for indexed sequential access method). Paradox, dBASE, FoxPro, and Clipper are examples of programmable desktop ISAM RDBMSs. These products are characterized by their use of individual files for tables, indexes, and application programs. In addition to their native programming languages, some desktop RDBMSs support SQL for creating queries. All data-manipulation operations occur at the workstation when files are shared in server directories. Most desktop RDBMSs rely on network security features to control permissions for tables. Software license charges for multiuser applications created with these products vary widely; most publishers offer runtime versions of their applications, if needed, so that developers can distribute multiple copies of complete applications without paying license fees for each copy.

■ A client-server RDBMS provides a proprietary database file structure designed to be installed on a dedicated server computer. Microsoft and Sybase SQL Server, ORACLE, Informix, and Digital Equipment's Rdb are typical implementations of the client-server model. Tables, indexes, and low-level applications (stored procedures) are included in a single file. All client-server products use SQL to create, modify, and query tables in the database. Queries are processed by the server and the selected data is returned to the workstation over the network. Database security is maintained by the RDBMS using SQL statements. Database applications usually are created with third-party software; the data manipulation and display capabilities of client-server RDBMSs, for the most part, are rudimentary. License charges are based on the number of workstations that may simultaneously use the client-server RDBMS.

■ A client-server front-end is an application that usually provides access to several different client-server database file structures. You can create data-manipulation and display applications that use previously created tables attached from a variety of client-server and desktop RDBMSs. PowerBuilder, Forest and Trees, and Pioneer Software's Q+E Database Editor are typical client-server front-end applications for Windows. All front-ends support SQL's data query, manipulation, and transaction-processing language (DQL, DML, and TPL) commands; and most can create new tables with SQL's data definition language (DDL). Some front-ends are designed for end users and employ a simple script language to create applications; others include a complete programming language, usually with proprietary (non-standard) syntax. Client-server front-ends traditionally require a license for each workstation on which they are installed, called a *per-seat* charge. Now that low-cost desktop RDBMSs, such as Access, can create client-server front ends, dedicated front-end generators with per-seat charges are likely to become an endangered species.

Access presents an interesting amalgam of the desktop RDBMS and the client-server model. Access employs a unique file structure that expands the single-file approach of client-server RDBMS; everything you need for a database application is contained in one .MDB file. Access's security system, which determines the ability of users to read and update data as well as to modify database objects, is based on the client-server techniques employed by Microsoft and Sybase SQL Server. Access combines the features of desktop RDBMSs and database front-ends; you can choose to use Access's proprietary file structure or attach files created by other desktop RDBMSs or client-server databases. The process for creating queries is identical for both Access's native tables and those attached from other RDBMSs.

From a business standpoint, one of the most significant features of Access is Microsoft Corporation's licensing policy for the product. For a one-time charge of $495, the Access 2.0. Development Toolkit (ADT, which replaces the Access 1.1 Distribution Kit or ADK) allows you to use and distribute as many copies of your Access applications as you want. In this book, computers on which the runtime version of Access is installed are called workstations.

This chapter begins with an analysis of what's new in Access 2.0, with special emphasis on the significance of new and improved features for Access database developers. It then goes on to explain why database developers, whether in-house or independent consultants, should choose Access 2.0 as a database-application development environment. The first edition of this book included a section that described "The Downside of Access 1.x." The "Downside" section is missing from this second edition, because the vast majority of the problems developers experienced with Access 1.x have been overcome by Access 2.0. The chapter ends with an introductory analysis of Access as a front-end for client-server databases and a description of the Access Developer's Toolkit, plus a section describing the PC resource requirements for Access 2.0.

What's New in Access 2.0 for Access 1.x Developers

Access 2.0 is the first major upgrade to Microsoft Access. (Access 1.1 is better classified as a "maintenance release" for version 1.0 than as an upgrade.) The new and improved features of Access 2.0 are directed at entry-level users and developers alike; however, Microsoft aimed the majority of the significant alterations to the developer community. The sections that follow describe the improvements made to Access 2.0 that are of greatest interest to developers. (This book assumes that you're familiar with running Access 2.0 and have at least skimmed its accompanying documentation, so the changes to the user interface to bring Access into conformance with the interface of other Microsoft applications are not included in the discussion of "What's New in Access 2.0 for Access 1.x Developers.")

Referential Integrity Is Maintained on Attached Access 2.0 Tables

Access enables the developer to combine application objects (queries, forms, reports, macros, and modules) and database objects (tables) in a single .MDB file. However, it is a generally accepted database-design practice to create two separate .MDB files for these objects. Using a separate file for tables enables you to upgrade the application elements without having to import the tables from the version you're replacing into the new version's .MDB file. In a multiuser environment, running the application .MDB file on workstations and attaching shared tables in an .MDB file on the server improves performance and reduces network traffic.

Access 2.0 maintains referential integrity on attached Access tables through a mechanism called *inherited relationships.* The default relationships you create through Access's new Relationships window, shown in Figure 1.1, are stored in a new system file, MSysRelations, that is stored in the table database. Thus, referential integrity now is enforced at the table level, rather than at the application level. This new feature makes Access 2.0 more closely resemble client-server RDBMSs, virtually all of which provide referential integrity enforcement on the server (often called the *back-end.*)

FIGURE 1.1.

Access 2.0's new graphical Relationships window.

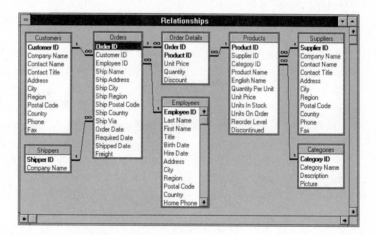

Automatic Cascading Deletions and Updates

Having Access, rather than your application, enforce referential integrity is a good database-design practice. However, you may need to delete a primary record (on the "one" side) that has dependent records (on the "many" side). An example is deleting records for out-of-date orders in a primary or base table that have dependent line-item records in a related table. When you enforce referential integrity between the orders and line-items tables, you have to delete all of the line items before you can delete the order record. In Access 1.x, you had to write a macro or Access Basic code to perform the deletion of related records, then delete the primary record. Using Access Basic was the preferred method, because you could apply *transaction processing* methods to the operation. Transaction processing, using the Access Basic **BeginTrans**, **CommitTrans**, and **Rollback** instructions, lets you test the ability to complete a transaction prior to making changes to the data in the affected tables. If for some reason you could not delete all of the line items, the **Rollback** instruction would undo the entire deletion process. The Access Basic code required to perform transaction processing is straightforward but not trivial.

Access 2.0 gives you the option of performing *cascading deletions* of and *cascading updates* to records of tables for which referential integrity is enforced. Figure 1.2 shows Access 2.0's new Relationships dialog box, in which you set the cascading options. In Figure 1.2, the option check boxes are ticked but disabled, because the Orders and Orders ID tables are attached, and the options have been set in the database containing the attached tables. Cascading operations apply to the deletion of primary records or changes to the value of the primary key field(s) on which related records depend. A cascading deletion begins a transaction, attempts to delete all of the dependent related records, and then attempts to delete the primary record. If the deletions are successful, the transaction is committed and the records are deleted permanently. If any of these attempts fail, the transaction is rolled back, and Access restores all of the records to their original state. The 4MB size limit for transactions in Access 1.x is increased to the size of your computer's available memory plus disk space for the temporary transaction file.

FIGURE 1.2.

The Relationships dialog box for attached tables with cascading updates and deletions.

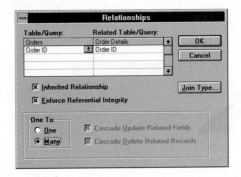

Cascading updates are more difficult to perform because of a dichotomy that occurs when you attempt to change the value of the primary key field(s): 1) You cannot change the foreign key value of the related records because no primary record exists with that key value; and 2) You cannot change the primary key value because related records depend on the primary key. This dichotomy becomes apparent when, for example, you attempt to change an employee ID number and you have related records in an orders or commissions table for the employee. Access 2.0's automatic cascading updates solve this dichotomy for you by temporarily removing the referential integrity constraint during the update process.

> **NOTE**
>
> It is not a good database-design practice to allow changes to primary key values in a completed application. If you use the Counter field data type as a primary key (as in the Employees table of NWIND.MDB), you cannot change the value. There are occasions during database development or during the importation of data from another database type when you might want to change primary key values.

Domain Integrity Is Enforced at the Table Level

The ability to enforce domain integrity with validation rules (often called *business rules*) is a feature of all popular desktop RDBMSs. The domain of a field is the set (enumeration) or range of all values that constitute valid entries for the field. For example, the domain of a foreign key field of a related table is the set of values of the corresponding primary key field of the base table. (In this case, domain integrity is maintained by enforcing referential integrity, not by validation rules.) Another example of a validation rule is [Shipped Date] >= [Order Date]; a shipping date entry must be on or after the date an order is received.

The validation rules of Access 1.x tables applied only to updates made in datasheet view; you had to add validation rules to each bound control on every form to maintain domain integrity. One of the cardinal rules of RDBMS design is that the database itself, not the application, enforces domain integrity. Access 2.0 now enforces domain integrity at the table level. This means that you need only enter the validation rule once and your application objects, such as forms and update queries, cannot override the domain integrity rules.

In order to implement this important new feature, Microsoft elected to separate field-level validation rules that depend only on the value of the field from table-level validation rules that depend on other values, such as values of other fields or domain aggregate functions. Figure 1.3 illustrates the new Table Properties window with the text box to add a table ValidationRule property value. Access 1.x allowed validation rules, such as [Shipped Date] >= [Order Date], as field-level rules. References to field names are no longer permitted in field-level validation rules, so you must alter the non-conforming validation rules of your Access 1.x tables during the migration to Access 2.0. Access aids this process by providing an Expression Builder that you can invoke by clicking the ellipsis button to the right of the ValidationRule text box. Access 2.0 also eliminates the need to add the Is Not Null expression to validation rules by providing a Required property. An additional new property, AllowZeroLength, enables you to prevent updating of records with an empty string (" ") in a text field. The new `InputMask` property is described in the following section.

FIGURE 1.3.

*Access 2.0's new
Field Properties
pane and Table
Properties window.*

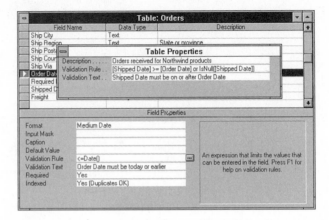

Input Masks for Formatted Data Entry

One of the most frequently-requested enhancements sought by Access 1.x developers was an equivalent of Visual Basic's masked edit control (albeit without the bugs that plague the Visual Basic 3.0 and earlier versions). Access 2.0's `InputMask` property answered these requests, providing an improved variant of xBase's `PICT(URE)` modifier. Access includes an Input Mask Wizard (actually a multi-step builder), shown in Figure 1.4, to help you learn the syntax for input masks. As an example, the `(999) 000-0000` input mask automatically formats telephone numbers in standard North American style. The Wizard has 10 predefined masks for commonly used data entry formats, such as Social Security number.

FIGURE 1.4.

*The first dialog box
of the Input Mask
Wizard.*

Object Linking and Embedding 2

Microsoft has staked the future of Windows and Windows NT on the successful implementation and evangelization of (OLE) 2.0. (Microsoft employees who aid third-party software publishers in adopting the company's new "industry standards" are called *technical evangelists*.) OLE 2.0 provides a variety of enhancements to the creation and editing of compound documents, but its most important feature for developers is OLE Automation (OA). OLE Automation lets OLE 2.0 client applications *programmatically* manipulate objects created by OLE 2.0 server applications. Programmatically is a Microsoft euphemism for "with many lines of code." OLE 2.0 is implemented by a variety of new Windows dynamic link libraries (DLLs). OLE 2.0 is backwardly-compatible with OLE 1.0; OLECLI.DLL and OLESVR.DLL remain in \WINDOWS\SYSTEM for use by OLE 1.0 applications.

Only a few applications were fully OLE 2.0-compliant by the time this edition was written: Microsoft Excel 5.0, Word 6.0, and Project 4.0, plus Shapeware Corp.'s Visio 2.0. Word 6.0 does not comply fully with the OLE Automation specification; like Visio 2.0, it is not an OLE 2.0 client. (You can use Word 6.0's Word.Basic object with OA clients to execute Word Basic menu commands, and OA clients can manipulate Visio 2.0 objects.) Microsoft Graph 5.0, included with Access 2.0, is an OLE 2.0 server applet; you only can activate MSGraph5 from within an OLE 2.0 client application.

Excel 5.0 and Project 4.0 both can serve as OA clients and servers because these applications use Visual Basic for Applications (VBA, also called Visual Basic Applications Edition) as their application programming language. A dialect of *Object Basic* is required in order for applications to act as OLE 2.0 servers. Object Basic is the root language of all of Microsoft's new application programming languages for Windows: Access Basic, Visual Basic, and VBA. Object Basic is the subject of a section that follows later in this chapter.

Access 2.0 is an OLE 2.0 client application only, just as Access 1.x provided only OLE 1.0 client capabilities. This means you can take advantage of the new features of OLE 2.0 and OLE Automation only if you have other OLE 2.0-compliant applications. Therefore you and your clients or employer must upgrade to OLE 2.0 applications as they appear in order to benefit from OLE 2.0's new features. What OLE 2.0 offers developers is described briefly in the sections that follow. A more extensive description of the features of OLE 2.0 appears in Chapter 14, "Understanding OLE 2.0."

In-Place Activation of Embedded Source Documents

One of Microsoft's objectives in developing OLE 2.0 was to make the editing of *compound documents* a seamless operation. A compound document is an object created by one application that contains an object created by another application. A Word 2+ document that contains an Excel worksheet or a Paintbrush image is a compound document. In OLE 2.0 terminology, the Word document is an OLE container object. (OLE 1.0 referred to container objects as destination documents.) Fields of the OLE Object type in Access tables are individual OLE containers. OLE 2.0 enables you to edit nested compound documents. As an example, you can edit an Excel 5.0 worksheet contained in a Word 6.0 document that, in turn, is contained in an Access OLE Object data cell; just keep double-clicking the objects to activate them.

If you embed an OLE 2.0 source object (document) that supports in-place activation (also called *in-situ editing*) in an OLE Object field and then double-click the object when it is displayed in a bound object frame of an Access 2.0 form, the source object's application takes over the client application's menus. The source application's toolbars, if any, appear as floating windows on top of the client application's window. Figure 1.5 shows an Excel 5.0 worksheet embedded in the Picture field of the Categories table of NWIND.MDB and displayed in the Categories form. Notice that the menu bar and the choices displayed in the Format menu are Excel 5.0 commands, not Access 2.0 menu choices. Having the source object's server application take over the operation of the client application during the editing process facilitates the seamless editing of compound documents. OLE 2.0's new Insert Object dialog box includes an explanation of how the insertion process works. (Attempting to edit the miniature worksheet that is constrained to more or less fit the confines of a small object frame, such as that shown in Figure 1.4, is a exercise in futility.) In-place activation is implemented with embedded documents, but not with linked documents.

OLE Automation

OLE Automation is designed to accomplish two objectives: 1) Enable developers to create applications that use OLE 2.0 objects as building blocks; and 2) Eliminate the use of DDE as the primary means of inter-application communication in Windows. The first objective is directed to object-oriented programming (OOP). The goal of OOP is to minimize the duplication of programming effort by creating sets of standardized *programming objects* that can be reused in a variety of applications. A programming object can range in complexity from a simple dialog box to a major-scale application server like Excel 5.0. Programming objects are treated like "black boxes;" you only need to know the properties of the box and the methods applicable to the box, not the code that is contained in the box.

FIGURE 1.5.

An Excel 5.0 worksheet activated in the Picture object frame of the Categories form.

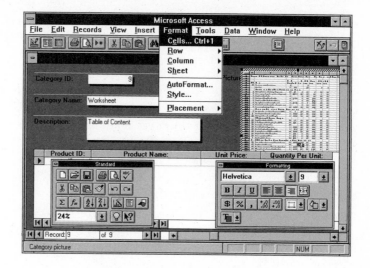

Several major new operating systems are planned for introduction in 1994 and 1995: Microsoft Windows 4.0 (Chicago), Windows NT 3.? (Daytona), Windows NT 4.0 (Cairo), Apple/IBM Taligent (formerly Pink) for the PowerPC, and Sun/NeXT OpenStep (derived from NextStep). The principal competition between these operating systems will be based on how well the products implement OOP and how easily the user can interchange objects created from one operating system to another operating system. The ease of storing objects in a repository database and of transporting objects over networks also will play an important role in the success of these new operating systems.

OLE 2.0 is the cornerstone of all of Microsoft's future operating systems, and OLE Automation is the foundation for managing programming objects. Currently, the OLE 2.0 client and server applications must reside on the same computer, although the source files for documents that are based on files can reside on a network server. Microsoft and Digital Equipment have formed an alliance to expand OLE 2.0's capabilities to transport objects over networks. It is expected that at least one of the new Windows versions will support transportable objects. A competing proposed standard for object manipulation is Apple Computer's OpenDoc. At the time this edition was written, only OLE 2.0 was available in shrink-wrapped software. Being first with an operable object standard that is implemented in mainstream applications and having an installed base of about 50 million copies of Windows assures Microsoft Corp. of the preeminent market position in OOP for the foreseeable future.

OLE Automation operates by *exposing* the properties of and the methods applicable to a set of OA server application objects, called an *object collection*, to an OA client application. Exposing an object means that you can read and set the values of properties of the object and apply methods to the object using the client applications' programming language. To create an application object in Access Basic, you can use the **GetObject**() method of a variable of the new **Object** data type, if the application object is based on a file. Alternatively, the **CreateObject**() method opens an empty application object, such as a blank Excel 5.0 worksheet or Word 6.0 document. Once you've assigned a value to the object variable, you have access to all of the object's methods and properties. Unlike DDE, the instance of the server that exposes the objects does not appear in Windows' Task Manager list, but you can make the server's window appear if you want. Just a few of the several hundred properties and collections of Excel 5.0 objects appear in the Excel's Object Browser dialog box, shown in Figure 1.6. Examples of Access Basic code for typical OA applications using Excel 5.0 and Word 6.0 as servers are provided in Chapter 16, "Using Access as an OLE Automation Client."

FIGURE 1.6.

One of the sets of objects exposed by Excel 5.0.

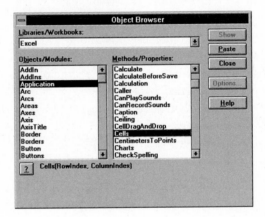

Visual Basic for Applications

Visual Basic for Applications is an interpretive application-programming language implemented as a DLL. VBA.DLL and its associated localization file for U.S., Canadian, and British English dialects, VBAEN.DLL, implements VBA for all Windows applications that employ it. Each application uses a DLL to connect to VBA. VBA is a typical OOP building block; the application sends the VBA code you write in modules to VBA, which, in turn, executes the code line by line. Thus the reserved words of VBA are identical for all applications that share VBA.DLL. The host application exposes its (native) objects to VBA so that you can program the application's own objects. Therefore there is very little difference in the VBA code to manipulate native objects or to manipulate objects created from another application's repertoire.

This book does not cover Visual Basic for Applications because Access is not an OLE Automation server, and therefore, VBA cannot manipulate Access database objects. However, Access 2.0 supports almost all of the reserved words of VBA. (One notable exception is VBA's With...Do structure for setting values of object properties; Access 2.0 does not support named arguments.) It is quite likely that the next major release of Access will substitute VBA for Access Basic, paving the way for Access to become an OA server, as well as a client. In addition, you may be able to select "FoxPro for Applications" (FPA?) as your Access programming language. This was promised by 1995 by the designers of Access in an article that appeared in a 1991 issue of *DBMS* magazine. Presumably, you could choose VBA to program FoxPro for Windows applications. When this occurs, the primary difference between Access and FoxPro will be the database engine, so Windows RDBMSs ultimately will end up as "plug and play" applications created from a set of user-interface, programming-language, and database-engine objects.

OLE 2.0 Common Controls

The OOP building-block approach isn't limited to using objects supplied by shrink-wrapped, OLE 2.0-compliant software products. You can create your own OLE 2.0 objects and use them as common control objects contained in Access forms and reports. Common controls are similar in concept to the common dialog boxes introduced with Windows 3.1 and implemented with COMMDLG.DLL. As with common dialog boxes, you can use common controls with any application that supports them by providing COMMCTRL.DLL. Unlike the common dialogs, however, you don't need to declare and call API functions to use common controls; instead you manipulate the common control as an **Object** variable. The new Microsoft operating systems are expected to make widespread use of OLE 2.0 common controls.

Access 2.0 is the first Microsoft application to offer compatibility with OLE 2.0 common controls. This feature answers developers' pleas for compatibility between Access and Visual Basic's custom controls in Access. Instead of using .VBXs, Access jumped a step beyond Visual Basic 3.0 and implemented OLE 2.0 common control compatibility. Future versions of Visual Basic are expected to accommodate both .VBXs and OLE 2.0 common controls, but common controls are the wave of the future.

The Access Developer Toolkit includes several examples of OLE 2.0 controls and the source code used to create them. You'll need to write programs in Microsoft Visual C++ 1.5+ and acquire the new OLE 2.0 Control Development Kit to create OLE 2.0 controls yourself. However, it is expected that a lively third-party market for OLE 2.0 controls will develop as soon as the CDK is available. The CDK provides a Visual Basic-like user interface that enables C programmers to quickly design and implement the code framework of simple controls. (Writing an OLE 2.0 application from scratch in C or C++ is a daunting project.) Visual C++ is compatible with most Visual Basic custom controls, so it is conceivable that the current publishers of .VBXs will simply add an OLE 2.0 "wrapper" to their existing product line to make the custom controls available to Access developers. Figure 1.7 illustrates one of the example custom controls included with the Access Developer Toolkit. The example controls of the ADT are one of the subjects of Chapter 18, "Introducing OLE 2.0 Custom Controls."

FIGURE 1.7.

The calendar custom control included in the Access Developers Toolkit.

Fewer "Read-Only in Run Mode" Properties

If you wanted to change the size, location, caption, or just about any other property of an Access 1.x control object with Access Basic code, it was a major exercise. It was necessary to switch to design mode, change the property values of an object, and then return to run mode. This process often was accompanied by brief appearances of objects (or white holes representing unpainted objects) that you could not prevent from appearing with the **DoCmd** Echo **False** instruction. Chapter 24 of this book, "Using Access Wizard Functions," provides an example of this programming methodology, which remains necessary if you want to create new forms, reports, or controls with the **CreateReport**(), **CreateForm**(), or **CreateControl**() methods.

Access developers who had cut their Windows programming eye teeth with Visual Basic were accustomed to manipulating the position, content, and appearance of objects with Visual Basic code. There was a Greek chorus of complaints about form, report, and control properties that were "read-only in run mode" (AKA "cast in concrete"). Here again, Microsoft answered the call by making these properties "programmatic." Now if you want to create a continuous subform to accommodate the result set of user-definable queries, you can simply add as many text boxes to the subform or subreport as might conceivably be necessary, then hide the ones you don't need. You can position and size the text boxes that remain to format the display or report for the appropriate number of columns. This process is discussed in Chapter 9, "Designing Decision-Support Forms for Management," and as an alternative approach to using design mode in Chapter 24.

New Events

Access developers who were accustomed to the variety of events that could be triggered on (or by) Visual Basic form and control objects complained about the lack of a similar collection of events for Access 1.x forms, reports, and controls. Visual Basic offers a high degree of event granularity (that is, the ability to distinguish between a variety of events), whereas Access 1.x did not. Microsoft rectified this deficiency by providing more events for Access 2.0 forms and controls than are offered by most of their Visual Basic 3.0 counterparts. Access 2.0 offers so many new properties and events that it was necessary to redesign the Properties window to display them in groups. Figure 1.8 shows the 15 events that a simple bound text box can trigger. Microsoft calls events "event properties" for reasons that are explained in Chapter 18, which discusses OLE 2.0 controls. This book uses the Visual Basic term, "event," except when referring to OLE 2.0 controls.

FIGURE 1.8.

Access 2.0's new Properties windows displaying the event properties for a bound text box.

Code Behind Forms

If you have concluded at this point that the development environment of Access 2.0 now duplicates that of Visual Basic 3.0 almost totally, it should come as no surprise that Access 2.0 has also adopted Visual Basic's event-handling coding methodology. Microsoft calls this new addition to Access 2.0 *code behind forms*, or CBF for short. CBF enables you to write Access Basic event-handling subprocedures for events that are triggered on (or by) forms and controls on forms. As is the case with Visual Basic, CBF source code is stored as an integral part of the Access 2.0 form. Therefore if you create a set of standard form objects that you use in a variety of applications, when you import a copy of the standard form, the event-handling code comes with the copy. CBF qualifies Access forms as OOP building blocks. (You still cannot import Visual Basic forms into Access 2.0 applications, however.)

Figure 1.8 shows [Event Procedure] as the value of the Before Update event "property." To open the code editing window for writing a CBF "event procedure," click the ellipsis button of a selected event to display the Choose Builder dialog. Choose Code Builder to display the Form.*FormName* module that contains your source code for the event, as illustrated by Figure 1.9. Like Visual Basic, the Access 2.0 Code Builder creates a subprocedure stub, **Sub** *ObjectName_EventName*...**End Sub.** You can create common subprocedures and function stubs by entering **Sub** *ProcName* or **Function** *FuncName* anywhere in the code editing window. Functions you've written in Access Basic module objects and assigned as event handlers with =*FuncName*() entries in event text boxes are unaffected when you migrate to Access 2.0, and you can continue to use event-handling functions, if you choose.

FIGURE 1.9.

A CBF event-handling stub created by the Code Builder.

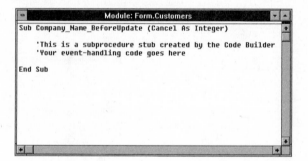

New Data Access Objects

Much of the power of the Access database engine was unavailable to Access 1.x developers; only a few of the data access objects defined by the Jet engine were exposed to Access Basic. Whereas Visual Basic 3.0 offers the **CreateDatabase**() method to create new databases and the TableDefs and Fields collections to add new tables to a database, Access 1.1 required the use of MSADDL11.DLL and a substantial amount of Access Basic code to create a table. Many operations, such as setting values of options, required cumbersome **SendKeys** commands that slowed opening of your Access 1.x applications.

Access 2.0 now exposes all of the objects created by the Jet 2.0 database engine in OLE 2.0-compatible form. You can perform many of the operations that required **DoCmd** DoMenuItem or **SendKeys** statements in Access 1.x by programming these new objects. The hierarchy of the collections of objects exposed by Access 2.0 is described briefly in the following list:

- The **Application** object refers to the currently-open Access 2.0 application. You now can apply the **GetOption**() and **SetOption**() methods to the **Application** object to read and set the values of options for your application. The MenuBar property enables you to name a macro to designate a special menu bar for your application. (You still need to use macros to define custom menus.)

- The new **DbEngine** master object has a Workspaces collection with a **Workspace** object for each current *session* of the Jet engine. A session is an instance of the Jet engine; you can open multiple sessions, each with its own **Workspace** object. Your application opens the default **Workspace** object, Workspaces(0).

- The **Workspace** object include Databases, Users, and Groups collections for programmatic control of entries in SYSTEM.MDA for secure Access applications.

- The **Database** object contains TableDefs, QueryDefs, Recordsets, Relations, and Containers collections. The default **Database** object, formerly **CurrentDB**(), is DbEngine.Workspaces(0).Databases(0) in Access 2.0. **QueryDef** objects in Access 2.0 are identical to those of Access 1.x. **Recordset** objects replace Access 1.x's **Dynaset** and **Snapshot** objects, but the **Dynaset** and **Snapshot** reserved words continue to be supported. **Database** objects refer to objects that you open with the Access Basic **Open*ObjectName*()** methods, while Document objects, described later in this list, refer to objects saved in a .MDB file.

- The **TableDef** object contains the Fields and Indexes collections of **Field** and **Index** objects. You add a new **TableDef** object to a database, or a **Field** or **Index** object to a table, with the **Append** method. Reserved words in Access 2.0's new SQL Data Definition Language (DDL) also enable you to create new tables, fields and indexes, add fields and indexes to existing tables, as well as to alter and delete tables and indexes with SQL statements.

- The Containers collection stores Documents collections. Documents consist of collections of databases and objects stored in database files: TableDefs, QueryDefs, Relationships, Forms, Reports, Scripts (macros), and Modules containers. These collections, with the exception of Relationships, contain the objects listed in the Database window (now called the Database *Container*).

Exposing all of the objects created by Access, plus those created by the Jet engine, is necessary for the future compatibility of Access with Visual Basic for Applications. Chapter 5 of this book, "Understanding Access 2.0's Data Access Objects," explains how you write Access Basic code to take advantage of these new objects.

New Access Basic Reserved Words and Macro Actions

Access 2.0 adds more than 200 new elements to Access Basic and macros. Many of the new reserved words and keywords of Access Basic are the names of newly-exposed objects (reserved words) and collections (key words), and the properties of and methods applicable to these new objects and collections. New events, which are duplicated in Microsoft's list of new language elements as "event properties," also are reserved words. Five new macro actions, `DeleteObject`, `OpenModule`, `OutputTo`, `SendObject`, and `ShowToolbar`, have been added to bring the total number of Access 2.0 actions close to 50. `OutputTo` sends the contents of your table, query, form, or report to a file. `SendObject` is similar to `OutputTo`, but creates an attachment to a Microsoft Mail message instead of to a named file. The marginal Access 2.0 icon identifies new reserved words and keywords used in the code examples of this book.

One of the most useful new events of Access 2.0 is `Error`. The `Error` event is triggered by any error that occurs with a form or report active. You can write an error-handling subprocedure, **Sub** `Form_Error` or **Sub** `Report_Error`, to trap the `Error` event so that you can handle the error with Access Basic code or display a custom message box. The `Error` event is triggered only from forms and reports, not from errors that result from executing Access Basic code.

Extensions to Access SQL

There are about 30 new SQL reserved words in Access 2.0. Some, like `TOP` and `OLEOBJECT`, are specific to Access SQL, while others, such as `MATCH`, `ALL`, and `ANY`, are part of ANSI SQL-92. The most important additions to Access 2.0's version of SQL are the Data Definition Language (DDL) keywords, **CREATE TABLE**, **CREATE INDEX**, **DROP TABLE**, and **ALTER TABLE**. These DDL keywords can create, modify, or delete tables in Access and client-server databases for which you have the required permissions. Using the new DDL keywords is one of the subjects of Chapter 24, "Using Access Wizard Function." Along with the added SQL reserved words, Microsoft has improved the SQL window; it's now a conventional MDI child window (instead of a dialog box) that you select by a mode control button (SQL View) in the Query Design toolbar.

Access 2.0 SQL also adds the UNION reserved word and enables you to create SQL subqueries. UNION queries combine records from more than one query in a single query-result set. SELECT subqueries, which were implemented to a limited extent by nested queries in Access 1.x, are now fully supported by Access 2.0 SQL.

A new concept in SELECT queries is Access 2.0's TOP *n* and TOP *nn* PERCENT queries, which return only the first *n* rows or first *nn* percent of the rows generated by a SELECT query. These new Access SQL modifiers let you dispense with the minutiae and display only the significant information that you specify with a GROUP BY clause. TOP *n* and TOP *nn* PERCENT queries don't run any faster than a conventional SELECT query, but you can minimize network traffic by only returning rows with significant data.

> **NOTE**
>
> Access SQL reserved words also are keywords in Access 2.0, and you should not assign object or Access Basic variable names that are the same as Access SQL reserved words. Using the object and variable naming conventions in Appendix B of this book will solve potential conflicts.

Native SQL Pass-Through for Client-Server Databases

SQL pass-through enables you to send SQL statements directly to a client-server database or to any other type of database or document to which you can connect via the Open Database Connectivity (ODBC) API. The advantage of SQL pass-through is that you can use server-specific SQL dialects, such as Transact-SQL for Microsoft and Sybase SQL Server, or execute stored procedures on the server database. Stored procedures are pre-compiled and optimized queries, stored in the server database, that can accept parameters to alter their behavior. Complex queries often run much faster when executed as stored procedures, rather than by sending SQL statements to the server. Under some circumstances, using SQL pass-through can reduce network traffic.

You had to declare and call the functions in Access 1.1's MSASP110.DLL to pass queries through the Jet engine unaltered for server execution. (Without pass-through, the Jet engine attempted to execute on the server as much of a query as it believed the server could handle.) MSASP110.DLL created a persistent table, then appended records to the table, one at a time, as the query-result set was returned from the server. This was not a fast process, especially when the query returned a large number of rows to a table with many columns. As with MSADDL11.DLL, using MSASP110.DLL required a significant amount of Access Basic code.

Visual Basic 3.0 was the first application to offer SQL pass-through as an option for executing SELECT and action queries. Access 2.0 now provides the same feature. Pass-through query-result sets now appear as (non-updatable **Recordset**) objects. **Recordset** objects are stored in memory (to the extent of available memory), so pass-through is accelerated (greatly in some cases) in Access 2.0.

Customizable Toolbars for Applications

One of the new common objects of Microsoft applications is the generic toolbar object. New and upgraded Windows applications introduced by Microsoft since late 1993 use COMMTB.DLL to implement toolbars, just as almost all Windows applications use COMMDLG.DLL for common dialogs and newer applications use or will use COMMCTRL.DLL for common controls. (In Access 1.x, Access toolbars were stored as forms in UTILITY.MDA.) You can expect to see an increasing variety of common objects, each type implemented by a single DLL, as Microsoft's new operating systems emerge. Although the use of common objects does not greatly reduce the size of mainstream windows applications, which now require, on the average, about 20MB to 30MB of disk space for a full installation, it's a step in the right direction. Using common objects also conforms to good object-oriented programming practices (GOOPPs).

Access 2.0 gives you the option of displaying the standard or a customized version of the Access application toolbar, or of creating special toolbars for your application. Custom application toolbars are stored in your application's system files and are visible only in the application in which you create the custom toolbar. The Customize Toolbars dialog box makes creating application toolbars a quick and easy process. You can use your own bitmapped images for toolbars, and change the buttons description in the status bar and in the new ToolTips captions that appear when you leave the mouse pointer on a button for more than about a half-second. Chapter 26, "Customizing Access Applications with Special Menus and Toolbars," describes how to use this developer-oriented feature of Access 2.0.

Performance Optimization

The overall performance of Access 2.0 is an improvement when compared with Access 1.x. You can expect your Access applications to have more "snap" when run under version 2 of MSACCESS.EXE and MSARN200.EXE than when executed with versions 1.1 of these programs. This book was written using beta versions of Access 2.0, which often contain debugging code and which were not fully optimized for performance. Therefore it is difficult to predict just how much improvement you'll see. In many cases, the speed of Access operations is constrained by Windows itself, rather than by the efficiency of MSACCESS.EXE, MSARN110.EXE, or your application's code.

Microsoft has expended a great deal of time and energy to improve the performance of version 2.0 of the Jet database engine. Rushmore Technology, a query-optimization methodology imported from FoxPro, improves the speed of execution queries against large tables that have the appropriate indexes. Better optimization of queries against client-server databases is another benefit of using Access 2.0. Designing queries for Access client-server front-ends is one of the subjects of Chapter 20, "Front-Ending Client-Server Databases."

New Add-Ins, Wizards, and Builders

Access 2.0 sports 37 add-ins, wizards, and builders; search for Builders in Access 2.0's help system to display a complete list. Most wizards and builders are designed to assist new users of Access 2.0 in creating their first applications, so these features are not given substantial coverage in this book. The Menu Builder, shown in Figure 1.10, however, is oriented to the development community. The Menu Builder, similar in appearance to the Menu Design dialog box of Visual Basic, creates custom menu macros for you automatically. You launch the Menu Builder by clicking the ellipsis button for the MenuBar property of a form or report or by choosing Add-Ins from the File menu, then Menu Builder from the submenu.

FIGURE 1.10.

Access 2.0's Menu Builder.

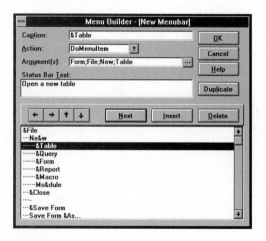

Add-ins and the Add-In Manager also are designed for developers and are similar in concept to Microsoft Excel's .XLA Add-Ins for worksheets. "Add-in" is Access's new term to describe Access libraries designed to perform operations that differ from those of wizards; wizards create database objects for you, while add-ins usually perform operations on existing objects. You choose the add-in you want from the list presented by the Add-In Manager. This simplifies management of add-in libraries supplied by independent software vendors (ISVs.) Add-In Manager, shown in Figure 1.11, automatically makes the required entries in the [Libraries] section of MSACC20.INI, the replacement for MSACCESS.INI of version 1.x. (You need to create your own entries for the [Menu Add-Ins] section and restart Access to make the add-ins operable.) Menu add-ins now appear in the submenu for the Add-Ins choice of the **F**ile menu, rather than as choices of the **H**elp menu.

FIGURE 1.11.

Access 2.0's new
Add-In Manager.

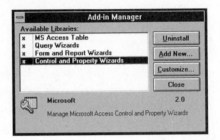

The four add-ins supplied with Access 2.0 are as follows:

■ *Database Documenter*, which provides a printed data dictionary for all of the objects in your Access 2.0 database. Database Documenter replaces the Database Analyzer library (ANALYZER.MDA), supplied with Access 1.x, with a full-featured version. Using Database Documenter is described briefly in the next chapter and in more detail in Chapter 27, "Documenting Your Access Applications."

■ *Attachment Manager*, which enables you to manage the reattachment of attached tables that you or others have moved from their original disk drive or directory to another location.

■ *Import Database*, which automatically imports all of the objects from another database, including Access 1.x databases. This enables you to quickly change the ownership of all of the objects in a database for which you have the appropriate permissions.

■ *Menu Builder*, which creates custom menu macros automatically and which is described earlier in this section.

Most suppliers of Access 1.1 add-ins provide upgraded versions of their libraries, which take advantage of the new features of Access 2.0.

Expanded Documentation for Database Developers

Access 1.x included a small (166-page) booklet, *Introduction to Programming*, that described Access Basic programming methods and used Access Basic code snippets as examples. The ADK included two brief pamphlets, one explaining how to create distribution diskettes for Access applications and the other devoted primarily to describing how to use the `Create...()` functions to develop your own wizards. This documentation was adequate for experienced Visual Basic programmers, but not for those unfamiliar with programming in the Windows environment.

Access 2.0's *Building Applications*, a 400+ page book, replaces *Introduction to Programming*. Building Applications includes chapters describing how to design applications, write Access Basic code, use OLE Automation, secure Access applications, use Access libraries and Windows DLLs, and use the Add-In Manager. The Access Development Toolkit comes with *Advanced Topics*, a complete manual for developing applications that use the runtime version of Access. The Access Basic *Language Reference*, however, is *not* included in the retail version of Access 2.0.

ODBC Driver for Access 2.0 Database Files

Other members of the Microsoft Office suite, such as Microsoft Word 6.0, Excel 5.0, and Project 4.0, rely on ODBC drivers for database connectivity to desktop databases and Microsoft SQL Server. The versions of the drivers supplied with the initial retail versions of Word 6.0 and Excel 5.0 are compatible with Access 2.0 .MDB files. Access 2.0 includes a new ODBC driver for use with Microsoft Office applications that replaces SIMBA.DLL. Microsoft is expected to release a general-purpose ODBC driver for Access 1.1 and 2.0 databases later in 1994.

The Access Developer's Toolkit

Microsoft changed the name of the runtime Access product from the Access Distribution Kit (ADK) to the Access Developer's Toolkit (ADT), because the Access 2.0 ADT contains more than just runtime Access (MSARN200.EXE), the Microsoft Help Compiler (HC31.EXE), and instructions for their use. The additions to the ADT include:

■ A new Setup Wizard for creating distribution diskettes for your runtime applications. The structure of the setup information files for distribution diskettes has undergone a drastic change, which makes manually editing these files difficult. Fortunately, the ADT's Setup Wizard now lets you include as many additional files as you need to complete your applications.

- Several example applications, including versions of Access Wizards that contain commented code. The comments are terse, however, and the structure of the new Form and Report Wizards is even more convoluted than their predecessors. If you fully comprehend the code for the Access Wizards, you qualify as an Access Basic expert.

- Three OLE Custom Controls: Calendar, Scrollbar, and Data Outline. The Calendar and Scrollbar Custom Controls are distributable; that is, you can include them with your runtime applications. The Data Outline Control (AKA "Navigator") has distribution restrictions. (Refer to the license agreement for the ADT.) The OC1016.DLL file, required to use Microsoft and third-party OLE Custom Controls also is provided and is a distributable component.

- A new version of Visual Basic 3.0's VBDB300.DLL that provides Visual Basic developers with a *mapping layer* between Visual Basic 3.0 and Access 2.0's revised .MDB file structure. The mapping layer detects whether the .MDB file is version 1.1 or 2.0, and automatically uses the appropriate Jet DLLs for the .MDB. The Jet DLLs required by Visual Basic 3.0 developers also are included in the ADT. At the time this edition was written, purchasing the ADT was the only means for Visual Basic developers to be able to write applications that manipulate Access 2.0 .MDB files.

- The *Language Reference,* which is no longer included as a component of the Access 2.0 documentation. The Language Reference is indispensable for Access 2.0 developers because of the many new reserved words and keywords added to version 2.0 of Access Basic. You can purchase the *Language Reference* manual directly from Microsoft Corp. if you want to experiment with Access Basic but do not want to purchase the ADT.

- An *Advanced Topics* book describes how to design Access applications for the runtime environment, as well as how to use the components of the ADT. Expanded coverage of using Access with other database types, including client-server databases, is provided. *Advanced Topics* briefly describes how to use the new OLE 2.0 custom controls with Access 2.0 applications.

The Microsoft Access Solutions Pack

Microsoft has published a set of four Access 2.0 applications, called the Microsoft Access Solutions Pack, that you can use as is or modify to suit your own needs. The Access Solutions pack is not included with Access 2.0 or the Access Developer's Toolkit; it is marketed as a Microsoft product. Access developers will find the applications in the solutions pack to be useful in demonstrating the capabilities of Access

2.0 to prospective clients or employers. The Access Solutions Pack also demonstrates interesting approaches to application design; macros predominate in some of the applications, while others rely on Access Basic code for event handling.

Following is a brief description of each of the four Access Solutions Pack applications:

- *Microsoft Access Sales Manager* stores data on sales contacts, tracks sales opportunities, and finds information on both contacts and opportunities. Sales Manager has a built-in time scheduling system, enables you to maintain a history of customer contacts, and can generate mailing lists for form letter preparation with Microsoft Word. Sales Manager demonstrates drill-down methods in transaction-processing applications.

- *Microsoft Access Registration Desk* automates the registration process for seminars, training programs, and similar events. You can preregister attendees and add on-site registrations, and account for paid and owing registration fees. Registration Desk enables you to print badges for attendees and create a mailing list to send letters to registrants and attendees. You also can compile an on-line survey of attendee responses to the event.

- *Microsoft Access Asset* Tracker maintains records and values of fixed assets. You can use Asset Tracker to determine the location and condition of fixed assets, such as computers and peripheral equipment. Asset Tracker also enables you to maintain records on maintenance cost, depreciation, and asset status.

- *Microsoft Access Help Desk* is an application that maintains a log of service requests and their disposition. The sample data supplied with Service Desk is PC-related, but you can use this application for any service-related activity or business.

Why Choose Access 2.0 as a Desktop Database Development Platform?

Developers often do not have the opportunity to choose the desktop RDBMS they use; clients or employers make the choice for them. You may find yourself faced with developing a full-scale Access application for at least one of the following reasons:

- Your client or firm is a "Microsoft-only house" and acquires licenses for new Microsoft products as they are released. In this case, you may be able to make the choice between using Microsoft Access or FoxPro 2.5 for Windows.

- Upper management has adopted Access as the "standard" database application for the firm. You are locked in.

- Your client or supervisor has acquired a copy of Access and has decided to try a pilot or production application to determine whether Access is an appropriate choice for future RDBMS development. You have the opportunity to dissuade him or her from trying Access and instead continuing to use the current RDBMS that is your bread-and-butter product (but only at your peril).

Firms that use client-server RDBMSs, such as SQL Server or ORACLE, may elect to use Access as a replacement for front-end applications that require a per-workstation licensing fee. With the purchase of a $495 Access Developer's Toolkit, developers can create applications for use on an unlimited number of workstations. When this book was written, Access 2.0 and FoxPro 2.5 for Windows had the lowest per-user cost of any networked Windows RDBMS, based on use of the distribution kits available for each product. The present cost advantage of Access may be diminished as competitors lose additional market share to Access 2.0. It is unlikely, however, that PowerBuilder or similar front-end applications will ever reach the pricing point at which they compete head-to-head with Access on the basis of fully-amortized cost per workstation.

If your client or firm enables you to choose the RDBMS for an application, the following sections should be helpful. They supply the reasons that you should select Access rather than a competitive Windows RDBMS as your primary Windows database development platform. If you don't get to choose and you'll be working with Access, the information in these sections may temper your disappointment in having the choice made for you. In the following sections, there is some unavoidable duplication of the information contained in the preceding "What's New" sections, because the new features of Access 2.0 also are incentives to adopt Access as your primary (or only) desktop database and client-server front-end development platform.

Access Minimizes RDBMS Development Cost

The most challenging task facing developers of database applications is estimating the time required to develop, debug, document, and install the application. If you're an independent developer, you need to submit a competitive proposal that includes a realistic application-completion date. Similarly, if you are creating in-house applications, management is likely to insist on a time budget and a deadline for installation of an operable product. In some cases, you'll be working from a detailed specification; in less formal situations, which are common in small firms, you may receive only a vague description of the desired result.

Once you acquire basic skills in designing Access forms and reports, using Access can reduce the time required to create an industrial-strength RDBMS application by a factor of two or better (compared with the equivalent application developed with a conventional character-based RDBMS running directly under DOS). Some of the reasons for this time reduction are as follows:

- Creating forms and reports with control objects selected from Access's toolbox is fast. New Access wizards make creating complex controls, such as combo boxes, list boxes, and option groups, even faster. Drag-and-drop techniques let you link control objects to fields of tables and queries. You can create a prototype form for a complex transaction-processing operation in less than 30 minutes. Simple decision-support forms, including graphs, ordinarily require less than one hour of programming time for all design and testing activities.

- Queries are quick to design and test because of Access's drag-and-drop graphical *query by example* (QBE) methodology. You don't need to use structured query language (SQL) to create Access queries; Access writes the SQL statements for you in a subset of ANSI SQL (with a number of Access-specific SQL keywords added). Access 2.0's new Query Builder appears when you click the ellipsis button of the RowSource property text box of list and combo boxes. You use graphical QBE to create the query, then the Builder inserts the SQL statement for you in the RowSource text box.

- Macros that respond to events with one or more actions that you pick from a drop-down combo box can take the place of Access Basic code in about 95 percent of your applications. On the average, one macro action takes the place of five to 10 lines of xBase or ObjectPAL code. Macros are easy to debug, but not so easy to document. If you prefer writing code, you can use most of the macro actions in Access Basic modules. Access 2.0 displays the Macro Design window when you select Macro Builder from the new Choose Builder dialog box.

- When you use Access Basic code, you'll find that it takes far fewer lines of code to respond to Access events than to perform the equivalent activity with xBase or oPAL code. Much of the structuring of your Access Basic code is imposed by Access itself. This is because you write individual event-handling functions to respond to mouse clicks on command buttons and menus or a change of Windows' focus from one control object to another. When you use the Code Builder to write event-handling subprocedures, Access 2.0 creates the subprocedure stubs for you.

- You add default values and establish validation rules at the table level. Default values are table properties and validation rules are table methods.

Properties and methods of tables are inherited by the queries, forms, and reports that are based on the tables. No code is required to set table properties and methods. You don't need to write VALID statements or functions in Access Basic.

If you're a FoxPro developer and you have the choice of using either FoxPro or Access, you are faced with the decision of whether to port your code to FoxPro 2.5 for Windows, or start from scratch with Access. Form and report design in Access is simpler and faster than in FoxPro. On the other hand, applications written in FoxPro are likely to perform somewhat faster than Access applications, especially with large tables. The difference in performance is less with Access 2.0, because version 2 includes FoxPro's Rushmore indexing technology, which speeds queries on large tables. A full analysis of the trade-offs between the use of FoxPro 2.5 for Windows and Access is beyond the scope of this book. Even the most dedicated FoxPro developers should evaluate Access for creating database applications from the ground up, especially client-server front-end applications.

The choice is likely to be simpler for Paradox 3.x developers who have not yet made the commitment to Paradox for Window. You'll need to rewrite your PAL code to conform to ObjectPAL syntax of Paradox for Windows. Thus you need to decide whether to adopt Paradox for Windows, with its myriad of individual files that make up a database, or switch to Access with its "one file holds all" concept. You are likely to find that the time required to become proficient in using either Paradox for Windows or Access is about the same. Paradox for Windows comes with about six inches of documentation; Microsoft supplies about three inches with Access. Some reviewers have stated that Access's documentation is insufficient. If you need more help in learning Access than the manuals provide, there is a surfeit of introductory-level Access tutorials in almost every bookstore.

Many firms standardize on Microsoft applications for Windows because of price inducements offered with software suites. Software suites are collections of several mainstream Windows applications sold at a deep discount from retail prices. Microsoft Office was one of the first examples of suite-selling and consistently appears on best-selling Windows software lists. Current releases of Windows applications from Microsoft provide tighter integration of cross-application functions with OLE 2.0, as well as greater standardization of the user interface (UI) of suite products. Word 6.0 has built-in query capability and Excel 5.0 includes Microsoft Query, which is derived directly from the graphical QBE features of Access. The more closely Windows applications resemble one another, and the more common programming elements they contain, the flatter your learning curve for developing your own Windows applications.

Object-Oriented Applications and Programming Are Here to Stay

"Object-oriented" is the buzzword of the 1990s for computer programming languages and applications. As mentioned earlier in this chapter, the principal benefit of object-oriented programming (OOP) languages is the ability to reuse blocks of code in a variety of different applications. OOP techniques minimize the duplication of effort when many programmers work on the same application. Using OOP, you reduce the cost of developing applications (at least in theory). Object-oriented programming languages provide the capability to encapsulate properties (characteristics, represented by data) and methods (behavior, usually implemented as programming code) in a single element, a programming object. The object is considered a "black box" with defined properties and methods; you don't need to understand or even see the code or what the code does to the data to use the programming object in an application.

Objects are arranged in hierarchies of classes and subclasses. If you define a class called Persons, you can then define subclasses of the Persons class, such as Employees and Applicants. Your subclasses of the Persons class inherit properties that apply to people, such as name, address, telephone number, and educational background. Subclasses also inherit the class's methods; all members of the Persons class must have at least a first and last name, an address and a telephone number that includes an area code, and a social security number in order to be included. Members of the Employees subclass have additional properties, such as date hired and date terminated, and methods such as the calculation of benefit entitlements. Applicant members might have properties relating to the result of interviews and methods that determine how applicants are ranked in competition for a job opening. Figure 1.12 shows a typical hierarchy of objects for Persons.

FIGURE 1.12.

A typical hierarchy of programming objects.

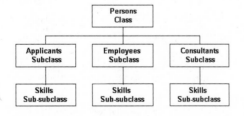

The Skills class shown in Figure 1.12 might be the same function for each of the subclasses of Persons, or you can overload the functions so that the properties of skills or the methods used to categorize skills are different for members of the Applicants, Employees, and Consultants classes.

Programming objects have a third characteristic, *polymorphism*, derived from the Greek word for "having many shapes." Polymorphism enables you to employ different versions of methods, depending upon the status of your application while it is running (this is called *late binding* in some languages). C++ also allows you to overload functions, which means you can have more than one function with the same name. The classic example of overloading is a set of functions with the same name that are capable of performing calculations on different data types. If you declare different arguments for each function, C++ will figure out which function is needed based on the arguments you supply. You cannot overload functions in Access, but Access's `Variant` data type enables you to write code that accomplishes the same objective as overloading. The `Variant` data type is discussed later in this chapter.

Access is not an object-oriented database management system (OODBMS), but Access 2.0 is a truly object-oriented development environment. The full hierarchy of the objects new to Access 2.0 appears earlier in this chapter. `Table` objects, for example, encapsulate properties and methods, and many of these properties and methods are inherited by other database objects that rely on tables, such as queries, forms, and reports, that employ the tables. You can override some table property values, such as `Format`, with properties assigned at the form or report object level; this creates an elementary form of polymorphism.

Even an abbreviated hierarchy of Access database objects is not as simple as that of Persons (shown previously in Figure 1.12). The `Database` object class is a container for all open Access database objects, but the relationship between `Database` objects in Access, illustrated by Figure 1.13, does not follow the top-down structure of Persons. `Table` objects can include embedded or linked OLE objects, which in turn have their own subclasses, determined by the OLE server that created the object. Queries (`QueryDef` objects) inherit properties and methods of the tables on which they are based, but forms and reports can be based either on tables or queries. Control objects, for the most part, are identical for forms and reports, but certain control objects, such as text boxes, inherit different methods (behavior) when used in forms than when employed in reports.

Macros and modules do not appear in the object hierarchy of Figure 1.13 because macros and code in modules supply the methods employed by classes and subclasses of database objects. You can use macros and Access Basic code to alter some of the properties of most database objects (after establishing the default values of object properties), or to determine the methods that control how the objects behave. Access classifies macros and modules as database objects, but you will be better served by considering macros and modules to supply methods to the objects shown in Figure 1.13. Bear in mind that macros cannot be attached directly to table and query objects, but the AutoExec macro (or a macro named on Access's start-up command line), supplies methods to the new **Application** object. The full hierarchy of Access 2.0 objects is described in Chapter 5, "Understanding Access 2.0's Data Access Objects."

FIGURE 1.13.

The hierarchy of some of the Database *objects of Access 2.0.*

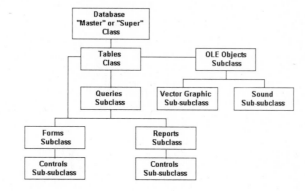

Object Basic, the subject of the next section, provides a new data type, **Variant**, that eliminates the necessity to overload functions to accommodate different data types. The **Variant** data type accommodates any one of nine subtypes, ranging from dates to strings. This makes up for the fact that you can't declare or use multiple functions (or procedures) with the same name in an Access Basic database.

Object Basic: the *Lingua Franca* of Microsoft Applications for Windows

Access Basic, like Visual Basic and Word Basic, is a dialect of Object Basic, the root application-programming language of Microsoft's mainstream software products for Windows. There is no Object Basic language, *per se*; Access Basic, Visual Basic, and Visual Basic for Applications all are dialects of Object Basic. (The Word Basic macro language of Word 6.0 is not yet a truly object-oriented application-programming language.) Bill Gates, Chairman and CEO of Microsoft, has decreed that *all* Microsoft applications that need an embedded programming language will use Microsoft's flavor of BASIC (Embedded Basic was the name given to Access Basic in the early development stage of Access). This is not surprising, considering that Mr. Gates built his Microsoft empire on the foundation of a BASIC interpreter that would run on 4KB of RAM on early microcomputers, such as the original Altair.

Fortunately for xBase and PAL developers, the syntax of Object Basic does not differ greatly from these two languages. All are derived from original Dartmouth BASIC, with keywords added to simplify database operations. All the same flow control statements are available, with just minor modifications (**End If**, instead of ENDIF, for example). Familiar database keywords, such as xBase's **Seek**, perform identical operations in Object Basic and xBase, but Object Basic enables you to qualify **Seek** with operators, such as > or <.

Object Basic, xBase, and PAL were each designed for line-by-line interpreters, not compilers, so you are allowed to commit programming heresies—such as creating variables "on the fly" by implicit declaration—in all three languages. Although Access uses the term "compile" in module menus, compilation in Access means conversion of your source code to a tokenized pseudo-code (p-code) that the Access Basic interpreter can process quickly. The Access Basic interpreter is remarkably fast; the speed of execution of Access Basic code rivals that of equivalent executable code created by C++ compilers.

The scope of variables and their visibility is much like that of xBase and Clipper variables. Object Basic's **Global** keyword substitutes for PUBLIC. Variables declared within procedures (**Sub** or **Function** in Access Basic) are PRIVATE, and values are lost between successive instances of a procedure unless the variable is declared **Static**. Variables declared in the declarations section of a module are visible to all procedures within that module. Note that the convention in Object Basic is upper- and lowercase keywords, not the strict uppercase of the traditional xBase languages.

Microsoft is now in the process of regularizing the dialects of Object Basic. Visual Basic 3.0 and Access Basic resemble one another quite closely; Visual Basic 2.0 introduced data types for database tables and queries (**Dynaset** and **Snapshot** objects). Visual Basic 3.0 includes the Access 1.1 database engine; thus you can develop Access applications in Visual Basic 3.0 Professional Edition or Access 2.0, but you'll need to use attached tables in Access 1.1 format or use the Access ODBC driver if you plan to use both Access 2.0 and your present version Visual Basic 3.0 with Access databases. Visual Basic won't support Access 2.0 databases until Microsoft releases a future version of Visual Basic or provides an upgrade for version 3.0. You choose the development platform based on the unique features it offers that are most significant to your applications. You'll also be able to attach Access 2.0 tables to other applications that support the ODBC API. The Microsoft ODBC Desktop Database Drivers kit provides an ODBC driver that works with Access 1.0 or 2.0 databases. The ODBC driver for Access, RED110.DLL, also is included with Excel 5.0 and Word 6.0.

Microsoft Excel 5.0 and Project 4.0 now use Visual Basic for Applications, one of the Object Basic dialects. All future releases of Microsoft's premier Windows applications, and possibly new Microsoft operating systems, will incorporate dialects of Object Basic, primarily VBA. Word 6.0 users can expect a future upgrade to Word

Basic (the new name for Word 1.x's WordBASIC) that substitutes VBA. Word 6.0 already includes built-in "hooks" to the Access database engine through the ODBC API. Other applications are likely to follow suit. If not, you'll be able to write Object Basic code to add the hooks yourself.

For Access developers, the upshot of this process of regularizing the dialects of Object Basic and implementing Visual Basic for Applications is that much of your code will be reusable, at least with other Microsoft applications for Windows. Thus, if you write a user-defined function in Access Basic, you can import the code into Excel, Visual Basic, or a future version of Word and then use it without significant alteration. Even now, you can import large chunks of Visual Basic 2+ code into Access Basic, and vice-versa, with only minor modifications required. Once you get used to the idiosyncrasies of Object Basic, you'll be ready to program in Excel, Project, and a future version of Word. Microsoft has implemented VBA on the Apple Macintosh versions of Excel and Project, so it's likely that a version of Word with VBA and Visual Basic for the Macintosh will appear in the not-too-distant future.

Access Macros Are a Different Breed of Script

Access macros represent a new approach to application-programming techniques. Traditionally, you create application macros by recording a series of keystrokes and menu choices, and then save the code that represents the actions in a file. When you run the macro from the file, the macro regurgitates the actions, emulating the original keyboard entries and mouse clicks. Applications that employ macros provide macro editors so that you can modify the macros you record, or write macros from scratch.

Macros are called scripts in many applications, including Paradox, and you occasionally see the term "script" used in Access to refer to macros. (The macros you save are referred to in Access 2.0 as the **Scripts** collection.) You cannot record macros in Access; instead, you pick the actions you want the macro to perform from a combo box of available actions. The procedure has similarities to picking WordPerfect macro commands from the list that appears when you press Ctrl+PgUp in WordPerfect for DOS's macro-editing mode. Most Access macro actions require a specific set of qualifiers, called arguments, to determine the object to which the action applies and to specify what the action is to do. Macros in Excel 5.0 and Project 4.0, however, are implemented as VBA code that these two applications write for you. Whether macros and actions will remain in future version of Access or be converted to the Excel and Project approach remains to be seen.

OLE 2.0 and OLE Automation Predict the Future of Windows Applications

Microsoft Corporation published a "white paper" in late 1991 that outlined the firm's strategy to automate complex tasks that require more than one Windows application for completion. One of the elements of Microsoft's strategy is a *common macro language* (CML) for applications, a macro Esperanto. Originally, CML was planned with a menu command-oriented syntax, similar to Word Basic; this concept was replaced by Visual Basic for Applications. OLE 2.0, formally released as a beta version in mid-1993, establishes the framework, called OLE Automation (OA), to implement a considerably-revised version of CML based on VBA. Applications that support OLE 2.0 as servers expose application objects that other OLE 2.0 client applications can manipulate with VBA or other Object Basic dialects. As mentioned earlier in the chapter, Microsoft Graph 5 (included in Access 2.0), Excel 5.0, and Project 4.0 are OLE Automation servers, and Word 6.0 can be used as an OA server, although it is not fully OA-compliant. Access 2.0, Visual Basic 3.0, Excel 5.0, and Project 4.0 are OA clients. The official Microsoft name for objects created by OA-compliant servers is *programmable objects*.

As an example of object programmability, you can write Access Basic code that automatically alters the values of specified cells in a series of Excel worksheets that are linked to OLE Object fields of individual records in an Access Database. Extracting data from a linked or embedded worksheet is a cumbersome, manual process with OLE 1.0. There are a number of other interesting features of OLE 2.0, such as *in situ* editing, that are discussed in Chapter 15, "Embedding and Linking Objects with OLE." Microsoft claims that more than 150 independent software vendors (ISVs), including Apple Computer Inc., Borland International, Aldus Corporation, and Lotus Development Corporation, participated in the development of Microsoft's OLE 2.0 standard for Windows.

In early 1993, Novell, Apple, and IBM formed a coalition to create a different OLE specification in an attempt to prevent Microsoft's OLE 2.0 from becoming a de facto industry standard. Apple, IBM, and Borland are members of the Object Management Group (OMG), an industry organization composed of more than 250 software publishers and user organizations, which published the specification for the Common Object-Request Broker Architecture (Corba) in 1991. Corba determines how objects communicate between applications or over networks, but within a single operating system, such as UNIX. The interchange of objects between different operating systems, such as NeXTStep/OpenStep and Windows/Windows NT, is a future OMG objective. OMG claims that Corba is being supported by more than 50 major firms, but Microsoft is not among them. OLE 2.0 appears to be firmly established as the basic specification for object manipulation in future versions of Windows and Windows NT. With about 50 million copies of Windows in use and OLE 2.0 becoming available for Apple Macintosh systems, it's likely that the Microsoft standard will predominate. While this chapter was being written, Microsoft and Digital Equipment concluded an agreement to create a multi-platform, transportable, object environment based on Digital's ObjectBroker technology.

If you, your clients, or your firm are committed to using Microsoft applications for Windows, you can gain experience with the future "look and feel" of mainstream Windows applications and Microsoft operating systems by using Access. Learning Object Basic programming and becoming comfortable with OLE Automation will pay future dividends when OLE 2.0 becomes an integral component of Windows 4.0 (Chicago) and Windows NT (Cairo).

Access Can Import or Attach a Variety of File Types

Access can import files in dBASE III, dBASE IV, Paradox 3.x and 4.x, Btrieve, Excel, Lotus 1-2-3, and ASCII/ANSI text formats. The ability to import Paradox 4.x is a new feature of Access 2.0. Importing files is a satisfactory solution for a "one-shot" migration from an existing RDBMS application to Access. Most RDBMS applications allow you to import a variety of file formats. Imported worksheet and text files, however, are seldom in the normalized form suitable for relational tables. Normalizing worksheet and text files can be a time-consuming process, especially if you need to update tables with imported data.

In the real world faced by Windows RDBMS developers, single-step migration to an Access application is the exception rather than the rule. You are likely to be called upon to create Windows replacements for existing DOS database applications, often with substantial added functionality. If the existing application is used by several workstations, you need to develop a migration strategy that allows simultaneous operation of the new and existing application during the changeover. This necessitates attaching, rather than importing, files to your new Access database. In the case of client-server databases, you attach only tables.

Attaching dBASE III and dBASE IV .DBF files with .NDX and .MDX indexes is straightforward with Access. Similarly, attaching Paradox 3.x and 4.x .DB files with .PX primary key indexes is easy. The xBase driver of Access 2.0 lets you attach FoxPro indexes. You can import or attach Btrieve files if you have a copy of Novell's WBTRCALL.DLL, a component of the firm's Btrieve for Windows application, or a Btrieve toolkit, such as Smithware's DDF Builder for Windows. Access, however, does not maintain .NTX index files created by Clipper; this is a serious problem for the migration of Clipper applications. Microsoft has announced that its priority for developing new DLLs to manipulate PC RDBMS files is Paradox for Windows and Clipper, in sequence.

> **TIP**
>
> If you need to attach files with Clipper indexes now, consider using the ODBC API with third-party drivers supplied by Pioneer Software, Inc., with its ODBC Driver Pack. You'll have to pay a license fee for each workstation that uses the drivers, but the ability to work with existing database file formats may compensate for the cost. Pioneer's ODBC drivers are discussed in the section, "Current and Future ODBC Drivers," later in this chapter.

If the current application is compiled with Clipper and uses .NTX files, and you have access to the source code and Clipper 5.x, you can substitute DBFNDX.LIB or DBFMDX.LIB to create conventional dBASE .NDX or .MDX files, respectively. You may find that the performance of the Clipper application suffers slightly as a result of using the dBASE indexes. Your Access application is likely to be considerably slower than the Clipper application it replaces, so an interim degradation in the speed of SEEK operations in the DOS version should not be a major consideration.

Attaching Btrieve .DAT files to Access databases requires the availability of the associated Xtrieve FILES.DDF data dictionary file, as well as INDEX.DDF and FIELDS.DDF files for the database. If all the necessary data dictionary files are not available, if the tables are not in the directory specified by FILES.DDF, or if the indexes do not match the field specifications, you receive a "File is corrupt or is not an Access database" message. Chapter 2, "Developing a Design Strategy for Access Applications," includes assistance with problems that occur when attaching Xtrieve databases.

You use the ODBC Administrator application to attach client-server databases to front-end applications that you create with Access. Database front-ends and the ODBC API are the subject of a topic near the end of this chapter and are described in depth in Chapter 20, "Front-Ending Client-Server Databases."

Access Basic Enables You to Use Windows API and Third-Party DLL Functions

Microsoft Windows consists of a relatively small executable application and a collection of dynamic link libraries (DLLs) that Windows applications call upon to obtain necessary services, such as creating a window and positioning the mouse pointer. DLLs contain a collection of functions, written in C, that Windows executable applications call by name. There are more than 500 individual DLL functions that constitute the application programming interface (API) of Windows 3.1. Windows DLLs are similar to executable (.EXE) Windows applications but do not include a main (WinMain) procedure. For example, GDI.EXE, in your \WINDOWS directory, provides the graphic device interface of Windows. Although GDI.EXE has an extension that indicates that it is an executable file, GDI.EXE is really a DLL; you cannot execute GDI.EXE, or any other Windows DLL file, as a stand-alone Windows application.

The advantage of Windows DLLs is that one copy of the DLL serves any number of applications that are running simultaneously. DOS object code libraries must be linked with object code compiled from your source code to create an executable (.EXE) application. Thus, your .EXE file contains a permanent copy of the library. When a Windows application calls a function contained in a Windows DLL, the application attaches an instance (a temporary copy) of the DLL in memory. The attachment is released when the application terminates.

You need to specify the DLL functions that your application will use before you call the function. This process is called declaring function prototypes and is accomplished by adding **Declare Function** or **Declare Sub** statements to the declarations section of your Access Basic modules. All function prototype declarations are global; a function declared in one module is available for use in any other module of your database. Declaring function prototypes is one of the subjects of Chapter 22, "Using the Windows API with Access Basic."

Access Basic Libraries Emulate DLLs

Third-party extensions add new capabilities, such as creating charts and displaying graphic images, that are not offered by xBase RDBMSes. For example, a variety of libraries are available to Clipper programmers in the form of object code that you link with the object code compiled from your own source code. Access offers a similar but more flexible capability in the form of database libraries that carry the extension .MDA. The Wizards that you use to create forms, reports, and graphs are contained in the WZFRMRPT.MDA library supplied with Access 2.0. Builders are included in WSBLDR.MDA, and WZTABLE.MDA contains the basic elements of the Table Wizard.

Access libraries are similar to the Windows DLLs described in the preceding section, but Access libraries do not require that you declare the functions they contain. Instead, you enter a line in the [Libraries] section of your MSACC20.INI file that specifies the name and location of the library and whether you need read-only or read-write access to the library. Access libraries represent the ultimate in late binding of functions (discussed earlier in this chapter); you bind the functions independently of your code. Unlike polymorphic functions of C++, however, you cannot have function names in libraries that duplicate function names in your Access Basic code. When you attach an Access library, the functions it contains are attached to Access itself, not a specific database. Thus, the functions in an attached Access library are available to any database you open.

Access Wizards are libraries that create and manipulate new form, report, and control objects in the open database. Wizards employ Access Basic design-mode methods, such as `CreateForm()`, `CreateReport()`, and `CreateControl()`. The *Advanced Topics* booklet, included in the documentation that accompanies the Access Developer's Toolkit, explains the syntax of these "wizard" method functions. Chapter 24, "Using Access Wizard Functions," shows you how to use these functions to create custom-designed forms and reports.

Access libraries can include any type of `Database` object except macros. The most common use of libraries is to contain Access Basic modules with user-defined functions that are applicable to multiple databases. If you create a variety of database applications that use the same forms or reports, you can include the common forms or reports in a library and make them available to all your database applications. Libraries let you reuse code, and creating libraries can lead to substantial cost savings in developing Access applications. How you create Access libraries is the subject of Chapter 23, "Developing Access Libraries and Add-Ins." A variety of useful third-party libraries are available for Access. Some of the currently-available libraries are described in Chapter 3, "Using Libraries, Wizards, Builders, and Add-Ins," and are listed in Appendix A, "Access Resources."

OLE Simplifies the Incorporation of Non-Traditional Data Types in Databases

Version 1.0 of the Object Linking and Embedding API, abbreviated OLE and pronounced as in the Spanish ¡Olé!, was formally introduced with the release of Windows 3.1. (Before OLE 1.0 was formally announced, several Microsoft applications, including Excel and PowerPoint, incorporated OLE functions to embed graphic images, such as charts and graphs, in worksheets and slides.) Access uses OLE 1.0 or 2.0 to incorporate nontraditional data types, principally graphic images and multimedia objects, in OLE Object fields of Access tables and in unbound object frame controls on forms and reports. Some Windows RDBMSs, such as Paradox for Windows and Superbase, have a field data type specifically devoted to bitmapped graphics. These graphic field data types allow you to incorporate data in a variety of common bitmapped graphics file types, such as .PCX, .GIF, .TIF, and .BMP, in tables. Access does not provide such a graphics field data type, nor does it directly support binary large objects (BLOBs) that may contain data of any type. The simplest method of incorporating graphics in Access is by means of an application that can embed or link a graphic image as an OLE object in a table field of the OLE Object data type.

You need to take Access's extensive use of OLE into account when you are developing applications for clients or your firm. Windows Paintbrush, an OLE 1.0 server, can embed or link graphics files only in .BMP (Windows bitmap) or .PCX (ZSoft) formats. You need an OLE-compliant image-editing application, such as Micrografx Picture Publisher or Corel PhotoPaint, to embed or link bitmapped graphics files with other formats. If you plan to store vector-based graphics, such as images contained in .WMF, .DRW, or .CDR files, in your tables, or to use vector-based images in unbound object frames, you need an OLE-compliant drawing application. Microsoft Draw, (supplied with Word 2.0, but not with Word 6), Micrografx Windows DRAW! 3+ with OLE, and CorelDRAW! 4+ are candidates. Chapter 15, "Embedding and Linking Objects with OLE," describes the use of OLE with Access and how to avoid some of the pitfalls that using OLE entails.

You can embed or link waveform (digital) audio files by using the Sound Recorder applet supplied with Windows 3.1. To incorporate other multimedia objects, such as MIDI music (.MID) and Video for Windows (.AVI) files, you need to replace the Windows 3.1 version of Media Player with the new Microsoft Media Player 3.1. Media Player 3.1 is included on the accompanying diskette. Third-party OLE 1.0 server applications for a variety of graphic and multimedia objects are now available for use with Access, and OLE 2.0 versions of these applications are likely to be available in 1994. Figure 1.14 illustrates linking a Video for Windows (.AVI) clip to an OLE Object field of an Access table.

FIGURE 1.14.

Linking a Video for Windows file with the Media Player 3.1 OLE 1.0 server.

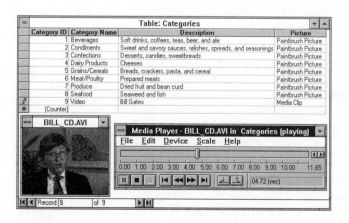

> **TIP**
>
> Each workstation that is used to display graphics or play multimedia objects needs its own copy of the OLE server that is used to embed or link the image to the OLE Object field or to unbound object frames on forms and reports. You can eliminate the necessity for local copies of OLE graphic servers by converting editable OLE graphics objects to static "pictures" in Access. You cannot, however, play multimedia objects without a local copy of the appropriate OLE server. Be sure to include the purchase cost of the necessary OLE server applications when you are preparing a proposal or cost estimate for Access database applications.

The registration database of Windows 3.1 is the key to determining the types of files assigned to OLE servers and how an OLE object responds when you double-click its presentation in a form's bound object frame. To make OLE objects behave the way you want, you need to know how to use the Registration Database Editor (REGEDIT.EXE) in verbose mode. OLE 2.0 makes extensive use of REG.DAT to identify OLE 2.0 servers and their capabilities. Chapter 14, "Understanding OLE 2.0," explains the significance of REG.DAT entries and how to change them with RegEdit.

You can use the OLE Object field to store any type of binary data, such as data from graphics files in any format you choose, if you're willing to write some heavy-duty Access Basic code. Thus, OLE Object fields can become BLOB fields; just disregard the "Invalid Object" presentation in table datasheet view and don't bind the BLOB field to a object frame. Storing data, other than that for OLE Objects in OLE Object fields, is not officially approved by Microsoft, but you can use this technique for special-purpose applications. Chapter 25, "Stretching the Limits of Access," explains how to use OLE Object fields to store and export BLOBs.

Access Is a Powerful DDE Server

Access can use Windows dynamic data exchange (DDE) to obtain data from or supply data to other Windows applications. OLE Automation is designed to replace DDE with a more robust method of inter-application communication. It is likely that your most extensive use of DDE will be to interchange data with spreadsheet applications, such as Excel 4.0, Lotus 1-2-3, and Quattro Pro, none of which support OLE Automation. Access acts as a DDE client when it receives data from another application, called the DDE server. DDE clients and servers have the same relationship as clients and servers in client-server RDBMSs. If you have used earlier versions of Excel or Word as DDE clients, you'll find that Access DDE client operations are quite similar.

Access includes two client DDE functions, DDE() and DDESend(), that can be used to import data from a DDE client to a text box on a form or to poke unsolicited data from a text box to a client. The DDE() and DDESend() functions, however, have very limited flexibility. Using Access Basic DDE functions, such as **DDEInitiate**() and **DDERequest**(), in modules is the recommended approach to implementing DDE. Using DDE, rather than OLE 1.0, enables you to specify the data items, such as a row-column selection or a named range in a worksheet, that are to be imported when you use Access as a DDE client. OLE 2.0 makes DDE a feature that is required only for networked Access applications that require inter-application communication and backward compatibility with non-OA-compliant applications. Therefore, the chapter on DDE in this book is included in Section VI, "Networked and Client-Server Applications."

Where Access stands apart from other database applications is as a DDE server to DDE client applications. Access is not an OA server, so you need to use DDE from other applications to obtain data directly from Access databases. Access has a rich set of commands that DDE clients can use to obtain data from Access database applications. As an example, you can open an Access database and run a query, written in SQL, on the tables it contains, returning selected records from the result of the query to the client application. You use the familiar **DDERequest**() syntax for these operations, not the complex **DDEExecute** statements required by many other DDE servers. You can specify a macro to execute, using a simple **DDEExecute** command; the macro can run a query, execute Access Basic code, or perform any other operation provided by macro actions. Chapter 21, "Employing Access as a DDE Client and Server," explains how to use Access as both a DDE client and server with a variety of other Windows applications.

TIP

If you plan to use either OLE or DDE in your applications, make sure that the workstations on which your applications will run have sufficient memory to execute both Access and the other participating application(s) efficiently. See the section called "System Requirements for Access" at the end of this chapter for some recommendations.

Access Was Designed for Networks and Workgroups

Microsoft released Windows for Workgroups about two weeks before the debut of Access 1.0. Access now has its first major upgrade; Windows for Workgroups 3.11, released in late 1993, is a minor upgrade that provides improved file security and several new (but not compelling) features. The first edition of this book was written under Windows for Workgroups 3.1, and this edition was written under version 3.11. A more significant event that occurred between the first and second editions of this book was the retail release of Microsoft Windows NT Advanced Server and Microsoft SQL Server for Windows NT, both of which are used to demonstrate the client-server database features of Access 2.0 in this edition.

Access is designed for use in a multiuser environment and has specific features that make sharing files among members of designated workgroups a simple process for users of your applications. Smaller firms may find that the need to share Access database files among employees provides the incentive to install a network. Windows for Workgroups is the ideal "starter" network operating system (NOS) for two to about 20 workstations. For developers, the advantage of Windows for Workgroups is that you can install it quickly and easily on existing computers, and the cost for each workstation is quite low, especially if you use conventional thin Ethernet (also called 10BASE2 or "thinnet") cabling.

If your client or firm has a Microsoft LAN Manager, Windows NT Advanced Server, Novell NetWare, or Banyan VINES network installed, Windows for Workgroups can provide local peer-to-peer file and printer sharing under the existing network. Windows for Workgroups also includes network versions of File Manager and Print Manager, a simplified version of Microsoft Mail for workgroup messaging, Schedule+ (a workgroup scheduling application), a couple of utilities for determining network utilization, and a four-handed Hearts game designed to be played from four different workstations. Access 2.0 now is mail-enabled; that is, you can send the data contained in a table, returned from a query, or from a form or report as an attachment to a Microsoft Mail message with a menu choice (**F**ile Sen**d**) or from Access Basic code. You can create Access applications that interact with Schedule+ using Microsoft's Schedule+ Access Library (SAL) that you can download from the Windows Extensions Forum (GO WINEXT) on CompuServe as SAL.ZIP.

One of the most important features of Windows for Workgroups is the capability to transfer data stored in the Windows Clipboard over the network. This enables you to conduct NetDDE operations with applications installed on other workgroup computers. Prior to the release of Windows for Workgroups, DDE operations were limited to application topics (files) residing on a single computer. Using NetDDE is one of the subjects covered in Chapter 21.

Whether your firm or your client uses a peer-to-peer or a server-based network, the technique for creating workgroups that share one or more database applications is the same. The database(s) and the SYSTEM.MDA file associated with the database(s) are placed in a shared directory on the designated server. Access 2.0 includes an improved version of Access 1.x's Change Workgroups application called the Workgroup Administrator. Your application's .MDB file stores the permissions that are granted to workgroup members to read and edit data, as well as to run queries and macros. Permissions are assigned by members of the Admins (administrators) group to members of the Users and Guests (occasional users) groups. You can combine the security features provided by Access with those afforded by the network operating system to maintain strict control over those who can use your database application. Chapter 19, "Networking Secure Access Applications," explains how you set up Access on a network and how to implement a secure Access database.

WARNING

Do not use the security features of Access until you have a full understanding of how these features work. It is possible to lock yourself out of the database you are creating. Make diskette backup copies of your SYSTEM.MDA and database files before you add security features. Chapter 19 provides additional details on how to circumvent accidental implementation of security features that prevent you from opening or modifying your own applications.

Power Users Can Develop Their Own Queries, Forms, and Reports

One of the principal reasons that many firms have chosen Access as their "standard" RDBMS is the capability of users to create their own applications to query tables in existing databases or to create their own databases by importing data from existing applications. Power users of other Windows applications, such as Excel, have demonstrated that they can learn the basics of Access and start attaching tables and running queries in less than one day. Off-loading development of simple *ad hoc* queries from application support groups to the end user is one of the objectives of the downsizing process.

Most power users are able to create simple Access forms and reports, but they are unlikely to have the time to develop full-scale Access applications for their own use.

There are two opportunities for available to independent and in-house developers in this case:

■ The creation of Access database "shells" to attach and provide appropriate permissions for tables in external databases. Users who write their own queries or applications should have their own database to contain the objects they create. In most cases, tables will be attached from other databases.

■ The completion of applications begun by power users, especially members of management. Once a user has created the skeleton of the application and determined that the query design returns the desired result, you, the developer, can turn the skeleton into an industrial-strength application by adding necessary macros and Access Basic code, and dressing up the design of forms and reports.

Independent developers can expect a substantial portion of their revenue from Access to derive from the completion and expansion of user-initiated designs.

Access Applications as Client-Server Front-Ends

The trend toward downsizing mainframe database applications to client-server databases running on PC and now RISC (reduced instruction set computing) servers has created a substantial market for Windows front-end development applications. Most of these front-end development applications accommodate a variety of back-ends (servers), but some are designed specifically for a single software publisher's product, such as SQL Server or ORACLE. Access uses Microsoft's Open Database Connectivity (ODBC) API to attach client-server database tables.

The ODBC API, announced by Microsoft in November 1991, is a set of functions designed primarily to allow you to navigate (browse) client-server databases and to create queries based on their tables. The ODBC was the first component of the Windows Open Services Architecture (WOSA); Microsoft released version 1.0 of the ODBC API in the form of a software development kit (SDK) in November 1992, and ODBC 2.0 was in the beta test stage at the time this book was written. The ODBC functions comply with standards created by the SQL Access Group's (SAG) Call Level Interface (CLI) specification established in 1991. SAG is an industry association of about 40 major firms that publish and use client-server database products. Conformance to SAG's CLI specification is now *de rigeur* for all client-server front-end applications. Figure 1.15 shows the new ODBC Administrator application supplied with Access.

FIGURE 1.15.

*The ODBC
Administrator
window, used to
add new data
sources.*

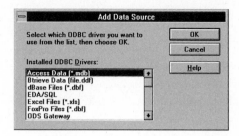

Microsoft's ODBC API supports both ISAM and client-server databases with individual drivers for each type of database from which you want to attach tables. The ODBC driver manager loads the driver that you specify in the ODBC Administrator's window for an individually named data source. The data source includes information on the tables to be attached, the RDBMS in which the tables reside, and the network used to connect to the RDBMS. The ODBC driver submits SQL statements to the data source, then returns results to Access.

Current and Future ODBC Drivers

Only one ODBC driver is included with the retail version of Access 2.0, the driver for Microsoft and Sybase SQL Server. Access 1.1 added an ODBC driver for ORACLE databases; however, Oracle Corp. has taken over the support and development of ODBC drivers for its RDBMSs. Microsoft has released ODBC drivers for Access, Paradox, Btrieve, and dBase III and IV databases, as well as Excel and text (ASCII) files in the Microsoft ODBC Desktop Database Drivers kit.

Pioneer Software, probably best known for its Q+E database application (which was included with Microsoft Excel versions prior to 5.0), supplies an ODBC Driver Pack that includes ODBC-compliant drivers for more than 40 desktop and client-server RDBMSs. If you need an ODBC driver that Microsoft does not supply, Pioneer Software is the logical source. Suppliers of other ISAM and client-server databases often provide ODBC drivers for their products. For example, drivers are available for IBM DB2/2, Watcom SQL, MicroRim R:BASE SQL Engine, QuadBase SQL, and DataEase Express for Windows. See Appendix A, "Access Resources," for further details on Pioneer's ODBC Driver Pack and other third-party ODBC drivers.

Competitors in the Client-Server API Arena

The only serious competition on the horizon for Microsoft's ODBC API is Borland International's Integrated Database API (IDAPI), previously known as the Object Database API (ODAPI). ODAPI was an element of the proposed Borland Object

Component Architecture (BOCA) announced in early 1992, apparently in reaction to Microsoft's WOSA white paper. ODAPI was originally intended to create a standard API for Borland's Interbase database, which is currently available in versions that run under UNIX and on Digital Equipment Corporation's VAX systems. IBM, Novell, Oracle, Computer Associates, WordPerfect Corporation, and 16 other firms joined with Borland to support ODAPI, rechristening the pending specification IDAPI.

The still-forthcoming IDAPI product appears to duplicate Microsoft's ODBC; IDAPI is based on the same SAG CLI as the ODBC API and promises to provide access to both client-server and ISAM databases. Pioneer Software states that its ODBC-compliant drivers are also IDAPI-compliant, despite the fact that the IDAPI specification had yet to be published at the time this edition was written. Competition between the ODBC API and IDAPI appears to be following the same pattern as that for forthcoming e-mail standards. Microsoft offers their Messaging API (MAPI), which is used in Microsoft Mail and Windows for Workgroups; Lotus, together with many of the same members of the IDAPI axis, is attempting to garner industry support for its Vendor-Independent Messaging (VIM) API. Access 2.0's mail-enabling features include support for VIM.

The Access Developer's Toolkit

The Access Developer's Toolkit (ADT) is a necessity for developers of Access applications. In addition to the runtime executable version of Access 2.0, MSARN200.EXE, the ADT includes the Microsoft Help Compiler (HC31.EXE, a DOS application), documentation that describes how to write help files for Windows applications, and the syntax of the Access wizard functions. It also includes a runtime version of GRAPH5.EXE that lets the user display (but not create or edit) graphs. SETUP.EXE, STFSETUP.EXE, and the required supporting files for installing your Access application enable you to emulate the standard Microsoft setup procedure for applications such as Access, Excel, and Visual Basic. The new features of the ADT are described earlier in this chapter.

Designing Access Applications for Distribution

The Access runtime executable file, MSARN200.EXE, substitutes for MSACCESS.EXE, supplied with the retail version of Access. MSARN200.EXE hides the design view of windows for all database objects. (The windows exist, but they are not displayed.) The Database window is minimized and its icon is hidden. Thus, any application that you distribute with the ADT requires an AutoExec macro (or a macro specified on the command line for MSARN200.EXE) in order to open the startup form. MSARN200.EXE removes the toolbars and deletes menu choices that relate to design operation. You can use custom toolbars, menu macros, and the `DoMenuItem` macro action to perform menu commands that do not appear in the default runtime menus. You can employ the techniques described in Chapter 26, "Customizing Access Applications with Special Menus and Toolbars," to create your own custom toolbars, and then set the Show Toolbar option to Yes with an Access Basic routine that sets the properties of the **Application** object to display the toolbars.

When you supply database applications with runtime Access, you create a special version of the MSACC200.INI file with a new name. This prevents your application from overwriting the existing MSACC200.INI files of users who have installed the retail version of Access. MSARN200.EXE adds a new section, `[Runtime Options]`, to your application's private .INI file and recognizes three options in this section, `TitleBar=`, `Icon=`, and `HelpFile=`. These option lines specify, respectively, the text that appears in the title bar of the MDI parent window of your application, an icon (in the form of an .ICO file) that appears when your application is minimized, and the name of the help file for your application.

You don't need to distribute a SYSTEM.MDA file with your application, because the Setup application creates a unique SYSTEM.MDA file for each installation. Using the security features of Access ensures that users cannot accidentally or intentionally modify your database objects. Chapter 29, "Distributing Runtime Versions of Your Databases," provides details on the security concepts applicable to Access applications that are designed for distribution.

Command-line parameters to compact and repair databases have been added to the syntax for running MSARN200.EXE. You can create a Program Manager program item that users can double-click to defragment a database with the syntax `msarn200.exe database.mdb /Compact`. Substitute or add `/Repair` to the command line to repair a damaged .MDB file.

Creating Help Files for Applications

You need to create at least a minimal help file for your distribution application so that the Help menu choices are operable and so that pressing the F1 key does not result in an error message. At the minimum, you need a single contents window. You display a copyright message in a form in response to the About... choice of the Help menu with a form and Access Basic code.

The Microsoft Help Compiler for the Windows 3.1 WinHelp engine, HC31.EXE, compiles help text files in rich text format (.RTF). Thus, you need a word processing application, such as Word 2.0 or 6.0, that can save files in .RTF format. Word 1.x creates .RTF files that are incompatible with some of the features of HC31.EXE, so you need to upgrade if you are still using Word version 1.x.

There are several commercial applications that can aid you in writing WinHelp files. You should not even consider writing a help file with more than 10 or 20 windows without the aid of a "help crutch." Chapter 28, "Writing Help Files for Access Applications," uses WexTech Systems' Doc-to-Help 1.5 application to show you how to create commercial-quality help files without becoming lost in footnotes and context ID strings.

Using STFSETUP.EXE

If you've ever wondered about the specifications for the SETUP.INF or STFSETUP.INI files that are included on the distribution diskettes for Windows applications, you'll have the chance to translate them with the aid of the ADT's documentation. Installation of a runtime application requires a specific collection of files on distribution diskettes 1 and 2. MSARN200.EXE and a number of other required files, as well as your .MDB and private .INI file, can be supplied on any diskette you choose. You can supply compressed versions of the files (use COMPRESS.EXE on your .MDB file), and STFSETUP.EXE will expand them automatically. STFSETUP.EXE installs the OLE 2.0 DLLs that are required to run Access 2.0 applications. Chapter 24 of this book supplements the ADT documentation with tips for optimizing Access applications for distribution.

System Requirements for Access

The Microsoft Access User's Guide for Access 1.1 stated that Access could be used with computers having 2MB of RAM, but that 4MB "is recommended." You can launch Access 2.0 on a computer with 4MB of RAM, but that's about all you can do. Even with the recommended 6MB of RAM, an uncommon configuration, you may find the performance of Access 2.0 to be unsatisfactory, especially with large applications or those applications that employ DDE or that use OLE servers with graphic and multimedia objects. 8MB of RAM is the practical minimum for Access developers, and 16MB is recommended for development (especially if you use OLE Automation).

Disk space requirements differ for retail versions of Access that are installed on computers used for application development and for workstations on which the runtime version of Access is installed. These requirements are discussed in the two sections that follow. Using a permanent Windows swap file on computers running Access in enhanced mode improves performance, especially with large tables. (Chapter 29 provides recommendations for the size of permanent swap files.)

The files that are used for adding features of Windows 3.1 that are required by Access to existing installations of Windows 3.0 (COMMDLG.DLL, DDEML.DLL, OLECLI.DLL, OLESVR.DLL, SHELL.DLL and VER.DLL) total about 300K. If Windows 3.1 is installed, existing versions of these files in \WINDOWS\SYSTEM will be overwritten by the new versions on the distribution diskettes. Otherwise, Setup adds these files to the \WINDOWS\SYSTEM directory. The OLE 2.0 files total about 1.5MB. In the sections that follow, it is assumed that Windows 3.1 is installed on the workstations and development computers.

Minimum Requirements for Workstations

Installation of the runtime version of Access on workstations requires free disk space in the designated application directory approximately equal to the minimum installation of Access, about 5MB plus the space required by your .MDB and .HLP file(s). In addition, you need about 1.6MB in the \WINDOWS\MSAPPS\MSGRAPH5 directory for the runtime version of GRAPH5.EXE (if the retail version of GRAPH5.EXE has not been installed). For program installation, about 10MB of free disk space, plus the .MDB and .HLP space requirement, is a safe number. If you've already installed an OLE 2.0 application, deduct about 1.5MB from the preceding numbers.

> **TIP**
>
> If your application requires using an OLE server to manipulate graphics or multimedia objects, the server's disk space requirement must be included in your computations.

Most workstations can execute small runtime Access 2.0 applications (.MDB files 1MB or less in size) satisfactorily with 8MB of RAM, if users do not have any other mega-apps open. Install 12MB to 16MB of RAM if your application uses DDE, employs OLE servers, or otherwise requires that more than one mega-app (an application with an .EXE file exceeding 1MB in size) be run simultaneously. Although firms usually are loathe to upgrade workstations, the cost of an additional 4MB of RAM is less than $200 at today's street prices. The investment in additional RAM is repaid quickly by efficiency increases. 12MB or 16MB of RAM also is recommended for workstations that attach very large client-server tables. This enables you to increase the size of the buffer memory that is dedicated to Access applications. Chapter 29 includes recommendations for buffer allocation for large Access or attached tables.

All workstations running Access applications should be equipped with VGA displays, preferably with a maximum dot pitch of 0.28 mm. The default font size for Access's datasheet views is 8 points. Using a small font allows more data to be presented in a window. Conventional VGA mode, 640-by-480 pixels with 16 colors, is adequate for applications that do not involve bitmapped images with 256 or more colors. 8-point type is quite readable on conventional 13- and 14-inch VGA displays at normal viewing distances (approximately 18 inches) by all but the most myopic of users. Noninterlaced displays are recommended, because they reduce flicker-induced fatigue. However, most organizations are even more reluctant to upgrade workstation displays than to add additional memory. They fear that replacing a monochrome with a color display or providing a larger display for one operator will result in similar requests from all others, regardless of need.

> **TIP**
>
> Do not install 256-color drivers for SVGA adapters if you do not need the 256-color palette for graphic objects. Unless a windows accelerator card is installed on the workstation, using the 256-color palette slows the redrawing of windows appreciably. You can demonstrate the difference in performance by using the Visible property to show and hide forms in your application. Showing a hidden form requires about twice the time with the 256-color driver than with the 16-color driver.

Recommendations for Development Systems

You need a minimum of about 20MB to install the retail version of Access on computers that are presently running Windows 3.1 if you have not installed another OLE 2.0-compliant application, such as Excel 5.0. A total of 30MB to 40MB of free disk space is a safe figure for computers that will use the retail version of Access with all of its features.

Developers also need to install the runtime version of Access so that they can test applications designed for distribution with the ADK. Runtime Access requires an additional 5MB or so of disk space, bringing the total requirement to about 25MB for developers, plus the space required to hold the sizable .MDB files you create. You'll need additional free disk space to hold images of the distribution diskettes for your

Access applications, too. Chapter 29 provides tables that list disk space requirements for these files.

The absolute minimum for developers is 8MB of RAM, and you may find that you want to install 12MB so that you can increase Access's buffer size to the maximum of 4MB with the MaxBufferSize= entry in the [ISAM] section of MSACCESS.INI when you are dealing with large attached tables, complex queries, or forms that you hide rather than close (to speed performance).

You'll find that one of the best investments you can make as an Access developer is a larger video display unit. Moving and aligning control objects on forms and reports requires precise positioning of the mouse pointer. A 17-inch noninterlaced display with 0.28-mm dot pitch or smaller, operated in VGA mode (640-by-480), gives you the resolution you need to select control objects easily. Using 800-by-600 mode with a 17-inch display enables you to cascade multiple windows and still read the 8-point MS Sans Serif font. You can speed development operations by installing a Windows graphics accelerator card or employing a computer with local bus video (LBV) that conforms to the Video Electronics Standards Associations (VESA) specifications.

> **TIP**
>
> Remember that you need to develop applications that are compatible with the lowest common denominator of Windows workstations, 640-by-480 VGA on 13- and 14-inch displays. Be especially careful when adding special effects, such as shadows, to text boxes and object frames. Your shadow may not appear the same in 640-by-480 mode as it did in 800-by-600 or 1024-by-768 mode. Test all applications fully in plain vanilla VGA mode before you release them.

2

Developing a Design Strategy for Access Applications

To develop a successful Access database application for your clients or your firm, you must plan thoroughly before you create the first table or form. Because Access is designed for rapid application development (RAD), the planning process may take more of your time and effort than implementing the application. The retail version of Access 1.x came in a box that referred to it as "the database that's hard-working without the hard work." Implementing a well-designed information system founded on one or more properly structured relational databases is easier with Access than with Access's DOS or Windows competitors, but implementation is only one of the elements involved in creating a database application. The really hard work consists of designing the database application so that the application achieves the objectives you and your client or firm establish, then testing the application to make sure that these objectives are met. This chapter describes the database design process and explains how the characteristics of Microsoft Access and the Access Developer's Toolkit (ADT) affect the design and implementation of your database application.

Understanding the Database "Life Cycle"

The process of developing an Access database application—or any other information system—involves the following four main steps:

1. Defining your objectives.
2. Determining a plan to achieve the objectives.
3. Executing the plan.
4. Evaluating the results to determine whether execution of the plan met your original objectives.

In the field of computer software development, this process commonly is formalized into a five-step software life cycle, as follows:

1. Specify your objectives.
2. Design the application to meet your objectives.
3. Implement the design, in this case with Access database objects.
4. Test your implementation and verify that data integrity is maintained.
5. Maintain and upgrade the production application.

Commercial application software for Microsoft Windows (such as Access, Word, and Excel) consists of an executable file and supporting components, such as Windows dynamic link libraries and help files. Developers of application software don't have to worry about the specific needs of individuals who will use the software; the application simply must satisfy the requirements of most users (or potential users) of the application. It is up to each person who buys the software to install the application and then create the data structures, such as worksheets or word processing documents, with the application.

The software life cycle for a specific database application is more complex than for the application software. The developers, not the users, of database applications most often are responsible for creating the database structure and the application elements (forms and reports) that make up the application. Developers are responsible for creating and maintaining virtually all multiuser database applications. In most cases, the database developer is responsible also for installing the application, training users or support personnel, and verifying that the application operates correctly. Thus, the database life cycle consists of the following seven basic steps:

- Specify the objectives of the database application. The specification should be a carefully crafted statement of the purpose of the application, the benefits expected to be obtained through use of the application, and the anticipated cost of application development. This phase of the database life cycle is often called "systems planning and analysis." The specification phase may involve investigation of the overall needs of the firm for information management and how the database application integrates with the firm's goals.

- Design the database structure and the methods of entering, editing, and viewing the data contained in the database. The three phases of database application design are to create a conceptual model (schema) of the database, to apply (map) the conceptual model to the RDBMS that will be used, and to lay out the sequence and content of the forms and reports based on the data. You create the data dictionary for the application during the third phase.

- Implement the design by creating the necessary database(s) and tables, queries, forms, and reports. Implementation includes writing the macros (or, preferably, Access Basic code) that control data flow, enforce relational integrity (if necessary), and maintain domain integrity in the application.

- Test the application with a prototype database to verify that the application meets the stated objectives and that data integrity is maintained. Generally, you involve prospective users of the application in the test phase to get independent verification that user expectations are met. Online help systems usually are created during the testing stage because you can determine the areas of the application with which users need help. The test phase often takes more time and effort than the implementation phase.

■ Install the production version of the application at the site. With multiuser applications, you need to install runtime Access on each client workstation and install the database on a peer-to-peer or dedicated file server. The network or database administrator establishes network security restrictions and database permissions for users during the installation phase. If your application is to be installed at remote sites, you create a Setup application to automate the installation process.

■ Train the users and administrators of the application. Database developers often are responsible for training users or support personnel to operate the application. Large firms often require formal training sessions that only you, the developer of the application, are qualified to conduct. To establish a secure database system, database administrators need to understand fully the labyrinthine security features of Access.

■ Maintain the application after its release as a production database. The three categories of application maintenance are corrective (eliminating bugs in the application), adaptive (modifying the application to conform to changes in the operating environment), and perfective (adding new features to the application, based on requests by users). The maintenance phase also includes periodic review and analysis to determine whether the application meets the stated objectives. Maintenance costs of large commercial database applications often reach 50 percent of the lifetime project cost.

The seven database life cycle phases constitute the principal items of a proposal or budget for the database application. The ability to estimate accurately the time needed to complete each phase of the life cycle can be gained only through experience. You can increase the accuracy of the estimate by breaking each phase of the database life cycle into individual elements, each with its own milestones and resource requirements. You may also need to reiterate a series of steps in one life cycle several times before your application is truly bulletproof. By using computer-aided software engineering (CASE) tools to create the conceptual design and by mapping the design to an Access database, you can save a substantial amount of time in the first two phases of the database life cycle. Later in this chapter, you learn about using CASE tools with Access.

The most uncertain part of your estimate is likely to be the implementation phase, especially if you are in the process of learning Access. If this is your first venture into the Windows environment, but previously you have used CA-Clipper or Paradox to develop character-based database applications for DOS, base your budget or proposal on the time needed to create the equivalent DOS-based application. After you become familiar with Access, you are likely to find that the implementation phase for an Access database application takes about half the time needed for an equivalent DOS product.

TIP

Project management applications, such as Microsoft Project, simplify the development of a proposal or budget for creating or migrating database applications. Project management applications quickly enable you to create PERT charts and Gantt diagrams that describe the development process in a time-based format. And project management applications can provide periodic performance reports that compare achievements to targeted milestones and actual costs to budgeted costs.

If you're converting an existing database application to Access, you may be tempted to bypass the specification and design stages of the application life cycle. Many database applications have been developed without the formal methodology of the database life cycle. These database applications often lack proper documentation; some databases may lack a data dictionary that fully describes the tables contained in the database and the way the tables relate to one another. Ad hoc maintenance of the application is likely to result in data structures that do not comply fully with the normalization rules of relational databases. Converting (often called migrating) a database application to a new RDBMS gives you the opportunity to correct deficiencies in the structure and documentation of the application and to create a professional, maintainable product.

Designing the Database Structure

The theory of the relational database model first appeared in Dr. E. F. Codd's paper, "A Relational Model of Data for Large Share Data Banks," published in the June 1970 issue of *Communications of the ACM*, a journal of the Association for Computing Machinery. Ever since the publication of this paper, controversy has raged about the benefits of the relational model versus the CODASYL (Committee for Data Systems Languages) network model versus the hierarchical model (such as IBM's IMS, which uses the DL/I language). Although the overwhelming majority of new DBMS installations are based on the relational model, many network and hierarchical databases are still used on mainframe and minicomputers. Many of these network and hierarchical databases are called legacy databases. Most legacy database programs are written in COBOL, a language developed by the Committee for Data Systems Languages.

IBM's San Jose Research Laboratory began work on a language called SEQUEL (for Structured English QUery Language) shortly after Dr. Codd, an IBM employee at the time, published his famous paper. The prototype SEQUEL language ultimately evolved into a final IBM version called SQL. IBM's first commercial relational database product, released in 1981 and called SQL/DS, used SQL as its application programming interface (API). (The pronunciation of the term SQL is the subject of some debate—most database developers use "sequel" or "seekel," but purists insist on "ess cue ell," to distinguish SQL from SEQUEL.)

The mathematical theory of relational databases and the details of the process required to normalize data to meet the five normal forms of relational tables are beyond the scope of this book. Many tutorial books and college-level texts are available on the subject of relational database design. In this book, however, most of the examples that involve queries emphasize the use of SQL. The reason for the emphasis on SQL rather than on graphical QBE becomes clear when you reach the section called "Creating Ad Hoc Queries for Runtime Applications," later in this chapter. The sections that follow describe the elemental principles of database design, not the step-by-step details for implementing an Access relational database structure.

Formalized Database Design Procedures

Most experienced database application developers can design an adequate relational database structure without going through a formalized design process. Data structures that are applicable to the most common types of databases for commercial application are remarkably similar. The structure of the Northwind Traders sample database is similar to thousands of other databases used by brokers, distributors, and manufacturers. All that is missing is an Invoices and Invoice Details table, so that Northwind can bill its customers when the order is shipped and place unfilled items on back order. Often, however, explaining the design of the database to a client or supervisor who is not conversant with database theory is quite difficult. Primary and foreign keys, relationships, tuples, domains, constraints, and the other esoteric terms commonly used in relational database design have little or no meaning in the real world of business and commerce. If you speak "Relational" and your clients or co-workers do not, getting meaningful information from clients or co-workers to ensure an artful database design can be equally difficult.

NOTE

The Northwind Traders sample database is not normalized optimally. For example, the Orders table includes a shipping address that, for about 90 percent of the records, duplicates the billing address fields of the Customers table. Data in the Ship Address, Ship City, Ship Region, Ship Postal Code, and Ship Country fields is duplicated for every order placed by the customer. Although Northwind seems to deal primarily with small firms, some of Northwind's customers might open an additional location or even expand to become a mini-chain of delicatessens. If orders are placed from and billed to a central location, you need to be able to create more than one shipping address for the same Customer ID. To create a new Shipping Locations table with the Customer ID and the Ship Address fields for customers whose shipping addresses differ from their billing address, follow these steps:

1. Replace the Ship Address field of the Orders table with Null values where the shipping and billing address are the same.

2. Create a code, such as CustomerID plus "01," for firms whose billing and shipping addresses differ, add the code for each entry to the Shipping Locations table, and make the field containing the code the primary key field.

3. Add the corresponding code to the Ship Address field of records of the Orders table.

4. Delete the Ship City, Ship Region, Ship Postal Code, and Ship Country fields.

Duplicated data is a typical problem that arises when you fail to use formalized database design procedures.

As a database developer, you need to give other participants in the database specification and design process a view (perspective) of the data that they can understand. By using a formalized procedure and a set of English-language constructs, such as ServerWare, Inc.'s Formal Object-Role Modeling Language (FORML), you can describe in everyday English the content of tables, the relations between tables, and constraints on field values, at least during the specification and design stages of the database life cycle. The five views of data, based on Asymetrix Inc.'s definitions in *A Guide to FORML*, and the relationship of each view to the phases or elements of the database life cycle are listed in Table 2.1.

Table 2.1. A formal representation of the views of a database application.

View	Definition
External	A view of the data common to everyone involved with the database, from upper management to people who are not employed by the client or firm but have a role in the database system (such as employees of supplier firms). The external view is independent of the database application, the characteristics of the database management system, and the type of computer on which the application runs. You must be able to express an external view of the data in natural, everyday English. The external view and the objectives of the specification phase of the database life cycle often are identical.
Conceptual	A view of the data that is common to participants in the database design process: information system managers, developers, and end users. The conceptual view defines, as a set of facts, the requirements of the firm and the users of the database application. These facts can be articulated in structured, formal English terms and in diagrams called conceptual schema. The conceptual view also is independent of the resources needed to implement the database application. The conceptual view is the first element of the design phase of the database life cycle.
Logical	A view of the data that the database developer uses to specify which tables to include in the database, the fields of the tables, the relations between the tables, and the constraints on the data values that may be contained in the fields. The logical view is dependent upon the classification of the database system, in this case a relational DBMS, but not on the specific database management system that is to be used. The expression of the logical view in relational terminology is a data dictionary. In diagrammatic form, the logical view is called a logical (or database) schema. The logical view is the second element of the design phase in the database life cycle.

View	Definition
Physical	A view of the data determined by the RDBMS chosen to implement the database application. The physical view of an Access database consists of the design view of each table in the database, and the properties and methods applicable to the table and its fields. Creation of the physical view of the database is the first element of the implementation of the database application.

These views define the set of steps that lead to the implementation of a relational database (Access or other) on a workstation or file server. The eight steps involved in database design using ServerWare's FORML are shown in Figure 2.1. The objects (more properly, object types) in Step 4 of Figure 2.1 are data entities and attributes; facts describe the relationships between the attributes and entities; constraints are the set of valid data values for an object. In Access databases, constraints are imposed on field (object) values by validation rules.

FORML expresses the conceptual database design in simple English sentences such as "Instructor (Id) teaches Course (Id)." Instructor is the object of the sentence and teaches Course is the predicate; Course is a predicate object. The converse of this structure is the reflexive form: "Course (Id) is taught by Instructor (Id)." The logical implementation of either of these sentences is two tables, Instructor and Course, each with a primary key field, Id, and a one-to-many relation between the Instructor.Id and Course.Id fields. FORML sentences are the basis of the object-role modeling (ORM) diagrams described later in the chapter.

Application and Database Diagrams

Several modeling and diagramming methodologies are available for designing relational databases. The following sections describe data-flow diagrams and entity-relationship diagrams, as well as a new approach to conceptual modeling of information systems. The sequence of the three sections that follow is the order in which the programming community adopted them, not the sequence in which you apply the diagrams during application design.

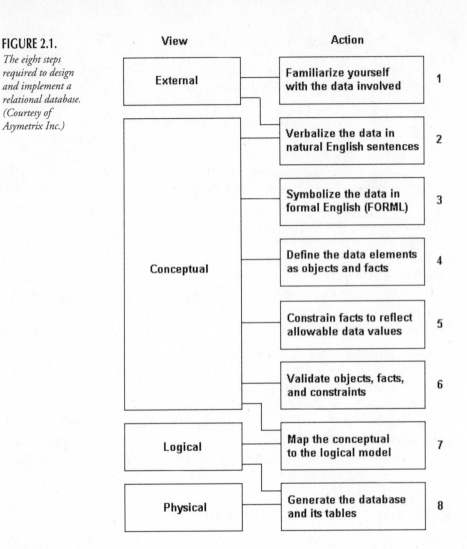

FIGURE 2.1.

*The eight steps
required to design
and implement a
relational database.
(Courtesy of
Asymetrix Inc.)*

Data-Flow Diagrams

Traditional data-flow diagrams can be used with any kind of computer program, not just database applications. Data-flow diagrams were introduced early in the history of computer programs; the symbols that are used have changed little since the 1950s. Data-flow diagrams are process-oriented, not data-oriented. They model the behavior of the database application by defining the sequence of events that lead to adding new records to a database or updating the existing records, displaying the data in a meaningful way, and printing useful reports from the data. Relationships between tables need not be identified in data-flow diagrams, but defining the queries on which forms or reports are based is helpful. Figure 2.2 shows an example of a typical data-flow diagram to print a report.

Data-flow diagrams are useful for defining the queries needed for explicit functions of the database application, such as data entry and report generation, and for explaining the operation of the database application to management and users. You can prepare preliminary data-flow diagrams before the logical design step by omitting references to specific tables and substituting "Database" as the title for the database symbol. After you develop the logical implementation of the database, you can fill in table names and specify the queries you need to create the report. During the application implementation stage, you apply final form and report names to screen and report symbols, respectively.

FIGURE 2.2.

A data-flow diagram that represents the preparation of a report.

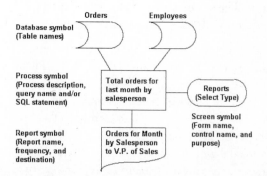

NOTE

You can use a variety of Windows applications to help create data-flow diagrams. Many CASE tools include advanced data-flow diagramming capability; some of these tools will write the SQL statement for the query on which each form or report is based.

Entity-Relationship Diagrams for Logical Schema

The most popular way to depict the logical schema of databases is the entity-relationship diagram, abbreviated as E-R, ERD, or EAR (entity-attribute-relationship). E-R diagrams combine the identification of database entities and the relations between the entities. Figure 2.3 is an E-R representation of the FORML sentences "Instructor (Id) teaches Course (Id)" and "Course (Id) is taught by Instructor (Id)," discussed earlier in the chapter. In E-R diagrams, rectangles represent data entities (tables) and ellipses designate data attributes (fields); diamonds show relationships between the attributes of entities. The "1" and "m" symbols in Figure 2.3 represent the "one" and the "many" sides of a one-to-many relationship between the Instructor.Id and Course.Id fields of the two tables.

FIGURE 2.3.

A simple E-R diagram for two tables with a one-to-many relationship.

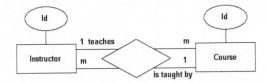

Because relationships between every attribute of every entity use a separate diagram, sets of E-R diagrams that depict the logical design of complex databases can become quite large. The advantage of E-R diagrams is that they are easy to create with simple Windows applications, such as Microsoft Draw. (Microsoft Draw was used to create Figure 2.3.)

Some database CASE tools can generate SQL data definition language (DDL) statements from a complete set of E-R diagrams. A CASE tool that can write the lengthy `CREATE TABLE` and `CREATE INDEX` statements can save an appreciable amount of time during the implementation phase of the database life cycle. Now that Access SQL supports SQL's DDL keywords, you can use CASE tools designed for creating client-server databases to generate Access 2.0 databases. You must add table- and field-level `ValidationRule` and `ValidationText` property values, because Access SQL does not include SQL reserved words to set these values.

Object-Role Data Modeling Diagrams

Object-role modeling (ORM) is a recent development that overcomes the limitations of E-R diagrams. ORM diagrams are based on NIAM (Nijssen's Information Analysis Methodology), developed by Professor G.M. Nijssen of the University of Queensland, Australia. Unlike E-R diagrams that depict the logical view of data, ORM diagrams display the conceptual view. In addition, ORM diagrams offer a wider variety of symbols to express constraints and other characteristics of the data entities. ORM diagrams are better suited than E-R diagrams for creating diagrams of the entire structure of the database. Figure 2.4 shows an example of a portion of an ORM diagram. (Figure 2.4 was created by using the instructor-student-course example included in Asymetrix Database Division's InfoModeler for Access CASE application, formerly InfoDesigner for Access, described in the next section.) The complete ORM diagram depicts objects and roles that result in the creation of 12 tables.

FIGURE 2.4.

A portion of an object-role modeling diagram for an instructor-course-student database.

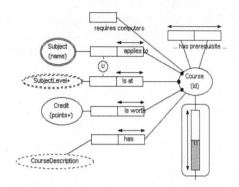

In ORM diagrams, ellipses indicate object types; rectangles depict facts that pertain to the objects. Solid object ellipses represent entities and dotted ellipses represent values. A fact with a single object—"Course (id) requires computers" in Figure 2.4—is called a unary role. A fact that connects two objects, such as "Subject (name) applies to Course (Id)" is a binary role; the fact rectangle is divided by a vertical line." Arrows above the fact predicates and dots on the periphery of an object symbol indicate that constraints apply to the data. One of the principal advantages of ORM diagrams is that the FORML statements on which the diagram is based can be compiled into a logical design which, in turn, can create the necessary data-definition language statements to create the final database structure.

Using CASE Tools to Create Access Databases

Developers of applications for client-server RDBMSs and mainframe database systems have a variety of computer-aided software engineering tools that can help create conceptual database schema and map the conceptual schema to a database structure. Advanced database CASE tools write SQL data-definition language (DDL) statements to create the tables for the database, define the relationships between the tables, and implement domain integrity rules. As mentioned earlier in this chapter, Access 1.x did not support DDL reserved words; you needed special versions of CASE tools in order to create Access databases automatically. Access 2.0's new DDL reserved words opens Access 2.0 to a variety of CASE tools.

In early 1994, the only commercially available CASE tool designed specifically for Access was Asymetrix Inc.'s InfoModeler for Access. Not surprisingly, InfoModeler for Access uses ORM symbols and FORML sentence constructs to create database entities and attributes. In Figure 2.5, the diagramming window of InfoModeler for Access displays a portion of the working version of the instructor-course-student tutorial example.

FIGURE 2.5.

*InfoModeler for
Access's conceptual
database diagram
window.*

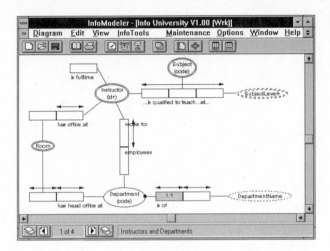

After you complete your conceptual design, validate your design by clicking the toolbar
button with the check mark. Then click the Relational Model Generation button of
the Diagram window's toolbar (the seventh button from the left in Figure 2.5—between the button with the check mark and the one labeled "DB") to compile the
FORML statements that underlie the conceptual diagram. FORML sentences with
proper grammar constitute source code for the compilation process that creates the
relational table design. In Figure 2.6, the Table Browser window of InfoModeler for
Access displays the fields and relations of five of the tables of the tutorial example in
condensed mode and three of the tables in minimized window mode.

FIGURE 2.6.

*The Table Browser
window of
InfoModeler for
Access.*

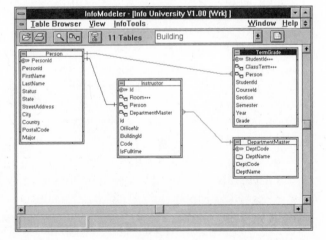

The InfoModeler for Access Table Browser uses a key symbol to designate primary key fields and a two-table symbol to identify foreign key fields of the tables. Relations between tables are shown by lines that connect table headers (representing the primary key field) and foreign key fields. In one-to-many relations, a perpendicular line segment designates the "one" side and a half-diamond indicates the "many" side of the relation.

To display the detailed structure of the table, you click the condensed version of the table diagram to select the table, then click the toolbar's Show Detail (magnifying glass) button. Figure 2.7 shows the Detail window for the Course table of Figure 2.6. Primary and foreign key fields are displayed in the Detail window's Key pane. InfoModeler creates indexes on foreign key field definitions. (Access automatically creates a no-duplicates index on the primary key field.) The Field pane enables you to alter field properties if you need to. InfoModeler also writes the Fact Text that becomes the Description property of each field.

FIGURE 2.7.

The Detail window for the Course table shown in Figure 2.6.

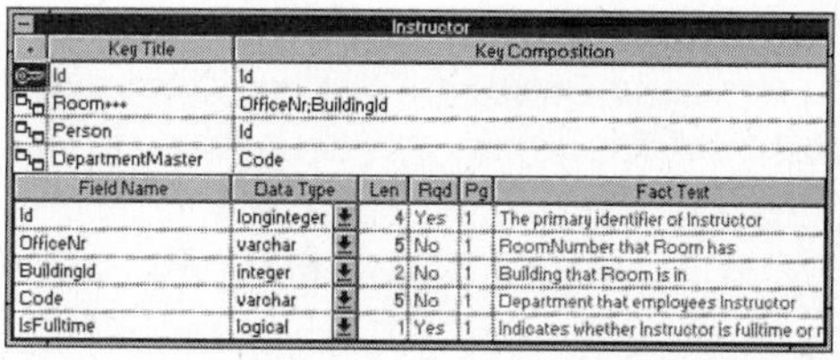

After you compile your conceptual diagram into a relational model, you create an Access database by clicking the Build Native Database button (the button with the "DB" caption in either the Diagrammer or Table Browser window). InfoModeler launches Access, creates a new database, and then builds each table for you, complete with all necessary table and field properties. You can use InfoModeler for Access also to write the "generic" SQL DDL statements needed to build the tables. The following code is a portion of the SQL text file that creates an InfoView database, then adds the Course table to the database:

```
CREATE DATABASE InfoView

/*  Table of Course  */

CREATE TABLE Course (
    CourseId     varchar (8) NOT NULL,
    Subject      datetime    NOT NULL,
    CourseDesc   text        NULL,
    CreditHours  integer     NOT NULL,
    SubjectLevel integer     NOT NULL,
    ReqComputer  logical     NOT NULL,
    PRIMARY KEY (CourseId),
```

```
    UNIQUE (Subject, SubjectLevel)
)
CREATE UNIQUE CLUSTERED INDEX CourseIdx
    ON Course ( CourseId )

CREATE UNIQUE INDEX CourseIdx2
    ON Course ( Subject, SubjectLevel )
```

You can get a separate module for InfoModeler that creates SQL DDL statements specifically designed for Microsoft and Sybase SQL Server and then runs SQL Server's ISQL utility to create the database and the tables. Although you can export Access tables to SQL Server databases, InfoModeler's SQL module gives you the added capability to establish relationships and attribute constraints that are missing when you export Access tables to client-server databases.

Generic Form Design Principles

After you have implemented your database design as Access tables, the next step is to develop the application elements of the Access database. The sections that follow outline the basic principles of form design for commercial Access database applications. (To learn how to create basic forms and reports, see the *Access User's Guide* or any beginning-to-intermediate book about Access.)

The balance of this chapter deals primarily with recommendations for the overall design of Access applications. Later chapters provide examples of advanced form and report design techniques for transaction processing and decision support. Many of the recommendations in the sections that follow represent developers' opinions and should not be interpreted as fixed rules for form design or construed as requirements imposed on form design by Access's methodology.

Defining the Main Form

All Access database applications need a main form. The main form can be just a collection of command buttons that open other forms. (Microsoft refers to a form with only command buttons as a switchboard.) Switchboards are used primarily with large integrated applications, such as accounting packages, that offer users a variety of options for entering or displaying data or printing reports. The Main Switchboard and Forms Switchboard forms of NWIND.MDB are typical (but gaudy) examples of switchboard forms. You can create a less obtrusive switchboard with a custom toolbar, either on your main form or as a pop-up floating toolbar, similar to the Palette or Toolbox forms of Access's design mode. (For more information about custom toolbars, see this chapter's "Menus and Toolbars for Runtime Applications" section and Chapter 26, "Customizing Access Applications with Special Menus and Toolbars.")

Another approach is to designate one of your forms as the main form, then add command buttons to close the main form and open other related forms. If the computers on which your applications run have at least 8MB of memory, you can open forms and then hide them instead of closing them. Use the `IsLoaded()` function, included in the Introduction to Programming Module of NWIND.MDB, to determine whether the form is loaded; if `IsLoaded()` returns **True**, show the form instead of opening it.

> **TIP**
>
> You can add a `HideFormOnClose=` entry to an [*AppName*] section you create in MSACCESS.INI or in another private .INI or .INF file to designate whether your applications close (0) or hide (1) forms. Then use the `ReadPrivateProfileInt()` Windows API function, described in Chapter 22, "Using the Windows API with Access Basic," to set a flag in your application that determines how the application handles opening and closing forms.

You can segment complex applications so that each user opens the form that relates to his or her specific role in the organization. Using an accounting application as an example, create individual macros that use the `RunCode` action to execute Access Basic functions that open the accounts payable, accounts receivable, order entry, and other elements of the application. Then modify the command line to launch Access to run the macro by adding the /x *MacroName* parameter. You will need to add a code that sets the value of a module-level or global variable to indicate which macro opened the form. The added code enables you to program the Quit button on the opening form to close Access or open a switchboard form, depending on the macro that executes when the user launches Access.

Opening and Closing Subsidiary Forms

In this book, forms that relate to or provide information to the main form of an application or a primary form opened by a selective macro are called subsidiary forms. Figure 2.8 shows a main form with two open subsidiary forms. (The Product Categories form is superimposed on the main form; two modal pop-up forms cannot be open at the same time.) Subsidiary forms come in the following three flavors:

■ Support forms, which include lookup tables that enable you, for instance, to pick values from a modal pop-up form rather than from a combo box, or to add a new entry to a lookup table. The Product Categories form shown in Figure 2.8 is an example of a lookup form.

■ Expanded data entry forms, typified by the modal pop-up Contact Details form of Figure 2.8. With expanded data entry forms, you can display more fields than you can in a continuous subform.

■ Other forms that might be primary forms for some users. Primary forms are usually, but not necessarily, modeless single forms, with or without subforms. For instance, by clicking the Products Form button of the main form shown in Figure 2.8, you open another primary form; this one is based on types of products rather than names of suppliers.

FIGURE 2.8.

A main form with two subsidiary forms open (a composite image).

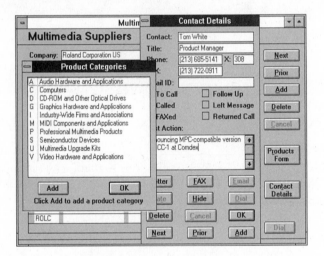

Although most main or primary forms are conventional modeless forms with the values of the PopUp and Modal properties set to No, treating all full-window forms as if they were modal pop-up forms is advisable in low-memory conditions in order to conserve resources. Thus, you might open and close large main or primary forms but show and hide smaller pop-up forms to improve performance. You can create the equivalent of the Show and Hide choices of the Window menu of retail Access with a custom menu that provides a choice for the main form and each primary form.

NOTE

If you use the approach described in the preceding section to launch Access with a different main window for individual classes of users, you need to write a different menu macro with AddMenu actions appropriate for the class of user.

Creating Separate Procedures for Transaction Processing and Decision Support

The forms you design for users ordinarily fit into two distinct categories: forms used to update data in tables and forms that simply display data. Users fit into similar categories: users who are allowed to make changes to the data and those who either are not authorized to update records or whose ordinary duties do not include data entry. You can improve the performance of decision-support applications, especially those that run on computers with less than 8MB of RAM, by opening databases in read-only mode instead of read-write mode. Add the /Ro (read-only) switch to the command line that launches your application for decision-support users. If the application also includes transaction-processing functions, segment the application by executing a special decision-support-only macro. (Refer to the section called "Defining the Main Form" in this chapter.) By segmenting your application, you avoid displaying "You are not authorized..." messages to upper-management users if you also limit permissions to Read Data.

An alternative approach is to create a separate database for decision-support applications and attach the tables of the transaction-processing database. Access has no provision for attaching tables in read-only mode; your only option is to open attached tables in Exclusive or Shared mode. Thus, you need to restrict permissions on the tables to read-only for decision-support database users; alternatively, open all forms in read-only mode. Potential problems associated with this alternative method of segmenting applications are described in the section called "Attaching Tables from an Access Database," later in the chapter.

Designing Access Database Applications for Distribution

With very few exceptions, commercial Access applications are designed to use the runtime version of Access (MSARN200.EXE, MSARN110.EXE for version 1.1) rather than the retail version of the executable file (MSACCESS.EXE). If you are developing applications for other people to use, you need the Access Developer's Toolkit (ADT). Even if you do not own the ADT, you need to design your applications so that they work with both MSACCESS.EXE and MSARN200.EXE. Failure to take into account the differences between the operating characteristics of the alternative operating environments for your database applications can result in many hours of drudgery as you redesign the applications.

The sections that follow describe (briefly) the ADT and explain the basic principles of application design for use with MSARN200.EXE. Methods of attaching tables to Access are categorized in this book as distribution-dependent because the technique you use to attach Access or other database tables is likely to be determined by how (and by whom) your applications are installed. Destination PC hardware issues are discussed here also because computer capabilities affect application design and performance.

The Access Developer's Toolkit

The Access Developer's Toolkit (formerly the Access Distribution Kit or ADK) enables you to distribute royalty-free versions of your Access applications; in this case, royalty-free means that users do not need to own a retail version of Access to use your application. Runtime Access hides all design windows, including the Database window and the query design window, and hides the menu choices that lead to design mode. By default, the value of the ShowToolbar property is set to No so that users cannot choose design mode from the standard Access toolbars.

The ADT includes the following components:

■ The runtime executable file, MSARN200.EXE, that substitutes for MSACCESS.EXE. Runtime Access uses the same dynamic link libraries supplied with retail Access.

■ A runtime version of GRAPH5.EXE, the new Microsoft Graph OLE 2.0 server installed in the \WINDOWS\MSAPPS\MSGRAPH5 directory. (The runtime version of MSGRAPH5.EXE does not overwrite the full version installed by retail Access, if the full version is present.)

■ Setup files that you use to install your application on users' computers. For information about using SETUP.EXE and STFSETUP.EX_ and creating files to support the setup operation, see Chapter 29, "Distributing Runtime Versions of Your Databases."

■ A Setup Wizard that helps you create the distribution diskettes and the setup information file required for your application.

■ The Microsoft Help Compiler (HC31.EXE), a DOS application you use to compile .RTF (rich text format) files created with a word-processing application, such as Microsoft Word 2+, to a format compatible with the WinHelp 3.1 engine. Chapter 28, "Writing Help Files for Access Applications," describes how to use HC31.EXE and its protected-mode counterpart, HCP.EXE.

■ A license to distribute, with each copy of your Access database file, one copy of MSARN200.EXE and the other components of retail Access needed for your Access database application to operate. You cannot distribute files from the retail version of Access that relate to Cue Cards or Access help files, or the retail version of MSGRAPH5.

■ Documentation for the ADT and HC31.EXE. The *Advanced Topics* book covers the general principles of designing Access 2.0 runtime applications using OLE 2.0 Custom Controls, and how to use the Setup Wizard to create distribution diskettes. The *Help Compiler Guide* provides the basics of creating help files for Access applications.

■ Example applications, including a sample wizard with fully documented source code and three OLE 2.0 common controls.

To use the ADT to distribute your applications, you must observe the precautions and design considerations discussed in the following two sections.

Error-Trapping Requirements of Runtime Applications

When you use MSARN200.EXE, all untrapped runtime errors are fatal. If your application encounters an untrapped error during the execution of a macro or in your Access Basic code, Access quits unceremoniously. Access 2.0 now provides the Error event that you can use to execute an error-trapping subprocedure, `Form_Error` and `Report_Error`, when an error occurs with a form active. Because you cannot trap errors that occur during macro execution, you need to avoid (as much as possible) using macros in applications designed for use with runtime Access. Using code rather than macros runs counter to Microsoft's promotion of Access as a "codeless" RDBMS. Writing code, however, has the advantage of providing built-in documentation for your applications. There is no search-and-replace feature for modifying macros, and macro documentation, even with Database Documentor, is cumbersome. Therefore using macros, other than AutoExec and menu macros, for production database applications can be a problematic choice. Your AutoExec or startup macro should contain a single `RunCode` action that calls an Access function to perform housekeeping duties and open your application's main form or switchboard. The only other macros that should appear in your runtime application are those needed to create custom menu bars and menu choices. Custom menus and toolbars are the subject of the next section.

All of your Access Basic functions and procedures, whether behind forms or in modules, need to include an error-handling code consisting of an **On Error GoTo** *LabelName* and a *LabelName:* statement followed by error-handling code appropriate to the function or procedure. You also can trap the Error event of forms and reports by executing a generic error handling procedure. Chapter 4 of this book, "Writing Access Basic Code," discusses Access Basic error-handling techniques.

> **TIP**
>
> If you have made extensive use of Access macros in an application and need to convert the macros to Access Basic code, use the Macro to Module Converter function of Andrew Miller's FIRSTLIB.MDA. The Macro to Module Converter creates (from your macros) text files you can import into a module. The necessary error-trapping features are added automatically to each function. By the time you read this edition, it is likely that an updated version of FIRSTLIB.MDA will be available.

Menus and Toolbars for Runtime Applications

The runtime version of Access modifies the menus of application objects, but you probably do not want users to have unrestricted access to the default menu choices. In most Access applications, command buttons on forms or a custom-designed toolbar for your application will supplement or replace menu choices. On the whole, toolbars are a better approach than switchboard forms for choosing the form or report you want to open, because toolbars have become a standard component of almost every mainstream Windows application. Thus you can dispense with most of the standard menu bar choices offered by runtime Access. Use the MenuBar property (previously the OnMenu event) of forms and reports to execute a set of menu macros that use the AddMenu action to create the custom menu structure for each of your application's forms and reports. Your standard menu might consist simply of an Exit and a Help menu bar; however, it is a good application-design practice to provide a menu choice that duplicates the action of each toolbar button.

> **NOTE**
>
> Unless you supply a custom Windows help file with your application, users receive a "Help isn't available for this command" message when they choose Contents or Search from the Help menu. To make your applications conform to Windows standards, however, you should retain the Help menu bar and add an About... choice to open a form that displays copyright and other information describing your application.

Creating custom toolbars for Access 2.0 applications is a much simpler process than for earlier Access versions. You can create a single custom toolbar for the entire application or design individual toolbars for each form or report you include. The custom toolbars you create are stored in your application's .MDB file. You can use any of Access's toolbar buttons in your custom toolbar or create new buttons with bit map images (.BMP) or icons (.ICO). You can show or hide toolbars using the new ShowToolbar macro action, which lets you specify the toolbar's name and if the toolbar is visible. You use the new Activate event to cause the toolbar to appear and both the Deactivate and Unload events to make the toolbar disappear.

When you design applications in the retail version of Access, the toolbar is present unless you have explicitly set the value of the ShowToolbar property to No in the Options dialog of the General category. Most commercial Access applications are designed to run in maximized window mode. If you design forms for a maximized window and then run your application without a toolbar, your forms gain an extra 3/8 inch of vertical display area. Often the result is an unwanted blank area at the bottom of the form, directly above the status bar. If your forms do not have a header, you can add a header with the Height property of the Header section set to 0.28 inch. With a standard 0.28-inch high header, the remaining height for the detail section of your form is approximately 7.16 inches.

An alternative to using Access 2.0 custom toolbars is to add command buttons that emulate toolbar buttons to your form. This approach was the best choice for Access 1.x applications; with Access 2.0, however, you lose the advantage of custom ToolTips. The header section of a form is the usual location for command buttons that emulate toolbar buttons. Figure 2.9 shows an example of a form opened in runtime Access with the default menu bars for forms. The form header includes a random group of toolbar buttons imported from the retail Access toolbars. For information about creating custom menus and toolbars, see Chapter 26, "Customizing Access Applications with Special Menus and Toolbars."

NOTE

If you use a floating toolbar or switchboard created with a pop-up form, you need to provide a "parking space" on your form so that the user can place the floating toolbar without obscuring other control objects. Provide a custom menu selection for a Window menu bar to Show or Hide the floating toolbar. Alternately, you can use Meliora Systems's "roll-up" toolbar, which is described in Chapter 12, "Looking at an Access Training Database."

FIGURE 2.9.
Toolbar buttons added to the header of an Access form.

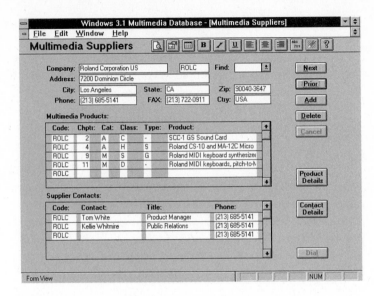

Creating Ad Hoc Queries for Runtime Applications

Because Access's design windows are not visible when you run your application under MSARN200.EXE, users cannot create their own queries with Access's QBE features. The lack of the query-design window does not interfere with applications that use only queries you define, either as SQL statements or as stored `QueryDef` objects. Often, however, because users of decision-support applications want to be able to create their own queries, you need to create an equivalent of Access 2.0's Query Builder, which generates an SQL statement to create `QueryDef` objects. The ad hoc `QueryDef`s serve as the `DataSource` property of forms, subforms, and reports. They also populate list or combo boxes and perform other duties, such as creating mailing lists or exporting data to text files or spreadsheet applications.

You need to master SQL, as well as Access Basic, to enable users of your database applications to create their own queries. The fastest way to learn the syntax of Access SQL is to choose SQL from the View menu whenever you create a new query with Access QBE. Review the SQL statement that Access stores as the SQL property of a `QueryDef` object, especially for queries that involve totals, groups of records, and crosstabs. A simple query wizard to create a mailing list is used as an example of ad hoc query generation in Chapter 9, "Designing Decision-Support Forms for Management." An *ad hoc* crosstab query wizard that creates its own custom subforms is described in Chapter 24, "Using Access Wizard Functions."

Separating Application and Data Objects

The capability to combine application objects (forms, reports, macros, and modules) with data objects (tables and queries) into a single database file is a unique feature of Access. Conventional desktop database systems maintain separate table, index, and application-related files. All major client-server RDBMSs include a rudimentary capability to create and display views of data interactively. Custom front-end applications for client-server RDBMSs designed for everyday use, rather than for database administration, are maintained as separate executable applications. Front-end applications can be stored on the server, but seldom are incorporated into the server database itself. (This statement does not apply to object databases, which are beyond the scope of this book. Object databases, unlike relational databases, encapsulate methods within tables.)

Combining data objects (database object properties) and application objects (database object methods) in a single database conforms to the object-oriented model. Using a single .MDB file with a designated SYSTEM.MDA file simplifies the creation and administration of multiuser database applications. Problems can arise with this structure, however, when you want to modify the application objects in an Access database without disturbing existing data stored in the tables of the database. Clearly this problem does not arise if your Access applications consist wholly of database front-ends. Another disadvantage of the single-file approach in a multiuser environment is that performance is degraded when users run the application from a server.

If you, the developer of the single-file database application, are also the administrator of the database, you can add or update application objects simply by importing new or modified forms, reports, macros, or modules into the single .MDB file for your application. You can delete the existing versions, then import the new objects from the development database. If you do not delete the objects to be replaced and your updated objects have the same names as existing objects, Access adds a version digit to the name of the newly imported object. Then you delete or rename the old versions and rename the new objects. If you are making a major upgrade, this process can be tedious.

Using the import, delete, and rename procedure to update or upgrade databases administered by others is fraught with potential danger. The database administrator might delete the wrong object(s) and not have a current backup. Purchasers of commercial Access applications expect to be able to upgrade their product by running an easy-to-use setup application. Off-site updates and upgrades are better handled by placing the application-related objects and query objects in one .MDB file and storing Access tables in another database file. The following sections describe some of the ramifications of using the two-file approach.

Attaching Tables from Access 1.x and 2.0 Databases

Most Access developers use the two-file approach to application design, and Microsoft employs separate application and data .MDB files in the applications included in the Microsoft Access Solutions Pack. As noted near the beginning of Chapter 1, Access 2.0 now enforces referential and domain integrity at the table level, so you no longer must write application macros or Access Basic code to enforce these constraints in every form updates tables. This is a major improvement over Access 1.x, which did not enforce the referential integrity of attached tables. Access's new Relationships window shows relationships inherited from attached tables, just as if the relationships were created in the application .MDB. Figure 2.10 shows the Relationships window for a database to which all of the tables of NWIND.MDB have been attached. When you add the tables to the Relationships window, the inherited relationships appear automatically.

FIGURE 2.10.

Inherited relationships shown in Access 2.0's Relationships window.

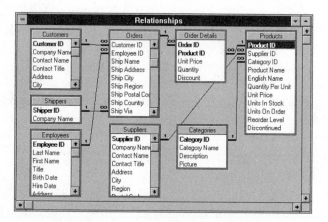

NOTE

You do not need to specify the relationships of attached tables in your application database; the relationships are inherited automatically. You only need to add relationships between the attached tables and any local tables that you include in your application database.

One of the other drawbacks of attaching tables in Access 1.1 was a problem that occurred when you relocated the tables. You had to delete the attachments that pointed to tables in the prior location, then reattach the tables from their new location. Access 2.0 overcomes this obstacle with the Attachment Manager add-in. The Attachment Manager, whose dialog box appears in Figure 2.11, simplifies the reattachment

of tables for clients and developers alike. To reattach tables from Access or other database types, choose Add-Ins from the File menu, then choose Attachment Manager
from the submenu. Tick the check boxes of the tables you want to reattach. The
Attachment Manager checks to see if the table exists in the specified location; if not,
an Attach Table (common FileOpen) dialog box opens, in which you specify the new
location for relocated tables.

FIGURE 2.11.

*The opening dialog
box of the
Attachment
Manager.*

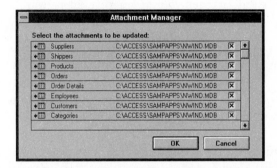

TIP

You should include an equivalent of the Attachment Manager add-in in any
application you create that uses attached tables, and instruct users to run the
attachment manager immediately after installing the application. (Microsoft
Wizards, which include the Attachment Manager, are not distributable
components as defined by the license agreement of the ADT.) This is
especially important for multiuser applications where the attached files are
located on network drives that are specified by drive letter, instead of by
UNC, the uniform naming convention for network drives (for instance, `d:\`
rather than `\\SERVER`). Network drive letters on workstations can change for
a variety of reasons.

Using Access Libraries to Store Application Objects

An alternative to the two-database approach is to incorporate all of your application
objects in an Access library. Chapter 3, "Using Libraries, Wizards, Builders, and Add-
Ins," and Chapter 23, "Developing Access Libraries and Add-Ins," describe how to
use and create Access libraries, respectively. Storing application objects in a library
attached to Access offers the following advantages:

■ The location of the database containing the data objects can be changed
   without the necessity of reattaching the tables.

■ Each user can be given only the application objects necessary for his or her duties.

■ Special-purpose tables, such as ZIP Code lookup tables, that are necessary for specific applications can be stored in the library database.

■ The use of local libraries and shared database files can improve performance in multiuser applications. If you use combo boxes to locate a specific record of a very large set, you can improve the performance of your application by using Access Basic code to fill the combo box.

The downside of storing application objects in libraries is that you cannot use bound controls on forms, nor can you fill combo or list boxes by using queries or an SQL statement as the value of the combo or list box RecordSource property. Because Access does not enable you to bind a form to a table or query located in another database, you need to write substantially more Access Basic code for the application. Chapter 8, "Optimizing Transaction-Processing Forms," includes an example of an application you can attach as an Access library. The library technique normally is used only for simple data-entry applications because of the incapability to bind forms, subforms, reports, or subreports to tables or queries in the current database.

Attaching Tables from Other Desktop Database Applications

Access database applications intended to replace existing multiuser desktop database applications often need to be phased into production use. In this situation, you have no alternative but to share the tables and their indexes with the existing database application during the phase-in period. The primary problem with sharing database tables is maintaining table indexes when new records are added to the table or the values of indexed fields are edited in the Access application. Access's index maintenance has the following limitations:

■ The xBase driver of Access 2.0, XBS200.DLL, does not support CA-Clipper .NTX indexes. If the existing application uses CA-Clipper .NTX indexes, you need to alter the source code and recompile the application to use conventional xBase .NDX indexes or dBASE IV .MDX multiple-field indexes.

■ Access 2.0 does not enable you to attach xBase indexes that use functions. If your xBase application includes indexes created with xBase statements such as INDEX ON cust_code + DTOS(order_date)—a common construct in CA-Clipper applications—you need to revise the source code of the existing application to eliminate dependence on indexes of this type.

■ Access does not recognize primary key fields in attached xBase tables, because xBase does not recognize primary key fields. Thus you cannot set a primary key field for an attached xBase table. Access does not use indexes, other than the primary key field index, to order records. Thus, you need to bind forms and reports to queries sorted on the table's indexed fields.

■ Access does not distinguish between xBase indexes created with SET UNIQUE ON or OFF. Access 1.x displays Yes (Duplicates OK) as the value of the Indexed field property for either type of xBase index. You need to write a macro or an Access Basic function to ensure that xBase fields used as primary key fields by existing applications do not contain duplicate values.

■ Access does not support Paradox secondary (query speed-up) indexes. Paradox applications that use query speed-up indexes may be affected by changes made to tables in Access applications.

■ Access automatically attaches Paradox 3.x and 4.x primary key index files (.PX). With Access, you cannot update a Paradox table that does not have a corresponding primary key index file.

■ Access uses the Paradox primary key index file in the same way it uses the no-duplicates index that Access automatically creates on the primary key fields of a native table. Thus, you cannot attach a Paradox table that includes null values in the primary key index file. You need to replace all null values in the primary key field of Paradox tables or delete the offending records.

■ To import, export, or read from and write data to an attached Novell Btrieve file, you need to have Novell's Btrieve for Windows WBTRCALL.DLL file in the \WINDOWS\SYSTEM directory. To distribute WBTRCALL.DLL with your Access database applications, you need a licensing agreement with Novell.

Rewriting and recompiling xBase applications to conform to Access's index maintenance limitations can be a time-consuming and expensive process. This is especially true if you did not write the source code for the application, the application has no documentation, and the author did not comment the code adequately.

The problem with the relocation of attached Access tables applies also to xBase, FoxPro, and Paradox files attached to your application. The fields of records that identify attached xBase tables appear in Figure 2.12. Access defines an attached "database" as the directory that contains the tables. Tables in foreign database formats require a connect string to identify the type of the attached table. Your application needs to alter only the values of the Database field and, optionally, the value of the Description field to specify a new database location.

FIGURE 2.12.

Records in MSysObjects for attached xBase tables.

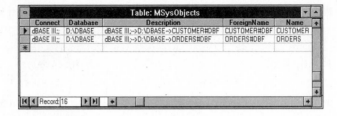

	Connect	Database	Description	ForeignName	Name
▶	dBASE III;;	D:\DBASE	dBASE III;->D:\DBASE->CUSTOMER#DBF	CUSTOMER#DBF	CUSTOMER
	dBASE III;;	D:\DBASE	dBASE III;->D:\DBASE->ORDERS#DBF	ORDERS#DBF	ORDERS
*					

Table: MSysObjects

Record: 16

Access specifies the indexes to be maintained for each table in the foreign "database" by a private initialization (profile) file, TABLENAME.INF, located in the same directory as the table. The index files need not be in the directory that contains the table. The content of the CUSTOMER.INF file that specifies two indexes for the CUSTOMER.DBF table shown in Figure 2.12 is as follows:

```
[dBASE III]
NDX1=D:\DBASE\CUST_CID.NDX
NDX2=D:\DBASE\CUST_ZIP.NDX
```

Indexes are identified by serial suffix digits. The following are examples of indexes for additional tables in the "database":

```
[dBASE III]
NDX3=D:\DBASE\ORDR_CID.NDX
NDX4=D:\DBASE\ORDR_OID.NDX
```

Attaching Tables of Client-Server RDBMSs

To attach tables contained in client-server databases, you must use the ODBC Administrator application supplied with Access and have a driver that supports the client-server RDBMS. Microsoft supplies an ODBC driver for the Microsoft (OS/2 and Windows NT) and Sybase (UNIX and NLM) versions of SQL Server. The ORACLE ODBC driver, supplied with Access 1.x, no longer is included with Access 2.0. If you are not using SQL Server, you need to get an ODBC driver from the publisher of the database system (such as Digital Equipment Corporation's driver for Rdb databases) or a third-party ODBC driver for the RDBMS. Chapter 20, "Front-Ending Client-Server Databases," describes how to use the ODBC Administrator application to attach tables of client-server RDBMSs.

> **NOTE**
>
> Oracle Corp. now develops, supports, and distributes ODBC drivers for its database products. The ODBC driver for ORACLE 7 databases was in the development stage as this edition was being written. The ORACLE 6 ODBC driver supplied with Access 1.x can be used with Access 2.0 applications.

If the tables attached from the client-server database contain many records, network traffic increases dramatically when you attach the tables upon opening your application and when you traverse the table. The process of moving from a record at the beginning to a record at the end of a large table (or to the tentative append record) causes a surge of network traffic and can be frustratingly slow.

NOTE

Take seriously Microsoft's recommendation that you set to `DataEntry` the value of the `DefaultEditing` property of forms used for transaction processing when your application just adds records to a table. `DataEntry` mode does not display existing records of a table or a query and greatly improves performance.

WARNING

Do not use aggregate functions, such as `SUM()` or `AVG()`, in Access queries against large attached tables. Aggregate functions require Access to process all records in the attached table. The only exception to this rule is the use of `COUNT()` to return the number of records that meet the query criteria. The `COUNT()` function is useful for determining whether your query will return an excessive number of records.

Using SQL Pass-Through with Client-Server and Mainframe RDBMSs

You can minimize the network traffic and performance problems described in the preceding sections by creating an Access **Recordset** object from a query processed on the server or by the mainframe RDBMS. This process is called *SQL pass-through*; the query is sent directly to the server, bypassing the Jet database engine's query parser and optimizer. With this process, you do not have to attach the remotely located tables to Access; only the query-result set is returned to your database. A query-result **Recordset** created from a remote database is the counterpart of an Access **Snapshot** object; you cannot update the data stored on the server.

Access 1.x created a persistent **Table** object from the query-result set returned by an SQL pass-through query executed on the server. You had to use the SQL pass-through dynamic link library (SPT.DLL for Access 1.0 or MSASP110.DLL for 1.1) to send to the server the SQL statement that creates the query. Using SQL pass-through with Access 1.x involved writing a substantial amount of Access Basic code.

Access 2.0 now provides SQL pass-through as an option of the **OpenRecordset**() method that replaces Access 1.*x*'s **CreateDynaset**() and **CreateSnapshot**() methods. If your client-server RDBMS supports stored procedures, you can specify a precompiled query in lieu of the SQL statement. The RDBMS executes the query on the server and returns the query rows to a non-updatable **Recordset** in your application's database. You also can use SQL passthrough to cause the RDBMS server to execute action queries that do not return rows. Action queries return the number of rows affected by the query. SQL pass-through is one of the subjects of Chapter 20, "Front-Ending Client-Server Databases."

> **NOTE**
>
> You're not limited to using SQL pass-through with client-server databases. There are several suppliers of ODBC drivers for the network and hierarchical databases that are commonly encountered in the mainframe environment. (These products are often called *legacy* databases.) As an example, Information Builders, Inc., offers EDA/Extender for Microsoft ODBC, which, in conjunction with its EDA/Link for Windows and EDA/SQL products, provides access to a multitude of mainframe database types.

The Influence of the Destination Hardware on Application Design

As of early 1994, the ideal platform for Access application development is a 66-MHz 80486DX2 or Pentium computer with 16MB of RAM. A VESA local bus with a 32-bit Windows accelerator video adapter card (1MB of VRAM) and a 32-bit IDE or SCSI-2 adapter card connected to a 13-ms or faster fixed disk helps minimize the time needed for the hourglass mouse pointer to disappear. If you use a 66-Mhz Pentium CPU, your Access applications may run almost as fast as Clipper-compiled xBase applications under DOS on a 80386DX-25. A noninterlaced display, 17 inches for 800-by-600-pixel or 21 inches for 1,024-by-768-pixel UVGA, is useful for presentation purposes, as well as applications that involve high-resolution graphic images. Unfortunately, most users of your applications will not be blessed with PCs that conform to these ideal specifications. Users are likely to have conventional 13- or 14-inch VGA displays with 16-color, not 256-color, drivers installed. Even worse, many users may run your applications on laptop PCs with monochrome VGA displays.

Destination Computer Memory Requirements

Although Access database applications will run under MSARN200.EXE or MSACCESS.EXE on 386SX or 386DX computers with 4MB of RAM, application performance will be slow. If you have large tables in your database or many forms and reports, virtual memory paging to the Windows swap file may take up most of the destination PC's resources. If you make extensive use of OLE objects, such as graphs and charts, it is likely that your applications will not run on computers with only 4MB of RAM, and even with 8MB, performance may suffer. Increasing the destination computer's RAM to 8MB provides the greatest improvement in performance for the least cost, and 12MB to 16MB is recommended for power users. The street price for adding 4MB of RAM to 66-MHz computers was about $90 as of early 1994. Increasing memory on 80486 computers, at least to 12MB, usually provides a greater improvement in performance than upgrading the processor to a faster clock rate.

NOTE

The performance of Access applications that are run on computers with less than 8MB to 12MB of RAM improves when you use a permanent swap file for virtual memory paging. Most Windows installations use the default temporary swap file. Depending on the fragmentation of the disk partition in which a temporary swap file resides, paging from RAM to a permanent swap file can be up to twice as fast as paging to a temporary file. Microsoft recommends a total of 25MB of RAM plus permanent swap file. A total of 20MB appears to be adequate for most Access 2.0 applications. You may need to run a disk defragmentation application, such as Norton SpeedDisk, on the partition to get 4MB of contiguous clusters for the permanent swap file. (Permanent swap files require all disk clusters to be contiguous.)

Access front-end applications for client-server databases may need additional RAM to hold substantial portions of large tables in memory. If your application runs Access queries against large tables attached from the server database, the client workstation may need 16MB of RAM to provide acceptable performance.

Display Limitations

In the commercial and institutional environment, most PCs that run Windows applications use the conventional 16-color, 640-by-480-pixel VGA operating mode provided by Windows 3.1's built-in generic VGA display driver. Most VGA displays have 13- or 14-inch (diagonal measurement) CRTs, and many displays have 0.35mm or greater dot pitch rather than the present standard of 0.28mm. You need to design your application for the lowest-common-denominator display—plain vanilla VGA. If you design your application in 800-by-600-pixel (SVGA) mode or, worse, in 1,024-by-768-pixel (UVGA) mode, parts of large forms will disappear when users run your application in conventional VGA mode.

Running Access Applications with Fixed-Disk Data-Compression Utilities

Fixed disk-drive capacity can be a major constraint when users create large Access databases. Fixed-disk data-compression utilities, such as Stacker 3.1 and the Double-Disk derivative supplied with DOS 6.x, can nearly double the capacity of disk drives. Stacker 3.1, for example, compresses the average Access database by a factor of between 2.0 and 2.5. The compression ratio increases when your database contains graphic images stored as Windows bitmaps (.BMP or .DIB format) in OLE Object fields. Increased compression ratio compensates, in part, for the size of embedded OLE presentations of linked graphic images, as discussed in Chapter 15, "Embedding and Linking Objects with OLE."

> **TIP**
>
> Encrypted Access database files do not compress significantly, either with disk data-compression utilities or with archiving utilities such as PKWare's PKZIP.EXE. Compression algorithms used by data-compression utilities substitute tokens for repeating groups of bytes. The encryption algorithm that Microsoft uses with Access databases removes most repeating groups of bytes.

Little or no degradation in performance occurs with computers whose disk drives have average seek times of 18-ms or more. The time saved by reading fewer bytes from the hard disk compensates for the time the CPU takes to decompress the data. All sample applications for this book were created and tested on a 486DX2-66MHz computer with local bus video and a 32-bit local bus IDE fixed disk drive using Stacker 3.1. No difference was detected in the performance of the applications with Access and the database application run from compressed or uncompressed disk partitions.

> **NOTE**
>
> Data-compression utilities do not significantly compress many types of multimedia data embedded in or linked to OLE fields. Waveform audio (.WAV) and digital video (.AVI) files compress at a very low ratio or do not compress at all. (Long periods of silence in .WAV files compress if the signal-to-noise ratio of your audio adapter card is very high.) The compression ratio of animation data varies according to whether the data has already been compressed by RLE (run-length encoding).

3

Using Libraries, Wizards, Builders, and Add-Ins

One of the most useful features of Microsoft Access is the ability to extend Access's capabilities with libraries. Libraries consist of databases that you attach to Access with an entry in the MSACC20.INI file. Once you've attached a library, your Access applications can execute any Access Basic function contained in the library, just as if the function were included in a module in your application itself. Access 2.0 libraries can contain any type of database object, including macros, and can display forms and print reports. (Access 1.x did not let you execute macros in library databases.) As noted in the preceding chapter, using macros in library databases is discouraged because macros do not provide the error-trapping capabilities of Access Basic.

Wizards are a special form of library that create database objects in your application. The Wizards included with Access 2.0 are typical examples; the Access Wizards use a special set of Access Basic methods to create forms, reports, and graphs in databases you develop. Wizards, by definition, have multiple windows (forms) that lead you, step-by-step, in the creation of the new database objects. A builder is a special category of Access library that returns a value to a property. You launch builders by clicking the ellipsis button that is added to the property text box when a builder for the property is available. Builders usually have a single window. Add-ins are libraries whose functions you call with choices that appear in the File Add-Ins submenu; Access 2.0's new Database Documenter and Attachment Manager are examples of very useful add-ins. Add-ins may have a single window or display a succession of windows. Access 2.0's Menu Builder is both an add-in and a builder.

This chapter describes some of the libraries, wizards, builders and add-ins available for Access and how you use them to aid in developing commercial Access applications. Chapter 23, "Developing Access Libraries and Add-Ins," describes how to write libraries for use by your clients or employer, and Chapter 24, "Using Access Wizard Functions," explains how to use the `CreateForm()`, `CreateControl()`, and other `Create...()` functions to develop your own wizards and to generate user-definable forms and reports in design mode.

Understanding Access Libraries

At the minimum, Access libraries consist of one or more functions written in Access Basic code. You execute Access Basic library functions by either of the methods that you use to call functions contained in a module of the open database, or by an additional method that is applicable to add-in libraries only. The four methods of calling a function in an Access 2.0 library are as follows:

■ Assign the function name as the argument of a `RunCode` action in an Access macro. As an example, you can call a library function with a key combination by adding the combination, such as Shift+F12, as the +{F12} macro of

the AutoKeys macrogroup, and then assign this macro the `RunCode`
FunctionName() action.

■ Enter an equal sign followed by the function name as the value in the text
box of the appropriate event in the Properties window of a form, report, or
control object.

■ Call the function from an Access Basic function or subprocedure from an
Access module or an event-handling subprocedure behind a form or report.

■ Choose the name (alias) assigned to the function in the **F**ile Add-Ins
submenu. Adding **F**ile Add-Ins submenu choices to execute functions is
described in a forthcoming section of this chapter. (Access 1.x used **H**elp
menu choices to call entry-point functions in libraries.)

Each function included in an Access library is registered automatically when you
launch Access. Any Access database that you open can call any function in the library, except functions preceded by the **Private** reserved word. Functions in a library that initiate execution of a specific library routine are called *entry-point functions.* If you call a function, other than a function designated as the entry point, you
may encounter an unexpected result or a runtime error. An untrapped runtime error
that occurs in a library results in the message shown in Figure 3.1. The term "permission" in the dialog box is a misnomer, because you cannot view modules in a library (even if you are the owner of the module object or a member of the Admins
group). In most, if not all, cases it is futile to click the Continue button of the runtime
error dialog box; you simply see another instance of the same dialog box. Clicking
the Reinitialize button executes an error handler that closes the dialog box.

FIGURE 3.1.

*The error message
that results from a
runtime error in an
attached Access
library.*

All users can share a single copy of an Access library that is installed on a network
server, thus saving the disk space required by multiple copies. SYSTEM.MDA and
UTILITY.MDA are both Access libraries; both SYSTEM.MDA and
UTILITY.MDA, or their surrogates, are required to start Access. Microsoft chose
the file extension .MDA to designate databases designed to be attached as libraries;
however, developers are free to choose any file extension they want for libraries.

After you attach a library to Access, you can no longer open the library with the Open Database choice of the File menu. If you attempt to open an attached library, you receive a message box that reads, "The database 'LIBRARY.MDA' is already open as a library database," as shown in Figure 3.2. Notice that this message box, along with many others that appear when you encounter Access errors, is not a standard message box; there is no value documented for the *Type* argument of the **MsgBox**() function that corresponds to "Display OK and Help buttons."

FIGURE 3.2.

The message that occurs when you attempt to open an attached library as a database.

NOTE

Although you cannot open an attached Access library, you can import objects contained in the attached library with the Import choice of the File menu. You cannot import Access Basic modules from the library, because of a restriction against loading functions with duplicate names (as discussed in the section of this chapter called "Limitations of Access Libraries"). You can, however, import forms, reports, and other database objects contained in attached libraries. You may encounter runtime errors if you display a form or report imported from an attached library in run mode. Importing and modifying objects from attached libraries is not a recommended practice.

Forms contained in libraries that are opened by functions in library modules are, most of the time, modal pop-up forms that emulate Windows dialog boxes. Modal pop-up forms retain the focus in your application until you close them. This prevents the user from performing other operations on the application until the library function has completed its assigned task or the user clicks a Cancel button. Access Form Wizards and Report Wizards are examples of the modal pop-up form design that is typically used in libraries. Libraries that add additional toolboxes to Access use modeless pop-up forms. Modeless pop-up forms remain on top of all other windows, but they lose the focus when you click the surface of another window or make a menu selection.

Access libraries fall into two basic categories: those intended to assist users and developers of Access applications, and those designed to add functionality to commercial Access databases. This chapter concentrates on describing libraries, wizards, and builders designed specifically for the development of Access applications. As mentioned in the introduction to this chapter, libraries and wizards that you attach to the commercial database applications that you create for your clients or employer are described in Chapter 23 and Chapter 24.

Attaching Access Libraries

Access libraries, like the Windows dynamic link libraries described in Chapter 22, "Using the Windows API with Access Basic," are examples of late binding of functions. You bind the Access library to your copy of Access by adding an entry in the [Libraries] section of your MSACC20.INI initialization file, as in the following example:

```
[Libraries]
wzlib.mda=rw
wzTable.mda=rw
wzQuery.mda=rw
wzfrmrpt.mda=rw
wzbldr.mda=rw
;firstlib.mda=ro
```

On startup, Access reads MSACC20.INI and attaches the files listed in the [Libraries] section; thus the term "late binding." The technicalities involved in the early and late binding of functions are discussed in Chapter 22. If Access is loaded, you need to close and reopen Access in order for the changes you make in MSACC20.INI to take effect.

NOTE

To prevent a library listed in the [Libraries] section of MSACC20.INI from being attached to Access, precede the entry with a semicolon. This is similar to the method used to "comment out" an entry in your WIN.INI or SYSTEM.INI file. Commenting out the attachment of a library enables you to quickly reattach it by deleting the semicolon. In the preceding example of the [Libraries] entries, the FIRSTLIB.MDA library is commented out.

The Setup application adds the first four entries in the preceding example to your MSACC20.INI file when you install the retail version of Access. Additional entries that you make attach other special-purpose libraries. For example, entering firstlib.mda=ro attaches Andrew R. Miller's FIRSTLIB.MDA library, which is discussed later in this chapter. The only limit to the number of libraries you can attach to Access is the amount of memory available in your computer. If the library is not located in your \ACCESS directory, you need to add the well-formed path to the name of the library file.

The =ro expression appended to the library file name opens the library as read-only. Entering =rw (or just the equal sign) opens the library for read-write operations. Most libraries are designed for read-only use; read-only libraries open faster than read-write libraries. However, you need read-write capability if your application modifies an object contained in the library. For example, you must attach WZTABLE.MDA as a read-write library with wztable.mda= or wztable.mda=rw because your application can customize the example tables contained in WZTABLE.MDA.

> **NOTE**
>
> Libraries designed to be used as Form Wizards or Report Wizards to create forms or reports, or to add control objects to forms or reports, require a special [Form Wizards] or [Report Wizards] section of MSACC20.INI and an entry to identify the name and entry-point function of the wizard library. These two entries are required by Access 2.0 in order to display the names of wizards in the list boxes that appear in the "Which Wizard" dialog box. Access automatically passes two parameters, the name of the table or query that serves as the data source for the form or report, and an integer WizardID value. The syntax of the entries required for wizards is described in Chapter 23.

The SYSTEM.MDA and UTILITY.MDA libraries that are required by Access are attached by entries in the [Options] section of MSACC20.INI and use a slightly different syntax. If you are a member of a workgroup that shares database files and a common SYSTEM.MDA file on a network, you alter the SystemDB= entry to point to the shared system library database, as in SystemDB=g:\sales\salessys.mda. You can rename SYSTEM.MDA whatever you like in order to identify the file as the system library database for a particular workgroup. Sharing system library databases is one of the subjects of Chapter 19, "Networking Secure Access Applications."

Entries in MSACC20.INI for Standard Wizards and Builders

The entry-point functions to launch the standard collection of Access wizards and builders are defined in the following sections of MSACC20.INI:

- `[Table Wizards]` defines the entry-point function for the Table Wizard, WZTABLE.MDA, and `[Table Wizard Data Files]` specifies the database that contains the sample tables, WZTBLDAT.MDT.

- `[Query Wizards]` specifies the entry-point functions for each of the special types of queries created by the Query Wizard, WZQUERY.MDA.

- `[Form Wizards]` provides the entry-point functions for the five standard Form Wizards.

- `[Report Wizards]` defines the entry-point functions for the seven standard Report Wizards.

- `[Control Wizards]` supplies the entry-point functions for the four Control Wizards contained in WZBLDR.MDA.

- `[Property Wizards]` specifies the entry-point function of the seven standard builders provided with Access 2.0. Although the heading is `[Property Wizards]`, the name of each of the functions has a "`Builder`" suffix.

The standard entries for the `[Control Wizards]` section of MSACC20.INI are:

```
[Control Wizards]
MSCommandButtonWizard=CommandButton,Command Button Wizard,BW_ENTRY,w
MSListBoxWizard=ListBox,List Box Wizard,LST_ENTRY,w
MSComboBoxWizard=ComboBox,Combo Box Wizard,CMB_ENTRY,w
MSOptionGroupWizard=OptionGroup,Option Group Wizard,OGrp_ENTRY,w
```

The general syntax of the preceding entries is as follows:

```
WizardName=strControlType, strWizardCaption, strEntryPoint, strParameter
```

These entries are used internally by Access to launch the Control Wizards. Similar syntax is used to open the Property "Wizards."

Adding Menu Choices to Execute Library Functions

Another method of executing a function contained in a library is to add a descriptive name for the function to appear as a menu choice of the **F**ile Add-Ins submenu and to add the name of the entry-point function to the [Menu Add-ins] section of your MSACC20.INI file. The following example shows four menu choices for functions contained in two add-in libraries described in sections later in this chapter. The first five entries provide Access 2.0's standard add-in menu choices.

```
[Menu Add-ins]
&Add-in Manager==Wm_Entry()
&Database Documentor==Doc_PrintDataBase()
A&ttachment Manager==Am_Entry()
Im&port Database...==Doc_ImportDatabase()
&Menu Builder==CustomMenuBuilder()
Domain &Function Wizard==StartDomainWizard()
F&orm Design Tools==flib_OpenFDTools()
Mac&ro to Module==flib_ConvertMacros()
&New Procedure==flib_NewProc()
```

The syntax to add an add-in menu choice is the text of the menu choice followed by a double equal sign (used in C as the identity operator) and the entry-point function name with following parentheses. Access treats the part of the entry after the first equal sign as a command, similar to the *=FunctionName()* syntax used to assign a function in a module to an event. To execute a function from an event, you need to prefix an equal sign to the command (thus the two equal signs). Figure 3.3 illustrates the Help menu choices added by the preceding [Menu Add-ins] section entries.

FIGURE 3.3.

Add-In submenu choices that execute functions contained in Access libraries.

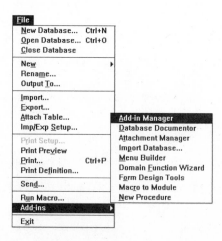

You can pass literals as arguments of the functions, if you need them. If you want to call an entry-point function in a form or report wizard from an Add-In submenu choice, you need to supply a quoted string argument that contains the name of the table or query on which the form or report created by the wizard is based, together with a wizard identification number. Access automatically passes the name of the table or query and an integer wizard ID number to libraries designated as form or report wizards. Therefore, form or report wizard entry-point functions must include designated arguments to receive these values. The syntax of the [Menu Add-ins] entry for custom form or report wizards is as follows:

```
[Menu Add-ins]
AddInMenuEntry==EntryPoint("TableOrQuery",WizardID)
```

The requirement that you pass the table or query name as a string literal restricts the form or report wizard called by an Add-In submenu choice to the data source you specify as the value of **TableOrQuery**. However, you can add as many Add-In submenu choices as you want that call the same function with different argument values. Automating the creation of entries in the **[Menu Add-Ins]** section of MSACC20.INI is discussed in the section called "Using Access 2.0's Add-In Manager," near the end of this chapter.

Limitations of Access Libraries

Access libraries have two limitations: The debugging operation of a library is not always easy while the library is attached, and the names of functions contained in library modules must not duplicate function names in any module of the database to which the library is attached. Access 2.0's new ability to open Access Basic procedures contained in library databases, as discussed in the section called "Viewing and Debugging Code in a Library Database" near the end of this chapter, makes debugging code in libraries a simpler process. Now that Access 2.0 supports macros in libraries, you can use the Add Menu action within a library to change menu choices.

The duplicate function-name problem is more difficult to overcome. All function names, including those in the modules of libraries, are stored in a global symbol table in Access. For example, if a developer uses the IsLoaded() function in an Access library and you attempt to load NWIND.MDB, which also includes an IsLoaded() function, you receive the message box shown in Figure 3.4.

FIGURE 3.4.

The message box announcing the duplication of a library function name in the database you just opened.

If this problem occurs, you need to give the function in the library another name, called an alias. You cannot short-cut the process by renaming the function in the database module, because you receive the same error message when you attempt to view the module's code. The best approach is to change the name of the function in the library. To rename a function in a library, follow these steps:

1. Close Access and comment out the attachment line for the offending library in the [Libraries] section of MSACC20.INI.

2. Reopen Access and open the library file as a database. (You need to enter the .MDA extension manually; Access does not include a library-file type in the List Files of Type drop-down list.)

3. Open the module (or any one of the modules) contained in the library.

4. Choose **R**eplace from the **E**dit menu. Type IsLoaded in the Find What text box and an alias for the module name, such as mod_IsLoaded, as shown in Figure 3.5. (Use a mnemonic abbreviation for the module name as the *mod_* prefix.) If there is more than one module in the library, click the Loaded Modules option button. Click the Replace All command button to make the changes. (Clicking the Verify button is a more conservative method.)

5. Choose **Co**mpile Loaded Modules from the **R**un module to check to see that all instances of references to IsLoaded (including instances where the code sets the return value of the function) are replaced.

6. If the module contains a test form, or you have added an Add-In submenu choice to execute the entry-point function that calls *mod_*IsLoaded(), execute the function to check for the absence of runtime errors.

7. Choose **S**ave from the **F**ile menu to save the changes to your module.

8. Close Access, reattach the library, launch Access, and try again. You must repeat the preceding steps if there are additional duplicate names in the database and the library.

The preceding steps are valid also for changing the names of duplicate global constants and variables.

> **TIP**
>
> As a rule, it is a better policy to change duplicate function names in the library module rather than in your application. If you use macros to call functions, you must rename the function call in each macro in your application. Regardless of where you change the offending function name, you must find the events of all objects that call the function. There currently is no simple means of doing this in Access; Access 2.0 lacks a search-and-replace function for properties and events of objects.

FIGURE 3.5.

Renaming an offending function name in an Access library.

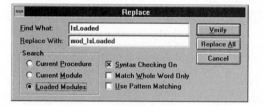

Some authors of modules go to extremes to prevent duplicating Access Basic function names in libraries, but they forget to do the same for Windows API functions and global constant declarations. The function names, variables, and constants in wizard libraries often are prefixed with zw. Windows API function prototypes that are declared in the Declarations section of library modules, such as `GetOpenFileName()`, `GetSaveFileName()`, and `lstrcpy()`, often appear in other libraries and modules of databases. You may need to alias these functions to make the Database Analyzer operable with a database application. Aliasing Windows API functions is a special case. For more information, refer to Chapter 22.

A more insidious problem is the duplicate definition of global constants or variables. Access 1.x's ANALYZER.MDA, for example, contains the line `Global Const DefaultMessage = "Select an object button to display a list of those objects"` in the Localization Constants module. This appears to be a rather innocuous line of code, but it results in a runtime error if a module in the open database declares a `Global Const DefaultMessage = "Verboten!"` (You substitute localization constant modules for applications published in different languages.) In this case, you receive a runtime error when a function in either module requests the value of `DefaultMessage`. You get the rather abrupt runtime error message box that is shown in Figure 3.6. If the request for the value of `DefaultMessage` is buried deep in the code, you receive only the error message under a particular set of circumstances. (This usually occurs when you are demonstrating the final version of your application to your client or supervisor.) The solution here is to add a prefix and create a name—such as `engDefaultMessage` or `deuDefaultMessage`—that is less likely to be duplicated in other code.

FIGURE 3.6.

The message box that appears when a global constant or variable is defined in a library and a database.

Security Issues with Access Libraries

The majority of Access Libraries available at the time this book was written were created by members of the Microsoft development, quality-assurance, and product-support staff for Access. Authors of books on Access and independent Access developers also contribute libraries, mostly freeware, to the MSACCESS forum on CompuServe. (Freeware is a term used to describe applications that may be copyrighted by their developers but payment of license or usage fees is not expected.) Often, these freeware libraries are used to demonstrate ingenious Access Basic coding techniques or combo-box marvels, so you have full permission to view and modify the database objects that the libraries contain.

On the other hand, publishers of commercial Access libraries, including Wizards, usually restrict permissions to view and modify the Access Basic code in their modules. Restricting the viewing of code in modules is accomplished by clearing the check box for Read Design, Modify Design, and Administer permissions of the Users Group for each module in the library, making sure that the owner of the database objects is not Admin, and verifying that there is no member of the Admins users group named Admin with an empty password when the final distribution version of the product is created. Furthermore, commercial publishers usually encrypt the database. Securing Access Basic code and other database objects in commercial database applications is one of the subjects of Chapter 29, "Distributing Runtime Versions of Your Databases." Distributing an application with MSARN200.EXE does not preclude the purchaser from running the product under MSACCESS.EXE.

When a runtime error occurs with a secure library database, the problem of duplicate definitions increases in severity. In this case, the "permissions" term in the message in the dialog box of Figure 3.1 (earlier in this chapter) is correct; you do not have permissions to view the code in the module. Therefore you need to alter the code in the database application to alias the offending function, constant, or variable names. If the code in the database application is secure (an unlikely occurrence), you are out of luck.

Using Freeware Access Libraries for Developers

Non-commercial Access libraries serve three purposes for developers:

- ■ Speeding the creation of Access applications by providing automatic shortcuts for tedious manual operations, such as creating menu macros.
- ■ Adding new features to Access applications, such as the ability to make multiple selections in a list box.
- ■ Demonstrating Access Basic coding techniques that you can use in your database applications or to create your own libraries.

The sections that follow describe two libraries, both written by members of the Access team at Microsoft Corporation, that you can use to improve your Access application-development productivity. These early libraries portend commercial libraries and wizards that will be created by ISVs (independent software vendors) to aid developers of Access applications, paralleling the third-party development tools now available for popular DOS DBMSs and compilers such as dBASE, Clipper, FoxPro, and Paradox.

NOTE

You can use most Access 1.x libraries with Access 2.0 without the need to convert the *LIBRARY.MDA* file to Access 2.0's format. However, libraries that you or others create with Access 2.0 cannot be attached to Access 1.x applications running under version 1.x of Access. If you attempt to attach an Access 2.0 library to an Access 1.x application, you receive an "Incompatible database version" message box followed by a message that reads, "Some library database modules could not be loaded. Click OK or press Enter to continue." Your Access 1.x application runs, but library functions are not accessible.

FIRSTLIB.MDA: A Multipurpose Add-In for Access Developers

An example of a library designed primarily for Access 1.1 developers is Andrew R. Miller's FIRSTLIB.MDA. You can download FIRSTLIB.MDA as FIRST.ZIP from Library 15, Third Party, of the MSACCESS Forum on CompuServe. The version of FIRSTLIB.MDA that was available at the time this book was written contains four basic tools you can launch with key combinations. The documentation file, FIRSTLIB.TXT, included in FIRST.ZIP, provides a complete description of how to install and use each of the four functions in FIRSTLIB.MDA. Three of the four tools are described briefly in the sections that follow.

> **NOTE**
>
> The Menu Builder of FIRSTLIB.MDA and parts of the Form Design Tool Palette have been incorporated into Access 2.0's WZBLDR.MDA library and into Access 2.0 itself. The Menu Builder of FIRSTLIB.MDA uses the `BuilderFormOnMenu` function that is no longer supported by Access 2.0. (The `OnMenu` event of Access 1.x is the `MenuBar` property of Access 2.0 forms and reports.) Therefore, the Menu Builder of FIRSTLIB.MDA is not included in the discussion that follows.

FIRSTLIB.MDA is a "borderline wizard" because it creates module objects and it modifies objects that are contained in your forms and reports. FIRSTLIB.MDA does not, however, create new form or report objects, so it is classified as an add-in library, not a wizard. This library contains quite sophisticated code, typical of that found in commercial wizards. Some of the more interesting elements of the code, which uses Access 1.x conventions, are examined in the following sections.

> **NOTE**
>
> You need to import the AutoKeys macro that is included in FIRSTLIB.MDA into your database in order to activate the four key combinations that are defined in the AutoKeys macrogroup with `RunCode` `EntryPoint()` functions. If you already have an AutoKeys macro, the AutoKeys macro of FIRSTLIB.MDA will import as AutoKeys1. If this occurs, rename your old AutoKeys macro to another name, then rename AutoKeys1 to AutoKeys. Alternately, you can run any of the functions except Menu Builder from the Immediate window by entering `? EntryPoint()`, or use the Help menu choices method described earlier in this chapter.

The Form Design Tool Palette

The Form Design Tools Palette, launched with Shift+F12, displays a modeless pop-up toolbox form, shown in Figure 3.7, with two rows of six tools to assist in the design of forms. Modeless pop-up forms are used to create floating toolboxes or menus that always remain on top of other windows. Tools to create shadowed and sunken frames around controls, to size and align control objects, and to bring control objects to the front or send them to the back are included in the palette. Many of these functions are now standard features of Access 2.0, but the Form Design Tools Palette is an interesting example of a wizard with readable Access Basic code. The entry point of the Form Design Tools function is `flib_OpenFDTools()`.

FIGURE 3.7.

The modeless pop-up form of the Form Design Tools Palette.

Figure 3.7 demonstrates a creative use of bitmaps to replace the caption text of command buttons. Designing and applying bitmaps to command and toggle buttons is one of the subjects of Chapter 26 of this book, "Customizing Access Applications with Special Menus and Toolbars." You can add floating toolboxes to serve as navigation tools for your applications. For example, if your Access application involves a series of nested forms that users display with Next and Back command buttons, you can provide a set of shortcut buttons in a floating toolbox to show a specific form. In most cases, however, using Access 2.0's new custom toolbars provides a simpler approach.

NOTE

Examples of the use of Access Basic code in libraries appear in this section and in the sections that follow. If you're not familiar with programming languages, skip over the code examples for now. Finish reading Part III, "Using Access Basic," and then return to this point. However, if you've programmed in xBase, PAL, or Object PAL (OPAL), it's likely that you'll be able to understand most of the examples.

The code associated with the Form Design Tools Palette employs some seldom-seen Access Basic reserved words and code constructs. When you click the Uniform Size button (the fourth button from the left in the top row of the FDTools form), the Make Controls Uniform Size dialog box appears, as shown in Figure 3.8. The `flib_CreateControlList()` function creates an array of the names and types of control objects contained in the active form. The number of control objects on a form is returned by the `iMax = Forms(iFrm).Count` expression, where `iFrm` is the number of the form. You need this value to determine the size of the array to hold the names and types of the control objects. The peculiar-appearing expression, `Forms(iFrm)(iCtl).ControlName`, returns the control name of the control in the position on the form object, `Form(0)` for instance, determined by the value of `iCtrl`, which is an array subscript.

```
Function flib_CreateControlList (iFrm As Integer) As Integer
    Dim iCtl As Integer
    iMax = Forms(iFrm).Count
    If (iMax > 0) Then
        ReDim ControlList(0 To (iMax - 1))
        For iCtl = 0 To iMax - 1
            ControlList(iCtl).stName = _Forms(iFrm)(iCtl).ControlName
            ControlList(iCtl).stType = _
            ➥flib_StControlType(Forms(iFrm)(iCtl))
            ControlList(iCtl).iSelList = -1
        Next iCtl
    End If
    flib_CreateControlList = iMax
End Function
```

FIGURE 3.8.

The dialog box that appears when you click the Uniform Size button of the Form Design Tools Palette.

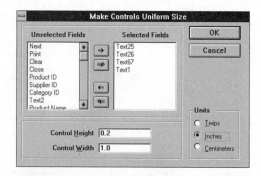

newly saved form with any of the tools in the Form Design Tools palette. The AutoKeys macro contained in FIRSTLIB.MDA behaves normally when you open FIRSTLIB.MDA as a database.

The function call to the `flib_stControlType()` function passes the control object, **Forms**(iFrm)(iCtl), as an argument of the **Control** data type. The `flib_StControlType()` function returns a string corresponding to the **TypeOf** of the control. A portion of the code of `flib_stControlType()` follows:

```
Function flib_StControlType (c As Control) As String
    If TypeOf c Is BoundObjectFrame Then
        flib_StControlType = "BoundObjectFrame"
    ElseIf TypeOf c Is CheckBox Then
        flib_StControlType = "CheckBox"
    ElseIf TypeOf c Is ComboBox Then
        flib_StControlType = "ComboBox"
        ...
    ElseIf TypeOf c Is TextBox Then
        flib_StControlType = "TextBox"
    ElseIf TypeOf c Is ToggleButton Then
        flib_StControlType = "ToggleButton"
    Else
        flib_StControlType = "Rectangle"
    End If
End Function
```

The **TypeOf** Access Basic reserved word did not make it into the Access 1.1 Basic Language Reference, either under **TypeOf** or **Is**. The Language Reference states that the **Is** operator "appears only with the Null reserved word." The **Is** operator, however, also is used with the **Select Case** construct and the **TypeOf** reserved word. **TypeOf** is discussed in the *Introduction to Programming* booklet. You are likely to encounter many undocumented or semidocumented functions, reserved words, constants, and other gems in libraries designed for Access developers, especially libraries written by Microsoft personnel.

The Macro To Module Converter

The Macro To Module Converter (Ctrl+F12) converts macros to their equivalents in Access Basic code. This library function is especially useful when you decide to create a library from a database application that includes macros. The Converter creates a text file from the macro that you import into your module with the Load Text choice of the File menu. `flib_ConvertMacros()` is the entry-point function. Figure 3.9 shows the Macro To Module Converter's form.

FIGURE 3.9.

*The form for
FIRSTLIB.MDA's
Convert Macro To
Module function.*

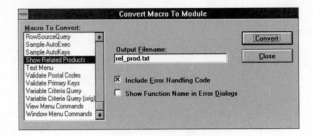

The flib_LstMacrosInit procedure of the DlgMacToMod module creates an array of names of macros by running an SQL query against the MSysObjects table. Comments are added to the code of the flib_LstMacrosInit procedure in the following listing:

```
Sub flib_LstMacrosInit ()
    Dim db As Database
    Dim ds As Dynaset
    Set db = CurrentDB()

    'Return a Dynaset consisting of the rows containing the Names
    'of macros from the MSysObjects table to fill the list box
    stSQL$ = "SELECT Name FROM MSysObjects WHERE Type = " +
    ➥Format$(idMACROOBJ) + " ORDER BY Name;"
    Set ds = db.CreateDynaset(stSQL$)
    If (ds.RecordCount = 0) Then
        cMacros = 0
        ds.Close
        db.Close
    End If

    'Count the number of records to obtain the UBound() of the _array
    ds.MoveLast
    cMacros = ds.RecordCount
    ds.MoveFirst

    'Create the array of macro names to populate the list box later
    ReDim rgstMacros(1 To cMacros)
    For i% = 1 To cMacros
        rgstMacros(i%) = ds!Name
        ds.MoveNext
    Next i%

    'Clean up
    ds.Close
    db.Close
End Sub
```

The value of idMACROOBJ is obtained from the declaration Const idMACROOBJ = - 32766 in the Declarations section of the DlgMacToMod module. The use of the

MSysObjects table to obtain data on objects and how the values in the Type field of MSysObjects correspond to database objects are two of the subjects of Chapter 27, "Documenting Your Access Applications."

The values of the elements of the array are used by the flib_LstMacros() function to add the entries shown in the Macro To Convert list box of the Convert Macro To Module form that is shown in Figure 3.9. The following code listing is an example of using a function as the RowSourceType property of a list box or combo box. Open the DlgMacToMod form of FIRSTLIB.MDA in design mode, then select the Macro To Convert list box. When you open the Properties window, the entry =flib_LstMacros() appears as the value of the RowSourceType property.

When you specify a function as the RowSourceType property of a list or combo box, Access automatically creates five pointers to arguments for the function: the control object (fld), a unique ID number supplied by the function (id), the row number (row), column number (col) and a value ranging from 0 to 6 (code) that indicates what information is to be returned by the function. The function you create must include placeholders for these arguments. Access automatically calls the function repeatedly to obtain the information necessary to fill the list or combo box. The code of flib_LstMacros() appears in the following listing:

```
Function flib_LstMacros (fld As Control, id, row, col, code) As _Variant
    Select Case code
        Case 0                         'Initialize.
            flib_LstMacrosInit          'Create the rgstMacros() array
            flib_LstMacros = True       'Advice array is valid
        Case 1                         'Open the instance of the _control.
            flib_LstMacros = Timer      'Unique ID number for control.
        Case 3                         'Number of rows.
            flib_LstMacros = cMacros
        Case 4                         'Number of columns.
            flib_LstMacros = 1
        Case 5                         'Column Width.
            flib_LstMacros = -1         'Use default width.
        Case 6                         'Get data.
            flib_LstMacros = rgstMacros(row + 1)
    End Select
End Function
```

Each call to flib_LstMacros increments the value of code by 1 until code = 6. The data returned by flib_LstMacros is determined by the **Select Case...End Select** structure. Access calls flib_LstMacros with code = 6 until the values for the number of rows specified when code = 3 have been returned. This is a rather arcane method of passing values from an array, but the method overcomes the problem of the inability of Access Basic to pass an array as the value of an argument of a Windows DLL.

Figure 3.10 illustrates the text file of the `ShowRelatedProducts()` function that the Converter creates automatically from the Show Related Products macro of NWIND.MDB. (Word wrap is enabled in Figure 3.10 so that the entire **DoCmd** `OpenForm` statement is visible.)

FIGURE 3.10.

The text file of a function created from a macro by the Convert Macro To Module function of FIRSTLIB.MDA.

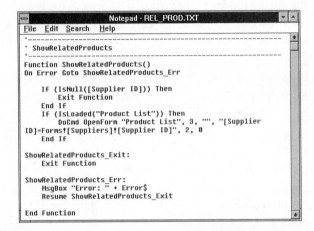

```
'---------------------------------------------------------
' ShowRelatedProducts
'---------------------------------------------------------
Function ShowRelatedProducts()
On Error Goto ShowRelatedProducts_Err

    If (IsNull([Supplier ID])) Then
        Exit Function
    End If
    If (IsLoaded("Product List")) Then
        DoCmd OpenForm "Product List", 3, "", "[Supplier
ID]=Forms![Suppliers]![Supplier ID]", 2, 0
    End If

ShowRelatedProducts_Exit:
    Exit Function

ShowRelatedProducts_Err:
    MsgBox "Error: " + Error$
    Resume ShowRelatedProducts_Exit

End Function
```

NOTE

If you use the Macro To Module Converter with macrogroups, make sure that the macro name appears on a line by itself, without a designated action. If the line contains the macro name and an action, the **Function** *FunctionName*`()` line does not appear in the resulting text file.

The Extended New Procedure Dialog

The Extended New Procedure Dialog (F12) adds standardized headers and error-handling code to Access Basic functions or procedures. The entry-point function is `flib_NewProc()`. This tool, which uses the **SendKeys** statement of Access Basic to create the function stub, can save a substantial amount of typing when you are writing many Access Basic functions. The Macro To Module Converter uses the Extended New Procedure code that creates the strings used for function or procedure stubs. Figure 3.11 shows the New Procedure dialog box in the process of creating a function stub. Figure 3.12 displays the resulting `BogusFunction()` stub.

FIGURE 3.11.

The New Procedure dialog box of FIRSTLIB.MDA.

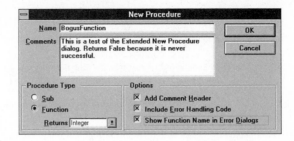

The `flib_AddNewProc` procedure of the ModBasicUtils module exercises the gamut of the **SendKeys** statement. Writers of WordPerfect macros will feel a twinge of nostalgia when reviewing code that makes extensive use of **SendKeys**. You can add the statement **"{TAB}" &**, shown in bold type in the code listing that follows, to indent the **On Error GoTo** ... line.

```
Sub flib_AddNewProc (stName$, iType%, stRetVal$, stComments$, _fHdr%,
➡fErr%, fFxnNames%)

    'Move to the end of the current function, and type
    'the keyword "Function" or "Sub.
    If (iType = 1) Then
        SendKeys "^{END}Sub "
    Else
        SendKeys "^{END}Function "
    End If

    'Send the function name, argument list, and
    'press {ENTER} to seal the deal.
    SendKeys stName$
    SendKeys "()"
    If (iType = 2) Then
        If (stRetVal$ <> "<None>") Then
            SendKeys " As " + stRetVal$
        End If
    End If
    SendKeys "{ENTER}"

    'If user wants error handling, add it for him automatically.
    If (fErr%) Then
        SendKeys "{TAB}" & flib_StParseSk(flib_StProcHdr(stName$)) +
        ➡"{ENTER}"
        SendKeys "{ENTER}"
        SendKeys "{ENTER}"
        SendKeys flib_StParseSk(flib_StProcFtr(stName$, iType%,
        ➡fFxnNames%))
    End If

    If (fHdr) Then
        SendKeys "^{HOME}{ENTER}^{HOME}{END}{- 60}{ENTER}"
```

```
    SendKeys " " + stName$ + "{ENTER}"
If (stComments$ <> "") Then
    SendKeys "{ENTER}"
    stComments$ = flib_StBlockTxt(stComments$, 55)
    While (InStr(stComments$, Chr$(13)) > 0)
        SendKeys "    " + flib_StParseSk(Left$(stComments$,
    ➥InStr(stComments$, Chr$(13)) - 1)) + "{ENTER}"
        stComments$ = Mid$(stComments$, InStr(stComments$,
    ➥Chr$(13)) + 2)
    Wend
    SendKeys "    " + flib_StParseSk(stComments$) +
    ➥" {ENTER}"
End If
SendKeys "{- 60}"
SendKeys "{HOME}{DOWN 4}"
    End If
End Sub
```

> **NOTE**
>
> You can replace the **While...Wend** structure of BASIC with the modern Object Basic variant **Do While...Loop**. The advantage of **Do While...Loop** is that you can use the **Exit Do** statement to escape from within the loop.

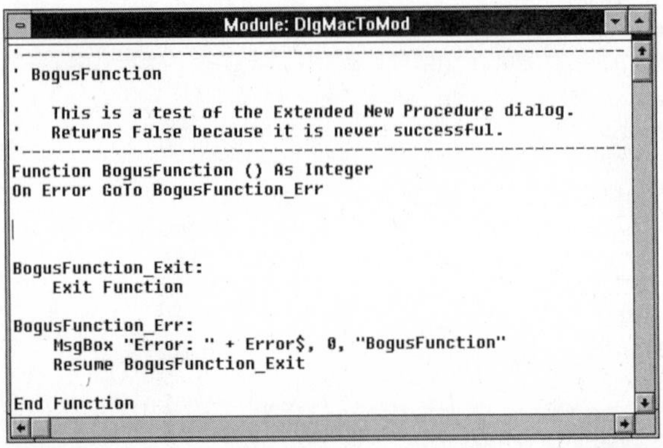

FIGURE 3.12.

The function stub created from the New Procedure dialog entries of Figure 3.11.

```
'----------------------------------------
' BogusFunction
'
'    This is a test of the Extended New Procedure dialog.
'    Returns False because it is never successful.
'----------------------------------------
Function BogusFunction () As Integer
On Error GoTo BogusFunction_Err


BogusFunction_Exit:
    Exit Function

BogusFunction_Err:
    MsgBox "Error: " + Error$, 0, "BogusFunction"
    Resume BogusFunction_Exit

End Function
```

> **WARNING**
>
> Do not attempt to run the Extended New Procedure function by opening DlgNewProc while FIRSTLIB.MDA is open as a database. If you click the OK button of the New Procedure form, the **SendKeys** statement sends key strokes to whatever object it can find with the focus (the New Procedure dialog box, initially). You are guaranteed to receive an unexpected result.

DOMAIN.MDA: A Tool for Using the Domain Aggregate Functions

DOMAIN.MDA is a library, created by Dan Madoni when he was a member of Microsoft Product Support Services, that creates domain aggregate function syntax for you. Dan is the author of the ANALYZER.MDA that was distributed with the retail version of Access 1.x. Analyzer has been replaced with the Database Documenter add-in of Access 2.0. You can download DOMAIN.MDA as DOMAIN.ZIP from Library 15, "3rd Party," of the MSACCESS Forum on CompuServe

Although Dan calls DOMAIN.MDA the "Aggregate Wizard," DOMAIN.MDA is categorized here as an Access add-in. To qualify as a wizard in this book, the library must create a form, a report, or a control object on a form or report, in your database. DOMAIN.MDA, however, is a good example of a multistep Access library tool. You follow these steps after launching the Aggregate Wizard to create the aggregate function statement:

1. Choose the domain aggregate function you want by clicking the appropriate option button, and then click the Next button to display the table/query list box. The `Domain_SetDWhichWizard()` function creates a **Snapshot** of the tables and queries in your database from the MSysObjects table and then adds only the table and query names to an array.

2. Select the table or query that contains the field whose data is used in the aggregate function from the list box filled with the array elements created in Step 1. Click the Next button to display the fields of the table or query in a list box. The `Domain_SetDFunctionTable()` function creates a **Snapshot** of the fields of the selected table or query with the **ListFields** method and places the data from the **Snapshot** into another array.

3. Select the field that provides the data to the aggregate function from the list box that is filled with the values from the array created in the preceding step. Click the Next button to display the form to enter optional filter criteria.

4. Specify the filter criteria you want, and then click the Next button. The domain aggregate function syntax appears as shown in Figure 3.13.

5. Click the Copy Domain Function to clipboard button, then close the window with the Cancel button or by double-clicking the document control box. Use Ctrl+V to paste the function into your Access Basic code, preceded by an equal sign, in the Control Source property of a text box.

FIGURE 3.13.

The last window of the Aggregate Wizard, before the domain aggregate function syntax has been copied to the clipboard.

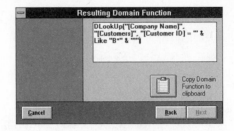

One of the principal design elements of a multistep Access library tool or wizard is the use of Next and Back command buttons for navigation, plus a Cancel button that allows the user to exit the sequence and close the form at any point in the action. The code in the Domain_WizardCode module of DOMAIN.MDA is quite typical of that which you might use to choose tables, queries, and fields to create libraries for applications that create SQL statements from user-defined choices. In DOMAIN.MDA, Dan uses the **ListFields** method to populate the field list box of DomainWizardForm2, as shown in the listing of Domain_SetDFunctionTable that follows:

```
Function Domain_SetDFunctionTable (SetTo As String)
    ' Set Global table name variable
    DFunctionTable = Trim(SetTo)

    DoCmd Hourglass True

    'Open VT objects
    Dim Domain_UserDatabaseObject As Database
    Dim Domain_Snapshot As Snapshot
    Set Domain_UserDatabaseObject = CurrentDB()
    Set Domain_Snapshot =
➡Domain_UserDatabaseObject.ListFields(DFunctionTable)

    'Copy dynaset to array
    DNumOfItems = 0
    Domain_Snapshot.MoveFirst
    Do Until Domain_Snapshot.EOF
        DItems(DNumOfItems, 1) = Domain_Snapshot!Name
        DItems(DNumOfItems, 2) = Trim(Str(Domain_Snapshot!Type))
        DNumOfItems = DNumOfItems + 1
        Domain_Snapshot.MoveNext
    Loop

    If Len(Trim(DFunctionField)) = 0 Then
        DFunctionField = DItems(0, 1)
    End If

    DoCmd Hourglass False
```

```
    execfunc = Domain_GenericClose()
    DoCmd OpenForm "DomainWizardForm2"
End Function
```

Methods that return the properties of databases, such as **ListTables**, **ListIndexes**, and **ListFields**, are Access 1.x methods used primarily in conjunction with wizards and developer libraries, as well as for documenting your databases. These methods have been replaced in Access 2.0 by the preferred method of enumerating the TableDefs collection and the properties of **TableDef** objects. The List... methods remain in Access 2.0 for backward compatibility. Using these methods to document your database applications is one of the subjects of Chapter 27.

Using Access 2.0's Add-In and Wizard Manager

Access's Add-In Manager is designed to make installation of new add-ins and the removal of existing add-ins easy for the Access user. In this and the sections that follow, the term "libraries" is used in lieu of "add-Ins," because the Add-In Manager also installs and uninstalls wizards. A better name for the Add-in Manager of Access might be Library Manager. Add-In Manager was chosen to conform to the terminology used by other Microsoft Applications, such as Excel, which also have an Add-In manager or the equivalent.

Libraries have a special system table, USysAddIns, that identifies the library to Add-In manager as a legitimate, version 2.0 add-in library or wizard. The first of the following sections describes how you use the Add-In Manager to install the Access 2.0 version of FIRSTLIB.MDA, created as FIRSTLI2.MDA by converting a renamed version 1.1 copy of FIRSTLIB.MDA. A USysAddIns table added to FIRSTLI2.MDA provides the required information for the Add-In Manager. (Chapter 23 describes how to create the USysAddIns table and add the necessary records.) The last section of this chapter describes how you customize add-ins.

> **NOTE**
>
> When you convert an Access database file from version 1.x to 2.0, the name of the converted file must be the same as the name of the file being converted (thus the need to rename the file to be converted if you want to retain the Access 1.1 version).

Installing and Uninstalling Add-Ins

Installing a library consists of adding an entry for the add-in to the [Libraries] section of MSACC20.INI, and then adding entries to the [Menu Add-Ins] section for add-ins and to the appropriate [...Wizards] section(s) if the library contains wizards. Uninstalling the add-in removes the corresponding entries from each affected section. To install or uninstall a library, follow these steps:

1. Choose Add-Ins from the **F**ile menu, then choose **A**dd-In Manager from the Add-Ins submenu to display the Add-In Manager dialog box. Before the dialog box appears, the Add-In Manager opens each library database with an .MDA extension in your \ACCESS directory and reads the data from the USysAddIns table, if the table exists.

2. Select the add-in or wizard you want to install or uninstall in the Available Libraries list box. The first four items in the list box shown in Figure 3.14 are default entries for the Access 2.0 wizards and builders. The FIRSTLIB entry is for the Access 1.1 version of FIRSTLIB.MDA, which does not have a USysAddIns table. The last entry is for FIRSTLI2.MDA, a new library.

FIGURE 3.14.

Add-In Manager displaying libraries in the \ACCESS directory.

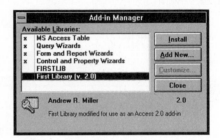

3. If you select a library that has not been installed (that is, there is no "X" to the left of the library's assigned name), the caption of the top button of the dialog box is "Install"; if the library is currently installed (there is an "X" in the installed column), the button's caption reads "Uninstall." To install First Library (v. 2.0), select its entry and click the Install button.

4. Click the Close button to return to Access. A message box appears, advising that you must restart Access for the entries to take effect. (This is because Access attaches library databases specified in MSACC20.INI during the launch process.) (See Figure 3.15.)

FIGURE 3.15.

*The notice that you
must relaunch
Access to activate
changes made by
the Add-In
Manager.*

Customizing Add-Ins

The Add-In Manager gives you the option of altering the content of libraries that offer customization features. If a library database is customizable, the Customize command button is enabled. When you click the Customize button, Add-In Manager calls a different entry point function whose name is specified in the FunctionToCallOnCustomize record of the USysAddIns table. All of the libraries supplied with Access 2.0, except the Query Wizards, have at least one customizable feature.

If you or your clients use special mailing labels that are not included in the standard list of labels offered by the Mailing Label (Report) Wizard, you can add your own label definition to the list by adding a new label to the Wizard's repertoire. Each of the 107 standard labels is specified by a record in the LabelSizes table included in WZFRMRPT.MDA, and records for labels you define are added to the UserSizes table. The Mailing Label Wizard is used as an example of a customizable wizard, because it demonstrates a library database that is a self-contained transaction-processing application.

To add a new record to the UserSizes table of the Mailing Label Wizard, follow these steps:

1. Select the Form and Report Wizards item in Add-In Manager's Available Libraries list box. (See Figure 3.16.) Click the Customize button to display the Customize Add-In dialog.

2. Double-click the Customize Mailing Label Sizes item in the Customize list box to display the User Label Sizes dialog box shown in Figure 3.17. (The Form and Report Wizards must be installed to customize a mailing label.) The description list box is empty if you have not added a custom label definition.

FIGURE 3.16.

Selecting the Form and Report Wizard for customizing.

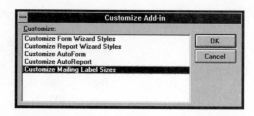

FIGURE 3.17.

The User Label Sizes dialog box before adding a custom mailing label.

3. Click the New button to display the New Mailing label dialog box. Give the label a descriptive name in the Label Name text box; then enter the dimensions of the label and the number of labels across in the text boxes provided. (The layout of the dimension entry area of the dialog box is an example of how good graphic design can turn otherwise complex data entry forms into easy-to-use application components.)

4. Enter the dimensions of your custom label in the text boxes bound to fields of the User Sizes table, as shown in Figure 3.18. Click the OK button when you've entered values for each dimension.

5. Your new user-defined mailing label appears in the User Label Sizes as shown in Figure 3.19.

FIGURE 3.18.

Adding the required dimensions for a user-defined mailing label.

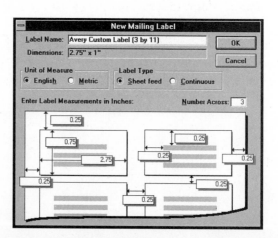

FIGURE 3.19.

The new user-defined mailing label entry in the User Label Sizes list box.

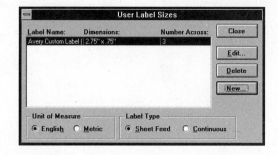

Chapter 23, "Developing Access Libraries and Add-Ins," describes how to design customizable wizards for use with commercial Access applications.

> **NOTE**
>
> The mailing-label customization process departs from the norm of standard Access wizards by dispensing with the Next and Back buttons, as well as by eliminating the other graphic elements, such as the swash bit map, associated with Microsoft-supplied Wizards. Thus the mailing label customizing process is more akin to an add-in application than a wizard. Add-ins such as a mailing label "customizer" are excellent candidates for inclusion in a library database because mini-applications of this type can be used with a variety of full-scale Access applications.

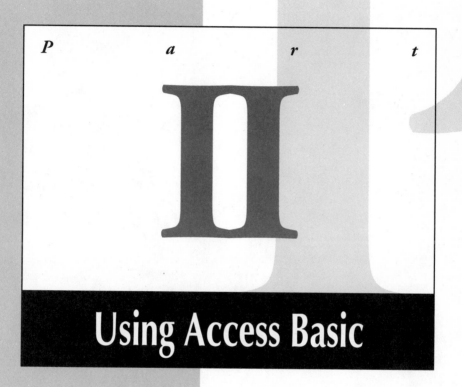

II

Using Access Basic

P

II

4

Writing Access Basic Code

You can create a functioning Access database application without writing a single line of Access Basic code. It is unlikely, however, that such a codeless application would satisfy the requirements of the majority of your clients or co-workers. Although the 50 actions you can execute with Access 2.0 macros are surprisingly versatile, the vast majority, if not all, of the applications you create for other people need at least a few functions written in Access Basic. Even the simple Country Filter.Open macro, attached to the OnOpen event of NWIND.MDB's Customer Mailing Labels form, needs the user-defined IsLoaded() function of the Utility Functions module. Distributing runtime versions of Access applications makes using Access Basic code instead of macros a virtual necessity. As pointed out in the preceding chapter, any error encountered in the execution of a macro run without an active form or report with error trapping is fatal—only errors you trap with Access Basic code are survivable. Thus, this book contains few examples of the use of macros. Refer to Access 2.0 documentation and introductory Access books for examples of the use of macros. (It should be noted that the AutoExec and menu macros are needed by all commercial Access applications.)

As mentioned in the introduction to this book, readers are expected to be familiar with the basic concepts of computer programming and to have some experience in writing programming code in a procedural (third-generation or 3GL) language, such as dBASE or its derivative xBase dialects, the Paradox Application Language (or ObjectPAL), or one of the many flavors of BASIC. Experience in writing more complex Excel or Word macros also prepares you for the content of this chapter. Where comparisons of the syntax of programming languages are made, xBase is used as the standard because xBase applications dominate the DOS desktop RDBMS marketplace.

The purpose of this chapter is to provide the foundation you need in generic Object Basic to develop commercial Access database applications. Most of the Object Basic syntax examples in this chapter apply equally to Access Basic, Visual Basic, Visual Basic for Applications, and, in all likelihood, the next generation of Word Basic. The next chapter introduces you to Object Basic features and keywords that are unique to Access Basic. The remaining chapters of this book provide increasingly complex examples of Access Basic coding techniques. Many of these examples will be applicable to other dialects of Object Basic as Microsoft releases additional applications with Visual Basic for Applications as their programming language.

NOTE

Microsoft does not officially acknowledge the existence of "Object Basic," but the term has been in widespread internal use in Redmond since the disappearance of "Embedded Basic," which was originally intended to describe Visual Basic for Applications. In the early beta versions of Access 1.0, Access Basic was called "Embedded Basic." When all of Microsoft's mainstream Windows applications adopt Visual Basic for Applications, the term "Object Basic" will become obsolete.

Adopting Object Basic as Your Application Development Language

Database developers who have experience with one of the dialects of xBase or PAL will have little difficulty adopting the syntax of Object Basic. Both of these languages have roots in BASIC. Object Basic includes most of the commands and functions available to xBase and PAL programmers. Many Object Basic commands and functions, however, are disguised by a naming convention that extends back in history to the original line-numbered Dartmouth BASIC (Beginner's All-purpose Symbolic Instruction Code). To change from `IF...ELSE...ENDIF` commands in xBase to **`If...Then...Else[If]...End If`** structures in Access Basic, you simply must break old typing habits, not learn a new programming language. Adapting to the object-oriented, event-driven environment of Windows programming is likely to pose more problems than remembering the minor syntactical differences in commands and functions. The extent to which Object Basic truly is object-oriented is a matter of debate, but there is no question that Object Basic is event-driven. The event-driven aspects of Object Basic and its Access Basic dialect are the subject of Chapter 7, "Using Access Objects, Methods, and Events."

NOTE

Examples of command and function syntax appear in monospace type in this book. Object Basic reserved words and keywords are mixed-case (following the convention for Object Basic); reserved words are boldface in this book, for emphasis and to make reading code examples easier. Keywords of syntax examples for other programming languages, except C and C++, are uppercase (the convention for xBase, PAL, and SQL).

If you have created Visual Basic applications, you are already an Object Basic programmer. Both Visual Basic and Access Basic are dialects of Object Basic, the root language destined to become the application-programming language of all future Microsoft mainstream applications for Windows. All Microsoft Object Basic dialects will gravitate to the Visual Basic for Applications standard. The 2.0 version of Access Basic is almost totally compliant with Visual Basic for Applications (VBA). Some of the features of VBA, such as named arguments (which are present in the current version of Word Basic) and the `With...Do...End With` structure have not yet found their way into Access Basic. Microsoft representatives have stated publicly that in the future, FoxPro users will be able to choose between using the FoxPro dialect of xBase and a derivative of Object Basic to program their Windows applications. Microsoft has a firm grasp on the market for mainstream Windows applications. Thus, independent or in-house developers who intend to base their livelihood on Windows applications need an equally firm grasp of Object Basic programming techniques.

> **NOTE**
>
> Visual Basic for Applications truly is a *standard* application-programming language. VBA is implemented for all applications that support VBA as a single windows dynamic link library, VBA.DLL. Localization (spoken-language independence) is implemented by a separate DLL; examples are VBAEN.DLL for English and VBAIT.DLL for Italian. With a single DLL, you can rest assured that the key words and reserved words of VBA for all applications are identical. What changes are the application objects that the application exposes to VBA.

Access Basic and Code Behind Forms Modules

In Access 1.x Access Basic code was contained only in **Module** objects, called *modules* in this book. Access Basic modules are related to dBASE procedure and PAL library files that contain collections of user-defined functions (UDFs), event-handling functions, and subprocedures. A single Access Basic module can contain a multitude of individual UDFs, event-handling functions, and subprocedures. The discussion that follows relates only to Access Basic code in modules, not code behind forms (except when necessary to distinguish between the two). Code behind forms (CBF) is Object Basic code that is stored with the form or report for which you write the code. The distinction between Object Basic CBF code and Access Basic code in modules is important. You use functions (**Function** *FuncName*...**End Function** structures) for event-handlers in modules, while CBF event-handing code uses subprocedures (**Sub**

ProcName...**End Sub**). Using subprocedures as event-handlers, as in Visual Basic programming, is the convention for Object Basic.

Because Access Basic functions and subprocedures stored in modules have global (public) scope, each function or subprocedure in any module of your application must have a unique name. (You can explicitly declare procedures to be **Private** and have module-level scope. The scope of variables, constants, and procedures is discussed later in this chapter.) If you attempt to create a function or procedure with a name that duplicates that of an existing function or procedure in any module of your application, you receive a "Duplicate procedure name" error message. Subprocedures and functions you declare in CBF have form- or report-level scope; that is, CBF code is only visible when the form or report is active. Thus you can have a Form_Error subprocedure in every form and report you design.

The following three sections describe the elements of Access Basic code that you incorporate in modules and Object Basic CBF code. The term *container* is used to describe the storage mechanism for CBF code.

The Declarations Section

Each module and CBF container has a Declarations section, which contains the elements of your code that apply to all the code in the module or CBF container. The following statements appear in the Declarations section:

- Options that apply to all the code in the module or container. These options are called environmental variables. The most important one is the **Option Explicit** statement, which establishes the requirement that you declare a variable before assigning the variable a value. **Option Compare** lets you choose between case-sensitive (**Binary**) and case-insensitive (**Text**) string comparisons. Access adds a third comparison option, **Database**, so that you can use the Database sort order in string comparisons.

- Declarations of variables and constants using the **Dim** *VarName* and **Const** *ConstName* statements. Variables and constants that you declare in the Declarations section are visible to (can be used by) all functions and procedures in the module or container.

- Declarations of global variables and constants using the **Global** *VarName* and **Global Const** *ConstName* statements. These variables and constants are visible to all code in your application.

- Prototype declarations for functions contained in Windows dynamic link libraries. Function prototype declarations use **Declare Function** and **Declare Sub** statements. Declaring function prototypes is one of the subjects of Chapter 22, "Using the Windows API with Access Basic." The names of function prototypes, like other Access Basic functions and procedures, are global in scope.

■ Comments, preceded by **Rem** or an apostrophe (`'`), that describe the purpose of the module and the code in the module. Copyright, version, revision, and other comments often are included in the Declarations section. Comments are optional, but strongly encouraged.

The Declarations section of a module or CBF container is similar in purpose and content to a header (.H) file for a C or C++ source code (.C or .CPP) file. When you compile a C or C++ application, the compiler assigns a memory location to each variable, constant, and function you declare in the header. The Access "compiler" (an interpreter) assigns memory locations to variables and constants declared in the Declaration section, but does so only when you first execute one of the procedures in the module or container.

> **NOTE**
>
> Examples of the source code for many of the sample functions and procedures in this chapter are included in the Object Basic module of the AB_EXAMP.MDB database from the accompanying disk. To test the examples, import the module or form and the associated database object (usually a **QueryDef**) into the Northwind Traders sample database.

Access Basic Functions

Functions written in Access Basic modules serve two purposes: to return values to expressions (user-defined functions, UDFs) and to create methods that respond to events which occur when you run your application. In CBF, functions serve only to return values, because event-handling code is contained in subprocedures. The code that makes up the working portion of the function is located between **Function** *FunctionName*() and **End Function** statements. You enclose arguments of functions in the **Function** keyword's terminating parentheses and use commas to separate multiple arguments. The process of declaring and using UDFs in Access Basic, Object Basic, and xBase is almost identical. The code for a user-defined Access Basic or CBF function that determines price discounts based on the number of a specific item that gets ordered is as follows:

```
Function sngDiscount (wOrderQuan [As Integer]) [As Single]
    Select Case wOrderQuan
        Case Is >= 1000
            sngDiscount = .25
        Case Is >= 500
```

```
            sngDiscount = .20
        Case Is >= 250
            sngDiscount = .15
        Case Is >= 100
            sngDiscount = .1
        [Case Else
            sngDiscount = 0]
    End Select
End Function
```

The optional **As Integer** and **As Single** clauses that specify the data type of the wOrderQuan argument and the return value of the sngDiscount() function are discussed in the next section, "Variables and Variable Typing in Object Basic." Enclosing statements in Roman (not bold) square brackets indicates that the statement is optional. The **Case Else** sngDiscount = 0 statement also is optional, because the default value returned by a function is 0 unless you explicitly assign a different value to the function's name.

To use the sngDiscount() function to calculate the value of a query's field that is based on the Order Details table of NWIND.MDB, you type **Net Price:[Unit Price] * (1 - sngDiscount([Quantity]))** in the Fields row of the query. The sngDiscount() function and the associated qryDiscount query are included in AB_EXAMP.MDB.

> **NOTE**
>
> Access Basic code in modules requires that you use a function, not a subprocedure, as the entry point to Access Basic code that you write to create methods to respond to events (the subject of the next chapter). The entry point is the function you specify as the value in the text box for the event in the Properties window of a form or report, or that you specify as the argument of the RunCode macro action. Using CBF code for handling events that occur on forms and reports is the preferred programming method for Access 2.0 applications.

Subprocedures

When you do not need to return a value to the procedure or event that executes the procedure, you can use subprocedures to contain code. Subprocedure code is contained between **Sub...End Sub** statements. The following is an example of the sngDiscount() function that has been converted to subprocedure form:

```
Sub Discount (sngDiscount [As Single], wOrderQuan [As Integer])
    Select Case wOrderQuan
        Case Is >= 1000
```

```
            sngDiscount = .25
        Case Is >= 500
            sngDiscount = .20
        Case Is >= 250
            sngDiscount = .15
        Case Is >= 100
            sngDiscount = .1
        [Case Else
            sngDiscount = 0]
    End Select
End Sub
```

> **NOTE**
>
> Functions and subprocedures are referred to collectively as procedures in this book. The term subprocedure distinguishes `Sub...End Sub` structures from functions. Object Basic has no "Main" procedure corresponding to the main program of xBase that you execute on start-up of the xBase application. The "Main" program of Object Basic is the application in which the code is contained, Access in this book. Until you create an executable Visual Basic application, VB.EXE is the "Main" program in Visual Basic, although you can create `Sub` Main that executes when you launch your Visual Basic application. There is no direct equivalent in Access Basic of Visual Basic's `Sub` Main. You use a RunCode action in your AutoExec macro to call your startup function that must be located in a module. (There is no form or report open at this point, so CBF code is not visible.)

You can execute a subprocedure simply by entering the name of the subprocedure as a command; the DO command of xBase, or its equivalent, is not required. If you use the optional Object Basic `Call` *ProcName* statement to execute a subprocedure, you need to enclose the parameters of the subprocedure in parentheses. If you do not include the `Call` keyword, you use a space to separate the parameters from the procedure name. Almost all of the examples of subprocedures in this book and on the accompanying disk use the `Call` statement. The `Call` statement explicitly identifies the following elements as invoking a subprocedure. The two sample functions that follow call the preceding Discount subprocedure:

```
Function sngGetDiscount (wOrderQuan As Integer) As Single
    Dim sngPercent As Single
    Discount sngPercent, wOrderQuan
    sngGetDiscount = sngPercent
End Function

Function sngCallDiscount (wOrderQuan As Integer) As Single
```

```
    Dim sngPercent As Single
    Call Discount(sngPercent, wOrderQuan)
    sngCallDiscount = sngPercent
End Function
```

You need to add the **Dim** statement to declare the local sngPercent variable and then assign the value of sngPercent, calculated by the Discount subprocedure, to sngGetDiscount to return the value to the calling expression. In Access Basic and CBF, you cannot use the function name as an argument of a function or a parameter of a subprocedure in the function itself.

The only difference between Access Basic or CBF and xBase syntax for declaring and calling procedures is substitution of keywords: **Sub** for PROCEDURE, **End Sub** for RETURN, and **Call** for DO.

NOTE

Although you can use subprocedures in Access Basic for purposes other than returning a value, most Access developers use functions exclusively. In cases where the function does not need to return a value, a common practice is to return **True** (-1) if the function is successful and **False** (0) if an error is encountered during execution of the function. You can use the **True** or **False** return value in an **If...End If** structure, such as the following:

```
If SomeFunction(Argument) Then
    [Do something]
Else
    [Do something else]
End If
```

The Access Basic and CBF Programming Interface

The user interface for writing Access Basic and CBF code is similar in all Microsoft products that have been upgraded to incorporate a dialect of Object Basic. Menu choices differ between applications, but the process of editing or creating new procedures is basically the same. Because Visual Basic applications are self-contained, you can run the code you write from a menu choice. Other applications, such as Access, in which procedures can be executed only as the result of an event that occurs in another object, do not provide the Run menu choice. Debugging techniques are similar in all Object Basic implementations; however, Visual Basic and VBA have a more sophisticated version of the Immediate window, called the Debug window, to accompany their enhanced debugging capabilities.

You can create a new procedure in an Access Basic module by opening an existing or new module, then clicking the New Procedure button of the toolbar or choosing New Procedure from the **E**dit menu to display the New Procedure dialog. You choose Function or Subprocedure, then enter the name of the procedure (see Figure 4.1). To create a new CBF subprocedure, you select the event for the procedure, click the ellipsis button, and choose Code Builder from the Choose Builder dialog box. Access 2.0 automatically names the CBF event-handling subprocedures for you, combining the name of the object that triggers the event with the event name, separated by an underscore (_) character. A subprocedure for the On Change event of a combo box named cboCustomer is **Sub** `cboCustomer_Update`. (The "On" is dropped from the name of the event in CBF procedures.) Alternatively, you can create new procedures by typing **Function** *FuncName*( ) or **Sub** *ProcName*( ) anywhere in the window of any procedure in your module or CBF container. When you create a new procedure, Access creates a procedure stub. A stub consists of the **Function...End Function** or **Sub...End Sub** statements without intervening code.

FIGURE 4.1.

*Creating a new
Access Basic
procedure in an
Access module.*

Other menu choices enable you to "compile" the source code in your procedures, use debugging features to correct errors in your code, and get context-sensitive help for Access Basic keywords. One of Access's features is syntax checking of source code as you enter it. When you complete a line and press the Enter key, the Access interpreter tests for typing errors, such as missing parentheses and quotation marks, and corrects many errors automatically—changing ENDIF to **End If**, for example.

> **NOTE**
>
> You can turn off Access Basic syntax checking by choosing Options from the View menu, selecting the Module Design category, and setting the value of the `SyntaxChecking` property to `No`. In Visual Basic you turn syntax checking on or off with a menu option.

To display the help window for a keyword, you place the caret (Windows terminology for the cursor or insertion point) in front of the first letter of the keyword (or select the keyword) and then press F1. Figure 4.2 shows the Access Basic help window for the **OpenRecordset**() method. Click the See Also hot-spot to display a pop-up window from which you can choose related topics or on the Example hot-spot to open a window that contains an example of the syntax for the keyword you selected. The 2.0 hotspot indicates that the reserved word or keyword was introduced by Access 2.0.

FIGURE 4.2.

The Access Basic context-sensitive help window.

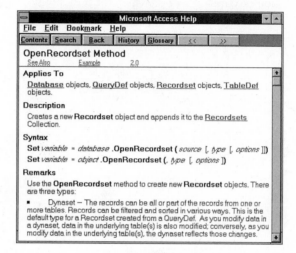

The following two sections describe the debugging features of Object Basic modules.

The Immediate Window

You can use the Immediate window to execute Access functions, examine the value of variables, or execute the functions and subprocedures you write. The Immediate window is a pop-up modeless window that remains on top of the module window as long as the module window is open (or until you close the Immediate window). Figure 4.3 shows the Immediate Window for an Access Basic module. You open this window by clicking the Immediate window of the toolbar or by choosing **I**mmediate Window from the **V**iew menu. To execute a function or display the value of a variable, type **?** (an abbreviation for the **Print** command) and the name of the function or the variable. For functions and subprocedures, you must supply the values of the function's arguments, if any.

Setting Breakpoints and Stepping Through Code

The extent of the debugging features for Object Basic code is determined by the application in which the code is used. Access enables you to set breakpoints in your code that cause execution of the code to halt after the line immediately preceding the line with the breakpoint. To set breakpoints in Access, place the caret on the line of code in which you want the breakpoint, then press F9, click the Breakpoint button of the toolbar or choose **T**oggle Breakpoint from the **R**un menu. Setting a breakpoint applies the bold attribute to the source code on the breakpoint line. Before your application executes the line on which the breakpoint is located, execution of the code halts and Access displays the module or CBF window with the breakpoint line highlighted. (Refer to Figure 4.3.)

FIGURE 4.3.

The Immediate window of Access modules and CBF containers.

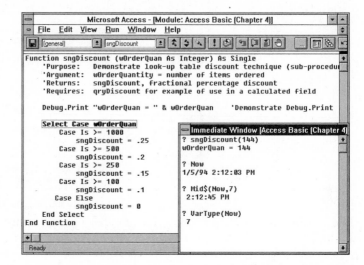

After the breakpoint has opened the module or CBF window, open the Immediate Window and examine the values of variables in your procedure. You can single step through the code from the breakpoint position by repeatedly pressing the F8 key, clicking the toolbar's Step Into button, or choosing **S**tep Into from the **R**un menu. You can jump to the next procedure in your code by pressing Shift+F8, clicking the Step Over button, or choosing Ste**p** Over from the **R**un menu. After you finish with the breakpoints, you can remove all breakpoints from the module by choosing **C**lear All Breakpoints from the **R**un menu. The menu choices for setting breakpoints and stepping through code are similar in all Object Basic dialects.

You can automate the process of displaying variable values by adding the line, **Debug.Print** *VarName*, at the location in your code where you want to test the value of *VarName*. When you open the Immediate Window, the value appears, as shown in the second line of the code in the Immediate Window in Figure 4.3. If you use more than one **Debug.Print** statement in your code, you can identify the variable with the statement **Debug.Print** "VarName = "; *VarName*. In **Debug.Print** statements, the semicolon serves the same purpose as the **&** concatenation operator (which also works). If you concatenate variables with a comma (,) instead of an ampersand (&), the variables appear left-justified in 14-character-wide fields.

Variables and Variable Typing in Object Basic

Computer languages that you compile and link to create executable files (COBOL, C, and Pascal are examples) are called strongly typed languages. You need to declare the name and data type of each named variable you intend to use before you assign the variable name a value. Interpreted computer languages, such as BASIC and xBase, are loosely typed languages—you can create a variable by assigning a value to a name without previously making the variable's presence known to the interpreter. Loosely typing variables leads to loosely-written programs; thus COBOL, Pascal, and especially C programmers denigrate BASIC and its interpreted relatives. The technicalities of compiling, linking, and interpreting applications in the Windows environment are among the subjects of Chapter 22.

All dialects of Object Basic give you the opportunity to use strong data typing by adding the `Option Explicit` line to the Declarations section of your module, as mentioned earlier in this chapter. When you add `Option Explicit`, you need to declare the name of the variable and its data type with a `Dim` VarName `As` *VarType* or `Global` VarName `As` *VarType* statement before you assign a value to the variable in your code. If you do not assign a data type with the `As` clause, Object Basic declares a variable of the default `Variant` data type discussed shortly.

The four advantages to using strong data typing in Object Basic are as follows:

- ■ Your Object Basic code executes faster when you pre-declare variables and specify a string or a particular numeric data type instead of accepting the default `Variant` data type.

- ■ You are less likely to encounter bugs in the execution of your code caused by typographical errors when you write variable names. If you do not specify `Option Explicit`, Object Basic creates a new `Variant` variable with the misspelled name, instead of referring to the intended variable.

- ■ When applications that can compile Object Basic source code to executable files become available, you do not have to rewrite your applications to comply with the `Option Explicit`'s requirement.

- ■ Your source code is easier to read and for others to follow when you pre-declare variables. The line on which you declare the variable is a good place to add a comment that describes the purpose of the variable.

> **NOTE**
>
> Default assignment of the **Variant** data type to variables declared without a
> data-type identification clause (or data-type identification character) applies
> only to true Object Basic dialects, such as Visual Basic 2+ and Access Basic
> 1+. The default data type of Visual Basic 1.0 and Word for Windows 2.0 is
> **Single**.

Fundamental Numeric and String Data Types

Object Basic has a richer set of fundamental data types than xBase, PAL, or other
desktop RDBMSs. For example, dBASE IV offers a string data type and two numeric
data types: BCD (type N, the only numeric data type of earlier versions of dBASE)
and Float (type F, floating point, introduced in dBASE IV). Table 4.1 lists the
conventional string and numeric data types available in Object Basic, as well as the
minimum and maximum values of each data type. The database field data type that
corresponds to the Object Basic data type is listed also. (Field data types and Object
Basic data types are two related but distinctly different items.)

Table 4.1. The conventional numeric and string data types of Object Basic.

Data Type	BASIC Symbol	Field Data Type	Minimum Value	Maximum Value
Integer	%	Byte, Integer, Yes/No	-32,768	32,767
Long	&	Counter, Long Integer Long Integer	-2,147,483,648	2,147,483,647
Single	!	Single	-3.402...E+38 1.401...E-45	-1.401...E-45 3.402...E+38
Double	#	Double	-1.797...E+308 4.940...E-324	4.940...E-324 1.797...E+308
Currency	@	Currency	-922,337,203, 685,477.5808	922,337,203,685, 477.5807
String	$	Text	0 characters (empty)	65,500 characters (+/-)

> **NOTE**
>
> The use of symbols to specify the data type of BASIC variables has been carried over into Object Basic from earlier versions of BASIC for the purpose of backward compatibility with existing code. Most Access developers use the **As** clause to specify data types, including explicit declaration of the **Variant** data type with the **As Variant** clause. The code examples in this book and on the accompanying disk—except those drawn from other sources—use the **As** *VarType* clause instead of using type declaration symbols. Object data types, such as **Table** or **QueryDef**, do not have corresponding data type symbols.

Object Data Types

Because of the importance of database connectivity to all mainstream Windows applications and the advent of Access 1.0, Microsoft Corporation added several new database-related data types to its Embedded Basic language to create the first version of Object Basic that appeared in Access 1.x and Visual Basic 2.0. Table 4.2 lists the original Object Basic object data types of Access 1.0 and Visual Basic 2.0. The objects listed in Table 4.2 are the most commonly-used subset of the data access object set, commonly called data access objects (DAOs), of Access 2.0.

Table 4.2. The database-related object data types common to the first Object Basic dialects.

Object Data Type	*Database Object*
Database	Access (and other types of databases in applications other than Access 1.x). **Database** objects contain the other objects described in this table.
Table	Tables contained in a **Database** object (including tables attached from foreign databases in Access).
QueryDef	The definition of a query against tables of an Access **Database** object, expressed in Access SQL.
Dynaset	A virtual table (memory image) of a **Table** object, created from the result set returned by a SQL statement (any data-base) or from a **QueryDef** object (Access databases only). All **Dynaset** objects based on tables, and some **Dynaset** objects based on SQL statements

continues

Table 4.2. continued

Object Data Type	Database Object
	and `QueryDef` objects can be updated. `Dynaset` objects are dynamic (thus the name) and reflect changes that others make to the data in tables of databases shared in a multiuser environment. Access 2.0 substitutes an updatable `Recordset` object for the `Dynaset` object, but the `Dynaset` object remains supported.
SnapShot	A virtual table equivalent to a frozen image of a `Dynaset` object. `SnapShot`s cannot be updated and do not reflect changes to data made after the `SnapShot` is "taken." A `Snapshot` object is a non-updatable `Recordset`.

All applications that use the Object Basic application language should support at least the common object data types listed in Table 4.2. `Table`, `Dynaset`, and `SnapShot` objects collectively were called recordsets; now `Recordset` is an object in its own right. `Table`, `Dynaset`, and `Snapshot` objects now are types of `Recordset` objects that you specify as the value of the *intType* argument of the `OpenRecordset`(str*Source*, *intType*, *intOptions*) method of Access 2.0. Visual Basic 3.0 introduced the `TableDef` object that lets you create new tables with Object Basic code. Access 2.0 incorporates a wide range of new objects, including `TableDef` objects, in anticipation of its reincarnation as an OLE Automation server in a future version. The OA-oriented object hierarchy of Access is the subject of the next chapter, "Understanding Access 2.0's Data Access Objects."

Shortcuts, such as menu choices that let you open database files, dialogs with list boxes from which you can choose fields to create queries, and other features that minimize the amount of Object Basic code you need to write, vary with the application.

> **NOTE**
>
> The `Form`, `Report`, and `Control` object data types are specific to dialects of Object Basic for applications that contain such objects. Visual Basic 2+, for example, has `Form` and `Control` objects, but not `Report` objects. You can create arrays of `Control` objects in Visual Basic, but not in Access Basic. Chapter 7, "Using Access Objects, Methods, and Events," covers the Access `Form`, `Report`, and `Control` objects and explains how to declare and assign values to variables of the object data types.

When you create a variable of an object data type, you create an *instance* of the object. An instance is a reference to the object—in the form of a pointer. An instance is not a copy of the object. A pointer is an integer (usually a **Long**) that specifies a location in memory which holds the object or a fixed reference to the location of the object. Thus, you can declare several variables that refer to the same object; each variable is an instance of the object. **Table** and **QueryDef** objects are persistent objects. In other words, they are a physical entity stored as components of your .MDB file. Recordset objects, on the other hand, are virtual (impersistent) objects; they exist only in your computer's memory. If, for example, you create two variables of the **Table** object type by using the same table, you can position the record pointer of each variable (instance of the table) to a different record in the variable's virtual table. An Access 1.x **Table** object is a **Recordset** object of the table type in disguise.

In early versions of BASIC, you had to use the LET keyword to assign a value to a named variable, as in LET x = 10. Later versions of BASIC made the use of LET optional; LET is seldom seen today, but Object Basic includes the **Let** keyword for backward compatibility. In Object Basic you must use the keyword **Set** to create an instance of (a pointer to) an object. The following example, using Access 1.x syntax, creates an instance of a **Table** object contained in a **Database** object:

```
Dim dbNWind As Database
Dim tblEmployees As Table
Set dbNWind = OpenDatabase("c:\access\nwind.mdb")
Set tblEmployees = dbNWind.OpenTable("Employees")
```

You need to create an instance of the container in which the object you want is located, in this case a **Database** object is the instance of the container. After you create the **Table** object, you can refer to the properties of the instance of the source table or execute methods applicable to the object with code like the following:

```
varLastName = tblEmployees.[Last Name]   'Value of a field
tblEmployees.MoveNext                     'Move to next record
tblEmployees.Close
dbNWind.Close
```

The next chapter explains how to use Access 2.0 object syntax, the properties of variables of Access 2.0 object data types and how to apply methods to Access 2.0 object variables.

Field Data Types of Database Objects and the *Variant* Data Type

The present incarnation of Object Basic provides for 11 different field data types, all of which can accommodate almost all field data types encountered in both desktop and client-server databases, except BLOB (binary large object) fields. BLOB fields (the image data type in SQL Server) are used primarily to store graphic images in a variety of data formats. Table 4.3 lists the Object Basic field data types identified by the value of the **Long** Integer returned as the value of the Type field of the **SnapShot** recordset created by the **ListFields** method for a **Table** object. Comments indicate the field data types of a desktop RDBMS and Microsoft or Sybase SQL server that are converted to the Object Basic field data type.

Table 4.3. The 11 common field data types supported by Object Basic.

Field Type ID	Object Basic Field Data Type	Comments and Data Types in Other Database Systems
1	Yes/No (Integer)	Logical fields in xBase; bit in SQL Server
2	Number (Byte)	Can also represent a single ASCII character using Chr$(Value); tinyint in SQL Server
3	Number (Integer)	Short number in Paradox, not available in xBase; smallint in SQL Server
4	Number (Long)	Not available in xBase or Paradox; integer in SQL Server
5	Currency	Not the same as the Paradox Currency field data type; money in SQL Server (smallmoney is not supported)
6	Number (Single)	Float in SQL Server
7	Number (Double)	Numeric fields in xBase and Paradox tables; real in SQL Server
8	Date/Time (Microsoft date/time format)	Date fields in Paradox and xBase tables; datetime and smalldatetime in SQL Server
9	(Reserved)	(Constant is DB_BOOLEAN)
10	Text (String)	Character fields in xBase, Alphanumeric fields in Paradox; char and varchar fields of SQL Server
11	OLE Object	Can also be used to store BLOBs; size limited by maximum table size
12	Memo (String)	Memo fields of xBase and Paradox 4+ tables; text fields of SQL Server, except maximum size is 32,000 characters

The Binary field data type (SQL's varbinary data type), a field that lets you store up to 255 bytes of data of any type, is not officially supported in Access 1.x or 2.0. Microsoft uses fields of this type to store system Ids (SIDs) of users, passwords, and other information that is to be withheld from Access users. If you need to store varbinary or BLOB data (varbinary data without a length restriction), you use an OLE Object field and disregard the "Invalid Object" method that appears. Using the OLE object field for purposes not intended by Microsoft is discussed in Chapter 25, "Stretching the Limits of Access."

> **NOTE**
>
> All applications do not support OLE object fields directly. For example, Visual Basic can display images stored in Windows bit map (.BMP and .DIB) or metafile (.WMF) formats only. Access displays only images created with such OLE server applications as Windows Paintbrush, Microsoft Graph, CorelDRAW!, or Visio 2.0. Access adds a special "wrapper" around OLE objects; you can unwrap the object and display it in a Visual Basic 3.0 OLE control by a method described in Chapter 15, "Embedding and Linking Objects with OLE" or use a commercial imaging application, Media Architects' ImageKnife/VBX 1.3, to display Access OLE objects in Visual Basic 3.0. You can embed sound files (.WAV or .MID) in OLE Object fields.

The *Variant* Data Type

When Microsoft decided to add the database-related objects to Embedded Basic, then represented by Visual Basic 1.0, the following three elements were missing:

■ The capability to handle **Null** field data values returned by client-server and some desktop RDBMSs. **Null** field values indicate that no data is present in the data cell of a table.

■ A mechanism to use and create indexes on table fields of different data types without requiring explicit data-type conversion (also called type-casting) functions.

■ A means to return a value to a variable without knowing the data type of the value in advance. This is primarily a requirement of OLE 2.0 and OLE Automation.

Microsoft created the **Variant** data type to solve these problems, as well as to make programming easier for beginners by eliminating concerns with data type consistency.

Values of all data cells of recordset objects are one of nine subtypes of the **Variant** data type. Table 4.4 lists the nine subtypes of the **Variant** data type, as well as the **Variant** subtype identifier returned by the **VarType**(var*VarName*) function. The Empty **Variant** subtype ID is reserved to **Variant** variables that have been declared but have not been assigned a value by your code.

Table 4.4. Variant data subtype IDs and the field data types with IDs that return them.

Variant SubType ID	Field Data Type ID	How Variant Data is Handled
0	(None)	Empty (uninitialized)
1	(None)	**Null** (unknown, no valid data)
2	3, 1, 2	**Integer** (2 bytes); Logical and Byte field data types also return subtype 2 **Variant**s
3	4	**Long** Integer (2 bytes)
4	5	**Single** (single-precision floating point, 4 bytes)
5	6	**Double** (double-precision floating point, 8 bytes)
6	7	**Currency** (fixed point, four decimal places)
7	8	Date/Time (fixed point, Microsoft date/time format)
8	10, 11, 12	**String** (conventional Basic string, up to 65,500 bytes long); Memo and OLE Object field values return subtype 8 **Variant**s

> **NOTE**
>
> The addition of the **Variant** data type to Object Basic provides the advantages of polymorphism without the need to provide overloaded functions. Polymorphism is one of the characteristics that defines an object-oriented programming language. In C++, for example, you can have several functions with the same name. Multiple functions with the same name, which are not permitted in Object Basic, are called overloaded functions. Depending on the data types and other characteristics of the arguments the function call supplies, the C++ application chooses the appropriate function to return the type of value you want.

Using Operators with *Variant* Data Types

One of the purposes of the **Variant** data type is to let you manipulate values of different data types without first having to convert one of the values to a compatible data type. To create a message that displays a numeric value with conventional data types, for example, you need to use an expression such as strMessage = "List Price = $" + **Str$**(curListPrice) to convert the number to a string value. If the list price variable is a Variant of subtype 6, however, you can create a string with the statement strMessage = "List Price = $" + varListPrice. Figure 4.4 shows the result of the concatenating strings with the + operator, with and without data type conversion.

> **NOTE**
>
> You need to add a temporary apostrophe to "comment out" the **Option Explicit** statement in the Declarations section of the module if you want to declare implicit variables in the module's Immediate Window. In Figure 4.4, **Option Explicit** is disabled. Field type identifier characters are required to specify a data type (except the **Variant** data type) because you cannot enter a **Dim...As** statement in the Immediate Window. Notice the space inserted in front of the string returned by the **Str$**() function (to provide space for a minus sign, when necessary). When you concatenate a **Variant** variable with a string, no padding for a missing minus sign is provided.

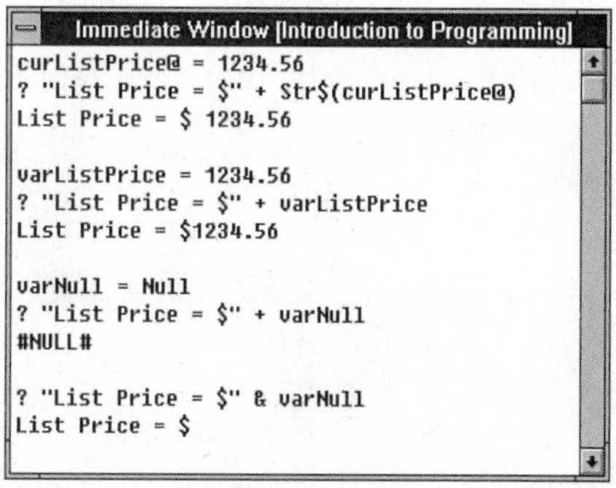

FIGURE 4.4.

Using the Variant data type to avoid type conversion and differences between the + and & operators.

```
 ═  Immediate Window [Introduction to Programming]
curListPrice@ = 1234.56
? "List Price = $" + Str$(curListPrice@)
List Price = $ 1234.56

varListPrice = 1234.56
? "List Price = $" + varListPrice
List Price = $1234.56

varNull = Null
? "List Price = $" + varNull
#NULL#

? "List Price = $" & varNull
List Price = $
```

> **NOTE**
>
> Object Basic has duplicates of every built-in function that returns string values. One function, for example **Str$**(), returns a conventional Basic string. The duplicate function, **Str**(), returns a subtype 8 **Variant**.

Introducing the **Variant** data type with its **Null** type to Object Basic also made adding a new string concatenation symbol, **&**, to the language necessary. (**&** is the standard concatenation symbol of SQL.) Previously, the + sign did double duty as the arithmetic addition and string concatenation operator. **Variant** data made the + operator ambiguous as a string concatenation operator, however. A **Null** value is defined as "unknown" or "no valid data." A **Null** value + any other value, by definition, is **Null**. The third example in Figure 4.4 returns #NULL#, the Immediate Window's representation of the intrinsic constant **Null**, when you use + to concatenate a string with a **Null** value. If you use the **&** concatenation symbol, Object Basic treats a string with the **Null** value as the equivalent of the empty string ("").

> **TIP**
>
> Skip fields with **Null** values when you use Access Basic code, rather than aggregate functions, to sum field values. If you add a **Null** value to a running sum, the sum becomes and remains **Null**. Perform the summation in an **If Not IsNull**(*FieldName*) **Then ... End If** structure to avoid unintentional **Null** totals.

Object Basic attempts to assign the **Variant** data type of the lowest-valued subtype ID when your code initializes **Variant** variables. When you use the mathematic operators (except +) on two **Variant** variables, Object Basic assigns the greater of the two **Variant** subtype IDs to the result. Thus a subtype 2 **Variant** (**Integer**) multiplied by a subtype 5 **Variant** (**Double**) returns a subtype 5 **Variant**. The + operator behaves differently. If you concatenate a subtype 8 **Variant** (**String**) with a numeric **Variant**, the + operator converts the subtype 8 **Variant** to a numeric value, if it can, then sums the two numbers. The first three examples in Figure 4.5 illustrate this behavior of the + operator.

FIGURE 4.5.

*Using the + and &
operators with
Variant data.*

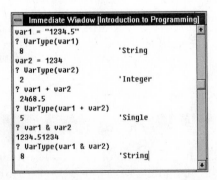

NOTE

Use the **VarType()** function in the Immediate Window to determine the type ID of the **Variant** variables you create.

The fourth example in Figure 4.5 illustrates the result of concatenating **Variant** variables with the **&** operator. The **&** operator first converts numeric **Variant** operands to strings, then concatenates the two strings. Thus, use the **&** operator when you want to ensure that your concatenation expression returns a string. This book uses the **&** operator for all string concatenation operations.

Date and Time *Variant* Variables and Functions

The recommendation that you convert **Variant** variables to conventional Object Basic data types does not apply to date and time values. Object Basic date and time values are subtype 7 **Variant** variables that use Microsoft date and time format (MDTF). MDTF is a double-precision numeric format in which the integer portion of the number represents the number of days since December 30, 1899. (Midnight January 1, 1900, has the value 2.0.) The first two examples in Figure 4.6 show the value returned by the **Now()** function, the DOS system date and time, as a formatted string and as an MDTF value. The **CVDate()** function converts to a subtype 7 **Variant** a numeric or string value that represents a date. The decimal fraction represents the time of day, with .0 representing 00:00 (midnight). The fourth example in Figure 4.6 shows the MDTF date and time numeric value returned by **CVDate(2.5)**. The **CDbl()** function returns negative values for dates before December 30, 1899.

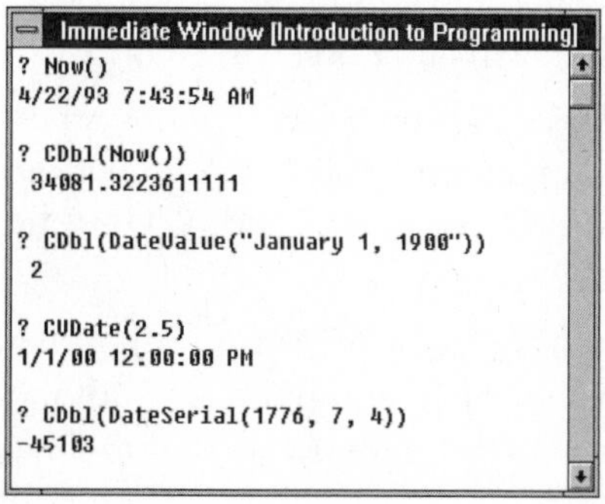
Immediate Window [Introduction to Programming]
? Now()
4/22/93 7:43:54 AM
? CDbl(Now())
34081.3223611111
? CDbl(DateValue("January 1, 1900"))
2
? CVDate(2.5)
1/1/00 12:00:00 PM
? CDbl(DateSerial(1776, 7, 4))
-45103

FIGURE 4.6.
Object Basic date and time values and conversion functions.

Object Basic includes a variety of other functions to create or manipulate **Variant** subtype 7 date and time variables: **Date()**, **Time()**, **IsDate()**, **DateAdd()**, **DateDiff()**, **DatePart()**, **Day()**, **Month()**, **Weekday()**, and **Year()**. These functions are well documented in the Microsoft Language Reference that accompanies retail Access applications; syntax examples are not repeated here.

Data Type Conversion Functions

You can force conversion of a variable of any Object Basic data type to another data type by using the data type conversion functions: **CCur()**, **CDbl()**, **CInt()**, **CLng()**, **CSng()**, **CStr()**, and **CVar()**. The data type conversion functions are said to coerce **Variant** values to the designated data type. The following limitations apply to data type conversion:

■ If a numeric value exceeds the maximum allowable value for the new data type, you incur a runtime error message, Overflow.

■ A runtime error message, Invalid Use of Null, results if you attempt to convert a subtype 1 (**Null**) **Variant** to any other data type.

> **NOTE**
>
> Object Basic's data type conversion functions have their counterpart in the CAST...AS expression of SQL-92. For example, if the field type of *Table.Field* is numeric, you can change the data type to a string with the CAST (*Table.Field* AS STRING) statement.

When you convert a **Single** or **Double** variable to an integer value, you can use one of the following three functions:

■ **CInt()** rounds numbers to the nearest even integer. Thus, **CInt(0.5)** returns 0 (rounds down) and **CInt(1.5)** returns 2.0 (rounds up).

■ **Int()** truncates (removes) the fractional portion of a numeric argument, returning an integer less than the numeric argument (if the numeric argument contains a decimal fraction). Thus, **Int(2.5)** returns 2 and **Int(-2.5)** returns -3.

■ **Fix()** behaves exactly like **Int()** for positive numbers, but returns an integer greater than the numeric argument with the decimal fraction if the numeric argument is negative. **Fix(2.5)** returns 2 and **Fix(-2.5)** returns -2.

CInt() returns the **Integer** data type, whereas **Int()** and **Fix()** return the same data type as the numeric argument. If the argument of any of these three functions is a subtype 8 (String) **Variant** that Object Basic can convert to a numeric value, **CInt()**

returns a type 2 (**Integer**) Variant, whereas **Int**() and **Fix**() return a subtype 5 (**Double**) **Variant**.

Intrinsic Constants in Object Basic and Access

Object Basic provides three intrinsic (predeclared) logical symbolic constants: **True** (-1), **False** (0), and **Null**. **True** and **False** are of the **Integer** data type and **Null** is a subtype 1 **Variant**. You can use these constants with commands and operators that accept logical values.

NOTE

Although the intrinsic constant **True** returns the value -1 (the two's complement, **&HFFFF**, of 0, **&H0000**), the actual definition of **True** is **Not False**. A variable with any value other than 0 is considered to be true when evaluated by a logical operator or when used in an expression that relies upon a logical result, such as **If** *VariableName* **Then...End If**. Statements following **If** *VariableName* **Then** are executed if *VariableName* has a value other than zero. Hexadecimal notation, using the **&H** operator, is discussed in the section called "User-defined Data Types as Structures" in Chapter 22.

Programmers use intrinsic symbolic constants to represent values that specify a property of an object, to indicate the status of an object or variable, and for other system-related purposes. The use of symbolic constants in place of the literal value of constants is intended to ensure that changes to values of the constant in subsequent releases of an application do not cause errors in code written in earlier versions. The Windows API (application programming interface), for example, uses hundreds of predefined symbolic constants. Microsoft can change the values of these constants in future versions of Windows. This means developers will not have to rewrite their code (or at least the portion of the code that uses the constants) for the new version.

The use of symbolic constants, rather than their values, has another advantage: names, rather than numbers, make your code easier to read and understand. The line, **If VarType**(*varName*) = V_CURRENCY **Then** is more expressive than **If VarType**(*varName*) = 6 **Then**. Table 4.5 lists the intrinsic symbolic **Integer** constants you can use to specify **Variant** subtypes.

Table 4.5. Intrinsic symbolic constants for `Variant` subtypes.

Symbol	Value	Symbol	Value
V_CURRENCY	6	V_DATE	8
V_DOUBLE	5	V_EMPTY	0
V_INTEGER	2	V_LONG	3
V_NULL	1	V_SINGLE	4
V_STRING	8		

Access defines 29 intrinsic symbolic constants with the prefix DB_ that specify the properties of database objects. Intrinsic constants are defined by Access itself; you do not need to declare these constants as **Global Const** DB_*WHATEVER* in the Declarations section of an Access Basic module. (Visual Basic 3.0, however, requires that you declare these constants, included in.) Table 4.6 lists these intrinsic constants; constants added to Access 2.0 (intrinsic) and Visual Basic 3.0 (declared) are marked with an asterisk (*). You use these **Long** constants, for example, to evaluate data contained in the **SnapShot** object created by the **ListFields** method of a **Table** object, an obsolescent (Access 1.x) method that is now replaced by iterating members of property collections. Property collections are discussed in the next chapter.

Table 4.6. Access intrinsic symbolic constants.

Constant Class	Symbol	Value (Long)	Description
Field Data Types	DB_BOOLEAN	1	Logical or Yes/No field
	DB_BINARY	9	(Reserved)
	DB_BYTE	2	Byte (8 bits)
	DB_CURRENCY	5	Currency
	DB_DATE	8	Date and Time
	DB_DOUBLE	7	Double
	DB_INTEGER	3	Integer
	DB_LONG	4	Long (integer)
	DB_MEMO	12	Memo (text)
	DB_OLE	11	OLE Object

Constant Class	Symbol	Value (Long)	Description
	DB_TEXT	10	Text (variable length)
Field Properties	DB_AUTOINCRFIELD	16	Field is a counter field (Long data type)
	DB_UPDATABLEFIELD	32	Values in field can be updated
	DB_FIXEDFIELD	1	Values in field cannot be updated
Index and Sorting	DB_NONULLS	8	Null values not allowed in index
	DB_PRIMARY	2	Index is on the primary key field
	DB_IGNORENULL	4	Ignore null values in index
	DB_UNIQUE	1	Index is unique
	DB_DESCENDING	1	Descending sort on field
Recordset Types	DB_ATTACHEDODBC	4	**Table** object is attached by an ODBC driver
	DB_ATTACHEDTABLE	6	**Table** object is attached by the Jet engine
	DB_QUERYDEF	5	Object is a **QueryDef**
	DB_SYSTEMOBJECT	-2147483646	**Table** object is a system table
	DB_TABLE	1	**Table** object is an Access database table

continues

Table 4.6. continued

Constant Class	Symbol	Value (Long)	Description
Recordset Options	DB_DENYWRITE*	1	Prevent others from writing to underlying table(s)
	DB_DENYREAD*	2	Prevent others from reading underlying table(s)
	DB_READONLY*	4	Non-updatable (Snapshot)
	DB_APPENDONLY*	8	Updatable (Dynaset) with no read privileges
	DB_INCONSISTENT*	16	Allow updates on one side of one-to-many query
	DB_CONSISTENT*	32	No updates on one side of one-to-many query
	DB_SQLPASSTHROUGH*	64	Send SQL statement directly to server
QueryDef Types	DB_QACTION	240	**QueryDef** is an action query
	DB_QAPPEND	64	Append **QueryDef**
	DB_QCROSSTAB	16	Crosstab **QueryDef**
	DB_QDELETE	32	Delete **QueryDef**
	DB_QMAKETABLE	80	Make-table **QueryDef**
	DB_QUPDATE	48	Update **QueryDef**

> **NOTE**
>
> Although intrinsic symbolic constants are not reserved words in Object Basic, they exhibit some of the same properties. You cannot declare a function or procedure that uses the name of an intrinsic symbolic constant. Microsoft has not documented all the intrinsic symbolic constants. If you receive a message that reads "Procedure name conflicts with global constant or global variable" when you create a procedure, you probably have discovered an undocumented intrinsic constant.

> **WARNING**
>
> You cannot declare a variable with **Global** scope that has the same name as an intrinsic constant, but you can overwrite intrinsic constant values with **Dim** statements in Access Basic 1.x modules. For example, if you attempt to enter **Global** db_binary **As Long** in the Declarations section of a module, you receive a Duplicate definition error message. But you can declare a variable of module-level scope with **Dim** db_binary **As Long** without incurring an error. You can assign a value to db_binary in your code without encountering a runtime error. If you use DB_BINARY elsewhere in the code of this module to determine whether a field data type is Logical, an unexpected result might occur.

Conversion of Foreign Database to and from Object Basic Field Data Types

The Jet (formerly JET, for Joint Engine Technology) database engine developed for Access is expected to be an integral element of most, if not all, all dialects of Object Basic. Thus you can expect to be able to open and use tables in any of the database formats supported by the Jet engine. In the 1.1 version, the Jet engine supported Access, xBase (dBASE III+, dBASE IV, and FoxPro 2+), Btrieve and Paradox 3+ database files and the index structures for each of these database types. The 2.0 version of Jet also supports Paradox 4.x table files. Access 2.0 lets you create **Recordset** objects from tables in or queries against client-server databases with Microsoft's Open Database Connectivity (ODBC) API and an ODBC driver for a specific type of database. ODBC data types are based on the SQL data types specified in the SQL-89 and SQL-92 standards.

Table 4.7 lists the relationship between the Object Basic field data types (which are based on terminology used for Access databases) for the database types supported by the Jet engine and the ODBC driver manager.

Table 4.7. Field data type conversion among databases supported by Object Basic.

Object Basic and Access	xBase	Paradox	BTrieve	SQL-92	ODBC
Yes/No	Logical		Logical		SQL_BIT
Number (Byte)			Integer (1-byte)		SQL_TINYINT
Number (Integer)		Short number	Integer (2-byte)	SMALLINT	SQL_SMALLINT
Number (Long)			Integer (4-byte)	INTEGER	SQL_INTEGER
Currency			Money		
Number (Single)			Float or bfloat (4-byte)	REAL	SQL_REAL
Number (Double)	Number, Float	Number, Currency	Float or bfloat (8-byte), decimal, numeric	DOUBLE PRECISION, FLOAT, DECIMAL, NUMERIC	SQL_FLOAT, SQL_DOUBLE, SQL_DECIMAL, SQL_NUMERIC
Date/ Time (MDTF)	Date		Date, time	DATE, TIME, TIMESTAMP	SQL_DATE, SQL_TIME, SQL_TIMESTAMP
Text (String)	Character	Alpha-numeric	String, lstring, zstring	CHAR, VARCHAR <=(255)	SQL_CHAR, SQL_VARCHAR
OLE Object			Lvar	BIT, BITVARYING	SQL_LONGVARBINARY
Memo (String)	Memo	Memo	Note	VARCHAR >= (256)	SQL_LONGVARCHAR

> **NOTE**
>
> The field size properties of numeric data types of SQL databases are implementation-defined. Implementation-defined means that publishers of client-server databases can determine the number of bytes and the precision of numeric data types such as INTEGER, SMALLINT, NUMERIC, DECIMAL or FLOAT. Some SQL RDBMSs let you specify NUMERIC(p,s), DECIMAL(p,s), and FLOAT(p), in which p represents the precision and s represents a scale in the range of the data type.

User-Defined Data Types

Object Basic enables you to define your own, user-defined data types that comprise elements of other data types. User-defined data types are called structures (struct) in C and records in Pascal. Before the inclusion of data access capability in Object Basic, the only way to process data in xBase or other database table formats was by creating a user-defined data type that matched the structure of the records of a random-access file. (A number of third-party add-in applications for processing xBase, Paradox, and other popular database table formats have been available since the introduction of Visual Basic 1.0.) The capability of creating user-defined data types is not a common feature of desktop RDBMSs.

You create a user-defined data type with **Type...End Type** structures contained in the Declarations section of your module. Each element (called a field) of a user-defined data type must be one of the conventional data types of Object Basic or a Variant. You cannot include object data types in a user-defined data type. Strings in user-defined data types usually are declared fixed length by specifying the number of characters with an asterisk (*) followed by a literal or a named constant. Following is the definition of a user-defined data type that includes a variety of data types:

```
Type tagUDT
    strFixed As String * 20
    intNumber As Integer
    curMoney As Currency
    varDate As Variant
    varTime As Variant
End Type
```

After you define a user-defined data type, you need to declare a variable of the user-defined type with a Dim statement, such as **Dim** udtRecord **As** tagUDT. You then assign values to the fields of udtRecord with a set of statements such as the following:

```
udtRecord.strFixed = "Now is the time"
udtRecord.intNumber = 12345
```

```
udtRecord.curMoney = 12345.67
udtRecord.varDate = Date()
udtRecord.varTime = Time()
```

Records in Object Basic are most commonly used to emulate the C structures that are necessary to declare and use Windows API function that require structures as arguments. Chapter 18 contains an example of the creation of a structure for the serial data communication functions of Windows.

Object Basic Arrays

The current versions of most desktop RDBMS applications enable you to create multidimensional arrays of the data types the applications support. Object Basic enables you to create arrays with up to 32,767 elements. Object Basic arrays can have as many as 60 dimensions, but two-dimensional arrays are the most common. In Object Basic, you must declare an array before you use it in your code, even if you omit the **Option Explicit** statement. You can fix the number of dimensions and elements of your array when you declare it in the Declarations section of a module with an expression such as **Dim** rgwNumbers(10, 10) **As Integer**, which creates an empty 10-by-10-element array that accepts **Integer** values.

Alternatively, you can declare a dynamic array in the Declarations section or in a procedure with the **Dim** *ArrayName*() **As** *DataType* statement (omitting the array's dimensions). Then use the **Redim** statement to specify the dimensions, as in **Redim** *ArrayName*(10, 10). The advantages of a dynamic array are twofold: you can declare an array without knowing in advance how many elements it needs, and you regain the memory consumed by the array, either when you exit the procedure or by adding a **Redim** *ArrayName* (0, 0) statement when you finish using the array. Use the **UBound**(*ArrayName*, *Dimension*) and **LBound**(*ArrayName*, *Dimension*) functions to determine the value of the upper and lower bounds, respectively, of each dimension of the array. You can omit the *Dimension* argument when *ArrayName* is a one-dimensional array.

TIP

Object Basic retains the Option Base environmental variable that lets you determine whether the default value of the lower bound of arrays you declare is 0 (the default) or 1. A good programming practice is not to use the **Option Base** 1 statement in the Declarations section of your modules. In the case of arrays created by Access control objects, you need the 0th element of the array. If you want to save the small amount of memory occupied by an unneeded 0th element, use the **To** keyword in the array declaration, as in **ReDim** *ArrayName*(1 **To** 10, 1 **To** 10).

Before the **Variant** data type was introduced, the only way to create an array that contained different data types was to create an array of variables of the user-defined data type. Arrays of user-defined data types whose fields correspond to the field data types of a record of a database file often were used in Visual Basic programs to create memory images of the content of database tables. Such arrays emulate Object Basic **SnapShot** objects created from **Table** objects. Now you can create an equivalent multidimensional array of the **Variant** data type with the first dimension equal to the number of fields and the second dimension equal to the number of records of a table (or vice versa). Arrays of **Variant** data types are somewhat larger and slower in operation than arrays of conventional Object Basic variables. Object Basic's recordset data types have minimized or eliminated the necessity of creating array images of database tables.

> **NOTE**
>
> The normal limit of the size (the total number of elements times the number of bytes that compose the elements) of an Object Basic array is 64KB. Arrays larger than 64KB are called huge arrays. The limits on the size of huge arrays are 1MB for Windows running in standard mode, and 64MB in enhanced mode. You cannot create huge arrays that contain variable-length strings or object data types.

You can create arrays of other objects, such as Control, Form, and Report objects, if the application supports these object types. With some applications, such as Access, which create intrinsic arrays of objects, you need to create arrays of objects yourself. The use of object arrays (more property called collections) in Access Basic to reference Form, Report, and Control objects is one of the subjects of the next chapter.

Data Types of Functions and Their Arguments

Functions return values of the **Variant** data type unless you explicitly declare the data type of the function's return value with the **As *DataType*** clause, as in the statement, **Function** *FunctionName(Argument(s)...)* **As *DataType***.

When you pass arguments to functions, you need to declare the data types of the arguments in the function declaration, unless the values of the arguments have been declared in the Declarations section of the module in which the function appears or unless they are global variables declared in another module of your application. The **Function** sngDiscount (wOrderQuan **As Integer**) **As Single** statement, near the beginning of this chapter, declares the wOrderQuan argument to be of the **Integer** data type and the return value of the `sngDiscount()` function to be of the **Integer** data type. If you pass wOrderQuan to `sngDiscount()` as a **Double**, for instance, you receive a "Parameter type mismatch" error message when you execute the function.

If you want to call a function that expects an argument of one data type but the variable whose value you want to pass has a different type, you can pass the argument as an expression by enclosing the argument in parentheses, as shown in the following example. You do not receive a "Parameter type mismatch" error with the following code, which calls the `Discount` subprocedure that expects the first parameter to be of the **Integer** data type:

```
Function sngCallDiscount (wOrderQuan As Variant) As Single
    Dim sngPercent As Single
    Call Discount(sngPercent, (wOrderQuan))
    sngCallDiscount = sngPercent
End Function
```

Alternatively, you can use the **ByVal** keyword to specify that the procedure use a copy of the value of the argument or parameter, rather than use the reference (pointer) to the argument or parameter, as in **Sub** Discount (sngDiscount **As Single**, **ByVal** wOrderQuan **As Integer**).

When you specify that arguments or parameters be passed either as expressions or by value, the called procedure cannot alter the value of the variable in the calling procedure. By converting sngPercent to an expression in the calling statement or applying **ByVal** to the sngPercent parameter in the Discount subprocedure, however, you defeat the purpose of calling the Discount subprocedure; sngPercent remains 0 regardless of the value of wOrderQuan.

Object Basic Variable Naming Conventions

In most of the code examples in this book, variable names begin with a three-letter, lowercase prefix that specifies the variable data type. These abbreviations are based on the variable-naming conventions for Access Basic proposed by Greg Reddick and Stan Leszynski of Kwery Corp., publishers of commercial applications and development tools for Microsoft Access.

Including identification of the data type in the name of a variable or a function makes the Object Basic code you write more readable. Data type identification helps to minimize errors that arise when you attempt to apply a method to a variable that is not appropriate either to the variable's data type or to the operator that executes the function. Adoption of a common variable-naming convention by Object Basic developers helps other people understand how the Object Basic code you write works (or is supposed to work). Another advantage is that when you want to use code written in one dialect of Object Basic in an application that uses another dialect, you can use the module window's searching features to locate variables with data types that are not supported in the destination dialect.

Most prefixes for variable and function names are derived by combining the first letter of the data type with two subsequent consonants. Thus, **Table** objects are identified by the prefix tbl and **Form** objects use the prefix frm. In many cases, this book uses prefixes derived from C and Windows data types, such as w (word), instead of int, for **Integer**; dw (double-word) for the **Long** data type; and rg (regular group) followed by the data type for arrays (as in rgw, which specifies an array of the **Integer** data type). Appendix B, "Naming Conventions for Microsoft Access," includes a complete list of the prefixes proposed at the time this book was written and an explanation of how the prefixes are applied to variable names.

The Scope of Object Basic Variables and Procedures

The xBase language provides two keywords, PUBLIC and PRIVATE, you can use to declare variables and define their scope. The scope of a variable, sometimes called visibility, determines whether you can refer to a variable in a module or procedure without first declaring the variable with a Dim statement. The four sections that follow describe the scope of Object Basic variables, constants, and procedures.

Global Variables and Constants

Object Basic's **Global** keyword is similar to xBase's PUBLIC. If you substitute **Global** for **Dim** when you declare variables or prefix **Global** to **Const** when you declare constants, you can refer to these variables in any procedure contained in any module of your application. After you assign a value to a global variable, the value of the variable can be altered by any procedure contained in any module or CBF container. Thus, you need not pass global variables as arguments or parameters to procedures. The variable retains the last value assigned until you exit from your application. The period during which a variable retains its value is called the lifetime or duration of the variable. You can declare a global variable or constant in the Declarations section of any module of your applications.

> **NOTE**
>
> You can prevent a procedure from modifying the value of a globally declared variable by passing the global variable argument or parameter by value, using the **ByVal** keyword, as described earlier.

Module-Level Variables and Constants

If you declare variables with a `Dim` statement or constants with a `Const` statement in the Declarations section of a module, these variables and constants have module-level scope. Module-level variables are visible to all procedures contained in the module; any procedure can alter the value of module-level variables. The lifetime of module-level variables and constants is the same as that of their global counterparts; only the visibility of the variable or constant is affected by declaring a variable or constant at the module level. You do not save memory by declaring module-level variables and constants. Compared to the use of global constants, declaring module-level variables and constants has an advantage: you do not have to worry about unintentional changes to the value of variables that, by coincidence or oversight, have the same name as a variable in another module.

Object-Level Variables and Constants

Variables declared with the `Dim` *VarName* `As` *VarType* statement in the Declarations section of a CBF container have the scope of the container. A variable declared in the Declarations section of a `Form` object is visible when the form is active, but at no other time. The same is true for variables declared in the Declarations section of a `Report` object; the variable is visible only while the report is being previewed or printed.

Local Variables and Constants

Any variable or constant that you declare in a procedure has local scope. Local scope is the equivalent of declaring xBase variables with the PRIVATE keyword. The visibility of the local variable or constant is limited to the procedure in which the variable or constant is declared. The lifetime of the variable or constant begins when it is declared and ends with execution of the procedure's `End Function` or `End Sub` statement. You conserve memory by using local variables, because the memory locations occupied by local variables are freed when you exit the procedure.

You can preserve the values of individual local variables between successive executions of the procedure by declaring the variables with the `Static` keyword instead of `Dim`. The `Static` keyword changes the lifetime of the variable to the equivalent of a global or module-level variable but does not affect the visibility of the variable. You can declare all the variables in a procedure to be static by preceding `Function` or `Sub` with `Static`.

Private Procedures

By default, the names of all functions and subprocedures in your application's Object Basic modules have global scope. You can restrict the visibility of a procedure to the module in which it is located by preceding the **Function** or **Sub** keywords with the **Private** keyword. **Private** can be combined with the **Static** keyword, as in **Private Static Function** *FuncName*. By declaring a procedure as **Private**, you can duplicate the procedure's name in other modules of your application.

"Compiling" Your Object Basic Source Code

Before your application can execute Object Basic source code, the Object Basic interpreter converts the text of the code to pseudocode. Pseudocode (sometimes called p-code) substitutes symbols for Object Basic keywords, assigns variables to memory addresses, and performs other housekeeping chores that make your source code execute faster. In most dialects of Object Basic, this process is called "compiling" your source code. Chapter 18 discusses the difference between the traditional use of the term compile and the pseudocode compilation process.

The Access interpreter makes a final syntax check, tests to determine that all variables have been declared before use (if **Option Explicit** is set), and attempts to verify that all variables and constants have data types appropriate to their use. Errors the interpreter reports during this process are called compile-time errors; you need to correct all compile-time errors before you can execute your code. Most compile-time errors involve declaration of variables and assignment of their values. Most syntax errors are detected by Access's source-code parser, which checks the current line of your code when you press Enter.

When you execute the code, the Access interpreter first tests to determine whether you have made any changes to the code since the last time it was compiled. If the code in a module has been altered in any way, the interpreter automatically compiles the module before execution.

> **TIP**
>
> Explicitly "compile" your Object Basic code before you attempt to execute it. In Access, choose **C**ompile Loaded Modules from the **R**un menu. By checking for compile-time errors before you attempt to execute your code from an event of an Access form or report or the RunCode action of a macro, you can save a great deal of time during the testing process.

You can execute all or portions of your code, depending on the code's structure, by typing the name of a function or procedure in the Immediate Window. Substitute literal values for arguments or parameters of the function or procedure. You need to precede the function name with the ? symbol to provide a placeholder for the return value of the function. (Subprocedure calls do not need the ? symbol.) A quick Immediate Window test of each function or procedure after you complete the coding process pays debugging dividends.

> **NOTE**
>
> To execute code (in the Immediate window) that includes references to other objects of your application, such as forms or reports, an instance of each referenced object must exist before the line that contains the reference can be executed. If an instance of the object is not open, you receive an "Invalid reference to Object Type 'Object Name'" error message. You cannot declare variables of any of the object data types in the Immediate window.

Handling Runtime Errors in Object Basic

In early versions of BASIC, line numbers (not procedure names) identified blocks of code. If you wanted to create the equivalent of a procedure in line-numbered BASIC, you wrote GOSUB *LineNumber* (*LineNumber* was the number of the line of code in which the procedure began). When the capability to use labels was added to early BASIC, the situation improved slightly because you could use GOTO *LabelName* and GOSUB *LabelName* statements. Code that made extensive use of the GOTO keyword was called spaghetti code because a diagram of the execution of the code resembled a plate of pasta.

The introduction of procedural versions of BASIC, such as Microsoft's QuickBASIC, enabled you to identify procedures by name, instead of by line number or label. Procedural BASIC eliminated much of the use of GOTOs and GOSUBs among BASIC programmers, but the capability to use line numbers remained for backward compatibility with the millions of lines of existing line-numbered BASIC code. At this point, BASIC programmers could abandon GOSUB, but GOTO remained for handling errors. By preserving the **On Error GoTo *LabelName*** statement needed to trap runtime errors in Object Basic, Microsoft has engraved GOTO on the Basic tablets of stone. The **On Error GoTo *LabelName*** statement is similar to dBASE IV's ON ERROR DO *ProcName* command. With dBASE IV, you can write an error-handling procedure; with Object Basic, the error-handling code must be included in the procedure that contains the **On Error GoTo *LabelName*** statement. Table 4.8 lists the three optional forms of the **On Error** statement in Object Basic.

Table 4.8. The three basic forms of the `On Error` statement.

Statement	*Code Execution after Encountering Error*
`On Error GoTo` *`LabelName`*	Executes next line after *`LabelName`*: (No error message box is displayed)
`On Error Resume Next`	Executes next line after line that caused the error, disregarding the error (No error message box is displayed)
`On Error GoTo 0`	Disables error trapping and resumes display of error message boxes

> **NOTE**
>
> The use of `GoTo` *`LabelName`* statements to control program flow is not considered a good programming practice. In Object Basic programs, use of the `GoTo` *`LabelName`* statement should be restricted to error-handling procedures.

The *Error* Event

Access 2.0 includes the new `Error` event (On Error "property") that is triggered when an error occurs with a **Form** or **Report** object open. You can write an error handling procedure for each form or report, or you can call a "central" error handling procedure for all forms and reports in an Access Basic module. Whichever method you choose, you need to write your own **Select Case...End Case** structure with **Case** statements that execute whatever action is necessary to eradicate the error so that execution of your application can continue. If you do not trap errors of forms or reports that you open with macros, your application will unceremoniously close when you execute the application under MSARN200.EXE and encounter an error.

Writing Object Basic Procedures with Error-Handling Routines

When the Object Basic interpreter encounters a runtime error caused by a bug in your code or the failure of an element external to your application to behave as anticipated, the interpreter tests for the last **On Error** statement in the code executed by the interpreter. The previously executed code that leads to the currently executing procedure is called the invocation path of the procedure. If no **On Error** statement was executed on the invocation path or if the last **On Error** statement encountered was **On Error GoTo 0**, the interpreter displays a runtime error message box.

> **NOTE**
>
> The environment in which your application is operating determines what happens after an untrapped runtime error occurs. An untrapped runtime error that occurs in an Access application operating under the runtime version of Access, for example, causes your application to quit unceremoniously (the equivalent of executing the Exit action).

The standard structure of Object Basic procedures that include error trapping appears in the following example of a codeless (except for error-handling) function:

```
Function FunctionName () [As Integer]
    'Comments describing the function

    On Error GoTo ErrorHandler      'Branch on error

    'Code for the function

    [FunctionName = True] 'Return value indicating success
    [On Error GoTo 0] 'Require each function to have its own handler
    Exit Function    'Required to bypass ErrorHandler

ErrorHandler:          'Must begin in first column and end with a colon

    'Error handling code
    [Call ErrorProc]  'Execute a centralized error-handling
    ➥procedure

    [FunctionName = False] 'Return value indicating failure
    [On Error GoTo 0] 'If you use Exit Function
    {Resume¦Resume Next¦Resume Labelname¦Error Err¦Exit Function}
    ➥'Choose one statement
End Function
```

Following are rules and suggestions for creating procedures with error-handling capability:

- The structure of subprocedures with error trapping is identical to that of functions; substitute **Sub** for **Function** in the preceding example.

- The **On Error GoTo** statement should follow the descriptive comments for your procedure. Some programmers place the first **On Error GoTo** statement after **Dim** statements that declare local variables. Runtime errors in **Dim** statements are unlikely.

■ You can have more than one error handler in a procedure. Add another **On Error GoTo** *LabelName* statement at the point at which you want to handle an error differently and use a unique LabelName:.

■ You can use the value returned by a function to the calling procedure that indicates whether the function completed without an error or whether the error was resolved by the error-handling routine. Add a *FunctionName* = **True** statement before the error handler's label. Alternatively, if your code previously set the function's return value, add a *FunctionName* = **False** (or 0) statement in the error-handling routine.

■ Add an **Exit Function** (or **Exit Sub**) statement before the first error-handling label so that the interpreter skips the error-handling code if the procedure executes correctly.

■ To prevent execution of the last error handler on the invocation path if you want to disable error trapping temporarily in the procedure, add an **On Error GoTo 0** statement immediately before the **Exit Function** statement.

■ All label names in Object Basic must start in the first column of the code and must end with a colon.

■ You can create a common error-handling procedure and call that procedure from your code's error-handling section.

■ Add one of the five statements listed in Table 4.9 to the end of your error-handling code. If you choose the **Exit Function** statement to terminate the error-handling routine and you want to disable error trapping, you need to add another **OnError GoTo 0** statement immediately before **Exit Function**.

Table 4.9 lists the five alternatives for completing an error-handling routine. If one of these statements does not precede your procedure's **End Function** or **End Sub** statement, a compile-time error occurs. If your procedure has more than one error-handling routine, each routine must have its own exit statement.

Table 4.9. Alternatives for completing an error-handling routine.

Error Completion Statement	*Execution after Error Handling*
Resume	Returns to and re-executes the line that caused the error
Resume Next	Returns to the line following the line that caused the error; continues execution from that line
Resume *LabelName*	Jumps to a label, *LabelName*, and continues execution of subsequent lines

continues

Table 4.9. continued

Error Completion Statement	Execution after Error Handling
`Error Err`	Re-creates the runtime error that caused the error. Interpreter searches invocation path for the immediately preceding error handler and executes the error-handling routine if such a routine exists. If no active error handler is found in the search, the interpreter displays an error message box.
`Exit {Function¦ Sub}`	Exits the procedure

Other Error-Related Keywords

Table 4.10 lists the six other Object Basic keywords commonly used in error-handling routines. The `MsgBox` statement and `MsgBox()` function are included in Table 4.10 because you normally need to indicate to the user that an error has occurred.

Table 4.10. The six remaining Object Basic keywords commonly used in error-handling routines.

Keyword	Description of Error-Related Keyword
`Err`	A function (`wError = Err`) that returns an integer code which represents the type of the last error encountered. `Err` is set to 0 after execution of any of the five error-routine completion statements listed in Table 4.9.
`Err`	A statement (`Err = wError`) that lets you set the value of `Err` to emulate a runtime error.
`Error$`	A function that returns a string variable which describes the last error that occurred. `Error$` returns the empty string (`" "`) if no error has occurred. You can return the description of an error by supplying an integer argument. For example, `Error$(10)` returns `Duplicate definition`. Omitting the string symbol (`$`) returns a subtype 8 `Variant`.

Keyword	*Description of Error-Related Keyword*
`Error` *Code*	When you execute `Error` as a statement with an integer error code as a parameter, you create a runtime error. If *Code* equals an Object Basic error code, a message box with the corresponding error message appears; otherwise, the message box displays `User-defined error`. The most common syntax, `Error Err`, is used to complete an error-handling routine.
`MsgBox`	A statement that displays a message box with a user-supplied message and title. You can specify the icon for the message box and a limited number of combinations of buttons with captions. The default statement for error handlers is `MsgBox Error$, 16,` *AppName* (*AppName* is the name of your application). The message box displays the standard error message for the error that occurred. Type 16 message boxes display a red stop sign and an OK button. If you omit *AppName*, the name of the application, such as `Microsoft Access`, appears.
`MsgBox()`	A function that returns an integer value indicating the button on which the user clicked. Otherwise, the syntax of the `MsgBox()` function is identical to the `MsgBox` statement.

NOTE

`Erl` is a function that returns the line number on which the error occurred (or the line number of the immediately preceding line, in some cases). `Erl` is provided for backward compatibility with earlier versions of BASIC and is not used in Object Basic.

Resolving Runtime Errors

Your error-handling routine must either take corrective action to resolve the error that caused execution of the routine or terminate the procedure. If the error is fatal to your application's operation, you might want to exit the application after giving users the opportunity to save files. Thus, you might want to preserve the value of `Err` by assigning its value to a variable you pass to another procedure that shuts down the application in an orderly way.

You can disregard some types of runtime errors without affecting the continued operation of your code. When the runtime errors that can occur are not fatal to continued operation of your procedure, you can disable error messages by preceding a block of code with **On Error Resume Next** and then resume trapping errors with an **On Error GoTo** *LabelName* statement. An example of the safe use of **On Error Resume Next** follows:

```
Dim dbNWind As Database
Dim qdfEmployees As QueryDef
On Error GoTo OpenError
Set dbNWind = OpenDatabase("c:\access\nwind.mdb")
On Error Resume Next
dbNWind.DeleteQueryDef("Employees")
On Error GoTo CreateError
Set qdfEmployees = dbNWind.CreateQueryDef("Employees", "SELECT * FROM
➥Employees;)
```

You need to delete a **QueryDef** object before you create a new **QueryDef** object with the same name. When you run the application the first time, no **Employees QueryDef** exists and a runtime error occurs. Use the **On Error Resume Next** to disregard the runtime error and continue execution at the next line, which activates error trapping with an **On Error GoTo** CreateError statement.

5

Understanding Access 2.0's Data Access Objects

All of Microsoft Corp.'s new mainstream Windows applications make use of the features of OLE 2.0. Some of these new applications, such as Excel 5.0, are themselves OLE 2.0 objects. (Excel 5.0 workbook files are OLE 2.0 objects, .XLS files with an OLE 2.0 "wrapper.") The current crop of OLE 2.0-compliant applications have varying degrees of support for OLE 2.0 functions; all of the new applications include drag-and-drop embedding and in-place activation of embedded OLE 2.0 objects. Excel 5.0 and Project 4.0 are full-scale OLE 2.0 applications; these products can act as OLE 2.0 container (*client* in OLE 1.0) and server applications. Both use Visual Basic for Applications (VBA) as their application programming language and support OLE Automation for interapplication communication. Word 6.0 doesn't use VBA, but you can execute WordBasic commands using OLE Automation (OA) methods; Word 6.0 is an OLE Automation server, although Word presently does not comply fully with the OLE 2.01 specification. Access 2.0 is an OLE Automation client-only application.

Windows 4.0, called Chicago and in the alpha test stage when this chapter was written, will make extensive use of OLE 2.0 features. OLE 2.0 is incorporated within the operating system, which replaces DOS, and the applets supplied with Windows 4.0 will consist primarily of OLE 2.0 *custom controls*, an extension of the concepts of the common dialog boxes of Windows 3.1, the common toolbars of recently-released Windows applications, and Visual Basic 3.0 .VBX custom controls. (OLE 2.0 custom controls use the .OCX extension.) Access is the first Microsoft application to afford developers a first look at how OLE 2.0 Custom Controls will be implemented in Windows 4.0, Daytona (a future upgrade to Windows NT 3.1), and Cairo (Windows NT 4.0, the fully object-oriented version of Windows NT expected to be released in 1995).

> **NOTE**
>
> Microsoft has not confirmed that the retail version of Chicago will be named "Windows 4.0" or that Cairo will be "Windows NT 4.0." It is likely, however, that these version numbers will be used. Features of Chicago, Daytona, and Cairo that are described in this chapter and elsewhere in this book are based on reports that have appeared in the computer press.

Chapter 14 of this book, "Understanding OLE 2.0," provides an in-depth analysis of the impact of OLE 2.0 on the future of Windows applications, including your Access database applications. Chapter 16, "Using Access as an OLE Automation Client," and Chapter 18, "Introducing OLE 2.0 Custom Controls," describe how you take advantage of OA to manipulate other applications' objects and use OLE custom controls in your Access applications. The reason for introducing the subject of OLE 2.0 at this point in the book is that OLE 2.0 requires that applications rigidly conform to the object definition rules of the Microsoft OLE 2.01 specification, called the Component Object Model (COM). Microsoft offered in late 1993 to make the OLE 2+ specification an "industry standard;" however, Microsoft's competitors have so far evidenced little or no enthusiasm nor expressed their gratitude for this offer.

The database object structure of Access 1.x constituted a step toward OLE 2.0 COM compliance. Visual Basic 3.0, an OLE 2.0 client application, took the next step by adding the TableDefs collection, which lets you add new tables to databases with Visual Basic code. Access 2.0's data access object structure, based on collections of objects, complies with OLE 2.0's essential requirements for the COM. Version 2.0 of Access, however, does not expose its collections of objects to other applications; therefore Access 2.0 cannot act as an OA server. It is likely, however, that future versions of Access will have OA server capabilities.

This chapter describes Access 2.0's data access objects (DAOs) within OLE 2.0 Component Object Model framework. Chapter 7, "Using Access Objects, Methods, and Events," shows you how to use the data access objects described here in your Access applications. This chapter also discusses the relationship between data access objects and such Access 2.0 application objects as forms, reports, and modules. (Application object classes are called containers in OLE 2.0 parlance.) You can gain a better understanding of the OLE 2.0 terminology used in this chapter by reading the first few sections of Chapter 14. It is not necessary, however, to understand all of the intricacies of OLE 2.0 to comprehend the hierarchy and use of Access 2.0's data access objects.

Defining Access 2.0 Data Access Objects and Collections

The Access Basic code examples in the preceding chapters use Access 1.x conventions for declaring and setting the values of database object variables. The object at the top of the Access 1.x DAO's hierarchy is the **Database** object, which could be assigned a pointer to **CurrentDB**( ), the currently-open database, or **CodeDB**( ), which points to the currently-executing library database. Access 2.0 defines additional levels in the DAO hierarchy, above and below the **Database** object. Data access objects are members of DAO collections; an object collection is similar to an array in which the elements of the array consist of pointers to locations of member objects. This book uses the term *member* when referring to collections and the term *element* when referring to conventional arrays. The sections that follow describe the characteristics of collections of DAOs.

Technically, collections represent the enumeration of member objects of a particular class of objects. OLE 2.0 requires that collections be named as the common-usage plural version of the object type name; thus a collection of `Axis` objects is named `Axes`. (Microsoft Graph5 includes the `Axis` object and the `Axes` collection.) The members of some collections point to instances of objects, objects that are open in your application; others point to persistent objects stored as components of a .MDB file, which may or may not have been opened. Figure 5.1 shows the hierarchy of Access 2.0 data access objects. A collection of persistent objects is called the `Containers` collection, which departs from the rule that collections be named for its member objects' class; the `Containers` collection actually contains `Documents` collections. (An OLE 2.0-compliant document object is defined as being a container; thus Access 2.0 substitutes the term Database *Container* for Access 1.x's Database *Window*.) The document objects of Access 2.0 are discussed near the end of this chapter.

FIGURE 5.1.

The hierarchy of collections of Access 2.0 data access objects.

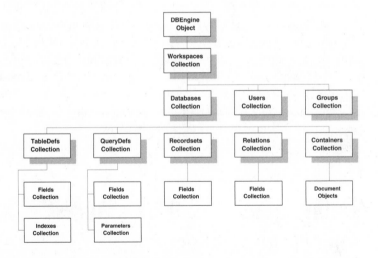

Collections of the Database Engine Object

Following are the characteristics of the upper three tiers of data access objects, beginning with the "chief executive officer" of the DAO corporation, `DBEngine`:

■ The `DBEngine` object is at the top rung of the hierarchy of data access objects and thus is not a member of a collection. There is only one instance of the `DBEngine` object, which corresponds to the instance of the Jet database engine that Access opens on launching. The `DBEngine` object contains only the `Workspaces` collection.

- The `Workspaces` collection contains **Workspace** objects. **Workspace** objects represent instances of the `DBEngine` object, called *sessions*. The first **Workspace** object of the collection, `Workspaces(0)`, is the workspace for the current session that is opened automatically by Access when you open a database. You can open more than one session, which are referred to as `Workspaces(1)`...`Workspaces(n)` in the order in which you open the sessions, with the new **Append** method that is applicable to most DAOs. **Workspace** objects contain **Databases**, **Users**, and **Groups** collections. Access 2.0's transaction-processing methods, **BeginTrans**, **CommitTrans**, and **Rollback** are limited in scope to a single **Workspace** object. Visual Basic 3.0 first implemented control of the Workspace object with its `SetDataAccessOption` and `SetDefaultWorkspace` statements, neither of which are supported by Access 2.0.

- The `Databases` collection contains the **Database** objects for the active **Workspace** object. When you open an Access database after launching Access, the current database is assigned to `Databases(0)`. Thus the appropriate Access 2.0 syntax is **Set** `dbName` = **dbEngine**.`Workspaces(0)`.`Databases(0)`, not Access 1.1's **Set** `dbName` = **CurrentDB()**. (Old habits die hard, so you see many instances of the use of **CurrentDB()** in the Access Basic code for the wizards supplied with Access 2.0.) **Database** objects contain a variety of object collections that are discussed later in this chapter. You can add a new database to your current `Workspace` object by applying the **Append** method.

- The `Users` and `Groups` collections are related to secure Access databases in networked workgroup environments. These two collections are discussed briefly in this chapter and are discussed in greater detail in Chapter 19, "Networking Secure Access Applications."

NOTE

Objects whose names are reserved words (object data type names used in **Dim** `objName` **As** *ObjectDataType* expressions) in Access Basic are set in bold monospace type, as are other Access Basic reserved words, such as **For...Next**. Names of collections, which are Access Basic keywords, are set in normal-weight monospace type.

All of the preceding collections are new to Access 2.0; the `Databases(0)` member **Database** object, formerly pointed to by **CurrentDB()**, behaves identically to its Access 1.x predecessor, but it has more collections. For Access developers, the significance of the addition of these objects is the ability to create new databases, then to add objects such as tables to the databases with Access Basic code, a process that Microsoft calls creating objects "programatically." You could not create a new database with version 1.x of Access Basic, and you had to use a tack-on library (MSADDL110.DLL), declare its functions, then call the functions with code. This was not a trivial task, and MSADDL110.DLL did not win any awards for stability. Creating DAOs programatically is discussed later in this chapter.

Collections of the Database Object

The **Database** object is familiar to anyone who has written Access Basic 1.x code or used Visual Basic 3.0's database extensions that hook to the Jet 1.1 database engine. The following list describes the collections contained in each **Database** object of Access 2.0:

■ The TableDefs collection consists of **TableDef** objects that define the design of Access tables. The value of the Name property of each **TableDef** object appears in the Database Container (DBC) when you click the Tables tab. **TableDef** objects are the approximate equivalent of the table design grid. (**Table** objects, which are a type of document object, correspond to table datasheet view.) **TableDef** objects were introduced by Visual Basic 3.0 and are used to modify the design of existing persistent **Table** objects or to append new **Table** objects to the TableDefs collections. **TableDef** objects contain Fields and Indexes collections that are essentially identical to the Fields and Indexes collections of Access 1.x Table objects.

■ The QueryDefs collection should be familiar to Access 1.x developers. **QueryDef** objects are persistent SELECT and action queries stored in .MDB files. **QueryDef** objects are stored in the form of SQL statements that have been optimized, when necessary, by the Jet database engine's query optimizer. **QueryDef** objects contain Fields (more properly called *columns* in a query-result set) and Parameters collections.

■ The Recordsets collection substitutes for Access 1.x's **Dynaset** and **Snapshot** objects, which were not members of a collection. You open an updatable **Recordset** object, which is equivalent to a **Dynaset** object, by assigning the value of the intrinsic global constant DB_OPEN_DYNASET to the int*Options* argument of the **OpenRecordset**() method in a statement such as rs*Name* = **OpenRecordset**(str*Name*[, int*Options*]) or by omitting the int*Options* argument. You open a non-updatable **Recordset** object by using the DB_OPEN_SNAPSHOT intrinsic global constant. The **OpenDynaset**() and **OpenSnapshot**() methods remain in version 2.0 of Access Basic for backward compatibility. Microsoft recommends using (and this book uses)

`OpenRecordset`(); you may, however, find an occasional lapse in the examples that follow this chapter as well as in the code Microsoft wrote for the Access wizards.

■ The `Relations` collection contains **Relation** objects, which define the relationships between members of the `Fields` collection of **TableDef** objects. **Relation** objects are valid only for tables of **Database** objects contained in the same **Workspace** object. **Relation** objects let you specify primary and foreign key fields as property values, and you can specify if cascading updates and cascading deletions are to be performed. The `Relations` collection might have been more aptly named the "Relationships" collection, because the term "relation" is equivalent to the term "table" when used in relational algebra. The `Relations` collection is not included in Visual Basic 3.0 because **Workspace**-scope relationships are not supported by the Access 1.1 database engine.

■ The `Containers` collection, not surprisingly, contains `Container` objects, which in turn contain collections of **Document** objects of a common document type. The `Documents` collection has a member **Document** object for each of the persistent objects of the parent **Database** object, plus the parent **Database** itself; the values of the `Name` property of the **Document** objects of type **Table**, **QueryDef**, **Form**, **Report**, **Script** (macro), and **Module** appear as items in the list box of the DBC. (**Table** and **QueryDef** objects are combined in the `Tables` Document.) **Document** objects differ from the preceding objects that refer to instances of (open) objects; **Document** objects refer to the persistent objects that are stored in the .MDB file of the parent **Database** object. Visual Basic 3.0 does not have a direct equivalent of the `Containers` collection.

Creating New Data Access Objects with Access Basic Code

Creating new data access objects with the Access user interface is considerably simpler than creating DAOs with Access Basic code. In fact, there are relatively few instances in which developers need to create DAOs "programatically." The most common type of object you may need to create are new **User** objects when you distribute applications where the user is to employ the same login ID and password for a client-server database and for Access. (The tables in SYSTEM.MDA are read-only in Access 2.0, so adding a new **User** object now is the only practical method of accomplishing this.) Creating new users "programatically" is covered in Chapter 19, "Networking Secure Access Applications."

Regardless of how infrequently you need to use Access Basic to create new DAOs, a *Developer's Guide* for Access 2.0 would be incomplete without leading you though the DAO creation thicket. The sections that follow describe the methods you use to create DAOs with Access Basic.

Declaring Object Variables

You must precede the use of the **Set** statement with a variable declaration of the object type in the declarations section (module-level or global scope) or in a procedure of an Access Basic module or CBF event-handler. (You cannot create intrinsic *ad hoc* object variables, even if you omit the **Option** Explicit statement.) The general syntax for declaring object variables is

```
{Global¦Dim¦Static} objName As ObjectDataType
```

You replace *ObjectDataType* with the data type of the object you want, such as **Workspace**, **Database**, or **TableDef**. Like other Object Basic variables, variables of object data types can have global, module-level, form-level, report-level, and local scope. You cannot, however, create arrays of any object data type, nor does Access Basic support Visual Basic's control arrays. Collections are an adequate approximation of arrays of objects for most programming purposes.

The *Create*ObjectType*()* and *Open*ObjectType*()* Methods

You create new database objects in the current Workspace object with one of the **Create*ObjectType*** () methods listed in Table 5.1. The syntax for the **Create*ObjectType***() method is

```
Set objName = ParentObject.CreateObjectType(Argument[s])
```

Using the **OpenDatabase**() or **OpenRecordset**() methods automatically appends an existing **Database** or new **Recordset** object to the **Databases** or **Recordsets** collections, respectively. The general syntax of the **Open*ObjectType***() method is identical to that for **Create*ObjectType***():

```
Set objName = ParentObject.OpenObjectType(Argument[s])
```

The obsolete **CreateDynaset**() and **CreateSnapshot**() methods do not have corresponding "Dynasets" and "Snapshots" collections; using these obsolete methods in Access 2.0 applications violates the consistency of relationships between objects and collections. The Object Type column in Table 5.1 also includes the prefix for object variable names that indicates the type of object to which the variable points. Appendix B, "Naming Conventions for Microsoft Access " explains the L-R (Leszynski-Reddick) naming conventions for object and other variables used in this book.

Table 5.1. Object Type, Object Variable Prefixes, and Syntax for Creating and Opening DAOs.

Object Type and Prefix	*Syntax for Set objName = statement*
Workspace wks	**DBEngine.CreateWorkspace**(str*Name*, str*UID*, str*PWD*)
Group grp	{wks*Name*¦usr*Name*}**.CreateGroup**([str*Name*[, str*PID*]])
User usr	{wks*Name*¦grp*Name*}**.CreateUser**([str*Name*[, str*PID*[, str*PWD*]]])
Database db (new)	**DBEngine.CreateDatabase**(str*FileName*, int*Locale*, int*Options*)
Database db (existing)	wks*Name*.**OpenDatabase**(str*FileName*[, f*Exclusive* [, f*Readonly* [, str*Source*]]])
TableDef tdf (new)	db*Name*.**CreateTableDef**([str*Name* [, lng*Attributes* [,str*Source* [,str*Connect*]]]])
Field fld	tdf*Name*.**CreateField**(str*Name*[, int*Type*[, int*Size*]])
Index idx	tdf*Name*.**CreateIndex**([str*Name*])
Relation rel	db*Name*.**CreateRelation**([str*Name* [, str*TableName* [, str*ForeignTableName* [, lng*Attributes*]]]])
QueryDef qdf	db*Name*.**CreateQueryDef**(str*Name*, str*SQL*)
Recordset rs	db*Name*.**OpenRecordset**(str*Source*, int*Type*, int*Options*)
Recordset rs	{tdf*Name*¦qdf*Name*¦rs*Name*}.**OpenRecordset**(, int*Type*, int*Options*)
Dynaset ds (obsolete)	db*Name*.**CreateDynaset**([str*Source* [, f*Exclusive* [, f*Inconsistent*]]])
Snapshot ss (obsolete)	db*Name*.**CreateSnapshot**(str*Source*)
Property prp	obj*Name*.**CreateProperty**(str*Name*, var*Value*)

continues

Table 5.1. continued

Object Type and Prefix	*Syntax for Set objName = statement*
Workspace wks	**DBEngine.CreateWorkspace**(str*Name*, str*UID*, str*PWD*)
Group grp	{wks*Name*¦usr*Name*}.**CreateGroup**([str*Name*[, str*PID*]])
User usr	{wks*Name*¦grp*Name*}.**CreateUser**([str*Name*[, str*PID*[, str*PWD*]]])
Database db (new)	**DBEngine.CreateDatabase**(str*FileName*, int*Locale*, int*Options*)
Database db (existing)	wks*Name*.**OpenDatabase**(str*FileName*[, f*Exclusive* [, f*Readonly* [, str*Source*]]])
TableDef tdf (new)	db*Name*.**CreateTableDef**([str*Name* [, lng*Attributes* [,str*Source* [,str*Connect*]]]])
Field fld	tdf*Name*.**CreateField**(str*Name*[, int*Type*[, int*Size*]])
Index idx	tdf*Name*.**CreateIndex**([str*Name*])
Relation rel	db*Name*.**CreateRelation**([str*Name* [, str*TableName* [, str*ForeignTableName* [, lng*Attributes*]]]])
QueryDef qdf	db*Name*.**CreateQueryDef**(str*Name*, str*SQL*)
Recordset rs	db*Name*.**OpenRecordset**(str*Source*, int*Type*, int*Options*)
Recordset rs	{tdf*Name*¦qdf*Name*¦rs*Name*}.**OpenRecordset**(, int*Type*, int*Options*)
Dynaset ds (obsolete)	db*Name*.**CreateDynaset**([str*Source* [, f*Exclusive* [, f*Inconsistent*]]])
Snapshot ss (obsolete)	db*Name*.**CreateSnapshot**(str*Source*)
Property prp	obj*Name*.**CreateProperty**(str*Name*, var*Value*)
Workspace wks	**DBEngine.CreateWorkspace**(str*Name*, str*UID*, str*PWD*)
Group grp	{wks*Name*¦usr*Name*}.**CreateGroup**([str*Name*[, str*PID*]])

Object Type and Prefix	Syntax for Set objName = statement
User usr	{wksName¦grpName}.**CreateUser**([strName[, strPID[, strPWD]]])
Database db (new)	**DBEngine.CreateDatabase**(strFileName, intLocale, intOptions)
Database db (existing)	wksName.**OpenDatabase**(strFileName[, fExclusive [, fReadonly [, strSource]]])
TableDef tdf (new)	dbName.**CreateTableDef**([strName [, lngAttributes [,strSource [,strConnect]]]])
Field fld	tdfName.**CreateField**(strName[, intType[, intSize]])
Index idx	tdfName.**CreateIndex**([strName])
Relation rel	dbName.**CreateRelation**([strName [, strTableName [, strForeignTableName [, lngAttributes]]]])
QueryDef qdf	dbName.**CreateQueryDef**(strName, strSQL)
Recordset rs	dbName.**OpenRecordset**(strSource, intType, intOptions)
Recordset rs	{tdfName¦qdfName¦rsName}.**OpenRecordset**(, intType, intOptions)
Dynaset ds (obsolete)	dbName.**CreateDynaset**([strSource [, fExclusive [, fInconsistent]]])
Snapshot ss (obsolete)	dbName.**CreateSnapshot**(strSource)
Property prp	objName.**CreateProperty**(strName, varValue)

The majority of the optional arguments of the **CreateObjectType**() and **OpenObjectType**() methods are identical. The arguments that are not included in Table 5.1 through Table 5.7, are described in the following list:

■ The strName argument of the **CreateDatabase**() method follows the same format as the strName argument of the **OpenDatabase**() method.

■ The strName argument of the **CreateProperty**() method enables you to create a user-defined **Property** object that you can append to any object other than the **DBEngine** object. The value of the strName argument must not conflict with the name of the predefined "offical" property of the object.

■ The str*DataType* argument of the **CreateProperty**() method enables you to specify the **Variant** data type of the property by the numeric identifier of the **Variant** subtype.

■ The f*Exclusive* and f*Readonly* arguments of the **OpenDatabase**() method are set **True** to open the database for exclusive read-only access. The default value of these arguments is **False**.

■ The f*Exclusive* argument of the obsolete **CreateDynaset**() method, when set **True**, opens the table(s) underlying the **Dynaset** object for exclusive access. **False** is the default.

■ The str*Source* argument of the **OpenRecordset**() method is required only when you open a **Recordset** object from the **Database** object. You omit the str*Source* argument when you create a **Recordset** based on a **TableDef**, **QueryDef**, or another **Recordset** object. The type of **Recordset** object is, by default, table for **Recordset** objects based on **TableDef** objects, and, if possible, a dynaset (updatable **Recordset**) when the **Recordset** object is created from the **QueryDef** or another **Recordset** object.

■ The f*Inconsistent* argument of the **CreateDynaset**() method, when set **True**, allows updates to fields of the primary (base) table that underlies the "one" side of a one-to-many relationship. **False** is the default.

Table 5.2 lists the values for the str*Name* and str*Source* arguments of the **OpenDatabase**() method. Table 5.3 specifies the global intrinsic constants required to set the CollatingOrder property of the database to that for the language of your locale. Table 5.4 lists values for the int*Option* argument of the **CreateDatabase**() and **OpenRecordset**() methods, and Table 5.5 provides values for the int*Type* argument of the **OpenRecordset**() method.

Table 5.2. Values for the strName and strSource Arguments of the OpenDatabase() Method.

Database Type	strName	strSource
Access	`"d:\path\filename"`	(none)
Btrieve	`"d:\path\filename.DDF"`	`"Btrieve;"`
dBASE III	`"d:\path"`	`"dBASE III;"`
dBASE IV	`"d:\path"`	`"dBASE IV;"`
FoxPro 2.0	`"d:\path"`	`"FoxPro 2.0;"`
FoxPro 2.5	`"d:\path"`	`"FoxPro 2.5;"`

Database Type	strName	strSource
ODBC	`""` (zero-length string)	`"ODBC;DATABASE=`*defaultdatabase*`;UID=`*username*`;PWD=`*password*`;DSN=`*datasourcename*`;"`
Paradox 3.x	`"d:\path"`	`"Paradox 3.x;"`
Paradox 4.x	`"d:\path"`	`"Paradox 4.x;"`

Table 5.3. Values for the `intLocale` Argument of the `CreateDatabase()` Method.

Locale Constant	Languages
`DB_SORT_GENERAL`	English, German, French, Portuguese, and Italian
`DB_SORT_SPANISH`	Spanish
`DB_SORT_DUTCH`	Dutch
`DB_SORT_SWEDFIN`	Swedish, Finnish
`DB_SORT_NORWDAN`	Norwegian, Danish
`DB_SORT_ICELANDIC`	Icelandic
`DB_SORT_NORDIC`	Nordic countries (Access 1.0 only)

Table 5.4. Values for the `intOption` Argument of the `CreateDatabase()` and `OpenRecordset()` Methods.

Object	intOption	Purpose of Option
Database	`DB_ENCRYPT`	Encrypt the new database
	`DB_VERSION10`	Create an Access 1.0 format database
	`DB_VERSION11`	Create an Access 1.1 format database
	`DB_VERSION20`	Create an Access 2.0 format database (default)
Recordset	`DB_DENYWRITE`	Prevent others from making changes to any records in the underlying table(s) while the **Recordset** is open.

continues

Table 5.4. continued

Object	intOption	Purpose of Option
	`DB_DENYREAD`	Prevent others from reading any records in the underlying table(s) while the **Recordset** is open. This option should be used for administrative purposes only.
	`DB_READONLY`	Do not allow updates to records in the table. Read-only access increases the speed of some operations.

Table 5.5. Values for the `intType` Argument of the `OpenRecordset()` Method.

Object	intType	Description of Type
Field		See Table 5.3
Recordset	`DB_OPEN_TABLE`	Table (default value for **TableDef** source)
	`DB_OPEN_DYNASET`	Dynaset (default value for **Database**, **QueryDef**, **Recordset**, or an attached **TableDef**)
	`DB_OPEN_SNAPSHOT`	Snapshot (not updatable)

Table 5.6 lists the intrinsic global constants that serve as the values of the *lngAttributes* field for **TableDef**, **Field**, **Index**, and **Relation** objects. Attribute values are flags, so you can combine the intrinsic constant values with the **Or** operator to specify more than one attribute.

Table 5.6. Values of the Intrinsic Constants for the `intAttributes` argument.

Object	intAttributes	Description of Attribute
Field	`DB_FIXEDFIELD`	Fixed field size (default for Numeric fields)
	`DB_VARIABLEFIELD`	Variable field size (Text fields only)
	`DB_AUTOINCRFIELD`	Counter field data type (auto-incrementing)
	`DB_UPDATABLEFIELD`	Updates to field values are allowed

Object	intAttributes	Description of Attribute
Index	DB_DESCENDING	Use descending index
Relation	DB_RELATIONUNIQUE	One-to-one relationship
	DB_RELATIONDONTENFORCE	Don't enforce referential integrity
	DB_RELATIONINHERITED	Relationship is inherited from attached tables
TableDef	DB_ATTACHEXCLUSIVE	An attached table opened for exclusive use
	DB_ATTACHSAVEPWD	Save the user ID and password for the attached table with the connection data
	DB_SYSTEMOBJECT	The table is a system table
	DB_HIDDENOBJECT	The table is a hidden table (for system use)
	DB_ATTACHEDTABLE	The table is an attached table from another database (except by ODBC)
	DB_ATTACHEDODBC	The table is attached by ODBC

Table 5.7 lists the allowable values of int*Type* and int*Size* for the **Field** object and int*Type* for the **Property** object. You need only specify a value for the int*Size* argument when you specify the Text field data type.

Table 5.7. Allowable values of the `intType` and `intSize` arguments.

intType	intSize	Field Data Type
DB_BOOLEAN	1	Yes/No (logical, boolean)
DB_BYTE	1	Byte
DB_CURRENCY	8	Currency
DB_DATE	8	Date/Time
DB_DOUBLE	8	Double
DB_INTEGER	2	Integer
DB_LONG	4	Long
DB_LONGBINARY	0	Long Binary (OLE Object)

continues

Table 5.7. continued

intType	intSize	Field Data Type
DB_MEMO	0	Memo
DB_SINGLE	4	Single
DB_TEXT	1 to 255	Text

Using the *Append* Method to Add Objects to Collections

The **Append** method is the key to creating new database objects with Access Basic code. If you wondered why Microsoft used the **AddNew** method, instead of **Append**, to add a new record to a **Table** or updatable **Recordset** object, it is because **Append** is reserved in Object Basic to add new objects to collections. (The **For Append** mode clause in the **Open** instruction for sequential file output operations, however, is retained for compatibility with earlier versions of Object Basic and various DOS BASIC dialects.)

With the Append method, you can add a newly-created object to any collections for which you have the appropriate (Modify Design) permissions for the parent object of the collection or where the parent object is an object you created. You can use the Append method to add objects to the following collections, subject to the restrictions noted:

- Workgroups and two of the child collections of Workgroups—Users and Groups.

- TableDefs, Relations, and QueryDef collections of a database that you have added to the Databases collection with the **CreateDatabase**() or **OpenDatabase**() methods.

- Fields of updatable **TableDef** objects. You cannot, for example, add a field to an attached table because you are not allowed by Access to change the structure of an attached database. You can, however, create a new table in an attached database with Access's new SQL Data Definition Language (DDL) reserved words, **CREATE TABLE**.

- Indexes of updatable **TableDef** Objects. The same restrictions apply to adding indexes to attached tables. However, you can add an index to an attached table using Access SQL's **CREATE INDEX** reserved words.

- Properties of **Database**, **Index**, **QueryDef**, and **TableDef** objects, and of **Field** objects in the Fields collections of **QueryDef** and **TableDef** objects.

Properties you append to the `Properties` collection of an object are called *user-defined* properties. The ability to create your own user-defined properties enables you to document the objects you create or to assign the objects a code. You cannot append a user-defined property that has the same name as a member of the `Properties` collection of an object.

Before you can use the **Append** method, you must have created the new object to append with the **Create*ObjectType*()** methods described in the preceding sections. As mentioned earlier, when you use the **Open*ObjectType*()** method, the object, either a **Database** or **Recordset** object, automatically is appended to the corresponding collection. The general syntax of the **Append** method is

ParentObject.CollectionName.**Append** obj*Name*

Deleting and Closing Objects

You can delete most appended objects from a collection with the **Delete** method, which uses the same general syntax as the **Append** method:

ParentObject.CollectionName.**Delete** obj*Name*

The exceptions are `Workspace` objects and objects that you open with the **Open*ObjectType*()**, **CreateDynaset()**, and **CreateSnapshot()** methods. You delete **Workspace**, **Database**, **QueryDef**, and **Recordset** objects with the **Close** method, as in the following:

obj*Name*.**Close**

Experimenting with the *CreateObjectType()*, *OpenObjectType()*, and *Append* methods

Microsoft has included a number of examples of code that use the **Create*ObjectType*()**, **Open*ObjectType*()**, and **Append** methods. For instance, the example code for the help topic for the **Create*ObjectType*()** method creates, appends, and closes a new **Workspace** object. You can save a substantial amount of typing if you use the example code instead of writing your own functions or subprocedures to experiment with the methods that are used to create new DAOs.

To use the Access Basic code that appears in the pop-up windows when you click the Example hot-spot for an Access Basic reserved word or keyword, follow these steps:

1. Choose **S**earch from the **H**elp menu and type the reserved word or keyword you want to find, in this case, **CreateWorkspace**.

2. Click the Example hot-spot to display the help window with example Access Basic code.

3. Click the Copy button of the window to open the Copy dialog box. Highlight only the code content of the example, excluding any material that does not appear in the Courier typeface. (See Figure 5.2.)

4. Click the Copy button to copy the code to the Clipboard and close the Copy dialog. (Using Ctrl+C doesn't close the Copy dialog box.)

5. Open a new module in your database. If the example includes **Function...End Function** or **Sub...End Sub** statements, use Ctrl+V to paste the code anywhere in the module. If these statements are missing, enter **Function** *FunctionName*() or **Sub** *SubName* to create a new function or subprocedure stub, then paste the code between the two stub statements.

6. Choose **C**ompile Loaded Modules from the **R**un menu to check the syntax conformance of the example code. In the case of the **CreateWorkspace**() example, you need to comment out the pair of ellipsis surrounding the 'Use Special Workspace as desired' statement

7. Choose **I**mmediate Window from the **V**iew menu and type the name of the procedure in the Immediate Window. Precede a function name with **?**. Press enter to execute the procedure. You may need to change user IDs or passwords if you encounter runtime errors. For example, it is probable that the "SomethingSpecial" value of the Password property will not conform to your current password, which is likely to be "" (empty). You can alter the user name and password arguments of the **CreateWorkspace** () statement to read "Special", "Admin", "", the default values for str*UID* and str*PWD*, respectively, if you aren't running a secure version of Access. (If you make the preceding changes, comment out the MyWorkspace.UserName and MyWorkspace.Password lines that set the value of these two properties, as shown in Figure 5.3.)

8. Set a breakpoint at the last line of the code, or on the line that includes the **Close** or **Delete** methods so that execution stops before the new object is removed from the collection. The examples use object variables of local scope, so the object disappears after execution of the **End Function** or **End Sub** statements.

FIGURE 5.2.

Selecting example code to copy to an Access module.

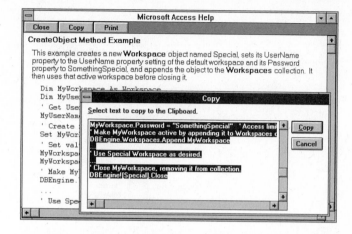

FIGURE 5.3.

Executing and testing the code in the Immediate Window.

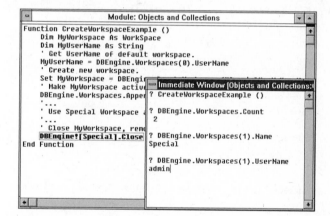

NOTE

The code examples of help topics for Access Basic code in this chapter and elsewhere in this book are from beta versions of Access 2.0 (called *Test Releases* by Microsoft.) The code examples may differ in the retail version of Access 2.0.

While the new object is visible, you can experiment with reading the values of the object's properties, as shown in the Immediate Window of Figure 5.3. The example code for the **CreateWorkspace()** function, EnumerateWorkspace(), provides an example of using the **Debug** object to print the values of properties to the Immediate Window, as shown in Figure 5.4.

FIGURE 5.4.

*Running the
Enumerate
Workspace()
function from the
Immediate
Window.*

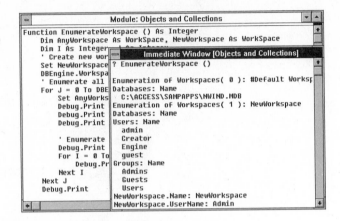

Modifying DAOs with Access Basic

You can add new tables to existing databases and new fields to existing tables with the **CreateTableDef**() and **CreateField**() methods, respectively. You also can add an index to a table with the **CreateIndex**() method. Alternatively, you can use the **CreateObject*Type***() method with the appropriate int*Type* constant to modify the structure of existing DAOs.

The EnumerateTableDef() function that serves as the Example1 code for the **TableDef** object's help topic adds a new table to your current database using the **CreateObject*Type***() method, adds a field to the new **TableDef** object, then removes the **TableDef** object from the **TableDefs** collection with the **Delete** method. Figure 5.5 shows a portion of the code for the EnumerateTabelDef() function and the result of executing this function in the Immediate Window.

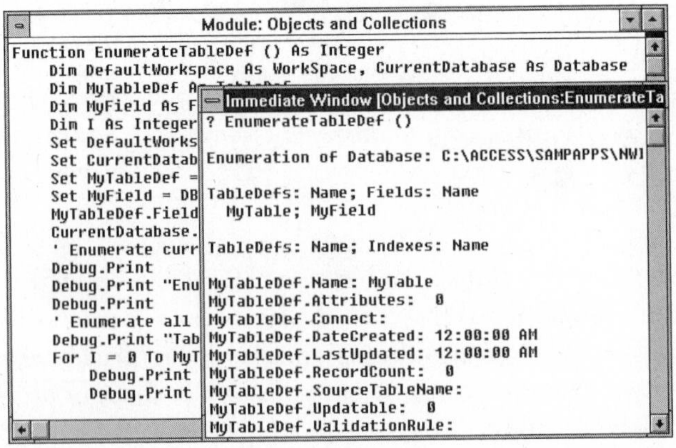

FIGURE 5.5.

*Running the
Enumerate
TableDef()
function from the
Immediate
Window.*

You can add fields to existing tables with the **CreateField**() method, but you cannot delete existing fields of existing tables with the **Delete** method. This restriction follows the rules of the SQL DDL ALTER TABLE statement, which lets you add but not delete fields of tables. The reason for this restriction is that the field(s) you want to delete may (and are very likely to) contain data that will be lost when the field is deleted. To delete a table field, you must use the DROP TABLE statement, an operation with potentially serious consequences, then reconstruct the table with a new CREATE TABLE statement. The example code for the **CreateField**() method is an incomplete fragment that adds a Phone field to the first **TableDef** object (TableDefs(0)) of your current database (**DBEngine**.Workspaces(0).Databases(0)).

Using the *Containers* Collections

The primary purpose of the Containers collection is to provide access to information about the **Document** objects that constitute the persistent objects of an Access application. The Database Documenter add-in, for example, iterates the **Document** objects of all members of the Containers collection to create a printed data dictionary. A corollary benefit of the Containers collection is that you can change the ownership of **Document** objects with Access Basic code instead of having to import the objects into a new database. Changing the ownership and permissions of **Document** objects is one of the subjects of Chapter 19, "Networking Secure Access Applications."

The Containers collection includes a **Container** object for each type of **Document** object: Databases, Tables (combined with queries), Relationships (not Relations), Forms, Reports, Scripts (macros), and Modules. A hidden **Container** object, SysRel, stores the layout of the Relationships window. You can address property values of **Document** objects with the following syntax:

DBEngine.Workspaces(0).Databases(0).Containers(*i*)[.Documents(*j*)].*Property*

wherein *i* is the index of the Container object, ranging from 0 (Databases) to 7 (Tables), and *j* is the index of the **Document** object in the **Container** object. If you've assigned a pointer to the current database to db*Name*, you can use an alternate syntax, as follows:

db*Name*.Containers(str*Container*).Documents(*j*).*Property*

to read or set the value of a property of a specific **Document** object, wherein str*Container* is the name of a **Container** object, such as "Tables." Properties of a **Document** object are listed in Table 5.8. All values of properties are returned in the **Variant** data type.

Table 5.8. The Properties of Document Objects.

Property	Access	Description
Name	Read-only	Name of the **Document**, such as Orders Form
Owner	Read-write	Owner name of the **Document**; to set a new owner name, you must have permissions for the document and the value of Owner must be a valid **User** or **Group** name
Container	Read-only	The value of the Name property of the **Container** in which the **Document** object is located, such as Forms
UserName	Read-write	Used to set the permissions for a **User** or **Group**; see Chapter 19
Permissions	Read-write	An integer flag that sets permissions for the user or group specified by UserName; see Chapter 19
DateCreated	Read-only	The date and time when the **Document** was created
DateUpdated	Read-only	The date and time when the **Document** was last modified

The example code for the Containers help topic, the EnumerateDocuments() function, enumerates the Containers collection and the **Document** objects contained in each of the **Container** objects. If you import the Enumerate Documents() code into a new module in NWIND.MDB and execute the function in the Immediate Window, you get a very long list of **Document** objects and the values of properties of these objects. The size of this list exceeds the buffer capacity of the Immediate Window, so the initial lines are lost. Figure 5.6 shows part of the output of the Enumerate Documents() function.

FIGURE 5.6.

Enumerating Document objects in the Immediate Window.

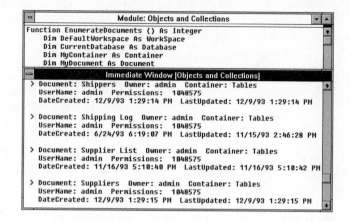

```
Module: Objects and Collections
Function EnumerateDocuments () As Integer
      Dim DefaultWorkspace As WorkSpace
      Dim CurrentDatabase As Database
      Dim MyContainer As Container
      Dim MyDocument As Document

                 Immediate Window [Objects and Collections]
> Document: Shippers  Owner: admin  Container: Tables
  UserName: admin  Permissions:  1048575
  DateCreated: 12/9/93 1:29:14 PM  LastUpdated: 12/9/93 1:29:14 PM

> Document: Shipping Log  Owner: admin  Container: Tables
  UserName: admin  Permissions:  1048575
  DateCreated: 6/24/93 6:19:07 PM  LastUpdated: 11/15/93 2:46:28 PM

> Document: Supplier List  Owner: admin  Container: Tables
  UserName: admin  Permissions:  1048575
  DateCreated: 11/16/93 5:10:40 PM  LastUpdated: 11/16/93 5:10:42 PM

> Document: Suppliers  Owner: admin  Container: Tables
  UserName: admin  Permissions:  1048575
  DateCreated: 12/9/93 1:29:15 PM  LastUpdated: 12/9/93 1:29:15 PM
```

Understanding the Application Object

OLE Automation server applications, and those that are designed for ultimate use as OA servers, require an **Application** object that points to the current instance of the application. Instances of OA applications that are initiated by the **CreateObject**() or **GetObject**() OA functions do not appear in Windows' Task Manager's list but nevertheless are current instances of the application that consume your computer's resources. The **Application** object is the highest member of the hierarchy of application-related objects. In the case of Access 2.0, the **Application** and **DBEngine** objects essentially are coequals. The following two sections describe the use of the Application option and its three methods.

Characteristics of the Application Object

The Access 2.0 **Application** object is unlike the DAOs described in this chapter. The **Application** object has no properties and contains no collections. The **Application** object has the following three purposes:

■ It provides an alternative to the **DoCmd** DoMenuItem macro action that invokes the **F**ile E**x**it menu choice with the **Quit** method that employs the general syntax, **Application.Quit** [, *intOptions*]. The allowable values for the optional *intOptions* argument are: A_PROMPT (prompt to save unsaved objects); A_SAVE (save unsaved objects without prompting, the default); and A_EXIT (quit without saving or prompting).

■ It enables the values of application options to be set in accordance with the currently logged-in user of the application. Access 2.0 lets you set the values of the options in each of the categories displayed by the Options dialog box. Reading and setting option values is the subject of the next section.

■ It provides the `Application.Quit` method for OLE Automation (in a future version of Access), which closes the application and frees the resources consumed by the OA-initiated server instance of the application.

Reading and Setting Option Values with the *GetOption()* and *SetOption* Methods

You can read the current values of options with the `Application.GetOption` (str*OptionName*) statement or set new option values with the `Application.SetOption` str*OptionName*, var*OptionValue* statement. Access 1.x offered no method of determining the current value of option settings that were set by the Options dialog box opened by the **View Options** menu choice. Access 2.0 solves this problem with the `GetOption()` and `SetOption()` methods. Option values are stored in a record created for each user in the MSysPreferences table of SYSTEM.MDA.

The values of str*OptionName* must be character strings that exactly match the name shown in the Items list box of the option category you select. (The match is not case-sensitive, however.) Items that include parenthetical units in their description require that you include the parenthetical expression in str*OptionName*. Values returned by the `GetOption()` method are of the **Variant** data type. Values returned by items with drop-down lists are integers representing the position of the current selection in the list sequence, the value of the `ListIndex` property. (The first list item is 0.) The general syntax of the `GetOption()` method is

var*OptionValue* = `Application.GetOption`(str*OptionName*)

You set the values of options with the **SetOption** method. Using **Application.SetOption** is a substantially simpler process than the very chancy **SendKeys** statements required by Access 1.x to change option values. An additional benefit is that the brief, but distracting, appearance of display artifacts does not occur when you use the **SetOption** method. The values of str*OptionName* are the same as for the `GetOption()` method. The value of var*OptionValue* is the entry you make in a text box or the ListIndex value of a selection in a drop-down list. The general syntax of the **SetOption** method is

`Application.SetOption`(str*OptionName*, var*OptionVaue*)

Figure 5.7 illustrates the use of the **GetOption**() and **SetOption** methods through entries in the Immediate Window. If your application changes the values of options, you should preserve the original values and reset the options to the original values before closing the application with the **Application.Quit** method. You can create a three-dimensional **Variant** array of the option names, the original values, and your new values, then iterate the array upon opening and before exiting Access. (The option methods also accept **Variant** values for option names.)

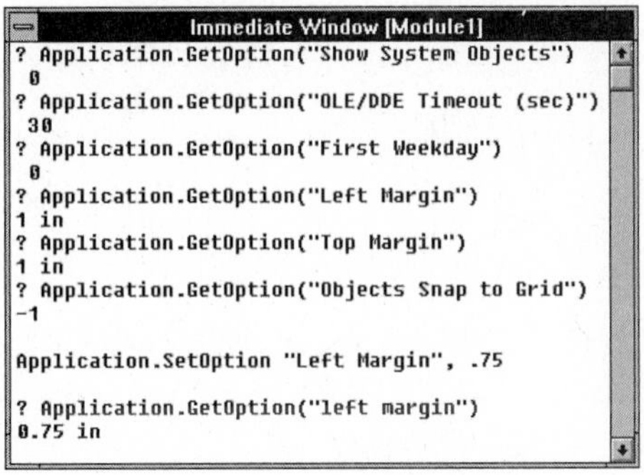

FIGURE 5.7.

Experimenting with the GetOption() and SetOption methods.

```
                Immediate Window [Module1]
? Application.GetOption("Show System Objects")
  0
? Application.GetOption("OLE/DDE Timeout (sec)")
  30
? Application.GetOption("First Weekday")
  0
? Application.GetOption("Left Margin")
1 in
? Application.GetOption("Top Margin")
1 in
? Application.GetOption("Objects Snap to Grid")
-1

Application.SetOption "Left Margin", .75

? Application.GetOption("left margin")
0.75 in
```

6

Creating and Using Object Variables

Object Basic is destined to be the lingua franca of Microsoft's mainstream Windows applications. Ultimately, it is likely that all Microsoft productivity applications, including Visual Basic itself, will use Visual Basic for Applications (VBA) as its application programming language. However, each category of product that currently uses a dialect of embedded Object Basic has one or more object data types that are unique to the application's category. Visual Basic 3.0 has forms and its own version of the Access 1.1 data access object. Access 2.0 has forms (which differ from the structure of Visual Basic forms), reports, and an extended version of the Jet 2.0 database engine's data access object. Excel 5.0 uses the spreadsheet object model with a very complex hierarchy of more than 100 objects. Thus, additional keywords that refer to special object types, and the properties and methods applicable to special object types, need to be added to product-specific dialects of Object Basic. These added keywords are not a part of the root Object Basic language. This chapter explains the syntax of Object Basic reserved words that apply primarily to database-related objects. The next chapter describes the use of the keywords added to Access Basic that apply specifically to Access application objects, such as tables, queries, forms, and reports.

Object Terminology

Object-oriented programming languages enable you to combine (encapsulate) data and code that acts on the data into a single programming object. The data elements are called the properties of an object; you implement methods that determine the behavior of an object with the code. Programming objects are arranged in a hierarchy of classes. The preceding chapter concentrated on data access objects (DAOs), most of which are defined by the Jet 2.0 database engine. Figure 6.1 shows a detailed view of the hierarchy of Access-specific object types, Container and Document objects. Objects lower in the hierarchy are descendants of objects above them, which are called ancestors. Descendants inherit properties and methods from their ancestors but also have their own properties and methods. In most cases, the ancestor serves as a container for descendant objects; the container provides the context of the objects it contains. Access **Control** objects, for example, can be contained in either **Form** or **Report** objects. A **Control** object in a **Form** container has a different context (display) than the same **Control** object in a **Report** container (printer). The **Control** object inherits its context from its container. The context of an ancestor object determines many of the properties and methods of the descendant objects that the ancestor contains.

NOTE

Although the `Section` property and **Control** objects appear in Figure 6.1 for the `Forms` and `Reports` containers' **Document** objects, neither is accessible from the **Document** object. These elements of forms and reports are accessible only when the form or report is open. **Document** objects refer to saved objects, which, except for `Relationships` and `SysRel` documents, appear in the Database window. (`SysRel` defines the appearance of the Relationships window.) `Tables` documents contain information on both **TableDef** and **QueryDef** objects. The `Scripts` collection refers to macros; programmers commonly call macros of the type used by Access *scripts*.

FIGURE 6.1.

A view of the hierarchy of Access Container and Document objects.

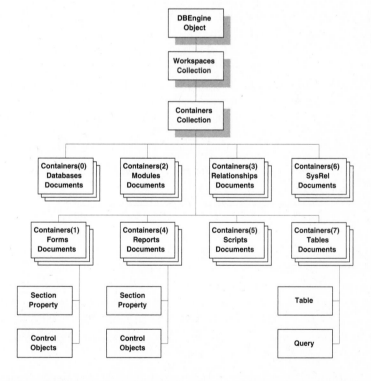

Much of the terminology for the application-specific objects of Access 2.0 is derived from the OLE 2.0 specification. Collections, containers, and documents are key constructs of OLE 2.0. Although Access 2.0 does not expose objects for manipulation by OLE 2.0 client applications that support OLE Automation, it is likely that future versions of Access will be capable of acting as OLE 2+ servers. Similarly, the structure and terminology of Access 2.0 database objects follows the OLE 2.0 rules.

The Jet 2.0 database engine is the forerunner of Microsoft's 32-bit "Unified Database Engine," which the March 7, 1994, issue of *PC Week* magazine reported will be the basis of Microsoft's Information Exchange mail server for Windows NT.

The single .MDB file structure of Access database applications is the container for both application-related objects, such as forms and reports, as well as traditional database-related objects, tables. The class of database objects is represented by the **Database** object type, a container for **TableDef**, **QueryDef**, **Recordset**, **Relation**, and **Container** objects in the TableDefs, QueryDefs, Recordsets, Relations, and Containers collections, respectively. Although Access 2.0 supports the **Table**, **Dynaset**, and **Snapshot** object data types of Access 1.x for backward compatibility, these object data types are obsolescent; these data types may not be supported in future versions of Access.

Access 2.0 **Recordset** objects can be specified to be of the Table, Dynaset, and Snapshot type. When you open an Access table in datasheet mode, Access is said to create an updatable **Recordset** object of the Dynaset type *over the table* and displays the **Recordset** object in a datasheet window that has a design unique to Access. If the table is not updatable, for instance because the database in which the table is located was opened in read-only mode, Access creates a non-updatable **Recordset** object of the Snapshot type. You also can open a **Recordset** of the Table type. **Recordset** objects of the Table type enable the use of the **Seek** method on indexed fields. The **Seek** method usually is faster than using the **Find...** methods that are applicable only to **Recordset** objects of the **Dynaset** or **Snapshot** types.

The datasheet window is an application-specific view of a **Recordset** object. **TableDef** and **QueryDef** objects share the datasheet window and have many properties in common; therefore, Microsoft included both tables and queries in the Documents collection of the Tables container. Access displays the records of **Recordset** objects in the specified sort order for queries, if a sort order is specified, or the order of the primary key of a table, if a primary key exists; otherwise, the records are displayed in entry order. The Datasheet view of a **Recordset** object also includes a record number, which is not a property of a **Recordset** object. A **Recordset** object of the **Snapshot** type is simply a **Dynaset** type in a static context; the updating methods applicable to **Dynaset** types are missing from the **Snapshot** type.

Although Access refers to a **QueryDef** as an object, **QueryDef** objects are better defined as methods (queries) applied to **Table** objects. A **QueryDef** method applied to **Table** objects results in a **Recordset** object of the **Dynaset** type, if the query-result set is updatable and of the **Snapshot** type if the result is not updatable. Macros and Access Basic code contained in modules provide methods for objects to which the macro or Access Basic function is attached. Although you can substitute a `QueryDef` object for a `Table` object in Access SQL statements (thus creating a nested query), the Jet engine first executes the `QueryDef` object, then executes the remainder of the Access SQL statement. `QueryDef`s, macros, and modules retain their object terminology in this book for consistency with the Microsoft documentation. Both macros and modules are containers for methods, but macros and modules inherit a very limited number of properties from their respective containers.

In object-oriented terms, actions are predefined methods that are specific to the application that defines them. Thus, actions are not an element of the core Object Basic language. The conventional Object Basic syntax to execute a method of an object is *ObjectName*.*MethodName*, as in `SomeTable.MoveNext`. To use actions as methods in Access Basic Code, you prefix the name of the action with the keyword, `DoCmd`. In most cases, you specify the name of the object, and then provide additional arguments for the action as required.

Actions let you apply methods to objects that exist in Access, such as menus, rather than in the objects of your Access application. (Access forms, unlike Visual Basic forms, cannot have their own menus. Access forms are MDI child windows of the Access MDI parent window. Only the parent window has a menu.) The statement, `DoCmd DoMenuItem A_FORMBAR, A_EDITMENU, A_SELECTRECORD`, selects the current record of a form; this statement emulates choosing the Select Record option of Access's Edit menu. The three parameters of `DoMenuItem` are Access intrinsic global action constants with the prefix "A_"; action constants are related to the `DB_` database intrinsic constants (described in the preceding chapter).

Names of Access actions are not set in bold in the code examples of this book because action names are neither reserved words nor keywords; action names are a parameter of the `DoCmd` statement. The means by which Microsoft added application-specific methods to Access is similar in concept to the CA-Clipper feature that enables you to add new commands to Clipper's xBase dialect.

A macro is a method that comprises an ordered set of one or more Access actions. An Access Basic function is an ordered set of statements that also creates a method. You can attach methods to certain properties by assigning the name of a macro or an Access Basic function, such as the `OnClick` (formerly `OnPush`) event of a command button, as the value of the property. Properties that accept names of methods constitute the events that are applicable to the object. In this book, the term "action" is used in conjunction with macros, for consistency with Microsoft conventions; "method" replaces "action" in the context of Access Basic code.

Distinguishing Object Basic and Access Basic

The terms "reserved word" and "keyword" often are used interchangeably to describe the collection of instructions and functions that constitute a programming language. In Access Basic and other application-specific versions of Object Basic, keywords that are not reserved words can be considered intrinsic global variables. The application in which Object Basic is embedded defines these global variables; thus the term "intrinsic." For example, the keyword Forms in Visual Basic and Access Basic is an intrinsic multidimensional global array, Forms(), of the **Form** data type whose elements include handles (Windows pointers or references) to the instance of a specific form of the application, the name of the form, and the values of its properties. Intrinsic variables are created by application-defined functions, equivalent to a user-defined function that executes when you launch the application. Microsoft calls all intrinsic global arrays of object data types "collections." An object is represented in the collection specified by its object type, such as QueryDefs or Forms, only after you have created an instance of the object; you create an instance of the object by opening it, either in the Database window or in your Access Basic code. The exception to this rule is the collection of Document objects of the Containers collection, discussed earlier in the chapter.

> **NOTE**
>
> You can use the Dim statement to distinguish keywords that are reserved words and application-specific keywords in Access Basic. Typing Dim Open As String results in a message box, "Expected: Shared or variable," when you press Enter. Open is an Access Basic (and Object Basic) reserved word used to open conventional text or binary, not database, files. Access enables you to enter the line Dim Forms As String or Dim Reports As String; both Forms and Reports are collections. In the case of collection keywords, you receive a "Duplicate definition with [sic] existing Object" message when you attempt to "compile" the module. You can declare and use a variable with the name of an action; Dim DoMenuItem As String does not generate a compile-time error. Declaration and use of the DoMenuItem variable does not interfere with the execution of a DoCmd DoMenuItem statement. DoMenuItem is neither a keyword nor a reserved word.

According to Microsoft, the syntax of the Object Basic language is defined by the syntax of Visual Basic. Visual Basic 2.0 introduced the **Variant** and object data types. The Professional Edition of Visual Basic 2.0 includes the Open Database Connectivity (ODBC) Administrator application and an ODBC driver for Microsoft SQL Server. (Only the SQL Server ODBC driver was certified when Microsoft released Visual Basic 2.0.) Thus, you could create Visual Basic 2.0 database applications for SQL Server without using a third-party add-in product. Visual Basic 3.0 added the ODBC driver for Oracle databases, plus the Access Jet database engine. You still need third-party ODBC drivers to connect to other client-server databases, such as Digital Equipment's Rdb, IBM's DB2, Ingres, Informix, and Gupta SQLBase.

In Visual Basic 1.0, properties of objects, such as forms, were reserved words. In Visual Basic 2+, properties are keywords. Each object has a collection of properties that is contained in an intrinsic global variable. The object's context determines which members of the set of properties are valid for an object. For example, Access text box controls have **BeforeUpdate**, **AfterUpdate** and other event properties in the form context but do not possess any event properties in the report context. The **BeforeUpdate** and **AfterUpdate** events are used primarily in the context of a text box that is bound to a field of a recordset. Visual Basic distinguishes between events and properties, but Access considers events to be properties. This book maintains the distinction between properties and events in all cases.

> **NOTE**
>
> When new keywords are added to a dialect of Object Basic, code for the prior version may contain objects with names identical to a new keyword. Visual Basic 2+, and thus Object Basic, have the ability to explicitly specify a value as the name of an object by enclosing the value within square brackets. For example, if your Visual Basic 1.0 application includes a form named OpenDatabase, a compile-time error results under Visual Basic 2+. You eliminate the compile-time error by enclosing the form name in square brackets, as in the statement, `[OpenDatabase].Width = 7660`. Using square brackets to create an explicit reference to a named object enables names of Access objects to include spaces and other punctuation that otherwise would cause compile-time errors in Object Basic.

The version of Basic that is embedded in Access 2.0 now offers most of the reserved words of the most advanced dialect of Object Basic, Visual Basic for Applications (VBA). Access Basic does not yet conform to all the syntactical rules (grammar) of VBA. For example, Access Basic does not support the `With {Object¦UserDefinedType}...End With` structure, because Access Basic does not support VBA's `:=` operator to specify values of named arguments. (Named arguments, to which you assign values with statements such as `CommandName NamedArg1:=Value`, were introduced to Object Basic by Word Basic with the `CommandName .ArgName = Value` syntax.) Future versions of Access are expected to incorporate "standard" embedded Object Basic, which more closely resembles VBA's implementation, or to use VBA itself, with Access-specific extensions.

Creating Data Access Object Variables

You can create instances of existing data access objects and create new database access object types with Access Basic code using methods that are defined by Object Basic. Methods that open application objects using Access's **DoCmd** *Action* syntax, discussed in the next chapter, are restricted to opening objects that are contained in the currently open database. Object Basic, however, lets you open data access objects and then assign one or more instances of the objects to named variables of the appropriate data access object type. The following sections discuss how to create object variables and obtain the values of their properties.

Declaring and Opening Data Access Objects

Before you can assign an instance of a data access object to a database object variable, you need to declare the data access object variable by a **Dim** statement with an appropriate **As** *DataType* clause, using one of the five Access 2.0 data access object data types, as shown in the following examples:

```
Dim wspName As Workspace    'new with Access 2.0
Dim dbName As Database
Dim tdfName As TableDef    'new with Access 2.0
Dim qdfName As QueryDef
Dim rsName As Recordset    'new with Access 2.0
```

A **Workspace** object, whose parent is the **DBEngine** object, represents an instance of the Jet 2.0 database engine. Microsoft calls each **Workspace** object a *session*. The term session commonly is used in conjunction with terminals, such as the classic IBM 3270, running database applications on a mainframe. As with multiple sessions on a 3270 terminal, you can run several simultaneous and totally-independent instances of the Jet engine. The value of the Name property of the default **Workspace** object, Workspaces(0), is #DefaultWorkspace#.

You assign the default workspace to a variable of the **Workspace** data type with the following statement that uses the **Set** reserved word for assigning values to object variables:

```
Set wspName = DBEngine.Workspaces(0)
```

The primary use for the **Workspace** object is to specify the domain of databases for transaction processing, using the Access Basic **BeginTrans**, **CommitTrans**, and **Rollback** methods. Use of these methods are discussed in Chapter 8, "Optimizing Transaction-Processing Forms," and Chapter 25, "Stretching the Limits of Access." By making transaction-processing methods applicable to the **Workspace** object, in which you can open multiple databases, Access 2.0 has the potential for applying transaction methods across tables contained in *distributed databases*. Distributed databases are databases that contain related information but are located on different servers, often in widely dispersed locations. It remains to be seen how Access developers will utilize multiple Jet 2.0 sessions in production database applications.

You can open any type of database supported by Access or by the ODBC Administrator within a **Workspace** object with Access's **OpenDatabase**() method, which accepts an additional str*Connect* argument. This book uses the term "foreign" to describe databases that consist of tables from other RDBMSs, such as dBASE IV or SQL Server, to distinguish between such databases and native (Access .MDB) databases. You can open a foreign database as a **Database** object only with Access Basic code; Access 2.0 does not enable you to open a foreign database with the **O**pen choice of the **F**ile menu or by specifying the name of a foreign database as a command-line parameter.

Opening a database with the **Set** reserved word assigns a value to a **Database** object variable; the value is a pointer to an instance of the database object you specify. There are three different ways to open a database in Access 2.0:

```
Set dbName = wspName.OpenDatabase(strDatabaseName[, fExclusive[,
➥fReadOnly[, strConnect]]])
Set dbName = wspName.Databases(0)
Set dbName = DBEngine(0)(0)
Set dbName = CodeDB()
```

Table 6.1 describes the arguments of the Object Basic methods for creating new instances of database objects using the **OpenDatabase**() method.

Table 6.1. Arguments for methods to create database objects.

Argument	Value	Domain
strDatabaseName	A string value consisting of the full path and, in some cases, the name of a database; you can use the UNC name of a database on a server	Database types supported by the JET engine and ODBC drivers; can be "" (empty) for ODBC databases
fExclusive	A flag (**Integer**) that determines the mode of opening the database	**False** = Shared **True** = Exclusive
fReadOnly	A flag that determines the editing mode of the database	**False** = Read/Write **True** = Read-Only
strConnect	A string value that specifies the type of database to open	"" (empty), dBASE III; dBASE IV;, Paradox 3.x;, Btrieve;, FoxPro 2.0;, and FoxPro 2.5;, or ODBC (see Table 6.2)

Table 6.2 lists the values that are valid for strDatabaseName and strConnect for the types of foreign databases supported by Access 2.0. The value of strConnect is the same as the value that is used to specify the type of database file when you attach foreign tables to Access databases. Access assumes that all dBASE, Paradox, and FoxPro files in the same directory are part of the same database. You need a *Table*.INF file in the directory specified by strDatabaseName if you want to read or update indexes of dBASE or FoxPro index files. The section called "Attaching Tables from Other Desktop Database Applications" in Chapter 2, "Developing a Design Strategy for Access Applications," describes how Access creates *Table*.INF files.

For client-server databases that use the ODBC driver manager, an empty strDatabaseName with strConnect = "ODBC;" displays the ODBC Data Sources dialog from which you can choose a list box of previously installed ODBC data sources.

Using the ODBC Administrator application to install and maintain ODBC data sources is covered in Chapter 20, "Front-Ending Client-Server Databases."

Table 6.2. Values of `strDatabaseName` and `strConnect` for databases supported by Access 1.1.

Database Type	strDatabaseName	strConnect *(Literal)*
Access	*Drive:\Path\FileName*.MDB	(Omit)
dBASE III	*Drive:\Path*	dBASE III;
dBASE IV	*Drive:\Path*	dBASE IV;
Paradox 3.x	*Drive:\Path*	Paradox 3.x;
Paradox 4.x	*Drive:\Path*	Paradox 4.x;
Btrieve	*Drive:\Path\FileName*.DDF (Btrieve data definition file)	Btrieve;
FoxPro 2.0	*Drive:\Path*	FoxPro 2.0;
FoxPro 2.5	*Drive:\Path*	FoxPro 2.5;
ODBC	ODBC data source name	ODBC;

DSN=*ServerName*; UID=*UserName*; PWD=*Password*; LoginTimeout=*Seconds*

In Access 1.x, `OpenDatabase()` was a function; in Access 2.0, `OpenDatabase()` is a method of the Workspace object. Access 1.x used the `CurrentDB()` function to create a pointer to the currently-open database of an Access application. Access 2.0 replaces `CurrentDB()` with the default `Database` object (Databases(0)) of the Databases collection of the specified `Workspace` object. The shortcut syntax, `DBEngine(0)(0)`, is the most common Access 2.0 replacement for Access 1.x's CurrentDB() function. Use of the `CodeDB()` function, which returns a pointer to an attached library database in which the `CodeDB()` function is executed, instead of the application database, is identical in Access 1.x and 2.0. Using the `CodeDB()` function is one of the subjects of Chapter 23, "Developing Access Libraries and Add-Ins."

You can use Access 2.0's shortcut syntax to return or set property values of database objects at any level of the data access object hierarchy. For example, setting the **Workspace** and **Database** objects and then executing ? DBEngine(0)(0)(0)(0).Name in the Immediate Window returns the name of the default (first) field of the default (first in alphabetic order) table of the default database and workspace. You need to set the **Database** object variable before executing the statement so that an instance of the default database object exists. Examples of using the Immediate Window to experiment with object variables are shown in Figure 6.2. Use of shortcut syntax, other than **DBEngine(0)(0)**, however, is uncommon.

FIGURE 6.2.

Using shortcut syntax in the Immediate Window.

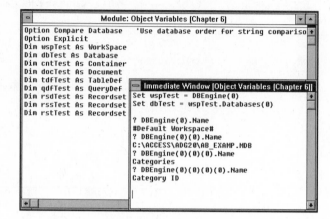

```
Module: Object Variables [Chapter 6]
Option Compare Database    'Use database order for string compariso
Option Explicit
Dim wspTest As WorkSpace
Dim dbTest As Database
Dim cntTest As Container
Dim docTest As Document
Dim tdfTest As TableDef
Dim qdfTest As QueryDef            Immediate Window [Object Variables [Chapter 6]]
Dim rsdTest As Recordset   Set wspTest = DBEngine(0)
Dim rssTest As Recordset   Set dbTest = wspTest.Databases(0)
Dim rstTest As Recordset
                           ? DBEngine(0).Name
                           #Default Workspace#
                           ? DBEngine(0)(0).Name
                           C:\ACCESS\ADG20\AB_EXAMP.MDB
                           ? DBEngine(0)(0)(0).Name
                           Categories
                           ? DBEngine(0)(0)(0)(0).Name
                           Category ID
```

Once you have created a **Database** object variable, you can create other object variables that represent the content of the **Database** object container. Following is the syntax of the Object Basic methods that assign pointers to existing objects to variables of data access object types:

```
Set tdfName = dbName.TableDefs(strTableName)
Set qdfName = dbName.QueryDefs(strQueryName)
Set rsName = dbName.OpenRecordset(strSource[, intType[, _intOptions]])
Set rsName = {tdfName¦qdfName¦rsName}OpenRecordset([intType[,
➡intOptions]])
Set rsClone = rsName.Clone()
Set rsClone = frmName.RecordsetClone
```

> **NOTE**
>
> You can substitute the **Integer** ordinal value (index) of the **TableDef** or **QueryDef** object for the object name (str*TableName* or str*QueryName*) when you use the TableDefs or QueryDefs collections. Using the ordinal value is uncommon, except when iterating collections, because the ordinal value of a member of the object collection may change when you add or delete objects from the collection.

The value of the str*Source* argument of the **OpenRecordset()** method can be the name of an existing **TableDef** or **QueryDef** object, or an Access SQL statement that returns a query result set. You also can open a **Recordset** object on an object variable of the

TableDef, QueryDef, or Recordset type; in this case, you omit the *strSource* argument. The allowable values for the *intType* argument of the OpenRecordset() method are listed in Table 6.3 and values for the *intOptions* argument are listed in Table 6.4. (These tables appear in the preceding chapter as Table 5.4 and Table 5.5, and are repeated in this chapter for convenient reference.)

Table 6.3. Allowable values of the intType argument of the OpenRecordset() method.

Database Constant	Result
DB_OPEN_TABLE	Opens a **Recordset** object of the Table type. The **Recordset** object is updatable if the user has read-write access to the table.
DB_OPEN_DYNASET	Opens a **Recordset** object of the Dynaset type. Whether the **Recordset** object is updatable depends on the underlying object.
DB_OPEN_SNAPSHOT	Opens an non-updatable Recordset object of the Snapshot type.

Table 6.4. Allowable values of the intOptions argument of the OpenRecordset() method.

Database Constant	Applies To	Result
DB_DENYWRITE	Table	
	Dynaset	
	Snapshot	Other users cannot modify or add records to the underlying tables.
DB_DENYREAD	Table	Other users cannot view records.
DB_READONLY	Table	
	Dynaset	You cannot update, delete, or append records; other users can do so.
DB_APPENDONLY	Dynaset	You can only append new records.
DB_INCONSISTENT	Dynaset	Inconsistent updates are allowed. (You can update values on the "one" side of a one-to-many relationship.)

continues

Table 6.4. continued

Database Constant	Applies To	Result
DB_CONSISTENT	Dynaset	Only consistent updates are allowed. (You cannot update values on the "one" side of a one-to-many relationship.)
DB_FORWARDONLY	Snapshot	You can only scroll forward through the Recordset object.

NOTE

Access 2.0 supports the **OpenTable**(), **CreateDynaset**(), and **CreateSnapshot**() methods for compatibility with applications created using Access 1.x. Access 2.0 Basic continues to support the **Table**, **Dynaset**, and **Snapshot** data types required to use these three methods. Using the **OpenRecordset**() method and specifying the type of **Recordset** object you want with the int*Type* argument is now the preferred syntax.

You can use the **Clone**() method to create an identical copy of an existing **Recordset** object of any type. The purpose of the **Clone**() method is to enable you to have two instances of the same **Recordset** object with different record pointer positions that you can specify with the Bookmark property. The use of the Bookmark property to specify the position of the record pointer is discussed in the section called "Using the Bookmark and Bookmarkable Properties as a Substitute for RECNO( )," later in this chapter. Using **Clone**() is simpler and faster than creating a new **Recordset** object and enables the original and the clone to share Bookmark values. You create a clone **Recordset** object of the table or query bound to a **Form** object with the **RecordsetClone** method. The properties and methods of these two types of clone **Recordset** objects are identical.

The only persistent Access data access object that you could create with Access 1.x Basic code was a **QueryDef** object. A persistent Access object is an object that you identify with a "proper name" that appears in one of the list boxes of the Database window and is a member of the Documents collection of one of the Container objects. Persistent Access objects are classified in this book as application-specific objects. Only persistent Access database objects can serve as the **RecordSource** property for bound objects. For example, Access does not enable you to set the value of the

RecordSource property of a bound text box to the name of a field of a **Recordset** object that you create with the **OpenRecordset**() method.

Access 2.0 lets you create new database objects with the **CreateDatabase**() method of the **Workspace** object and provides two methods of creating new tables: using the **CreateTableDef**() method of the **Database** object, and the **CreateField**() and **CreateIndex**() methods of the **TableDef** object; or using Access 2.0's new SQL Data Definition Language CREATE TABLE and CREATE INDEX statements. Using the **Create*ObjectType*()** methods is described in the preceding chapter.

TIP

You cannot create an Access **QueryDef** object in a foreign database; if you attempt this, you receive a "Feature not available" message. You can create the nonpersistent equivalent of a **QueryDef** object by using the OpenDynaset() method with a valid Access SQL statement as the str*Source* argument. The **Dynaset** object that you create is identical to that created by a **QueryDef** object.

Using Properties of *Recordset* Objects

Table 6.3 lists the properties that apply to **Recordset** objects. The syntax for evaluating and setting these properties is as follows:

```
varProperty = rsName.PropertyName
rsName.PropertyName = varProperty
```

Some of the properties of **Recordset** objects, such as BOF and EOF, are read-only. Unless indicated otherwise in the Description column, you can get and set the value of the property as a **Variant** of the subtype appropriate to the value. Most of the properties listed in Table 6.3 apply to all recordsets. Properties that apply only to a particular type of records (such as **Index**, which is only a property of **TableDef** objects) are so identified in the Description column of Table 6.5. Many of the properties of Access recordset objects are related to or equivalent to xBase and Paradox functions; xBase equivalents are noted in the Description column. The methods referred to in the Description column of Table 6.5 are described in the section called "Applying Methods to Database Objects," later in the chapter. Property names in Table 6.5 that are followed by an asterisk are newly-added and are only supported by Access 2.0.

> **TIP**
>
> Square brackets identify the enclosed value as a field name when used in conjunction with an object variable. You need to enclose the field name if the field name contains spaces or punctuation other than the underscore. In the unlikely event that a field of a table has the same name as an Access Basic property or an event, enclose the field name in square brackets to specify the field name, rather than the property or method.

Table 6.5. Properties of recordset objects.

Property	Description
BOF, EOF	BOF, and EOF are read-only properties that return **True** when the record pointer attempts to move to a position before the first record or to a position after the last record of a recordset, respectively. The BOF and EOF properties are equivalent to the BOF( ) and EOF( ) functions of xBase.
Bookmark	
Bookmarkable	Bookmark returns a subtype 8 **Variant** that you can use to identify and return to a specific record of a recordset object. The read-only Bookmarkable property returns **True** for recordset objects in which you can set and return to a Bookmark. You use Bookmark for many of the same purposes as xBase's RECNO( ) function. (See the section called "Using the Bookmark and Bookmarkable Properties as a Substitute for RECNO( ).")
CacheSize*	
CacheStart*	CacheSize specifies the number of records to be stored in local memory to improve the performance of operations on **Recordset** objects with large numbers of records. CacheStart specifies the Bookmark value of the first record of the local cache. Both of these properties are valid only for tables attached from ODBC data sources.

Property	Description
DateCreated	
LastUpdated	DateCreated and LastUpdated are read-only properties that return a subtype 7 `Variant` representing the date and time of the computer when creating and updating a table, respectively. `LastUpdated` is similar to a timestamp value, except that `LastUpdated` applies to a table, not to an individual record.
Filter	Sets or returns a valid Access SQL `WHERE` clause that restricts the records that appear in a recordset object. The SQL statement consists only of the operands and the operator(s), without the `WHERE` keyword and the trailing semicolon. `Filter` is similar in usage to the `SET FILTER TO` command of xBase.
Index	Sets or returns the name of the index used to order the records of a **TableDef** object or a **Recordset** object of the **Table** type only. If the specified index does not exist, a runtime error occurs. `Index` is related to the `SET INDEX TO` command of xBase. (For additional information, see the section called "Using the Index Property," later in this chapter.)
Last Modified*	Contains the value of the `Bookmark` for the last record modified (read-only).
LockEdits	Sets or returns the type of record locking used for shared tables. **True** (the default) sets pessimistic locking; the **Table** page containing the current record is locked from the time you use the **Edit** method until you apply the **Update** method. **False** applies optimistic locking. The page is locked only during the period of time that the **Update** method requires to make the change to the **Table** values.
Name*	Returns the name of the object (read-write for most data access objects, read-only for other objects.)

continues

Table 6.5. continued

Property	Description
NoMatch	A read-only value that returns **False** if a record is found when you apply any of the **FindRecord** methods or the **Seek** method. Otherwise, NoMatch returns **True**. NoMatch is the converse of the xBase FOUND( ) function and is the equivalent of testing EOF( ) after a xBase SEEK command.
PercentPosition*	Indicates the approximate current position of the record pointer as a percentage of the total number of records.
RecordCount	A read-only subtype 3 (**Integer**) or subtype 4 (**Long**) **Variant** value that often returns the exact number of records in a recordset. The conditions under which RecordCount returns incorrect values are discussed in the text. Under most conditions, RecordCount is the equivalent of the RECCOUNT( ) function of xBase.
Restartable*	**True** if the **Recordset** object supports the Requery method that re-executes the SQL statement on which the query is based. (**False** for the Table type.)
Sort	Sets or returns a valid Access Basic SQL ORDER BY clause that determines the sort order of records of a **Recordset** object of the **Dynaset** or a **Snapshot** type. The SQL statement consists only of the operands and the operator(s), without the ORDER BY keywords and the trailing semicolon.
SQL	Sets or returns a valid Access Basic SQL statement that defines a **QueryDef** object. You set the SQL property of a **QueryDef** object if you do not provide the SQL statement as the optional strSQL argument of the **CreateQueryDef**( ) method. SQL requires a terminating semicolon.
Transactions	A read-only property that returns **True** if the recordset supports transaction processing with the **BeginTrans**, **CommitTrans**, and **Rollback** methods.
Type*	Returns the **Integer** value corresponding to the type of the Recordset object. (See Table 6.3)

Property	Description
Updatable	A read-only property that returns **False** if any of the fields in a **Recordset** object are not updatable. The **Updatable** property of a recordset that contains a Counter field returns **False**.
ValidationRule*	An expression that evaluates **True** or **False** used to validate entries in fields of tables. Also applies to the **TableDef**, **QueryDef**, and **Field** objects.
ValidationText*	The text that appears in the message box when the ValidationRule evaluates **False**.

> **NOTE**
>
> Although properties of objects in Object Basic are keywords, not reserved words, properties are set bold in this book to aid in distinguishing between properties and field names.

Using the Bookmark and Bookmarkable Properties as a Substitute for *RECNO()*

Developers of xBase and Paradox applications have complained that there is no direct equivalent of the RECNO() function in Access. Using xBase as an example, RECNO() is a computed value obtained by determining the offset of the record pointer (distance in bytes) from the beginning of the data in an xBase table file and dividing the offset value by the number of bytes in a single, fixed-width record. The value of RECNO() is determined by the order in which the records are added to a table and is independent of any associated index. There is no practical method of calculating a RECNO() equivalent for recordsets with the variable-length fields used by client-server, Btrieve, and Access databases. Adding a Counter (auto-incrementing) field to an Access table does not solve the problem, because values of Counter fields are not adjusted to compensate for deleted records. (Counter field values are not updatable.)

Access uses the Bookmark property as a substitute for RECNO( ). To return to a specific record in a Bookmarkable **Recordset**, you assign the Bookmark value to a **Variant** variable, move the record pointer where you want it with the **MoveRecord** methods, and then set the Bookmark value to that of the variable to return the record pointer to its original position in the recordset. Because of its ability to return a value and perform an action, Bookmark combines the characteristics of a property and a method. A bookmark is quite useful to return the record pointer to its prior location after applying one of the **FindRecord** methods or the **Seek** method. The following code fragment shows a typical application for the Bookmark property:

```
Dim varPosition As Variant
...
If tblName.Bookmarkable Then
    varPosition = tblName.Bookmark     'Save the current record's
                                       ➥position
    tblName.MoveLast                   'Go to the last record
    ...
    tblName.Bookmark = varPosition     'Return to original record
Else
    'Use another technique, such as saving a unique field value and
    ➥finding it
End If
```

NOTE

Although the Bookmark property returns a **Variant** subtype 8 (string) variable, there is no observable relation to the content of the **Bookmark** string and the values of the fields of the corresponding record. As an example, the four characters in the string returned by the **Bookmark** property of the first record of the CUSTOMER.DBF table have ASCII values of 1, 0 (null), 0, and 0. The second record returns ASCII values of 2, 0, 0, and 0. The last record in the table returns 90, 0, 0, 0. There are 90 records in the CUSTOMER.DBF table. This might lead you to conclude that you could compute an equivalent to a RECNO() value by manipulating the bytes returned by the Bookmark property. The actual value returned by the Bookmark property is undocumented and therefore may change in future versions of Access. For this reason, it is inadvisable to use manipulated values of the Bookmark property in commercial Access applications.

The preceding Object Basic code, less the Bookmarkable test, is equivalent to the following xBase code example:

```
PRIVATE position
position = RECNO()
GO BOTTOM
...
GOTO position
```

Using the Index Property

The **Index** property determines the active index for a **Recordset** object of the **Table** type. The Access database engine or the client-server RDBMS maintains index integrity when you alter the values of indexed fields. Valid expressions to set the value of the **Index** property are as follows:

- ■ *tblName*.**Index** = "PrimaryKey" for tables that have an index on the primary key value. Paradox table files have an associated primary key index file, Table.PX, that is the primary key index. Most Access, Btrieve, and client-server tables are indexed on the primary key. You cannot specify a PrimaryKey index for dBASE III, dBASE IV, FoxPro 2.0, or FoxPro 2.5 files.

- ■ *tblName*.**Index** = "FieldName" of an indexed field for Access, Btrieve, and client-server tables. (You do not need an INDEX.DDF file to use Btrieve indexes. Index information is included in the FIELD.DDF data dictionary file.) This expression is equivalent to the TAG tagname clause of an xBase SET INDEX TO command, if the name of the TAG is the same as the field.

- ■ *tblName*.**Index** = "IndexName" where *IndexName* is the name assigned to an Access composite index. Composite indexes are indexes created on more than one field.

- ■ *tblName*.**Index** = "IndexName" where *IndexName* is the name of a dBASE III (.NDX), dBASE IV (.MDX), or FoxPro (.IDX or .CDX) index file, less the file extension, that must be included in the *Table*.INF file that is located in the database directory. This example is equivalent to the SET INDEX TO *indexname* command of xBase.

You can substitute a variable of the **String** type or **Variant** subtype 8 for the literal values shown in the preceding expressions. The section called "Transaction Processing and Record Locking Methods," later in this chapter, includes code that employs a field value to specify the name of an index.

TIP

You can create a *Table*.INF file for a dBASE III, dBASE IV, FoxPro 2.0, or FoxPro 2.5 database by attaching each of the .DBF table files to an Access database. Choose the associated index files from the file list in the Attach Index File dialog box. When you delete the attached files in the Database window, the *Table*.INF file you create for each table with an associated index remains in the database directory.

WARNING

Access uses the PrimaryKey index, if a primary key index exists, when you open a table from the Database window, apply the OpenTable macro action, or execute the **DoCmd** OpenTable method in your Access Basic code. If you open a table with the tbl*Name*.**OpenTable**() method, the records appear in the order in which the records were entered, unless you set the value of the **Index** property to a valid index name. The differences between opening a **Recordset** with the rs*Name*.**OpenRecordset**() method and the application-specific **DoCmd** OpenTable method are discussed in the section called "Opening Access Application Objects," later in this chapter.

TIP

Make sure that you associate all index files of xBase tables that you attach to Access or open as a database object for read-write operations with an entry in the *Table*.INF file. If you modify the values of an indexed field of a record and the index file is not associated, you receive an "Index does not match database" or similar error message from your xBase application. Also verify that Access correctly updates xBase indexes based on complex expressions such as VAL(SUBSTR(*fieldname*, 3, 6)) with a test file before you place an application that updates the field into production.

NOTE

When you create a **Recordset** object from an indexed table, the sequence of records is in the order of the index. You can alter the record order by

opening a **Recordset** object that uses an Access SQL statement with an
ORDER BY clause that specifies the desired sort order.

Collections Contained in *Recordset, TableDef,* and *QueryDef* Objects

Access 2.0 introduces two new collections, Fields and Indexes, that are contained
in data access objects. The **TableDef** object contains both the Fields and Indexes
collections. The **QueryDef** object contains Fields and Parameters collections.
Recordset objects contain only one collection, Fields. The following sections describe these three collections.

The *Fields* Collections of *Recordset, TableDef,* and *QueryDef* Objects

The Fields collection contains one **Field** object for each field contained in a
Recordset, **TableDef**, or **QueryDef** object. You assign a pointer to a **Field** object with
the following statements:

```
Dim fldName As Field
Set fldName = objName.Fields(strFieldName)
```

where *objName* is an object variable of the **Recordset**, **TableDef**, or **QueryDef** data type.
Table 6.6 lists the properties of the **Field** object.

Table 6.6. Properties of the Field Object

Property	Description
AllowZeroLength	**True** if zero-length strings are allowed in a field of the Text field data type; **False** otherwise.
Attributes	Returns a value indicating the attributes of the field. (See Table 5.6 of Chapter 5.)
CollatingOrder	Specifies the sort order of the **Field** object. (See Table 5.3 of Chapter 5.)
DataUpdatable	**True** if the **Field** object is updatable; **False** otherwise.
DefaultValue	Returns the default value for the field or **Null** if no default value has been specified.

continues

Table 6.6. continued

Property	Description
ForeignName	Specifies the field name of a foreign table that is related to the primary key field of the table.
Name	Returns the name of the field.
OrdinalPosition	Returns the relative position of the field in the object, with 0 as the leftmost field.
Required	**True** if a value is required to be entered in the field; **False** otherwise.
Size	The size of fields of numeric data types or the maximum length of fields of the Text field data type. Size returns 0 for fields of the OLE Object and Memo field data types. (Use the **FieldSize()** method to obtain the size of OLE Object and Memo fields.)
SourceField	The original name of the field of an attached table that serves as the data source for a field of a query.
SourceTable	The original name of the table of an attached table. As an example, the value returned by SourceTable for a table attached from SQL Server is dbo.*TableName*, which is translated to dbo_*TableName* when the table is attached to an Access database.
Type	The field data type of the field. (See Table 5.7 of Chapter 5.)
ValidateOnSet	**True** if validation is tested when the field value is entered; **False** if validation is deferred until the record is updated.
ValidationRule	An expression that tests the value of the field and evaluates to **True** or **False**.
ValidationText	The text that appears in the message box if the ValidationRule expression evaluates **False**.
Value	The value of the data cell specified by the field and the current position of the record pointer. (Value is the default property of the **Field** object.)

The *Indexes* Collection of *Field* Objects of *TableDef* Objects

If a table represented by a **TableDef** object has one or more indexes, **Index** objects for each indexed field are included in the Indexes collection of the **TableDef** object. You assign a pointer to an **Index** object with the following statements:

```
Dim fldName As Field
Dim idxName As Index
Set fldName = objName.Fields(strFieldName)
Set idxName = fldName.Indexes(strIndexName)
```

The properties of the **Index** object are listed in Table 6.7.

Table 6.7. Properties of the **Index** Object

Property	Description
Clustered	Returns **True** if the index for a table attached to an Access database is clustered; **False** otherwise. (Access databases do not support clustered fields.)
Foreign	Returns **True** if the index is for a foreign key; **False** otherwise.
IgnoreNulls	Returns **True** if the search on an index ignores **Null** values in the field.
Name	Returns the name assigned to the index.
Primary	Returns **True** if the index is for the primary key field of the table; **False** otherwise.
Required	**True** if a value is required to be entered in the field (other than fields of the Counter field data type); **False** otherwise.
Unique	Returns **True** if the index requires that the field values be unique for each record of the table; **False** otherwise. (**True** for primary key indexes.)

The Parameters Collection of *QueryDef* Objects

If a query represented by a **QueryDef** object has one or more parameters, **Parameter** objects for each indexed field are included in the Parameters collection of the **QueryDef** object. You assign a pointer to a **Parameter** object with the following statements:

```
Dim qdfName As QueryDef
Dim prmName As Parameter
Set qdfName = objName.QueryDefs(strQueryName)
Set prmName = qdfName.Indexes(strParameterName)
```

The properties of the **Parameter** object are listed in Table 6.8.

Table 6.8. Properties of the Parameter Object

Property	Description
Name	Returns the name of the parameter (the text that appears in the Enter Parameter dialog box).
Type	Returns the field data type of the parameter value as the number corresponding to the **Variant** subtype.
Value	Returns the value supplied to the parameter in the text box of the Enter Parameter dialog box.

Applying Methods to Data Access Objects

Table 6.6 lists the methods that you can apply to instances of **Recordset** objects that you have created with **OpenRecordset()** method. Table 6.9 also lists methods applicable to **Workspace** and **QueryDef** objects.

Table 6.9. Object Basic methods that are applicable to Access Recordset objects.

Method	Syntax and Purpose
AddNew	**AddNew** adds a tentative append record to the recordset (equivalent to APPEND BLANK in xBase).
AppendChunk	
GetChunk	**AppendChunk** and **GetChunk** enable you to handle OLE Object fields whose lengths are greater than 32KB or let you manipulate data in Memo or OLE Object fields in pieces (chunks). See Chapter 25, "Stretching the Limits of Access," for an example of using these two methods.

Method	Syntax and Purpose
BeginTrans **CommitTrans** **Rollback**	Placing a wsp*Workspace*.**BeginTrans** line before a set of updates and a wsp*Workspace*.**CommitTrans** after the updates causes all updates that occur during the execution of the intervening code to be treated as a single transaction. You use wsp*Workspace*.**Rollback** to cancel the transaction in the event of an error.
Clone()	Creates a clone of a **Recordset** object.
Close	**Close** closes the specified object. Applies to all object variables, including **Database** objects.
Delete	**Delete** deletes the current record. Not applicable to **Recordset** objects of the **Snapshot** type or to **QueryDef** objects whose **Updatable** property is **False**. The **Delete** method is identical to the xBase DELETE command.
Edit	**Edit** prepares the current record for updating its values. Not applicable to **Recordset** object of the **Snapshot** type or **QueryDef** objects whose **Updatable** property is **False**. Follow the **Edit** method with the **Update** method to apply the changes to the underlying table(s). The combination of the **Edit** method, an expression to change the value of the field, and the **Update** method is the equivalent of xBase's REPLACE *fieldname* WITH *value* command.
Execute	*qdfName*.**Execute** runs a previously defined action **QueryDef**, *qdfName*. The **Execute** method is available only for **QueryDef** objects that do not return result sets.
FieldSize()	*rsName*!*FieldName*.**FieldSize()** returns the length of an OLE Object or Memo field name specified by the *FieldName* identifier as a subtype 3 (integer) or subtype 4 (long integer) **Variant**. If *FieldName* is not an OLE Object or Memo field, you receive a "Can't perform operation; it is illegal" message. Microsoft classifies **FieldSize()** as a method, although **FieldSize()** behaves as a read-only property.

continues

Table 6.9. continued

Method	Syntax and Purpose
FillCache*	Fills all or part of a local cache (set by the CacheSize property) for tables attached by the ODBC API only.
FindFirst FindLast FindNext FindPrevious	*rsName*.**FindRecord** *strSQLWhere* sets the record pointer of **Recordset** objects, except of the **Table** type, to the first, last, next, or previous record meeting the criteria of a valid SQL Where clause, *strSQLWhere*. Omit the WHERE keyword and the trailing semicolon from the value of *strSQLWhere*. The **NoMatch** property is set **False** if the **FindRecord** method is successful. The **FindFirst** method is similar to xBase's LOCATE FOR condition command and **FindNext** resembles CONTINUE following a LOCATE FOR statement in xBase.
MoveFirst MoveLast MoveNext MovePrevious	Positions the record pointer at the first, last, next, or previous record in a recordset. If you apply the **MovePrevious** method when the **BOF** property is **True** or the **MoveNext** method when the **EOF** property is **True**, a runtime error occurs. The four MoveRecord methods are equivalent to xBase's GO TOP, GO BOTTOM, SKIP, and SKIP-1 commands, respectively.
Requery	Re-executes the query underlying a **QueryDef** object or a Recordset object whose *strSource* argument is an SQL statement.
Seek	*rsName*.**Seek** *strOperator*, *typValue1*[, *typValue2*[, *typValue3*]] finds the first occurrence of *typValue* that meets the criteria of *strOperator* and *typValue1* in an indexed field of a **Recordset** object of the Table type only. If *strOperator* is "=", the **Seek** method is the equivalent of the SEEK *value* command of xBase. See further details in the text.
Update	*rsName*.**Update** makes an update to a record permanent. Use the **Update** method after the **AddNew** or **Edit** methods, but not after the **Delete** method. A runtime error occurs if another user has the table or the same page locked when you attempt to use the **Update** method.

Transaction Processing and Record Locking Methods

In database terminology, a transaction is a collection of updates to tables that must be completed as a unit. If all the updates cannot be completed successfully, those updates to tables that were made prior to the problem that prevented completion of the transaction must be undone. A common example used to demonstrate transaction processing is an electronic funds transfer (EFT) from your bank account to the account of a merchant from whom you make a purchase. If your account has insufficient funds to cover the transaction, your bank is unlikely to want to credit the merchant's account with the amount of the purchase. Therefore, the debit to your account must succeed for the credit to the merchant's account to be executed. This example is a transaction between two databases connected by a wide-area network (WAN). The same rule applies to tables within the same database and to tables in databases shared on a local-area network (LAN).

There are two reasons for using transaction processing with Access databases:

■ Preserving the validity of data of the two (or more) tables that take part in a transaction, as illustrated by the preceding example. Transaction processing is necessary in a multiuser environment, because there is the chance that a user may have temporarily locked the table or, more commonly, locked the page of the table during an update. Object Basic enables you to perform transaction processing with attached tables and tables in multiple databases, but you should use transaction processing only if the value of the **Transactions** property of each of the participating tables is **True**.

■ Speeding the processing of bulk updates to a table. Using the **AddNew** or **Edit** methods together followed by the **Update** method ordinarily writes the new or updated record to the database file that contains the table(s) affected. When you use transaction processing, Access attempts to lock each of the pages of the table that contain the records being updated. If all the locks succeed, all updates are made permanent. If, for example, another user has one of the pages locked for editing, the transaction fails and any changes actually made to the table are undone (rolled back).

Access employs transaction processing for all its action queries. When you run a delete query, for example, Access counts the number of records affected and attempts to place a temporary lock on each page of the participating tables. If all the locks succeed, a message box appears indicating the number of records to be deleted. When you click the OK button, Access commits the transaction, making the changes to the table permanent. Access also uses a form of transaction processing to enforce referential integrity. When you attempt to delete a record in a primary or base table, Access applies the equivalent of the **Seek** or **Find** method to the foreign key field of the related table to determine whether the related table contains dependent records. If related records are found, the transaction is rolled back.

> **TIP**
>
> You can use transaction processing with Access tables in conjunction with tables attached from foreign databases, regardless of whether the attached tables support transaction processing. If the attached tables do not support transaction processing (tbl*Name*.**Transactions = False**), you cannot undo changes to the attached tables when you roll back changes to the Access tables. Client-server RDBMSs support transactions; use Access 2.0's new SQL Pass-through feature, described in Chapter 20, "Front-Ending Client-Server Databases" and Chapter 25, "Stretching the Limits of Access," to transmit SQL statements directly to the client-server RDBMS.

You can implement transaction processing only with Access Basic code. To group more than one update to a table in a single transaction, you precede the code that performs the update with the **BeginTrans** method of the **Workspace** object and an **On Error GoTo** *LabelName* statement. *LabelName* is the name of a special error-handling routine for transactions that includes the **Rollback** method. Applying the **Commit** method follows the updating code block. The following code fragment illustrates the use of these three reserved words for transaction processing—in this case, deleting all the records of a table:

```
wspCurrent.BeginTrans
    On Error GoTo UndoTrans          'Set transaction error handler
    tblCurrent.MoveFirst             'Go to the first record
    Do While Not tblCurrent.EOF
        tblCurrent.Delete            'Delete the record
        tblCurrent.MoveNext
        DoEvents                     'Give other applications a chance
    Loop
wspCurrent.CommitTrans               'Make the deletions permanent,
_if no error
On Error GoTo Somewhere              'Reset the error handler
    ...
Exit Function

UndoTrans:
    On Error GoTo UndoError
    wspCurrent.Rollback              'Undo the transaction on an error
    'Message box advising that transaction has been rolled back
    Exit Function
UndoError:
    'Message box indicating a problem in the rollback operation.
    Exit Function
```

It is traditional to indent updating code between statements containing **BeginTrans** and **CommitTrans** methods to identify the code constituting a transaction. A simple action **QueryDef** object with its SQL property set to DELETE * FROM *TableName*; provides the same result as the 20 lines of code in the preceding example. The execution speed of the action query is about the same as the execution speed of the preceding code fragment for tables with a few hundred records. The time required to create and save the persistent **QueryDef** object is much greater than the time needed to delete the records with the SQL DELETE statement.

The **BeginTrans**, **CommitTrans**, and **Rollback** methods are similar to dBASE IV's BEGIN TRANSACTION, END TRANSACTION, and ROLLBACK commands, and similar transaction error trapping is employed in xBase code. You use the xBase COMPLETED() function to determine whether a transaction succeeded and the ROLLBACK() function to indicate whether the ROLLBACK command was successful. There is no direct equivalent to the ROLLBACK() function in Access Basic. Both the preceding code fragment and the **QueryDef** perform the same function as xBase's ZAP command, but both take longer than ZAP to delete all records.

The wTestIndex() function shown in Listing 6.1 that follows opens a dBASE III file (strSrcTable) with an associated index (strIndex) located in a database directory (strSrcDir), and transfers the data to an Access table (strDstTable) having the same structure as the dBASE III file. All records in the destination table are deleted with a temporary action **QueryDef** object before adding new records. Transaction processing is used with the **AddNew** and **Update** methods to append records to the table. The wTestIndex() function is included in the Object Variables module of the AB_EXAMP.MDB example database of the accompanying diskette. You can test the wTestIndex() function with the dBASE III files and indexes that also are included on the accompanying diskette and are installed your C:\ACCESS\ADG20 directory. Empty tblCustomer and tblOrders tables are included in AB_EXAMP.MDB. To use CUSTOMER.DBF with the CUST_ZIP.NDX ZIP Code index, execute ? wTestIndex ("c:\access\adg20", "customer", "cust_zip", "tblCustomer") in the Immediate window. You can try a larger file, ORDERS.DBF, with about 1,000 records indexed by customer ID by executing ? wTestIndex ("c:\access\adg20", "orders", "ordr_cid", "tblOrders").

NOTE

Access 2.0 supports the statement version of **BeginTrans**, **CommitTrans**, and **Rollback** for backward compatibility with Access 1.x applications. The statement version of these reserved words does not require a wsp*Workspace* object prefix. Access 2.0 also supports the Access 1.x **ListFields**() and

`ListIndexes()` methods that create a **Snapshot** object that describe the fields and indexes of a table. (You cannot create a **Recordset** object of the Snapshot type with the **List...()** methods.) Listing 6.1 demonstrates the backward compatibility of Access 2.0 with Access 1.x and shows how the `ListFields()` and `ListIndexes()` methods can be used. In keeping with the obsolescent status of these methods, the content of CUSTOMER.DBF and ORDERS.DBF were obtained from the Access 1.1 version of NWIND.MDB. Chapter 27, "Documenting your Access Applications," includes an example of using the properties and collections of **TableDef** and **QueryDef** objects, rather than the Access 1.x **List...()** methods.

Listing 6.1. A function to create an Access table in indexed order from a dBASE table.

```
Function wTestIndex (strSrcDir As String,
                     strSrcTable As String,
                     strIndex As String,
                     strDstTable As String) As Integer
    'Purpose:   Open a dBASE III database with an index
    'Arguments: strSrcDir = path to location of dBASE III database
    '           strSrcTable = name of source table in database
    '           strIndex = name of dBASE III index file (less the
                ➥extension)
    '           strDstTable = name of destination table in current
                ➥database
    'Called by: ? wTestIndex in the Immediate window
    'Returns    True if successful, False on failure

    'Set initial error handler
    On Error GoTo Bombed

    'Utility variables
    Dim varRetVal As Variant
    Dim wCtr As Integer

    'Declare local object variables and assign destination table

    Dim dbCurrent As Database
    Dim tblCurrent As Table
    Dim ssCurrent As Snapshot
    Dim qdfCurrent As QueryDef
    Dim ds1 As Dynaset

    Set dbCurrent =
    Set tblCurrent = dbCurrent.OpenTable(strDstTable)
    Set ssCurrent = tblCurrent.ListFields()

    'Declare foreign object variables and assign source table and
    ➥index
```

```
Dim dbForeign As Database
Dim tblForeign As Table
Dim ssForeign As Snapshot

Set dbForeign = OpenDatabase(strSrcDir, False, False, "dBASE _III;")
Set tblForeign = dbForeign.OpenTable(strSrcTable)
Set ssForeign = tblForeign.ListFields()

'Set the index to be used
tblForeign.Index = strIndex

'Trap the error that occurs if the destination table has no _records
On Error Resume Next
tblCurrent.MoveFirst
On Error GoTo Bombed

'Set the status bar to display what's happening
varRetVal = SysCmd(1, "Deleting " & strDstTable, 100)

'Execute a delete all records query
Set qdfCurrent = dbCurrent.CreateQueryDef("qdfTemp", "DELETE *
➥FROM " & strDstTable & ";")
qdfCurrent.Execute
qdfCurrent.Close
dbCurrent.DeleteQueryDef ("qdfTemp")

'Set up the status bar to display deletion progress
tblForeign.MoveLast                       'Assure an accurate
➥record count
If tblForeign.RecordCount < 32000 Then
    varRetVal = SysCmd(1, "Recreating " & strDstTable,
    ➥tblForeign.RecordCount)
    wCtr = 1
Else
    varRetVal = SysCmd(1, "Recreating " & strDstTable, 100)
End If

'Recreate the records in the current database's table
BeginTrans
    On Error GoTo UndoTrans               'Set the error handling
                                          ➥routine
    tblForeign.MoveFirst
    Do While Not tblForeign.EOF
        'Debug.Print tblForeign.zip_code 'For debugging
        ➥purposes
        If wCtr > 0 Then
            varRetVal = SysCmd(2, wCtr)   'Update the progress bar
            wCtr = wCtr + 1
        End If
        tblCurrent.AddNew                 'Append a blank record
        ssCurrent.MoveFirst               'Reset the field list
        ➥record pointers
```

continues

Listing 6.1. continued

```
                    ssForeign.MoveFirst
                    Do While Not (ssCurrent.EOF Or ssForeign.EOF)
                        'Update the value of the field of the appended _table
                        ➥with the
                        'value of the same field of the foreign table
                        'Note: This method of specifying a field name is
                        ➥undocumented in Access
                        tblCurrent(ssCurrent!Name) = _tblForeign(ssForeign!Name)
                        ssCurrent.MoveNext
                        ssForeign.MoveNext
                    Loop
                    tblCurrent.Update                       'Tentatively update the
                                                            ➥table

                    tblForeign.MoveNext
                    'DoEvents                               'For safety during
                    ➥debugging
                Loop
            CommitTrans                                     'Commit the updates

            On Error GoTo Bombed                            'ReSet the error handler
            varRetVal = SysCmd(1, "Opening " & strDstTable, 100)

            DoCmd OpenTable strDstTable                     'Display the resulting
            ➥table

            'Close everything
            tblCurrent.Close
            dbCurrent.Close
            tblForeign.Close
            dbForeign.Close
            VarRetVal=SysCmd(5)
            Exit Function

    UndoTrans:
        'Transaction did not complete
        On Error GoTo UndoError
        Rollback
        MsgBox Error$, 32, "Transaction Rolled Back"
        Exit Function

    UndoError:
        'Rollback failed
        MsgBox Error$, 32, "Rollback Error"
        Exit Function

    Bombed:
        'Some other error occurred
        MsgBox Error$, 16, "Error in Source/Destination"
        Exit Function
    End Function
```

The wTestIndex() function uses many of the methods listed in Table 6.6 earlier in the chapter. You use the **Execute** method to run action **QueryDef** objects that do not return records. The **SysCmd()** function lets you create a custom status bar with Access Basic code. Further examples of using the **SysCmd()** function of Access are given in Chapter 24, "Using Access Wizard Functions." It's simpler, however, to import the foreign table to your Access database and then create the required indexes on the table manually.

> **NOTE**
>
> You can demonstrate the substantial difference in performance achieved by using transaction processing by "commenting out" the **BeginTrans**, **EndTrans**, and **Rollback** instructions of the wTestIndex() function by preceding the three reserved words with an apostrophe. Using transaction processing speeds up the bulk updating process by at least a factor of 20, depending on the amount of memory and speed of your computer and the performance of your fixed disk drive.

Finding a Record in a Recordset

The **FindRecord** methods emulate the operation of the Find dialog box that you open by choosing Find from the Edit menu in table or query run mode. The **FindRecord** methods apply to **Dynaset** and **Snapshot** objects, including **Dynaset** objects created by a **QueryDef**. You can employ any of Access's comparison operators as literals in the SQL WHERE clause. Following are examples of the syntax of three of the most commonly used **FindRecord** methods:

```
Recordset.FindFirst "FieldName = Value"
Recordset.FindNext strFieldName & " Between " & varDateBeg & " And " &
➡varDateEnd
Recordset.FindPrior strFieldName & " Like " & Chr$(34) & strFind &
➡Chr$(34)
```

> **NOTE**
>
> You need to enclose string expressions used with the **Like** and **Between** operators between literal double quotation marks created with the **Chr$(34)** function. Alternately, you can "nest" the double quotation marks within two double quotation marks, as in "Like" & """ & StrFind & """. If you use **Between** with date values, each date value must be enclosed within # signs, as shown in Listing 6.3 that follows.

Listing 6.3 uses the **FindFirst** and **FindNext** methods to print the Customer ID code for orders received within a range of dates in the Immediate window. The code tests whether the **FindFirst** operation was successful by evaluating the **NoMatch** property; if a matching record is found, a loop with the **FindNext** prints all of the matching records. To return to the first matching record in the table, you save the **Bookmark** value before you apply the **FindNext** method, then set the **Bookmark** value to the saved value after the loop executes. To use this example, attach the Orders table from NWIND.MDB to AB_EXAMP.MDB, then execute ? wFindDates( ) in the Immediate window.

Listing 6.3. An Access Basic function that uses the FindFirst and FindNext methods.

```
Function wFindDates () As Integer
    'Purpose:    Demonstrate the use of the FindFirst and FindNext
    ➥methods
    '            with date Variants (subtype 7)
    'Returns:    True if successful, False on failure

    'Declare local variables
    Dim varBookmark As Variant
    Dim varDateBeg As Variant
    Dim varDateEnd As Variant
    Dim strFind As String

    'Set date values
    varDateBeg = #1/1/94#
    varDateEnd = #1/31/94#

    'Create the find string
    strFind = "[Order Date] Between #" & varDateBeg & "# And #" &
    ➥varDateEnd & "#"

    'Declare and set object variables
    Dim dbCurrent As Database
    Dim rsOrders As Recordset
    Set dbCurrent = DBEngine(0)(0)
    Set rsOrders = dbCurrent.OpenRecordset("SELECT * FROM ORDERS")

    'Find first order
    rsOrders.FindFirst strFind
    If rsOrders.NoMatch Then
        MsgBox "No entries found for '" & strFind & ".", 32,
        ➥"Find Record"
    Else
        'Set the bookmark to the first record found
        varBookmark = rsOrders.Bookmark

        'Print the first and succeeding values to the Immediate window
        Debug.Print rsOrders("Customer ID") & " " &
        ➥rsOrders("Order Date")
```

```
    Do While Not rsOrders.NoMatch
        rsOrders.FindNext strFind
        Debug.Print rsOrders("Customer ID") & " " &
        ➥rsOrders("Order Date")
        DoEvents
    Loop
    rsOrders.Bookmark = varBookmark

    'Prove that the bookmark worked
    Debug.Print rsOrders("Customer ID") & " " &
    ➥rsOrders("Order Date")
    wFindDates = True
End If
End
```

Figure 6.3 shows the values printed in the Immediate window when you execute the **wFindDates()** function. The **Debug.Print** method is useful to verify proper operation of your code when the instructions act on nonpersistent database objects. To test more sophisticated applications, you may need to create a persistent **Table** object whose contents you can examine carefully in Datasheet view.

FIGURE 6.3.

The result of executing the wFindDates() function from the Immediate window.

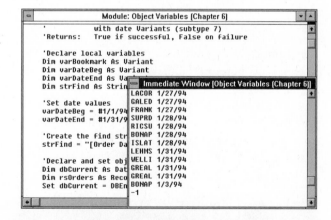

Using the *Seek* Method with *Recordset* Objects of the *Table Type*

The **Seek** method of Access is more flexible than the SEEK command of xBase. The most common syntax of the **Seek** method for a **Recordset** of the Table type whose active index is based on a single field (PrimaryKey or *FieldName* for Access tables) is as follows:

tbl*Name*.**Seek** "=", *typValue*

You can specify any one of the other arithmetic operators, <, <=, >=, or >, as a literal value in place of the "=" operator. If you don't use a **Variant** *typValue*, the value you are seeking, the data type of the *typValue* argument must correspond to the field data type. As with the **FindRecord** methods, the parameter of the **Option** Compare statement in the declarations section of the module that contains the **Seek** statement must be Text if you don't want the **Seek** operation to be case-sensitive.

When you use an index created on more than one field (composite *Primary Key* or Index1...Index5 for Access tables), you need to supply a value for each of the fields applicable to your search. The expression tbl*Name*.**Seek** "=", *typValue1*, *typValue2* finds the first occurrence of a record with the two first indexed field values equal to *typValue1* and *typValue2*.

Seek is much faster than any of the **FindRecord** methods with tables that contain a large number of records, although version 2.0 of the Jet database engine uses indexes for the **FindRecord** methods when possible. **Seek**, however, finds only the first occurrence of the match; no provision is made to find successive matches. If you need to process a group of records that have the same field value, create a **Recordset** object of the Dynaset type over the **Table** object and use one or more of the **FindRecord** methods. Alternately, you can **Seek** the first instance of the value, then compare the values in the field of successive records until no further records match.

> **NOTE**
>
> The **Seek** method is valid only for use with **Recordset** objects of the Table type with the Index property set to a valid index for the table. A runtime error occurs if you attempt to use the **Seek** method on any other type of **Recordset** or if the **Index** property is **Null**.

Addressing Database Objects to Get and Set Values

When you create a database object variable with the **Set** instruction, you specify the object's container and its identity within the container. To get or set the value of an object, when setting the object's value is permissible, you use the same technique. The preferred syntax for obtaining or updating the value of a field of a table, the only object value you can set, is as follows:

```
varValue = tblName(strFieldName)
tblName("FieldName") = varValue
```

The advantage of using the preceding syntax is that you can use either a variable or a literal to specify the field name. You need not (and cannot) use square brackets to specify field names that include spaces or illegal punctuation in the preceding syntax.

The alternate literal syntax of the following examples is more commonly seen in Access Basic examples, because this syntax is used almost exclusively in the User's Guide and Language Reference that accompany retail Access:

```
varValue = dsName!LiteralName
varValue = dsName![Literal Name]
```

Both of the preceding expressions return the same **Dynaset** field value to varValue. In this case, you must supply the literal value of the field name (without the quotation marks) after the bang (!) qualifying operator. Access 2.0 now supports the somewhat redundant Visual Basic syntax dsName!LiteralName.Value property

NOTE

The use of the period separator (.) in place of the bang separator (!) to specify field names of **Recordset** objects was accepted by Access 1.x if the field name was not identical to a property name. (In this case, you receive the property value, rather than the field value you expected.) Access 2.0 is not forgiving of the use of the period separator. Use the bang separator to refer to field names if you use the alternate explicit syntax.

7

Using Access Objects, Methods, and Events

Access application objects consist of tables, forms, queries, reports, and control objects on forms and reports. Macro and module objects are classified as support objects in this book, because macros and modules consist of collections, or more properly enumerations, of methods that apply to objects. This chapter introduces the terms *Access object* and *Access method* to distinguish application-specific objects and methods from the Object Basic database objects and methods discussed in the preceding chapter. You use Access methods, which Microsoft calls "actions," to respond to events that are triggered by Access objects.

Access 2.0 now rivals Visual Basic 3.0's repertoire of properties, methods, and events. In the case of forms used for updating tables, Access 2.0's bound text boxes provide much finer granularity of data-related events than those of Visual Basic 3.0. Following is a list of the changes to Access objects in version 2.0 that are most important to Access developers:

- You can now change the value of the properties of forms and reports, as well as control objects on forms and reports in run mode. This brings Access 2.0 into closer conformance with Visual Basic 3.0's programming model.

- A variety of new properties have been added to Access objects.

- Many new events have been added to forms, reports, and control objects. The majority of these events relate to mouse and keyboard operations. Most of the added events will be quite familiar to Visual Basic programmers.

- Seven new methods have been added that replace or supplement actions. As an example, you now can replace **DoCmd** GoToControl str*ControlName* statements with *objName*.**SetFocus**.

- Five new actions have been added. SendObject, ShowToolbar, and OutputTo implement the new mail-enabling, toolbar, and output-to-file features of Access 2.0. DeleteObject makes it easier to delete temporary objects, and OpenModule lets you search all modules for a specified procedure, then display the procedure in the code editing window.

This chapter focuses on Access objects, methods, and events in your Access Basic code. Much of the information presented here also is applicable to Access macros. Unless you can write "bulletproof" macros, however, using Access Basic code with thorough error-trapping is the safest approach for applications that you create for others to use.

Trading Access Basic Code for Macros

An Access macro consists of one or more "actions" executed by attaching the name of the macro to an event property of a form, report, or control object. When the event occurs, Access executes the macro. The present objective of Access macros is to allow users to create applications without the need to write programming code. Whether Microsoft achieved the "codeless database" objective depends upon how one defines programming. If multiaction macros with conditional execution and looping capability are not considered programs, then Microsoft achieved its objective (at least for marketing purposes). Otherwise, writing macros simply is programming in a command language whose keywords are limited to the 40-some predefined Access actions. It is, however, remarkable that this limited number of actions can be combined to create very sophisticated Access applications that require little or no Access Basic Code.

If you are developing applications for use with runtime Access, you ordinarily use Access macros only for the following purposes:

- Opening the main form of your application with the AutoExec macro.
- Assigning short-cut keys with the AutoKeys macro.
- Creating custom menus for your application with the Menu Builder.
- Creating custom toolbars for your forms.

You use Access Basic functions in conventional modules or procedures in form or report modules to respond to all events. The reason for using Access Basic code instead of macros to respond to events is that you can trap runtime errors in Access Basic code, but you cannot trap errors in macro execution. An untrapped error in the execution of a macro or an Access Basic function results in an abrupt exit from your application when run with MSARN200.EXE. Thus, this chapter concentrates on describing how you use macro actions in Access Basic code to open Access application objects and to respond to events. Chapter 8, "Optimizing Transaction-Processing Forms," gives an example of an Access transaction-processing application, originally implemented almost entirely with macros, and explains how to convert the macros in such an application to Access Basic code.

This book uses the term "Access method" to refer to actions used in Access Basic code. In object-oriented programming terminology, objects have properties and methods, not "actions." The "action" terminology is retained, however, when discussing Access macros.

Opening and Addressing Access Objects

An Access object is any element of your application that can appear in a window of your application in run mode. Thus Access objects consist of tables, queries, forms and reports. You cannot display **Recordset** objects that you create with Object Basic in a window of your application. You use a special set of Access methods to open Access objects. Once the object is open, you refer to (address) the object with a special syntax reserved for objects. The sections that follow describe how to open and address Access objects with Access Basic code.

Opening Access Objects

You open an Access object with one of the five application-specific **DoCmd** *OpenObject* methods. The significance of the **DoCmd** keyword is discussed in the section, "Applying Access Methods to Access Objects," later in this chapter. Access objects include application-specific views of **Recordset** objects that underlie bound forms and reports. Unlike Visual Basic, you cannot manipulate the record pointer of these application-specific **Recordset** objects by applying the **Find...** or **Move...** methods in Access Basic code. The Access Basic syntax for opening application objects using the **DoCmd** *OpenObject* methods is as follows:

```
DoCmd OpenTable strTableName[, wView[, wDataMode]]
DoCmd OpenQuery strQueryName[, wView[, wDataMode]]
DoCmd OpenForm strFormName[, wView[, strFilterName[, strSQLWhere[,
➥wDataMode[, wWindowMode]]]]]
DoCmd OpenReport strReportName[, wView[, strFilterName[, _strSQLWhere]]]
DoCmd OpenModule {strModuleName, strProcedureName¦strModuleName¦,
➥strProcedureName}
```

NOTE

Square brackets in the preceding syntax indicate arguments that are optional. If you omit the value of an optional argument, but specify the value of a succeeding argument, the intervening commas must appear, as in **DoCmd** OpenForm "Employees", , , , A_ICON to open the Employees form in minimized window mode. The use of brackets in the preceding examples differs from that in the Language Reference. Enclosing an individual argument within square brackets, as in [, Argument], infers that the comma and the argument value are optional. In the case of OpenModule, you must supply one or both of the arguments. If the strModuleName argument is empty, Access searches all loaded modules for strProcedureName. If you omit strProcedureName, Access opens the strModuleName module and displays the Declarations section.

Table 7.1 lists the arguments for the preceding five **DoCmd** *OpenObject* methods. The domain column describes or lists values that are valid for the argument. Default values for the intrinsic global action constants (prefix A_) are shown in bold type. The

A_FORMDS value is applicable only to forms. Opening a report in A_NORMAL view prints the report. Opening an action query with the **DoCmd** OpenQuery method executes the action query.

Table 7.1. The arguments of the DoCmd OpenObject application-specific methods.

Argument	*Value*	*Domain*
str*ObjectName*	The name of the object expressed as a string literal or variable	Any object of the specified class in the opened database
w*View*	An integer that represents how the object is displayed when opened	**A_NORMAL** A_DESIGN A_PREVIEW A_FORMDS
str*FilterName*	The name of a query used to create a filter for the form	Saved queries that include all the fields that are bound to controls
str*SQLWhere*	A string expression that constitutes a valid SQL WHERE clause	Must include a valid operator, but does not include WHERE or a trailing semicolon
w*DataMode*	An integer that represents the DefaultEditing property of a form	**A_EDIT** A_ADD A_READONLY
w*WindowMode*	An integer that represents the mode in which the object opens	**A_NORMAL** A_HIDDEN A_ICON A_DIALOG
str*ModuleName*	The name of a currently-loaded module	
str*ProcedureName*	The name of a procedure in a currently-loaded module	

NOTE

The syntax for the use of actions in Access macros is identical to the syntax for application-specific methods in Access Basic, with the exception of the precedent **DoCmd** statement. When you create a macro, Access stores the values of arguments that you select from combo boxes as either string literals or integers that represent the index of the selection in the list box; the top selection of the combo box is 0. You can substitute the literal value of the index for the corresponding A_ constant in most cases.

Opening an Access object using an Access method opens an MDI child window with the window mode that you specify by the value of the *wWindowMode* property. When Access opens a form or report, Windows supplies a window handle (reference) to the object; you can obtain the value of the window's handle with the **hWnd** property. You use the **hWnd** property, an unsigned integer (word) in Windows treated as an **Integer** in Access Basic, only in conjunction with Windows API functions. Chapter 22, "Using the Windows API with Access Basic," gives examples of the use of the **hWnd** property. Access makes use of the **hWnd** property for processing Windows messages, the subject of the last major section of this chapter.

NOTE

The capability to open Access objects specified by the value of a variable is related to xBase's macro feature that lets you substitute a variable name for an unquoted literal in a command. The xBase command, SET FORMAT TO &*formname*, is equivalent to Access Basic's **DoCmd** OpenForm str*FormName* method.

When you open a table or query, or a form or report that is bound to a table or query, Access creates an instance of the database objects that underlie the Access object. As mentioned earlier in this chapter, Access does not allow you to directly address the underlying database objects in your code and apply actions such as **MoveNext** or **FindFirst**. These and other Object Basic actions are applicable only to instances of database objects that you open in your Access Basic code. The instance of a **Table** object that you open with the **OpenRecordset**(str*TableName*, DB_OPEN_TABLE) method of Access 2.0 (or the **OpenTable**() method of Access 1.x) is not the same instance as an instance of the table that you open with the Access **DoCmd** OpenTable method. Unlike database objects, you can open only one instance of an Access object.

During the opening process, Access adds a new element to the collection for the object type. If the object contains control objects, Access adds a collection of the controls that appear on the object. (Access removes the elements and reorders the collection when you close an object.) The data necessary to fill these collections is stored in the system tables (with names prefixed by "MSys") of your database. Thus, when you open a form, Access reads the records in the system tables for the form and the controls on the form, and then places the field values of the records in the collection. This is one of the reasons that hiding and showing forms is faster than closing and re-opening forms.

NOTE

Although you can use the **DoCmd** SelectObject method (with the InDatabaseWindow argument set to **True**) to set the focus to the name of a form that is not open, the **DoCmd** SelectObject method does not open the form. Thus you cannot address (nor apply methods, such as **SetFocus**, or actions, such as GoToControl, to) an unopened object selected in the Database window.

When you open a table using the application-specific **DoCmd** OpenTable method, records are displayed in the sequence of the primary key, if a primary key exists. Otherwise, the records appear in the sequence in which they were added to the table (called entry order). Paradox tables have intrinsic primary key fields; xBase and Btrieve tables do not. You specify the primary key field(s) of an xBase or Btrieve table, if an index on the field(s) exists, in Access 2.0's new Select Unique Record Identifier dialog box that appears after you specify the indexes for an attached table. The only method of displaying records in the order of an index that is not created on the primary key field is to create a query from the table that is sorted on the same field or combination of fields that constitute the table's index.

TIP

Many developers favor the use of queries, rather than tables, as the RecordSource for all bound Access objects. The advantage of using queries for the RecordSource is that you can change the table names, field names, and the structure of the tables that underlie the query, then modify the query to reflect the changes. Using this approach eliminates the problem of having to change many references to a changed object name in forms, reports, controls, and Access Basic code.

Addressing Access Objects

Once you have opened an object, you can create a reference to the instance of it in your Access Basic code and return the values of the properties of the object to a variable or to a property of another Access object. You can set the values of properties of Access objects that are not specified as "read-only in run mode" in the Access Language Reference. You can apply those Access methods that are applicable to the object. You create references to (address) instances of Access forms and reports by using values stored in the collections, Forms(), Form(), Reports(), and Report(), whose names have been disclosed in the documentation. The Form() and Report() collections are arrays of control objects, similar to the control arrays used in Visual Basic programming, that refer to the specified form or report.

Figure 7.1 illustrates the collections applicable to forms of the Northwind Traders sample database. Only one of the properties of the Forms() and Form() collections and two properties of the Section() collection are shown in Figure 7.1. Other members of the collections and property values of the members are included in additional rows and columns of the tables that are represented by dotted lines.

Access offers the following four methods of referring to Access form and report objects, and to refer to control objects on forms and reports:

■ By the string value of the proper name of the object, also included in the collection

■ By the integer value of the index to the representation of (pointer to) an object in a collection

■ By explicit reference using the proper name of the object, enclosing the name of the object within square brackets if the name contains spaces or illegal punctuation

■ By using one of the three intrinsic screen objects of Access, **Screen.ActiveForm**, **Screen.ActiveReport**, and **Screen.ActiveControl**, to specify the active window and the control with the focus

FIGURE 7.1.

Collections for forms represented as a set of related tables.

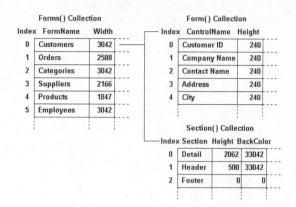

There is only one method by which you can obtain the value of a field of a table or column of a query for the current record of a bound form or report with this syntax: address a control object that is bound to the table field or query column. The following sections describe each of four ways to address Access form, report, and control objects.

The Preferred Access Object Reference Syntax

The preferred method to refer to Access objects in Access Basic code is by supplying the name of the object as a literal string or a variable of the **String**, or the **Variant** subtype 8 data type as the index to the collection array. When Access detects a string index value instead of the expected integer, Access searches the specified collection for a case-insensitive match. If a match is not found, you receive a message that reads "Invalid Reference to Form 'FormName'." Examples of the preferred syntax to get and set values and properties of forms and control objects on forms follow:

varPropVal = Forms("*FormName*").*PropertyName* returns the value of a property of the entire form. You can set the Visible property of a form to False to hide the form, and then display the form by setting the Visible property to True.

varPropVal = Forms("*FormName*").Section(*wSect*).*PropertyName* returns the value of a property of a section of a form that you specify with the index of the section (*wSect*). The correspondence of the index value and the sections of forms and reports is shown in Table 7.2 that follows. Properties of sections of forms are read-only at runtime.

varCtrlVal = Forms(str*FormName*).Form("*ControlName*") returns the value of a control on a form. Use of the *varCtrlVal* = Forms(str*FormName*).Form("*ControlName*").Value syntax is optional in Access 2.0.

`Forms(str`*`FormName`*`).Form("`*`ControlName`*`") = var`*`CtrlVal`* sets the value of a control on a form. If the control is bound to a field of a table or column of a query, the value of the field or column of the current record is updated to the value of var*CtrlVal* when the control loses the focus. Here, too, adding the `Value` property is optional.

var*CtrlPropVal* =
`Forms("`*`FormName`*`").Form(str`*`ControlName`*`).`*`PropertyName`* returns the value of a property of a control object on a form. Access 2.0 lets you read and set the values of most properties of controls on forms and reports. You also apply methods with this syntax.

var*SubformVal* =
`Forms(str`*`FormName`*`).Form(str`*`SubformName`*`).Form("`*`FieldName`*`")` returns the value of the *FieldName* field of the current record of a subform. You can set the value of *FieldName* by reversing the order of the expression.

var*SubformProp* =
`Forms(str`*`FormName`*`).Form(str`*`SubformName`*`).`*`PropertyName`* returns the value of a property of a subform.

var*SubformVal* =
`Forms(str`*`FormName`*`).Form(str`*`SubformName`*`).Form(str`*`FieldName`*`).`*`PropertyName`* returns the value of a property of the field of a subform.

NOTE

To fully comply with conventional object-oriented syntax, Access enables you to explicitly specify the value of an object with the `Value` property. Visual Basic 3.0, for example, uses the `Text` and `Value` properties to return the values of text boxes and other control objects, respectively. Access objects do not have a `Text` property.

You can test the preferred object addressing syntax using the Immediate window by following these steps:

1. Open the Orders form of NWIND.MDB in run mode. The first record, an order from Valley Store, appears.

2. Open the Utility Functions module and display the Immediate window.

3. Execute `? Forms ("Orders").Visible;` -1 **(True)** is returned.

4. Execute `? Forms("Orders").Section (0).Height;` 5280, the height of the form in twips, is returned.

5. Execute ? `Forms("Orders").Form("Address")`; the Immediate window displays `Via Monte Bianco 34`, if the record pointer is on the first record.

6. Execute ? `Forms ("Orders").Form ("Address").Enabled`; 0 (**False**) is returned.

7. Execute ? `Forms ("Orders").Form ("Orders Subform").Form("Product Name")`; the Immediate window displays `Alice Mutton`.

8. Execute ? `Forms("Orders").Form("Orders Subform").Form("Product Name").Visible`; the Immediate window displays `-1`.

Using the preferred object addressing syntax has the advantage of providing consistency with the OLE 2.0 object naming conventions and consistency across current and future dialects of Object Basic. Note, however, that Access Basic is presently the only dialect of Object Basic that includes subforms.

> **NOTE**
>
> You can use an alternative syntax to specify a control on a form that is similar to the **DBEngine**`(0)(0)` shorthand syntax that substitutes for **DBEngine**`.Workspaces(0).Databases(0)`. As an example, `Forms(strFormName)(strSubformName).Form(strFieldName)` returns the value of the field specified by str*FieldName*.

The syntax for addressing reports and objects of reports is identical: substitute **Reports** for **Forms** and **Report** for **Form**. The cascade syntax used to refer to elements of subforms is appropriate, because a subform is an object contained in a form, and a field is an object contained in the subform. Microsoft refers to objects contained in another object as a property of the container object. You use the period (`.`) qualifying operator with the preferred syntax. If you use the bang (`!`) operator in the preceding examples, you receive an "Invalid object reference" message.

> **NOTE**
>
> You do not need to declare an object variable of the data type **Form**, **Report**, or **Control** or use the **Set** instruction to open or refer to an Access object in your Access Basic code. You can, however, assign a form or report to a declared object variable with, for example, **Set** `cboComboBox = `**Forms**`("FormName").`**Form**`("ControlName")`. Then use the object variable, cbo*ComboBox*, as a shorthand method of referring to the Access object.

TIP

When you use form or report modules to contain event-handling procedures use the new **Me** self-reference reserved word to refer to form or report in which the code is contained. Using **Me**, instead of Forms(str*FormName*) is faster and requires much less typing.

Table 7.2 lists the index values for the sections that can appear on forms and reports. You specify the index value as the argument of the Sections() collection; Sections() does not accept a **String** argument.

Table 7.2. Section index values for form and report sections.

Index	Form Section	Report Section
0	Detail	Detail
1	Header	Header
2	Footer	Footer
3	Page Header	Page Header
4	Page Footer	Page Footer
5		Group-level 1 header
6		Group-level 1 footer

Additional group-level headers and footers, if any, are added to the collection in pairs, beginning at index 7.

NOTE

You can obtain the number of the section in which a control is located with the Section property, omitting the trailing parenthesis. The syntax shown in the above example is required when you use **Section**() as a property of form and report objects.

Using the Index to the Collection

You can refer to forms by the index value that specifies the location of the form in the collection. This is the fastest method of specifying a particular form, report, or control object in your code, except for the **Me** self-reference in form and report modules. The downside is that you need to know the sequence of opening the Access objects in advance, because the collection is ordered in the sequence in which your application or the user opens the forms.

The `Forms()` collection has only one property, `Count`, that specifies the number of open forms in your application. The `Forms` collection has no properties that you can address with Access Basic. Thus you cannot determine explicitly the number of controls on a form. You can use the following syntax to refer to forms, reports, and controls by index values:

```
wPropVal == Forms..Count (collection property)
varPropVal == Forms(wFrm)..PropertyName (form property)
varPropVal == Forms(wFrm)..Section(wSect)..PropertyName (section
➥_property)
varCtrlVal == Forms(wFrm)..Form(wCtrl) (get control value)
Forms(wFrm)..Form(wCtrl) == varCtrlVal (set control value)
varCtrlPropVal == Forms(wFrm)..Form(wSbf)..PropertyName (control
➥_property)
varSubformVal == Forms(wFrm)..Form(wSbf)..Form(wC) (subform control
➥_value)
varSubformProp == Forms(wFrm)..Form(wSbf)..PropertyName
varSubformProp == Forms(wFrm)..Form(wSbf)..Section(wSect)..PropertyName
(subform section property)
varSubformVal = Forms(wFrm).Form(wSbf).Form(wC).PropertyName (subform
control property).
```

The index values for forms (*wFrm*), sections of forms (wSect), controls (*wCtrl*), and subforms (*wSbf*) in the preceding syntax examples range from zero to one less than the number of objects in the collection. For example, `Forms(0).Form(0)` refers to the first control you added to the form that you or your application first opened. The `IsLoaded()` function in the Utility Functions module of NWIND.MDB uses the index addressing method to determine whether a particular form is open. The listing that follows is a version of `IsLoaded()` that has been modified to comply with the conventions used in this book:

```
Function wIsOpen (strFormName As String) As Integer
    'Purpose:   Determines if a form is loaded
    'Argument:  strFormName = Name of form to test
    'Returns:   True if specified the form is open
    '           False if the specified form is not open

    On Error GoTo ErrHandler
    Dim wCtr As Integer

    For wCtr = 0 To Forms.Count - 1
        If Forms(wCtr).FormName = strFormName Then
            wIsOpen = True
            Exit Function
```

```
        End If
    Next wCtr
    Exit Function

ErrHandler:
    MsgBox Error$, 32, "wIsOpen() Error"
    Exit Function
End Function
```

> **NOTE**
>
> Although it is unlikely that an error can occur in the execution of wIsOpen(), it is a good programming practice to add an error-handling routine to each Access Basic function or procedure. Trapping errors prevents your runtime application from abruptly closing when an error occurs.

Controls are added to the collection in the sequence of their creation. If you delete a control and then replace it with another control, the sequence of the controls in the collection changes. The number that Access automatically appends to the name of an unbound control, as in Box 38, does not refer to the index of the control. You can mix combinations of the preferred syntax and the index reference method.

> **TIP**
>
> Using the index of the object in a collection is not a recommended practice, unless your application opens all forms and users hide, rather than close, all forms during the application's lifetime. Otherwise, you may find that your index value refers to the wrong form or to an undesired control, depending upon user actions or design changes to forms. This note also applies to controls on reports. Using a variable or a literal value with the preferred syntax also makes your code easier to read.

Literal Reference to Access Objects

The most common method of referring to Access objects in the Access documentation is literal reference that requires you to use the proper name of each object. If the name of an object includes spaces or illegal punctuation, you must enclose the name within square brackets. This method of referring to Access objects commonly is called *bang syntax*. The bang operator (!) preceding a proper name explicitly identifies the proper name as a form, report, or control name, rather than the name of a property of the object that precedes the ! operator. (This is why you cannot use the ! operator with the preceding two methods of referencing Access objects.) Bang syntax usually executes faster than the preferred syntax described earlier in the chapter, but is less flexible, because you can't use variables for object names. The following are examples of literal reference syntax:

```
varPropVal = Forms!FormName.FormProperty
varPropVal = Forms!FormName.Section(wSect).SectionProperty
varCtrlVal = Forms!FormName!ControlName
varPropVal = Forms!FormName![Control Name].ControlProperty
varCtrlVal = Forms![Form Name]![Subform Name].Form.SubFormProperty
varSubformVal = Forms![Form Name]!SubformName.Form![FieldName]
varSFPropVal = Forms!FormName![Subform Name].Form![Control
➥Name].ControlProperty
```

Literal reference syntax is most commonly employed with macros and, in some cases, must be used as the argument of an Access method (when the syntax specifies that the argument value must be the name of a control on the active form).

Using the Intrinsic Screen Objects

You can obtain the property values of the active form or report by addressing the object as **Screen.ActiveForm** or **Screen.ActiveReport**. The control object with the focus is identified by **Screen.ActiveControl**. If you write a single multipurpose function to respond to the OnClick (formerly the OnPush) event of several command button controls, you can determine which control is active by testing the value returned by **Screen.ActiveControl.ControlName**.

> **NOTE**
>
> You can open a form and then open a module and use the Immediate window to experiment with each of the Access Basic naming conventions, except when you use the intrinsic **Screen** object. When you make the Immediate window the active window, the intrinsic **Screen** objects are no longer valid objects.

Properties of Access Objects and the *TypeOf()* Function

There are about 200 properties that apply to Access objects. It is not possible to make an accurate count of the properties of Access 2.0 objects, because all properties are not disclosed in the documentation that accompanies retail Access and the Access Developer's Toolkit (ADT). For example, the *Language Reference* does not explain the Data property of a graph object. This property is used by the Access Graph Wizard. Fortunately, you no longer need to use the Data property of a graph object to create user-defined graphs with Microsoft Graph 5.0.

The two properties of Access control objects that are likely to appear most frequently in your code are `Visible` and `Enabled`. Now that you can change the `Caption` property of labels and other control objects with a caption property in run mode, Caption is probably a close third. When the operation of a command button or other control object is inappropriate for the present condition of your application, you set the control object's `Enabled` property to **False**. Controls whose `Visible` or `Enabled` property is **False** do not trigger events.

> **NOTE**
>
> Developers new to Access may wonder why superimposed control objects and use of the `Visible` property is so common in existing Access applications. Access 1.x developers who wanted to change the appearance of a label or the purpose of a command button, had to create two superimposed labels or command buttons, then alternate display of the two superimposed controls by hiding one control by setting its `Visible` property to **False**, and showing the other control by setting its `Visible` property to **True**.

You can declare local **Form**, **Report**, and **Control** object variables in your Access Basic code, and then pass these object variables as arguments to other functions and subprocedures that can evaluate the object's properties. Following is a code fragment for a function that passes a variable of the **Control** object type to another function:

```
Function wPassControl () As Integer
    Dim txtControl As Control
    Set txtControl = Forms("frmForm").Form("txtControl")
    If wCatchControl (txtControl) Then
        ...Do something
    End If
    ...
End Function

Function wCatchControl (typControl As Control) As Integer
    If TypeOf typControl Is TextBox Then
        ...typControl has a value
    Else
        ...typControl may have a value
    End If
    ...
End Function
```

If wCatchControl() is a general purpose function, you can use the **If TypeOf** *typControl* **Is** *ControlType* **Then ... End If** structure to determine the object type of *typControl*, and then get or set the values of its properties accordingly. The **TypeOf** function does not have a separate entry in the Language Reference, but appears in

conjunction with the **If** statement. The permissible values of *ControlType* are
BoundObjectFrame, CheckBox, ComboBox, CommandButton, Label, Line, ListBox,
ObjectFrame (for embedded and linked unbound object frames and graphs),
OptionButton, OptionGroup, PageBreak, Rectangle, SubForm, SubReport, TextBox, or
ToggleButton. The **TypeOf** function is restricted to use with the **If** or **ElseIf** state-
ments, the **Is** operator and a control type, so you cannot use the **Select Case...End
Select** structure with **TypeOf**. Use the **ElseIf TypeOf** *typControl* **Is** *ControlType*
instead.

NOTE

As mentioned in the preceding chapter, the properties of an object depend
upon the context (container) of the object. Control objects, such as text
boxes, on forms have a different set of properties than control objects on
reports. If you write a general-purpose function that evaluates properties of
control objects, make sure that the function takes into account the context
of the control objects with which the function deals.

The **Parent** property applies only to **Form** or **Report** objects that are sub-forms or
reports. The value of the **Parent** property refers to the main form or report on which
the sub-object is a control. Thus if you have an orders subform, you can refer to a
control on the main form with the syntax Parent.[*ControlName*]. However, the main
form must be the active window and the subform must be the active control to prevent an "Invalid object reference" message from occurring when you are debugging
your Access Basic code. The problem of focus changes while debugging is discussed
in the section that follows.

The SourceObject property of a form or report identifies the name of a subform or
subreport. For example, executing ? Forms("Orders").Form("Order
Details").SourceObject with the Orders form open returns Order Details. A more
useful purpose of the **SourceObject** property is to return the full path and file name
of an object that is linked to a bound object frame. If you have linked a .WAV file to
a bound object frame, executing ? Forms(frmMultimedia).Form(bofSound) might
return a value such as c:\windows\tada.wav in the Immediate window.

Access **Form** objects that are bound to **Table** or **QueryDef** objects have a pair of properties, RecordsetClone (formerly Dynaset) and Bookmark, that you employ to create
a clone of the **Recordset** object that underlies forms and subforms. The use of the
RecordsetClone and Bookmark properties of forms is discussed in the section, "Creating and Synchronizing a Recordset Clone," that follows later in the chapter.

Applying Access Methods to Access Objects

Access methods, for the most part, emulate processes that you can perform manually in Access's run mode. The traditional method of creating simple application macros is to record menu choices, keystrokes, and decisions made in dialogues. Recorded macros in Windows applications are ordered collections of events. Events are the subject of the section, "Understanding Event-Driven Coding Methods," that appears later in this chapter. When you execute the recorded macro, the macro reproduces the recorded events. Early macro editors let you expand the usefulness of recorded macros by adding decision and loop structures. Ultimately, macro editing methods evolved into full-scale, application-specific programming languages, such as Word Basic.

When Microsoft Corp. decided to standardize on Object Basic as the core application programming language for its mainstream applications, a means of providing methods for application-specific objects, such as worksheets and word processing documents, was needed. Excel 5.0, which uses Visual Basic for Applications (VBA) as its programming language, uses methods to manipulate application objects. Microsoft Word 6.0 employs commands derived from menu choices to manipulate its objects with Word Basic. For Access, Microsoft added the keyword, **DoCmd** to identify the subsequent word as an instruction to apply an application-specific method to an application object. It is likely that the **DoCmd** reserved word will disappear when a future version of Access adopts VBA as its programming language.

Access methods fall into two general categories: those that involve manipulation of windows and control objects and those that apply only to tables, queries, and the **Recordset** objects that underlie forms and reports. The following sections describe these methods and how you create a database object that you can relate to the **Recordset** object that underlies a form.

Methods Applicable to Windows and Control Objects

The majority of Access macro actions perform the same function as methods in Access Basic code as when the actions are used in a macro. You cannot use the macro actions listed in Table 7.3 with the **DoCmd** keyword in Access Basic code. With the exception of the Add Menu action, Access Basic provides an alternative syntax to emulate applicable actions with reserved words.

Table 7.3. Macro actions that cannot be used with the DoCmd keyword in Access Basic.

Action	*Access Basic Alternative*
AddMenu	There is no capability of adding menu items with Access Basic commands or functions. Chapter 26, "Customizing Access Applications with Special Menus and Toolbars," describes how to use the AddMenu macro action.
SetValue	Set the value of the property in your code.
MsgBox	Use the Access Basic **MsgBox** statement or **MsgBox()** function.
SendKeys	Use the Access Basic **SendKeys** command.
RunCode	Execute an Access Basic function from within your code.
StopMacro	Not applicable.
StopAllMacros	Not applicable.
RunApp	Use the **Shell**() function.

TIP

You can use a **DoCmd** RunMacro "*[MacroGroup.]MacroName*", [, *wRepeatCount*[, *wRepeatExpression*]] method to run a macro from Access Basic code. The primary application for the **DoCmd** RunMacro action is to apply the AddMenu action, which you cannot execute directly from Access Basic. It is a poor programming practice to execute macros from Access Basic code for other purposes.

There are two methods that are particularly important in Access Basic functions that employ the **DoCmd** FindRecord method, described in the section that follows, and other Access methods that rely on the value of the active control. **DoCmd** SelectObject makes the specified object the active object. **DoCmd** GoToControl lets you select the control object on the active object. The syntax of these two commands, which direct Windows' focus to the specified object or control, is as follows:

```
DoCmd SelectObject wObjectType, strObjectName, [fDBWindow]
DoCmd GoToControl strControlName
```

Table 7.4 lists the allowable values for the arguments of the **DoCmd** SelectObject and **DoCmd** GoToControl methods.

Table 7.4. The values of arguments for the DoCmd `SelectObject` and DoCmd `GoToControl` methods.

Argument	Value	Domain
wObjectType	An Integer constant that specifies the type of object. You ordinarily do not select macros and modules in Access Basic code.	A_TABLE = Table A_QUERY = Query A_FORM = Form A_REPORT = Report (A_MACRO = Macro) (A_MODULE = Module)
strObjectName	A **String** literal or variable that specifies the name of the object.	The name must appear in the appropriate Database window list box.
fDBWindow	Specifies if the object is to be selected in the Database window.	**False** = select from open objects. **True** = select from the Database window.
strControlName	A **String** literal or variable that specifies the name of a control on the active object.	Use a quoted string literal of string variable, not the control object reference syntax.

TIP

Use the new Access SetFocus method to set the focus to a form or a control on a form. {*Form¦FormContol*}.**SetFocus** is faster in operation and easier to type than either of the preceding methods.

You use the **DoCmd** SelectObject and **DoCmd** GoToControl methods in Access Basic code when you test and debug code. When you use the Immediate window in the testing process, the Immediate Window has the focus. Thus you need to apply the **DoCmd** SelectObject method before you use methods that apply only to the active object, such as **DoCmd** FindRecord. To select the current field for searches other than on all fields of the selected object, you need to apply the **DoCmd** GoToControl method to set the focus to the appropriate field. If you fail to add these methods before you use the **DoCmd** FindRecord method, for example, you receive a "Command not available" message. The following code fragment illustrates the use of these three **DoCmd** methods in sequence to find the first record in the Company Name field of the Customers form of NWIND.MDB that matches the value of strCompany:

```
DoCmd SelectObject A_FORM, "Customers"
DoCmd GoToControl "Company Name"
DoCmd FindRecord strCompany
```

After testing, you can comment out the **DoCmd** SelectObject line if your code executes only when the Customers form is active, and you can do the same for the **DoCmd** GoToControl line if your code executes from an event of the Company Name text box. You incur little speed penalty in the execution of your code by leaving these two lines active, however.

> ### TIP
>
> The change of focus problem applies to the use of the **Form** property without a preceding form name identifier to refer to the active form in Access Basic code. When you test your code, the form is no longer active; either the module window or the Immediate window is active. Thus you receive an "Invalid object reference" message when you reach the line on which frmForm.PropertyName appears. The solution is to specify the proper name of the form with the preferred syntax or to declare an object variable of the **Form** object type, then use the frmForm.PropertyName syntax to get or, if applicable, set the value of PropertyName.

Methods Applicable to Recordset Objects

Many of the Access methods applicable to forms bound to tables or queries **Recordset** objects correspond to the database methods of Object Basic and xBase commands. Access record manipulation methods and their equivalents in Object Basic and xBase are listed in Table 7.5.

Table 7.5. Correspondence of Access, Recordset, and xBase methods for data manipulation.

Access Method	Recordset Method	xBase Command
DoCmd FindRecord	*Recordset.***FindFirst**	LOCATE
DoCmd FindNext	*Recordset.***FindNext**	CONTINUE
DoCmd GoToRecord , , A_FIRST	*Recordset.***MoveFirst**	GO TOP
DoCmd GoToRecord , , A_LAST	*Recordset.***MoveLast**	GO BOTTOM
DoCmd GoToRecord , , A_NEXT	*Recordset.***MoveNext**	SKIP
DoCmd GoToRecord , , A_PREVIOUS	*Recordset.***MovePrevious**	SKIP -1
DoCmd GoToRecord , , A_NEWREC	*Recordset.***AddNew**	APPEND BLANK

Recordset objects do not have a "RecordNumber" property, but Access creates a record number that identifies the position of the current record of a table or query. Thus, you can use the Access method

```
DoCmd GoToRecord A_FORM, strFormName, A_GOTO, dwOffset
```

to position the current record to the record specified by the **Long** integer dwOffset. This rather cumbersome syntax is similar in effect to the xBase GOTO *recno* command, except that the record number you specify as the offset value of the GoToRecord method is determined by the position of the record in the current view of the query or table. (The dwOffset value that specifies a record number in Access methods begins with 1 as the offset of the first record). In xBase, record numbers are defined by the sequence in which the records were added to the database file (unless the file is restructured by the SORT ON ... TO command). Access record numbers are relative, whereas xBase record numbers are fixed. Access and xBase record numbers correspond only when a table has no primary key and a query based on a table with no primary key is not sorted.

The **DoCmd** FindRecord method emulates the Find dialog of Access, shown in Figure 7.2. The Access Basic syntax of the **DoCmd** FindRecord method is as follows:

```
DoCmd FindRecord varWhat[, wWhere[, fMatch[, wDirection[, wFormatted[,
➡wIn[, fFirst]]]]]]
```

The allowable values of the arguments of the **DoCmd** FindRecord Access method are listed in Table 7.6.

Table 7.6. The allowable values of the arguments of the `DoCmd FindRecord` method.

Argument	Value	Domain
varWhat	A value or an expression that evaluates to a value (Find What text box)	Any value that corresponds to types of values in the table
wWhere	An **Integer** constant that specifies all or the part of the field to be matched (Where list box)	**A_ENTIRE** = Like "varWhat" A_ANYWHERE = Like "*varWhat*" A_START = Like "varWhat*"
fMatch	An **Integer** flag that specifies if the match is to be case-sensitive (Match Case check box)	**False** True
wDirection	An **Integer** constant that specifies the direction of the search (Direction option buttons)	**A_DOWN** = search from current record to end A_UP = search from current record to beginning
fFormatted	An **Integer** flag that specifies if varWhat is formatted (Search Fields as Formatted check box)	**False** = wData corresponds to data as stored in the field True = wData corresponds to the format specified for the field
wIn	An **Integer** constant that specifies if values in the current or all fields are to be searched	**A_CURRENT** = search only in the current field A_ALL = search all fields (Search in for a match option buttons)
fFirst	An **Integer** flag that specifies where to begin the search (related to the Find First and Find Next command buttons)	**True** = start at the beginning of the recordset (Find First) False = start at the current record

FIGURE 7.2.

*The Find in field
dialog box for the
Customer ID field
of the Customers
table.*

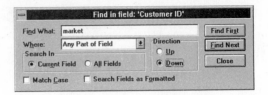

The statement equivalent to the values shown in the Find in field: 'Customer ID'
dialog of Figure 7.2 when you click the Find First command button is as follows:

```
DoCmd FindRecord "market", A_ANYWHERE, False, A_DOWN, False,
➥A_CURRENT, True
```

The structure of the **DoCmd** FindRecord statement is closely related to the EditFind
statement of a Word for Windows' Word Basic macro statement that appears as follows:

```
EditFind .Find = "A_ANYWHERE", .WholeWord = 0, .MatchCase = 1,
➥.Direction = 1, .Format = 0
```

Excel 5.0's Find dialog box, illustrated by Figure 7.3, that searches cells of worksheets
for matching values or formulas, is similar to the Find dialog box of Access and Word
for Windows 2+. The Excel VBA macro, recorded by choosing **F**ind from Excel's
Edit menu, making the choices shown in Figure 7.3, and clicking the OK button,
appears as follows:

```
Sub FindMacro()
    Cells.Find(What:="front-ending", After:=ActiveCell, LookIn:=
        ➥xlFormulas, LookAt:=xlPart, SearchOrder:=xlByRows,
        ➥SearchDirection:=xlNext, MatchCase:=False).Activate
End Sub
```

The equivalent Excel 4.0 function, =FORMULA.FIND("front-ending",2,2,2,1,FALSE)
is much more like the structure of the FindRecord action. Excel 4.0 macro keywords
are functions that return values, although the returned value is disregarded in many
cases.

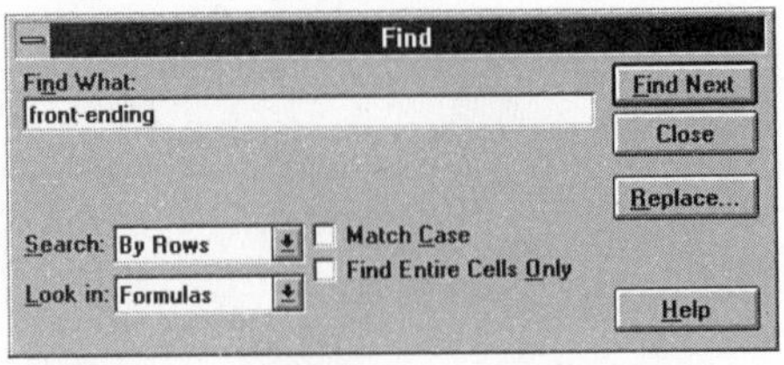

FIGURE 7.3.

*Excel 5.0's Find
dialog box.*

Each of the constants and flags of the preceding **DoCmd** FindRecord statement represents the default value, so you can abbreviate the preceding Access Basic statement as follows:

DoCmd FindRecord "market"

If you want to start the search at the current record, the equivalent of the initial click on the Find Next button in the Find in field dialog box the first time, you need to add the intervening placeholder commas to indicate that the default values of the arguments are to be used, as in:

DoCmd FindRecord "market", , , , , , **True**

Once you've entered a value in the Find in field dialog and clicked the Find First or Find Next button, clicking the Find Next button is equivalent to applying the **DoCmd** FindNext method. **DoCmd** FindNext takes no arguments. Thus, you need to apply a **DoCmd** FindRecord method before you can apply the **DoCmd** FindNext method.

The formal syntax of the **DoCmd** GoToRecord method is as follows:

DoCmd GoToRecord [w*ObjectType*, str*ObjectName*[, w*WhichRecord*[,
➥dw*Offset*]]]

Types and domains of values for the **DoCmd** GoToRecord method are listed in Table 7.7.

Table 7.7. Values for the arguments of the DoCmd GoToRecord method.

Argument	Value	Domain
w*ObjectType*	An Integer constant that specifies the type of object. If you include str*ObjectName*, you must include w*ObjectType*.	A_TABLE = Table A_QUERY = Query A_FORM = Form
str*ObjectName*	A **String** literal or variable that specifies the name of the object. If you do not provide values for wObjectType and strObjectName, the active object is the default.	The object must be a table, query, or form object, and the name must appear in the appropriate Database window list box.

continues

Table 7.7. continued

Argument	Value	Domain
wWhichRecord	An **Integer** constant that specifies the record to become the current record.	A_NEXT = Next record A_FIRST = First record A_LAST = Last record A_PREVIOUS = Prior record A_NEWREC = Tentative append record A_GOTO = go to record specified by dwOffset
dwOffset	A **Long** integer that specifies the record number to become the current record (1 = the first record).	From 1 to the number of records in the table or query.

> **NOTE**
>
> Access methods are commands; thus, Access methods do not return values. From a programmer's standpoint, it would be preferable to implement Access methods in the form of functions that return values, such as the record number of the current record when you apply the **DoCmd** GoToRecord method, or an integer to represent success in finding a matching record with the **DoCmd** FindRecord method. Alternatively, functions such as xBase's RECNO() or FOUND() functions that are operable with Access methods would be useful, but such functions are not available in Access 2.0.

Creating and Synchronizing a Recordset Clone

As mentioned earlier in this chapter, you cannot manipulate the **Recordset** object that underlies an Access table, query, form, or report with the Object Basic database methods. You can create a clone of the underlying **Recordset** object, however, by using the RecordsetClone property of an open form or report in a **Set** statement. You use the value of the Bookmark property of the **Form** or **Report** object to set the value of the Bookmark property of the clone. This positions the record pointer of the clone to the record that corresponds to the current record of the form or report. Following is a code fragment that creates a clone of the **Recordset** object underlying a form and sets the record pointer of the **Recordset** object to the form's current record:

```
Dim rsClone As Recordset
Set rsClone = Forms(strFormName).RecordsetClone
rsClone.Bookmark = Forms(strFormName).Bookmark
```

Add the declaration statement for rsClone to the Declarations section of your module so that the object variable has module-level scope. You set the value of rsClone immediately after you execute the OpenForm action for strFormName. You need to execute the Bookmark statement each time your code or the user changes the current record of a form. You can synchronize the clone **Recordset** by "attaching" a simple user-defined function wSyncClones() to the OnCurrent event of the form.

NOTE

When you add a record to or delete a record from a table, it is advisable to create a new clone.

The following function, wSyncClones(), illustrates how you synchronize clones of both the main form and subform **Recordset** objects. The wSyncClones() function and the remaining code examples in this chapter are included in the Access Objects and Methods module of the AB_EXAMP.MDB database of the accompanying diskette.

```
Function wSyncClones () As Integer
    'Purpose:   Synchronize two clone recordsets to a form/subform's
    ➥Recordset
    'Returns:   True if no error, False on an error

    On Error GoTo SyncError

    'Note: You can use the other forms of addressing here
    'Set the bookmark from the main form
    rsOrders.Bookmark = Forms("Orders").Bookmark

    'Set the bookmark from the subform
    rsOrdDtls.Bookmark = Forms("Orders").Form("Order
    ➥Details").Form.Bookmark

    wSyncClones = True
    Exit Function

SyncError:
    MsgBox Error$, 16, "Synchronization Error"
    Exit Function
End Function
```

The function wOpenOrders() of the listing that follows demonstrates the use of the **DoCmd** OpenForm and the **DoCmd** GoToRecord methods, and how to create and manipulate records in clone **Recordset** objects independently of the **Recordset** objects that underlie forms and subforms. The wOpenOrders() function employs the wSyncClones() function to maintain the two sets of **Recordset** objects in synchronization. Import the Access Objects and Methods module into NWIND.MDB and open the module, then open the Immediate Window. Run the wOpenOrders function by executing ? wOpenOrders() in the Immediate window.

```
Function wOpenOrders () As Integer
    'Purpose:    Open the Orders form with the Order Details _subform
    '            Create clone recordsets of the form and subform
    '               ➡recordsets
    '            Synchronize and manipulate the two clone recordsets
    'Calls:      wSyncClones() (bookmark synchronization)
    'Returns:    True if successful, False on failure

    On Error GoTo OpenError

    Dim strOrders As String
    strOrders = "Orders"

    'Test to determine if the form is already open
    If Not wIsOpen(strOrders) Then
        DoCmd OpenForm strOrders
    End If

    'Assign values to object variables declared in Declarations _section
    Set rsOrders = Forms(strOrders).RecordsetClone
    Set rsOrdDtls = Forms(strOrders).Form("Orders
    ➡Subform").Form.RecordsetClone

    'Synchronize the form and subform clones
    If wSyncClones() Then
        'Go to the second record of Orders (which has several line
        ➡items)
        DoCmd GoToRecord A_FORM, strOrders, A_GOTO, 2

        'Position the record pointers of the clones
        If Not wSyncClones() Then
            'An error occurred
            Exit Function
        End If

        'Print the order number and date as a test
        Debug.Print rsOrders.[Order ID] & " " & rsOrders.[Order _Date]

        'Find the first line item of the order in the Order Details clone
        'Note: Specify the table, if you compare fielrs of two tables
        rsOrdDtls.FindFirst rsOrdDtls.[Order ID] = rsOrders.[Order ID]
```

```
    If rsOrdDtls.NoMatch Then
        'No line items were found
        MsgBox "No line items entered for order " &
        ➥rsOrders.[Order ID] & ".", 32, "Order Problem"

    Else
        'Print the details from the rsOrdDtls clone for testing
        Do While Not rsOrdDtls.NoMatch
            Debug.Print rsOrdDtls.[Order ID] & " " &
            ➥rsOrdDtls.[Quantity]
            rsOrdDtls.FindNext rsOrdDtls.[Order ID] =
            ➥rsOrders.[Order ID]
        Loop
    End If

    'Reposition the record pointers of the clones
    If Not wSyncClones() Then
        Exit Function
    End If

    wOpenOrders = True
  End If
  DoCmd OpenModule "Access Objects and Methods (Chapter 7)",
  ➥"wOpenOrders"
  Exit Function

OpenError:
  MsgBox Error$, 16, "Error Opening Form"
  Exit Function
End Function
```

The advantages of creating a clone **Recordset** object and using the database methods to manipulate data are as follows:

■ You can determine the number of records in the **Recordset** underlying a form or report by applying the **MoveLast** method and storing the value of the **RecordCount** property to a **Long** integer variable. You can use the value of the **RecordCount** property to limit the value of the dwOffset argument of **DoCmd** GoToRecord, thus preventing "Can't go to specified record" error messages.

■ You can obtain values of fields of the current record that are not bound to controls on the form. This eliminates the inconvenience of adding hidden text boxes to forms to make field values available to your Access Basic code.

■ You can transfer data from the current record to tables in another database. An example is archiving a record in a table of another database before you delete the current record in your database.

■ You can use the clone **Recordset** to add a record to a transaction log when a user adds, deletes, or edits a record in the underlying tables of a form. Transaction logs are always located in a database other than the current database, and the log database is usually located on a computer that is not used to store the main database. The next chapter, "Optimizing Transaction-Processing Forms," discusses why and how you create Access transaction logs.

■ Manipulating data in the clone **Recordset** with database methods usually is faster than performing the same operation with Access methods. This is especially the case when the manipulation requires repainting of the current window.

> ### WARNING
>
> The Transactions property of clone tables created by using the RecordsetClone property of a form is **False** for Microsoft Access databases. This contradicts the statements in the *Language Reference* that all Access tables, including attached tables, support transactions. You cannot roll back changes made to the underlying tables of **Recordset** objects created with the RecordsetClone property of a form. The Transactions property for all other **Table** and **Recordset** objects created from Access tables and queries returns **True**.

Understanding Event-Driven Coding Methods

Developers of RDBMS applications in languages such as xBase or COBOL are accustomed to writing code in a top-down, hierarchical structure. Creating Windows RDBMS applications in Access requires a completely different view of the application programming process. If you have Written windows applications in Visual Basic, Borland, Microsoft C++, or one of the other application languages designed for Windows, you might want to skip to the section titled "Classifying Events of Form, Report, and Control Objects." The sections that follow contrast application development in character-based (DOS) and Windows environments, and provide some of the definitions of Windows objects to assist DOS developers in adapting to the Windows GUI.

The Structure of Menu-Driven DOS RDBMS Applications and the Windows Message Loop

The code listings presented in this and the previous chapter do not differ significantly in structure from conventional functions and subprocedures that character-based database developers write in xBase, PAL, or C for use with DOS. Some of the syntax of Access Basic may appear peculiar to xBase or PAL programmers, but it is not difficult for any person with RDBMS programming experience to fathom the purpose of the function or subprocedure. Executing functions and procedures from the Immediate window is not appreciably different from interactively executing xBase functions and procedures from the dot prompt. The only programming element that's missing is the main program, MAIN.PRG (or whatever), which calls the example functions and subprocedures.

The classical structure of the main or entry program of a multifunction DOS RDBMS application consists of a DO WHILE .T....ENDDO loop. Inside the loop, a DO CASE...ENDCASE structure calls one of a multitude of procedures as result of a choice made by the user. A typical main program code construct, written in xBase, that implements the first level of a hierarchical menu structure appears in the following listing:

```
*main.PRG
...Screen painting code
DO WHILE .T.
   choice = INKEY()
   DO CASE
      CASE CHR(choice) = "1"
         DO proc1 .............. PROCEDURE proc1
      CASE CHR(choice) = "2"      * Display a form
         DO proc2                 RETURN
      CASE CHR(choice) = "3"
         Do proc3 .............. PROCEDURE proc3
         ...                      * Display a different form
      CASE CHR(choice) = "0"      RETURN
         EXIT
   ENDCASE
ENDDO
```

One or more of the called procedures, proc1...procN, might have its own DO WHILE...ENDDO structure with DO CASE...ENDCASE calling to other procedures in the next lower level of the hierarchy. The lowest level of the hierarchy contains procedures that display forms to display or enter data, or print reports.

You do not create a main program for Access applications; Access itself is the main program. Windows applications created with application languages dispense with the need to create menu loop structures; Access, not the code you write, calls the equivalent of proc1...procN procedures in at all levels of the menu hierarchy. With Windows application languages, you can forever dispense with writing INKEY()...DO WHILE .T....ENDDO structures, or the equivalent, for menu hierarchies. The Windows application provides the loop structure, called the Windows application message loop, for you. When you launch Access or MSARN110.EXE with your application's database, Access becomes a part of the main Windows message loop that permits multitasking of Windows applications. Other application languages, such as Visual Basic and Word Basic, use the same programming methodology. The details of the application message loop and the Windows message loop, and its effect on how you structure your Access Basic code, are discussed shortly.

> **NOTE**
>
> C and C++ programmers writing code for Windows applications are not so fortunate as programmers who employ application languages. According to the originators of the C language, C was intended to be a programming language with which to write operating systems, not applications. In C and C++ you need a main program (referred to as WinMain), and you must create the program's message loop. The message loop consists of a large collection of nested switch...break expressions that respond to Windows messages. The recent crop of C++ compilers, typified by Microsoft Visual C++, provide prefabricated WinMain routines that you can modify to suit your application.

Access's Multiple Document Interface Windows

Access, like other Microsoft applications such as Excel and Word, makes extensive use of Windows' multiple document interface (MDI). In Access, each form and report is an MDI child window; Access's main window is the parent window of the MDI children. Access classifies these MDI child windows as forms and reports, but the Windows environment makes no such distinction. When you open a form or report in Run mode, you create a new MDI child window; when you close the form or report, the MDI child window disappears. The main window of MSACCESS.EXE or MSARN200.EXE is the parent window.

Many child windows can coexist within the parent window, but only one child window can be the active window at any instant. You choose which child window is active by clicking its surface with the mouse or choosing the name or number of the window from the Window menu of the parent. There is no hierarchical relationship between these MDI child windows; all form and report windows in Access are siblings. Subforms and subreports, however, are MDI children of the main form, indicated by the fact that the **Parent** property of a subform or subreport returns the name of the main form or report.

User input to your application, such as mouse clicks and keystrokes, is directed to the active window. If no child window is open, as is the case when you open Access without specifying a database, the parent window is the active window. The active window is indicated by a title bar with a specified color (dark blue when you use Windows' default color scheme). The active Window is said to have the focus. Only one window can have the focus at any instant; open windows without the focus have a title bar of a contrasting color (white with Windows' default colors). The exception to this rule is the parent window: the menu of the parent window is active, without the focus, regardless of whether an MDI child window is open. If only one MDI child window is open, the only child always has the focus unless the parent or MDI child window opens a new window. The last window you open has the focus until an event occurs that changes the focus.

Styles and Modes of Windows

There are six window styles modes from which you can choose. Each of the styles and modes is a property of the window, but not all the window properties can be set as values of properties of forms and reports. Some of the modes you can specify as values of properties of forms and reports, such as Popup and Modal, can be combined. The six basic windows styles and modes are as follows:

- ■ Normal windows have sizable borders. You can resize the parent window by dragging the window's borders with the mouse. Normal MDI child windows can appear only within the confines of the parent window, with the exception of modeless pop-up windows (Windows dialogs). Technically, dialogs are not MDI child windows, but the dialog is associated with the child window that caused the dialog to appear. You can cascade or tile normal MDI child windows. When you reopen Access, the parent window opens in the mode of the parent window when you last closed Access.

- ■ Maximized windows occupy the entire active area of your display and lack visible borders. When you first launch Access, Access's parent window opens in maximized mode. You can maximize the parent window, but the MDI child windows that you open in the parent window can be either normal or maximized windows. The mode of one child window applies to all its siblings; if you maximize one MDI child window, all the sibling windows, except pop-up windows, open in maximized mode. You cannot minimize a maximized window by clicking a button; you need to display the Document Control menu box, and then choose Minimize. Alternately, you can click the Normal button of the maximized window, and then click the Minimize button of the normal mode window.

■ Minimized windows are represented by an icon that appears by default near the lower-right corner of the window. Each of the six types of Access windows has its own icon. A minimized window can be made the active window and thus receive the focus. You double-click the icon to restore the window to its previous dimensions, or click the icon to open the Document Control menu and then click the Maximize choice.

■ Hidden MDI child windows cannot be made active and thus cannot receive the focus. You can hide a minimized window, but when you show the minimized window, it reopens as a normal window (unless another MDI child window is open in maximized mode). You cannot hide the parent window. You hide and show forms by setting the value of the form's Visible property to No and Yes, respectively. The Database window and all design windows are hidden when you run your database application with MSARN200.EXE.

■ Pop-up windows remain on top of any other windows that you open. Examples of pop-up windows are the Access toolbars, toolbox, Properties and Field List windows, and the palette. You can move or close Access MDI child windows when you set the value of their Popup property to yes, but you cannot resize or minimize pop-up windows you create in Access. (You can use Windows API functions to resize pop-up windows.) You can, however, resize the Properties and Field List pop-up windows that appear in form and report design mode. When you minimize the parent window, modeless pop-up windows disappear.

■ Modal windows monopolize the focus and remain the active window until you close them. Thus, you can open only one modal window at a time. (But you can open a modal window from another modal window. The next chapter provides an example of this behavior.) Modeless windows, Access's default, enable you to change the focus to other open windows at will. Windows dialog boxes that you create with Access forms usually are modal pop-up windows. Windows that you create in DOS RDBMS applications usually are the equivalent of dialogs, modal pop-up windows. You can display modal pop-up windows outside the boundaries of a normal-mode parent window. Modal pop-up windows maintain their predetermined dimensions, regardless of whether other MDI child windows are open in normal or maximized mode. Opening a modal pop-up window causes the parent window to become inactive; modal conventional windows allow you to make menu choices that are applicable to the window while the modal window is open.

NOTE

When you hide a modal window by setting the `Visible` Property of the form to **False**, Access makes the window modeless before hiding the form. When you set the `Visible` property of the form to **True**, the window appears in its original modal window mode. As mentioned earlier in this chapter, showing and hiding a modal form is considerably faster than opening and closing the form.

In addition to the six basic window styles and modes, the Access documentation specifies "views" of tables, queries, forms, and reports. In this book, datasheet view, form view, and report view are called, collectively, run mode. Design view is referred to as design mode. Run mode for reports is print preview, which is not a basic windows mode. Print preview is a window that has a set of predefined properties determined primarily by the values that you establish in the Print Setup dialog. In the case of reports, you have only the choice of whether to print the report as soon as the print preview window opens.

Using the *Shell()* Function to Open Another Windows Application

When you use the **Shell**() function to launch another application from within your Access application, you can specify the mode in which you want the application to open with the *wStyle* argument as shown in the following syntax:

```
hTask = Shell(strCommand, wStyle)
```

The **Shell**() function returns the windows task handle (hTask) of the application that you launch with the value you assign to the strCommand argument. Every application that you open in Windows has a task handle. The *wStyle* argument is a set of flags, similar to those used to specify the icon and number of buttons. Table 7.8 lists valid values for the *wStyle* property of the **Shell**() function.

Table 7.8. Valid integer values of the wStyle argument of the Shell() function.

Value	Window Style	Focus
1, 5, or 9	Normal	Yes
2	Minimized	Yes
3	Maximized	Yes
4 or 8	Normal	No
6 or 9	Minimized	No

Thus the statement, hTask = **Shell**("c:\excel\excel.exe /e", 2) opens Excel, without the default Sheet1, minimized to an icon with the focus. When you launch a new application, the application joins the Windows message loop. With the **SendKeys** command, your Access application can send keystrokes to a window of another application that temporarily has the focus. You can execute menu commands and perform other operations in the application that has the focus, depending upon what keystrokes you send. Using the **SendKeys** command is one of the subjects of the next chapter.

> **TIP**
>
> The mode in which Access opens, normal or maximized, is determined by the Maximized= entry in the [Microsoft Access] section of MSACC20.INI. If Maximized=1, Access's parent window opens in maximized mode; if Maximized=0, the parent window opens in normal mode. Access alters the value of the Maximized= entry when you quit Access.

Windows Events and Messages

Windows is an event-driven messaging environment. All communication between objects in Microsoft Windows takes place in the form of Windows messages. Windows messages are identified by a WM_ prefix, such as WM_MOUSEMOVE. Most Windows messages have two elements, called parameters, that constitute the content of the message. In the case of the WM_MOUSEMOVE message, the first parameter (wParam) specifies which mouse button, if any, was clicked and whether the Control or Shift keys were depressed when the mouse was moved. The second parameter (lParam) supplies the horizontal (x-axis) and vertical (y-axis) coordinates of the position of mouse, relative to the upper-left corner of the active window.

Some Windows messages, such as WM_KEYDOWN and WM_KEYUP, usually are directed to a control object with the focus. The most common exception is an Alt+*Key* combination that represents an accelerator (also called a hot key) that emulates a mouse click on a command button or a menu element. (Ctrl+*Key* combinations that invoke menu commands, such as Ctrl+C for **E**dit **C**opy, are called shortcut keys.) Pressing the accelerator key combination for a command button bypasses the control with the focus and activates the corresponding command button. Windows has a variety of methods of indicating that a control object has the focus. For example, a command button with the focus has a dark border and the caption is enclosed in a dotted rectangle.

Windows messages are directed to the message queue. When you move the mouse, a large number of WM_MOUSEMOVE messages are added to the message queue. Windows itself intercepts these messages and moves the mouse pointer to the location specified by lParam. The application with the focus also intercepts the messages and can take a specific action. When Windows Paintbrush, for example, intercepts WM_MOUSEMOVE messages with wParam indicating that the right mouse button is depressed, Paintbrush sets pixels in the active window to black at the locations specified by lParam. After Windows and the active application receive the message, the message is removed from the message queue. Thus the message queue is called a first-in, first-out (FIFO) stack. The message being processed is at the top of the stack, and new messages are placed at the bottom of the stack in order of their occurrence.

Classifying Events of Form, Report, and Control Objects

Windows messages can be divided into two categories: messages that result directly from user actions such as clicking a menu choice or a command button, or pressing a key, and messages that result when a change of state occurs in an active application. Access responds to specific Windows messages with a particular set of parameter values by translating the Windows messages into corresponding events. This book classifies events into two types, user-initiated and application-initiated. The sections that follow describe these two classes of Access events.

> **NOTE**
>
> The names of properties and events listed in the Properties window include spaces between the preposition and the object of the preposition that constitute the name of an event. Such spaces are not included in the names of events (properties) in the Access Language Reference documentation. This book omits such spaces in all references to names of events.

User-Initiated Events

Control objects on forms and reports occupy a position and size specified by the control's Left, Top, Height, and Width properties. If, for example, the mousepointer is positioned within the area occupied by a command button, and you click and release the left mouse button, Access receives a WM_LBUTTONUP message. Access tests the lParam value, determines that the click occurred within the confines of the command button, and then triggers the OnClick event. If the value of the OnClick event of the command button on a form is the name of a macro, an Access Basic function in a module, or [Event Procedure] (indicating an event-handling subprocedure in a form or report module), Access executes the macro or Access Basic procedure. If the value of the Visible or Enabled property of a control is **False**, Access disregards the occurrence of the event. Table 7.9 lists the primary events that are applicable to control objects on forms.

Table 7.9. User-initiated events associated with control objects located on Access forms.

Event	When the Event Occurs
OnClick	Upon release of the left mouse button after clicking a control or upon depressing the access key for the control. (Holding down the access key creates repeated OnClick events.)
OnDblClick	Double-clicking a control with the mouse.
OnEnter	Immediately prior to a control receiving the focus.
OnGotFocus	When the control receives the focus.
OnExit	Immediately prior to a control losing the focus.
OnLostFocus	When the control loses the focus.
BeforeUpdate	After you have changed the value of a control but before the change to the value of the control is made permanent.

Event	*When the Event Occurs*
AfterUpdate	After a change to the value of a control is made permanent.
OnChange	When a change occurs in the value of a calculated control or you select an item from a drop-down list or a combo list.

NOTE

There are no user-initiated events for control objects located on reports. Control objects located on reports do not trigger events and none of the above events are included in the Properties window for control objects of reports.

You use the OnEnter, BeforeUpdate, or OnExit event of a control object to test whether the value of an individual control complies with domain integrity rules for the field to which the control is bound before the change to the value of the control is made permanent. Write an individual domain test event handler, either in the form of a macro or an Access Basic function, for each field whose value you need to test. Execute the event handler from one of the three events. The BeforeUpdate event is triggered only if the user changes the value of the control. Neither the OnEnter nor the OnExit event depends on the user changing the value of the control; these events result from the control obtaining and losing the focus, respectively. If you use the OnExit event, your event-handling code should include a GoToControl action to return the focus to the noncompliant control object.

TIP

You cannot rely on the OnEnter, BeforeUpdate, or OnExit events to ensure enforcement of domain integrity rules for fields or columns of updatable recordsets. The BeforeUpdate event is not triggered if the user does not change an existing invalid value. If the user changes to a new record without having changed the focus to each control object (by repeatedly pressing either the Enter or Tab keys), OnEnter and OnExit events for controls can be skipped. You need to use the OnCurrent event, described in the next section, and write an associated event handler that tests the value of each bound control on the form for which a domain integrity rule applies.

Application-Initiated Events

This book classifies application-initiated events as events that are triggered by methods, such as opening a form, or that arise as a consequence of the user-initiated events listed in the preceding section. An example of a consequential event is the BeforeUpdate event of a form that results from updating a value of a control object bound to the **Recordset** on which the form is based. Although the BeforeUpdate event might be triggered by the user clicking the Next Record navigation button, the BeforeUpdate event occurs only if preceded by a BeforeUpdate and AfterUpdate event of a bound control object. Table 7.10 lists the most commonly-used events that are applicable to forms and reports, only to forms, and only to reports.

Table 7.10. Application-initiated events that apply to forms and/or reports.

Event	*When the Event Occurs*
OnOpen	Upon opening a form or report, but before the form or report becomes visible and before the control objects on the form are accessible to macros or Access Basic code.
OnClose	Before closing a form or report.
OnCurrent	Upon opening a form or moving to another record of a form, before the new record becomes current, if the form is based on a **Recordset** (table or query). The OnCurrent event is triggered when you open any form, even if it is not bound to a table or query.
BeforeUpdate	After you have changed the value of at least one column of a **Recordset** on which the form is based but before the change to the **Recordset** is made permanent.
AfterUpdate	After you have changed the value of at least one column of a **Recordset** on which the form is based and after the change to the **Recordset** is made permanent.
OnDelete	Immediately after receipt of an instruction to delete a record from the **Recordset** on which the form is based, but before the record is deleted from the **Recordset**.
OnInsert	Immediately after you commence typing into any field of the tentative append record of the **Recordset** on which the form is based, but before the record is added to the **Recordset**.

Event	When the Event Occurs
OnEnter	Immediately before the first control in the tab order of a form receives the focus (same as the OnEnter event for a control, except that this event applies only to the control with tab order 0). Although this event is an event of a control object, it is included here because of its importance as the event that indicates when the control objects on a form are valid objects.
OnFormat	After determining the values for control objects located in a section of a report, but before creating the layout for printing of the section of the report.
OnPrint	After formatting the layout of a section but before printing that section.

NOTE

Only the OnOpen and OnClose events are shared by both forms and reports. The OnCurrent, BeforeUpdate, AfterUpdate, OnDelete, OnInsert, and OnEnter events apply to forms only. The OnFormat and OnPrint events apply only to individual sections of reports.

You can use the OnCurrent event to test each value of a field or column of a recordset for which you want to enforce domain integrity rules. Write an event handler executed by the OnCurrent event that uses the RunMacro action to execute each domain test macro or, in the context of this chapter, write an Access Basic function that calls each domain test function. This process slows moving through records, but testing each field is the only technique to assure that all domain integrity rules are enforced for each record traversed by the application. Writing validation functions for transaction processing applications is one of the subjects of the next chapter.

NOTE

You can emulate triggering an application-initiated event with Access Basic code by using the **Eval** function in an expression such as var*Temp* = **Eval**(**Mid**(Forms("*FormName*").Form("*ControlName*").OnClick)) if the

OnClick event of `ControlName` contains the name of a function. The `Mid()` function is required to strip the leading equal sign from the function call. This statement serves to demonstrate that events can return a value, but little else. It is simpler to call the function specified as the value of the `OnClick` event.

Responding to Events with Access Basic Procedures

The Access Basic code you write for an application is another collection—in this case, a collection of event-handling procedures contained in one or more modules. This book uses the term *procedure* to include both functions (`Function FunctionName()`) and subprocedures (`Sub SubprocedureName()`). As discussed in Chapter 4, "Writing Access Basic Code," Access 2.0 enables you to write event-handling code in either of the following ways:

- You can specify the Access Basic event-handling function contained in a module to be executed in response to the event by typing an equal sign (=) followed by the name of a function (=FunctionName()) in the text box associated with the name of the event. The function you specify in the event text box is called the entry point to your code. When an event calls your entry-point function, the function's return value is disregarded. You cannot use a subprocedure as the entry point to Access Basic code contained in modules. This is the traditional method of writing Access event-handling code.

- You can specify that an event-handing subprocedure be used to store your event-handling code in a module contained in the form or report in which the event occurs. This approach is used exclusively by Visual Basic. Microsoft refers to modules contained within forms or reports as code-behind-forms (CBF). As with Visual Basic, Access automatically names the subprocedure for you: Form_EventName for events that originate on forms, and ControlName_EventName for events that originate from controls. In this case, you use the Code Builder to open a subprocedure stub.

If you write an event-handling procedure that is to be used by several controls on the same or different forms, the most efficient approach is to use an event-handling function contained in a conventional Access Basic module. Another advantage to the use of event-handling functions is that all of these functions in all of your modules are loaded into Access's symbol table before your first form opens. This slows the opening of your application, but speeds opening of forms once your application has opened its first form. Form opening is slowed because of the additional overhead added by code-behind-forms. If your application has only one form, such as the Order Entry form of the MSA_OLTP.MDB example database, described in Chapter 25, "Stretching the Limits of Access," there is no appreciable difference between the performance of applications that use either location for event-handling code.

> **NOTE**
>
> You must include the equal sign and the trailing parenthesis when you specify a function to respond to an event. If you omit either the equal sign or the parenthesis, Access reformats your entry to a field reference or interprets your entry as a macro name, and you receive an error when you trigger the event.

Although your application may have a hierarchical design, in which clicking a command button on one form leads to display of another form, Windows applications do not recognize this hierarchy. All forms and Access Basic entry-point functions that respond to events on the form exist at the "top level" in Windows. The only exceptions to this rule are the Windows 3.1 common dialogs for opening and saving files, printing and printer setup, choosing fonts, and color selection. Chapter 25 describes how to use the common dialogs in your applications. If your Access Basic function requires values of control objects on another form, the form with the control objects that supply the values must be open, but can be hidden, when you execute that function. Unlike events, values of the properties of hidden forms are active; you can obtain and set property values of forms that are hidden.

The following sections describe some of the characteristics of Windows and Access Basic that you should consider when you write Access Basic event-handling functions.

Foreground and Background Processes in Functions and Procedures

Once you execute an entry-point function in response to an event, Access executes the code in the function until execution reaches the **End Function** statement of the entry-point function. At this point, Windows returns to the idle state, awaiting the next event. Windows is a multitasking environment, thus two or more functions can be executing code at the same instance. Multitasking can occur, for example, if you click a command button to execute one function while another function is in the process of executing a bulk transfer of records to another table or database. Multitasking is an important factor for DOS RDBMS programmers to consider; the majority of desktop DOS RDBMS applications do not provide multitasking capabilities.

> **NOTE**
>
> Windows NT offers a threaded, multitasking and multiprocessing environment in which multiple applications designed for use with 32-bit Windows can execute simultaneously. You can obtain increased performance with Windows NT by adding additional CPU chips, assuming your computer's motherboard has sockets for them. Unfortunately, Access 2.0 is not a 32-bit application, so Access cannot yet take full advantage of the performance enhancement offered by the Windows NT environment.

This book divides processes performed by your Access Basic code into two categories:

- Foreground processes that deal with Access objects. Foreground processes include Access methods executed by the **DoCmd** keyword or code that changes property values of control objects on forms and reports. Foreground processes send and receive Windows messages to and from your Access objects.

- Background processes that act on objects which you create with Access Basic. All code that manipulates database objects, including a clone **Dynaset** of the **Dynaset** that underlies a form or report, is a background process. Background processes do not send Windows messages to your Access objects.

Functions can contain both foreground and background processes. Background processes with complex loops can interfere with the performance of your foreground process. It is possible to lock up your application if you create an infinite loop in a background process. Execution of the infinite loop consumes virtually all the resources of your computer, preventing Windows messages, such as pressing Ctrl+Break to halt execution of your code, from reaching your application. Thus, you need to add **DoEvents** statements within loops of background processes so that Windows can process messages that accumulate in the message queue. This is the reason that you see **DoEvents** statements in many of the code examples in this book. Placing **DoEvents** statements in **Do While**, **Do Until**, and **For...Next** loops is especially important when you are testing newly written code.

Starting Your Application

You start applications that use Access Basic code in place of all avoidable macros with an AutoExec macro that contains one action, RunCode "OpenFunction()". OpenFunction() opens the main form of your application with a **DoCmd** OpenForm action. From that point, you control the opening and closing of all forms and reports, or hiding and showing forms, with Access Basic code. You can think of OpenFunction() as the "main program" of a DOS RDBMS application.

Alternately, you can open the application and execute a macro other than AutoExec with the /x MacroName command-line parameter, as discussed in Chapter 2's section, "Defining the Main Form." This gives you the opportunity to alter the behavior of your application for specific users or groups of users.

Setting the Values of Global and Module-Level Variables

Access Basic assigns default values to the global variables that you declare with the **Dim** statement in the Declarations section of your modules when you open the application database. Module-level variables come into existence the first time you execute code contained in the module. The default value of numeric variables is 0; for String variables the default is the empty string (""). **Variant** variables that have not received values are subtype 0 (Empty). You cannot initialize the value of global and module-level variables in the Declarations section.

If other functions or procedures depend on the values of global and module-level variables, you need to execute a function that assigns values to these variables before the dependent functions or subprocedures execute. The most straightforward methods of setting the values of such variables are as follows:

- Initialize the values of variables in the function that you execute with the RunCode action of the AutoExec macro (`OpenFunction()`)
- Initialize the values of variables in a subprocedure that you **Call** from any of the functions that are executed by the macros you specify on the command line of your application with the /x parameter
- Add a RunCode action that executes a function devoted to initializing the values of global and module-level variables

Visibility of Objects When Opening Forms

Applications that combine macros to open forms and Access Basic code that refers to values of control objects opened by a macro action can encounter problems that cause "Invalid object reference" or "Object has no value" messages when your Access Basic code executes. The most common cause of these errors is the use of the OnOpen event of the form to execute a function that refers to the value of a control object on the form. The OnOpen event is triggered before the form is opened; thus neither the form nor the control objects on the form have values when your code executes. Use the OnEnter event of the control object that is first in the tab order (receives the focus when the form opens) to execute the Access Basic function, rather than the OnOpen event of the form.

> **NOTE**
>
> It is a better programming practice to open forms with **DoCmd** OpenForm action in Access Basic than to combine OpenForm macro actions and Access Basic functions that interact with the form.

Passing Parameters to Access Basic Event-Handling Functions

You can pass literal numeric and character values, and values of control objects that possess values, to Access Basic entry-point functions. Passing parameters in your entry-point function call is useful to identify which event called a multipurpose function. You can pass form names, control names, or values of control objects as parameters of entry point functions. You need to write your entry-point function so that it accepts the arguments, and each time you call the function, you need to supply the same number of arguments. (Access Basic does not provide for optional arguments of functions and parameters of subprocedures, although most intrinsic Access Basic functions and statements have optional arguments or parameters.)

For example, you can use the same function to respond differently to each of two or more superimposed command buttons by supplying the caption of the command button as an argument to the event-handler. Type `=FunctionName("Caption")` or `=FunctionName(Screen.ActiveControl.Caption)` in the text box for the `OnClick` event. Your entry-point function, **Function** *FunctionName* (strCaption **As String**) takes the appropriate action based on the value of strCaption.

NOTE

Most event-handling subprocedures do not receive argument values through parameters. Those that do, such as the `Form_MouseMove()` subprocedure, have parameter values specified by and supplied by the event. Thus event-handling functions are more flexible than event-handling subprocedures. On the other hand, writing an event-handler to emulate the `Form_MouseMove()` subprocedure is a major exercise, involving declaring and calling many Windows API functions.

III

Creating Effective Forms and Reports

P

III

8

Optimizing Transaction-Processing Forms

This book defines transaction-processing applications as any applications that can add new records to tables or edit the values contained in the fields of an existing table. Decision-support applications, the subject of the next chapter, read but do not write to tables. Another method of differentiating between the two applications is how you open databases or tables with your application. Transaction-processing applications require read-write permissions; decision-support applications use read-only permissions. If you are using Access to create client-server front-end applications, the majority of your forms are likely to be the decision-support type. Database administrators often are unwilling, at least initially, to trust the integrity of data on the server to applications created with a new desktop RDBMS. The reluctance remains, even if data integrity is enforced primarily by stored procedures and triggers that are part of the database on the server. If you are designing new Access applications, however, the pendulum swings in the transaction-processing direction. When you create the application, you are likely to be the initial database administrator, and therefore you can do with your data what you will. This chapter describes how to design forms and write Access Basic code to optimize transaction processing, ensure referential and domain integrity, and assist in maintaining data accuracy. The chapter closes with a demonstration of how to create Access transaction logs that enable you to reconstruct data that is lost in the event of a fixed-disk hardware failure.

Designing Forms for Transaction-Processing Applications

The majority of Access transaction-processing applications run in online mode rather than the more traditional batch mode. Online transaction-processing (OLTP) means that the records in the tables of the database are updated immediately upon entry of new or revised data. In batch mode, your application creates a set of records containing new or revised records. After a validity test, the application adds or updates the records to the tables by the equivalent of append and update queries, respectively. All the examples presented in this chapter are OLTP applications (except the transaction log example at the end of the chapter, which involves batch transactions).

> **NOTE**
>
> You can emulate batch-mode operation by writing an application that delays execution of the `CommitTrans` statement until completion of a specified set of entries, or until the operator clicks a command button. Unless you save the entries in a temporary table, the entries will be lost in the event of a system crash or power failure.

The majority of online transaction-processing forms fall into the following three categories:

■ *Interactive forms,* which combine transaction processing with the ability to review previously entered information. Personal information management (PIM), scheduling, and other types of list-processing applications fall into this category. Interactive forms often are used for live data entry, such as telephone-order entry and reservation systems. Live data-entry systems usually include subforms, or their equivalent, to list available items.

■ *Input-only forms,* which are used for heads-down data entry. The term "heads-down" means that data-entry operators concentrate their attention on a document that represents the source of the data, rather than on the video display unit (VDU). The epitome of a heads-down data-entry system is the almost-obsolete IBM 029 keypunch, which had only a keyboard and bins for blank and punched cards.

■ *Data-validation forms,* which are used to inspect and correct errors in imported or other batched data. The source data for these forms may be created by exception testing; only those records that fail domain integrity or other data validity tests are included in the set of records to be reviewed and edited.

The sections that follow give examples of the principles applicable to designing each of these three general types of forms for Windows applications.

Forms for Interactive Data Entry

Figure 8.1 depicts an OLTP form to maintain a list of multimedia-related products for Windows 3.1. The form (frmSuppliers) and two subforms (frmProductDetails and frmContactDetails) are based on three underlying tables. These tables contain information on multimedia hardware and software suppliers (tblSuppliers) and products (tblProducts), and supplier contacts who can provide information about new and upgraded products (tblContacts). The Multimedia Suppliers form and the Access Basic code that supports its operation is included in the MULTIMED.MDB database on the accompanying diskette. The tables for the form are attached from the DMM_DATA.MDB database. The Multimedia Suppliers form and its supporting database objects are used in the majority of the form-design and code examples presented in this chapter. A previous version of MULTIMED.MDB and DMM_DATA.MDB appeared in the April 1993 issue of *Access Advisor* magazine. (For more information about this magazine, see Appendix A, "Access Resources.")

> **NOTE**
>
> The linkage to the tables attached to MULTIMED.MDB requires that DMM_DATA.MDB be located in C:\ACCESS\ADG20. If you place DMM_DATA.MDB in a directory other than C:\ACCESS\ADG20, use the Attachment Manager to change the linkage to the current location. You also need to change the value of the global LOOK_UPS_DB constant in the Declarations section of the Suppliers module to point to the location of the LOOK_UPS.MDB file.

FIGURE 8.1.

An online transaction-processing form for multimedia suppliers and products.

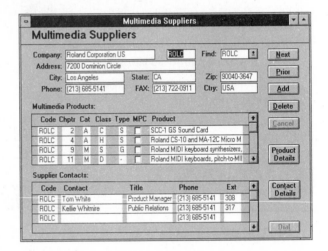

A four-letter code is assigned to each supplier firm based on the first three characters of the first word and the first character of the second word of the firm's name. The code is the primary key field of tblSuppliers. Products are classified by a three-letter key, consisting of category, class, and type. Each record in tblProducts includes the supplier code in a foreign key field. There is no primary key field for tblProducts because suppliers often produce a variety of products of a given type.

In addition to the main form and two subforms, the Multimedia Suppliers form has a number of subsidiary forms that show data contained in lookup tables. Modal pop-up forms display information from lookup tables for book chapters (frmChapter, based on tblChapter) and product categories (frmCategories), classes (frmClasses), and types (frmTypes), all of which use tblCategories as their data source. Two additional modal pop-up forms (frmProductDetails and frmContactDetails) enable you to add additional information about products and supplier contacts (see Figure 8.2.).

FIGURE 8.2.

The Contact Details and DMM Chapters modal pop-up forms.

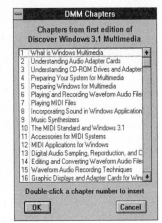

Substituting Command Buttons for Record Selectors

Record-selector keys are the only choice for traversing records of tables and queries in datasheet view. When you design forms, the default record-selector buttons offer simplicity at the expense of usability. Record-selector buttons are small and thus are a difficult target to hit for those unaccustomed to using a mouse. The VCR symbols to choose the first, previous, next, and last records underlying a form or a subform are not intuitive for all users. Adding a new record by clicking the "fast forward" and then the next-record button is even less intuitive. Thus the majority of developers dispense with Access's default record-selector buttons and substitute Next, Previous, and Add command buttons for basic record manipulation.

There is seldom a need to add First and Last buttons on transaction-processing forms; you normally want to add a record or find a specific record quickly. In most cases, Access's versatile combo-box control is the answer to finding a record. Using a pre-defined query object, rather than an SQL statement, as the value of the RowSource property can speed operation of the combo box, because the predefined query eliminates the time necessary to create an internal **QueryDef** from the SQL statement each time you open the combo box.

> **TIP**
>
> Hide Access's default record navigation buttons and do not add First or Last buttons to forms that are based on tables with a very large number of records. Traversing the entire recordset causes each record in the table to be processed. Moving from the top to the bottom of a recordset based on large tables causes a burst of traffic on networks and can interfere with the performance of other users' networked applications.

Grouping Controls for Ease of Use

Another reason for using command buttons rather than record selectors, especially on full-screen forms, is that considerable mouse movement is required to reach the record navigation buttons at the bottom left of the form. When quickly scanning a form to determine its content, the user initially focuses at the upper-left of the form, and then scans the form as if reading text in a book. (Arabic speakers are likely to focus at the upper-right corner.) Thus, the text boxes that contain the information that identifies a record should be grouped in the upper-left corner of the form.

Record-manipulation command buttons also should be grouped, either in a column at the right of the form, or in a row at the top or bottom of the form. The bottom of the form is the conventional position for a row of buttons; this position does not interfere with top-to-bottom scanning. The Multimedia Suppliers form uses the column approach. The combo box to select a record is adjacent to the Next button so a minimum of mouse movement is required to find the next or previous record if you choose the wrong code.

Providing Accelerator Keys for Command Buttons

Many users prefer the keyboard to the mouse as the primary means of selecting control objects on forms. Requiring the user to remove his or her hands from the keyboard to click a command button reduces data-entry efficiency. Therefore you should specify a unique accelerator-key combination for every command button on your form. Windows accelerator keys (Alt+Key combinations) are related to short-cut key (Ctrl+Key) combinations that substitute for menu choices. Accelerator keys are particularly important for the heads-down data-entry forms that are discussed in a section that follows shortly.

You specify an accelerator key by preceding a letter or number of the caption of the command button with the ampersand (&) character. The accelerator key is indicated by an underlined character. It is traditional to use the first letter of the command button's caption as the accelerator key, when possible. Using arbitrary combinations of keys to create single-handed accelerator-key combinations is discussed in the section of this chapter devoted to heads-down data entry.

> **TIP**
>
> You can specify an accelerator key for control objects with associated labels by specifying the accelerator key in the label for the control. Accelerator keys are assigned to each of the text boxes and the combo box of the Multimedia Suppliers form. Some ingenuity is required in the selection of accelerator

keys for objects whose labels have initial letters that are the same as those of the captions of command buttons.

Setting the Tab Order

Using the Tab key to shift the focus to control objects in a specific sequence is a standard feature of Windows. You choose the control object that receives the focus when the window opens as well as the sequence in which control objects receive the focus with the Tab Order dialog. Only controls whose TabStop property is set to Yes are included in the Tab Order dialog. You open the Tab Order dialog with the Tab Order choice of the Edit menu. The tab order for the controls of the Multimedia Suppliers form is shown in Figure 8.3.

FIGURE 8.3.

A portion of the tab order for the Multimedia Suppliers form.

The first control object in the tab order, the record-selection combo box (cboCodes), receives the focus when you open the form. The position of the combo box and the Next and Prior buttons enables these controls to be grouped in a logical sequence to manipulate the record pointer. The two subforms are the next most commonly used control objects, so they are next in the tab order. When you click the Add button to add a new supplier, you need to enter the company name first so that the application can calculate and test a new code for uniqueness. Therefore the cmdAddSupp, txtCompany, and txtCode controls follow in tab order.

NOTE

Once you tab your way into a subform, the focus remains within the subform. When the focus is in a subform control object, press Ctrl+Tab to move out of the subform to the next control object. Shift+Tab and Ctrl+Shift+Tab execute the tab order in reverse sequence.

Adding the Default and Cancel Properties to Command Buttons

Command buttons have two properties that are shared by no other control objects: `Default` and `Cancel`. Pressing the Enter key on a form that has a command button with its `Default` property set to `True` causes the button's `OnClick` event to be triggered. The event triggers even if a text box has the focus; the Enter key completes the update to the text box and then triggers the command button's `OnClick` event (formerly OnPush in Access 1.x). If you set the `Cancel` property of a command button to **True**, pressing the Escape key triggers the button's `OnClick` event. The Multimedia Suppliers form has no default command button; the `Cancel` property of the Cancel button is set to **True**, as one might expect.

Only one command button can have its `Default` or `Cancel` property set to **True**. You can set both the `Default` and `Cancel` properties of a single command button to **True**, however. You use this combination on forms that make permanent changes to a record. If a command button's `Visible` or `Enabled` properties are set to **False**, events that ordinarily would be triggered by buttons with `Default` or `Cancel` properties set to **True** are inhibited.

Using Continuous Subforms

When you create a form/subform combination with the FormWizard, the default view of the subform is set to datasheet. Using the datasheet view of subforms results in inelegant form designs. In addition, the record-selector buttons of the subform occupy vertical space on the form that could be used to display another subform record. Few, if any, commercial applications employ datasheet views of subforms.

Creating continuous subforms to replace the default datasheet view is labor-intensive, but it is well worth the effort. Your forms gain a consistent appearance and you gain the ability to use versatile text boxes, rather than a fixed datasheet grid, to display data. Table 8.1 lists the recommended properties settings for subforms. These settings are employed in the sbfProducts and sbfContacts subforms of the Multimedia Suppliers form (frmSuppliers).

Table 8.1. Recommended settings for subform properties.

Property	Setting	Comments
DefaultView	ContinuousForms	Adds style and flexibility.
DefaultEditing	AllowEdits	Unless not needed.
AllowEditing	Available	Unless subform is read-only.
AllowUpdating	DefaultTables	Allow edits to bound table.
ScrollBars	VerticalOnly	Eliminate record selectors.

Property	Setting	Comments
ViewsAllowed	Forms	Prevents change to datasheet view.
BackColor	Same as form	For all sections of form.
BackColor	Same as text boxes	For text boxes that you can edit; otherwise the same BackColor as the form.
Border	**False**	For text boxes; borders are distracting.
RecordSelectors	**False**	Use code to select the record.
NavigationButtons	False	Use command buttons and code to manipulate the record pointer.
Width	Same as subform	Manually setting the control width of the subform to that of the subform control makes layout easier.

NOTE

Access 2.0 enables you to specify a horizontal scrollbar without displaying the navigation buttons. This was not possible in Access 1.x.

Replacing Command Buttons with the *OnDblClick* Event

If you add command buttons to forms, and especially to headers or footers of continuous subforms, your form becomes cluttered with buttons. An excessive number of buttons on a form is distracting to users and causes "choice crises" when an action is required. Another problem arises when you want to open a form or take other action that is dependent on the position of the caret in the grid of a subform.

TIP

The Multimedia Suppliers application and the majority of the other database applications in this book use functions contained in modules to handle events that occur on forms. Access 2.0 provides the option of using form or report modules (code-behind-forms) in which you can write event-handling subprocedures, a process similar to that used by Visual Basic. Adding substantial amounts of code to form or report modules slows the opening of the form or report. On the other hand, opening conventional (global) modules slows the opening of your application. Slowing the opening of the application usually is preferable, because the user only opens the application once, whereas forms and reports may be opened and closed many times during use of the application.

You can use the double-click event of a text box to take an action that is specific to the content of the text box. For example, double-clicking the Code field of a record in either of the subforms of Multimedia Suppliers opens a message box that enables you to choose to delete the underlying record. Double-clicking the Chapter field of the Products subform opens the DMM Chapters modal pop-up form. Double-clicking the name of a contact opens the Contact Details form with details for the specified contact displayed. Both these subsidiary forms are illustrated in Figure 8.2, which appeared previously. The OnDblClick event of the Contact field of sbfContacts executes the mms_OpenToContact() function. The code for the mms_OpenToContact() function is as follows:

```
Function mms_OpenToContact ()
    'Purpose:   Open the Contact Details form to the selected contact
    'Called by: OnDblClick event of the Contact field of sbfContacts
    'Note:      Original version created by Andrew Miller's Macro to
    '           Module converter function of FIRSTLIB.MDA (edits
    '           ➥required)

    On Error GoTo mms_OpenToContact_Err

    'Test for an entry in the Contact field
    If IsNull(Forms![frmSuppliers]![sbfContacts].Form![Contact]) Then
        DoCmd Beep
        MsgBox "A record with a valid contact name is required.", 32,
        ➥"Contact Details Open Error"
        Exit Function
    Else
        'Save changes made to the underlying record (File Save Changes)
        'MSA20: Save Record is not enabled in Access 2.0 unless record
        ➥is altered
        'DoCmd DoMenuItem 0, 0, 4, 0
    End If
```

```
    If IsLoaded("frmContactDetails") Then
        'Show the hidden form
        Forms!frmContactDetails.Visible = True
        'Requery to set the proper (current) record
        DoCmd Requery
    Else
        'Open the form and apply a filter to specify the record
        DoCmd OpenForm "frmContactDetails", 0, "",
    ➡"[Code]=Forms![frmSuppliers]![Code] And
    ➡[Contact]=Forms![frmSuppliers]![sbfContacts].Form![Contact]",
    ➡1, 0
    End If
    'Display the short version of the form
    DoCmd MoveSize , , , 5328

    'Shift focus to the Hide button (used to demonstrate a phenomenon)
    DoCmd GoToControl "cmdHide"

    'Set the contact status check and text boxes
    wRetVal = mms_SetContactStatus()

mms_OpenToContact_Exit:
    Exit Function

mms_OpenToContact_Err:
    MsgBox "Error: " + Error$
    Resume mms_OpenToContact_Exit
End Function
```

NOTE

New!

The MULTIMED.MDB application was created with Access 1.1. Alterations to version 1.1 code that are required in order to conform to Access 2.0 programming standards are noted in all of the code examples of this book by a comment that begins with 'MSA20:. In the preceding listing, the **DoCmd DoMenuItem 0, 0, 4, 0** statement that saves the current record prior to opening a subsidiary form has been commented out. Access 2.0's File Save Record menu choice is enabled only if you alter the data in the current record. Access 1.1 enables you to save a record at any time. To find the code changes made in the modules for the Multimedia application to accommodate Access 2.0, search for MSA20: in All Loaded Modules.

NOTE

Many of the functions included in the Suppliers module of MULTIMED.MDB are converted from an original set of macros that performed similar operations. The functions were created with the Macro to Module Converter component of Andrew Miller's FIRSTLIB.MDA library, as described in Chapter 3, "Using Libraries, Wizards, Builders, and Add-Ins." Functions converted from macros have an additional label prior to the first **Exit Function** statement. Converted functions use literal references to forms and control objects. The macros from which the functions were created are included in the Suppliers macrogroup of DMM_DATA.MDB.

The critical line in the `mms_OpenToContact()` function begins with **DoCmd** `OpenForm`, which is executed when you open the form. In this case, a filter is applied to the **DoCmd** `OpenForm` method so that the record that underlies the form corresponds to the current record. When you hide and then show the form, the **DoCmd** `Requery` method sets the underlying record to the current record of the subform. The **DoCmd** `MoveSize` method shortens the form to hide the Next, Prior, and Add buttons that are not applicable when you display a form for a specific individual. These buttons are visible when you open frmContactDetails with the Contact Details button.

TIP

You can set the `AutoCenter` property of the form to **True** in order to cause the form to be centered horizontally within Access 2.0's window upon opening. The form is not centered vertically, however. The top margin is set to one half the size of the bottom margin; one third of the vertical "white space" appears above the form and two thirds appears below the form. (Access 1.1's problem with progressive vertical relocation of forms when showing and hiding them has been eliminated in Access 2.0.)

Setting the Enabled Property of Command Buttons

Only those command buttons that are appropriate for the present status of the form need be and should be enabled. Therefore the Cancel button of the Multimedia Suppliers form is enabled only after you click the Add button to add a new record to tblSuppliers. The Prior button should be disabled when the first record is displayed, and the Next button disabled when the last record is current. This takes a bit of doing, because you want to detect when the current record is the first record or the last record of the underlying **Recordset** object.

> **NOTE**
>
> You can use the mcrAutoOpen macro of MULTIMED.MDB to open the Multimedia Suppliers form instead of double-clicking frmSuppliers in the Database window. The mcrAutoOpen macro uses the RunCode action to call the mms_AutoOpen() function that opens frmSuppliers. The OnOpen event of the frmSuppliers form executes the mms_wInitialize() function that creates the clone **Recordset**, and establishes the initial values of the **Bookmark** variables for the first and last record of the clone **Recordset**. The values of these variables are lost when you recompile or reinitialize the code. Run mcrAutoOpen or close and reopen frmSuppliers to re-create these variables. Rename the mcrAutoOpen macro to AutoExec if you want the form to open automatically when you load MULTIMED.MDB.

To properly control the **Enabled** property of the Prior and Next buttons, you first need to create a clone **Recordset** object and store the values of the Bookmark properties of the first and last records of the **Recordset**. Access 2.0's RecordsetClone property replaces the Dynaset property of a form. (The Dynaset property is retained for compatibility with Access 1.1 code.) Moving from the first to the last record violates the maxim that was mentioned earlier in this chapter: "Don't traverse all records in large recordsets." With a table that contains less than 1,000 or so records, you can use a procedure such as mms_GetBookmarks, as follows:

```
Sub mms_GetBookmarks ()
    'Purpose:   Create a clone of the Dynaset that underlies the form
    '           Get the Bookmark values of the first and last records
    'Called by: mms_AutoOpen(), mms_AddSupp(), and mms_CnclSupp()
    'Note:      dsClone, varFirstCode, and varLastCode have module-level
               ➥scope

    Set dsClone = Forms("frmSuppliers").RecordsetClone
    dsClone.MoveFirst
    varFirstCode = dsClone.Bookmark
    dsClone.MoveLast
    varLastCode = dsClone.Bookmark
End Sub
```

> **NOTE**
>
> You can test **Forms**("FormName").EOF or **Forms**("FormName").BOF, except that the Enabled property of the buttons should be set when the record pointer reaches the first or last record. If you use the EOF or BOF properties for the test, the buttons remain enabled even if the record pointer is on the first or last record. If you use EOF or BOF, you also need to move the record pointer back to the first or last record. Use an EOF test rather than the last record Bookmark value to avoid the record-traversal problem mentioned previously.

Each function that can move the record pointer needs to test whether the current record is the first or last record. You use code such as that contained in the mms_TestPrevSupp procedure for position testing:

```
Sub mms_TestPrevSupp ()
    'Purpose:    Test if the current record is the first record
    'Called by: cmdPriorSupp button and use of cboCodes
    '           Also called when adding or deleting records

    If Forms!frmSuppliers.Bookmark <> varFirstCode Then
        'Blank the combo box if you move off a selected record
        Forms!frmSuppliers![cboCodes] = Null
        Forms!frmSuppliers!cmdNextSupp.Enabled = True
    Else
        'Disable the Prior button when you reach the first record
        DoCmd GoToControl "cmdNextSupp"
        Forms!frmSuppliers!cmdPriorSupp.Enabled = False
    End If
End Sub
```

You call mms_TestPrevSupp from the event handler for the OnClick event of the Prior button, mms_PrevSupp(), the listing for which is as follows:

```
Function mms_PrevSupp ()
    'Purpose:    Event handler for Prior record pushbutton

    On Error GoTo mms_PrevSupp_Err

    'Move the previous record
    DoCmd GoToRecord 2, "frmSuppliers", 0

    'Enable the Prior button
    Forms!frmSuppliers!cmdPriorSupp.Enabled = True

    'Check to see if you're on the first record
    Call mms_TestPrevSupp

mms_PrevSupp_Exit:
```

```
    Exit Function

mms_PrevSupp_Err:
    MsgBox "Error: " + Error$
    Resume mms_PrevSupp_Exit
End Function
```

Short procedures that handle the OnClick event of command buttons, such as the two preceding functions, are logical candidates for inclusion in forms. Placing the code of the two preceding examples in the frmSuppliers module enables you to substitute the self-referencing reserved word **Me** for the explicit designation of the form, Forms!frmSuppliers or Forms("frmSuppliers"). The ability to use **Me** to refer to the underlying form minimizes typing. Variables in conventional modules that have module-level scope must be assigned **Global** scope so that these variables are visible to the modules behind your forms. The following cmdNextSupp_Click subprocedure in the frmSuppliers module is the equivalent of the mms_NextSupp() function in the Suppliers module:

```
Sub cmdNextSupp_Click ()
    On Error GoTo mms_NextSupp_Err

    'Go to the next record
    DoCmd GoToRecord 2, "frmSuppliers", 1

    'Enable the Prior button
    Me!cmdPriorSupp.Enabled = True

    'Don't do it if you're on the last record
    Call mms_TestNextSupp

mms_NextSupp_Exit:
    Exit Sub

mms_NextSupp_Err:
    MsgBox "Error: " + Error$
    Resume mms_NextSupp_Exit

End Sub
```

When you make a choice of a supplier from the Find combo box (cboCodes), the new supplier that you choose could be either the first or the last supplier in the list. Following is the listing for the mms_FindCode() function, which makes the record for the supplier code that is chosen from the combo box the selected record:

```
Function mms_FindCode ()
    'Purpose:    Make the record selected in the combo box the current
    ➥record

    On Error GoTo mms_FindCode_Err

    'Set the focus to the Code text box (or somewhere else)
    DoCmd GoToControl "txtCode"

    'Find the record with the value of the code selected in cboCodes
    DoCmd FindRecord Forms("frmSuppliers").Form.[cboCodes], 1, 0, 1, 0,
    ➥0, -1

    'Set the Enabled property of both buttons to True
    'Note: This prevents errors that occur on moving the focus to a
    ➥disabled control
    Forms!frmSuppliers!cmdPriorSupp.Enabled = True
    Forms!frmSuppliers!cmdNextSupp.Enabled = True

    'Check the button status and set the Enabled property accordingly
    If Forms!frmSuppliers.Bookmark = varFirstCode Then
        Forms!frmSuppliers!cmdPriorSupp.Enabled = False
    Else
        Forms!frmSuppliers!cmdPriorSupp.Enabled = True
    End If
    If Forms!frmSuppliers.Bookmark = varLastCode Then
        Forms!frmSuppliers!cmdNextSupp.Enabled = False
    Else
        Forms!frmSuppliers!cmdNextSupp.Enabled = True
    End If

mms_FindCode_Exit:
    Exit Function

mms_FindCode_Err:
    MsgBox "Error: " + Error$
    Resume mms_FindCode_Exit
End Function
```

The event-handling subprocedure version of the mms_FindCode() function is given in the following listing:

```
Sub cboCodes_AfterUpdate ()
    'Purpose:    Make the record selected in the combo box the current
    ➥record

On Error GoTo mms_FindCode_Err
```

```
    If IsNull(Me![cboCodes]) Then
        Exit Sub
    End If

    'Set the focus to the Code text box
    DoCmd GoToControl "txtCode"

    'Find the record corresponding to the value of the code selected in
    ➥cboCodes
    DoCmd FindRecord Me.[cboCodes], 1, 0, 1, 0, 0, -1

    'Set the Enabled property of both buttons to True
    'Note: This prevents errors that occur on moving the focus to a
    ➥disabled control
    Me.cmdPriorSupp.Enabled = True
    Me.cmdNextSupp.Enabled = True

    'Check the button status and set the Enabled property accordingly
    If Me.Bookmark = varFirstCode Then
        Me!cmdPriorSupp.Enabled = False
    Else
        Me!cmdPriorSupp.Enabled = True
    End If
    If Me.Bookmark = varLastCode Then
        Me!cmdNextSupp.Enabled = False
    Else
        Me!cmdNextSupp.Enabled = True
    End If

mms_FindCode_Exit:
    Exit Sub

mms_FindCode_Err:
    MsgBox "Error: " + Error$
    Resume mms_FindCode_Exit

End Sub
```

Using the **Me** reserved word to refer to the form is particularly efficient in this case. Both varFirstCode and varLastCode must be declared as **Global** variables in the Declarations section of the Suppliers module so that the variables are visible to the form module.

TIP

If you're converting Access 1.1 code to Access 2.0, you can copy the code between **Function...End Function** to the Clipboard, then paste it into the event-handling subprocedure stub for the event. You need to delete the existing function call (=mms_FindCode() in the preceding example), then click the ellipsis button and select Code Builder in the Choose Builder dialog box. Paste the code between the **Sub** *ControName_EventName*...**End Sub** statements. Access automatically changes any instances of **Function** in your code to **Sub**.

You need to call mms_GetBookmarks to create an updated clone **Recordset** when you add or delete a record from tblSuppliers. The mms_AddSave() function, called by the OnClick event of the cmdAddOK button, creates a new set of bookmarks for the first and last records of the form's **Recordset**. You need to save the record, then apply the **DoCmd** Requery method to the form or use the Select All Records choice of the Records menu with the **DoCmd** DoMenuItem method to reposition the added record from its temporary location at the end of the **Dynaset** to its permanent place in the order of the primary key. The listing for the mms_AddSave() function is as follows:

```
Function mms_AddSave ()
    'Purpose:   Save the added record and recreate the bookmarks
    'Called by: OnClick event of the cmdAddOK button

    Dim strCode As String

    On Error GoTo mms_AddSave_Err

    'Save the record and the code
    strCode = Forms("frmSuppliers").[Code]
    DoCmd DoMenuItem A_FORMBAR, A_FILE, A_SAVERECORD

    'Disable repainting of the form
    Forms("frmSuppliers").Painting = False

    'Place the record in sequence of the primary key (Show All Records)
    DoCmd DoMenuItem A_FORMBAR, A_RECORDSMENU, 5

    'Make the added record the current record
    DoCmd GoToControl "txtCode"
    DoCmd FindRecord strCode, A_ENTIRE, False, A_DOWN,
    ➥False, A_CURRENT, True

    'Enable repainting of the form
    Forms("frmSuppliers").Painting = True

    'Reset the bookmarks (You may have added a first or last record)
    Call mms_GetBookmarks

    'Hide the OK button and show the Add button (enabled)
    Forms("frmSuppliers").cmdAddOK.Visible = False
    Forms("frmSuppliers").cmdAddSupp.Visible = True
    Forms("frmSuppliers").cmdAddSupp.Enabled = True
```

```
    Call mms_EnableBtns(True)
    Exit Function

mms_AddSave_Err:
    MsgBox "Error: " & Error$
    Exit Function
End Function
```

> **NOTE**
>
> The Painting property of a form does not appear in the Properties window for forms. Setting the Painting property of a form to **False** is similar to applying the **DoCmd** Echo False method. The Painting property applies only to a single form, whereas the **DoCmd** Echo False method freezes the display of all the open forms of your application.

Optimizing Form Design for "Heads-Down" Data Entry

All the preceding recommendations for interactive transaction-processing forms also apply to forms designed for high-speed, heads-down data entry. Following are a few recommendations to help achieve maximum data-entry efficiency:

■ Choose a monospace rather than a proportionally spaced typeface, in at least a 10-point font, for data-entry text boxes. Apply the bold attribute to the text boxes to increase legibility. The advantage of monospace typefaces is that the characters "i," "l," and "1," for example, are easier to distinguish.

■ If you base the heads-down form on an interactive form design, remove all unneeded buttons and fields from the new form. The ideal data-entry form has two buttons: Save (the record) and Cancel (the addition).

■ If you use subforms to add records to related tables, use the value of the primary key field as the default value of the foreign key field of the related tables.

■ Use single-handed accelerator key combinations that do not require the data-entry operator to place his or her hand in an unnatural position. Neither of the Alt keys on a conventional 101-key keyboard are in an ideal location. Some operators will prefer the left and some will prefer the right Alt key. If you use attached tables, you can create two databases with forms that differ only in the accelerator-key combinations, in case the choice of which Alt key to use becomes an issue. Optimizing accelerator-key combinations helps to minimize occurrences of Carpel Tunnel Syndrome.

■ If the form is to be used exclusively for entering new records, set the value of the **DefaultEditing** property of the form to DataEntry. DataEntry mode restricts both the form and subforms, if any, from displaying existing records; only the tentative append record of the underlying table(s) appears. DataEntry mode is much faster than AllowEdits mode for adding new records to tables with a large number of records.

■ Keep the form as small as possible, consistent with adequate area to contain text boxes, and open the form as a normal (rather than a maximized) window. This enables the data-entry operator to reposition the form on the display; the capability to change the position of the form minimizes fatigue.

■ Do not set the **Default** property of any command buttons on the form to **True**. Most data-entry operators are accustomed to completing field entries with the Enter key. If the **Default** property of a command button is set **True**, pressing the Enter key executes the command button's OnClick event, instead of completing the entry for a field.

Figure 8.4 shows a simple, high-speed, data-entry-only form using the Courier New typeface in a 10-point bold font. When you use DataEntry editing, you need only the Save and Cancel buttons. Add a Close or a Quit button if you don't use a menu choice to exit the application.

Designing Data-Validation Forms

Data-validation forms combine features that are applicable to both interactive and high-speed data-entry forms. In many cases, the tables bound to data-validation forms store data that is imported from other sources, such as worksheets or text files, in a temporary file. Once the validation process is complete, you append the validated data to production tables with append queries and then delete the records from the temporary tables. Alternately, you can use a Yes/No field to flag unvalidated records in the tables, and then use a filter in the **DoCmd** OpenTable method to display only the unvalidated records.

FIGURE 8.4.

A simple data-entry form for heads-down use.

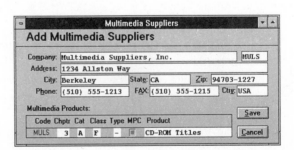

Data validation usually does not involve adding new records to tables; only the editing of existing records is permitted. There is no simple method in Access, such as setting a subform property, to restrict the adding of new records to tables that are bound to subforms. To prevent addition of new records to subforms, you need to create a non-updatable query. For example, to preclude the addition of new records to tblProducts in the sbfProducts subform, you create a query in which the Code field is from the tblSuppliers file, and the balance of the fields are from tblProducts. Then change the **RecordSource** property of sbfProducts to the non-updatable query. The qryValidation query included in MULTIMED.MDB is an example of a non-updatable query.

> **NOTE**
>
> In the context of the preceding paragraph, an updatable query is a query to which you can add a new record. You can edit data of fields of records that are contained in the table on the many sides of most non-updatable one-to-many queries. Technically, the term "non-appendable" is more accurate than "non-updatable" for describing queries to which you cannot add new records.

Separating Transaction-Processing and Decision-Support Applications

Decision-support applications usually do not make changes to values of tables; therefore, precautions that are necessary when updating database records do not apply to decision-support applications. Some Access database applications may contain both transaction-processing and decision-support functions. It is advisable to separate the two types of database applications, for the following reasons:

- The user can open databases in read-only mode for most decision-support applications. This reduces the memory requirements of your application and often speeds data access, especially with large tables. All **Recordset** objects created from databases opened in read-only mode are of the **Snapshot** type.

- Access to transaction-processing applications can be controlled at the network level. This avoids the complex security issues associated with granting specific users or groups permissions on individual objects within databases. Corporate officers often become irate when they receive messages that read "You do not have permission to view this object." You can avoid such messages by allowing network access to data-entry applications only to those persons who are authorized to enter data.

■ Decision-support functions from multiple dual-purpose databases can be combined into a single decision-support database.

■ The size of a transaction-processing database is reduced by the removal of decision-support elements. This reduces the memory requirements of the transaction-processing database and can speed operations, especially on computers with less than 8MB of RAM.

■ Large lookup tables that are used to maintain data accuracy need not be included in decision-support applications. If lookup tables are included in libraries, you need not attach the library when users run decision-support applications. Lookup tables are the subject of the section called "Using Lookup Tables to Enforce Data Accuracy," later in this chapter.

The following sections describe the methods that you can use to separate dual-purpose databases into individual transaction-processing and decision-support applications. These methods also apply to optimizing the design of both transaction-processing and decision-support databases, so the methods appear in this chapter, rather than in the next chapter, which deals solely with decision-support applications.

Removing Decision-Support Elements from a Dual-Purpose Database

It is a common practice among Access developers to include all database objects that are used with a particular set of related tables in a single Access database. This practice simplifies the installation and maintenance of the database. As users add new entries to the tables and you add new features to the application, the size of the Access database grows. As the database increases in size, performance begins to deteriorate, especially when users run the application on computers with less than 8MB of memory. Users then complain that data-entry efficiency is decreasing, but management is often reluctant to authorize memory or CPU upgrades to users' computer hardware. When members of management complain that the decision-support elements of your application are "bogging down," you need to take immediate action.

The most direct approach to separating transaction-processing and decision-support applications is by following these steps:

1. Create a new decision-support database.

2. Import the objects that are required for decision support from the dual-purpose database to the new database. You can delete unneeded decision-support objects from the transaction-processing database.

3. Attach the necessary tables to the decision-support database from the transaction-processing database. Make sure that the attached tables are located in the directories that will be used when the application goes into production. Alternatively, you can alter the attachment specification when the application reaches the production stage.

4. Delete the macros and macrogroups that are no longer needed in each of the databases. Alter the AutoExec macro (or the start-up macro that you specify on the command line with the /x parameter) of each database to execute the appropriate entry-point function.

5. Delete the functions and subprocedures that are not required by each of the databases. You may need to alter the code to provide separate entry-point functions for each of the databases. Alternatively, use the code library approach described in the next section.

6. Alter the design of the switchboard or main form in each database to remove options that are no longer applicable.

7. Change the command-line parameters in the Program Item Properties dialog of the icon for the decision-support database. Specify the location and name of the new database, and add the /ro parameter to open the database in read-only mode.

You now have two independent databases that share common tables. If your application involves very large tables, the improvement in the performance of decision-support applications is much greater than that achieved for transaction-processing applications.

> **WARNING**
>
> If you make changes to the structure of tables (such as adding or deleting a field) that are attached to other databases, the changes may not be reflected automatically in the databases to which the tables are attached. You must delete the attaching link and reattach the tables in each of the other databases before the new structure becomes effective for the attached table.

Maintaining Common Access Basic Code

The problem with separating transaction-processing and decision-support applications is that you are likely to have modules in each of the databases that contain functions required by both of the databases. Having two copies of Access Basic code causes a version-control problem when you alter code that is included in modules contained in each of the two databases.

You can solve this problem by moving all the code from the original database into an Access library and then attaching the library to each of the databases. Access stores code in a fairly compact manner in modules; thus, unneeded code does not add significantly to the memory requirement of either of the databases. For example, all the code required for the Multimedia database (MULTIMED.MDB) used as an example in this chapter occupies less than 100KB. Access libraries are one of the subjects of Chapter 3, "Using Libraries, Wizards, Builders, and Add-Ins," and creating libraries is the subject of Chapter 23, "Developing Access Libraries and Add-Ins." Users can share library databases in the same manner that users can share conventional Access databases. Access automatically opens library databases in shared mode.

> **TIP**
>
> If you elect to use the library method described in this section to contain code that is common to one or more applications, you should make the decision early in the development process. You can employ a combination of event-handling subprocedures in form or report modules, or you can rely entirely on functions contained in conventional Access modules. The best compromise is likely to be using form modules to hold application-specific code and using Access modules to contain common code.

> **TIP**
>
> Make sure that your code is fully tested before you move the code to an Access library. Once you attach the library, you can no longer open the modules that contain the code. If you are creating applications for use with runtime Access, move the code to the library just before you create the final version to run under MSARN110.EXE.

Take the following steps to move the code from the dual-purpose database to an Access library, and attach the library to both applications:

1. Create a new library database with a conventional filename and the extension .MDA. (.MDA is the standard extension for Access library databases.)
2. Import the modules from the dual-purpose database into the library database.
3. Delete the modules from the dual-purpose database after you verify that the modules have imported correctly. If you fail to delete these modules, you

receive error messages that read "Tried to load duplicate procedure 'ProcedureName'" when you open the database with the library attached.

4. Use Windows' Notepad to add the line *FileName*.MDA=ro as the last entry of the [Libraries] section of MSACCESS.INI. If you locate the library in a directory other than your \ACCESS directory, precede *FileName* with a well-formed path to the file. The significance of the =ro (read-only) element of the entry is discussed in Chapter 12.

5. Close and relaunch Access. Changes to MSACCESS.INI take effect only when you open Access. Access attaches the library during its loading process, before loading the specified .MDB file.

NOTE

If you are using the Access Developer's Toolkit (ADT), you can specify a custom .INI file, *AppName*.INI, that MSARN200.EXE reads when you open runtime Access. Custom .INI files enable you to choose which libraries are attached when the user launches your application with runtime Access. Chapter 29, "Distributing Runtime Versions of Your Databases," describes how to substitute *AppName*.INI files for MSACC20.INI.

This procedure applies not only to Access Basic code but also to macros. Access 2.0 enables you to run macros contained in attached library databases. In the majority of cases, you need not make any changes to your code or macros in order to make them operable from an attached library database.

NOTE

Using a library to store Access Basic code is especially effective when you create high-speed data-entry or data-validation forms from copies of interactive transaction-processing forms. You may want to use many of the same event-handling functions and subprocedures for all variations of the form. If you place each type of form in its own database, you can maintain the same form name for the counterparts in the original design. Then you can attach the Access Basic code library to each database containing a related form or set of forms and reuse your code. Reusable code is one of the primary features of object-oriented programming techniques.

Using Access Basic Code to Ensure Data Integrity

Maintaining data integrity is (or should be) the primary objective of a transaction-processing application. Field values of records in a database in which data integrity is enforced from its inception accurately reflect the real-world objects that the records represent. Ensuring data integrity when users add or edit records of tables requires that you enforce rules that maintain the following:

■ *Referential integrity.* Access 2.0 automatically enforces the referential integrity of native and attached Access tables. However, if you are using attached tables created by another desktop RDBMS, such as dBASE, FoxPro, or Paradox, you need to write code to enforce referential integrity. Access 2.0 and most client-server databases automatically enforce referential integrity at the database level. Access 2.0 also provides optional automatic cascading deletions and cascading updates to maintain referential integrity on Access 2.0 tables. (Cascading deletions and updates are not available if you attach Access 1.1 tables to an Access 2.0 application.)

■ *Domain integrity.* Access enables you to add validation rules to fields of tables and to bound text boxes on forms in order to maintain domain integrity. Enforcing domain integrity at the table level by using Access 2.0's new validation methods is by far the better approach. Access applies the rules that you add only if the user changes the value of the field.

■ *Data accuracy.* Ensuring data accuracy is not possible in all cases. For example, you can test the validity of U.S. city-name and ZIP-code entries against values in a lookup table of reasonable size. Testing street addresses, however, requires gigabytes of data derived from the 1990 census data.

The following sections discuss typical methods of enforcing referential integrity, domain integrity, and data accuracy rules with Access Basic code.

Enforcing Referential Integrity with Attached Tables

When you attach tables from desktop databases other than Access, Access does not automatically enforce referential integrity rules. Enforcing referential integrity requires that all foreign key fields of related tables have a corresponding value in the primary key field of the corresponding base or primary table. Records in related tables that fail this test are called "orphan records." This rule also requires that you delete all records in related tables with foreign key values that match the value of the primary key of a record in a base or primary table that you want to delete. Most client-server databases enforce referential integrity on the server. If your RDBMS enforces referential integrity, you need not implement the macro or Access Basic function in the paragraph that follows. (You need to trap the error that is returned by the ODBC driver when you attempt to violate the referential integrity rule if you are using runtime Access.) You can enforce referential integrity for a set of related tables with two macros or two Access Basic functions.

Assuring Validity of Key Fields

You execute the first macro or function with the BeforeUpdate event of the text box that is bound to the foreign key field of the related table. The macro uses the FindRecord action to test the primary key field to verify that the proposed value exists; you use the CancelEvent action to prevent the update if the value is missing. Access Basic is more flexible than macros for testing primary and foreign key field validity. You can use the Access Basic **Seek** method to perform a faster test of the base or primary table, because all primary key values are indexed. Another approach is to use the domain aggregate function, **DCount**(), to test for the existence of the supplier code.

The four-letter supplier code is specified as the value of the DefaultValue property for the Code field of records added to the tblProducts and tblContacts tables that underlie the subforms of the Multimedia Suppliers form. Therefore, you need not test the validity of the code when you add a new record to tblSupplier or tblContact with the subforms. When you add a new supplier firm, however, you need to create a unique code for the supplier. The mms_CreateCode() function calculates a new supplier code from the value you enter in the txtCompany text box. The code tests the new supplier code for duplication against entries in the clone **Recordset** with the **FindFirst** method. If a duplicate supplier code is encountered, a message box instructs the user to choose a new code for the supplier. The Access Basic code for the mms_CreateCode function appears in Listing 8.1.

Listing 8.1. Access Basic code to create automatically a unique primary key for appended records.

```
Function mms_CreateCode ()
    'Purpose:   Create a supplier code when new records are added
    '           Test the code for uniqueness (to avoid Duplicate
    '           ➥Primary key errors)
    '           Allow editing of the supplier code during this
    '           ➥process
    'Called by: OnExit event of txtCompany (to create code)
    '           AfterUpdate event of txtCode (to verify changes)
```

continues

Listing 8.1. continued

```
On Error GoTo mms_CreateCode_Err

If IsNull(Forms("frmSuppliers")![Code]) Then
    'Create a code from the first three letters of the first
    ➥word of Company
    'and the first letter of the second word of Company

    Forms("frmSuppliers").txtCode.Locked = False
    Forms("frmSuppliers").txtCode =
    ➥UCase(Left(Forms("frmSuppliers").[txtCompany], 3) &
    ➥Mid(Forms("frmSuppliers").[Company],
    ➥(InStr(Forms("frmSuppliers").[txtCompany], " ") + 1), 1))
End If

'Test the code for uniqueness in the clone recordset
dsClone.FindFirst "Code = " & Chr$(34) &
➥Forms("frmSuppliers").Code & Chr$(34)
If dsClone.NoMatch Then
    'Code is OK, lock the field to prevent further changes
    Forms("frmSuppliers").txtCode.Locked = True
    Forms("frmSuppliers").cmdAddSupp.Visible = False
    Forms("frmSuppliers").cmdAddOK.Visible = True
    DoCmd GoToControl "txtAddress"
Else
    'Referential integrity violation message
    MsgBox Forms("frmSuppliers").[Code] & " duplicates existing
    ➥code. Please choose another.", 32, "Integrity Error"
    Forms("frmSuppliers").txtCode.Locked = False
    DoCmd GoToControl "txtCode"
End If

mms_CreateCode_Exit:
    Exit Function

mms_CreateCode_Err:
    MsgBox "Error: " & Error$
    Resume mms_CreateCode_Exit
End Function
```

> **NOTE**
>
> The Locked property of the text box that displays the four-letter code for the current supplier is set **True**, except when you add a new supplier record. This prevents users from changing existing supplier codes; changing a supplier code creates orphan records in related tables. Values of the Code field in the subforms are set from the value of txtCode, the Code text box of the main form.

Performing Cascade Deletions

You execute the second macro or Access Basic function, called a cascade deletion, only when you are deleting records with forms that are based on a primary table or on a query that includes fields of a primary table. Use the `BeforeUpdate` event of the form or run the macro or Access Basic function from another macro or function that is executed by the `OnClick` event of a Delete button. In this case, you search the foreign key field of the related table for a value corresponding to the primary key that you want to delete. If the user confirms the deletion, you delete each record in the related table that has a corresponding primary key field value, and then you delete the record in the base or primary table. This two-step procedure gives rise to the term "cascade."

> **NOTE**
>
> If your database application uses Access 2.0 tables and you have established relationships between the tables, enforcing referential integrity and specifying cascading deletions in the Relationships dialog, you don't need to add the deletion code contained in the `mms_DelSupp()` function. However, you may want to use code to perform these functions so you can customize the message box that appears prior to the deletion.

The `mms_DelSupp()` function in Listing 8.2 provides a message box that displays a count of the number of related records that will be deleted before deleting the record in the base table. More than half the code of `mms_DelSupp()` is devoted to creating a question in proper English that reflects the correct number of a verb ("is" or "are") and two nouns ("record" or "records"). The **DoCmd** RunSQL method executes delete queries against the two related tables.

Listing 8.2. Access Basic code to perform a cascade deletion.

```
Function mms_DelSupp ()
    'Purpose:    Delete supplier record and any related records
    '            Using executable SQL statement for cascade deletion
    'Called by: Delete button of frmSuppliers

    On Error GoTo mms_DelSupp_Err

    Dim varProdRecs As Variant
    Dim varContRecs As Variant
    Dim strSQL As String
```

continues

Listing 8.2. continued

```
'Get count of related records, if any, that will be deleted
varProdRecs = DCount("[Code]", "tblProducts", "[Code] =
➥Form.[Code]")
varContRecs = DCount("[Code]", "tblContacts", "[Code] =
➥Form.[Code]")

'Prepare a deletion confirmation message using proper English
strMsg = ""
If (varProdRecs + varContRecs) > 0 Then
    'Create first phrase
    If varProdRecs > 0 Then
        strMsg = strMsg & varProdRecs & " Product record"
        If varProdRecs > 1 Then
            strMsg = strMsg & "s "
        Else
            strMsg = strMsg & " "
        End If
        If varContRecs > 0 Then
            strMsg = strMsg & "and "
        End If
    End If

    If varContRecs > 0 Then
        'Create second phrase
        strMsg = strMsg & varContRecs & " Contact record"
        If varContRecs > 1 Then
            strMsg = strMsg & "s "
        Else
            strMsg = strMsg & " "
        End If
    End If

    'Choose verb of proper number
    If varContRecs > 1 Or varContRecs > 1 Or (varContRecs > 0 _And
    ➥varContRecs > 0) Then
        strMsg = "There are " & strMsg
    Else
        strMsg = "There is " & strMsg
    End If

    'Complete the message
    strMsg = strMsg & "for " & _ Forms("frmSuppliers").[txtCompany]
    If Right$(Forms("frmSuppliers").[txtCompany], 1) = "." Then
        strMsg = strMsg & " "
    Else
        strMsg = strMsg & ". "
    End If
    strMsg = strMsg & "Confirm deletion of all records for " &
    ➥Forms("frmSuppliers").txtCompany & "?"
Else
```

```
        strMsg = "Confirm deletion of record for " &
        ➥Forms("frmSuppliers").txtCompany & "?"
    End If

    'Create the confirmation message box
    If MsgBox(strMsg, 36, "Supplier Record Deletion") = 6 Then

        'Turn off system warnings
        DoCmd SetWarnings False

        If varProdRecs > 0 Then
            'Cascade deletion required
            strSQL = "DELETE DISTINCTROW tblProducts.Code
            FROM tblProducts WHERE tblProducts.Code = "
            strSQL = strSQL & Chr$(34) &
            Forms("frmSuppliers").txtCode &
            Chr$(34) & " WITH OWNERACCESS OPTION;"
            'Run the delete query
            DoCmd RunSQL strSQL
            'Refresh the subform so the deleted records disappear
            DoCmd Requery "sbfProducts"
        End If

        If varContRecs > 0 Then
            strSQL = "DELETE DISTINCTROW tblContacts.Code   FROM
            ➥tblContacts WHERE tblContacts.Code = "
            strSQL = strSQL & Chr$(34) &
            Forms("frmSuppliers").txtCode &
            Chr$(34) & " WITH OWNERACCESS OPTION;"
            DoCmd RunSQL strSQL
            DoCmd Requery "sbfContacts"
        End If

        'Delete the supplier record by an alternative method
        DoCmd DoMenuItem 0, 1, 7, 0      'Select the record
        DoCmd DoMenuItem 0, 1, 6, 0      'Delete the record

        'Requery the underlying form to get rid of the record
        DoCmd Requery
        'Requery the cboCodes combo box to update the combo box
        DoCmd Requery "cboCodes"

        DoCmd SetWarnings True

        'Recreate the bookmarks (first or last record may be deleted)
        Call mms_GetBookmarks
        Call mms_TestPrevSupp

    End If

mms_DelSupp_Exit:
    Exit Function
```

continues

Listing 8.2. continued

```
mms_DelSupp_Err:
    MsgBox "Error: " & Error$
    Resume mms_DelSupp_Exit
End Function
```

You need to apply the **DoCmd** Requery method to each of the subforms from which records are deleted so that the deleted records disappear. Alternatively, you can use the **DoCmd** DoMenuItem method to execute the Show All Records choice of the Records menu.

> **TIP**
>
> You need to apply the **DoCmd** Requery method to combo boxes that are used to select records after deleting records. Otherwise, the code for the records remains in the combo box. If you choose a code for a deleted record, the current record does not change. There is no equivalent of the NoMatch property for the result of applying the **DoCmd** FindRecord method. You can, however, test the value of a temporary **Bookmark** to determine whether the **DoCmd** FindRecord method changes the position of the record pointer.

Maintaining Domain Integrity

The domain of a field, also called the constraints applied to a field, is the set of all values that are valid for a field. The domain of a Yes/No (logical) field is **True** or **False**. (Access applies the default value 0 (**False**) to Yes/No fields; **Null** values are not allowed in Yes/No fields.) The domain of a ZIP code field for the U.S. is the set of valid ZIP codes recognized by the U.S. Postal Service. In the case of ZIP codes, the **Null** value constitutes a "don't know" or "hasn't been entered" condition. **Null** ZIP code values represent a condition for which you might test records in a data-validation procedure. Maintaining domain integrity requires that all field values comply with the constraints on the field values. Complying with domain integrity rules does not ensure data accuracy; however, failing to maintain domain integrity *guarantees* the presence of inaccurate data.

> **NOTE**
>
> Access 2.0's validation rules differ from those of Access 1.1. Field-level validation rules (*FieldName*.ValidationRule) apply only to the field value

itself and cannot reference another field of the table in a validation expression. You use table-level validation rules (`TableName.ValidationRule`) if you need to compare values to data in other table fields. Unlike Access 1.1, which allowed form-level validation rules (`BoundControlName.ValidationRule`) to override rules established for tables, Access 2.0 enforces field-level and table-level validation rules at all times that the table is in use.

Access does not enforce the domain-integrity rules that you apply to fields of tables or text boxes of forms by setting the `ValidationRule` property unless you update (change) the value of the field. For example, the `ValidationRule` property of the Company, Address, City, State, and ZIP code fields of the tblSuppliers table is **Is Not Null**. The `ValidationRule` and the `ValidationText` properties of table fields are propagated through queries to forms that update the tables. You can add a new supplier record, however, with the Multimedia Suppliers form that includes **Null** values in any field except the supplier Code field. (Code is the primary key field, and Access does not permit **Null** values in primary key fields.) Unless you write a function that explicitly tests the value of each field when you click the OK button to save an added record, the loss of domain integrity may go undetected by Access.

NOTE

When you apply a validation rule to a field or a table in Access 2.0 and the table contains records, Access checks all existing records to determine if the records conform to the proposed validation rule. Access reports existing violations of the proposed rule with a message box.

Your first step is to write a test function for each of the fields for which domain integrity testing is necessary. The test function can be as simple as the expressions you otherwise would use as the `ValidationRule` property of the field. You add a **DoCmd** CancelEvent method to return the focus to fields that do not pass the domain integrity test. To ensure that fields are tested when the operator tabs through the fields on the form, you can execute the individual domain test function with the OnExit event, rather than the BeforeUpdate event. This lets the function test fields that have not been updated

Once you've written the test functions for individual fields, you have the following choices in applying the functions in multiple-field domain integrity tests (listed in order of increasing effect on the performance of your application):

■ Test only records that you add to tables with the form. This is the fastest method. All records previously added to tables must have passed the current domain-integrity tests in order for domain integrity to be enforced. You execute the function that tests all fields for domain integrity from the OnClick event of the button that saves the added record.

■ Test each record that you update with the form. Unless you make a change to a field, domain integrity is compromised. The BeforeUpdate event of the form executes the all-fields test function. The user cannot move to another record without correcting the domain-integrity violation.

■ Test each record you display in the form. This provides the most effective insurance against domain-integrity violations. Depending upon the extent of the testing process, checking each record you display can slow manipulation. Use the form's OnCurrent property to execute the all-fields test function. Using the OnCurrent event, however, does not prevent the user from disregarding the warnings and proceeding to the next record.

The mms_TestEntries() function of MULTIMED.MDB (see Listing 8.3) is a typical procedure that checks all fields for domain-integrity violations. In this case, the test is simply a check for **Null** values. You can add more sophisticated tests, such as those described in the next section, for specific fields. It is more efficient to check all fields for illegal **Null** values first, and then test specific fields for valid data.

Listing 8.3. Access Basic code to test the domain integrity of multiple fields.

```
Function mms_TestEntries () As Integer
    'Purpose:   Test each field for domain integrity
    'Called by: OnClick property of cmdAddOK, or BeforeUpdate or
    ➥OnCurrent
    '           property of form
    'Note:      Unless a lookup table is attached, this function only
    '           tests for null values

    Dim wCtr As Integer
    Dim strControl As String

    On Error GoTo TestEntries_Err

    'Loop to test each supplier field for Null values
    For wCtr = 1 To 7
        Select Case wCtr
            Case 1
                strControl = "txtCompany"
            Case 2
                strControl = "txtCode"
            Case 3
```

```
                    strControl = "txtAddress"
            Case 4
                    strControl = "txtCity"
            Case 5
                    strControl = "txtState"
            Case 6
                    strControl = "txtZipCode"
            Case 7
                    strControl = "txtCountry"
        End Select
        If IsNull(Forms("frmSuppliers").Form(strControl)) Then
            'DoCmd CancelEvent does not work in this case
            'DoCmd SetWarnings False doesn't work, either

            'Inform the user of the problem
            strMsg = Mid$(strControl, 4) & " field cannot be empty. "
            strMsg = strMsg & "Please enter valid data."
            MsgBox strMsg, 32, "Domain Integrity Violation"

            'Set the focus to the offending control object
            DoCmd GoToControl strControl
            Exit For
        End If
    Next wCtr

    If fLookUp And Forms("frmSuppliers").txtCountry = "USA" Then
        'Test the city, state, and ZIP code functions
        wRetVal = mms_TestZipCode()
        wRetVal = mms_TestCity()
    End If
    Exit Function

TestEntries_Err:
    MsgBox "Error: " & Error$
    Exit Function
End Function
```

NOTE

The **DoCmd** CancelEvent method does not apply to the OnClick event of command buttons. If you execute the mms_TestEntries() function from the BeforeUpdate event of a form that occurs in response to clicking the Next or Prior buttons, you receive the message that reads "Can't go to specified record," regardless of the existence of a **DoCmd** CancelEvent method in your domain-testing code. Using the **DoCmd** SetWarnings False method does not inhibit the appearance of the "Can't go to specified record" message.

Using Lookup Tables to Enforce Domain Integrity and Test Data Accuracy

Domain-integrity tests can ensure that values with limited domains, such as state abbreviations, are valid. However, in the case of ZIP codes in the U.S. and postal codes in other jurisdictions, domain-integrity testing requires the use of lookup tables for city names and postal codes. You can search a table containing a list of valid city names and ZIP codes to confirm the values of city and ZIP-code fields. The LOOK_UPS.MDB database on the accompanying diskette contains records with ZIP code, city, and state values for several northeastern U.S. states (ZIP codes 01000 thru 11980). The data for LOOK_UPS.MDB is derived from the U.S. Postal Service's ZIP code data files.

> **NOTE**
>
> The code examples and the code in the Suppliers module of MULTIMED.MDB specify that LOOK_UPS.MDB be located in your C:\ACCESS\ADG20 directory. If you place these databases in a different directory, open the Declarations section of the Suppliers module and change the value of the LOOK_UPS_DB global constant as necessary.

Independently testing city, state, and ZIP-code fields does not ensure that the ZIP-code or state value is valid for a particular city. Similarly, using a table of telephone area codes to test area-code values does not ensure that an area-code entry is valid for the location of the subscriber. You can design functions that perform domain-integrity testing and do data-validity checks at the same time. The sections that follow describe how to write Access basic code for lookup-table searches.

Finding and Validating a ZIP Code in a Lookup Table

The mms_TestZipCode function (see Listing 8.4) is executed by the BeforeUpdate or OnExit events of the txtZipCode control (fFromForm = **False**) or, via the mms_TestEntries() function, the OnCurrent or BeforeUpdate event of the form (fFromForm = **True**). The mms_TestZipCode function does more than simply test for the existence of a valid ZIP code. If you enter city and state values, and there is only one ZIP code for the city, the ZIP code value is entered automatically. If more than one ZIP code exists for the city, you receive a message box with a list of valid ZIP codes (if there are less than 30 ZIP-codes for the city). Thus, a non-**Null** city entry is required. Following is the code listing for the mms_TestZipCode function of the Multimedia module:

Listing 8.4. Access Basic code to test entries against an attached lookup table.

```
Function mms_TestZipCode (fFromForm As Integer) As Integer
    'Purpose:    Test for valid ZIP code from lookup table
    '            Provide list of valid ZIP codes for city/state
    '            Insert ZIP code if there is only one code for the _city
    'Called by: BeforeUpdate or OnExit event of txtZipCode
    '           mms_TestEntries() function

    If Not (fLookUp And Forms("frmSuppliers").txtCountry = "USA") Then
    Exit Function
    End If
    If IsNull(Forms("frmSuppliers").txtCity) Then
        Exit Function
    End If

    Dim dbLookUps As Database    'Lookup tables in LOOK_UPS.MDA when not
                                 ➥attached
    Dim tblZipCodes As Table     'ZIP code table in dbLookups
    Dim frmSuppliers As Form

    Dim strTestCity As String    'Uppercase version of city
    Dim strZipCode As String     'StrZero version of ZIP code
    Dim strZipList As String     'List of valid ZIP codes
    Dim wZipCtr As Integer       'Number of ZIP_ codes in city
    Dim dwTestZip As Long        'ZIP code as Long integer

    On Error GoTo TestZip_Err

    'If LOOK_UPS.MDB is attached as a library, use = CodeDB()
    Set dbLookUps = OpenDatabase("c:\access\adg20\look_ups.mdb")
    Set tblZipCodes = dbLookUps.OpenTable("tblZipCodes")
    Set frmSuppliers = Forms("frmSuppliers")

    'Convert city to upper case
    strTestCity = UCase$(frmSuppliers.txtCity)

    If IsNull(frmSuppliers.txtZipCode) Then
        'ZIP code not yet entered
        If IsNull(frmSuppliers.txtState) Then
            MsgBox "Please enter state abbreviation before ZIP code.",
            ➥32, "Entry Error"
        Else
            'Find the city and create list of valid ZIP codes
            tblZipCodes.Index = "PrimaryKey"
            tblZipCodes.Seek ">=", strTestCity, 0&
            If tblZipCodes.NoMatch Or tblZipCodes.City <> strTestCity
            ➥Then
                MsgBox "Entry error in city field.", 32, "Entry Error"
            Else
                Do While tblZipCodes.City = strTestCity
```

continues

Listing 8.4. continued

```
                If tblZipCodes.State = frmSuppliers.State Then
                    'Only add ZIP codes for the city/state
                    ➥combination
                    strZipCode = Trim$(Str$(tblZipCodes.ZipCode))
                    If tblZipCodes.ZipCode < 10000 Then
                        strZipCode = "0" & strZipCode
                    End If
                    If InStr(strZipList, strZipCode) = 0 Then
                        'Do not duplicate ZIP code values
                        wZipCtr = wZipCtr + 1
                        If wZipCtr > 30 Then
                            Exit Do
                        End If
                        strZipList = strZipList & strZipCode & ", "
                    End If
                End If

                tblZipCodes.MoveNext
                'DoEvents    'Safety
            Loop

            If wZipCtr < 30 And Len(strZipList) > 4 Then
                If wZipCtr = 1 Then
                    'Supply the zip code automatically
                    frmSuppliers.txtZipCode = strZipCode
                    strMsg = ""
                Else
                    'Create message for user
                    strZipList = Left$(strZipList, Len(strZipList) -
                    ➥2)
                    strMsg = "Valid ZIP code(s) for " &
                    ➥frmSuppliers.City & ", "
                    strMsg = strMsg & frmSuppliers.State &
                    ➥" are " & strZipList & "."
                End If
            Else
                strMsg = "More than 30 ZIP codes for " &
                ➥frmSuppliers.City & ", " & frmSuppliers.State & "."
            End If
            If Len(strMsg) > 0 Then
                MsgBox strMsg, 32, "ZIP codes"

            End If
        End If
    End If
If fFromForm Then
    DoCmd GoToControl "txtZipCode"
Else
    DoCmd CancelEvent    'Works for BeforeUpdate, OnExit, etc.
End If
```

```
    Else
        'Convert ZIP code value to Long integer and seek the ZIP code
        dwTestZip = CLng(Left$(frmSuppliers.txtZipCode, 5))
        tblZipCodes.Index = "ZipCode"
        tblZipCodes.Seek "=", dwTestZip
        If tblZipCodes.NoMatch Then
            MsgBox "ZIP code " & frmSuppliers.txtZipCode &
            " not found.", 32, "ZIP code Error"
            If fFromForm Then
                DoCmd GoToControl "txtZipCode"
            Else
                DoCmd CancelEvent
            End If
        Else
            If tblZipCodes.City <> strTestCity Or
            tblZipCodes.State <> frmSuppliers.txtState Then
                strMsg = "ZIP code " & frmSuppliers.txtZipCode &
                " is for "
                strMsg = strMsg & tblZipCodes.City & ", " &
                tblZipCodes.State
                If Not (IsNull(frmSuppliers.txtCity) Or
                IsNull(frmSuppliers.txtState)) Then
                    strMsg = strMsg & ", not " & frmSuppliers.txtCity &
                    ", " & frmSuppliers.txtState
                End If
                strMsg = strMsg & "."
                MsgBox strMsg, 16, "ZIP code Error"
                If fFromForm Then
                    DoCmd GoToControl "txtZipCode"
                Else
                    DoCmd CancelEvent
                End If
            End If
        End If
    End If
    tblZipCodes.Close
    dbLookUps.Close
    Exit Function

TestZip_Err:
    MsgBox "Error: " & Error$
    Exit Function
End Function
```

Much of the code of the mms_TestZipCode() function is devoted to creating message boxes that inform the user of problems with the ZIP-code value or lists of valid ZIP codes for the city and state. Testing only the domain integrity, without regard to data validity, would require only a simple **Seek** operation on the ZipCode field. A list of the ZIP codes that `mms_TestZipCode()` returns for Springfield, MA, when you enter a **Null** (blank) ZIP code value is shown in Figure 8.5.

FIGURE 8.5.

A message box displaying valid ZIP codes for a city.

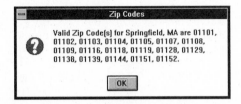

> **NOTE**
>
> All the "traps" have not been removed from the test functions. If you change the state abbreviation for a city with a ZIP-code value, you need to delete the city name, change the state to the correct value, and then re-enter the original city name. This trap was deliberately left in the code to demonstrate a cycle, which is an error condition in a program from which you cannot escape without knowing the secret work-around or exiting the application.

Seeking Partial Values of Composite Keys

The composite primary key index for tblZipCodes is City;ZipCode. The ZipCode field also has a duplicates-allowed index. xBase databases enable you to seek any portion of a single-field or composite key. You cannot use a partial key with the **Seek** method on an Access composite index; you must specify a value for each indexed field. Thus, to **Seek** a City value without knowing one of its ZipCode values, you need to specify **0&** (**Long**) as the value of the ZipCode field and use the >= operator to find the first record that matches the City value, regardless of the first ZipCode value. This technique is used in the `mms_TestZipCode()` function described in the preceding section and in the other domain-integrity and data-validity test functions in MULTIMED.MDB.

Once you have located the first record for a city, you can process all records for the city in a **Do While...Loop** structure conditioned on the equality of city-name values. You can test the values of other fields, such as State, to add records to a list of values that are valid for a selected city. This technique is used to create the list of valid ZIP codes for a city, an example of which is found in Figure 8.5, shown previously.

> **WARNING**
>
> The **Not** NoMatch property requires an additional qualifier to indicate a valid match of a partial composite key value when using the >= or > operators. The NoMatch = **False** condition can occur even if there are no records that match the partial key value. If you apply the **Seek** method to tblZipCodes with the operands ACUSHNA, 0&, a **Not** NoMatch condition occurs with ACUSHNET (MA) as the City value of the current record. You need to verify that the current record contains a value matching the first **Seek** operand. The line **If** tblZipCodes.**NoMatch Or** tblZipCodes.City <> strTestCity **Then** in the preceding Listing 8.4 for the mms_TestZipCode() function provides this test. You need to test both conditions, because tblZipCodes.City returns a **Null** value when the **EOF** property is **True**. **Null** values do not return expected results when used with comparison operators.

Size Considerations for Lookup Tables

Lookup tables can become exceedingly large. Some of the largest lookup tables in existence are the tables used for credit-card verification; these files contain millions of records. The dBASE III+ file used to create tblZipCodes originally contained about 80,000 records and occupied 8.5MB of disk space. Converting the dBASE III+ file to an Access table cut the size by approximately one half as a result of Access's use of variable-length text fields. Access indexes also occupy less disk space than dBASE III+ .NDX files; an Access composite index on City;ZipCode is only about 25 percent of the size of the same index created with dBASE III+.

The original dBASE III+ file contained fields for the name of the post office serving the ZIP-code area and the county in which each ZIP code is located. These fields, which are not necessary to verify city names and ZIP codes, were removed from the tblZipCodes table. Removing unneeded fields decreased the table size by about 50 percent. Using a **Long** integer, rather than a Text field data type for ZipCode, slightly decreases the size of the table and indexes created on the ZipCode field. Originally, the table was indexed on ZipCode;City with a second index added on the City field. Changing the primary key to City;ZipCode and adding a ZipCode index reduced the index size by about 10 percent. The sizes of the tables and indexes of LOOK_UPS.MDB for each stage of the table conversion process for tblZipCodes are listed in Table 8.2.

Table 8.2. Sizes of U.S. ZIP-code tables of different types and structures.

Operation	Table Only	Index(es)	Total Size
Original .DBF and .NDX files	8,566,462	8,093,184	16,659,646
Imported as tblZipCodes to LOOK_UPS.MDB	4,784,128	Not Indexed	Not Indexed
Remove unneeded fields, index on ZipCode;City	2,424,832	2,064,384	4,489,216
Replace ZipCode Text field with Long	2,326,528	1,933,312	4,259,840
Add index on City	2,326,528	3,047,424	5,373,952
Change to primary key index City;ZipCode and add index on ZipCode	2,326,528	2,719,744	5,046,272

The effect of the size of lookup tables on performance depends primarily on external conditions. City and ZIPcode lookup operations using a 80486DX2 66MHz computer with 16MB of RAM are virtually instantaneous. With a fast computer with 8MB or more of RAM and local tables, the time required for most lookup operations is virtually imperceptible to the user. When the lookup table is shared on a network server, lookup performance is affected by network traffic conditions and the size of the disk cache on the server. Using large lookup tables with applications that are run on 80386DX computers with 4MB of RAM is slowed by the swapping of memory to temporary disk files.

Removing Primary Key Violations from Lookup and Other Imported Tables

The tblZipCodes table is a base or primary table. By tradition, base or primary tables have unique primary key fields. The tblZipCodes table has no related tables, so a primary key is not necessary in this case. Code in the data-validity checking functions of the Multimedia module prevents duplicate ZIP codes and state abbreviations in lists of valid ZIP codes and states for a particular city. You can create a composite Index1 index that allows duplicate values of city name and ZIP code combinations. To use a composite, non-primary-key index, substitute "Index1" for "PrimaryKey" as the value of the **Index** property of the table.

When you want to ensure that a lookup table (or any other table) contains unique values for the search key, you need to create a primary key field. Duplicate primary key values prevent you from creating the required no-duplicates index on primary keys of Access tables. Unfortunately, Access does not create the equivalent of Paradox's KeyViols table, which is created when Paradox encounters a duplicate primary key value. You need to write an Access Basic procedure to identify and delete records with duplicate primary key values. Listing 8.5 shows the code used by the wKeyViols() function of the Lookup Tables module in the LOOK_UPS.MDB database, which moves duplicate records from tblZipCodes to tblKeyViols.

Listing 8.5. Access Basic code to remove records with duplicate key fields.

```
Function wKeyViols () As Integer
    'Purpose:    Detect primary key duplications and send them to the
    '            KeyViols table, then delete duplicate values from the
    '            ➥table
    'Note:       Run this function with LOOK_UP.MDB open as a database
    '            Index1 is a composite index on ZipCode;City

    Dim dwRecno As Long
    Dim dwRecPct As Integer
    Dim varRetVal As Variant
    Dim varIndexKey As Variant
    Dim dbCurrent As Database
    Dim tblZipCodes As Table
    Dim tblKeyViols As Table

    'MSA20: Access 1.1's CurrentDB() function is replaced by
    ➥dbEngine.Workspaces(0).Databases(0)
    '        DBEngine(0)(0) is shorthand for the Access 2.0 expression
    'Set dbCurrent = CurrentDB()
    Set dbCurrent = DBEngine(0)(0)
    Set tblZipCodes = dbCurrent.OpenTable("tblZipCodes")

    'Set the index to the composite ZipCode;City index
    tblZipCodes.Index = "Index1"

    Set tblKeyViols = dbCurrent.OpenTable("tblKeyViols")

    tblZipCodes.MoveFirst
    dwRecno = 1

    'Add a progress indicator to the status bar
    varRetVal = SysCmd(1, "Testing", 100)
```

continues

Listing 8.5. continued

```
'Use transaction processing to improve speed
BeginTrans
    Do While Not tblZipCodes.EOF
        'Set the value of the key for which you are testing
        varIndexKey = tblZipCodes.ZipCode & tblZipCodes.City

        'Move to the next record to see if it's a duplicate
        tblZipCodes.MoveNext

        'You need this test to prevent a "No current record"
        ➥message at the end of processing
        If tblZipCodes.EOF Then
            Exit Do
        End If


        If tblZipCodes.ZipCode & tblZipCodes.City = varIndexKey
        ➥Then
            'If a duplicate is found, inform the user
            MsgBox "Found duplicate " & tblZipCodes.ZipCode & " in "
            ➥& tblZipCodes.City & ".", 64, "Key Violation"

            'Add a record to the key violations table
            tblKeyViols.AddNew
            tblKeyViols.ZipCode = tblZipCodes.ZipCode
            tblKeyViols.State = tblZipCodes.State
            tblKeyViols.City = tblZipCodes.City
            tblKeyViols.Update

            'Delete the record from the ZIP codes table
            tblZipCodes.Delete

            'Move to the next record
            tblZipCodes.MoveNext
        End If

        If dwRecno Mod 100& = 0& Then
            'Show the progress (based on 80,000 records)
            varRetVal = SysCmd(2, CInt(dwRecno \ 800))
        End If
        dwRecno = dwRecno + 1
    Loop
    CommitTrans
    wKeyViols = True
    Exit Function

OpsError:
    Rollback
    MsgBox Error$, 16, "Operations Error"
    Exit Function
End Function
```

There was one duplicate record in the original dBASE III+ table for Fishers Island (in Long Island Sound), whose jurisdiction is divided between the states of Connecticut and New York. Fishers Island has only one ZIP code, but records exist for two states. The state field is not included in the primary key field; therefore, a primary key violation occurs. You can test the wKeyViols() function by running the qryAppendKeyViols query, included in LOOK_UPS.MDB, which adds the offending record from tblKeyViols to tblZipCodes. You need to delete the primary key from tblKeyViols before running qryAppendKeyViols, and then add the Index1 composite index on the ZipCode;City fields. Type ? wKeyViols() in the Immediate window to execute the function. The use of transaction processing (**BeginTrans...CommitTrans**) greatly speeds the operation of the wKeyViols() function.

Attaching Lookup Databases as Libraries

Lookup tables are logical candidates for inclusion in library databases that you attach to applications which require them. You can minimize the amount of duplicated Access Basic code in your applications by moving domain-validation and data-accuracy enforcement code to modules in the library. City, state, and ZIP-code validation procedures are especially good choices for inclusion in library databases. Address verification procedures are similar for all database applications.

If you maintain consistent names for the text boxes of forms that contain, for example, city, state and ZIP code fields, you can hard-code the control object names in your library code. Hard-coding means referring to the control object by a literal reference to its Name property (formerly ControlName in Access 1.1), as in Forms!frmSuppliers!txtCity. Moving code to a library database, however, is likely to be an afterthought. Therefore, you need to use the preferred syntax to specify form and control names by string variables. You pass the form name to a module-level variable, such as strFormName, in the library code by calling the initialization function of the library code. The initialization function includes a **Set** dbLookUp = **CodeDB**() line to specify that the library module uses its own tables, not those of the currently open database. You can pass the names of the control objects to module level variables, such as strCity, strState, and strZipCode, during the initialization process. Alternatively, you can pass the names of control objects as values of arguments of individual validation function calls that you add as the values of the appropriate events. If your validation function refers only to one control object, you can use **Screen.ActiveControl.** Name to pass the name of the control object that you want to test.

> **WARNING**
>
> Avoid using `Screen.ActiveControl. Name` or `Screen.ActiveForm.Name` in Access Basic code. You cannot debug code that includes either of these two objects. When your module occupies the active window, neither the current form nor the active control has the focus. You receive "Invalid object reference" messages when you step through such statements in your code.

Creating Transaction Logs

Almost all client-server RDBMSs create transaction logs that identify the date, time, and changes to the tables of the database. The purpose of transaction logs is to enable the database administrator to restore the tables of the database in the event of a media (fixed disk) failure or other catastrophe affecting the contents of the tables. Records of transaction logs represent the changes to the tables that occur after the last backup of the database. Most transaction logs are of the write-ahead type, which adds the log record before changes are made to table records. If a hardware failure occurs, the database administrator restores the database from the backup tape or writable CD-ROM, and then updates the tables with the records of the transaction log. Client-server systems include procedures to automate this bulk-updating process. The content of transaction logs is transitory; to conserve disk space, the system administrator dumps (that is, copies) the log, often to a special backup device, every time a new backup of the database occurs. Then the administrator deletes all the records of the log.

The sections that follow describe the basic design features required of a transaction-logging file and how you implement a transaction log with Access Basic code.

Considerations in Designing Transaction Logs

Access does not include a built-in transaction log. You can, though, write an Access Basic function, executed by the `AfterUpdate` event of each form in your database, to add records to a transaction log. However, it is easier to create a log that consists of individual entries for each update to a control object with the AfterUpdate event. Figure 8.6 shows a typical transaction log that provides sufficient information to reconstruct changes to tables that underlie forms.

You need the name of the table or query that underlies the transaction-processing form and the key field value(s) so that you can identify the record that is updated. Additional fields identify the name of the field of the table or query that is updated and the new value assigned to the field. Additions are made to the transaction log in date/time sequence, so the last change to a field in the transaction log table represents the last change to the field value of the form's table or query. You assign a special code, such as that shown in the last record of Figure 8.6, to indicate records that are deleted. You can then create a series of action queries or write a relatively simple Access Basic function to update a backup copy of the table to the last entry made.

FIGURE 8.6.

A simple transaction log table.

Computer	UserN	DateU	TimeU	TableName	KeyField1	FieldName	UpdateValue
OakLeaf1	Admin	5/6/93	13:24	qrySuppliers	TRAT	Company	Transaction Test Entry
OakLeaf1	Admin	5/6/93	13:24	qrySuppliers	TRAT	Address	123 Elm Street
OakLeaf1	Admin	5/6/93	13:24	qrySuppliers	TRAT	City	Oakland
OakLeaf1	Admin	5/6/93	13:24	qrySuppliers	TRAT	State	CA
OakLeaf1	Admin	5/6/93	13:24	qrySuppliers	TRAT	Zip Code	94610
OakLeaf1	Admin	5/6/93	13:24	qrySuppliers	TRAT	Telephone	5108885151
OakLeaf1	Admin	5/6/93	13:24	qrySuppliers	TRAT	FAX	510888-5160
OakLeaf1	Admin	5/6/93	13:26	qrySuppliers	TOSA	Address	9740 Irvine Boulevard
OakLeaf1	Admin	5/6/93	13:26	qrySuppliers	TRYM	Address	2166 W. Broadway, Suite 330
OakLeaf1	Admin	5/6/93	13:55	qrySuppliers	ARCF	Address	530 West 25th Street
OakLeaf1	Admin	5/6/93	13:56	qrySuppliers	ARCF	Zip Code	10010
OakLeaf1	Admin	5/6/93	13:56	qrySuppliers	ARCF	Zip Code	10020
OakLeaf1	Admin	5/6/93	13:56	qrySuppliers	ARCF	Zip Code	10001
OakLeaf1	Admin	5/6/93	13:56	qrySuppliers	ARCF	Zip Code	
OakLeaf1	Admin	5/6/93	13:57	qrySuppliers	ARCF	City	G P O, NY
OakLeaf1	Admin	5/6/93	13:57	qrySuppliers	ARCF	Zip Code	10001
OakLeaf1	Admin	5/6/93	13:57	qrySuppliers	ARCF	Zip Code	
OakLeaf1	Admin	5/6/93	13:57	qrySuppliers	ARCF	City	G P O
OakLeaf1	Admin	5/6/93	13:57	qrySuppliers	ATIT	Address	3761 Victoria Park Ave.
OakLeaf1	Admin	5/6/93	13:57	qrySuppliers	AUSC	Address	10300 Metric Boulevard
OakLeaf1	Admin	5/6/93	14:29	qrySuppliers	AIMC	[Record]	[Delete]

Table: tblTransLog — Record: 1

Transaction-Processing Limitations of Access

You need to use transaction processing to add records to transaction logs, because you want to commit the changes if the record is updated (triggering the AfterUpdate event of the form) or roll back the changes if the update to the form is not executed. Transaction processing in Access must occur within one instance of a procedure, however. This means that you cannot execute a **BeginTrans** statement and then repetitively execute a second procedure that uses the **Update** method to accumulate records for the transaction and finally execute a **CommitTrans** statement in a third procedure to cause the transaction to proceed. As a result of this limitation, you cannot add transaction records to the transaction log table directly, because multiple records may be appended by several instances of a function called by the AfterUpdate event of control objects (for example, when you add a new record). If you cancel the addition of the new record, the **Rollback** method does not prevent the addition of the accumulated records to the transaction log table.

The preceding limitation on Access's transaction-processing methods requires that you create a temporary table to hold the records that result from updates to each field. Then you append the records of the temporary table to the transaction log when you update the form. You can use Access' transaction-processing methods for this second step, because here the **BeginTrans**, **Update**, and **CommitTrans** methods can be contained within a single instance of a single function. Appending groups of records from a temporary holding file is an example of batch-mode processing.

> **NOTE**
>
> One of the advantages of the temporary table is that if the transaction cannot be completed, the records remain in the temporary table and are appended to the transaction log table on the next occurrence of an update. This is an important consideration when users share the transaction log table. You need to index the transaction log table on date and time in a multiuser environment, because the records of a rolled-back transaction (usually the result of locking contention) that is completed at a later time are added to the transaction in a non-time-sequential manner.

Locating Transaction Log Files on Separate Computers

For a transaction log to survive a total media failure, the log must be contained in a database that is stored on a fixed disk drive other than the one which stores the database being logged. This necessitates that you open two databases simultaneously; the only method of opening more than one database is to use Access Basic code. You can include the module that creates log entries in your application or in a library attached to each copy of Access that updates tables in the logged database(s).

Single-user applications that update tables containing important business information also benefit from the insurance provided by a transaction log. If you have more than one partition on your fixed disk, maintain the transaction log in a partition other than the one which stores the critical database. Each partition has its own file allocation table (FAT), so a read failure of one partition's FAT does not affect the ability to read the other partition (unless the failure is in the boot sector of your C: drive). Disk-compression utilities, such as Stac Electronic's Stacker, create multiple partitions. Space permitting, store your transaction-log database on the uncompressed volume if your database resides on the compressed volume. Another advantage to using transaction logs is that you can back up a transaction-log database to diskette(s) more quickly than you can back up a large main database.

The Transaction Log Module of MULTIMED.MDB

The Transaction Log module of MULTIMED.MDB consists of the Access Basic code for a simple transaction-logging application. This application appends records to a local table in MULTIMED.MDB's tblTempLog table and then transfers the temporary records from tblTempLog to the tblTransLog table of the LOOK_UPS.MDB database. In a production application, you create a separate TRANSACT.MDB database, located on a computer other than the server that stores the logged databases.

The tl_wAddTrans() function, shown in Listing 8.6, adds a record to the tblTempLog table each time it executes. The AfterUpdate event of the control objects on the form that are bound to the qrySuppliers query execute the tl_wAddTrans() function. The mms_DelSupp() function also calls tl_wAddTrans, but with an empty string as the value of strControlName to indicate the deletion of a record.

Listing 8.6. Access Basic code to create a transaction log.

```
Function tl_wAddTrans (strControlName As String) As Integer
    'Purpose:    Add transaction record to temporary table
    'Arguments:  strControlName supplied by event's function call
    '            If strControlName is empty, the record has been deleted
    'Called by: AfterUpdate event of each control on the form
    '            mms_DelSupp() function when deleting a supplier record
    'Note:       Transaction processing is not effective here

    On Error GoTo AddTrans_Err

    tblTempLog.AddNew

    'Enter user ID and time/date
    tblTempLog.ComputerName = strComputerName
    tblTempLog.UserName = CurrentUser()
    tblTempLog.DateUpdated = Date
    tblTempLog.TimeUpdated = Time

    'Enter record source (may be a table or a query)
    tblTempLog.TableName = Forms(strFormName).RecordSource

    'Enter the key field values, if applicable
    If Len(strKeyField1) > 0 Then
        tblTempLog.KeyField1 = Forms(strFormName).Form(strKeyField1)
    End If
    If Len(strKeyField2) > 0 Then
        tblTempLog.KeyField2 = Forms(strFormName).Form(strKeyField2)
    End If
    If Len(strKeyField3) > 0 Then
        tblTempLog.KeyField3 = Forms(strFormName).Form(strKeyField3)
    End If

    If Len(strControlName) > 0 Then
        'Enter the new value and append the record
        tblTempLog.FieldName =
        ➡Forms(strFormName).Form(strControlName).ControlSource
```

continues

Listing 8.6. continued

```
        tblTempLog.UpdateValue = Forms(strFormName).Form(strControlName)
    Else
        'If no control name is specified, the record has been deleted
        tblTempLog.FieldName = "[Record]"
        tblTempLog.UpdateValue = "[Delete]"
    End If

    'Execute the update to the record
    tblTempLog.Update
    Exit Function

AddTrans_Err:
    MsgBox "Error: " & Error$
    Exit Function
End Function
```

The tl_wTransferLog function uses Access' transaction-processing methods to append all the records of the tblTempLog table in MULTIMED.MDB to the tblTransLog table of LOOK_UPS.MDB. If the transaction fails because of locks placed on the pages of the tblTransLog table by other users, records accumulate in the temporary table until the next occurrence of an update or when you close the form. The tl_wTransferLog() function is executed by the AfterUpdate event of the form via the tl_CommitTrans() function, by the OnClose event of the form via the tl_wCloseLogDB() function, and by the mms_DelSupp() function. In the preceding three cases, the fDoTransfer flag is set **True**. When you click the Cancel button after adding a new record, the mms_CnclSupp() function sets fDoTransfer to **False** and calls tl_wTransferLog(); in this case, the records in tblTempLog simply are deleted. Figure 8.7 shows the Properties window for the Multimedia Suppliers form with two function calls for transaction logging and two calls to domain-integrity and data-validity checking functions. (The mms_wInitialize() function executed on opening the form also calls the tl_wInitialize() function.) Listing 8.7 shows the code for the transaction-processing function, tl_wTransferLog():

FIGURE 8.7.

The Properties window for the frmSuppliers form.

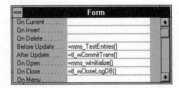

Listing 8.7. Access Basic code to append transaction log records.

```
Function tl_wTransferLog (fDoTransfer As Integer) As Integer
    BeginTrans
        On Error GoTo RollBack_On_Error
        tblTempLog.MoveFirst
        Do While Not tblTempLog.EOF
            If fDoTransfer Then
                tblLog.AddNew
                tblLog.ComputerName = tblTempLog.ComputerName
                tblLog.UserName = tblTempLog.UserName
                tblLog.DateUpdated = tblTempLog.DateUpdated
                tblLog.TimeUpdated = tblTempLog.TimeUpdated
                tblLog.TableName = tblTempLog.TableName
                tblLog.FieldName = tblTempLog.FieldName
                tblLog.KeyField1 = tblTempLog.KeyField1
                tblLog.KeyField2 = tblTempLog.KeyField2
                tblLog.KeyField3 = tblTempLog.KeyField3
                tblLog.UpdateValue = tblTempLog.UpdateValue
                tblLog.Update
            End If
            tblTempLog.Delete
            tblTempLog.MoveNext
            'DoEvents      'Safety
        Loop
    CommitTrans
    Exit Function

RollBack_On_Error:
    Rollback
    MsgBox Error$, 16, "Transaction Error"
    Exit Function
End Function
```

NOTE

In a multiuser environment, you should include a test that is the equivalent of the mms_AddSupp() function to make sure that the temporary log table is empty before permitting the addition of a new record. Otherwise you might delete records for prior changes that have not been transferred successfully to the transaction log table.

For the most part, the remaining functions of the Transaction Log module perform housekeeping duties, such as opening and closing databases and tables. The code shown in the preceding listings for creating transaction logs is typical of that which you use for any Access batch-processing operation.

Transaction Logs for Related Tables

You create transaction logs for related tables that are updated by entries in subforms with methods that are similar to those used for transaction logs for primary or base tables. When more than one table is involved in a transaction, you open and close the tables in your function that adds entries to the temporary log file, instead of opening and closing the form. To accurately re-create updates to related tables with transaction-log entries, the related tables require a unique primary key. If you cannot create a unique primary key from data in the fields of the related table, you need to add a counter field, or its equivalent, to the related table. Both the tblProducts and tblContacts tables of MULTIMED.MDB need an added counter field to identify their records for transaction-logging purposes.

9

Designing Decision-Support Forms for Management

The preceding chapter, "Optimizing Transaction-Processing Forms," defined decision-support database applications as those applications that are operable with tables opened in read-only mode or with databases in which decision-support users do not possess modify-data permissions for table objects. Some applications, such as the creation of mailing lists in Word for Windows or other mail-merge formats, also are considered part of the decision-support category because such applications create external text files, not records in database tables. Thus, this chapter includes examples of applications that use existing data to create text and worksheet files.

The majority of the users of decision-support applications are supervisory or management personnel who need the information provided by the decision-support application for performance evaluation and short- or long-term planning purposes. The current trend, especially among larger firms, is to provide all supervisory and management personnel with workstations connected to networked databases. This trend has expanded the opportunities for developers to create customized decision-support applications. Software publishers, in turn, have flooded the market with database-application generators designed to speed development of decision-support applications. An application generator is a program that creates macro scripts (or their equivalent) or programming code based on user choices made from list boxes, combo boxes, and command buttons. Many application generators, such as Channel Computing's Forest & Trees, are designed specifically for end users and do not require programming. Others, like Powersoft's Power Builder, are directed toward skilled programmers. As a developer, you can use Access as your own application generator. Better yet, you can create Access decision-support applications that rival or surpass end-user oriented application generators. The QueryWizard application described in this chapter is an example of the latter option.

Design Criteria for Decision-Support Forms

The recommendations that apply to interactive transaction-processing forms described in the preceding chapter also are valid for decision-support forms. Some of the more important design principles for decision-support forms are as follows:

■ Remember that the audience for your decision-support applications (that is, the users) view their computer as a tool, rather than as a device that is critical to their livelihood. Keep decision-support applications as simple and intuitive as possible so that upper-echelon users do not need to read documentation or help files. Use labels on the form, where necessary, to explain the purpose of control objects and how to use the controls.

■ Adopt the design style that your audience expects. Marketing and sales executives expect to see the firm's logo and bright, colorful presentations of a limited amount of data. In such cases, your form design might bear more resemblance to a bulleted PowerPoint slide than to a conventional Access form with its standard 8-point MS Sans Serif font. Financial and accounting people, on the other hand, are more accustomed to ledger-like presentations.

■ Employ a familiar model for your application. If the users of your application are accustomed to running spreadsheet applications, design your applications to emulate Excel, Lotus 1-2-3, or Quattro Pro. Emulating Excel 5.0, for instance, necessitates displaying tables and query results in a continuous subform or grid of text boxes, rather than in Access's table or query datasheet view. You can use menu macros to create a set of custom menus that follow the general pattern of Excel 5.0's menus, or you can provide a custom toolbar to make the application easier to use. (See Chapter 26, "Customizing Access Applications with Special Menus and Toolbars," which describes how to use Access 2.0's new toolbar feature.)

■ Give users the chance to work with the data they view in your Access application within spreadsheet or related applications. Letting users manipulate the data in a familiar environment is much easier than writing the Access Basic code necessary to create "what-if " scenarios in your application. A simple example that creates an Excel worksheet from a user-defined query is given later in this chapter. Chapter 24, "Using Access Wizard Functions," includes a more sophisticated method to create Excel .XLS or Lotus 1-2-3 .WK? files.

■ Use Access graphs and charts to depict the information that your application delivers. The higher your users have risen on the management ladder, the more likely they are to want broad-brush graphs, not rows and columns of numbers. Employ drill-down techniques, as described later in this chapter, to display numerical data that underlies the graph or chart. If your users have fast computers (80486DX25 or better) with at least 8MB of memory, your opening form can be a graph created with Microsoft Graph 5.0. On slower computers, it is advisable to let users choose whether to display a graph or chart because of the time required by your application to create the underlying query and for Microsoft Graph to display the image. Creating Access graphs and charts is the subject of Chapter 17, "Charting Data with Microsoft Graph 5.0." Alternatively, you can use the OLE Custom Control version of Pinnacle Publishing's Chart application to speed the creation of graphs and charts. The Chart OLE Control is described in Chapter 18, "Introducing OLE 2.0 Custom Controls."

■ Use command buttons rather than the default record navigation buttons of Access forms for record navigation, and design subforms to use continuous forms as opposed to datasheet views. These principles are especially important for first-time or occasional users of database applications. The Access Basic functions for record manipulation in decision-support applications are much simpler than the functions described in the preceding chapter for transaction-processing forms.

■ Consider adding icons to a Program Manager application group as a substitute for or as a supplement to a main switchboard form. Create a macro for each of the icons that executes the function to open a specific form or to specify the query that underlies the form. Use the /x *MacroName* parameter in the command line of the Program Item Properties dialog box to specify the macro that runs when you open retail or runtime Access with the decision-support database.

■ Do not rely on opening read-only databases or restricting user permissions to preclude attempts at entering data in decision-support applications. Members of upper management might take offense at messages informing them that they are precluded from taking specified actions or do not have "permission" to modify an object (unless these management personnel are accustomed to receiving such messages from client-server database systems). Your Access Basic code should be designed to prevent the occurrence of these types of messages.

■ Consider using Visual Basic 3.0's Professional Edition with Access databases to create simple decision-support applications. You'll find that you need to write more code for most Visual Basic database applications than for their Access equivalents. Visual Basic 3.0, however, provides added flexibility by letting you open an Access database in read-write mode and then open the database tables in read-only mode. With Visual Basic applications, you can attain better performance with slower computers or computers having less than 8MB of RAM. The advantages and limitations of Visual Basic's data access functions are detailed at the end of this chapter.

Most of these topics are discussed at greater length in the sections that immediately follow. The remainder are discussed later in the chapter or elsewhere in the book, as noted.

> **TIP**
>
> Be careful how you employ colors on forms. Forms that use saturated colors to distinguish between objects may make elements of your form unreadable on laptop PCs with monochrome LCD or even plasma displays. If you expect users of your application to employ laptops, stick with black, light gray, and white on your forms. If you use colors, match their intensity to the lighter of the two shades of gray available in Access's palette. Test applications on a laptop with the lowest-common-denominator monochrome LCD display (the passive-matrix type that is not backlit) before you release the applications for production.

Attaching Tables to Decision-Support Applications

The preceding chapter recommended that you create separate databases for decision-support and transaction-processing applications. In the majority of applications that use Access tables, you include the tables in the database devoted to transaction processing. Many Access decision-support applications use tables in a foreign desktop RDBMS format, such as xBase or Paradox, or they depend on tables of a client-server database. Thus the data underlying decision-support forms and reports usually involves attached tables. Most of the considerations you need to take into account when using attached tables appear in the section called "Separating Application and Data Objects" of Chapter 2, "Developing a Design Strategy for Access Applications." Chapter 20, "Front-Ending Client-Server Databases," discusses the use of the Open Database Connectivity (ODBC) API to attach client-server RDBMS tables.

Access 2.0 does not give you the option of attaching tables in read-only mode; the `Updatable` property of **TableDef** objects is read-only. You can control the opening mode of tables attached from Access and client-server databases by granting only read-data permissions for the source database tables to decision-support users. You set the value of the `AllowUpdating` property to `NoTables` to emulate read-only access to the tables. Setting `AllowUpdating` to `NoTables` also increases the speed of most queries. If your forms include a combo box to select a specific record, you need to open the form with the value of the `DefaultEditing` property set to `AllowEdits`. Otherwise, the user cannot type an entry into an unbound combo box (such as cboCodes on the frmSuppliers form of MULTIMED.MDB) to shortcut the process of finding a record in large tables. If the user does not need to type entries, you can set the value of the `DefaultEditing` property of the form to `ReadOnly`.

> **NOTE**
>
> Access applies the read-only attribute to all objects in the database when you open a database in read-only mode. Therefore, you cannot create new database objects, such as custom **QueryDef** objects, when you open databases in read-only mode. When you open the database in read-write mode, all tables are opened in read-write mode. As is the case for attached tables, your forms (and the Access Basic code behind the forms) control whether the application can update unsecured tables.

Create a **Recordset** object cloned from the RecordsetClone property of the table or query that underlies the main form, as described in the section, "Setting the Enabled Property of Command Buttons," of the preceding chapter. Use the Bookmark property of the first and last records of the cloned **Recordset** to toggle the value of the Enabled property of the Prior, Next, and any other record navigation command buttons on your form. You don't need to update the clone **Recordset** during the user's session in the majority of decision-support applications. Alternatively, you can detect that the user has selected the last valid record by examining the value of the key field and disable the Next button if the key field value is **Null**.

In most cases, you can set the value of the DefaultEditing property of subforms to ReadOnly. You do not need to base the subform on a non-updatable query, as described in the preceding chapter's "Designing Data Validation Forms" section, because you don't allow the editing of existing data with decision-support forms. The appearance of the Multimedia Suppliers form modified for use as a decision-support form is shown in Figure 9.1. The Cancel, Add, Product Details, and Contact Details buttons are removed, but decision-support users can display the modal pop-up lookup forms, frmCategories, frmChapters, frmClasses, and frmTypes, and they can dial the firm's primary number (by clicking the Dial button) or the direct line to a contact at the firm (by double-clicking the contact's telephone number). Setting the value of the DefaultEditing property of both subforms to ReadOnly eliminates the tentative append record for products and contacts.

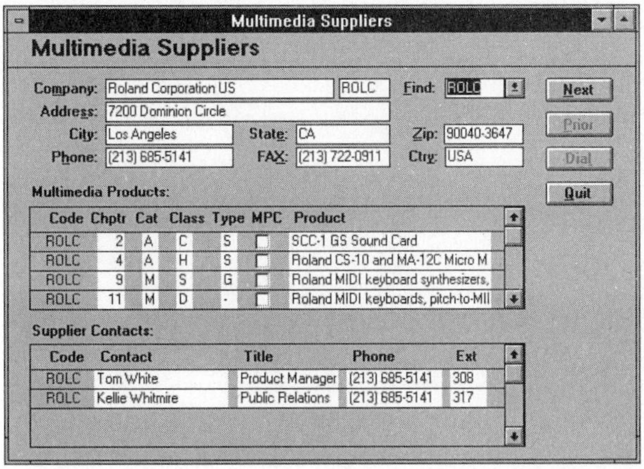

FIGURE 9.1.

*The frmSuppliers
form of
MULTIMED.MDB
modified for
decision-support
use.*

NOTE

The decision-support version of the Multimedia Suppliers form is included
in the DEC_SUPT.MDB database on the accompanying diskette. As with
the original version in MULTIMED.MDB, the DMM_DATA.MDB
database that contains the attached tables for frmSuppliers must be located
in your C:\ACCESS\ADG20 directory. If DMM_DATA.MDB is elsewhere, use the Attachment Manager add-in to reattach the tables from
DMM_DATA.MDB.

Drill-Down Techniques

Decision-support applications that present an initial "broad-brush" visualization of
data from tables and queries usually require the capability to display the detailed
information that underlie the summary data. Displaying selected detail elements of
summaries is called *drilling down* into the data. For example, when you display a graph
based on a crosstab query in the opening form of a decision-support application, such
as that shown in Figure 9.2, and add a Data button to the form to display the crosstab
query result set of Figure 9.3, you've created a single-level drill-down form. The forms
shown in Figure 9.2 and Figure 9.3 are modified versions of the custom crosstab graph
and data forms described in Chapter 24.

FIGURE 9.2.

*A "broad-brush"
graph of sales of
beverages for a two-
year period.*

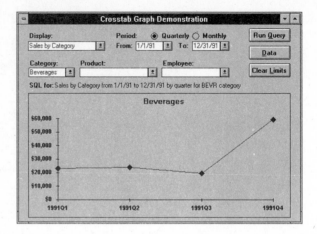

Once you display the subform, you open a Pandora's box of opportunities to drill deeper into the data. The double-click event of bound and unbound text boxes is the logical event to use for drill-down purposes. For example, you might use the DblClick event of the fields of the subform shown in Figure 9.3 to display the following types of data in the third drill-down level:

- An English Name header text box, to open a modal pop-up form that displays a list created from the Product Name and Supplier Name fields of the Products table for every product in the Beverages category.

- English Name detail fields, to open a modal pop-up form that displays other information about the product, such as the supplier's name, packaging data, cost and list prices, and discount schedules.

- 1991Q1-1991Q4 header text boxes, to display a list of customers who purchased products in the Beverages category during the quarter.

- 1991Q1-1991Q4 detail fields, to display a list of each invoice issued for the corresponding product during the quarter.

- 1991Q1-1991Q4 footer totals text boxes, to display a list of invoices issued for any product in the Beverage category for the quarter.

- Totals column detail fields, to display a list of every invoice issued for the product during the one-year period covered by the crosstab query.

- The grand total footer column, to display a list of every invoice for every product during the period of the crosstab query.

FIGURE 9.3.

The data that underlies the graph of Figure 9.2.

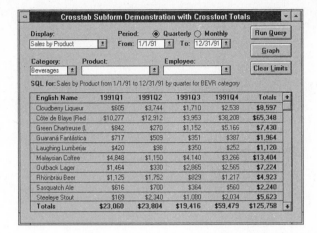

English Name	1991Q1	1991Q2	1991Q3	1991Q4	Totals
Cloudberry Liqueur	$605	$3,744	$1,710	$2,538	$8,597
Côte de Blaye (Red	$10,277	$12,912	$3,953	$38,208	$65,348
Green Chartreuse (L	$842	$270	$1,152	$5,166	$7,430
Guaraná Fantástica	$717	$509	$351	$387	$1,964
Laughing Lumberjac	$420	$98	$350	$252	$1,120
Malaysian Coffee	$4,848	$1,150	$4,140	$3,266	$13,404
Outback Lager	$1,464	$330	$2,865	$2,565	$7,224
Rhönbräu Beer	$1,125	$1,752	$829	$1,217	$4,923
Sasquatch Ale	$616	$700	$364	$560	$2,240
Steeleye Stout	$169	$2,340	$1,080	$2,034	$5,623
Totals	$23,060	$23,804	$19,416	$59,479	$125,758

Each of the lists that result from double-clicking a field on the subform can open other forms, such as a form to display a particular invoice or provide details on customer purchases. The possibilities for the use of drilling down into the data are virtually limitless, even with a form as simple as that shown in Figure 9.3. Each drill-down form that you open should be provided with a button that lets the user return to the preceding level or jump back to the original form from which the drilling commenced.

You use Access Basic functions similar to those used to open subsidiary forms or lookup lists in the Multimedia Suppliers interactive transaction-processing form described in the preceding chapter. You may want to open conventional modeless forms for drill down applications so that the user can choose to redisplay any previously opened form.

Designing a General-Purpose QueryWizard

Many decision-support applications require that the user be allowed to create his or her own queries to choose the data that will be displayed on a form or transferred to a spreadsheet or word-processing application. It is unlikely that you'd want to grant users of your applications unfettered access to the tables in your database applications with the query-by-example design feature of retail Access. If your application runs under MSARN200.EXE, the query-design feature is not available. You cannot distribute the Microsoft wizards with your runtime applications (due to the terms of the ADT license agreement), so you can't use the Access 2.0 Query Wizard to create queries.

NOTE

Theoretically, it is possible to use Microsoft Query (MSQuery) with an Access application to return data to an Access Recordset. MSQuery is a server that uses DDE to communicate with applications, such as Microsoft Word 6.0 and Excel 5.0. A substantial amount of Access Basic code is required to use MSQuery, and the benefits of providing a graphical query tool are not likely to compensate for the programming effort. Further, users of your applications would need to have one of the members of Microsoft Office 4.0 that include MSQuery and the ODBC drivers that accompany MSQuery, plus the special ODBC driver required for MSQuery to connect to Access 2.0 .MDB files.

To enable users to make their own selections of data within the limits that you set, you must provide users with a simple wizard to substitute for Access's query-design window. The term "wizard" describes a self-contained subapplication that creates a component of an application for users through a series of predetermined steps. The QueryWizard qualifies as a wizard, because the QueryWizard creates a persistent `QueryDef` object that appears in the Database window. Chapter 24, "Using Access Wizard Functions," describes more sophisticated wizards that you can use to create custom forms.

Wizards usually consist of a series of modal pop-up forms (the equivalent of dialog boxes) in which users make selections of the parameters that determine the properties of an object. You use the FieldWizard and QueryWizard forms, described in the following two sections, in sequence to determine the `SQL` property of a `QueryDef` object. Users pick the fields of a table to include in the query-result set and the sort order in list boxes on the FieldWizard form, and then they add criteria in a similar set of list boxes on the QueryWizard form. Access Basic code underlying the forms creates an Access SQL statement from the user's choices and displays the statement in an adjoining text box. Users receive two benefits from the QueryWizard: they create their own queries and they learn simple SQL grammar simultaneously.

NOTE

You need to open the database in which the QueryWizard is located in read-write mode, because the QueryWizard creates a persistent `QueryDef` object that appears in the Database window. (The name of the `QueryDef` object is the table name prefixed with "qry.") You cannot create or modify any persistent database object, such as a form or a table, in a database that you open in read-only mode.

Designing and Writing the Code for the FieldWizard Form

The basic tenet of wizard design is simplicity; successful wizards are easy to use. Another rule for wizard design is to minimize the number of choices you offer on a single form. Although you can incorporate the four list boxes of both the FieldWizard and the QueryWizard on a single form, the natural process of creating an SQL query is first to choose the fields you want to include in the query-result set and the sort sequence of the set. Then apply criteria to select the records you want from the sorted set. Thus, the QueryWizard consists of two forms: frmFieldWizard and frmQueryWizard.

The frmFieldWizard form incorporates two list boxes, lstFields and lstSort, which complete the SELECT statement and the ORDER BY clause, respectively, of the query's SQL statement. Command buttons are provided to do one of the following: add fields to the SQL statement (cmdAddField), delete the last field added (cmdDelLastField), delete all the fields added (cmdDelAllFields), proceed to the QueryWizard form (cmdQuery), or cancel query creation (cmdCancel). To minimize the number of buttons on the form, a toggle button (tglSort) determines whether the Add Field, Delete Last, and Delete All command buttons act on the SELECT statement (tglSort = **False**) or on the ORDER BY statement (tglSort = **True**). Once you've chosen the fields that you want in the query and selected the sort order, you click the Query button to close the frmFieldWizard form and open the frmQueryWizard form. The design of the frmFieldWizard form is depicted in Figure 9.4.

FIGURE 9.4.

The design of the FormWizard dialog.

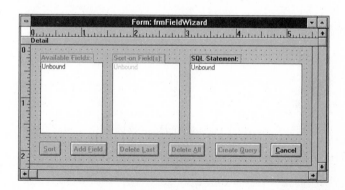

The following sections list and describe the Access Basic code for the frmFieldWizard form. Much of the code is devoted to controlling the enabled property of the list box labels and command buttons so that the actions available to the user are indicated by labels and buttons with black captions. Enabling and disabling controls also results in simpler Access Basic functions; you don't have to write code to test the status of other controls to determine whether each event-handler function should execute.

NOTE

The frmFieldWizard and frmQueryWizard forms, together with the Field and Query Wizard module, are included in the DEC_SUPT.MDB database on the accompanying diskette. Attach or import the Customers table from the Northwind Traders sample database to DEC_SUPT.MDB to provide the data for the custom query. Open the frmField Wizard form from the Database window to initiate operation of the QueryWizard.

The Declarations Section of the Field and Query Wizards Module

In contrast to many of the other examples in this book, the majority of the variables for the QueryWizard application are declared with module-level scope. This is necessary because the event-handling functions for most list-box selections and for command and toggle-button actuation need to know the status of the selection process. These event handlers are executed by events on the form, so arguments supplied by the function call that you enter as the value of events are not appropriate in this case.

Following are the declarations of the module-level variables for the Field and Query wizards:

```
Option Compare Database    'Use database order for string
                           ➥ comparisons
Option Explicit            'Declare all variables before use

'Module-level variable declarations for FieldWizard and QueryWizard
➥forms

Dim frmFields      As Form     'frmFieldWizard form
Dim frmQuery       As Form     'frmQueryWizard form
Dim lstField       As Control  'selected field from frmFieldWizard
Dim lstSort        As Control  'selected sort field on
                               ➥ frmFieldWizard
Dim txtSQLText     As Control  'txtSQL on both forms
Dim lstOperator    As Control  'lstOperators
Dim txtCompare     As Control  'txtCriterion

Dim strSQL         As String   'SQL statement to be executed
Dim strSQLSelect   As String   'SELECT DISTINCTROW statement
Dim strSQLFrom     As String   'FROM clause
Dim strSQLWhere    As String   'WHERE clause
Dim strSQLOrderBy  As String   'ORDER BY clause
Dim strSQLSort     As String   'ORDER BY statement
Dim strSQLRule     As String   'WHERE statement
Dim strSQLEnd      As String   'WITH OWNERACCESS OPTION;

Dim strLastField   As String   'Last field added to SELECT
```

```
Dim strLastSort      As String   'Last field added to ORDER BY
Dim strLastRule      As String   'Last rule added to WHERE
Dim strThisRule      As String   'Current rule being added to WHERE

Dim wNumFields       As Integer  'Number of fields in SELECT
Dim wNumSorts        As Integer  'Number of fields in ORDER BY
Dim wNumRules        As Integer  'Number of rules in WHERE
Dim fIsSort          As Integer  'True if tglSort pushed
Dim fIsField         As Integer  'True if frmFieldWizard active
Dim fIsStarted       As Integer  'True if frmQueryWizard has opened
Dim wRetVal          As Integer  'General-purpose return value

Dim strTableName     As String   'Name of table underlying query
Dim rgstrFields()    As String   'List of fields and data types
```

The Entry-Point Function, *fw_StartSQL()*

All wizards require an entry-point function that initializes the values of global and module-level variables. To avoid the necessity of using the Immediate window or a File Add-In menu choice to launch the QueryWizard, the OnOpen event of the frmFieldWizard form executes the fwStartSQL() function. When you incorporate the QueryWizard in an application, you call fw_wIntialize("*TableName*") from an event. The fw_wInitialize() function is the entry-point function for the QueryWizard that opens the frmFieldWizard form and fills an array of field information. Executing entry-point functions in libraries by File Add-In menu choices is one of the subjects of Chapter 24.

> **TIP**
>
> When debugging code associated with events that occur on pop-up forms (either modal or modeless), temporarily set the values of both the PopUp and Modal properties to No. If you encounter an error in your code when a modal pop-up form is active, the focus moves to the newly opened module window. However, you cannot close a modal pop-up form to examine your code unless you choose Reinitialize from the Run menu to halt execution of the code and reset all variables.

```
Function fw_StartSQL (strTableName)
    'Purpose:   Assign default valuables to module-level variables
    'Argument:  Name of table passed as literal
    'Called by: OnOpen event of frmFieldWizard
    'Returns:   Nil

    'MSA20: You can set the value of the RowSource property only
    '          in a function or procedure called by the Open event of a form
```

```
    If strTableName = "" Then
        strTableName = "Customers"
    End If
    Forms("frmFieldWizard")!lstFields.RowSource = strTableName
    Forms("frmFieldWizard")!lstSortFields.RowSource = strTableName

    'Initialize SQL variables
    strSQLSelect = "SELECT DISTINCTROW"
    strSQLFrom = " FROM " & strTableName & " "
    strSQLWhere = "WHERE "
    strSQLOrderBy = "ORDER BY"
    strSQLEnd = " WITH OWNERACCESS OPTION;"
    strLastField = ""
    strSQL = ""
    strSQLSort = ""
    strSQLRule = ""
    strLastRule = ""
    wNumFields = 0
    wNumSorts = 0
    wNumRules = 0
    fIsField = True
    fIsSort = False
End Function
```

The value of the RowSourceType property of both list boxes is FieldList, and the value of the RowSource property is set to the value of the strTableName argument you pass to the fw_StartSQL() function. If you specify =fwStartSQL("Customers"), when you open the form, both list boxes are filled with the names of fields of the Customers table. RowSource, like many other properties of Access 1.x forms, reports, and controls, was read-only in Access 1.x's run mode. Access 2.0, however, lets you set most properties in run mode. The section called "Filling List Boxes and Combo Boxes with an Access Basic Function," later in the chapter, shows you an alternate method to fill the two list boxes with the field names of the table specified by strTableName using the rgstrFields() array created by the fw_wInitialize() function.

> ### NOTE
>
> The prefix fw_ added to the names of functions identifies the association of the function with a form. The prefix also serves to add uniqueness to the name of the function so that duplicating the names of functions in other modules is unlikely. Creating unique names for wizard functions is important because most wizards are attached to Access as libraries. Chapter 23, "Developing Access Libraries and Add-Ins," discusses the subject of aliasing function names with unique prefixes.

Adding a Field to the *SELECT* and *SORT* Statements

Before you can add a field to the SQL SELECT statement or ORDER BY clause, you need to choose a field from the active list box, as determined by the status of the tglSort toggle button. If you select a field with a single-click on a field name in either of the list boxes, the fwEnableAdd() function enables the Add Field button.

```
Function fw_EnableAdd ()
    'Purpose:   Enable cmdAddField when a selection is made
    'Called by: AfterUpdate event of lstFields and lstSortFields
    'Returns:   Nil

    Forms!frmFieldWizard!cmdAddField.Enabled = True
End Function
```

Alternately, you can add a field to the SQL statement by double-clicking the field name in the enabled list box. Clicking the Add Field button or double-clicking the name of a field executes the fw_wAddField() function. If the Sort button (tglSort) is depressed, the fw_wAddField() function executes the fw_wAddSort() function, whose listing follows. The fw_wAddField() function tests to determine whether the field you selected is already included in the SELECT statement and issues an error message upon detecting a duplicate field with the **InStr**() function.

If the field name contains one or more spaces, square brackets are added to the beginning and the end of the field-name variable, strLastField. The name of the last field that was added is stored in a variable so that clicking the Delete Last button can replace the value of strLastField with "". When you add a new field, the prior value of strLastField is made a permanent part of the SQL SELECT statement. Then the fw_wAddField() function calls the fw_SQLText procedure to display the resulting SQL statement in the txtSQL text box. **DoCmd** GoToControl methods return the focus to the active list box, and a **SendKeys** statement automatically moves the selection to the next field name in the list box.

Listing 9.1. Access Basic code to add a field name to an SQL statement.

```
Function fw_wAddField () As Integer
    'Purpose:   Add a field to the SQL query
    '           Enable and disable appropriate pushbuttons
    'Called by: OnClick event of cmdAddField button
    '           OnDblClick event of lstFields list box
    'Returns:   True if successful, False on error

    If fIsSort Then
        'Add field to the ORDER BY clause
        wRetVal = fw_wAddSort()
        Exit Function
```

continues

Listing 9.1. continued

```
End If

Set frmFields = Forms!frmFieldWizard
Set lstField = frmFields!lstFields

'Test if added field is duplicated in query
If Len(strSQL) > 0 And InStr(strSQL, lstField) > 0 Then
    GoTo FieldError
End If
If Len(strLastField) > 0 And InStr(strLastField, lstField) > 0
    ➥Then
    GoTo FieldError
End If

If wNumFields > 1 Then
    'Add the last field to the SQL statement
    strSQL = strSQL + ", " + strLastField
Else
    If wNumFields = 0 Then
        'Add SELECT ...
        strSQL = strSQLSelect
    Else
        'Add the last field to the SQL string
        strSQL = strSQL + " " + strLastField
    End If
End If

'Add brackets around field names with spaces
If InStr(lstField, " ") > 0 Then
    strLastField = "[" & lstField & "]"
Else
    strLastField = lstField
End If

wNumFields = wNumFields + 1

'Paint the SQL statement text box
Call fw_SQLText

'Return the focus to the appropriate list box and move cursor
If fIsSort Then
    DoCmd GoToControl "lstSortFields"
Else
    DoCmd GoToControl "lstFields"
End If
SendKeys "{Down}"

'Enable all the buttons
frmFields!cmdDelLastField.Enabled = True
frmFields!cmdDelAllFields.Enabled = True
```

```
    frmFields!cmdCreateQuery.Enabled = True
    frmFields!tglSort.Enabled = True

    fw_wAddField = True
    Exit Function

FieldError:
    MsgBox "Field '" & lstField & "' already selected.", 32, "Field _
           ➡Error"
    fw_wAddField = False
    Exit Function
End Function
```

The `fw_wAddSort()` function is similar in structure and operation to the `fw_wAddField()` function. The `fw_wAddSort()` function uses the **InStr**() function to detect that a field chosen for sorting is not included in the selected fields. A message box enables the user to accept or reject sorting on a hidden field.

Listing 9.2. Access Basic code to add a sort criterion to an SQL statement.

```
Function fw_wAddSort () As Integer
    'Purpose:   Add a field to the ORDER BY clause
    '           Enable and disable appropriate pushbuttons
    'Called by: fw_wAddField If tglSort = True
    '           OnDblClick event of lstSortFields
    'Returns:   True if successful, False on error
    'Note:      Same structure as fw_wAddField (thus only changes
    '           ➡commented)

    Set frmFields = Forms!frmFieldWizard
    Set lstSort = frmFields!lstSortFields
    Dim strMsg As String

    If IsNull(lstSort) Then
        'Prevents execution if a field is not selected
        Exit Function
    End If


    'Error on duplicate sort fields
    If Len(strSQLSort) > 0 And InStr(strSQLSort, lstSort) > 0 Then
        GoTo SortError
    End If
    If Len(strLastSort) > 0 And InStr(strLastSort, lstSort) > 0
            ➡Then
        GoTo SortError
    End If
```

continues

Listing 9.2. continued

```
'Detect sort on unselected field and request confirmation
If InStr(strSQL, lstSort) + InStr(strLastField, lstSort) = 0
        ➡Then
    strMsg = "'" & lstSort & "' is not in field list. "
    strMsg = strMsg & "Use hidden field for sorting?"
    If MsgBox(strMsg, 36, "Hidden Sort Field") <> 6 Then
        Exit Function
    End If
End If


'Create the ORDER BY clause
If wNumSorts > 1 Then
    strSQLSort = strSQLSort + ", " + strLastSort
Else
    If wNumSorts = 0 Then
        strSQLSort = strSQLOrderBy
    Else
        strSQLSort = strSQLSort + " " + strLastSort
    End If
End If


If InStr(lstSort, " ") > 0 Then
    strLastSort = "[" & lstSort & "]"
Else
    strLastSort = lstSort
End If


wNumSorts = wNumSorts + 1
Call fw_SQLText

DoCmd GoToControl "lstSortFields"
SendKeys "{Down}"

frmFields!cmdDelLastField.Enabled = True
frmFields!cmdDelAllFields.Enabled = True
frmFields!cmdCreateQuery.Enabled = True
fw_wAddSort = True
Exit Function

SortError:
    MsgBox "Sort field '" & lstSort & "' already selected.", 32,
            ➡"Field Error"
    fw_wAddSort = False
    Exit Function
End Function
```

Determining the Visible and Enabled Properties of Controls

The setting of the tglSort button determines whether clicking the Add Field, Delete Last (field), or Delete All (fields) buttons applies to values of the SQL SELECT statement or the ORDER BY clause. You can toggle the tglSort button at any time after you have added at least one field to the SELECT statement. As you add fields to the SELECT statement, you can click the tglSort button to add a field to the ORDER BY clause, and vice versa. Thus a good deal of testing and housekeeping is required of the fwTestSort() function when you click the tglSort button so that the proper command buttons are enabled.

Listing 9.3. Access Basic code to set control properties.

```
Function fw_TestSort ()
    'Purpose:    Enable the list boxes, depending on value of tglSort
    '            Display or hide the gray label (indicating
    '            ➥disabled)
    '            Enable appropriate buttons for field or sort
    '            ➥selection
    'Called by: AfterUpdate event of tglSort button
    'Returns:    Nil

    Set frmFields = Forms!frmFieldWizard

    If frmFields!tglSort Then
        'The Sort toggle button is pushed; set fIsSort flag
        fIsSort = True
        frmFields!lstFields.Enabled = False
        frmFields!lblFields.Visible = True
        frmFields!lstSortFields.Enabled = True
        frmFields!lblSort.Visible = False
        If IsNull(frmFields!lstSortFields) Then
            frmFields!cmdAddField.Enabled = False
        End If
        If Len(strSQLSort) > 0 Then
            frmFields!cmdDelAllFields.Enabled = True
        Else
            frmFields!cmdDelAllFields.Enabled = False
        End If
        If Len(strLastSort) > 0 Then
            frmFields!cmdDelLastField.Enabled = True
        Else
            frmFields!cmdDelLastField.Enabled = False
        End If
        DoCmd GoToControl "lstSortFields"
    Else
        'Sort toggle button is not pushed
        fIsSort = False
```

continues

Listing 9.3. continued

```
        frmFields!lstFields.Enabled = True
        frmFields!lblFields.Visible = False
        frmFields!lstSortFields.Enabled = False
        frmFields!lblSort.Visible = True
        If Len(strSQL) > 0 Then
            frmFields!cmdDelAllFields.Enabled = True
        Else
            frmFields!cmdDelAllFields.Enabled = False
        End If
        If Len(strLastField) > 0 Then
            frmFields!cmdDelLastField.Enabled = True
        Else
            frmFields!cmdDelLastField.Enabled = False
        End If
        DoCmd GoToControl "lstFields"
    End If
End Function
```

Deleting Fields from Query

The `fw_DelLastField()` and `fw_DelAllFields()` functions delete the last field and all the fields, respectively, from the SQL SELECT statement or ORDER BY clause, depending on the setting of the tglSort button. When you delete the last remaining field with `fw_DelLastField()` or all the fields with the `fw_DelAllFields()` functions, these functions reset the Enabled status of the appropriate command buttons.

Listing 9.4. Access Basic code to remove a field entry.

```
Function fw_DelLastField ()
    'Purpose:    Delete last field entered if tglSort = False
    '            Delete last sort field entered if tglSort = True
    '            Enable and disable appropriate pushbuttons
    'Called by: OnClick event of cmdDelLastField button
    'Returns:    Nil

    Set frmFields = Forms!frmFieldWizard
    Set txtSQLText = frmFields!txtSQL

    If fIsSort Then
        'Delete the last ORDER BY field
        strLastSort = ""
        wNumSorts = wNumSorts - 1
        If wNumSorts = 0 Then
            strSQLSort = ""
        End If
        DoCmd GoToControl "lstSortFields"
```

```
    Else
        'Delete the last SELECT field
        strLastField = ""
        wNumFields = wNumFields - 1
        If wNumFields = 0 Then
            strSQL = ""
        End If
        DoCmd GoToControl "lstFields"
    End If

    'Update the SQL statement text box
    Call fw_SQLText

    'Reset the status of the buttons
    frmFields!cmdDelLastField.Enabled = False
    If (wNumFields = 0 And Not fIsSort) Or (wNumSorts = 0 And
    ➥fIsSort) Then
        frmFields!cmdDelAllFields.Enabled = False
        frmFields!cmdCreateQuery.Enabled = False
        frmFields!tglSort.Enabled = False
    End If
End Function

Function fw_DelAllFields ()
    'Purpose:    Delete the SQL statement if tglSort = False
    '            Delete the SQL ORDER BY statement if tglSort = True
    '            Enable and disable appropriate pushbuttons
    'Called by: OnClick event of cmdDelAllFields button
    'Returns:    Nil

    Set frmFields = Forms!frmFieldWizard
    Set txtSQLText = frmFields!txtSQL

    wNumSorts = 0
    strSQLSort = ""
    strLastSort = ""
    If fIsSort Then
        'Delete only the ORDER BY clause
        txtSQLText = strSQL & strSQLFrom
        DoCmd GoToControl "lstSortFields"
    Else
        'Delete the entire SQL statement
        wNumFields = 0
        strSQL = ""
        strLastField = ""
        txtSQLText = ""

        'Reset button status
        frmFields!tglSort = False
        frmFields!tglSort.Enabled = False
        frmFields!lstFields.Enabled = True
        frmFields!cmdCreateQuery.Enabled = False
```

continues

Listing 9.4. continued

```
        DoCmd GoToControl "lstFields"
    End If

    'Reset the delete fields buttons' status
    frmFields!cmdDelAllFields.Enabled = False
    frmFields!cmdDelLastField.Enabled = False
End Function
```

Creating or Canceling the Query

Once you've added at least one field to the SQL SELECT statement, you proceed to the next form, frmQueryWizard, to add criteria to the WHERE clause of the SQL statement and execute the query. The fw_CreateQuery() function adds the last field to the SQL SELECT statement and the last sort field (if any) to the ORDER BY clause, closes the frmFieldWizard form, and opens the frmQueryWizard form.

Listing 9.5. Access Basic code to create the SQL statement.

```
Function fw_CreateQuery ()
    'Purpose:    Complete the SQL statements, close frmFieldWizard
    '            Open frmQueryWizard
    'Called by: OnClick event of the cmdCreateQuery button
    'Returns:    Nil

    'Add the last field to the SELECT field list
    If wNumFields > 1 Then
        'Add trailing comma
        strSQL = strSQL + ","
    End If
    strSQL = strSQL & " " & strLastField

    'Add the last sort field to the ORDER BY field list
    If wNumSorts > 1 Then
        'Add trailing comma
        strSQLSort = strSQLSort + ","
    End If
    strSQLSort = strSQLSort & " " & strLastSort

    'Reset the last field values
    strLastField = ""
    strLastSort = ""

    'Launch the Query Wizard form
    DoCmd Close A_FORM, "frmFieldWizard"
    DoCmd OpenForm "frmQueryWizard"
End Function
```

You can terminate the QueryWizard at any time by clicking the Cancel button to clear the variables and close the frmFieldWizards form.

```
Function fw_Cancel ()
    'Purpose:   Close frmFieldWizard, empty the SQL strings
    'Called by: OnClick event of the cmdCancel button
    'Returns:   Nil

    strSQL = ""
    strSQLSort = ""
    strLastField = ""
    strLastSort = ""

    DoCmd Close A_FORM, "frmFieldWizard"
End Function
```

Displaying the SQL Statement

The fw_SQLText procedure displays the current SQL statement in the txtSQL text box. The fw_SQLText procedure updates the contents of the txtSQL text box each time you modify the statement with controls located either on the frmFieldWizard or on the frmQueryWizard form. The fw_SQLText procedure concatenates the individual components of the SQL statement because you do not create a final SQL statement until you click the Run Query button of the frmQueryWizard form. The fw_SQLText procedure adds commas to punctuate lists of fields as required by SQL grammar.

Listing 9.6. Access Basic code to display the SQL SELECT statement.

```
Sub fw_SQLText ()
    'Purpose:   Display the current SQL statement in the text box
    'Called by: fw_wAddField, fw_wAddSort, fw_wDelLastField,
                ➥fw_wDelAllFields
    '           and similar functions of frmQueryWizard
    'Returns:   Nil

    Dim strSQLText As String

    If wNumFields > 0 Then
        strSQLText = strSQL
        If Len(strLastField) > 0 Then
            'Add the last SELECT field to the statement
            If wNumFields > 1 Then
                'Add a trailing comma
                strSQLText = strSQLText & ", " & strLastField
            Else
```

continues

Listing 9.6. continued

```
                    strSQLText = strSQL & " " & strLastField
            End If
        End If
        strSQLText = strSQLText & strSQLFrom & strSQLRule &
                    ➥strLastRule & strSQLSort

        If Len(strLastSort) > 0 Then
            'Add the last ORDER BY field to the statement
            If wNumSorts > 1 Then
                'Add a trailing comma
                strSQLText = strSQLText + ", " & strLastSort
            Else
                strSQLText = strSQLText + " " & strLastSort
            End If
        End If
        strSQLText = strSQLText + strSQLEnd
    Else
        strSQLText = ""
    End If

    'Replace the text in the text box (prevents flashing during
    ➥string construction)
    If fIsField Then
        Forms!frmFieldWizard!txtSQL = strSQLText
    Else
        Forms!frmQueryWizard!txtSQL = strSQLText
    End If
End Sub
```

> **NOTE**
>
> Functions that are common to both frmFieldWizard and frmQueryWizard arbitrarily are included in the FieldWizard module.

Figure 9.5 shows the frmFieldWizards form on completion of the first phase of creating a query that might be used to create a mailing-labels report or a mail-merge text file.

FIGURE 9.5.

Using the FieldWizard to create an SQL statement without criteria.

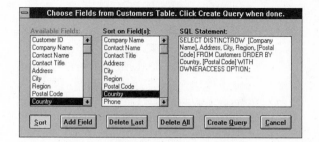

NOTE

To fix the position of a form on the display when the form opens, open the form in run mode and then click the title bar and drag the form to the position you want. Choose **S**ave Form from the **F**ile menu. Access saves the coordinates of the upper-left corner of the form's window as the values of two hidden properties of the form, Left and Top. Alternatively, you can set the value of the AutoCenter property of the form to Yes in order to center the form horizontally and position it vertically above the centerline of Access's window.

Designing and Coding the QueryWizard Form

The frmQueryWizard form is similar in appearance to the frmFieldWizard form. Another guiding principle of wizard design is to maintain a consistent style for all the forms that constitute the wizard. The frmQueryWizard form lets you add multiple criteria to the form by using the AND and OR SQL operators. Thus, the frmQueryWizard form needs two additional elements, an option group (grpAndOr) that lets you choose whether to use the AND or the OR operator, and a text box (txtCriterion) in which you enter the operand. The design of the frmQueryWizard form appears in Figure 9.6. The command buttons on the frmQueryWizard form perform similar duties to the buttons in similar positions on the frmFieldWizards form. The Run Query button creates the final query by applying the **DoCmd** CreateQueryDef method with the SQL statement that appears in the SQL text box.

NOTE

The frmQueryWizard form makes extensive use of superimposed labels to indicate the status of the two list boxes. This was necessary with Access 1.x because, unlike with Visual Basic, you could not change the ForeColor or

BackColor properties of labels and text boxes or the Caption property of labels in Access 1.x's run mode. Under the left option button and label (And) shown in Figure 9.6 are three labels: lblOperand (Is:, black), lblIs (Is:, dark gray), and lblAndGray (And, dark gray). A substantial portion of the code in the preceding listings is devoted to showing and hiding the appropriate label to indicate the status of the two list boxes.

FIGURE 9.6.

The design of the frmQueryWizard form.

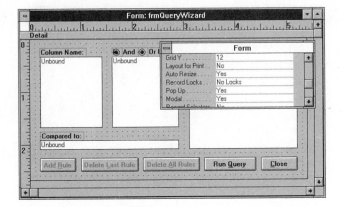

Initializing the Code for the frmQueryWizard Form

When you open the frmQueryWizard form, you need to know the field data type of the fields of the table so that the appropriate punctuation is applied to operands. For example, operands of the SQL LIKE operator and other **String** operands need to be enclosed within double quotation marks in Access SQL, whereas numeric operands do not. Therefore, you need to create a two-dimensional array consisting of table names and the **Long** integer value of the field data type, stored as a **String**.

The Access 1.1 version of qw_StartQuery() function employed the **ListFields**() method of the **Table** object specified by strTableName to create a **Snapshot** object that contained records with the values of the Fields collection of the table. You can continue to use the **ListFields**() method with Access 2.0, but you need to declare and create a **Dynaset** object over the table, then declare and create a **ListFields**() **Snapshot** object. Neither of these object types are recommended for use with Access 2.0.

You use the **Field** object of Access 2.0's **TableDef** object to return information about the fields in tables. The TableDefs collection is contained in the **Database** object and the Fields collection is contained in the **TableDef** object. The code beginning at the line Dim dbCurrent As Database of Listing 9.7 creates the array and assigns the name and field data type of the fields to the array's elements.

TIP

Code is included in the qw_StartQuery() function to let you test the frmQueryWizard form independently of prior entries in the frmFieldWizard form. The addition of test code can speed development of forms that depend on values created by previously executed code. Once you've tested your code thoroughly, you can remove the test code from the function.

Listing 9.7. Access Basic code to initialize the QueryWizard.

```
Function qw_StartQuery ()
    'Purpose:   Assign initial values for frmQueryWizard
    'Called by: OnEnter event of lstFields (cannot use OnOpen event of
            ➥form)
    'Returns:   Nil

    If fIsStarted Then
        'Do not repeat execution on successive entry to lstFields
        Exit Function
    End If

    'The following statements let you test without opening
            ➥frmFieldWizard
    'Delete these statements after testing is complete
    If strSQL = "" Then
        strSQL = "SELECT DISTINCTROW [Company Name], Address, City,
            ➥Region, [Postal Code] FROM Customers "
        wNumFields = 5
    End If
    If strSQLSort = "" Then
        strSQLSort = "ORDER BY Country, [Postal Code] "
        wNumSorts = 2
    End If
    If strTableName = "" Then
        strTableName = "Customers"
    End If
    strSQLEnd = " WITH OWNERACCESS OPTION;"

    'All statements from this point on are required
```

continues

Listing 9.7. continued

```
wNumRules = 0
fIsField = False
strSQLWhere = "WHERE "
Set frmQuery = Forms!frmQueryWizard
Call fw_SQLText
fIsStarted = True

Dim dbCurrent As Database
Dim tdfSource As TableDef    'Use the Fields property of a TableDef
        ➥object
Dim wCtr As Integer

Set dbCurrent = DBEngine(0)(0)
Set tdfSource = dbCurrent.TableDefs(strTableName)

ReDim rgstrFields(tdfSource.Fields.Count, 2)   'Get number of fields
        ➥in table

For wCtr = 1 To tdfSource.Fields.Count           'Get the name and type
        of each field
    rgstrFields(wCtr, 1) = tdfSource.Fields(wCtr - 1).Name
    rgstrFields(wCtr, 2) = Trim$(Str$(tdfSource.Fields(wCtr -
        ➥1).Type))
Next wCtr

'Close the temporary object
dbCurrent.Close
End Function
```

> **NOTE**
>
> You can avoid the necessity of casting (also called coercing) the field values of the array to a conventional data type (**String** in this case) by declaring the array **As Variant** in the **Dim** statement. Elements of arrays of the **Variant** data type can contain any **Variant** subtype. The capability to declare **Variant** arrays is one of the principle features that distinguish Object Basic from its predecessor, Visual Basic 1.0.

> **NOTE**
>
> The Access 1.x code using the **ListFields**() method is contained in the
> `qw_ListFields()` function in the Field and Query Wizards module. If you
> compare the code that is required for using the **ListFields**() method with
> that for using **Field** objects, you can see that using the
> `TableDefs(strName).Fields(intNumber).Property` method simplifies the
> code.

Adding *WHERE* Clause Rules to the SQL Statement

Adding a WHERE clause to the SQL statement is a two- or three-step process. First,
you select a column of the query in the lstFields list box. The AfterUpdate event of
the lstFields list box executes the qw_AddOperator() function that displays a dark gray
label (lblFields) in place of the default label of the lstFields list box that disappears
when you disable the list box. The default label for the lstOperators list box appears
if no prior rules have been applied; otherwise, the grpAndOr option group with its
associated labels is displayed.

```
Function qw_AddOperator ()
    'Purpose:   Force focus to operators list box
    '           Display criterion text box
    'Called by: AfterUpdate event of lstFields
    'Returns:   Nil

    Set frmQuery = Forms!frmQueryWizard
    frmQuery!lblAndGray.Visible = False
    frmQuery!lblOrIsGray.Visible = False
    If wNumRules > 0 Then
        frmQuery!grpAndOr.Visible = True
        frmQuery!lblAnd.Visible = True
        frmQuery!lblOrIs.Visible = True
        frmQuery!grpAndOr.Enabled = True
    End If
    frmQuery!lblIs.Visible = False
    frmQuery!lstOperators.Enabled = True
    frmQuery!txtCriterion.Visible = False
    DoCmd GoToControl "lstOperators"
    frmQuery!lstFields.Enabled = False
    frmQuery!lblFields.Visible = True
End Function
```

When you choose an operator from the lstOperators list box, the AfterUpdate event
executes the qw_AddCriterion() function. If the criterion is neither "Is Null" or "Is
Not Null," the qw_AddCriterion() function displays the txtCriterion text box so that
you can enter the required operand for the operator. The qw_AddCriterion()

function also resets the labels to indicate that neither the lstFields or lstOperators list boxes are active at this point.

```
Function qw_AddCriterion ()
    'Purpose:    Display criterion text box if not a null operator
    'Called by: AfterUpdate event of operators text box
    'Returns:    Nil

    Set frmQuery = Forms!frmQueryWizard

    If InStr(frmQuery!lstOperators, "Null") > 0 Then
        'No criterion is required for Is Null or Not Is Null
        frmQuery!cmdAddRule.Enabled = True
        DoCmd GoToControl "cmdAddRule"
    Else
        frmQuery!txtCriterion.Visible = True
        DoCmd GoToControl "txtCriterion"
    End If

    'Reset the labels
    If wNumRules > 0 Then
        frmQuery!lblAnd.Visible = False
        frmQuery!lblOrIs.Visible = False
        frmQuery!lblAndGray.Visible = True
        frmQuery!lblOrIsGray.Visible = True
    Else
        frmQuery!lblIs.Visible = True
        frmQuery!lstOperators.Enabled = False
    End If
End Function
```

The qw_wTestCriterion() function conducts a series of tests on the txtCriterion entry. The majority of the tests are based on the formatting necessary to take into account the field data type. If, for example, the field data type is Date/Time, you need to add # symbols to the entry. The qw_wTestCriterion() function also tests for the presence of And in the txtCriterion entry when you use the Between operator.

Listing 9.8. Access Basic code to test SQL WHERE clause values.

```
Function qw_wTestCriterion () As Integer
    'Purpose:    Test and format the entry in the criterion text box
    'Called by: OnExit event of txtCriterion
    'Returns:    True if successful, False on failure

    Dim strMsg As String        'Error message
    Dim wCtr As Integer         'General-purpose counter
    Dim strFieldType As String  'Field data type of selected field
    Dim wAndPos As Integer      'Position of "And" in "Between"
                                ➥argument
```

```
Dim strChar As String        'Replacement character

Set frmQuery = Forms!frmQueryWizard
Set lstField = frmQuery!lstFields
Set lstOperator = frmQuery!lstOperators
Set txtCompare = frmQuery!txtCriterion

'Test for errors in choosing a field and an operator
'This test can be removed if you correctly enable the other
        ➡controls
If IsNull(lstField) Then
    MsgBox "You must choose a field before adding an operator.", 48,
        ➡              "Rule Error"
    DoCmd GoToControl "lstFields"
    Exit Function
End If
If IsNull(lstOperator) Then
    MsgBox "You must add an operator if you choose a field.", 48,
        ➡              "Rule Error"
    DoCmd GoToControl "lstOperators"
    Exit Function
End If


'Test for errors in the operand text box
If IsNull(txtCompare) And InStr(lstOperator, "Null") = 0 Then
    strMsg = "You must add an operand after adding an operator
        ➡(except Null and Not Null.)"
    GoTo RuleError
End If
If lstOperator = "Between" And InStr(UCase$(txtCompare), "AND") =
        ➡0 Then
    strMsg = "You must include 'And' between two operands."
    GoTo RuleError
End If


'Find the field name in the ListFields array to get the data
        ➡type
'(This array is created in qw_StartQuery)
For wCtr = 1 To UBound(rgstrFields)
    If rgstrFields(wCtr, 1) = lstField Then
        strFieldType = rgstrFields(wCtr, 2)
        Exit For
    End If
Next wCtr

'Add brackets around field names with spaces
If InStr(lstField, " ") > 0 Then
    strThisRule = "[" & lstField & "]"
Else
    strThisRule = lstField
End If
```

continues

Listing 9.8. continued

```
'Test for numeric values compared to string fields (use Val())
'or numeric values compared to date fields (use #'s)
If Val(txtCompare) > 0 Then
    'Note: Field data type values have no relationship
        ➥to Variant type values
    If strFieldType = "10" Then 'Field is Text
        'Use Val() if txtCompare is numeric
        strThisRule = "Val(" & strThisRule & ")"
    ElseIf strFieldType = "8" Then  'Field is Date
        'Add #'s to dates
        txtCompare = "#" & txtCompare & "#"
    End If
End If


'Test the string if the operator is "Like" or if
'the field type is text and the operator is "=" or "Between"
If lstOperator = "Like" Or (strFieldType = "10" And
➥(lstOperator = "=" Or lstOperator = "Between") And
➥Val(txtCompare) = 0) Then
    'Fix the Like string, if quotes are missing
    If Left$(txtCompare, 1) <> Chr$(34) Then
        txtCompare = Chr$(34) & txtCompare
    End If
    If Right$(txtCompare, 1) <> Chr$(34) Then
        txtCompare = txtCompare & Chr$(34)
    End If
End If


'Fix the intervening quotes or #'s for "Between...And"
        ➥operators
If lstOperator = "Between" And Left$(txtCompare, 1) = Chr$(34) Or
        ➥Left$(txtCompare, 1) = "#" Then
    'Get position of "And" (assumes spaces fore and aft)
    wAndPos = InStr(UCase$(txtCompare), "AND")
    'Test the length of the string and case "aNd" to "And"
    If Len(txtCompare) > wAndPos + 6 Then
        txtCompare = Left$(txtCompare, wAndPos - 1) &
        ➥"And" & Mid$(txtCompare, wAndPos + 3)
        If strFieldType = "8" Then
            strChar = "#"
        Else
            strChar = Chr$(34)
        End If
        'Replace the first missing character, if necessary
        If Mid$(txtCompare, wAndPos - 2) <> strChar Then
            txtCompare = Left$(txtCompare, wAndPos - 2) &
        ➥strChar & Mid$(txtCompare, wAndPos - 1)
        End If
        'Replace the second missing character, If necessary
        If Mid$(txtCompare, wAndPos + 5) <> strChar Then
```

```
                txtCompare = Left$(txtCompare, wAndPos + 4) &
            ➥strChar & Mid$(txtCompare, wAndPos + 5)
            End If
        Else
            strMsg = "There is something missing in your 'And'
            ➥criteria."
            GoTo RuleError
        End If
    End If


    'Enable and give the Add Rule button the focus
    Forms!frmQueryWizard!cmdAddRule.Enabled = True
    DoCmd GoToControl "cmdAddRule"

    qw_wTestCriterion = True
    Exit Function

RuleError:
    MsgBox strMsg, 48, "Rule Error"
    qw_wTestCriterion = False
    'This is a workaround for the inability to force the focus back
    'to the control that presently has the focus
    DoCmd GoToControl "lstOperators"
    Exit Function
End Function
```

WARNING

There are many records in the Customers table of NWIND.MDB that contain **Null** values in the Postal Code field. If you attempt to use the **Val( )** function with a **Null** argument, you receive an error message. When you test an SQL statement that uses an operator with the Postal Code field, precede the Postal Code criterion with a Country = "USA" criterion.

The last step in creating a WHERE criterion is to click the Add Rule command button to create the value of strLastRule. The qw_AddRule( ) function adds the WHERE statement to the SQL WHERE clause on its first execution, and then concatenates the value of strLastRule on successive executions.

```
Function qw_AddRule ()
    'Purpose:   Add the last rule to the SQL statement, if one
               ➥exists
    '           Create a new "last rule" for the statement
    'Called by: OnClick event of Add Rule button
    'Returns:   Nil
```

```
    Set frmQuery = Forms!frmQueryWizard

    If wNumRules = 0 Then
        'Create the WHERE clause
        strSQLRule = " WHERE "
    Else
        'Add the last rule to the WHERE clause
        strSQLRule = strSQLRule & " " & strLastRule
    End If

    'Create the new last rule
    If wNumRules > 0 Then
        'Add AND or OR from button
        If frmQuery!grpAndOr = 1 Then
            strLastRule = " AND (" & strThisRule
        Else
            strLastRule = " OR (" & strThisRule
        End If
    Else
        strLastRule = "(" & strThisRule
    End If

    wNumRules = wNumRules + 1

    'Update the SQL statement text box
    strLastRule = strLastRule & " " & lstOperator & " " & _
                ➥txtCompare & ") "
    Call fw_SQLText

    'Reset the labels
    frmQuery!lstFields.Enabled = True
    frmQuery!lblFields.Visible = False
    DoCmd GoToControl "lstFields"
    frmQuery!cmdDelLastRule.Enabled = True
    frmQuery!cmdDelAllRules.Enabled = True
    frmQuery!cmdAddRule.Enabled = False
    Forms!frmQueryWizard!lstOperators.Enabled = False

    'Hide the "Is:" label and display the And..Or option group
    'with gray labels until you choose another rule
    frmQuery!lblIs.Visible = False
    frmQuery!lblOperators.Visible = False
    frmQuery!grpAndOr.Visible = True
    frmQuery!lblAnd.Visible = False
    frmQuery!lblOrIs.Visible = False
    frmQuery!lblAndGray.Visible = True
    frmQuery!lblOrIsGray.Visible = True

    'Clear the criterion text box and show it
    frmQuery!txtCriterion = Null
    frmQuery!txtCriterion.Visible = False
End Function
```

Deleting Rules

The `qw_DelLastRule()` and `qw_DelAllRules()` functions behave identically to the `fw_DelLastField()` and `fw_DelAllFields()` functions. The principal difference between the two sets of functions is the resetting of the labels on the frmQueryWizard form.

```
Function qw_DelLastRule ()
    'Purpose:    Delete the last rule entered
    'Called by: OnClick event of the Delete Last Rule button
    'Returns:    Nil

    Set frmQuery = Forms!frmQueryWizard
    strLastRule = ""
    wNumRules = wNumRules - 1
    If wNumRules = 0 Then
        'All rules have been deleted, reset buttons accordingly
        strSQLRule = ""
        frmQuery!cmdDelAllRules.Enabled = False
        frmQuery!lblOperators.Visible = True
        frmQuery!grpAndOr.Visible = False
    End If

    'Update the SQL statement text box
    Call fw_SQLText

    DoCmd GoToControl "lstFields"
    frmQuery!cmdDelLastRule.Enabled = False
End Function

Function qw_DelAllRules () As Integer
    'Purpose:    Delete the SQL WHERE statement
    '            Enable and disable appropriate pushbuttons
    'Called by: OnClick event of cmdDelAllRules button
    'Returns:    Nil

    Set frmQuery = Forms!frmQueryWizard

    wNumRules = 0
    strSQLRule = ""
    strLastRule = ""
    DoCmd GoToControl "lstFields"
    frmQuery!cmdDelAllRules.Enabled = False
    frmQuery!cmdDelLastRule.Enabled = False
    frmQuery!lblOperators.Visible = True
    frmQuery!grpAndOr.Visible = False
    frmQuery!grpAndOr = 1

    Call fw_SQLText
End Function
```

Creating the QueryDef Object or Canceling the Query

When you click the Run Query button, its OnClick event executes the qw_wRunQuery function, which completes the SQL statement and creates the **QueryDef** object from the SQL statement.

```
Function qw_wRunQuery () As Integer
    'Purpose:    Create a QueryDef from the SQL statement and
                 ➥display it
    'Called by: Run Query button
    'Returns:    True if successful, False on failure

    On Error GoTo RunQueryError

    Dim strSQLQuery As String   'The SQL statement to execute
    Dim strQueryName As String  'The name of the query (see note
                                ➥below)
    Dim dbCurrent As Database   'Set up database objects
    Dim qdfQuery As QueryDef
    Set dbCurrent = DBEngine(0)(0)

    If Left$(strTableName,3) = "tbl" Then
        strQueryName = "qry" & Mid$(strTableName, 4)
    Else
        strQueryName = "qry" & strTableName
    End If

    'Delete the existing QueryDef, it exists
    On Error Resume Next
    dbCurrent.DeleteQueryDef (strQueryName)
    On Error GoTo RunQueryError

    strSQLRule = strSQLRule & strLastRule
    strSQLQuery = strSQL & strSQLFrom & strSQLRule & strSQLSort &
                  ➥strSQLEnd
    strLastRule = ""
    strThisRule = ""

    Set qdfQuery = dbCurrent.CreateQueryDef(strQueryName, strSQLQuery)
    'Note: Using Error$(Err) gives uninformative error messages

    DoCmd Close A_FORM, "frmQueryWizard"

    'Open the query in datasheet view (for demonstration purposes only)
    'Note: You cannot use an expression, such as '"qry" & strTableName'
           ➥     '        as the argument of an Access action
    DoCmd OpenQuery strQueryName
```

```
    'Close the temporary objects
    qdfQuery.Close
    dbCurrent.Close
    Exit Function

RunQueryError:
    MsgBox "Error: " & Error$
    Exit Function
End Function
```

You can execute the `qw_Close()` function at any point during the final query design by clicking the Close button. The statements that clear the **String** variables are useful when you are testing the frmQueryWizard form and its associated Access Basic code.

```
Function qw_Close () As Integer
    'Purpose:   Close the Query Wizard form
    'Called by: OnClick event of the Close button
    'Returns:   Nil

    strSQLWhere = ""
    strSQL = ""
    strSQLRule = ""
    strLastRule = ""
    wNumRules = 0
    Forms!frmQueryWizard!txtSQL = ""
    DoCmd Close A_FORM, "frmQueryWizard"
End Function
```

The purpose of the `qw_NotStarted` function, which is executed by the OnClose event of the frmQueryWizard form, is to reset the fIsStarted flag to **False** upon closing the form. The fIsStarted flag is used to determine whether the OnEnter event of the lstFields list box executes the code of the `qw_StartQuery()` function.

```
Function qw_NotStarted ()
    'Purpose:   Reset Not Started flag on closing form
    'Called by: OnClose event of frmQueryWizard
    'Returns:   Nil

    fIsStarted = False
End Function
```

Figure 9.7 shows the frmQueryWizard form with an SQL statement having two criteria in the WHERE clause. When you click the Run Query button, the **DoCmd** OpenQuery method displays the result of the query.

FIGURE 9.7.
*An SQL statement
created by the
QueryWizard.*

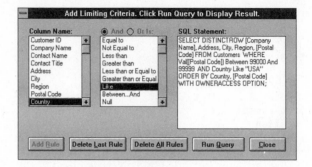

Filling List Boxes and Combo Boxes with an Access Basic Function

If you wanted to fill an Access 1.x list box with the field names of any table that you would specify by the value of `strTableName`, you needed to use a special type of Access Basic function that filled list or combo boxes with values other than those that are available as standard choices for the value of the `RowSource` property (`Table/Query`, `ValueList`, and `FieldList`). This process is no longer required for changing table names dynamically because Access 2.0 lets you alter the value of the `RowSource` property in run mode. However, there are many occasions when you want to fill a list box or a drop-down combo list or box with values other than those offered by the three `RowSource` property choices.

Access does not use the conventional `AddItem` method of Visual Basic to add new entries to list boxes. Access list boxes, combo boxes, and most of the other Access control objects are not conventional Windows objects. Microsoft decided to use bitmapped emulations of these objects to conserve resources. Microsoft's original objective was to make Access operable with computers having 2MB of RAM. Perhaps you *could* load Access 1.0 with a 2MB computer, but that's about all you could do with either Access or your computer. Version 2.0 now officially recommends at least 6MB of RAM installed. To achieve acceptable performance with moderate- to large-scale Access applications, users should have 8MB of RAM installed.

To use an Access function to fill a list or a combo box, you substitute the name of the function that you plan to write for the value of the `RowSourceType` property and leave the value of the `RowSource` property empty. In this case, you do not prefix a = symbol to the function name, nor do you include the trailing set of parentheses. When your application opens the form on which a custom combo box or list box is located, Access automatically calls the list-filling function 10 times or more, obtaining a different piece of data or a **Null** value with each call. The data is transferred to Access by the return value of the list-filling function.

The Field and Query Wizards module includes the fw_varFillBoxes() function to fill the lstFields list boxes of the frmFieldWizard and frmQueryWizard forms, and the lstSortFields list box of frmFieldWizard. You must provide receptors for the five argument values supplied by Access's internal function call, despite the fact that your function does not use the ctlControl argument. The first argument must be specified as being of the **Control** data type. The remaining four arguments are of the default **Variant** data type, so you don't need to specify their data type in your function. Following is the listing of the fr_varFillBoxes() function:

```
Function fw_varFillBoxes (ctlControl As Control, varID, varRow, varCol,
        ➥varCode) As Variant
    'Purpose:  Fill the list boxes with field names from the
              ➥rgstrFields array
    '          created by the fw_wInitialize function
    'Returns:  Values determined by value of varCode
    'Called by:lstFields and lstSortFields list boxes on
              ➥ frmFieldWizard
    '          lstFields on frmQueryWizard

    Dim strMsg As String          'Error message when form opened
                                  ➥directly

    On Error GoTo FillBoxes_Err

    'Standard case statement for filling list and combo boxes
    Select Case varCode
        Case 0  'Initialize the fill routine by returning True
            fw_varFillBoxes = True
        Case 1  'Return an unique (random) number
            fw_varFillBoxes = Timer
        Case 3  'Return the number of rows
            fw_varFillBoxes = UBound(rgstrFields)
        Case 4  'Return the number of columns
            fw_varFillBoxes = 1
        Case 5  'Return True to use default column width
            fw_varFillBoxes = True
        Case 6  'Return the data (called the 'number of columns'
                ➥times)
            fw_varFillBoxes = CVar(rgstrFields(varRow + 1, 1))
    End Select
    Exit Function

FillBoxes_Err:
    'Reminder to start from the Immediate window, not to open the form
    strMsg = "You must open frmFieldWizard from the Immediate window "
    strMsg = strMsg & "with a ? fw_Initialize('TableName') statement."
    MsgBox strMsg, 16, "Open Error"
```

```
        Exit Function
End Function
```

To use the `fw_varFillBoxes()` function to fill the list boxes, you need to create the `rgstrFieldList` array before opening the frmFieldWizard form, because Access fills the list boxes when you open the form. Therefore, you call the added `fw_wInitialize` function that uses the code from the `qw_StartQuery()` function to assign values to the `rgstrFieldList` array before you open the form. You no longer need to create this array in the `qw_StartQuery()` function, so `qw_wInitialize` replaces `qw_StartQuery` as the function called on triggering the `OpenForm` event of frmQueryWizard. Listings for these two functions are not included here because the code is copied from the original versions of the functions, whose code is listed previously in this chapter.

You need to change the properties of the list boxes of the frmFieldWizard and frmQueryWizard forms to specify `fw_varFillBoxes()` as the `RowSourceType` property. Table 9.1 shows the changes you need to make to the design of the two forms to implement the list-filling function.

Table 9.1. Changes to the values of properties required to use the `fw_varFillBoxes()` function.

Form	Object	Property	Original Value	Replacement Value
frmFieldWizard	lstFields	RowSourceType	Table/Query	fw_varFillBoxes
	lstFields	RowSource	Null	Null (leave empty)
	lstSortFields	RowSourceType	Table/Query	fw_varFillBoxes
	lstSortFields	RowSource	Null	Null (leave empty)
frmQueryWizard	lstFields	RowSourceType	Table/Query	fw_varFillBoxes
	lstFields	RowSource	Null	Null (leave empty)
	lstFields	OnEnter	=qw_StartQuery()	qw_wInitialize()

To start the QueryWizard with function-filled list boxes, type ? `fw_wInitialize("Customers")` in the Immediate window. If you open the frmFieldWizard form from the Database window, you receive a "nocando" reminder message caused by the error created in `fw_varFillBoxes()`. If you don't include this error handler, Access returns the misleading message, "Argument count mismatch," which can cause you to believe that you can't count five arguments. The correct message is "Array subscript out of range," the result of not issuing the **ReDim** statement in the `fw_wInitialize()` function before attempting to read the values in the array.

> **NOTE**
>
> You can attach other tables from NWIND.MDB or other databases to DEC_SUPT.MDB and execute the `fw_wInitialize()` function with the name of the alternate table as the value of the `strTableName` argument. If you use attached tables, you need to substitute **Set** db*Name* = **OpenDatabase**(str*DBName*) for **Set** db*Name* = **CurrentDB**() to set the value of the **Database** object variable. Access does not consider an attached table a member of the set of tables in the current database.

Using the Query Wizard to Create a Mail-Merge List or a Worksheet File

You can use the QueryWizard to create a mail-merge data file for Word for Windows 2+ or an Excel 2.1 or Lotus 1-2-3 worksheet file by executing the SQL statement for a make table query to create the persistent **Table** or **QueryDef** object that is necessary to export data which is not in native Access table format. Then you substitute the appropriate **DoCmd** TransferText or **DoCmd** TransferSpreadsheet method for the **DoCmd** OpenQuery method in the qw_wRunQuery() function. The syntax for these two methods is as follows:

```
DoCmd TransferText wType, strSpecName, strTableName, strFileName,
        ➡fFieldNames
DoCmd TransferSpreadsheet wImpExp, wType, strTableName, strFileName[,
        ➡fFieldNames[, strRange]]
```

Table 9.2 lists the arguments for the **DoCmd** TransferText and **DoCmd** TransferSpreadsheet methods. Table 9.3 lists the values of the *wType* arguments of both methods and the Access intrinsic constants, where applicable.

Table 9.2. Arguments for the DoCmd TransferText and DoCmd TransferSpreadsheet methods.

Argument	Purpose
wImpExp	Import (A_IMPORT) or export (A_EXPORT) for **DoCmd** TransferSpreadsheet only
wType	Type of operation for **DoCmd** TransferText; type of worksheet file for **DoCmd** TransferSpreadsheet (see values in Table 9.3)

continues

Table 9.2. continued

Argument	Purpose
str*SpecName*	Name of import/export specification (required for fixed-width text file import/export)
str*TableName*	The name of the table from which the file is exported or to which the data in the file is imported
str*FileName*	The path and filename of the text or spreadsheet file
f*FieldNames*	**True** if first row of data contains or is to contain field names; otherwise **False** (default)
str*Range*	A valid worksheet range name to which the data is to be exported (for export only)

Table 9.3. Values of the *wType* argument for the `DoCmd TransferText` and `DoCmd TransferSpreadsheet` methods.

Value	DoCmd **TransferText**	DoCmd **TransferSpreadsheet**
0	A_IMPORTDELIM	Microsoft Excel
1	A_IMPORTFIXED	Lotus 1-2-3 (.WKS)
2	A_EXPORTDELIM	Lotus 1-2-3 (.WK1)
3	A_EXPORTFIXED	Lotus 1-2-3 (.WK3)
4	Word for Windows Merge	(Not used)

The `qw_wCreateFile()` function, called by the `qw_wRunQuery()` function, creates an Excel worksheet (in Excel 2.1 file format) and a Word for Windows 2+ mail-merge text file from a temporary table, tblTemp, that is created by a make table **QueryDef** object. The listing for the `qw_wCreateFile()` function follows.

```
Function qw_wCreateFile (strQueryName As String) As Integer
    'Purpose:   Create a worksheet or mail-merge file from a query
    'Argument:  Name of QueryDef created by QueryWizard
    'Called By: qw_CreateQuery()
    'Returns:   True if successful, False on failure

    Dim dbQuery As Database
    Dim qdfMakeTable As QueryDef
    Dim strMTSQL As String
```

```
    On Error GoTo CreateFile_Err

    'Turn on the Hourglass mousepointer
    DoCmd Hourglass True

    'Create the make-table SQL statement
    strMTSQL = "SELECT DISTINCTROW * INTO tblTemp FROM "
    strMTSQL = strMTSQL & strQueryName & " WITH OWNERACCESS
           ➥OPTION;"

    Set dbQuery = CurrentDB()

    'Turn off error checking in case the file exists
    On Error Resume Next
    Set qdfMakeTable = dbQuery.CreateQueryDef("qryTemp", strMTSQL)

    'Execute the query without warnings
    DoCmd SetWarnings False
    qdfMakeTable.Execute
    DoCmd SetWarnings True

    'Turn error-checking back on
    On Error GoTo CreateFile_Err

    'Create a worksheet file
    DoCmd TransferSpreadsheet A_EXPORT, 0, "tblTemp", "query.xls", True

    'Also, create a Word for Windows mail-merge data file
    DoCmd TransferText 4, "", "tblTemp", "maillist.txt", True

    'Turn off the Hourglass Mouse Pointer
    DoCmd Hourglass False

    'Close open objects
    dbQuery.DeleteQueryDef ("qryTemp")
    dbQuery.Close
    Exit Function

CreateFile_Err:
    DoCmd Hourglass False
    MsgBox "Error: " & Error$, 16, "Create File Error"
    Exit Function
End Function
```

Remove the apostrophe preceding the line wRetVal = qw_wCreateFile(strQueryName) in the qw_wRunQuery() function in order to execute the qw_wCreateFile() function when you click the Run Query button of the frmQueryWizard form. Figure 9.8 shows the Excel worksheet, and Figure 9.9 illustrates the Word for Windows mail-merge data file created by the qw_wCreateFile() function. The Word for Windows mail-merge format replaces spaces in file names with underscores to comply with Word's mergefield naming requirement.

	A	B	C	D	E
1	Company Name	Address	City	Region	Postal Code
2	Village Food Boutique	2782 - 92nd Ave.‖Suite 1	Los Angeles	CA	90071
3	La Tienda Granda	12345 - 6th St.	Los Angeles	CA	91406
4	Rite-Buy Supermarket	P.O. Box 4421	Berkeley	CA	92701
5	Dollarwise Convenience S	98 N. Hyde Dr.	San Francisco	CA	94103
6	Let's Stop N Shop	87 Polk St.‖Suite 5	San Francisco	CA	94117
7	Gruenewald Delikatessen	3344 Byerly St.‖Suite 5	Berkeley	CA	94701
8	Caesar's Mediterranean In	9308 Dartridge Ave.	San Francisco	CA	94965
9	Oceanview Quickshop	Franklin Mall‖231 N. Uki	Aloha	OR	97006
10	The Big Cheese	89 Jefferson Way‖Suite	Portland	OR	97201
11	Lonesome Pine Restaurar	89 Chiaroscuro Rd.	Portland	OR	97219
12	Lillegard's Old Country Del	89 Rain Way	Portland	OR	97219
13	Lee's Oriental Food Mart	44 McKnight Rd.	Portland	OR	97229
14	Live Oak Hotel Gift Shop	7384 Washington Ave.	Portland	OR	97229
15	Great Lakes Food Market	2732 Baker Blvd.	Eugene	OR	97403
16	Frugal Feast Comestibles	Evans Plaza‖531 - 2nd /	Eugene	OR	97403
17	O'Connor's Town Store	45 E. 23rd St.	Drain	OR	97435

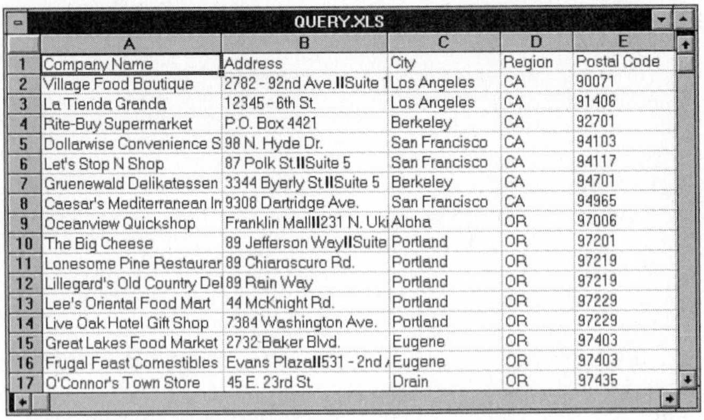

FIGURE 9.8.
An Excel 4.0 worksheet created with the `DoCmd TransferSpreadsheet` *method.*

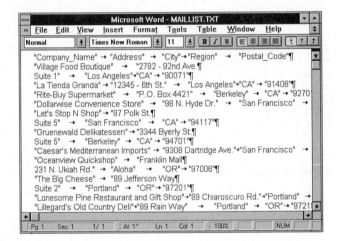

FIGURE 9.9.
A Word for Windows 2.0 mail-merge data file created by the `DoCmd TransferText` *method.*

Using Visual Basic 3.0 for Decision-Support Applications

The Professional Edition of Visual Basic 3.0 includes the Access database engine that lets you manipulate data in Access, xBase, Paradox, and Btrieve databases. Visual Basic 2+ connects to client-server databases with the ODBC API. Visual Basic 3.0 offers somewhat better flexibility in setting the values of the properties of its forms and control objects in run mode. Some of the other advantages of using Visual Basic rather than Access to create decision-support applications are as follows:

- The overhead and resource requirements of Visual Basic applications are substantially less than those required for the equivalent Access application.

You usually can achieve better performance with an application created in Visual Basic than with Access, especially on computers with less than 8MB of RAM.

■ The Graph custom control of Visual Basic is much faster than the Microsoft Graph 5.0 OLE 2.0 server used by Access 2.0. However, the Graph OLE Custom Control described in Chapter 17, "Charting Data with Microsoft Graph 5.0," is almost as fast as the Graph custom control.

■ Visual Basic offers a rich selection of custom controls, available both from Microsoft and from third-party publishers. At the time this edition was published, there were few retail versions of OLE 2.0 Custom Controls available. (Most publishers of Visual Basic .VBX custom controls are expected to release .OCX versions in 1994 and 1995.)

■ Visual Basic provides programming aids, such as the ability to create control arrays and to create multiple instances of forms. In some cases, because of these features, the amount of code required to create Visual Basic database applications can be less than that for Access 2.0 applications.

The downside of using Visual Basic is that Visual Basic 3.0 does not incorporate Access 2.0's flexible report writing features and does not directly support the OLE Object field data type of Access tables. The graphic control objects of Visual Basic support only Windows bitmap (.BMP and .DIB) and Windows metafile (.WMF) formats. Third-party custom controls and DLLs are available to support other graphic formats. You need to include a field in your Access table that specifies the linkage to the graphic file that you embed in or link to the OLE Object field. Another disadvantage of Visual Basic is that you need to implement subform data manipulation with code; Access's built-in subform functions are not yet available in Visual Basic. Visual Basic emulations of Access applications usually are more appropriate for decision-support applications than for interactive transaction-processing applications. (However, there are several third-party, data-aware custom controls available for Visual Basic 3.0 that emulate Access's Datasheet View.)

NOTE

You still need your retail version of Access in order to implement Access's security features on objects contained in Access databases that are used by Visual Basic applications. Another reason for continuing to use Access in a Visual Basic programming environment is that it is easier to create new Access databases and the tables the databases contain with Access's graphic tools. You need to write a substantial amount of Visual Basic code to create database objects "programatically."

If you have made a large investment in learning Access Basic and writing code in Access modules, all is not lost if you decide to try a Visual Basic implementation of your application. Just as Visual Basic 3.0 code can be imported into Access 2.0 modules, you can export much of your Access Basic 2.0 code to the Professional Edition of Visual Basic 3.0. You can export event-handling procedures for forms directly to Visual Basic event-handling modules. Export the statements of Access Basic functions that respond to events to the **Sub** *ControlName_EventName* ... **End Sub** structures that Visual Basic creates for you. Import the remainder of your code to Visual Basic *.BAS modules. You'll need to do some "tweaking" of your code because Visual Basic database-related control objects do not have all the events of their Access counterparts. Each **DoCmd** *ActionName* statement needs to be converted to an equivalent Object Basic method. Expect to spend a few hours learning how to manipulate subform data with Visual Basic code.

Extensive instruction on designing forms and writing code in Visual Basic 3.0 in order to emulate Access applications is beyond the scope of this book. If you are interested in exploring the possibilities of re-creating Access decision-support applications with Visual Basic, acquire the Professional Edition of Visual Basic 3.0 and a copy of this author's book, *Database Developer's Guide with Visual Basic 3.0*, (Indianapolis, IN, 1994, Sams Publishing, ISBN 0-672-30440-6) to help guide you in the conversion process.

10

Generating Meaningful Reports

Predictions made in the late 1980s that the "paperless office" would become a reality by the mid-1990s were, as it turns out, grossly optimistic. Computers are capable of quickly generating voluminous reports, especially from information stored in databases. Laser printers quietly churn out billions of pages of forms and reports every year. True, computer-based imaging systems make storing and retrieving documents more efficient, but the source documents remain paper. There is little likelihood that images on a video display unit will replace a substantial percentage of printed reports in the foreseeable future.

Microsoft Access includes a fast and versatile report generator that surpasses the report-preparation capabilities of character-based DOS database-management applications. Windows' printer drivers accommodate all the major brands and models of laser, ink-jet, and dot-matrix printers, as well as the now uncommon daisy-wheel printers. Therefore, unless you are using a fixed-pitch printer, you need not be too concerned with the type of printer that users employ with your Access database applications. It is Windows' responsibility to handle the hardware; this is one of the major benefits that accrue to DOS developers when they make the transition to developing Windows applications.

Access 2.0 brings no revolutionary changes that apply specifically to generating reports. Following are some of the evolutionary improvements offered by Access 2.0 reports:

- The new KeepTogether property gives you the option of avoiding page breaks within the middle of a group.

- Reports have gained a Pages property that you can use to print something such as "Page 1 of 422" in the footer of your reports. The Pages property returns an **Integer** representing the total number of pages of the report.

- The Application.**GetOption**() and Application.**SetOption** methods let you read and set the values of user-defined options, such as default printing margins, typeface families, and font sizes. The Application.**SetOption**() method replaces cumbersome SendKeys macro actions or **SendKeys** statements in Access Basic to change the values of user-defined options.

- Enhanced control sizing and spacing features speed the design of reports. You now can select a group of controls and size them to match the narrowest, shortest, widest or tallest member of the group. You also can equalize the spacing between selected controls.

- If you are creating a large number of different reports for a client who desires a particular report style, you can customize the Report Wizards to apply the style to all the reports you create with the wizards.

■ The AutoReport button of the toolbar invokes the AutoReport Wizard, which creates a simple tabular report from a table or a query-result set. It's unlikely, however, that you'll be able to make use of an AutoReport without extensive changes to the Wizard's default design.

This chapter does not cover the details of how to design reports; the documentation accompanying retail Access and beginning- to intermediate-level books about Access give you the basic information that you need in order to design reports. Instead, this chapter focuses on deciding whether to print datasheets or reports, using Access Basic functions to control the appearance of reports, and creating text and other types of files from reports.

Printing *Ad Hoc* Reports from Tables and Queries

Supervisory and management personnel are prone to requesting a multitude of *ad hoc* reports. You can save the time necessary to design simple reports that list the contents of a table or query by printing the datasheet view of the table or query. The resulting hard copy has minimal formatting; only the margins are adjustable. Access does not print dates or page numbers when you print from the datasheet view. Unless you change the default typeface and font size, your reports are printed in the typeface that your printer substitutes for MS Sans Serif. (PostScript printers substitute ITC Avant Garde, not Linotype Helvetica, because Avant Garde is the first PostScript font—alphabetically—that matches MS Sans Serif's attributes.) The sections that follow describe how to set printing preferences and how to change the typeface and font size when you print *ad hoc* reports from tables and queries.

TIP

If you know the Adobe PostScript page description language and your client or firm's printers have PostScript capability, you can use the low-level file functions of Access Basic to add lines to create page headers and page footers for printed versions of tables and queries. You print the table to a PostScript (.PS) text file, then parse the file to find the beginning and end of each page, recreating a new version of the file with the added lines for the headers and footers. Then you use DOS commands or Windows API functions to copy the modified .PS file to the printer. This is not a simple task, and a description of the required code is beyond the scope of this book. It is possible, however, to write a generic Access Basic function that can add headers and footers to any PostScript file created by printing tables or queries.

Setting Default Margins for Reports with *Application.SetOption*

You can set the default margins that your copy of Access uses to print reports from tables or datasheets by changing the values of the four margin options that appear when you choose Options from the View menu, then select Printing from the Category list box. The new values you set for the `Left Margin`, `Top Margin`, `Right Margin`, and `Bottom Margin` options appear as the default margins when you choose Print Setup from the File menu to print tables or queries or when you create a new report. The default margin values do not affect the printing margin of Access reports that you created before setting the new default margins. Setting default printing margins is useful primarily when you print *ad hoc* reports from datasheets or create custom Report Wizards for your applications. The default printing margins apply to all *ad hoc* reports you print directly from datasheets.

> **NOTE**
>
> User-defined options in Access 2.0 are not properties of the Application object. The Application does not have a `Properties` collection. You receive an error message if you execute **? Application.Properties.Count** in the Immediate window. Option names are shown in monospace type in this book because options are quite similar to properties. If future versions of Access become OLE Automation servers, it is likely that the user-defined options will become members of a `Properties` collection.

To test the `GetOption`() method in the Immediate window, enter ? `Application.GetOption("Left Margin")`. This expression returns `1 in`. The literal argument of the `GetOption`() method must match, character-for-character, the name that appears in the Items list of the Options window, including spaces. (It is not, however, case sensitive.) You should use the `GetOption`() method to create an array of the user's option preferences prior to changing the option values with code. As in the following example, you can declare a **Global** or **Static** three-dimensional variant array, `varOptions(n, 3)`, then store the names, new values, and original values as elements:

```
ReDim varOptions(n, 3)   'n = number of option values to be set and reset
varOptions(0, 0) = "Left Margin"
varOptions(1, 0) = "Right Margin"
varOptions(2, 0) = "Top Margin"
varOptions(3, 0) = "Bottom Margin"
```

```
For intCtr = 0 To n
   varOptions(n, 2) = Application.GetOption(varOptions(n, 0))
Next intCtr
```

To change the default printing margins for new reports you create in Access 2.0 from the default 1 inch to 1/2 inch, execute the following code:

```
varOptions(0, 1) = "0.5 in"
varOptions(1, 1) = "0.5 in"
varOptions(2, 1) = "0.5 in"
varOptions(3, 1) = "0.5 in"

For intCtr = 0 To n
   varOptions(n, 1) = Application.SetOption varOptions(n, 0),
   ➥varOptions(n, 1)
Next intCtr
```

Setting Datasheet Style, Typefaces, and Font Sizes

The style (gridlines on or off), type family, font size, and attributes of data printed in *ad hoc* reports is inherited from the default values assigned to the Datasheet options. Access's default is the MS Sans Serif 8-point font with no attributes. You can change these values for *ad hoc* reports with the **SetOptions** method using a code similar to that for default margins. As an example, to turn gridlines off, use the following:

```
varOptions(4, 0) = "Default Gridlines Behavior"
varOptions(5, 0) = "Default Font Name"
varOptions(6, 0) = "Default Font Size"
varOptions(7, 0) = "Default Font Weight"

varOptions(4, 1) = False
varOptions(5, 1) = "Courier New"
varOptions(6, 1) = 12
varOptions(7, 1) = 6

For intCtr = 4 To n
   varOptions(n, 2) = Application.GetOption(varOptions(n, 0))
Next intCtr

For intCtr = 4 To n
   varOptions(n, 1) = Application.SetOption varOptions(n, 0),
   ➥varOptions(n, 1)
Next intCtr
```

TIP

Use the Immediate window to test the data type returned by the **GetOption**() method for each option value you plan to alter. As the preceding example illustrates, it is difficult to predict the **Variant** data subtype expected by many options. As an example, the `Default Font Weight` option is set by the position of the selection in the drop-down list, but the value of the first selection in the list, Extra Light, is one, not zero. Zero is the most common value for the initial selection of an Access drop-down list.

Figure 10.1 shows the datasheet view of the Order Information query of NWIND.MDB with 12-point Courier New (the TrueType equivalent of pica) bold as the default font. When you print this datasheet by choosing Print from the File menu, the printed version employs the same font.

FIGURE 10.1.

A query datasheet display in a 12-point Courier New font.

Order ID	Custome	Company Name	Address	City	Reg
10000	FRANS	Franchi S.p.A.	Via Monte Bia	Torino	
10001	MEREP	Mère Paillarde	43 rue St. La	Montréa	Québ
10002	FOLKO	Folk och fä HB	Åkergatan 24	Bräcke	
10003	SIMOB	Simons bistro	Vinbæltet 34	Københa	
10004	VAFFE	Vaffeljernet	Smagsløget 45	Århus	
10005	WARTH	Wartian Herkku	Torikatu 38	Oulu	
10006	FRANS	Franchi S.p.A.	Via Monte Bia	Torino	
10007	MORGK	Morgenstern Ges	Heerstr. 22	Leipzig	
10008	FURIB	Furia Bacalhau	Jardim das ro	Lisboa	
10009	SEVES	Seven Seas Impo	90 Wadhurst R	London	
10010	SIMOB	Simons bistro	Vinbæltet 34	Københa	
10011	WELLI	Wellington Impo	Rua do Mercad	Resende SP	
10012	LINOD	LINO-Delicatese	Ave. 5 de May	I. de M	Nuev

Record: 1   of 1078

Using Access-Defined Properties to Format Datasheets for Printing

Using Access-defined properties is an alternative to employing the `GetOption()` and `SetOption` methods to format datasheets for printing. Access-defined properties, described in Chapter 5, "Understanding Access 2.0's Data Access Objects," and Chapter 6, "Creating and Using Object Variables," are not visible until you append the property by name to an object. `TableDef`, `QueryDef`, and `Field` objects of `TableDef` and `QueryDef` objects have Access-defined properties that you can use to format reports. Table 10.1 lists the Access-defined properties of these three objects. It is clear from the number of Access-defined properties that using these properties to format datasheets for printing offers much more flexibility than setting user-defined options.

Table 10.1. Access-defined properties of `TableDef`, `QueryDef`, and `Field` Objects.

TableDef *Objects*	QueryDef *Objects*	Field *Objects*
DatasheetFontHeight	DatasheetFontHeight	Caption
DatasheetFontItalic	DatasheetFontItalic	ColumnHidden
DatasheetFontName	DatasheetFontName	ColumnOrder
DatasheetFontUnderline	DatasheetFontUnderline	ColumnWidth
DatasheetFontWeight	DatasheetFontWeight	DecimalPlaces
Description	Description	Description
FrozenColumns	FrozenColumns	Format
RowHeight	LogMessages	InputMask
ShowGrid	RecordLocks	
	RowHeight	
	ShowGrid	

Listing 10.1 shows the Access Basic code required to create and set the values of the `DatasheetFontName`, `DatasheetFontHeight`, `DatasheetFontWeight`, and `ShowGrid` properties of a **QueryDef** object, and the `ColumnWidth` property of each field of the **QueryDef** object. This example is included in the Access-Defined Properties (Chapter 10) module of AB_EXAMP.MDB on the accompanying diskette. The code is equally applicable to **TableDef** objects.

Listing 10.1. Code to set the values of Access-defined properties.

```
'Declarations Section

Dim dbCurrent As Database    'Workspaces (0)(0)
Dim qdfTest As QueryDef      'QueryDef object
Dim fldTest As Field         'Field object of QueryDef
Dim prpTest As Property      'Property object of QueryDef or Field object

Global varProps() As Variant  'Array to hold names, data types, and
➥values

Function TestDSProps ()
    'Reference: Chapter 10, "Generating Meaningful Reports"
    'Purpose:   Test the use of Access-defined properties in conjunction
    '           with formatting datasheets

    Dim intCtr As Integer    'General-purpose counter
```

continues

Listing 10.1. continued

```
ReDim varProps(4, 3)

varProps(0, 0) = "DatasheetFontName"
varProps(0, 1) = DB_TEXT
varProps(0, 2) = "Courier New"
varProps(1, 0) = "DatasheetFontHeight"
varProps(1, 1) = DB_INTEGER
varProps(1, 2) = 12
varProps(2, 0) = "DatasheetFontWeight"
varProps(2, 1) = DB_INTEGER
varProps(2, 2) = 700
varProps(3, 0) = "ShowGrid"
varProps(3, 1) = DB_BOOLEAN
varProps(3, 2) = False

Set dbCurrent = DBEngine(0)(0)
Set qdfTest = dbCurrent.OpenQueryDef("Order Information")

'Delete prior instances of the query properties, if they exist
On Error Resume Next
For intCtr = 0 To 3
    qdfTest.Properties.Delete varProps(intCtr, 0)
Next intCtr
On Error GoTo 0

'Append the new properties and values to the collection
For intCtr = 0 To 3
    Set prpTest = qdfTest.CreateProperty(varProps(intCtr, 0),
    ➡varProps(intCtr, 1), varProps(intCtr, 2))
    qdfTest.Properties.Append prpTest
Next intCtr

'Delete existing ColumnWidth properties of the fields
On Error Resume Next
For intCtr = 0 To qdfTest.Fields.Count - 1
    Set fldTest = qdfTest.Fields(intCtr)
    fldTest.Properties.Delete "ColumnWidth"
Next intCtr
On Error GoTo 0

'Add new ColumnWidth property to each field, Set to "best fit"
For intCtr = 0 To qdfTest.Fields.Count - 1
    Set fldTest = qdfTest.Fields(intCtr)
    Set prpTest = fldTest.CreateProperty("ColumnWidth", DB_INTEGER, -2)
    fldTest.Properties.Append prpTest
Next intCtr
End Function
```

Note that the code to delete existing Access-defined properties from the `Properties` container precedes the `For...Next` loop structures. The only way of changing the value of an Access-defined property, once you have created the property, is to delete the property and then recreate and append the property with a new value.

> **NOTE**
>
> Using the correct datatype constant, `DB_TYPE`, is necessary to cause the revised value for an Access-defined property "to take." For instance, if you specify `DB_INTEGER`, instead of `DB_BOOLEAN`, as the data type for the `ShowGrid` property, the grid continues to appear when you open the query datasheet.

Using Access Basic Functions in Reports

The documentation that accompanies retail Access devotes almost an entire chapter to using macros to print reports. If you intend to run your Access 2.0 database application under MSARN200.EXE, you need to minimize the number of macros that you use because of the lack of error trapping during macro execution. In most cases, you can use the Macro To Module converter of Andrew Miller's FIRSTLIB.MDA library, which is described in Chapter 3, "Using Libraries, Wizards, Builders, and Add-Ins," to ease the burden of converting macros to Access Basic functions.

The sections that follow describe properties of reports and tables that you can set in Access Basic functions to control the printing of reports and the appearance of query printouts. These properties were undocumented in retail Access 1.x, but were discussed briefly in the *Secrets of Access Wizards* booklet that accompanied the Access 1.1 Distribution Kit.

Obtaining and Setting the Device Mode and Printing Option Values

When designing commercial applications that include reports or printed copies of tables or queries, you often want to alter the values set by the Print Setup dialog. Your application, not the user, needs to change these values because you can't (and shouldn't) rely on the user to choose the proper settings. Reports have two properties, `PrtDevMode` and `PrtMip`, for changing the print setup; these properties are not documented in the Language Reference that accompanies retail Access. Microsoft exposed the `PrtDevMode` and `PrtMip` properties in the booklet, the *Secrets of Access Wizards*. Exposing a property, method, or action means that the heretofore hidden keyword is now documented and supported by Microsoft. Both of these properties are used by the ReportWizard functions that are contained in WZFRMRPT.MDA. You can use the `PrtDevMode` and `PrtMip` properties to return or set the values that appear in the Print Setup dialog, shown in Figure 10.2. Using the `PrtDevMode` and `PrtMip` properties is much easier than adding a **DoCmd** DoMenuItem action preceded by a long **SendKeys** statement to set the values in the Print Setup dialog.

TIP

The `PrtDevMode` property is especially important when you design a single application to print invoices on preprinted, multiple-part manifold forms with an impact printer (dot-matrix or daisy-wheel type) and print other reports with a laser printer. If you are creating a new invoice, you want to print the invoice with the impact printer. When you need copies of an invoice for review purposes, you print the invoice on the laser printer. Similarly, if your firm or client has a laser printer with multiple paper bins, you might want to select paper in a specific bin for different types of reports. Setting the values of the fields of the `PrtDevMode` property lets you set up the printer as needed for a particular report.

FIGURE 10.2.

The Print Setup dialog of Access with default property values.

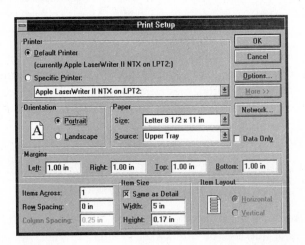

The `PrtDevMode` property represents the portion of the Print Setup dialog that appears when you initially open the form. The `PrintMip` property includes the additional margin and item values that appear when you click the More button.

The `PrtDevMode` and `PrtMip` properties are fixed-length string representations of the values of the fields of C structures (user-defined data types in Access Basic). This peculiar method of getting and setting values of fields of a structure is necessary because Access Basic limits the values of properties to values that can be expressed as one of the **Variant** data subtypes. Structures are user-defined data types, so structures, by definition, cannot be of the **Variant** data type.

The *PrtDevMode* Property

The `PrtDevMode` property is a 64-character fixed-length string whose content corresponds to the Windows `DEVMODE` (device mode) structure, which defines the current Windows printer driver in use. The first 32 characters of the string are reserved for the field that stores the name of the printer driver. The remaining 32 characters represent the values of 15 **Integer** fields and one **Long** value that specify the settings shown in the pane of the Print Setup dialog above the Margins group. The `PrtDevMode` property includes several field values, such as `Scale`, that you cannot set from the Print Setup dialog.

You need to declare two structures in the Declarations section of a module to accommodate the `PrtDevMode` property. The following two declarations are derived from the declarations included in the zwAllGlobals module of WZFRMRPT.MDA. You cannot declare two user-defined data types with the same name, so the original zwt tag is changed to `prt` to prevent the occurrence of an error if you attach WIZARD.MDA to an application that declares these data types. Otherwise, the names of the structures and their fields preserve their original names assigned in WIZARD.MDA.

```
Type PrtDevModeStr
    rgb As String * 64
End Type
```

> **NOTE**
>
> The value of the `PrtDevMode` property is assigned to a user-defined data type with a single fixed-length string field so that you can use Access Basic's **LSet** instruction to obtain and set the value of the individual fields of the `prtDeviceMode` structure with the corresponding values contained in the `PrtDevModeStr` structure. **LSet** is a very powerful but often overlooked instruction. The code examples that follow show how to use the **LSet** instruction to transfer values between two structures.

```
Type prtDeviceMode
    dmDeviceName As String * 32
    dmSpecVersion As Integer
    dmDriverVersion As Integer
    dmSize As Integer
    dmDriverExtra As Integer
    dmFields As Long
    dmOrientation As Integer
    dmPaperSize As Integer
    dmPaperLength As Integer
    dmPaperWidth As Integer
    dmScale As Integer
    dmCopies As Integer
    dmDefaultSource As Integer
    dmPrintQuality As Integer
    dmColor As Integer
    dmDuplex As Integer
End Type
```

Table 10.2 describes the purpose of each field of the `prtDeviceMode` structure. Some of the enumerations of valid values for the fields, such as the list of values that correspond to all possible paper sizes (`dmPaperSize`), are incomplete in Table 10.2. Refer to the description of the `DEVMODE` structure in the documentation that accompanies the Windows 3.1 Software Development Kit (SDK) for a complete listing of the values.

Table 10.2. Description of the fields of the `prtDeviceMode` structure.

Field of `prtDeviceMode`	*Purpose of Field*
`dmDeviceName`	The name of the printer device driver as it appears in the Printer combo box, padded to a length of 32 characters with spaces
`dmSpecVersion`	The version number of Windows for which the printer driver is designed (`&H030A` for Windows 3.1)
`dmDriverVersion`	The driver version number assigned by the author of the printer driver
`dmSize`	The size in bytes of the length of the structure (equal to `Len`(`prtDeviceMode`))
`dmDriverExtra`	The size in bytes of an optional `dmDriverData` structure, if the structure is used; otherwise 0

Field of `prtDeviceMode`	Purpose of Field
`dmFields`	The **Long** integer value of the combination of a set of flags shown in Table 10.3; these flags indicate which of the following fields of `ptrDevMode` are applicable to the driver
`dmOrientation`	1 = Portrait or 2 = Landscape
`dmPaperSize`	An integer representing one of the standard paper sizes supported by the printer: 1 = 8.5 x 11 inches; 5 = 8.5 x 14 inches
`dmPaperLength`	The length of the paper in twips (overrides the `dmPaperSize` value)
`dmPaperWidth`	The width of the paper in twips (overrides the `dmPaperSize` value)
`dmScale`	A factor (`dmScale`/100) that determines the size of the printed image; a `dmScale` value of 50 causes the image to be printed at 50 percent of original size
`dmCopies`	The number of copies to be printed
`dmDefaultSource`	An integer representing the paper bin (1 = upper (primary); 2 = lower; 3 = middle; 4 = manual; 5 = envelope)
`dmPrintQuality`	The print resolution (-4 = high; -3 = medium; -2 = low; -1 = draft)
`dmColor`	Specifies whether a color printer prints in color (1) or in monochrome (2) mode
`dmDuplex`	Specifies whether the printer prints both sides of a sheet (2 = horizontal and 3 = vertical duplex); use 1 for simplex (one-sided) printers

Table 10.3 supplies the value of the flags (constants) that indicate whether values are provided for the properties specified by the 10 fields that follow the `dmFields` field of `prtDeviceMode` in Table 10.2. The value of the mFields property is the sum of the applicable constant values created by combining each of the applicable constant values with the **Or** operator.

Table 10.3. Values of the `dmFields` constants.

dmFields *Constant*	*Value*	*dmFields* *Constant*	*Value*
DM_ORIENTATION	&H00000001	DM_PAPERSIZE	&H00000002
DM_PAPERLENGTH	&H00000004	DM_PAPERWIDTH	&H00000008
DM_SCALE	&H00000010	DM_COPIES	&H00000100
DM_DEFAULTSOURCE	&H00000200	DM_PRINTQUALITY	&H00000400
DM_COLOR	&H00000800	DM_DUPLEX	&H00001000

The *PrtMip* Property

The structures for the `PrtMip` property and `prtMarginInfo` structure that let you set and return the four margin values, plus the other properties for reports that appear below the Margins group in Figure 10.2, follow:

```
Type PrtMipStr
    rgb As String * 24
End Type

Type prtMarginInfo
    xLeftMargin As Integer
    yTopMargin As Integer
    xRightMargin As Integer
    yBotMargin As Integer
    fDataOnly As Integer
    xFormSize As Integer
    yFormSize As Integer
    fDefaultSize As Integer
    cxColumns As Integer
    xFormSpacing As Integer
    yFormSpacing As Integer
    radItemOrder As Integer
End Type
```

Table 10.4 lists the associations of the fields of the `prtMarginInfo` structure with the controls on the Print Setup dialog. All dimensions specified for fields whose names are prefixed with x (horizontal) and y (vertical) are in twips.

Table 10.4. Correspondence of fields of the `prtMarginInfo` and Print Setup dialog entries.

Field of prtMarginInfo	Corresponding field of Print Setup dialog
xLeftMargin	Margins, Left text box
yTopMargin	Margins, Top text box
xRightMargin	Margins, Right text box
yBotMargin	Margins, Bottom text box
fDataOnly	Default Size check box (**True** if checked, **False** if empty)
xFormSize	Item Size Width text box
yFormSize	Item Size Height text box
fDefaultSize	Same as Detail check box (**True** if checked, **False** if empty)
cxColumns	Items Across text box; number of columns for multiple-column reports
xFormSpacing	Column Spacing text box; the space between detail columns
yFormSpacing	Row Spacing text box; the space between detail rows
radItemOrder	Item Layout option group (1 = horizontal; 2 = vertical)

Displaying the Values of the *PrtDevMode* and *PrtMip* Properties

You can use the Immediate window to display the values of the fields of the prtDeviceMode structure assigned from the PrtDevModeStr structure with the following wShowDevMode() function:

```
Function wShowDevMode (strReport As String)
    'Purpose:   Display all fields of prtDeviceMode in the Immediate
    ➥window
    'Argument:  Literal name of report open in Print Preview mode
    'Returns:   True if successful, False on Failure

    'Declare the variables of the user-defined types
    Dim dmStruct As prtDeviceMode
    Dim dmString As PrtDevModeStr
```

```
'Quit if report does not return a value for PrtDevMode
If IsNull(Reports(strReport).PrtDevMode) Then
    Exit Function
End If

'Assign the value of PrtDevMode to the dmString structure
dmString.rgb = Reports(strReport).PrtDevMode

'Assign the value of the dmString to the dmStruct structure
LSet dmStruct = dmString

'Print the fields of dmStruct to the Immediate window
Debug.Print "Driver name", dmStruct.dmDeviceName
Debug.Print "Windows ver.", Hex$(dmStruct.dmSpecVersion)
Debug.Print "Driver ver.", Hex$(dmStruct.dmDriverVersion)
Debug.Print "Size", Str$(dmStruct.dmSize)
Debug.Print "Driver data", Str$(dmStruct.dmDriverExtra)
Debug.Print "Fields", Hex$(dmStruct.dmFields)
Debug.Print "Orientation", Str$(dmStruct.dmOrientation)
Debug.Print "Paper size", Str$(dmStruct.dmPaperSize)
Debug.Print "Paper length", Str$(dmStruct.dmPaperLength)
Debug.Print "Paper width", Str$(dmStruct.dmPaperSize)
Debug.Print "Scale", Str$(dmStruct.dmScale)
Debug.Print "Copies", Str$(dmStruct.dmCopies)
Debug.Print "Source ", Str$(dmStruct.dmDefaultSource)
Debug.Print "Quality ", Str$(dmStruct.dmPrintQuality)
Debug.Print "Color ", Str$(dmStruct.dmColor)
Debug.Print "Duplex ", Str$(dmStruct.dmDuplex)

    wShowDevMode = True
End Function
```

To run the wShowDevMode() function, import the Report Printing Functions module from the AB_EXAMP.MDB database into NWIND.MDB, and then open a report, such as Catalog, in Print Preview mode. Open the Report Printing Functions module and type ? wShowDevMode("Catalog") in the Immediate window. The wShowDevMode() function reports the values of each field of the prtDeviceMode structure as shown in Figure 10.3.

The wShowMarginInfo() function displays the field values of the prtMarginInfo structure in a manner similar to that of the preceding wShowDevMode() function, as follows:

```
Function wShowMarginInfo (strReport As String)
    'Purpose:   Display all fields of prtMarginInfo in the Immediate window
    'Argument:  Literal name of report open in Print Preview mode
    'Returns:   True if successful, False on Failure

    'Declare the variables of the user-defined types
    Dim miStruct As prtMarginInfo
    Dim miString As PrtMipStr
```

```
    'Quit if report does not return a value for PrtMip
    If IsNull(Reports(strReport).PrtMip) Then
        Exit Function
    End If

    'Assign the value of PrtMip to the miString structure
    miString.rgb = Reports(strReport).PrtMip

    'Assign the value of the miString to the miStruct structure
    LSet miStruct = miString

    'Print the fields of miStruct to the Immediate window
    Debug.Print "Left margin", , miStruct.xLeftMargin
    Debug.Print "Top margin", , miStruct.yTopMargin
    Debug.Print "Right margin", , miStruct.xRightMargin
    Debug.Print "Bottom margin", , miStruct.yBotMargin
    Debug.Print "Data only?", , miStruct.fDataOnly
    Debug.Print "Item width", , miStruct.xFormSize
    Debug.Print "Item height", , miStruct.yFormSize
    Debug.Print "Same as Detail?", miStruct.fDefaultSize
    Debug.Print "Items across", , miStruct.cxColumns
    Debug.Print "Column spacing", miStruct.xFormSpacing
    Debug.Print "Row spacing", , miStruct.yFormSpacing
    Debug.Print "Item layout", , miStruct.radItemOrder

    wShowMarginInfo = True
End Function
```

TIP

If you use commas to specify that the fields of the Debug.Print statement are to be printed in separate print zones, you don't need to convert the values of non-**String** variables to **String** variables. Print zones are 14 characters wide. Use multiple commas to align data in the appropriate print zone.

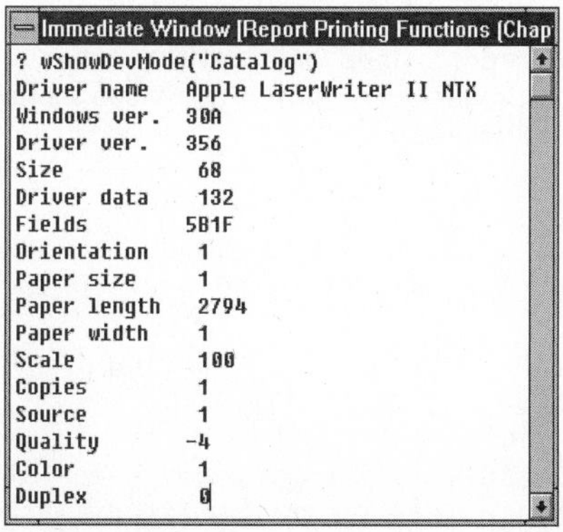

FIGURE 10.3.

Values of fields of the PrtDevMode property for the Catalog report.

```
Immediate Window [Report Printing Functions [Chap
? wShowDevMode("Catalog")
Driver name    Apple LaserWriter II NTX
Windows ver.   30A
Driver ver.    356
Size           68
Driver data    132
Fields         5B1F
Orientation    1
Paper size     1
Paper length   2794
Paper width    1
Scale          100
Copies         1
Source         1
Quality        -4
Color          1
Duplex         0
```

When you execute ? wShowMarginInfo("Catalog") in the Immediate window, the values of the fields of the prtMarginInfo structure appear as shown in Figure 10.4.

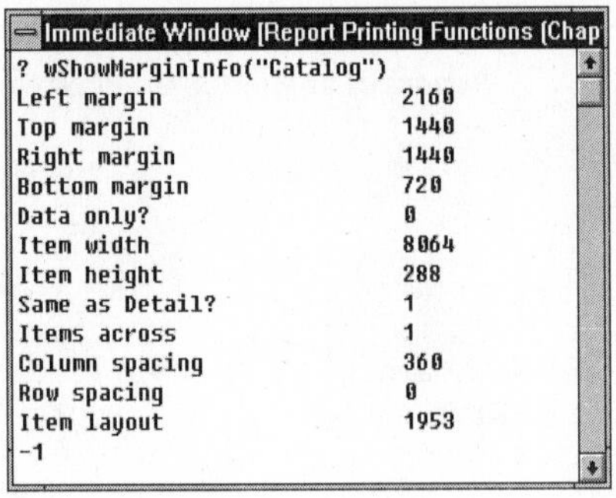

FIGURE 10.4. ·

Values of fields of the PrtMip property for the Catalog report.

```
═ Immediate Window [Report Printing Functions [Chap]
? wShowMarginInfo("Catalog")
Left margin                    2160
Top margin                     1440
Right margin                   1440
Bottom margin                  720
Data only?                     0
Item width                     8064
Item height                    288
Same as Detail?                1
Items across                   1
Column spacing                 360
Row spacing                    0
Item layout                    1953
-1
```

Using the *PrtDevMode* and *PrtMip* Properties

As with many other properties of Access objects, you only can set the values of the PrtDevMode and PrtMip properties in design mode; thus, PrtDevMode and PrtMip are not set bold in the code listings of this chapter. The wSetDevMode() function, whose listing follows, sets the printer driver to the Generic/Text Only driver and changes the scale at which the report is printed. The wSetDevMode() function uses the **LSet** instruction to left-justify the name of the printer driver in the 32-character fixed-length string, as well as to return the value of dmStruct back to dmString to set the value of the PrtDevMode property.

```
Function wSetDevMode (strReport As String) As Integer
     'Purpose:   Set value fields of prtDeviceMode
     'Argument:  Literal name of report open in Design mode
     'Returns:   True if successful, False on Failure

     'Declare the variables of the user-defined types
     Dim dmStruct As prtDeviceMode
     Dim dmString As prtDevModeStr

     'Quit if report does not return a value for PrtDevMode
     If IsNull(Reports(strReport).PrtDevMode) Then
         Exit Function
     End If

     'Assign the value of PrtDevMode to the dmString structure
     dmString.rgb = Reports(strReport).PrtDevMode

     'Assign the value of the dmString to the dmStruct structure
     LSet dmStruct = dmString

     'Assign values to the commonly-used fields of dmStruct
     'Use LSet to left align the literal string in the fixed-width
     ➡string
```

```
    LSet dmStruct.dmDeviceName = "Generic / Text Only"
    dmStruct.dmDriverVersion = &H30A
    dmStruct.dmDriverExtra = 8
    dmStruct.dmFields = &HC202
    dmStruct.dmOrientation = 1
    dmStruct.dmPaperSize = 1
    dmStruct.dmScale = 75
    dmStruct.dmCopies = 1

    'Now use LSet to return the new values to dmString (PrtDevMode)
    LSet dmString = dmStruct
    Reports(strReport).PrtDevMode = dmString.rgb

    wSetDevMode = True
End Function
```

To experiment with the wSetDevMode() function, open the Catalog report of NWIND.MDB in design mode. Then execute ? wSetDevMode("Catalog") in the Immediate window. You need to close the Catalog report, save the changes, reopen the Catalog report in Print Preview mode, and finally click the Setup button to see the effect of the modifications. Click the Options button of the Print Setup dialog box to see the change to the printing scale.

Creating Files from Reports

If you want to incorporate a report in a word-processing document or a worksheet, you need to create a compatible file from the report. Access isn't an OLE server, so you can't embed the report in a compound document. The two methods currently available to create files that you can import into word-processing documents and spreadsheets are described in the sections that follow.

Using the Generic/Text Only Printer

You can create text files from Access reports by installing the Windows Generic/Text Only printer driver and connecting the installed printer to FILE rather than to an LPT# line-printer port. The print-to-text-file technique is important because it is the only method by which you can include the text of subforms or subreports that are incorporated in your reports. Few Windows users employ the Generic/Text Only printer, because Windows 3.1 includes printer drivers for virtually every type and model of printer. You use the Generic/Text Only printer driver to create text files because this driver generates the fewest control codes that attempt to format the printed output. The filename of the Generic/Text Only printer driver is TTY.DRV; TTY is the abbreviation for teletype. Teletype printers print 10 characters per horizontal inch at six lines per vertical inch and have only two methods of formatting their output: via spaces and via newline pairs.

To install the Generic/Text Only printer driver, have the distribution disks for Windows 3.1 or Windows for Workgroups ready and follow these steps:

1. Launch Windows' Control Panel and double-click the Printers icon to open the Printers dialog.

2. Click the Add button of the Printers dialog to display the List of Printers list box. Select Generic/Text Only, then click the Install button. Figure 10.5 shows the Printers dialog with the Generic/Text Only printer selected.

3. Insert the requested distribution disk into a disk drive, then click the OK button to install the driver. (The Generic/Text Only printer driver is on disk #8 among the Windows for Workgroups 3.1 disks.)

4. Click the Connect button to display the Connect dialog, as shown in Figure 10.6, and choose FILE: from the Ports list box; then click the Fast Printing Direct To Port check box, if necessary, to mark the box. This check box lets you bypass Print Manager and print the report directly to the file you specify. Click the OK button to return to the Printers dialog.

5. Click the OK button of the Printers dialog to close the dialog, then close Control Panel.

Testing the Generic/Text Only Printer Driver

Once you've installed the Generic/Text Only printer driver, you need to test the driver to determine whether it is operable on your computer. Testing the Generic/Text Only printer driver with an Access form also lets you see the report-design problems that you need to solve before you can use the driver to create a clean text file. Figure 10.7 shows the original design of the List of Products by Category report of the Northwind Traders database.

FIGURE 10.5.

The Printers dialog of the Windows Control Panel applet.

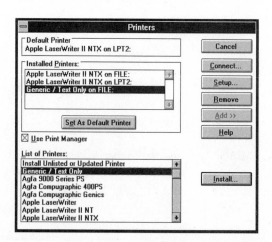

FIGURE 10.6.

Using the Connect dialog to specify printing directly to a file.

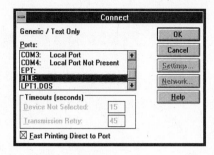

FIGURE 10.7.

The original design of the List of Products by Category report of NWIND.MDB.

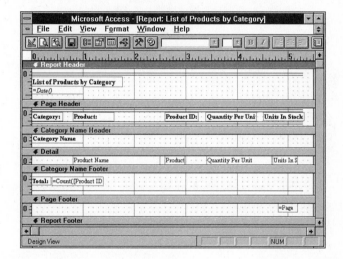

To print the List of Products by Category report to an ASCII (not ANSI) text file, do the following:

1. Open the report in Print Preview mode from the Database window. Then click the Print Setup button to display the Print Setup dialog.

2. Choose the Generic/Text Only on FILE: printer from the Printer combo box.

3. Set all the margins to 0. (You don't need to be concerned with the printable area of a text file.) Your Print Setup dialog appears as shown in Figure 10.8.

4. Click the OK button to close the Print Setup dialog. Then click the Print button of Access's Print Preview window to display the Print to File dialog.

5. Enter the name of the text file in the Output File Name text box of the Print to File dialog. Then click the OK button to create the text file.

FIGURE 10.8.

Choosing the Generic/Text Only printer and setting margins.

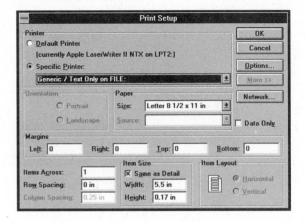

To view the text file created from the report, open the text file in Windows' Notepad. Figure 10.9 illustrates the result. The repeated groups of words (or portions of words) are an attempt by the Generic/Text Only printer driver to mimic the boldface attribute by overprinting the same text multiple times. ASCII characters that are not supported in the ANSI character set of Windows 3.1 appear as black rectangles in the text. The text representation of several elements of the report is truncated. Clearly, the text file shown in Figure 10.9 is a mess; you need to do a substantial amount of manual clean-up work to make the file usable.

FIGURE 10.9.

The text file created by the original design of the List of Products by Category report.

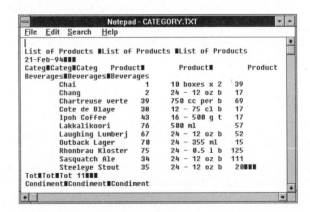

Modifying the Report Design to Generate a Clean Text File

The problems associated with the text file illustrated by Figure 10.9 primarily relate to the dimensions of labels and list boxes. The Generic/Text Only printer driver is designed to print 12-point (pica) type at a fixed pitch of 10 characters per inch. Access's tiny default report font, 8-point Arial, requires about half the line width of 10-character/inch pica in order to print the average word. You need to modify the design of your form to take into account the change in font. A generalized procedure for modifying standard Access reports to create ASCII text files involves these steps:

1. Open the report in design mode and choose Select All from the Edit menu to select all the control objects on the report.

2. Click the Bold button of the toolbar twice to remove the bold attribute from all labels and text boxes.

3. Open the FontName combo box and select the Courier New typeface. (The term "font" is improperly used in this case; you choose the type family or typeface in the FontName text box, and then pick a type size and add the attributes you want, such as bold italic. The combination of type family, size, and attributes determines the font.) Figure 10.10 shows the limited number of typefaces that are available with the Generic/Text Only printer driver installed.

4. Open the FontSize combo box and type 12, corresponding to 12-point pica type. The pica type family is defined as a 10-character/inch (monospace), exclusively 12-point typeface. The italic, bold, strike-through, and underline attributes are available for pica type.

5. Open the Form Properties window and set the `GridX` value (pitch) to 10 and the `GridY` value to 6. (There are six lines of pica type to the vertical inch.)

6. Choose **A**lign from the F**o**rmat menu, and then click Si**z**e to Fit. This procedure sets the height property of all text boxes to suit the 12-point font and sets the widths of labels to allow display of the full text of their `Caption` property.

7. Adjust the location and size of the text boxes to provide sufficient line width to display the content of the field, if possible.

8. Remove all graphic elements (such as lines and rectangles) from the report and delete all page-break controls, if they appear in the design.

9. Close up each section of the report by moving the controls so that the top edge of the control is adjacent to the bottom of the section divider bar, then move the next section divider bar up to the bottom edge of the controls.

The left part of the design of the List of Products by Category report, with the preceding modifications applied, appears in Figure 10.10. Figure 10.11 shows a part of the modified report in Print Preview mode. Although some of the product names are truncated, a sufficient number of characters appears so that the products are identified uniquely.

Figure 10.12 shows the cleaned-up text file created by the modified report design of Figure 10.11 displayed in Notepad. You can import this file to any word-processing or spreadsheet application. Unfortunately, you need to take another series of steps to format the report in a word-processing application or to move the elements of the report to worksheet cells.

FIGURE 10.10.

Modifying the design of a report for printing to a text file.

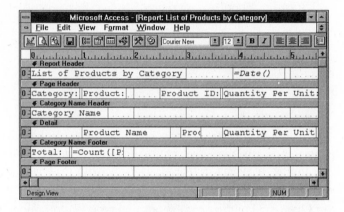

FIGURE 10.11.

The modified report in Print Preview mode.

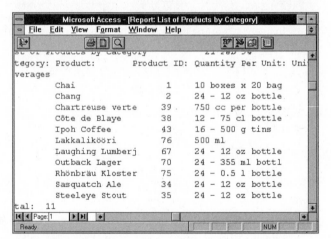

FIGURE 10.12.

The text file resulting from the modified form design of Figure 10.10.

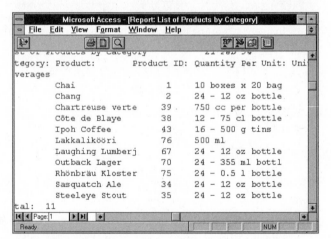

TIP

If you want to create text files of reports destined for tables of word-processing applications or to be imported into spreadsheet applications, modify the content of your text boxes to include a special character, such as the tilde (~), to represent a tab character in a tab-separated text file. Then write a program in Access Basic that uses the low-level sequential file features of Access Basic to remove spaces between the special character and the next valid character in the line. Next, replace the tildes with Chr$(9). The fields of your text file then import correctly into successive columns of word-processing tables or spreadsheets. Chapter 25, "Stretching the Limits of Access," and Chapter 27, "Documenting Your Access Applications," explain how to use the low-level (binary) file commands of Access Basic.

Using Output To to Create Files from Reports

Access 2.0 offers the Output **T**o choice of the **F**ile menu in order to create files from tables, queries, forms, and reports. This feature replaces the OUTPUTAS.MDA and OUTPUTAS.DLL add-in combination used by Access 1.x to print reports to files. Access 2.0's Output To feature has been enhanced to generate cleaner .RTF and .TXT files than OUTPUTAS.MDA; however, Output To remains incapable of including the content of subreports in the files.

Creating a file from a report with Output To involves these steps:

1. Open the report, then choose Output **T**o from the **F**ile menu to display the Output To dialog shown in Figure 10.13.

2. Select the type of file you want to create in the Select Format list box. Click OK to display the second Output To dialog.

3. Select the location for your file and give the file a name with the appropriate extension, as shown in Figure 10.14. If you tick the AutoStart check box, the application associated with the file extension opens to display the content of the file.

4. Click OK to create the file. The CATEGORY.TXT file created from the modified List of Products by Category report appears in Notepad. (See Figure 10.15.)

FIGURE 10.13.

Choosing a report to save as a file.

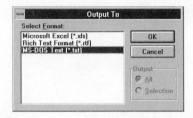

FIGURE 10.14.

Specifying the filename for the report.

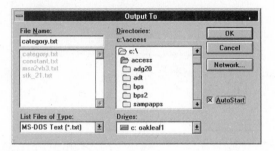

Figure 10.15 shows part of the ASCII text file you created in the preceding steps opened in Notepad. Output To spaces the text to prevent truncation; therefore, the width of the fields is greater than the text file created by printing to a file with the Generic/ Text Only printer. The Generic/Text Only printer converts special ANSI characters to their ASCII equivalent. Thus, "Côte de Blaye" becomes "Cote de Blaye" in the text file. Output To does not make this conversion and Notepad does not accommodate special ANSI characters; the special characters are replaced by black rectangles.

FIGURE 10.15.

An ASCII text file of a report displayed in Notepad.

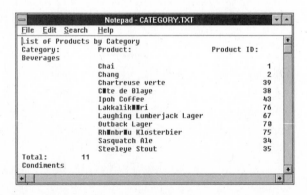

Output To also is capable of creating files in Microsoft rich-text format (.RTF). RTF files are text files that include embedded formatting commands to specify typefaces, font size and attributes, line spacing, and page layout. RTF files even can incorporate representations of bitmaps and vector image files. Word 6.0 uses RTF as an intermediary file format when Word converts files created by other word-processing applications to its native format. Figure 10.16 shows an .RTF file created by Output To displayed in Word 6.0 with paragraph and tab symbols displayed.

FIGURE 10.16.

An .RTF file created by Output To and displayed in Word 6.0.

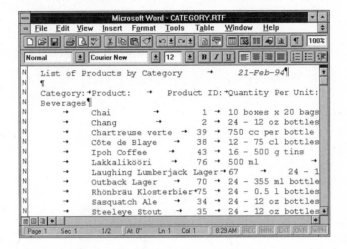

The Excel BIFF (.XLS) files created by Output To give the most useful result. Figure 10.17 shows the List of Products by Category report imported into Excel 5.0. None of the text is truncated, and for the most part, the data for groups of products correctly appears in conterminous cells. The report header does not appear, and the totals line is missing. No matter how you reformat the report, the totals for each category do not appear. Although the outlining feature of Excel is turned on by the .XLS file, when you collapse the outline by clicking the 1 button, only the group header lines appear.

FIGURE 10.17.

A report saved in BIFF format, then imported into Excel 5.0.

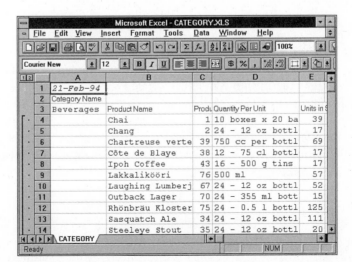

Using Excel as an intermediary is the most effective method of importing data created by Output To to tables in word-processing documents. Figure 10.18 shows the result of selecting all the cells of the worksheet of Figure 10.17, copying the cells to the clipboard, and pasting the cells into Word 6.0.

FIGURE 10.18.

The Excel worksheet of Figure 10.17 pasted into a Word 6.0 document.

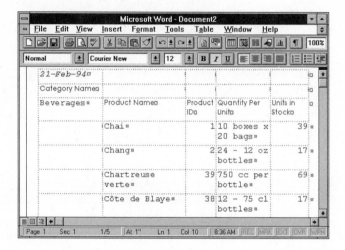

On the whole, Output To is useful but is not yet ready for prime-time use in most commercial Access applications. Failure to include total lines in .XLS files, the inability to incorporate data from subreports, and peculiar formatting features in complex .RTF files require that you design reports specifically for use with Output To. Therefore, if your production applications need to create files that emulate the output of reports, your best choice at present is to create tab- or comma-delimited text files with Access Basic code.

Printing Reports to Encapsulated PostScript Files

If you need to include images of your reports in documentation for your application, you can print the file to an Encapsulated PostScript (.EPS) file, then import the .EPS file into your Word 6.0 document. Your printer does not need to have PostScript capability for Windows to create an .EPS file. Although the information in this section might appear better suited to inclusion in Chapter 27, "Documenting Your Access Applications," it is presented here so that this chapter can consolidate all the methods of printing reports to files.

To create an Encapsulated PostScript file from an Access report, follow these steps:

1. If you have not installed a PostScript driver, follow the steps outlined in the preceding section, "Using the Generic/Text Only Printer," to install a new Windows printer driver. In this case, choose the Apple LaserWriter II/NTX printer driver rather than the Generic/Text Only printer driver. Use the Connect dialog to set the Port to LPT1 or LPT2, not FILE:.

2. Open the report that you want to save to an .EPS file in Print Preview mode and click the Setup button to display the Print Setup dialog.

3. Choose the PostScript printer in the Printer combo box and click the Options button to display the Options dialog.

4. Click the Encapsulated PostScript File option button of the Options dialog and enter the filename with an .EPS extension in the Name text box.

5. Click the None button to remove the margins from the image in the .EPS file. Make sure that the Send Header With Each Job check box is marked. If you want to change the scale of the image at this point, enter the scaling percentage in the Scaling (%) text box. (The Scaling text box contains the value of the `dmScale` field of the `prtDeviceMode` structure, as discussed earlier in this chapter.) Alternately, you can scale the image in your word-processing application. The Options dialog with entries to create an .EPS file of the Catalog report of NWIND.MDB is shown in Figure 10.19.

6. Click the OK button of the Options dialog, and then click the OK button of the Printer Setup dialog to return to the Print Preview window.

7. Click the Print button of the Print Preview window for the report to display the Print dialog. Choose the page of the report to print. Do not mark the Print to File check box. Your Print dialog appears as shown in Figure 10.20. Click the OK button to print the report to the .EPS file, in this case CATALOG.EPS.

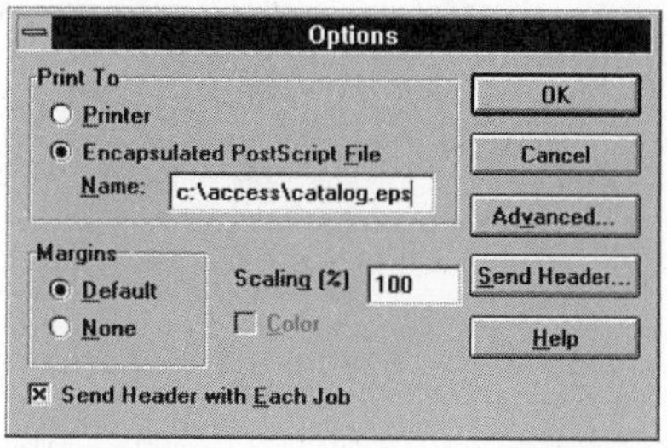

FIGURE 10.19.

The Options dialog with the settings to create an Encapsulated PostScript file.

FIG 10.20.

The Print dialog setting to print a single page of a report as an Encapsulated PostScript file.

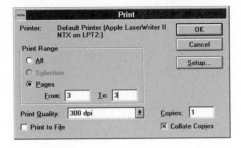

To insert the image of the report page in a Word 6.0 document, choose **P**icture from Word's **I**nsert menu to display the Picture dialog. Choose your .EPS file from the File Name list box. Word displays the .EPS file as a frame, with the filename as the title. (See Figure 10.21.) You can scale the illustration by selecting the EPS frame and choosing Picture from the Format menu. Figure 10.22 shows a printed page of a Word for Windows document with an embedded EPS image of page 4 of the Catalog report scaled to 75 percent.

FIGURE 10.21.

The appearance of an encapsulated PostScript file in Word 6.0.

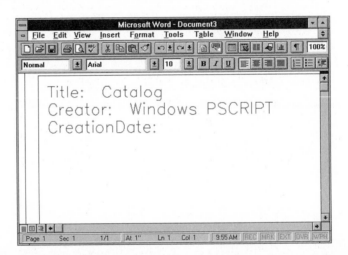

NOTE

If you intend to use your application manual to create a Windows help file with the Doc-To-Help application described in Chapter 28, you need to convert the .EPS file to a Windows bitmap .BMP file. Windows illustration applications, such as CorelDRAW! 4, are capable of opening .EPS files, scaling the image as necessary, and converting the .EPS vector image to a .BMP file.

FIGURE 10.22.
A printed page of a Word 6.0 document with an embedded .EPS image of an Access report.

Beverages

Soft drinks, coffees, teas, beer, and ale

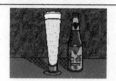

Product Name:	*Product ID:*	*Quantity Per Unit:*	*Unit Price:*
Chai	1	10 boxes x 20 bags	$18.00
Chang	2	24 - 12 oz bottles	$19.00
Chartreuse verte	39	750 cc per bottle	$18.00
Côte de Blaye	38	12 - 75 cl bottles	$263.50
Ipoh Coffee	43	16 - 500 g tins	$46.00
Lakkalikööri	76	500 ml	$18.00
Laughing Lumberjack Lager	67	24 - 12 oz bottles	$14.00
Outback Lager	70	24 - 355 ml bottles	$15.00
Rhönbräu Klosterbier	75	24 - 0.5 l bottles	$7.75
Sasquatch Ale	34	24 - 12 oz bottles	$14.00
Steeleye Stout	35	24 - 12 oz bottles	$18.00

Condiments

Sweet and savory sauces, relishes, spreads, and seasonings

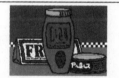

Product Name:	*Product ID:*	*Quantity Per Unit:*	*Unit Price:*
Aniseed Syrup	3	12 - 550 ml bottles	$10.00
Chef Anton's Cajun Seasoning	4	48 - 6 oz jars	$22.00
Genen Shouyu	15	24 - 250 ml bottles	$15.50
Grandma's Boysenberry Spread	6	12 - 8 oz jars	$25.00
Gula Malacca	44	20 - 2 kg bags	$19.45
Louisiana Fiery Hot Pepper Sauce	65	32 - 8 oz bottles	$21.05
Louisiana Hot Spiced Okra	66	24 - 8 oz jars	$17.00
Northwoods Cranberry Sauce	8	12 - 12 oz jars	$40.00
Original Frankfurter grüne Soße	77	12 boxes	$13.00
Sirop d'érable	61	24 - 500 ml bottles	$28.50
Vegie-spread	63	15 - 625 g jars	$43.90

Northwind Traders Products - Spring 1994

Page 3

Using Access Basic to Create Report Files

You can use the low-level file functions of Access Basic to create the text equivalent of reports that you can import into a word-processing or spreadsheet application and then print. Chapter 25 explains how to use the low-level file functions of Access Basic. You need to write a substantial amount of Access Basic code in order to generate a report surrogate that includes subreports, but the process is no more lengthy or tedious than employing the same low-level file methods in xBase dialects. In this case, however, xBase has the edge on Access, because you can use the REPORT FORM command of xBase with the TO FILE clause to create an ASCII text file of the report.

> **TIP**
>
> If your report displays data from only one record of an underlying table or query per page, or if it alternates blank and printed pages, the culprit may be null characters in your data. Null characters (ASCII 0 or `Chr$(0)`) in text box values cause unpredictable results in the printing of your forms. For example, the `SQL` property of many `QueryDef` objects created in query design mode often include one or more null characters. These characters are ignored when you display the value of the `SQL` property in a text box on a form. However, when you attempt to print a report that includes multiple `qdfQueryName.SQL` values, your report contains alternating pages with one record and pages that are blank. If you encounter abnormal formatting, execute `? Instr(strVariable, Chr$(0))` in the Immediate window to check your text box values for null characters. If null values are present, add a `Do While Instr(strVariable, Chr$(0)) > 0` loop to your code and replace the null values with spaces.

IV

Exploring Commercial
Access Applications

11

Examining an Access Accounting Application

by Gerry Novreske

Other chapters of this book cover the techniques of using all the various objects found in Access, including in-depth analysis and using macros and modules. This chapter looks at putting it all together to create an aesthetically pleasing, user-friendly application using only Access.

The MTX Accounting SDK was developed as an accounting application base for end-user solutions. The SDK is designed to provide the "hooks" for vertical applications to extract data from the database, or for data to be added to the database from add-on applications such as Inventory or Order Entry/Billing applications. The goal of the SDK is to help the developer or consultant provide a cost-effective, customized solution to an end-user through the combination of the SDK, add-ons developed by others or by the developer, and minor customization.

Many of you may not have decided whether to develop an industrial-strength application. This chapter looks at the factors involved in making that decision using Microsoft Access, based on the experience of MTX. You can follow the development process with an emphasis on the following:

■ Application requirements

■ Application audit controls

■ The look and feel of the application

■ Developing standards

■ Creating a user-friendly interface

■ Meeting the needs of the user

The Decision to Use Microsoft Access

MTX International, Inc. was incorporated in 1976 to provide management consulting services for small- and medium-sized businesses, and it has provided computerized accounting solutions to the small business marketplace since 1980. Its first accounting application was written in CBasic under the CP/M operating system. As technology advanced, the software was continuously updated (based not only on technology but also on the results of annual user surveys).

The first major update was from a single-user CP/M system to a multiuser application under the TurboDos operating system. The second major update was to port the application to MS-DOS and then to Novell networks. Throughout the life of the application, it continued to be enhanced, based on the requests of the users. However, after 14 years, the software began to look old and tired.

A substantial effort would be required to port the software to another platform in order to meet the desires of the customers (and the marketplace in general). Users were becoming more computer literate and demanded the capability to customize the software—or at least to generate customized reports. One option was to completely rewrite the application to include the latest technologies using a 4GL language. The high cost of a complete rewrite demanded the right choice of an operating platform so that the software would have the longest possible life expectancy.

Along came Microsoft Windows 3.0. The quick market acceptance of Windows convinced developers worldwide that they might be looking at the next universally-accepted operating platform. Then came Windows 3.1 and the decision was made—the MTX Accounting application would be rewritten to the new Windows standard. Then the search was on for a language that would be compatible with the Windows standard and fulfill the other requirements for a Relational Database Management System. The solution: Access.

Access was much more than a Windows database front end or an end-user report generator. Access was an in-depth, powerful development environment. A bonus would be the ability to use the new software as a front end for an SQL server. The accounting package could function in a client/server environment. Access provided the tools to meet all the objectives of MTX.

Application Requirements

Much of the development of an accounting application is dictated by Generally Accepted Accounting Practices (GAAP). Data security is a mandatory requirement. The challenge of a good accounting package is to meet all the requirements of the accounting profession and yet meet the end-users' desires for ease of use and intuitive operation. Security requirements meant designing the general navigational structure (menu system) of the application so that various activities could be logically grouped (to the various accounting processes assigned to different user groups or personnel) and restricted where necessary. The system administrator then would be able to restrict access to the various menu forms as needed.

In order to create complete end-user solutions, "hooks" must be provided to allow the easy attachment of add-on applications. Form-design standards must be developed to ensure a consistent "look and feel" throughout the application, including any add-ons or customization.

The Menu System

The menu system is designed to allow easy access to the various functions provided in the application and to allow the implementation of a simple security scheme. Entry to the Main Menu is from the copyright notice shown in Figure 11.1. The copyright notice is the only intimidating form, error message, or informational message in the application.

FIGURE 11.1.
*The copyright
message and entry
to the menu system.*

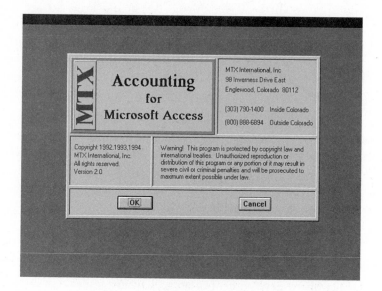

If possible, a message should never tell the user that he or she did something wrong. Instead, messages should simply inform the user of what can be done to correct whatever mistake may have been made. You want to guide the user through the application in a friendly manner; users never need to be scolded or told that they have made a serious mistake. The user must believe that any error can be easily corrected. (Of course, you have to make sure that this is true.) The application may be the first Windows business software that your user will ever be required to master, so it's worth the time to make it friendly and inviting.

The Main Menu

The Main Menu (see Figure 11.2) provides access to all the various submenus. In addition, buttons on the Main Menu can launch applications not included in the accounting application. Access allows permissions to be granted or restricted to individual objects as the first level of security. The system administrator can selectively restrict access to the various submenus by restricting access to one or more of the submenu forms. For example, the administrator might allow only the accountant access to the Month End (see Figure 11.3) and Payroll Menu; an accounting clerk might be able to use only the General Ledger and People Places Things menus; the billing clerk may have rights to only the Accounts Receivable Menu. It is useful to consider how your end-user might run his or her business and design the menu system to meet the requirements of specific job descriptions or typical office work groups. Using this thought process to design your menu system can make the job of the system administrator much easier.

FIGURE 11.2.
The Main Menu provides access to submenus.

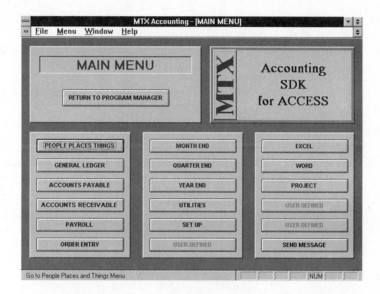

FIGURE 11.3.
The Month End Menu is accessed from the Main Menu.

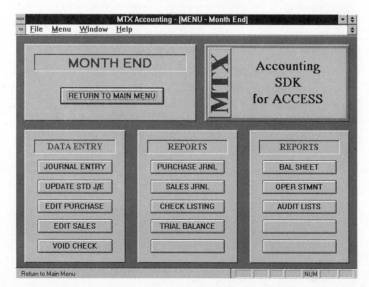

Application Controls

Two tables have been included to provide records of the activities that take place during the use of the application. These tables are shown in Figure 11.4 and Figure 11.5.

The function of these two tables is to provide information regarding who has used the application, what the user did, and when he or she did it. This information, contained in the System Activity Log (see Figure 11.4), may then be used in performing system diagnostics (to reconstruct the sequence of events leading up to a problem) or to determine whether problems may be originating in certain forms or by certain users. A search of this table will also show whether any forms have been opened but not closed. (This information may indicate an error that caused a form to close abnormally.)

The System Batch Numbers table (see Figure 11.5) is used to record the totals for a number of transactions (known as a batch), entered during a single session. When a user opens a form for the addition of transactions to any of the accounting tables, this table is searched for the next batch number, and the time, date, and user are recorded on the table. Every transaction entered has this batch number recorded on each record added to it. The table records the total of the transactions when the entry of the transactions is completed. In the future, if any of the transactions for the batch are edited (changed), the date and the user are recorded, as is the revised batch total (if applicable). For auditing purposes, a report for any batch may be printed using the Audit List menu step provided on the Month End Menu.

FIGURE 11.4.

The System Activity Log shows who has been in the system and when.

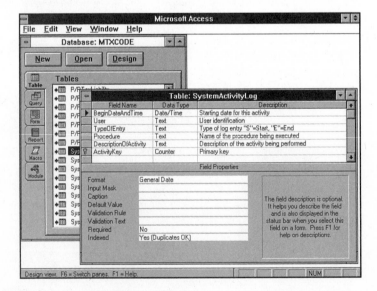

In addition to the Activity Log and the Batch Numbers tables, for supplemental auditing purposes each primary record contained in the system tables also carries fields for both the creation and modification of date/time and user ID. These fields are automatically updated when records are initially created or subsequently modified.

FIGURE 11.5.

The System Batch Numbers table logs the batches of data entered by various users.

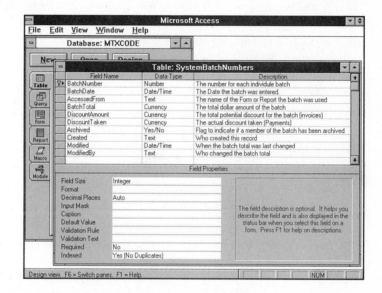

Turning Data into Information

Data stored in the database must be easily accessible by users as they do their day-to-day tasks. Most of the accounting data in a database is usually associated with the various entities (customers, suppliers, and employees) with whom the users deal. Much of this information is needed on demand when answering or asking questions about these entities.

Once you determine the most useful information that may be required by your user, you may want to develop a toolbar to make accessing the information easy. All of the new versions of the Microsoft Office applications include "Tool Tips." Now with Access 2.0, you can provide Tool Tips as part of your application. The new MouseMove event is generated continually as the mouse pointer moves over objects. To show a Tool Tip, simply set a text box to "visible" as the mouse moves over the various icons or buttons.

The MTX Toolbar shown in Figure 11.6 is an example of how a toolbar may be used to access information commonly needed while using the MTX Accounting application. This toolbar is found at the top of every primary form. The user always knows where to look for it when additional information is needed. The appropriate information is displayed on a pop-up form by simply pushing a button. The "additional information" buttons are located on the top and include memos, telephone numbers, billing addresses, and credit information as well as access to other Microsoft Office applications. The Toolbar form may be copied and pasted onto each new form as you create it. As a new form is developed, you can modify the Toolbar as necessary for your individual application. Using the copy-and-paste method will ensure that each of your forms has a standardized look.

FIGURE 11.6.

The MTX Toolbar is used for immediate access to associated information as well as to various pushbuttons that initiate other procedures.

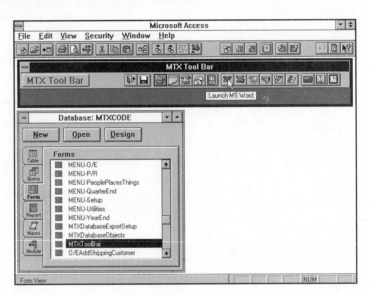

One of the icons is used to call a print command for the data on the primary form. If printing is not used on a particular form, the icon's enabled property can be set to enabled=no to gray the icon out.

Another icon calls a memo pop-up form for the entity (customer, supplier, or employee) displayed on the primary form. A memo field has been provided on every primary record in the database. Because Access uses only as many bytes on a record as there is data, you are not using any more storage than is necessary by using memo fields. Using memo fields enables the user to record any information desired. The information is always available at the push of a button.

Another of the icons requests telephone numbers. The envelope icon requests a mailing address and the CR icon requests credit information for the entity displayed on the primary form.

Other icons are used to call standard Windows applets, such as clock, calendar or schedule+ (if Windows for Workgroups is used), the calculator, and Microsoft Office applications. You may want to create different icons to represent and call other applets or to initiate other procedures.

Buttons may be placed on the left side of the Toolbar to initiate any function desired for your application.

The Toolbar is used throughout the accounting application when entering or querying data. Examples of the uses of the Toolbar are shown later in this chapter as the primary forms are reviewed.

People, Places, and Things

One of the goals of an RDBMS is to eliminate the duplication of information and to reference only the required data as needed. In a typical business-accounting application, almost all data is associated with a particular entity (customer, employee, or supplier). In some cases, an employee can also be a customer and/or a supplier. One table is created to contain the basic information for every entity. Additional tables are created to contain only the information specific to a particular kind of entity.

The People Places and Things (PPT) Editor form (see Figure 11.7) in the MTX Accounting application may be accessed from the Setup Menu or from any form that requires information for an entity. This is done by double-clicking the control (field) where the information is needed. Double-clicking the field opens the PPT Editor so that the user may enter the necessary data.

The Memo and Telephone buttons on the PPT Editor are specific to the record in the PPT table. The memo buttons on the Customer, Supplier and Employee tables, however, access a separate memo field for each record. In other words, each entity may have as many as four separate memo fields: one for entity, one for customer, one for supplier, and one for employee. Examples of the uses of these memo fields will be shown later in the chapter.

When you close the PPT Editor, the Customer, Supplier, or Employee Editor forms are opened (depending upon which primary form called for the setup of a new entity) so that additional data may be entered. See Figure 11.8 for the A/R Customer Editor form. After closing this supplemental form, the user is returned to the original calling form.

FIGURE 11.7.

The PPT Editor is the form used to set up each entity with whom the user deals.

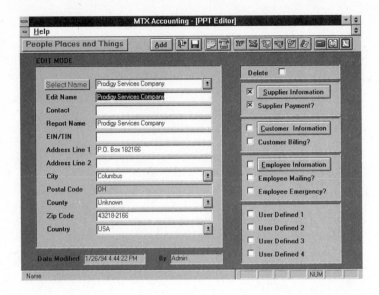

The A/R Customer Editor (see Figure 11.8) contains only the information specific to a customer. The information shown in the Name, Address, and Telephone Number areas of the form is from the PPT table. The Credit and Accounting Info are used only for the Customer. Any information on this form may be changed as necessary, however. The memo field accessed from the Toobar button is a separate memo field for the customer record of this entity. The Accounting Info area provides combo boxes to select default general-ledger account numbers for the customer. These general-ledger numbers are used as defaults when entering invoices in the Accounts Receivable section of the accounting application.

In addition to the Customer Editor, the application includes similar forms for suppliers and employees. These forms are used for entering only the supplemental information required for specific kinds of entities.

Another advantage of a single table for all entities is the ability to easily get selective labels or reports for specific uses.

The user may select one, many, or all of the items shown in the form in Figure 11.9. The selections are then used to filter the PPT table to produce labels or reports for specific activities (such as Christmas cards, customer newsletters, employee communications, or supplier notices).

On the basis of the selection criteria, a complex SQL dialog is created in Access Basic for the query required to filter the PPT file for the user's request.

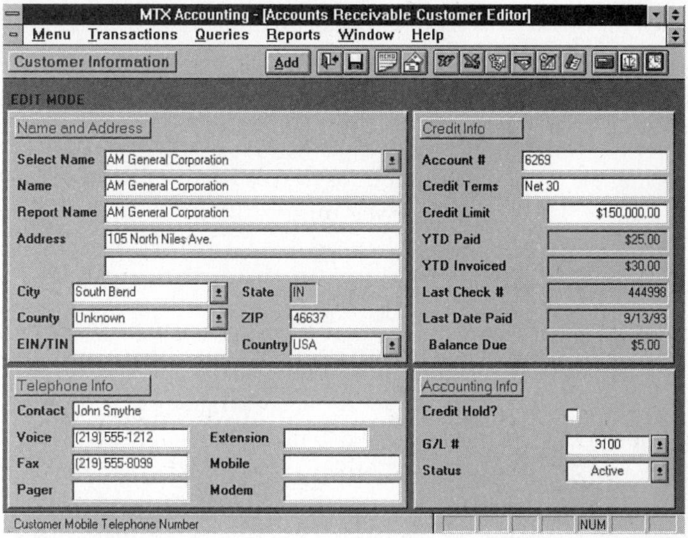

FIGURE 11.8.

The A/R Customer Editor form is used to enter additional information if the entity is a customer.

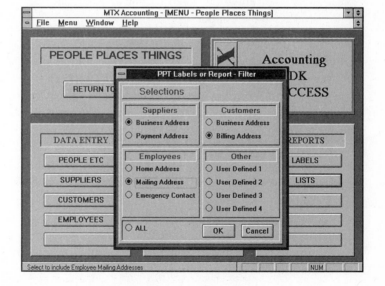

FIGURE 11.9.

The SYS PPT Report is an example of using a form to create complex select queries.

The Look and Feel of "User Friendly" Applications

A "user friendly" Windows application is something entirely different from a character-based application. Developers using the Windows environment have given us many new or rewritten applications. Many of these applications are fun to use and easy on the eyes. You have seen examples of poorly designed interfaces, however, that attempt to use every kind of object, color, and font on the same screen. Some applications just don't look or feel right.

Before windows, programming traditional character-based applications only required that all the necessary questions or instructions be displayed on the screen using good grammar. The use of color was minimal and font size and weight was of little concern. The programmer didn't need to think of a screen as anything more than a piece of paper with text and a few boxes.

Windows and the graphical environment, coupled with ever-increasing hardware power, have made applications more creative in how the user is prompted or provided with information. In addition, the programmer no longer dictates the sequence of operations. The users now dictate the operations to be performed and their sequence. The programmer's job is to present objects to the user and then respond to the users' actions on those objects. The goal of the developer is to logically group objects so users may easily find the ones they need. The tools that are available in the Access development environment enable you to quickly and easily and create a graphical user interface for the application.

If you are new to designing a graphical user interface, a good way to start is to use a Form Wizard to get all the fields on the screen with some consistency. The next step is to arrange the controls and labels logically (see Figure 11.10), which means grouping similar information. You may want to create or copy your custom toolbar to the form at this point. Keep in mind that the users' eyes will initially go to the upper-left side of the form when it first appears. The identification or instructions for use of the form therefore should be in the upper-left corner. A way to shift the eye of the user to another part of the form is by using color or large fonts. Overuse of color or large fonts can be very tiring for users because their eyes are constantly on the move. These techniques should be used only to identify logical groups of objects so that users can quickly find the needed area of the form. Another thought to keep in mind: in general, because the eye scan of the user goes from upper-left to lower-right, the most important objects should be in the upper-left corner and the least important or last objects in the lower-right corner.

After all the objects have been located in the general area of the form that you want, the next step is alignment. Your goal should be to provide a symmetrical layout with consistent spacing between controls and borders. Using rectangles around your object groupings enables users to quickly focus only on the area they need without having to read every label or look at every control. Alphanumeric fields need to be left-justified and numeric fields need to be right-justified. (See Figure 11.10.) That goes for column headings, too. There are exceptions to this rule, but you must use good judgment.

FIGURE 11.10.

The A/P Invoice form resembles an actual input document and uses many of Access's GUI controls.

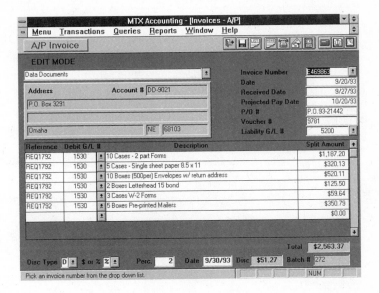

With most forms, you will have data that is informational and cannot be changed, and controls that may be empty or contain data that can be changed. You must differentiate between them so that users can quickly get to the task at hand. One way to accomplish this is to set the control background to light gray for those with information that can't be changed and set the background to white for those controls in which the data may be changed. In addition, to prevent the user from going to the unchangeable control, you need to set the enabled property to enabled=no and locked=yes. Setting the Enabled property to "no" means that the control may never have the focus. Setting the locked property to "yes" means that the information in the control may not be edited. By setting the two properties in this manner, the control will have a normal appearance; you may not, however, "move to" or select the control. If the colors of the control are set to black letters on a grey background, this effect will be produced.

The buttons on the toolbar enable the user to obtain or update other information on an as-needed basis. Pressing a button on the toolbar results in a pop-up form for a specific purpose. The basic form should allow for the entry of all the required data, whereas the use of the toolbar pop-ups would be for the exceptional data.

List boxes and combo boxes need to be used wherever possible to provide easy access to information the user needs in order to complete a task with the minimum chance of error. List boxes should be used even if it seems as though the proper input would be self-evident. For example, if the required data might be only "Yes" or "No," using a list box (with the Limit To List property set to "yes") enables the user to select a correct response—without having to worry about whether it is case sensitive, whether it should be spelled out, or whether it should be just the first character. If the response is limited to the list, there is no chance of error. Combo boxes provide choices for the user that eliminate the need to look up information on printouts or to precode data on an input document. Access allows input of one or more characters in a combo box, and then automatically goes to the first match in the list. The user may then scroll to the desired item.

FIGURE 11.11.

Using a calendar that is an OLE 2.0 embedded object is an easy way to enable the user to select a date that may be needed in one of the fields on your data entry form.

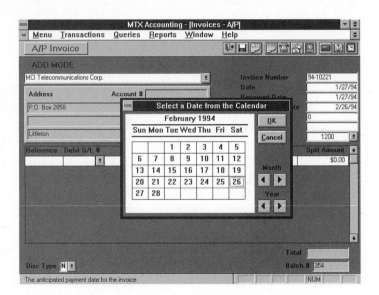

Access 2.0 implements the use of embedded OLE 2.0 objects, such as a calendar. When the user is required to enter or select a date, one of the usual steps in doing it is to look at a calendar. This eliminates the confusion sometimes caused by non-work days such as weekends or holidays. The Calendar object (see figure 11.11) pops up after a double click in the date field. The user then selects the appropriate date by clicking. The selected date is then automatically inserted into the calling field on the form and the calendar object is closed.

Another technique to keep a form uncluttered is to overlay controls using the visible properties. The combo boxes on the subform of the Payroll Tax Deduction Specification form (shown in Figure 11.12) is an example of this technique. There are actually five sets of combo boxes for the tax jurisdictions, one on top of the other. Each of the radio buttons for the various tax jurisdictions requires a set of combo boxes specific to that jurisdiction. For instance, if state withholding taxes are required for the selected employee, the radio button for State is checked and a macro is executed that makes the State combo boxes visible (and all others for the tax jurisdictions invisible). Clicking the down arrow for the combo box then displays a list of states from which the user may choose. This technique (using the `visible=yes/visible=no` property) is used on forms throughout the MTX Accounting SDK when information is required to be entered only under certain conditions, as determined by the user's selections.

FIGURE 11.12.

The Payroll Tax Deduction Specification form is an example of using overlaid combo boxes to keep a form uncluttered.

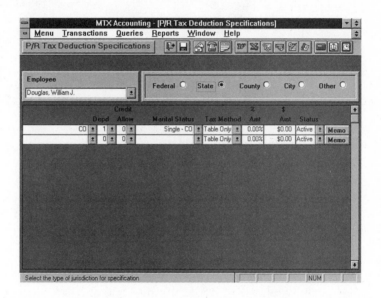

Another feature of Access is the ability to use forms and subforms. A wizard is provided to help set up correct subforms. An example of the effective use of a subform is shown in Figure 11.13. The A/P Inquiry Payment History form is used for information regarding paid supplier invoices. As an example of its use, consider a supplier's inquiry about what he shows as an unpaid invoice. The user can select the supplier name from the combo box and the subform will then show all paid invoices for that supplier. (If there are more invoices than can fit on the form, the user may use the scroll bar on the right side of the subform to bring additional invoices into view.) In keeping with the goal to turn data into information, this form not only shows the paid invoices but also shows the check number, check date, and the number of days from the invoice date to the check date. It also calculates the average numbers of days needed to pay all of the invoices on file for the selected supplier.

FIGURE 11.13.

The A/P Inquiry Unpaid form shows effective use of a subform to present additional information to the user.

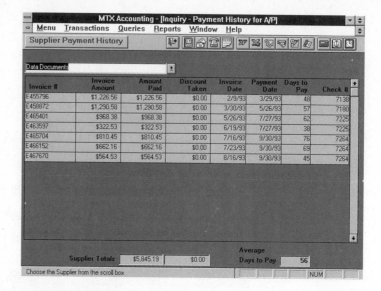

Putting It All Together

What's an effective way to know whether you have designed a pleasing form? Ask some other programmers, "How do you like it?" If they say it looks better than prior versions but are unable to tell you quite what it was that changed, you will know that you are very close to a good form design. Many of the elements of good form design (right- and left-justification, balances of copy mass, appropriate use of bold and normal characters) are almost imperceptible. The result? It just looks better.

Figures 11.14 through 11.18 demonstrate how a well-designed application enables the user to perform a job simply and effectively. These figures show how a typical accounts-receivable task, such as collections, can take advantage of the available data using intuitive forms.

After selecting the UNPAID menu item on the Accounts Receivable menu, the collector can choose to view all accounts that are past due. The collector uses the A/R Inquiry Unpaid form (see Figure 11.14) to review the account status of those customers with past-due invoices.

The Memo button on the Toolbar is then pushed to pop up the Memo form shown in Figure 11.15. The memo indicates all prior conversations with the customer and may prompt another telephone call.

Pushing the Telephone button on the Toolbar pops up the telephone numbers. (See Figure 11.16.) During the telephone conversation, the collector may decide to review the account with the customer and push the Credit button on the Toolbar. This pops up the Customer Credit Information form (see Figure 11.17), which shows the amount of the last payment, the payment date, and the check number. (Other useful information on this form shows the credit terms that were granted to the customer and the dollar amount of business done with the customer.) The collector may then record the results of the collection call, including the credit review, on the memo form.

FIGURE 11.14.

The A/R Inquiry screen shows the account status of a selected customer and can be used in collection efforts.

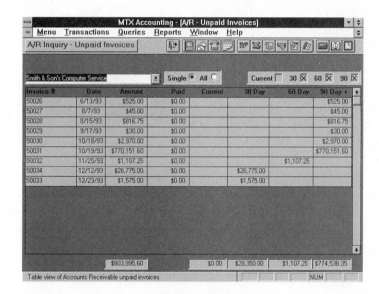

FIGURE 11.15.

The A/R Customer Memo is a pop-up form that may be used to record the conversations and results of a collection call.

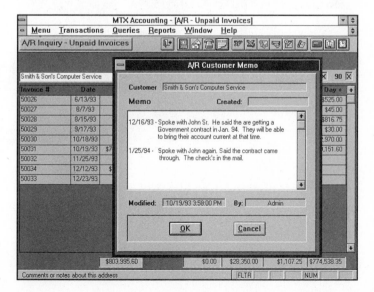

FIGURE 11.16.

The SYS PPT Telephones is a pop-up form called from the Toolbar and includes all customers' telephone numbers.

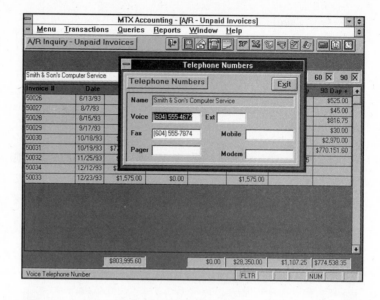

FIGURE 11.17.

The Customer Credit Information form is a pop-up form called from the Toolbar and shows important credit information for the selected customer.

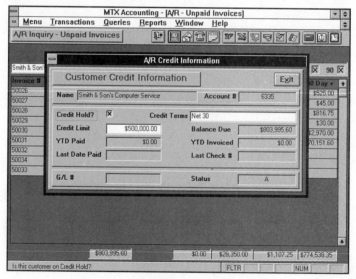

Further review of customer accounts may be accomplished using the Customer Payment History form. (See Figure 11.18.) The payment history form shows not only all the paid invoices on file but also the days to pay for each invoice and the average number of days to pay for each customer.

Thinking like a user who must perform daily business tasks will give you the insight to create an application that makes these tasks easier and more productive.

FIGURE 11.18.

The Customer Payment History is used to analyze a customer's payment habits.

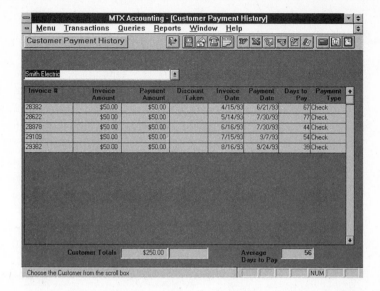

You need to keep in mind that your job is not only to provide an application that accumulates data and prints reports, but also presents that data as useful information that is easily accessible.

Correcting Errors

A well-designed application will have plenty of error trapping at the data-input level. Using default information, such as general-ledger number defaults carried on supplier and customer records, "limit to list" list boxes, and embedded data validation expressions will certainly reduce the number of data-entry errors. Providing batch control totals to compare to adding-machine control tapes will also help reduce errors. If errors are found when comparing control totals, the user must have an easy way to make the necessary corrections through an editing process.

Unfortunately, not all errors can be trapped, and some will show up only at a later time (such as month end during the review of various journals and reports). You need to provide an easy way to find and correct these errors.

One of the most common errors that occurs in an accounting system is posting a transaction to the wrong general-ledger account. This error is usually caught when reviewing a purchase or sales journal; the accountant may find, for example, the utility bill posted to the telephone expense general-ledger account. The developer must provide a simple way to correct this kind of error. Figure 11.19 is the Edit Purchase Journal form, which shows a list of all the transactions for a selected date range. Although all transactions in the MTX Accounting SDK are carried in their appropriate tables for as long as the user wishes, the transaction amount is updated to total fields on the general-ledger account table for a specific accounting period. Therefore the Edit Purchase Journal list indicates whether each transaction has been previously updated. If a transaction has not been updated, the user may change the general-ledger account as necessary without being required to reverse and reenter the transaction. If the transaction has been updated, the entry will have to be reversed and reentered. A similar form is provided for the sales journal. For accounting-data integrity, you need to consider carrying a flag on each transaction indicating update status if appropriate and only allow modification of transactions prior to update.

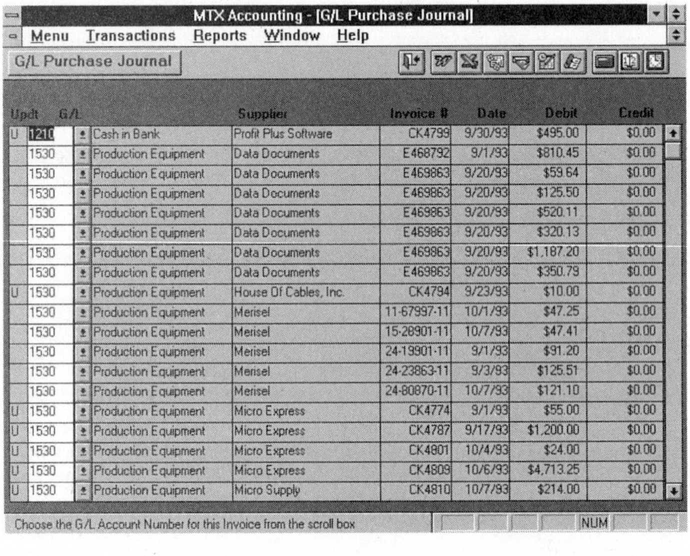
MTX Accounting - [G/L Purchase Journal]
Menu Transactions Reports Window Help
G/L Purchase Journal
Updt G/L Supplier Invoice # Date Debit Credit
U 1210 Cash in Bank Profit Plus Software CK4799 9/30/93 $495.00 $0.00
1530 Production Equipment Data Documents E468792 9/1/93 $810.45 $0.00
1530 Production Equipment Data Documents E469863 9/20/93 $59.64 $0.00
1530 Production Equipment Data Documents E469863 9/20/93 $125.50 $0.00
1530 Production Equipment Data Documents E469863 9/20/93 $520.11 $0.00
1530 Production Equipment Data Documents E469863 9/20/93 $320.13 $0.00
1530 Production Equipment Data Documents E469863 9/20/93 $1,187.20 $0.00
1530 Production Equipment Data Documents E469863 9/20/93 $350.79 $0.00
U 1530 Production Equipment House Of Cables, Inc. CK4794 9/23/93 $10.00 $0.00
1530 Production Equipment Merisel 11-67997-11 10/1/93 $47.25 $0.00
1530 Production Equipment Merisel 15-28901-11 10/7/93 $47.41 $0.00
1530 Production Equipment Merisel 24-19901-11 9/1/93 $91.20 $0.00
1530 Production Equipment Merisel 24-23863-11 9/3/93 $125.51 $0.00
1530 Production Equipment Merisel 24-80870-11 10/7/93 $121.10 $0.00
U 1530 Production Equipment Micro Express CK4774 9/1/93 $55.00 $0.00
U 1530 Production Equipment Micro Express CK4787 9/17/93 $1,200.00 $0.00
U 1530 Production Equipment Micro Express CK4801 10/4/93 $24.00 $0.00
U 1530 Production Equipment Micro Express CK4809 10/6/93 $4,713.25 $0.00
U 1530 Production Equipment Micro Supply CK4810 10/7/93 $214.00 $0.00
Choose the G/L Account Number for this Invoice from the scroll box
NUM

FIGURE 11.19.
The Edit Purchase Journal form is used to quickly correct the most common errors; for example, wrong general-ledger numbers on a transaction.

Summary

Although this chapter has concentrated on the look and feel of an application, you should keep in mind that you can develop as complex an application as you want. The MTX Accounting SDK demonstrates that a diligent developer can build a complex, industrial-strength application using Access.

12

Looking at an Access Training Database

by Michael Gilbert

This chapter examines the development of Ingenium for Windows, a commercial application from Meliora Systems, Inc., a Rochester, New York consulting firm. Now in its second major release, its purpose is to help a company's training coordinators track the skills and training needs of employees within their organizations. Ingenium for Windows began life as a consulting project within the Access Early Developers program, but eventually it was revamped and marketed as a stand-alone application. It is a relevant case study for our purposes, because much of the wisdom in these pages has come from this attempt to transform a highly customized database solutions for a single client into a commercial-quality application. This chapter describes the development of an Access application from both the consulting and commercial points of view. It discusses the unique aspects of Ingenium for Windows, its evolutionary history, and the challenges involved in marketing an Access application. The chapter also includes several tips for query creation, the interface standards used, and sample code that demonstrates some of the unique features of Ingenium for Windows.

Ingenium for Windows Satisfies the Need for Effective Training Management

In brief, Ingenium for Windows is a database application that manages an organization's skills and training needs. In reality, it does much more than that. The program tracks trainees' skill inventories and needs based on three criteria: (1) the job they hold, (2) the group or organization they work for, and (3) the individual assessments of managers. Courses and class information also is stored, including which skills each course teaches and what grade is required to acquire those skills. Future versions will include facilities management and advanced budgeting features. Both training companies and corporations can use Ingenium for Windows to assess which employees need what training, how much it's going to cost, and (through student class histories and grade levels) how effective the training is.

Ingenium for Windows (originally called Skil-Trak, a name that was eventually dropped due to possible trademark conflicts) began as a consulting project for a division of Xerox Corporation in El Segundo, California. The division's training coordinator was looking for a system to help her manage what had become a cumbersome task. She was responsible for making sure that the division's 300 technical-service representatives got the advanced training they required. The division's training regimen involved maintenance and troubleshooting for high-speed laser printing systems as well as a myriad of interfaces and software. Add to this the management and personal-skills training for supervisors and administrators, provided by nearly 100 internal and external sources, and the result was a mountainous task.

At this firm, the typical process of coordinating an employee's training started with an interview with the employee when he or she first arrived. This resulted in a checklist of the skills the employee thought he or she had mastered. A tentative needs assessment could then be developed based on the skill requirements of the employee's work group. (Job descriptions were not used as a basis for skill needs.) Decisions on a course schedule for the employee were usually made by the training coordinator, the employee, and the employee's manager based on their personal knowledge of what each course had to offer. This was, however, never quantified, so employees often found themselves repeating courses or enrolled in different courses that covered the same material. When you consider that the average cost for a day of training was about $500, including expenses (not to mention the opportunity cost of taking an employee off the job for that time), it is clear that this approach was highly inefficient. At the time, the training coordinator was using a combination of hand-written notes, various course catalogs, and even several Microsoft Excel spreadsheets.

To better organize the training process, Meliora Systems offered to design a database system using the then-unreleased Access. The result was Skil-Trak.

NOTE

For the purposes of this chapter, all references to Skil-Trak refer to the program originally developed for Meliora's consulting client. The first commercial release of Ingenium for Windows (version 1.0) began shipping in October 1993, version 2.0 in April 1994. While I was the primary developer of Skil-Trak and Ingenium 1.0, the development of version 2.0 was considerably more complex. It was performed by a team of developers lead by Ingenium's new product manager, Karen Jaskolka.

Although functional, Skil-Trak was far from being a textbook example of an Access application. It was an excellent vehicle, however, for exploring the capabilities and limitations of the database and its development tools. Also, researching the marketplace and showing the result to others served to validate our perception that the application satisfied a critical corporate need.

Meliora's primary client base is made up of Fortune 1000 corporations in the financial and manufacturing industries. Given the rate of technological change in these industries and the competitive necessity of keeping employees up-to-date, the training costs for such organizations can reach well into the millions of dollars. The sheer volume of data that must be tracked can overwhelm training coordinators. Inefficient training methodology costs companies not only the expenses incurred during training classes but also in lost productivity due to employees being off the job. Yet despite these compelling factors, there are still many companies that have not been able to establish cost-effective training programs.

Meliora's Development Process

Skil-Trak, in its original, somewhat crude form, represented the foundation of the commercial product. At this point in its evolution, the application that became Ingenium for Windows was being viewed as a one-time consulting project. As is standard with most of our projects, the development process was broken down into these six phases:

1. Functional requirements analysis
2. Database schema specification
3. Query design and testing
4. Screen and report design
5. User interface construction
6. Testing, documentation, and training

The next several sections will explain how we went through each phase. Where applicable, these sections will also discuss how the transformation of Skil-Trak into a commercial application altered the results of the development process.

Extracting the Functional Requirements

Once the consulting agreement was signed, the first step was to develop a conceptual database design or schema. Typically, this involved interviews with the application's users and an extensive examination of any existing inputs and outputs, either manual or computerized. Unfortunately, the situation did not allow these luxuries. Our agreement with the client was to build the system at a reduced rate (essentially at cost) in exchange for the rights to publicize the application. No provisions were made for travel and, to this day, the two sides in this arrangement have never met face-to-face. (The closest we came was a customer interview played on Microsoft's DevCast satellite telecast.) The solution was to provide the user with paper forms that roughly amounted to a database-design questionnaire. A sample form is shown in Figure 12.1. The training coordinator filled out one form for each entity in the data model, describing her view of its attributes and relationships. The end result was a layperson's depiction of the system's data model.

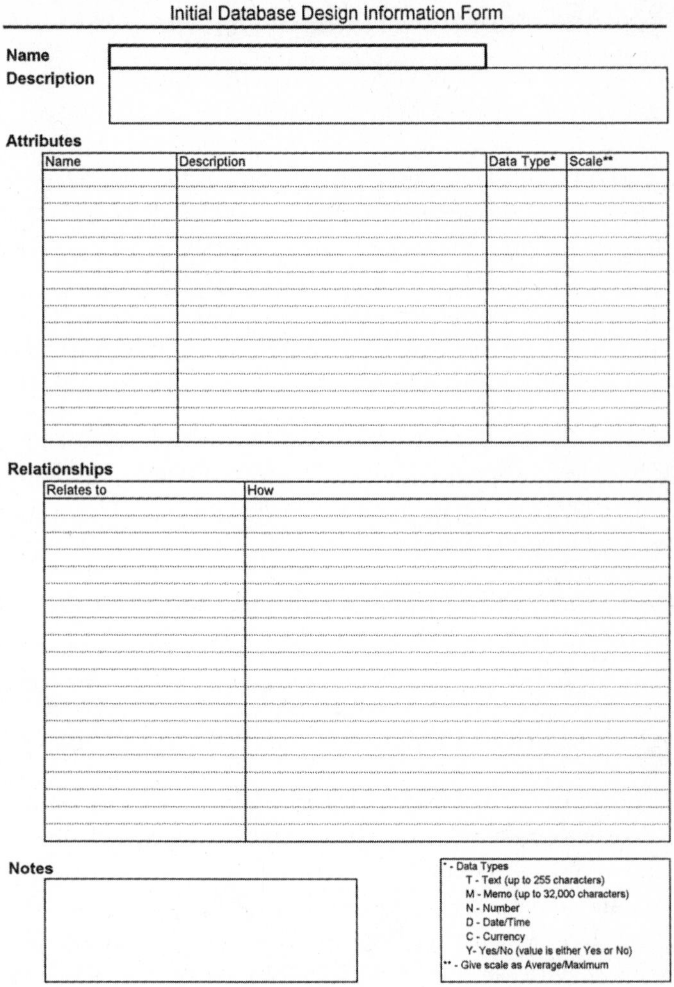

FIGURE 12.1.

A sample database design question-naire.

Initial Database Design Information Form

Name

Description

Attributes

Name	Description	Data Type*	Scale**

Relationships

Relates to	How

Notes

```
* - Data Types
     T - Text (up to 255 characters)
     M - Memo (up to 32,000 characters)
     N - Number
     D - Date/Time
     C - Currency
     Y- Yes/No (value is either Yes or No)
** - Give scale as Average/Maximum
```

The forms were designed to insulate the respondent from technical terms such as "entity" and "primary key." Instead, the instructions asked her to list and describe the major "things" that she wanted to track, how they could be identified, and how they related to one another. This worked surprisingly well in providing a foundation of knowledge about the application. It allowed for the generation of a basic design, which was later refined by more in-depth questioning.

The All-Important Database Design

It has always been our belief that the single most important element in any project of this type is a good database design. The design dictates what data elements the system will store as well as the flexibility and quality of information that can be retrieved. Theoretically, the design is implementation-independent, so it matters little which RDBMS and interface tools you use. It is usually quite difficult, however, to stop midstream and modify the underlying design to any great extent. Access can be forgiving in some situations, should this become necessary; for example, a field can be added to a table that contains data. Finding a mistake in your normalization techniques, on the other hand, can mean plenty of reworking, no matter which tools you use.

The logical schema for Ingenium for Windows was generated using ERWin/SQL from Logic Works, a portion of which is shown in Figure 12.2. ERWin/SQL's strengths are in database design and documentation for server-based SQL databases. It can build the required DDL (Data Definition Language) SQL statements for a variety of database platforms. I highly recommend the use of such a tool if you relate well to the graphical representation of concepts. (If you're developing in Windows and Access, you probably qualify.) ERWin/SQL also helps out with the design to a small degree by automatically creating dependent primary keys and foreign keys when appropriate. I don't consider it a complete CASE tool, however, and we used it primarily for diagramming and documenting Ingenium for Windows's data model.

One thing you'll notice right away (provided that you can understand the symbols used by ERWin/SQL) is the abundance of dependent tables formed by the intersection of many-to-many relationships. This design is necessitated by the interaction among the application's main data elements: students (formerly "employees" in version 1), courses, job descriptions, skills, and organizations (formerly "work groups"). Almost every element relates to at least one occurrence of every other element. This design offers a great deal of flexibility in viewing data. The user can, for example, look at one student and the skills she has, or isolate one skill and all the students that have or require it.

FIGURE 12.2.
Creating the logical data model with ERWin/SQL.

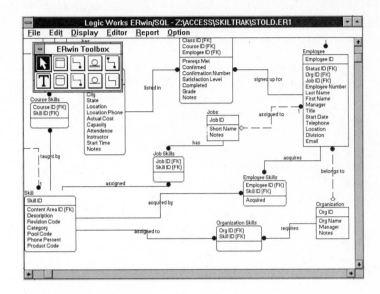

Table and Query Implementation

Our plan was to first implement all the tables called for in the design. This would enable us to start entering test data immediately. The next part of the plan was to develop the queries necessary to extract the data for data-entry forms and reports. The multitude of many-to-many relationships called for a large number of multi-table joins.

This represents one instance in which a fully normalized data model hurts more than it helps. For a typical main/subform design, you need two separate queries, one for the main form and one for the subform. In fact, one Ingenium for Windows form has four separate subforms. If the relationship is many-to-many, at least one query will involve a join. Finally, if you've implemented nice interface features such as list boxes, you've probably got a few more queries driving those as well. This can really put a drain on interface performance in a stand-alone application. You should carefully consider whether the use of these attractive features really adds enough value to the application to compensate for the degradation in performance.

One way to overcome performance barriers is by using Access Query objects. Query objects are excellent tools to use when developing an application because they are easy to create and, since Access optimizes them before saving, they are very fast compared to regular SQL statements. Nonetheless, they are sometimes underutilized, since some users forget that they can do more than just return data. When developing your applications, examine your use of code routines using dynaset methods. Many of these can be replaced with action queries that greatly increase performance. See the section called "Working with Access SQL," later in this chapter, for additional comments and tips on using query objects.

> **TIP**
>
> A rule of thumb for planning your queries is a minimum of three queries for each one-to-many relationship in your model. This translates into one query for the one side (for the main Access form), one for the many side (for a subform), and one combined query for a report that displays the same information. Thus, a many-to-many relationship would require six queries to represent completely. (Fortunately, you get to conserve a query if an entity participates in more than one relationship of this type.)

The Ingenium for Windows User Interface

After the tables and queries were completed, we began work on the application's user interface. An attractive and functional user interface is an important component of any application. Beyond its role as an instrument to accomplish the user's tasks, it can facilitate user acceptance of the application as a whole, as well as attract the attention of potential customers. As developers, we need to be concerned with the performance and integrity of the database and the functionality of the tools we provide for the user. The user, on the other hand, is often more impressed with the "look and feel" of the application and how simple it is to operate. We cannot afford to overlook this aspect of the design process. This section discusses the choices we made and the standards we set while developing Ingenium for Windows.

Many Access applications feature a form that acts as a main menu or home base for the program's functions. (The Forms Switchboard in the Northwind Trader's database is one example.) In fact, because custom Access menus are tied to forms, this is the only real way to create a user interface. Figure 12.3 shows Ingenium for Windows's main menu.

Ingenium for Windows makes extensive use of icons to concentrate the functionality on the main menu. Our customer base is made up of people in the training community who are, on the whole, visually oriented. Most quickly identify the main program functions based on its associated icon. The text labels are used primarily for new or infrequent users. The list box in the center of the main menu form displays the many reports that are available to the user. A special Access table containing report information drives the contents of the list. Using a table of information enables us to take different actions based on the specific report chosen. For example, we use special pop-up forms to capture query criteria before certain reports are run. The options buttons below the report list enable the user to view reports grouped by subject area, such as courses or students, instead of viewing all the reports at once. Selecting an option button requeries the report list, limiting the reports displayed. This helps make the larger list more manageable.

FIGURE 12.3.

Ingenium for Windows's main menu form.

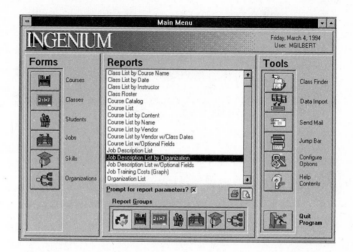

Like many Windows Multiple Document Interface applications, Ingenium is designed to enable users to do what they want, when they want. As such, users do not have to return to the main menu before opening other forms. To help them navigate through various functions, Ingenium features a pop-up "Jump Bar," shown in Figure 12.4, which provides easy access to many forms. Users open the Jump Bar by clicking on that button on the main menu and can keep it open while working in Ingenium. The form is also one of the many "collapsible" forms used in Ingenium for Windows. The method for creating such forms is explained later in this chapter along with a description of one of Ingenium for Windows's most unique features, the Class Finder form.

FIGURE 12.4.

The Jump Bar.

Interface Design Standards

Figure 12.5 shows the Ingenium for Windows Courses form, which is representative of all the data-entry forms in the application. All the data-entry forms share a set of common characteristics and standard features. Some of the guidelines we developed for constructing Access forms are explained in the following paragraphs.

FIGURE 12.5.

The Courses form.

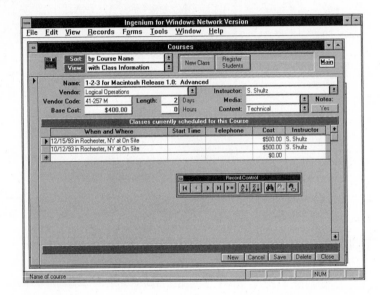

Form Size. Because all the main data entry forms contained at least one subform as well as many other fields, we decided to size them to closely fit in a whole VGA (640×480) screen. Obviously some forms have more extra space than others, but we decided that a consistent interface was more important than optimal use of space. Supporting forms are sized as necessary to fit the controls.

Background Color. All forms use light gray as their background color. This muted hue makes the white background of the edit controls stand out. It also allows you to make the best use of Access's "3-D" controls.

Font Size. The controls on each form were all designed using the 8-point, MS Sans Serif typeface with a height of 0.17 inches. With the grid granularity set to 16×16 (the finest level at which the dots are displayed), you can position the controls so that they are separated by a small space.

Label Color. Field labels use white, boldface type. The background color varies with the context of the control. All fields that are directly tied to data in the database and editable by the user have dark blue labels. Dark cyan labels are used to indicate data and information that is either not editable or is related to system functions. All subform labels also have dark cyan backgrounds.

Icon Designation. An icon representing the data source of the form is embedded on the upper-left corner of each data entry form. This is the same icon used on the main menu and throughout the application. This provides a visual reminder to the user of which data they are using.

Dynamic Sorting. Forms have several filters that can be applied to change the sort order of the data. Each form has a combo box in the header section that lists possible sort orders. When the user selects an option from the list, Ingenium for Windows applies the appropriate filter.

Dynamic Subforms. Ingenium for Windows uses subforms to represent the various one-to-many relationships in the data model. To maximize the use of available screen space and maintain a consistent interface, only one subform is displayed at a time. Each form has a combo box that enables the user to choose which subform to view. See the section titled "Creating Dynamic Subforms" for details on how this behavior is achieved.

Default Values. Whenever a system control was created with a default value, Access Basic code was attached to the OnDblClick event of the control to re-establish this default. The combo boxes described in the preceding two paragraphs use this feature to restore the default sort order and subform view, respectively.

Main Menu Return Icon. Each form has an icon in the upper-right corner that displays the main menu form when the user clicks on it with the mouse. This is facilitated by a transparent command button covering the icon.

You are encouraged to develop standards like these for your own applications. Be prepared to spend some time thinking about them beforehand, since making changes midstream can be very time consuming.

Working with Access SQL

After the initial design was completed for Skil-Trak, the ancestor of Ingenium for Windows, we began creating the queries that would become the basis for the program's forms and reports. We especially liked Access's QBE grid for query definition, but we found Microsoft's adaptation of SQL somewhat cumbersome. We are experienced in other host-based RDBMSs. (We even teach a course in ANSI SQL under contract for a national training firm.) We were quietly disappointed, however, in the particular flavor of the language Access uses. For example, the simple ANSI SQL query

```
SELECT s.LastName, k.Skill
    FROM Students s, Skills k, StudentSkills sk
    WHERE s.StudentID = sk.StudentID AND sk.SkillID = k.SkillID;
```

would need to be transformed into the following Access SQL statement when using the QBE grid:

```
SELECT DISTINCTROW Student.[Last Name], Skills.Skill
    FROM Student, [Student Skills], Skills,
    Student INNER JOIN [Student Skills] ON
        Student.[Student ID] = [Student Skills].[Student ID],
    Skills INNER JOIN [Student Skills] ON
        Skills.[Skill ID] = [Student Skills].[Skill ID]
    WITH OWNERACCESS OPTION;
```

This unique syntax was not a major issue for those queries we designed using the QBE grid and saved as Access query objects, since we rarely had cause to even look at the generated SQL. Conversely, creating SQL statements in Access Basic became quite a chore. We quickly adopted the practice of building queries with the QBE grid and then copying the SQL text to a Module window. The statements required subsequent editing, but this was considered more efficient than typing Access SQL statements from scratch. One nice improvement in Access 2.0 is the use of a full-window text editor for creating SQL. This is more convenient than the old method, a modal dialog box, because you can switch to other windows while the SQL text is still being displayed.

Using Subqueries and the ANSI IN Operator

One drawback of Access 1.x SQL became readily apparent as we began to code one of the key features of Skil-Trak—the lack of nested subqueries. Users of Ingenium for Windows (and Skil-Trak) are usually able to answer the question, "What skills does a particular student have?" Most firms keep some type of records to this effect, even if they're in the form of index cards. A more difficult, yet significantly more useful, question is, "What skills does that employee need?", and furthermore, "What courses are available to teach those skills, and when are they being offered?" When the application was developed using Access 1.x, we had to create a series of complex queries to answer these questions. Access 2.0's support for nested subqueries enabled us to replace these with a single, more simple query.

Students interact with skills in two ways: Some skills they have, and some they need. What we really wanted to ask, conceptually speaking, was which skills in the student's *need* table were NOT in the student's *have* table. Briefly, what this required us to do in Access 1.x was create a series of queries, as follows:

1. First, we created a query listing the skills a student already had from the Student Skills table.

2. A second query was created from one of the required skills tables (Organization Skills or Job Skills). It listed the skills required by the student's organization or job.

3. The second query was then joined in a LEFT OUTER JOIN to the skill ID numbers in the first query. Skill deficiencies were revealed where there were no skills in the output set from the first query (the fields were null).

Sound complicated? It is. What we eventually did after upgrading to Access 2.0 was use a nested subquery such as the one shown in Figure 12.6.

FIGURE 12.6.

A query that uses a nested subquery.

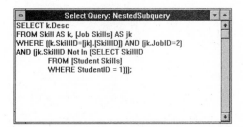

WARNING

With most RDBMSs, you should try to avoid this type of query, because the database's optimizer often does not use any indexes on the tables in the NOT IN clause; thus your query performance will be poor. It is, nonetheless, a convenient approach for small operations on a database that supports it.

Figure 12.7 shows the output of the query. While this example shows missing skills, nested subqueries can be used in virtually any inventory-oriented application where you need to create a list of items that either appear in or are missing from another list of similar items.

FIGURE 12.7.

The results of the nested subquery.

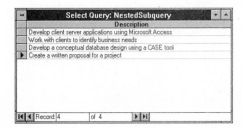

Using Pop-Up Helper Forms: The Class Finder

The inclusion of these types of queries was essential to implementing one of the key components of Ingenium for Windows, the Class Finder form. This pop-up form, shown in Figure 12.8, enables the user to determine the skill requirements for any student in the database. The user can then schedule that student for any one of the classes that teach the required skills by utilizing an intuitive, point-and-click interface.

FIGURE 12.8.

The Class Finder form.

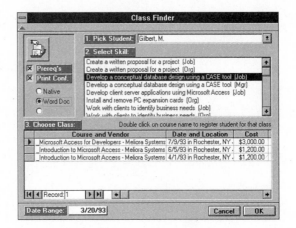

The Class Finder form was designed as a pop-up, nonmodal form. This means that the user can open it whenever necessary and leave it displayed on the screen, "floating" on top of other forms. To keep the form from obscuring other information on the screen, Class Finder has a special roll-up feature that collapses the form down to about 1/2-inch tall by 1-inch wide, or about 50×100 pixels on a VGA screen. How this was accomplished is described in the section called "Creating a Collapsible Floating Pop-Up Form" that appears later in this chapter.

Users can access the Class Finder from Ingenium for Windows's main menu from the Jump Bar, or via a button on the Student data-entry form. The latter method automatically configures Class Finder to display the skill requirements of the current student. Either way, the user can select any student in the database from the combo box at the top of the Class Finder form.

The form itself consists of three major controls: the combo box, which displays a list of students; a list box, which shows the skill requirements for that student; and a subform that lists the available courses and classes that are designated as teaching each particular skill.

Class Finder's Unique Features

There are a number of interesting things about the Class Finder form and its underlying functionality. As stated on the form itself, to register a student for one of the displayed classes the user simply double-clicks the mouse on the course name in the subform. An Access Basic function is attached to the OnDblClick event of the Courses Name field that inserts a record into the Employee Class table.

When the user selects a class, he or she has the option of using two additional features: automatic prerequisite verification and printed confirmation sheets. The two check boxes on the left side of the form control these features.

The prerequisite feature enables the user to make sure that a student has completed all required courses before registering him or her for the course in question. Version 1 of Ingenium for Windows simply provided a binary response. That is, the student either had or had not passed all the prerequisites. Based on feedback from those who had used that version, we modified Ingenium for Windows version 2 to provide a list of all the prerequisites and an indicator for each one. Selecting this option now opens a pop-up form listing each prerequisite course name and shows the text "Completed" or "Required."

The second option available to the user is to print a confirmation form for the student confirming that he or she has been registered for a particular class. Ingenium for Windows currently provides two methods of producing the form. The first is a native Access report that prints a memo from the training coordinator listing the pertinent information such as class name, date, location, and so forth. This report is quite interesting itself, as several of the field values are actually stored in an .INI file rather than the database and are read each time the report is printed. The second method produces a similar memorandum in Microsoft Word for Windows. A Word template containing the text of the memo is stored on disk. To create the report, Ingenium for Windows launches Word, loads a copy of the template, and inserts the appropriate information into the document using DDE to trigger Word Basic commands such as EditGoto and Insert. An example of the finished product is shown in Figure 12.9. Eventually a third option was added: the capability to send an electronic mail note via Microsoft Mail or other MAPI-compliant mail system.

In the bottom-left corner of the Class Finder form there is an unbound text field labeled Date Range. Using this field, the user can limit the classes displayed in the subform to those that fall on or after a given date. (The default is the current date.) This helps to make the list a little more manageable. The query driving the subform actually refers to this field in its criteria (for example, Forms![frmClassFinder]![txtDateSpec]). Attached to the AfterUpdate event of the text box is a small piece of code that forces a requery of the subform's dynaset. As an added feature, there is another bit of code attached to the text box's `OnDblClick` event that resets the value of the field to the current date and requeries the subform.

FIGURE 12.9.

A class confirmation memo created using Microsoft Word.

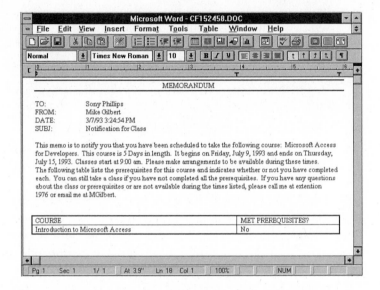

Some Access developers frown on the use of Access datasheets in an application. The Class Finder subform uses this view mode for a number of reasons. First and most importantly, it provides a familiar interface for the user. By now, most potential users of Ingenium for Windows have been exposed to Windows spreadsheets that employ the same format as Access datasheets. That is, they have the same row and column headings, gridlines, and sizable columns. Additionally, Access, like Microsoft Excel, enables users to reorder the columns to suit their particular viewing needs. Second, the datasheet view is aesthetically pleasing and blends in with Ingenium for Windows's use of light gray forms. Too many colored labels can distract the user, especially on a form like Class Finder that packs a lot of functionality into a small space.

Linking a Subform to an Unbound Text Box

Unlike many forms you'll develop in Access that have subforms, the Class Finder form is not bound to a table or query to supply a LinkMasterField to the subform. Instead, a hidden text box on the main form contains the value to which the subform is linked. The text box is updated every time the user selects a new skill from the list box. This is accomplished by a fairly simple bit of Access Basic code attached to the AfterUpdate event of the list box. This code, shown below, is called using the syntax `=UpdateSkillID(`**Form**`)`.

```
Function UpdateSkillID(frmAny As Form)
    'Set value of hidden text box equal to ID number of skill
    frmAny.txtSkillID = frmAny.List
End Function
```

The keyword `Form` passes the function a reference to the form from which the code is called as a parameter. This is a simple alternative to using the extended syntax, that is, `Forms!FormName`, and we've found it safer than using the global `Screen.ActiveForm` object in our code. Although we could have simply passed the value of the list box to the function, we chose to pass a reference to the entire form because it enables us to validate the contents in the control, if necessary, before proceeding. This is not much of a problem with list boxes, but some controls, such as text boxes, can be troublesome if they contain a null value. Because Access generates an error message ("Invalid use of Null") when you try to pass a null value to a function that expects a data type other than `Variant`, passing a form or control reference enables us to check for this condition. The following code framework demonstrates this:

```
Function UseValueOfControl(frmAny As Form)
    If IsNull(frmAny![Some Control Name]) Then
        'Either exit function or display some message
    Else
        'Perform your actions
    End If
End Function
```

Creating a Collapsible Floating Pop-Up Form

Ingenium for Windows incorporates a number of nonmodal utility forms that the user can keep open while he or she works with the application. Some of them, like the Class Finder form, are large enough that they obscure most of a VGA screen when in use. Rather than force the user to search for a menu or button to open and close the form, we decided to make the forms collapse to occupy a smaller area. The user can then expand them as necessary. This is similar to the Roll-Up windows in CorelDRAW! 3.0.

Building the Form

The forms are initially displayed expanded with a small, red, upward-pointing arrow in the upper-left corner. This arrow indicates to the user that the form may be collapsed by clicking on it. The collapsed Class Finder form is shown in Figure 12.10. After collapsing, the form displays a green, downward-pointing arrow to indicate that the form can be expanded.

FIGURE 12.10.
The collapsed Class Finder form.

The arrows themselves are simply bitmaps embedded on the form's header section. A transparent command button placed over the buttons actually triggers the collapse.

> **NOTE**
>
> When designing a form like this, make sure that the arrow images overlay each other closely so that they appear as a single object when toggled.

Accomplishing this effect requires four steps: (1) determine whether the form needs to be collapsed or expanded, (2) adjust the size of the form accordingly, (3) hide and unhide the arrow bitmaps to correspond with the new state, and (4) enable or disable the controls on the form. The last action is required because when the form is collapsed the user could still conceivably tab to other controls, hiding the header section. This would prohibit the user from expanding the form. The required Access Basic code is shown as follows.

```
'Windows API function and user-defined type declarations
'must appear in the Declarations section of the module.
Declare Function GetSystemMetrics Lib "USER" (ByVal nIndex
➡As Integer) As Integer
Declare Sub GetWindowRect Lib "USER" (ByVal hWnd As Integer,
➡lpRect As RectType)
Declare Sub MoveWindow Lib "USER" (ByVal hWnd As Integer,
➡ByVal x As Integer, ByVal y As Integer,
➡ByVal cx As Integer, ByVal cy As Integer, ByVal bRepaint As Integer)
Declare Function GetDC Lib "USER" (ByVal hWnd As Integer)
➡As Integer
Declare Function ReleaseDC Lib "USER" (ByVal hWnd As Integer,
➡ByVal hDC As Integer) As Integer
Declare Function GetDeviceCaps Lib "GDI" (ByVal hDC As Integer,
➡ByVal iCapacity As Integer) As Integer

Type RectType
    left As Integer
    top As Integer
    right As Integer
    bottom As Integer
End Type

Global Const SM_CYBORDER = 6
Global Const SM_CYCAPTION = 4
Global Const LOGPIXELSX = 88
Global Const LOGPIXELSY = 90
```

```
Function FormRollup (frmAny As Form, sUpX As Single, sUpY As Single,
    ➡sDownX As Single, sDownY As Single)
    'Purpose:  Collapse or expand pop-up form
    'Calls:    GetWindowRect()      (Windows API)
    '          GetSystemMetrics()   (Windows API)
    '          InToPix()
    '          EnableFloatControls

    If Not frmAny.Popup Then Exit Function

    Dim lpRect As RectType
    Dim cxForm As Integer, cyForm As Integer, cyCaption As Integer
    Dim cxNew As Integer, cyNew As Integer

    'Get the window location and dimensions
    Call GetWindowRect(frmAny.hWnd, lpRect)
    cxForm = lpRect.right - lpRect.left
    cyForm = lpRect.bottom - lpRect.top
    cyCaption = GetSystemMetrics(SM_CYMENU) -
    ➡GetSystemMetrics(SM_CYBORDER)

    'Decide which action to take based on which arrow is visible
    If frmAny![xUpArrow].Visible Then
        frmAny![xDownArrow].Visible = True
        frmAny![xUpArrow].Visible = False
        If sUpX = 0 Then cxNew = cxForm Else cxNew =
        ➡InToPix(frmAny, sUpX, LOGPIXELSX)
        If sUpY = 0 Then cyNew = cyForm Else cyNew =
        ➡InToPix(frmAny, sUpY, LOGPIXELSY) + cyCaption
        Call EnableFloatControls(frmAny, False)
    Else
        frmAny![xUpArrow].Visible = True
        frmAny![xDownArrow].Visible = False
        If sDownX = 0 Then cxNew = cxForm Else cxNew =
        ➡InToPix(frmAny, sDownX, LOGPIXELSX)
        If sDownY = 0 Then cyNew = cyForm Else cyNew =
        ➡InToPix(frmAny, sDownY, LOGPIXELSY) + cyCaption
        Call EnableFloatControls(frmAny, True)
    End If
    'Use MoveWindow to set the new size, retaining current position
    Call MoveWindow(frmAny.hWnd, lpRect.left, lpRect.top, cxNew, cyNew,
    ➡True)
End Function

Sub EnableFloatControls (frmAny As Form, bEnable As Integer)
    'Purpose:  Enables or disables all but selected controls on a form

    For c% = 0 To frmAny.Count - 1
        s$ = frmAny(c%).ControlName
        If Left$(s$, 1) <> "x" Then frmAny(c%).Visible = bEnable
    Next
End Sub
```

```
Function InToPix (frmAny As Form, sInches As Single, nAxis As Integer)
➥As Integer
    'Purpose:  Coverts inches to screen pixels
    'Calls:    GetDC()    (Windows API)
    '          GetDeviceCaps()     (Windows API)
    '          ReleaseDC()    (Windows API)
    'Returns:  Number of pixels in specified inches

    Dim hDC%, wRatio%, i%

    hDC = GetDC(frmAny.hWnd)
    wRatio% = GetDeviceCaps(hDC, nAxis)
    i = ReleaseDC(frmAny.hWnd, hDC)
    InToPix = CInt(sInches * wRatio)

End Function
```

The *FormRollup()* Function

The function attached to the button on the form is FormRollup(). This accepts a Form variable and four Single variables as arguments. The four numbers represent the width and height of the form, in inches, when the form is collapsed and expanded, respectively. FormRollup() begins by calling the Windows API function GetWindowRect() to place the form's dimensions, in pixels, into the lpRect structure. The GetSystemMetrics() function is then used to compute the height of the form's caption bar.

The main If...Then...Else block in the function determines which way to resize the form based on which arrow bitmap is visible. If the Up arrow is visible, the form is collapsed, and if the Down arrow is visible, the form is expanded. The additional If statements within the main block determine the new size of the form in pixels. If the arguments are set to 0, then the current size is retained by setting cxNew and cyNew to cxForm and cyForm.

After determining the new form size, the controls on the form are made invisible (so that the user cannot tab to them) if the form is to be collapsed, or visible if the form is to be expanded. The form is finally resized using the Windows API MoveWindow() function.

The Supporting Functions

FormRollup() calls two user-defined "helper" functions. The InToPix() function converts a form dimension from inches to screen pixels. Because the scaling factor depends on the display adapter and the Windows system font that is installed, the function must call three Windows API functions to determine the exact value. The GetDeviceCaps() function returns the device capabilities of a given device or, more specifically, a device context. A device context is a logical representation of a device such as a video display or printer. The `GetDeviceCaps()` function can return the number of logical pixels per inch for both the x and y dimensions. Because it bases its assessment on a given display context, the `GetDC()` and `ReleaseDC()` functions are used to supply the display context of the current form (by using the forms handle).

The `EnableFloatControls` subroutine selectively enables controls on a given form. It uses a `For...Next` loop to set the `Visible` property of each control. Note, however, that it excludes controls that have names beginning with the letter x. This allows you to protect the enabled status of the command button on the form that triggers this whole process.

Creating Dynamic Subforms

As I mentioned earlier, Ingenium forms concentrate a large amount of data in one place by using subforms that are selectively displayed and hidden as needed. Exactly how this is done will be explained in this section.

If you re-examine the Courses form shown previously in Figure 12.5, you'll notice a drop-down list labeled "View" in the upper left-hand corner. Opening this list presents a number of options, such as "with Class Information" and "with Student Information." Selecting one of these options displays the appropriate subform showing how the current course relates to the listed entity. (For example, selecting "with Student Information" would show all students who have taken the course.)

With Ingenium 1.0, we were forced to design the form so each related subform appeared on the form in design view. Each subform's Visible property was toggled in run view to display the appropriate information. This arrangement was less than optimal, not only because it made designing the main form quite tedious, but because it destroyed system performance, since Access ran the queries associated with each subform regardless of whether the subform was visible.

Access 2.0 enabled us to streamline the process a great deal because of its ability to change the `SourceObject` property of subform objects at runtime. Now each form contains a single subform control object rather than multiple objects, one for each subform. Making a selection from the drop-down list runs code similar to the following:

```
Sub cboView_AfterUpdate ()
    MySubForm.SourceObject = cboView
End Sub
```

CboView is the name of the combo box object. Its bound column contains a list of subform objects as they appear in the database window. I think you'll agree this is much simpler than hiding or displaying a series of subforms. In addition, it speeds load time as Access runs only one subform query. The query associated with other subforms is run when the SourceObject property is changed to point to that subform.

Loading Data into Ingenium

One truism with new computerized systems is that users always have existing data they want to incorporate. (After all, we've existed in the Information Age for quite a while.) Users of Ingenium are no exception. Most have personnel data stored on mainframe or minicomputer systems and some have already begun to track employee skills using tools like dBase, Paradox, and Excel. This section discusses our approach to data import.

When developing a commercial product, you strive to be as generic as possible, broadening the potential market for your product. Data import is one area where a generic approach is critical. You cannot place very many restrictions on the format or layout of imported data without making the process cumbersome and thus unappealing to prospects and users. Ingenium for Windows uses a point-and-click interface to help users through the process of importing almost any kind of data. Ingenium's Data Import form is shown in Figure 12.11 and is explained in the next few paragraphs.

FIGURE 12.11.

Ingenium's Data Import interface.

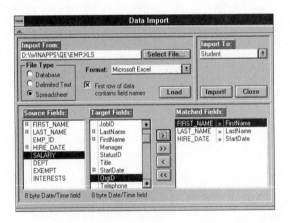

The Data Import form is divided into three main sections. The first, in the upper-left corner, enables the user to specify a source for the imported data. He or she can choose from all the database and spreadsheet formats supported by Access as well as delimited text. Which format they use is selected from the combo box. The Select File button opens a dialog box where the user can choose a file to import. Pressing the Load button causes Ingenium to display the data file's structure in the list box in the form's lower-left corner. If a spreadsheet or text file is used, Ingenium imports it into a temporary Access table before proceeding.

Before continuing with the import, a user must select the target Ingenium table that will hold the incoming data. This is done by selecting it from the combo box in the upper right corner of the form. After the user chooses both a source and a target, he or she can specify how the data is to be imported.

The lower portion of the form is devoted to linking fields in the source data file to fields in the target table. Ingenium uses Access 2.0's Data Access Object (DAO) methods to retrieve the field names and types and displays the names in the two list boxes marked *Source Fields* and *Target Fields* respectively. Selecting a field name causes its data type and size to be displayed below each list box.

Users create a link between two fields by selecting them in the appropriate list box and clicking one of the buttons in the center of the section. These buttons work much like those in Access Wizard dialogs boxes; the top button moves one set of fields from the left-hand list boxes to the right, and so on. The form also has a "fast forward" button, which simply moves down each list in order, moving matching fields to the *Matched Fields* list. This last box shows the user the selections he or she has made. Finally, after making all their choices, users click the Import button to complete the process.

Exchanging Data with Other Applications: The Export Tool

We realized early on in the development of Ingenium for Windows that in addition to importing, users would want to exchange the information stored in the database with other people and other applications. This can become complicated, however, if you are developing for the runtime version of Access, because your users may not have access to the normal file-transfer facilities.

Ingenium for Windows's answer to this is the Data Export tool shown in Figure 12.12. This pop-up form is activated by a button on the main menu. You'll notice from the arrow icon in the upper-left corner that this, too, is a collapsible form.

The tool enables the user to choose from a finite set of data elements (which are simply Access queries) and export the resulting dataset to a variety of formats. The user can choose from all the database, spreadsheet, and text file formats supported by Access. More interesting, however, is the ability to export to other Windows applications directly using DDE.

FIGURE 12.12.

*The Data Export
tool pop-up form.*

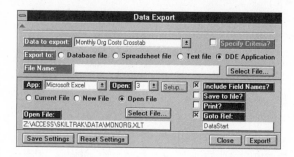

Figure 12.12 shows the export form configured for output to Microsoft Excel. There are a number of options available from which to choose. Ingenium for Windows can export to either a new, existing, or the currently loaded document. It can also optionally save the resulting document to a new file, include field names in the output, and go to a given reference in the output document before exporting.

What makes this tool truly unique is the fact that the DDE commands for each application are not hard-coded into the Access Basic functions, but are instead stored in an Access table that the user can update. Selecting the Setup button on the Data Export form opens the DDE Specification form shown in Figure 12.13.

FIGURE 12.13.

*The DDE
Specification Setup
form.*

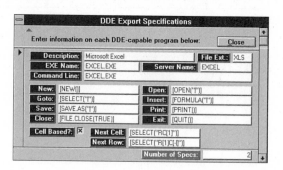

This form enables the user or system administrator to add the appropriate command strings for any application that supports DDE. Those of you familiar with Excel will recognize the macro commands shown in the figure. Letting the user configure the DDE commands for new applications adds to Ingenium for Windows's flexibility while eliminating the need for the developer to support a multitude of programs. The export facility is also completely dynamic, automatically compensating for the number and type of fields in the output queries. Meliora Systems is currently considering making the data-export tool available to other developers as an Access library.

Adding Flexibility to Reports

Printed reports remain the most common output of database systems. Despite the fact that most people have access to computers, they have not lost their love of seeing the results on paper. Besides, nobody wants to drag their desktop computer to a conference room for a meeting. As such, one challenge for developers of complex, commercial applications like Ingenium for Windows is keeping up with users' desires for many and varied reports.

When developing version 1 of Ingenium for Windows, we decided on a middle-of-the-road approach between a fixed set of reports and a completely *ad hoc* report designer like Access' ReportWizard. Figure 12.14 shows Ingenium's Report Parameter, which enables users to specify what data should appear in the many Ingenium report formats.

FIGURE 12.14.

Ingenium's Report Parameters form.

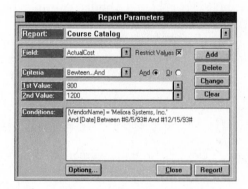

Ingenium for Windows enables users to apply their own filters to each of the stock reports that ship with the product. They use the form shown in Figure 12.14 to specify the criteria that define the filter. Ingenium's main menu form, shown previously in Figure 12.3, features a check box beneath the list of reports. When a user checks this option, Ingenium opens the Report Parameters form instead of directly printing the selected report.

At the top of the form is another list of reports. If opened from the main menu form, the correct report is already highlighted. After a report is selected, the user can start defining a filter for that report's data. He or she begins by selecting a field from that combo box. This control lists each field contained in the query upon which the report is based. Ingenium uses Access DAO methods to populate the list. Once a field is chosen, the user then selects a comparison operator from the next combo box and either selects or enters a value in the final two combo-box controls. Depending on which operator a user chooses, the form will display two (**Between...And**), one (**Equal**), or no (**Is Null**) value combo boxes.

After selecting a field from the first list, Ingenium runs the report's RecordSource query and places each resulting value in the two 'value' combo boxes. This makes it easy to specify criteria that are guaranteed to produce at least one record, because the values in the list come directly from the underlying database. When the Restrict Values check box is checked, Ingenium applies all previously defined criteria (shown in the list box at the bottom of the form) before populating the combo boxes. The net result is a list of values that gets smaller and smaller as more and more criteria are applied. Alternatively, if a user does not want to use the combo boxes (or is using an operator like **Like**), he or she can type a value into the control directly.

Buttons on the right side of the form help users manage individual criteria. They can add, remove, or change individual criteria or clear all conditions at once. As each new criterion is added, users have the option of combining it with those already defined using either the **And** or **Or** operators. Ingenium displays criteria in the list box at the bottom of the form. When all criteria have been defined, the user clicks the Report button and Ingenium for Windows opens the report using all the criteria as a filter. An additional feature of this tool is the capacity to save sets of criteria for reuse.

Developing Stand-Alone Applications

Creating stand-alone applications, either for commercial sale or mass distribution within an organization, is not a trivial undertaking. The final sections of this chapter will try to convey some of the things we learned during the process of developing Ingenium for Windows.

Plan Your Application with Flexibility in Mind

Microsoft Access is a very efficient and flexible interface and application-building tool. Although it also has its own very capable database engine, you will find that many of your potential customers and/or users will have existing data they wish to use with your application. Here, too, Access is a powerful tool, but there are several things you should consider during the initial stages of development.

First, if you plan to integrate external data sources such as FoxPro or SQL Server, remember that their database and field-naming schemes may differ from those used by Access. Try to choose the lowest common denominator that you expect to encounter. For example, do not use spaces in your table or column names, even though Access supports them. This enables you to use the same queries with other databases that do not.

Avoid creating Access Basic routines that use Access-specific properties and methods such as `Index` and `Seek`. These features cannot be used with attached tables and therefore will have to be rewritten if you use them. Stick to the dynaset methods such as `FindFirst`.

Finally, even if you are not going to use attached tables, you must provide a way for users to import existing data. This will also affect the design of the tables in your database. For example, does the existing data use different key fields than your application? How will relation tables be populated when new data is imported? The capability to use or import existing data will add to the appeal of your application, so be sure to consider this during its design.

Develop a System to Insure the Integrity of Attached Tables

The Access Developer's Toolkit recommends using at least two databases for each application, one for the data and one for the interface and reporting elements. Because the full path to attached tables is stored in the application databases, you will need to develop some method to update this if the files are moved. The method you devise should insulate users from the mechanics of manually deleting and then reconnecting attached tables, perhaps through a form-based interface.

If you use multiple databases, you will be unable to specify default relationships for attached tables. If you are not using the runtime version of Access and your users will have access to the QBE window, think about how this will affect those users who do not understand joins. You may need to provide built-in queries for them that perform the joins on related tables.

Making the Leap from Consultant to Software Marketer

As consultants, we sometimes become too narrowly focused on the project at hand without considering its wider appeal. The result is a lot of re-engineering of an application if we attempt to modify it for mass distribution. Although from a features standpoint Ingenium for Windows version 1 represented only a moderate improvement over Skil-Trak, it actually required more than twice as much time to complete. If you have any indication that a project may have wider applicability, take the time to consider how this will affect its design. Aim for modularity in your Access Basic code so that portions can be easily swapped in and out of applications. Carefully track all elements of the application that are specific to your client so that they can be easily removed later on. Also, make sure that the ownership of code and marketing rights are clear.

Marketing and pricing issues should also be contemplated fairly early on in the development cycle. This is a much trickier issue for commercial applications than it is for consulting projects. The first thing potential customers will likely want to know about your application is how much it will cost. Try to find competing or similar products and examine their pricing strategies. Are they copy- or user-based? Is there a discount structure for volume purchases? Are there site licenses available? What about support? Is it per-call or are there yearly maintenance programs? Do they sell through resellers or directly? Try to develop a rough estimate of expected costs and cash flows. Beginning this process early will let you reply with confidence to customer queries and focus more of your efforts toward developing a robust product.

13

Analyzing an Access Time and Billing System

by William J. Serrahn

Microsoft Access 1.x was a tremendous sales success in its first year of release, with over 1 million copies sold. Microsoft initially positioned the product as an end-user Windows RDBMS and encouraged professional developers to consider FoxPro 2.5. Many business applications developers, realizing the significance of the Access technology, ignored the Microsoft marketing position, viewing it as something akin to the original Microsoft/IBM proposition that suggested Windows be used on 2MB computers while OS/2 should be used on 4MB and larger machines.

WorkGroup Solutions released WorkGroup Billing/EIS, a time and billing application, shortly after the release of Access 1.0. One year later, armed with the knowledge it had gained from its versions 1.x, its customers and prospects, and a few thousand hours of Access development experience, the company was ready to develop the next version of its product.

Data Access Objects and Microsoft Access Objects

The big story in Microsoft Access 2.0 is the unveiling of Microsoft's data access object (DAO) and Microsoft Access objects (MAOs) technology. Microsoft Access and the other Microsoft applications are no longer stand-alone applications with similar but incompatible coding syntax to support isolated data and object models. The various Windows operating systems will universally provide data and object handling services to these global application objects.

All of the data-access technology and much of the new basic and object-addressing standards have come out of the Access development, so it is not much of a stretch for developers who are familiar with Access Basic, dynasets, and object addressing to operate globally in the new, object-oriented Microsoft productivity application environment.

Using DAO, MAO, and Wizard technology, entire applications can quickly be generated or customized. It's incredible that not only can all of the objects in an application be generated, but they can be generated under transaction management, allowing a commit or rollback of object and data transactions. The implications of this technology for applications developers are immense. With a little imagination, it is possible to see how the DAO-MAO technology will serve as the cornerstone of Microsoft's future strategy, with plenty of growth potential for new client-server technologies and object databases.

Assessing the New Features in Microsoft Access Version 2.0

Although we at WorkGroup Solutions were in awe of the new DAO-MAO technology, we believed that some of the other Access 2.0 improvements and features offered immediate gains as well. The most important of these features in our redevelopment effort for WorkGroup Billing were the following:

CBF (Code Behind Forms)

We began writing our first Access 1.x application using more macros than Basic code, but we quickly found that writing Access Basic functions gave us much more flexibility and control over event handling. Our programming style evolved to tying most of our functions to objects and events. The inability to trap runtime errors in macros when using runtime access also forced us to rethink the "codeless" macro outlook.

Code behind forms (CBF) makes creating the relationships between objects and code a very natural process, much like writing event-handling subprocedures in Visual Basic. Simply launch the Code Builder from a form, report, or control object and you open an editing window with a properly-named basic subroutine in which you can create the instructions for the event. The advantages to this approach are as follows:

- The form or report's event code is closely tied to the object and moves with it.

- The coding effort is usually reduced—both in time and actual number of coded lines.

- Implicit addressing makes referring to the object and its controls a very simple and natural process. Instead of `Forms!Customer!CustomerID`, you simply state it as `CustomerID`. The form that initiates the code is simply the `Me` form, so its properties can be accessed as `Me.Property` instead of as `Forms!Customer.Property`.

- The CBF code loads with the form or report and not when the database is opened, so initial startup time is reduced. Any module-level variables use memory only while the form or report is open.

Updateable Properties

One of the biggest disappointments with Access 1.x in the developer community was that nearly all control properties for the form and report objects were read-only in run mode. Even a button caption or a border color couldn't be changed programmatically. With Access 2.0, almost every property is updateable at runtime. You can even change the RecordSource property of forms and subforms on-the-fly.

Larger Event Model

If you have ever had two forms open with the same records and needed to guarantee the changes would be saved in one form before moving to the other, you will appreciate the following new events: OnGotFocus and OnLostFocus. OnOpen and OnClose have been supplemented by OnLoad, OnUnload, OnActivate, and OnUnactivate. It also was clear that WorkGroup Billing would benefit from the new timer and mouse events.

New Methods

The two most necessary yet difficult-to-control **DoCmd** actions in Access 1.x were GotoControl and Requery. These two actions have been replaced by the **SetFocus** and **Requery** methods. You can now easily requery any form or control or move to any form or control by simply setting these properties.

Many developers relied upon **SendKeys** code to interact with the available menu options. The new application methods Application.GetOption and Application.SetOption enable you to read and set options with one statement or macro.

Menu Builder

Drop-down menus for forms are still implemented with the AddMenu macro action. The good news is that you can now have submenus and application menus, plus Access 2.0 provides a new Menu Builder add-in to help you create all of your menus. The Menu Builder add-in of Andrew Miller's FIRSTLIB.MDB for Access 1.1 undoubtedly saved Access developers (who knew where to find it) thousands of hours building menu bar and menu macros. Shipping the Menu Builder as an Access 2.0 add-in is another step in making Access 2.0 a complete development environment.

Table-Level Validation

You can now specify validation rules within tables that remain in force regardless of how the tables are accessed. Like client-server RDBMSs, Access 2.0 business rules are enforced by the database itself, not by application code. You may still want to create supplemental validation routines within forms when the validation requires lookup of data within other tables. Form-level validation rules no longer override the validation rules you specify for fields and tables.

Cascading Updates and Deletes

Our customer table is related to at least a dozen other tables. With Access 1.x, we didn't even attempt to allow changes to values in primary key fields. With Access 2.0, we specify cascading deletions for all relationships, and primary key value changes are now updated in all related tables.

The *UNION* Operator

The volume of time detail records in our application can become huge. For better performance, we would like to archive closed time periods and keep the record count for active time detail files as small as possible. With the new SQL UNION operator, we can do analysis on the active and archived time detail records as if they were in one table. An example demonstrating this is provided in this chapter. Access 1.x forced us to make a table from the invoice detail and time detail attached to invoices before we could print data from the two tables as one merged invoice. Now we can place a UNION over the two tables and print them as one.

Data Definition Queries and SQL Pass-Through

Data definition queries and SQL pass-through were beyond the scope of our initial development, but they will become more important when the application is ported to Microsoft or Sybase SQL Server, or to other client-server RDBMSs, using the ODBC API.

OLE Custom Controls

Access 2.0 has implemented OLE 2.0 custom controls. We believe Access 2.0 is the prototype for future implementation of OLE custom controls in all Microsoft productivity applications. Three OLE 2.0 custom controls are supplied with the Access Developer's Toolkit. We have had a lot of fun with the data outline control and have only now begun to find ways to use it. A Project Outline using the data outline control is illustrated in this chapter. We also experimented with the calendar control and believe that it will be useful in future implementations of WorkGroup Billing. We haven't found a suitable use for the scrollbar control yet.

Custom controls will change the way that you design applications. After using the data outline control, you may completely overhaul the methods by which you present data to your users. Other Microsoft and third-party controls are certain to offer additional functionality to your applications as the developer community gains a fuller understanding of the OLE 2.0 paradigm, and Microsoft and third-party suppliers develop OCX versions of Visual Basic's VBX custom controls.

Microsoft Graph 5.0

Microsoft Graph 5.0 offers a number of improvements over the prior Microsoft Graph 3.0 and has a new look inherited from the graphing features of Excel 5.0. In-place activation makes customizing graphs and charts a snap. The most important advantage of Microsoft Graph 5.0 is the ability to manipulate embedded graph objects with Access Basic code through OLE Automation. On the other hand, access to the data series of Microsoft Graph 5.0 presently remains next to impossible, because Microsoft Graph 5.0 expects its data in Excel 5.0's BIFF format. Microsoft Graph 5.0 is a heavy-hitter when it comes to system resources, so many Access developers will opt for BPS/Pinnacle's Graph OCX OLE Custom control described in Chapter 18, "Introducing OLE 2.0 Custom Controls."

Built-In and Custom Toolbars

We had hoped to eliminate our application toolbar and rely on the Microsoft toolbars. The Access team would have probably preferred to make this process more programmable, but undoubtedly the developers had to implement the Microsoft cross-application toolbar DLLs. We at WorkGroup Solutions would have preferred a toolbar object, similar to form or report objects, with which we could monitor the toolbars that were open. The inability to include buttons with custom bitmaps makes the built-in and custom toolbars difficult to use as application toolbars for our products, although they are very useful and welcome additions. We've added new buttons to our forms to show and hide the built-in toolbars and custom toolbars.

Access Developer's Toolkit

One of the best features of the Access Developer's Toolkit (ADT) is that we now can create a setup program for our applications without having to include the runtime DLLs. The Setup Wizard has also been refined, allowing us to include as many add-ins and other ancillary files as we need. The most important feature, however, is that Microsoft has maintained its policy of unlimited run-time licensing when you purchase the ADT. The price of the ADT remains at $495, but you also receive the sample OLE Custom Controls, two of which are distributable, and supplementary documentation in the form of the Access Basic *Language Reference*, an *Advanced Topics* manual, and the *Help Compiler Guide*.

Establishing Overall Design Objectives for WorkGroup Billing 2.0

The main objectives of WorkGroup Billing/EIS version 1.x were to record the employees' time on forms resembling conventional time cards, create and print invoices for time and material, monitor accounts receivable, and provide tabular and graphical sales analyses.

The initial target market for WorkGroup Billing 1.x was small consulting, accounting, and legal firms. Among these, the product had been modestly successful in small consulting firms, and a sprinkling of accountants, lawyers, and other professionals had adopted it as well. One of the objectives of WorkGroup Billing 2.0 was to expand the market for the application to larger firms and, ultimately, to the client-server model.

WorkGroup Solutions discovered that many of its clients and prospective clients had an interest in a more sophisticated project model and required that time and expenses be logged to project phases and tasks. These clients typically use project-planning software such as Microsoft Project to plan the projects, estimate time and material requirements, make schedules, and allocate resources. Thus we needed to plan for connectivity to Microsoft Project 4.0 in future versions of WorkGroup Billing using OLE Automation.

Each industry has its own terminology for the same concepts—for example, *projects*, *jobs*, *matters*, and *engagements* are essentially the same. Firms in different industries also have diverse coding systems and billing methods. CPAs need a sophisticated write-up/write-down capability to adjust the actual time spent on an engagement to match the amount that they decide to bill for it. Consultants and others bill agreed-upon amounts at project milestones. The flexibility afforded by Access 2.0's newly programmable properties was important to implement such changes.

Many of the potential customers for time and billing software have distributed workforces armed with laptop computers. They want to enter time and expenses on their laptops, mail them to the billing administrator, and receive client and project maintenance in their return mail. Windows for Workgroups' Remote Access Services (RAS) with Access 2.0's SendObject action provides this capability.

We knew that WorkGroup Billing 2.0 would have to meet the preceding requirements without complicating the lives of those customers whose primary interest was simply getting their invoices in the mail. The new application would be mail enabled to meet the needs of a distributed work force. The Project data model would be a fixed, three-tier table structure (Project>Phase>Task), compatible with Microsoft

Project 4.0. These tables and the other tables would have a limited number of standard fields, allowing the user to determine the field definitions for each table via the Wizard and data access object technology. We decided that the application would be shipped with examples of Excel time sheets, as well as project and sales analysis via the Excel 5.0 pivot tables. If our users find these features to be useful, we'll add the necessary OLE Automation code to implement them within a future version of WorkGroup Billing.

WorkGroup Billing 2.0 Application Forms

When the WorkGroup Billing application is opened, the user is presented with either a client/project display or time card display depending on their last selection before exit. Figure 13.1 shows the client selection window. Clients, Projects, Contacts, Rates, Notes, and Time forms can be directly accessed and maintained from the initial display. The user can select a subset of these tables by setting the criteria through the use of command buttons located at the bottom of the window.

FIGURE 13.1.

The main Client window of WorkGroup Billing 2.0.

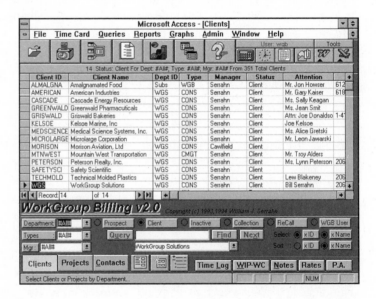

The application is designed to give the project manager all of the information that he or she needs with the minimum of searching through menus. You can easily find and select a client, display all projects for the client, and then press the form button displaying active projects, phases, tasks, and assignments. Figure 13.2 shows simulated active projects for WorkGroup Solutions.

FIGURE 13.2.

*WorkGroup
Solution's Projects
window.*

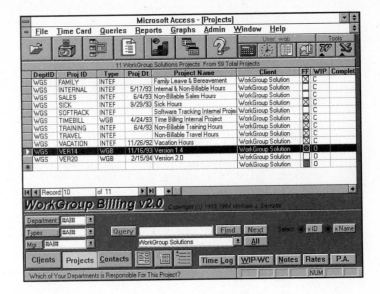

Each time new client, project, or contact-selection criteria are selected, a new RecordSource for the clients, projects, or contacts subform is generated, as illustrated in Listing 13.1.

Listing 13.1. Creating the client subform's RecordSource.

```
Sub Sub_Clients (ByVal SelectMode)
    Dim strRS As String,
    Dim strWhere As String, Dim strOr As String, strAnd As String
    strWhere = "Where "

    If Not IsNull(srchtxt) Then      'If Searchtext criteria ignored
        strRS = "SELECT DISTINCTROW Client.* FROM Client "
        If Srchbykey Then
            strRS = strRS & strWhere & "ClientID Like '" & srchtxt &
            ➡"*' "
            strWhere = "": strOr = "or "
        End If
        If SrchbyName Then
            strRS = strRS & strWhere & strOr & "Name Like '" & srchtxt &
            ➡"*' "
        End If
    Else      'Build SQL Criteria From Selections
        strRS = "SELECT DISTINCTROW Client.* FROM Client "
        strRS = strRS & "INNER JOIN [WGS Client Status] "
        strRS = strRS & "ON Client.Status <> [WGS Client Status].Status "
        If Not IsNull(DeptID) And DeptID <> "#ALL#" Then
```

continues

Listing 13.1. continued

```
            If DeptID = "#NA#" Then
                strRS = strRS & strWhere & strAnd & "DeptID is null "
            Else
                strRS = strRS & strWhere & strAnd & "DeptID='" & DeptID
            ➥& "' "
            End If
            strWhere = "": strAnd = "And "
        End If

        If Not IsNull(CType) And CType <> "#ALL#" Then
            strRS = strRS & strWhere & strAnd & "Type='" & CType & "' "
            strWhere = "": strAnd = "And "
        End If
        If Not IsNull(MgrID) And MgrID <> "#ALL#" Then
            strRS = strRS & strWhere & strAnd & "MgrID='" & MgrID & "' "
            strWhere = "": strAnd = "And "
        End If

        If Optsort = 1 Then
            strRS = strRS & " Order by ClientID ;"
        Else
            strRS = strRS & " Order by Name, ClientID ;"
        End If

        Clients.Form.Recordsource = strRS
End Sub
```

In order to identify if a record had been changed with Access 1.x, it was necessary to compare the prior and current values of each bound control. Testing for a change with Access 2.0's the **Dirty** property makes this process much easier, as illustrated in Listing 13.2.

Listing 13.2. Using the Dirty property.

```
Sub Form_BeforeUpdate (Cancel As Integer)
    If Dirty Then
        MB_Msg = "Accept Changes To The Client Record?"
        Beep
        If MsgBox(MB_Msg, MB_ICONSTOP + MB_OKCancel + MB_DefButton1,
        ➥"Record Changed") = IDCancel Then
            DoCmd CancelEvent
            SendKeys "{Esc}"
            Exit Sub
        End If
    End If
End Sub
```

The DeptID combo box must be populated with all of the departments plus an additional entry for all departments (#All#). Using Access 1.x, we had to populate the list box with a very complex and memory-intensive listbox function. With Access 2.0's updateable properties, it is possible to update the RowSource property to a string containing all of the values. (This tip comes from Scott Barker of Applications Plus in Woodinville, WA.) It is much simpler, faster, and more flexible than the old list box functions. If attached to the OnEnter event, as shown in Figure 13.3, the process doesn't consume CPU time until the user enters the control. Listing 13.3 shows how to create a **String** variable to load a combo or list box with a set of static values.

FIGURE 13.3.

Properties of the DeptID combo box.

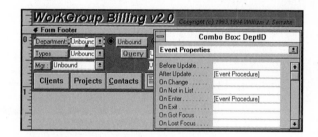

Listing 13.3. Updating a Combo Box's **RowSource**.

```
Sub DeptID_Enter ()

    Dim db As Database, Dept As Recordset, LBSource As String
    Set db = dbengine(0)(0)
    Set Dept = db.OpenRecordset("Department", DB_Open_SnapShot,
    ➥DB_ForwardOnly)

    LBSource = "DeptID;Department"
    LBSource = LBSource & ";#All#;All Departments"

    Do Until Dept.EOF
        LBSource = LBSource & ";""" & Dept!DeptID & """"
        LBSource = LBSource & ";""" & Dept!Department & """"
        Dept.MoveNext
    Loop
    Dept.Close

    DeptID.RowSourceType = "Value List"
    DeptID.RowSource = LBSource
End Sub
```

WorkGroup Billing 2.0 Client Forms

If you select a client from the application form and press the Form button, a more detailed client form is displayed, as shown in Figure 13.4. In this case, the client form contains subforms for projects, client departments or ship-to addresses, contacts, and notes. To save form loading time, the client form contains only one subform container. Each time an option button is pressed for projects, departments, contacts, or notes, the subform's `SourceObject` property is updated to the form corresponding to the button pressed. The property values of other controls, such as the open form command button's caption property, are also updated. Listing 13.4 shows the code used to update the RowSource of combo boxes, and control the visibility and set the captions of command buttons.

FIGURE 13.4.
A detailed Client form.

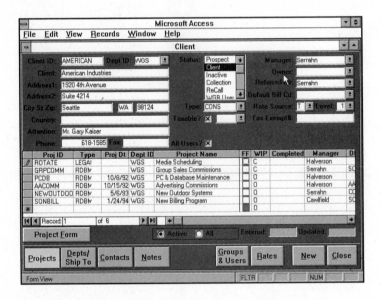

Listing 13.4. Updating a combo box's `RowSource` property and setting command button properties.

```
Sub sfOpt_AfterUpdate ()
    Select Case Me.sfOpt           'Me. is not necessary
      Case Is = 1
        Sf.SourceObject = "Client Projects SF"
        Me.btnForm.Visible = True
        Me.btnForm.Caption = "Projects &Form"
        Me.SelProjectID.Visible = False
        Me.SelActive.Visible = True
      Case Is = 2
        Sf.SourceObject = "Client Departments SF"
```

```
      Me.btnForm.Visible = True
      Me.btnForm.Caption = "Department &Form"
      Me.SelProjectID.Visible = False
      Me.SelActive.Visible = False
    Case Is = 3
      Sf.SourceObject = "Client Contacts SF"
      Me.btnForm.Visible = True
      Me.btnForm.Caption = "Contacts &Form"
      Me.SelProjectID.Visible = False
      Me.SelActive.Visible = False
    Case Is = 4
      Sf.SourceObject = "Client Notes SF"
      Me.btnForm.Visible = True
      Me.btnForm.Caption = "Notes &Form"
      Me.SelProjectID.Visible = False
      Me.SelActive.Visible = True
    End Select
End Sub
```

WorkGroup Billing 2.0 Project Forms

As mentioned earlier in the chapter, WorkGroup Billing 2.0 was designed with a new project model containing phases, tasks, and assignments. Compatibility is maintained with Microsoft Project 4.0 column headings so that data can be easily imported and exported, pending use of OLE Automation to integrate this operation. Figure 13.5, Figure 13.6, and Figure 13.7 show the Project form with the project's phases, tasks, and assignments displayed, respectively.

FIGURE 13.5.

The Project form with phases displayed.

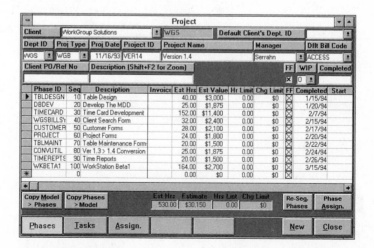

FIGURE 13.6.

*The Project form
with tasks
displayed.*

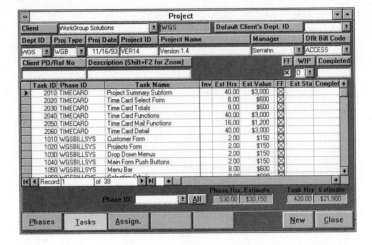

FIGURE 13.7.

*The Project form
with assignments
displayed.*

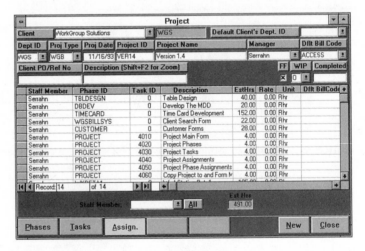

Very few projects are designed from scratch. Project managers tend to develop new projects and estimates from prior work that they have done. WorkGroup Billing enables you to save prior projects as Project Model templates and retrieve these templates when developing new projects. Figure 13.8 shows a typical template in a Project Model form.

FIGURE 13.8.

The Project Model form used to define and save phases of a project.

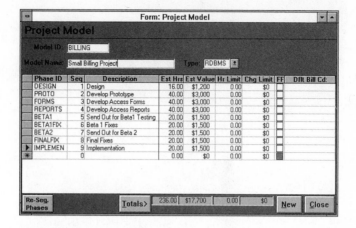

WorkGroup Billing 2.0 Rate Hierarchy

Implementing a universal rate system among a diverse group of consulting, accounting, legal, architectural, and various other companies was an interesting challenge. We found that some companies bill a combination of hours and professional days depending on the identity of the client or of the staff member. Some companies issue invoices based strictly on the staff type or class, while others bill for time of individual staff members. Some companies charge a different rate for specific services rendered by a single staff member.

Rate-overrides for specific clients, projects, phases, and tasks are always possible. Figures 13.9, 13.10, and 13.11 show how we implemented rates for staff types, staff members, and special client rates, respectively. Special project rates are implemented together with the project assignments.

FIGURE 13.9.

Staff Type form for assigning billing rates.

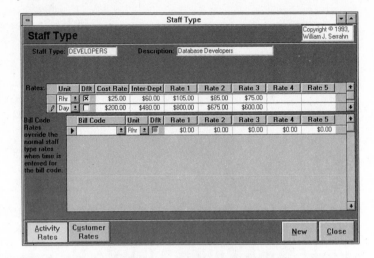

FIGURE 13.10.

Staff Member billing rate form.

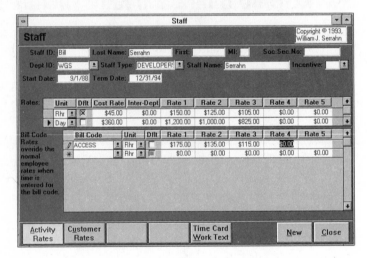

FIGURE 13.11.

*Client Rates
assignment form.*

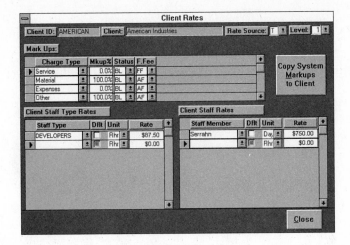

WorkGroup Billing 2.0 Time Card

WorkGroup Billing opens either to the Clients, Projects, and Contacts form, illustrated earlier in the chapter, or to the last time card selected. If the user has never selected a time card, a time-card selection form, similar to that shown in Figure 13.12, is presented.

FIGURE 13.12.

*Time Card
Selection form.*

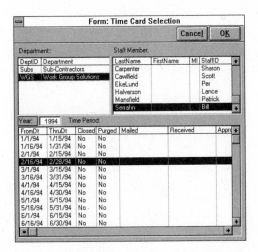

Each time-card view represents one complete time period for one staff member. Time periods can be weekly, biweekly, semi-monthly, or monthly. The top of the time card displays the ID and name of the staff member and the specified period. Each day of the period is represented by an option button, as shown in Figure 13.13. A subform displays time project summaries by `DeptID`, `Client`, `ProjectID`, `PhaseID`, `Bill Code`, `Client DeptID`, `Unit`, and `Status`. Hours can be entered directly into the project summary or can be entered into the time detail form illustrated later in this chapter.

FIGURE 13.13.

Bill Serrahn's time card for February 16 through 28.

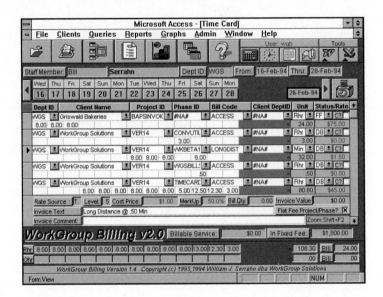

Using Access 1.x, we were unable to implement the day buttons with an option group because we could not update the button's captions to subsets of the the day numbers, 01 through 31. With Access 2.0, the day and days-of-the-week buttons are easily updated with the code shown in Listing 13.5.

Listing 13.5. Updating the time card's day option buttons.

```
Sub Sub_GetDisplayDays ()
    Dim i As Integer, varDate As Variant

    For i = 1 To 16              'Up to 16 days Can be Displayed
        varDate = DateAdd("d", i - 1 , TC_DisplayFromDt)
        If varDate <= TC_DisplayThruDt Then        'If it's within
        ➥Display 'limits, show it.
          Me("WD" & i).Visible = True
          Me("WD" & i) = Format(varDate, "ddd")        'Mon,Tue... Etc.
          Me("btn" & i).Visible = True
          Me("btn" & i).Caption = DatePart("d", varDate)
          ➥ 'Day 01 - 31
          Else                                   'if no day such as
                                                 'Febrary 29,30,31
```

```
            Me("WD" & i).Visible = False              'Don't show it.
            Me("btn" & i).Visible = False
        End If
    Next
End Sub
```

There are two ways to address access objects. You can reference a control as
Forms![*FormName*]![*ControlName*] or just [*ControlName*] in CBF code. You can alternately address objects as Forms("*FormName*")("*ControlName*") or just
Me("*ControlName*") in CBF code. The second method provides greater flexibility, as
illustrated by the code in Listing 13.5. In this example, we update controls WD01
through WD16 with the days of the week and btn01 through btn16 with the day numbers for the displayed period and also hide the unused day buttons.

WorkGroup Billing 2.0 Time Detail

The time card illustrated above enables you to enter time on a summary basis just as
you would fill out a time sheet. Some companies are not interested in detail, so the
summary is all that is necessary. The time card and time detail forms are two coop-
erating objects that are constantly maintained in synchronization. Whenever you enter
time on the summary form, a time detail record is updated or created via transaction
management. Whenever time detail is entered or changed, the summary is updated
accordingly. Listing 13.6 shows how a time entry on the time card creates or updates
time detail records behind the scenes and adds the net change to the time card totals.

Listing 13.6. Updating detail records with time card changes.

```
Sub TC_AddDayQty (DayNo)
    If TCClosed Or TCPurged Then Exit Function

    If n(InvNo) <> 0 Or Closed = True Then
        Beep
        MsgBox "Record Has Been Invoiced or Closed To Edits
        ➥ - Operation Canceled."
        DoCmd CancelEvent
        DoCmd DoMenuItem A_Formbar, A_Edit, A_Undo
        Exit Sub
    End If

    Dim Unit As Variant, inttotdx As Integer
    Unit = Unit
    intdx = DayNo
```

continues

Listing 13.6. continued

```
inttotdx = intdx

If intdx > 16 Then inttotdx = inttotdx - 16
Dim dblQty As Double, x As Integer

dbldayqty = n(aryQty(intdx))
Sub_TC_QtyRangeCheck Unit

If MB_Msg <> "" Then Exit Sub
Dim db as database, S As Recordset
Dim i As Integer, InvNo As Long
Dim strCriteria As String

strCriteria = "StaffID='" & tfrm!StaffID & "'"
strCriteria = strCriteria & " and DeptID='" & DeptID & "'"
strCriteria = strCriteria & " and CustomerID='" & CustomerID & "'"
strCriteria = strCriteria & " and ProjectID='" & ProjectID & "'"
strCriteria = strCriteria & " and PhaseID='" & PhaseID & "'"
strCriteria = strCriteria & " and BillCode='" & BillCode & "'"
strCriteria = strCriteria & " and CustDeptID='" & CustDeptID & "'"
strCriteria = strCriteria & " and Unit='" & Unit & "'"
strCriteria = strCriteria & " and InvStatus='" & InvStatus & "'"
strCriteria = strCriteria & " and WorkDt =#" & tfrm!SelectDt & "#"
Set db = dbengine(0)(0)
Set S = db.OpenRecordSet("Select * From [Time Detail] WHERE " &
➥StrCriteria & " ;")

Dim QtyChg As Double, BillQtyChg As Double

If S.Eof Then
    If dbldayqty <> 0 Then
        S.AddNew
        S!YR = tfrm!YR
        S!Period = tfrm!Period
        S!StaffID = tfrm!StaffID
        S!DeptID = DeptID
        S!CustomerID = CustomerID
        S!ProjectID = ProjectID
        S!PhaseID = PhaseID
        S!BillCode = BillCode
        S!CustDeptID = CustDeptID
        S!Unit = Unit
        S!InvStatus = InvStatus
        S!WorkDt = tfrm!SelectDt
        S!CostPrice = CostPrice
        S!Qty = dbldayqty: QtyChg = dbldayqty
        If InvStatus = "DB" Or InvStatus = "NC" Then
            S!BillQty = 0
        Else
            S!BillQty = dbldayqty: BillQtyChg = dbldayqty
```

```
            End If
            S!MarkUpPct = MarkUpPct
            S!Price = n(Price)
            S!DetlDesc = InvDesc
            S.Update
        End If

        If Unit = "Rhr" Then
            tfrm!RegHrs = tfrm!RegHrs + QtyChg
            tfrm!BillRegHrs = n(tfrm!BillRegHrs) + BillQtyChg
            aryTRhr(inttotdx) = n(aryTRhr(inttotdx)) + QtyChg
        End If

        If Unit = "Day" Then
            tfrm!RegHrs = n(tfrm!RegHrs) + (QtyChg * 8)
            tfrm!BillRegHrs = n(tfrm!BillRegHrs) + (BillQtyChg * 8)
            aryTRhr(inttotdx) = n(aryTRhr(inttotdx)) + (QtyChg * 8)
        End If

        If Unit = "Ohr" Then
            tfrm!OvtHrs = n(tfrm!OvtHrs) + QtyChg
            tfrm!BillOvtHrs = n(tfrm!BillOvtHrs) + BillQtyChg
            aryTOhr(inttotdx) = n(aryTOhr(inttotdx)) + QtyChg
        End If
        Qty = n(Qty) + QtyChg
        BillQty = n(BillQty) + BillQtyChg
Else

BeginTrans
    Dim TxTot As Integer
    Do Until S.Eof
        If n(S!InvNo) <> 0 Or S!Closed Then    'Invoiced?
            i = 9999
            InvNo = S!InvNo
            Exit Do
        End If

        If S!Qty <> S!BillQty And dbldayqty <> 0 Then
            If (S!InvStatus <> "DB" And S!InvStatus <> "NC") Or
            ➥S!BillQty <> 0 Then
                i = 9998
                Exit Do
            End If
        End If

        If i < 1 Then
            QtyChg = QtyChg - S!Qty
            BillQtyChg = BillQtyChg - S!BillQty

            If dbldayqty <> 0 Then
                S.Edit
```

continues

Listing 13.6. continued

```
                    S!Qty = dbldayqty: QtyChg = QtyChg + dbldayqty
                    If InvStatus = "DB" Or InvStatus = "NC" Then
                        S!BillQty = 0
                    Else
                        S!BillQty = dbldayqty: BillQtyChg = BillQtyChg +
                        ➥dbldayqty
                    End If
                    S.Update
                Else
                    S.Delete
                End If

        End If
        i = i + 1
        S.MoveNext
    Loop

    If i = 1 Then
        CommitTrans
        S.Close
        If Unit = "Rhr" Then
            tfrm!RegHrs = n(tfrm!RegHrs) + QtyChg
            tfrm!BillRegHrs = n(tfrm!BillRegHrs) + BillQtyChg
            aryTRhr(inttotdx) = n(aryTRhr(inttotdx)) + QtyChg
        End If

        If Unit = "Day" Then
            tfrm!RegHrs = n(tfrm!RegHrs) + (QtyChg * 8)
            tfrm!BillRegHrs = n(tfrm!BillRegHrs) + (BillQtyChg * 8)
            aryTRhr(inttotdx) = n(aryTRhr(inttotdx)) + (QtyChg * 8)
        End If
        If Unit = "Ohr" Then
            tfrm!OvtHrs = n(tfrm!OvtHrs) + QtyChg
            tfrm!BillOvtHrs = n(tfrm!BillOvtHrs) + BillQtyChg
            aryTOhr(inttotdx) = n(aryTOhr(inttotdx)) + QtyChg
        End If
        Qty = n(Qty) + QtyChg
        BillQty = n(BillQty) + BillQtyChg
    Else
        Rollback
        S.Close
        DoCmd CancelEvent
        DoCmd DoMenuItem A_Formbar, A_Edit, A_Undo

        intTDSetColVisIP = True
        If i < 9999 Then
            If i = 9998 Then
            MsgBox "Time Detail Hour Qty Differs From Bill Qty...
        Else
            MsgBox "Multiple Records or Both Regular Hours...
        End If
```

```
        Else
            MsgBox "Hour Total Previously Invoiced on Invoice...
        End If
    End If
End Sub
```

WorkGroup Billing 2.0 Time Detail Form

Pressing the day button on the time card enables time detail records to be entered and displayed. The time detail can be filtered by date, client, project, and phase. It can be configured to enter start and stop times or hour quantities. In addition, time expenses and other charges can be entered. In Figure 13.14, the operator clicked the day button for February 25th, and the detail is displayed for the entire day.

FIGURE 13.14.

Bill Serrahn's time detail for February 25.

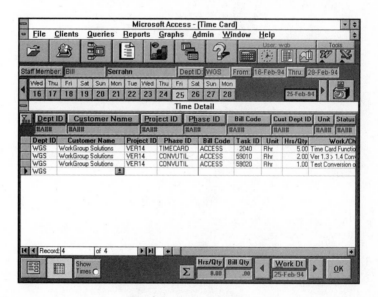

Listing 13.7 shows the CBF code on the day button option group that displays the time detail. It also shows typical use of the new Requery and Setfocus methods. Columns on the time detail subform are hidden or shown according to the filters selected. If the detail is selected for a particular day, the day column in the detail is hidden. The new ColumnHidden property enables you to show and hide columns without using the Visible property, which had unwanted side effects in Access 1.x.

Listing 13.7. CBF code for the `OptDisplayDay` control.

```
Sub OptDisplayDay_AfterUpdate ()
    'Calculate the Date for The Day Option Button Pressed

    SelectDt = DateAdd("d", OptDisplayDay - 1, TC_DisplayFromDt)

    If isloaded("Time Detail") Then         'if the form is not
        DoCmd OpenForm "Time Detail"         'open, open it.
    Else                                     'if it's hidden,
        Forms![Time Detail].Visible = True    're-display it and
        Forms![Time Detail].Requery          'requery for the
    End If                                    'new date

    Dim sfrm As Form                         'Assign form var
    Set sfrm = forms![Time Detail]![Sf].Form 'to Time Detail's sf.
    sfrm.SetFocus                            'Set Focus to Subform
                                             'and select new rec.
    DoCmd DoMenuItem A_Formbar, A_RecordsMenu, 1, 4

    'Set focus at the first non-hidden control

    If Screen.ActiveControl.ControlName = "DeptID" Then
        If sfrm!WorkDt.ColumnHidden Then
            sfrm!CustomerID.SetFocus
        Else
            sfrm!WorkDt.SetFocus
        End If
    End If
End Sub
```

Figure 13.15 shows a view of time detail with the date filter set to Off, showing all of the detail for the entire period.

FIGURE 13.15.

Bill Serrahn's time detail for entire period.

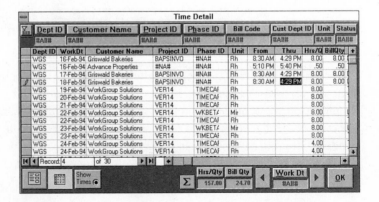

Mailing Time and Other Data from WorkGroup Billing 2.0

Many workforces today no longer work in a central office. Today, distributed workforces corresponding with their office via e-mail are becoming more common. WorkGroup Billing 2.0 is designed to allow staff members in the field to receive client, project, and other maintenance information with their regular Microsoft mail. They can also submit their time and expenses to a special mailbox form; project managers or billing administrators automatically receive the time and incorporate it into a central database.

Access 2.0 is mail-enabled, allowing data contained in persistent Access objects to be transmitted as attachments to messages. You can send mail by choosing Send from the File menu or executing the SendObject action in a macro or Access Basic code. We expect to see the entire Simple MAPI instruction set implemented by built-in commands or thru OLE Automation in future versions of Access or Microsoft Mail client applications.

Using Access 2.0, we still found it necessary to research and implement the Simple MAPI DLL interface within the WorkGroup Billing application to give us programmatic access to Compose, Read Mail, Open and Select From the Mail Address book, Attach and Detach Files, and to retrieve time data from groups of time cards that had been mailed. We gleaned the MAPI code from the Microsoft Workgroups (GO MSWRKGRP) forum on CompuServe, the Microsoft Developer Network CD-ROMs, and a very interesting product from Microsoft called WorkGroup Templates (available from Microsoft sales for $39.95). The WorkGroup Template code can be used in your applications. It still took us a couple of weeks to understand Simple MAPI, and much more time to integrate Simple MAPI functions in our application code. Listing 13.8 shows the declarations section we added to a module just to accommodate Simple MAPI.

Listing 13.8. MAPI declarations from MSWRKGRP forum.

```
Option Compare Database    'Use database order for string comparisons

'MAPI Message holds information about a message
Type MAPIMessage
    Reserved As Long
    Subject As String
    NoteText As String
    MessageType As String
```

continues

Listing 13.8. continued

```
        DateReceived As String
        ConversationID As String
        Flags As Long
        RecipCount As Long
        FileCount As Long
End Type


'MAPIRecip holds information about a message
'originator or recipient
Type MapiRecip
        Reserved As Long
        RecipClass As Long
        Name As String
        Address As String
        EIDSize As Long
        EntryID As String
End Type


'MapiFile holds information about File Attachments
Type MapiFile
        Reserved As Long
        Flags As Long
        Position As Long
        PathName As String
        FileName As String
        FileType As String
End Type


'    FUNCTION Declarations
Declare Function MAPILogon Lib "MAPI.DLL" (ByVal UIParam&, ByVal
➥UserName$, ByVal Password$, ByVal Flags&, ByVal Reserved&, Session&)
➥As Long
Declare Function MAPILogoff Lib "MAPI.DLL" (ByVal Session&, ByVal
➥UIParam&, ByVal Flags&, ByVal Reserved&) As Long
Declare Function BMAPIReadMail Lib "MAPI.DLL" (lMsg&, nRecipients&,
➥nFiles&, ByVal Session&, ByVal UIParam&, MessageID$, ByVal Flag&, ByVal
➥Reserved&) As Long
Declare Function BMAPIGetReadMail Lib "MAPI.DLL" (ByVal lMsg&, Message
➥As MAPIMessage, Recip As MapiRecip, File As MapiFile, Originator As
➥MapiRecip) As Long
Declare Function MAPIFindNext Lib "MAPI.DLL" Alias "BMAPIFindNext"
➥(ByVal Session&, ByVal UIParam&, MsgType$, SeedMsgID$, ByVal Flag&,
➥ByVal Reserved&, MsgId$) As Long
Declare Function MAPISendDocuments Lib "MAPI.DLL" (ByVal UIParam&, ByVal
➥DelimStr$, ByVal FilePaths$, ByVal FileNames$, ByVal Reserved&) As Long
Declare Function MAPIDeleteMail Lib "MAPI.DLL" (ByVal Session&, ByVal
➥UIParam&, ByVal MsgId$, ByVal Flags&, ByVal Reserved&) As Long
Declare Function MAPISendMail Lib "MAPI.DLL" Alias "BMAPISendMail"
➥(ByVal Session&, ByVal UIParam&, Message As MAPIMessage, Recipient As
➥MapiRecip, File As MapiFile, ByVal Flags&, ByVal Reserved&) As Long
```

```
Declare Function MAPISaveMail Lib "MAPI.DLL" Alias "BMAPISaveMail"
➥(ByVal Session&, ByVal UIParam&, Message As MAPIMessage, Recipient As
➥MapiRecip, File As MapiFile, ByVal Flags&, ByVal Reserved&, MsgId$) As
➥Long
Declare Function BMAPIAddress Lib "MAPI.DLL" (lInfo&, ByVal Session&,
➥ByVal UIParam&, Caption$, ByVal nEditFields&, Label$, nRecipients&,
➥Recip As MapiRecip, ByVal Flags&, ByVal Reserved&) As Long
Declare Function BMAPIGetAddress Lib "MAPI.DLL" (ByVal lInfo&, ByVal
➥nRecipients&, Recipients As MapiRecip) As Long
Declare Function MAPIDetails Lib "MAPI.DLL" Alias "BMAPIDetails" (ByVal
➥Session&, ByVal UIParam&, Recipient As MapiRecip, ByVal Flags&, ByVal
➥Reserved&) As Long
Declare Function MAPIResolveName Lib "MAPI.DLL" Alias "BMAPIResolveName"
➥(ByVal Session&, ByVal UIParam&, ByVal UserName$, ByVal Flags&, ByVal
➥Reserved&, Recipient As MapiRecip) As Long

'CONSTANT Declarations
Global Const SUCCESS_SUCCESS = 0
Global Const MAPI_USER_ABORT = 1
Global Const MAPI_E_FAILURE = 2
Global Const MAPI_E_LOGIN_FAILURE = 3
Global Const MAPI_E_DISK_FULL = 4
Global Const MAPI_E_INSUFFICIENT_MEMORY = 5
Global Const MAPI_E_BLK_TOO_SMALL = 6
Global Const MAPI_E_TOO_MANY_SESSIONS = 8
Global Const MAPI_E_TOO_MANY_FILES = 9
Global Const MAPI_E_TOO_MANY_RECIPIENTS = 10
Global Const MAPI_E_ATTACHMENT_NOT_FOUND = 11
Global Const MAPI_E_ATTACHMENT_OPEN_FAILURE = 12
Global Const MAPI_E_ATTACHMENT_WRITE_FAILURE = 13
Global Const MAPI_E_UNKNOWN_RECIPIENT = 14
Global Const MAPI_E_BAD_RECIPTYPE = 15
Global Const MAPI_E_NO_MESSAGES = 16
Global Const MAPI_E_INVALID_MESSAGE = 17
Global Const MAPI_E_TEXT_TOO_LARGE = 18
Global Const MAPI_E_INVALID_SESSION = 19
Global Const MAPI_E_TYPE_NOT_SUPPORTED = 20
Global Const MAPI_E_AMBIGUOUS_RECIPIENT = 21

Global Const MAPI_ORIG = 0
Global Const MAPI_TO = 1
Global Const MAPI_CC = 2
Global Const MAPI_BCC = 3

'FLAG Declarations
Global Const MAPI_LOGON_UI = &H1
Global Const MAPI_NEW_SESSION = &H2
Global Const MAPI_DIALOG = &H8
Global Const MAPI_UNREAD_ONLY = &H20
Global Const MAPI_ENVELOPE_ONLY = &H40
Global Const MAPI_PEEK = &H80
```

continues

Listing 13.8. continued

```
Global Const MAPI_GUARANTEE_FIFO = &H100
Global Const MAPI_BODY_AS_FILE = &H200
Global Const MAPI_AB_NOMODIFY = &H400
Global Const MAPI_SUPPRESS_ATTACH = &H800
Global Const MAPI_FORCE_DOWNLOAD = &H1000

Global Const MAPI_OLE = &H1
Global Const MAPI_OLE_STATIC = &H2

'Global variables used by MapiDemo only
Global MapiSession&
Global rc As Long
Global MsgId$
Global Recips() As MapiRecip, Files() As MapiFile
Global PopupErrors As Integer
```

Figure 13.16 shows the form that tells the user which time card will be sent with the Microsoft Mail message. The Access Basic code necessary to compose the message appears in Listing 13.9.

FIGURE 13.16.
Mail table data form.

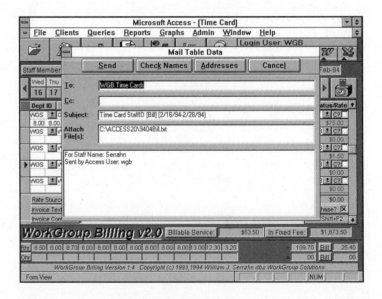

Listing 13.9. `MAPI_Compose` function from MSWRKGRP forum.

```
Function MAPI_Compose (SubJectText, ToText, CCText, BlindCCText,
AttachmentsText, MessageText) As Integer
```

```
'NOTE: only 10 attachment files may be specified
Dim s As String
Dim Mapi_Msg As MAPIMessage
Static toR(0 To 9)  As String
Static ccR(0 To 9)  As String
Static bccR(0 To 9)  As String
Static AttachFilename(0 To 9)  As String

ReDim Mapi_Recip_Desc(0 To 0) As MapiRecip
ReDim Mapi_File_Desc(0 To 0) As MapiFile

'Default the Subject field, if one is not entered
'Default the To field, if one is not entered
If (Len(SubJectText) = 0) Then
    SubJectText = "#NA#"
End If
If (Len(ToText) = 0) Then
    ToText = CurrentUser()
End If

'Pull out the "TO:" field and build up recipient structures
iTo = 0
iPos% = 1
Do While (iPos% <> 0)
    toR(iTo) = StringToken(iPos%, (ToText), ";")
    iTo = iTo + 1
Loop

'Pull out the "CC:" field and build up recipient structures
icc = 0
If (Len(CCText) <> 0) Then
    iPos% = 1
    Do While (iPos% <> 0)
        ccR(icc) = StringToken(iPos%, (CCText), ";")
        icc = icc + 1
    Loop
End If

'Pull out the "BlindCC:" field and build up recipient structures
ibcc = 0
If (Len(BlindCCText) <> 0) Then
    iPos% = 1
    Do While (iPos% <> 0)
        bccR(ibcc) = StringToken(iPos%, (BlindCCText), ";")
        ibcc = ibcc + 1
    Loop
End If

'Pull out the "Attachments:" field and build up file enclosure
➥structures
iencl = 0
```

continues

Listing 13.9. continued

```
If (Len(AttachmentsText) <> 0) Then
    iPos% = 1
    Do While (iPos% <> 0)
        AttachFilename(iencl) = StringToken(iPos%,
        ➥(AttachmentsText), ";")
        iencl = iencl + 1
    Loop
End If

'Allocate enough recipient structures
ReDim Mapi_Recip_Desc(0 To iTo + icc + ibcc - 1)

'Set up the "TO:" recipient structures
If (iTo <> 0) Then
    For i = 0 To iTo - 1
        Mapi_Recip_Desc(i).Name = toR(i)
        Mapi_Recip_Desc(i).RecipClass = MAPI_TO
    Next i
End If

'Set up the "CC:" recipient structures
If (icc <> 0) Then
    For i = 0 To icc - 1
        Mapi_Recip_Desc(iTo + i).Name = ccR(i)
        Mapi_Recip_Desc(iTo + i).RecipClass = MAPI_CC
    Next i
End If

'Set up the "BlindCC:" recipient structures
If (ibcc <> 0) Then
    For i = 0 To ibcc - 1
        Mapi_Recip_Desc(iTo + icc + i).Name = bccR(i)
        Mapi_Recip_Desc(iTo + icc + i).RecipClass = MAPI_BCC
    Next i
End If
Mapi_Msg.RecipCount = iTo + icc + ibcc

'Build up the file enclosure descriptors
Mapi_Msg.FileCount = 0&

If (iencl > 0) Then
    ReDim Mapi_File_Desc(0 To iencl - 1)
    For i = 0 To iencl - 1
        Mapi_File_Desc(i).FileName = ""
        Mapi_File_Desc(i).FileName = ""
        Mapi_File_Desc(i).PathName = AttachFilename(i)
        Mapi_File_Desc(i).Position = -1
        Mapi_File_Desc(i).FileType = ""
    Next i
```

```
        Mapi_Msg.FileCount = iencl
    End If

   'Set the mail message fields
   Mapi_Msg.Reserved = 0&
   Mapi_Msg.Subject = SubJectText
   Mapi_Msg.NoteText = MessageText
   Mapi_Msg.MessageType = ""
   Mapi_Msg.DateReceived = ""
   Mapi_Msg.Flags = 0&

   'Send the mail, then destroy the compose window if the send was
   ➥successful
TryToSendMail:
   MapiRtnVal& = MAPILogon(0, "", "", MAPI_LOGON_UI, 0, MapiSession&)
   If MapiRtnVal& <> SUCCESS_SUCCESS And MapiRtnVal& <>
   ➥MAPI_E_TOO_MANY_SESSIONS Then
       Debug.Print "Send Mail"
       Debug.Print MapiRtnVal&
       Debug.Print MapiSession&
       GoTo EndFuncCompose
   End If

   MapiRtnVal& = MAPISendMail(MapiSession&, Screen.ActiveForm.hWnd,
   ➥Mapi_Msg, Mapi_Recip_Desc(0),    Mapi_File_Desc(0), 0&, 0&)

   'Can't Step though the above module code since a "No Report is
   ➥active" message is issued.
   'Focus is on the Module Window ("OModule") during debug step process
   ➥and not the Report Window.
   'Use a Window Inspector to get the current handle to "OReport" and
   ➥change the argument as in the
   'statement below to correct handle. Exceute the Rem'ed statement
   ➥below and cheat.

   'MapiRtnVal& = MAPISendMail(MapiSession&, 15924, Mapi_Msg,
Mapi_Recip_Desc(0), Mapi_File_Desc(0), 0&, 0&)

   If MapiRtnVal& <> SUCCESS_SUCCESS Then
       Debug.Print "Send Mail"
       Debug.Print MapiRtnVal&
       Debug.Print MapiSession&
       GoTo EndFuncCompose
   End If

EndFuncCompose:
   MAPI_Compose = MapiRtnVal&

End Function
```

Using *UNION* Queries

UNION queries are a necessity when you must combine archived and current data for data from similar tables such as the WorkGroup Billing time detail and invoice detail. Figure 13.17 illustrates how we combined the archived 1992 project data with the current 1993 project data for a specific client via the UNION query. You must write your own SQL statements for UNION queries, but you can cut-and-paste most of the statement from conventional Access select queries. Figure 13.18 shows the SQL statement behind the UNION query datasheet of Figure 13.17.

FIGURE 13.17.

American Industries 1992/1993 data created with a UNION query.

Yr	ClientID	ProjectID	Hrs	BillHrs	Amount	AdjAmount
1992	American	AACOMM	0.5	0.5	$20.00	$0.00
1993	American	AACOMM	2	2	$107.00	$0.00
1993	American	AR	26	26	$996.50	$0.00
1992	American	BILLING	113	113	$3,904.00	$0.00
1993	American	BILLING	164.25	164.25	$5,916.50	$0.00
1992	American	CHARTING	11	11	$374.00	$0.00
1993	American	CHARTING	1	1	$34.00	$0.00
1992	American	CORPNET	62	58	$2,320.00	$0.00
1993	American	CORPNET	1509.5	1509.5	$55,001.50	$0.00
1992	American	FINANCIALS	69.5	62.5	$2,173.00	$0.00
1993	American	FINANCIALS	67.25	67.25	$2,333.00	$0.00
1992	American	HRMS	49.5	49.5	$1,980.00	$0.00
1993	American	HRMS	58	58	$2,515.00	$0.00
1992	American	LEASE	4.5	4.5	$153.00	$0.00
1993	American	LEASE	20	20	$715.00	$0.00
1992	American	LEDGER	18.25	18.25	$620.50	$0.00
1993	American	LEDGER	34	34	$1,206.00	$0.00

Record: 1 of 110

FIGURE 13.18.

The SQL statement for the UNION query result set of Figure 13.17.

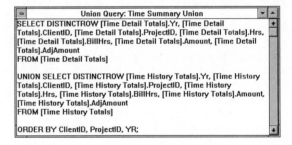

```
SELECT DISTINCTROW [Time Detail Totals].Yr, [Time Detail
Totals].ClientID, [Time Detail Totals].ProjectID, [Time Detail Totals].Hrs,
[Time Detail Totals].BillHrs, [Time Detail Totals].Amount, [Time Detail
Totals].AdjAmount
FROM [Time Detail Totals]

UNION SELECT DISTINCTROW [Time History Totals].Yr, [Time History
Totals].ClientID, [Time History Totals].ProjectID, [Time History
Totals].Hrs, [Time History Totals].BillHrs, [Time History Totals].Amount,
[Time History Totals].AdjAmount
FROM [Time History Totals]

ORDER BY ClientID, ProjectID, YR;
```

The Data Outline Custom Control

The Data Outline Control is one of the most exciting OLE Custom Controls for Access 2.0. The Data Outline Control is included in the ADT, along with simple Calendar and Scrollbar Controls. Figure 13.19 shows one way in which we initially used the data outliner to display a hierarchy of Clients, Projects, Phases, and Tasks. The ADT incorporates an example application, OUTLINE.MDB, that demonstrates more sophisticated implementations. Further details on how to use the Data Outline Control are provided in Chapter 18.

FIGURE 13.19.

Client project outline.

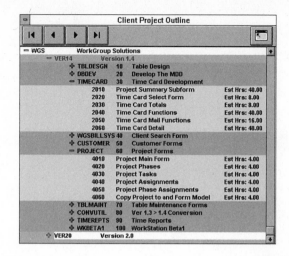

WorkGroup Billing 2.0 Invoicing and Accounts Receivable

WorkGroup Billing's invoicing, accounts receivable, and analysis functions illustrated in the the first edition of this book. As of this writing, these features had not yet been updated for Access 2.0. Plans for invoicing and accounts receivable features include a user-interface upgrade, a more intuitive form design, more sophisticated write-up/write-down processes, and new invoice formats.

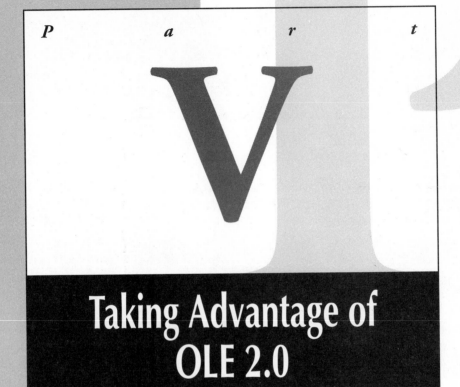

Taking Advantage of OLE 2.0

14

Understanding OLE 2.0

Access 2.0 is the first Windows database-application generator to provide Object Linking and Embedding (OLE) 2.0 compatibility. Access 2.0 is an OLE 2.0 client application, and it can manipulate objects exposed by OLE 2.0 server applications using OLE Automation. Access 2.0 also is the first Windows application to support the new OLE Custom Controls that are destined to replace the .VBX (Visual Basic Extension) custom controls of Visual Basic 3.0 and earlier. This chapter introduces you to the basic concepts of OLE in the Windows 3+ environment. The succeeding chapters of this section go into the details of using Access 2.0's object frames as OLE 2.0 containers on forms and reports, using OLE Automation, and employing the few OLE Custom Controls that were available at the time this book was written.

When Microsoft Chicago, which was in the alpha test stage when this edition was written, ultimately is introduced as Windows 4.0, 32-bit OLE 2.0 is likely to be part of the operating system itself. Many, if not all, of the applets that accompany Windows 4.0 probably will be OLE 2.0 mini-servers. Thus, learning at least the basic elements of OLE 2.0, including the new OLE 2.0 terminology, gives you a head start on understanding future versions of Windows and Windows NT.

If you are an experienced user of Windows word-processing or spreadsheet applications, you've undoubtedly employed OLE 1.0 for a variety of purposes, such as adding graphs or charts to documents with Microsoft Graph 3.0, or embedding bitmapped or vector-based images using Windows Paintbrush or Microsoft Draw, respectively. If you've made extensive use of OLE 1.0, you might be tempted to skip over the general description of OLE that begins this chapter. The information in the sections that follow is important for all users of OLE, because these first sections define the new object terminology employed by OLE 2.0. You can expect this new terminology to also be used in the documentation for upgraded versions of OLE 1.0 applications.

> **NOTE**
>
> The sections early in this chapter that describe the features of OLE 2.0 and elements of the registration database are adapted from the author's *Database Developer's Guide with Visual Basic 3.0* (Sams Publishing, 1994, ISBN 0-672-30440-6). The implementation of Access 2.0's OLE 2.0 client features is quite similar to that of Visual Basic 3.0, and the manipulation of OLE 2.0 objects in Access 2.0's bound and unbound object frames with Access Basic is derived from Visual Basic 3.0. Access 2.0's object frames better comply with the OLE 2.0 standard than the MSOLE2.VBX custom control of Visual Basic 3.0. This is understandable, because Visual Basic 3.0 was

released before the official publication of the OLE 2.0 specification and the accompanying OLE 2.0 Software Development Kit (SDK).

Learning OLE Terminology and OLE 1.0 Methods

OLE 2.0 uses Microsoft's *component object model* (COM), the programming foundation on which OLE 2.0 applications are constructed. The terminology and descriptions of the general methodology of OLE 1.0 and 2.0 that are presented in the following sections are based on OLE 2.0 guidelines established by Microsoft's *Programmer's Guide* for OLE 2.01, part of the documentation that accompanies the OLE 2.01 SDK.

NOTE

Version 2.01 of OLE was current at the time this edition was written. OLE 2.01 corrects a number of minor problems associated with the files included in the initial release of the OLE 2.0 SDK. The OLE 2.0-related files included with retail Access 2.0 conform to OLE 2.01 standards.

OLE is a method of inter-process communication (IPC) for transferring *documents* between two Windows applications running on a PC under Windows 3.1, Windows for Workgroups 3.1+, or Windows NT 3.1, or between two applications running on an Apple Macintosh computer under System 7+. You also can use OLE as an IPC on a RISC-based computer that uses the MIPS or Digital Equipment Alpha MPU chips running Windows NT or Windows NT Advanced Server. The current versions of OLE, 1.0 and 2.01, are designed for use on a single computer. This means that both the OLE container (client) application and the server application must run simultaneously on your computer.

Future versions of OLE and products that are intended to compete with Microsoft's OLE standard are expected to be able to share OLE objects across networks. Microsoft Chicago (Windows 4.0) and Cairo (Windows NT 4.0) are expected to be capable of sharing OLE objects in a networked environment, with Chicago limited to acting as a network OLE client and Cairo acting as either an OLE 2.0 object server or a client. In December 1993, Microsoft Corp. and Digital Equipment Corp. entered into an agreement to incorporate OLE 2.0 into Digital's ObjectBroker technology, which is discussed later in this chapter.

The sections that follow describe the terminology applicable to all versions of OLE and discuss the methods you use to embed or link OLE objects you create with OLE 1.0 server applications.

Documents and OLE Containers

A document, in OLE terminology, is any object that is created by a Windows application and contains some type of data. A document can be a bitmapped image created with Windows Paintbrush, an Excel worksheet (or a range of worksheet cells), part or all of a portion of a Word for Windows document, a waveform audio (.WAV) file, a video clip (.AVI), or a MIDI music (.MID) file. Any data object created by an OLE-compliant server application that you can copy to the Windows clipboard constitutes an OLE-aware document.

The application that initiates the communication link to embed or link the OLE object is called the *container* application. The application that originally created or that supplies the linked object is called the *server* application. Container applications were called OLE *clients* and server applications were called OLE *servers* prior to the introduction of OLE 2.0. Container applications create *compound documents*. A compound document is a document in the container application's chosen format (called an object class) that contains a document object created by a server application. Figure 14.1 illustrates a three-level hierarchy of OLE documents. The source document can be a compound document, in which case it is said to have nested objects.

FIGURE 14.1.

A diagram of a compound document containing another compound document.

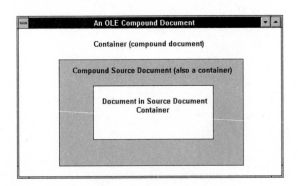

NOTE

You cannot edit a nested source document (the smaller white document in Figure 14.1) contained in a OLE 1.0 source container document (the document with the gray surface in Figure 14.1) that, in turn, is embedded or linked into your container application's compound document.

When you link or embed an OLE object from a source document into a container application's document, you create the compound document. The differences between documents that are embedded in or linked to a container document are as follows:

■ An *embedded* document object maintains a reference to (name of) the application that created the embedded object, but not to the data contained in the embedded document itself. Embedded objects become a permanent member of the container document. If you save the container object to a file, the file contains the data and application reference to each embedded object. You can only edit the content of the embedded object from within the container application. An example of an embedded object is an image created with Microsoft Draw embedded in a Word for Windows 2.0 document. Microsoft Draw can embed—but not link —a drawing object.

■ A *linked* document object requires the existence of a file to hold the document's data. The linked object maintains both a reference to the application that created the file and a reference to the file itself. The latter link is called the *link source*. You can edit the data of a linked object from within the container application *or* the server application. Linking objects ensures that your container application always has the latest version of an object that is subject to updates to its data. Linking objects also minimizes file size under most, but not all, conditions, because only the reference to the application and the link source is maintained. Depending on the type of document you link, the document is represented by an image or its server application's icon. The visible representation of a linked OLE object is called the object's *presentation*.

NOTE

Microsoft Draw is called an OLE *mini-server* application or applet. Mini-server applets are applications that do not offer the capability of saving their data to a file. Microsoft Graph 5.0 (called MSGraph5 in this book) is an

OLE 2.0 mini-server, as is Shapeware Corp.'s Visio Express. Other OLE mini-server applets include the OLE 1.0 applets supplied with Word for Windows 2+: Equation Editor and WordArt. The spelling checker and thesaurus of Word 6.0 are OLE 2.0 mini-server applets.

Depending on the container application, it may be not be readily apparent whether a source document is linked to or embedded in a compound document. As an example, Figure 14.2 shows two bitmapped images stored in Access 2.0 unbound OLE object frames. The image on the left is embedded; the image on the right is linked.

FIGURE 14.2.

The presentation and OLE-related properties of embedded and linked Paintbrush pictures.

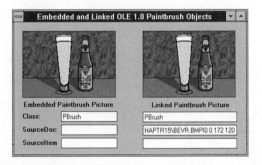

TIP

In the case of graphic images created by most OLE server applications, you do not save disk space by linking instead of embedding the image. This is because creating the presentation of the image requires the same data as is stored in the file. The presentation of OLE images is a Windows metafile. If the presentation contains a bitmap, your application can clip or scale the metafile that contains the bitmap, but the size of the original data remains the same. You need specialty applications, such as Lenel Systems' MultiMedia Works or Watermark's Discovery edition, that create *thumbnail* images in order to take advantage of the disk-space savings accorded by linking. A thumbnail image is an miniature version (not a scaled version) of the original image, usually about the size of an application icon.

Linked objects can be updated to current data values by either an *automatic* or a *manual* link. An automatic link refreshes the presentation by opening and reading the file designated by the link. A manual link requires that you make a menu choice or click a command button to update the presentation. You can link the entire file (a complete object) or only a range of cells (a partial or *pseudo object.*)

Activating OLE 1.0 Applications

You can edit embedded and linked documents. When you *activate* an OLE 1.0 object, either by double-clicking the object's presentation or choosing **E**dit or **P**lay (for multimedia objects) from a menu, the server application's window opens to display or play the data of the embedded or linked object. The representation of most multimedia objects is an icon that represents the OLE server. Figure 14.3 is a composite illustration that shows embedded (left) and linked (right) Media Clip objects created from the CANYON.MID MIDI file included with Windows 3.1. The version of Media Player shown in Figure 14.3 is the OLE server applet supplied with Windows for Workgroups and the multimedia (OEM) version of Windows 3.1+ that is distributed by original equipment manufacturers (OEMs) with their audio adapter cards.

FIGURE 14.3.

Media Player 3.1's icon and window for an embedded waveform audio object.

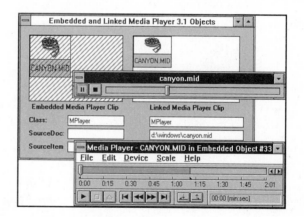

When you double-click the icon for Media Player the sound plays but Media Player's window does not appear. Instead, a control bar with a slider, and pause and stop/start buttons enables you to control playback of the music. When you activate an embedded application with an OLE 2.0-compliant client application, the background of the presentation is hatched with diagonal blue lines. (If the server application is not already running when you double-click the object, OLE activation causes Windows to launch the server application.) The server's application's window, in this case the control bar, receives the focus. To edit a multimedia object, you select the OLE object frame and click the right mouse button to display a floating menu. Choose **E**dit to display Media Player's editing window, shown at the bottom of Figure 14.3.

When you've completed your editing or playing of the data, choose Exit from the File menu or double-click the application control-menu box to close the server application's window and return the focus to the container application's window. If you have modified the data in an OLE 1.0 server application, a message box appears to ask if you want to save the changes. Any changes you make to an embedded object are saved in the container application, while alterations to linked objects are preserved in the updated disk file specified by the link source.

Understanding OLE 2.0

The component object model of OLE 2.0 extends the capabilities of OLE 1.0 with the following new features:

- In-place activation of OLE 2.0 server applications
- Object programmability
- Drag-and-drop transfer of source document objects
- Support for nested objects
- Transforming objects to match container properties
- Object type emulation and conversion
- Less-important but nonetheless useful utility features, including extended object layout, searching and spell-checking of embedded and linked documents, OLE version management, and adaptable links

Each of these features, with the exception of object programmability, is discussed in the sections that follow. Chapter 16, "Using Access as an OLE Automation Client," describes the new object programmability feature of OLE 2.0, how you program objects with Access Basic, and how Visual Basic for Applications (Object Basic) fits into the OLE 2.0 picture. The effect of OLE 2.0 on your registration database file (REG.DAT), the new and improved Insert Object and Paste Special dialog boxes of OLE 2.0, and how Access 2.0 interacts with OLE 2.0 server applications are discussed later in this chapter.

In-Place Activation of OLE 2.0 Server Applications

As mentioned earlier in the chapter, an OLE 1.0 server application opens its own window when you edit or play a linked or embedded object. If the OLE 2.0 application supports in-place activation (also called in-place editing), the behavior of an embedded source document differs from the norm for OLE 1.0. OLE 2.0's in-place activation feature has four defined states:

1. *Inactive.* An inactive object is defined as being neither activated nor selected, neither by itself nor as an element of an extended selection. OLE 2.0 indicates an embedded object with a solid border. Linked objects are identified with a dashed border. The dashed border is displayed as inactive (gray) if the data from a link is not guaranteed to be current, either as the result of specifying a manual link or because an automatic link did not succeed.

2. *Selected.* A selected object is identified by a solid border surrounding the object. An alternate method of identifying a selected object is to add a dotted border inside a solid border. Some applications provide eight sizing handles to scale the dimensions of the object. If a single object is selected, you can choose to edit or play the object, usually by an **O**bject menu choice from the **E**dit menu that displays a submenu with the *verbs* that are applicable to the object. (OLE verbs are discussed in a forthcoming section.)

3. *Active.* An active OLE 2.0 object is identified by a diagonal hatched border. You activate an object by double-clicking the object or choosing **E**dit from the **O**bject menu choice. If the object was created by an OLE 2.0 server application, the server application's menus (except the File and Window menus) are *grafted* onto the container application's window. (Play usually results in simply playing a sound without activating the server application's window.) Grafting means that existing Windows elements are replaced (menu choices) or supplemented (scroll bars) by elements of the server application. (Vertical and horizontal scroll bars and components associated with the scroll bars are called *adornments.*) The server application may replace the container application's toolbars, when applicable, and add floating menus that you access with the right mouse button. You can edit the data in the source document and use the source document's menu choices and toolbars as if those elements were elements of your container application.

4. *Open.* Both OLE 1.0 and 2.0 support the Open verb. When you activate an OLE 1.0 application, the server application opens its own window appropriate to the object class. OLE 2.0 usually requires that you specifically execute the Open verb to open a new window for the server application, most often from a menu choice. If the available presentation area is insufficient for an OLE 2.0 server application or an inappropriate scaling mode is in effect, the server application opens, instead of activating. An Open OLE 2.0 application is an *alternate viewing window* for the object; changes you make in the viewing window are reflected immediately in the presentation of the object in the container document. Therefore, applications don't need to present the message box that asks if you want to save the changes you made when you close the viewing window.

> **NOTE**
>
> OLE 2.0 servers can create *outside-in* and *inside-out* objects. Outside-in objects require the user to double-click the object or select Activate from a menu to activate the object. Inside-out objects are active at all times; they can be edited in place and can remain in the active state when the input focus moves to another control or form. Inside-out objects behave as if they were part of the container document itself, rather than as objects created by another application. Microsoft's criteria for server applications that create inside-out objects is that the server must load in no more than half a second. Thus, *mega-apps* (applications with .EXE files exceeding 1MB, such as Excel 5.0, Word 6.0, and Project 4.0) need not apply for inside-out status.

OLE applications of any type register the verbs that control the actions your container application can apply to the source object and server application. The most common verbs are Edit and Play; however, server applications can register special verbs, such as Slide Show (PowerPoint), Edit Package and Activate Content (Object Packager), and Open (Microsoft Excel 5.0 Chart). OLE server applications register their verbs in the registration database file, REG.DAT, in your \WINDOWS directory. OLE 2.0's REG.DAT entries are discussed later in this chapter.

> **NOTE**
>
> In-place activation applies only to OLE 2.0 source objects that are embedded in your container document. When you double-click a linked source object, the application's window that is appropriate for the object appears as a separate window. Linked source objects don't support the active mode; you open linked source objects rather than activate them.

Drag-and-Drop Creation of Source Document Objects

One of the simplest methods of embedding or linking an OLE object to create a compound document is to select all or a portion of the document and copy the selection to the Clipboard, and then use the Paste **S**pecial choice of the **E**dit menu to embed or link the object in your container document. When you choose Paste **S**pecial instead of **P**aste, a dialog box enables you to select between embedding and linking the object. (**P**aste automatically embeds the object.) OLE 2.0 adds a new way of creating a compound object: dragging a selection from an open source document into the region defined by your container document and dropping it where you want it.

Support for Nested Objects

Figure 14.1, near the beginning of this chapter, illustrated a hierarchy of compound documents that contained other compound documents (nested objects). The note associated with Figure 14.1 mentioned that you can only edit the first level of source documents with OLE 1.0. OLE 2.0 enables you to edit compound documents created with OLE 2.0 server applications that are nested as deeply as you want. This is because OLE 2.0 treats compound documents as containers at each level of embedding or linking. You can open the application that created the source document in your container document, and then open the application that created the source document in the next (deeper) object layer. You return to your own container application by successively choosing Exit from the File menu of the server application that created each of the nested objects.

Transforming Objects to Match Container Properties

When you create an OLE 1.0 compound document in a container application, the properties of the source document, such as the font type used to display data, is determined by the source document. If you link a spreadsheet to a word processing document, the word processing document's font (11-point Palatino, for example) and the font used by the spreadsheet (say 9-point Helvetica) may not be compatible from a stylistic standpoint. If you alter the font of the spreadsheet, the change becomes a permanent part of the source document file. Changing the spreadsheet font may make the spreadsheet's appearance inconsistent with other members of its class.

OLE 2.0 solves this dilemma by providing compound documents with container *property inheritance.* Property inheritance enables the source document to inherit the values of the container's properties, such as the font used for the object's presentation. Thus, the presentation of a spreadsheet object takes on the appearance of the word processing container document and gives the illusion of being an integral part of the container document. OLE 2.0 objects that support property inheritance are called *smart* OLE objects.

Object Type Emulation and Conversion

OLE 2.0 is designed for multiplatform applications that use a variety of operating systems and graphical environments. At present, OLE 2.0 is supported by Windows 3.1, Windows for Workgroups 3.1+, Windows NT, and Apple's System 7. This means that objects you create on PC, Macintosh, and RISC computers for which Windows NT is available need to be operable on each type of computer. It is likely that IBM will update OS/2 version 2.1 to provide OLE 2.0 compliance, so as to retain full compatibility with Windows 3.1 and prepare for Windows 4.0 applications. The objective of OLE 2.0's object-type conversion and emulation is to make objects created by a server that is resident on one platform behave in the same manner when you manipulate the objects with a different server on another type of computer. The two methods by which OLE 2.0 accomplishes this feat are as follows:

- *Type emulation* lets the object temporarily assume the characteristics of another object type, but retain its original object name and data format. Thus, you should be able to use future versions of OS/2 and Lotus 1-2-3 for OS/2 to activate and edit a linked Excel spreadsheet or chart. If you have an OLE 2.0- and POSIX-compatible UNIX OLE 2.0 word processing application, you could use such an application to edit a Word for Windows 6.0 document. OLE 2.0 provides the mechanism for object emulation through a Convert dialog box that offers the Convert As option. If the container application supports type emulation (or type conversion), you open the Convert dialog box from a Convert choice that appears on the same menu as the object's verbs.

- *Type conversion* permanently changes the characteristics of an object when you choose the Convert To option of the Convert dialog box. For example, you use type conversion when you have a new and improved server application to manipulate a specific class of source documents embedded in your container document.

The type of an OLE object is defined by entries in the registration database that equate a file extension and a programmatic identifier (ProgID), such as `.xls=Excel.Sheet.5`. In turn, another entry converts the type designator to a description (long name) of the object class, as in `Excel.Sheet.5=Microsoft Excel 5.0 Sheet`. If you have additional `.xls=ObjectType.Class` entries, these ProgID entries represent your type emulation or conversion options for .XLS files.

Other OLE 2.0 Features

OLE 2.0 offers four additional features that fall into the category of utility functions. The descriptions of the four utility functions follow:

- *Extended object layout* adds formatting features to multi-page source objects in container documents. If, for example, you link a large Excel 5.0 worksheet to a Word for Windows 6.0 container document, you can use extended object layout to cause the column headings, which only appear once in the worksheet, to display at the top of each Word document page that spans the worksheet's presentation.

■ *Source document searching and spell-checking* allows OLE 2.0 utility applications to include source documents within their sphere of influence. Thus, if you embed a Microsoft Word 6.0 document within a Word container document, Word's spelling checker will parse the text of both the container and source document. Similarly, Word 6.0's Find function will search all of the source documents in a container document, no matter how deeply the source documents are nested.

■ *Version management* tests source documents to determine if the source document is an object created by the current version of the source application with which the object type is associated in your REG.DAT file. If, for example, you have a compound document with embedded source documents created by Word 2.0 and you install Word 6.0, the Convert dialog box appears in order to give you the type emulation or conversion option.

■ *Adaptable links* provide automatic updates to source link values when you move a file to which a container document is linked. OLE 1.0 requires that you manually update the source link data if you move a linked file to a different location. The capability of the present implementation of adaptable links is relatively limited; it is likely that you'll have to wait for the release of Windows 4.0 or Cairo for a truly satisfactory solution to the relocated source file problem.

NOTE

When you install Access 2.0, a message box asks if you want to automatically update graphs and charts created by Microsoft Graph 3.0, the OLE 1.0 version supplied with Access 1.x and Word for Windows 2.0. Clicking Yes implements the autoconvert feature of OLE 2.0. If you want to retain your application's compatibility with Access 1.1, you click the No button. Later, you can install the Microsoft Graph AutoConvert applet to turn on the version management feature.

Potential Competition for Microsoft's OLE 2.0 API

Object Linking and Embedding 1.0 immediately became the *de facto* standard for creating Windows compound documents when Microsoft formally introduced OLE 1.0 as one of the new features of Windows 3.1. (Excel 3.0 and PowerPoint 1.0 had

OLE features built in to their .EXE files before OLE 1.0 was announced. Word for Windows 2.0, which predated the release of Windows 3.1, added OLE capability to Windows 3.0 during the installation process.) All suppliers of mainstream Windows applications, particularly publishers of word processing, spreadsheet, and graphics products, had to scramble to add OLE 1.0 client and server compliance to their applications.

> **NOTE**
>
> Access 1.x included the required files, OLECLI.DLL, OLESVR.DLL, and SHELL.DLL, to update Windows 3.0 installations for OLE 1.0. Access 2.0, in both the retail and runtime versions, requires that Windows 3.1 or later be installed before you can install Access. If Windows 3.1+ is not installed, you receive a message that reads "This product requires Microsoft Windows 3.1." Access 2.0 includes the myriad files required to upgrade Windows 3.1+ to OLE 2.0-compliant status. The distribution diskettes for runtime Access 2.0 applications with the Setup Wizard install the OLE 2.0 files on the recipients fixed disk. Table 29.2 and Table 29.3 of Chapter 29, "Distributing Runtime Versions of Your Databases," include the names and descriptions of the OLE 2.0 update files.

Adding OLE 1.0 capabilities to complex applications turned out not to be a simple process. Adding OLE 2.0 compatibility to major productivity applications is an even greater undertaking, although Microsoft has made the process somewhat less daunting for C++ programmers by adding standard 16-bit OLE 2.0 programming objects to Microsoft Application Frameworks 2.5, a component of the Professional Edition of Microsoft Visual C++ 1.5. Support for the 32-bit version of OLE 2.0, which should improve the performance of OLE 2.0 greatly, is expected to be included in the next version of Visual C++.

Many software publishers resented the fact that Microsoft had a head start as a result of having developed the OLE methodology. The envy deepened when the trade press published favorable reviews of OLE 2.0 and made references to OLE 2.0 as a "new object standard." OLE 2.0 is not considered to be an "open standard," because it was developed by Microsoft and not by a committee of computer-industry object pundits and major software publishers. Thus, many of Microsoft's principal competitors have attempted to prevent Microsoft from gaining a similar advantage with OLE 2.0. The following sections describe the major contenders for industry-standard status in the object manipulation realm at the time this edition was written.

> **NOTE**
>
> The terms "open system" and "open standard" appear commonly in the trade press and software publishers' press releases. The exact definition of open systems and standards is elusive; the most common interpretation appears to be "Not developed by Microsoft" and "For use with various flavors of UNIX. " (There are almost as many flavors of UNIX as of ice cream.) Open standards are written by committees and thus are subject to the inevitable publication delays engendered by the bureaucratic process. Microsoft is attempting to redefine "open standard" by its full disclosure of the internally developed Common Object Model's programming environment and by providing tools to developers in order to make adding OLE 2.0 features to Windows applications easier. In both the short and long term, Microsoft's approach appears the more likely to succeed.

OMG's Common Object Request Broker Standard

The Object Management Group (OMG), a consortium principally comprising major players in the UNIX market, has defined an alternate object standard called the Common Object Request Broker Architecture (CORBA). OMG is dominated by Sun Microsystems (which sponsored JOSS, the Joint Object Services Submission, which is expected to be incorporated in CORBA), IBM (promoting their Distributed Systems Object Model, DSOM, based on the Systems Object Model of OS/2), and Hewlett-Packard (with the Distributed Object Management Facility, DOMF, based on the Open Software Foundation's DCE, Distributed Computing Environment). The final version of the CORBA standard for interoperability of objects created by different firms and applications had not been released at the time this edition was written. Applications that conform only to the CORBA standard are unlikely to find a substantial PC market; such applications may be relegated to the much smaller UNIX market because of the question of inter-vendor object communication.

Digital Equipment Corp.'s ObjectBroker Technology

Digital Equipment Corp. defines ObjectBroker as a "cross-platform, object-to-object communications mediator." The purpose of ObjectBroker 2.5, the current version at the time this edition was written, is to enable programming objects to be shared on networks and to be used by applications running under different operating systems. Objects that can traverse networks and are operable on different platforms are called *distributed objects*. Object Broker 2.5 is based on the CORBA standard and currently supports seven different operating systems, including Windows NT, Digital's VMS and Ultrix.

As mentioned earlier in this chapter, Digital and Microsoft have concluded an agreement to incorporate Microsoft's Common Object Model for OLE 2.0 into Digital's ObjectBroker technology. Inter-application communication with distributed objects will be based on a proposed standard called Distributed Computing Environment/ Remote Procedure Call (DCE/RPC). If successful, the Digital-Microsoft enterprise will enable Windows and UNIX applications to be constructed from a set of distributed-object building blocks resident on one or more network servers.

The Proposed OpenDoc Standard

More recently, Apple Computer, Borland International, IBM, Novell, and WordPerfect Corp. joined to promote a new OpenDoc "standard." OpenDoc is proposed as an OLE 2.0 substitute for a variety of computer architectures (PCs, PowerPCs, and Macs) and several operating systems (OS/2 2+, Windows 3.1+, System 7+, and Taligent, with support for UNIX sometime in the future). According to an article by Robin Raskin titled "OLE by Committee?" in the September 14, 1993, issue of *PC Magazine*, OpenDoc has gone through several iterations at Apple, starting out as Jedi, renamed Exemplar, and finally called Amber, before being publicly announced as OpenDoc. The OpenDoc consortium has committed to support OLE 2.0. Because of the ubiquity of Windows 3.1+ in the PC market, it is likely that any widely accepted industry standard will support most, if not all, of the features of OLE 2.0. At the time this edition was written, the final OpenDoc standard had not been published.

Borland's Object Exchange DDE Methodology

Borland announced its Object Exchange (OBEX) engine in late 1994. OBEX is a module that uses DDE to transport objects over networks by means of shared files or via e-mail protocols such as Microsoft Mail, Lotus's Vendor-Independent Messaging (VIM) API, or Novell's Mail Handling Service (MHS). Each application that uses OBEX needs an extension product, called the Exchange Desktop, to make the connection between the application and the OBEX transport engine.

The first commercial implementation of OBEX and the Exchange Desktop appears in Borland's Quattro Pro 5.0 for Windows and Paradox 4.5 for Windows. OBEX is designed for use in the Windows environment only. Lotus, MCI, Novell, and WordPerfect Corp. are reported to be planning for the inclusion of OBEX in future versions of their products. Whether OBEX will gain significant market share, at the expense of OLE 2.0, remains to be seen. In the meantime, Borland was reported in the February 14, 1994 issue of *PCWeek* magazine to be developing a product called OpenPorts, a "superset of OLE 2.0 and OpenDoc technologies," and Object Automater, a Windows application-development environment similar to Visual Basic. Object Automater is likely to use OpenPorts and the ObjectPAL (OPAL) application (scripting) language, which Borland is promoting as an embedded macro language alternative to Visual Basic for Applications.

Installing OLE 2.0 Applications and the Registration Database

When you install an OLE server application, the setup application for the new software adds entries to your registration database (REG.DAT) file. The purpose of REG.DAT is to provide a persistent source of information on the associations between the file type, specified by a unique file extension, and the OLE object type. REG.DAT also provides the information that File Manager needs in order to associate an application with a file extension so that, for example, dragging a text file icon from File manager and dropping it on Print Manger's icon causes Notepad to open and print the file.

> **NOTE**
>
> One of the common ways to add entries for new or updated OLE server applications is to merge (not append) the data for the required entries with the existing REG.DAT file. For example, Excel 5.0 merges EXCEL5.REG with REG.DAT to register Excel's object types. Merging inserts the new entries at the beginning of REG.DAT so that the newest entries are encountered first when an application reads REG.DAT. Access 2.0 adds its entries to REG.DAT from the SETUP.INF file when you install retail Access or a runtime Access application created with the Setup Wizard. Access 2.0 does not include a "MSACC20.REG" file for merging with REG.DAT.

Windows provides the Registration Info Editor Application (RegEdit), which enables you to view and modify entries in REG.DAT. The data in REG.DAT is stored in a binary format that appears primarily as gibberish when loaded into Notepad or a hex editor application. Depending on the version of Windows 3.1 you are using, RegEdit may not appear in a program group. (In such cases, create a new program item for \WINDOWS\REGEDIT.EXE.) When you launch RegEdit with the standard command line, RegEdit's window appears as illustrated in Figure 14.4. The long names (descriptions) of OLE server applications and non-OLE applications appear in the list. You'll find no major differences between the appearance of the standard RegEdit window for OLE 1.0 and OLE 2.0 applications. RegEdit's standard window enables you to edit only the application's command-line parameters that are used by File Manager to display or print a file. File Manager uses DDE to open the application and execute the desired action.

FIGURE 14.4.

RegEdit's standard window.

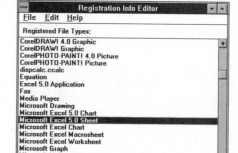

To prevent Windows novices from bollixing REG.DAT entries for OLE server applications, Microsoft requires that you add the /v (verbose) parameter to the command line in order to display the information necessary to register OLE servers and the other OLE objects introduced with OLE 2.0. When you launch RegEdit in verbose mode, RegEdit displays OLE 2.0 REG.DAT data in the format shown in Figure 14.5. Entries in RegEdit have a tree-like hierarchical structure similar to the DOS subdirectory structure. The \ symbol denotes the root of the registration database. Each REG.DAT entry has a path that is specified relative to the root.

FIGURE 14.5.

RegEdit's verbose display after merging Excel 5.0's registration data.

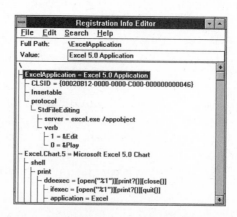

If you have used the verbose mode of RegEdit to view registration entries for OLE 1.0 servers, you will observe major changes to the appearance of REG.DAT in RegEdit after you add an OLE 2.0-compliant application, such as Excel 5.0. You will see new entries, such as CLSID= and Insertable, which are specific to OLE 2.0 applications. The sections that follow describe the entries in the REG.DAT file for both OLE 1.0 and OLE 2.0 server applications. The examples of the structure and syntax of entries in REG.DAT are complete to the extent that the entries are of consequence in Access Basic programming. Some of the more arcane entries have been omitted.

> **WARNING**
>
> Make sure you back up your REG.DAT file regularly. You should make a diskette backup along with copies of your WIN.INI and SYSTEM.INI files before installing any new OLE 2.0-compliant applications. The size and complexity of REG.DAT after adding OLE 2.0 applications make it very difficult to reconstruct REG.DAT if it becomes corrupted. If REG.DAT becomes unreadable for any reason, you are likely to find that you need to reinstall all of your OLE 1.0 and 2.0 applications to restore entries that previously appeared in the Insert Object and Insert New dialog boxes of your OLE 1.0 client and OLE 2:0 container applications.

File and Object Type Association

Traditionally, file extensions have been used to identify the data type of DOS files. Prior to the advent of OLE 1.0 and REG.DAT, Windows 3.0 used entries in the [Extensions] section of WIN.INI file to create associations between file extensions and applications, such as txt=notepad.exe ^.txt, which creates an association between .TXT files and Windows' Notepad. Windows 3.1's OLE 1.0 and enhanced File Manager required more information than was practical to add to the already-overcrowded WIN.INI file. Therefore, Windows 3.1 substitutes registration database for the WIN.INI [Extensions] entries. File-type association entries in REG.DAT are similar to those in WIN.INI. For example, .bmp = PBrush associates bitmap (.bmp) files with Windows' Paintbrush application (PBrush). PBrush is the programmatic identifier (ProgID) for Paintbrush.

As Windows applications have increased in sophistication, using file extensions to specify object types has become a problem. For example, Excel 5.0 .XLS files now contain Workbook, Sheet, Chart, and Excel Basic Module objects. The ProgID value for all file types of prior versions of Excel 5, .XLA, .XLM, .XLL, etc., except .XLC, is Excel.Sheet.5. .XLC files are associated with the Excel.Chart.5 object. Saving all of the objects supported by an application in a single file type, such as Access .MDB database files, makes applications simpler to use. On the other hand, the "single file contains all" approach complicates that portion of your life devoted to protecting your code. If, for example, you link an Excel Sheet object to an Access object frame, the user can activate the object, open a module, and modify the code it contains. You need to take special security precautions in Excel to prevent users from opening your VBA modules, just as protecting the code in your Access Basic modules requires you to implement a secure Access database.

Programmatic ID Registration in REG.DAT

The general syntax and structure used to register OLE 1.0 and 2.0 servers appears in the following example. This is the only information about an OLE server that appears when you execute RegEdit in standard mode. Additional information added to the ProgID section of REG.DAT as a result of registering an OLE 2.0 application appears in bold type. Replaceable items appear in italic type. Items without an equal sign (=) specify either the existence of a specific property of the object or constitute a REG.DAT "subdirectory" name.

```
.ext = ProgId (used to establish the server's ProgID for the file type)
ProgId = MainUserTypeName (long name that appears in standard RegEdit)
    Insertable (indicates insertability into an OLE 2.0 container)
    Protocol
        StdFileEditing (indicates insertability into an OLE 1.0 container)
            Verb
                0 = primary verb (usually &Edit)
                1 = secondary verb(s) (often &Play)
                ...
            Server = d:\path\servname.exe (path to server executable file)
            RequestDataFormats = Native, CF_TEXT, METAFILEPICT, etc.
            SetDataFormats = Native, CF_TEXT, METAFILEPICT, etc.
    CLSID={ClassID value} (object class identifier)
        Ole1Class=OLE 1.0 class name
        ProgId=OLE 1.0 class name
    Shell (used by File manager to open server or print a file)
        Open
            ddeExecute = open instructions with replaceable parameter (%1)
                Application = DDEServiceName
                Topic = DDETopicName (usually "system")
            Command = d:\path\servname.exe [parameter(s)]
        Print
            ddeExecute = open, print, and close instructions (with %1)
                Application = DDEServiceName
                Topic = DDETopicName (usually "system")
```

Insertable appears only in entries for OLE 2.0 servers; if **Insertable** is present, the *MainUserTypeName* value appears in the Insert New dialog boxes of OLE 2.0 applications. A **CLSID** (object class identifier) is required for any server that is capable of inserting objects into OLE 2.0 container documents. The StdFileEditing entry is required in order for *MainUserTypeName* to appear in an OLE 1.0 client application's Insert Object dialog box. Therefore, both OLE 1.0 and OLE 2.0 servers require StdFileEditing and **CLSID** entries. **Ole1Class** and **ProgID** (under **CLSID**) are used when OLE 1.0 objects are inserted into OLE 2.0 container documents; thus, these entries are made for OLE 2.0 servers. (One or both of the entries appear the first time you insert an OLE 1.0 object into an OLE 2.0 container document.) The **Application** and **Topic** information provides File Manager with explicit DDE service (application) name and topic name information for the application.

Many of the values in the preceding example appear in RegEdit's Modify File Type dialog box, which you open with the **M**odify File Type choice from the **E**dit menu when RegEdit is running in standard mode. The Modify File Type dialog box displaying the DDE execute commands required to print an Excel 5.0 worksheet from File Manager is shown in Figure 14.6. You can edit the values that appear in text boxes, but it is seldom necessary to do so.

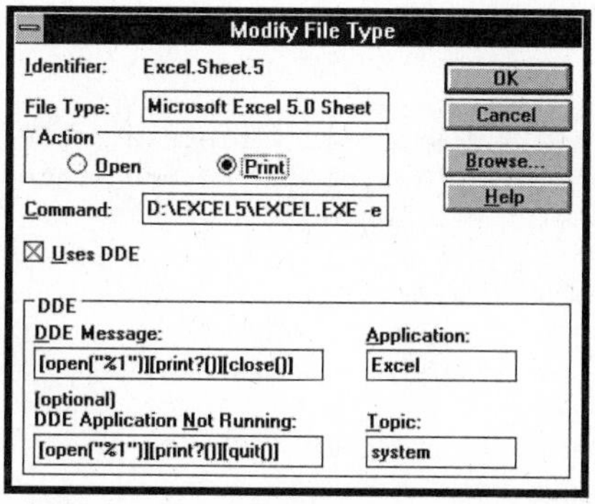

FIGURE 14.6.

RegEdit's standard-mode Modify File Type dialog.

Hidden \CLSID Information for OLE 2.0 Servers in REG.DAT

The *real* registration data needed by OLE 2.0 applications is hidden from casual users of RegEdit. OLE 2.0-compliant server applications provide the OLE 2.0 registration data in the \CLSID subdirectory that is identified by the value of the CLSID value established by the unique **CLSID={ClassID value}** entry shown in the example of the preceding section. The user never sees ClassID values in the course of OLE 2.0 operations. Figure 14.7 illustrates the \CLSID entry for an Excel 5.0 Sheet (worksheet) object. The ClassID value for an Excel 5.0 Sheet object is highlighted in Figure 14.7. ClassID values conform to the Open Software Foundation (OSF) DCE standard; CLSIDs are displayed in RegEdit as groups of 4, 8, or 12 hexadecimal characters separated by hyphens.

FIGURE 14.7.

*The \CLSID data
for an Excel 5.0
worksheet object.*

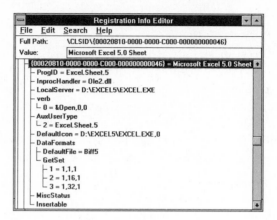

The syntax of the \CLSID entries that appear in RegEdit's verbose mode and that you are likely to find for the majority of OLE 2.0 servers is shown in the following example. All of these entries are new with OLE 2.0, so bold emphasis is not used in this example.

```
CLSID = MainUserTypeName
    ProgID = ProgID value
    LocalServer = d:\path\servname.exe (same as OLE 1.0's Server = )
    InprocServer = d:\path\dllname.exe (uncommon for insertable objects)
    InprocHandler = d:\path\dllname.exe (usually Ole2.dll)
    Verb
      -3 = verb to hide window (usually Hide, n, n)
      -2 = verb to open in separate window (usually Open, n, n)
      -1 = verb to open in preferred state (usually Show, n, n)
       0 = primary verb (usually &Edit, appears on menu)
       1 = secondary verb(s) (usually &Play, also on menu)
    AuxUserType
       2 = ShortName (often the same as the ProgID value)
       3 = LongName (an alternate name for the application or class)
    DataFormats
       DefaultFile = format (Biff5 for Excel 5.0)
       GetSet (similar to RequestDataFormats and GetDataFormats)
          0 = metafile formats supported
          1 = Excel (BIFF) formats supported
          2 = Rich text format (RTF) formats supported
    MiscStatus (use default status for aspects unless indicated below)
    Insertable (presence causes class to appear in OLE 2.0 Insert Object
    ➥dialogs)
    TreatAs = {CLSID} (CLSID of class for emulation)
    AutoConvertTo = {CLSID} (CLSID of class for automatic conversion)
    Conversion (provides information for the Convert options dialog)
       Readable
          Main = format(s)
       Readwritable
```

```
     Main = format(s)
DefaultIcon = d:\path\servname.exe, IconIndex (icon to display)
```

The EXCEL5.REG file that creates the preceding entries is a readable text file in which each entry is preceded with `HKEY_CLASSES_ROOT`. An equal sign divides the REG.DAT path from the value. You can use Windows' Notepad to display the entries in XLAPP.REG. A typical entry in XLAPP.REG is: `HKEY_CLASSES_ROOT\CLSID\{00020812-0000-0000-C000-000000000046}` = Excel 5.0 `Application`, which corresponds to the entry in the first line of the preceding REG.DAT syntax example.

Hidden \CLSID Entries for OLE 2.0 Member Functions

When you install Access 2.0, Excel 5.0, or another OLE 2.0-compliant application, the setup process also merges OLE2.REG with REG.DAT. OLE2.REG registers the interface objects (member functions beginning with the letter "I" contained in the OLE 2.0 DLLs). A typical entry from OLE2.REG is `HKEY_CLASSES_ROOT\Interface\{00020400-0000-0000-C000-000000000046}` = `IDispatch`, which registers the `IDispatch` member function. Figure 14.8 illustrates the appearance of a few of the entries that OLE2.REG creates when it is merged with your REG.DAT file. Microsoft has assigned each of the interface objects a unique CLSID value. These interface objects need to be registered, because your OLE 2.0 container and server applications use these objects as intermediaries when you create or edit container documents or use OLE Automation features in your applications.

FIGURE 14.8.

A few of the OLE 2.0 interface objects registered by OLE2.REG.

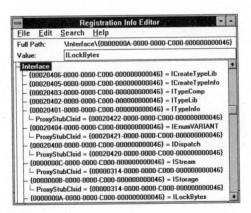

Interface object entries added to your REG.DAT file for OLE 2.0 member functions fall into two basic categories:

■ OLE 2.0 classes for creating and manipulating compound documents (all of the entries whose values begin with "I" that are not included in the OLE

Automation classes). Most of these functions are incorporated into OLE2.DLL.

■ OLE Automation classes: `IDispatch`, `IEnumVARIANT`, `ITypeInfo`, `ITypeLib`, `ITypeComp`, `ICreateTypeInfo`, and `ICreateTypeLib`. These interface objects, which are components of OLE2DISP.DLL and TYPELIB.DLL, provide the mechanism to expose and manipulate the objects of OLE Automation applications.

You'll see some of the member functions of the `IDispatch` object class when you use Excel 5.0's or the Microsoft Office Developer's Kit's Object Browser to display a list of the objects in Access 2.0's STDOLE.TLB in Chapter 16, "Using Access as an OLE Automation Client."

Using Access 2.0's Object Frames to Contain OLE 2.0 Objects

The process of embedding or linking OLE 2.0 objects with Access 2.0's bound or unbound object frames does not differ dramatically from the methods you use with OLE 1.0 server applications. OLE 2.0 is backward-compatible with OLE 1.0 applications. Access does not have a single, native document format, such as a worksheet (BIFF5 format) or a word-processing document (Word format), so Access 2.0 is not easily adaptable to OLE 2.0 server status.

> **NOTE**
>
> You need to use Microsoft's Windows 3.1 or Apple Computer's System 7 to take advantage of the features of OLE 2.0, including in-place activation, OLE Automation, and Object Basic. For PCs, you need to load SHARE.EXE before running Windows, unless you are using Windows for Workgroups 3.1+ in 386 enhanced mode. Windows for Workgroups loads VSHARE.386 when running in 386 enhanced mode; VSHARE.386 takes the place of the DOS TSR, SHARE.EXE, and disables SHARE.EXE if it is loaded. Access 2.0 installs SHARE.EXE and modifies your AUTOEXEC.BAT file to load SHARE.EXE with 500 locks (`SHARE.EXE /L:500`) if the setup application does not detect the presence of Windows for Workgroups.

The following sections describe the properties and the one event of Access 2.0 object frames that are specific to OLE 2.0 operations, and then show you how to create an OLE container with an unbound object frame. Properties, methods, and events of the OLE container control that are shared with the majority of other Access 2.0 control objects, such as `GotFocus`, `LostFocus`, `Click`, and `DblClick`, are not discussed in this chapter. There is only one event, `Updated`, that is unique to the OLE container object.

Properties of the OLE 2.0 Container Control

Table 14.1 lists each OLE-related property of the OLE control that appears in the Properties window of bound and unbound object frames, and describes the purpose of the property. The first four properties are the primary properties you need to set in order to create an OLE object, and are listed in the order in which the properties typically would be assigned values in a Access Basic procedure. The remaining properties, beginning with `AutoActivate`, are optional and are listed in alphabetical order. Unless otherwise indicated, all properties listed in Table 14.1 are read-write in design and run modes.

Table 14.1. OLE-Related Properties of Access 2.0 object frames.

Property Name	Purpose
Class	The value of ProgID that identifies the application that has created an existing object or that is to create a new, empty object. Setting the `Class` value overrides file-extension associations established in REG.DAT.
SourceDoc	The well-formed path and *FILENAME.EXT* of the file that contains existing source data for a linked or embedded object. Leave the `SourceDoc` property empty to open an empty object, such as a blank Excel worksheet.
SourceItem	Determines the portion of the data within the source file to link. Leave `SourceItem` empty if you want to link the entire contents of the file or if you embed the object.
Action	Determines the operation that the OLE controls. Table 14.2 lists the valid integer values that specify the 14 actions that you currently can perform with the OLE control. The default value is 0, `OLE_CREATE_EMBED`. You

continues

Table 14.1. continued

Property Name	Purpose
	can only set the value of the Action property with Access Basic code.
AutoActivate	Specifies if the source document is to be activated manually (by setting the value of the Action property to 7, OLE_ACTIVATE), automatically (when the OLE control receives the focus), or by double-clicking.
AutoVerbMenu	**True** to specify that right-clicking on the surface of the object in the inactive state displays a pop-up menu with the list of verbs applicable to the object; **False** for no menu. The default value is **True**.
DisplayType	Determines if the presentation of an OLE object is the object's data (**False**) or an icon representing the application (**True**). The default value is **False**.
ObjectVerbsCount	The number of verbs supported by the OLE object, used to iterate the ObjectVerbs collection.
ObjectVerbs	A collection of **Integer** values that correspond to verbs supported by the OLE object. (See the Verbs entry in Table 14.3.)
OleTypeAllowed	Specifies whether you can link (0), embed (1), or either link or embed (2) an OLE source object with the control. The default value is 2.
SizeMode	Determines if the presentation of the object is to be clipped (0) or stretched (1), or if the OLE control is to be autosized to fit the image (2). The effect of applying these attributes is similar to their effect on Image objects.
UpdateOptions	Determines if the OLE object is updated automatically whenever the value of the data changes (0), updated only when updated data is saved to a file (1, called *frozen*, 1), or manually (2, by setting the value of the Action property to 6, OLE_UPDATE).
Verb	Activates the object in its default mode (0), activates the object for editing (-1), opens the object in an alternate viewing window (-2), hides the server applications window (-3). See Table 14.3 for additional values of the Verb property.

> **NOTE**
>
> Access 2.0 does not support many of the properties of OLE objects whose values are accessible to Visual Basic programmers using the MSOLE2.VBX custom control. For example, Access 2.0 does not directly support the `Data` property of an object frame, nor are the `HostName` or `MiscFlags` properties accessible.

You can determine the operation that the OLE control is to perform when you use Access Basic code to manipulate an OLE container (object frame) by setting the value of its `Action` property. Table 14.2 lists the global constant name, value and purpose of each action that the OLE control can perform. CONSTANT.TXT in the \ACCESS directory contains the declarations for the `OLE_*` symbolic global constants; you need to import these constants into the Declarations section of an Access Basic module to use the symbols, rather than integers, to evaluate or set the values of properties of object frames with code. Where the name is missing in the Action Constant column, the value is not valid for Access 2.0.

Table 14.2. Global constant name, value, and purpose of valid values of the Action property.

Action Constant	Value	Purpose
OLE_CREATE_EMBED	0	Creates an embedded OLE object (same as `OLE_CREATE_NEW` of the OLE 1.0 control). Requires a value for the `Class` property and `OleTypeAllowed` = 1 (embedded) or 2 (either embedded or linked).
OLE_CREATE_LINK	1	Creates a linked OLE object (same as `OLE_CREATE_FROM_FILE` of the OLE 1.0 control). Requires a value for the `SourceDoc` property and `OleTypeAllowed` = 1 (embedded) or 2 (either embedded or linked).
	2	Reserved.
	3	Reserved.
OLE_COPY	4	Copies the OLE object to the Clipboard.

continues

Table 14.2. continued

Action Constant	Value	Purpose
OLE_PASTE	5	Copies data from the Clipboard to the OLE object. If the operation was not successful, the OleType property is set to 3.
OLE_UPDATE	6	Updates the OLE object with the current source data.
OLE_ACTIVATE	7	Activates the OLE object for editing (the default) or in one of the modes specified by the previously set non-zero values of the Verb property shown in Table 14.3.
	8	Reserved.
OLE_CLOSE	9	Closes an embedded object and terminates the association with the server application. (Does not apply to linked objects.)
OLE_DELETE	10	Deletes the OLE object and frees resources consumed by the object. (Same effect as closing the form on which the OLE control is located.)
	11	Not used. In Visual Basic 3.0, saves the object's data and linkage information to a file.
	12	Not used. In Visual Basic 3.0, creates an OLE object from data in an open .OLE file.
	13	Reserved (possibly due to superstition).
OLE_INSERT_OBJ_DLG	14	Opens the Insert Object dialog box to enable the user to insert an object of his or her choice.
OLE_PASTE_SPECIAL_DLG	15	Opens the Paste Special dialog box that enables the user to paste a previously copied object from the Clipboard.
	16	Reserved.
OLE_FETCH_VERBS	17	Updates the list of verbs that are supported by the object. (Verbs with values < 0 may not appear in the list.)

Action Constant	Value	Purpose
	18	Not used. In Visual Basic 3.0, saves the object to an .OLE file in OLE 1.0 format.

Table 14.3 lists the global constant names, the values, and the effects of applying the values to the `AutoActivate`, `DisplayType`, `MiscFlags`, `OLETypeAllowed`, `SizeMode`, `UpdateOptions`, and `Verb` properties.

Table 14.3. Global constants and values for other properties of OLE objects.

Property and Constant	Value	Effect
AutoActivate		
OLE_ACTIVATE_MANUAL	0	Requires `Action = 7` (`OLE_ACTIVATE`) to activate the object.
OLE_ACTIVATE_GETFOCUS	1	Object activates when the OLE control receives the focus. (Applies only to OLE servers that support inside-out activation. See note that follows.)
OLE_ACTIVATE_DOUBLECLICK	2	User activates object with a double-click.
DisplayType		
OLE_DISPLAY_CONTENT	0	Presentation of the object appears as the default mode of the server.
OLE_DISPLAY_ICON	1	The presentation is an icon representing the server.
OLETypeAllowed		
OLE_LINKED	0	Only linked objects are allowed.
OLE_EMBEDDED	1	Only embedded objects are allowed.
OLE_EITHER	2	Either linked or embedded objects are allowed.
SizeMode		
OLE_SIZE_CLIP	0	Elements of the object beyond the confines of the OLE control do not appear.

continues

Table 14.3. continued

Property and Constant	Value	Effect
OLE_SIZE_STRETCH	1	The presentation of the object is scaled to fit the OLE control's dimensions.
OLE_SIZE_AUTOSIZE	2	The dimensions of the OLE control are altered to fit the size of the object, if not limited by the size of the form.
UpdateOptions		
OLE_AUTOMATIC	0	Presentation of object is updated whenever data changes.
OLE_FROZEN	1	Updates to presentation occur only when changed source data is saved to a file.
OLE_MANUAL	2	Updates occur only when Action = 6.
Verb		
VERB_PRIMARY	0	The default verb for the object (usually &Edit).
VERB_SHOW	-1	Activates the object for editing.
VERB_OPEN	-2	Opens the server's window as a secondary viewing window.
VERB_HIDE	-3	Hides the server's window.
VERB_INPLACEUIACTIVATE	-4	See note that follows.
VERB_INPLACEACTIVATE	-5	See note that follows.

NOTE

The VERB_INPLACEUIACTIVATE and VERB_INPLACEACTIVATE values apply only to the Verb property of objects that support *inside-out* activation. The difference between conventional outside-in and the new inside-out activation technique is described in the section called "In-Place Activation of

Server Applications," earlier in this chapter. If you have an inside-out server, you can use either of the two values (-4 or -5) for the Verb property.

If the object has floating toolbars or other pop-up paraphernalia, you can specify VERB_INPLACEUIACTIVATE to make the toolbars automatically appear when the object appears. More than one visible object can have VERB_INPLACEACTIVATE as the value of the Verb property, but only one object can use the VERB_INPLACEUIACTIVATE value at a time. Set the value of the Verb property of an OLE object to either of the preceding values, and then set the value of the Action property to OLE_ACTIVATE to change to inside-out activation. Setting the value of the object's AutoActivate property to OLE_ACTIVATE_GETFOCUS, has the same effect as using the OLE_ACTIVATE action with the VERB_INPLACEUIACTIVATE Verb property value.

The OnUpdated Event of Object Frame Controls

The OnUpdated event is triggered whenever the data or the status of the source object of an OLE container control changes. The syntax of the event-handling subprocedure for the OnUpdated event of object frame controls is

Sub *ControlName*_Updated (int*TypeOfChange*)

The required int*TypeOfChange* parameter (Access supplies the argument name Code) accepts one of the four values shown in Table 14.4 to indicate whether a change to the OLE data or to the status of the OLE object triggered the Updated event.

Table 14.4. The values of the parameter of the OnUpdated event handler.

Constant	Value	Purpose
OLE_CHANGED	0	Indicates that a change to the OLE data triggered the event.
OLE_SAVED	1	Indicates that the OLE data was saved to a file by the application that created the object.
OLE_CLOSED	2	Indicates that the OLE server that created the application has closed.
OLE_RENAMED	3	Indicates that the name of the file containing linked OLE data has changed.

> **NOTE**
>
> The four global symbolic constants listed in Table 14.4 were not included in the version of the CONSTANT.TXT file at the time this chapter was written. If your CONSTANT.TXT file does not include these entries and you want to use the symbol names rather than Integer values, add the constants of Table 14.4 to the declarations section of the module that contains the other OLE constants imported from CONSTANT.TXT.

The OLE 2.0 Common Dialog Boxes

When you add an OLE 2.0 container control to a form in design mode, the Insert Object dialog box shown in Figure 14.9 appears. OLE 2.0 includes a set of standard dialog boxes, similar in concept to the common dialog boxes of Windows 3.1, for inserting, converting, and emulating objects. The standard Insert Object dialog box gives you the option of creating a new (empty) embedded object or an object linked to a file.

To open the Insert Object dialog box, create a new unbound form and choose Insert Object from Access 2.0's Edit menu. You can choose any of the OLE 1.0 or OLE 2.0 server applications that are registered in REG.DAT from the Object Type list box. The Object Type list box displays the *MainUserTypeName* values corresponding to the *ProgID* entries in REG.DAT.

FIGURE 14.9.

The standard OLE 2.0 Insert Object dialog box.

If you choose to create a new embedded object, the default design-mode presentation of the object type you chose appears. When you click the right mouse button, a floating menu shows the choices available to you at this point in the creation of your

OLE 2 container object. Figure 14.10 shows an empty Excel 5.0 Sheet object embedded in an unbound object frame with the floating menu activated. Selecting either **E**dit or **O**pen from the Spreadsheet **O**bject menu choice opens Excel 5.0 in its own window and enables you to add data to the Sheet object, if you wish. Choosing **C**hange to Picture breaks the link with the OLE Server, leaving you with a static (in this case, empty) presentation.

FIGURE 14.10.

An embedded Excel 5.0 worksheet in design mode with the floating menu for a Spreadsheet Object activated.

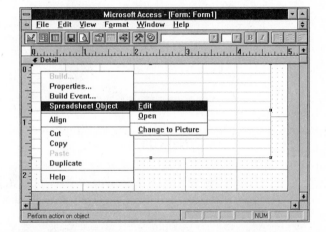

> **NOTE**
>
> Although Access refers to the embedded object as a Spreadsheet object, Excel 5.0 assigns the name Sheet to worksheet objects. The object-name terminology of Excel 5.0 and other OLE 2.0 server applications that expose objects for manipulation by OLE Automation is used in this and the remaining chapters of this book.

By default, the value of the Enabled property of Access object frames is **False** and the value of the Locked property is **True**. To try in-place activation of your empty Excel 5.0 Sheet object, set the Enabled property of the object frame to **True** and the Locked property to **False**. Change to run mode and double-click the surface of the empty spreadsheet presentation to activate Excel 5.0 in place. Excel's menu replaces most of the menu bars of Access 2.0. Excel's toolbars become floating toolbars. If you select a cell and then click the right mouse button, Excel's floating menu appears, as shown in Figure 14.11. Clicking the surface of the form outside of the active area of the object frame deactivates the object.

FIGURE 14.11.

In-place activation of the empty Excel 5.0 worksheet.

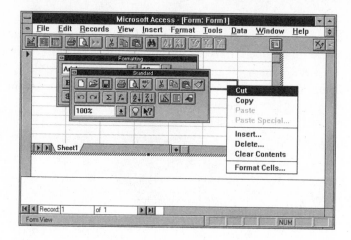

You can use the Paste **S**pecial choice of the **E**dit menu to insert an object whose data you previously pasted to the Clipboard. In this case, you must open the OLE server application independently of Access, select the data you want to embed in or link to the new object frame, and then copy the data to the Clipboard. Return to Access and choose Paste **S**pecial from the **E**dit menu to display the standard OLE 2.0 Paste Special dialog box. (See Figure 14.12.) Make sure that the Paste option button is selected, because you cannot activate a linked OLE 2.0 object in place. Click the OK button to insert an unbound object frame containing the embedded data in your form.

FIGURE 14.12.

The standard OLE 2.0 Paste Special dialog box for an Excel 5.0 Sheet object.

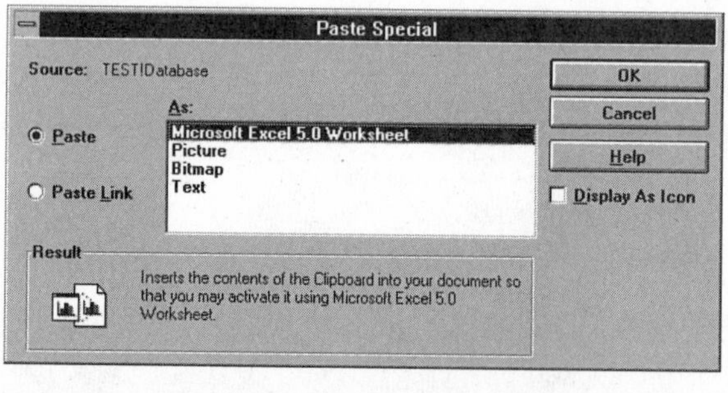

> **NOTE**
>
> The processes for creating new unbound object frames described in this section also apply to objects created by OLE 1.0 servers. The principal distinction between objects created by OLE 1.0 and OLE 2.0 servers is that you cannot activate OLE 1.0 objects in place. The other differences, discussed early in this chapter, also apply, but in-place activation is the primary

distinction between embedded OLE 1.0 and OLE 2.0 objects. The behavior of linked OLE 2.0 objects is essentially identical to that of embedded or linked OLE 1.0 objects.

Set the Enabled property to **True** and the Locked property to **False**, and then change to run mode. The data appears in the default presentation for Sheet objects. Double-click the presentation to activate Excel 5.0 in place. (See Figure 14.13.)

FIGURE 14.13.

An Excel 5.0 Sheet object activated in place with all its adornments visible.

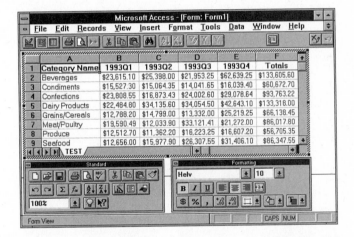

NOTE

The position of the object frame in the form and other minor modifications have been made to the object frame in design mode to assure that all of the adornments of the object appear in or around the object frame. Dealing with adornments of OLE 2.0 objects activated in place is one of the subjects of the next chapter, "Embedding and Linking Objects with OLE."

15

Embedding and Linking Objects with OLE

This chapter describes how to use OLE 2.0 to embed and link graphic images and other objects to your Access applications. The chapter begins with an explanation of how Access stores OLE data in table fields of the OLE Object field-data type and in unbound object frames. Later in the chapter, you are shown the specific steps to take to embed and link graphic images and multimedia objects in your Access tables, forms, and reports.

Understanding How Access Stores OLE Objects

The OLE 2.01 specification fully defines the structure of the data that constitutes an object that complies with the Component Object Model (COM). Objects created with OLE 1.0 servers do not comply with the Component Object Model, but OLE 2.0 is backwardly-compatible with OLE 1.0. As mentioned in the previous chapter, OLE 2.0 includes the capability to convert many types of OLE 1.0 objects into OLE 2.0's COM format. A simplified definition of any OLE object is an ordered set of data elements that provides at least the following information:

- The name of the OLE server application that created the object, specified by its programmatic identifier. As an example, the programmatic identifier (ProgID) of Windows Paintbrush is PBrush. The main user-type name, the executable file name, and the path to the OLE server are specified by entries for the server in the registration database, REG.DAT. Paintbrush's main user-type name is Paintbrush Picture and is used by Access to identify any object created by Paintbrush; for example, the main user-type name appears in the data cells of OLE Object fields of Access tables. OLE server entries in REG.DAT are discussed in the preceding chapter.

- The well-formed path and file name of the file containing the OLE data, if the OLE object is linked rather than embedded. This information appears as the value of the SourceDoc property of an object frame that displays a linked object.

- The specification of the subset of the original object's data that is included in the OLE object, if the entire object is not linked or embedded. For objects that define ranges by methods such as Microsoft Excel's R1C1...R#C# or Word's bookmarks, the range name appears as the value of the SourceItem property of an object frame for both embedded and linked objects.

- The type of data, expressed as one of the standard clipboard formats. Text, bitmap, Windows metafile, and native are four of the most common clipboard formats. Native designates a format that is specific to the application, such as BIFF5 for Excel 5.0.

■ The presentation style of the object, which determines how the object appears in the inactive state in an object frame. For example, the presentation of an Excel worksheet object is a grid that displays the content of the Sheet object's cells. In the case of bitmaps and metafiles, the presentation consists of the object's data. The presentation of a bitmap is the bitmap contained within a metafile. If you link or embed a part of a bitmap or metafile graphic, the entire object is included, but only the selected area of the image appears. (The presentation metafile clips the image.) The presentation of video and animation objects is the first frame of the data. Some objects that cannot be displayed, such as waveform audio and MIDI files, use the OLE server application's icon as their presentation.

■ The data for the object, if the object is embedded. The data for linked metafile and bitmap objects is included, because the data is necessary to create the presentation. The issue of the surprisingly large size of Access databases that contain linked graphic objects is discussed later in this chapter. Unlike Visual Basic 3.0, Access does not provide direct access to the object's data with a Data property for object frames.

■ The status of linked objects relating to the concurrency of the presentation, similar to a "dirty" flag. If the linked source data was changed by another application after the presentation was created, the presentation may no longer be valid. The UpdateOptions property determines if the presentation is updated automatically when the source data changes, or you need to use the **L**inks choice of the **E**dit menu to update the presentation manually.

The OLE 2.01 specification defines OLE 2.0 objects by sets of programming interfaces to the objects that are of interest primarily to C and C++ programmers. The Uniform Data Transfer interfaces, IDataObject, IViewObject, and IDataAdviseHolder, provide OLE 2.0-compliant applications such as Access 2.0 with access to the data elements of an OLE 2.0 object. OLE 2.0 also provides a set of Structured Storage Interfaces that enable you to store OLE objects in and read OLE objects from individual files. As noted in the preceding chapter, Access 2.0 does not support this feature of OLE 2.0. The storage of OLE objects in Access objects is the subject of the next two sections.

> **NOTE**
>
> You can manipulate OLE data in Access as a subtype 8 **Variant** (**String**) variable using the **GetChunk** and **AppendChunk** methods. You need a comprehensive knowledge of the structure of the OLE data in order to modify OLE

data. It is possible to modify the file name and/or location of linked OLE data with Access Basic code by searching for the first occurrence of the : \ combination in the OLE data. You can parse the OLE data at this point to substitute a new path or file name.

Access bound and unbound object frames are used to display the presentation of OLE objects and to activate the objects for editing. Bound and unbound object frames have an almost identical collection of properties and events. The primary difference is that bound object frames have a `ControlSource` property and unbound object frames do not. The following two sections briefly describe how OLE objects are stored in Access 2.0 containers and displayed in bound or unbound object frames.

Storing OLE Objects in Tables

Newer versions of client-server and DOS database-management systems provide a BLOB (Binary Large OBject) data type that can accommodate any type of non-traditional data, ranging from bitmap images to formatted text generated by word-processing applications. Paradox 4.0 and Paradox for Windows go one step further and provide specific field-data types for bitmaps, formatted text, and other unclassi-fied data (BLOBs.) Microsoft and Sybase SQL Server use the `image` field-data type to store BLOB data.

Access puts all its special data-type eggs in the OLE basket. Therefore, as a devel-oper, you need to become an Access expert and an OLE 2.0 guru at the same time. You may need to gain some computer graphic-arts skills in the process so that you can convert your client's artwork to a file format and a design that is compatible with Access. Access adds its own "wrapper" around OLE objects stored in tables. The wrapper supplies the main user-type name that appears in the data cells of fields of the OLE Object type and tests the object's data integrity by comparing a stored checksum with a checksum calculated from the object's data. Chapter 25, "Stretch-ing the Limits of Access," describes how you can store non-OLE data, such as data obtained directly from graphics files, in OLE Object fields of Access tables. When you use an OLE Object field to store non-OLE objects, "Invalid Object" replaces the main user-type name in the data cells.

NOTE

If you use Visual Basic 3.0 to store OLE data in an OLE Object field of an Access database, the Access OLE wrapper is missing. Thus, Access considers the object to be invalid. You can convert Visual Basic 3.0 OLE objects to Access's format using a Visual Basic 3.0 application, OLEACCDM.MAK, derived by Marshall Kosten from the OLE2DEMO.MAK application included as one of the sample applications with Visual Basic 3.0. You can download Mr. Kosten's application from Library 10 of the MSBASIC forum on CompuServe as OLEACC.ZIP. The author's *Database Developer's Guide with Visual Basic 3.0* (Sams Publishing, 1994, ISBN 0-672-30440-6) includes an expanded version of Mr. Kosten's application, MSA2VB3.MAK, together with a description of the Access OLE wrapper. Both OLEACCDM.MAK and MSA2VB3.MAK are compatible with Access 2.0 .MDB files when you use the Access 2.0 Compatibility Layer for Visual Basic 3.0 that is included in the Access Developer's Toolkit (ADT).

NOTE

Access 2.0 enables you to store and retrieve OLE objects in Access's OLE Object format in SQL Server 4.2's `image` fields using the SQL Server ODBC driver. For example, you can export the Employees and Categories tables of NWIND.MDB to an SQL Server database, then attach the tables to NWIND.MDB and change the value of the `RecordSource` property of the Employees form to `dbo_Employees` to display the photos. You receive an error indication in the Employee ID, First Name, and Last Name text boxes of the Employees form because the SQL Server driver replaces spaces in field names with underscores. Chapter 20, "Front-Ending Client-Server Databases," provides additional information on using the ODBC API and SQL Server with Access 2.0.

At the time this edition was written, Access's bound object frame was the only container in which you could display (or play) OLE Objects contained in Access tables. It is likely, however, that many of the publishers of Visual Basic custom controls for image editing will convert their .VBXs to OLE Custom Controls. Image editing controls, such as Media Architect's ImageKnife/VBX, enable you to use many different graphics file formats and provide a wide range of image editing capabilities.

> **NOTE**
>
> Technically, Access tables that contain OLE Object fields are not OLE 2.0 containers or compound documents. A compound document must display one of the two presentations offered by OLE objects: a visual representation of the object, or the icon of the object's server. Instead, Access displays the main user-type name. Although you can activate the object's server by double-clicking the data cell, in-place activation does not occur with embedded OLE 2.0 objects.

Storing Objects in Forms and Reports

Unbound object frames are containers for OLE objects whose data is not stored OLE data in OLE Object fields of tables. The OLE data for unbound object frames is stored with the other data that defines the form and its controls in fields of the Long Binary Data type of the MSysObjects table. All of the operations that are valid for inserting objects into table fields of the OLE Object field data type also are valid for OLE objects stored in unbound object frames. Unbound object frames are used primarily for displaying static graphic images, and charts and graphs created by Microsoft Graph 5.0 (MSGraph5).

> **NOTE**
>
> Visual Basic 3.0 defines field type 11 as the Long Binary Data type, but Access defines field type 11 as OLE Object. Binary (type 8) and Long Binary Data fields are used only in system files in Access, and the content of these fields in system fields is meaningful only to internal operations of Access.

OLE Custom Controls (OCXs) are a special type of OLE 2.0 object that support OLE Automation (OA). Only unbound object frames can be used as containers for OCXs. OCXs add their own collection of properties to the default properties of unbound object frames that appear in the Properties window, and they also possess their own sets of methods and events that you manipulate with OA statements in Access Basic code. OCXs are described in Chapter 18, "Introducing OLE 2.0 Custom Controls."

Displaying Graphic Images in Object Frames

As mentioned earlier in this chapter, one of the primary applications for OLE objects in Access is to display graphic images, primarily of the bitmapped type. Object frames also can display vector-based images created by drawing, illustration, and charting applications. The sections that follow describe how Access displays graphic images in bound and unbound object frames, and how you can add graphics capability to your Access 2.0 applications.

How Access Displays Graphic Images

The Northwind Traders sample database includes examples of OLE objects embedded in the OLE Object field of tables (Employees and Categories) as well as in forms (Main Switchboard and Forms Switchboard) and reports (the first page of Catalog). Figure 15.1 shows the Employees form that uses a bound object frame control to display a color snapshot of each employee. In this case, the form is the container document, because the table's OLE Object field simply stores the OLE data.

FIGURE 15.1.

A bitmap displayed in a form's bound object frame.

Illustrations that constitute decorative components of forms and reports are displayed in unbound object frames. Images in unbound object frames are linked or embedded to the form or report in which they appear. The Main Switchboard form, shown in Figure 15.2, includes three unbound object frames with bitmap images: the lighthouse logo, the Northwind Traders stylized type, and the textured background surrounding the command buttons. These OLE objects have been converted to static bitmaps that no longer are linked to the OLE server that supplied the objects. When you display the Data Properties of static bitmap objects in design mode, the value of the OLEClass property is Picture (Device-Independent Bitmap) (DIB) and the value of the Class property is StaticDib, one of the standard Clipboard data formats. (See

Figure 15.3.) If you attempt to activate the unbound object frame that contains a DIB, you receive a message that reads "This Picture does not support the attempted operation."

FIGURE 15.2.

Sixteen-color bitmapped images in three unbound object frames.

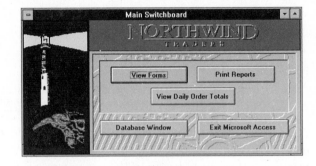

FIGURE 15.3.

Properties of an OLE object converted to a static bitmap.

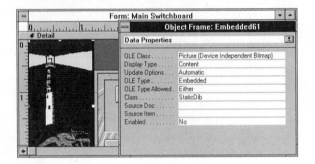

You can add illustrations to your reports as easily as you can add them to forms. Figure 15.4 shows a black-and-white version of the Northwind Logo embedded in an unbound object frame (selected) on the first page (Report Header section) of the Northwind Traders Catalog report. The OLEClass property value is the main user-type name (Microsoft Drawing) and the Class property is the programmatic identifier of the OLE object (MSDraw). The RowSourceType, RowSource, and ColumnCount properties of the unbound object frame are used to pass information to specific OLE servers, usually MSGraph5, launched by the graph tool or the Graph Wizard. The LinkChildFields and LinkMasterFields properties are used to link the content of unbound object frames that appear on subforms.

FIGURE 15.4.

A monochrome bitmap displayed in a report's unbound object frame.

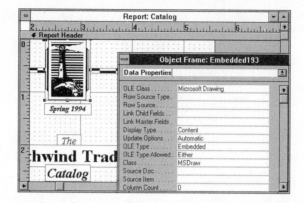

> **NOTE**
>
> When you display the data properties of the logo of the Catalog report, it is likely that the OLEClass property value will be empty. The Microsoft Drawing entry in the OLEClass property text box shown in Figure 15.4 was added by copying the illustration in Microsoft Draw to the Clipboard, then using Paste Special to reinsert the object into the report.

When you double-click an object frame in design mode, the main window of the server that supplied the object appears. In-place activation of OLE 2.0 objects is not available in design mode. If you have Microsoft Draw installed on your computer, the bitmap of the Northwind Traders lighthouse logo (with a few vector-based embellishments) appears, as illustrated by Figure 15.5. Images created by Microsoft Draw are Windows metafiles, which can contain embedded bitmaps.

FIGURE 15.5.

The Microsoft Draw OLE applet displaying the logo for the Catalog report.

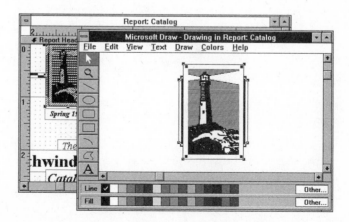

TIP

Use monochrome bitmaps or vector drawings on reports whenever possible. Few of your clients will have color printers. Conventional laser and ink-jet printers differ widely in the methods they use to differentiate colors by varying the dot density. Those clients that have color printers are unlikely to use them for printing Access reports because of the cost of consumables (ink cartridges or thermal transfer supplies).

You set the ControlSource property of bound object frames on forms and reports, like other bound controls, to the name of the OLE Object field in the table or query that serves as the data source for the form. Figure 15.6 shows a bound object frame that will contain a color picture symbolizing the product category. Access creates a bound object frame for you when you drag an OLE Object field from the field list window to the surface of your form or report. The Picture object has been converted to a bitmap for use in the report. Unlike unbound object frames, bound object frames do not display an image in design mode. Bound object frames do not possess the RowSourceType, RowSource, or ColumnCount properties, and unbound object frames in reports lack other properties related to activation of the object.

FIGURE 15.6.

A bound object frame in the Category Name Header section of the Catalog report.

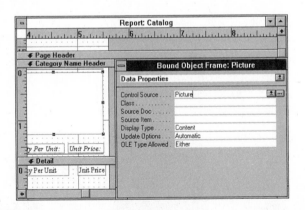

TIP

If you plan to use Access to display graphic images of significant size with more than 256 colors, it is recommended that you use a 486DX50 or faster computer with a minimum of 12MB of RAM and install a Windows graphics accelerator card. Alternately, use a 486DX50 (or faster) computer with VESA (Video Electronics Standards Association) local-bus video capability. Otherwise, manipulating large graphic images of substantial color depth created by OLE servers can be a painfully slow process.

Embedding Versus Linking OLE Objects

OLE offers the choice of embedding or linking OLE objects in a destination document. When you embed an OLE object, the destination document includes a copy of the OLE object's data. The data for the embedded OLE object may be from a file, created in the server application, or copied to the server application from the Windows Clipboard. You need not (and, with some OLE applications, you cannot) save the data you intend to embed to a file.

Linking an OLE object requires that the data for the source document originate in a file. When you link an OLE object, you insert a reference to the file name and its location, a well-formed path (WFP, the drive letter followed by the path) to the disk or CD-ROM drive and directory that contains the file.

Embedding OLE objects has the advantage of ensuring that the object's data is available within the compound document, regardless of whether the original source of the data has disappeared. If, for instance, you link an OLE object and later move the file to a new directory or erase the file, you no longer can edit it (or, in the case of multimedia objects, play it). If the object is a graphic image, however, you can still see the image because the OLE presentation of the object (the subject of a section later in this chapter) is stored together with the file linking reference. Embedding OLE objects is useful for creating archival copies of an object, such as the data in a worksheet that is updated monthly. For example, you might embed a copy of each month's worksheet data in an OLE Object field of an Access table so that you can create a history of monthly changes to the data.

Linking an OLE object is the better choice when the object is likely to be updated from time to time and you want to obtain the latest version of the data. If you need to maintain the source data in a file, you can avoid doubling the disk space required to store the data by linking, instead of embedding, the file. You do not, however, save disk space when you link a graphic image to an Access table or form; the presentation occupies the same or more disk space than the data in the file.

Conventional OLE Graphic Servers

Conventional OLE server "paint" applications, such as Windows Paintbrush, can be used to create, import, or edit bitmap graphic images. Paintbrush is limited to dealing with bitmap files in four formats:

■ Standard Windows bitmap files (.BMP)

■ Device-independent bitmap files (.DIB, similar to .BMP format; .BMP and .DIB are standard Windows Clipboard formats)

■ ZSoft-format bitmap files (.PCX), which use a form of run-length encoding (RLE) to conserve disk space

■ Files created by the version of Paintbrush supplied with releases of Microsoft Windows prior to 3.0 (.MSP)

Figure 15.7 shows Windows Paintbrush with the image of the first record of the Photo field of the Employees table ready to be edited. You launch the OLE server in Access, as with most other OLE client applications, by double-clicking the image or other visual representation of the object. In the case of Access tables, you can display an image only by employing the server to do so. Images in forms and reports can be displayed in the form of pictures, rather than OLE objects, by choosing to embed the object as a picture; doing so breaks the link to the OLE server that was used to embed the image. A picture is an image that does not contain a linkage to the OLE server that created the image. As mentioned earlier in the chapter, you cannot edit an OLE source document (in this case, an image) that has been embedded as a picture.

FIGURE 15.7.

The Windows Paintbrush OLE server displaying a bound OLE object.

NOTE

The photographs in the Employees table are 16-color bitmaps, so they appear the same whether you use the standard Windows 16-color VGA driver or the 256-color SVGA driver supplied with your video adapter card. A process called color dithering was used to create these bitmaps. Color dithering simulates colors in an image that are not included among Windows' 16 standard colors (the colors available using the Palette tool in form or report design mode) by alternating different colors in adjacent pixels.

OLE-compliant image-editing applications, such as Micrografx Picture Publisher and Corel PhotoPaint!, support a much wider variety of bitmap file formats, such as TIFF (Tagged Image File Format, .TIF), which is the standard file format for most image-scanning devices. Picture Publisher also supports newer formats, such as images compressed using the JPEG (Joint Photographic Experts Group) compression algorithm (.JPG files) and Kodak's Photo CD format (.PCD files). Figure 15.8 shows Picture Publisher 3.1 displaying an enlarged version of the application's logo in 16 colors. (Picture Publisher dithers colors that are not available in the 16-color palette.)

FIGURE 15.8.

Micrografx Picture Publisher 3.1 displaying a linked bitmap image.

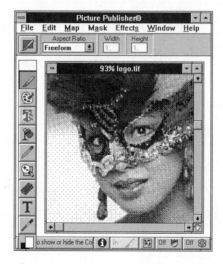

> **TIP**
>
> If your applications involve the display of bitmap graphics stored in file formats other than .BMP or .PCX, you and your client will need an OLE-compliant image-editing application to link or embed them in object frames. Clients seldom want to change the format of large numbers of bitmap images solely to accommodate a new application. If your client has not yet accumulated a large number of image files, consider the use of .JPG compression. The advantage of the .JPG format is that you can control the degree of compression of color image files.

OLE-compliant drawing applications that create and manipulate vector-based images can be used to link or embed specialized images, such as maps and mechanical-design drawings, in OLE Object fields. Commercial drawing applications, including Micrografx's Designer and Windows Draw! with OLE, and Corel Systems' CorelDRAW!, are typical of servers that create vector-based images. You can import drawings created by AutoCAD and other computer-aided design and drafting applications in .DXF format into most commercial drawing applications. The most common vector-image file formats are as follows:

- Windows metafiles (.WMF), the vector format native to Windows, a standard Clipboard format
- Files created by Micrografx Designer and Windows Draw! (.DRW)
- CorelDRAW! files (.CDR)
- Computer graphic metafiles, another standard vector format (.CGM)
- Drawing exchange files, the standard format for exchanging CAD files (.DXF)
- Encapsulated PostScript files (.EPS)
- Animation files created by AutoDesk Animator (.FLC and .FLI)

The Microsoft Draw applet includes filters that can import .WMF, .CGM, .DXF, and .DRW files, along with files in HPGL (Hewlett-Packard Graphic Language) formats used with H-P plotters. You also can use the drawing features of Microsoft Word 6.0 as a substitute for Microsoft Draw. Word 6.0 pictures support several more graphics file formats than does Microsoft Draw. The object type is Microsoft Word 6.0 Picture.

NOTE

The version of the MS Draw filter that was available at the time this book was written cannot import some .DRW files created with Micrografx Windows Draw! 3.0 and Windows Draw! with OLE. If you are using either of these applications, save the images in .WMF format if you want to import them to MS Draw. Alternatively, copy the image to the Clipboard and paste the image from Draw! into MS Draw. This problem has been corrected in the .DRW filter for Microsoft Word 6.0 Picture objects.

TIP

Vector-based drawings usually provide better images than do bitmaps when the image must be scaled to fit the confines of the display area available on a form or report. Unless you scale bitmaps by powers of 2 (25 percent, 50 percent, 200 percent, and so forth) the bitmap image will usually be distorted and its contrast is likely to change. Try to obtain vector images of logos and other client artwork, if possible in .WMF format.

WARNING

When using vector-based client artwork that includes type, make sure that you have the identical typeface families used to create the artwork available on your computer. If you do not have the typeface available, Windows will attempt to substitute a face that Windows believes is the closest to your client's typeface. Select the type in the image (preferably on the client's computer) and use the Convert-to-Curves menu option of a commercial drawing application to change the selected type from a typeface outline to the Bezier curves used for other elements of the drawing. The Convert-to-Curves option is not available in Microsoft Draw.

OLE Graphic Server Applets

Microsoft Graph 3.0, supplied with Access 1.x and several other earlier releases of Microsoft applications, is an example of a category of OLE 1.0 server called an *OLE server applet*. OLE server applets are mini-servers in OLE 2.0 terminology. (MSGraph5 is an OLE 2.0 mini-server.) Unlike conventional Windows applications, you cannot run an OLE server applet or mini-server with the **R**un choice from Program Manager's **F**ile menu. If you try, you receive a message box stating "This application can run only within another application." Microsoft Draw and WordArt give similar messages when you try to run them ("Sorry, Microsoft Draw can run only within a destination application.") You cannot save the data imported into or created with an OLE applet to a file. The data can be embedded only in the client document.

> **TIP**
>
> You can save data created in an OLE applet if you have a commercial drawing or image-editing application. Drawing applications are capable of importing both bitmap and vector images. Image editors handle bitmaps only. Select the image or portion of the image you want to save, copy it to the Clipboard, and then paste it into the drawing or image-editing application. You can save the file in the application's native format or one of the standard formats that the application offers. Another way of saving data created in an OLE applet is to copy the image to the Clipboard, then use Windows Clipboard application (Clipbook in Windows for Workgroups) to copy the image to a .CLP file. Later you can open the .CLP file, copy the image to the Clipboard, and paste it into the OLE server applet.

The Presentation of OLE Graphic and Other Objects

As mentioned at the beginning of this chapter, OLE servers also embed an image, called a presentation, in addition to a copy of or a link to the data for the OLE Object. The presentation consists of a Windows metafile that is used to create the image that appears in your client's compound document. A Windows metafile rather than a Windows .DIB file is used because the image needs to be scalable. When you alter the scale factor of a metafile containing a bitmap, the bitmap changes scale too. Scaling images is discussed in the forthcoming section called "Adding Graphics to Forms and Reports."

Presentations of Unsupported and Non-Graphic Data Formats

If the client application does not support displaying the type of data employed by the server, the server substitutes an icon to display. Access, for example, does not support Word for Windows' native Clipboard data format; therefore, the WinWord icon is displayed in a bound object frame on a form rather than as an image of the document. Audio files, which have no visual content, display the icon of the server with which they were linked or embedded. When you double-click the icon, the sound plays. Alternately, you can make changes in Windows 3.1's registration database so that the server's window is displayed for editing. If you use Media Player 3.1, you have several options to control the presentation during playback of linked multimedia files. These options are described in the next chapter.

Dealing with Bitmap Presentations

The OLE presentation of a bitmap image is the entire bitmap in Windows DIB format, scaled to the desired size by the server or from instructions to the server from the client application. The storage space required for the presentation depends upon the size and number of colors of the bitmap. Table 15.1 shows the number of bytes required to store DIB-format bitmaps of varying size and color depth. Even if you have the default 16-color Windows VGA display driver installed, 256-color bitmaps will consume the storage space shown in Table 15.1. Depending on the OLE server used and the display driver installed, presentations with color depth greater than 256 colors may occupy the storage space shown for 16-color or 24-color images.

Table 15.1. Storage requirements, in bytes, of images in DIB format as a function of size and color depth.

Image Size	Display	16 Colors	256 Colors	16-bit Colors	24-bit Colors
160×120	1/16 VGA	9,600	19,200	38,400	57,600
320×240	1/4 VGA	38,400	76,800	152,600	230,400
640×480	VGA	152,600	307,200	614,400	921,600
800×600	SVGA	240,000	480,000	960,000	1,640,000
1,024×768	UVGA	393,216	786,432	1,572,864	2,359,296

> **NOTE**
>
> Access cannot display bitmaps with more than 256 colors in object frames. If you need the greater color depth, you must launch the OLE server that embedded or linked the image in order to view the picture in its 16-bit or 24-bit glory.

You may be surprised by the increase in size of your Access .MDB file when you embed an image from a .PCX file that contains large fields of a single color. The .PCX file is run-length encoded so that repeating groups of pixels with the same color are replaced by the color value and number of repetitions. It is not uncommon, under these circumstances, for the presentation to require twice the data space of the file from which the object was embedded. Other compressed file formats for bitmap images, such as .GIF, .JPG, and .TIF, give similar storage-requirement expansion ratios. The storage requirements for OLE graphics presentations in compound documents are about the same for any client application; you can observe the same effect when you embed compressed images into Word for Windows or Excel as in Access.

You may be dismayed, however, when you link large graphic images to an Access table and find that the file has increased in size by the same amount as if the data from the file were embedded. Here again, the OLE presentation created by the server is the culprit. Conventional OLE servers are not designed to provide a user-scalable presentation with a choice of color depth. OLE presentation storage requirements are seldom a problem in applications other than image databases, because only a few images are likely to be linked to a word-processing document, such as a chapter in a book, or a worksheet. Databases, on the other hand, may need to contain thousands of linked images.

If you are creating an image database with linked graphics files in Access, you have only the following three choices to keep database size within reason:

■ Use Lenel's MultiMedia Works graphics' server (described in Appendix A, "Access Resources"), which provides for a user-scalable thumbnail presentation image.

■ Create your own thumbnail image to link or embed and add a text field that includes a well-formed path and the file name of the originating image.

■ Link the file with Object Packager so that the presentation is Object Packager's icon. Object Packager's icon is a very small (32×32-pixel) bitmap included within a Windows metafile, so the bitmap is scalable.

Two of these approaches are described in the following paragraphs; using Object Packager to embed and link images is discussed in a separate section of this chapter that follows shortly.

Lenel's approach is clearly the simplest, therefore it is listed first. Figure 15.9 shows three bitmapped images from CorelDRAW! 4.0 linked to an OLE Object field of an Access table using MultiMedia Works's graphic object type. The presentation of the image displayed in the bound object frame is a 32×32-pixel Windows metafile that contains the thumbnail bitmap. When you double-click the thumbnail presentation on the form, the original, full-size image appears in MultiMedia Works' window. MultiMedia Works enables you to control the default position, size, and window characteristics of the image displayed in MultiMedia Works's window. Figure 15.10 shows the dialog box to choose display properties. The only limitation of MultiMedia Works is that you cannot edit the image when you double-click to display the image in MultiMedia Works' window. In most cases, however, you do not want the user to edit images; this process is better left to the experts.

FIGURE 15.9.

Thumbnail presentations of three images linked to an Access table and MultiMedia Works' display window.

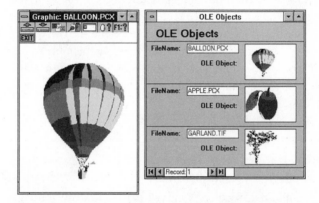

FIGURE 15.10.

MultiMedia Works' Display Window Configuration dialog box.

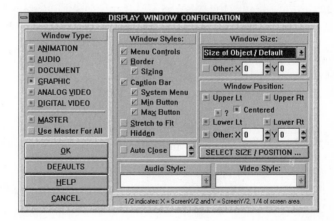

An alternate approach is to create a thumbnail image yourself by scaling the bitmap with an image-editing application. If the image uses more than 256 colors, you can use the color-reduction option that most image editors offer to reduce the color depth to the 256-color palette supported by Access. Because you will not be interested in editing the thumbnail image, you can choose Paste Special from the Edit menu and paste the image into the OLE Object field as a picture rather than as an editable OLE image. Objects pasted as pictures consist of the presentation without the link to the OLE server; thus, pictures are not editable.

> **TIP**
>
> If you are dealing with Kodak Photo CD images in Access files, you can embed the thumbnail image from a .BMP file as a picture (not editable) using the Kodak Photo CD Access application (not a relative of Microsoft Access) or Picture Publisher 3.1 to make the conversion from .PCD to .BMP format. In this case, add fields to the table to identify both the Photo CD title and the filename. A message box that instructs the user to place the appropriate Photo CD in the CD-ROM drive avoids "file not found" messages.

Palette Issues

If you were using a display driver that provides 256 or more colors, Access 1.x used the standard 256-color Windows palette to display images in bound and unbound object frames. Thus, the colors of 16-bit and 24-bit images were mapped to the closest color available in the standard 256-color Windows palette when viewed in object frames. Access 2.0 enables you to specify a filename as the value of the `Palette` property that provides a custom palette for a form. A custom palette is useful for images that contain photographs of people; in this case, the palette assigns more colors to represent flesh tones. You can specify a palette (.PAL) file with a custom Windows palette, or use the palette associated with a bitmap (.BMP or .DIB) or icon (.ICO) file. To create your own palette files, you need a palette-editing application, such as PAL Edit, the palette editor supplied with Microsoft Video for Windows.

If a graphic OLE object has its own palette, you can specify that the value of the `ObjectPalette` property of the object in the bound or unbound object frame be used for the `PaintPalette` property of a form or report with code similar to the following:

```
Forms(strFormName).PaintPalette =
Forms(strFormName).objObjectFrame.ObjectPalette
```

When you specify a `PaintPalette` property value, the value of the `Palette` property of the form is set to `Custom`.

> **NOTE**
>
> Although Access 2.0 enables you to change the palette together with the image, the change applies to all objects on the form. This limitation is imposed because palette conflicts occur when more than one image appears simultaneously on a continuous form. (Windows can use only one palette at a time in the active window.) Even if you display only one image on a single form, loading a new palette for each image to be displayed can slow the movement between records to a less-than-tolerable rate.

Performance Problems with Complex Vector Images

Complex vector images, such as maps used in geographic information systems (GIS), embedded or linked to an OLE Object field, can seriously delay movement between records in a table. As you move from one record to another in a form, the presentation (in BMP format) must be created from the vectors contained in the metafile that provides the data for the image. Even small vector images that contain many individual elements may slow the display of successive records to a crawl.

As with bitmap presentations, you can elect to use an OLE-compliant drawing application, such as Windows Draw! or CorelDRAW!, to convert all or part of a vector image to a small bitmap, then embed the bitmap as a picture in an OLE Object field to provide the presentation. Next, use Object Packager to create the link to the source file of the vector image. You need two bound object frames in this case—one to display the thumbnail and another to display Object Packager's icon that you can double-click to launch the application that created or can display the vector image.

Lenel MultiMedia Works again provides a simpler alternative. When you create the presentation using MultiMedia Works' Thumbnail button, you can choose to create a scaled bitmap from the vector image, as shown in Figure 15.11.

FIGURE 15.11.

Three thumbnail bitmap presentations of complex vector images (.WMF files) created in CorelDRAW! 4.0.

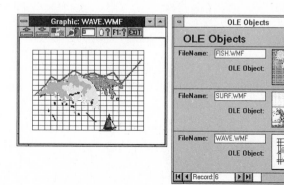

Using Object Packager to Create OLE Objects

You can use the Object Packager application supplied with Windows 3.1 to embed or link OLE objects in Access tables. The primary use for Object Packager is to create source documents with Windows applications that are not OLE-compliant. You can, however, use Object Packager to reduce the storage requirement of the presentations of graphic images to that of the icon of the application used to link or embed them. Another advantage of using Object Packager is that you can control whether multimedia objects play when you double-click the icon or display the window of the application used as the methods component of the package.

You can use Object Packager to link or embed the data (properties) for OLE Objects in destination documents, but the package created by Object Packager is always embedded. The linking procedures and the embedding procedures for Object Packager are quite different. Each method is described in the sections that follow.

Embedding Objects with Object Packager

Embedding objects with Object Packager does not save disk space compared with using the OLE server applications for the object type. For example, when you embed a bitmapped or vector graphic image, the presentation consists of the embedded data; therefore, there is no significant difference in the storage requirements of an image embedded with an OLE server or Object Packager. However, if you want to embed MIDI music files in your Access tables and you do not have Media Player 3.1, Object Packager is your only choice. Similarly, embedding word-processing files created with non-OLE-compliant applications requires Object Packager.

> **TIP**
>
> You can use Object Packager to speed the scanning of records that contain graphic images if you are willing to forego the full or thumbnail image. In the case of large vector images, the increase in speed may be quite significant. You can view the image by double-clicking the icon to launch the OLE server that created or that can display the image.

To embed an object with Object Packager, follow these steps:

1. Position the caret (cursor or insertion point) in the location at which you want to insert the packaged object. In the case of Access, a field with the OLE Object type must be selected.

2. Choose Object from the appropriate main menu selection of your application. In the case of Access, choose Insert Object from the Edit menu, and a list of the available OLE servers appears in the Insert Object dialog box as shown in Figure 15.12.

3. Choose Package from the Object Type list box and click the OK button. Access offers you the optional shortcut of clicking the File button to choose a file to supply the data for the package, but Object Packager does not have file-type associations. Therefore, using the File button is not appropriate in this case. File-type associations were discussed in the preceding chapter. Object Packager's window appears, as shown in Figure 15.13.

FIGURE 15.12.

Choosing the Package object type as the value of an OLE Object field in Access.

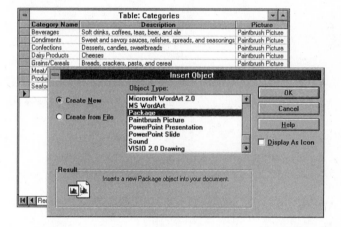

FIGURE 15.13.

Object Packager's window before choosing a file to embed.

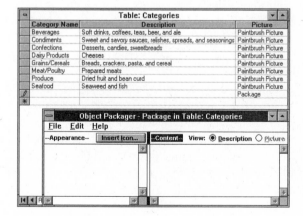

4. Select the Content pane of Object Packager's window (if it is not already selected), and then choose **I**mport from the **F**ile menu. The Import common file dialog box appears. Choose the file whose data you want to embed.

5. If an association exists for the type of file you select, the icon of the application with which the file is associated (methods) appears in the appearance pane and a description of the data (properties) of the packaged object appears as illustrated in Figure 15.14. The associated application need not be an OLE server.

FIGURE 15.14.

Choosing the properties and methods for a packaged object.

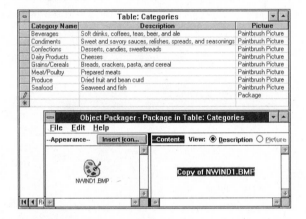

6. Choose **C**opy Package from the **E**dit menu to copy the package to the Clipboard. Then choose E**x**it from the **F**ile menu to close the instance of Object Packager.

7. Click Yes when asked whether you want to update Microsoft Access.

8. When you double-click the presentation of the packaged application, the window of the application appears as shown in Figure 15.15.

Notice that the identification of objects in the title bar of the application used to display or edit them differs from objects embedded by OLE servers. When you embed a bitmap image directly with Paintbrush, the identification is "Paintbrush Picture in *Table*:*Categories*." Packaged objects are identified by ~PKG, a four-character serial number in hexadecimal format, and the extension of the file type from which the object was created, in this case .BMP.

FIGURE 15.15.

*The main window
of the application
used to embed the
packaged object.*

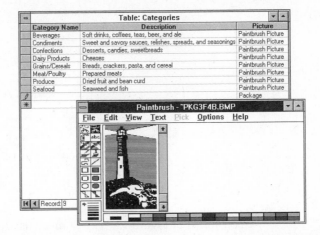

NOTE

The presentation of OLE objects in table and query datasheet mode is the name of the object type that was displayed in the Object Type list box in Step 1 of the foregoing procedure. The presentation of objects created with Object Packager is "Package," regardless of the type of object the package contains. Add fields to your table to describe the type of object and the file that contains the data for the object when you use Object Packager to embed graphic images.

Linking Objects with Object Packager

You use Object Packager, in the majority of cases, to minimize the storage requirements for presentations and to improve the speed of traversing records in a table or query. Minimizing storage requirements of graphic images requires that you link the file containing the properties of the packaged object. You may have wondered about the purpose of the Copy to Clipboard option that can be selected from the Copy command of the File menu of File Manager. You are about to discover why this option exists.

To link a file with Object Packager, follow these steps:

1. Launch File Manager from the Main Windows application group.
2. Select the file to which you want to create a link, as shown in Figure 15.16. (The improved File Manager application supplied with Windows for Workgroups appears in this figure.)

FIGURE 15.16.

Choosing a file to link with Windows for Workgroups's File Manager.

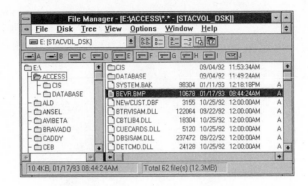

3. Choose **C**opy from the **F**ile menu and click the Copy to Clipboard option button, as illustrated in Figure 15.17, and then click the OK button. File Manager copies the name of the file and its location (a well-formed path to the file) to the Clipboard.

FIGURE 15.17.

Copying the file specification for a bitmapped image to the clipboard.

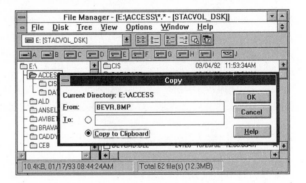

4. Open Object Packager and choose Paste Link from the Edit menu. A link to the file whose reference you copied to the Clipboard appears in the Content pane, as shown in Figure 15.18.

5. Choose Copy Pac**k**age from the **E**dit menu to place a copy of the package in the Clipboard. Then choose E**x**it from the **F**ile menu to close the instance of Object Packager.

6. Return to your source document application (Access in this case) and position the caret where you want to embed the packaged object. Choose Paste **S**pecial from the **E**dit menu to embed the package with the link to the file.

7. Double-click the associated application's presentation to verify that the link was created, as shown in Figure 15.19.

FIGURE 15.18.

Creating a link to a file in Object Packager.

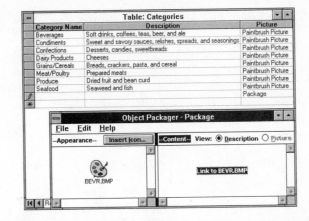

TIP

You distinguish a linked object from an embedded object in most OLE server windows by the contents of the window's title bar. Linked objects display the filename (see Figure 15.19), whereas embedded objects display a message similar to "Object in Microsoft Access" or a code that represents the embedded object. (See Figure 15.14, shown previously.)

FIGURE 15.19.

Displaying an embedded package linked to a bitmapped image file.

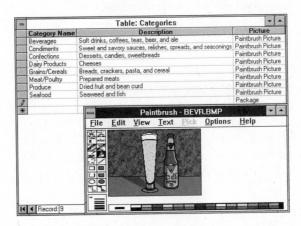

> **NOTE**
>
> You cannot edit the link to the content file for a packaged object by choosing Package Object from Access's Edit menu. The Change Link choice of the fly-out submenu is disabled (gray) because packaged objects are embedded, even if the package contains a link to its data source.

Embedding or Linking Graphics in OLE Object Fields

Embedding data stored in graphics files as values of OLE Object fields of Access tables creates a copy of the data contained in the file. Subsequent editing of the originating file does not change the embedded image. You can embed OLE objects in one of the following two ways:

Choose Insert Object from the **E**dit menu, and then select the type of object you want to embed from the Object Type list box of the Insert Object dialog box. If the source of data for the object is a file, click the File button and select the file whose data you want to embed in the Insert Object from File dialog box. If you are using an OLE server applet, such as Microsoft Draw or WordArt, click OK to open the applet's window in which you can create the drawing you want to embed. If you copy a graphic image to the Clipboard, you can paste it into Microsoft Draw and then edit the image as necessary. Choose Exit from the server's File menu, then click Yes when asked if you want to update Microsoft Access.

or

Open the OLE server independently of Access, select the image or portion of the image you want to embed, and then copy the selected image to the clipboard. Most image-editing and drawing applications (other than Paintbrush) have a Select **A**ll choice in their **E**dit menu, so you can select the entire image to copy to the clipboard. Activate Access, select the OLE Object field of the record, and choose Paste from Access's Edit menu. Alternately, you can choose Paste **S**pecial from the **E**dit menu to display the Paste Special dialog box shown in Figure 15.20. The Paste Special dialog box enables you to embed (Paste) any object or link (Paste Link) objects whose data source is a file.

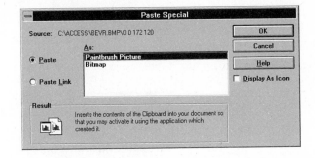

If you select Picture or Bitmap from the Data Type list box, you create a static image that has no link to the OLE server that you used to embed the image. Therefore, you cannot display or edit the image with the originating server. There is no significant file-size reduction if you choose the Picture or Bitmap option. If, however, you are adding images to a table from an OLE server, such as Microsoft Word, in which the images were inserted as pictures (not OLE objects), your only choice is to embed a Picture, Device-Independent Bitmap, or a standard Windows Bitmap.

Linking graphic data enables you to display the latest version of a graphics file in a bound object frame. Access 2.0 bound object frames, however, do not have "hot link" or "warm link" capability; that is, the presentation of a linked graphic image displayed in a bound object frame is not updated automatically when the linked file is edited. Automatically updating linked objects in tables creates a number of performance problems in both the client and server applications.

To ensure that you display the latest version of a linked file, you need to select the object frame in Form View, then choose Links from the Edit menu to display Access 2.0's new Update Links dialog box, shown in Figure 15.21. The Links dialog box enables you to manually update, open the server (source) of the object, change the source of the object, or break the link with the server, creating a static presentation.

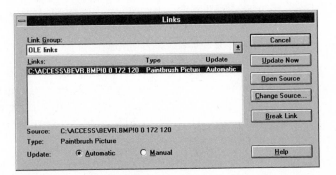

Linking an object requires that you open the OLE server independently of Access using the same procedure as shown in the second option for embedding objects. To link rather than embed the image, choose Paste Link from the Edit menu or choose Paste Special, and then click the Paste Link button in the Paste Special dialog box.

> **TIP**
>
> Do not change the location of linked files without giving the matter a great deal of thought. You need to change the link data for each record that contains a field whose value is a linked object when you move the linked data source. It is possible to change the link by replacing the value of the SourceDoc property of the object frame with a well-formed path to the new location of the file.

Adding Graphics to Forms and Reports

Up to this point, the discussion of OLE in this chapter applies to the creation of compound documents in any OLE client application. Access 2.0 complies with almost all the requirements for client applications of OLE Specification 2.01 published by Microsoft Corporation. However, at the time this edition was written, there were few OLE 2.0-compliant graphics server applications. Shapeware Corp.'s Visio 2.0 is an OLE 2.0-compliant, template-based drawing application that was used to create most of the diagrams in this edition. Visio 2.0 offers OLE Automation capabilities and is discussed in the next chapter, "Using Access as an OLE Automation Client." Shapeware Corp. also offers a mini-server version called Visio Express.

Displaying Graphics in OLE Object Fields of Tables

As noted earlier in the chapter, OLE objects embedded or linked to OLE Object fields of tables are displayed in bound object frames (the object is "bound" to the field you choose as the value of the ControlSource property). You can create a bound object frame in one of two ways, as follows:

> Select the field in the Field List window, drag the field icon to the form, and drop the icon in the desired location. Size the resulting bound object frame as necessary for the form or report that contains it. An object frame bound to the Picture field of the Categories table, created by the field drag-and-drop method, is shown in Figure 15.22.

or

Display the toolbox and click the bound object frame tool (with the "xyz" in the top border). Position the object-frame mouse pointer at the position where you want the upper-left corner of the frame and click the left mouse button. Size the bound object frame as required.

FIGURE 15.22.

A bound object frame created by dragging and dropping an OLE Object field to a form.

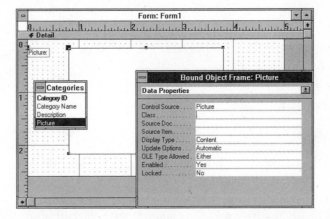

TIP

If you want to prevent users of your application from editing the image in a bound object frame, set the `Enabled` property of the object frame to **False**. You can allow users to display the object with the originating server by setting both the `Enabled` and `Locked` properties to **True**. Preventing editing by unauthorized persons is particularly important if the object is linked to the original file.

Bound object frames are usually located in the detail section of forms and reports. You can also place bound object frames within group headers of reports.

TIP

If you attempt to edit a linked OLE Object whose data source file is read-only, such as images stored on CD-ROMs, you receive an error message. Tables that include OLE Objects linked to read-only or removable data sources should include a field that indicates the media type. Attach a `MsgBox` macro action to the `OnDoubleClick` event of the bound object box to notify the user that the data cannot be edited or that you need to insert the source media before proceeding. You can set the `Enabled` property of bound object frames that display objects linked to read-only or removable media files (such as files on CD-ROMs) to **False** by a conditional `SetValue` macro action or with an Access Basic function.

Displaying Static Graphics on Forms and Reports

OLE objects that constitute the artwork used for embellishing forms or reports are contained in unbound object frames. As for bound object frames, there are the two methods for creating unbound object frames, as follows:

1. To embed an illustration in your form or report, click the unbound object frame tool of the toolbox, then position the unbound-frame mouse pointer where you want the upper-left corner of the frame, and click the left mouse button. A shaded representation of the unbound object frame is added to your form or report and the Insert Object dialog box appears automatically. Alternatively, you can choose Insert Ob**j**ect from the **E**dit menu to insert an unbound object frame of standard dimensions. Select the type of object and click the File button if the data source for the object is a file. Size the frame to fit the image. Figure 15.23 shows an embedded object created by this method, with the `Scaling` property set to `Zoom`. Scaling graphic images is the subject of the next section.

2. To link an OLE object to an unbound object frame, open the OLE server application independently of Access, import the desired file, select the image, and copy the selected image to the Clipboard. Open the form design window in Access, then choose Paste Special, then click the Paste Link option button of the Paste Special dialog box. The linked OLE object appears as shown in Figure 15.24.

The default value of the `Enabled` property for both embedded and linked images in unbound object frames is **False**. The properties applicable to linked objects differ greatly, however, from those applicable to embedded objects. The difference is apparent when you compare the Properties window for the unbound object frames in Figure 15.23 and Figure 15.24. The Properties window for a linked object includes the location and name of the file as the value of the `SourceObject` property and a set of numeric values for the `SourceItem` property. In the case of bitmapped graphic objects, the `SourceItem` value is the value, in twips, of the upper-left and lower-right limits of the selection, separated by spaces.

FIGURE 15.23.

An embedded OLE object in an unbound object frame.

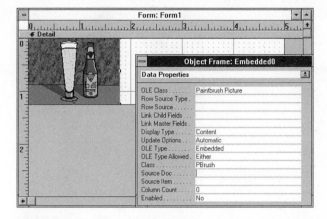

FIGURE 15.24.

An OLE image linked to an unbound object frame.

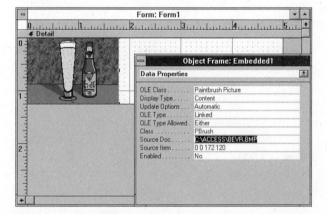

NOTE

The values of `SourceObject` and `SourceItem` cannot be changed by altering entries in the text boxes for these properties. Changes you make to these values do not affect the object in any way.

Scaling Graphics Images

Access offers three types of scaling methods for graphics images: the `Clip`, `Stretch`, and `Zoom` values of the `SizeMode` property. (Access 1.x called `Stretch` the `Scale` value.) The scaling methods are equally applicable to bound and unbound object frames. Figure 15.25 illustrates the differences between the three scaling methods.

FIGURE 15.25.

Three scaling methods applied to the same bitmap image.

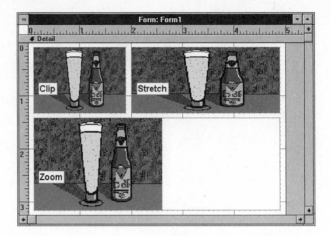

The criteria for the three scaling methods available in Access 2.0 are as follows:

- ■ *Clip* displays that portion of the image that will fit within the object frame, using the upper-left corner of the image as the reference point (datum). If the object frame is larger than the image size, blank areas appear below and to the right of the edge of the image.

- ■ *Stretch* shrinks or stretches the horizontal and vertical dimensions (x and y axes) of the image so that the image fills the object frame. If the aspect ratio (the ratio of width to height) of the object frame does not match the aspect ratio of the image, the image is distorted when it is displayed.

- ■ *Zoom* shrinks or stretches either the horizontal or vertical dimension of the image to fill one axis of the object frame without changing the aspect ratio of the image. Unless the object frame has exactly the same aspect ratio as the image, blank areas will appear in the frame.

Access does not enable you to scale and crop images with the flexibility offered by Aldus PageMaker, Microsoft Word, or other Windows word-processing and desktop-publishing applications.

Exporting Graphics to OLE Client Applications

Access 2.0 is not an OLE server, so you cannot embed an object contained in an OLE Object field or displayed in a bound or unbound object frame directly from a client application. You can, however, export an object by selecting the object, copying it to the Clipboard, and then pasting the object into the destination document. Alternately, you can create a file from the embedded image with an OLE-compliant paint or image-editing application. Exporting graphic images is usually not a consideration when the image is linked to a file, because the file is the basic source of the image, not the table, form, or report in which the link to the file is stored.

Using Other OLE 2.0 Full Servers with Access 2.0

An OLE 2.0 *full server* is a stand-alone executable Windows application that enables you to save the objects you create as files. Microsoft Excel 5.0, Word 6.0, and Project 4.0, Corel Systems' CorelDRAW! 5.0, and Shapeware's Visio 2.0 are examples of OLE 2.0 full servers. In addition to providing the benefits of in-place activation and the other user-interface features associated with OLE 2.0, these applications support OLE Automation. (CorelDRAW! 5.0 was in the final beta testing stage at the time this edition was written.) The following sections describe how you can use Excel 5.0 and Word 6.0, both members of the Microsoft Office software suite, in your Access 2.0 applications.

Adding Excel Spreadsheet Objects to Forms

Version 5.0 of Excel, which offers OLE 2.0 compatibility, in-place activation, and programmable objects for use with OLE Automation, has many added features that make the use of Excel 5.0 with Access 2.0 much easier than using earlier versions of Excel. You can insert an Excel 5.0 Sheet or Chart object into bound or unbound object frames, or into cells of the OLE Object type in Access tables. The examples in the following sections require familiarity with the basics of using Excel 5.0. The following sections describe the manual methods of using Excel 5.0 with Access 2.0. The next chapter describes how to program Excel 5.0 objects with Access Basic using OLE Automation.

Embedding an Excel Worksheet in a Form

You can embed an entire Excel worksheet in an unbound object frame with the process described in this section. The presentation of an Excel worksheet without a range specified as the value of the SourceItem property is the entire content of the worksheet. Large embedded worksheets occupy considerable disk space and may require a significant length of time to display their presentation.

The following process embeds an Excel worksheet in an unbound object frame of a new form. To try this example, you need a relatively simple Excel worksheet, similar to that shown at the end of the preceding chapter. This example uses the

OUTPUT.XLS workbook created by saving a crosstab query whose result set is 1993 quarterly sales of Northwind products by category. (OUTPUT.XLS is included on the accompanying diskette.)

1. Create a new blank form about 2.5 inches high by 6 inches wide. Set the properties of the form to provide a single form without scroll bars, record selectors, or navigation buttons.

2. Select the unbound object frame tool and create an unbound object frame with the left corner at about 0.5 inches to the left of the form's left edge and about 0.25 inches from the top. (The dimensions of these margins are important; the margins leave room for Excel's window adornments.) When you release the mouse button, the Insert Object dialog box appears.

3. Click the Create from File option button and type `c:\access\adg20\output.xls` (or the name of any other Excel 5.0 workbook file you want to embed) in the File text box, and then click OK. (See Figure 15.26.)

FIGURE 15.26.

Inserting an unbound object from an Excel 5.0 workbook file.

4. After a few seconds of disk activity, the presentation of the Excel 5.0 worksheet appears in the unbound object frame. Select the frame and drag the right border to about 5.6 inches. Drag the bottom border to about 2.3 inches. (See Figure 15.27.)

5. Select Data Properties and set the value of the Enabled property to **True** . If you don't enable the object frame, you can't activate the object. Select Other Properties and set the Locked property to **False**. If the object is locked, you can't edit the values in the worksheet.

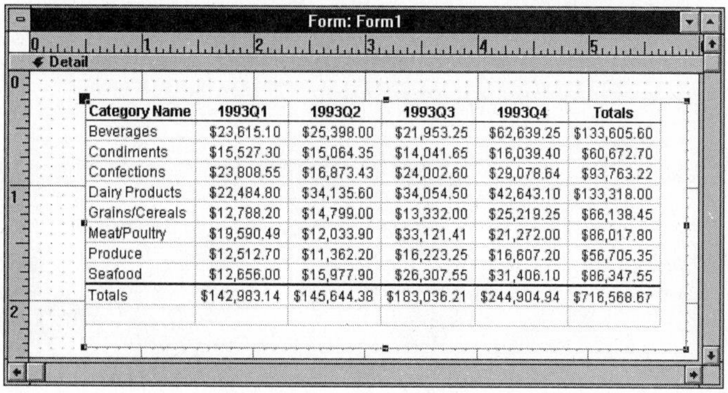

Category Name	1993Q1	1993Q2	1993Q3	1993Q4	Totals
Beverages	$23,615.10	$25,398.00	$21,953.25	$62,639.25	$133,605.60
Condiments	$15,527.30	$15,064.35	$14,041.65	$16,039.40	$60,672.70
Confections	$23,808.55	$16,873.43	$24,002.60	$29,078.64	$93,763.22
Dairy Products	$22,484.80	$34,135.60	$34,054.50	$42,643.10	$133,318.00
Grains/Cereals	$12,788.20	$14,799.00	$13,332.00	$25,219.25	$66,138.45
Meat/Poultry	$19,590.49	$12,033.90	$33,121.41	$21,272.00	$86,017.80
Produce	$12,512.70	$11,362.20	$16,223.25	$16,607.20	$56,705.35
Seafood	$12,656.00	$15,977.90	$26,307.55	$31,406.10	$86,347.55
Totals	$142,983.14	$145,644.38	$183,036.21	$244,904.94	$716,568.67

FIGURE 15.27.
The presentation of an Excel `Sheet` *object in design mode.*

6. Switch to run mode, then choose Size to Fit Form from the Windows menu. (See Figure 15.28.) If only part of a column displays, return to design mode and adjust the width of your object frame so that a full column is displayed with a 0.25-inch border at the right. You also may need to adjust the height of the form to provide a 0.25-inch border at the bottom. The borders inside the object frame are necessary to display the vertical and horizontal scroll bars.

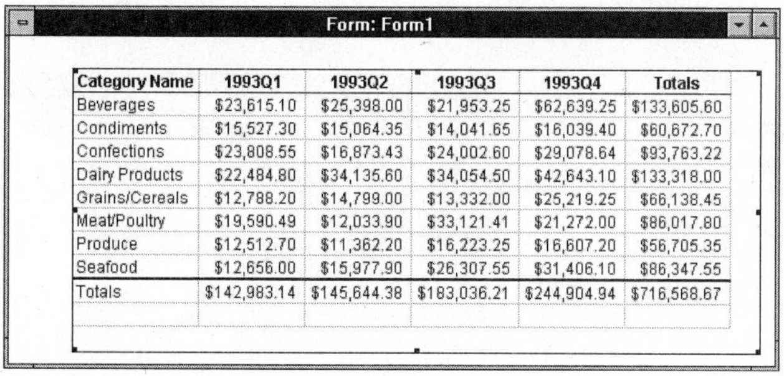

Category Name	1993Q1	1993Q2	1993Q3	1993Q4	Totals
Beverages	$23,615.10	$25,398.00	$21,953.25	$62,639.25	$133,605.60
Condiments	$15,527.30	$15,064.35	$14,041.65	$16,039.40	$60,672.70
Confections	$23,808.55	$16,873.43	$24,002.60	$29,078.64	$93,763.22
Dairy Products	$22,484.80	$34,135.60	$34,054.50	$42,643.10	$133,318.00
Grains/Cereals	$12,788.20	$14,799.00	$13,332.00	$25,219.25	$66,138.45
Meat/Poultry	$19,590.49	$12,033.90	$33,121.41	$21,272.00	$86,017.80
Produce	$12,512.70	$11,362.20	$16,223.25	$16,607.20	$56,705.35
Seafood	$12,656.00	$15,977.90	$26,307.55	$31,406.10	$86,347.55
Totals	$142,983.14	$145,644.38	$183,036.21	$244,904.94	$716,568.67

FIGURE 15.28.
The presentation of a worksheet in an unbound object frame in run mode.

7. Double-click the object frame to activate the worksheet in place. If you correctly set the left and top positions of your object frame and provided the proper internal borders, your activated worksheet appears as shown in Figure 15.29. Excel 5.0's **E**dit and **V**iew menus replace Access's **E**dit and **V**iew menus, and Excel's **I**nsert, F**o**rmat, **T**ools, and **D**ata menus are added to Access's menu. The toolbars that normally appear when you open Excel are floating toolbars in Access 2.0. Activated mode is indicated by a blue hashed border around the object frame.

You can execute any Excel 5.0 menu command when the object is activated, except commands that require use of Excel's **F**ile menu, such as saving the workbook to a file or printing the worksheet.

FIGURE 15.29.

The OUTPUT.XLS worksheet activated in place.

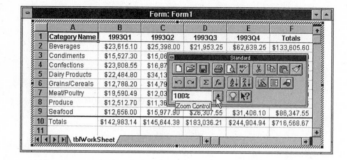

8. Click outside the bound object frame to deactivate the object and return to presentation mode so that Access's menu bar is active.

9. Choose Spreadsheet O**bj**ect from Access's **E**dit menu, and then choose Open from the submenu to open Excel 5.0's window with the embedded data as the source of Excel's current workbook. (See Figure 15.30.) When you open Excel, you can print the worksheet or save the embedded workbook to a file.

FIGURE 15.30.

Opening Excel 5.0 in its own window (from presentation mode).

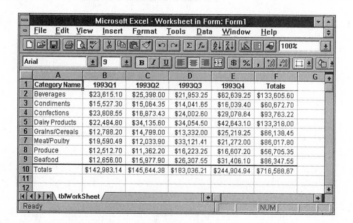

10. Choose E**x**it from Excel's **F**ile menu to close the instance of Excel and return to presentation mode.

> **NOTE**
>
> Two sets of important factors determine the visibility of adornments when you activate an object in place. The top of the object frame must provide room for the column selector buttons in the form area (0.25 inches above the object frame), and the left position of the frame must provide space for the row selector buttons (0.4 to 0.5 inches outside the object frame). The visibility of the horizontal and vertical scroll bars is determined by the internal margin of the object, the space between the edge of the worksheet presentation and the bottom and right edge of the object frame (0.25 inches each inside the object frame). If all of the adornments that appear in Figure 15.28 do not appear after setting these margins, position the mouse pointer on the upper-left corner of the activation border and drag the corner diagonally downward to reduce the size of the activation frame. You may need to make repeated adjustments to the size of the object frame and the activation frame to ensure that all the adornments appear.

Extracting Values from an OLE Object

You can copy individual numeric or text values from a linked or embedded Excel 3+ OLE object and insert these values in an unbound text box, as follows:

1. Add an unbound text box to the form, and set the value of the Scrollbars property to Vertical.

2. Double-click the unbound object frame to activate the workbook object.

3. Select the cell or range of cells you want to import to a text control object.

4. Choose **C**opy from the **E**dit menu, or press Ctrl+C to copy the selection to the Clipboard.

5. Select the text box, which deactivates the object frame, and then press Ctrl+V or choose Paste **S**pecial from Access's **E**dit menu to display the Paste Special dialog box. When you copy data items from an embedded object, you only have the option of pasting them as text. If you chose the Paste **S**pecial approach, click OK to close the Paste Special dialog box.

6. The pasted data items appear in the text box as shown in Figure 15.31. The vertical bars that separate the values in the text box represent the tab characters that Excel uses to separate data columns in a row. Rows are separated by newline pairs.

FIGURE 15.31.

*Pasting a selection
from an embedded
Excel worksheet
into a text box.*

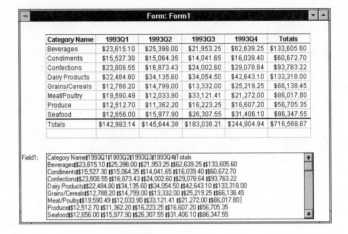

If you add bound text boxes with a numeric data type, you can paste a number from a selected single cell to each text box and update the fields of the table to which the text box is bound. A more efficient method, however, is to use OLE Automation or Access Basic `Recordset` instructions to update values in tables with data from another application. OLE Automation is the subject of the next chapter, and using Access Basic to implement DDE is described in Chapter 21, "Employing Access as a DDE Client and Server."

Linking to a Range of Cells of an Excel Worksheet

Embedding Excel objects is useful if you want to use in-place activation or employ OLE Automation to transfer data from a `Recordset` object to an empty embedded worksheet. In most cases, however, creating an OLE link to all or a range of cells in a worksheet is a more common practice. This is because linking to the file enables you to display or edit the most recent version of the worksheet's data from its source file. Any changes you make to the data in Access are reflected when you close Excel (if you save the changes).

The usual process of linking an Excel 5.0 file in an OLE 2.0 environment is similar to that for using OLE 1.0 to link graphics files. (In-place activation is not available with linked objects.) The following steps create a link to a range of cells in an existing Excel file:

1. If you created the embedded object frame in the preceding section, make a copy of the form. Otherwise, open a new, blank Access form.

2. Launch Excel independently of Access.

3. Choose **O**pen from Excel's **F**ile menu, and in Excel's Open dialog box, select the file you want to link. This example uses OUTPUT.XLS.

4. Select the cells of the worksheet to be included in your Access table; then copy the selected cells to the Clipboard with Ctrl+C.

5. Return to Access and choose Paste **S**pecial from Access's **E**dit menu to display the Paste Special dialog box. Click the Paste Link option button. Unlike embedded objects, your only data-type choices for a linked object are the object or the text contained in the selected data items. If you selected all of the data cells, the data source, tblWorkSheet!R1C1:R10C6, appears in the Source label. (See Figure 15.32.)

FIGURE 15.32.

The Paste Link dialog box for a linked range of cells in an Excel worksheet.

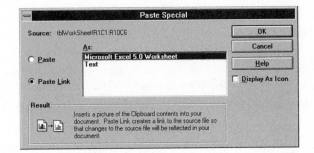

6. Click OK to create the unbound object frame containing the presentation of the selected cells. You don't need to provide for margins in the design because in-place activation is not available with linked objects. If you made a copy of the form and you selected the object frame with the embedded copy, Access adds the new frame below the original.

7. Set the value of the Enabled property of the new frame to Yes and the Locked property of the frame to No.

8. Return to run mode and double-click the presentation of the worksheet to launch Excel in its own window with the linked cells selected.

9. Choose E**x**it from Excel's **F**ile menu to return the focus to Access. If you have made changes to the data, you can elect to save the changes at this point.

Inserting Word 6 Documents in Object Frames

One of the major uses of word-processing applications is the creation of documents, such as contracts, from a collection of individual files containing components of various types of documents. These components often are referred to as *boilerplates*.

In the case of contracts, the boilerplate files may change depending on the jurisdiction of the contract. Although adoption of the Uniform Business Code has reduced the differences in contract provisions between states, there remain many statutory variations in contract law, especially as it relates to express and implied warranties, among the states. Keeping track of large numbers of components of documents and ensuring that a component is correct for the purposes of the destination document can be an awesome challenge. It is very easy to forget the relationship between a source document's 8.3 DOS filename and its contents. Windows NT's long filenames, which are available only when you use the New Technology File System (NTFS), can provide a better description of the contents of files. Database systems, however, are the best approach to providing access to a variety of document components.

Applications that track and maintain the revision history of documents are classified as *document-management systems.* Document management systems differ from image-management systems; image-management systems process static bitmapped images (usually created by page scanners), rather than the actual contents of the document, which is editable data. Access 2.0's OLE 2.0 compatibility makes Access a logical choice for creating document-management database applications.

You can create a simple Access 2.0 document-management system by designing a table with a field of the OLE Object data type to contain embedded documents or links to individual document files. You need two other fields—one to identify the source file name of the document and the other to provide a document description. Additional fields can be added to indicate who originated the document, the owner of the document, the document's status, key terms for searching, and to control who can view and modify the document. Figure 15.33 shows the design of a table that stores the manuscript of this edition of *Access 2 Developer's Guide* in the form of individual chapters in Microsoft Word 6.0 format. The table contains two OLE Object fields: ChapterMS, the original manuscript for the chapter, and ChapterAR, the files that contain changes made by the publisher's editors and final revisions by the author. The data for the table was imported from an Excel 5.0 worksheet that was used to maintain the current status of the manuscript and the corrections and additions made during the editing and author-review process. (See Figure 15.34.)

FIGURE 15.33.

The design of an Access table for a simple document-management system.

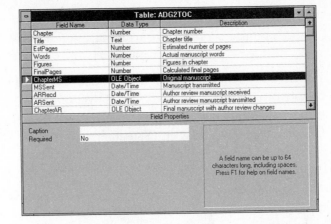

FIGURE 15.34.

Data for the document-management table imported from an Excel 5.0 worksheet.

Chapter	Title	EstPages	Words	Figures	FinalPag
	Introduction		6406	0	
1	Viewing Access 2.0 from a Developer's Perspective	50	19004	15	
2	Developing a Design Strategy for Access Applications	40	11234	12	
3	Using Libraries, Wizards, Builders, and Add-ins	30	8507	19	
4	Writing Access Basic Code	48	13957	6	
5	Understanding Access 2.0's Data Access Objects	30	6273	7	
6	Creating and Using Object Variables	45	11646	3	
7	Using Access Objects, Methods, and Events	60	14713	3	
8	Optimizing Transaction Processing Forms	56	15699	7	
9	Designing Decision Support Forms for Management	54	12091	9	
10	Generating Meaningful Reports	36	8001	22	
11	Examining an Access Accounting Application	24	5225	19	
12	Looking at an Access Training Database	32	10323	14	
13	Analyzing an Access Time and Billing System	38			
14	Understanding OLE 2.0	35	10683	14	
15	Embedding and Linking Objects with OLE	46			
16	Using Access as an OLE Automation Client	30			
17	Charting Data with Microsoft Graph 5.0	30			
18	Introducing OLE 2.0 Custom Controls	20			
19	Networking Secure Access Applications	36	10973	24	
20	Front-Ending Client-Server Databases	28	10616	22	
21	Employing Access as a DDE Client and Server	45	9225	15	
22	Using the Windows API with Access Basic	48	12805	7	

Record: 1 of 34

TIP

It is a better practice to embed, rather than link, documents in a document-management system. If you link the document, there is no assurance that the person who modifies the document updates the other fields of the table to reflect the changes. If all editing is done on the embedded objects, the likelihood of the document's editor updating the other fields is much higher. If all users share the database that contains the document table, changes are reflected immediately. With linked objects, it's necessary to manually update the link so that the presentation contains the newly edited data.

Embedding or Linking a Word 6.0 Document in a Table

To embed or link a Word 6.0 document in an OLE Object field of a table with a design similar to that shown in Figure 15.34, follow these steps:

1. Place the caret in the OLE Object field, and choose Insert Object from the **E**dit menu to open the Insert Object dialog box.

2. To link or embed an existing document, click the Create From File option button and then click OK. (You don't need to select Microsoft Word 6.0 Document when you insert an object from a file; the file extension determines the server used in this case.) The Object Type list box changes to the File text box.

3. You can type the path and filename in the File text box or click the Browse button to display the Browse dialog box. (See Figure 15.35.) Select the file you want to use in the File Name list, and then click OK to close the Browse dialog box and return to the Insert Object dialog box. (See Figure 15.36.)

FIGURE 15.35.

Selecting the Word 6.0 document file to embed in the table.

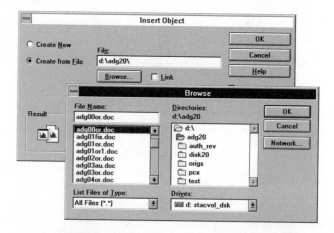

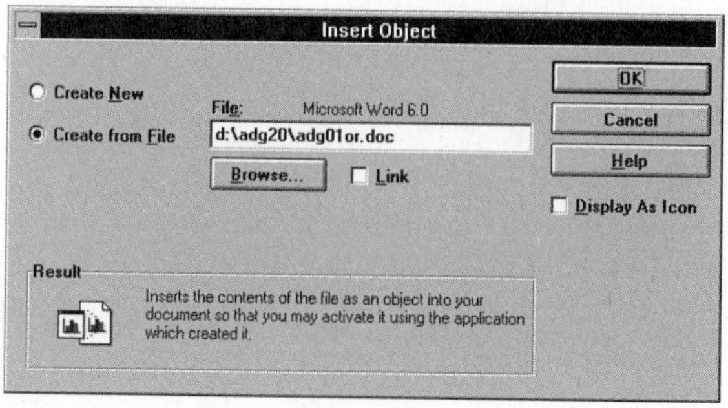

FIGURE 15.36.

The Insert Object dialog box with the document file specified.

4. The file you selected in the preceding step appears in the File text box. You can select between linking and embedding the file; this example uses embedded objects to demonstrate in-place activation. If you want to link the file, tick the Link check box. Click OK. A Microsoft Word 6.0 Document entry appears in the OLE Object field of the selected record.

5. Position the record selector of the table to a different record to save the embedded object or link to the object's file in your table, together with its OLE presentation.

Repeat the preceding steps for each document you want to add to the table. You can activate the document object in Word 6.0's window by double-clicking the OLE Object cell. (See Figure 15.37.) Viewing the documents you insert in the table lets you verify that the contents correspond to the description.

FIGURE 15.37.

Viewing the embedded document in Word 6.0.

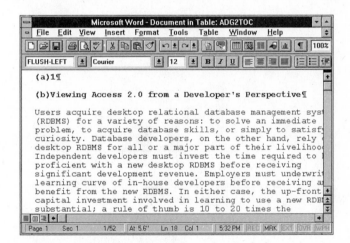

Creating a Form to Display the Document

If your table contains only a few fields, the AutoForm Wizard quickly creates a simple form to display and edit your linked or embedded object. The following steps create the document display form:

1. Open the New Form dialog box and select the table that contains your linked or embedded documents, then click the Form Wizards button to display the Form Wizards dialog box.

2. Double-click the AutoForm item in the Which Wizard Do You Want? list to create the new form.

3. Change to design mode and relocate and resize the controls as necessary.

Your bound object frame should occupy most of the display area. To view the entire document in its original format, set the `Height` property of the object frame to 11 inches and the `Width` property to 8.5 inches.

4. Return to run mode to display the presentation of the document. Figure 15.38 shows the presentation of the initial version of the manuscript for the first chapter of this edition. The presentation of Word 6.0 Documents is the page-layout view of the document. The size of the bound object frame of Figure 15.38 is about 3.5×6 inches.

FIGURE 15.38.

The presentation of a Word 6.0 document in run mode.

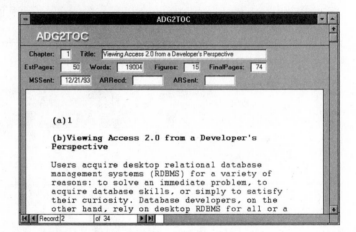

5. Double-click the surface of the object frame to activate the document object. If you embedded the document, activation adds Word's toolbars to the display as floating toolbars. Word's menu choices take over Access's **E**dit and **V**iew menus, and Word adds its **I**nsert, **F**ormat, **T**ools, and T**a**ble menus to the menu bar. (See Figure 15.39.) You view the entire document with the Page Up and Page Down keys. All of the editing features of Microsoft Word 6.0 are available when the document object is activated.

6. Click the surface of the form, outside of the area of the bound object frame, to deactivate the object and return to presentation view of the document.

7. To save the document to a file, alter the page layout, or print an embedded document, choose Document **O**bject from the **E**dit menu, and then choose **O**pen from the submenu. Word's window gains the focus and you can save the document to a file.

8. Choose **C**lose and Return to *FormName* from the **F**ile menu to close Word's window and return to Access.

FIGURE 15.39.

A Word 6.0 document activated in place.

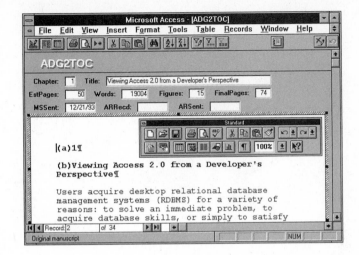

You can insert additional document objects directly in the form instead of adding the documents in the table's Datasheet View. Use the navigation buttons to position the record pointer on the blank (tentative append) record. An empty presentation appears in the bound object frame. Choose Insert Object from the Edit menu and follow steps 2 through 5 of the preceding section to embed or link additional document objects.

16

Using Access as an OLE Automation Client

OLE Automation and Object Basic (now called Visual Basic for Applications, or VBA, by Microsoft) are the most significant new features to be added to Microsoft Windows applications subsequent to Microsoft's introduction of Windows 3.0 in May 1990. As mentioned in Chapter 14, "Understanding OLE 2.0," Windows 3.1 marked the official release of OLE 1.0, but many of the features of OLE 1.0 had been imbedded in versions of Microsoft Excel, Word for Windows, and PowerPoint before Windows 3.1 appeared in retail stores. In the case of OLE 2.0, however, Microsoft was not the first to release a retail version of a fully OLE 2.0-compliant application. This honor goes to Shapeware Corp.'s Visio 2.0 template-based drawing application. Visio 2.0, which features both in-place activation and OLE Automation, began to appear on software retailers' shelves in November 1993. One of the examples in this chapter shows Visio 2.0 in action, in conjunction with an Access 2.0 OLE Automation application.

OLE 2.0 provides the framework for the future of truly object-oriented and 32-bit Windows applications. Entire books can (and undoubtedly will) be devoted to OLE Automation and Visual Basic for Applications, both on Intel 80x86 and Macintosh platforms. Windows NT extends OLE 2.0 capabilities of 16-bit Windows applications to RISC-based workstations, such as Digital Equipment Corp.'s Alpha series, and to the IBM-Apple PowerPC product line. For the moment, you'll need to run the applications that participate in an OLE Automation process on a single computer. The next iterations of Windows (Chicago, or Windows 4.0) and Windows NT (Cairo, expected to be called Windows NT 4.0) are likely to include 32-bit versions of OLE 2.0. The addition of OLE 2.0 compliance to a future version of Digital Equipment Corp.'s ObjectBroker technology, discussed in Chapter 14, will enable you to manipulate OLE Automation objects across networks.

OLE Automation is an interprocess communication (IPC) methodology that enables one OA-compliant application to manipulate members of the collection of objects that are *exposed* by another OA-compliant application. Exposing an application's objects means making members of the application's object collection available to be declared as object variables in another application. Thus, one application can alter properties of, and apply methods that are applicable to, the member objects of another application. OLE Custom Controls, the subject of the next chapter, are special versions of OLE 2.0 mini-servers that expose *events*, in addition to properties and methods, of their objects.

Visual Basic for Applications is the long-awaited common macro language (CML) for Windows applications, derived from Visual Basic 3.0. VBA enables you to use a dialect of Object Basic to manipulate members of the collection of OA objects of the application itself or member objects of another OA-compliant application. Ultimately, application-specific dialects of VBA will replace the existing macro and programming languages of all Microsoft applications for Windows 3.1+ and Apple's System 7+, including Access Basic. An OLE 2.0 application, however, does not need to support VBA to be a participant in an OA process. Microsoft Word 6.0 and Shapeware's Visio 2.0 are examples of OLE 2.0-compliant applications that support OA without using VBA as their application-programming language. OLE 2.0 applications that don't yet support VBA are limited to acting as OA servers. Microsoft Excel 5.0 and Project 4.0 are fully compliant OA clients and servers.

The upshot of OLE 2.0 and OLE Automation is that mainstream Windows applications become building blocks from which you can easily construct customized, multipurpose applications. In the past, Access programmers were forced to use **DDEExecute** instructions to manipulate *data* in documents of DDE server applications. Now you can use Access Basic, Excel VBA, or Project VBA (each a dialect of Object Basic) to orchestrate *objects*, not just data. Word 6.0's Word Basic is not an Object Basic dialect, but you can use Word 6.0 as a OLE Automation server with Access 2.0.

The documentation accompanying the retail version of Access 2.0 and the Access Developer's Toolkit (ADT) does not provide detailed information on using OA with Access 2.0. The Visual Basic 3.0 manuals also contain very little information on using OA. (Visual Basic 3.0 was released before Microsoft released the OLE 2.0 specification.) This chapter fills the OA void in the Microsoft documentation with a discussion of the following major topics:

- Using OLE Automation techniques to manipulate the objects exposed by applications that support OLE Automation, such as Microsoft Excel 5.0 and Word for Windows 6.0.
- Using the Microsoft Excel dialect of Visual Basic for Applications.
- Converting VBA code to Access Basic code to manipulate programmable objects.

The next chapter, "Charting Data with Microsoft Graph 5.0," describes how to use the new OLE 2.0- and OA-compliant version of Microsoft Graph supplied with Access 2.0.

> **NOTE**
>
> Much of the material in this chapter has been adapted from Chapter 16, "Using OLE Automation and Visual Basic for Applications," of the author's *Database Developer's Guide with Visual Basic 3.0* (Sams Publishing, 1994, ISBN 0-672-30440-6). Manipulating objects in Access 2.0's unbound object

frames and using Visual Basic 3.0's MSOLE2.VBX custom control in OLE Automation client applications are almost identical processes. The Access Basic code you write to manipulate objects that are not displayed in object frames is identical to Visual Basic 3.0 code.

Taking Advantage of OLE Automation

Microsoft designed OLE Automation to accomplish the following three basic objectives:

- To enable an application to expose collections of its application-specific objects that other applications can manipulate. Excel 5.0, for instance, exposes Workbooks, Worksheets, and Charts collections, to name just a few.

- To manipulate objects exposed by other OLE 2.0 applications that support OLE Automation. You can declare members of object collections of OA server applications as objects of your OA client application, and then get and set the values of properties of the object, as well as apply a set of predefined methods to the object.

- To enable developers to create external programming tools that manipulate objects in OA applications. Other possibilities for external programming tools are object browsers, embedded macro languages in OA applications (including, but not limited to VBA), and even compilers. Visual Basic 3.0 applications are used as external programming tools in this book.

Applications that incorporate VBA or an equivalent application programming (macro) language can manipulate their own objects. If an OA-compliant application does not have its own macro language, you can use Access Basic or Visual Basic 3.0 as an external programming tool to fill the gap. For example, you can create a database application that animates Visio 2.0 objects in an unbound object frame while playing MIDI music and WAVE file narration, stored in OLE Object fields of tables, in the background.

Technically, OLE Automation objects are instances of a class that consist of member-function pairs that you can use to get and set the properties of an OA object, and member functions that you use to apply a set of methods to the object. Figure 16.1 is a greatly simplified diagram that shows how an Access Basic external programming tool (the OA client) interacts with Excel 5.0 and Visio 2.0 (OA servers).

FIGURE 16.1.

Interaction of participants in an OLE Automation process.

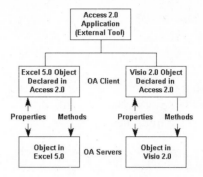

Many OA-compliant applications include a built-in object browser tool that displays a list of the object collections and member objects that the application exposes. When you choose a collection or member object, list box(es) display the methods and properties applicable to that collection or member object. Figure 16.2 shows Excel 5.0's Object Browser, which you open by selecting **O**bject Browser from the View menu after you open a VBA module.

FIGURE 16.2.

Excel 5.0's Object Browser dialog box.

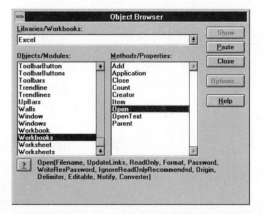

NOTE

The Microsoft Office Developer's Kit (ODK), which was in the final beta test stage at the time this chapter was written, includes a stand-alone Object Browser application (MSPOB.EXE). MSPOB.EXE enables you to browse the objects of all of the OA-compliant full-servers and mini-servers registered in REG.DAT. MSPOB.EXE uses the help file for the server in the directory specified in the HELPDIR entry in REG.DAT. Using MSPOB.EXE eliminates the need to open Excel 5.0 and then a module to browse objects. MSPOB.EXE alone justifies the modest price of the ODK.

When you choose a property or method in Excel's Methods/Properties list, the syntax for the object's method or property appears adjacent to the help (?) button. Clicking the help button displays the help window for the property or method. Figure 16.3 shows the help window for the `WorkbookObject.Open()` method. You can see from Figure 16.3 that the syntax of the `Workbook` object's `Open()` method is quite similar to that of Access's **OpenDatabase**`()` method. All OA applications that support storing and retrieving data from files support the `Open()` method.

> **NOTE**
>
> `Open()` is not printed in boldface type in this book because the `Open()` method is not a member of Access 2.0's collection of reserved words. `Open()` is a reserved word in Visual Basic for Applications.

FIGURE 16.3.

Excel 5.0's help window for the `Open()` *method that applies to the Workbooks collection.*

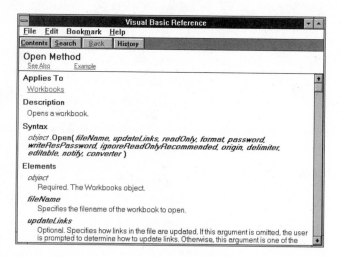

The following sections introduce you to the terminology of OLE Automation.

> **NOTE**
>
> The sections that follow draw heavily on the pre-release version of *Creating Programmable Applications,* which is a component of the Microsoft documentation for the first release of the OLE 2.0 SDK. The current version of OLE 2.0 at the time this edition was printed was OLE 2.01, but there were no major differences between the OLE 2.0 and 2.01 versions of the information contained in the sections that follow. The full text of *Creating*

Programmable Applications appears in the "OLE 2.0" group in the "Product Documentation" section of the Winter 1994 edition (Disk 6) of the Microsoft Developer Network CD-ROM. Readers who are interested in delving deeper into the intricacies of OLE Automation are advised to acquire the OLE 2.01 SDK or join the Microsoft Developers Network, if only to obtain the OLE 2.01 documentation that is included on the CD-ROM.

OLE Automation Terminology

As mentioned in Chapter 14, OLE Automation is built on Microsoft Corp.'s Component Object Model (COM) for OLE 2.0. Applications that support OA expose *programmable objects*. A programmable object is an application-specific object, such as an Excel Worksheet object, whose properties can be manipulated by code contained in another OA-compliant application. The application that manipulates the programmable object is called the OA client, and the application that supplies the object or provides the framework to create the object is called the OA server. This terminology is consistent with DDE, but conflicts with OLE 2.0's use of "destination" to specify the OLE 2.0 client and "source" to identify the OLE 2.0 server application.

External programming tools *dispatch an action* to the OA application. Dispatching an action is the OLE 2.0 equivalent of sending DDEExecute or **LinkExecute** instructions to a DDE server. You dispatch actions through the IDispatch interface of OLE 2.0 applications. The following are typical actions you dispatch from an Access 2.0 OA client application to OA servers:

- ■ Creating a new object of an application-specific class
- ■ Opening an existing object from a file
- ■ Getting the current values of the properties of the object
- ■ Setting the values of the properties of the object
- ■ Applying methods to the object
- ■ Responses to events triggered by OLE Custom Control objects

Complex OA applications, such as Excel 5.0, may have a total of several hundred collections, member objects, properties, and methods that are exposed to OA client applications. Developers of OA applications use the IClassFactory interface to define objects of application-specific classes. Collections are handled by OLE 2.0's IEnumVARIANT interface. (Values passed between OA applications are always of the

`Variant` data type.) The identities of the exposed objects, as well as their properties and methods, are contained in the application's *object type library*. For example, the object library for Excel 5.0 is XLEN50.OLB (about 400KB), which is located in the \EXCEL directory. Excel's and ODK's Object Browsers display entries contained in XLEN50.OLB when you choose Excel from the Libraries drop-down list box of the Browser.

Each OA-compliant application has its own object hierarchy. The name of the application, such as `Excel`, `Word`, or `Visio`, specifies the base class of the programmable objects. Most, but not all, OA-compliant servers use the name `Application` to specify the top member of the application-specific object class structure. Thus, `Excel.Application` or `Visio.Application` specifies a programmable object class that encompasses all of the programmable objects that are exposed by Excel 5.0 or Visio 2.0. Word for Windows 6.0 uses `Word.Basic` to specify the highest member of the class hierarchy. The `Excel.Application`, `Visio.Application`, and `Word.Basic` programmable object classes correspond to the `Application` object class that is the topmost member of the class of Access 2.0's application objects.

Documents correspond to the next lower level of object class. Here, the term "documents" refers to the general type of documents, not the `Documents` collection of Access 2.0 **Container** objects. Excel 5.0's document hierarchy consists of `Workbook` documents (members of the `Workbooks` collection), which contain `Worksheet` objects (members of the `Worksheets` collection) and `Module` objects (members of the `Modules` collection) that are stored in a single .XLS file. Like the tables contained in **Database** objects, you open a `Workbook` object from a file to make the programmable objects, such as members of the `Worksheets` collection contained in the `Workbook` object, accessible to your client application. `Worksheet` objects have a vast collection of properties and methods. Some properties of `Worksheet` objects, such as `Cells()`, are actually objects that have their own set of properties and methods.

Excel also has two types of programmable document objects that you can specify directly: `Excel.Sheet` and `Excel.Chart`. Visio 2.0 has a `Documents` collection that includes each `Document` (drawing or template) object open in Visio. (Microsoft Word 6.0 does not have a programmable document object. Word 6.0 exposes the `Word.Basic` object discussed later in this chapter.) Examples of the uses of the collections and member objects discussed in this section appear in the section titled "Visual Basic 3.0 Syntax for OLE Automation Instructions," later in this chapter.

> **NOTE**
>
> You obtain the names of objects exposed by OA-compliant OLE 2.0 servers and the properties of and methods applicable to these objects in the documentation and/or online help file that accompanies the server application. Many OA-compliant applications also provide an object browser, such as that for Excel 5.0, shown in Figure 16.2 earlier in the chapter. An object browser is the most convenient method of determining the programmable objects available and the syntax for getting and setting the properties of and applying methods to the programmable objects.

Files Required for OLE 2.0 and OLE Automation Applications

To take advantage of the programmable objects of OA applications, you need to have the files listed in Table 16.1 in your \WINDOWS\SYSTEM directory. Like MSARN200.EXE and the other components required for runtime Access applications, these library files are distributable; that is, developers can include these files on the installation diskettes of applications that use OLE 2.0 and OLE Automation. The files listed in Table 16.1 are replacements for the OLESVR.DLL and OLECLI.DLL libraries that support OLE 1.0 in Windows 3.1+. OLE 1.0 support is built into the OLE 2.0 libraries.

Table 16.1. Files required by applications that support OLE 2.0 and OLE Automation.

OLE 2.0 File	Purpose of File
OLE2.DLL	Supplies OLE 2.0 functions that are used by OLE objects and containers.
COMPOBJ.DLL	Provides functions that support creation of and access to an OLE 2.0 object creation.
OLE2DISP.DLL	Includes the IDispatch... functions required to get and set properties and to invoke methods of programmable objects.
OLE2PROX.DLL	Supplies the functions that enable you to access objects across intra-application processes and between different OLE 2.0 applications.

continues

Table 16.1. continued

OLE 2.0 File	Purpose of File
OLE2CONV.DLL	Provides conversion services for QuickDraw (.PCT files from Macintosh PICT files) to a format compatible with the Windows GDI.
TYPELIB.DLL	Provides access to object type libraries for individual OA applications.
OLE2.REG	Registers OLE 2.0 and OLE Automation data in REG.DAT.
STORAGE.DLL	Provides functions for the storage of objects and compound documents.
OLE2NLS.DLL	Provides translation facilities for string variables for localized applications. This file is needed only if your applications support multiple languages.
OC1016.DLL	Supports DLL for OLE Custom Controls. (OC1016.DLL is required only for applications that use OLE Custom Controls.)

WARNING

Well-behaved applications use VER.DLL to compare the version number, file-creation date, and file size of distributable files before overwriting existing files. Changes were made to several of the files in Table 16.1 while this book was being written. If you install an OLE 2.0 application that does not use VER.DLL to determine if the OLE 2.0 support file being installed is a newer version than the existing OLE 2.0 support file, versions of the OLE 2.0 support files that are incompatible with some or all of your OLE 2.0 applications may be installed. If you back up the files listed in Table 16.1 to diskettes before installing a new OLE 2.0 application, you can restore your known-good files if a problem occurs. This recommendation is especially important for the OC1016.DLL file, for which version control has not always been implemented.

In addition to the files required by all applications that use OLE 2.0 and OLE Automation, Access 2.0 requires several additional files that serve as intermediaries between Access 2.0 and the OLE 2.0 DLLs. These files are discussed in Chapter 29, "Distributing Runtime Versions of Your Databases."

Access Basic Syntax for OLE Automation Instructions

Creating and using programmable objects exposed by OA applications follows the pattern established in Access 2.0 for the member objects of the data access object. The primary difference between programmable objects and data access objects is that you can easily create a new or empty programmable object with the **CreateObject**( ) function. (Creating new databases and tables with Access Basic code requires a major programming effort.) Once you've assigned a value to a programmable object variable, you can set or get the values of properties of the object and apply methods to the object using the same techniques that apply to data access objects. The sections that follow describe how you declare and assign values to programmable object variables, and how you manipulate the programmable objects with Access Basic code.

> **NOTE**
>
> Close all open applications except Access 2.0 when running OLE Automation code. Using mega-apps, such as Excel, as OA servers to mega-app clients, such as Access 2.0, consumes a substantial amount of your computer's resources. In some cases, you may need more than 8MB of RAM for adequate performance with Access 2.0 OA operations. The computer used to write and execute the OA applications in this chapter is an 80486DX2-66 with 16MB of RAM and an 8-ms fixed disk. You may not be able to execute the example applications with a computer that delivers substantially lesser performance.

Declaring and Using Programmable Object Variables

The **Object** data type of Access 2.0 is the data type for variables that point to application-specific programmable objects exposed by OA-compliant applications. You can create a new object type of an application-specific class with the **CreateObject**( ) function or open an object whose data is stored in an existing document file with the **GetObject**( ) function. Both of these functions can be considered methods of the generic Access Basic programmable object, just as **OpenDatabase**( ) is treated in this book as a method of the abstract data access object of Access 2.0.

> **WARNING**
>
> The names of many of the object types and classes used in the code examples of this and the following two chapters are for beta versions of the OLE 2.0 server applications and OLE Custom Controls. The names of object types and classes may change in the retail versions or updated (bug-fix) versions of these products. Review the documentation that accompanies the OLE 2.0 server application or check the contents of your REG.DAT file (in the verbose mode) to verify the object type or class name if you encounter a problem with the `CreateObject()` or `GetObject()` functions. In most cases, you don't need to specify the object class of objects you open with the `GetObject()` function.

To create a new object, you use the following pair of statements:

```
Dim objObjectVar As Object
Set objObjectVar = CreateObject(strApplicationName.strObjectType)
```

Thus, to create an object variable, `objXLApp`, that points to `Excel.Application`, you would write the following two lines of code:

```
Dim objXLApp As Object
Set objXLApp = CreateObject("Excel.Application")
```

These two lines create a new object in much the same manner as adding a new unbound object frame with the default Create New option button selected in the OLE 2.0 Insert Object dialog box, described in the preceding two chapters. Listing 16.1 is an example of a subprocedure that uses OA instructions to create an Excel `Application` object, open an existing .XLS file, and print the values of a few of the rows of each `Worksheet` object of the `Workbook` object in the Debug window.

> **TIP**
>
> You must enclose the `Quit` method, applied to an Excel `Application` object, with square brackets to prevent the Access Basic interpreter from testing the source code to Access Basic syntax; in Access Basic, you can only apply the `Quit` method to the Access Application object.

> **NOTE**
>
> The following function is contained in the OLE Automation module (Chapter 16) of the AB_EXAMP.MDB database on the accompanying diskette. This example and the examples that follow rely on the existence of the STOCKS5.XLS file in the default C:\ACCESS\ADG20 subdirectory. If STOCKS5.XLS is located in a different directory, change the code accordingly.

Listing 16.1. Code to create and manipulate an `Excel.Application` object.

```
Function CreateNewObject () As Integer
    'Purpose:   Test the CreateObject() function

    Dim intRow As Integer        'Row counter
    Dim intCol As Integer        'Column counter
    Dim intCtr As Integer        'Worksheet counter

    Dim objXLApp As Object       'Excel.Application object
    Dim objXLSheet As Object     'A worksheet object

    'Create the application object
    Set objXLApp = CreateObject("Excel.Application")

    'Open an existing .XLS file and add it to the Workbooks collection
    objXLApp.Workbooks.Open ("c:\access\adg20\stocks5.xls")

    On Error Resume Next 'Prevent error on Null value

    'Loop through each of the Worksheet objects
    For intCtr = 1 To objXLApp.Worksheets.Count
        Set objXLSheet = objXLApp.Worksheets(intCtr)
        Debug.Print objXLApp.Worksheets(intCtr).Name

        'Print the cell values for a few rows to the Debug object
        For intRow = 1 To 5
            For intCol = 1 To 6
                If Err Then
                    Debug.Print "Null",
                    Err = 0
                Else
                    Debug.Print objXLSheet.Cells(intRow, intCol).Value,
                End If
            Next intCol
```

continues

Listing 16.1. continued

```
          'Add a blank line to the Debug window display
          Debug.Print
      Next intRow
  Next intCtr

  If Not Err Then
      CreateNewObject = True
  End If
  'Turn on error processing
  On Error GoTo 0

  'Close the application and release local memory
  objXLApp.[Quit]
  Set objXLSheet = Nothing
  Set objXLApp = Nothing
  If Not Err Then
      CreateNewObject = True
  End If
End Function
```

NOTE

If you receive a message that reads "OLE server cannot create object" when you run the preceding example, a timeout may have occurred due to the time required to load Excel 5.0 when several add-ins are loaded also. Open the Add-In Manager and temporarily disable all of the add-ins. Then try running the preceding example again.

FIGURE 16.4.

Values from an Excel 5.0 worksheet displayed by the code in Listing 16.1.

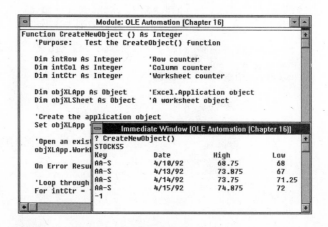

> **NOTE**
>
> When you create and manipulate a programmable object, you launch an instance of the OLE 2.0 server application. The OLE 2.0 server application is invisible and the server name does not appear in the Windows task manager's list. Invisible execution of OLE 2.0 servers is accomplished by adding a parameter to the command line that executes the server. The value of the `LocalServer` entry in REG.DAT for the CLSID corresponding to `Excel.Application` (Microsoft Excel 5.0 Application) is `C:\EXCEL\EXCEL /automation`. The `/automation` parameter causes Excel 5.0 to execute without opening a window.

You can open an OA-compliant application with a specified document by using the `GetObject()` function with the following syntax. Using the `GetObject()` function is more efficient than the preceding example when you want to open an existing file.

```
Dim objObjectVar As Object
Set objObjectVar = GetObject("d:\path\filename.ext"[, strObjectClass])
```

The preceding code fragment is related to the creation of a new unbound object frame when you select the Create From File option button of the Insert Object dialog box and then type *d:\path\filename.ext* in the file text box. The syntax also parallels that for the `OpenDatabase()` function (a method of the data access object).

> **NOTE**
>
> If you omit the optional `strObjectClass` argument, the server specified in the file-extension association entry of REG.DAT, `.ext = ObjectClass`, determines the server that is used. If you've installed Excel 5.0, files with an .XLS extension specify the `Excel.Sheet` object class. You can override the default association with the `strObjectClass` argument. If you want to create a programmable object from an OA-compliant application that is currently running, you substitute a comma for the path and filename argument and specify the object class.

To open an existing Excel 5.0 `Worksheet` object, use the following two lines:

```
Dim objXLSheet As Object
Set objXLSheet = GetObject("c:\access\adg20\stocks5.xls")
```

Listing 16.2 uses the `GetObject()` method to return the values of cells contained in the first few rows of a `Worksheet` object. You obtain the same result if you omit the

Excel.Sheet argument of the **GetObject**() method, because the default object for a .XLS file is a Worksheet object. The active Worksheet object is the one that was opened last in the Excel workbook.

Listing 16.2. Code that uses the GetObject() method to open a Worksheet object.

```
Function GetExistingObject () As Integer
    'Purpose:    Test the GetObject() function

    Dim intRow As Integer        'Row counter
    Dim intCol As Integer        'Column counter
    Dim objXLSheet As Object     'A worksheet object

    Set objXLSheet = GetObject("c:\access\adg20\stocks5.xls",
    ➥"Excel.Sheet")

    'Print the active worksheet name
    Debug.Print objXLSheet.Name

    'Print the cell values for a few rows to the Debug object
    For intRow = 1 To 5
      For intCol = 1 To 6
          'Substituting .Formula for .Value returns dates in number
          ➥format
          Debug.Print objXLSheet.Cells(intRow, intCol).Value
      Next intCol
      Debug.Print
    Next intRow
    Debug.Print
    objXLSheet.Parent.Saved = True
    objXLSheet.Application.[Quit]
    Set objXLSheet = Nothing
End Function
```

TIP

If you omit the line objXLSheet.Parent.Saved = True, Excel's "Save Changes?" message box appears, despite the preceding code having made no changes to the data in the worksheet. (Excel sets the "dirty" flag, in this case erroneously.) You can trick Excel into believing that you have saved the file by setting the Saved property of the Workbook object in which the Worksheet object is located to True. To refer to the next member upward in the object hierarchy, you specify the Parent property. You can refer to the Application object for any object in Excel's collection with the Application property of the object.

In most cases, opening the application with the **CreateObject**() method and then opening a file is the better method of manipulating programmable objects. The code example in Listing 16.1 opens the .XLS file as a Workbook object (the sole member of the Workbooks collection). Thus, you can open and manipulate any programmable object contained in the Workbook object. When you use the **GetObject**() method, most applications limit you to manipulating a single object. If you use "Excel.Application" as the value of the str*ObjectClass* argument when you use the **GetObject**() method, you receive an error message that reads "OLE Automation server cannot create object."

Using the Object Property of Object Frames

When you add an object frame to a form and select an object type supplied by an OA-compliant application, the Object property of the OLE container control points to the programmable object. When you add an object frame whose content is created from a file, the object frame applies the **GetObject**(str*FileName*) method for you. Figure 16.5 illustrates using Visual Basic 3.0's Debug Window to get or set the properties of the selected Worksheet object, Stocks3.

> **NOTE**
>
> You need to declare the object variables with **Dim** obj*Name* **As Object** statements in the Declarations section of the form on which the OLE container control is located, or with **Global** obj*Name* **As Object** statements in a module, before you type the **Set** obj*Name* = ... statements in the Debug Window.

FIGURE 16.5.

Using the Debug Window to experiment with the Object property.

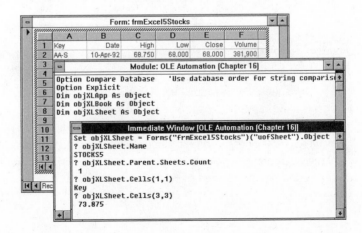

> **NOTE**
>
> You need to activate the OLE object in an OLE container control before you
> refer to the object with Visual Basic code, which you enter in the Debug
> Window or execute in a subprocedure. You activate the OLE object by
> double-clicking the OLE control or by executing the statement
> `oleObject.Action = 7` or `oleObject.Action = OLE_ACTIVATE`. However, if
> you activate the object when a module has the focus, in-place activation does
> not occur. Instead, Excel's main window appears.

Figure 16.6 illustrates how to use the `Cells(R, C).Value` reference to change data or
enter new data in cells of an Excel `Sheet` object. You also can employ a formula as a
String literal that complies with Excel's formula syntax. Using the Debug Window
to experiment with programmable objects is quicker and easier than writing and testing
OA code that is executed in subprocedures.

FIGURE 16.6.

*Setting the values
of object variables
with the
`Object.Application`
reference.*

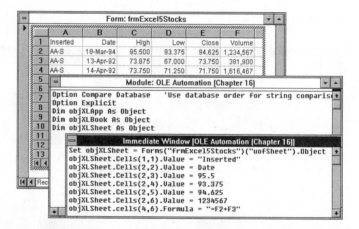

> **NOTE**
>
> The **Set** statement in Figure 16.6 uses a shorthand method of referring
> to form and report control objects that is not used elsewhere in
> this book. Using the `Forms(strFormName)(strControlName)` or
> `Reports(strReportName)(strControlName)` syntax to refer to a control
> object is similar to the use of **DBEngine(0)(0)** notation to refer to the
> currently open **Database** object.

If you add a new (empty) Excel 5.0 object to a form, Visual Basic applies the **CreateObject**("Excel.Application") method to the control. When you open a new Excel 5.0 object in an OLE container control, the default Workbook object, Book1, contains one empty Worksheet object, Sheet1. The Application object class of the OLE container Object gives you access to all of the properties and methods of the programmable objects of the application. You can set the Name property of these new objects with a **String** literal or variable.

When you open a new Workbook object in an OLE container with the Open method, the new Workbook object is added to the Workbooks collection. The original Workbook object, with the single empty Worksheet object, is Workbooks(1) or Workbooks("Book1"), and the new Workbook object opened from the file is Workbooks(2). You refer to the three Worksheet objects in Workbooks(2) either as Worksheets(1)...Worksheets(3) or by name, as in Worksheets("Stocks3"). References to programmable objects and their member objects follow the same conventions as the naming rules applicable to data access objects.

Creating a New Excel Worksheet with OLE Automation

You can emulate the Output To feature of Access 2.0 with Access Basic. The advantage of substituting OA for the Output To feature of Access is that you have complete control over the formatting of the resulting worksheet. (Formatting an Excel worksheet is discussed in the section titled "Worksheet Macros and Excel VBA," later in this chapter.) The disadvantage is that using OA is much slower than using Output To, as shown in Figure 16.7. The CreateOrders() function of Listing 16.3 creates a new Workbook object and then transfers data from the Orders table to a Worksheet object named Orders. When the process is complete, the new Workbook object is saved in the current directory (C:\ACCESS) as ORDERS.XLS.

Listing 16.3. Access Basic code to create a new Worksheet object.

```
Function CreateOrders() As Integer
    'Purpose: Create new Excel 5.0 worksheet from the Orders table

    'Declare local variables (Object variables are module-level)
    Dim dbNWind As Database      'Current database
    Dim tdfOrders As TableDef    'TableDef for Orders
    Dim rstOrders As Recordset   'Dynaset Recordset over Orders
    Dim intRow As Integer        'Row counter
    Dim intCol As Integer        'Column counter
    Dim objXLSOrders As Object   'Orders worksheet
    Dim sngTimer As Single       'Timer
```

continues

Listing 16.3. continued

```
    'Assign DAO pointers
    Set dbNWind = DBEngine.Workspaces(0).Databases(0)
    Set tdfOrders = dbNWind.TableDefs("Orders")
    Set rstOrders = dbNWind.OpenRecordset("Orders")

    DoCmd Hourglass True          'This process takes some time
    sngTimer = Timer              'Set the starting progress timer

    'Create a new Excel Worksheet object
    Set objXLSOrders = CreateObject("Excel.Sheet")
    DoEvents

    'Give the new worksheet a name
    objXLSOrders.Name = "Orders"

    'Add the column headings
    intRow = 1
    For intCol = 1 To tdfOrders.Fields.Count
        objXLSOrders.Cells(intRow, intCol).Value =
        ➥tdfOrders.Fields(intCol -1).Name
    Next intCol

    intRow = 2
    rstOrders.MoveFirst              'Go to the first record (safety)
    Do Until rstOrders.EOF
        'Loop through each record
        For intCol = 1 To rstOrders.Fields.Count
            'Loop through each field
            objXLSOrders.Cells(intRow, intCol).Value =
            ➥rstOrders.Fields(intCol - 1)
        Next intCol

        If rstOrders.Fields(0) Mod 100 = 0 Then
            'Display the progress
            Debug.Print rstOrders.Fields(0).Value & Chr$(9) & (Timer -
            ➥sngTimer)
        End If

        rstOrders.MoveNext
        intRow = intRow + 1
        'DoEvents                    'For safety, delete after testing for
        ➥speed
    Loop

    DoCmd Hourglass False

    objXLSOrders.SaveAs ("orders.xls")
    objXLSOrders.Parent.Parent.[Quit]
    Set objXLSOrders = Nothing       'Not required, but a good practice
End Function
```

Run the function shown in the preceding listing by entering ? CreateCust() in the Immediate Window. Then go have a cup of coffee or a sandwich. The Immediate Window of Figure 16.7 shows the value of the Order ID field, followed by the time in seconds required to complete the transfer of data to the worksheet for each 100 records. The first entry for order 10000 indicates the time in seconds required to open the **TableDef** and **RecordSet** objects and to open Excel 5.0 as an OA server. Figure 16.8 shows the ORDERS.XLS workbook with part of the Orders worksheet created by the CreateOrders() function opened in Excel 5.0.

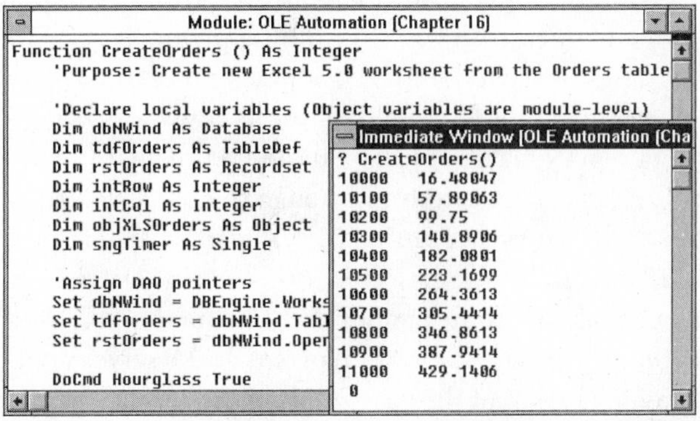

FIGURE 16.7.

Time, in seconds, required to open Excel and to create the ORDERS.XLS workbook.

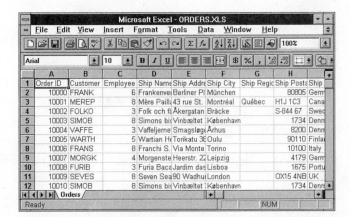

FIGURE 16.8.

Part of the Orders worksheet of the ORDERS.XLS workbook.

NOTE

Access 2.0's Output To feature uses functions contained in SOA200.DLL to transfer data in Excel BIFF5 format directly to a workbook file. Output To requires about 33 seconds to complete the same operation as the code in Listing 26.3, which requires about seven minutes to execute. Using OLE

> Automation involves transferring data through functions contained in many layers of libraries. If you plan to create large worksheets from data contained in Access tables, it is faster to use Output To to create the worksheet and then use Access Basic OA code to modify the worksheet as necessary.

Closing Objects and Quitting Applications

When you open an OA server application with Visual Basic code, the server application remains open until you close it by applying the obj*Application*.[Quit] method (or the equivalent method if the application does not support the Quit method). If you do not apply the Quit method (or its equivalent) when you are finished manipulating a programmable object, you can eventually run out of memory when opening other OA server applications. Although the *Building Applications* manual that accompanies Access states that setting the value of an Application object to **Nothing** closes the OLE server, testing has shown this is not always true. Exiting your application does *not* apply the equivalent of the Quit method. Closing (but not hiding) a form that contains an OLE control closes the OA server application in most cases, but explicit application of the Quit method, if the Application object supports it, is the safest approach.

NOTE

> Programmable Word.Basic objects you create in Access 2.0 are an exception to the preceding rule. Unlike other programmable objects, Word.Basic objects close when the procedure that uses the Word.Basic object completes its execution.

Object variables can consume a significant amount of memory. You do not regain the memory consumed by object variables you declare with local scope when the subprocedure in which the variables are declared finishes executing or when you use the Quit method. To recover the memory used by object variables, always set the value of the variables to the **Nothing** reserved word when you have finished using them.

Manipulating Programmable Objects with Code

The purpose of the simple code examples given in the preceding sections is to illustrate the techniques you use to declare and assign values to object variables in Access

Basic. As noted earlier in this chapter, each OA application has its own set of programmable objects, and each object has a specific set of properties and applicable methods. The programmable objects, properties, and methods exposed by Microsoft applications that use Visual Basic for Applications as their macro language are, as a whole, the same objects, properties, and methods that are manipulated by the macro language.

OLE Automation server applications that do not incorporate VBA have sets of programmable objects, properties, and methods that reflect the nature of the application. The base object class of both Microsoft Word for Windows 6.0 and ShapeWare Visio 2.0 is the Application object. Unlike Excel 5.0 and Microsoft Project 4.0, both Word 6.0 and Visio 2.0 are OA servers only.

The section that follows describes the changes you need to make to VBA code that you import from Excel 5.0 and Project 4.0 into Access Basic procedures. Subsequent sections give examples of the use of Word Basic instructions in Visual Basic 3.0 applications and of creating macros for Visio 2.0 with OLE Automation.

Programming Microsoft Excel 5.0 and Project 4.0 Objects with VBA Code

Microsoft applications that incorporate Visual Basic for Applications expose the same objects, properties, and methods to OA client applications as those accessible to the application's dialect of Object Basic. Both Excel 5.0 and Project 4.0 incorporate VBA. Excel 5.0 is used for most of the examples in this chapter because Excel is likely to be the most common OA server used with Visual Basic 3.0 database applications. Project 4.0 was in the final beta test stage at the time this book was written, and was not expected to be released by Microsoft until after this edition's publication date.

Space limitations preclude a full discussion here of the Access Basic programming methods for programmable objects exposed by the OA server applications that were available at the time this edition was published. Fortunately, you can use the VBA documentation that accompanies the OA server application and the server's online help system to guide you in writing Access Basic OA client code. Similarly, you can modify code examples in VBA manuals and third-party books on VBA for use in Access OA applications. The syntax for variable declaration and assignment, conditional execution statements, loops, and most other program flow control instructions is identical in Access Basic and VBA. You can copy VBA code from an OLE server application's module, paste the code into an module behind a form, modify it to conform to Access Basic syntax, and execute the code with Access 2.0.

> **TIP**
>
> Use code-behind-forms (CBF) modules, rather than conventional Access Basic modules, to hold the VBA code you import from existing applications or adapt from examples in manuals and books. VBA makes extensive use of the Me self-reference to containers and direct reference to objects. Substantially fewer modifications are required for VBA code that is added to CBF modules than that added to conventional Access modules.

To execute VBA code in Access Basic, you are likely to need to modify the imported code as follows:

- Declare the object variables you need in the Declarations section of a form module. (There was no equivalent in OLE 2.0 servers of a **Report** object at the time this edition was written.) In most cases, you can copy the declarations from the VBA application's Declarations section(s). As an example, you need to replace references to Active*Object* (for example, ActiveSheet in Excel's VBA) with an object variable. Thus, you need to declare an obj*Sheet* object variable to supply the proper reference.

- Add the **Set** objAppName = **CreateObject**("AppName.Application") statement to point to the application object. VBA applications use the **CreateObject**() and **GetObject**() methods only to set the values of programmable object variables from external OA-compliant server applications.

- Depending on the method by which the VBA code references objects, you may need to precede methods and properties with the object variable. VBA enables you to refer to objects in subclasses of the active object with simple statements such as Cells(1,1) = 1234.

- Convert all arguments that use positional notation to conventional Visual Basic 3.0 format, substituting commas for missing argument values. Positional arguments are discussed in the section called "Contrasting Visual Basic for Applications with Visual Basic 3.0," later in this chapter.

- Some VBA reserved words and constructs, such as For Each...In...Next and With...End With, are not supported by Access Basic. (All VBA reserved words and constructs are expected to be supported by the next version of Access.)

Using VBA code in Visual Basic 3.0 applications is discussed in the section called "Contrasting Visual Basic for Applications with Visual Basic 3.0," later in this chapter.

Manipulating Word for Windows 6.0 Documents

Version 6.0 of Microsoft Word is an OLE Automation client only. The Word Basic macro language of Word 6.0, which is not a dialect of Object Basic, cannot open programmable objects of other OA server applications. Thus, Word Basic retains its status as a macro language, as opposed to an application programming language such as VBA. As noted in the introduction to this chapter, you can use Word 6.0 as an OA server to your Access 2.0 client applications. It is possible, for example, to create an Access application that generates complete Word 6.0 documents from names, addresses, boilerplates, and graphic images that are stored in one or more Access databases.

> **NOTE**
>
> To use Access to manipulate Word 6.0 documents, you need the Microsoft Word Developer's Kit (WDK). The WDK is a separate product that you purchase from Microsoft Corp. The WDK documents all of the reserved words, commands, and other keywords of Word Basic, and provides examples of programming Word Basic macros. The full text of the WDK documentation and the example macros are included in the Microsoft Office Developer's Kit.

When you use Word 6.0 as an OA server application, almost all of the instructions in the Word Basic macro language are available to your Access OA client application. Thus, an Access 2.0 application can employ the **CreateObject**(`"Word.Basic"`) method to launch Word 6.0 as an application and gain access to the Basic object of Word 6.0. Basic is the only object that Word 6.0 exposes; the Basic object does not have conventional, object-oriented properties and methods. Therefore, you *cannot* use the **GetObject**(`"docname.doc"`) method to open an existing Word 6.0 document from a file. Instead, you execute Word Basic instructions as if these instructions were methods of the Basic object you create in your Access application. This book uses the term *pseudo-method* to describe macro language instructions that are exposed by OLE Automation.

To open an existing Word document using OA, you use the following three statements:

```
Dim objWWApp As Object
Set objWWApp = CreateObject("Word.Basic")
objWWApp.FileOpen "d:\path\filename.doc"
```

Once you've opened the file, you can apply any Word Basic instruction as a pseudo-method of the objWWApp object. Word Basic includes many instructions that append the string object-type identifier symbol ($) to indicate that the instruction returns a string. References to Word Basic pseudo-methods that include the $ symbol should be enclosed within square brackets ([ ]) in your code. The use of square brackets in Visual Basic 3.0 to normalize nonconforming OA syntax is the same as the use of square brackets to enclose table, field, and **QueryDef** names of Access database objects that incorporate spaces or other impermissible characters.

For example, to return the value of a bookmark in a Word 6.0 document pointed to by objWWApp to a **String** variable, you use the following syntax:

```
Dim strBookmark As String
strBookmark = objWWApp.[GetBookmark$]("BookmarkName")
```

When you embed a Word 6.0 document in a Visual Basic 3.0 OLE container control, you use the following statements to gain access to the OLE container control's Basic object:

```
Dim objWWApp As Object
Set objWWApp = oleControl.Object.Application.WordBasic
```

In this case, the WordBasic object descriptor does not include a period between Word and Basic, because WordBasic is the (only) object exposed by the Application object class of the OLE container control's Object "property." As is the case with any object embedded in an OLE container control, you need to activate the object before you refer to the Object "property."

NOTE

When you embed an object in an unbound object frame, the data for the object is stored in the form object on which the control appears. As noted in Chapter 14, in-place activation is available only with embedded (not linked) OLE objects. Word documents with embedded bitmapped graphics in OLE container controls can result in *very* large .MDB files. For example, the size of the .MDB file for Figure 16.7 is more than 1MB, because the manuscript for this chapter, which was written using Word 6.0, included all of the figures for the chapter as embedded bitmaps. Unless you have a specific need to edit Word 6.0 documents in a Visual Basic 3.0 application, you are likely to be better served by using the **GetObject**() method to operate on large Word 6.0 documents and to manipulate large Excel 5.0 worksheets.

It is probable that the next major upgrade to Microsoft Word will incorporate Visual Basic for Applications. Most Word Basic developers had expected that Word 6.0 would incorporate VBA. Changing from the template-oriented Word Basic macro language, the progenitor of Object Basic, to object-oriented VBA contained in modules constitutes a major change in the development environment for Word applications. Major alterations of this scope often are called *paradigm shifts.* Publishers of high-volume, mainstream Windows mega-apps take a very conservative approach to instituting paradigm shifts. This conservatism is understandable when hundreds of millions of dollars in revenue hinge on the success of the application in a highly competitive market.

The versions of WordPerfect for Windows and AmiPro that were newly announced at the time this book was written do not offer *any* OLE 2.0 or OLE Automation features. Therefore, Microsoft can take an incremental approach that includes the in-place activation features of OLE 2.0 and can add OA features that preserve backward compatibility with existing Word Basic macros, while opening up the ability to write the equivalent of Word Basic macros in Access Basic. This approach lets Microsoft reserve full VBA compliance for the next battle in the word processing feature war.

NOTE

Developers of Word Basic applications should seriously consider using Access 2.0 and OA for document-management applications that involve Word 6.0. This is especially recommended for any Word 6.0 application that requires access to databases, a subject that is discussed later in this chapter. Just as you can import VBA code to Access Basic, you can export a substantial percentage of your Access Basic OA code to VBA modules. The principal limitation of VBA is that it doesn't have the rich complement of control objects provided by Access's form-design toolbox and OLE Custom Controls. VBA currently limits you to displaying dialog boxes with only a few standard Windows controls. To the extent possible, use controls in Access OA applications that also are available in Word 6.0 and Excel 5.0 dialog boxes. Design your Access Basic code for Word 6.0 applications so that event handlers call subprocedures contained in modules and explicitly address all Access control objects. This design method will minimize the amount of restructuring you'll need to do to your Access Basic code when you import it into VBA modules in the next version of Word.

Contrasting Visual Basic for Applications with Access Basic

Currently, only Microsoft applications offer Visual Basic for Applications, because Microsoft decided in mid-1993 not to license VBA to other software publishers. However, anyone who can fathom the contents of Microsoft's *Programmer's Reference* for OLE 2.0 and is willing to suffer the agony of adding and debugging the required C++ code can create or update applications to support OLE Automation. Competitive pressures will force spreadsheet, database, and word processing software publishers to include OLE Automation. If Microsoft continues its policy of refusing to license VBA to others, a Tower of Basic Babel will arise in the industry. Lotus Development Corp., for instance, has announced that Lotus Script, originally developed for the firm's Improv spreadsheet product, will be converted to a Basic-like language and will be included in future versions of other Lotus products.

Visual Basic for Applications consists of the following elements:

■ The core VBA language, which is both a subset and a superset of Visual Basic 3.0. VBA is intended to replace the diverse collection of macro languages in Microsoft's mainstream Windows and to add programmability to Microsoft's Macintosh applications that previously lacked a macro language or whose macro language had a limited vocabulary.

■ A macro recording feature that translates menu choices, keystrokes, and other user input into VBA code. The ability to record macros and then import the VBA code into an Access form, report module, or conventional Access Basic module can minimize the time you spend looking up the VBA syntax for a variety of application-specific operations.

■ Application-specific extensions to VBA, usually in form of methods that have names related to menu choices or the equivalent. If the menu choice leads to a dialog box, the selections you make in the controls of the dialog box become the values of arguments of the method.

■ Application-specific intrinsic global constants.

■ A code editor that is an amalgam of the Word Basic macro editor and Visual Basic 3.0's code-editing windows. The VBA code editor includes debugging features, such as breakpoints and watchpoints, that are similar to the debugging features of Access 2.0.

■ Application-specific objects, properties, and methods. Technically, application-specific objects are OLE Automation functions and are not components of VBA. However, the Microsoft documentation for Excel 5.0

treats these OA functions as components of VBA. The documentation for Project 4.0 is expected to follow a similar format. For the purposes of the present discussion, this chapter conforms to the Microsoft documentation conventions.

■ An object browser that uses list boxes to display the objects, properties, and methods of the active object, the application itself, and VBA. Figure 16.2, at the beginning of this chapter, shows the object browser display for Excel 5.0.

■ Modal dialog boxes to provide an interactive user interface (UI) for VBA code. Application dialog boxes have a limited repertoire of control objects, and the control objects that are available have few associated events (usually only one). VBA dialog boxes lack the flexibility that developers have come to expect from Access form objects.

■ A dialog editor that lets you create modal dialog boxes using drag-and-drop methods, similar to those of Access, to add control objects to the dialog box.

VBA also is a subset of Access Basic because the root Object Basic language does not include reserved words and keywords for application-specific objects, such as Access 2.0's data access object and Access application objects. The current applications that support VBA restrict you to the use of modal dialog boxes. The application to which VBA is attached also is responsible for providing tools that assist you in writing VBA applications, such as Excel 5.0's Object Browser. The dialogs and control objects supplied by the host application trigger a much smaller collection of events than Access's forms, reports, and controls.

VBA is a superset of Visual Basic 3.0 because it enables you to create user-defined functions (UDFs) that act directly on the application's native document format. Each application that embeds VBA includes properties and methods that apply to the elements of the host application's document. As an example, Excel's implementation of VBA includes a `Range` object that has `Column`, `Formula`, `Height`, and `WrapText` properties, among others. In total, Excel specifies about 120 different classes and collections of objects. Excel-specific methods for VBA replace the familiar functions of Excel 4.0 macros.

OLE Automation and Object Basic dialects are very closely related. The objects that OLE Automation applications expose so that other applications can orchestrate their behavior are the same objects that you address with embedded VBA. The sections that follow describe how VBA differs from Access Basic and how you use Excel's macro recording capability to create VBA code that you can modify for use in Access Basic OA code.

> **NOTE**
>
> An understanding of the basic principles of writing VBA code is necessary if you intend to make use of OA in Access 2.0 applications. As mentioned earlier in this chapter, the manuals that accompany OA-compliant Microsoft applications provide only brief explanations and code snippets to demonstrate how to program the objects exposed by other applications. To gain insight into OA programming methods for Excel 5.0 and Project 4.0 objects, you need to be able to translate the VBA examples in the manuals and third-party books about these applications, as well as VBA code you create by recording macros, into Access Basic OA client code.

VBA Syntax Currently Not Supported by Access Basic

Visual Basic for Applications introduces a number of features and structures that are not available yet in Access Basic. The following sections describe the most important differences in syntax between VBA and version 2.0 of Access Basic.

References to Named Arguments

Visual Basic for Applications enables you to refer to named arguments of instructions and functions without regard to the position of the argument in the instruction's or function's argument list. For example, in Word Basic, the full syntax of the EditFind instruction is as follows:

```
EditFind .Find = "Developer's", .WholeWord = 0, .MatchCase = 1,
➥.Direction = 0, .Format = 0
```

In Word Basic and VBA, you can accept the default value, usually **0** or **Null**, for an argument by omitting the variable from the collection, as in the following example:

```
EditFind .Find = "Developer's", .MatchCase = 1
```

Access does not enable you to use named functions, nor can you omit intermediate optional arguments of VBA or Word Basic instructions and functions that accept named arguments. In Access Basic, the required syntax is

```
objXLApp.EditFind "Developer's", 0, 1
```

Word Basic requires that you specify the intermediate **0** value for the .WholeWord argument. Default values of arguments that trail the last argument that has a non-default value can be omitted in Access Basic statements.

> **NOTE**
>
> Microsoft refers to named arguments as positional arguments in the *Microsoft Excel Visual Basic User's Guide.* A better description of named arguments is *appositional* arguments, because named arguments are members of a parameter collection of the receiving function that the receiving function iterates by name, rather than by position.

The *With...End* With Structure

Visual Basic for Applications introduces a new programming structure, `With...End With`, which you can use to simplify reading and setting the value of multiple named arguments of a property of an object variable. This new structure is quite similar to the nested `Begin...End` structures, which identify the relationships and properties of objects when you save a Visual Basic 3.0 form to an ANSI (text) file. The syntax of the `With...End With` structure is as follows:

```
With Object.Property
    .Argument1 = Value1
    .Argument2 = Value2
    .Argument3 = Value3
    ...
    .Argument# = Value#
End With
```

You need to substitute conventional Access Basic argument values, described in the preceding section, for named arguments when you import VBA code that uses `With...End With` structures. It is likely that future versions of Access will include the `With...End With` structure. Including the `With...End With` structure would require that Access Basic support named arguments.

The *For Each...Next* Structure

The `For Each...Next` structure is designed to iterate member objects of a collection. You also can use the `For Each...Next` structure of VBA to iterate all elements of an array of values of the **Variant** data type. The syntax of the `For Each...Next` structure is as follows:

```
For Each Member In Collection
    Statement
    [...]
    [Statement]
Next Member
```

You need to substitute a conventional `For...Next` loop when importing VBA code that incorporates the `For Each...Next` structure into Access Basic modules. It also is likely that the next version of Visual Basic will incorporate the `For Each...Next` structure.

Visual Basic for Applications Code Modules

The user interface of embedded VBA code modules combines features present in the code-editing windows of Word Basic templates with those in the Access Basic dialect of Object Basic. The modules in which you create and store Object Basic code resemble the template workspace of Word Basic. Embedded modules, like Word Basic templates, can contain multiple functions and subprocedures. Unlike with Access Basic and Visual Basic 3.0, separate code-editing windows are not created for the Declarations section, or for the individual functions and subprocedures that are included in the module. Instead, the Declarations section of an Object Basic module is defined as the region of the code-editing window above your first `Sub ProcName` or `Function FunctionName` statement. You can add as many procedures as you want following the declaration of Windows API function prototypes, and any global or module-level variables you need.

Worksheet Macros and Excel VBA

Microsoft Excel 5.0 has adopted VBA as the preferred method of creating new macros to automate Excel applications. Although Excel 5.0 is backwardly compatible with conventional Excel function-style macros, any new macros you record will generate VBA code in a module, unless you explicitly choose to create Excel 4.0 function macros. The process of creating Excel VBA macros is virtually identical to the method used by Word to create macros. You can use VBA statements to execute existing macros and user-defined functions (UDFs) that were created with earlier versions of Excel.

If you want to use Access Basic OA code to modify the worksheets you create, recording Excel macros is the easiest method of finding the name of and syntax for Excel-specific objects and methods. The following example creates a VBA macro to format the Orders worksheet of the ORDERS.XLS workbook described earlier in the chapter. Once you've created the macro, you can add the code to that of Listing 16.3, or create a separate function that formats the worksheet.

1. Launch Excel 5.0 and open the ORDERS.XLS workbook.
2. Choose **R**ecord Macro from the **T**ools menu, and then **R**ecord New Macro from the submenu to open the Record New Macro dialog box. Type a descriptive name, such as `FormatOrders`, in the Macro Name text box and

click OK. (See Figure 16.9.) A floating toolbar with a single Stop (recording) button appears.

FIGURE 16.9.

Assigning a name to a recorded Excel VBA macro.

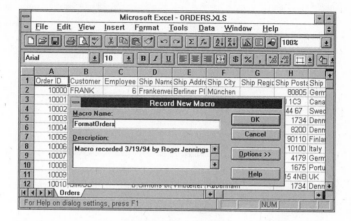

3. With cell A1 selected, press Ctrl+Shift+End to select the entire worksheet, and then choose AutoFormat from the Format menu to display the AutoFormatDialog. Select the format you want, and then click OK. (See Figure 16.10.) If the "Selection too large, continue without Undo" message box appears, click OK to apply the new format.

FIGURE 16.10.

Selecting a standard Excel format for a worksheet with the AutoFormat dialog.

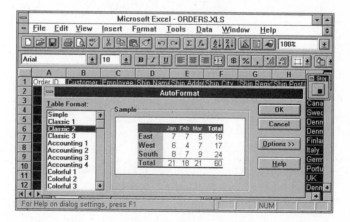

4. Select cell A1, and then click the Stop button to halt the recording process. Your worksheet, with Excel's Classic 2 style applied, appears as shown in Figure 16.11.

FIGURE 16.11.

The Orders worksheet with the Classic 2 format applied.

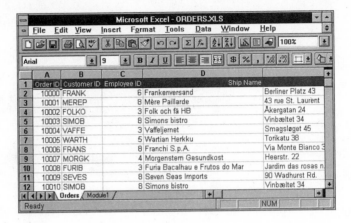

5. Click the Module1 tab to open the module that contains the recorded macro. (See Figure 16.12.) Select the subprocedure and copy the code, without the comments, to the Clipboard.

FIGURE 16.12.

The VBA code created by the recorded Excel macro.

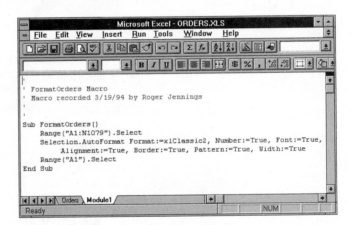

6. You need to verify that values have been provided for each of the arguments of the `Selection.AutoFormat` method. Select the `AutoFormat` method name and press F1 to display the Help topic for the method. AutoFormat is applicable to `Chart` and `Range` objects, so click the Range hotspot to display the Help topic for `Range.Autoformat`. (See Figure 16.13.) Although the syntax shown in Figure 16.13 shows that `AutoFormat` requires parentheses around its arguments, this is not correct.

FIGURE 16.13.

The Help topic for the AutoFormat *method.*

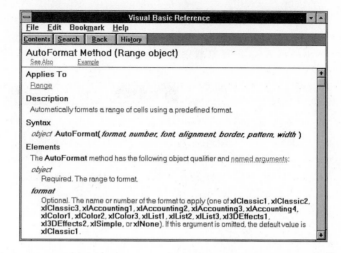

7. Verify that values for each of the arguments of the AutoFormat method are provided by the named arguments of the method in the code, and that the sequence of the named argument values corresponds to the sequence of the argument names in the help topic.

8. The Format:=xlClassic2 argument refers to an Excel-specific intrinsic global constant, xlClassic2. To obtain the **Integer** value of xlClassic2, press Ctrl+G, or choose Debug Window from the View menu to open the Debug Window. Execute ? xlClassic2 in the upper pane of the Debug Window, which returns the value 2. (See Figure 16.14.)

FIGURE 16.14.

Obtaining the value of an Excel intrinsic global constant in the Immediate pane of the Debug Window.

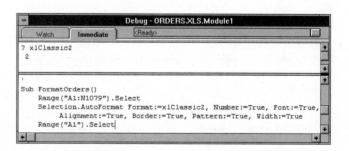

Excel Basic's Debug window differs substantially from the Immediate Window of Access and the Debug Window of Visual Basic 3.0. You choose between the Immediate window and the Watch window by clicking the Immediate or Watch folder tabs. The split window enables you to easily paste expressions from the module code in the lower pane to the upper pane, where you edit and execute the expressions.

9. Give Access the focus and paste the code into an Access module to create the Access Basic `FormatOrders()` subprocedure that you modify to conform to the requirements of Access Basic OA syntax and operations on Excel objects.

NOTE

Neither the Excel or VBA help file provides the values of Excel intrinsic constants. The ODK, however, provides XLCONST.BAS, a Visual Basic 3.0 module that contains the **Global Const** declarations for a late beta version Excel 5.0. The XLCONST.TXT file, included on the accompanying diskette and installed in your C:\ACCESS\ADG20 directory, contains all of the `xl...` constants from XLCONST.BAS, sorted in alphabetic order.

Listing 16.4 shows the code for the stand-alone version of the `FormatOrders()` subprocedure. To apply a method, such as `AutoFormat`, to an Excel object, you must first create an object variable and give it a pointer to the type of object appropriate to the method. As shown in the help topic for `AutoFormat`, the `AutoFormat` method is applicable only to `Range` objects. (`Selection` is a property, not an object, and therefore is not accessible to OA code.) To apply the `AutoFormat` method, you create an object variable, `objXLROrders`, and give it a pointer to the range (in this case, the entire active content of the worksheet) specified by the literal `"A1:N1079"` argument of the `Range` method. Once you've created the object, you can apply any applicable Excel method to the object.

Listing 16.4. Access Basic code to format an Excel `Range` object.

```
Sub FormatOrders ()
    'Purpose:  Format the Orders worksheet with Excel Classic 2 style

    Dim objXLSOrders As Object  'Orders worksheet
    Dim objXLROrders As Object  'Range in Orders worksheet

    'Launch Excel, open ORDERS.XLS, and select the range
    Set objXLSOrders = GetObject("c:\access\orders.xls", "Excel.Sheet")
    Set objXLROrders = objXLSOrders.Range("A1:N1079")

    objXLROrders.AutoFormat 2, True, True, True, True, True, True

    objXLSOrders.Parent.Save
    objXLSOrders.Application.[Quit]

    Set objXLROrders = Nothing    'Not required, but a good practice
    Set objXLSOrders = Nothing
End Sub
```

> **NOTE**
>
> The code in Listing 16.4 is specific to the 14-column, 1079-row Orders worksheet created earlier in the chapter. You need to create the string that specifies the range with code that determines the number of columns and the number of rows, and that translates these values into *RC* format.

Deciding When to Use VBA or Access Basic as the External Programming Environment

If you intend to create an application that involves the interaction of two applications that are OA-compliant and incorporate VBA, your choice for the programming environment for your application will come from the following two options:

- Write an Access OA client application that uses the `CreateObject()` method to create *Server*.`Application` object variables for the two OA servers.
- Write a Visual Basic for Applications client application that applies the `CreateObject()` method in the VBA code of one of the servers to use the other OA-compliant application as an OA server.

Access 2.0 isn't an OA server, so the second choice is not available to you if you are using Access 2.0 and only one other OA server application. However, if your application involves access to one or more databases, writing an Access OA client application is the obvious choice. Using Access 2.0's data access object to open and manipulate database objects is more straightforward than employing the somewhat cumbersome database extensions of Excel 5.0 and Word 6.0.

You have another choice, however, if the OA server uses VBA. You can write VBA subprocedures and execute the VBA subprocedures from Access Basic with the `objXLApp.Run()` method. You can execute VBA functions using *Variable* = `objXLApp.Run()` statements. Thus, you have the choice of writing Excel-specific code either in Access Basic or in the Excel flavor of VBA.

Word 6.0 developers currently are limited to using `DDEExecute` instructions to manipulate objects of other applications that are not components of a Word 6.0 document. As mentioned earlier in the chapter, Word Basic programmers who need to manipulate programmable objects in other OA-compliant applications can gain control more easily over the other applications' objects by using Visual Basic 3.0 OA client applications.

Excel developers are likely to favor VBA code, because the Excel worksheet is a familiar development environment and creating references to Excel objects is simpler in VBA. When you program Excel objects with Access Basic, however, you are not limited to using Excel 5.0 modal dialog boxes to interact with the user of your application. Thus, your Excel application can take full advantage of the variety of window modes and control objects offered by Access 2.0.

17

Charting Data with Microsoft Graph 5.0

One of the first features added to basic spreadsheet applications was the ability to create graphs and charts from spreadsheet data. The current Windows versions of Microsoft Excel, Lotus 1-2-3, and Borland Quattro Pro provide quite sophisticated graphing and charting capabilities. Excel 5.0 includes a ChartWizard to aid users in the creation of colorful, three-dimensional charts; Lotus 1-2-3 and Quattro Pro also provide automated assistance for the creation of charts. Access 1.x included Microsoft Graph 3.0, which was derived from the code for the embedded chart engine of Excel 4.0. Access 2.0's graphing features are implemented by an OLE 2.0 version of Microsoft Graph that also is OLE Automation-compliant.

Microsoft Graph 5.0 (abbreviated MSGraph5 in this book) is an OLE 2.0 mini-server application that is almost indistinguishable from the graphing application embedded in the executable code of Excel 5.0. Access 2.0 is the first Microsoft application to include the MSGraph5 mini-server; it is likely that future versions of all Microsoft productivity applications will use MSGraph5 to supply graphing and charting capabilities. The Graph Wizard included with Access 2.0 is almost identical to the ChartWizard of Excel 5.0. This chapter describes how to use Access 2.0's Graph Wizard to add MSGraph5 graphs and charts to Access 2.0 forms and reports, and how to use OLE Automation (OA) to manipulate graphs and charts contained in unbound object frames.

Creating Crosstab Queries for Graphs and Charts

The majority of graphs and charts you create with Access are based on summarized information, such as orders received, product sales volume, and gross margin, for a set of discrete time periods. In this book, these graphs and charts are referred to as the *time-series* type. Another common summary graph compares sums or averages of category values for grouped data; an example is a graph of sales for the year for categories of products grouped by employee or sales region. This book refers to such graphs as the *comparative-performance* type. Regardless of whether you create time-series or comparative-performance graphs, you are likely to use a crosstab query to summarize the data that underlies the graph.

> **NOTE**
>
> The terms *graph* and *chart* often are considered synonyms. This book defines a graph as a collection of points or a series of lines connecting points that represents the relation of one or more independent variables (sales or gross

margin) to a dependent variable, such as the quarters of years. Charts, in this book, use surfaces, rather than lines, to depict the relationships between variables. Chart types include two- and three-dimensional bar, column, and area charts, plus three-dimensional surface charts.

The basic data for the crosstab queries for Access graphs and charts usually derives from tables that store entries from source documents (such as sales orders and invoices). This source data often is called *line-item* data. Very large firms can accumulate several million line-item records in a single year, so larger firms usually aggregate line-item source data in tables; aggregation greatly improves the performance of queries at the expense of disk space. Aggregated data are referred to as *rolled-up* data or *rollups*. Rolling up data from relational tables violates one of the guiding principles of relational theory: Don't store calculated values in tables. Tables and even databases that consist solely of rolled-up data are very common in mainframe environments.

The examples of Access graphs and charts in this chapter are based on two crosstab queries: qryOrders1993Quarterly, a time-series query, and qryOrders1993Employees, a comparative-performance query. Both of these queries are included in the AB_EXAMP.MDB database on the accompanying diskette. Both queries rely on tables attached from NWIND.MDB that AB_EXAMP.MDB expects to be located in your C:\ACCESS\ADG20 directory. (Refresh the attachments with the Attachment Manager add-in if you located the example applications elsewhere.) The Design View of the qryOrders1993Quarterly query is shown in Figure 17.1.

FIGURE 17.1.

The design of the qryOrders1993 Quarterly query.

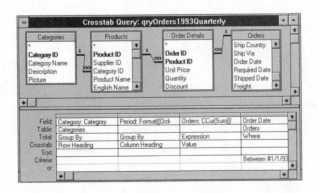

Following is the SQL statement for qryOrders1993Quarterly defined by the design in Figure 17.1. The **CCur(Sum**([Order Details].[Unit Price]*[Order Details].[Quantity]*(1-[Order Details].[Discount]))) expression calculates the net (discounted) value of the orders based on line-item records in the Order Details table. The `CCur()` function converts the **Double** value returned by the **Sum()** aggregate function to the **Currency** data type. The INNER JOIN syntax is quite convoluted and is easier to understand if you refer to Figure 17.1 while attempting to follow the JOINs. Figure 17.2 shows the result set of qryOrders1993Quarterly.

```
TRANSFORM CCur(Sum([Order Details].[Unit Price]*
    [Order Details].[Quantity]*(1-[Order Details].[Discount])))
    AS Orders
SELECT Categories.[Category Name] AS Category
    FROM Orders
    INNER JOIN ((Categories
    INNER JOIN Products ON Categories.[Category ID] = Products.[Category
    ➡ID])
    INNER JOIN [Order Details] ON Products.[Product ID] =
        [Order Details].[Product ID]) ON Orders.[Order ID] =
        [Order Details].[Order ID]
WHERE ((Orders.[Order Date] Between #01/1/93# And #12/31/93#))
    GROUP BY Categories.[Category Name]
PIVOT Format([Order Date],"yyyy\Qq")
WITH OWNERACCESS OPTION;
```

FIGURE 17.2.

The query result set of the qryOrders1993Quarterly time-series query.

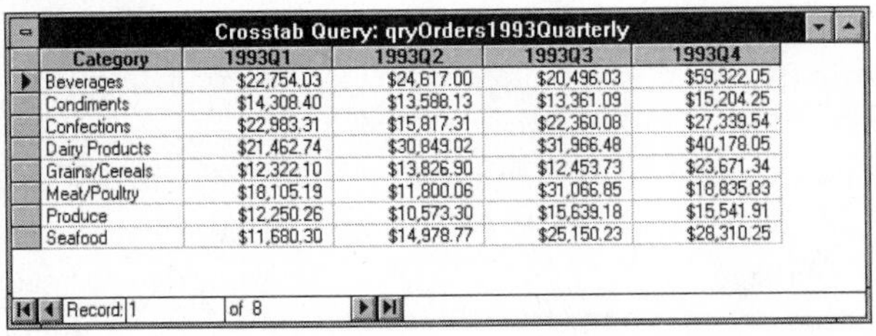

Category	1993Q1	1993Q2	1993Q3	1993Q4
Beverages	$22,754.03	$24,617.00	$20,496.03	$59,322.05
Condiments	$14,308.40	$13,588.13	$13,361.09	$15,204.25
Confections	$22,983.31	$15,817.31	$22,360.08	$27,339.54
Dairy Products	$21,462.74	$30,849.02	$31,966.48	$40,178.05
Grains/Cereals	$12,322.10	$13,826.90	$12,453.73	$23,671.34
Meat/Poultry	$18,105.19	$11,800.06	$31,066.85	$18,835.83
Produce	$12,250.26	$10,573.30	$15,639.18	$15,541.91
Seafood	$11,680.30	$14,978.77	$25,150.23	$28,310.25

Crosstab Query: qryOrders1993Quarterly — Record: 1 of 8

The qryOrders1993Employees query is complicated by the addition of the employees table, as shown in Design View in Figure 17.3. The INNER JOIN syntax shown in the SQL statement that follows borders on the bizarre. As demonstrated by the query result set of Figure 17.4, however, the JOIN statements succeed. (You can prove this by totaling the order amounts for each query result set and comparing the two sums.)

```
TRANSFORM CCur(Sum([Order Details].[Unit Price]*
    [Order Details].[Quantity]*(1-[Order Details].[Discount])))
    AS Orders
SELECT Categories.[Category Name] AS Category
    FROM Employees
    INNER JOIN (Orders
    INNER JOIN ((Categories
    INNER JOIN Products ON Categories.[Category ID] = Products.[Category
    ➡ID])
    INNER JOIN [Order Details] ON Products.[Product ID] = [Order
Details].[Product ID])
        ON Orders.[Order ID] = [Order Details].[Order ID])
```

```
    ON Employees.[Employee ID] = Orders.[Employee ID]
WHERE ((Orders.[Order Date] Between #01/1/93# And #12/31/93#))
    GROUP BY Categories.[Category Name]
PIVOT Employees.[Last Name]
WITH OWNERACCESS OPTION;
```

FIGURE 17.3.

Design of the qryOrders1993Employees comparative-performance query.

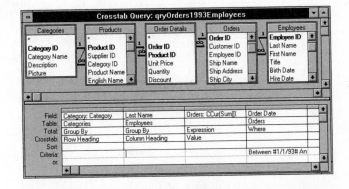

FIGURE 17.4.

The query result set of the qryOrders1993Employees.

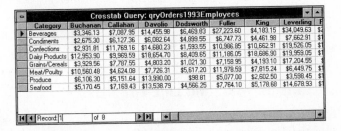

Using the Graph Wizard to Design Graphs and Charts

Although it's possible to create a graph or chart using the Insert Object method and selecting the Microsoft Graph 5.0 object type in the Insert Object dialog box, the Query Wizard makes the process of creating a graph much faster. You can use the Query Wizard to create two different classes of graphs and charts, defined thusly:

■ *Unbound.* Unbound (also called *un-linked* or *non-linked*) line graphs display a line for each of the rows of your query. You can also create un-linked stacked column charts and multiple-area charts.

■ *Bound.* A bound (linked) graph or chart is bound to the current record of the form on which it is located and displays only a single set of values from one row of your table or query at a time.

The three sections that follow describe how you create unbound line graphs based on queries, how to display alternative presentations of your data in the form of bar and area charts, and how to create a graph linked to a specific record of a query result set.

Creating an Unbound Line Graph

The following process uses the Graph Wizard to create an unbound graph that displays the data from the qryOrders1993Quarterly query:

1. Open a new blank form without selecting a table or query. Display the toolbox and make sure that the Wizard's toggle button is on (depressed).

2. Click the Graph toolbox button. Position the caret at the upper left of the form, click the left mouse button, and drag the rectangle for the graph's unbound object frame to about 3x7 inches.

3. When you release the mouse button, the opening dialog box of the Graph Wizard appears. Click the Queries option button, and then select the qryOrders1993Quarterly query. (See Figure 17.5.) Click the Next button to continue the graph-building process.

4. Click the line-graph button (the third from the left in the top row of the buttons that display MSGraph5's available graph styles). A miniature view of your graph displays the quarter names in the legend, but Category Names should appear in the legend. Click the Rows option button in the Data Series In group to transform the rows and columns. A miniature version of

your graph appears, with considerable distortion, as shown in Figure 17.6. Click the Next button to display the final Graph Wizard dialog box.

FIGURE 17.5.

Selecting the data source in the Graph Wizard's opening dialog box.

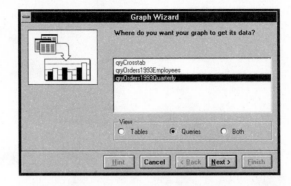

FIGURE 17.6.

Selecting a graph style and data orientation in the second dialog box.

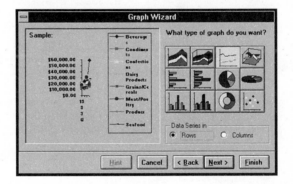

5. Type `Quarterly Orders for 1993 by Category` in the text box to add a title to your graph, then click the Yes option button to display the Category Name legend. (See Figure 17.7.)

6. Click the Finish button to display your graph in design mode, as shown in Figure 17.8.

7. Open the Properties window, select Data Properties, and set the value of the `Enabled` property to **True** so you can activate the graph in run mode. Select Other Properties and set the value of the `Locked` property to **False** so you can change the design of the graph object in run mode.

8. Choose Select Fo**r**m from the **E**dit menu, then select the form's Layout Properties. Set the `ScrollBars` property to `Neither` and the `RecordSelectors` and `NavigationButtons` properties to **False**.

9. Change to run mode. Access reruns the query and redisplays the graph. The graph is the only control on the form, so it receives the focus at all times. (See Figure 17.9.)

FIGURE 17.7.

Adding a title and legend to the graph.

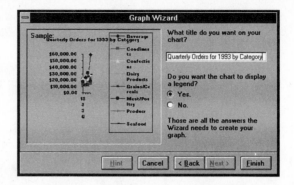

FIGURE 17.8.

The Wizard's default graph in design move.

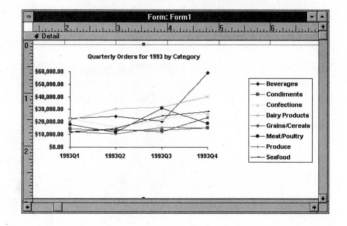

FIGURE 17.9.

The graph in run mode with the focus.

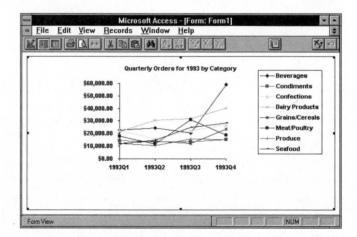

Modifying the Design of Your Graph in Run Mode

Although the Graph Wizard has created your graph style, added the data source, and applied a legend for you, the default graph design leaves much to be desired. MSGraph5 is an OLE 2.0 mini-server, so you can activate MSGraph5 in place and modify the design of your graph. MSGraph5 also supports OLE Automation, so you can use Access Basic code to automate design changes. Using OLE Automation with MSGraph5 is discussed later in this chapter. This section shows you how to use MSGraph5 to edit the design of the graph and how to change the line graph to an area or column chart.

> **NOTE**
>
> You can modify the design of the graph in either run or design mode. Run mode offers the advantage of in-place activation. In-place activation enables you to view the graph as it will appear to the user while you make your design changes.

The following process activates your graph in place and uses MSGraph5 to enhance its design:

1. Double-click the graph to activate MSGraph5 in place. A diagonally-hashed border surrounds the graph. MSGraph5's menus replace or supplement those of Access 2.0. (See Figure 17.10.)

FIGURE 17.10.

Activating the graph in place.

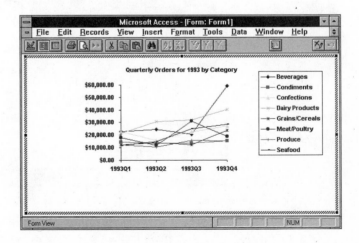

2. The decimal fraction of the y-axis labels is superfluous, so double-click the y-axis or select the y-axis and choose Selected Axis from the Format menu to open the Format dialog box. Click the Numbers tab and select a currency format that does not display cents (see Figure 17.11), then click OK to close the dialog box.

FIGURE 17.11.

Selecting a format for the y-axis values.

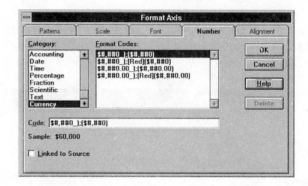

3. The size of the default graph is much smaller than the available area, so click within the area of the graph (but not on a data series line) to display the sizing rectangle. Drag the sizing handles of the graph to maximize the size of the graph within the available area, as shown in Figure 17.12.

FIGURE 17.12.

Adjusting the size of the graph.

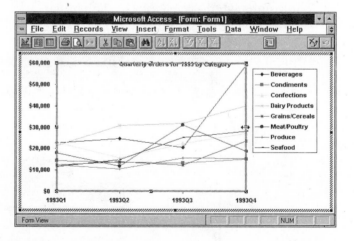

4. Horizontal gridlines aid the user in determining the value of data points. Select the graph title, then press Delete to remove it. Choose **G**ridlines from the **I**nsert menu to display the Gridlines dialog box. Tick the Major

Gridlines check box of the Value Axis (y-axis) group to add horizontal gridlines to the graph. (See Figure 17.13.) Click OK to close the Gridlines dialog box.

Using a label for the graph title rather than using the built-in title of the graph can conserve space and makes altering titles easier when you change the data source for the graph.

FIGURE 17.13.

Adding horizontal gridlines to the graph.

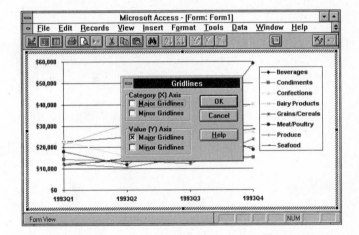

5. You can change the type family and font size of your chart's labels and legend. Double-click the y-axis to display the Format dialog box, then click the Font tab. Set the size of the y-axis labels to 11 points, then click OK. Repeat the process for the x-axis, as shown in Figure 17.14.

    Type families are limited to TrueType and bitmapped system fonts, such as MS Sans Serif. PostScript and other scalable, outline-style fonts are not supported. Make sure you choose a type family that all users of Windows 3.1 possess, such as Arial (the default type family for MSGraph5).

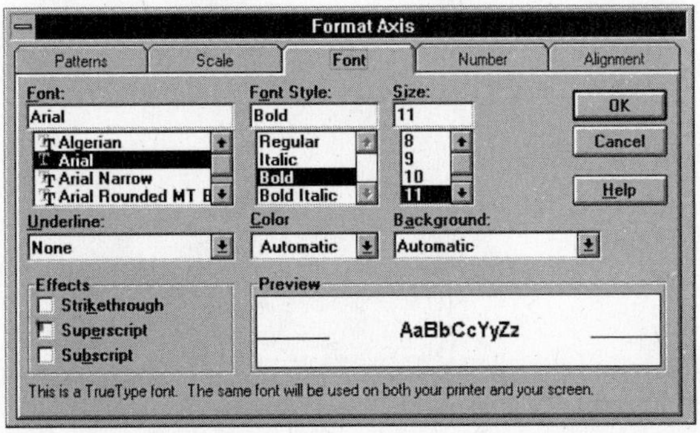

FIGURE 17.14.

Changing the font size of the graph labels.

6. The light colors used for the Confections and Dairy Products data series are difficult to read against the stark white background of the graph. Most Access applications use the default light-gray background for forms. To change the background color of the graph, select the entire graph by double-clicking an inactive area of the graph, such as below the legend, to display the Format Chart Area dialog box. Click the Patterns tab, then click the light-gray button of the Colors group to add the gray background. (See Figure 17.15.)

FIGURE 17.15.

Adding a light gray background to the graph.

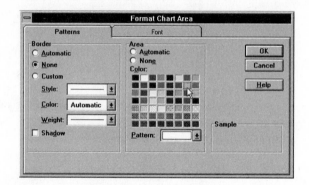

7. The border around the legend is distracting and the legend needs to be repositioned for graphic balance. Double-click the legend to display the Format Legend dialog box and click the None button of the Border group, then close the dialog box. Click and drag the legend to balance its position with respect to the data area of the graph. Your completed graph appears as shown in Figure 17.16.

FIGURE 17.16.

The graph with design modifications completed.

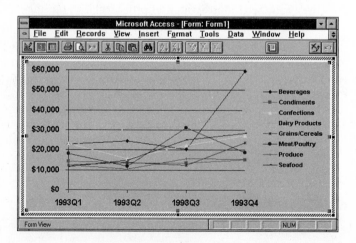

8. Return to design mode, add a label to the form, and set the BackColor property of the label, unbound object frame, and the detail section of the form to light gray. Set the Enabled property of the object frame to **False** to prevent users from activating the graph. Set the Name of the unbound object frame to uofChart. The completed graph in run mode appears in Figure 17.17.

FIGURE 17.17.

The final graph in run mode.

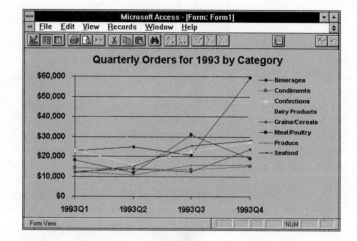

Changing the Graph to a Chart

MSGraph5 offers a variety of graph and chart types. Area charts, for example, are used to display the contribution of individual product categories to total sales. To change the line graph to another type of chart, follow these steps:

1. Return to design mode and double-click the unbound object frame to display MSGraph5's main window. (See Figure 17.18.)

2. Choose **C**hart Type from the F**o**rmat menu to open the Chart Type dialog box.

3. Select the Area chart image in the Chart Type dialog box. (See Figure 17.19.) Click OK to change your line graph into an area chart. The contribution of each category appears as an individually-colored area, and the uppermost line segment represents total sales.

4. The default colors applied to the areas by MSGraph5 are designed for 256-color VGA displays. Many users are unlikely to have 256-color capability or, if they do, may be using the default 16-color display driver to improve

performance. To change the colors of the area chart to one of Windows'
standard 16 colors, double-click each area to display the Format Data Series
dialog box, click the Patterns tab, and click a button in the color group.
Your area chart appears as shown in Figure 17.20.

FIGURE 17.18

*MSGraph5's main
window activated.*

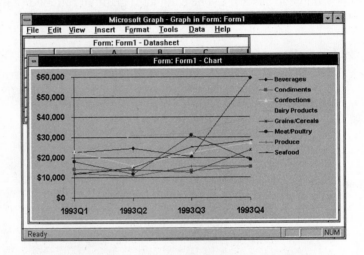

FIGURE 17.19.

*Selecting the area
chart type.*

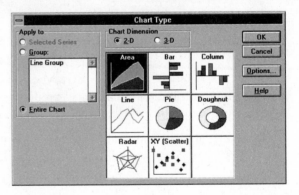

5. An alternative to the area chart is the multiple-column chart shown in Figure
   17.21. Multiple-column charts are useful only when you have relatively few
   members in the y-axis data set.

FIGURE 17.20.

The area chart using eight of Windows' 16 standard colors.

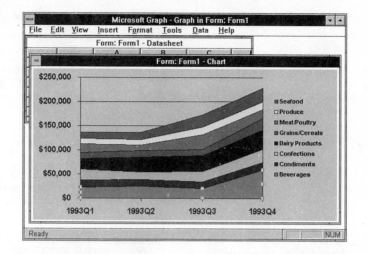

FIGURE 17.21.

A multiple column chart.

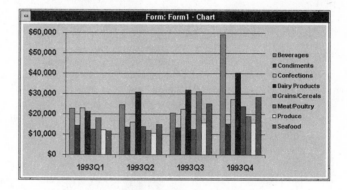

6. A more practical column chart type is the stacked column chart. To change the multiple-column chart to a stacked column chart, click the Options button of the Chart Type dialog box to display the Format Column Group dialog box. Click the stacked column chart button (see Figure 17.22), then click OK. The stacked column chart appears as shown in Figure 17.23.

7. Another subtype of the area chart and the stacked column chart is the *percentage distribution* chart. To create a distribution-of-orders graph, repeat Step 6, but select the percent column picture in the Format Column Group dialog box. Because you set the format of the y-axis previously to eliminate the decimals, you need to change the format of the y-axis to Percent manually. To reduce the number of horizontal gridlines, click the Scale tab of the Format Axis dialog box and replace 10 with 20 as the value of the Major Unit scale. (See Figure 17.24.) Your percentage distribution of orders graph appears as shown in Figure 17.25.

FIGURE 17.22.

Selecting a column chart subtype in the Format Column Group dialog box.

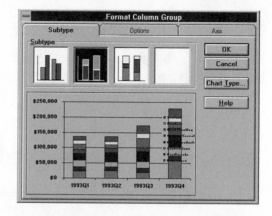

FIGURE 17.23.

A stacked column chart.

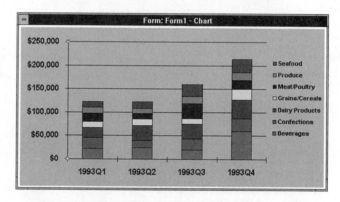

FIGURE 17.24.

Changing the number of horizontal gridlines.

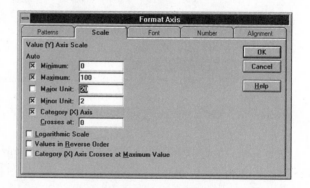

FIGURE 17.25.

A percentage distribution chart.

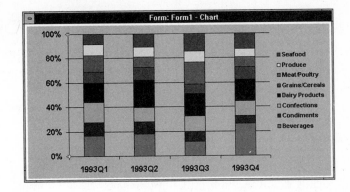

8. Select the final type of graph or chart you want, add a Caption to the form, and save your form with a descriptive name, such as **frmOrders1993Quarterly**. The form shown in run mode in Figure 17.26 is included in the AB_EXAMP.MDB.

FIGURE 17.26.

The completed Quarterly Orders for 1993 by Category area chart.

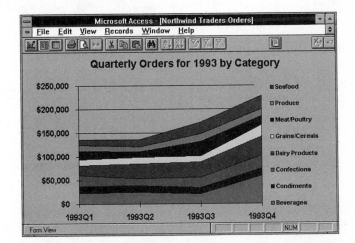

TIP

The default SizeMode property for graphs and charts created by the Graph Wizard is Zoom. To prevent changes to the presentation of your graph and fonts used for labels and legends, change the SizeMode property to Clip.

> **NOTE**
>
> The process of adding an unbound graph to an Access report is almost identical to that used for forms. Unless you have a color printer, select a line-graph subtype that identifies data points with a different symbol for each category. For area and stacked-column charts, select hatched patterns to differentiate the product categories.

MSGraph5 offers many additional formatting features that were not described in the preceding example. Publishing limitations preclude a complete description of each type of graph provided by MSGraph5. One of the problems with MSGraph5, however, is performance. Each time you change from Design View to Form View, Access runs the query, launches MSGraph5 in the background, and passes the query data to MSGraph5. This process, using the qryOrders1993Quarterly query, takes about 12 to 15 seconds on a 80486DX2-66 computer with a video local bus and an 18-ms fixed disk drive. The operation of the graph custom control of Visual Basic is much faster than MSGraph5.

Another problem with MSGraph5 is that you cannot easily transfer data to MSGraph5's datasheet with Access Basic code. (MSGraph5 does not expose its `DataSeries` object for manipulation by OLE Automation.) Bits Per Second Ltd.'s Graph OCX OLE Custom Control, described in the next chapter, provides considerably faster operation and gives you access to the data series. Bits Per Second Ltd. developed the Graph custom control included with the Professional Edition of Visual Basic 3.0. Graph OCX also has a Hotspot event that you can use for drill-down purposes. You need to write a considerable amount of Access Basic code, however, to use a third-party graphing tool such as Graph OCX.

Binding a Graph to a Single Record of a Table or Query

You create a bound graph or chart by setting the values of the MSGraph5 object's `LinkChildFields` and `LinkMasterFields` properties. The binding is similar to that between a form and a subform. A bound graph displays the data series from the current row of the table or query that serves as the `RecordSource` of the form. As you move the record pointer, the graph is redrawn to reflect the data values in the selected row. Thus the graph behaves similarly to a linked subform.

The following process changes the frmOrders1993Quarterly form to accommodate a graph bound to the qryOrders1993Employees query:

1. Open frmOrders1993Quaterly in design mode, then select Data Properties. Type `Categories` as the value of the `RecordSource` property of the form; this binds the form to the Categories table.

2. Select Layout Properties of the form and set the value of the `NavigationButtons` property **True** and the value of the `ScrollBars` property to `Horizontal`. You need navigation buttons, or the equivalent, to select the record to graph; the horizontal scroll bar prevents a contrasting white space from appearing at the lower right of your form.

3. Select the object frame and type `Category Name` as the value for the `LinkMasterFields`, and type `Category`, the corresponding value of the graph, as the value for the `LinkChildFields` property. This binds the graph to the current record of the form. (See Figure 17.27.) Set the `Enabled` property to **True** so you can modify the design of the graph in run mode. Save the form as **frmOrders1993Employees**.

FIGURE 17.27.

Binding the chart to a common field of the form's RecordSource property.

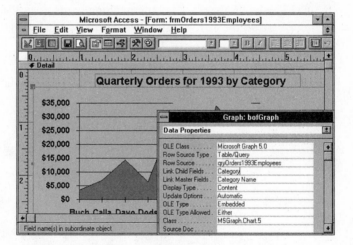

4. Test your linked graph in run mode. Your graph appears as shown in Figure 17.28. It is clear that some major graphic facelifting is required. Double-click the chart to activate MSGraph5.

5. Delete the unneeded legend, then expand the chart to as wide as possible. Change the font size of the x-axis labels to 6 or 7 points, depending on which size permits all names to appear. Then change the chart type to a line graph.

FIGURE 17.28.

The first cut at a bound graph.

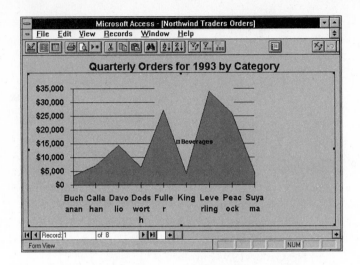

6. The single line appears a bit anemic for a graph of this size, so double-click anywhere on the line to display the Format Data Series dialog box. Open the Weight drop-down list, and choose the second thickest line it offers. To change the data-point marker, open the Style drop-down list and select the type you want. Use the drop-down lists to set the Foreground and Background colors of the marker to a contrasting hue, such as white and blue. (See Figure 17.29.) Click OK to close the dialog box.

FIGURE 17.29.

Changing the line and data marker properties.

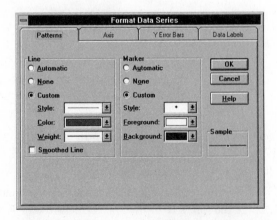

7. You need to change the label caption as the category name changes when you move the record pointer. Add a text box bound to the Category Name field and set its Visible property to **False**. Create a SetValue macro and type [Forms]![frmOrders1993Employees]![Text1].[Caption] as the Item

(Text1 is the name of the label) and `"Quarterly " &`
`[Forms]![frmOrders1993Employees]![Field2].[Value] & " Orders for`
`1993"` as the Value. (Text2 is the name of the text box.) Save the macro as
mcrCategoryName. Attach mcrCategoryName to the OnCurrent event of the
form. When you change to run mode, your graph appears as shown in
Figure 17.30.

FIGURE 17.30.

*The graph with a
synchronized
caption.*

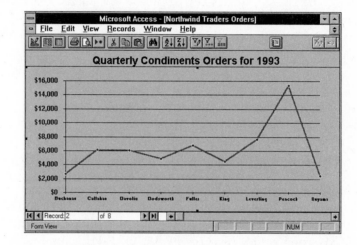

8. You can smooth the data series line by activating the graph and double-
   clicking the line. Mark the Smoothed Line check box in the Line frame, and
   then click OK. Your graph now appears as shown in Figure 17.31.

FIGURE 17.31.

*Smoothing the line
connecting data
points.*

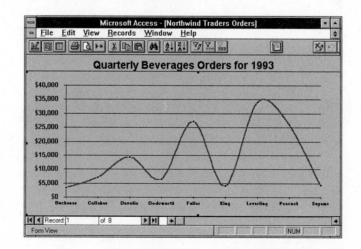

Using Microsoft Graph 5.0 as an OLE Automation Server

You can use OLE Automation to modify *some* of the features of MSGraph5 charts and graphs with Access Basic code. Unfortunately, you cannot access the data series OA. The data series that Access 2.0 and other applications that use MSGraph5 transmit to the graph is in Excel BIFF5 data format. At the time this edition was written, neither Microsoft nor a third party had provided a DLL to convert text or numeric Access Basic values to BIFF5 and send the data directly to MSGraph5. You can, however, substitute SQL statements for the RowSource property of an unbound object frame using Access Basic. This, however, is the limit of the present ability to customize the data series for MSGraph5. The sections that follow introduce a few of the OLE Automation features of MSGraph5.

Obtaining Online Help for MSGraph5 OLE Automation

MSGraph5 exposes an extraordinary number of objects in a variety of collections. Figure 17.32 displays a few of the objects and collections in the Object Browser of the Office Developer's Kit. At the time this edition was written, the help file for MSGraph5's OA features, VBA_GRP.HLP in \WINDOWS\MSAPPS \MSGRAPH5 was incomplete, and VBA_GRP.HLP is not included in the retail version of Access or the Access Developer's Toolkit (ADT).

FIGURE 17.32.

Some of MSGraph5's objects listed in the ODK's Object Browser.

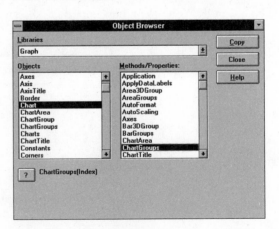

NOTE

An updated, but not yet completed, version of VBA_GRP.HLP should be available in the MSACCESS forum on CompuServe by the time this edition is published. Search all libraries for VBAGRP.HLP. As the Microsoft Graph product group completes VBA_GRP.HLP, you can expect updated versions to appear. Most of the help topics of the version of VBA_GRP.HLP that was available when this edition was written were not synchronized with the ODK's Object Browser, so pressing F1 or clicking the ? button resulted in a "Help topic does not exist" message. This problem is likely to be remedied in later versions of VBA_GRP.HLP.

Most of the objects, properties, and methods, however, correspond to the chart-related objects of Microsoft Excel 5.0. Therefore, you can use Excel 5.0's VBA help file, VBA_XL.HLP, as a resource to aid in programming MSGraph5. Unfortunately, the code examples for most of the chart-related objects of Excel 5.0 are less than illuminating. One of the more interesting examples from the VBA_XL.HLP online help file is the topic for the `ChartTitle` property and the example VBA code shown in Figure 17.33. The help topic states that `ChartTitle` is read-only, but the example code sets its `Text` value, as well as its font size and attributes. (The example, not the topic, is correct, as demonstrated later in the next section. `ChartTitle` is an object, not a property.)

FIGURE 17.33.

A help topic and VBA example code for a chart object property in VBA_XL.HLP.

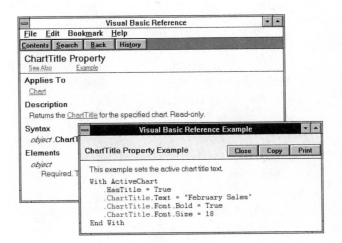

Experimenting with MSGraph5 OLE Automation Code

As with other less-well-documented features of Access 2.0, the best method of learning programming techniques with MSGraph5 is to use the Immediate Window. Figure 17.34 displays the required object variable declaration in a module and some of the MSGraph5 objects you can manipulate with OA code in the Immediate Window.

FIGURE 17.34.

Using the Immediate Window to experiment with MSGraph5's OLE Automation features.

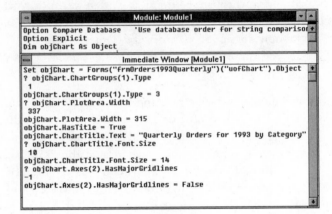

```
                        Module: Module1
Option Compare Database    'Use database order for string comparison
Option Explicit
Dim objChart As Object
```

```
                  Immediate Window [Module1]
Set objChart = Forms("frmOrders1993Quarterly")("uofChart").Object
? objChart.ChartGroups(1).Type
  1
objChart.ChartGroups(1).Type = 3
? objChart.PlotArea.Width
  337
objChart.PlotArea.Width = 315
objChart.HasTitle = True
objChart.ChartTitle.Text = "Quarterly Orders for 1993 by Category"
? objChart.ChartTitle.Font.Size
  10
objChart.ChartTitle.Font.Size = 14
? objChart.Axes(2).HasMajorGridlines
 -1
objChart.Axes(2).HasMajorGridlines = False
```

1. Open the frmOrders1993Quarterly form in run mode.

2. Open a new module and declare an object variable, objChart, then open the Immediate Window.

3. Assign the Object property of the unbound object frame to objChart to establish a pointer to the Chart object.

4. You can have multiple chart groups in MSGraph5. The default ChartGroup is the first member of the ChartGroups collection, ChartGroups(1). You can change the type of graph by setting the value of the ChartGroups(1).Type property. Setting Type to 3 changes the graph to a multiple-column type. (See Figure 17.35.)

5. The chart now overlaps the legend. The Width property of the PlotArea object controls the width of the actual chart. Set the Width property to 315 points. (Access Basic uses twips as the default unit of measurement, while MSGraph5 uses points.) Figure 17.36 shows the effect of the change.

FIGURE 17.35.

The effect of changing the ChartGroups(1).Type *property to 3.*

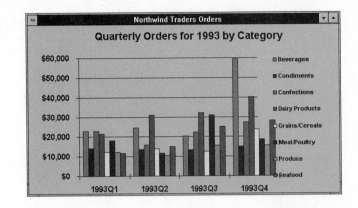

FIGURE 17.36.

The appearance of the chart after reducing the width of the PlotArea *object.*

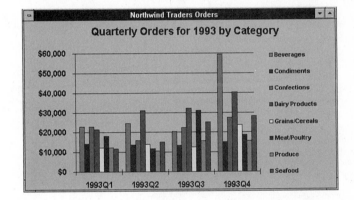

6. The chart currently does not have a title, so create a default title by setting the HasTitle property to **True**. You then can set the Text property of the ChartTitle object to a literal or an Access Basic **String** variable. Set the size of the font to 14 points by assigning 14 to the Size property of the ChartTitle's Font object.

7. You can remove the horizontal gridlines from the chart by setting the HasMajorGridlines property of the second member of the Axes collection to **False**. (The first member of the Axes collection is the x-axis.)

The effect of all of the preceding operations is shown in Figure 17.37. The primary application for OLE Automation with MSGraph5 is to alter the appearance of user-defined graphs and charts based on the information the graphs and charts contain. Once you understand the relationship between the objects and collections of MSGraph5, OA operations are straightforward. Gaining such an understanding from the documentation that was available for MSGraph5 at the time this edition was written would not have been easy.

FIGURE 17.37.

The modifications made by executing the OA statements shown in Figure 17.34.

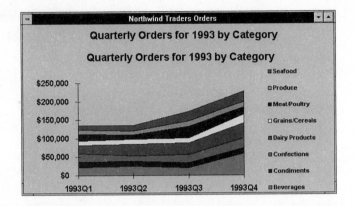

NOTE

The section called "Creating a Graph from a User-Defined Query" of Chapter 24, "Using Access Wizard Functions," makes use of OA to manipulate user-defined charts created with MSGraph5.

18

Introducing OLE 2.0 Custom Controls

Access 2.0 is the first Microsoft application to support OLE 2.0's Custom Control capabilities. Rumors that Microsoft was developing OLE Custom controls began to surface in the computer trade press in early 1994, well after the official release of the OLE 2.0 Software Development Kit (SDK) and the retail availability of OLE 2.0-conforming applications. The updated OLE 2.01 specification, issued in early 1994, doesn't mention OLE Custom Controls. Microsoft officially announced the existence of 16-bit OLE Custom Control technology on March 28, 1994 at the Microsoft Tech*Ed '94 conference in New Orleans. However, the OLE Custom Control Development Kit (CDK) for Microsoft Visual C++ 1.5, required by programmers to create these objects, was just entering the beta stage when the announcement was made. Thus, the availability of OLE Custom Controls, called OCXs (after their file extension), was very limited when this edition was written.

OLE Custom Controls ultimately will have a profound effect on the design of custom productivity applications for Windows. OLE Custom Controls, like the original Visual Basic Extension custom controls (VBXs), are a major step toward implementing the "building block" approach to creating specialized applications. VBXs were limited in scope to Visual Basic applications. (Although Visual C++ 1+ accommodates VBXs, few developers used VBXs in production C++ code.) At the time this was written, Access 2.0 was the only application that accommodated OCXs. It is reasonable to assume that all future versions of Visual Basic, FoxPro, Excel, Word, and other Microsoft programming and productivity applications will provide an OCX-compliant environment. The extent to which competing software publishers will add OCX "hooks" to their products remains to be seen.

This chapter introduces you to the three OLE Custom Controls included with the Access Developer's Toolkit (ADT), and to one of the first third-party OCX products, Bits Per Second Ltd's Graph OCX Custom Control. Bits Per Second is the UK company that created the graph custom control for the Professional Versions of Visual Basic 2.0 and 3.0. Graph OCX was in the beta stage when this edition was written. You need the ADT to use OCXs, because the library required to implement OCXs, OC1016.DLL, is a component of the ADT. The three sample OCXs included with the ADT were the only OLE Custom Controls available as commercial products when this edition was written.

Comparing OCXs, Mini-Servers, and VBXs

OLE Custom Controls are a special variety of OLE 2.0 mini-server, called *in-process servers*, that support OLE Automation (OA) and provide additional features not available from mini-servers. Like mini-servers such as Microsoft Graph 5.0 (MSGraph5), you embed OCX objects in object frames. The most common container for OCX objects is an unbound object frame on a single form. (Access 2.0 does not support multiple instances of OCX objects in continuous forms, and you should avoid the use of OCXs in subforms.) Unlike mini-servers, OCXs do not need to use OLE 2.0's LRPC (Lightweight Remote Procedure Call) protocol to communicate with their container object; OCXs are more tightly bound to their container than local servers. (The term *local server* includes both full- and mini-servers, but not OCXs.) OCXs are inside-out OLE objects that are activated when they appear in their container; most local servers are conventional outside-in objects that you activate by double-clicking. Local servers ordinarily register themselves in REG.DAT during the installation process. Before you can use an OCX, however, you must manually register the OCX in the registration database, REG.DAT.

The presentation of an OCX is an instance of the control object. Unlike mini-servers, OCXs don't have their own menu choices that replace or supplement those of the container application when the server is activated. Instead, you gain access to the properties and methods of the object through *Property Pages* or OA code you write in Access Basic. Property Pages appear when you click the object frame with the right mouse button in design mode, choose the **Object**'s name, and then choose **P**roperties from the submenu. Property Pages substitute for the properties window of VBX and supplement the standard entries for bound and unbound object frames in Access 2.0's Properties window.

Another feature of OCXs that distinguish them from OLE 2.0 mini-servers is a collection of additional events that appear in the object frame's Procedures drop-down list in the module window. Simple controls may add only a few events or trigger existing events of object frames, such as the AfterUpdate event. More complex controls, such as Graph OCX, add several new events, such as HotHit. The HotHit event triggered when you click or double-click an element of a chart, and it returns the index to the data point. The Data Outline Control, described later in this chapter, has a multitude of events.

The sections that follow describe how you register OCXs, the entries OCXs create in REG.DAT, and the properties, events, and methods of a typical OCX.

> **WARNING**
>
> Before registering any OCX or modifying REG.DAT with REGSVR.EXE (described in the next section), make a backup copy of your REG.DAT file in the \WINDOWS directory, as REG.BK1 or the like. (Do not use REG.BAK, because some applications create a REG.BAK file during the

registration process.) There is always the possibility that a problem will occur during the registration process that results in a corrupted REG.DAT file. Corrupted REG.DAT files are very difficult to repair or re-create. It is a good practice to make backup copies of REG.DAT before you install any new OLE 2.0 server.

Registering OLE Custom Controls

As mentioned earlier in this chapter, all OLE servers, including OCXs, must be registered in the registration database, REG.DAT. The Microsoft Foundation Classes (MFC) for Visual C++ now include a new object class called COleControl. The COleControl class provides a standard entry point that the container application can call the first time you use an OCX to provide automatic registration. Access 2.0, however, does not register OCXs automatically. You manually register OCXs in REG.DAT with the following process:

1. Open a new, blank, unbound form.
2. Choose Insert Object from the **E**dit menu to open the Insert Object dialog box.
3. Click the Insert Control option button. If you have not previously registered an OCX, the Control Type list is empty. (See Figure 18.1.)

FIGURE 18.1.
The Add Control dialog box with no OLE Custom Controls registered.

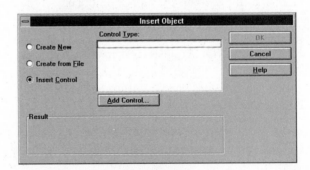

4. Click the Add Control button to open the Add Control dialog box.
5. OLE Custom controls commonly use the .OCX extension, but some may use .DLL or .EXE as the extension. (See Figure 18.2.) MSACAL20.OCX is the file for the Calendar Control supplied with the ADT.

FIGURE 18.2.

Selecting the OCX to register.

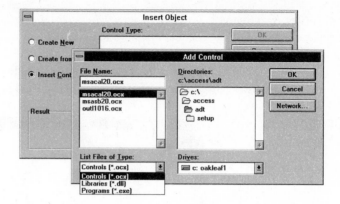

6. Select the file you want to use and then click the OK button to close the Add Control dialog box. Access adds registration entries to REG.DAT for the control. The OLE Control you added appears in the Control Type list. (See Figure 18.3.)

FIGURE 18.3.

The Add Control dialog box after registering an OCX.

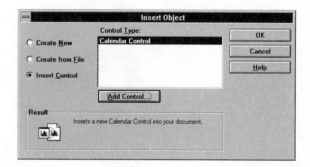

7. Click the OK button of the Insert Object dialog box to insert the OCX into your unbound object frame, or click Cancel to register the control. Figure 18.4 shows the Calendar Control in design mode.

The primary entry in REG.DAT for each OCX you add appears at the top of REG.DAT. (See Figure 18.5.) The first entry identifies the main user type name of MSACAL20.OCX, Calendar Control, provides the CLSID of the control that provides a pointer to other entries for the control in REG.DAT, and specifies the OLE TypeLib (type library) of the control. The additional entries, located in the OLE (Part 1 of 5) section of REG.DAT, also are added during the registration process. (See Figure 18.6.) These additional entries provide the CLSID of the Property Page, the

ProgID (programmatic ID) of the control, MSACAL20.CCalendarCtrl, and other information needed by the client application to utilize the control. The ToolboxBitmap entry points to the location of the bitmap resource that will be added to the toolbox of a future version of Visual Basic that supports OCXs. Chapter 14, "Understanding OLE 2.0," discusses REG.DAT entries for OLE 2.0 servers in detail.

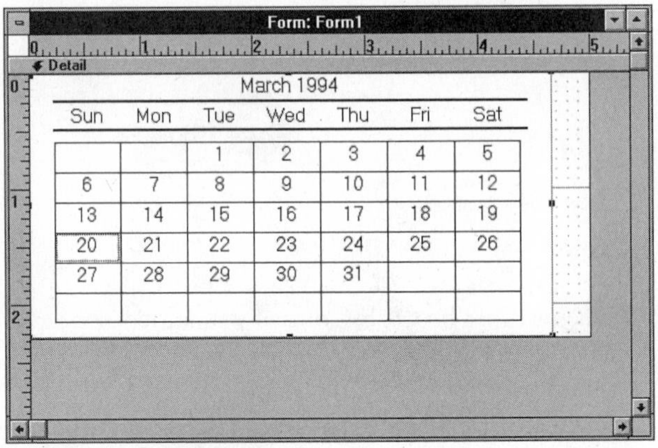

FIGURE 18.4.

The default Calendar Control in design mode.

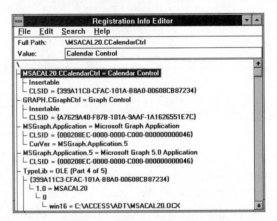

FIGURE 18.5.

Primary entries for the Calendar Control in REG.DAT.

> **NOTE**
>
> There is no provision built into Access 2.0 to remove the registration entries for OCXs. To delete the registration entries for OCXs, you need a Windows application, REGSVR.EXE, that is expected to be available for downloading in the MSACCESS forum as REGSVR.ZIP. (Search for REGSVR in all libraries.) To remove the registration entries for an OCX, execute

regsvr /u *d:\path\filename*.ocx in the Command Line text box of Program Manager's Run dialog. The /u parameter unloads the registration entries. You can register an OCX by omitting the /u parameter, but registration using the Add Control dialog is the recommended method for registering OCXs.

FIGURE 18.6.

Additional entries for the Calendar Control in the OLE section (Part 1 of 5) of REG.DAT.

Properties, Methods, and Events of OCXs

All commercial OLE Custom Controls are likely to include online help files that provide lists of objects exposed by the OCX, and the properties, methods, and events applicable to the objects. You also can use the Object Browser of the ODK, described in the preceding chapter, to display objects, methods and events of OCXs. Figure 18.7 shows the properties and methods for the Calendar Control in the ODK's Object Browser. If the help file for the OCX is specified in REG.DAT and the help context ID for the help file is included in the properties page of the .OCX file, you can click the ? button to display the help topic for the property. (The versions of the OCXs supplied with the ADT that were available when this book was written do not contain a help file entry in REG.DAT.)

To use Excel's Object Browser with OCXs, follow these steps:

1. Launch Excel and choose Macro from the Insert menu. Then choose Module from the submenu to create an empty Module1.

2. Choose References from the Tools menu to open the References dialog. OCXs do not provide a name for the Available References list box, but the path to and name of the OCX file appears in the Group frame. Check each

of the <no name specified> items in the Available References list box (see
Figure 18.8), and then click OK to close the dialog box.

FIGURE 18.7.

*Displaying the
objects, properties,
and methods of the
Calendar Control
in the ODK's
Object Browser.*

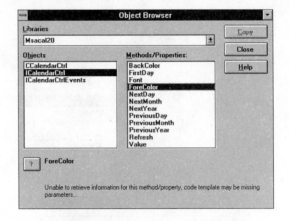

FIGURE 18.8.

*Adding references to
registered OLE
Custom Controls.*

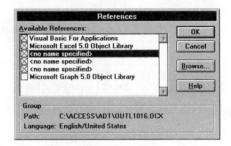

3. Press F2 or choose Object Browser from the **V**iew menu to display Excel's
    Object Browser dialog box. Figure 18.9 shows a few of the many events of
    the Navigator (Data Outline) control, OUTL1016.OCX, included with the
    ADT. The syntax for the event appears under the Objects/Modules list box.
    For example, `AfterCollapse Level` translates to an event-handling
    subprocedure, `ObjectName_AfterCollapse (Level As Integer)`.

You set the values of static properties, such as foreground and background colors, in
properties dialogs whose controls set the values of properties included in the OCX's
Property Page. Some OCXs have only a single properties dialog, General, others have
several properties dialogs that you select from a drop-down list. Setting the values in
properties dialogs is discussed in the sections devoted to each of the three Microsoft
Access Custom Controls, later in this chapter.

FIGURE 18.9.

Displaying a list of and the syntax for OCX events in Excel 5.0's Object Browser.

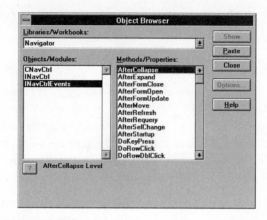

Troubleshooting Registration Problems

The following problems can result from missing entries in or corruption of your registration database file:

■ If you attempt to open a form that contains an OCX that you have not previously registered, you receive an error message that reads "There is a problem in the registration database." You usually can correct this problem by registering the OCX by the process described in the preceding section.

■ If your registration database has become corrupted, or you have made an improper modification of REG.DAT using RegEdit, you may receive the "Problem in the registration database" error message or a "Registration database is corrupted" message.

■ To determine the extent of the corruption, attempt to open REG.DAT with RegEdit using the verbose mode. (See Chapter 14 for details on how to use RegEdit.) If you can open REG.DAT with RegEdit, it is likely that the entries for the OCX are a problem. Remove the registration entries with REGSVR.EXE (discussed earlier in this chapter) and re-register the control. If this does not solve the problem, contact the supplier of the OCX.

■ If you cannot open REG.DAT with RegEdit, you have a major scale problem. You need to copy REG.DAT from the distribution diskette for you version of Windows and recreate RegDat. Some OLE 2.0 full-servers and mini-servers, including Access 2.0, automatically register themselves on launching, if the application does not detect its required entries in REG.DAT. Others, such as Excel 5.0 and Word 6.0, provide .REG files (EXCEL5.REG and WINWORD6.REG) that you can merge with REG.DAT using the **M**erge Registration File choice of RegEdit's **F**ile menu.

You also need to register OLE 2.0 with OLE2.REG that is located in the \WINDOWS\SYSTEM directory.

■ If your REG.DAT file contains a spurious entry or is missing an entry for an OCX, you may receive a message such as "Internal error (-4); the Control Name had an internal error and will stop." This message is likely to be followed by a GPF. Messages of this type also result from a corrupted copy of OC1016.DLL or installation of the incorrect version of OC1016.DLL for the OCX. In this case, contact the supplier of the OCX to determine the source of the problem. Be prepared to send a copy of your REG.DAT file and the size and date of your OC1016.DLL file to the supplier.

The last problem in the preceding list is likely to occur only to Access developers that have installed beta versions of OLE 2.0 servers or OCXs, or have installed OCXs from a variety of suppliers. The technology for creating OCXs was in a relatively early stage when Access 2.0 was released, and it is likely that OC1016.DLL and the .OCX files will go through several update releases in 1994. The MSACCESS forum is the best source of continuing information on the currency of OC1016.DLL and OCXs for Access 2.0.

> **NOTE**
>
> You will receive the first error in the preceding list if you attempt to open the CALENDAR.FRM form included in AB_EXAMP.MDB without having first installed the ADT and the Calendar and Scrollbar controls, MSACAL20.OCX and MSASB20.OCX.

Using the Calendar and Scrollbar Controls

The Calendar (MSACAL20.OCX) and Scrollbar (MSASB20.OCX) Controls included with the ADT are distributable components; you can include these controls in runtime Access applications you distribute with MSARN200.EXE. The following two sections describe the characteristics of these two controls; the third section shows how to program these controls with OLE Automation code in a form module.

The Access 2.0 Calendar Control

The Calendar Control provides a simple perpetual calendar. You can change the size, background and foreground colors, and the font that displays the month, year, and days. With the exception of the size of the control, which you determine by the size of the object frame container, all other property settings can be set through entries in Property Pages or by OLE Automation code in Access Basic. This section describes the use of Property Pages to set property values. The "Controlling the Calendar with Scrollbars" section describes how to apply methods and interact with events of the Calendar control.

The online help file, MSACAL20.HLP, that accompanies MSACAL20.OCX provides a complete listing of the properties, methods, and events of the Calendar Control object, and individual help topics provide the syntax for getting and setting the values of these properties. Figure 18.10 shows the main help topic for properties of the Calendar Control. The help file contains an Overview topic that describes the control, but the primary purpose of the help file is to aid in writing OA code.

FIGURE 18.10.

The main help topic for the Calendar Control's properties.

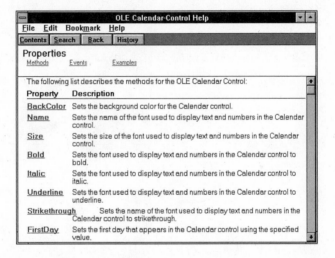

To open the Property Pages, click the right mouse button with the mouse pointer on the unbound object frame to open the floating menu (see Figure 18.11), choose Calendar Control **O**bject, then choose **P**roperties from the submenu. The main (General) Property Page of the Calendar control appears in Figure 18.12. You can set the date (`Value` property) and choose the first day of the week (`FirstDay` property) in this sheet.

Select Colors in the drop-down list at the top of the sheet to set the `BackColor` and `ForeColor` properties of the Control. You can select from one of the 16 standard Windows colors, or select one the Windows System colors, which change with the setting of the system colors in the Desktop function of Control panel, as the value of these two properties. (See Figure 18.13.)

FIGURE 18.11.

Floating menu choices for the Calendar Control object.

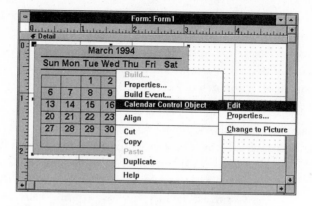

FIGURE 18.12.

The General Property Page of the Calendar Control.

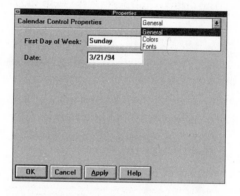

FIGURE 18.13.

Setting the BackColor property of the Calendar Control.

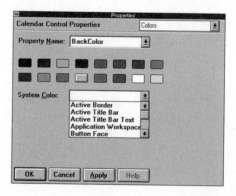

The third Property Page, Fonts, lets you select the typeface (Font, the value of the Name property), font size (Size property), and attributes (Bold and Italic properties). You also can add other attributes to the font, such as Strikeout and Underline properties. (See Figure 18.14.) Figure 18.15 shows the effect of the settings shown in Figure 18.12 and Figure 18.13 on the calendar control in run mode.

FIGURE 18.14.

Setting the properties of the typeface used by the Calendar Control.

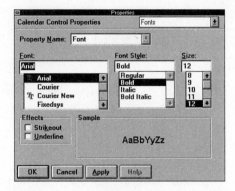

FIGURE 18.15.

The Calendar Control in run mode with new property values set.

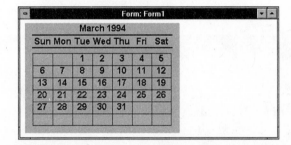

TIP

Make sure the Enabled property of the control is set **True**; if it is **False**, you cannot change the date by clicking the day of the month. The Locked property does not affect operation of the control.

You set the date that is returned by MSACAL20.OCX as a subtype 7 **Variant** to the Value property by clicking a date rectangle on the calendar. When you change the date, MSACAL20.OCX triggers the OnUpdated event. You can experiment with the interaction between the Value property, the OnUpdated event, and the methods applicable to the Calendar Control in the Immediate Window. Open the form module for the form on which your Calendar Control and add the statement **Debug.Print Format**(uofCalendar.Object.Value, "dddddd") to the uofCalendar_Updated (Code **As Integer**) subprocedure stub. The first four dates shown in the Immediate Window of Figure 18.16 result from clicking the first four days of the month of March. The two remaining dates appear as a result of applying the NextMonth and NextYear methods to the Control.

FIGURE 18.16.

Experimenting with the Updated event and the Value property in the Immediate Window.

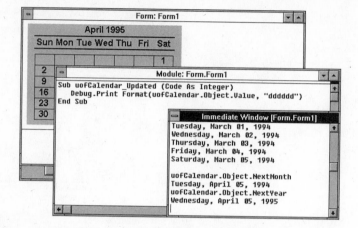

> **NOTE**
>
> Methods of OLE Custom Controls are not printed in bold face in this book because methods of OCXs, like methods of OLE Automation objects, are not reserved words in Access 2.0. If a method for an OCX is identical to an Access method, you need to enclose the name of the method in square brackets, as shown for the objName.Application.[Quit] statement in the preceding chapter.

The Scrollbar Control

Visual Basic programmers will recognize the Scrollbar Control immediately on its appearance on a form in design mode. The Scrollbar Control, MSASB20.OCX, is a direct descendent of the vertical and horizontal scroll bar controls of Visual Basic 3.0. The two scroll bar controls are native to Visual Basic, so there is no corresponding custom control file, such as "MSSCROLL.VBX," required to implement these controls. The properties, methods, and events of the MSASB20.OCX are almost identical to those of the two Visual Basic scroll bars. The most significant difference between the two implementations is the ability to change the orientation of the MSASB20.OCX scroll bar from vertical to horizontal in the properties window. Add a Scrollbar control to the form with the Insert Object object dialog, then click the right mouse button with the mouse pointer on the control. Figure 18.17 shows a horizontal Scrollbar Control added to the Calendar Control form with the Property Page activated.

FIGURE 18.17.

Adding a horizontal Scrollbar Control to the form.

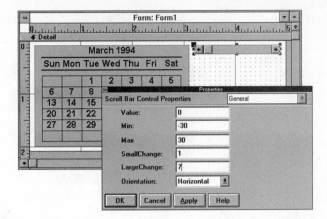

The Scrollbar Control has only one Property Page. The property settings shown in Figure 18.17 are designed to provide a Value ranging between –30 and +30 depending on the position of the slider. This range of values is designed to let you change the date one day at a time by clicking the Min and Max buttons of the scroll bar, vary the date up to a month in either direction with the slider (SmallChange property), or click the area between the slider and the Min or Max button and the slider (LargeChange property) to alter the date by a week. This slider is used in conjunction with the OA code to control the Calendar with Scrollbar Controls in the following section.

Controlling the Calendar with Scrollbars

The Calendar and Scrollbar Controls are quite simple elements, but they serve to demonstrate the interaction between OCXs that you can achieve on a single form or between forms. Figure 18.18 shows the design of a form in which two Scrollbar Controls, uofDayWeekSB and uofMonthQuarterSB, change the day and week, and month and quarter displayed by the Calendar Control, uofCalendar. The Today command button, cmdToday, resets the date to your computer's DOS date. The values of the properties of the uofDayWeekSB Control are shown in Figure 18.17. The property values of the uofMonthQuarterSB are: Value = 0, Min = -12, Max = 12, SmallChange = 1, and LargeChange = 3. The event handling code to control the date displayed in the text box and set as the current date of the Calendar Control is provided in Listing 18.1.

FIGURE 18.18.

*The design of the
interactive
Calendar-Scrollbar
Control form.*

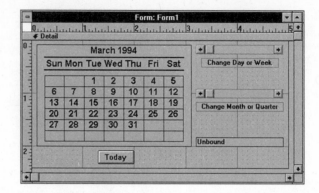

Listing 18.1. Code to change the date of the Calendar Control with Scrollbar Controls and a command button.

```
Sub uofCalendar_GotFocus ()
   'Purpose:   Update the date text box on start-up
   txtDate.Value = Format(uofCalendar.Object.Value, "dddddd")
End Sub

Sub uofCalendar_Updated (Code As Integer)
   'Purpose:   Update the date text box on a change of date
   txtDate.Value = Format(uofCalendar.Object.Value, "dddddd")
End Sub

Sub cmdToday_Click ()
   'Purpose: Reset calendar to today
   uofCalendar.Object.Value = Date
End Sub

Sub uofDayWeekSB_Change ()
   'Purpose: Move day or week with Day/Week scrollbar
   uofCalendar.Object.Value = Date + uofDayWeekSB.Object.Value
End Sub

Sub uofMonthQuarterSB_Change ()
   'Purpose:   Change the date by one month or a quarter
   uofCalendar.Object.Value = DateAdd("m", uofMonthYearSB.Object.Value,
Date)
End Sub
```

Figure 18.19 shows the interactive controls in run mode. The scrollbar sliders enable you to alter the Calendar Control's date plus or minus 30 days or 12 months. Clicking the scroll bar buttons changes the date by one day or one week. Clicking between the slider and a button changes the date by one week or one quarter. Clicking the Today button resets the Calendar to the DOS system date.

FIGURE 18.19.

The design of the interactive Calendar-Scrollbar Control form.

Exploring the Data Outline Control

The Data Outline Control, OUTL1016.OCX, is derived from the outline custom control, MSOUTLIN.VBX, included with the Professional Edition of Visual Basic 3.0. During its development phase, the Data Outline Control was called Navigator, and that term is used in this chapter for brevity. Navigator provides a hierarchical view of relational data stored in Access tables as an expandable (and collapsible) outline. You also can display the data in a separate form designed for each level of the hierarchy. Unlike the Calendar and Scrollbar Controls, which you can distribute with runtime Access applications, the distribution license for Navigator requires that each user of Navigator possess a copy of retail Access. This restriction reflects the investment that Microsoft made in the development of a very complex OCX, and Microsoft's desire to obtain a nominal return on that investment.

An extensive online help file, OUTLINE.HLP, provides an overview of Navigator, and documents each property, method, and event of the Control. You also can use the Object Browser of the ODK or Excel 5.0 to display the properties, methods, and events of Navigator, together with their syntax. Figure 18.20 shows just a few of the properties and methods of the Navigator Control.

FIGURE 18.20.

The syntax for the MoveSync() method of the Navigator Control shown in the ODK's Object Browser.

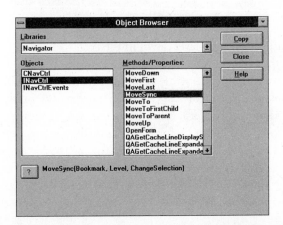

Exploring the Navigator Control with OUTLINE.MDB

The ADT includes a sample application, OUTLINE.MDB, that demonstrates the use of Navigator. OUTLINE.MDB, which uses tables attached from NWIND.MDB as the data source for each of six example applications you select from the list box that appears in the Northwind Explorer Switchboard form when you open OUTLINE.MDB. (See Figure 18.21.) Double-clicking the Help File Example item opens the Help Example form that initially displays the first level of the hierarchy. The Help File Example application is a three-level hierarchy of Customers, Orders, and Order Details. When you double-click a customer name, the Customers form opens and displays additional data for the selected customer. (See Figure 18.22.)

FIGURE 18.21.

Selecting an example Navigator application in the opening window of OUTLINE.MDB.

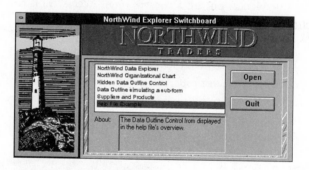

To display the next level down in the hierarchy, orders for a specific customer, you click the plus symbol adjacent to the customer name. The plus symbol turns into a minus symbol, indicating that the outline is expanded at this level and can be collapsed. Orders for the customer appear indented and in a smaller font size, indicating their lower level in the hierarchy, as shown in Figure 18.23. When you double-click the order information text, the Orders form appears with the details of the selected order. (See Figure 18.24.)

FIGURE 18.22.

Displaying customer information in the first level of the hierarchy.

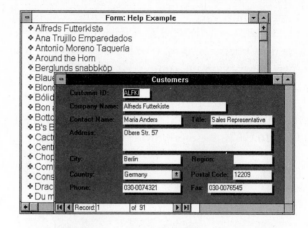

FIGURE 18.23.

Displaying the second level of the hierarchy, customer orders.

FIGURE 18.24.

The Orders form that appears when you double-click order information text.

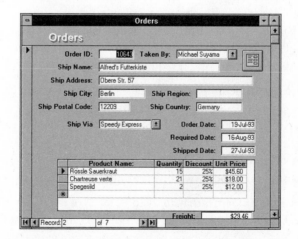

The third and final level of the hierarchy, order details, appears when you double the plus symbol adjacent to the order information. Double-clicking one of the detail items displays the Orders Subform. (See Figure 18.25.) Clicking the plus or minus symbols toggles expansion and contraction of the outline level. The methodology of the Navigator's outlining feature is identical to that employed by MSOUTLIN.VBX. The lowest level in the hierarchy corresponds to the leaf level of MSOUTLIN.VBX. Unlike MSOUTLIN.VBX, you cannot display the folder and page symbols; OUTL1016.OCX does not provide replaceable bitmaps for the outline symbols.

FIGURE 18.25.

Displaying the lowest (leaf) level of the hierarchy.

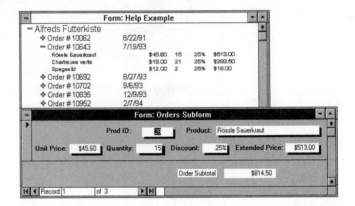

Properties and Methods of the Navigator Control

You can implement Navigator's basic features with little or no Access Basic code. For example, the Northwind Organization chart example, which displays the hierarchy of Northwind Employees, requires only three lines of code. It is possible to create Visual Basic 3.0 applications similar to the example applications of OUTLINE.MDB. Using Visual Basic 3.0 to duplicate the relatively simple Help File Example, however, would require hundreds of lines of Visual Basic code.

The secret to the simplicity of creating custom hierarchical data outlines with Navigator lies in its Property Pages. To display the Property Pages of the Navigator Control of the Help File Example application, open the Help File form in design mode, click the right mouse button on the unbound object frame, choose Data Outline Control from the floating menu, and Properties from the submenu. The General Property Page appears, as shown in Figure 18.26.

You set the properties that apply to all levels of the hierarchy in the General Property Page. Unlike other Access 2.0 controls, you can assign a special online help file to the Navigator Control. Navigator has a variety of events triggered by mouse clicks and keyboard operations; you can selectively enable these events by ticking the Send Mouse

Events and Send Keyboard Events check boxes. When you use the Property sheets, Navigator internally implements the required methods to perform its basic data outlining operations.

FIGURE 18.26.

The General Property Page for the Navigator Control of the Help File Example application.

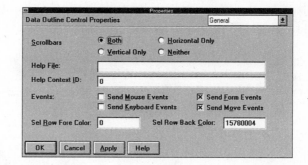

You can select Property Pages for up to 16 hierarchical levels, the maximum supported by Navigator, in the drop-down list at the upper right of the General Property Page. The Level One Property Page appears in Figure 18.27; this sheet specifies the RecordSource property for the first level of the outline, an SQL statement that returns all of the records of the Customers table. Tables and queries also can serve as the RecordSource property of a level. You specify the field that appears in the outline with an entry the Display Fields text box; each level can have its own typeface, font size, and font attributes. The entry in the Form Name text box determines the form that appears when you double-click the text at the first outline level. The Link Master Fields text box contains the field name on which the Customers form is linked to the outline entry.

FIGURE 18.27.

The Level One Property Page for the Customer Name entries.

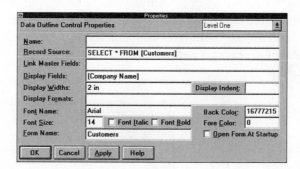

The Level Two Property Page, shown in Figure 18.28, uses a parameterized SQL statement to return the records for orders placed by the customer selected at level 1. The full SQL statement that comprises the RecordSource property at level 2 is:

```
PARAMETERS [p0] Text;
SELECT DISTINCTROW "Order # " & [Order ID] AS Expr1,
    Orders.* FROM Orders WHERE [Customer ID] = [p0];
```

The parameter, p0, passed to the statement is the value of the Customer ID field of the level 1 record, thus the parameter's data type is Text. The Orders form is linked to the outline by the Order ID field.

FIGURE 18.28.

The Level Two Property Page that selects the orders to display.

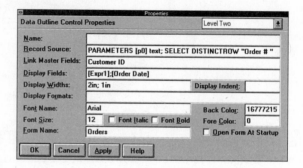

The third level of the hierarchy, which displays the order details for an order selected at level 2 uses the following SQL statement as the RecordSource property. The DOCParam0 parameter is the value of Order ID selected at level 2, thus its field data type is Long (Integer).

```
PARAMETERS [DOCParam0] Long;
SELECT * FROM [Order Details Extended]
WHERE [Order Details Extended].[Order ID] = [DOCParam0]
```

Figure 18.29 shows the Level Three Property Page. You specify the width of and the format for each field in the Display Widths and Display Formats text boxes. The syntax for the Display Widths field is identical to that for the ColumnWidths property of combo and list boxes. You format fields with the str*Format* values that are applicable to the **Format$()** function. Currency format is equivalent to the $#,##0.00 format value.

FIGURE 18.29.

The Level Three Property Page that displays order line items.

Properties

Data Outline Control Properties   Level Three ▼

Name:	
Record Source:	PARAMETERS [DOCParam0] Long;SELECT * FROM [Order De
Link Master Fields:	Order ID
Display Fields:	[Product Name];[Unit Price];[Quantity];[Discount];[Extended Pr
Display Widths:	2.5 in;.5 in;.375 in;.375 in;.6667 Display Indent:
Display Formats:	;Currency;0;0%;Currency
Font Name:	Arial Back Color: 16777215
Font Size:	10 ☐ Font Italic ☐ Font Bold Fore Color: 0
Form Name:	Orders Subform ☐ Open Form At Startup

OK   Cancel   Apply   Help

You can program the Navigator Control with OLE Automation code in Access Basic forms or modules to customize the Control's behavior. The extent to which Access developers utilize Navigator in production applications remains to be seen. One of the primary advantages of using Navigator in your applications is its fast operating speed; you don't need to open additional forms to obtain a drill-down view of relational data.

Examining BPS's Graph OCX

Bits Per Second Ltd's (BPS) Graph OCX Control is designed to replace MSGraph5 in applications where operating speed and full programmability are primary requirements. Graph OCX, which is derived from BPS's ChartBuilder custom control for Visual Basic, is an extended version of the BPS graph custom control Microsoft includes with the Professional Edition of Visual Basic 3.0. BPS also publishes the Graphics Server SDK, a general-purpose graphing tool for Windows applications, which includes support for Windows NT and an OLE Automation server. BPS distributes its products in the UK and Europe; Pinnacle Publishing, Inc. distributes Graph OCX and other BPS products in the Americas.

Graph OCX was in the final beta testing stage when this edition was published. Figure 18.30 shows a beta version of the Sales Graphs form of SALES.MDB, an example Access 2.0 application created by BPS to demonstrate programming techniques for Graph OCX. The Sales and Sales Analysis charts are interactive. When you click a column in the Sales chart, the Sales Analysis pie chart displays the sales distribution for the month.

FIGURE 18.30.

The Sales Graphs form of SALES.MDB with Sales and Sales Analysis charts.

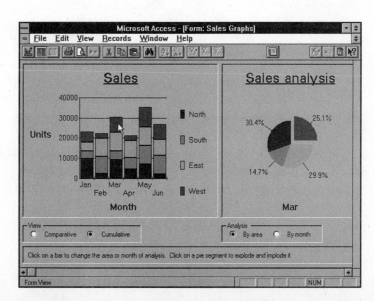

The primary advantages of the Graph OCX Control over MSGraph5 are as follows:

■ The operation of Graph OCX is much faster than MSGraph5. Opening a form containing two Graph OCX charts (see Figure 18.30) whose data is derived from tables or simple queries requires about three seconds, compared with at least 15 seconds for a form containing two MSGraph5 charts. Redrawing a graph or chart usually requires one second or less.

■ You have direct, programmatic access to the data series of Graph OCX. Thus you can change the values displayed by graphs and charts without redrawing the entire presentation in the object frame. Response to changes in data values is virtually instantaneous.

■ You can initiate drill-down operations by clicking a data element of a graph or chart. The HotHit() event returns **Integer** indexes, HitSet and HitPoint, to the data set and data point of the element you click. Thus you can use the HotHit() event for drill-down processes that display detailed information for the specified element.

■ All properties and methods apply to the Graph object itself; thus you need not deal with the rather arcane object hierarchy of MSGraph5 described in the preceding chapter. Figure 18.31 shows some of the events for the Graph object and the syntax for the HotHit() event displayed in the ODK's Object Browser.

FIGURE 18.31.

Some of the events and the syntax for the Graph OCX's HotHit() event.

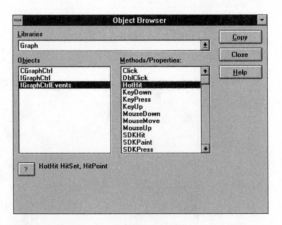

Figure 18.32 shows how the Sales Graphs form uses the HotHit() event to redraw the Sales Analysis pie chart based on the column (March) and data set (North) you click in the Sales chart. Listing 18.2 shows the OA code for the DrawPieChart subprocedure that creates the a new Sales Analysis pie chart.

FIGURE 18.32.

Intercepting the HotHit() event to redraw the Sales Analysis pie chart.

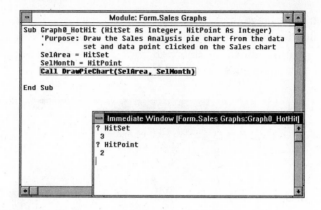

Listing 18.2. The code required to draw a pie chart.

```
Sub DrawPieChart (a As Integer, m As Integer)
    PieChart.DataReset = 9

    If Field9.Value = 1 Then
        PieChart.NumPoints = BarGraph.NumSets
        PieChart.BottomTitle = BarGraph.Label(m)

        For i% = 0 To PieChart.NumPoints - 1
            BarGraph.ThisSet = i%
            PieChart.Data(i%) = BarGraph.Data(m)
            ' PieChart.Legend(i%) = BarGraph.Legend(i%)
        Next i%

    ElseIf Field9.Value = 2 Then
        PieChart.NumPoints = BarGraph.NumPoints
        PieChart.BottomTitle = BarGraph.Legend(a)
        BarGraph.ThisSet = a

        For i% = 0 To PieChart.NumPoints - 1
            PieChart.Data(i%) = BarGraph.Data(i%)
            ' PieChart.Color(i%) = a + 1 + 8
            ' PieChart.Pattern(i%) = i% + 2 + 64
            PieChart.Legend(i%) = BarGraph.Label(i%)
        Next i%

    End If

    PieChart.GraphStyle = 4
    PieChart.DrawMode = 3

End Sub
```

You can change the Sales chart type from a stacked column chart to a comparative multiple-column chart and the Sales Analysis pie chart from analysis by area to analysis by month, as shown in Figure 18.33. The alteration to both charts requires less than one second on an 80486DX2-66 computer.

FIGURE 18.33.

Alternative presentations of the Sales and Sales Analysis Charts.

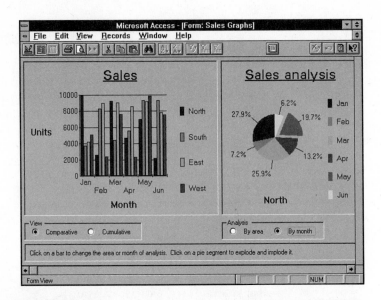

NOTE

The names of the properties, methods, and events of Graph OCX are identical to those for BPS's ChartBuilder custom control. Chapter 12, "Graphing Summary Data Created with Crosstab Queries," of the author's *Database Developer's Guide with Visual Basic 3.0* (Sams Publishing, 1994, ISBN 0-672-30440-6) provides extensive explanations and listings for programming graphs and charts with Visual Basic 3.0. The examples use Access tables as the source of the data for the graphs and charts. With minor changes to delete the references to MDI child forms and to accommodate the `Object` property of Access 2.0's unbound control frame, this code can be imported directly into Access 2.0 modules.

VI

Networked and Client-Server Applications

P VI

19

Networking Secure Access Applications

Most of the Access database applications you develop will be installed on networked PCs. Even if your client or employer does not use a local area network (LAN) when you develop the Access applications, industry sources project that about 75 percent of all commercial and institutional users of Windows will have LANs installed by the end of 1994. The desire to share Access database applications among multiple users may be the incentive your client or employer needs to install a network operating system (NOS). Windows for Workgroups 3.11 is an example of an inexpensive and easy-to-use NOS that is ideal for sharing Access database applications among as many as 10 to 25 PCs. Windows NT includes similar peer-to-peer networking capabilities with more security features than are offered by Windows for Workgroups 3.11. Windows NT Advanced Server 3.1+ is an economical, high-performance NOS for enterprise-wide LANs. Using Access applications in a network environment involves two distinct elements: network operations and Access security features. This chapter discusses the ramifications of using the retail and runtime versions of Access on a network and unlocks the secrets of creating secure Access database applications.

Installing Access in a Network Environment

If your client or employer has an operational network, you need to determine how to install retail or runtime Access on the network server (if one exists), in a shared directory of a peer-to-peer server, or on the local fixed disks of workstations. This decision may be made for you by the network administrator (if your client or employer has appointed a person to this position). If you are the one who must decide how to install Access on the network, consider the issues in the following sections when you make your decision.

Network Traffic Considerations

Network traffic increases greatly when you run Access from a dedicated network server or from a shared directory of a peer-to-peer server. Network traffic, in this case, consists of requests from the client workstation to the server to provide the content of the executable file and any additional files necessary to run the application. Then the content of these files is sent over the network to the requesting workstation, creating an instance of the application on the workstation. The increase in network traffic is due not only to the large size of MSACCESS.EXE or MSARN200.EXE, but also to Access's extensive use of DLLs to provide most of the services Access needs to manipulate database objects and run Access Basic code.

Applications that do not make extensive use of DLLs, such as Word 6 and Excel 5, simply load a copy of their .EXE file in the workstation's memory. WINWORD.EXE and EXCEL.EXE are much larger files, consuming 3.5MB and 4.2MB respectively, than either MSACCESS.EXE or MSARN200.EXE (1.9MB). After Word or Excel is loaded, it generates little additional network traffic; therefore its performance is not affected greatly by locating the .EXE file on a network server. Access, on the other hand, makes frequent calls to its MSABC200.DLL, MSAEXP200.DLL, MASAJT200.DLL, and MSAJIN200 .DLL libraries, among others, in the \WINDOWS\SYSTEMS directory, and to MSAIN200.DLL and MSAJU200.DLL in the \ACCESS directory. When a local instance of Access releases the DLL and then needs to use the DLL again, Access must request that the server send a fresh copy of the DLL to the workstation.

> **TIP**
>
> Workstations that run Windows from a dedicated file server should specify storage of temporary files on the workstation's local fixed disk to minimize network traffic. Make sure that each workstation's AUTOEXEC.BAT file includes the line `TEMP=c:\temp`, or its equivalent. If you do not include this line, temporary files for each user will be created on the server.

If Windows is installed on a dedicated network server rather than on individual workstations, the network administrator probably will want to install Access on the server also. The advantage of installing applications on the server is version control; when you update the server copy of Windows or Access, all workstations use the new version. By placing Windows and Access on the server, you avoid having to install updates on each workstation that uses these applications, thereby minimizing application-support duties. The disadvantage of this method is that the traffic resulting from workstations requesting services from Windows, Access, and other server-installed applications, such as Word and Excel, may over-tax the capabilities of the network; this results in extremely poor performance, especially with Access applications.

> **NOTE**
>
> You can install a copy of retail or runtime Access on the network server, then install copies of either version of Access on each workstation from the server copy. This is a faster process than installing Access from the distribution disks. Use the /n option to specify installation from a server copy of Access,

as in d:\access\setup /n. (d is the drive designator assigned by the workstation to the server directory containing MSACCESS.EXE or MSARN200.EXE.) In this case, the files that are used to install Access are stored on the server in a compressed format. For information about the use of MSACCESS.EXE installed on network servers, see the Microsoft License Agreement that accompanies the retail version of Access.

The network traffic issue becomes even more important when you share Access database applications that contain large tables or attach tables contained in client-server RDBMSs. Each workstation that shares an Access database creates substantial amounts of traffic when opening the database and conducting queries against the tables it contains. Similarly, queries against attached client-server tables require that Access open the ODBC DLLs stored on the server and create several connections to the client-server RDBMS. Queries that return many rows also generate substantial amounts of network traffic. If the network on which you plan to install Access currently has or is expected to have many workstations connected to a client-server RDBMS, installing local copies of Access on the workstation is likely to be a more effective approach.

TIP

You can minimize the amount of network traffic by using Access 2.0's new native SQL Pass-through feature with SQL client-server RDBMSs and the ODBC Application Programming Interface (API). Using SQL Pass-through (described in Chapter 20, "Front-Ending Client-Server Databases") bypasses Access's query parsing and optimization system and sends SQL statements you write directly to the SQL RDBMS, creating a **Recordset** object from the rows returned by the query.

Access DDE and OLE Operations on Networks

Applications that make extensive use of DDE and OLE deserve special consideration in a network environment. After you activate a DDE server, its instance remains available on the local workstation until you deliberately close the instance with a SendKeys macro action or the Access Basic **SendKeys** statement. If the workstation has less than 8MB of RAM, you probably will need to close the DDE application after use—especially if your application also uses OLE servers—to maintain adequate performance of your Access application. Having to reload the DDE server slows subsequent DDE operations.

> **NOTE**
>
> Access database applications that use DDE server applications, such as Microsoft Excel, whose .EXE files are located on a server rather than on a local fixed disk, should be given a private .INI file that includes the location of the DDE server's .EXE file. This enables you or the network administrator to change the location of DDE server applications or the workstation's drive designator corresponding to the location of the DDE server. Make sure that Windows for Workgroups users do not inadvertently change the drive designator of shared peer-to-peer server directories by altering the shared directory list with the Networks function of the Control Panel. Private .INI files for DDE applications are discussed in Chapter 21, "Employing Access as a DDE Client and Server."

The registration database file, REG.DAT, takes care of specifying the location of OLE servers, whether local or on-network servers. If the workstations run Windows from a dedicated server, REG.DAT may be located on the server or in a local \WINDOWS directory. Third-party OLE servers needed for special-purpose applications, such as multimedia databases, may be operable only from a local disk drive.

> **NOTE**
>
> If you plan to create multiuser multimedia databases that rely on files stored on CD-ROMs, and a dedicated network server is installed, your client or employer may need a special CD-ROM drive networking application to make the CD-ROM drive appear to be a server. CD-ROM drive networking applications for Novell Netware, Microsoft LAN Manager, and Banyan VINES are available from several third-party sources. See Appendix A for a partial list of suppliers of CD-ROM drive networking applications. Windows NT, Windows NT Advanced Server, and Windows for Workgroups enable you to share CD-ROM drive directories with other workstations.

The Effect of Server Performance on Access (and Vice Versa)

One of the advantages of using a dedicated network server is the server's ability to store the most recently used files in its cache memory. Server cache memory works like Windows' SMARTDRV.EXE, but dedicated servers usually have substantially more RAM than workstations. Therefore, server caches often can forward the data contained in disk files over the network to workstations faster than workstations can read the data from a local drive. One of the major influences on your application's performance is the size of the server's cache when network traffic is light. With large server caches, the speed of the network interface cards (NICs) installed in the server and workstations usually becomes the performance bottleneck. Today's most common NIC operating speed is 8 to 16 megabits/second (1MB to 2MB/second). Speeds of up to 100 megabits/second with unshielded twisted-pair (UTP) wiring are achieved with newer LAN protocols and hardware.

When many workstations simultaneously request data from the server's disk drive, speed may suffer (especially if a client-server database shares the disk drive with the file server). The server's cache is not likely to accommodate large database tables and Windows files at the same time. As a general rule, if your client or firm uses a PC server with an 80486DX CPU and a client-server RDBMS is stored on the server, workstations should run Windows and Access from a local fixed disk drive.

It is uncommon to run applications from directories shared by peer-to-peer servers, such as Windows for Workgroups (WfW), Windows NT, Lantastic, or NetWare Lite. But shared directories on peer-to-peer server drives often store workgroup files, such as multiuser Access tables-only .MDB files. When several PCs on a peer-to-peer network are actively sharing large Access files, the performance of applications being run on the PC sharing the directory deteriorates. With WfW, the trade-off between local and network performance is determined by the Performance Priority setting in the Startup Settings dialog box (shown in Figure 19.1), which appears when you click the Startup options button of WfW's Control Panel.

> **NOTE**
>
> The workstation whose Startup Settings dialog box is shown in Figure 19.1 is connected as a client (OAKLEAF1) to a Windows NT Advanced Server domain (OAKLEAF). If you are using Windows for Workgroups, the entries in the Options for Enterprise Networking section of the dialog box do not appear.

FIGURE 19.1.

The Startup Settings dialog box of the Networks function of the Windows for Workgroups 3.11 Control Panel applet.

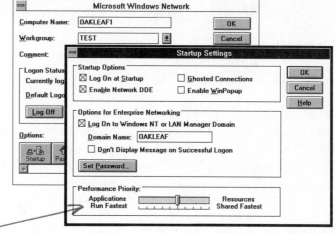

— WfW —
Determine
local & network
performance

Often, the frustrated user of a PC sharing a popular file moves the Performance Priority pointer to the far left, causing the speed of Access applications to deteriorate. With dedicated file servers, you can minimize the frustration by adding more memory to peer-to-peer server PCs and increasing the amount of memory dedicated to SMARTDRV.EXE's cache. The parameters that control the amount of memory dedicated to a local disk cache are explained in the *Microsoft Windows User's Guide* and the *Windows for Workgroups Resource Kit*.

TIP

When you install the retail version of Access under Windows 3.1, the Setup application adds the line `share.exe /l:200` to your AUTOEXEC.BAT file. This installs the DOS SHARE application that is required for several Access functions, including attaching, importing, or exporting Paradox files. Windows for Workgroups includes its own Windows version of SHARE.EXE. If you convert from Windows 3.1 to Windows for Workgroups 3.11, and you do not need SHARE.EXE for DOS applications run by workstations using WfW, you can eliminate the line (add `rem` at the beginning of the line) to save valuable memory.

Creating Workgroups to Share Access Applications

Develop a departmental framework.

A workgroup consists of users of networked computers who share computer resources to achieve a common objective. Most often, membership in workgroups follows a departmental framework. Thus, a firm might have Marketing, Financial, Personnel, Research, and Production workgroups. It is common also to form *ad hoc* workgroups, such as New Products, that involve members chosen from standing workgroups. Members of workgroups share information in the form of files stored in a designated workgroup directory of a file server. If information from an RDBMS is involved in the workgroup's activities, workgroup members share information from the database tables appropriate to their needs. Workgroups often share printers, modems, scanners, and other resources for which networking applications are available. Shared workgroup directories can be created on dedicated file servers, on peer-to-peer servers, or on both types of servers. Having user-maintained workgroups established with Windows for Workgroups running under a Novell NetWare or Microsoft LAN Manager network is common.

Access Workgroups and SYSTEM.MDA

An Access workgroup is defined as a group of users who share one or more Access applications and who attach a common (shared) SYSTEM.MDA library to their copy of Access. The shared database(s) and the accompanying SYSTEM.MDA file usually are stored in a single, shared workgroup directory that looks like a drive letter to other workstations, but it is not necessary that a single directory be employed. As an example, members of a workgroup might share a database located in their own workgroup directory and attach tables from a database located in another workgroup's directory or from a client-server RDBMS running on a dedicated server.

A member of a workgroup is identified by adding his or her user name—often called a logon ID—to the shared SYSTEM.MDA file. It is the shared SYSTEM.MDA file that distinguishes an Access workgroup from an aggregation of users who simply share an Access database. SYSTEM.MDA stores user names, passwords, and a unique System ID (SID) in a table called MSysAccounts. The operating preferences chosen by each user (in the Options dialog box opened by choosing **O**ptions from the **V**iew menu) are stored in the AccessPreferences table. (User names, passwords, and SIDs are discussed in the section called "Establishing Secure Access Applications," which follows shortly.)

The SYSTEM.MDA library that attaches to Access when a user launches his or her copy of Access is determined by the line `SystemDB=` in the `[Options]` section of your MSACC20.INI file, located in the \WINDOWS directory. The default entries in this section, assuming that you installed Access in the C:\ACCESS directory, are as follows:

```
[Options]
UtilityDB=c:\access\utility.mda
SystemDB=c:\access\system.mda
```

You change the SYSTEM.MDA entry to point to the location of the shared SYSTEM.MDA file for the workgroup. If the workgroup directory for a workstation is designated as drive G, the options section is as follows:

```
[Options]
UtilityDB=c:\access\utility.mda
SystemDB=g:\system.mda
```

Creating and Joining Workgroups by Editing MSACC20.INI

Basically, creating a new Access workgroup involves creating the shared workgroup directory on the dedicated or peer-to-peer network server and adding the shared SYSTEM.MDA file to the directory. To establish an Access workgroup, follow these steps:

1. On the network server, create a new directory with a name appropriate to the function of the workgroup.

2. Copy SYSTEM.MDA to the new workgroup directory. The specific version of SYSTEM.MDA to copy to the workgroup directory depends on membership and security issues (which are discussed in a forthcoming section of this chapter).

3. Copy the Access database file to be shared to the new workgroup directory, unless the file is already in a shared directory.

4. Designate the directory as shareable by other network users with read-write access. The degree of control you can exercise over who on the network can share the files in the directory depends on the network operating system in use.

5. In the `[Options]` section of the MSACC20.INI file of each workstation that is to join the workgroup, change the `SystemDB=` entry to point to the location of the shared SYSTEM.MDA file.

6. Use Program Manager to create a new program item with a command-line parameter that identifies the shared Access database file. An example of a

typical command-line entry is `c:\access\msaccess.exe e:\orders.mdb` for the retail version of Access. Command-line parameters for applications designed for use with runtime Access are described in Chapter 29, "Distributing Runtime Versions of Your Databases."

Using the Workgroup Administrator to Create a New Workgroup

Access 2.0 includes a new application, Microsoft Access Workgroup Administrator, that performs the preceding steps 2 through 5 for you. Workgroup Administrator, WRKGADM.EXE, replaces the Change Workgroup applications (STFSETUP.EXE /W) of Access 1.x.MSACC20.INI. After you install Access 2.0, the Workgroup Administrator icon appears in your Microsoft Access program group. The command line to run the Change Workgroups version is `c:\access\stfsetup.exe /w`. You can use the Workgroup Administrator to create a new workgroup or to join an existing workgroup. The series of steps that follow create a new workgroup, Sales, whose SYSTEM.MDA file is located in the ...\SALES directory of the server:

1. Create the directory on the server to hold SYSTEM.MDA and the .MDB database files for the workgroup. You can share this directory as a server share or as a subdirectory of a server share. You must create the shared workgroup directory *before* launching the Workgroup Administrator.

2. Double-click the Workgroup Administrator icon in the Microsoft Access program group to launch WRKGADM.EXE. The opening dialog box of the Workgroup Administrator appears as shown in Figure 19.2.

FIGURE 19.2.

The opening dialog box of the Workgroup Administrator.

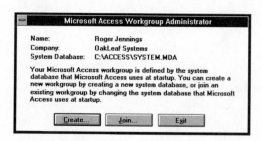

3. Click the Create button to open the Workgroup Owner Information dialog box. (See Figure 19.3.) You enter your name, company, and an optional Workgroup ID. The Workgroup ID creates a unique SID for the workgroup. (Workgroup ID replaces the personal identification number— PIN—used to identify Access 1.x workgroups.)

FIGURE 19.3.

The Workgroup Owner Information dialog box of the Workgroup Administrator.

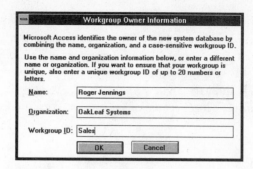

4. Click the OK button to display the Workgroup System Database dialog box. (See Figure 19.4.) Enter the path to the server share, relative to the workstation that you are using, and the name of the SYSTEM.MDA file to use for the workgroup.

> **TIP**
>
> If you do not want to create the workgroup's SYSTEM.MDA file by copying the SYSTEM.MDA file located in your \ACCESS directory, do not use the Workgroup Administrator application to create the SYSTEM.MDA file. Rather, manually copy to the workgroup directory the SYSTEM.MDA file with which you want to start the workgroup.

FIGURE 19.4.

Using the Workgroup System Database dialog box to specify the location of the SYSTEM.MDA file.

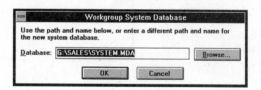

5. Click the OK button to display the Confirm Workgroup Information dialog box. (See Figure 19.5.)

> **WARNING**
>
> Create System Database overwrites an existing SYSTEM.MDA file in a workgroup without warning. Make sure that you keep a current backup of each SYSTEM.MDA file. If you accidentally overwrite the workgroup's

SYSTEM.MDA file and you do not have a current backup, you may need to re-create the SYSTEM.MDA file from scratch, duplicating each user's login ID and PIN exactly as originally typed. If you have not kept a record of login IDs and PINs, you cannot re-create the required SIDs to enable users to regain their lost permissions for the workgroup database(s).

FIGURE 19.5.

Confirming the information for the new workgroup and its location.

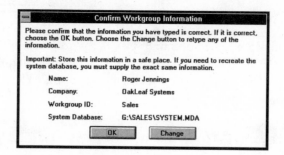

6. If the information shown in the dialog box is correct, click the OK button to return to the Workgroup Administrator dialog box. If the directory of the location you specified for the system database exists, you receive the message shown in Figure 19.6. If not, you receive an error message.

FIGURE 19.6.

The message box confirming that SYSTEM.MDA has been copied to the specified location.

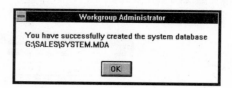

7. If you want to join the new workgroup you just created, click the Exit button of the Workgroup Administrator dialog box to close the application.

WARNING

What the message box of Figure 19.6 does *not* tell you is that the Workgroup administrator also has changed the SystemDB= entry of the [Options] section of MSACC20.INI to point to the new SYSTEM.MDA file you created. Unless you want to join this workgroup, you need to change workgroups to return to using the SYSTEM.MDA file in your \ACCESS directory.

Using the Workgroup Administrator to Change Workgroups

After you add a SYSTEM.MDA file to the new workgroup directory, launch the Workgroup Administrator application, if necessary. Click the Join button of the Workgroup Administrator's opening dialog box to display the Workgroup System Database dialog box. You can enter the path to the workgroup directory manually or click the Browse button to display the Select Workgroup System Database dialog box that displays files of the type *.MDA. SYSTEM.MDA is the default File Name entry. (See Figure 19.7.) When you click the OK button, the new location of the SYSTEM.MDA for the chosen workgroup appears in the Workgroup System Database dialog box and you receive the confirmation message shown in Figure 19.8. Click OK to accept the change and then click the Exit button of the Workgroup Administrator dialog box to close the application.

FIGURE 19.7.

Choosing the SYSTEM.MDA file to use for the workgroup you want to join.

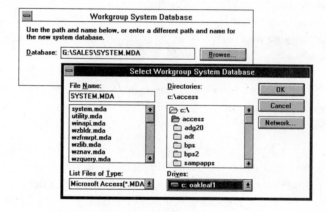

FIGURE 19.8.

Confirming a change to a new workgroup SYSTEM.MDA file.

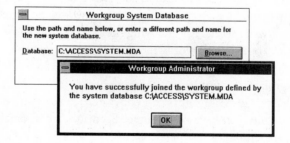

> **NOTE**
>
> What the message box of Figure 19.8 does *not* tell you explicitly is that you must restart Access for the change of workgroup SYSTEM.MDA files to become effective. The need to restart Access, however, can be inferred from the text ("...on startup...") of the Workgroup Administrator's dialog box that appears after you click OK.

Establishing Network-Level Security   *first level*

The network operating system itself provides the first level of security in a multiuser application. The NOS enables you to assign rights for users to share server directories. As mentioned in the preceding section, the degree of control you can exercise over rights to share the files in the workgroup directory depends on the NOS. All network operating systems let you control which individual network users can gain access to the shared directory. With Novell NetWare, Microsoft LAN Manager, Windows NT, and Windows NT Advanced Server network operating systems, you can determine whether specific users have read-write or read-only rights to individual files in the directory. Sophisticated NOSs have several levels of rights; read-write access does not imply the right to copy or delete a file, for example.

Network rights: read/write: not copy or delete.

If you are sharing a directory under Windows for Workgroups, all users on the network can share the files in that directory unless you password-protect the directory. The shareable directory appears in File Manager's Connect Network Drive list of all other workstations running Windows for Workgroups and connected to the network. You can restrict access to files in the directory by requiring that users enter a password to open the shared files. Separate passwords can be required to allow read-only and read-write access by employing the Depends on Password option for the shared directory, but the passwords for either type of right are common to all users who hold the right. Passwords known by several users are seldom secure. Windows for Workgroups does not let you assign rights for individual files in the directory. Users who have read-write rights can copy, delete, move, or otherwise wreak havoc on database files you have not secured. Securing Access database files is the subject of the next section.

Generally, you want to have two categories of workgroup members at the network security level: members who can modify the data in the database (read-write rights) and those who can only view the data (read-only rights). If your NOS enables you to assign these rights on a file-by-file basis, assign read-write rights for SYSTEM.MDA to all users so that they can change their passwords and option preferences. Assign read-only or read-write rights to database files as necessary. For files shared by

Windows for Workgroups servers, you need to establish a secure Access application to control users' rights to the database file. You cannot, however, prevent users of Windows for Workgroups 3.1 who have read-write rights to a shared directory from using File Manager to copy, delete, or overwrite an Access database file in the directory.

> **WARNING**
>
> Make sure that you maintain current backups of database files you share with Windows for Workgroups. The network system administrator usually handles backing up files located on dedicated network servers. The possibility of a disgruntled employee deliberately deleting or otherwise maiming a database file shared by a Windows for Workgroups user cannot be taken lightly. Unintentional injury to database files is another possibility. Network administrators, as a rule, are not assigned the responsibility for backing up locally shared files. Appoint a workgroup member to back up workgroup database files regularly.

Establishing Secure Access Applications   *second level*

The second level of security is provided by the database application itself. The four basic circumstances in which you need to implement Access's features are as follows:

- You want to prevent unauthorized people from viewing or modifying database applications you create on your computer, whether for your own use or for use by clients or co-workers. Unless you store your database applications in a private subdirectory of a server, you need a secure Access database.

- Your runtime Access application is designed for distribution to users who may have the retail version of Access. You do not want these users to be able to view your Access Basic source code or the designs of your forms, reports, macros, and queries.

- Your application is installed on a network server that cannot assign rights file-by-file. You want all workgroup members to be able to change their passwords and preferences, but only some users to be able to modify the data contained in the tables.

- Your application is installed on any type of network server and you want to restrict the ability of some users to view the contents of tables containing sensitive data, such as payroll information.

Access's security methodology is derived from security systems used by client-server database systems such as Microsoft SQL Server. Access's labyrinthine security system is, for the most part, well thought out, but the security model is, to be charitable, not intuitive. When you first start Access, its security features are placed in operation but the security system is hidden from view. The sections that follow describe how to establish a secure Access database system.

Access Owners, Groups, and Users

The concept of classifying into groups those individuals who can open an Access database is fundamental to Access's security strategy. In the discussion that follows, the term *account* means the combination of a database user's logon ID (user name) and PIN that results in a unique system ID (SID). By combining the logon ID and PIN, more than one user can have the same logon ID and still have a unique SID, thanks to a different PIN. To be a member of a group, you must have an account. Permissions—including the ability to view database objects, run macros, execute Access Basic code, and modify database objects—are granted to accounts to act on database files. The term *rights*, in this book, is reserved to network security measures.

Upon installation, Access establishes the following default groups:

Default groups:
1. owners
2. users
3. admin
4. guest.

■ *Owners* of databases and objects contained in databases. The database owner is the account that creates a new Access database by choosing **N**ew Database from Access's **F**ile menu. (Internally, Access calls the owner of a database object its *creator*.) The owner of a database object is the account holder who added the object to the database. The owner of a database usually, but not always, is the owner of the objects contained in the database. Information on database ownership is stored in the database file, not in SYSTEM.MDA. Owners are not an official Access group, but this chapter treats them as if they were. Permissions of owners of databases and of objects created by owners cannot be revoked by any account, including accounts in the Admins group.

■ *Users* of databases. With the exception of members of the Guests group, all accounts in any group must have accounts in the Users group also. When you install Access, accounts in the users group have full permissions for database objects. (The implications of full permissions is discussed in the section that follows.) Information on groups and accounts is stored in the MSysAccounts table of SYSTEM.MDA.

■ *Admins* (administrators) of database applications. Accounts in the Admins group are accounts in the Users group also. In addition to the permissions granted to accounts in the Users group, accounts in the Admins group can add new accounts to any group. Accounts in the Admins group also can transfer ownership of databases and the database objects they contain. When you install Access, you automatically are assigned an account with the logon ID, Admin, and you are made a member of the Admins and Users group. Admins must contain at least one account at all times.

■ *Guests.* Guests are database users who are not members of the Users group. By default, account holders in the Guests group can view database objects only. When you install Access, Guests has one user, Guest, whose account Admins cannot delete.

Each account and group has its own name and SID stored in the MSysAccounts table SYSTEM.MDA. The Access systems tables (using the MSys prefix) in SYSTEM.MDA no longer appear in the Database window when you open a copy of SYSTEM.MDA in Access 2.0. Instead, Access 2.0 lets you obtain information about groups and users through security objects in the Data Access Object hierarchy. Using Access Basic to manipulate the security features of Access 2.0 is discussed in a section that follows later in the chapter.

You cannot enter a logon ID with the same name as the name of a group. Passwords and SIDs are encrypted so that you cannot read them. The entries for Admin and Guest represent the encryption of an empty password. The SID for the Admins group is created by Access during installation. Other groups do not need SIDs. Unique SIDs are not created for accounts until you enter a password for the account.

> **WARNING**
>
> When you install Access, you are requested to enter your name and your company's name. This information is copied to the files on the setup disk. Access uses your name and company entries (in case-sensitive form), combined with the serial number of the Access Setup disk, to create a unique SID for the Admins group. Thus, if another person uses your distribution disks to install a copy of Access, the person's Admins SID is the same as yours. Any account in the other person's Admins group has full permissions for databases for which you have permissions. This situation does not occur when you install individual copies of Access on workstations from a network installation, because each workstation user enters his or her name during the installation process. This creates a unique SID for the local SYSTEM.MDA used by the workstation copy of Access.

Install Access on a workstation from the network installation.

Assigning New Accounts and Securing Access Logon

To create secure database objects, you must first add a new account for yourself in the Admins group and then delete the default Admin account. You delete the Admin account, because the SID for the Admin account is the same for every copy of retail Access 2.0. Thus any user who logs in as the default Admin user with no password would have full privileges for all objects in your application. Although you can simply choose **C**hange Password from the **S**ecurity menu and add a password to the Admin account, the accepted approach is the one described in the first sentence. To establish logon security, follow these steps:

1. Close Access (if it is running), then use File Manager to make a backup copy of SYSTEM.MDA to a diskette. Place the diskette in a secure location. When you delete the Admin account, you need a backup copy of the original SYSTEM.MDA to use in case you accidentally lock yourself out of Access.

2. Launch Access, open any database, then choose **C**hange Password from the **S**ecurity menu. The Change Password dialog box for the Admin user appears. (See Figure 19.9.) You need to add a password to the Admin account so that the logon dialog box appears when you reopen Access.

FIGURE 19.9.

The Change Password dialog box of Access's security system.

3. Press the Tab key to bypass the Old Password text box and type any password in the New Password text box. Retype the same password in the Confirm text box and press Enter or click the OK button.

4. Close and relaunch Access to activate the logon procedure. The Logon dialog box appears when Access's window opens. (See Figure 19.10.) Type Admin in the upper text box and the password you entered in Step 2 in the lower text box, then click the OK button or press Enter to open Access in "semisecure" mode.

FIGURE 19.10.

The Logon dialog box that appears when you launch Access after adding a password to your Admin account.

5. Open any database, then choose **U**sers from the **S**ecurity menu to open the Users dialog box. Click the New button to open the New User/Group dialog box shown in Figure 19.11. In the text boxes, type the logon ID you will use and a four-digit personal identification number (PIN). Then press Enter or click the OK button. Make a written note of your user name (including its capitalization) and the PIN number you assigned yourself. You now have an account in the Users group.

FIGURE 19.11.

The New User/ Group dialog box opened from the Users dialog box.

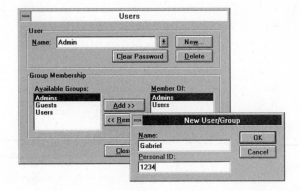

6. Select the Admins group in the Available Groups list box, if it is not selected by default. Click the Add >> button to add your new account to the Admins group. This is a *critical* step; the Member Of list box should display both Users and Admins. (See Figure 19.12.) If you fail to add your account to the Admins group, you will not be able to delete the Admin account later. Click the Close button.

FIGURE 19.12.

The Users dialog box after adding a new user account to the Users and Admins groups.

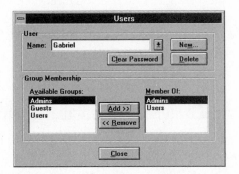

7. Close and relaunch Access and type your new logon ID in the Name text box of the Logon dialog box. Leave the Password text box blank and click the OK button or press Enter. You are now logged on to Access with your new logon ID and an empty password.

8. Open any database and choose **C**hange Password from the **S**ecurity menu. Type the password you plan to use for future logon operations, confirm the password, and click OK or press Enter.

9. Choose **U**sers from the **S**ecurity menu to open the Users dialog box. Select the Admin user from the User Name combo box if it is not currently selected. Click the Delete button, then confirm the deletion with a click on the OK button of the confirmation message box that appears.

You have deleted the Admin account; your logon name, password, group membership(s), and SID have been added to the MSysAccounts table in the SYSTEM.MDA file that was attached to Access when you made the changes.

WARNING

You must make similar changes to other SYSTEM.MDA files you created for workgroups if the default Admin user account with no password was present when you created the workgroup files. If you fail to delete the Admin account, anyone can gain access to and modify or delete objects in the *DATABASE*.MDB you created using the Admin account with no password.

NOTE

The AccessPreferences table of the current SYSTEM.MDA stores the system options you specify in the Options dialog box displayed by the Options choice of the View menu. When you create and attach a new SYSTEM.MDA library, your preferences revert to Access's default values. You need to reestablish your system preferences for each new SYSTEM.MDA library you attach to Access.

Transferring Ownership of Databases and Database Objects

The database applications you created while logged on to Access with the Admin account are not yet fully secure. The SIDs of the Admin and Guest user accounts of all copies of Microsoft Access are the same. Thus, if you create a database when logged on as Admin (the default), Admin is the owner of the database and all of your database objects. Anyone with a retail version of Access has full permissions for your database and its objects, because his or her Admin account SID is the same as yours.

To fully secure your database applications, you need to transfer ownership of each object in your database to a new database you open with your newly created Admins-Users account. Then you archive and delete the unsecure database file. The following sections describe how to change the ownership of a database and all of the objects it contains, or selected objects in a database.

Changing Ownership of All Database Objects

Access 2.0 includes a new add-in, Import Database, that makes changing the ownership of all objects in an existing database a quick and easy process. To transfer ownership of a database and the objects it contains to a different account with the Import Database add-in, follow these steps:

1. Log on to Access with the logon ID for the account that is to become the owner of the database and its objects.

2. Choose **N**ew Database from the **F**ile menu and give your database a new name (or specify the same name, but use a different directory). The default db1.mdb filename usually is satisfactory, because you will rename the new database after you delete the original version. Click the OK button. Your logon account becomes the owner of the new database.

3. Choose Add-Ins from the **F**ile menu, then choose Im**p**ort Database from the submenu to display the Import Database dialog box. (See Figure 19.13.) Double-click the source database file to start the import process. The length of time required to import the objects into your new database depends on the size and number of objects, the speed of your fixed disk drive, and, to a lesser extent, the speed of your computer's CPU. You receive a confirming message box when the import process is complete.

FIGURE 19.13.

Selecting the .MDB file to import by using the Import-Database add-in.

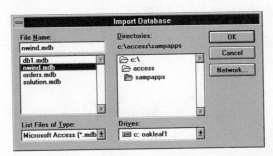

4. To make sure that your current Admins account has full permissions for the objects the new database contains, test it by making minor modifications to the design of an object in each class without saving the changes. Permissions is the subject of the next section of this chapter.

5. Save a copy of the original database to disk before you delete the original database, just in case there is an undiscovered problem with your security settings.

> **TIP**
>
> If you want to change ownership and convert an Access 1.1 database to Access 2.0 format, using the Import Database add-in accomplishes both objectives in a single step. Using Import Database eliminates the need to use the Convert choice of the File menu to convert the Access 1.1 .MDB file to 2.0 format before you change the ownership of the .MDB and the objects it contains.

Your new database is now secure because other people cannot view or modify the database objects unless you give them permission to do so. A person with a copy of your original SYSTEM.MDA file no longer qualifies as the owner of the database and its objects. This step is particularly important for developers of Access database applications and libraries who want to prevent clients from viewing Access Basic source code or other database objects contained in a commercial product.

> **NOTE**
>
> With the retail version of Access, any user of a database can add objects to the database. The Access security system has no provision to prevent users from adding database objects. The only way you can prevent users with retail versions of Access from adding objects to databases is by denying them rights to open the database in read-write mode. The toolbar and menu choices that enable users to add new objects are hidden in the runtime version of Access. The only way to prevent users with read-write rights from adding objects to your databases is to use MSARN200.EXE.

Changing Ownership of Individual Objects in a Database

Access 2.0 adds a new choice, Change **O**wner, to the **S**ecurity menu so that you can change the ownership of individual database objects without the need to create a new database and import the objects. Figure 19.14 shows the Change Owner dialog box in the process of changing the ownership of the Customers, Order Details, Orders, and Products tables of NWIND.MDB from the Admin account to the Erendira account. You can transfer ownership of any or all of the objects of a single type by selecting the objects in the Objects list box. (Press the Ctrl key and click the object to make a multiple selection.) You also can change the ownership objects to a group; assigning ownership rights to a group gives full permissions on the objects to every member of the group.

FIGURE 19.14.

Using the Change Owner Dialog box to change ownership of individual database objects.

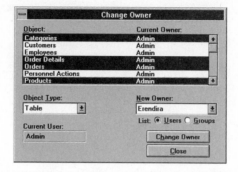

Assigning Permissions and Adding New Accounts

Permissions enable database users to manipulate database objects. You grant and revoke specific permissions for groups and users by choosing Permissions from the Security menu to display the Permissions dialog box shown in Figure 19.15. (GRANT and REVOKE are SQL keywords, but they are not capitalized here, because Access SQL does not use SQL Data Control Language (DCL) statements to alter permissions.) Permissions apply only to objects in the current database, and permissions are stored in the MSysACEs table of the current database. Groups are granted a default set of permissions by Access. Specific permissions granted to or revoked from groups and users using the Permissions dialog box apply only to the database that is open when you modify the permissions (because permissions for each group and user account are stored in the database file, not in SYSTEM.MDA).

> **NOTE**
>
> Unlike the MSys... tables of SYSTEM.MDA, you can view the content of the MSys... tables of the current database by choosing **O**ptions from the **V**iew menu and setting the value of the Show System Objects option in the General options category to Yes.

FIGURE 19.15.

Default permissions for the Users group displayed in the Permissions dialog box.

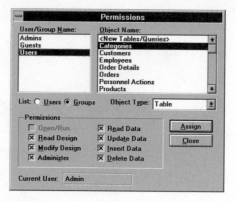

Access's 2.0's security system has the following nine types of permissions, four of which are new to Access 2.0:

■ *Read Design* (formerly *Read Definitions*) permission enables accounts to view objects contained in the database.

■ *Read Data* permission lets accounts view the data contained in tables, queries, and forms. To restrict specific accounts from viewing objects that display sensitive data, revoke the accounts' Read Data and Read Design permissions for these objects.

■ *Open/Run* (formerly *Execute*) permission enables accounts to use reports and forms and to run macros. Open/Run permission does not affect the capability to run code in Access Basic modules. Ordinarily, Read Definitions, Read Data, and Open/Run permissions are granted to all accounts in the Users group.

■ *Open Exclusive* permission (a new feature), which appears only for the Database object type, enables a user to open an .MDB file for exclusive use. You need not remove this permission for an application .MDB if the user has his or her own local copy of the application database. However, Open Exclusive permission should not be granted to any user, other than to the database administrator, for shared .MDB files.

■ *Update Data* (formerly *Modify Data*) lets accounts edit data in tables, queries, and forms. Update Data permission, as well as the preceding three and following two permissions, are granted to data-entry operators and other accounts that need to edit, delete, or add new records to tables.

■ *Insert Data* (new, formerly included in *Modify Data*) lets accounts add new records to tables.

■ *Delete Data* (new, formerly included in *Modify Data*) lets accounts delete records from tables.

■ *Modify Design* (formerly *Modify Definitions*) enables accounts to replace and delete objects. Accounts with Modify Design permissions automatically are granted Read Definitions permissions. Modify Definitions permission usually is granted only to developers of Access applications.

■ *Administer* (formerly *Full Permissions*) assigns all permissions and includes the ability to modify permissions of other accounts.

Some permissions are not applicable to specific classes of database objects. For example, Modules have only Read Design, Modify Design, and Administer permissions. Permission check boxes that are not applicable to a class of database objects are disabled in the Permissions dialog box.

Implicit, Default, and Explicit Permissions

Implicit permissions are required to permit other permissions to operate. Thus, if you assign an account Read Data or Modify Design permissions, Read Design permission is implied. For example, if you revoke all permissions for an object and an account and then add Read Data permissions, Access automatically places a mark in the Read Design check box.

Access establishes default permissions for each group. The Admins and Users groups have full permissions for all objects in the database. Guests have only Read Design, Read Data, and Open/Run permissions by default. The only way you can restrict access to database objects is to revoke all permissions for the object by the Users and Guests groups. You grant or revoke permissions for groups by clicking the Groups option button, then choosing the group you want from the list in the User/Group Name list box. Mark or clear the check box for the applicable permission(s) for the group for each object in the database.

> **NOTE**
>
> Many Access developers believe that Microsoft erred in granting full (Administer) permissions by default to Users group accounts. Full permissions for the Users group means that you must explicitly revoke the Users group's permissions for each database object to establish groups, other than Admins, that you don't want to have these permissions. (All accounts, except Guest, must be members of the Users group.)

You grant explicit permissions to individual accounts in order to permit actions not granted by membership in a group. As an example, if you grant only Read Design, Read Data, and Execute permissions to the Users group for a database object, these permissions are implicit to all Users group accounts. To explicitly grant Update Data and Insert Data permissions to accounts that need to edit or enter new data, you click the Users option button and then choose the logon ID for the account from the list in the Name combo box.

> **NOTE**
>
> Implicit permissions inherited by individual accounts from group membership in Users and Guests do not appear as marks in permissions check boxes when you display the permissions for individual accounts. Only the permissions you grant explicitly to individual Users and Guests accounts cause the check boxes to be marked. Permissions inherited by members of the Admins group are displayed, but permissions of the Admins group itself are not displayed.

Adding New Groups and Users

You need to develop a strategy for the security techniques to be used with the databases you create before you add new groups and users to the SYSTEM.MDA library to be used with the database. For most developers, the first element of the strategy is to explicitly revoke Update Data, Insert Data, Delete Data, and Modify Design privileges from the Users group for existing objects so that all Users group accounts do not inherit these privileges implicitly. In addition, you might want to revoke Read Design permissions for modules.

> **TIP**
>
> Access 2.0 makes the process easier if you plan ahead for security features of your applications. When you create a new database, each object type in the database has only a single entry in the Permissions dialog box, <New ObjectNames>. Once you set the permissions for each group, all new objects you add to the database carry the default permissions you set.

The next step is to determine how you want to grant specific accounts permissions to edit and add new table records and to permit other developers to modify some or all of the objects in the database. Often, you want developers to be able to modify the design of forms or reports but not be able to change the data in the tables. In this case, you do not give developers Modify Data or Modify Definitions permissions for tables. In the second stage of your security strategy, you use either of the following approaches:

- ■ Maintain the default group structure of Access. With this approach, you need to assign to each user account explicit permissions for Update Data, Insert Data, Delete Data, or Modify Design for each object, according to job duties.

- ■ Create new groups, such as Data Entry and Developers, to which you explicitly grant all Data and Modify Design permissions, respectively. By adding new groups, you minimize the number of steps required to grant appropriate permissions to specific accounts. This is the best approach to follow when many accounts share the database.

To create a new group in the currently attached SYSTEM.MDA library, follow these steps:

1. Choose **G**roups from the **S**ecurity menu to display the Groups dialog box.

2. Click the New button to open the New User/Group dialog box. (See Figure 19.16.)

FIGURE 19.16.

Adding a new group with the New User/Group dialog box.

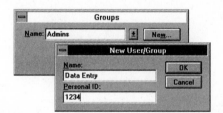

3. Enter the name of the group (Data Entry, in this example) and the group's PIN in the text boxes; then press Enter or click the OK button to add the new group to SYSTEM.MDA.

4. Repeat Steps 2 and 3 to add another group, such as Developers. Click the Close button of the Groups dialog box to return to Access.

Now follow these steps to grant explicit permissions for each group you added to each database object:

1. Choose Permissions from the Security menu to display the Permissions dialog box.

2. Choose the object class and the object for which the explicit permissions of the new group are applicable.

3. Click the Groups option button in the User/Group frame and select the name of the new group from the list in the User/Group Name list box. No permissions check boxes are marked because the new group has only implicit permissions inherited from the Users group.

4. Tick the check box next to the explicit permission for the object you want to grant to accounts that are members of this group. As an example, click the Update Data, Insert Data, and Delete Data check boxes for the Data Entry group. Your Permissions dialog box for a new database now looks like the one in Figure 19.17. The marks in the Read Design and Read Data check boxes are created because these permissions are implied by the Update Data permission. (Note that the Read Design and Read Data permissions already exist because they were inherited from the Users group.)

FIGURE 19.17.

Adding explicit permissions for a newly added group.

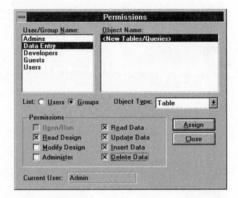

5. Click the Assign button to add the new group permissions for the object in the current database.

6. Repeat Steps 3 through 5 for any additional groups you added.

The preceding process requires one set of entries for each class of objects in each new group when starting with a new database. With existing databases containing many objects, the preceding process is tedious, because the Access security system has no provision for adding default permissions for new groups you define.

Now you can add accounts to the new groups by following the same steps you took earlier in this chapter to add the new account that replaced the default Admin account. If specific developers are to be allowed to modify the structure of tables, you can grant these developers explicit Modify Design for the tables. Figure 19.18 shows the MSysAccounts table after two new groups and three new accounts appear there.

The MSysAccounts table is attached from the current SYSTEM.MDA file. Although you cannot view system objects by opening a copy of SYSTEM.MDA, you can attach the tables from SYSTEM.MDA and view their contents.

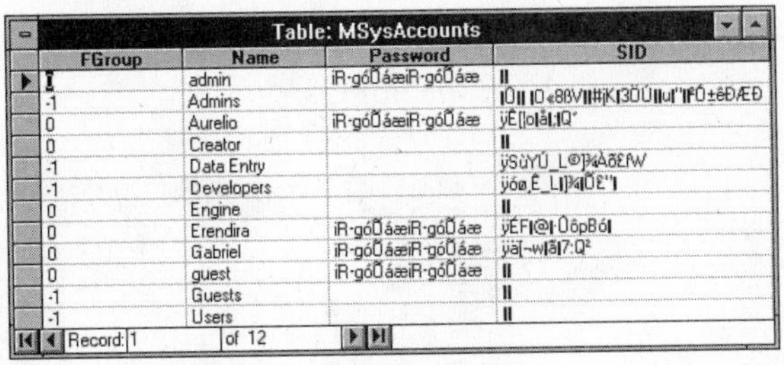

FIGURE 19.18.

The MSysAccounts table reflecting three new users and two groups added to SYSTEM.MDA.

FGroup	Name	Password	SID
	admin	iR·góŨáæiR·góŨáæ	‖
-1	Admins		ÎÛ‖ ‖◌‹88V‖#‖K[3ÛÜ‖ù‖'ÏÍÖ±ëÐÆÐ
0	Aurelio	iR·góŨáæiR·góŨáæ	ÿÈ‖◌ìÄ‖Q˜
0	Creator		‖
-1	Data Entry		ÿSùYÛ_L®p̧ÀðÊĪW
-1	Developers		ÿóֆ‚É_L‖p̧ÛÈˆ‖
0	Engine		‖
0	Erendira	iR·góŨáæiR·góŨáæ	ÿÉFî@‖Ûôp̧Bóı
0	Gabriel	iR·góŨáæiR·góŨáæ	ÿäֱ‖~wÏ8ֱ7:Q¹
0	guest	iR·góŨáæiR·góŨáæ	‖
-1	Guests		‖
-1	Users		‖

Record: 1 of 12

> **WARNING**
>
> If you want to view the contents of SYSTEM.MDA, create a copy of SYSTEM.MDA in another directory or with a different name, then attach the tables from the copy of SYSTEM.MDA. If you attach tables from the copy of SYSTEM.MDA that is attached to your current database, you can't delete the attachment. You receive a message that reads "Couldn't lock table 'MSysAccounts'; currently in use." In this case, you need to close Access, attach a different copy of SYSTEM.MDA, and then delete the attachment.

Creating a Query to Display Objects, Users, and Groups

You can create a query that displays the names of all groups and users with permissions for objects in your database by following these steps:

1. Set the value of the Show System Objects option to Yes.
2. Open the Permissions dialog box, select the MSysACEs table, and tick the Read Data check box.
3. Attach the MSysAccounts table from your SYSTEM.MDA library to the current database.
4. Open a new query and add MSysACEs, MSysAccounts, MSysObjects to the query.
5. Drag the Name field of the MSysObjects table to the first column of the query-design grid and add the alias Object:.
6. Drag the Name field of the MSysAccounts table to the second column and give the field the alias User or Group:.

7. Create an inner join between the SID fields of the MSysACEs and MSysAccounts tables.

8. Create an inner join between the ObjectID field of MSysACEs and the Id field of MSysObjects, as shown in Figure 19.19.

9. Run the query to display the list of objects and the users and groups who have permissions for the objects.

FIGURE 19.19.

The design of the objects, groups and users query.

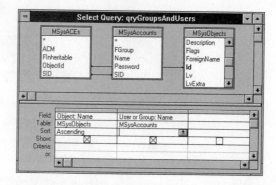

You can minimize the number of duplicate rows returned by your query by changing the DISTINCTROW keyword to DISTINCT, as in the following SQL statement used to generate the query result shown in Figure 19.20:

```
SELECT DISTINCT MSysObjects.Name AS Object,
           ➥MSysAccounts.Name AS [User or Group]
FROM (MSysACEs INNER JOIN MSysAccounts ON MSysACEs.SID =
➥MSysAccounts.SID)
➥INNER JOIN MSysObjects ON MSysACEs.ObjectId = MSysObjects.Id
```

FIGURE 19.20.

The result set of the Objects, Groups, and Users query design of Figure 19.19.

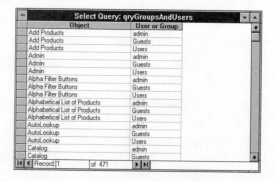

Exploring the *Groups* and *Users* Collections of the DAO

Access 2.0's Data Access Object lets you manipulate Groups and Users with Access Basic code. Any operation you can perform with the **P**ermissions, **U**sers, **G**roups, **C**hange Password, and **C**hange Owner choices of the Security menu can be duplicated by code in Access Basic modules. The key to user and group management with Access Basic is the access granted to the Groups and Users collections of the current **Workspace** object. Although you might expect the Users collection to be below the Groups collection in the DAO hierarchy, this is not the case. The Users and Groups collections are co-equals. Just as a **Group** object has a Users collection, **User** objects have a Groups Collection.

The most effective way to become familiar with the Groups and Users collections is to use the Immediate Window to test a few simple expressions that return information about the two collections. You need to declare an object variable to point to the current **Workspace** object before you attempt to read or set the values of members of the Groups or Users collections with a statement such as **Set** wsCurrent = **DBEngine**(0), the shorthand method of specifying **DBEngine**.Workspaces(0). As with other DAO collections, the Groups and Users collections have only one property, Count, that you use to limit the iteration of the members of the collection. Figure 19.21 shows how you manually iterate the Name property of the five groups of the current **Workspace** object. (The Data Entry and Developers groups were added to the default groups, Admins, Guests, and Users, earlier in this chapter.) The Group object has only two properties, Name and PID (personal identifier, related to PIN). The Name property is read-only and the PID property is not accessible, except when you are creating a new **User** object; when you create a new **User** object, both Name and PID are write-only properties.

FIGURE 19.21.

Iterating the Name property of the Groups collection in the Immediate Window.

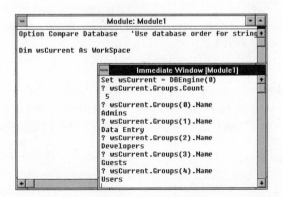

You also can determine all of the users registered in the copy of SYSTEM.MDA attached to the current instance of Access by iterating the Users collection. The Users collection of the current Workspace object includes a member **User** object for each user, regardless of group membership. Figure 19.22 shows the value of the Name property of five of the seven **User** objects in the Users collection of the current **Workspace** object. **User** objects have Name, Password, and PID properties. Like **Group** objects, Name is read-only, and Password and PID are write-only when you create a new **User** object and are otherwise inaccessible.

FIGURE 19.22.

Iterating the Name property of the Users collection in the Immediate Window.

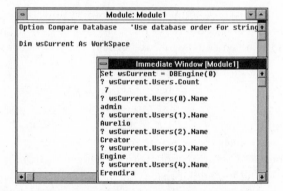

NOTE

The PID and Password properties are not the equivalent of write-only memory (the fictional WOM, memory that you can write to but you can never again read). Access can read the values of PID and Password, but you cannot. As an example, Access substitutes the values of the Name and Password property in the connect string (ODBC; DSN=*DataSourceName*; UID=*Name*; PWD=*Password*; DATABASE=*DatabaseName*) that is first sent to client-server databases attached by ODBC. If *Name* and *Password* aren't recognized by the server database, then you are requested to log on to the client-server database with your assigned user name and password.

If you have Administer privileges, you can delete groups (other than Admins, Guests, and Users), and existing users (other than the last user in the Admins group and the Guest user) by applying the **Delete** method to the Groups or Users collection. To add a new user or group, you first create a new **User** or **Group** object with the **CreateUser** or **CreateGroup** method, then use the **Append** method to add the new user or group to the collection. The general syntax of these methods is:

```
Dim wsCurrent As Workspace
Dim usrNewUser As User
Dim grpNewGroup As Group

Set wsCurrent = DBEngine(0)

Set usrNewUser = wsCurrent.CreateUser([strName[,strPID, [strPassword]]])
[usrNewUser.Name = strName]
[usrNewUser.PID = strPID]
[usrNewUser.Password = strPassword]
wsCurrent.Users.Append usrNewUser

Set grpNewGroup = wsCurrent.CreateGroup([strName[, strPID]])
[usrNewGroup.Name = strName]
[usrNewGroup.PID = strPID]
wsCurrent.Groups.Append usrNewGroup
```

The most efficient method of adding the new group or user is to assign the name (strName), personal identifier (strPID), and password (strPassword, for users only) when applying the **CreateUser**() method. You can, however, assign these property values *prior* to adding the new user or group to the collection by assigning values to the properties, as shown in the preceding statements enclosed with square brackets.

You also can obtain the identity of users in a particular group or the group membership of users by using the ambidextrous strName = wsWorkspace.Groups(i).Users(j).Name and strName = wsWorkspace.Users(i).Groups(j).Name statements, respectively. Figure 19.23 shows how you iterate the members of the Users collection, wsCurrent.Users(4), of the current **Workspace** object in the Immediate Window.

FIGURE 19.23.

Iterating the Name property of Users in the Users group in the Immediate Window.

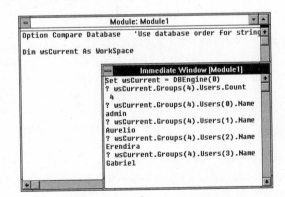

Using the *Owner* Property of *Document* Objects in the *Containers* Collection

The Access Basic equivalent to the Change Owner dialog box is the Owner property of a **Document** object. **Document** objects are members of Documents collections, which are members of the Containers collection. The Name property values of the eight members of the Containers collection (and thus of the Documents collections), in the order of their index, are as follows: Databases, Forms, Modules, Relationships, Reports, Scripts (macros), SysRel (the design of the Relationships window), and Tables.

Figure 19.24 shows typical entries in the Immediate Window to explore the properties of **Container** and **Document** objects. You must declare a variable of the **Database** object type, then **Set** and use the variable to obtain the properties of the **Database** object's Containers and Documents collections. The **DBEngine** object (Engine) is always the owner of the current **Databases** container; however, the database owner (creator) is the owner of all other containers and the current database, called MSysDb, that you address with the statement dbCurrent.Containers(0).Documents(0). (Executing ? dbCurrent.Containers(0).Documents(0).Name in the immediate window returns MSysDb.)

FIGURE 19.24.

Iterating members of the Containers and Documents collections in the Immediate Window.

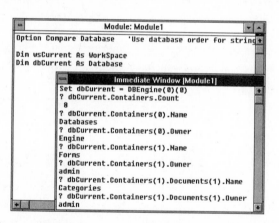

If you are the owner of a **Document** object or you have Administer privileges for the **Document** object, you can alter the value of the Permissions property of the **Document**. As an example, the default value of the Permissions property of the Categories form of NWIND.MDB is 1048575 (&HFFFFF, representing all or Administer permissions). Executing ? dbCurrent.Containers(1).Documents(1).Permissions returns 1048575 and ? Hex$(1048575) returns FFFFF. You use Access 2.0's intrinsic global

DB_SEC_... constants to set the value of the Permissions property to reflect the settings in the Permissions dialog box. Typing ? DB_SEC_FULLACCESS returns 1048575. If you are determined to set user permissions using Access Basic statements, the names of the DB_SEC_... constants are provided in the online help topic for the Permissions property.

Maintaining Security and Sanity Simultaneously

Access's security system was referred to as "labyrinthine" earlier in this chapter. "Byzantine," or even "Machiavellian," might be a more apt description. Following are some tips to guide you through the security maze and to avoid a few pitfalls.

The only way to really understand the security strategy of Access and to implement Access's security features properly with your database applications is to experiment. Create a new directory and add a copy of your SYSTEM.MDA to the directory. Verify that the SystemDB= entry of the [Options] section of MSACC20.INI points to the new copy of SYSTEM.MDA. Create a new database in the directory, import some objects from another database, then go through the procedures of adding your new Admins group account and deleting the Admin account. Revoke the Modify Data and Modify Definitions permissions for the User group, then create a couple of new user groups with explicit permissions. Add a bogus account to each user group. Then try logging on as the bogus user and testing the result of your changes. This may involve an hour or two of work but will pay dividends in the long run.

Revoke the Users group's Read Design permission for MSysObjects so that accounts in the Users group cannot display the SIDs of the Admins group or members of the Admins group. If an account other than a member of the Admins group can read the SIDs, the user probably can copy his or her SID to the Clipboard and then paste the copy as a replacement for the SID of the database owner and the SIDs of the owners of objects in the database. Copying and pasting a SID in this way is not always successful, but when it does work, it causes a major breach of security. Be sure to test your database application by logging on with a logon ID for a member of the Users group. If your application uses Access's Load From Query capability of Access filters, you receive a message that reads "No Permissions for 'MSysObjects'." Consider a workaround to eliminate the use of the Load From Query feature.

Be sure to test any database application or library that you want to distribute as a secure product on a computer running the retail version of Access installed from distribution diskettes other than yours. This is the only sure way to determine that clients cannot gain access to the database objects you want to secure. If, on the other hand, you want clients to have full access to all of your database objects, and you created the database while logged in as an account other than the default Admin account, you need to re-create the database logged in as default Admin. You may need to use DECOMP.EXE to create a plain vanilla SYSTEM.MDA from the compressed copy on the distribution diskettes. Attach this library to Access, then create a new database and import all the objects from the secure database.

Using the Run With Owners Permission (RWOP) option (which adds WITH OWNERACCESS OPTION to the Access SQL statement) when you create queries can lead to problems if other developers are adding query objects to your databases. Permissions to execute the query are those of the person who created the query, not the owners of the underlying tables. If the owner of an RWOP query has Read Definitions permission but not Read Data permissions on one of the tables used by the query, neither the owner of the query nor an account in the Admins group can execute the query, because the query owner's permissions prevail.

> **WARNING**
>
> Access's system tables are considered "officially undocumented" by Microsoft Corporation. This means that the structure and content of tables with the prefix MSys may change in future releases of Access. The examples in this chapter were tested with the beta versions of Microsoft Access 2.0 and the Access Developer's Toolkit. The retail release of Access 2.0 may yield different results.

20

Front-Ending Client-Server Databases

One of today's fastest-growing software markets is for Windows applications that manipulate and display data stored on a client-server RDBMS. These applications are called front-ends because the client-server RDBMS commonly is referred to as the back-end. Traditionally, front-ends are distinguished from conventional desktop database applications by the front-ends' lack of a native RDBMS. Front-end applications rely on the RDBMS back-end to process queries, enforce referential and domain integrity, and maintain database security. This chapter begins by defining the terms used in client-server database systems, then goes on to show you how to use Access as a front-end for client-server databases with the Open Database Connectivity (ODBC) application supplied with the retail version of Access. The chapter concludes with a demonstration of Access 2.0's new SQL Pass-through query feature and how to use the ODBC Connect String Builder to create ODBC connect strings for SQL Pass-through queries.

This chapter uses Microsoft SQL Server for Windows NT running under Windows NT Advanced Server as the model of a client-server database, but the examples apply equally to Sybase SQL Server using the SQL Server driver supplied with Access 2.0. Similar methods are employed with other client-server databases, such as Oracle, InterBase, and Informix, that run on UNIX servers or as NetWare Loadable Modules (NLMs) running under Novell NetWare.

Defining the Client-Server Environment

One of the reasons for the high growth rate of the front-end market is the downsizing of multiuser mainframe database systems to networked PCs. Downsizing involves moving the information stored in a mainframe or large minicomputer database to an RDBMS located on a PC-based or a UNIX server, then creating decision support and transaction-processing applications that run on networked client workstations. The primary incentive for downsizing is to cut costs—operating expenses as well as the capital investment required for mainframe hardware. Both PC-based and UNIX servers cost substantially less than mainframe computers. Only time will tell whether client-server databases are less costly in the aggregate, with application development and software support costs added.

Another objective of downsizing is to make important business information readily available in electronic form to those who need the information for making business decisions. Traditionally, mainframe-resident business information has been distributed in the form of predefined reports, usually in printed form. Recipients of the reports extract the information they need (which is often buried in irrelevant data), then manually enter the data in a spreadsheet application for analysis. Access 2.0 offers two methods of transferring server data directly to spreadsheets: saving the data to an Excel or Lotus 1-2-3 spreadsheet file, or creating a new Excel workbook with OLE Automation.

Usually, the mainframe database system being downsized is called a *legacy* database. Legacy databases generally do not conform to the relational model used by Access and most client-server RDBMSs; most legacy databases use the network or hierarchical model of the 1970s and early 1980s. Legacy database systems and their associated applications most commonly are programmed in COBOL (COmmon Business-Oriented Language). SQL is the application (high-level) language used for client-server databases. SQL has become the *lingua franca* for relational database applications, not only for client-server RDBMSs but also for relational mainframe databases, such as IBM's DB2.

Another application for database front-ends is manipulating and displaying data stored in modern relational database systems on mainframes and large minicomputers. You can gain direct or indirect access to information stored in IBM DB2 and Digital Equipment Rdb databases through gateways that make a direct connection to the database or use an intermediary, such as Microsoft or Sybase SQL Server, to deliver information to workstation clients. Other gateways, such as Information Builders, Inc.'s EDA/SQL provide the ability to use SQL with a variety of non-relational mainframe databases. Regardless of the exact method used to deliver the data, workstations transmit queries written in SQL over the network to the RDBMS, and the RDBMS returns query results (or error messages) to the workstations.

Client-server RDBMSs have an advantage over traditional desktop RDBMSs: The server processes SQL statements and returns only rows that represent the result of the query. Server processing of queries can greatly reduce network traffic compared with the same query run against shared xBase or Paradox files, for example, stored on a file server. The reduction in network traffic with client-server RDBMSs becomes more dramatic as the size of the desktop RDBMS files increases. The application on the workstation does all the work, sending thousands of instructions over the network to the file server in order to manipulate records in individual files that consist only of a single table with its associated index(es).

Most client-server databases can reduce network traffic even further and provide improved performance by using stored procedures. Stored procedures are self-contained applications that you write in the server's application language, then compile to object code so that they run faster. You create stored procedures when your applications repeatedly need to run the same or closely related queries. Database servers usually have one or more of the fastest 80x86 CPUs or RISC (Reduced Instruction Set Computer) processors, large amounts of RAM (much of which is devoted to disk-caching), and fixed disk drives with very fast seek times. Therefore, the performance of client-server systems often is better than that of a desktop RDBMS where the database file(s) are resident on the same disk drive as the application that uses them.

The majority of new applications designed to run on client workstations employ a graphical user environment (GUI). Windows 3.1 is the dominant GUI today. IBM's OS/2 and UNIX's X-windows and Motif compete with Windows 3.1 in the front-end market. Windows NT is gaining market share as an operating system for database servers and networking, at the expense of competing GUIs and operating systems. At the time this book was written, Chicago (32-bit Windows 4.0) was in the early beta stage, and Daytona (an upgrade to Windows NT) and Cairo (a full-scale makeover of Windows NT) were scheduled by Microsoft for release in 1994 and 1995 respectively. You can expect future versions of Access to be 32-bit Windows applications that run under Chicago, as well as Daytona and Cairo. When this occurs, be prepared for a substantial improvement in Access's operating speed—after you add another 8MB to 16MB of RAM to your computer.

How Access Fits into the Front-End Picture

Access is a unique desktop RDBMS for two reasons: Access uses a file structure similar to that used by client-server databases such as SQL Server, and Microsoft designed Access so that it provides virtually all of the features offered by the current crop of client-server application generators for Windows. Application generators are loosely classified as software language products that provide graphical drawing tools to create windows that display and manipulate data in a variety of client-server RDBMSs without coding in C or C++. Visual Basic 3.0, with its Jet database engine and added keywords for use with databases (many of which were taken directly from version 1.0 of Access Basic), now qualifies as a full-fledged application generator. In early 1994, about 300 Windows-based client-server application generators were available. Some of the more advanced application generators use proprietary languages that rival C and C++ in their complexity and obscure syntax.

Most large firms and institutions either have installed client-server database systems or plan to install client-server systems in the future. The primary reasons given by major firms for adopting Access as a company-wide application generator for client-server RDBMSs follow:

■ Access' low per-seat cost. Most client-server application generators require that your clients or employer pay a license fee for each computer (often called a *per-seat* charge) that runs applications you create with the product.

The $495 Access Developer's Toolkit lets you distribute as many copies of your Access applications as you want; no per-seat charges apply.

■ Access' wide-ranging RDBMS compatibility. Because Access uses the ODBC API for connecting to client-server databases, you can use Microsoft ODBC drivers for SQL Server databases, or third-party ODBC drivers for SQL Server and other RDBMSs. The ODBC API is available now, whereas competing client-server connectivity products (often called middleware), such as Borland's IDAPI, are currently under development. Users of application generators that do not use the ODBC API are limited to employing the product with databases for which the supplier provides proprietary drivers.

■ The short learning curve. Large firms make a substantial investment in training in-house developers to create and support database applications. Because the Access design tools are easy to use, employees need less time to become proficient in database application development.

■ Access' language compatibility. Organizations also face the cost of retraining applications programmers to use the application generator's programming language. COBOL programmers who learn Access Basic can quickly become proficient in other dialects of Object Basic, such as Visual Basic 3.0 and Visual Basic for Applications. The structure and syntax of all Object Basic dialects is virtually identical.

■ Future language extensibility. Microsoft designed Access so that Access itself is a client of a back-end "language server" (Access Basic's MSABC200.DLL in version 2.0). Microsoft personnel have stated in press interviews that users will be able to attach differing language modules to future versions of Access. This means that, ultimately, you will be able to write Access applications in Visual Basic for Applications, FoxPro, C++, and perhaps even in COBOL.

■ Early implementation of OLE 2.0. Microsoft Access 2.0, Excel 5.0, Word 6.0, and Project 4.0 use OLE 2.0 to simplify the editing of source documents in Access's OLE Object fields and in bound or unbound object frames. Access 2.0's implementation of OLE Automation (OA) lets you manipulate objects created by OA servers with Access Basic code. Unlike the OLE custom control of Visual Basic 3.0, which was released prior to the final OLE 2.0 specification, Access 2.0's object frames are fully compatible with OLE 2.0.

■ OLE Custom Controls. Access 2.0 is the first retail application to support OLE Custom Controls (OCXs). OCXs, like Visual Basic's VBX (Visual Basic Extension) custom controls, let you create applications with reusable control objects of considerable complexity. Ultimately, the user interface of many large-scale Access applications will consist of forms containing OLE Custom Controls, with only a smattering of controls added from the toolbox.

■ **The Microsoft advantage.** The dominance of Microsoft operating systems and productivity software on today's corporate desktops has been the subject of countless articles in the computer press. The success of the Microsoft Office software suite, and Access 2.0's inclusion in the Professional Edition of Microsoft Office, assures that Access will be a contender for the role of a "standard" corporate client-server front-end.

Not all of these reasons for adopting Access as a client-server application generator have immediate appeal to independent database developers. Many firms that have relied on outside developers will transfer more of the Access development effort in-house. Independent developers are likely to be called upon to design application shells that embody a basic program structure and templates for standardized forms and reports. In-house developers will then flesh out the templates and shell with control objects, macros, and Access Basic code for specific applications. Initially, independent developers may lose their traditional revenue source: packaged applications. The upside is that Access may greatly expand the market for Windows client-server front ends.

NOTE

Access is an ideal prototyping medium for client-server applications. The structure of Access .MDB files, automatic enforcement of referential integrity, table-level validation rules, and other features of Access databases and tables are similar to features incorporated into most client-server databases. Client-server databases differ in the way these features are implemented and they have different rules for table and field names. To emulate a client-server database, create your application with all the tables attached from another Access database. Establish default relations and enforce referential integrity in the table database (if the client-server database offers this capability). You can even attach Access databases with Microsoft's ODBC driver for Access, as discussed later in this chapter. You can emulate a client-server database attached with an ODBC driver with an Access database, if you don't have a direct connection to the server RDBMS.

Planning for Client-Server Migration

Even if your clients or employer have not yet implemented client-server technology, you should plan now for future conversion (migration) of applications that use Access .MDB files to client-server databases. The following sections discuss conversion from networks with peer-to-peer servers to those with dedicated servers, choosing a client-server database system, and moving Access databases to the client-server database. If your clients or employer already have a client-server database in operation, you may want to skip to the section called "Microsoft's Open Database Connectivity API."

Migrating from Peer-to-Peer to Server-Based LANs

The performance of multiuser Access applications that run on Windows for Workgroups or other peer-to-peer servers deteriorates as the amount of information contained in the shared databases grows. As files expand and more users join the network, you need to move the Performance Priority handle of Windows for Workgroups' Network Settings dialog box to the right. When you reach the Performance Priority's righthand limit, you have a dedicated server on a peer-to-peer network. The performance of Access applications run with the Performance Priority set to the Resources Shared Fastest limit is not acceptable.

The next step is to move your Access application files to a full-scale, dedicated-server network, such as Novell NetWare or Microsoft Windows NT Advanced Server. Another, more costly alternative, is a UNIX network. At this point, your client or employer needs to decide whether to simply move the .MDB file to a file server or bite the bullet and migrate your Access applications to a networked client-server database. If the shared database applications you have created are vital to your client's or employer's business operations, the added security and data-integrity features offered by client-server databases are a major incentive to make the change. Thus, you probably will make the conversion from a peer-to-peer network to a client-server database in a single step.

Choosing a Client-Server Database System

Some of the major players in client-server database systems are, in alphabetical order: Gupta, Informix, Ingres, Microsoft, Oracle, and Sybase. Borland's InterBase, Informix, Ingres, Oracle, and Sybase's SQL Server (now Sybase System 10) RDBMSs run on UNIX servers. Sybase System 10 is available also as a NetWare Loadable Module (NLM) for installation on NetWare servers. As a rule, an RDBMS that runs under UNIX or NetWare costs substantially more per user than an RDBMS that runs under DOS, Windows NT, or OS/2. Currently, Microsoft SQL Server for Windows NT running under Windows NT Advanced Server has the lowest per-seat cost of the major RDBMSs.

> **NOTE**
>
> The combination of Windows NT Advanced Server and SQL Server for Windows NT will operate on servers with 16MB of RAM. You can obtain a substantial improvement in the performance of SQL Server for Windows NT by increasing RAM to 24MB or, preferably, to 32MB. As with Access, increasing available RAM, at least up to 32MB, is more cost-effective than increasing the speed of the processor. 16MB of RAM, however, is adequate for initial testing purposes with a limited number of workstations using the server simultaneously.

Developers whose clients or employers are Microsoft-only users have a ready-made choice—their applications will run on Microsoft SQL Server for Windows NT or for OS/2. If you are part of a team responsible for selecting a client-server database, the safest choice for Access developers is Microsoft SQL Server for Windows NT (abbreviated SQLSNT in this book). The main reasons for choosing SQLSNT when you use Access as your front-end application generator are as follows:

■ The installation process for the combination of Windows NT Advanced Server (NTAS) and SQLSNT is simple and fast. If your network uses Windows for Workgroups 3.11 for its workstations, you can be up and running with tables attached from SQLSNT's "pubs" sample database to an Access 2.0 application on a workstation in less than one hour. (Plan on spending 90 minutes or so if you install NTAS from diskettes rather than CD-ROM.) You run SQLSNT as a process under NTAS; thus, you can automatically launch SQLSNT when you boot NTAS.

■ The Microsoft ODBC driver for SQL Server, which operates with the Windows NT and OS/2 versions of Microsoft and Sybase SQL Server, has had the most rigorous testing of any ODBC driver currently available for any RDBMS.

■ Microsoft gives priority to improving the SQL Server ODBC driver because the driver's performance influences not only the competitive position of SQL Server, but also the sale of other Microsoft products. Excel 5.0, Word

6.0, Project 4.0, and Visual Basic 3.0 access SQL Server databases through the ODBC API. The ODBC driver for SQL Server is likely to be the first 32-bit ODBC 2.0-compliant driver available.

■ Microsoft SQL Server is the first RDBMS designed specifically for operation under Windows NT 3.1 and thus has the longest operating history under Windows NT. The performance of SQL Server for NT is substantially better than the OS/2 version because of the NT version's multi-threaded design. Other RDBMS vendors have announced ports of their products for Windows NT, but none were available for testing at the time this edition was written. IBM, for example, has announced that it will port DB2 to Windows NT but has not committed to a firm date.

■ SQLSNT is *scalable*. Scalability means that you can improve the performance of SQLSNT by adding processors or moving NTAS and SQLSNT to a RISC server, such as one of the Digital Equipment Alpha series or a MIPS workstation.

■ SQL Server offers stored procedures (discussed earlier in this chapter) and triggers to maintain referential integrity. A trigger is a special type of stored procedure that executes when a specific event occurs. You can use triggers also to generate error messages and to send Microsoft Mail messages automatically to interested parties with the latest version of SQLSNT.

NOTE

The Microsoft ODBC driver for SQL Server is compatible with all Microsoft versions of SQL Server and Sybase SQL Server through version 4.9. You also can use the Microsoft ODBC driver with Sybase System 10 for UNIX, NetWare, or Windows NT, but many of the new features offered by Sybase System 10 are not accessible with the Microsoft driver. Sybase Corp. supplies its own ODBC drivers for System 10.

If you choose a client-server RDBMS other than Microsoft or Sybase SQL Server (for which Microsoft currently supplies the ODBC drivers), make sure that you test the proprietary or third-party ODBC driver with Access version 1.1 before you make a commitment to the database system. Third-party ODBC drivers are discussed later in this chapter. The section that follows discusses alternatives to using the ODBC drivers.

NOTE

Make sure that you upgrade to Access version 2.0 if you use or plan to use the ODBC Administrator application supplied with Access. Microsoft made a substantial number of improvements in the interface between Access and the ODBC Driver Manager, as well as changes to the SQL Server ODBC driver, in version 2.0. Access 2.0 also provides built-in SQL pass-through capability, which is discussed later in this chapter.

Migrating from Access to Client-Server Databases

Your principal consideration in planning for migration of .MDB files to a client-server database is to make sure that your applications comply with the rules of the client-server database you intend to use. As an example, most client-server databases do not allow spaces or punctuation characters in database, table, or field names. Therefore, you should not include spaces or punctuation in your Access table, field, or query names. You can alias the names that conform to client-server RDBMS conventions to more readable form with entries for their Caption property or rename attached tables to follow Access conventions, if necessary.

WARNING

Unlike in Access, all names in SQL Server databases are case-sensitive, unless you explicitly specify case-insensitivity for names when you install SQL Server. (It is an uncommon practice to install SQL server with the case-insensitive option set.) Case sensitivity applies to database, table, field, index, stored procedure, and trigger names. By tradition, object names for SQL Server databases are lower case, but it is not necessary that you follow this tradition. The most important issue in naming conventions for client-server database objects is to avoid the use of spaces. Substitute underscores for spaces to improve readability of object names.

You cannot alter the data type or field size of a field of an attached table. You can, however, control the appearance of data in attached client-server tables with the Format property of text boxes of forms. And you also can establish form-level DefaultValue, ValidationRule, and ValidationText property values for fields of attached client-server tables.

> **NOTE**
>
> Properties of fields of attached client-server tables whose values you cannot change are indicated by a message (the text is red) in the Properties pane of the table-design window. Access stores the values of fixed properties and the properties whose values you can set in Access's table-design mode in the .MDB file. If you delete the table attachment, you lose the property values you set previously.

Microsoft's Open Database Connectivity API

The ODBC API is a component of Microsoft's Windows Open Service's Architecture (WOSA), which includes other APIs for the Windows environment. Examples of these APIs include the following:

- MAPI, the Messaging API based on Microsoft Mail
- TAPI, the Telephony API, developed jointly by Microsoft and Intel Corp., for controlling voice and data messaging systems
- License Service API for application software license-fee management
- Windows SNA (System Network Architecture) for connectivity to IBM mainframes and AS/400 minicomputers
- Windows Sockets (WinSock) for UNIX-based applications
- Windows RPC (Remote Procedure Call) for use with the Open Software Foundation's DCE RPC standard
- WOSA Extensions for Real-time Market Data (RTX, a system designed to obtain market data, primarily for the financial services industry)

Currently, most of the members of WOSA in the preceding list are available as commercial products. Windows RPC and WOSA/RTX were in the testing stage at the time this edition was written.

The purpose of the ODBC API is to provide a standard interface between any type of RDBMS and Microsoft Windows applications. The standard interface consists of a set of functions that execute SQL statements on database tables (called the data source) and return data as rows when the application issues SQL SELECT statements. SQL statements must comply with the X/Open and SQL Access Group (SAG) specifications for SQL syntax. X/Open and SAG are industry associations comprising computer hardware manufacturers, database software publishers, and major users of client-server RDBMSs. Much of the X/Open-SAG specification has been incorporated into ANSI SQL-92, the current standard for SQL syntax used by client-server databases.

The X/Open-SAG 1991 SQL CAE 1991 draft specification and the ODBC API specify a set of core SQL grammar (reserved words) that all ODBC-compliant data sources should handle. The ODBC API specifies both a minimum SQL grammar that ODBC-compliant data sources must process and extensions to the core grammar. Extended functions support such data-source features as scrollable cursors. Scrollable cursors enable you to select a single row of a query result from an attached data source in the same way you select a row in an Access query on native Access tables. The ODBC API specifies conformance levels corresponding to the SQL grammar. Most ODBC drivers now conform to Level 1, which incorporates the core SQL grammar, and incorporate the elements of Level 2 that relate to scrollable cursors. At the time this edition was written, no ODBC drivers with full Level 2 conformance were available. Publishers of ODBC drivers certify their drivers to a specific level of conformance.

The ODBC API consists of a Driver Manager DLL (ODBC.DLL), which loads ODBC drivers designed specifically for the RDBMSs with which they are used. Figure 20.1 shows the relationships of Windows applications, the ODBC Driver Manager and ODBC database drivers, and the data sources (databases or table files) to which the ODBC database drivers connect. The sections that follow describe ODBC driver types and how Access uses ODBC drivers to attach client-server data sources.

FIGURE 20.1.

The hierarchy of Windows applications, ODBC API, and data sources.

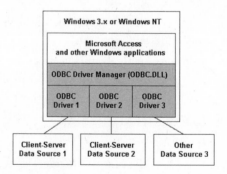

Types of ODBC Drivers

ODBC drivers perform most of the operations involved in obtaining data from an attached table. The two basic types of ODBC drivers are as follows:

■ Multiple-tier ODBC drivers pass SQL statements directly to the data source. The data source, not the driver, is responsible for processing low-level functions on the file in which the database is located. The focus of most of this chapter is on multiple-tier ODBC drivers.

■ Single-tier ODBC drivers process data in the attached table directly. This type of driver is used for processing xBase, Paradox, text, work-sheet and other database files. When you send an SQL statement to a single-tier ODBC driver, the driver itself translates the high-level SQL statement into low-level functions that operate on the file. Chapter 25, "Stretching the Limits of Access," describes the use of a single-tier xBase driver and typical low-level file functions.

The two sections that follow describe typical multiple-tier and single-tier drivers.

Multiple-Tier Microsoft ODBC Drivers

Figure 20.2 shows database clients and servers connected to a heterogeneous network. Heterogeneous networks connect clients and servers that use different operating systems. In Figure 20.2, the client workstations use Windows applications that operate under DOS. Microsoft SQL server operates under Windows NT or OS/2, and the Oracle RDBMS operates under UNIX. The most common multiple-tier ODBC driver is the two-tier type (SQL Server and Oracle 6 in Figure 20.2) in which the client workstation communicates over the network to a database server. To connect to a mainframe database, you need either a gateway server in a three-tier configuration (shown for IBM DB2 in Figure 20.2) or, for a wide-area network, a two-tier connection that emulates an IBM 3270 terminal.

FIGURE 20.2.

Two-tier and three-tier ODBC configurations.

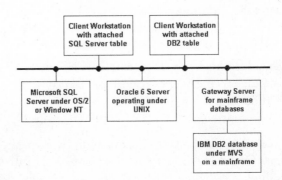

Single-Tier Microsoft ODBC Drivers

Microsoft released the ODBC Desktop Database Drivers application in July 1993. This product consists of the ODBC Administrator application, a master driver layer (SIMBA.DLL and SIMADM.DLL), and a collection of certified single-tier ODBC drivers for the following database and flat files. Subsequently, Microsoft included these drivers with Excel 5.0, Word 6.0, and Project 4.0 to provide enhanced database connectivity for these applications. (Excel, Word, and Project also include the Microsoft SQL Server driver.) The Desktop Database Drivers kit supports the following file types:

- Microsoft Access 1.1 .MDB files, with or without an associated SYSTEM.MDA system file. If you have applied Access security to the .MDB file, you need to specify the location and name of the system file to be used with the .MDB file.

- Borland/Aston-Tate dBASE and Microsoft FoxPro .DBF files with dBASE III+ (.NDX), dBASE IV (.MDX), and FoxPro 2+ (.IDX and .CDX) index files. All .DBF and index files that compose a database should be located in the same directory.

- Borland Paradox 3+ .DB files with Paradox primary index .PX files. Secondary index (query speed-up) files are not supported.

- Novell Btrieve .DAT files with their associated data dictionary (.DDF) files. The requirement for .DDF files is the same as that for directly attaching Btrieve files to an Access database. The Btrieve driver is not included with Excel 5.0, Word 6.0, or Project 4.0.

- Microsoft Excel 4.0 worksheet (.XLS) files. The advantage of using the Excel ODBC driver rather than importing Excel worksheet files into an Access database is that you can execute queries directly against records (rows) contained in named Excel database ranges. The Excel ODBC driver eliminates the importing step and assures that you run your query against the current version of the worksheet. The Excel driver is not included with Excel 5.0, Word 6.0, or Project 4.0.

- Delimited (.CSV or .TSV) and fixed-length (.TXT) files. As with .XLS files, you can execute queries against the data contained in fields of text files without importing the files into an Access database. The text-file driver is not included with Excel 5.0, Word 6.0, or Project 4.0.

The Access 1.1, Excel 4.0, and text drivers are the most useful of these Microsoft single-tier ODBC drivers for Access developers. The dBASE, Paradox, and Btrieve drivers duplicate Access's ability to attach these files directly to Access databases. Therefore, there is little incentive to substitute an ODBC driver for Access's native file-type conversion capabilities. You incur little or no speed penalty, however, when you attach Access, dBASE, Paradox, or Btrieve files with the corresponding ODBC drivers.

> **NOTE**
>
> The retail version of Access 2.0 includes the ODBC driver for Jet 2.0, ODBCJT16.DLL, to provide Access 2.0 .MDB file compatibility for the other members of the Microsoft Office software suite and Microsoft Project 4.0.

> **NOTE**
>
> Microsoft includes a new ODBC driver for Access 2.0 databases with the retail version of Access 2.0. The new driver was not available for testing at the time this edition was written. Microsoft also was expected to release an upgrade to the ODBC Desktop Drivers kit in mid-1994 to provide connectivity to Excel 5.0 workbook files.

The Access ODBC driver is especially handy for testing Access applications that use Access 2.0's new SQL pass-through feature to create **Recordset** objects from queries executed by the back-end server application. Prior versions of Access required that you use a separate DLL (SPT.DLL for version 1.0 or MSASP110.DLL for version 1.1) to take advantage of SQL pass-through. You can emulate client-server databases with an Access database and SQL passthrough because the single-tier Access driver passes your SQL statement directly to the server, without intervening processing. Using SQL pass-through with SQL Server and the Access ODBC driver is discussed later in this chapter.

> **TIP**
>
> Use conventional ANSI SQL syntax when creating SQL statements with Access Basic that are to be executed by the Access ODBC driver. If, for example, you add Access SQL's terminating semicolon for SQL statements, you receive an error message from the Access driver. Use conventional SQL WHERE clauses to specify joins, rather than using [INNER¦OUTER] JOIN statements, because few client-server databases presently support the JOIN syntax. You'll find that the time required by the ODBC driver to create an Access **Recordset** object from an SQL Pass-through query is quite close to the time needed by Access to execute the equivalent query against attached Access tables.

Proprietary and Third-Party ODBC Drivers for Client-Server RDBMSs

Microsoft presently offers a certified ODBC driver for Microsoft SQL Server operating under Windows NT and OS/2, and for Sybase SQL Server through version 4.9. Version 1.1 of Access included a driver for ORACLE databases, but Oracle Corp. has now assumed the responsibility for supplying and supporting the ODBC drivers for its products. If you need to connect to a client-server database other than those for which Microsoft ODBC drivers are available, you need a proprietary ODBC driver, supplied by the publisher of the RDBMS software (if such a driver is available), or a third-party ODBC driver from an independent supplier.

Q+E Software (formerly Pioneer Software, Inc.) is the primary third-party supplier of ODBC drivers. Q+E Software is best known for their Q+E database application that provided a variety of database services for Microsoft Excel 4.0. By mid-1994, Pioneer had released certified Level 1 drivers with partial Level 2 conformance for ORACLE, SQL Server, SQL Base, Informix, dBASE, NetWare SQL, Allbase, Ingres, and OS/2 DBM databases, as well as for Excel, xBase, Paradox, and text files. Appendix A of this book, "Access Resources," includes a full list of Pioneer's ODBC database drivers.

Borland International has announced that its Integrated Database API (IDAPI, previously the Open Database API, ODAPI) will support ODBC, but it has not released details of the level of compatibility that will be included in IDAPI. If IDAPI is successful in challenging Microsoft's ODBC API, third-party ODBC driver suppliers, such as Q+E, are likely to provide IDAPI versions of their ODBC drivers.

Connecting to an Attached Data Source

When Access uses the ODBC API to obtain data from one or more attached tables in a database, the following processes take place:

1. Access requests a connection (also called a session) to the data source. Sometimes, more than one connection is required; Access may require up to three simultaneous connections to SQL Server. The ODBC Driver Manager opens the driver DLL for the source database. If the connection is established by the ODBC driver, a Windows handle to the connection is returned. A handle is an unsigned integer that uniquely identifies the connection.

2. Access sends one or more SQL statements, called requests, to the data source. The SQL statements can originate by executing a conventional query

from Access's query window or from a SQL statement you create with Access Basic code. The Driver Manager handles parameter and sequence validation for the ODBC calls.

3. Access defines memory locations (buffers) and data formats for the result of the SQL request(s). If read-write access to the server database is permitted and a unique index has been created on the server tables that participate in the query, Access creates an updatable **Recordset** of the **Dynaset** type by default. Otherwise, Access creates a non-updatable **Snapshot Recordset**. (All **Recordset** objects created by SQL pass-through queries are of the **Snapshot** type.)

4. If the preceding operations are successful and the query result set is not updatable, Access requests that any rows constituting the result of the SQL query be returned to the designated buffer (**Snapshot Recordset**). You can then manipulate the **Recordset** as if it had been created from Access tables.

5. If the query result set is updatable, a set of "bookmarks" (short tags that uniquely identify each record in the result set) is returned, together with the rows required to populate the first page of a datasheet. Access 2.0 then continues to request additional rows in the background (called a *background fetch* or *background chunking*). You can control the interval and the number of rows of background fetches by adding an MSysConf table to the server database and entering the appropriate values in the table. (Background chunking does not apply to **Recordset** objects you create with Access Basic code.)

6. If your application modifies data in the server tables and employs transaction control, Access asks the data source to perform a COMMIT TRAN or ROLLBACK TRAN operation, depending on the success of the attempted modification.

7. Access processes any errors that occur during the preceding steps. An error that occurs at any point in the process terminates the current activity, but it does not close an open connection.

8. Access terminates the active connections to the data source, but maintains a single inactive connection so that it is not necessary to open a new connection to the server each time you process a query. The inactive connection terminates after 10 minutes of inactivity (by default). You can change the timeout interval by changing the ConnectionTimeout=600 entry in the [OCBC] section of MSACC20.INI.

If the query involves more than one table in a data source, or if tables from more than one ODBC data source are involved in the query, multiple shared connections are established through the ODBC functions. Depending on the complexity of your query, you may need up to three connections to SQL Server. (Only a single connection is required to ORACLE servers.) Each connection has its own ODBC handle. With Access, you can run queries against multiple data sources on the same or different servers.

> **NOTE**
>
> Attachment of and connection to data sources are not the same. When you first attach a client-server table, you specify the data source. Access creates a temporary active connection to the source database; it obtains and stores the Field Name, Data Type, and Field Size properties of each field of the attached table; and then it closes the active connection. When you run a query based on the attached table(s), Access reopens one or more active connections to the table, processes the query by the method described in the preceding steps, and closes the active connection(s).

Using the ODBC Administrator and ODBC Drivers

To use the ODBC API, you need to install the ODBC Administrator application (ODBCADM.DLL and ODBCADM.HLP) when you install Access 2.0 (unless one of the other current versions of Excel, Word, or Project have already installed it for you). The ODBC Administrator application is installed by the Setup application only if you choose Custom Installation when installing Access 2.0. When you install the ODBC Administrator application, Setup also installs the ODBC driver for SQL Server.

> **NOTE**
>
> The ODBC Administrator application supplied with prior versions of Access (ODBCADM.EXE) was a conventional executable Windows application. Access 2.0's ODBCADM.DLL is a Windows Control panel applet. (Excel 5.0, Word 6.0, and Project 4.0 also install the Control Panel applet version of the ODBC Administrator.)

The following sections show you how to install the ODBC Administrator application supplied with Access 2.0 (if you did not install it when you initially installed

Access 2.0) and how to set up an SQL Server data source. If the ODBC Administrator application is already installed, skip to the "Creating an ODBC Data Source" section.

Installing the ODBC Administrator Application and Microsoft ODBC Driver

To install the ODBC Administrator if you did not install it during the original installation of Access 2.0 follow these steps:

1. If you have made changes to NWIND.MDB or other sample applications that you want to retain, make a backup copy of NWIND.MDB and other modified sample applications. (This is for safety only, in case the Setup application errs and runs a complete reinstallation.)

2. Open the program group you specified when installing Access and double-click the MS Access Setup icon to start the Setup application. After Setup tests for installed components, the first Microsoft Access 2.0 Setup dialog box appears.

3. Click the Add/Remove button to display the Microsoft Access 2.0 Maintenance Installation dialog box.

4. Select the ODBC Support item in the Options list box, then click ODBC Support to tick the check box. (See Figure 20.3.)

5. Click the Continue button to install ODBC.DLL, ODBCADM.DLL, and the other files associated with the ODBC Administrator and the SQL Server ODBC driver.

6. After installation is complete, open Control Panel to verify that the ODBC Administrator application is properly installed. (See Figure 20.4.)

FIGURE 20.3.

Installing the ODBC Administrator and SQL Server ODBC driver from Access 2.0's Setup application.

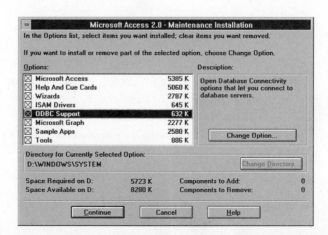

FIGURE 20.4.

The ODBC Administrator icon added to Control Panel.

Creating an ODBC Data Source

The next step after installing the ODBC Administrator application is to create an ODBC data source.

1. Double-click the ODBC icon in Control Panel to launch the ODBC Administrator. (See Figure 20.5.) If you have not installed data sources previously, the Data Sources (Driver) list box is empty. The Data Sources shown in Figure 20.5 were created during installation of Excel 5.0.

FIGURE 20.5.

The Data Sources dialog box before you add a client-server data source.

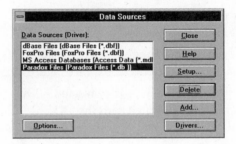

2. Click the Add button to install an SQL Server data source. The Add Data Source dialog box, shown in Figure 20.6, opens. If you have not installed the Data Access options of Excel, Word or Project, the Installed ODBC Drivers list box contains a single entry, SQL Server.

3. Double-click the SQL Server item to display the basic ODBC SQL Server Setup dialog box shown in Figure 20.7. Enter the Data Source Name, which usually is the same as the name of the database to which you want to con-nect, and a short description of the database. The Data Source Name (DSN) is the name by which Access refers to the server, not a specific database on the server.

4. Type the network name of the server in the Server text box. Do not precede the network name with the \\ used to identify the server when applying uniform naming convention (UNC) rules.

FIGURE 20.6.

Selecting the ODBC driver to use in the Add Data Source dialog box.

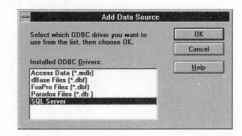

FIGURE 20.7.

The basic ODBC SQL Server Setup dialog box.

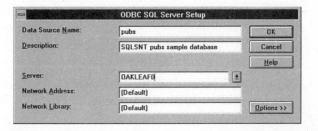

5. Accept "(Default)" as the value for the Network Address and Network Library unless you have reason to do otherwise. The named pipes network library, DBMNP3.DLL, is the default library for Banyan VINES, Microsoft Windows NT Advanced Server and LAN Manager, IBM LAN Server, and DEC Pathworks. Leave the (Default) entry in the Network Library unless you are using Sybase SQL Server or Oracle.

NOTE

You can use the DBMSVIN3.DLL network library for Banyan VINES or the DBMSSPX3.DLL library for NetWare networks. With VINES or NetWare, the Network Address entry is the same as the Server name specified as the server parameter of the network manager in use. With TCP/IP (UNIX) networks, you enter the IP (Internet Protocol) name of the server, a comma, and then the socket number.

6. Click the Options button to expand the SQL Server Setup dialog box so that it displays the Database Name, Language Name, and Translation controls. (See Figure 20.8.)

FIGURE 20.8.

The SQL Server Setup dialog box with added Options displayed.

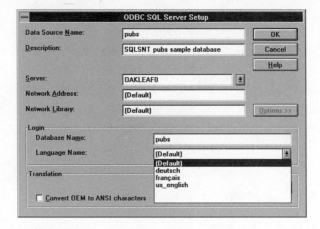

7. Type the name of the SQL Server database that contains the data you want to use in the Database Name text box. This entry is case-sensitive for SQL Server.

8. If you have SQL Server version 4.1 or higher, you can choose the national language used for localizing SQL Server. The available choices are U.S. English (the default), German, and French.

9. Translators are used to convert the character set used by SQL Server to that used by the SQL Server driver. You do not need to change the default setting (cleared) of the Convert OEM to ANSI Characters check box.

10. Click the OK button. Your new data source appears in the Data Sources (Driver) list box of the Data Sources dialog box shown in Figure 20.9.

FIGURE 20.9.

The Data Sources dialog box with a new SQL Server data source added.

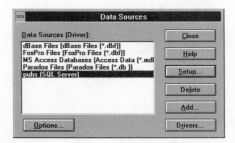

Configuring Microsoft SQL Server Versions 4.2 and Earlier

With Microsoft SQL Server for OS/2 versions 4.2 and earlier, you must run the SQL script file (INSTCAT.SQL) to set up the stored procedures that provide catalog information used by the ODBC API and Access. If you fail to install INSTCAT.SQL on versions of SQL Server that require it, you receive the following ODBC error message: `[Microsoft][ODBC SQL Server Driver] The ODBC catalog stored procedures installed on your server ServerName are version xx.xxxx; version xx.xx.xxxx is required to ensure proper operation. Please contact your system administrator.`

To install the catalog stored procedures, use SQL Server's ISQL (Interactive SQL) tool. You can run the ISQL tool from the MS-DOS command line at a client workstation or at the OS/2 command line of the server. To install INSTCAT.SQL with ISQL, type the following on a single line:

```
isql /U LogOnName /n /P Password /S ServerName /i d:\path\INSTCAT.SQL /o
➥d:\path\OutputFile
```

Following is an explanation of the parameters of the preceding ISQL command:

/U   Logon name for the system administrator (usually sa)

/n   Turns off line numbering and prompting for user input

/P   The case-sensitive password used by the system administrator

/S   The name of the target server database

/i   The drive and well-formed path to the SQL script file, INSTCAT.SQL, on your Access 2.0 distribution diskette

/o   Designates an output file for the result of the installation of INSTCAT.SQL, including any errors that may have occurred

An example of an ISQL command to install the necessary stored procedures from the distribution disk in drive A, a workstation connected to SQL Server named SQL_SERVER, and to write the results to INSTCAT.TXT in your Access directory would be as follows:

```
isql /U sa /n /P garcia /S main_server /i a:\instcat.sql /o
➥c:\access\instcat.txt
```

> **NOTE**
>
> Don't use the System Administrator Facility (SAF) utility provided with Microsoft SQL Server 4.2 in place of ISQL. Microsoft SAF for MS-DOS and OS/2 is limited to SQL script files with 511 lines or less of code. INSTCAT.SQL is an extremely large script file.

Tuning ODBC Performance with Entries in the [ODBC] Section of MSACC20.INI

You can add entries to the [ODBC] section of MSACC20.INI that establish the values of parameters used by the Jet engine to connect to ODBC data sources. Table 20.1, derived from the *Jet Database Engine ODBC Connectivity White Paper* by Neil Black of Microsoft's Jet Program Management and Stephen Hecht of Jet Development, lists the entries that are valid for version 2.0 of the Jet database engine. You use the Timeout entries to manage connections to the server. In most cases, the default values for [ODBC] entries shown in Table 20.1 are satisfactory.

> **NOTE**
>
> You can download the complete text of the *Jet Database Engine ODBC Connectivity White Paper*, in the form of a Word for Windows 2.0 document, from the ODBC library of the MSACCESS forum of CompuServe as JET2WP.ZIP.

Table 20.1. Valid entries in the [ODBC] section of MSACC20.INI

Entry	Value	Effect
TraceSQLMode	0	No Jet-level SQL tracing (default).
	1	Trace the SQL statements Jet sends to ODBC into the file, SQLOUT.TXT.
SQLTraceMode	0/1	Same as TraceSQLMode (for Access 1.x compatibility).
TraceODBCAPI	0	No ODBC API tracing (default).
	1	Trace ODBC API calls into the file, ODBCAPI.TXT.
DisableAsync	0	Use asynchronous query execution if possible (default). Asynchronous operation enables you to cancel a query using the Ctrl+Break key combination.
	1	Force synchronous query execution (required by some gateways).

Entry	Value	Effect
LoginTimeout	s	Cancel login attempts that don't complete in *s* seconds. (Default = 20 seconds.)
QueryTimeout	s	Cancel queries that don't finish in s seconds. (Default = 60 seconds.) This value generally is overridden by the query property "ODBC Timeout."
ConnectionTimeout	s	Close inactive cached connections after *s* seconds idle time. (Default = 600 seconds.)
AsyncRetryInterval	m	Interrogate server to determine if query is completed every *m* milliseconds. (Default = 500 milliseconds, DisableAsync= 0 only.)
AttachCaseSensitive	0	Attach to first table matching specified name, regardless of case (default). Does not apply to SQL pass-through queries.
	1	Attach only to table exactly matching specified name.
SnapshotOnly	0	Call SQLStatistics at attach time to allow updatable **Recordset** objects (default).
	1	Don't call SQLStatistics; forces non-updatable **Recordset** objects. (SQLStatistics determines the presence of a unique index on tables.)
AttachableObjects	string	List of server object types allowed to be attached. (Default = 'TABLE', 'VIEW', 'SYSTEM TABLE', 'ALIAS', 'SYNONYM.') Some gateways only enable you to attach tables.
TryJetAuth	1	Try Jet user ID (UID) and password (PWD) before prompting for user ID and passwords (default).
	0	Don't try Jet user ID and password before prompting.

continues

Table 20.1. continued

Entry	Value	Effect
PreparedInsert	0	Use custom INSERT that only inserts non-**Null** values (default).
	1	Use prepared INSERT that inserts all columns.
PreparedUpdate	0	Use custom UPDATE that only SETs columns that have changed (default).
	1	Use prepared UPDATE that updates all columns.

Following is an explanation of some of the [ODBC] entries listed in Table 20.1:

■ TraceSQLMode=1 maintains a perpetual log of the SQL statements that the Jet database engine has sent to the server. The log appears in SQLOUT.TXT, located in your Access application's current directory. This log is useful for debugging purposes, as well as for determining how the Jet engine partitions queries such that the server executes the bulk of the query, thus returning the minimum number of rows.

■ TraceODBCAPI=1 maintains a perpetual log of the ODBC API calls executed by Jet in ODBCAPI.TXT. This log can become exceedingly large. If you use either of the Trace... options, make sure to delete the .TXT files periodically. These files are recreated on the next entry after you delete them.

■ Some ODBC drivers have limited types of objects that you can attach to Microsoft Access databases or against which you can process SQL pass-through queries. As an example, version 2.1 of Information Builder Inc.'s EDA/Extender for Microsoft ODBC requires setting AttachableObjects='TABLE'; you only can attach a TABLE object with EDA/Extender.

■ If your Access application is secure, requiring a user ID and password to log in, Jet attempts to open a connection to the server database with these login values when TryJetAuth=1 (default). This feature eliminates the necessity of a dual login process with attached server tables, and is a convenience for your application's users. If ODBC login fails, the SQL Server Login dialog box appears.

■ PreparedInsert=1 and PreparedUpdate=1 (the default values) improves the speed of updating server tables by altering only those columns of the record(s) whose values are modified by the update.

Configuring Options for Server Databases

When you first open a connection to a server database, the Jet database engine looks for a configuration table called MSysConf in the database. The structure of the MSysConf table is defined by Table 20.2. If the Jet engine finds this table, it reads the Config and nValue fields of the table to obtain information about the database. (In version 2.0 of Jet, the chValue and Comment fields are ignored.) Adding this table to a server database is optional; if the Jet engine can't find the table, the default values shown in Table 20.3 are used. Table 20.2 and Table 20.3 also are derived from the *Jet Database Engine ODBC Connectivity White Paper*.

Table 20.2. The structure of the optional MSysConf table.

Field Name	SQL Datatype	Description
Config	SMALLINT	The number of the configuration option (see Table 20.3)
chValue	VARCHAR(255)	The text value of the configuration option (not used by Jet 2.0)
nValue	INTEGER	The integer value of the configuration option
Comment	VARCHAR(255)	A description of the configuration option (not used by Jet 2.0)

If the MSysConf table exists and errors are encountered when Jet attempts to read it, the Jet engine closes the connection and returns an error message. Table 20.3 lists the options for the MSysConf table that are defined by Access 2.0.

Table 20.3. Allowable values for the Config and nValue fields of the MSysConf table.

Config	nValue	Description
101	0	Don't allow storing userID and password in attachments
101	1	Allow storing userID and password in attachments (the default)
102	s	Access delays s seconds between each background chunk fetch (default = 10 seconds)
103	n	Access fetches n rows on each background chunk fetch (default = 100 rows)

Setting the value of the nValue column of the Config = 101 row to 0 results in disabling the "Save login ID and password locally" check box when you first attach a server table. Each time the application needs to use an attached table, the user must enter his or her user ID and password. The purpose of disabling the check box is to prevent unauthorized users from gaining access to data by using an Access application installed on another person's computer. Only the database administrator(s) should be allowed access to MSysConf.

Manipulation of the record pointer of attached tables in datasheet view often results in bursts of network traffic; a move to the last record of a large **Recordset** object of the **Dynaset** type requires that all of the bookmarks (keysets) between the original and the new position of the record pointer be sent to the workstation. Then the data to populate the datasheet is retrieved from the server. Bookmarks are relatively small compared to the size of the data in a row, and performance is greatly improved in comparison with a similar operation with a **Recordset** object of the **Snapshot** type (where all intervening data must be fetched).

As mentioned earlier in this chapter, Access 2.0 provides a background fetching (chunking) capability that can return additional rows from the current position of the record pointer forward in the keyset, while the record pointer is quiescent. The value in the nValue column of the Config = 102 row controls the time between successive background fetches of the number of rows specified by the nValue of the Config = 103 row. Setting the fetch delay to a high value reduces network traffic, but it slows moving to the last record in a datasheet, and vice versa. Background fetching does not occur with **Recordset** objects you create with Access Basic code.

Attaching Tables from an SQL Data Source to an Access Database

After you have created a data source, attaching client-server tables to your Access database is almost as simple as attaching tables contained in any other type of database. To attach tables from the SQL Server, follow these steps:

1. Choose Attach Table from Access's File menu, then choose <SQL Database> from the Data Source. Access's SQL Data Sources dialog box appears. (See Figure 20.10.) If you have added more than one data source, select the data source you want from the list, then click the OK button to display the SQL Server Login dialog box. (This example uses the "pubs" sample database of SQLSNT.)

FIGURE 20.10.

Selecting the data source that contains the tables from the basic SQL Data Sources dialog box.

2. Enter your Login ID and Password in the text boxes of the SQL Server Login dialog box (see Figure 20.11); then press Enter or click the OK button. (System administrator, sa, is the default login ID for SQL Server, and the default password is an empty string.) If you want to change the database that acts as the data source or change other options, click the Options button to expand the dialog box. (See Figure 20.12.)

FIGURE 20.11.

The standard version of the SQL Server Login dialog box.

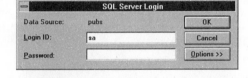

FIGURE 20.12.

The expanded version of the SQL Server Login dialog box.

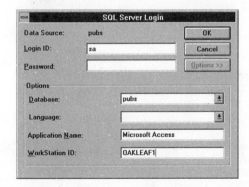

3. If you are not logged on to the network, or you enter an invalid database name or type an incorrect user name or password, you receive an error message with a brief explanation of the problem from the ODBC driver. If such a message appears, click OK, correct the problem, and try steps 1 through 3 again.

4. When you successfully log in to the data source, the Attach Tables dialog box appears. (See Figure 20.13.) Double-click the dbo.authors table to attach this table to your database. (dbo is the abbreviation for database

owner, the anonymous owner of the "pubs" database. Unlike Access, SQL Server identifies the name of the owner of the database and the tables it contains.)

FIGURE 20.13.

Access's Attach Tables dialog box for SQL Server databases.

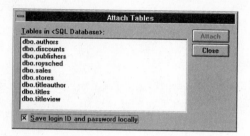

5. The message box shown in Figure 20.14 announces that you have Successfully Attached 'dbo_authors'. Access replaces the period that is not allowed in Access table names with an underscore. Click the OK button.

FIGURE 20.14.

The message box that indicates successful attachment of a table from the data source.

6. Repeat Steps 4 and 5 for the dbo.titleauthor (a relation file), dbo.titles, and dbo.publishers tables, at the minimum. Figure 20.15 shows the appearance of the Database window when you attach all of the tables of the pubs database.

FIGURE 20.15.

The Database window with all tables attached from the pubs sample database.

Creating a Conventional Select Query with SQL Server Tables

Queries you design with tables attached from SQL server are almost identical to those that use native Access tables. Primary key fields are identified with boldface names, and join lines appear between primary and foreign key fields of the same name in different tables. Access determines the existence of a primary key field by testing for a clustered, unique index on the table or, if a clustered, unique index does not exist, the first non-clustered index in alphabetical order of index name.

> **TIP**
>
> Clustered SQL Server indexes are indexes in which the pages of the data are arranged in the order of the index. It is a good database-design practice to create a clustered, unique index on the field(s) that serve as the primary key of SQL Server tables. Using a clustered, unique index, rather than a conventional unique index, on the primary key field(s) usually improves query performance—often significantly.

A query design that displays the names of authors, titles, and publishers is shown in Figure 20.16. To create this query, follow these steps:

1. Create a new query and add the dbo_authors, dbo_titleauthor, dbo_titles, and dbo_publishers tables to the query.

2. Drag the au_lname, title, and pub_name fields to the first three columns of the query.

3. Add an ascending sort to the au_lname field.

The result of the query is shown in Figure 20.17. Save the query so that you can use the SQL statement as the basis for the SQL pass-through you create in the next section.

FIGURE 20.16.

The design of the Authors/Titles/Publishers query.

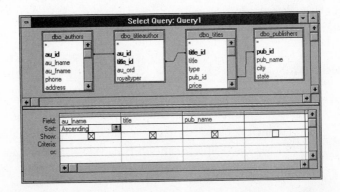

FIGURE 20.17.

The result of the query design of Figure 20.16.

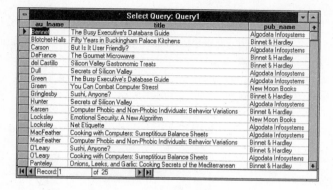

Queries that employ tables attached from SQL Server databases exhibit few differences from those that use attached Access tables. Depending on SQL Server tuning, server hardware performance, and network traffic, queries against attached SQL Server tables may run faster or slower than those against attached Access tables.

> **NOTE**
>
> Attaching tables from other SQL data sources, using proprietary or third-party drivers, follows a similar path, although the installation procedure for the driver may differ substantially from that shown for SQL Server. However, once you've attached the tables, the ODBC driver you use does not affect the design of your queries (although the choice of driver may affect query performance).

Creating an SQL Pass-through Query

Access 2.0's query-design menu offers a new **Q**uery menu choice: S**Q**L-Specific, with **P**ass-Through as a submenu choice. You cannot use the query-design window to create an SQL Pass-through query, but you can use the SQL statement from a preceding query as the basis for an SQL Pass-through query.

To create an SQL Pass-through query from the query you created in the preceding section, follow these steps:

1. Open the conventional select query you created in the preceding section and choose S**Q**L-Specific from the **Q**uery menu, then choose **P**ass-Through from the submenu. The SQL statement used by the Jet database engine to process your select query appears in the SQL Window. (See Figure 20.18.)

FIGURE 20.18.

The SQL statement for the conventional query design of Figure 20.16.

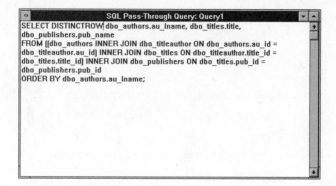

```
SQL Pass-Through Query: Query1
SELECT DISTINCTROW dbo_authors.au_lname, dbo_titles.title,
dbo_publishers.pub_name
FROM [[dbo_authors INNER JOIN dbo_titleauthor ON dbo_authors.au_id =
dbo_titleauthor.au_id] INNER JOIN dbo_titles ON dbo_titleauthor.title_id =
dbo_titles.title_id] INNER JOIN dbo_publishers ON dbo_titles.pub_id =
dbo_publishers.pub_id
ORDER BY dbo_authors.au_lname;
```

2. The SQL statement must comply with the syntax of SQL Server's Transact-SQL. Therefore, you need to delete the DISTINCTROW keyword, which is not supported by SQL Server.

3. Access renamed each of the tables to include the dbo_ prefix. Therefore, you need to remove this prefix from each of the table names to make the names correspond to those of tables in the SQL Server pubs database. (The dbo. prefix is not required by SQL Server.)

4. You can alias the column names in Transact-SQL queries by separating the alias from the field name with a space, as in SELECT authors_au_lname Authors, where Authors is the alias for the au_lname column. (Transact-SQL, like IBM DB2, does not support the AS reserved word for creating field or table name aliases.)

5. SQL Server for Windows NT version 4.2 does not support SQL-92's INNER JOIN syntax, so you need to replace the INNER JOIN statements with a WHERE clause to create the three equi-joins, as in WHERE authors.au_id = titleauthor.au_id AND titleauthor.title_id = titles.title_id AND titles.pub_id = publishers.pub_id.

6. You also must specify each of the table names in the FROM clause, FROM authors, titleauthor, titles, publishers.

7. SQL Server does not require the trailing semicolon as an SQL statement terminator, so remove the semicolon. (You may receive an error statement if you don't remove the semicolon.) Your final SQL statement in SQL Server's Transact-SQL is as follows:

```
SELECT authors.au_lname Authors,
    titles.title Titles,
    publishers.pub_name Publishers
FROM authors, titleauthor, titles, publishers
WHERE authors.au_id = titleauthor.au_id
```

```
    AND titleauthor.title_id = titles.title_id
    AND titles.pub_id = publishers.pub_id
ORDER BY authors.au_lname
```

8. Click the Run button of the toolbar to execute the SQL Pass-through query.

9. Select pubs in the SQL Data Source dialog box and click OK.

10. Enter your SQL Server login ID and password in the SQL Server Login dialog box box and click OK.

11. The query-result set appears as shown in Figure 20.19.

FIGURE 20.19.

The Transact-SQL statement for a SQL Pass-through query.

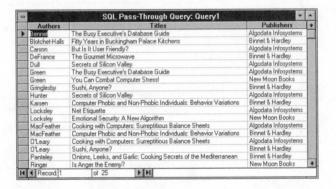

The query-result set shown in Figure 20.19 is identical to that of Figure 20.17, with the exception of the aliased column names. If you save both queries, then execute each while counting seconds, you'll find the pass-through query executes faster than the query against the attached tables, discounting the time required to select the data source and respond to the SQL Server Login dialog box.

Using the ODBC Connect String Builder to Create a Connect String

You can eliminate the appearance of the SQL Data Sources and SQL Server Login dialog box by using the SQL Connect String Builder to create a custom SQL connect string that becomes the value of the `Connect` property of the **QueryDef** object for the SQL Pass-through query. To use the SQL Connect String Builder, follow these steps:

1. In SQL view, choose Properties from the View menu to display the Query Properties window. (Query Design view is not available for SQL Pass-through queries.)

2. Place the caret in the ODBC Connect String text box. The ellipsis button to launch the ODBC Connect String Builder appears. (See Figure 20.20.)

FIGURE 20.20.

The Query Properties window for a SQL Pass-through query.

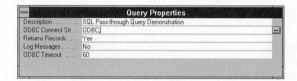

3. Click the ellipsis button to open the SQL Data Sources dialog box. Select pubs and click OK to display the SQL Server Login dialog box.

4. Enter your SQL Server login ID and password and click OK. The ODBC Connect String Builder displays a message box, shown in Figure 20.21, that offers you the opportunity *not* to violate the cardinal rule of database security: *Never* expose your password where anyone else can see it. Click Yes, in this case, to demonstrate the breach of security that occurs.

NOTE

When you create SQL Pass-through queries with Access Basic code, you can open a modal pop-up form to request the user's login ID and server password. You then pass the values from the text boxes to the `UID=` and `PWD=` elements of the connect string.

FIGURE 20.21.

The message box that offers you the choice of including your password in the ODBC connect string.

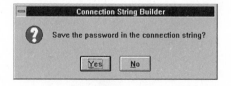

5. The ODBC Connect String Builder creates the connect string for the query in the ODBC Connect String text box of the Query Properties dialog box. (See Figure 20.22.) Close the Query Properties dialog box.

FIGURE 20.22.

The Query Properties window for a SQL Pass-through query with the completed ODBC connect string.

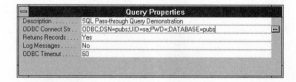

6. Click the Run button of the toolbar to execute the query. In this case, neither the SQL Data Sources nor the SQL Server Login dialog boxes appear when you execute the query. Your query result set is identical to that shown in the preceding Figure 20.19.

> **NOTE**
>
> All five of the connect string elements, ODBC;, DSN=*DataSourceName*;, UID=*UserID*;, PWD=*Password*;, and DATABASE=*DataBaseName* must be present to avoid the appearance of either or both of the SQL Data Sources and the SQL Server Login dialog boxes. (The sequence in which the entries appear is not significant, but each entry must be separated from the next by a semicolon.)

You'll find the capability of Access 2.0 to create SQL Pass-through queries using the SQL window to be a very handy feature when you use Access Basic to write SQL statements that are used to specify SQL Pass-through queries. You can test and modify the SQL statements by pasting the value of a strSQL variable that contains your SQL statement from the Immediate Window into the SQL window, then modifying the statement until the statement executes without error. Using Access Basic to write SQL statements is one of the subjects of Chapter 25, "Stretching the Limits of Access."

21

Employing Access as a DDE Client and Server

Dynamic Data Exchange (DDE) is one of the three real-time interprocess communication (IPC) methods offered by Access. OLE 1.0 provides the simplest method of communication between applications but does not provide a way to automatically update specific values in source documents (such as individual cells of Excel worksheets). The OLE Automation features of OLE 2.0 support transfer of selected data items between source and destination documents but, in mid-1994, only a few OLE 2.0-compliant server applications that supported OLE Automation had reached the commercial distribution state. Thus, if you want to transfer data stored in an Access database to or from specific cells of an Excel 4.0 or Lotus 1-2-3 worksheet or to a bookmarked section of a Word for Windows 2.0 document, as examples, you need to use DDE. If your application will interact solely with applications that are OLE Automation-compliant, such as Excel 5.0, Word 6.0, and Project 4.0, OLE Automation is the more reliable method of implementing IPC. OLE Automation is the subject of Chapter 16, "Using Access as an OLE Automation Client."

The DDE( ) function that returns data items from a DDE server, such as Excel, to text boxes on Access forms offers a simple but limited method of implementing Access DDE client operations. To take full advantage of DDE with Access, you need to use the Access Basic DDE statements and methods. This chapter shows you how to establish DDE communication between Access and Excel with Access Basic code and Excel macros, and from Word for Windows to Access by using Word Basic DDE instructions. Although Excel 4.0 and Word for Windows 2.0 are used as examples in this chapter, other Windows spreadsheet and word processing applications, such as Lotus 1-2-3, Quattro Pro, WordPerfect for Windows, and Ami Pro have similar DDE capabilities. To make the necessary changes in the syntax of the arguments of Access Basic DDE statements and functions, refer to the documentation for the application you intend to use as a DDE server with Access. You also can use Microsoft Excel 5.0, Word 6.0, and/or Project 4.0 as DDE clients and servers for the examples of this chapter.

Defining DDE Terminology and Methods

Interprocess communication between two Windows applications using DDE involves a DDE conversation. The conversation is initiated by the DDE client application by requesting that a DDE server application open a DDE channel over which to hold the conversation. DDE clients and servers are referred to occasionally as DDE destination and source applications, respectively, in order to parallel OLE terminology. A channel is identified by a unique integer, similar to the Windows handle used to identify a connection to a client-server database with the ODBC API.

The relationship between DDE clients and servers is similar to that between client workstations and database servers. The primary difference is that the DDE client and server applications both must be running on the same computer, because the transfer of data between applications takes place through the Windows Clipboard. The single-computer restriction does not apply if you use the Network DDE features of Windows for Workgroups.

DDE automates the copy and paste operations you use to copy data manually between applications. You can create DDE links that transfer data from other applications to unbound object frames on Access Basic forms by copying data from the client application to the Clipboard, choosing Paste **S**pecial from Access's **E**dit menu, and then selecting the Paste Link option button in the Paste Special dialog. As mentioned in the introduction to this chapter, you can use the built-in DDE( ) function to fill an unbound text box with data from a DDE server and you can send data to a DDE server from a bound text box with the DDESend( ) function. Although the DDE( ) function automates the Clipboard operations, this function basically is restricted to transferring a single piece of data at a time. When you use Access Basic DDE functions and statements, you can obtain a block of data from the server application, then write Access Basic code to parse the data and, for example, place it in an array or append the data to a **Recordset**.

In addition to transferring data from and to DDE server applications, you can execute instructions, usually as menu commands, in DDE servers that support the **DDE Execute** statement. This capability extends to OLE server applications that also support DDE. (Some OLE servers do not have **DDE Execute** capability.) Thus, you can retrieve data from an Excel worksheet linked to or embedded in a bound OLE object frame. The sections that follow describe DDE operations with Access as the client application. Using Access as a DDE server is discussed later in this chapter.

Initiating a DDE Conversation with Service and Topic Names

The DDE server that participates in the conversation is identified by its Service Name. (In versions of Windows earlier than 3.1, Service Name was called Application Name.) The Service Name is usually, but not always, the name of the application's executable file, without the .EXE extension. The Service Name is the name by which the Windows Task Manager recognizes the application. If the client request cannot get a DDE channel in a fixed time period, called the DDE timeout interval, you receive an error message.

> **NOTE**
>
> If the server application is not running, you need to launch the application with Access Basic's **Shell(**) function before you attempt to initiate a DDE conversation. Unlike Access' DDE( ) and DDESend( ) functions, which are not available in Access Basic, Access Basic's **DDEInitiate(**) function does not cause Windows to launch the application automatically. An example of Access Basic code to start an application if it is not already running is provided later in this chapter.

As with client-server databases, the client application requests data that is available in or available through the server application. Generally, the data of interest is contained in a document (file) you specify as the DDE Topic name. If the document is a file, you need to specify a well-formed path to the file and enter the file name as the Topic name. All DDE server applications are required to have a Topic name, "System," which returns information about the server, including the names of valid topics. By testing the values returned by the System topic, you can determine whether the file that constitutes the topic is presently open in the server application.

The syntax of the Access Basic **DDEInitiate(**) function used to initiate a DDE conversation by obtaining a DDE channel number follows:

```
wChannel = DDEInitiate(strServiceName, strTopicName)
```

If **DDEInitiate**( ) successfully opens a channel, the function returns a nonzero integer channel number. (Channel numbers can be negative integers, as well as positive ones.) If the function fails, it returns zero and you receive an error message corresponding to the type of error encountered. Table 21.1 lists the DDE error numbers (values returned by the **Err** function) and their corresponding messages (string values returned by the **Error$(Err)** function). Table 21.1 also includes errors returned by other DDE functions and statements discussed later in this chapter.

Table 21.1. Error values returned by the Err and Error$(Err) functions.

Err	Message Returned by the Error$(Err) Function
283	Can't open DDE channel; more than one application responded.
284	DDE channel is locked.
285	The other application won't perform the DDE method or operation you attempted.
286	Timeout while waiting for DDE response.

Err	Message Returned by the `Error$(Err)` Function
287	Operation terminated because Esc key was pressed before completion.
288	The other application is busy.
289	Data not provided when requested in DDE operation.
290	Data supplied in a DDE conversation is in the wrong format.
291	The other application quit.
292	DDE conversation closed or changed.
293	DDE method invoked with no channel open.
294	Invalid link format; can't create link to the other application.
295	Message queue filled; DDE message lost.
296	PasteLink already performed on this control.
297	Can't set LinkMode; invalid LinkTopic.
298	The DDE transaction failed. Check to ensure you have the correct version of DDEML.DLL.

To open a channel to an instance of Excel and the worksheet file DDE_TEST.XLS in the C:\DDE directory with literal values, you use the following Access Basic statement:

```
wChannel = DDEInitiate("Excel", "c:\dde\dde_test.xls")
```

If you want to obtain a list of the currently valid Topic names or send an instruction for the client application to execute, substitute `"System"` for *TopicName*. All DDE servers must respond to the `"System"` topic.

Requesting Data from the DDE Server with the Item Name

After you establish a channel over which to transfer data between the DDE client and server, you request data with the **DDERequest( )** function. The syntax of the **DDERequest( )** function is as follows:

```
strDDEData = DDERequest(wChannel, strItemName)
```

The *wChannel* argument is the channel number of the DDE conversation obtained from the return value of the **DDEInitiate( )** function. The *strItemName* argument is the method by which the server application specifies a particular piece or set of data, the data Item. When the server responds to a DDE request, it copies the requested data Item to the Clipboard. If the server is capable of handling several formats, it copies the requested data Item (in each format it supports) to the Clipboard. Access 2.0 supports only the Clipboard text format (called CF_TEXT by Windows) in DDE operations. Thus the data type of the return value of **DDERequest**( ) is **String** or type 8 **Variant**, depending on the data type you assign to strDDEData.

If you are using Excel as the DDE server, you specify the data Item by row and column coordinates ("R1C1" or "R1C1:RyCx") or a named range, such as "Database". The following statement returns a group of nine cells from the first three rows and three columns of an Excel worksheet:

```
strExcelData = DDERequest(wChannel, "R1C1:R3C3")
```

The string returned to strExcelData consists of three rows separated by newline pairs (**Chr$**(13) **&** **Chr$**(10)). In each row, columns are separated by tab characters (**Chr$**(9)). Thus, you need to parse strExcelData with Access Basic code to separate and identify the individual data elements.

You use a bookmark name to specify a data Item in Word documents. Bookmarks denote the beginning and end of a range of text in the Word document. If the bookmark specifies a Word table, the data in the table is returned in tab-separated columns and newline-separated rows. The syntax to return data from a table identified by the bookmark, "SalesTable", in a Word document is as follows:

```
strWordData = DDERequest(wChannel, "SalesTable")
```

If the Topic of your **DDEInitiate**( ) instruction is "System", you can get information on the capabilities of the DDE server by specifying in your **DDERequest**( ) instruction one of the data items in Table 21.2. Most, but not all, applications return each of the data items shown in Table 21.2. You need to request a list of SysItems from the application to determine which of the data items a specific server returns.

Table 21.2. Common valid data items for the DDE "System" topic.

Data Item	DDERequest() or DDE() Returns
SysItems	A tab-separated list of items supported by the topic "System", including SysItems
Format	A tab-separated list of the formats the server application can copy to the Clipboard
Status	Either "Busy" or "Ready"
Topics	A tab-separated list of all open document files, plus "System"

For example, Excel 4.0 returns the values listed in Table 21.3 when you initiate a conversation on the "System" Topic and use the values returned by SysItems to get Excel's DDE server capabilities and status. The Topics value listed in Table 21.3 include two worksheet files that were loaded in Excel when the DDE( ) function was executed previously. Unless you launch Excel with the /e command-line parameter, the default "Sheet1" is always a valid Excel topic. In addition to the common "System" Items listed in Table 21.2, Excel returns the file name and currently selected cell or range of cells, OLE protocols, and editable environmental items. "Selection" returns the name of the currently loaded worksheet and the location of the selection (cursor position) or the range of selected cells, separated by the "bang" symbol (!).

Table 21.3. Typical data returned by Excel 4.0 for valid data items.

Data Item	*DDERequest() or DDE() Returns*
SysItems	SysItems\<tab\>Topics\<tab\>Status\<tab\>Formats \<tab\>Selection\<tab\>Protocols\<tab\>EditEnvItems
Topics	F:\MADG\ADG_DISK.XLS\<tab\>F:\MADG\ADG_TOC1.XLS\<tab\> ➡Sheet1\<tab\>System
Status	Ready
Formats	XlTable\<tab\>Biff4\<tab\>Biff3\<tab\>SYLK\<tab\>Wk1\<tab\> ➡CSV\<tab\>Text\<tab\>Rich Text Format\<tab\>DIF\<tab\>Bitmap\<tab\>Picture
Selection	ADG_DISK.XLS!R5C2
Protocols	StdFileEditing\<tab\>Embedding
EditEnvItems	StdHostNames\<tab\>StdTargetDevice\<tab\> StdDocDimensions

You can use the DDE( ) function of Access to get the data shown in Table 21.3. The DDE( ) function is useful for experimenting with DDE techniques or obtaining data on the capability of DDE servers that is not readily available in the documentation that accompanies the application. The syntax of the DDE( ) function follows:

```
=DDE(strServiceName, strTopicName, strItemName)
```

The following entry as the control source of a text box obtains data from cell R3C5 of an Excel 4.0 worksheet, D:\MADG\ADG_DISK.XLS:

```
=DDE("Excel", "d:\madg\adg_disk.xls", "R3C5")
```

Figure 21.1 shows the design of the frmExcelDDE form that returns the data shown in Table 21.3. In this example, strTopicName is "System" and SysItem values are substituted for strItemName. The frmExcelDDE form is included in the AB_EXAMP.MDB database on the diskette that accompanies this book.

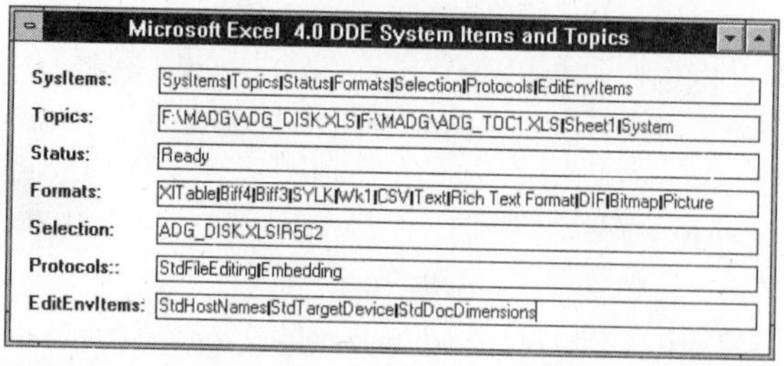

FIGURE 21.1.

A form design to return "SysItems" information from Excel 4.0 with the DDE() function.

NOTE

You cannot use Access's DDE( ) function in Access Basic code. Use of the DDE( ) function is limited to returning data to an unbound text box, option group, check box, or combo box. Data returned to option groups or check boxes must be numeric.

If Excel 4.0 is running or the directory containing EXCEL.EXE is on your DOS path when you run the frmExcelDDE form, the resulting data looks like that shown in Figure 21.2. (Excel 5.0 returns similar data, but includes workbook identifiers and additional supported formats.) If Excel 4.0 is not running, Access displays the "Remote data not accessible. Start application Excel?" message box. Click the OK button to start Excel. The vertical bars in Figure 21.2 represent the Tab character, which is not a printable character in the ANSI character set. Access displays all unprintable characters—except Chr$(0) (the Null character)—as vertical bars.

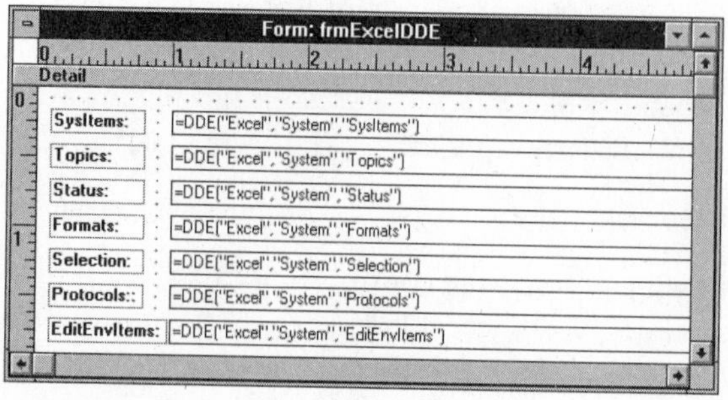

FIGURE 21.2.

The form design of Figure 21.1 in Run mode.

> **NOTE**
>
> For the DDE( ) function to succeed, the directory in which EXCEL.EXE is located must be on your DOS path or Excel must be running. Otherwise, you receive #Error values when you click the OK button of the "Remote data not accessible. Start application Excel?" message box.

Word for Windows 2.0 has a much more limited repertoire of SysItems than Excel 4.0. Figure 21.3 shows Word 2.0's SysItems, displayed in frmWinWordDDE. The frmWinWordDDE form is similar in design to frmExcelDDE (you substitute "WinWord" for "Excel" as the Service Name). The frmWinWordDDE form is also included in AB_EXAMP.MDB on the accompanying diskette.

FIGURE 21.3.

The values returned by Word for Windows for its "SysItems" Items.

> **NOTE**
>
> In addition to the paths to and names of open document files, Word returns the paths to and names of open document templates. NORMAL.DOT, the default global template, always appears in the Topics list.

Sending Data to the Server with the DDEPoke Statement

You use the Access Basic **DDEPoke** statement to send unsolicited data to the DDE server. The term unsolicited is used to distinguish data sent by the client to a server application from data sent from the server to the client. The syntax of the **DDEPoke** statement is as follows:

```
DDEPoke wChannel, strItemName, strData
```

The strData parameter of the **DDEPoke** statement must be in text format (**String** or type 8 **Variant** data type), no matter what the content of the data might be. It is the responsibility of the server application to translate string values representing integers, dates, or real numbers to the data type and format of the destination in the document. When the data consists of more than one element (a cell, in Excel), you use

Tab characters to separate the elements. The strData parameter must consist of a single string.

The following **DDEPoke** statement replaces the values in columns 2 and 3 of row 2 of an Excel worksheet with the values 6/5/93 and 123.82, respectively:

```
DDEPoke wChannel, "R2C2:R2C3", "6/5/93" & Chr$(9) & "123.82"
```

If the two cells that receive the data are formatted for dates and numbers, Excel translates the tab-separated string to a date and a numeric value. Alternatively, you can use the value of a control on a form to replace a single cell with a statement such as the one that follows:

```
DDEPoke wChannel, "R2C2", Forms!frmFormName!txtTextBox
```

The Access function DDESend( ) is the equivalent of Access Basic's **DDEPoke** statement. Like the DDE( ) function, DDESend( ) cannot be used in Access Basic and is limited to acting as the Control Source property of text boxes, option groups, check boxes, and combo boxes. The syntax of the DDESend( ) function follows:

```
=DDESend(strServiceName, strTopicName, strItemName, strData)
```

The following entry as the control source of a text box obtains data from cell R3C5 of an Excel worksheet, F:\MADG\ADG_DISK.XLS:

```
=DDESend("Excel", "f:\madg\adg_disk.xls", "R3C5", "AB_EXAMP.MDB")
```

Controls that use DDESend( ) are read-only in Run mode. Thus, to alter the value of strData, you must get the value of strData from another control, such as a bound text box, on a form. The frmWinWordDDESend form, whose design is shown in Figure 21.4. illustrates both methods of poking text to bookmarks in a Word document. The frmWinWordDDESend form is included in AB_EXAMP.MDB on the diskette that accompanies this book.

FIGURE 21.4.

The design of a form to use the DDESend( ) function with Word for Windows.

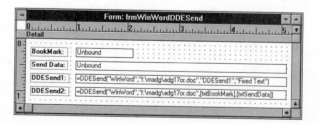

The expression in the DDESend1 text box uses string literals: "DDESend1" as the Item and "Fixed Text" for the data to be poked to the DDESend1 bookmark. DDESend2 uses the values of the txtBookMark and the txtSendData text boxes to identify the bookmark and to insert the text. If you use frmWinWordDDESend to test the DDESend( ) function, substitute the well-formed path and name of a Word document for the arguments of DDESend( ) and add the necessary bookmarks to the document before you run the form.

When you run frmWinWordDDESend by changing from Design to Run mode, Access executes the DDESend( ) expressions immediately. The DDESend1 expression succeeds because its arguments are literals valid for the Topic document. DDESend2 fails because txtBookMark contains a **Null** value. The #Error entry in the DDESend2 text box is the only indication of an error that you receive; Access does not display the expected "The other application won't perform the DDE method or operation you attempted" message box (error number 285). Figure 21.5 shows the result of opening frmWinWordDDESend with an empty txtBookMark text box.

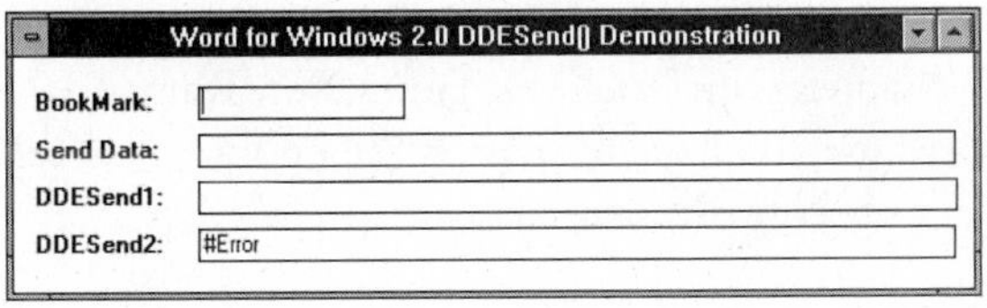

FIGURE 21.5.

The DDE error that results from using DDESend( ) with an empty Item value.

Access executes all DDE( ) and DDESend( ) functions that serve as the Control Source property of form control objects in the sequence of their Tab Order property when you open the form. Thus, you need to design your form and set the tab order so that each DDESend( ) function possesses valid argument values before it is executed. In most applications that use DDESend( ), you get the values of the Item and Data arguments from text boxes bound to a field of a table or query. When you edit either the txtBookMark or txtSendData text boxes, Access re-executes the DDESend( ) function when the OnExit event of the text box is triggered. Figure 21.6 shows the result of entering a valid bookmark name in the txtBookMark textbox.

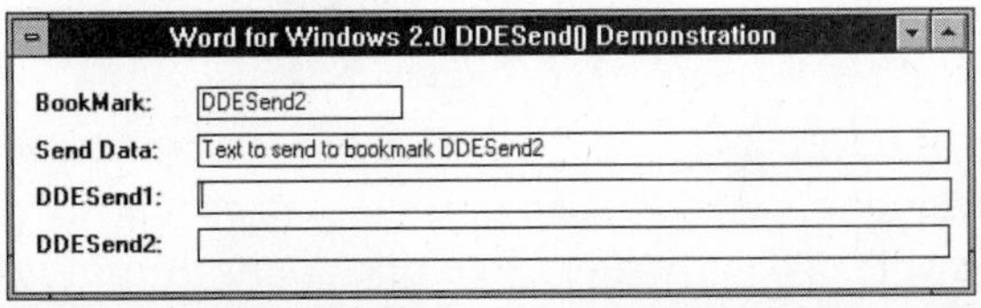

FIGURE 21.6.

Bookmark and text entries that result in successful execution of DDESend().

> **NOTE**
>
> Text boxes that contain DDESend( ) as their Control Source property display a value only if an error occurs in the execution of DDESend( ). Microsoft recommends that you set the value of the Visible property of DDESend( )

text boxes to No. If you follow this advice, however, you are not informed of any errors that might occur. You cannot add a macro that is triggered by the BeforeUpdate event of txtDDESend2 and tests for the #Error value, because txtDDESend2 is read-only in run mode and does not trigger events when its value changes. (You can, however, use the OnCurrent event to trigger the test macro when you move to a new record.) Thus, it generally is better policy to display the DDESend( ) text box. You might want to format the text box with a clear border and background, choose a large, bold font, and set the Text color property to red to emphasize the error.

Figure 21.7 shows the text inserted at the locations of the DDESend1 and DDESend2 bookmarks added to a Word document for this chapter's manuscript. The font used for Normal style in this document is PostScript Courier 12, but the text inserted by DDESend( ) appears in TrueType Times New Roman 10, the default font for Word. No matter how you have formatted the bookmarked selection, the text always appears in Times New Roman 10.

FIGURE 21.7.

Text inserted at two bookmarks in a Word document.

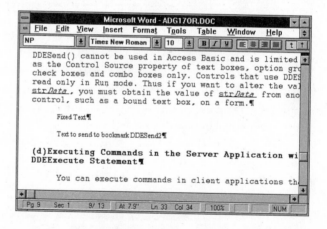

Although the DDE( ) and DDESend( ) functions are useful for learning the basics of DDE operations in Access, their purpose is to enable nonprogrammers to use DDE in a rudimentary way. To use DDE operations in commercial Access applications, use the Access Basic DDE statements and functions so that you have full control over the DDE conversation between Access and the server application.

Executing Commands in the Server Application with the *DDEExecute* Statement

To execute commands in client applications that support the DDE Execute commands, you use the Access Basic **DDEExecute** statement. **DDEExecute** commands often are menu choices or keywords in the application's macro language. No Access function equivalent to the **DDEExecute** statement exists. The syntax of the Access Basic **DDEExecute** statement is as follows:

DDEExecute *wChannel*, *strExecute*

With Excel, you can execute Excel functions such as Select( ) and New( ). With most DDE servers that recognize **DDEExecute** commands, you must enclose the commands in square brackets. The following statement creates a new Excel chart from data contained in columns 1 through 12 of row 2 of the Excel worksheet specified as the Topic argument of the **DDEInitiate**( ) function:

DDEExecute wChannel, "[Select(""R2C1:R2C12"")][New(2,2)]"

> **NOTE**
>
> The double quotation marks that enclose the selection coordinates in the preceding example are necessary; Excel requires that selection coordinates or range names be enclosed in single quotation marks. Double quotation marks in an Access Basic string denote a single literal quotation mark. Double quotation marks do not initiate or terminate an Access Basic string value.

You can execute any macro command of Excel and Word for Windows with the **DDEExecute** command. A single str*Execute* value contains multiple commands; each command is separated from the next by the enclosing square brackets. Commands are executed in the sequence in which they appear.

> **NOTE**
>
> You can emulate the **DDEExecute** statement for applications that do not support DDE Execute operations. Give the server application the focus. (You can use the Access Basic **AppActivate** statement to direct Windows' focus to the server application, even when that application is minimized.) Then use the **SendKeys** Access Basic statement to send a series of menu choices (and dialog box entries, if necessary) to the server application.

Terminating Open DDE Channels

Access Basic offers two statements, **DDETerminate** and **DDETerminateAll**, to close open DDE channels. **DDETerminate** closes the DDE channel specified by its single parameter, using the following syntax:

```
DDETerminate wChannel
```

DDETerminateAll closes all open DDE channels and does not require a parameter. Executing a **DDETerminateAll** statement to close any channels accidentally left open is common practice when your application has completed all of its DDE conversations.

> **TIP**
>
> When you are debugging DDE applications, reinitializing your program without executing the **DDETerminate** statement for the channels previously in use (before reinitialization) causes open DDE channels that no longer are active to accumulate. Periodically issue a **DDETerminateAll** statement from the Immediate Window to close any DDE channels left open.

> **NOTE**
>
> The DDE( ) and DDESend( ) functions automatically terminate the DDE channel that these functions open either when their execution is complete or when an error in execution occurs. No Access function equivalent to Access Basic's **DDETerminate** or **DDETerminateAll** statements exists.

Writing a Generic DDE Application in Access Basic

The procedure for opening a DDE channel to a DDE server that includes all of the required code to test the server's status is a candidate for a general-purpose set of functions that you can use with any Access application that employs DDE. The following sections describe the requirements for generic DDE Access Basic code, provide sample listings of the code, and show examples of how you can use the functions as components of Access Basic modules or as the values of the ControlSource properties of bound or unbound text boxes on forms.

Starting the Server Application and Opening the Topic

A general-purpose function to open a DDE channel to a server with a designated Topic needs to perform the following functions:

1. Test to determine whether the server is running on the local computer, by attempting to open a DDE channel with **DDEInitiate()** and the "System" topic.

2. If the server is not open, launch the server minimized to an icon with the **Shell()** function. If the server is not on the DOS path, add a well-formed path to the Service Name as the argument for **Shell()**. Open a DDE channel to the new instance of the server with the "System" topic.

3. Test to determine whether the Topic is available by using **DDERequest( )** to get a list of current topics and determining whether the Topic you want is included in the list.

4. If the Topic is not available, use the **DDEExecute** statement to open the Topic.

5. Close the DDE channel to the "System" Topic by using the **DDETerminate** statement.

6. Open a DDE channel to the topic with the **DDERequest( )** function and return the channel number to the calling function or procedure.

The generic function to open a channel must also provide descriptive error messages in the event of failure at any point in the process and must give status information to the user. The code for the wGetDDEChannel() function that follows is designed to meet the preceding requirements. To use the wGetDDEChannel() function, you need to supply four arguments: the Service name, the Topic name, the command string to open the Topic, and a well-formed path to the server (if the location of the server is not on the DOS path). You can call wGetDDEChannel() from the OnOpen event of a form that uses DDE to get values from the server application. But if you want to use text boxes that use =DDERequest( ) as the value of their ControlSource property, you need to add a text box with =wGetDDEChannel( ) as the value of its ControlSource property so that you can supply the DDE channel number argument to the **DDERequest()** function. The use of Access Basic DDE functions with forms is discussed in the "Obtaining Data from the Server" section, later in this chapter.

NOTE

For clarity, this book shows the arguments for wGetDDEChannel() on multiple lines. Enter the **Function** statement as one line in your code.

```vb
Function wGetDDEChannel (strServer As String,
                         strTopic As String,
                         strCommand As String,
                         strPath As String) As Integer
    'Purpose:   Open a DDE channel to a specified server with a
    ➡designated topic
    'Arguments: strServer = Service Name
    '           strTopic = Topic Name
    '           strCommand = Execute command string to open topic
    '           strPath = Well-formed path to server if not on DOS
    ➡path (e.g., network)
    'Returns:   DDE channel number, if successful, zero on failure

    Dim strStatus As String      'Status bar message
    Dim strMsgTitle As String    'Message box title
    Dim strErrMsg As String      'Message box error message
    Dim strOpenTopics As String  'List of server topics
    Dim wChannel As Integer      'DDE channel number
    Dim wRetVal As Variant       'Return value placeholder

    strServer = UCase$(strServer)
    strTopic = UCase$(strTopic)
    strPath = UCase$(strPath)
    strMsgTitle = strServer & " DDE Error"
    wChannel = 0
    wGetDDEChannel = 0
    wRetVal = SysCmd(1, "Opening DDE channel to " & strServer, 100)

    On Error Resume Next    'Handle errors with code

    'Attempt to open DDE channel to "System" topic
    wChannel = DDEInitiate(strServer, "System")

    If Err Then 'Server was not open, attempt to open it
        Err = 0
        'Use status bar for messages
        wRetVal = SysCmd(1, "Launching server " & strServer, 100)
        wRetVal = SysCmd(2, 10)

        If Len(strPath) > 0 Then    'Add path to server, If provided
            If Right$(strPath, 1) <> "\" Then
                strPath = strPath & "\"
            End If
            wRetVal = Shell(strPath & strServer, 6) 'Launch server
            ➡minimized
        Else
            wRetVal = Shell(strServer, 6)
        End If
        If Err Then
            strErrMsg = "Unable to start server " & strServer & "."
            GoTo DDEError
        End If
```

```
    'Attempt to open newly-launched server with "System" topic
    wChannel = DDEInitiate(strServer, "System")
    If Err Then
        strErrMsg = "Unable to open System topic. " & Error$(Err)
        GoTo DDEError
    End If
End If
wRetVal = SysCmd(2, 10) 'Update status progress bar (10%)

'Get list of current topics
strOpenTopics = DDERequest(wChannel, "Topics")
If Err Then
    strErrMsg = Error$(Err)
    GoTo DDEError
End If

'If topic is not open use DDEExecute() command to open it
If InStr(UCase$(strOpenTopics), strTopic) = 0 Then
    If Len(strCommand) > 0 Then
        wRetVal = SysCmd(1, "Executing " & strCommand, 100)
        wRetVal = SysCmd(2, 15)
        DDEExecute wChannel, strCommand
        If Err Then
            strErrMsg = Error$(Err) & " Unable to execute " &
            ➥strCommand & "."
            GoTo DDEError
        End If
    Else
        strErrMsg = "No DDEExecute command provided."
        GoTo DDEError
    End If
End If

DDETerminate wChannel    'Close channel to "System" topic
wRetVal = SysCmd(1, "Opening topic " & strTopic & ".", 100)
wRetVal = SysCmd(2, 25)

'Open channel to server with desired topic
wChannel = DDEInitiate(strServer, strTopic)
If Err Then
    strErrMsg = " Unable to open topic " & strTopic & ". " &
    ➥Error$(Err)
    GoTo DDEError
End If

'Function returns DDE channel number
wGetDDEChannel = wChannel
wRetVal = SysCmd(5)
Exit Function

DDEError:
    'Display message box with error message
    MsgBox strErrMsg, 48, strMsgTitle
```

```
'Re-initialize status bar
If wChannel <> 0 Then
    'Close the open channel
    DDETerminate wChannel
End If
wRetVal = SysCmd(5)
Exit Function
End Function
```

The `SysCmd( )` function displays a text message and an optional progress bar in the status bar of Access's main window. A full description of the syntax of `SysCmd( )` is included in Chapter 24, "Using Access Wizard Functions."

Terminating the DDE Conversation

You need to provide a function to terminate the DDE channel when you have completed the DDE conversation. You can call the `wCloseDDEChannel( )`, whose code follows, with a call from the `OnClose` event of your form that uses DDE.

```
Function wCloseDDEChannel (wChannel As Integer) As Integer
    'Purpose:    Close an open DDE channel
    'Arguments: wChannel = DDE channel number opened by wGetDDEChannel
    'Returns:    True if successful; False on failure

    wCloseDDEChannel = False
    On Error Resume Next
    DDETerminate wChannel
    If Err Then
        MsgBox "Unable to close DDE channel " & Str$(wChannel), 16,
        ➡"DDE Error"
    Else
        wCloseDDEChannel = True
    End If
End Function
```

Testing the *wGetDDEChannel( )* Function

Although you can test `wGetDDEChannel( )` by executing a `? wGetDDEChannel( )` statement in Access's Immediate Window, writing a simple function to supply the arguments required by `wGetDDEChannel()` can save a good deal of typing time in the long run. Following is the code for a sample function to test `wGetDDEChannel( )`:

```
Function wTestExcel () As Integer
    'Purpose: Test function for wGetDDEChannel() with Excel as server
    'Returns: DDE channel number

    Dim strServer As String      'Test Service Name
    Dim strTopic As String       'Test Topic Name
    Dim strCommand As String     'Test execute command string
```

```
    Dim strPath As String          'Path to Topic
    Dim wChannel As Integer        'DDE channel number
    Dim wRetVal As Integer         'Placeholder for function return
    ➥values

    'Substitute values applicable to your application
    strServer = "Excel"
    strTopic = "d:\madg\adg_disk.xls"
    strPath = "d:\excel"
    strCommand = "[OPEN(" & Chr$(34) & strTopic & Chr$(34) & ")]"
    wChannel = wGetDDEChannel(strServer, strTopic, strCommand,
    ➥strPath)

    'Add a call to your function that returns DDE data here

    'Close the open DDE channel
    If wChannel Then
        wRetVal = wCloseDDEChannel(wChannel)
    End If
    wTestExcel = wChannel
End Function
```

NOTE

After you terminate the DDE channel, the server application continues to run in the minimized window state. You can close an open server application by assigning the focus to the server with the **AppActivate**(*"ServerTitleBarText"*) function, sending the keystrokes required to close the application with the **SendKeys** statement, then returning the focus to Access with the **AppActivate**("Microsoft Access") function. You must match the title-bar text exactly (character for character, but not case-sensitive) for **AppActivate**( ) to succeed in changing the focus.

Creating a Private .INI File for Generic DDE Operations

You can include in your Access application code that specifies the values of all the arguments required by the wGetDDEChannel( ) function. If your application is designed for use with networked applications, however, the location of the server and the Topic file may change, depending on the current network topology. You can create a table to store this information and a form to alter the values of the strPath and strTopic arguments. A simpler alternative is to use a private .INI file, such as MSACC20.INI, to provide these values, and you won't have to create a form and table in each application that uses DDE operations.

The Windows API function, `GetPrivateProfileString( )`, reads entries in private .INI files and returns the value as a string to the right of the entry's = sign. To use Windows API functions in Access Basic code, you need to declare the function in the Declarations section of your module before you call the function. The next chapter, "Using the Windows API with Access Basic," describes the use of Windows API functions; the section called "Creating and Using Private Initialization Files" explains the syntax of Windows API functions used with private .INI files. Add the following function declaration on a single line to the Declarations section of your module:

```
Declare Function dde_GetPrivateProfileString Lib "Kernel"
    Alias "GetPrivateProfileString"
    (ByVal lpAppName As String,
    ByVal lpKeyName As String,
    ByVal lpDefault As String,
    ByVal lpReturnedString As String,
    ByVal nSize As Integer,
    ByVal lpFileName As String) As Integer
```

The `wGetDDEProfile()` function reads a section of a private .INI file designated by the `strAppName` argument. If entries in the [*strAppName*] section corresponding to the Service Name of the server, Topic, execute command, and path to the server exist, these values replace default values of their corresponding arguments supplied to `wGetDDEProfile( )` by the calling function. (The default values can be empty strings, if you want.)

Before running `wGetDDEProfile()`, you need to add the following section and entries in MSACC20.INI:

```
[DDE Test]
Server Name=Excel
Topic Name=d:\madg\adg_toc1.xls
Execute=[OPEN("d:\madg\adg_toc1.xls")]
Server Path=d:\excel
```

These entries—except `Topic Name`—correspond to the entries used in the `wTestExcel` ( ) function. Substitute appropriate topic names (including the value of the Execute entry) for your application.

Following is a listing of the code for the `wGetDDEProfile( )` function:

Listing 21.1. Access Basic code for `wGetDDEProfile()`

```
Function wGetDDEProfile (strAppName As String,
                         strServer As String,
                         strTopic As String,
                         strCommand As String,
```

```
                        strPath As String) As Integer
'Purpose:   Obtain arguments for wGetDDEChannel from private
➥.INI file
'Arguments: strAppName = name of .INI [Section]
'           Balance are the same as wGetDDEChannel (defaults)
'Returns:   True if successful, False on failure

Dim strKeyName As String          'Entry in .INI file
Dim strFileName As String         'Name of .INI file
Dim strRetString As String * 128  'Buffer for returned entry
                                  ➥value
Dim strKeyValue As String         'Variable-length entry value
Dim wRetVal As Integer            'Placeholder for Function _
                                  ➥return value
Dim wCtr As Integer               'General-purpose counter

'Use MSACC20.INI as the private .INI file
strFileName = "msacc20.ini"

'Obtain the values from the [strAppName] section of MSACC20.INI
For wCtr = 1 To 4
    'Specify the entry (key name) in the [strAppName] section
    Select Case wCtr
        Case 1
            strKeyName = "Server Name"
        Case 2
            strKeyName = "Topic Name"
        Case 3
            strKeyName = "Execute"
        Case 4
            strKeyName = "Server Path"
    End Select

    'Clear the buffer for the returned string
    strRetString = Space$(128)

    'Get the value of the returned string
    wRetVal = dde_GetPrivateProfileString(strAppName,
    ➥strKeyName, "", strRetString, 128, strFileName)

    If wRetVal Then     'Replace the default value with the
                        ➥returned value
        'Truncate the fixed-length string to the left of the Null
        ➥terminator
        strKeyValue = Left$(strRetString, (InStr(strRetString,
        ➥Chr$(0)) - 1))

        'Assign the value of strRetString to the appropriate
        ➥argument
        Select Case wCtr
```

continues

Listing 21.1. continued

```
                Case 1
                    strServer = strKeyValue
                Case 2
                    strTopic = strKeyValue
                Case 3
                    strCommand = strKeyValue
                Case 4
                    strPath = strKeyValue
                End Select
                wGetDDEProfile = True
            End If
        Next wCtr
End Function
```

Strings returned by GetPrivateProfileString( ) (and other Windows API functions) are conventional C-style lpsz null-terminated strings. Access Basic does not truncate null-terminated strings automatically. Hence, you need to determine the position of the null character, Chr$(0), in the string and terminate the string one character to left of the null character's position.

> **NOTE**
>
> You must declare strRetString as a fixed-length string to reserve a memory location large enough to accommodate the string returned by GetPrivateProfileString( ). If you declare strRetString as a conventional, variable-length string, you cause a fatal error in MSABC200.DLL when wGetDDEProfile( )—and Access terminates.

Add the following line to the wTestExcel( ) function:

```
wRetVal = wGetDDEProfile("DDE Test", strServer, strTopic, _ strCommand,
➥strPath)
```

immediately before the line

```
wChannel = wGetDDEChannel(strServer, strTopic, strCommand, strPath)
```

so that you can test operation of your wGetDDEProfile( ) function. Close Excel before you run the test to verify that the Service Name, Topic, execute command, and path specified in the [DDE Test] section of MSACC20.INI are correct.

Obtaining Data from the Server

Compared with opening a DDE channel to the server application, getting data from the server is simple. Use the **DDERequest( )** function, supplying the DDE channel number and the data item as arguments. After you open a DDE channel, you can return data to text boxes on your form by specifying `=DDERequest( )` as the value of the `ControlSource` property of the text boxes. Figure 21.8 shows the design of a form, frmGenericDDETest, that uses this methodology. The frmGenericDDETest form is included in AB_EXAMP.MDB on the accompanying diskette.

FIGURE 21.8.

The design of a form to use Access Basic's DDERequest( ) function.

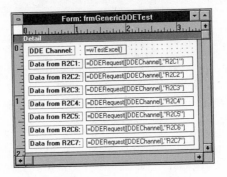

You need to comment out the following line:

```
wRetVal = wCloseDDEChannel(wChannel)
```

in the code for the wTestExcel( ) function by preceding the line with an apostrophe. If you do not comment out the line, wTestExcel( ) will terminate the conversation; execution of the **DDERequest( )** function will fail. To close the DDE channel when you close the form, add `=wCloseDDEChannel([DDEChannel])` as the value of the `OnClose` property of the form. Figure 21.9 shows the Generic DDE Test form in Run mode with data obtained from an Excel worksheet. (The worksheet for this figure was created by exporting the data in the Products table of ORDENTRY.MDB, a sample database supplied with Access, to the Topic worksheet PRODUCTS.XLS.)

It is possible to design a form that transfers data from a worksheet directly to records in a table or an updatable query. However, using Access Basic code to append or edit records in a table or query dynaset is a more flexible approach. One of the advantages of Access Basic is that you can get a substantial amount of data from a single call to **DDERequest( )** with a named range of a worksheet as the Item argument. You then use Access Basic parsing routines to get individual values to update the **Recordset**. Parsing arrays of data with Access Basic is faster than making repeated calls to **DDERequest( )** to return values of individual cells.

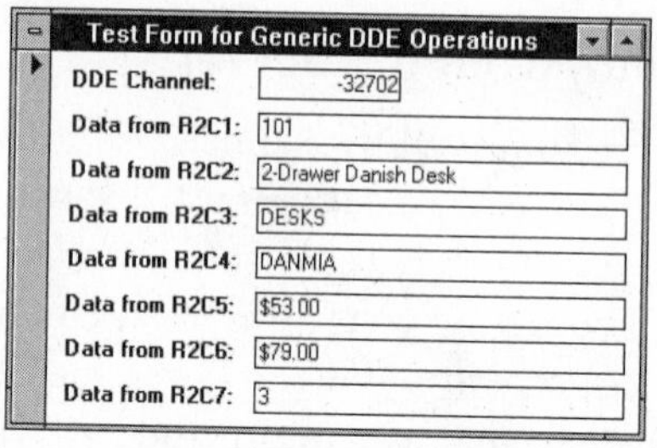

FIGURE 21.9.

The form design of Figure 21.8 in Run mode.

NOTE

When you write parsing routines for strings returned by **DDERequest( )**, make sure that you assign individual data values to a variable of the **Variant** data type. Use the **Variant** variable to update the value of the data cell of the **Recordset**. If you try to update the value of a field of Numeric field data type by using a **String** variable, you get a "Type Mismatch" error message.

You can write generic routines to parse worksheet data obtained by bulk transfers of data from DDE servers, placing the elements in a two-dimensional Access Basic array. You can calculate the required dimensions of an array by extracting the values from the row and column numbers of a "R1C1:RnCn" item. If you do not know the dimensions of a named range, you need to count the number of newline pairs in the returned string, then count the number of tab characters in the first row to obtain the dimensions of the array before you parse the string.

Access as a DDE Server

Access offers a rich set of DDE Topics when you use Access as a DDE server to other DDE client applications. You can transfer virtually any element of data from an Access database to applications such as Excel, Word for Windows, and other Windows applications that support DDE. Access is not an OLE server; until a future version of Access incorporates OLE 2.0 server functions, the only way to get data automatically from Access databases is to use Access as a DDE server. The sections that follow describe the five Topics Access supports as a DDE server and the valid Items for each topic. The five Topics Access supports are `"System"`, `"Database"`, `"Database;`*TableName*`"`, `"Database;`*QueryName*`"`, and `"Database ;` *SQLStatement*`"`. (For the Topics shown here in italic type, you must substitute appropriate literal values or variable names in your Access Basic code.)

NOTE

The examples of the use of Access as a DDE server in this chapter use Access Basic syntax for the DDE statements executed by the DDE client. The syntax of DDE commands in Word Basic is identical to the syntax of Access Basic and Visual Basic for Applications. Visual Basic 3.0, on the other hand, uses `Link`, rather than `DDE`, as the prefix for DDE functions and commands; substitute Visual Basic's `LinkRequest( )` function for **`DDERequest( )`**, for example. Excel macro functions omit the DDE prefix; thus, you substitute Excel's `=REQUEST( )` function for **`DDERequest( )`**.

The *"System"* Topic

`"System"` returns, in the same manner as other DDE server applications, information about the topics Microsoft Access supports. Table 21.4 lists the values of the `Item` argument that are valid for Access's `"System"` topic.

Table 21.4. Items that are valid for Access's `"System"` topic.

Item	Returns
SysItems	Items supported by the topic `"System"`
Formats	Formats that Microsoft Access can copy onto the Clipboard
Status	"Busy" or "Ready"
Topics	"System", a list of all open libraries except SYSTEM.MDA, and a list of open database(s)
MacroName	Runs an existing macro in the currently open database

> **NOTE**
>
> *MacroName* is shown as a valid topic for the "System" Topic because you can use an open DDE channel number for the "System" topic, then use *MacroName* as the value for the str*Execute* argument of a **DDEExecute** command. The problem with this technique is that a macro with the name *MacroName* must exist in the current database. If you do not specify a database as the Topic of the **DDEInitiate**( ) function, you cannot be sure which database is open or that *MacroName* exists.

The *"Database"* Topic

The value of the "Database" Topic is the file name of an existing Access database or of a library that is not attached to Access. The "Database" topic should include a fully qualified path to the file, but the .MDB extension is optional. You cannot use DDE to query the SYSTEM.MDA. After you use **DDEInitiate**( ), or the equivalent statement in the client's application language, to get a DDE channel number with Database as the topic, you can request a list of the objects in "Database" with **DDERequest** (or the equivalent statement). The lists you request are shown in Table 21.5.

Table 21.5. Valid Item names that return lists of objects in the Database specified as the Topic.

Item	Returns
TableList	A list of tables in "Database"
QueryList	A list of queries in "Database"
MacroList	A list of macros in "Database"
ReportList	A list of reports in "Database"
FormList	A list of forms in "Database"
ModuleList	A list of modules in "Database"

Figure 21.10 shows the design of a form you can use to get values of SysItems valid for the "System" topic; then you use these SysItems values to return additional information on Access's status as a DDE server. The frmAccessServer form, which uses Access's DDE( ) function, is included in AB_EXAMP.MDB. The design of Figure 21.10 demonstrates three ways to identify an Access database or library file. These

methods range from simply entering the database name, if the database is in the current directory, to a well-formed path and the file name, plus extension. You need to use the extension if you want to open an Access library (.MDA) file.

Form: frmAccessServer
Detail
SysItems: =DDE("MSAccess","System","SysItems")
Topics: =DDE("MSAccess","System","Topics")
Status: =DDE("MSAccess","System","Status")
Formats: =DDE("MSAccess","System","Formats")
Tables: =DDE("MSAccess","nwind","TableList")
Queries: =DDE("MSAccess","nwind.mdb","QueryList")
Forms: =DDE("MSAccess","e:\access\nwind.mdb","FormList")
Reports: =DDE("MSAccess","nwind","ReportList")
Macros: =DDE("MSAccess","nwind.mdb","MacroList")
Modules: =DDE("MSAccess","e:\access\nwind.mdb","ModuleList")

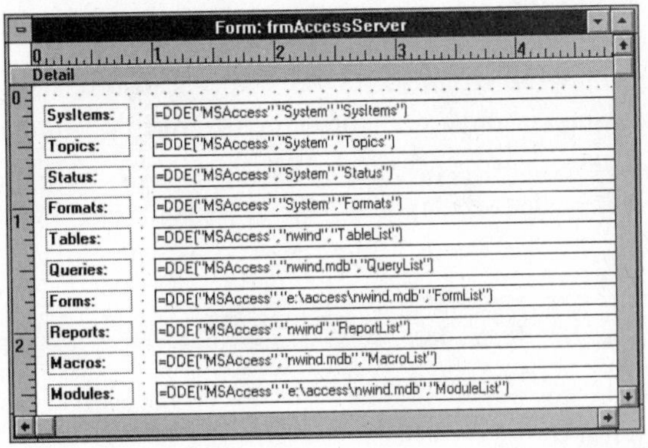

FIGURE 21.10.
The design of a form to display values returned by Access's SysItems values.

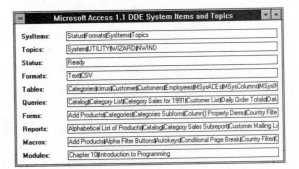

When you run frmAccessServer, the current instance of Access acts as a DDE server to itself. Figure 21.11 shows frmAccessServer with a typical result when NWIND.MDB is the open database. If you have attached libraries in addition to WIZARD.MDA, the names of the libraries (without the .MDA extension) appear in the Topics value. The current database is the last entry in the list. Some of the database objects in Figure 21.11 were added as this edition was being written.

Microsoft Access 1.1 DDE System Items and Topics
SysItems: Status|Formats|SysItems|Topics
Topics: System|UTILITY|WIZARD|NWIND
Status: Ready
Formats: Text|CSV
Tables: Categories|cirrus|Customer|Customers|Employees|MSysACEs|MSysColumns|MSysIN
Queries: Catalog|Category List|Category Sales for 1991|Customer List|Daily Order Totals|Dat
Forms: Add Products|Categories|Categories Subform|Column() Property Demo|Country Filte
Reports: Alphabetical List of Products|Catalog|Category Sales Subreport|Customer Mailing La
Macros: Add Products|Alpha Filter Buttons|Autokeys|Conditional Page Break|Country Filter|C
Modules: Chapter 10|Introduction to Programming

FIGURE 21.11.
The form design of Figure 21.10 in Run mode.

The *Database;TableName* and *Database;QueryName* Topics

The `Database;TableName` and `Database;QueryName` topics support the same items. When you request the contents of a table or the results of a query, you must specify the database the object is in, followed by a semicolon, the keyword TABLE (or QUERY), and then the name of an existing table or query.

The syntax for the `Database;TableName` and `Database;QueryName` topics for **DDEInitiate**( ) is as follows:

```
wChannel = DDEInitiate("MSAccess", "Database;TABLE TableName")
wChannel = DDEInitiate("MSAccess", "Database;QUERY QueryName")
```

To open a DDE channel to the Categories table or Category list query in the NWIND.MDB sample database, you type just the name of the database or the name of the database and a well-formed path to its location, as follows:

```
wChannel = DDEInitiate("MSAccess", "nwind;TABLE Categories")
wChannel = DDEInitiate("MSAccess", "c:\access\nwind.mdb;QUERY Category
➥List")
```

> **NOTE**
>
> Do not use square brackets to enclose the names of tables or queries that contain spaces or other punctuation.

After you have opened the DDE channel to the table or query, you can use the Items shown in Table 21.6 as the `strItemName` argument of **DDERequest**( ).

Table 21.6. Values of `Item` that are valid for the following topics: `Database;TableName`, `Database;QueryName`, and `Database;SQLStatement` topics.

Item	*Returns*
All	All the records in the table or rows in the query; the first row contains table field or query column names.
Data	All records in the table or rows in the query.
FieldNames	A list of field names of tables or column names of queries.
NextRow	The next record or row in the table or query. When you initiate a DDE channel, NextRow returns the first row. If the current row is the last record and you execute NextRow, you receive an error message.
PrevRow	The previous record or row in the table or query. If PrevRow is the first request after you initiate a DDE channel, PrevRow returns the last row of the table or query. If the current row is the first record, you receive an error message.
FirstRow	The data in the first record or row of the table or query.
LastRow	The data in the last record or row of the table or the query.
FieldCount	The number of fields in the table or columns in the query.

Examples of the use of the Item values listed in Table 21.6 are shown in Figure 21.12 in the next section.

The *SQLStatement* Topic

The SQLStatement topic returns the results of the specified SQL statement. The syntax to create a DDE channel with this topic follows:

```
wChannel = DDEInitiate("MSAccess", "Database;SQL Statement;")
```

The following database name and SQL statement open a DDE channel to a query that includes fields from the Employees table in the Northwind Traders sample database:

```
wChannel = DDEInitiate("MSAccess", "nwind;SQL SELECT * FROM Employees;")
```

To open a DDE channel to a query that returns only the values in the Last Name field of the Employees table, sorted in alphabetical order, use the following statement:

```
wChannel = DDEInitiate("MSAccess", "c:\access\nwind.mdb;SQL SELECT [Last
➥Name] FROM Employees ORDER BY [Last Name];")
```

> **NOTE**
>
> You need to terminate all Access SQL statements with a semicolon.

After you open the DDE channel to the query, use the **DDERequest( )** function with an Item chosen from the list in Table 21.6 to return the row of the query you want. Figure 21.12 shows the design of the frmAccessDDE form that uses the DDE( ) function to display the result of using the *Database;TableName*, *Database;QueryName*, and *Database;SQLStatement* topics with Item values chosen from Table 21.6. The frmAccessDDE form is included in the AB_EXAMP.MDB database.

FIGURE 21.12.

The design of a form for testing return of table and query values with the DDE( ) function.

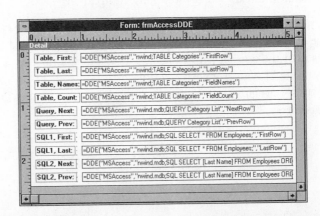

Figure 21.13 shows the result of running the frmAccessDDE form with NWIND.MDB as the open database. OLE Object fields are replaced with the entry "Long binary or text value." DDE( ) returns the entire content of memo fields, but the amount of the text you can view is limited by the dimensions of your text box, unless you add a vertical scrollbar. The text for Nancy Davolio's address is truncated at "20th Ave. E." because a newline pair follows in the text. The entire entry for Ms. Davolio appears if you increase the depth of the text box.

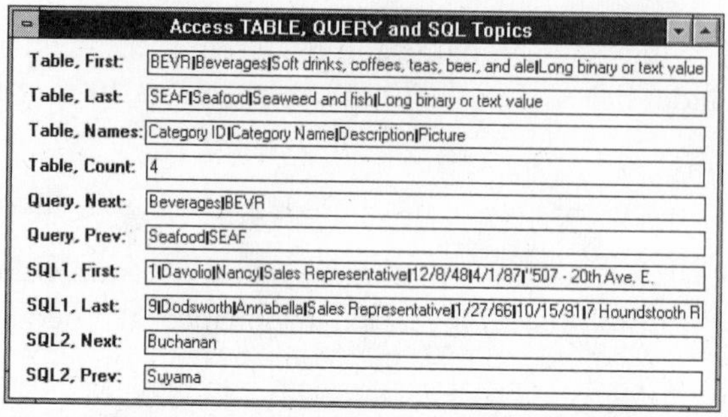

FIGURE 21.13.

The form design of Figure 21.12 in run mode.

Obtaining Data from Access for Excel 4.0 Worksheets

Figure 21.14 shows a simple Excel 4.0 macrosheet that returns the first three columns of the Categories table of NWIND.MDB. Excel's INDEX( ) function returns the value of an element of an array; you specify a range of cells or an array constant as the first argument, followed by the row and column numbers of the cell you want. (The row number is optional.) In DDE_MAC2.XLM, shown in Figure 21.14, the REQUEST( ) function returns a one-dimensional array of the columns of the table's first record. The FORMULA( ) function returns the value extracted by INDEX( ) to column B of the macrosheet. Three Excel macros (DDE_MAC1.XLM, DDE_MAC2.XLM, and DDE_MAC3.XLM) that demonstrate how to use Access as a DDE server are included in DDE_XL.ZIP on the accompanying disk.

Writing Excel macros is beyond the scope of this book. Readers experienced in the use of Microsoft Excel can create much more sophisticated and faster-running macros than the one shown in Figure 21.14. For example, you can transfer substantial amounts of data from Access tables or queries to Excel worksheets with a single REQUEST(Channel, "All") function that places all the data and the field names in an Excel array. Then use FORMULA( ) or other Excel functions to place the values of the array elements where you want them.

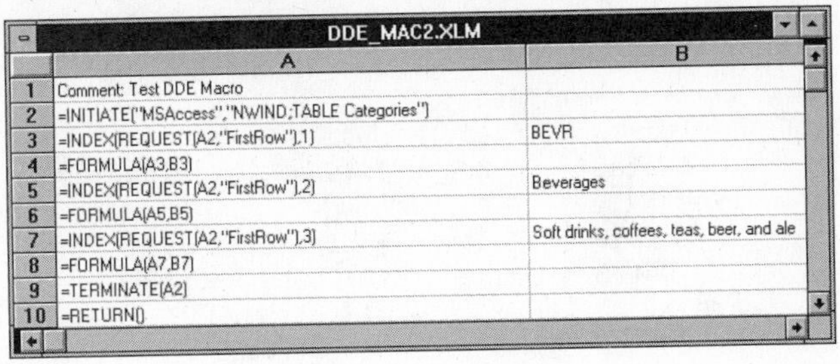

FIGURE 21.14.

A simple Excel macrosheet that uses the Database;TableName *topic.*

	DDE_MAC2.XLM	
	A	**B**
1	Comment: Test DDE Macro	
2	=INITIATE("MSAccess","NWIND;TABLE Categories")	
3	=INDEX(REQUEST(A2,"FirstRow"),1)	BEVR
4	=FORMULA(A3,B3)	
5	=INDEX(REQUEST(A2,"FirstRow"),2)	Beverages
6	=FORMULA(A5,B5)	
7	=INDEX(REQUEST(A2,"FirstRow"),3)	Soft drinks, coffees, teas, beer, and ale
8	=FORMULA(A7,B7)	
9	=TERMINATE(A2)	
10	=RETURN()	

Transferring Data from Access to Word for Windows

The Word Basic macro language of Word and Access Basic are quite similar. If you have Word 2+, you can create simple macros that insert the values from Access tables or queries as text at locations identified by bookmarks. In Figure 21.15, a Word for Windows 2.0 table has been filled with values returned by the "NWIND;SQL SELECT [Category ID], [Product ID], [Product Name], [English Name], [Unit Price] FROM Products;" Topic. The first cell of each row in the table is identified by a bookmark using Excel R1C1 syntax. For example, the bookmark name for the cell that contains "Record 3" in Figure 21.15 is "R4C1". The Word template, ACCS_DDE.DOT, is included on the accompanying disk as DDE_WORD.ZIP.

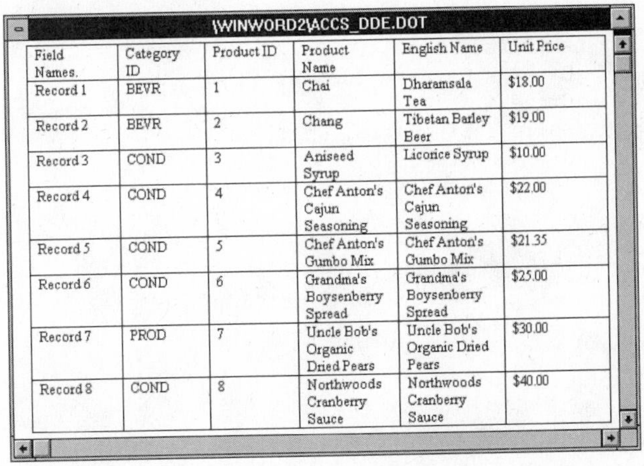

FIGURE 21.15.

A Word for Windows 2.x table filled with values returned by an SQL statement.

	\WINWORD2\ACCS_DDE.DOT				
Field Names.	Category ID	Product ID	Product Name	English Name	Unit Price
Record 1	BEVR	1	Chai	Dharamsala Tea	$18.00
Record 2	BEVR	2	Chang	Tibetan Barley Beer	$19.00
Record 3	COND	3	Aniseed Syrup	Licorice Syrup	$10.00
Record 4	COND	4	Chef Anton's Cajun Seasoning	Chef Anton's Cajun Seasoning	$22.00
Record 5	COND	5	Chef Anton's Gumbo Mix	Chef Anton's Gumbo Mix	$21.35
Record 6	COND	6	Grandma's Boysenberry Spread	Grandma's Boysenberry Spread	$25.00
Record 7	PROD	7	Uncle Bob's Organic Dried Pears	Uncle Bob's Organic Dried Pears	$30.00
Record 8	COND	8	Northwoods Cranberry Sauce	Northwoods Cranberry Sauce	$40.00

Following is the Word Basic code for the main procedure that processes the nine rows of data for the table. The first row of the table uses the "FieldNames" Item; column 1 of the remaining eight rows is filled with a record number identifier.

```
Sub MAIN
    SQLStatement$ = "SELECT [Category ID], [Product ID], [Product
➥Name], [English Name], [Unit Price] FROM Products;"
```

```
    Chan = DDEInitiate("MSAccess", "NWIND;SQL " + SQLStatement$)
    For Item = 1 To 9
        If Item = 1 Then
            List$ = "Field Names:"
            Data$ = DDERequest$(Chan, "FieldNames")
        Else
            List$ = "Record" + Str$(Item - 1)
            Data$ = DDERequest$(Chan, "NextRow")
        End If
        BookName$ = "R" + Right$(Str$(Item), 1) + "C1"
        EditGoTo .Destination = BookName$
        EndOfColumn 1      'Select to end of column
        Insert List$       'Replace selection with List$
        Call TableEntry Data$
    Next Item
    DDETerminate Chan
    BookName$ = "R1C1"
    EditGoTo .Destination = BookName$
End Sub
```

By identifying the position of Tab characters, the `TableEntry` subroutine parses the data returned from each row of the query. `TableEntry` uses Word's `NextCell` instruction to move the insertion point from the first column of a row to the succeeding columns. The code that parses the rows, shown in the following listing, is typical of that required to fill any Word table with data in tab-separated value format.

```
Sub TableEntry(Data$)
    If Len(Data$) > 1 Then
        Data$ = Data$ + Chr$(9) + " "
        Ctr = 1
        While InStr(Data$, Chr$(9)) > 0
            TabPos = InStr(Data$, Chr$(9))
            If TabPos > 0 Then
                Value$ = Left$(Data$,(TabPos - 1))
                NextCell
                Insert Value$
                Data$ = Mid$(Data$,(TabPos + 1))
            Else
                Data$ = ""
            End If
            Ctr = Ctr + 1
            If Ctr > 5 Then
                Data$ = ""
            End If
        Wend
    Else
        For I = 1 To 5
            NextCell
            Insert " "
        Next I
    End If
End Sub
```

Advanced Access Topics

P VII

22

Using the Windows API with Access Basic

Access macros and Access Basic code supply a rich set of programming resources with which to create database applications. In many cases, macros alone can accommodate your programming needs. When you need more flexibility than macros offer, Access Basic code does the job about 95 percent of the time. In some cases, however, you need to take control of the Windows environment or to incorporate functions that are not available in Access Basic. Dynamic link libraries (DLLs) enable you to use the functions contained within the Windows GUI itself, in DLLs designed specifically for use with Access, or in commercial DLLs that can be used with a variety of programming languages.

This chapter begins with a general description of how Windows applications employ DLLs and then gives examples of how to use the functions contained in Windows 3.1's DLLs with Access Basic code. Chapter 25, "Stretching the Limits of Access," provides examples of the use of functions contained in other types of windows DLLs with Access Basic code.

Understanding Windows Dynamic Link Libraries

The majority of programming languages in widespread use create executable (.EXE) files by compiling the source code you write to modules in an object (binary) language specific to the computer platform and operating system that will run the application. In the case of IBM-compatible PCs, the platform uses an Intel 80x86 CPU that requires object files to conform to the Intel object code standard and employs DOS as the operating system. You link the object (.OBJ) files with additional object code contained in one or more library (.LIB) files to create the final .EXE file. The object code in the library is said to be bound to the object code created from the source by linking.

Linking is a very familiar process for Clipper, COBOL, C, and Pascal programmers. These languages use static linking, sometimes called early binding, wherein the object code compiled from your source code and the object code resident in the libraries you specify become inextricable elements of the final product, an .EXE file. Each language requires its own set of libraries to perform input/output operations, mathematical manipulation, access to databases or tables, and other functions required of all programming languages. "Smart" linkers include only the library object code elements that your application needs in the resulting .EXE file. Figure 22.1 shows the sequence of events for creating a conventional DOS executable file.

FIGURE 22.1.

The steps in compiling and linking a DOS application.

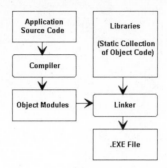

Windows' dynamic link libraries, on the other hand, are not bound to your code until you need to use the functions they contain; thus, the term *dynamic linking.* Windows .EXE files use a different format, the New Executable file format, than that employed by DOS .EXE files. You specify the name of the Windows DLL and the functions in the DLL needed by your source code. You can also refer to a function in a DLL by its ordinal number, related to the sequence of the function in the library. When you run your Windows application, the application creates a dynamic link, called a far pointer, to the entry point of each function you specify. When you link the object code compiled from your source code for a Windows application written in C, for example, you identify the functions you want to call in a header (.H) or definition (.DEF) file. A library of your C compiler that contains the names and ordinal numbers of all functions in the Windows application programming interface (API) translates the names of the functions to their ordinal numbers. The Windows header file takes care of creating the far pointers to the address of each DLL function for you.

The process of creating an executable file for use in a Windows application adds several steps to the compile and link process. The principal addition is the creation of a resource file that includes graphic elements, such as icons and bitmaps, as well as dialogs, menus, and other standard Windows object. You use the Resource Compiler to create a binary resource file (.RES) from the resource source code (.RC) files. Then you attach the .RES file to the .EXE file that you generate with your C compiler, libraries, and linker. Figure 22.2 shows the steps involved in creating a Windows executable file.

FIGURE 22.2.

The steps required to create an executable file for a Windows application.

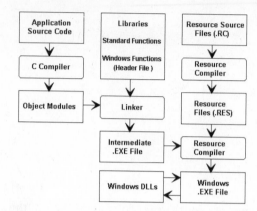

Interpreted Versus Compiled Windows Applications

Access Basic, Visual Basic, Visual Basic for Applications, Word Basic, and other forth-coming dialects of Microsoft's Object Basic are interpreted, not compiled, languages. QBasic, dBASE, and FoxPro also are interpreted programming languages. Each time you run an application written in an interpreted language, the interpreter processes each line of source code. Each line is checked for proper syntax, then converted to object code that is executable by your computer. Thus an application written in an interpreted language almost always runs more slowly than the same application compiled into an .EXE file. As an example, dBASE code in .PRG files compiled with CA-Clipper 5.2 to an .EXE file often runs several times faster than the same code executed by the dBASE interpreter.

Many interpreted programming languages offer runtime versions and compilers to speed execution of applications. The increase in speed is accomplished by dividing the interpretation process into two steps: syntax checking and code compression, followed by the execution of the compressed code. The Compile Loaded Modules choice of the **R**un menu of Access's Module window converts your Access Basic source code to pseudo-code, often called p-code. P-code substitutes binary codes (called tokens) for the reserved words of Access Basic; tokenizing speeds the execution of your application. At the same time, the interpreter checks to see that all the variables you employ have been declared with **Dim** statements, checks if you've added the **Option Explicit** instruction to the Declarations section of your module, and does internal variable type checking.

CA-Clipper and other compilers for interpreted programming languages accommodate declarations of *ad hoc* or implicit variables (variables that are not declared explicitly with a data type before they are used). CA-Clipper and other compilers for xBase code also must deal with xBase macros that substitute the value of a variable name for a variable. The .EXE files created by this type of compiler differ significantly from the .EXE file structure of conventionally-compiled code, such as C, where all variables are declared explicitly before compilation.

"Compiling" your Access Basic source code to a collection of tokens is a much faster process than compiling and linking a Windows application. Access has the further advantage of being an "incremental compiler" that only tokenizes code that has been added or changed since the last "compile." This further speeds the process of testing and debugging Access Basic applications.

Execution Speed: External Versus Internal Execution of Interpreted Code

externally executable require run time library

When you "compile" Visual Basic 3.0 code with VB.EXE, you create a Windows .EXE file. The Visual Basic .EXE file contains the resources (forms) you create and the tokenized code associated with the forms. The runtime library for Visual Basic 3.0, VBRUN300.DLL, contains all of the functions required to display the resources of your application and execute your tokenized code. .EXE files created by interpreted languages are classified as externally executable. These .EXE files do not fall into the "stand-alone" category typified by CA-Clipper files because externally executable files require a runtime library to function.

Visual Basic's custom controls (.VBX) are a special variety of Windows DLL that in most cases include a presentation in the form of a button to be included in an expanded Visual Basic toolbox. The OLE Customer Controls (OCXs) used by Access 2.0 are DLLs that are similar in function to VBXs, but differ markedly in structure. It is expected that future versions of Visual Basic will accommodate both OCX and VBX controls, but Access will continue to support only OLE Custom Controls.

Access takes an approach that is somewhat different from Visual Basic; MSACCESS.EXE includes the functions necessary to "compile" your Access Basic code to p-code and to process the resources incorporated into your forms and reports so that Windows displays them. Thus Access Basic code is internally executable. Access handles macros and Access Basic code much like the code for Word Basic macros contained in Microsoft Word template (.DOT) files that is executed by WINWORD.EXE. Applications, such as Excel 5.0 and Project 4.0, that use Visual Basic for Applications as their macro language use VBA.DLL to supply the programming language. As with Visual Basic and Visual Basic for Applications, Access Basic's runtime library is a DLL, MSABC200.DLL. Access uses a DLL similar in purpose to a Visual Basic custom control, CTL3DV2.DLL, to create three-dimensional effects for objects such as message boxes and dialog boxes. Other DLLs required to run Access 2.0 include:

- MSAEXP200.DLL, the Access expression-services DLL
- MSAIN200.DLL, which provides language-dependent functions (international versions)
- MSAJT200.DLL, the Access Jet database engine library that connects directly to Access .MDB files, as well as indirectly to xBase, Paradox and Btrieve files, in conjunction with a database driver such as XBS200.DLL that is used with Xbase files
- MSAJU200.DLL, the Jet database engine utilities library

Code in MSACCESS.EXE calls the functions contained in the preceding DLLs, as well as in several additional DLLs, as needed, for operations such as creating new database objects and running your applications.

The execution speed of interpreted Visual Basic 3.0 code rivals that of code compiled with C++. In many cases, execution speed of an application is limited by the Windows environment rather than how fast the application's interpreted or compiled code runs. The execution speed of your Access applications is influenced more by the time required to paint forms to the display and to obtain data from or update records in tables than by the execution speed of your Access Basic code.

> **TIP**
>
> The execution speed of an Access application is influenced greatly by the speed of your disk drive. The performance difference between a drive of 18-microseconds and a drive of 8-microseconds average seek time is easily discernible, especially with Access databases that contain large tables. Another major influence on performance is the degree of fragmentation of

the disk files that Access employs. Always use a permanent swap file with Access and use a disk optimizing utility periodically to defragment your databases. Compacting an Access database file improves performance by eliminating "holes" in the file, but compacting does not defragment the file.

Object Basic Syntax for Declaring DLL Function Prototypes

Access Basic and Visual Basic (including Visual Basic for Applications) use the Declarations sections of code modules for the same purposes as C's header files. You declare your intention to use a function contained in a DLL by registering its prototype in the Declarations section of a module. The prototype of a function consists of the Access Basic **Declare** and **Function** or **Sub** reserved word, followed by the function name, the keyword **Lib** followed by the name of the library that contains the function, and the arguments required by the function, if any. Most functions return values, so you also need to specify the data type of the return value. Word 6.0's Word Basic macro language does not have a separate Declarations section; you register the functions by adding their prototypes before the beginning of your **Sub Main** code. The generic syntax for registering a function prototype in any of these Object Basic dialects is as follows:

```
Declare {Function¦Sub} FunctionName Lib "DLLName[.{DLL¦EXE}]
➥[Alias "AliasName"] ([[ByVal] Argument1 As DataType[,
➥[ByVal] Argument2 As DataType[...]]]) [As DataType]
```

Functions that do not return values (called void functions in C) are declared as procedures (**Sub**s). You do not include the final **As** *DataType* expression, shown as optional, because there is no value for the type declaration. You must, however, include the set of empty parentheses that would surround arguments if no arguments are required. Adding the extension to *DLLName* is optional. Most Windows DLLs use the file extension .DLL; however, the DLLs that constitute the basic Windows functions, employed by all Windows applications, use .EXE as their extension. Windows functions are described in the section that follows.

Using the *Alias* Keyword to Call Functions by Another Name

The **Alias** keyword lets you substitute a *FunctionName* of your choosing to call a DLL function with the name *AliasName*. Function names declared in Access

Basic modules always have global scope; thus aliasing a function name is necessary if another component of your application has previously registered the function. As an example, if you attach an Access library that registers the Windows `WritePrivateProfileString()` function, you need to alias the function to another name, such as `WritePrivateINIString` or *prefix*`_WritePrivateProfileString()`. When you add a prefix to an alias, the conventional practice is to separate it from the function name by an underscore character. Your code then uses the *FunctionName* to call the aliased function of the sub-procedure you declare. Examples of aliased DLL function prototype declarations are provided in the sections called "Finding the Location of the Access Directory" and "Writing Code to Change Your SYSTEM.MDA File," later in this chapter.

TIP

Always use an *AliasName* for Windows API function calls employed in Access libraries. If your library declares a Windows API function with the same name as a function declared in a module of the database in use, you receive an error message saying "Tried to load procedure with duplicate name 'ProcedureName'" when you open the database.

NOTE

Function prototypes declared in form or report code modules have form- or report-level scope. These functions are visible only when the form or report that contains the declaration is loaded. Thus, it is possible to declare function prototypes with the same name in code behind several forms or reports. It is a more efficient programming practice to declare function prototypes use by more than one block of code in the declarations section of an Access Basic module.

Declaring Data Types of Arguments and Returned Values with the As and ByVal Keywords

A list of the arguments required by the function, if any, suffixed with a definition of their Object Basic data type (**As** *DataType*), follows the optional **Alias** statement. The **As** keyword provides data type checking; type checking assures that the data type passed to the DLL function is acceptable to the function. The most common data types used in function prototype declarations are **Integer**, **Long**, **Single**, **Double**, and **String**. You turn off data-type checking when different types of data are passed to the argument with the use of the **As Any** qualifier, depending upon the use of the function.

The optional **ByVal** statement that precedes argument names causes numeric arguments to be passed by value, rather than by reference. Passing an argument by its value precludes the DLL changing the value. Passing an argument by reference substitutes the location of (a pointer to) the value of the argument in memory. **ByVal** behaves differently with **String** variables; in this case, Basic creates a null-terminated string and passes a pointer to the location of the string in memory. The length of Basic strings is determined by a two-character value that precedes the ordered array of characters that compose the string. Thus the limit of 64KB (the maximum value that can be expressed in two 8-bit bytes) on the length of Basic strings. The length of null-terminated (also called ASCIIZ) strings used by C, the language in which most DLLs are written, is determined by the first null character (ASCII 0 or **Chr$(0)**) encountered as the DLL function sequentially reads the characters in the string. You do not use the **ByVal** keyword when passing arguments employing user-defined data types declared within **Type...End Type** structures. Basic's user defined data types substitute for C struct structures.

Excel 4.x uses the REGISTER() function to declare functions contained in DLLs. The syntax of the REGISTER() function is quite different from that of Microsoft's Object Basic languages. The Excel flavor of Visual Basic for Applications, however, uses Object Basic's **Declare** keyword and the preceding syntax.

> ### WARNING
>
> Do not use the **ByVal** keyword in conjunction with arguments of user-defined data types. DLLs need a pointer to the location of the structure in memory so that the DLL can read and modify the fields of the structure as necessary. Using the **ByVal** keyword with a user-defined data type results in a runtime error.

Declaring Functions Contained in Windows DLLs

Windows 3.x consists of a small executable file (WIN.COM, a binary file that DOS executes) and a myriad of DLLs. The Windows DLLs that compose the bulk of the functions used by all Windows 3.x applications are:

■ KERNEL.EXE, which is responsible for loading and executing applications, memory management, and controlling the simultaneous operation of multiple applications

■ USER.EXE, which handles all user-interface functions, including processing keyboard entries and controlling the appearance and state of individual windows

■ GDI.EXE, which processes the graphics that appear on the surface of windows and on printed output

These and the other DLLs, which include the 500-plus functions that constitute Windows 3.1, are located in your \WINDOWS\SYSTEM directory. When you specify a library with the **Lib** *"DLLName"* statement but do not include a well-formed path to the library file, Windows checks the \WINDOWS and \WINDOWS\SYSTEM directories, the working (application) directory, and then the directories on your DOS path to find the specified file. Some applications specify that their DLLs reside in the working directory of the application. If Windows cannot find the specified file in any of these locations, you receive an error message. Most applications terminate if a required DLL cannot be found.

Windows also includes a number of special purpose DLLs, many of which were added when Microsoft released Windows 3.1. Some of these DLLs include:

- OLECLI.DLL and OLESVR.DLL, which supply OLE 1.0 client and server functions to OLE 1.0-compliant applications. The functions provided by these DLLs are superseded by functions in OLE2.DLL, OLE2CONV.DLL, OLE2DISP.DLL, OLE2NLS.DLL, and OLE2PROX.DLL when you install Access 2.0 or other OLE 2.0-compliant applications. The OLE2... DLLs provide resources for additional features such as OLE Automation, for OLE 2.0 clients and servers.

- MMSYSTEM.DLL, responsible for orchestrating the multimedia functions of Windows 3.1, including sound, MIDI music, animation, and video components.

- SOUND.DLL, a lowly substitute for MMSYSTEM.DLL and a Windows-compatible sound card. SOUND.DLL uses your computer's speaker to play feeble, square-wave tones of different frequencies and durations.

- SHELL.DLL, which maintains data in your registration database (REG.DAT) and adds drag-and-drop features to Windows' File Manager.

One of the advantages to the use of DLLs is that you need not upgrade Windows itself to take advantage of new features, such as OLE 2.0. Another advantage of DLLs is that one copy of the .DLL file on your fixed disk can be used by several Windows applications simultaneously. The downside is that your \WINDOWS\SYSTEM directory becomes cluttered with obsolete DLLs; few applications have an uninstall feature that removes all of their components from your fixed disk drive. The Remove All option of the Setup application of recently-release Microsoft applications is a welcome feature that other software publishers are likely to duplicate.

The principal problem in using Windows DLLs is not declaring and using them, but determining which of the 500 or so Windows functions might accomplish your immediate programming objectives. The Access Developer's Toolkit (ADT) includes a cross-referenced WinHelp file, WIN31API.HLP, to help you find the function you need and the DLL that contains the function. If you haven't used the Windows API functions extensively, a Windows API programming reference book, such as Sams Publishing's *Developing Windows 3.1 Applications with Microsoft C/C++*, Second Edition, by Brent Rector, is a virtual necessity.

Windows API programming references and help files publish the syntax of Windows API functions in C format. The following is an example of the standard syntax for the GetPrivateProfileInt() function contained in KERNEL.EXE that reads a positive integer numeric value from a private .INI file and returns the value to the expression that contains the function:

```
WORD  GetPrivateProfileInt(lpApplicationName, lpKeyName, nDefault,
➡lpFileName)
```

WORD specifies the data type of the return value, in this case an unsigned 16-bit value. The replaceable arguments prefixed with lp are strings (LPSTR, lpsz in Hungarian notation, a long pointer to a null-terminated string). The n prefix refers to an integer (a signed 16-bit value). Substitution of Access Basic's **Integer** data type for C's WORD data type is discussed in the section that follows. You translate the preceding C syntax into the following Access Basic function prototype declaration:

```
Declare Function GetPrivateProfileInt Lib "Kernel" (ByVal
➡lpApplicationName As String, ByVal lpKeyName As String,
➡ByVal nDefault As Integer, ByVal lpFileName As String) As Integer
```

Because of the length of declaration statements, they are often typeset on multiple lines as in:

```
Declare Function GetPrivateProfileInt Lib "Kernel"
    (ByVal lpApplicationName As String,
     ByVal lpKeyName As String,
     ByVal nDefault As Integer,
     ByVal lpFileName As String) As Integer
```

When you enter the declaration statement in Access Basic, the entire statement must be contained on a single line. C compilers disregard white space, which includes tabs, extra space characters, and newline pairs. Access disregards tabs and closes up extra spaces in many instances, but Access interprets newline pairs as the end of a statement.

> **NOTE**
>
> Many books on Windows programming use bold monospace type to identify Windows functions, the data type of the returned values, and the data types of the arguments in code examples. This book uses bold monospace type only to identify Access Basic reserved words and symbols in both code examples and the text. Because Windows API functions are not reserved words in Access Basic, these functions are set in regular monospace type.

To minimize the length of the lines of code containing declarations, you can replace the **As** *Datatype* statements with Access Basic data type identification characters to reduce the number of keystrokes involved, as in:

```
Declare Function GetPrivateProfileInt% Lib "Kernel"
    (ByVal lpApplicationName$,
     ByVal lpKeyName$,
```

```
ByVal nDefault%,
ByVal lpFileName$)
```

The replaceable argument names in function prototype declarations serve only as placeholders; only the data type of arguments in these declarations are significant. You can use any argument names you like in the expression that calls the function, provided that the data types of the arguments correspond to those of the declaration statement. You also can substitute literals for arguments in the expression that calls the function. As an example, if you have an entry Baud Rate=2400 (lpKeyName) under the [Comm Settings] section (lpApplicationName) of a private .INI file, MSA_DIAL.INI (lpFileName), you can obtain the baud rate with the following statement:

```
wBaudRate = GetPrivateProfileInt("Comm Settings", "Baud Rate",
➡2400,"MSA_DIAL.INI")
```

The preceding statement will return 2400 to wBaudRate even if the Baud Rate=2400 line is missing, because 2400 was passed as the value of nDefault. If the value for Baud Rate= in MSA_DIAL.INI is a negative integer or is not an integer, GetPrivateProfileInt() returns 0, the equivalent of **False**.

NOTE

Many Windows API functions return a 0 (**False**) if unsuccessful. Some functions return positive integers on successful execution; negative integers correspond to an error value. Others return 0 to indicate success; any value other than 0 represents an error code. There does not appear to be any accepted convention for indicating the success or failure of the execution of functions contained in Windows DLLs. This means that you need to pay close attention to the return value specifications in the documentation for the DLL functions.

Translating C to Access Basic Data Types

Windows DLLs use C data types for return values and arguments. Thus you need to convert the C data types shown in the documentation for DLL functions to those available in Access Basic. Table 22.1 lists the ANSI (American National Standards Institute) C data type names (reserved words), the prefix commonly used for replaceable argument descriptors, the corresponding Windows data type, and the Access Basic data type you employ in the **As *DataType*** expression of function prototype declarations and user-defined data type (struct) declarations.

Table 22.1. ANSI C data types and their corresponding Windows and Access Basic data types.

C Data Type	Common Prefix	Windows Data Type	Access Basic Data Type
char	none	char	String * 1
unsigned char		BYTE	String * 1
int, short	n	int	Integer
		BOOL	
unsigned,	w	WORD	Integer
unsigned short	h	HANDLE	Integer
		handle	
long, long int	l	long	Long
unsigned long	w	DWORD	Long
	lp	tag FAR *	
float	varies	varies	Single
double	varies	varies	Double
long double	none	not used	none
Array of char	lp	LPSTR	String
	lpsz		

The char (-128 to + 127) and unsigned char (0 to 255) C data types (Windows char and BYTE data types) are employed in user-defined (aggregate) data types. Thus these data types are discussed in the next section that covers the use of structures in Windows API functions.

The BOOL Windows data type corresponds to the Yes/No field data type of Access tables and the Access Basic **Integer** data type. Many functions that return -1 (**True**) or any other non-zero integer if successful and 0 (**False**) if not successful use the BOOL data type for the return value.

> **NOTE**
>
> **True** and **False** are the only symbolic constants that are predefined by Access Basic for the values of data in fields of the Yes/No field data type. Other values, such as Yes, No, On, and Off, which are accepted in text boxes bound to Yes/No field data types, are not defined in Access Basic. **True**, Yes and On each are assigned the value -1 by Access; **False**, No, and Off have the value 0.

Windows makes extensive use of handles that identify Windows objects, such as individual windows, device contexts for graphic objects, and menus. Handles are unsigned integers with values determined by Windows' task manager. The most commonly used handles identify a specific window (hWnd) using the HWND Windows data type. You can obtain the handle to the active MDI child window for Access forms or reports with the **hWnd** property using either of the following statements:

```
hForm = Screen.ActiveForm.hWnd
hReport = Screen.ActiveReport.hWnd
```

Once you have the handle to the active window, you can obtain information about the window with the GetSystemMetrics(), IsZoomed(), and other related Windows API functions contained in USER.EXE. Examples of the use of window handles with other Windows API functions appear later in this chapter.

The Windows DWORD data type, an unsigned long (integer), is used for FAR * (long) pointers. Long pointers in Windows DLL functions are used primarily to identify the location of strings and user-defined data types in memory. When the pointer is to the location of a user-defined data type, the tag identifies the data structure. The C syntax of the SetCommState() function used to initialize a serial port connected to a modem is:

```
int SetCommState(lpDCB)
```

In this case, DCB is the tag (data type) you assign with a **Type** DCB ... **End Type** declaration. If you declare a variable, dcbCommState, of type DCB, the function prototype declaration statement is:

```
Declare Function SetCommState Lib "user" (dcbCommState As DCB) As
➡Integer
```

SetCommState() is one of several Windows API comm functions used in the AUTODIAL.MDA library, the subject of the next chapter.

NOTE

Some Windows API functions use long pointers to callback functions. Callback functions are functions in a Windows application that process Windows messages returned as a result of calling the API function. There is no provision for passing the address of the entry point of a function in Access Basic code. Therefore, you cannot declare and use Windows API functions that employ callback functions with Access. If you are a C or Pascal programmer, you can write your own DLL to handle callbacks. The MCI.VBX Visual Basic custom control for Windows' media control interface is an example of a DLL that processes callback functions.

C does not include an explicit string data type. Strings in C are arrays of type char. When you declare an array of characters in C with the statement

```
char rgb_char_array[] = "Char Array"
```

you don't declare the size of the array. (The brackets are empty.) The C compiler counts the number of characters, adds a null to terminate the string, and then automatically assigns the length of the string plus 1 to the array. When you declare an argument in a function prototype **As String**, Access creates a null-terminated string (sz) from the Access Basic string, then passes its location in memory (lpsz) as the value of the argument of the function.

You cannot pass Access Basic arrays as values for arguments of functions in DLLs; "As Array" is not a valid data type declaration. You can, however, pass a single element of an array to a function contained in a DLL. If you have a two-dimensional array declared as **Dim** rgbIniEntry(4,4) **As String** with the first dimension representing the [Section] of a private .INI file and the second dimension assigned to the lines (key names) within a section, the following syntax is valid:

```
wBaudRate = GetPrivateProfileInt(rgbIniEntry(3,0), rgbIniEntry(3,2),
➡0,"MSA_DIAL.INI")
```

User-Defined Data Types as Structures

Many Windows functions require structures, the C term for a user-defined data type, as arguments. As noted in the preceding section, Windows DLL functions expect a long pointer to the location of a variable of the specified structure. The C syntax for creating a typical structure (struct data type), in this case the communications-device control block (DCB), appears in Windows API documentation as the typedef statement that follows. The comm DCB structure is used in this example for two reasons: It contains a variety of data types, including the BYTE data type, and it is used in Chapter 23's AUTODIAL.MDA library.

```
typedef struct tagDCB {
    BYTE Id;
    WORD BaudRate;
    BYTE ByteSize;
    BYTE Parity;
    BYTE StopBits;
    WORD RlsTimeout;
    WORD CtsTimeout;
    WORD DsrTimeout;

    BYTE fBinary: 1;
    BYTE fRtsDisable: 1;
    BYTE fParity: 1;
```

```
      BYTE fOutxCtsFlow: 1;
      BYTE fOutxDsrFlow: 1;
      BYTE fDummy: 2;
      BYTE fDtrDisable: 1;

      BYTE fOutX: 1;
      BYTE fInX: 1;
      BYTE fPeChar: 1;
      BYTE fNull: 1;
      BYTE fChEvt: 1;
      BYTE fDtrFlow: 1;
      BYTE fRtsFlow: 1;
      BYTE fDummy2: 1;

      char XonChar;
      char XoffChar;
      WORD XonLim
      WORD XoffLim
      char PeChar;
      char EofChar;
      char EvtChar;
      WORD TxDelay;
} DCB;
```

You need to translate the data types contained in the structure to data types available in Access Basic. The only method of creating a char or BYTE data type in Access Basic is to use the **Chr$**() function, which returns a single character (1 byte) from the ASCII value of the character supplied as the argument of **Chr$**(). Thus you need to use a single-character fixed length string (**String * 1**) as the Access data type where Windows requires the char or BYTE data type in a structure.

The BYTE *fFlagName: n* fields of the DCB structure previously shown is the method used by C to set or read the value of the individual bits within an unsigned char byte. Here, *n* is the number of consecutive bits that constitute the field, with the most significant bit (MSB) first. Windows uses the individual bits as flags (prefix f) to set the mode of the COM port. If fRtsDisable is set (1), as an example, the status of the request-to-send (RTS) line is held low; if fRtsDisable is clear (0), RTS goes high when the COM device is opened and is set low when the device is closed.

Access does not provide a function that enables you to set the value of a single bit within a byte. In the case of DCB, however, the two bytes that contain the flags are contiguous. This means that you can replace the two bytes with an integer, then set the values of the individual bits of the integer by setting the numerical value of the integer with a mask. A mask, in this case, consists of the sum of the powers of two corresponding to the bits of the integer you want to set. Table 22.2 shows the relationship between the flag bits in the original BYTE data as they relate to the decimal and hexadecimal values you use for the flag. ABC in the hexadecimal column is an abbreviation for Access Basic code.

Table 22.2. Decimal values used for the mask of a two-byte integer.

Bit of Byte	Byte Number	Bit of Integer	Flag Name	Decimal Value	Hexadecimal Value (ABC)
MSB	1	15	fBinary	32768	&H8000
6	1	14	fRtsDisable	16384	&H4000
5	1	13	fParity	8192	&H2000
4	1	12	fOutxCtsFlow	4096	&H1000
3	1	11	fOutxDsrFlow	2048	&H800
2	1	10	fDummy (bit2)	1024	&H400
1	1	9	fDummy (bit1)	512	&H200
LSB	1	8	fDtrDisable	256	&H100
MSB	2	7	fOutX	128	&H80
6	2	6	fInX	64	&H40
5	2	5	fPeChar	32	&H20
4	2	4	fNull	16	&H10
3	2	3	fChEvt	8	&H8
2	2	2	fDtrFlow	4	&H4
1	2	1	fRtsFlow	2	&H2
LSB	2	0	fDummy2	1	&H1

If you want to set the mode of the COM port to disable the DTR line and use XON/XOFF receive and transmit flow control, add the values shown in Table 22.2 for fDtrDisable, fOutX, and fInX, 256 + 128 + 64 = 448. Thus you set the value of the integer that you substitute for the two BYTE fields to 448.

The one-byte Parity and StopBits fields of the DCB structure require the values supplied by Windows symbolic constants, the subject of the next section of this chapter.

The preceding DCB structure now translates to the Access Basic CommStateDCB structure that follows, with the wModeControl field representing the two flag bytes:

```
Type CommStateDCB
    bId            As String * 1    'Port Id from OpenComm
    wBaudRate      As Integer       'Baud Rate
    bByteSize      As String * 1    'Data Bit Size (4 to 8)
    bParity        As String * 1    'Parity
    bStopBits      As String * 1    'Stop Bits
```

```
    wRlsTimeOut   As Integer      'Carrier Detect Time "CD"
    wCtsTimeOut   As Integer      'Clear-to-Send Time "CTS"
    wDsrTimeOut   As Integer      'Data-Set-Ready Time "DSR"
    wModeControl  As Integer      'Mode Control Bit Fields
    bXonChar      As String * 1   'XON character
    bXoffChar     As String * 1   'XOFF character
    wXonLim       As Integer      'Min characters in buffer before XON
                                  ➥is sent
    wXoffLim      As Integer      'Max characters in buffer before XOFF
                                  ➥is sent
    bPeChar       As String * 1   'Parity Error Character
    bEofChar      As String * 1   'EOF/EOD character
    bEvtChar      As String * 1   'Event character
    wTxDelay      As Integer      'Reserved/Not Used
End Type
```

Once you've created the Access Basic structure for the user-defined data type required for the device control block, you need to declare a variable of the type `CommStateDCB` with a **Dim** `dcbCommState` **As** `CommStateDCB` in the declarations section, so that the structure and its fields have module-level scope. You set the field values of `dcbCommState` with code in a function or procedure in your Access Basic module, as in:

```
Sub InitCommState ()
    dcbCommState.wBaudRate = 2400
    dcbCommState.bByteSize = Chr$(8)
    dcbCommState.bParity = Chr$(0)
    dcbCommState.bStopBits = Chr$(0)
    dcbCommState.wRlsTimeOut = 0
    dcbCommState.wCtsTimeOut = 0
    dcbCommState.wDsrTimeOut = 0
    dcbCommState.wModeControl = 448
    dcbCommState.bXonChar = Chr$(0)
    dcbCommState.bXoffChar = Chr$(0)
    dcbCommState.bXonLim = Chr$(0)
    dcbCommState.bXoffLim = Chr$(128)
    dcbCommState.bPeChar = Chr$(0)
    dcbCommState.bEofChar = Chr$(0)
    dcbCommState.bEvtChar = Chr$(0)
    dcbCommState.wTxDelay = 0
End Sub
```

The values shown above set the default state of the COM port to 2400 bps, 8-bit bytes, no parity and 1 stop bit (2400-8/n/1) with DTR disabled and XON/XOFF flow control on both send and receive (`wModeControl`), and a 128-character limit on the size of the receive buffer (`bXoffLim`) before XOFF is sent. It is not necessary to include fields for which the value is 0, because Access initializes all numeric field values to 0 and string field values to the empty string ("") when you declare a variable of a user-defined data type. All of the fields of `dcbCommState` are shown in the preceding example for completeness.

> **NOTE**
>
> You use the `Asc()` function to read the numeric values of fields of Access Basic user-defined data types declared **As String** * 1. As an example, use the statement wByteLen = **Asc**(dcbCommState.bByteSize) to return the value of bByteSize to wByteLen, an integer.

Symbolic Constants for Windows APIs

Windows API functions use a substantial number of symbolic constants that represent numeric values of arguments. By convention, names of symbolic constants are entered in all uppercase letters; the two exceptions to this convention are the predeclared constants **True** and **False**. As an example, the constants for the bParity and bStopBits fields of dcbCommState might be declared with hexadecimal values by adding the following statements in the declarations section of your module:

```
Const NOPARITY = &H0
Const ODDPARITY = &H1
Const EVENPARITY = &H2

Const ONESTOPBIT = &H0
Const ONE5STOPBITS = &H1
Const TWOSTOPBITS = &H2
```

Alternately, you can substitute the decimal values of the constants as the value of the argument of the **Chr$**() expression that sets the values of bParity and bStopBits. Regardless of your approach, you need to know the values of the symbolic constants required by the Windows API functions you use. These values are seldom included in Windows API function documentation. If you can't find the required values in the documentation, you need to use the header file applicable to the DLL in which the values of the constants are provided. As an example, the following constants are defined in MSA_DDL.H, the header file for MSADDL11.DLL that was required to use the data definition language (DDL) functions of the Access 1.1 database engine. Constant declarations in C header files appear similar to the following:

```
#define ACCESSDDL_bitIndexUnique           0x00000001
#define ACCESSDDL_bitIndexPrimary          0x00000002

#define ACCESSDDL_ReferenceUnique          0x00000001
#define ACCESSDDL_ReferenceDontEnforce     0x00000002

#define ACCESSDDL_fieldtypeYesNo           1
#define ACCESSDDL_fieldtypeByte            2
```

```
#define ACCESSDDL_fieldtypeInteger      3
#define ACCESSDDL_fieldtypeLongInteger  4
#define ACCESSDDL_fieldtypeCurrency     5
#define ACCESSDDL_fieldtypeSingle       6
#define ACCESSDDL_fieldtypeDouble       7
#define ACCESSDDL_fieldtypeDateTime     8
#define ACCESSDDL_fieldtypeText         10
#define ACCESSDDL_fieldtypeOLE          11
#define ACCESSDDL_fieldtypeMemo         12
```

The `0x` prefix in C indicates that the characters following are in hexadecimal representation. It takes two hexadecimal characters to define a byte and integers comprise two bytes, so the `int` constant with a value of 1 is expressed by `0x0001`. In the preceding example, `0x00000001` represents 1 as a long int. Values without a preceding `0x` are assumed to be decimal values of integers. Alternately, C programmers can specify the decimal value of a `long int` by adding the suffix `L` to the decimal value, as in `1L`. To translate C hexadecimal constants to Access Basic constants, substitute **Const** for `#define` and `= &H` for the `0x` of C to define a hexadecimal constant. Append another `&` to the value to declare the constant as a **Long** integer, as in:

```
Const ACCESSDDL_bitIndexUnique = &H1&
Const ACCESSDDL_bitIndexPrimary = &H2&
```

If the C constants in the header file are integers, simply specify the values with an equal sign, as in:

```
Const ACCESSDDL_fieldtypeYesNo = 1
Const ACCESSDDL_fieldtypeByte = 2
```

Access Basic automatically assigns constants the most compact data type that matches the value of the constant. If the value of a constant includes a decimal fraction or a minus sign, C converts the value to a `float`. Access converts values with decimal fractions to the **Single** data type. If the values exceed those that can be accommodated by the **Single** data type, Access creates a **Double** constant.

NOTE

The use of long symbolic constant names in Access Basic increases the storage space requirement of your code. When you compile C source code that uses symbolic constants, the compiler substitutes a memory location for the constant's name. Access Basic, on the other hand, stores the name itself in a symbol table. Thus, you should declare only the symbolic constants you need in the declarations section of your module.

Error values returned by Windows API functions also are specified by symbolic constants, usually with mnemonic names. The following constant declarations define the values returned by the OpenComm() function if an error is encountered:

```
Const IE_BADID = -1       'Invalid or unsupported id
Const IE_OPEN = -2        'Device Already Open
Const IE_NOPEN = -3       'Device Not Open
Const IE_MEMORY = -4      'Unable to allocate queues
Const IE_DEFAULT = -5     'Error in default parameters
Const IE_HARDWARE = -10   'Hardware Not Present
Const IE_BYTESIZE = -11   'Illegal Byte Size
Const IE_BAUDRATE = -12   'Unsupported wBaudRate
```

If OpenComm() succeeds, it returns the COM port number, which will be 1 through 4 for Windows 3.1. OpenComm() is used in the preceding example because OpenComm() returns the value of **True**, even if the function fails because you supplied an invalid or unsupported bId value.

> **TIP**
>
> Do not declare Windows symbolic constant names with **Global** scope. Use **Const**, not **Global Const**, to declare these constants. If you create libraries containing Windows API function calls that require symbolic constants, and the library is attached when another Access database contains a module that includes declaration of the same global symbolic constant, you receive a runtime error.

Using Constants as Masks

Many Windows symbolic constants are used as masks so that you can determine whether one or more conditions is true by inspecting the individual bits of a value, usually an integer. An example is the group of the EV_ event constants that are used with the Windows GetCommEventMask() functions to detect the status of a COM port opened with OpenComm():

```
Const EV_RXCHAR = &H1     'Character received in buffer
Const EV_RXFLAG = &H2     'Event character received in buffer
Const EV_TXEMPTY = &H4    'Transmit buffer empty
Const EV_CTS = &H8        'Clear to send changed state
Const EV_DSR = &H10       'Dataset ready changed state
Const EV_RLSD = &H20      'Receive line signal detect changed state
Const EV_BREAK = &H40     'Break received
Const EV_ERR = &H80       'Line status error occurred
Const EV_RING = &H100     'Ring detected
Const EV_PERR = &H200     'Parity error occurred
```

```
Const EV_ALL = &H3FF       'Any event occurred
```

You set the mask to determine which events you want to test by adding the values of the constants in an expression such as:

```
wEventMask = &H20 + &H40 + &H80 + &H200
or:
wEventMask = EV_RLSD + EV_BREAK + EV_ERR + EV_PERR
```

This mask, when used with `GetCommEventMask()`, enables each of the events corresponding to the values shown.

```
wAPIError = SetCommEventMask(wCommHandle, wEventMask)
If wAPIError And EV_PERR Then
    [Code to handle a parity error]
End If
```

If a parity error occurs, `SetCommEventMask()` returns `&H200`. The **And** operation performs the following bitwise comparison:

```
Mask bit pattern 00000010 11100000
EV_PERR pattern  00000010 00000000
Result of And    00000010 00000000 = True
```

Thus, you can detect the occurrence of a change in the CD line, receipt of a break signal, a line status error, or a parity error by successive `If` wAPIError `And` EV_error `Then` ... `End If` structures.

Using Visual Basic Windows API Function and Constant Declarations in Access Basic

All is not lost if you do not have the Access Developer's Toolkit's WIN31API.HLP file or the Windows API function documentation. A widely-available text file, WIN31API.TXT, contains the function prototypes for the majority of the Windows 3.0 and 3.1 API functions, together with the symbolic constant and user-defined data type declarations required for the functions. The function prototypes were written for use in Visual Basic, but the syntax of these declarations is the same for all dialects of Object Basic. Use Windows Write or another text editor to copy and paste the declarations you need into the declarations section of your module; WIN31API.TXT is too large for Windows Notepad.

> **NOTE**
>
> Compressed as W31API.ZIP, WIN31API.TXT is available for downloading from Library 5 of the Microsoft Basic forum on CompuServe (GO MSBASIC). Browse the files in Library 5 by using the keyword "API" to

locate new and updated function prototype declaration files. You also can download the multimedia API function declarations as MMSYS.ZIP from Library 5.

Marshall Bostwick has created an application called APIHelper that makes the process of declaring Windows API function prototypes, user-defined data types, and symbolic constants even easier. AH30.EXE is a Visual Basic 2.0 application that automates the cutting and pasting of Windows API function declarations for you. APIHelper 3.0's window is shown in Figure 22.3.

FIGURE 22.3.

Choosing a Windows API function to paste to an Access module with APIHelper 3.0.

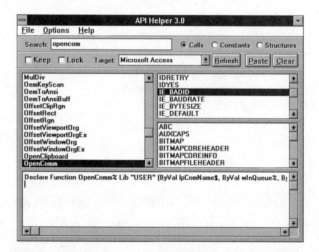

NOTE

You can download AH30.ZIP from Library 5 of the MSBASIC forum on CompuServe. Browse the files in Library 5 by using the "API" keyword to check for updated versions. AH30.EXE is a Visual Basic 2.0 application, so you also need VBRUN200.DLL, which you can download from the MSBASIC forum.

To use APIHelper with Access, expand AH30.ZIP with PKUNZIP.EXE, then follow these steps:

1. Open the Declarations section of the module into which you want to paste the declaration(s).

2. Launch APIHelper and select Access from the drop-down Target list box as the application into which you paste the declarations.

3. Select the function you want in the lefthand list box. The function prototype declaration appears in the text box. Constants and user-defined data types associated with the function appear in the two righthand list boxes.

4. Click the Calls option button, then the Paste button to paste the function prototype to your module.

5. Click the Constants option button, then select the constants you need for your function from the upper right list box. Click the Paste button to add the constants to your declarations section.

6. If you need a user-defined type declaration to accompany your function, click the Structures option button, select the constant, and click the Paste button. Make sure that you paste the user-defined type declaration above the function declaration in your module.

7. Mark the Keep check box to accumulate multiple declarations in APIHelper's text box, then paste the content of the text box as a group of declarations to your module.

NOTE

APIHelper uses an indexed database of function calls (API_CALL.DAT), constants (API_CONS.DAT) and structures (API_TYPE.DAT) to supply the data to the list boxes and the text box. The database functions are contained in QPRO200.DLL and the Visual Basic custom control is supplied by QPLIST.VBX. THREED.VBX is used to add the sunken appearance to the labels and button captions. QPRO200.DLL, QPLIST.VBX, and THREED.VBX must be located in your \WINDOWS\SYSTEM directory.

Using the WinAPI Library, WINAPI.MDA

The WinAPI library, WINAPI.MDA, that is included on the accompanying diskette uses Access to provide capabilities similar to APIHelper. WinAPI adds the following useful functions to those provided by APIHelper:

■ `Dim` statements to declare variables used with the functions

■ Statements you copy and paste into your modules to call the functions you declare

■ Optional alias prefixes for Windows API function names and function calls

■ Prefix conversion of *lp* to *str*, the prefix used for string variables in this book, and *n* to *w* for integer arguments; arguments declared **As Any** are declared **As Variant** in **Dim** statements

■ Constants declared with module-level, rather than global scope

The opening form of WINAPI.MDA is shown in Figure 22.4. The alias prefix *wa_* is added to the AnimatePalette() procedure declaration and **Call** statements so that these statements do not conflict with calls to the same Windows API functions in Access databases.

You choose constants for functions contained in all of the libraries by clicking the Constants button to display the modal pop-up Windows API Constants form shown in Figure 22.5. Double-click the constant name in the lefthand list box to add the constant to the text box on the right. The form uses a list box, rather than a combo box, because constants usually are added in groups.

FIGURE 22.4.
Windows API functions declared by WINAPI.MDA.

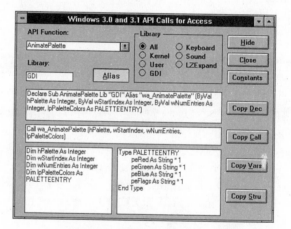

FIGURE 22.5.
Adding Windows API constants with WINAPI.MDA.

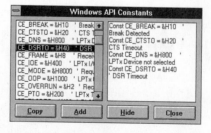

After you install WINAPI.MDA from the accompanying diskettes, follow these steps to attach and use WINAPI.MDA:

1. Close Access and add the line `c:\access\adg20\winapi.mda=rw` to the `[Libraries]` section of your MSACC20.INI file. For additional information on attaching libraries to Access databases, see Chapter 3, "Using Libraries, Wizards, Builders, and Add-ins."

2. Create an Add-In submenu entry to open the main WinAPI window by adding the line `&WindowsAPI==StartWinAPI()` to the `[Menu Add-ins]` section of MSACC20.INI.

3. Relaunch Access and open the Declarations section of your module. Position the caret where you want to insert the Windows API function declaration.

4. Open WinAPI by choosing WindowsAPI from the Add-Ins submenu. The main window of WinAPI opens.

5. Open the API Function combo box and choose a function to declare. The declaration statement, function call, variable declarations, and user-defined data type, if required, appear in the text boxes.

6. If you want to add an alias to the function name, click the Alias toggle button and enter a short alias, such as wa_, in the text box that appears above the button. WinAPI automatically re-creates your function call with the new prefix.

7. Click the Copy button for the component you want, then activate the Module window. Press Ctrl+V to paste the statement to your module. User-defined data types for declared functions must precede declarations of the function.

8. Click the Constants button to display the Windows API Constants form.

9. Double-click each constant that you want to add to your Declarations section to add it to the text box.

10. When your list of constants is complete, click the Copy button, activate your module, and press Ctrl+V to paste the constants to your Declarations section. Windows API Constants is a modal pop-up form, so you need to close or hide its window to return to the main WinAPI form.

11. If you plan to add several Windows API functions to your code, click the Hide button of the main WinAPI form, then reopen the form by choosing Windows API from the Help menu. Close the form when you have completed your Windows API function declarations.

The design methodology employed for WINAPI.MDA is discussed in the next chapter, "Developing Access Libraries and Add-Ins."

Using DLL Functions in Your Access Basic Code

Once you've declared the DLL functions and the user-defined data types and constants they require, you need to add the expressions to call the functions at the appropriate locations in your code. The sections that follow give the generalized syntax for DLL function calls and provide several examples of declaring and using some of the more popular Windows DLL functions.

Calling DLL Functions

Once you've declared the WinAPI functions, constants and user-defined data types you need, you use conventional Access Basic syntax to call the functions. If the API function returns a value, you use the conventional expression syntax:

```
wReturnValue = FunctionName (Argument1[, Argument2[, Argument#]])
```

Void functions that do not return values are declared as sub-procedures. This book uses the optional **Call** keyword as a preface to sub-procedure calls so that parameters of procedures are contained within parentheses; this duplicates the calling style for functions. Thus, the syntax for calling void API functions is as follows:

```
Call SubName (Argument1[, Argument2[, Argument#]])
```

Examples of function and sub-procedure calls are given in the sections that follow.

Creating Buffers for String Arguments and Parameters

A buffer is a location in memory that is reserved for storing the values of variables. In C and other compiled languages, you declare the size of the buffer to hold the value of a variable when you declare the variable in your code. In Access Basic, you can declare variables "on the fly" without declaring their existence with a Dim statement. Using *ad hoc* variables is not considered a "good programming practice," but Access Basic forgives this transgression by dynamically allocating memory to hold the value of the variables.

You must reserve sufficient memory to hold values that are returned by DLL functions. The majority of Windows API functions return values to their names; those functions that employ string variables often return a string to your application. A block of memory of the required size is automatically reserved by Access for variables of data types other than String when you declare the variables. When you declare a variable-length String variable, however, you only reserve enough memory to accommodate a pointer to the memory location of the first character of the string. If you do not reserve a block of memory large enough to hold the string that is returned by the DLL, you incur a runtime error.

You can reserve memory for the string by declaring the string as fixed length (with *
LenValue) or by explicitly creating a buffer with the **String**() function. The latter approach is used in this book because **String**() creates a variable-length string buffer of any size you need. Thus, if you expect the function to return a string no longer than 64 characters, use the following expression to create a 64-character buffer filled with spaces or null characters:

```
strArgString = String(64," ")
strArgString = String(64, 32)
strArgString = String(64, 0)
```

In the second expression, 32 is the ASCII value of the space character. The third expression uses nulls to fill the string. Examples of the use of buffers are given in the sections that follow.

> **WARNING**
>
> All strings in user-defined data types that substitute for structures used as arguments of DLL functions must be declared as fixed length strings with the * symbol. The length of the string must be expressed as an **Integer** or **Long** (but < 64KB) literal or a constant of the **Integer** or **Long** data type. You cannot use the value of a variable to set the length of a fixed-length string. You cannot pass an array as a field of an Access Basic user-defined data type, although you can assign the values of individual elements of an array to the fields of structures.

Creating and Using Private Initialization Files

Windows initialization (.INI) files store information employed by Windows and Windows applications to determine the user environment and for a variety of other purposes. Most entries in .INI files are related to network operating systems, your computer's hardware, location of required files, and allocation of memory. These entries are divided between WIN.INI and SYSTEM.INI, both located in your \WINDOWS directory. In the early days of Windows, all of the information related to Windows applications was stored in WIN.INI. As the number of applications adding entries to WIN.INI increased, WIN.INI grew to virtually unmanageable size. Thus modern Windows applications create their own initialization files, called private .INI files, to minimize new additions to WIN.INI. MSACC20.INI is a typical example of a private initialization file. Private .INI files are usually located in the \WINDOWS directory; however, some applications place their .INI file(s) in the same directory as the application's .EXE file.

The ability to read and create private .INI files is quite useful with Access. You can create a database to hold setup data, but the structure of .INI files is not well-suited to relational tables. Private .INI files also offer the advantage of being text files; you can use Windows Notepad to view and edit .INI files. The size of private .INI files and the code required to read and write them is usually quite small. As an example, you can dispense with WRKGADM.EXE, which occupies about 100KB of disk space to perform one function, once installation of Access is completed, changing a single line in MSACC20.INI to specify the location of SYSTEM.MDA. Creating a library that enables you to change workgroups occupies only 64KB of diskspace, but adding the code for reading or writing .INI files to your modules requires only 1KB or 2KB, at most. The following sections describe the syntax of the private .INI Windows API functions and show how to write a routine that alters the `SystemDB=` entry in your MSACCESS.INI file.

The Syntax of the Private Initialization File Functions

The Windows API includes functions to read and write sections of WIN.INI files (`GetProfileString()`, `GetProfileInt()`, and `WriteProfileString()`), and to create, read, and write private .INI files (`GetPrivateProfileString()`, `GetPrivateProfileInt()`, and `WritePrivateProfileString()`). The syntax for reading and writing WIN.INI and private .INI files is identical, except that you do not specify an .INI filename when you read from or write to WIN.INI. If you want to read entries in SYSTEM.INI, you need to use `GetPrivateProfileString()` or `GetPrivateProfileInt()`. This section deals exclusively with private .INI files.

The syntax for the three private initialization functions of the Windows API is:

```
Declare Function GetPrivateProfileString Lib "Kernel"
    (ByVal lpApplicationName As String,
     ByVal lpKeyName As String,
     ByVal lpDefault As String,
     ByVal lpReturnedString As String,
     ByVal nSize As Integer,
     ByVal lpFileName As String) As Integer
Declare Function GetPrivateProfileInt Lib "Kernel"
    (ByVal lpApplicationName As String,
     ByVal lpKeyName As String,
     ByVal nDefault As Integer,
     ByVal lpFileName As String) As Integer
Declare Function WritePrivateProfileString Lib "Kernel"
    (ByVal lpApplicationName As String,
```

```
ByVal lpKeyName As String,
ByVal lpString As String,
ByVal lpFileName As String) As Integer
```

The following is a description of the arguments used by these three functions:

- ■ *lpFileName* specifies the name of the private .INI file. You do not need to include a well-formed path to the private .INI file if it is located in the \WINDOWS directory.

- ■ *lpApplicationName* specifies the section header, [Section], of the .INI file. The term "application name" is a holdover from terminology used for reading and writing WIN.INI, where the section header for applications is the name of the application. Entries for Word for Windows 2.x in WIN.INI, as an example, use the [Microsoft Word 2.0] section. This book uses the term "section" to substitute for "application name." You do not include the square brackets when you specify a section name.

- ■ *lpKeyName* is the name of the line that contains the information you want to read or write. Entries in .INI files consist of a key name, an equal sign, and the value for the key name. The key name is the portion of the entry that precedes the equal sign. As an example, the key name of the line Baud Rate=2400 is "Baud Rate."

- ■ *lpReturnedString*, used by GetPrivateProfileString(), is the value of the key name, the characters following the equal sign. In the above example, *lpReturnedString* returns "2400."

- ■ *nSize*, an integer, specifies the maximum length of the string value returned by *lpReturnedString*. *nSize* is usually set to the size of the buffer you declare to receive the string. The necessity of declaring buffers is discussed in the preceding section. Setting *nSize* to a value equal to the length of your buffer prevents GetPrivateProfileString() from returning more than *nSize* characters to your application. This ensures against runtime errors resulting from buffer overflow.

- ■ *lpDefault* and *nDefault* are default values that are returned by the function if the specified *lpKeyName* is missing from the .INI file. If the specified *lpKeyName* is not present when you use GetPrivateProfileString() or GetPrivateProfileInt(), the default value is returned.

- ■ *lpString* is the value written to the specified lpKeyName by WritePrivateProfileString( ).

Each of the private .INI functions return different values when used in expressions:

- ■ GetPrivateProfileString() returns the length of the string copied to the lpReturnedString buffer, not including the terminating null. If you use the

expression wReturnValue = GetPrivateProfileString(...), you can trim
the string to the correct length with an expression such as strData =
Left$(*lpReturnedString*, wReturnValue).

■ GetPrivateProfileInt() returns the value of lpKeyName as a positive integer.
If the value of lpKeyName is 0, not a numeric value, or includes decimal
fractions, the return value is 0. The advantage of using
GetPrivateProfileInt() for integer values is the simplicity of its syntax
compared with GetPrivateProfileString().

■ WritePrivateProfileString() returns a Boolean integer; the return value is
zero if the function fails and a non-zero value if it is successful.

Finding the Location of the Access Directory

The Windows API contains a number of functions that you can use to determine
the location of files of Windows applications that are running concurrently on your
computers. To find the location of MSACCESS.EXE, or the .EXE file of another
application, on a fixed disk, you need to find the module handle of the application,
an integer assigned by Windows' Task Manager. Once you have the handle, hModule,
you can use the value of the handle to obtain a string that includes a well-formed
path to the file. The two Windows API declarations you need in the Declarations
section of your module, aliased to avoid conflict with other declarations of the same
function, are:

```
Declare Function gad_GetModuleHandle Lib "Kernel"
    Alias "GetModuleHandle"
    (ByVal lpModuleName As String) As Integer
Declare Function gad_GetModuleFileName Lib "Kernel"
    Alias "GetModuleFileName"
    (ByVal hModule As Integer,
    ByVal lpFileName As String,
    ByVal nSize As Integer) As Integer
```

Create a general-purpose function to retrieve the well-formed path and filename with
the following function:

```
Function strGetAccessDirectory (strModuleName As String)
    'Purpose:  Obtain path to Access directory with Windows API calls
    'Returns:  Path to directory name (String)
    'Argument: Module name ("msaccess" or "msaccess.exe" for Access)

    Dim wReturnVal As Integer
    Dim hModule As Integer
    Dim strFileName As String
    Dim wSize As Integer
    strGetAccessDirectory = ""
    hModule = gad_GetModuleHandle (strModuleName)
```

```
    If hModule = 0 Then
        MsgBox "Can't find handle for " & UCase$(strModuleName) & ".",
        ➥32, "Windows API Error"
    Else
        strFileName = String$(255," ") 'Create a 255-character buffer
        wSize = Len(strFileName)
        wReturnVal = gad_GetModuleFileName (hModule, strFileName, wSize)
        If wReturnVal Then
            strGetAccessDirectory = Left$(strFileName, wReturnVal)
        Else
            MsgBox "Can't find file for " & UCase$(strModuleName) & ".",
            ➥32, "Windows API Error"
        End If
    End If
End Function
```

You can test the function by running it in the Immediate Window of the module in which the function is located. Supply the strFileName argument to the function as a string literal; "msaccess" (the task name) or "msaccess.exe" (the filename) work equally well in this case. On the other hand, "msword" is the task name for Word, and "winword.exe" is Word's filename. The result when you execute ? strGetAccessDirectory( ) in the Immediate Window is shown in Figure 22.6.

FIGURE 22.6.

Testing a function in the Immediate Window.

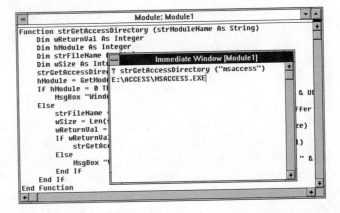

If you want to parse the returned filename so that strGetAccessDirectory includes only the well-formed path to the file, substitute the following code for the line that follows If wReturnVal Then:

```
Do While wReturnVal > 0
    strGetAccessDirectory = Left$(strFileName, wReturnVal)
    If Mid$(strFileName, wReturnVal, 1) = "\" Then
        Exit Do
    End If
    wReturnVal = wReturnVal - 1
Loop
```

If MSACCESS.EXE is in your E:\ACCESS directory, the modified function returns E:\ACCESS\.

> **NOTE**
>
> This procedure does not find the proper location of your MSACC20.INI file if you are running Access from a network directory. It will return the path to the server instead of the local \WINDOWS directory in which you store MSACC20.INI.

Writing Code to Change Your SYSTEM.MDA File

Changing workgroups by attaching SYSTEM.MDA files shared by a network or peer-to-peer server often is necessary in multi-user environments. Although the name of the SYSTEM.MDA for each workgroup is constant, the workstation directory that corresponds to the shared workgroup server directory may vary. As an example, when you use Windows for Workgroups, each workgroup adds shared directories with consecutive drive designators, usually beginning with d:. There is no guarantee, however, that all workstations will share the server's \\SERVERNAME\SALES directory with the same drive designator. Thus each workstation must have the capability of assigning a local drive letter and, perhaps, specify a directory to attach the correct SYSTEM.MDA library.

The function that you can use to replace WRKGADM.EXE to change the `SystemDB=` entry in the `[Options]` section of your MSACCESS.INI file is an example of the use of the `GetPrivateProfileString()` and `WritePrivateProfileString()` functions. In addition to declaring these two aliased Windows API functions, another utility function, `GetWindowsDirectory()`, is included to provide the location of the Windows directory. Using `GetWindowsDirectory()` is optional, because the private .INI functions test the Windows directory for the .INI file if a well-formed path is not included in the value of the *lpFileName* argument. The code for this module, Change Workgroups (Chapter 22), is included in the AB_EXAMP.MDB database on the accompanying diskette.

```
Declare Function cwg_GetPrivateProfileString Lib "Kernel"
     Alias "GetPrivateProfileString"
    (ByVal lpApplicationName As String,
     ByVal lpKeyName As String,
     ByVal lpDefault As String,
     ByVal lpReturnedString As String,
     ByVal nSize As Integer,
     ByVal lpFileName As String) As Integer
```

```
Declare Function cwg_WritePrivateProfileString Lib "Kernel"
     Alias "WritePrivateProfileString"
    (ByVal lpApplicationName As String,
     ByVal lpKeyName As String,
     ByVal lpString As String,
     ByVal lpFileName As String) As integer
Declare Function cwg_GetWindowsDirectory Lib "Kernel"
     Alias "GetWindowsDirectory"
    (ByVal lpBuffer As String,
     ByVal nSize As Integer) As Integer
```

The wChangeWorkGroup() function determines the location of the MSACC20.INI
or other .INI file you specify on the command line of MSARN200.EXE, the executable file for runtime Access. The SYSTEM.MDA file for a workgroup need not have
the standard name, but might be called SALES.MDA. Thus wChangeWorkGroup()
requires two arguments, strIniFile ("msacc20.ini") and strSystemFile
("system.mda") to make it applicable to the general case. Use of special .INI files with
runtime Access is discussed in Chapter 29, "Distributing Runtime Versions of Your
Databases."

When you type ? wChangeWorkGroup("msacc20.ini", "system.mda") in the Immediate Window and press Enter, the function confirms your local Access directory,
then opens the existing version of SYSTEM.MDA to read the current workgroup
directory. This information is used to create the message for an input box in which
you enter the new directory for the workgroup. If you change the workgroup directory, the function uses the low-level file functions of Access Basic to determine whether
the SYSTEM.MDA file exists in the location you specified and if you have read-write
privileges for the file. If the **Open** file statement is successful, wChangeWorkgroup()
attempts to write the new file name and path to the value of the SystemDB= entry in
MSACC20.INI. Using the low-level file functions of Access Basic is one of the subjects of Chapter 25, "Stretching the Limits of Access."

```
Function wChangeWorkGroup (strIniFile As String, strSystemFile As
➡String)
     'Purpose:    Change SystemDB= entry in [Options] section of
➡MSACC20.INI
     'Called By: Module or Macro RunCode action
     'Uses:       strGetAccessDirectory() function
     'Returns:    True if successful (even if workgroup not changed)

    Dim strBuffer As String
    Dim strApplicationName As String
    Dim strKeyName As String
    Dim strDefault As String
    Dim strReturnedString As String
    Dim wSize As Integer
    Dim strString As String
    Dim strMSADirectory As String
```

```
Dim strMessage As String
Dim strTitle As String
Dim wReturnVal As String

strApplicationName = "Options"
strKeyName = "SystemDB"
strDefault = ""
strMessage = "Enter a well-formed path to the new workgroup
➥directory. "
strMessage = strMessage & "Your present workgroup directory is:"
strTitle = "Change Access Workgroup"
wChangeWorkGroup = False


'Verify local Access directory
strMSADirectory = strGetAccessDirectory("msaccess")
If Len(strMSADirectory) = 0 Then
    Exit Function
End If


'Find Windows directory where MSACCESS.INI or other .INI file is
➥located
strBuffer = String$(255, 0)
wSize = Len(strBuffer)
wReturnVal = cwg_GetWindowsDirectory(strBuffer, wSize)
If wReturnVal = 0 Then
    MsgBox "Unable to find Windows Directory", 16, strTitle
    Exit Function
End If
strIniFile = Left$(strBuffer, wReturnVal) & "\" & strIniFile


'Find current WorkGroup directory by reading .INI file
strReturnedString = String$(255, 0)
wSize = Len(strReturnedString)
wReturnVal = cwg_GetPrivateProfileString(strApplicationName,
➥strKeyName, strDefault, strReturnedString, wSize, strIniFile)
If wReturnVal Then
    strReturnedString = Left$(strReturnedString, wReturnVal)

    'Strip file name from directory entry
    Do While wReturnVal > 0
        strReturnedString = Left$(strReturnedString, wReturnVal)
        If Right$(strReturnedString, 1) = "\" Then
            Exit Do
        End If
        wReturnVal = wReturnVal - 1
    Loop

    strMessage = strMessage & UCase$(Left$(strReturnedString,
➥Len(strReturnedString) - 1)) & " and is used as the default
➥entry. "
    strMessage = strMessage & "Your local Access directory is " &
➥Left$(strMSADirectory, Len(strMSADirectory) - 1) & "."
```

```
'Get new WorkGroup directory from InputBox
strString = InputBox$(strMessage, strTitle,
➥UCase$(Left$(strReturnedString, Len(strReturnedString) - 1)))

'Add trailing \ If missing
If Right$(strString, 1) <> "\" Then
    strString = strString & "\"
End If

If strString = strReturnedString Or Len(strString) < 3 Then
    wChangeWorkGroup = True
    Exit Function    'No change made or Esc pressed
End If

'Test to see if new SYSTEM.MDA or other system file exists
strString = LCase$(strString) & strSystemFile
On Error GoTo FileNotFound
Open strString For Input Access Read Shared As #1
On Error GoTo 0
Close #1

'Write the new WorkGroup location and file to the .INI file
wReturnVal = cwg_WritePrivateProfileString(strApplicationName,
➥strKeyName, strString, strIniFile)
If wReturnVal Then
    wChangeWorkGroup = True
    'Provide option to exit Access now or later
    strMessage = "Your workgroup file is now " &
    ➥UCase$(strString) & "." & Chr$(13) & Chr$(10)
    strMessage = strMessage & "Quit and restart Access Now?"
    wReturnVal = MsgBox(strMessage, 36, strTitle)
    If wReturnVal = 6 Then
        DoCmd Quit
    Else
        strMessage = "You must exit and restart Access later
        ➥to join the new workgroup."
        MsgBox strMessage, 64, strTitle
    End If
Else
    strMessage = "Unable to write to " & UCase$(strIniFile) &
    ➥". WorkGroup change canceled."
    MsgBox strMessage, 16, strTitle
End If
End If
Exit Function

FileNotFound:    'Error handler for missing or locked .MDA file
strMessage = "Unable to find or to open file " & UCase$(strString)
➥& " in shared mode. "
strMessage = strMessage & " WorkGroup change canceled."
MsgBox strMessage, 16, "System File Not Available"
Exit Function
End Function
```

The paths to the directories in the preceding function include trailing \'s. Thus there is considerable code devoted to stripping the trailing \'s from strings. In this book, well-formed paths include trailing \'s; other writers omit them. The choice is up to you, but once you decide on a style, it is wise to employ that style consistently in your code.

An input box, as shown in Figure 22.7, is used in the preceding function, but you can substitute text boxes contained in a form to display the current directories and enter the new workgroup directory. The advantage of using an input box is that the function is independent of a form contained in a specific application, and thus the function can be included in an Access library. Of course, libraries can contain forms, but in this case, the input box is an adequate substitute and requires little effort to create.

FIGURE 22.7.

The list box created by the wChangeWorkGroup () function.

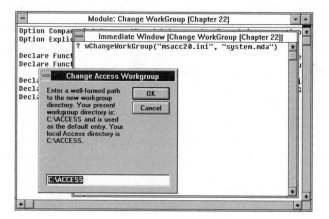

Calling Functions from an Add-In Submenu Choice

If you want to avoid repetitive typing of long function names and parameter values in the Immediate Window, you can add an Add-In submenu choice that calls the function. Add-In submenu choices ordinarily are used to call functions in Access libraries; however, Add-In submenu choices are not restricted to library functions. As an example, to add the Change Workgroups choice to the Add-In submenu, follow these steps:

1. Open MSACC20.INI in Windows' Notepad.

2. Add the line `Change Work&group==wChangeWorkGroup("msaccess.ini",` `"system.mda")` under the `[Menu Add-Ins]` section of MSACC20.INI.

3. Close and launch Access to make the change to MSACC20.INI effective.

4. Choose Change Workgroup from the Add-In submenu to execute the function.

Using an Add-In submenu choice to execute functions is a very handy way to test functions during the development and debugging stages. In the case of the `wChangeWorkGroup()` function, you can add several Add-In submenu choices if you use different *SYSTEM*.MDA names in shared workgroup directories.

Other Useful Windows DLL Functions

The following sections contain simple functions that employ Windows API functions to perform tasks that you cannot accomplish directly with Access Basic statements. The code examples that follow are based on articles contained in PSS-KB.HLP, a WinHelp file that you can download from Library 1, Index and Info, of the MSACCESS on CompuServe as PSS-KB.ZIP. The Microsoft Access Product Support Services (PSS) staff writes technical support articles that contain valuable tips, techniques and workarounds for developing Access applications. These articles are filed in the Microsoft Knowledge Base, another forum on CompuServe (GO MSKB). Members of the Access PSS periodically add newly written articles to PSS-KB.HLP, so you need to watch for the announcements that are posted when Microsoft updates the PSS-KB.ZIP file.

Displaying the Immediate Window at Any Time

If you use the **Debug.Print** instruction to display the value of variables in the Immediate Window, you may want to display the Immediate Window while you are running your application. Normally, you can only display the Immediate Window while a Module window is active. You can display the Immediate Window on command by declaring two Windows API functions and writing a simple function to use them. The following code for the ShowImmediateWindow() function is based on article Q89594, "How to Display Immediate Window without Module Window," of PSS-KB.HLP.

The declarations of the required Windows API functions, aliased so that this function can be contained in a library, and the constants for the FindWindow() and ShowWindow() functions are:

```
Option Compare Text
Option Explicit

Declare Function siw_FindWindow Lib "User"
    Alias "FindWindow"
    (ByVal lpClassName As Any,
```

```
        ByVal lpWindowName As Any) As Integer
  Declare Function siw_ShowWindow Lib "User"
      Alias "ShowWindow"
      (ByVal hWnd As Integer,
       ByVal nCmdShow As Integer) As Integer

  Const SIW_NULL = &H0&            'Declare null Constant

  Const SW_HIDE = 0                'Constants for ShowWindow()
  Const SW_NORMAL = 1
  Const SW_SHOWMINIMIZED = 2
  Const SW_SHOWMAXIMIZED = 3
  Const SW_SHOWNOACTIVATE = 4
  Const SW_SHOW = 5
  Const SW_SHOWMINNOACTIVE = 7
  Const SW_SHOWNA = 8
  Const SW_RESTORE = 9
```

The Windows API function and constant declarations are obtained from WINAPI.MDA, using the alias prefix siw_. Only SW_SHOW is required, because Access hides the Immediate Window when you double-click the window menu control box in the upper-left corner. Hiding (using SW_HIDE), instead of closing, the window retains your prior entries in the Immediate Window. Thus you use SW_SHOW, rather than SW_NORMAL, as the value of the wCmdShow argument of ShowWindow() in the function code that follows.

ShowImmediateWindow() demonstrates two important elements of Windows DLL function calls: use of the **Null** value and the **As Any** data type declaration. The *lpClassName* and *lpWindowName* arguments of FindWindow() function accept either a string or a null value. If you use a **Null** value for *lpWindowName*, FindWindow() returns the window handle (*hWnd*) of the first window it finds of the specified *lpClassName*. If you substitute a **Null** value for *lpClassName*, FindWindow() returns the first window in the window manager's list. Strings and **Null** values are of different data types; thus the arguments must be declared **As Any** to disable type checking. If you declare *lpWindowName* **As String** and then pass a **Null** value, you receive a type mismatch error message when you attempt to compile the code.

> **NOTE**
>
> When you need to use the **Null** value, declare a constant with the value &H0b. **Null** values in Windows are always of the **Long** integer data type. Preceding declaration of **Null** constants with &H is optional, but it is recommended to correspond to the 0x prefix used by C. The trailing & symbol is required to create a **Long** integer; if you don't add the trailing &, you receive a "Bad DLL Calling Convention" error when you execute the function.

The following function code for ShowImmediateWindow() is a modification of the code from the Microsoft Knowledge Base article. The changes are basically cosmetic so that the code conforms to the style used in this book. The function calls were obtained by copying the calls from WINAPI.MDA. The window class name of the immediate window is "OImmediate;" class names of Access windows are not documented by Microsoft.

```
Function ShowImmediateWindow ()
    'Purpose:  Show Immediate window during any Access operation
    'Returns:  Nil
    'Based On: Microsoft Knowledge Base Article Q89594

    Dim lpClassName As String
    Dim hWindow As Integer
    Dim wReturnVal As Integer
    Dim strMessage As String
    Dim strTitle As String

    lpClassName = "OImmediate"
    strMessage = "Open the Immediate window once before using this
    ➥function."
    strTitle = "Show Immediate Window"

    hWindow = siw_FindWindow(lpClassName, SIW_NULL)
    If hWindow Then
        wReturnVal = siw_ShowWindow(hWindow, SW_SHOW)
    Else
        MsgBox strMessage, 48, strTitle
    End If
End Function
```

ShowImmediateWindow() is included in AB_EXAMP.MDB on the accompanying diskette and is also incorporated in WINAPI.MDA. ShowImmediateWindow() is another candidate for a Help menu choice and the function can be included in a library of design tools. If you add the line &Show Immediate Window==ShowImmediateWindow( ) to the [Menu Add-Ins] section of MSACC20.INI, you can show the Immediate Window by choosing Show Immediate Window from the Help menu. (You must open the Immediate Window once before the ShowImmediateWindow() function will execute properly.)

23

Developing Access Libraries and Add-Ins

Access libraries provide Access developers with many of the benefits of Windows dynamic link libraries (DLLs), but they don't require that you learn C to write them. Like Windows DLLs, the functions contained in Access libraries are available to any database you open. Libraries can contain any type of database object, and Access 2.0 lets you execute macros contained in libraries. Creating Wizards, a special type of Access library, is described in Chapter 24, "Using Access Wizard Functions." This chapter explains how to write your own Access libraries and includes an example of a library, Access Autodialer, that you can use with a variety of Access applications.

Creating Libraries for Developers

The majority of Access libraries that were available at the time this edition was written are designed to assist the creation of Access applications. The MSACCESS Forum on CompuServe contains a variety of Access libraries that help you speed up development of applications for your clients or employer. Many of these libraries are related to Wizards; they would be categorized as Wizards if the libraries included the specialized Wizard functions described in Chapter 24.

Examples of Libraries for Access Developers

The libraries described in Chapter 3, "Using Libraries, Wizards, Builders, and Add-Ins," and WINAPI.MDA, which was used to create the Windows DLL function prototypes in the preceding chapter, are typical libraries designed for aiding the development of Access applications. Most commercial libraries and add-in products consist of code originally written for use with Visual Basic, adapted as necessary for use with Access Basic (a process called porting the code to Access). QuickPak Professional for Access and PDQComm for Access, both published by Crescent Software, Inc., are examples of ports of Visual Basic code to Access Basic. QuickPak Professional provides a collection of very useful subroutines that you can include in Access libraries. PDQComm is a full-featured communications application for Access with features similar to those provided by Visual Basic 3.0 Professional Edition's MSCOMM.VBX custom control. FMS, Inc.'s Total Access database documenter library for Access 2.0, described in Chapter 27, "Documenting your Access Applications," is an example of a library that is designed for Access end-user and developers.

The majority of Access developer libraries are presently freeware, contributed by developers to the MSACCESS Forum of CompuServe. You can use and distribute libraries that are designated by their authors as freeware or public-domain without restriction or payment. Thus, the prospect of creating a commercial enterprise based on the sale of Access libraries intended solely for developers is dim, at best. This caveat does not apply to full-scale commercial Access Wizards and related applications aimed at the developer and the end-user market. A lively market is developing in add-on products designed to help end-users create their own Access database applications.

Examining the content of libraries written by other Access developers is the best introduction to library design for development use, if the Access Basic code contains sufficient comments to make the code comprehensible to persons other than the author. It is virtually impossible to fathom the Access Basic code contained in WZFRMRPT.MDA, as an example, because WZFRMRPT.MDA is a very complex library and the code includes no explanatory comments. The commented versions of the Access wizards included with the Access Developer's Toolkit provide additional insight into the design of the Access Form and Report Wizards, but the comments are terse, at best. Members of the Microsoft Product Support Services (PSS) and Quality Assurance staff for Access write many of the libraries that appear in the MSACCESS Forum. Some of these libraries include comments that describe the more creative (obscure) coding techniques employed; others have relatively simple structures that you can comprehend by simply reading printed code.

Examining WINAPI.MDA and Converting Database Applications to Libraries

WINAPI.MDA, described in the preceding chapter and included on the accompanying diskette, contains three tables that supply Windows API function, structure and constant declarations. The content of these tables was created by importing the entire text of WIN31API.TXT into an Access table. A make-table query that detected "Declare" separated the function calls into the Declarations table, then a delete query was used to remove those records from the original table. The same process was used to create the Constants table. Finally, the remainder of the original file, which then contained only comments and structures, was processed with a delete query to remove blank lines and extraneous text. This process is typical of the steps required to create relational tables from organized text files.

The original version of WINAPI.MDA was a free-standing database that used a substantial number of macros, together with a main form and a modal popup form to display and copy Windows symbolic constants. With Access 1.1, the macros had to be implemented as Access Basic functions; Access 2.0 now supports running macros in libraries. The Macro-to-Module Converter of Andrew Miller's FIRSTLIB.MDA successfully converted the macros to functions. The next step was to replace the names of event handlers in the Properties window for the objects contained on both forms. The most important change was replacement of Access 1.1's CurrentDB() function, now **DBEngine**.Workspaces(0).Database(0) or **DBEngine**(0)(0), with CodeDB(), the subject of a section that follows. This process is typical of any conversion of a stand-alone Access database application to an attachable library.

WINAPI.MDA contains extensive comments that describe how the code functions, and why specific code constructs are employed where choices of methods to accomplish the same objective are available. As would be expected, WINAPI.MDA contains a substantial amount of text-parsing code; text parsing is one of the principal applications for Access Basic. The STUFF() function of xBase that makes changing one or more characters in a string a one-step process is, unfortunately, missing from Access Basic.

Libraries for Production Applications

Access libraries intended to be attached to applications designed for your clients or employer serve a wide range of purposes. A few examples where libraries can be employed in production Access applications are as follows:

- Providing a common set of special, user-defined functions required by multiple applications.

- Creating SQL statements for queries in runtime applications that use MSARN200.EXE, which hides the Query Design window from the user.

- Supplying generic procedures, such as opening and closing DDE channels, to several databases.

- Providing graphic assistance for users of your applications, either as a supplement to or a replacement for custom WinHelp (.HLP) files. You can design multistep library functions that emulate the Cue Cards included with the retail version of Access.

- Collecting data from multiple users in a single table for subsequent analysis. For example, you can create a log of when users open and close an application, then count the number of records added to or updated in a table or even count keystrokes, and add this information to the log table.

You can maintain and update common functions and procedures for all users of your applications by substituting a new shared library for the prior version. This is one of the principal advantages of the use of Access libraries, as opposed to including multiple copies of functions and procedures in modules incorporated in individual databases.

The majority of libraries designed to be attached to client applications consist primarily of Access Basic code and usually have only a few forms, if any. It is possible to create forms and reports with special wizards in applications designed for use with the runtime version of Access. However, wizards are designed primarily for assisting developers of applications, not users of transaction process or decision support databases.

Libraries for production applications must be "bullet-proof." Developers will forgive an occasional runtime error or other transgression in a library contributed to the MSACCESS Forum, but libraries attached to your transaction processing and decision support applications must meet professional quality assurance levels. Libraries that almost or usually work properly are seldom acceptable to clients or employers.

Design Considerations for Libraries

Unlike Windows DLLs, you do not need to register Access library function prototypes with **Declare Function** statements. Each function or subprocedure included in the Access Basic module(s) of an Access library is registered automatically when you launch Access. (This is not true of functions or subprocedures in modules contained in forms and reports; these functions and subprocedures are registered only when the form or report is loaded.) Thus, any database you open can call any function or subprocedure in the Access Basic modules of a library. Multiple users can share a single copy of an Access library that is installed on a network server, regardless of whether the users are running a local copy of Access or sharing a single copy of Access on a network. (SYSTEM.MDA and UTILITY.MDA are both Access libraries that commonly are shared by users.) Access libraries are automatically opened in Shared mode, regardless of whether the value of the Default Open Mode for Databases property of the Multi-user options is set to Exclusive or Shared.

Library Entry Points

Library functions that you call from your Access database are called entry points. You can pass arguments that represent the values of control objects on your forms and reports to library functions. Entry point procedures must be functions, not procedures, despite the fact that the function need not (and commonly does not) return a value. The entry point to the Access Autodialer library, described later in this chapter, receives a name, firm, and a telephone number from control objects, such as text boxes, in the calling application's form. You assign control values to the arguments of the =wAutoDial([*Name*], [*Firm*], [*Voice Phone*]) entry in the Properties text box for an event such as a DblClick on the Name text box in your form.

Complex libraries can have multiple entry points. For example, you can create a library that contains a collection of unrelated user-defined functions called by several applications. You can design your library so that common subprocedures serve a number of different entry point functions. A single library can contain forms and reports common to multiple databases. Creating a large multipurpose library has the advantage of minimizing the number of individual libraries you need to attach to user copies of retail or runtime Access. On the other hand, attaching large multipurpose libraries increase Access's memory requirement and slows its loading process.

Specifying Unique Names in Libraries

Access Basic function and subprocedure names have global scope. This means that you must take precautions to use distinctive function and subprocedure names in your libraries so that they do not duplicate names in database applications. If you duplicate a function or subprocedure name, you receive a "Tried to load procedure with duplicate name 'ProcName'" error message. Preceding function and subprocedure names with a code that is related to the library name is a useful technique. You are unlikely to find a duplicate of *xyz_FunctionName()* in the modules of database applications.

Aliasing the names of functions you use that are contained in DLLs is recommended when you call DLL functions from library code. This is especially important for Windows API functions, such as `GetModuleHandle()`, `GetPrivateProfileString()`, and other commonly-used functions. This book uses a two- or three-letter mnemonic code and an underscore as the alias for Windows API functions. Examples of using the **Alias** reserved word to create unique DLL function names are given in the preceding chapter.

The same precaution applies to names of global symbolic constants in libraries. In the case of constants, however, you have the opportunity to declare constants used in libraries with module-level scope. Thus, you should use **Const**, rather than **Global Const**, to declare symbolic constants in libraries whenever possible. The practice in Visual Basic is to declare all Windows API constants with global scope, but this practice is not recommended for Access Basic code. The Access Basic constant declarations created by WINAPI.MDA have module-level, rather than global scope.

Including Forms and Reports in Libraries

You design forms and reports for inclusion in libraries with the same techniques as used for database applications. Although Access 2.0 lets you execute macros contained in libraries, it is a more common practice to use Access Basic code to handle all events. You substitute Access Basic's **DoCmd** keyword, followed by the macro action name and its parameters, for the macros that you would ordinarily use in conjunction with forms and reports.

TIP

Be careful using the OnOpen event of a form or report to create variables of the **Form** or **Report** data type or to set the value of unbound controls. The OnOpen event occurs before the form is opened. If you create a reference to a control object in your even handler code for OnOpen, you may receive an "Object value not set" error message. There may be a significant delay between receipt of the OnOpen event and the presence of control objects on the form. The best approach is to create variables of database object types in the code for a user-initiated event, such as opening a combo box or clicking a command button on the form.

One of the most important considerations in using forms and reports in libraries is maintaining stylistic consistency. Creating standardized form and report styles for a client or employer is discussed in Chapter 2, "Developing a Design Strategy for Access Applications" and methods of using Wizards to maintain consistency in form and report design is a subject of Chapter 24. You may find that you need to redesign forms and reports included in your libraries so as not to contrast with the colors, control object special effects, and other design elements of the applications with which the library will be issued.

Using the *CodeDB()* Function to Refer to Library Databases

Access Basic's **DBEngine**.Workspaces(0).Databases(0) or **DBEngine**(0)(0) function that returns a pointer to the database in use is ambiguous when you attach a library: Which is the current database, that of the library or the application in use? The **CodeDB()** function solves this dilemma; the **CodeDB()** function returns a pointer to the database in which the code containing **CodeDB()** is executing. The rules for when to use **Set** dbVarName = **DBEngine(0)(0)** or **Set** dbVarName = **CodeDB()** in an Access library are:

- Use **DBEngine**(0)(0) to refer to the database that is running the database application employed by the copy of Access to which the library is attached.

- Use **CodeDB()** to refer to database objects contained in your library, if you include tables and queries in the library.

As mentioned earlier, **CodeDB()** returns the current database in which the code that calls **CodeDB()** is running. Thus, as an example, WINAPI.MDA uses the statement **Set** dbAPI = **CodeDB()** to specify that the tables for Windows API functions, structures and constants are resident in WINAPI.MDA, not the database with which you use WINAPI.MDA.

Viewing and Debugging Code in a Library Database

Access 2.0 lets you open Access Basic procedures in modules of library databases so you can view and debug your library code. (Access 1.x did not provide this feature.) You can set one or more breakpoints in your library code and trace the execution of library code. Access 2.0 does not implement this feature by default. You need to add the entry DebugLibraries=True to the [Options] section of MSACC20.INI to enable Access 2.0's integrated debugger. When you restart Access and open a module in your current database, you can use the View Procedures dialog to open modules in the library database. Figure 23.1 shows the Declarations section of the doc_Globals module of WIZLIB.MDA, that is used with the Database Documenter add-in, opened from the View Procedures dialog.

FIGURE 23.1.

Opening a module in a library database for debugging.

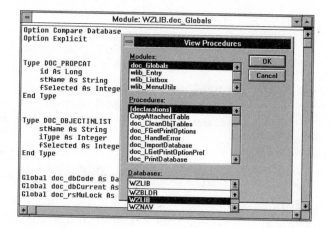

Creating an Autodialer Library for Access Applications

Access applications for marketing, purchasing or any other purpose that involves use of the telephone often need autodialing capability. Microsoft recognized this need by providing a simple built-in AutoDialer that uses your modem to dial a number contained in the text box with the focus. To use the Access 2.0 AutoDialer, you add the AutoDialer button from the Records category of the Customize Toolbars dialog to the Form or Datasheet View toolbar. Figure 23.2 shows the Access 2.0 AutoDialer activated and the Setup button clicked.

FIGURE 23.2.

*The AutoDial
dialog of the Access
2.0 AutoDialer.*

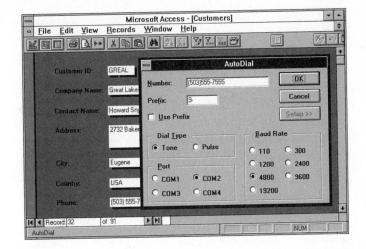

The Access 2.0 AutoDialer lacks a number of features that are required of an autodialer for a commercial application:

■ You must set the focus to the text box that contains the telephone number

■ There is no provision to strip your own area code from the number, so the user must delete his or her own area code in the AutoDial dialog's Number text box

■ No provision is made for sending a modem setup string to the modem; this may be necessary for some types of modems

■ You cannot launch the Access 2.0 AutoDialer and pass it the number to dial from an Access Basic procedure

The Access AutoDialer library described in the sections that follow overcomes the limitations of the Access 2.0 AutoDialer. Creating the autodialer library also provides new insights on the following subjects:

■ Declaring and using the Windows COMM API functions

■ Creating user-defined data types for data structures used as arguments of API functions

■ Aliasing Windows API functions

■ Using private .INI files to store setup data

■ Creating modal pop-up forms for dialing, COM port setup, modem control, and testing the library

■ Substituting user defined functions for the RunCode macro action

The Access Autodialer application is a modification of the original version that appeared in the March 1993 issue of the *Smart Access* newsletter published by Pinnacle Publishing, Inc., under the title, "An Access Autodialer Library." Much of the code in Access Autodialer was derived from COMMDEMO.BAS, a demonstration application written by Microsoft Corp., originally for QuickBASIC and later adapted to Visual Basic. Adapting Visual Basic code for use in Access is discussed in Chapter 25, "Stretching the Limits of Access." The remaining sections of this chapter describe the forms employed in the Access Autodialer and list the Access Basic code contained in the Autodialer module of AUTODIAL.MDA. Access Autodialer is presently in use in a variety of commercial Access 1.1 and 2.0 applications.

Forms Used in the Access Autodialer Library

The Access Autodialer library uses four modal pop-up forms, two of which are shown in Figure 23.3. The primary form, Access Autodialer, dials the number shown in the Dialing text box upon opening. You click the OK button to disconnect the modem from the line after you have lifted the receiver. The operation of Access Autodialer is similar to that of the autodialer of Windows' CardFile applet. The test form is used only when you have opened AUTODIAL.MDA as a database, not when AUTODIAL.MDA is attached to your database application. When you click the OK button of the test form, the test form passes the values of the Number to Dial, Contact Name and Company Name text boxes to the entry point function, `wAutoDial()`.

FIGURE 23.3.

The Autodial Test form and Autodialer form of the AUTODIAL.MDA library. (Courtesy of Smart Access.)

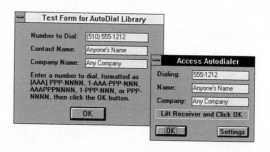

Click the Settings button of the Access Autodialer form opens the COM Port Settings form shown in Figure 23.4. The COM Port Settings form includes more functionality than is needed for an autodialer. The purpose of including the Data Bits, Parity, and Stop Bits unbound option group frames is to allow the same form and its associated code to be reused in conjunction with a general-purpose communications application for Access. When you click the Modem button of the COM Port Settings form, the Modem Setup form opens. The Modem Setup form, also illustrated in Figure 23.4, enables you to enter a modem initialization string, if necessary, control the operation of the speaker, set the hang-up string, and add your own area code so that the area code is removed from the dialing string of calls within your area. You can test the new modem setup without saving it by clicking the Use button. The Save button writes the modem setup data to the application's private .INI file.

FIGURE 23.4.

The forms used by Access Autodialer to set COM port and modem parameters.

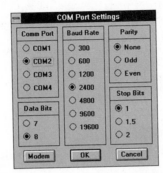
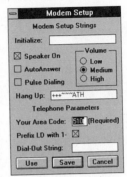

> **NOTE**
>
> Although modal pop-up forms retain the focus until you close them, a modal pop-up form can open another modal pop-up form that receives the focus. The Access Autodialer closes the open form before opening another form.

The Structure of the Access Autodialer Library

Figure 23.5 shows the structure of Access Autodialer in the form of a simplified program flow chart and lists the functions called by the buttons of the three forms that constitute the library's operating elements.

FIGURE 23.5.

The basic structure of the Access Autodialer code. (Courtesy of Smart Access.)

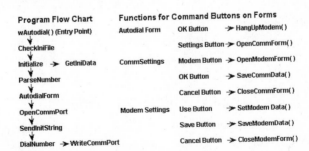

Only those procedures in Access Autodialer that need to return values, are called by your database application, or are used as methods for the OnClick event of command buttons are created as functions. The balance of the procedures are subprocedures created with the **Sub...End Sub** keywords. Table 23.1 lists all of the procedures and functions contained in the Autodialer module. Functions that return values use the type identification prefixes listed in Appendix B; wAutoDial(), for example, returns **True** if the number was dialed, **False** if not.

Table 23.1. The procedures and functions of the Access Autodialer application.

Procedures	*OnClick Functions*	*Called Functions*
CheckIniFile	wAutoDial( )	strReadCommPort( )
Initialize	HangUpModem( )	SetModemData( )
GetIniData	OpenCommForm( )	wIsOpen( )
ParseNumber	OpenModemForm( )	
OpenCommPort	SaveCommData( )	
WriteCommPort	CloseCommForm( )	
WinAPIErr	SetModemData( )	
SendInitString	SaveModemData( )	
DialNumber	CloseModemForm( )	
SetModemInit		

> **NOTE**
>
> The functions and procedures, other than Windows API functions, of this version of AUTODIAL.MDA have not been aliased with a unique prefix. If you find conflicts with functions and procedures in your database applications, add aad_ to the name of the offending function or procedure and the code that executes the function.

The MSA_DIAL.INI Autodialer Setup File

The settings you establish for the COM port and modem need to be preserved for future use. You could create a table and store the data in a single record of the table, but using a private .INI file to store initialization data is a simpler and more traditional technique. Access Autodialer uses MSA_DIAL.INI as its initialization file, so named because at least two other applications use AUTODIAL.INI for initialization purposes. The MSA_DIAL.INI file for a 2400 baud modem connected to COM1, created with `WritePrivateProfileString()` looks like:

```
[Modem Settings]
Hang-Up String=+++~~~ATH
Dial-Out String=
Init String=AT M1 L2 S0=0

[Telephone Data]
Your Area Code=510
Use LD Prefix=Yes
Use Pulse Dial=No

[Comm Settings]
COM Port Number=1
Baud Rate=2400
Data Bits=7
Parity=None
Stop Bits=1
```

One of the advantages of a private .INI file is that you can read the file with text editor, such as the Windows Notepad, to check the validity of your modem settings.

Declarations Section

The Declarations section of the Access Autodialer application incorporates a user-defined structure for the device control block required by the Windows API's Comm functions. This device control block is required to set the state of the serial port used by the modem. Single character strings (b*VarName* * n) substitute for the Byte (8-bit) data type that is not available in Access Basic. The prefix b is used to identify single-character strings used as the BYTE data type in Windows data structures.

> **NOTE**
>
> The **Type...End Type** declaration of data structures must precede the declaration of function prototypes in which arguments of the user-defined type defined by the structure are used.

Function prototype declarations for the eight Windows API functions that are required for serial data transmission under Windows 3.x follow the user-defined `CommStateDCB` type declaration. The three `PrivateProfile` functions required to read and write string values and read integers from MSA_DIAL.INI, described in

Chapter 22, are used to save and read modem and COM port setup data. (`ReadPrivateProfileInt()` is included as an example of its use.) As noted previously, function prototype declarations must be typed on a single line in the Module window; the stacked arguments are used to provide clarity in the text.

The remainder of the Declarations section is devoted to declaring constants required for error handling and event flag mask testing, plus module-level variables used by more than one procedure. The Declarations section of the Autodialer module appears as follows:

```
Option Explicit          'All variables are declared by type
Option Compare Text      'Disregard case in comparisons

Type CommStateDCB
     bId           As String * 1   'Port Id from OpenComm
     wBaudRate     As Integer      'Baud Rate
     bByteSize     As String * 1   'Data Bit Size (4 to 8)
     bParity       As String * 1   'Parity
     bStopBits     As String * 1   'Stop Bits
     wRlsTimeOut   As Integer      'Carrier Detect Time "CD"
     wCtsTimeOut   As Integer      'Clear-to-Send Time
     wDsrTimeOut   As Integer      'Data-Set-Ready Time
     wModeControl  As Integer      'Mode Control Bit Fields
     bXonChar      As String * 1   'XON character
     bXoffChar     As String * 1   'XOFF character
     wXonLim       As Integer      'Min characters in buffer before XON
                                   ➥is sent
     wXoffLim      As Integer      'Max characters in buffer before XOFF
                                   ➥is sent
     bPeChar       As String * 1   'Parity Error Character
     bEofChar      As String * 1   'EOF/EOD character
     bEvtChar      As String * 1   'Event character
     wTxDelay      As Integer      'Reserved/Not Used
End Type


'Windows Comm function prototypes

Declare Function aad_OpenComm Lib "User"
     Alias "OpenComm"
    (ByVal lpComName As String,
     ByVal wInQueue As Integer,
     ByVal wOutQueue As Integer) As Integer

Declare Function aad_CloseComm Lib "User"
     Alias "CloseComm"
    (ByVal nCid As Integer) As Integer

Declare Function aad_WriteComm Lib "User"
     Alias "WriteComm"
    (ByVal nCid As Integer,
```

```
    ByVal lpBuf As String,
    ByVal nSize As Integer) As Integer

Declare Function aad_ReadComm Lib "User"
    Alias "ReadComm"
    (ByVal nCid As Integer,
    ByVal lpBuf As String,
    ByVal nSize As Integer) As Integer

Declare Function aad_GetCommEventMask Lib "User"
    Alias "GetCommEventMask"
    (ByVal nCid As Integer,
    ByVal nEvtMask As Integer) As Integer

Declare Function SetCommEventMask Lib "User"
    Alias "SetCommEventMask"
    (ByVal nCid As Integer,
    ByVal nEvtMask As Integer) As Integer

Declare Function aad_SetCommState Lib "User"
    Alias "SetCommState"
    (lpDCB As CommStateDCB) As Integer

Declare Function aad_GetCommState Lib "User"
    Alias "GetCommState     (ByVal nCid As Integer,
    lpDCB As CommStateDCB) As Integer

'Functions for creating and reading the MSA_DIAL.INI file were added

Declare Function aad_GetPrivateProfileString Lib "Kernel"
    Alias "GetPrivateProfileString"
    (ByVal lpAppName As String,
    ByVal lpKeyName As String,
    ByVal lpDefault As String,
    ByVal lpReturnedString As String,
    ByVal nSize As Integer,
    ByVal lpFileName As String) As Integer

Declare Function aad_GetPrivateProfileInt Lib "Kernel"
    Alias "GetPrivateProfileInt"
    (ByVal lpAppName As String,
    ByVal lpKeyName As String,
    ByVal lpDefault As Integer,
    ByVal lpFileName As String) As Integer

Declare Function aad_WritePrivateProfileString Lib "Kernel"
    Alias "WritePrivateProfileString"
    (ByVal lpAppName As String,
    ByVal lpKeyName As String,
    ByVal lpString As String,
    ByVal lpFileName As String) As Integer
```

```
'COMM OPEN Error Constants
Const IE_BADID = -1       'Invalid or unsupported id
Const IE_OPEN = -2        'Device Already Open
Const IE_NOPEN = -3       'Device Not Open
Const IE_MEMORY = -4      'Unable to allocate queues
Const IE_DEFAULT = -5     'Error in default parameters
Const IE_HARDWARE = -10   'Hardware Not Present
Const IE_BYTESIZE = -11   'Illegal Byte Size
Const IE_BAUDRATE = -12   'Unsupported wBaudRate

'COMM Event Mask Flags
Const EV_RXCHAR = &H1     'Character received in buffer
Const EV_RXFLAG = &H2     'Event character received in buffer
Const EV_TXEMPTY = &H4    'Transmit buffer empty
Const EV_CTS = &H8        'Clear to send changed state
Const EV_DSR = &H10       'Dataset ready changed state
Const EV_RLSD = &H20      'Receive line signal detect changed state
Const EV_BREAK = &H40     'Break received
Const EV_ERR = &H80       'Line status error occurred
Const EV_RING = &H100     'Ring detected
Const EV_PERR = &H200     'Parity error occurred
Const EV_ALL = &H3FF      'Any event occurred

'Module-level COMM variables
Dim wCommHandle As Integer          'Handle to COM port
Dim wCommDeviceNum As Integer       'COM device
Dim strCommPortName As String       'COM1:, COM2:, etc.
Dim wCommPortNumber As Integer      '1...4
Dim wCommEventMask As Integer       'Event mask value
Dim dcbCommState As CommStateDCB    'Device control block
Dim wCommRBBuffer As Integer        'Size of receive buffer
Dim wCommTBBuffer As Integer        'Size of transmit buffer
Dim wCommReadInterval As Integer    'Read character timing

'Added module-level APIError and other general-purpose variables
Dim wAPIError As Integer            'Error number from the Comm functions
Dim strCrLf As String               'Newline pair
Dim wI, wJ, wK As Integer           'General purpose counters

'Modem parameter variables added
Dim frmModem As Form                'Modem form
Dim wSpeaker As Integer             'Speaker flag
Dim wAutoAnswer As Integer          'Auto Answer flag
Dim wPulseDial As Integer           'Pulse Dial flag
Dim wVolume As Integer              'Modem speaker volume setting
Dim strModemInit As String          'Modem initialization string
Dim strModemHangUp As String        'Modem hang-up string
Dim wUseLDPrefix As Integer         'Long distance prefix (usually 1-)
Dim strAreaCode As String           'Area code (three digits)
Dim strDialOut As String            'Dial-out prefix (e.g., 9-)

'Variables for MSA_DIAL.INI
```

```
Dim wDataLen As Integer            'Length of string from MSA_DIAL.INI
Dim strAppName As String           'Application name
Dim strKeyName As String           'Key name
Dim strRetString As String * 20    'Fixed length return string buffer
Dim wReturnInt As Integer          'Integer returned from MSA_DIAL.INI
Dim strFileName As String          'MSA_DIAL.INI for Autodialer
```

> **NOTE**
>
> The Windows API function prototype declarations shown in the preceding code example must appear on a single line in your module.

The *wAutoDial()* Entry Point Function

When you call the wAutoDial() function from your application, you need to pass the three parameters defined by the value OnClick event of the OK button of the Test Form, =wAutoDial([*Dial String*], [*Contact Name*], [*Company Name*]). The wAutoDial() entry point function calls all of the procedures used in the normal operation of AUTODIAL.MDA. The remaining functions contained in the AutoDial module respond to command buttons on the Access Autodialer forms or are called by other procedures.

```
Function wAutoDial (strDialString As String, strContact As String,
➥strCompany As String)
    'Purpose:   Main AutoDial procedure
    'Called by: RunCode AutoDial(Arguments) macro action or
    ➥=AutoDial(Arguments) as the On Push event of a command button or
    ➥the double-click event of a text box
    'Returns:   True if successful, False if not

    Dim wDialOK As Integer             'True if dialing test(s) met
    Dim strOrigString As String        'Copy of strDialString

    strOrigString = strDialString
    wCommHandle = -1                   'Initial invalid handle
    wCommDeviceNum = -1                'Initial invalid device
    strCrLf = Chr$(13) + Chr$(10)
    strAreaCode = ""

    strFileName = "MSA_DIAL.INI"       'Name of private .INI file

    If IsNull(strDialString) Or Len(strDialString) < 7 Then
        MsgBox "No Telephone Number Entered. Exiting Autodialer.", 8,
        ➥"Access Autodialer"
        wAutoDial = 0
        Exit Function
    End If
```

```
    Call Initialize                    'Set start-up values
    Call CheckIniFile(wDialOK)         'Test for previously-entered area
                                       ➥code
    wAutoDial = wDialOK                'Set return value of function
    If Not wDialOK Then
        Exit Function
    End If
    Call GetIniData                    'Read data from MSA_DIAL.INI
    Call ParseNumber(strDialString,_ wDialOK)    'Remove area code for
                                       ➥local calls
    If wDialOK Then                    'Proceed with dialing
        Call AutoDialForm(strDialString, strContact, strCompany)
        Call OpenCommPort
        Call SendInitString
        Call DialNumber(strDialString)
    Else
        MsgBox "Access Autodialer", 16, "Cannot Parse " & strOrigString
        ➥& "."
    End If
    wAutoDial = wDialOK
End Function
```

The *CheckIniFile* Procedure

The CheckIniFile procedure uses GetPrivateProfileString() to test if an area code has been entered by the user. If MSA_DIAL.INI does not exist or the area code is missing, the procedure opens the Modem Settings form to let you enter the area code. Clicking the Save Button of the Modem Settings form calls SaveModemData(), which uses WritePrivateProfileString() to create MSA_DIAL.INI, if necessary, and add your area code.

```
Sub CheckIniFile (wDialOK As Integer)
    'Purpose: Test for and create MSA_DIAL.INI if it doesn't exist
```

```
'Called by: AutoDial

wDialOK = True

If Val(strAreaCode) < 100 Then
    'Get your area code
    strAppName = "Telephone Data"
    strKeyName = "Your Area Code"
    strRetString = ""

    wDataLen = aad_GetPrivateProfileString(strAppName,
    ➥strKeyName, "", strRetString, 20, strFileName)

    If wDataLen > 0 Then
        strAreaCode = Trim$(strRetString)
    End If

    If Val(strAreaCode) < 100 Then
        wDialOK = OpenModemForm()
        MsgBox "Your area code is required.
Please enter your area code, click Save and then redial number.",
➥64, "Creating MSA_DIAL.INI"
        wDialOK = False
    End If
End If
End Sub
```

The *Initialize* Procedure

The Initialize procedure provides default values for the dcbCommState device control block structure. Initialize assumes that most users have assigned the modem to COM2 and that the modem is capable of sending at least 2400 bits per second. The usual 8/N/1 data bits, parity, and stop bits format is the default.

```
Sub Initialize ()
    'Purpose:' Provide comm and modem settings on startup
    'Called by: wAutoDial() function

    Dim wIndexTrans As Integer     'Index into transmit buffer
    Dim wIndexReceive As Integer    'Index into receive buffer

    wIndexTrans = 0
    wIndexReceive = 0

    'Default Port Settings
    strCommPortName = "COM2:"
    dcbCommState.wBaudRate = 2400
    dcbCommState.bByteSize = Chr$(8)
    dcbCommState.bParity = Chr$(0)
    dcbCommState.bStopBits = Chr$(0)
```

```
    'Default Line Settings
    wCommRBBuffer = 2048
    wCommTBBuffer = 2048
    dcbCommState.wRlsTimeOut = 0
    dcbCommState.wCtsTimeOut = 0
    dcbCommState.wDsrTimeOut = 0
    wCommEventMask = &H3FF
    wCommReadInterval = 500

    'Defaults for modem values
    wSpeaker = True
    wAutoAnswer = False
    wPulseDial = False
    wVolume = 2
    wUseLDPrefix = True
    strModemInit = "AT Z"
    strModemHangUp = "+++~~~ATH"

    'Read MSA_DIAL.INI values
End Sub
```

The *GetIniData* Procedure

GetIniData is a long procedure that reads MSA_DIAL.INI and translates the information in the [Comm Settings] section to data for the dcbCommState DCB. This procedure demonstrates the use of the **Chr$**() function to create byte values. This is necessary because Access Basic does not have a Byte data type. GetIniData also retrieves the values in the [Modem Settings] and [Telephone Data] sections of MSA_DIAL.INI.

```
Sub GetIniData ()
    'Purpose:   Read Comm and Modem settings from MSA_DIAL.INI
    'Called by: Initialize

    strFileName = "MSA_DIAL.INI"

    'Get Port Settings
    strAppName = "Comm Settings"

    'Get COM port number
    strKeyName = "COM Port Number"
    wReturnInt = aad_GetPrivateProfileInt(strAppName, strKeyName,
    ➡0, strFileName)

    If wReturnInt > 0 Then
        'Don't use if data not previously written to INI file
        wCommPortNumber = wReturnInt
        strCommPortName = "COM" + Trim$(Str$(wReturnInt)) + ":"

        'Get baud rate
```

```
    strKeyName = "Baud Rate"
    wReturnInt = aad_GetPrivateProfileInt(strAppName,
    ➡strKeyName, 0, strFileName)

    If wReturnInt > 0 Then
        dcbCommState.wBaudRate = wReturnInt

        'Get data bits
        strKeyName = "Data Bits"
        wReturnInt = aad_GetPrivateProfileInt(strAppName,
        ➡strKeyName, 0, strFileName)

        If wReturnInt > 0 Then
            dcbCommState.bByteSize = Chr$(wReturnInt)

            'Get parity
            strKeyName = "Parity"
            wReturnInt = _ aad_GetPrivateProfileString(strAppName,
            ➡strKeyName, "", strRetString, 20, strFileName)
            Select Case strRetString
                Case "None"
                    dcbCommState.bParity = Chr$(0)
                Case "Odd"
                    dcbCommState.bParity = Chr$(1)
                Case "Even"
                    dcbCommState.bParity = Chr$(2)
                Case Else
                    dcbCommState.bParity = Chr$(0)
            End Select

            'Get stop bits
            strKeyName = "Stop Bits"
            wReturnInt = _ aad_GetPrivateProfileString(strAppName,
            ➡strKeyName, "", strRetString, 20, strFileName)
            Select Case strRetString
                Case "1"
                    dcbCommState.bStopBits = Chr$(0)
                Case "1.5"
                    dcbCommState.bStopBits = Chr$(1)
                Case "2"
                    dcbCommState.bStopBits = Chr$(2)
                Case Else
                    dcbCommState.bStopBits = Chr$(0)
            End Select
        End If
    End If
End If

'Get modem settings (could be done in a loop, but this is more
➡readable)
strAppName = "Modem Settings"
```

```
'Get modem initialization string
strKeyName = "Init String"
strRetString = Space(20)
wDataLen = aad_GetPrivateProfileString(strAppName, strKeyName,
➥"", strRetString, 20, strFileName)
If wDataLen > 0 Then
    strModemInit = Trim$(strRetString)
End If


'Get modem hang-up string
strKeyName = "Hang-Up String"
strRetString = Space(20)
wDataLen = aad_GetPrivateProfileString(strAppName, strKeyName,
➥"", strRetString, 20, strFileName)
If wDataLen > 0 Then
    strModemHangUp = Trim$(strRetString)
End If


'Get telephone settings
strAppName = "Telephone Data"

'Get pulse dial data
strKeyName = "Use Pulse Dial"
strRetString = Space(20)
wDataLen = aad_GetPrivateProfileString(strAppName, strKeyName,
➥"", strRetString, 20, strFileName)
If strRetString = "Yes" Then
    wPulseDial = True
Else
    wPulseDial = False
End If


'Get your area code
strKeyName = "Your Area Code"
strRetString = Space(20)
wDataLen = aad_GetPrivateProfileString(strAppName, strKeyName,
➥"", strRetString, 20, strFileName)
If wDataLen > 0 Then
    strAreaCode = Trim$(strRetString)
End If


'Get modem dial-out string
strKeyName = "Dial-Out String"
strRetString = ""
wDataLen = aad_GetPrivateProfileString(strAppName, strKeyName,
➥"", strRetString, 20, strFileName)
If wDataLen > 0 Then
    strDialOut = Trim$(strRetString)
End If


'Get long-distance prefix used
strKeyName = "Use LD Prefix"
```

```
        strRetString = ""
        wDataLen = aad_GetPrivateProfileString(strAppName, strKeyName,
    ➡"", strRetString, 3, strFileName)
        If wDataLen > 0 Then
            If Trim$(strRetString) = "No" Then
                wUseLDPrefix = False
            Else
                wUseLDPrefix = True
            End If
        End If
End Sub
```

The *ParseNumber* Procedure

Parsing strings is one of the most common applications for Access Basic code. In the case of the `ParseNumber` procedure, the number to dial, `strDialString`, is tested to determine if it is a long-distance number (in one of several formats), an extended area number (prefixed with a 1- and no area code), or a local call. If the number includes your area code, the area code is stripped. This code makes extensive use of the `Instr()`, `Mid$()`, and `Left$()` functions to test and construct the final dialing string.

```
Sub ParseNumber (strDialString As String, wDialOK As Integer)
    'Purpose:   Parse various types of telephone numbers to area code
    ➡and number
    'Called by: wAutoDial

    Dim strArea As String
    Dim strNumb As String
    wDialOK = False

    If Left$(strDialString, 1) = "(" Then
        'Parse standard (AAA) PPP-NNNN
        strDialString = Mid$(strDialString, 2)
        If Mid$(strDialString, 4, 1) = ")" Then
            strArea = Left$(strDialString, 3)
            'Trim space between ) P
            strNumb = Trim$(Mid$(strDialString, 5))
        End If
    Else
        If InStr(strDialString, "-") > 0 Then
            'Hyphens are used instead of () as area code separators
            If Left$(strDialString, 2) = "1-" Then
                'Parse standard 1-AAA-PPP-NNNN or 1-PPP-NNNN
                If Len(strDialString) < 14 Then
                    'It's an extended area call
                    strArea = ""
                    strNumb = strDialString
                Else
                    'It's something else, delete the 1-
                    strDialString = Mid$(strDialString, 3)
```

```
                End If
            End If

            'Parse standard AAA-PPP-NNNN or 1-AAA-PPP-NNNN
            If Len(strDialString) > 10 Then
                strArea = Left$(strDialString, 4)
                strNumb = Mid$(strDialString, 5)
            End If
        Else

            'Parse numbers without hyphens 1AAAPPPNNNN, 1PPPNNN, etc.
            If Len(strDialString) > 7 Then
                'It's long distance or has a 1 prefix
                If Left$(strDialString, 1) = "1" Then
                    If Len(strDialString) > 8 Then
                        'It's long distance
                        strArea = Mid$(strDialString, 2, 3) & "-"
                        strNumb = Mid$(strDialString, 5, 3) & "-" &
                        ➥Mid$(strDialString, 8)
                    Else
                        'Extended area dialing
                        strNumb = Mid$(strDialString, 2, 3) & "-" &
                        ➥Mid$(strDialString, 5)
                        strNumb = "1-" & strNumb
                        strArea = ""
                    End If
                Else
                    'It's long distance without a 1 prefix, AAAPPPNNNN
                    strArea = Left$(strDialString, 3) & "-"
                    strNumb = Mid$(strDialString, 4, 3) & "-" &
                    ➥Mid$(strDialString, 7)
                End If
            Else
                'Local call
                strArea = ""
                strNumb = Left$(strDialString, 3) & "-" &
                ➥Mid$(strDialString, 4)
            End If
        End If
    End If

    'Reconstruct the string, deleting the area code if the same as
    ➥yours
    If Val(strArea) = Val(strAreaCode) Then
        strArea = ""
    End If
    If Len(strArea) > 0 And wUseLDPrefix Then
        strArea = "1-" & strArea
    End If
    strDialString = strArea & strNumb
    wDialOK = True
End Sub
```

The *AutoDialForm* Procedure

The `AutoDialForm` procedure opens the AutoDial form and sets the values of the text boxes from the values processed by the `wAutoDial()` function and the `ParseNumber` procedure.

```
Sub AutoDialForm (strDialString As String, strContact As String,
➥strCompany As String)
    'Purpose:   Opens the AutoDial Form
    'Called by: AutoDial function

    DoCmd OpenForm "AutoDial Form"

    'Set the values of the text boxes
    Forms![Autodial Form]![Dial Number] = strDialString
    Forms![Autodial Form]![Dial Contact] = strContact
    Forms![Autodial Form]![Dial Company] = strCompany
End Sub
```

The *OpenCommPort* Procedure

The `OpenCommPort` procedure uses the OpenComm() Windows API function to open a COM port and assign a Windows handle to the opened port, if the function is successful. **Call** `WinAPIErr("Open")` is an example of the use of a literal as the argument of a function.

```
Sub OpenCommPort ()
    'Purpose:   Open the comm port specified by strCommPortName
    'Called by: AutoDial()

    'Get a Windows handle to the CommPort
    wCommHandle = aad_OpenComm(strCommPortName, wCommRBBuffer,
    ➥wCommTBBuffer)
    wAPIError = wCommHandle

    If wCommHandle = -2 Then
        'The port is already open, close it and re-open it
        Call WinAPIErr("Open")
        wAPIError = aad_CloseComm(0)
        wCommHandle = aad_OpenComm(strCommPortName, wCommRBBuffer,
        ➥wCommTBBuffer)
    End If

    If wCommHandle < 0 Then
        'There's a problem with opening the port
        Call WinAPIErr("Open")
    Else
        'It's OK, set the event mask
        wCommDeviceNum = Val(Mid$(strCommPortName, 4, 1))
        wAPIError = SetCommEventMask(wCommHandle, wCommEventMask)
```

```
        If wAPIError < 0 Then
            Call WinAPIErr("Set Event Mask")
        End If

        'Send the device control block data
        dcbCommState.bId = Chr$(wCommHandle)
        wAPIError = aad_SetCommState(dcbCommState)
        If wAPIError < 0 Then
            Call WinAPIErr("Set Comm State")
        End If
    End If
End Sub
```

The *WinAPIErr* Procedure

The purpose of the WinAPIErr procedure is solely to display an error message that indicates what the problem is.

```
Sub WinAPIErr (APIErrType As String)
    'Purpose:   Display message box with error
    'Called by: OpenCommPort (WinComm API calls if error occurs)

    Dim strError As String

     'Translate the IE_* constants to English
    Select Case wAPIError
        Case Is = IE_BADID
            strError = "Invalid or unsupported ID"
        Case Is = IE_OPEN
            strError = "Device already open"
        Case Is = IE_NOPEN
            strError = "Device Not Open"
        Case Is = IE_MEMORY
            strError = "Unable to allocate queues"
        Case Is = IE_DEFAULT
            strError = "Error in default parameters"
        Case Is = IE_HARDWARE
            strError = "Hardware not present"
        Case Is = IE_BYTESIZE
            strError = "Illegal number of data bits"
        Case Is = IE_BAUDRATE
            strError = "Unsupported baud rate"
    End Select

    'Create the error message string
    strError = "Error (" & Str$(wAPIError) & ") " & strError
    strError = strError & strCrLf & "Comm Port: " & strCommPortName
    strError = strError & strCrLf & "Baud Rate:" &
➡Str$(dcbCommState.wBaudRate)
    strError = strError & strCrLf & "Byte Size:" &
➡Str$(Asc(dcbCommState.bByteSize))
```

```
strError = strError & strCrLf & "Parity:     " &
➡Str$(Asc(dcbCommState.bParity))
strError = strError & strCrLf & "Stop Bits:" &
➡Str$(Asc(dcbCommState.bStopBits))
strError = strError & strCrLf & strCrLf &
➡"Click Settings and change Comm parameters."

    MsgBox strError, 16, "Comm API " & APIErrType & " Error"
End Sub
```

The *SendInitString* Procedure

Some modems need an initialization string to set them up after being used for other communication purposes. If no initialization string is provided, WriteCommPort() sends the default AT Z instruction needed to reset the modem to its factory settings. After a short wait created by the **DoEvents** loop, SendInitString waits for the modem to respond with an OK message, indicating that the initialization string has been accepted by the modem.

```
Sub SendInitString ()
    'Purpose:  Send modem initialization string,
    ➡if one exists, otherwise reset
    'Called by: wAutoDial()

    Dim strInit As String        'Initialization string
    Dim strSend As String        'String sent to modem
    Dim strResponse As String    'Response from modem

    If IsNull(strModemInit) Then
        'Send AT Z to reset modem
        strSend = "AT Z" & Chr$(13)
        Call WriteCommPort(strSend)
    Else
        'Parse init string at spaces between commands
        strInit = Trim$(strModemInit)
        If InStr(strInit, "AT") > 0 Then
            strInit = Trim$(Mid$(strInit, InStr(strInit, "AT") + 2))
        End If
        strInit = strInit & " "
        Do While InStr(strInit, " ") > 0
            strSend = Left(strInit, InStr(strInit, " ") - 1)
            If Len(strSend) > 0 Then
                strSend = "AT " & strSend & Chr$(13)
                Call WriteCommPort(strSend)

                'Delay loop for modem to respond
                For wI = 1 To 20
                    strResponse = ""
                    strResponse = strReadCommPort(30)
        'Read up to 30 characters
```

```
                    DoEvents
                    If InStr(strResponse, "OK") > 0 Then  'OK _received
                        Forms![Autodial Form]![Action Box] = _
                        ➥Left$(strSend, Len(strSend) - 1) & "=OK"
                        Exit For
                    End If
                Next wI
            End If
            If Len(strInit) > InStr(strInit, " ") Then
                strInit = Mid$(strInit, InStr(strInit, " ") + 1)
            Else
                Exit Do
            End If
        Loop
    End If
End Sub
```

The *strReadCommPort()* Function

The strReadCommPort function returns a string that consists of the content of the
COM port's receive buffer. A more traditional form of this function might be
wReadCommPort (strReadData **As String**), which returns the length of the string
(wReadAmount). This would enable you to test whether data is available with an **If**
wReadCommPort (strReadData) **Then** instruction.

```
Function strReadCommPort (wReadAmount As Integer) As String
    'Purpose:   Read data from modem to buffer (checks for OK)
    'Called by: SendInitString
    'Returns:   Data read from COM port

    Dim wEventMask As Integer
    Dim wFound As Integer
    Dim strBuffer As String

    If wReadAmount < 1 Then
        strReadCommPort = ""
        Exit Function
    End If

    wEventMask = wCommEventMask
    wAPIError = aad_GetCommEventMask(wCommHandle, wEventMask)

    If wAPIError And EV_RXCHAR Then
        strBuffer = Space$(wReadAmount)
        wAPIError = aad_ReadComm(wCommHandle, strBuffer,
        ➥Len(strBuffer))

        If wAPIError < 0 Then
            MsgBox " aad_ReadComm API function failed (Error: " &
            ➥Str$(wAPIError) & ")", 3
```

```
                strBuffer = ""
            Else
                strBuffer = Left$(strBuffer, wAPIError)

                'Expand CR to CR/LF for "Text" box display
                wFound = 1
                Do
                    wFound = InStr(wFound, strBuffer, Chr$(13))
                    If wFound Then
                        strBuffer = Left$(strBuffer, wFound) & Chr$(10) &
                        ➥Right$(strBuffer, Len(strBuffer) - wFound)
                        wFound = wFound + 1
                    End If
                Loop While wFound
            End If
        End If

        If (wAPIError And EV_RING) And (wCommEventMask And EV_RING) Then
            MsgBox "Incoming RING detected", 8, "Access Autodialer"
            Beep
        End If

        strReadCommPort = strBuffer
End Function
```

The *DialNumber* Procedure

All of the preceding code leads up to the `DialNumber` procedure. `DialNumber` sends
the Hayes ATDT command, followed by the number to dial, to the modem with
the `WriteCommPort()` procedure.

```
Sub DialNumber (strDialString As String)
    'Purpose:   Dial the telephone number
    'Called by: AutoDial function

    Dim strSend As String

    'Create send string
    If wPulseDial Then
        strSend = "ATDP"
    Else
        strSend = "ATDT"
    End If
    If Not IsNull(strDialOut) Then
        strSend = strSend & strDialOut
    End If
    strSend = strSend & strDialString & Chr$(13)

    Call WriteCommPort(strSend)

    'Short Delay to display messages
```

```
    For wI = 1 To 10
        DoEvents
    Next wI
    If wIsOpen("Autodial Form") Then
        'Delay loop may still be running
        Forms![Autodial Form]![Action Box] = "Lift Receiver and Click
        ➥OK"
    End If
End Sub
```

The *WriteCommPort* Procedure

The WriteCommPort procedure uses the WriteComm() API function to send characters to the transmit buffer of the COM port. If you change WriteCommPort to a function, you can return the value of wAPIError to wWriteCommPort() for use by the calling procedure.

```
Sub WriteCommPort (strSend As String)
    'Purpose:   Write data to comm port
    'Called by: All procedures that write to comm port

    wAPIError = aad_WriteComm(wCommHandle, strSend, Len(strSend))
    If wAPIError < 0 Then
        Call WinAPIErr("Write")
    End If
End Sub
```

The *HangUpModem()* Function

The HangUpModem() function is used to send the required message to the modem to hang up the line (go on hook). If the telephone receiver is off the cradle when HangUpModem() is executed, the line stays off hook. On hook and off hook are holdovers from the days when telephones were wall-mounted and the receiver was suspended by a two-pronged hook when the telephone was not in use. HangUpModem() does not return a value; functions that do not return values are called void functions in C.

```
Function HangUpModem ()
    'Purpose:   Send HangUp string and close all
    'Called by: OnClick event of OK button of AutoDial form
    'Returns:   Nil

    Dim strSend As String

    If IsNull("strModemHangUp") Then
        strSend = "+++~~~ATH" + Chr$(13)
    Else
        strSend = strModemHangUp + Chr$(13)
```

```
        End If
        Call WriteCommPort(strSend)

        'Close the comm port
        Call CloseCommPort
        wCommHandle = -1
        wCommDeviceNum = -1

        'Close the form, if loaded
        If wIsOpen("Autodial Form") Then
            DoCmd Close A_FORM, "Autodial Form"
        End If
End Function
```

The *OpenCommForm()* Function

The OpenCommForm() function is executed by the OnClick event of the Settings button of the AutoDial form to close the Autodial form and display the COM Port Settings form. If the COM port is open, you have the opportunity to close the port by executing HangUpModem(). You can change COM port and other communications settings by clicking the option buttons of the form. It is not necessary to close the AutoDial form before opening the COM Port Settings form, but doing so eliminates the necessity of manually closing the AutoDial form.

```
Function OpenCommForm ()
    'Purpose:   Open Comm Settings form for changes
    'Called by: OnClick event of Settings button of AutoDial form
    'Returns:   Nil

    Dim wHangUp As Integer
    Dim frmComm As Form

    If wCommHandle > -1 Then
        wHangUp = MsgBox(Left$(strCommPortName, 4) + " is open.
        ➥Close it?", 35, "Access Autodialer")
        If wHangUp = 2 Then
            Exit Function
        End If
        If wHangUp = 6 Then
            wHangUp = HangUpModem()
            wCommHandle = -1
        End If
    End If

    DoCmd Close A_FORM, "AutoDial Form"
    DoCmd OpenForm "COM Port Settings"
    Set frmComm = Forms![COM Port Settings]

    'Set COM port
    wCommPortNumber = Val(Mid$(strCommPortName, 4, 1))
```

```
frmComm![Comm Port] = wCommPortNumber

'Set Baud Rate
frmComm![Baud Rate] = dcbCommState.wBaudRate

'Set Data Bits
frmComm![Data Bits] = Asc(dcbCommState.bByteSize)

'Set Parity
frmComm![Parity] = Asc(dcbCommState.bParity)

'Set Stop Bits
frmComm![Stop Bits] = Asc(dcbCommState.bStopBits)

End Function
```

The *OpenModemForm()* Function

The OpenModemForm() function is called by CheckIniFile, if settings are missing, or from the OnClick event of the COM Port Settings form. The function operates in a manner similar to the OpenCommForm() function. OpenModemForm() updates the values of text boxes and the option frame with current values read from MSA_DIAL.INI.

```
Function OpenModemForm ()
    'Purpose:   Open the Modem Settings form for data entry
    'Called by: CheckIniFile
    '           OnClick event of Comm Settings form
    'Returns:   Nil

    Dim wSaveData As Integer

    If wIsOpen("COM Port Settings") Then
        wSaveData = SaveCommData()
        DoCmd Close A_FORM, "COM Port Settings"
    End If
    DoCmd OpenForm "Modem Settings"

    Set frmModem = Forms![Modem Settings]

    If Not IsNull(strModemInit) Then
        'Check strModemInit string for prior settings
        If InStr(strModemInit, "M1") > 0 Or InStr(strModemInit, "M2")
        ➡Then
            wSpeaker = True
        End If
        If InStr(strModemInit, "M0") > 0 Then
            wSpeaker = False
        End If
        If InStr(strModemInit, "L") > 0 Then
            wVolume = Val(Mid$(strModemInit, InStr(strModemInit, "L")
            ➡+ 1, 1))
```

```
        End If
        If InStr(strModemInit, "S0=0") > 0 Then
            wAutoAnswer = False
        Else
            If InStr(strModemInit, "S0=") > 0 Then
                wAutoAnswer = True
            End If
        End If
    End If

    'Set text box values
    frmModem![Speaker On] = wSpeaker
    frmModem![Auto Answer] = wAutoAnswer
    frmModem![Pulse Dial] = wPulseDial
    frmModem![Set Volume] = wVolume
    frmModem![Init String] = strModemInit
    frmModem![HangUp String] = strModemHangUp
    frmModem![Area Code] = strAreaCode
    frmModem![DialOut String] = strDialOut
    frmModem![LD Prefix] = wUseLDPrefix
End Function
```

The *SaveCommData()* Function

The SaveCommData() function uses the WritePrivateProfileString() API function to create or change entries in the [Comm Settings] section of MSA_DIAL.INI. This function could be structured as a **For...Next** loop to minimize repeated typing of the long API function, but at the expense of readability of the code.

```
Function SaveCommData ()
    'Purpose:   Write Comm Data to INI file
    'Called by: OnClick event of OK button of COM Settings form
    '           OpenModemForm procedure (if COM Settings form is
    '           ➡loaded)
    'Returns:   Nil

    Dim strValue As String
    Dim wWriteOK As Integer
    Dim frmComm As Form
    Set frmComm = Forms![COM Port Settings]
    strAppName = "Comm Settings"

    'Save COM port number
    strKeyName = "COM Port Number"
    strValue = Trim$(Str$(frmComm![Comm Port]))
    wWriteOK = aad_WritePrivateProfileString(strAppName, strKeyName,
    ➡strValue, strFileName)

    'Save baud rate
    strKeyName = "Baud Rate"
    strValue = Trim$(Str$(frmComm![Baud Rate]))      'Remove the leading
    ➡space
```

```
wWriteOK = aad_WritePrivateProfileString(strAppName, strKeyName,
➥strValue, strFileName)

'Save data bits
strKeyName = "Data Bits"
strValue = Chr$(frmComm![Data Bits] + 48)
wWriteOK = aad_WritePrivateProfileString(strAppName, strKeyName,
➥strValue, strFileName)

'Save parity
strKeyName = "Parity"
Select Case frmComm![Parity]
    Case 0
        strValue = "None"
    Case 1
        strValue = "Odd"
    Case 2
        strValue = "Even"
End Select
wWriteOK = aad_WritePrivateProfileString(strAppName, strKeyName,
➥strValue, strFileName)

'Save stop bits
strKeyName = "Stop Bits"
Select Case frmComm![Stop Bits]
    Case 0
        strValue = "1"
    Case 1
        strValue = "1.5"
    Case 2
        strValue = "2"
End Select
wWriteOK = aad_WritePrivateProfileString(strAppName, strKeyName,
➥strValue, strFileName)
'Close the form
DoCmd Close A_FORM, "COM Port Settings"
End Function
```

The *SaveModemData()* Function

The SaveModemData() function is similar in structure to the preceding SaveCommData() function. A **For...Next** implementation of the call to WritePrivateProfileString() is equally applicable to this function.

```
Function SaveModemData ()
    'Purpose:   Save the modem data and close the form
    'Called by: OnClick event of Save button of Modem Settings form
    'Returns:   Nil

    Dim wWriteOK As Integer
    Dim strPulseDialer As String
```

```
    Dim strLDPrefix As String

    'Set the data from the form text box values
    wWriteOK = SetModemData()

    'Write modem settings
    strAppName = "Modem Settings"

    'Save modem initialization string
    strKeyName = "strInit String"
    wWriteOK = aad_WritePrivateProfileString(strAppName, strKeyName,
    ➥strModemInit, strFileName)

    'Save modem hang-up string (required)
    strKeyName = "Hang-Up String"
    wWriteOK = aad_WritePrivateProfileString(strAppName, strKeyName,
    ➥strModemHangUp, strFileName)

    'Save modem dial-out string
    strKeyName = "Dial-Out String"
    wWriteOK = aad_WritePrivateProfileString(strAppName, strKeyName,
    ➥strDialOut, strFileName)

    'Write telephone data
    strAppName = "Telephone Data"

    'Save pulse dial data
    strKeyName = "Use Pulse Dial"
    If wPulseDial Then
        strPulseDialer = "Yes"
    Else
        strPulseDialer = "No"
    End If
    wWriteOK = aad_WritePrivateProfileString(strAppName, strKeyName,
    ➥strPulseDialer, strFileName)

    'Save area code
    strKeyName = "Your Area Code"
    wWriteOK = aad_WritePrivateProfileString(strAppName, strKeyName,
    ➥strAreaCode, strFileName)

    'Save if long-distance prefix used
    strKeyName = "Use LD Prefix"
    If wUseLDPrefix = False Then
        strLDPrefix = "No"
    Else
        strLDPrefix = "Yes"
    End If
    wWriteOK = aad_WritePrivateProfileString(strAppName, strKeyName,
    ➥strLDPrefix, strFileName)
End Function
```

The *SetModemData()* Function

The SetModemData() function sets the modem settings to the values you establish in the option frames of the Modem Settings form and then closes the form. The data is saved to the [Modem Settings] and [Telephone Data] sections of MSA_DIAL.INI only when the SaveModemData procedure is executed.

```
Function SetModemData ()
     'Purpose:    Set modem variables with form text box values
     'Called by: On Push event of OK button of Modem Settings Form
     '           SaveModemData procedure
     'Returns:    Nil

     Set frmModem = Forms![Modem Settings]

     'Modem initialization string (optional)
     If Not IsNull(frmModem![Init String]) Then
         strModemInit = frmModem![Init String]
     End If

     'Modem hang-up string (required)
     If IsNull(frmModem![HangUp String]) Then
         MsgBox "Hang-Up string is required"
         Exit Function
     Else
         strModemHangUp = frmModem![HangUp String]
     End If

     'Your area code (required)
     If IsNull(frmModem![Area Code]) Then
         MsgBox "Area Code is required"
         Exit Function
     Else
         strAreaCode = frmModem![Area Code]
     End If

     'Dial-out string (optional)
     If Not IsNull(frmModem![DialOut String]) Then
         strDialOut = frmModem![DialOut String]
     End If

     'Use long-distance prefix
     If frmModem![LD Prefix] Then
         wUseLDPrefix = True
     Else
         wUseLDPrefix = False
     End If

     'Close the form
     DoCmd Close A_FORM, "Modem Settings"
End Function
```

The *SetModemInit()* Function

The SetModemInit() function ordinarily is called by the Use button of the Modem Settings form. If you change the modem initialization string in the InitString text box, this procedure is called by the text box's AfterUpdate event.

```
Function SetModemInit ()
    'Purpose:   Create modem initialization string, if necessary
    'Called by: Use button on frmModem form
    '           AfterUpdate event of init string settings
    'Returns:   Nil

    Dim wNewInit As Integer
    Dim frmModemSet As Form
    Set frmModemSet = Forms![Modem Settings]

    If frmModem![Speaker On] <> wSpeaker Then
        wNewInit = True
    End If
    If frmModem![Speaker On] Then
        wSpeaker = True
    Else
        wSpeaker = False
    End If
    frmModem![Set Volume].Visible = wSpeaker

    If frmModem![Auto Answer] <> wAutoAnswer Then
        wNewInit = True
    End If
    If frmModem![Auto Answer] Then
        wAutoAnswer = True
    Else
        wAutoAnswer = False
    End If

    If frmModem![Pulse Dial] <> wPulseDial Then
        wNewInit = True
    End If
    If frmModem![Pulse Dial] Then
        wPulseDial = True
    Else
        wPulseDial = False
    End If

    If frmModem![Set Volume] <> wVolume Then
        wNewInit = True
    End If
    wVolume = frmModem![Set Volume]

    If wNewInit Then
        strModemInit = "AT "
```

```
    If wSpeaker Then
        strModemInit = strModemInit & "M1 L" &
        ➡Trim$(Str$(wVolume)) & " "
    Else
        strModemInit = strModemInit & "M0 L0 "
    End If
    If wAutoAnswer Then
        strModemInit = strModemInit & "S0=2"
    Else
        strModemInit = strModemInit & "S0=0"
    End If
    frmModem![Init String] = strModemInit
    End If
End Function
```

The *CloseComForm()* Function

CloseComForm() and the following CloseModemForm() are housekeeping functions.
These functions could be replaced by **DoCmd Close** statements in the calling function
or procedure.

```
Function CloseComForm ()
    'Purpose:   Close the COM Settings Form
    'Called by: OnClick event of Cancel Button of COM Settings form
    'Returns:   Nil

    DoCmd Close A_FORM, "COM Port Settings"
End Function
```

The *CloseModemForm()* Function

```
Function CloseModemForm ()
    'Purpose:   Close the frmModem Settings form
    'Called by: OnClick event of Cancel button of frmModem Settings
    ➡form
    'Returns:   Nil

    DoCmd Close A_FORM, "Modem Settings"
End Function
```

The *CloseCommPort* Procedure

The CloseCommPort procedure uses the CloseComm() API function to close the COM
port opened by the OpenComm() API function.

```
Sub CloseCommPort ()
    'Purpose:   Close the open COM port
    'Called by: HangUpModem function
    'Returns:   Nil
```

```
    wAPIError = aad_CloseComm(wCommHandle)

    If wAPIError < 0 Then
        Call WinAPIErr("Close")
    End If

    wCommHandle = -1
    wCommDeviceNum = -1
End Sub
```

The *wIsOpen()* Function

The wIsOpen() function is a derivative of the IsLoaded() function of the Introduction to Programming module of the Northwind Traders sample data base. wIsOpen() tests to determine if a form whose name is passed as the argument is open (returns **True**) or closed (returns **False**).

```
Function wIsOpen (strTestForm As String)
    'Purpose:   Same as IsLoaded in NWIND.MDB, test if form is loaded
    'Called by: Any routine that needs it
    'Returns:   True if form is open, False if not

    wIsOpen = False
    For wI = 0 To Forms.Count - 1
        If Forms(wI).FormName = strTestForm Then
            wIsOpen = True
            Exit Function 'Quit function once form has been found.
        End If
    Next wI
End Function
```

Testing the Access Autodialer as a Database

Open AUTODIAL.MDA as a database, not as an attached library. Use the test form to debug the code thoroughly before you attach AUTODIAL.MDA. The first time you click the OK button of the Autodialer Test Form, the application detects that you have not entered your area code and requests that you do so. Test all of the command buttons and verify that the changes you make to values of the control objects in the COM Port Settings and Modem Settings forms are reflected in the [Modem Settings], [Telephone Data] and [Comm Settings] sections of MSACCESS.INI.

If the default COM2/COM4 interrupt (IRQ3) is occupied by another device, you receive an interrupt conflict message from Windows, followed by a message box similar to that shown in Figure 23.6. If this error message occurs, change the COM Port to COM1 or COM3.

FIGURE 23.6.

*The error message
that results from an
interrupt conflict on
the COM2 port.*

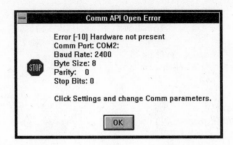

Attaching the Access Autodialer to Your Application

To attach the Access Autodialer library to your database application, add the line
`autodial.mda=ro` to the `[Libraries]` section of MSACCESS.INI. Enter
`=wAutoDial([DialString],[Contact],[Company])` as the method for the `OnClick` event
of an AutoDial command button or as the method for the `OnDblClick` event of a text
box on your form. Substitute the Control Name properties of the fields or control
objects that contain the `DialString`, `Contact`, and `Company` values.

24

Using Access Wizard Functions

The primary purpose of Access wizard functions is to create database objects with Access Basic code. Microsoft Corporation refers to this process as "creating objects programmatically." You can design applications that generate their own forms and reports with the four basic wizard functions: `CreateForm()`, `Create Report()`, `CreateControl()`, and `CreateReportControl()`. These functions let you design applications that generate their own forms and reports based on user-generated queries. WZFRMRPT.MDA employs the wizard functions, together with several other related functions and properties, to create elemental forms, reports, and graphs. Although this chapter concentrates on using wizard functions to create forms, the process described here is equally applicable to creating reports.

Using wizard functions is not limited to writing your own custom wizards, nor do wizards necessarily need to use these functions. As mentioned in Chapter 9, "Designing Decision-Support Forms for Management," this book defines a wizard as any form that enables users to create their own database objects. If you are using the ADT, you need a query wizard, because users of MSARN200.EXE cannot enter query-design mode (or any other design mode) from menu choices. Even if query-design mode were available to users of runtime access applications, most users would become hopelessly lost when attempting to design their own crosstab queries. Thus, this chapter also includes an example of how to create a crosstab query wizard, despite the fact that query wizards do not require use of the Access wizard functions.

Creating a Crosstab Query Wizard

Crosstab queries are a powerful feature of Access, but it takes an Access power user to design a crosstab query that returns a meaningful (or any) result. Crosstab queries form the basis of or appear in the majority of decision-support applications. Thus, you often need to provide users of your applications with the capability to create their own custom crosstab queries. The sections that follow describe how to create a general-purpose crosstab query wizard that you can include in your application databases or that you can attach to Access as a library.

Defining the User Interface for a Crosstab Query

You can use crosstab queries to return result sets from data contained in Access or attached tables. If you are working with Access or client-server tables, you may need to create multiple joins to obtain the crosstab data values. Data you obtain from mainframe and minicomputer databases, such as IBM's DB2, are often in the form of a single table (a flat file) created from a rollup of the source data, so joins are not required. Crosstab queries require, at the minimum, the following elements:

- *Data source(s)* that underlie the query and supply the value(s) to the ANSI SQL FROM statement. If more than one data source is involved in the query, joins are specified by the ANSI SQL-89 [LEFT¦RIGHT] INNER JOIN statement. You can use the WHERE clause to specify the joins, but using INNER JOINs creates a more easily readable SQL statement, reserving the WHERE clause for optional record-selection criteria. Using JOIN has the additional benefit of showing the join line when you examine your SQL statements in query-design mode.

- *Row Headings* that are usually derived from groups of records with a common attribute value determined by the ANSI SQL GROUP BY clause.

- *Column Headings* that group underlying records by another attribute, such as a range of dates, determined by the Access SQL PIVOT statement.

- *Values* created with one of the SQL aggregate functions, such as Sum( ), set by the Access SQL TRANSFORM statement.

First, you need to provide users with the facility to choose the type of crosstab to run; the crosstab type determines the data source(s) and the row headings of the query. Next, users need to be able to change the range of dates or other values that are used as column headings. Combo boxes are usually the most appropriate control for these user choices, because combo boxes consume the least amount of display "real estate." You set the LimitToList property of the combo boxes to Yes so that only the valid choices that you supply are available to the user. Your application uses the selections from the combo boxes to create the SQL statement that returns the desired result. Option groups or check boxes also are useful for choosing between alternate presentation formats.

Creating Complex SQL Statements in Access Basic

The Field and Query Wizard forms described in Chapter 9, "Designing Decision-Support Forms for Management," create simple SQL statements based on a single data source. If you have examined the SQL statement required to create a crosstab query, it is clear that the SQL syntax to create crosstab queries, especially if several data sources are involved, is not simple. Figure 24.1 shows a typical SQL statement created by the crosstab query wizard that is described in the following sections. The data sources for this example query are tables attached from the Northwind Traders sample database.

FIGURE 24.1.

A typical SQL statement for creating a multisource crosstab query.

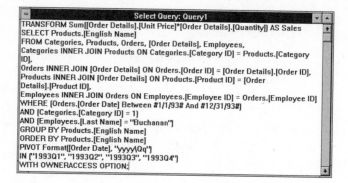

```
Select Query: Query1
TRANSFORM Sum([Order Details].[Unit Price]*[Order Details].[Quantity]] AS Sales
SELECT Products.[English Name]
FROM Categories, Products, Orders, [Order Details], Employees,
Categories INNER JOIN Products ON Categories.[Category ID] = Products.[Category
ID],
Orders INNER JOIN [Order Details] ON Orders.[Order ID] = [Order Details].[Order ID],
Products INNER JOIN [Order Details] ON Products.[Product ID] = [Order
Details].[Product ID],
Employees INNER JOIN Orders ON Employees.[Employee ID] = Orders.[Employee ID]
WHERE [Orders.[Order Date] Between #1/1/93# And #12/31/93#]
AND [Categories.[Category ID] = 1]
AND [Employees.[Last Name] = "Buchanan"]
GROUP BY Products.[English Name]
ORDER BY Products.[English Name]
PIVOT Format([Order Date], "yyyy\Qq")
IN ["1993Q1", "1993Q2", "1993Q3", "1993Q4"]
WITH OWNERACCESS OPTION;
```

Creating a crosstab query wizard is not as formidable a project as it would appear from the SQL statement shown in Figure 24.1. Fortunately, you usually do not need combo boxes or to write Access Basic code to create every element of the SQL statement for crosstab queries. You can "crib" much of the text of the SQL statement by cutting and pasting from Access's SQL dialog box, then use Access Basic to concatenate the pieces into a valid SQL statement. Following are some guidelines for each of the elements of SQL statements required to create crosstab queries:

■ The TRANSFORM statement is constant for a single class of queries. In the example of Figure 24.1, gross order values are derived by multiplying Quantity by Unit Price. You could add a pair of option buttons to choose between gross and net order values. If net order value is desired, the required SQL statement is TRANSFORM Sum([Order Details].[Unit Price]*(1 - [Order Details].[Discount])*[Order Details].[Quantity]) AS Sales. If you have multiple classes of queries, you need to provide the value of the TRANSFORM statement from another data source, such as a record in a table or an entry in a private .INI file. The AS clause provides an arbitrary column name; the column name does not appear in the query-result set.

■ The SELECT statement varies with the type of query. You provide the SELECT statement from a choice made by the user in a two-column combo or list box. The first column contains the description of the type of query, and the second column contains the value for the SELECT statement. If the SELECT statement consists of an expression, you should provide an alias for the query column name with the AS clause.

■ List all the tables that are used by any of the query types in the FROM statement, separated by commas. Access disregards tables that are not involved in a particular query type.

■ Add all the INNER JOINs between the tables in the FROM statement that are needed by all query types within your query class. Your query may take slightly longer to run than if only the INNER JOINs for the particular query type were specified. If you want row headings for all products, even if no values are returned, specify LEFT JOINs rather than INNER JOINs.

■ The WHERE clause adds record-selection criteria from choices the user makes in combo or list boxes. You can specify criteria based on fields that do not participate directly in the crosstab query-result set, provided that the field on which each criterion is based is included in the JOIN network.

■ The GROUP BY and ORDER BY clauses specify the content and sort-order of the row headings, respectively. Ordinarily, these values are the same as that of the SELECT statement, less the AS clause (if the SELECT field is aliased).

■ The PIVOT statement creates the column headings. The columns of most crosstab queries represent a range of dates, so you need to specify the date format that creates a common value for a specific week, month, quarter, or year. In the example of Figure 24.1, the Format([Order Date], "yy-q") statement creates column headings 93-1, 93-2, and so forth for the year 1993. This type of formatting is necessary to obtain columns in proper sequence when data for more than one year is desired. If you specify values from a field of a table (such as Employees, to obtain sales of product by employee) as the column headings, the column headings appear in alphabetical sequence.

NOTE

If you have a time-series crosstab, you need a minimum of three combo boxes: one each for query type, starting date, and ending date. Add one additional combo box for each additional criterion you need.

Designing a Crosstab Query Wizard

The crosstab wizard described in this chapter provides six different types of queries that display total order values. The objects required for the example crosstab wizard are as follows:

■ frmCrosstabQuery, the form used to create the query, shown in Figure 24.2.

■ tblReportTypes, a table with the names of the six report types and the value of SELECT statement for each type. The content of the table is shown in Figure 24.5.

■ tblReportMonths and tblReportQuarters that supply values to the combo boxes for the beginning and ending dates of the query. The primary key of both tables is the Start Date field. The four date combo boxes are filled from a table, rather than from fixed values, because new months and quarters need to be added to the combo boxes as the data becomes available.

■ Create Crosstab Query, the module that contains the Access Basic code to create and display the crosstab query in datasheet view.

> **NOTE**
>
> Users are likely to run the majority of their queries on the latest available information. Thus, you might want to set the value of the `RecordSource` property of the four date combo boxes to SQL queries with a sort in descending order so that most recent dates appear first in the list.

Each of these objects is included in the AB_EXAMP.MDB database on the accompanying diskette. Import each of these objects into NWIND.MDB or, preferably, attach the Categories, Employees, Order Details, Orders, and Products tables to AB_EXAMP.MDB to run the example application.

> **NOTE**
>
> AB_EXAMP.MDB includes attachments to the tables of NWIND.MDB required to make the crosstab wizard operable. The attachments assume that NWIND.MDB is in your C:\ACCESS\SAMPAPPS directory. If NWIND.MDB is located elsewhere, use the Attachment Manager add-in and refresh the attachments.

FIGURE 24.2.

The design of a typical user interface to create a crosstab query.

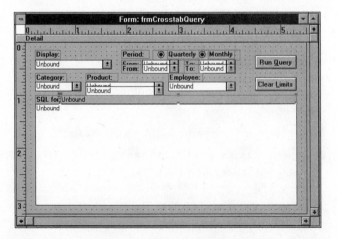

The frmCrosstabQuery form provides combo boxes to select the type of query (Display), beginning (From) and ending (To) dates for the values in the query-result set, and it also provides three combo boxes that enable you to add criteria to limit the values or the number of records displayed. The Period option group enables you to choose between quarterly and monthly data, so two sets of From and To combo boxes are necessary; one set is filled by tblReportQuarters and the other by tblReportMonths. Two Product combo boxes are provided: one lists all of the products (if no selection is made from the Category combo box, the list is filled from the Products table) and the other lists only those products in the selected category (filled by a query against the Products table). The SQL text boxes display the name of the query, derived from user choices, and the SQL statement generated by the choices. Buttons to run the query and clear choices in the combo boxes complete the form design at this point. The form design of Figure 24.2 in run mode, with a typical user-generated SQL statement, is shown in Figure 24.3.

FIGURE 24.3.

The demonstration version of the query wizard in run mode.

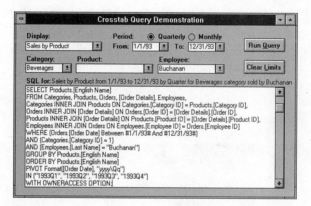

Writing Access Basic Code for the Crosstab Query Wizard

The Declarations section of the Create Crosstab Query module consists of declarations of module-level variables to eliminate the necessity of passing the values of the variables as arguments of functions. With few exceptions, the functions in this module are called by events triggered by control objects.

```
Option Compare Database        'Use database order for string
                               ➥comparisons

Option Explicit

'General purpose variables
Dim wRetVal As Integer         'Return value of functions
Dim strCrLf As String          'Newline pair
```

```
'SQL variables for a crosstab query
Dim strSQLTransform As String    'TRANSFORM statement (Values
                                 ➥expression)
Dim StrSQLSelect As String       'SELECT statement
Dim strSQLFrom As String         'FROM statement
Dim strSQLJoin As String         'INNER JOIN statement (standard)
Dim strSQLWhere As String        'WHERE clause (criteria)
Dim strSQLGroupBy As String      'GROUP BY clause (Row Headings)
Dim strSQLOrderBy As String      'ORDER BY clause (Sort sequence)
Dim strSQLPivot As String        'PIVOT clause (Column Headings)
Dim strSQLEnd As String          'WITH OWNERACCESS OPTION;
Dim strSQL As String             'SQL statement to be executed
Dim strQueryName As String       'Name of query (generated)

'Objects
Dim frmCTQ As Form               'The Crosstab Query Demonstration
                                 ➥form

'Flags
Dim fProdByCat As Integer        'True if products limited to
                                 ➥category
```

The following two sections provide listings of the functions that create the crosstab query SQL statement and determine the visibility of control objects on the form. All the functions in the Create Crosstab Query module are aliased with ctq_ to prevent conflicts with similarly named functions that you might create in specific applications. This lets you safely attach a library containing these functions to Access.

NOTE

The code of the Create Crosstab Query module includes the declaration of four variables, strTotalsCol, strTotalsRow, strTotalsColHdr, and strTotalsRowHdr, that are used in conjunction with creating crossfooted subforms, the subject of sections later in this chapter. The code examples in the following sections omit reference to these variables for the purpose of clarity of presentation.

The Primary Functions of the Create Crosstab Query Module

The functions that do the basic work of creating the SQL statement for the crosstab query appear in the following listings. The ctq_InitSQL() function assigns fixed values for those elements of the SQL statement that are constant for the query class and the SQL reserved word prefixes of the elements that are derived from the values of combo boxes. If you have a variety of crosstab query classes, consider replacing the code in this function with code that reads a private .INI file or reads data from a table that contains the values that apply to all classes of queries.

Listing 24.1. Access Basic code for the `ctq_InitSQL()` function.

```
Function ctq_InitSQL ()
    'Purpose:   Assign initial and default values of components of SQL
    ➥statement
    'Called by: ctq_CreateSQL
    'Returns:   Nil

    'Note: You could obtain these values from a private .INI file or a
    ➥table
    strSQLTransform = "TRANSFORM Sum([Order Details].[Unit Price]*
    ➥[Order Details].[Quantity]) AS Sales "
    strSQLSelect = "SELECT "
    strSQLFrom = "FROM Categories, Products, Orders, [Order
    ➥Details], Employees, "
    strSQLJoin = "Categories INNER JOIN Products ON
    ➥Categories.[Category ID] = Products.[Category ID], " & strCrLf
    strSQLJoin = strSQLJoin & "Orders INNER JOIN [Order Details] ON
    ➥Orders.[Order ID] = [Order Details].[Order ID], " & strCrLf
    strSQLJoin = strSQLJoin & "Products INNER JOIN [Order Details] ON
    ➥Products.[Product ID] = [Order Details].[Product ID], " &
    ➥strCrLf
    strSQLJoin = strSQLJoin & "Employees INNER JOIN Orders ON
    ➥Employees.[Employee ID] = Orders.[Employee ID] "
    strSQLWhere = "WHERE (Orders.[Order Date] Between "
    strSQLGroupBy = "GROUP BY "
    strSQLOrderBy = "ORDER BY "
    strSQLPivot = "PIVOT Format([Order Date], "
    strSQLEnd = "WITH OWNERACCESS OPTION;"
End Function
```

The `ctq_CreateSQL()` function completes the SQL statement and supplies the query name, based on values derived from selections made in the combo boxes. The `OnUpdate` events of each combo box call the `ctq_CreateSQL()` either through the `ctq_UpdateSQL` function or through functions dedicated to the specific control. Code is included in Listing 24.2 to remove the SQL AS clause, if it exists, when you employ the value of the SQL SELECT statement as the value for the GROUP BY and ORDER BY clauses.

Listing 24.2. Access Basic code for the `ctq_CreateSQL()` function.

```
Function ctq_CreateSQL ()
    'Purpose:   Create the SQL statement and the query name
    'Called by: ctq_UpdateSQL, ctq_RunQuery and other functions
    'Returns:   Nil

    Dim strSelectField As String
```

continues

Listing 24.2. continued

```
Dim strFormat As String
Dim strNameCriteria As String

Set frmCTQ = Forms(strFormName)
strCrLf = Chr$(13) & Chr$(10)

'Get the SELECT statement from the Display combo box
strSelectField = frmCTQ!cboDisplay.Column(1)

'Reinitialize the SQL statements
wRetVal = ctq_InitSQL()

'Create the SELECT statement
StrSQLSelect = StrSQLSelect & strSelectField & " "

'Create the WHERE statement
If frmCTQ!grpPeriod = 2 Then
    strSQLWhere = strSQLWhere & "#" & frmCTQ!cboFromMonth & "#
    ➥And "
    strSQLWhere = strSQLWhere & "#" & frmCTQ!cboToMonth & "#) "
    strFormat = "yy-mm"
Else
    strSQLWhere = strSQLWhere & "#" & frmCTQ!cboFromQuarter &
    ➥"# And "
    strSQLWhere = strSQLWhere & "#" & frmCTQ!cboToQuarter & "#) "
    strFormat = "yy-q"
End If

'Remove any alias from the SELECT statement
If InStr(UCase$(strSelectField), " AS ") > 0 Then
    'Remove alias from strSelect field for use in ORDER BY and
    ➥GROUP BY
    strSelectField = Left$(strSelectField,
    ➥InStr(UCase$(strSelectField), " AS ") - 1)
End If

'Add category or product restriction to the WHERE clause
If IsNull(frmCTQ!cboProduct) Then
    If Not IsNull(frmCTQ!cboCategory) Then
        'Add a restriction by category using default Column(0) of
        ➥combo box
        strSQLWhere = strSQLWhere & strCrLf & "AND
        ➥(Categories.[Category ID] = " & frmCTQ!cboCategory  & ") "

        strNameCriteria = DLookup("[Category Name]", "Categories",
➥"[Category ID] = Forms!frmCrosstabQuery!cboCategory") & " category "
    End If
Else
    'Add a restriction by product using fifth column of combo box
    strSQLWhere = strSQLWhere & strCrLf & "AND (Products.[English
```

```
➥Name] = " & Chr$(34) & frmCTQ!cboProduct.Column(4) &
➥Chr$(34) & ")"

    strNameCriteria = DLookup("[Category Name]", "Categories",
    ➥"[Category ID] = Forms!frmCrosstabQuery!cboCategory") & " "
End If

'Add employee restriction to the WHERE clause
If Not IsNull(frmCTQ!cboEmployee) Then
    'Add a restriction by employee using second column of combo
    ➥box
    strSQLWhere = strSQLWhere & strCrLf & "AND (Employees.[Last
    ➥Name] = " & Chr$(34) & frmCTQ!cboEmployee.Column(1) &
    ➥Chr$(34) & ")"
    strNameCriteria = strNameCriteria & "sold by " &
    ➥frmCTQ!cboEmployee.Column(1)
End If

'Create the GROUP BY and ORDER BY clauses from the SELECT
➥value
strSQLGroupBy = strSQLGroupBy & strSelectField
strSQLOrderBy = strSQLOrderBy & strSelectField

'Create the PIVOT statement from the quarter/month format
strSQLPivot = strSQLPivot & Chr$(34) & strFormat & Chr$(34)
➥& ") "

'Create the SQL statement from its components
'Note: Add newline pairs between statements to improve read
➥ability
strSQL = strSQLTransform & strCrLf & StrSQLSelect & strCrLf
➥& strSQLFrom & strCrLf & strSQLJoin & strCrLf
strSQL = strSQL & strSQLWhere & strCrLf & strSQLGroupBy
➥& strCrLf & strSQLOrderBy & strCrLf
strSQL = strSQL & strSQLPivot & strCrLf & strSQLEnd

'Display the SQL statement in the textbox
Forms(strFormName)!txtSQL = strSQL

'Create the query name
strQueryName = frmCTQ!cboDisplay & " from "
If frmCTQ!grpPeriod = 2 Then
    strQueryName = strQueryName & frmCTQ!cboFromMonth
    ➥& " to " & frmCTQ!cboToMonth
    strQueryName = strQueryName & " by month "
Else
    strQueryName = strQueryName & frmCTQ!cboFromQuarter
    ➥& " to " & frmCTQ!cboToQuarter
    strQueryName = strQueryName & " by quarter "
End If
strQueryName = strQueryName & "for " & strNameCriteria
```

continues

Listing 24.2. continued

```
      'Display the query name in the text box
      frmCTQ!txtQueryName = strQueryName
End Function
```

> **NOTE**
>
> The value of the global variable strFormName, is assigned by the line
> strFormName = "frmCrosstabQuery" in the Form_Load event handler of the
> frmCrosstabQuery form. Assigning the value of strFormName by this method
> enables the functions contained in the Create Crosstab Query module to be
> used by each of the four forms described in this chapter. The **DLookup**()
> function requires the explicit Forms![*FormName*]![*ControlName*] syntax, so
> the **DLookup**() function in the code for the ctq_CreateSQL() function is
> specified in a **Select Case...End Select** structure in the code on the
> accompanying diskette. A simplified form of the **DLookup**() function appears
> in Listing 24.2 for clarity.

The dtq_wRunQuery() function is provided primarily for testing purposes. The code
that you run when you click the Run Query button depends on the final design of
your application. In most cases, you do not want to display the query result in datasheet
view. Creating new subforms that correspond to the query you select is the subject of
a section later in this chapter.

Listing 24.3. Access Basic code for the ctq_wRunQuery() function.

```
Function ctq_wRunQuery ()
    'Purpose:   Runs the query based on the SQL statement generated
    '           Displays the result of the query
    '           This is the initial version for test purposes
    'Called by: OnClick event of Run Query button
    'Returns:   True if successful, False on failure

    'Test for required entries made
    If ctq_wTestEntries() Then
        DoCmd Hourglass True

        'Update the SQL statement and give it a chance to display
        wRetVal = ctq_CreateSQL()
        DoEvents

        'Create the necessary object pointers
```

```
    Dim dbCurrent As Database
    Dim qdfQuery As QueryDef
    Set dbCurrent = DBEngine(0)(0)

    'Delete the existing QueryDef, if it exists
    On Error Resume Next
    dbCurrent.DeleteQueryDef ("qryCrosstab")
    On Error GoTo QueryError

    'Create the query def
    Set qdfQuery = dbCurrent.CreateQueryDef("qryCrosstab",
    ➥strSQL)
    'Display the resulting query (temporary for testing)
    DoCmd OpenQuery "qryCrosstab"
    qdfQuery.Close
    dbCurrent.Close
    DoCmd Hourglass False
    End If
    Exit Function

QueryError:
    MsgBox Error$, 16, "Query Error"
    Exit Function
End Function
```

NOTE

The code for the ctq_RunQuery() function in the Create Crosstab Query module includes three arguments passed to ctq_RunQuery(). These arguments determine whether other functions, described later in this chapter, are executed. Only the code that is necessary to create the query is shown in the preceding listing.

Housekeeping Functions

The functions whose listings follow are classified as *housekeeping functions*. This is because they control visibility of superimposed controls on the form and test for required user-supplied inputs before creating the SQL statement. Most housekeeping functions can be implemented as macros. Using macros, however, precludes making a library of your application and adds to the documentation burden. If your application requires Access Basic code, the best practice is to use code in place of macros so that a text file created from your code includes all the event handlers for the application.

> **TIP**
>
> Don't forget to include the time necessary to implement housekeeping in your proposal or budget. The number of lines of code contained in housekeeping functions often exceeds the "working" code in a module, and the time required to design and write housekeeping code can easily exceed the time necessary to design the form and implement the working code. With Access 2.0, the housekeeping-to-working code ratio in the average module ranges from about 1.2 to 1.5.

The ctq_ClearLimits() function replaces the values in the Category (cboCategory), Product (cboProduct and cboAllProducts), and Employee (cboEmployee) combo boxes with **Null**. Alternately, you can provide each combo box with an optional **Null** value that the user can add as a choice. Clearing the combo boxes by setting their values to **Null** is the simpler approach. The ctq_ClearLimits() function is attached to the OnClick event of the cmdClearLimits button.

Listing 24.4. Access Basic code for the ctq_ClearLimits() function.

```
Function ctq_ClearLimits ()
    'Purpose:   Remove previously-entered limiting combo box values
    'Called by: OnClick event of Clear Limits button
    'Returns:   Nil

    Set frmCTQ = Forms(strFormName)

    'Clear the combo boxes and reset the visibility of the products
    ➡combos
    frmCTQ!cboCategory = Null
    frmCTQ!cboProduct = Null
    frmCTQ!cboAllProducts = Null
    frmCTQ!cboEmployee = Null
    frmCTQ!cboProduct.Visible = False
    frmCTQ!cboAllProducts.Visible = True
    frmCTQ!cmdClearLimits.Enabled = False
    DoCmd GoToControl "cboCategory"

    'Update the SQL text box
    wRetVal = ctq_UpdateSQL()
End Function
```

The BeforeUpdate event of the Category combo box (cboCategory) triggers the ctq_ShowProduct() function that determines which of the two superimposed Product combo boxes, cboAllProducts (the default) or cboProduct, is visible. The cboProduct combo box appears when the user chooses a category from the cboCategory combo box. You need to requery the cboProduct combo box each time it appears, because the category for the query that supplies the value of cboProduct's RowSource property may change.

Listing 24.5. Access Basic code for the `ctq_ShowProduct()` function.

```
Function ctq_ShowProduct ()
    'Purpose:   Display product list limited to category if
    ➥category chosen
    '              Otherwise, show all of the products in the list box
    'Called by: BeforeUpdate event of cboCategory
    'Returns:   Nil

    Set frmCTQ = Forms(strFormName)

    If IsNull(frmCTQ!cboCategory) Then
        frmCTQ!cboProduct.Visible = False
        frmCTQ!cboAllProducts.Visible = True
        fProdByCat = False
    Else
        frmCTQ!cboProduct.Visible = True
        frmCTQ!cboAllProducts.Visible = False
        fProdByCat = True
        'Reset entries in combo box list
        DoCmd Requery "cboProduct"
    End If

    'Update the SQL statement
    wRetVal = ctq_UpdateSQL()
End Function
```

The `ctq_TestPeriod` function is triggered by the BeforeUpdate event of the Period option group (grpPeriod). The `ctq_TestPeriod` function determines whether the monthly (cboToMonth and cboFromMonth) or quarterly (cboToQuarter and cboFromQuarter) combo boxes are visible from the OptionValue property of the Quarterly (1) and Monthly (2) option buttons.

Listing 24.6. Access Basic code for the `ctq_TestPeriod()` function.

```
Function ctq_TestPeriod ()
    'Purpose:   Choose which period combos to display based on
    ➥period chosen
    'Called by: BeforeUpdate event of grpPeriod
    'Returns:   Nil
```

continues

Listing 24.6. continued

```
    Set frmCTQ = Forms(strFormName)

    If frmCTQ!grpPeriod = 2 Then
        'Monthly periods
        frmCTQ!cboFromQuarter.Visible = False
        frmCTQ!cboToQuarter.Visible = False
        frmCTQ!cboFromMonth.Visible = True
        frmCTQ!cboToMonth.Visible = True
    Else
        'Quarterly periods (default)
        frmCTQ!cboFromQuarter.Visible = True
        frmCTQ!cboToQuarter.Visible = True
        frmCTQ!cboFromMonth.Visible = False
        frmCTQ!cboToMonth.Visible = False
    End If

    'Update the SQL statement
    wRetVal = ctq_UpdateSQL()
End Function
```

A change in any value of a combo box or option group on the form triggers the ctq_UpdateSQL() function. This test is necessary, because the user may delete a required combo box value by using the Delete or Backspace keys. If a required value is missing, the function clears the SQL text box. Although this function is similar to the ctq_wTestEntries() function (which follows), this function does not return messages. Therefore, the user can make an entry in the Display combo box (cboDisplay) when the form opens without encountering error messages that the remaining combo boxes with required entries are empty.

Listing 24.7. Access Basic code for the `ctq_UpdateSQL()` function.

```
Function ctq_UpdateSQL()
    'Purpose:   Check to determine if required combo boxes are
                ➥filled
    '           Display SQL if filled, blank SQL if not
    'Called by: On update event of combo boxes on form
    '           Functions of other controls' BeforeUpdate event
    'Returns:   Nil

    Set frmCTQ = Forms(strFormName)
    If IsNull(frmCTQ!cboDisplay) Then
        GoTo ClearSQL
    End If
    If frmCTQ!grpPeriod = 2 Then
        If IsNull(frmCTQ!cboFromMonth) Then
```

```
            GoTo ClearSQL
        End If
        If IsNull(frmCTQ!cboToMonth) Then
            GoTo ClearSQL
        End If
    Else
        If IsNull(frmCTQ!cboFromQuarter) Then
            GoTo ClearSQL
        End If
        If IsNull(frmCTQ!cboToQuarter) Then
            GoTo ClearSQL
        End If
    End If
    wRetVal = ctq_CreateSQL()
    Exit Function

ClearSQL:
    frmCTQ!txtSQL = ""
    frmCTQ!txtQueryName = ""
    Exit Function
End Function
```

The ctq_wTestEntries() function checks to determine whether required combo-box values are present before executing a query. Message boxes indicate the necessity for the missing value. The function also tests to verify that the To date is not less than the From date. The message box approach, instead of enabling or disabling the Run Query button, was chosen here so that the user can determine what's missing and correct the problem. The message approach is more appropriate when there are many required combo boxes to be filled before executing the query.

Listing 24.8. Access Basic code for the ctq_wTestEntries() function.

```
Function ctq_wTestEntries () As Integer
    'Purpose:   Test the required entries and return messages
    'Called by: ctq_CreateSQL
    'Returns:   True if all entries made, False otherwise

    Dim strMsg As String
    Set frmCTQ = Forms(strFormName)

    'Test for Display selection
    If IsNull(frmCTQ!cboDisplay) Then
        strMsg = "You must select a query to display"
        DoCmd GoToControl "cboDisplay"
        GoTo EntryError
    End If
```

continues

Listing 24.8. continued

```
    'Test for beginning and ending period selection
    If frmCTQ!grpPeriod = 2 Then
        'Quarterly data
        If IsNull(frmCTQ!cboFromMonth) Then
            strMsg = "You must select a starting month"
            DoCmd GoToControl "cboFromMonth"
            GoTo EntryError
        End If
        If IsNull(frmCTQ!cboToMonth) Then
            strMsg = "You must select an ending month"
            DoCmd GoToControl "cboToMonth"
            GoTo EntryError
        End If
        If DateValue(frmCTQ!cboFromMonth) >
        ➥DateValue(frmCTQ!cboToMonth) Then
            strMsg = "To month must be the same as or after From
            ➥month"
            DoCmd GoToControl "cboToMonth"
            GoTo EntryError
        End If
    Else
        If IsNull(frmCTQ!cboFromQuarter) Then
            strMsg = "You must select a starting quarter"
            DoCmd GoToControl "cboFromQuarter"
            GoTo EntryError
        End If
        If IsNull(frmCTQ!cboToQuarter) Then
            strMsg = "You must select an ending quarter"
            DoCmd GoToControl "cboFromQuarter"
            GoTo EntryError
        End If
        If DateValue(frmCTQ!cboFromQuarter) >
        ➥DateValue(frmCTQ!cboToQuarter) Then
            strMsg = "To quarter must be the same as or after From
            ➥quarter"
            DoCmd GoToControl "cboToQuarter"
            GoTo EntryError
        End If
    End If

    ctq_wTestEntries = True
    Exit Function

EntryError:
    'Display message box with name of missing entry
    strMsg = strMsg & " from the combo box."
    MsgBox strMsg, 32, "Query Entry Error"
    ctq_wTestEntries = False
    Exit Function
End Function
```

Testing Your SQL Statements

Tracking minor syntactical errors in SQL statements can be tedious. This is because you need to use the error messages returned by the Access query engine, not those returned by **Error$**, to determine the cause of the problem. To test your statement and proposed corrections, select the SQL statement in the SQL text box and copy it to the Clipboard. Then open a new query in design mode without adding a table, and click the SQL button or choose **SQL** from the **V**iew menu. Delete the default SELECT DISTINCTROW; line in the SQL window, and then paste the statement that you need to diagnose into the SQL text box. Click the OK button to check for syntax errors. Change the statement as necessary to eliminate the problems, then alter your code to revise the statement generation. Figure 24.4 shows the SQL statement of Figure 24.3, shown earlier in the chapter, in Access's query-design mode.

FIGURE 24.4.

The Access query design that results from the SQL statement shown in Figure 24.3.

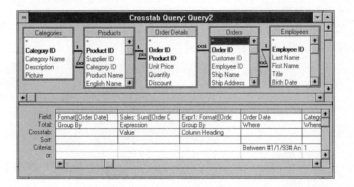

Figure 24.5 illustrates the query-result set from the SQL statement of Figure 24.3 and the query design of Figure 24.4. When creating crosstab query wizards, you need to have a sufficient amount of data available to test your SQL statement adequately. You may find it necessary to synthesize data to test a sufficient range of dates in order to validate your query design and the code that creates its SQL statement.

FIGURE 24.5.

The result set of the query design of Figure 24.4 and the SQL statement of Figure 24.3.

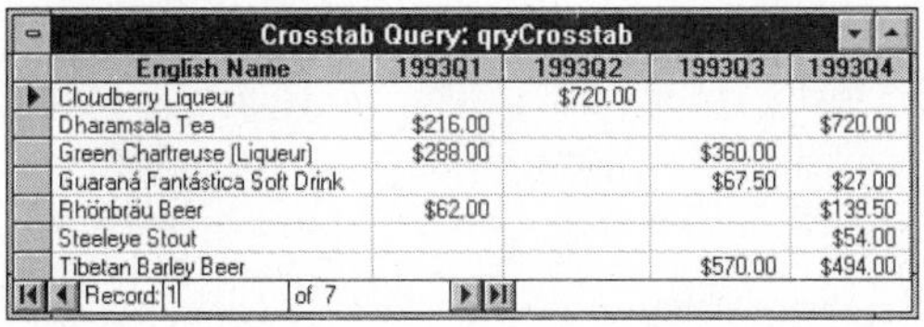

Using the Access SQL *IN* Operator to Create Fixed Column Headings and Graph Labels

Fixed column headings assure that all columns appear—whether values for the columns are available or not. Missing columns confound the users and result in spurious bug reports. Fixed column headings also greatly improve the performance of crosstab queries, especially when complex joins are involved. Fixed column headings also enable you to use more traditional formats, such as three-letter month abbreviations ("mmm yy"), without scrambling the sequence of the months by Access's automatic sorting of crosstab column names.

When you add fixed column headings to a crosstab query in Access's query-design mode, each of the headings appears as an argument of what appears to be Access's **In**() operator following the PIVOT statement. An SQL dialog box with an SQL statement with the IN() syntax used to specify fixed column headings is shown highlighted in Figure 24.6.

FIGURE 24.6.

*The Access In()
operator used to
create the SQL IN
clause.*

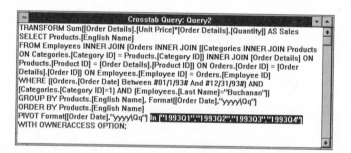

```
Crosstab Query: Query2
TRANSFORM Sum([Order Details].[Unit Price]*[Order Details].[Quantity]) AS Sales
SELECT Products.[English Name]
FROM Employees INNER JOIN [Orders INNER JOIN [[Categories INNER JOIN Products
ON Categories.[Category ID] = Products.[Category ID]] INNER JOIN [Order Details] ON
Products.[Product ID] = [Order Details].[Product ID]] ON Orders.[Order ID] = [Order
Details].[Order ID]] ON Employees.[Employee ID] = Orders.[Employee ID]
WHERE [[Orders.[Order Date] Between #01/1/93# And #12/31/93#] AND
[Categories.[Category ID]=1] AND [Employees.[Last Name]="Buchanan"]]
GROUP BY Products.[English Name], Format([Order Date],"yyyy\Qq")
ORDER BY Products.[English Name]
PIVOT Format([Order Date],"yyyy\Qq") In ("1993Q1","1993Q2","1993Q3","1993Q4")
WITH OWNERACCESS OPTION;
```

> **NOTE**
>
> In the grammar of SQL, the IN( ) operator is called the in-predicate. Other SQL predicates include the between-predicate ([NOT] BETWEEN *expression1* AND *expression2*), the like-predicate (LIKE *"literal"*), and the null-predicate (IS [NOT] NULL). The full syntax of the In( ) operator when used in SQL is the expression [NOT] IN (*expression-list*), where *expression-list* consists of a minimum of one expression, with additional expressions separated by commas. When Access operators are used as predicates in SQL, the operator name is capitalized to indicate SQL keyword status.

To create the Access SQL IN predicate, you need to use each of the values in the date tables, tblReportMonths or tblReportQuarters, within the range of dates specified by the From and To combo boxes. The code for the ctq_strFixedHeads function in

Listing 24.9 opens a **Recordset** object from the table appropriate to the date interval selected, and creates the column headings in the same format (strFormat) as that used in the PIVOT statement to define the columns.

TIP

You can create custom formats for date/time values in query-design mode that include literals with expressions such as Date:Format(DateField, yyyy"Q"q) to return data values formatted as 1993Q2. In Access Basic and SQL statements, however, format strings must be enclosed within quotation marks. To create the equivalent format statement in Access Basic, precede the quoted literal with a backslash, as in **Format$**(*DateField*, "yyyy\Qq"). If you apply a double set of double quotation marks (**Format**(*DateField*, "yyyy""Q""q"), in the **Format**( ) function of an SQL statement, Access removes the double quotation marks and substitutes the backslash.

Listing 24.9. Access Basic code for the `ctq_strFixedHeads()` function.

```
Function ctq_strFixedHeads (strFormat As String) As String
    'Purpose:   Create IN clause for fixed column headers
    'Called by: ctq_CreateSQL
    'Returns:   SQL IN predicate clause

    Dim strSQLIn As String
    Dim varLastDate As Variant

    'Create pointers to objects
    Dim dbCurrent As Database
    Dim tblDates As Table
    Dim cboFromDate As Control
    Dim cboToDate As Control

    Set frmCTQ = Forms(strFormName)
    Set dbCurrent = DBEngine(0)(0)

    'Set the objects for the time period selected
    If frmCTQ!grpPeriod = 2 Then
        'Monthly periods, format "mmm yy"
        Set tblDates = dbCurrent.OpenTable("tblReportMonths")
        Set cboFromDate = frmCTQ!cboFromMonth
        Set cboToDate = frmCTQ!cboToMonth
    Else
        'Quarterly periods, format "yyyy\Qq"
        Set tblDates = dbCurrent.OpenTable("tblReportQuarters")
        Set cboFromDate = frmCTQ!cboFromQuarter
```

continues

Listing 24.9. continued

```
        Set cboToDate = frmCTQ!cboToQuarter
    End If

    'Both tables have the Start Date field as their primary key
    tblDates.Index = "PrimaryKey"

    'Get the value of the last record in the table
    tblDates.MoveLast
    varLastDate = tblDates.[Start Date]

    'Set the record pointer to the starting date
    tblDates.Seek "=", cboFromDate

    If tblDates.NoMatch Then
        'This error should not occur
        Exit Function
    End If

    'Create the IN predicate
    strSQLIn = "IN ("
    Do While tblDates![Start Date] < DateValue(cboToDate)
        'Note: DateValue() is required because combo boxes return
        ➥type 8 variants
        strSQLIn = strSQLIn & Chr$(34) & Format$(tblDates.[Start
        ➥Date], strFormat) & Chr$(34) & ", "
        If tblDates.[Start Date] = varLastDate Then
            'Note: Match test used because EOF does not go True
                    ➥when
            '       the last record is reached ("No current record"
                    ➥error)
            'Note: Add a DoEvents method here when testing
            Exit Do
        End If
        tblDates.MoveNext
    Loop

    'Remove the trailing comma and space, add closing parenthesis
    strSQLIn = Left$(strSQLIn, Len(strSQLIn) - 2) & ")"

    'Close the database objects
    tblDates.Close
    dbCurrent.Close

    ctq_strFixedHeads = strSQLIn
End Function
```

You need to make some minor changes in the code of the ctq_CreateSQL function in order to implement the fixed column headings. Change the format for monthly columns from "yy-m" to "mmm yy" and for quarterly columns from "yy-q" to "yyyy q". Alter the line in the `ctq_CreateSQL` function that creates the value of the `PIVOT` statement (`strSQLPivot`) as follows:

```
'Create the PIVOT and IN statements from the quarter/month format
strSQLPivot = strSQLPivot & Chr$(34) & strFormat & Chr$(34) & ") " &
➥strCrLf & ctq_strFixedHeads(strFormat) & " "
```

> **NOTE**
>
> The newline pairs (`strCrLf`, `Chr$(13) & Chr$(10)`) added to the SQL statement are used to format the statement for better readability. Most SQL interpreters and compilers interpret spaces and newline pairs as white space. White space is disregarded when the SQL statement is processed by Access's query engine.

When you run the query with the `IN` predicate added, the SQL statement for the Sales By Category query type for the year 1993 by month appears, as shown in Figure 24.7. The query-result set for the SQL statement of Figure 24.7 is shown in Figure 24.8.

FIGURE 24.7.

The SQL statement for a crosstab query with fixed column headings.

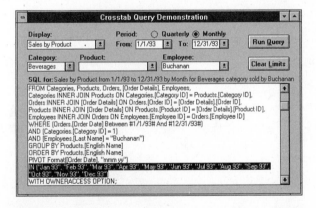

FIGURE 24.8.

Part of the query-result set from the SQL statement of Figure 24.7.

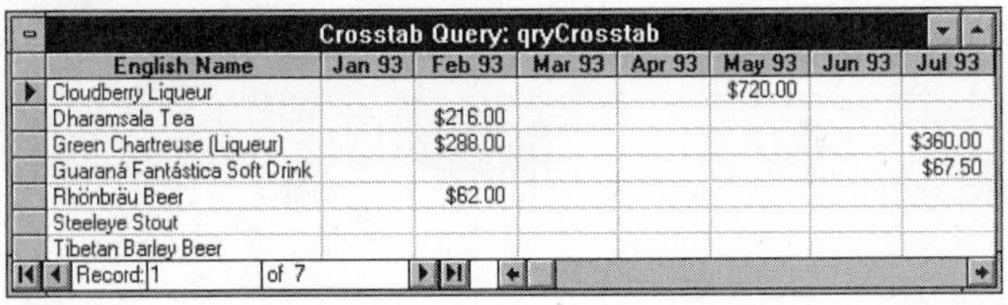

Creating a Graph from a User-Defined Query

Access 2.0's Microsoft Graph 5.0 OLE 2.0 mini-server, described in Chapter 17, "Charting Data with Microsoft Graph 5.0," makes creating graphs derived from user-definable queries a simple process. Access 1.x, which used Microsoft Graph 3.0 (an OLE 1.0 server applet), required extensive programming, using the **DeleteControl()** and **CreateControl()** wizard functions, and an undocumented property (the Data property of an object frame) and a DLL function (aliased as BiffMunge()), to display fully-formatted graphs. (The first edition of this book devoted 16 pages to the subject of creating formatted graphs.)

Microsoft Graph 5.0 (abbreviated as MSGraph5 in this book) retains the formatting property values you apply to the graph when you add the graph to your form and lets you manipulate the appearance of the graph to suit the query-result set using OLE Automation. As an example, if your query-result set has only a single row, you don't need to display a legend. Eliminating the appearance of the Legend object by setting its Height and Width property values to 0 lets you widen the graph and makes the display of the graphical data more readable, especially when you display a year's data by month. You also can alter the color and format of the legend and the chart axes, but you can't change the values of legend items or axis labels. (As mentioned in Chapter 17, the Legend and TickLabels objects do not have a writable Values property; these values are obtained by MSGraph5 from the RowSource property of the object frame.) Figure 24.9 shows one type of line graph you can create from user-defined queries.

FIGURE 24.9.

A graph created from a user-defined crosstab query.

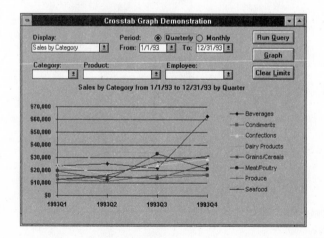

> **NOTE**
>
> If any of the following steps are unfamiliar, review Chapter 17, "Charting Data with Microsoft Graph 5.0." It provides a thorough grounding in the creation of unbound graphs and charts with MSGraph5.

The fastest method of adding a graph to the crosstab query form is to use Access 2.0's graph tool and the Graph Wizard that the tool activates. The following process adds a graph (uofGraph) superimposed on the SQL textbox (txtSQL) of the frmCrosstabQuery form:

1. Open frmCrosstabQuery in Design View, click the graph tool, and size the graph to the same dimensions as the SQL text box.

2. When you release the left mouse button, the first dialog box of the Graph Wizard appears. Click the Queries button and select qryCrosstab, the **QueryDef** object created by frmCrosstabQuery, in the list box. (See Figure 24.10.) Click the Next button.

3. Click the line graph command button and the Rows option button to create a multiple line graph with the DataSeries in rows. (See Figure 24.11.)

FIGURE 24.10.

Selecting qryCrosstab as the RowSource *property of the graph.*

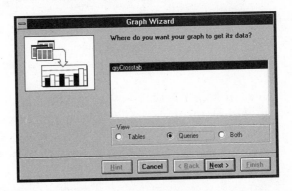

4. Click the Finish button to add the graph to your form.

5. Set the value of the Enabled property of the graph to Yes, so you can edit the graph in run mode, and type uofGraph as the value of the Name property of the unbound object frame that contains the Graph object. Set the BackColor property value to light gray.

6. Change to Form View to run the query and create a sample graph. Double-click the surface of uofGraph to activate the graph for editing. You can adjust the relative size of the graph and the legend by clicking the graph or legend and dragging the sizing handles. (See Figure 24.12.)

FIGURE 24.11.

Selecting the type of graph to create and the orientation of the DataSeries property.

FIGURE 24.12.

Sizing the graph's legend.

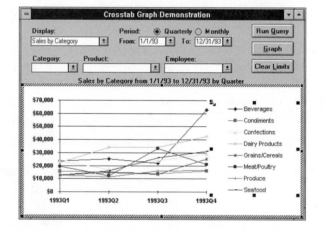

7. Double-click the abscissa (the y-axis) of the graph to display the Format Axis dialog box for the abscissa. Click the Number tab, then choose the first or second of the Format Codes in the list box to eliminate the decimal fraction of the abscissa labels. Click the OK button to close the dialog box.

8. Double-click the legend to display the Format Legend dialog box. Click the Patterns tab, if necessary, and click the None option button of the Area group to make the background of the legend transparent. Click OK to close the dialog box.

9. Click the surface of the form, outside the object frame, to de-activate the graph and check your work. You can make any additional adjustments you need to the graph by activating the graph with a double-click.

10. Open the Form_Load event-handler and add the line `strFormName = "frmCrosstabGraph"` to specify the name of your new form.

11. Save your form as **frmCrosstabGraph**.

Only two short event-handling procedures are required to create qryCrosstab and the graph based on qryCrosstab. The balance of the code necessary to create and run the query is contained in the Create Crosstab Query module.

> **NOTE**
>
> The frmCrosstabGraph form, with formatting applied in accordance with the preceding steps, is included in the Forms collection of AB_EXAMP.MDB on the accompanying diskette.

The *cmdRunQuery_Click* Event-Handler

The cmdRunQuery_Click event-handler in frmCrosstabGraph makes the txtSQL text box visible and creates the SQL statement for the qryCrosstab **QueryDef** object. (See Listing 24.10.) The attributes of the txtQueryName text box are altered to provide a title for the graph, so cmdRunQuery_Click resets these attributes to those used by frmCrosstabQuery.

Listing 24.10. The cmdRunQuery_Click event-handling procedure.

```
Sub cmdRunQuery_Click ()
    'Purpose:   Enable the Graph button after running a query
    '           Hide the SQL text box and make the graph visible

    DoCmd Hourglass True

    'Change the attributes of the query name for the query title
    txtQueryName.Left = .7021 * 1440      'All dimensions are in twips
    txtQueryName.Width = 4.6 * 1440
    txtQueryName.TextAlign = 1            'Left alignment
    txtQueryName.FontWeight = 400         'Normal font weight

    'Run the crosstab query without opening the datasheet
    If ctq_wRunQuery(1, "", "") Then
        uofGraph.Visible = False
        txtSQL.Visible = True
        cmdGraph.Enabled = True
    Else
        'Query failed
    End If
    DoCmd Hourglass False
End Sub
```

The *cmdGraph_Click* Event-Handler

The cmdGraph_Click event-handling subprocedure, shown in Listing 24.11, uses OLE Automation methods to cause the legend to disappear if the query returns only a single row. The Legend object has no Visible property, so you need to set the Legend object's Height and Width properties to 0 to prevent the legend from appearing when only one record is present. Although Access Basic uses twips (1,440 per inch) for setting dimensions, MSGraph5 uses points (72 per inch). The dimensions for the Legend and PlotArea objects in Listing 24.11 apply to the Graph object of the size incorporated in frmCrosstabGraph. If you are creating a larger or smaller graph, these dimensions will differ.

TIP

Use the Immediate Window to determine the position and size of your Legend and PlotArea objects before setting their size with code such as that shown in Listing 24.11. Place a breakpoint at the **If** rsGraph.RecordCount > 1 **Then** line to halt execution with objGraph set. Execute **?** objGraph.*Object*.*Property* to determine the values of dimensions to use when you want the legend to appear.

Listing 24.11. The `cmdRunQuery_Click` event-handling procedure.

```
Sub cmdGraph_Click ()
    'Purpose:    Create the graph from the updated QueryDef object
    '            Display the legend if the query returns more than 1
                 ↩record

    DoCmd Hourglass True

    'Declare and set data object variables
    Dim dbCurrent As Database
    Dim rsGraph As Recordset
    Dim objGraph As Object
    Set dbCurrent = DBEngine(0)(0)
    Set rsGraph = dbCurrent.OpenRecordset("qryCrosstab")

    If rsGraph.RecordCount > 0 Then
        'Change the attributes of the title
        txtQueryName.Left = 0
        txtQueryName.Width = Me.Width
        txtQueryName.TextAlign = 2
        txtQueryName.FontWeight = 700
        DoCmd Requery "txtQueryName"
```

```
    'Set the graph object variable for OLE Automation
    Set objGraph = uofGraph.Object
    rsGraph.MoveLast
    If rsGraph.RecordCount = 1 Then
        'Shrink the legend to nothing and expand the graph
        objGraph.Legend.Width = 0
        objGraph.Legend.Height = 0
        objGraph.Legend.Left = 0
        objGraph.PlotArea.Width = objGraph.ChartArea.Width
    Else
        'Show the legend and contract the graph accordingly
        objGraph.Legend.Width = 121
        objGraph.Legend.Height = 126
        objGraph.Legend.Left = 283
        objGraph.PlotArea.Width = objGraph.ChartArea.Width -
        ➥objGraph.Legend.Width
    End If

    'Hide the SQL text box
    txtSQL.Visible = False

    'Display the graph
    uofGraph.Visible = True

    'Update the graph's data
    DoCmd Requery "uofGraph"
Else
    'Query returned no rows
End If

DoCmd Hourglass False
End Sub
```

TIP

If you apply the Delete method to the Legend object, the legend is gone forever. Therefore, shrinking the legend to 0 Height and Width is by far the better approach.

To create the graph, set the criteria for your query in the combo boxes, then click the Run Query button. After the query has executed, click the Graph button to display the graph based on the new **QueryDef** object. Figure 24.13 shows the graph that results from a query-result set with a single row. Any line graph that consists of a single line or column or area chart that displays only one dependent variable set does not need a legend; the title suffices to define the graph.

FIGURE 24.13.

A legendless graph from a single-row query.

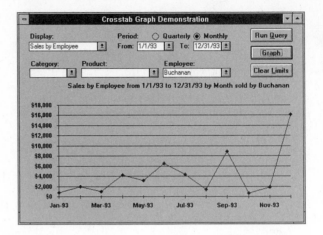

You can determine the type of graph to display either by choosing **C**hart Type from the F**o**rmat menu when the graph is activated in run mode, or by setting the value of the `Type` property of the first member of the `ChartGroups` collection, `ChartGroups(1)`. Table 24.1 lists the values of the `Type` property for the assortment of graph and chart styles provided by MSGraph5. Figure 24.14 shows an area chart created by setting the value of the ChartGroups(1).Type property to 1.

Table 24.1. Values of the `ChartGroups(1).Type` Property.

Type	Chart Style	Type	Chart Style
1	Area	10	3-D Bar
2	Horizontal bar	11	3-D Column
3	Vertical column	12	3-D Line
4	Line	13	3-D Pie
5	Pie	14	3-D Surface
6	Doughnut	15	Area
7	Radar	16	Area
8	Line	17	Horizontal Bar
9	3-D Area		

FIGURE 24.14.

An area chart created by setting ChartGroups(1).Type *= 1.*

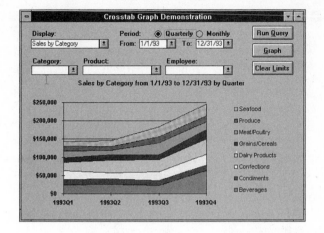

Creating Forms and Reports with Wizard Functions

The WZFRMRPT.MDA library employs a number of functions that are not extensively documented in the *Language Reference* that accompanies the ADT. The sections that follow show you how to create graphs and subforms programmatically using the four basic Wizard functions:

- **CodeDB()** is used with the **Set** statement to specify the library database rather than the application database. If you open the library as an application, the result of using **CodeDB()** is identical to using **DBEngine(0)(0)**.

- **CreateForm()** is used with the **Set** statement to create a new form based on the default form template (Normal), a template you have specified as the value of the Form Template property in the Form & Report Design Options, or a template form that you specify. The syntax of **CreateForm()** is **Set** frm*FormName* = **CreateForm**("[*FormName*]", "[*TemplateName*]"). In this syntax, the brackets are used to indicate that *FormName* and *TemplateName* are optional literals, but the double quotation marks must be present unless you substitute str*FormName* and str*TemplateName* variables. If you do not specify a *FormName* literal, your form automatically will be named Form1 (or the next number in sequence). If you omit *TemplateName*, the form is based on the default template. Once you have created the new form, you set the values of the form's properties with additional lines of code. The **CreateReport()** function uses the same syntax.

■ **CreateControl**() is used with the **Set** statement to create a new control in a specified section of the designated form. The basic syntax is **Set** *ctlControlName* = **CreateControl**(*strFormName*, *wControlType*). There are a variety of other properties that you can specify as arguments, but in most cases your code will be clearer if you explicitly set the property values with lines of code. An expanded discussion of the syntax of the **CreateControl**() function appears in the sections that follow. The **CreateReportControl**() function employs a similar syntax.

■ **DeleteControl** is a statement, not a function. The principal use of the **DeleteControl** statement is to delete a control prior to creating a new control with the same name. The syntax is **DeleteControl** *strFormName*, *strControlName*. The same syntax applies to the **DeleteReportControl** statement.

The preceding functions are valid in design mode only. Forms and reports created with the **CreateForm**() and **CreateReport**() functions are opened minimized to an icon in design mode. When you use the **CreateControl**() or **CreateReportControl**() functions with existing forms or reports, you must explicitly change to form or report design mode by executing a **DoMenuItem** action before adding or deleting the control, or changing the values of properties that are read-only in run mode. Each of these functions is used in the wizard code examples that follow.

Replacing Subforms with *CreateForm( )* and *CreateControl( )*

Displaying the result of user-defined queries in a subform that uses query datasheet view is a straightforward process. The graphic elements of the standard query datasheet view, however, usually conflict with the overall design of a well-designed form. If you want to display values from user-defined crosstab queries in custom-designed subforms that run in form view, you have two choices:

■ Create a new subform each time you make a change in the user-defined query parameters. You can create a template for the subform to save adding the code to define the subform's size, appearance, and other basic properties.

■ Delete the existing controls from the form based on values for the control name properties obtained before you delete the **QueryDef** from which the existing form was created.

Regardless of the approach you choose, you need to close and then reopen the form so that the new subform replaces the previous subform. The second choice is a bit faster than creating a new form for each new query, but it requires more complex code. The complexity results from code that you need to add to ensure that the names of controls on the subform are derived from values in the current query. The example that follows uses the first choice for coding simplicity. Housekeeping functions, such as hiding the SQL text box (txtSQL), are not implemented in this example. The subform simply is superimposed over txtSQL.

To execute the code example that follows, you need to add two objects and make two changes to the original version of the frmCrosstabQuery form (without the graph object):

1. Create a template for the subform (frmCTTemplate) similar to that shown in Figure 24.15. The template should have only a form header and detail section, both with a depth to accommodate a single label and text box, respectively.

2. Create a dummy subform based on the template (frmCTSubform). Copy frmCTTemplate to the Clipboard, then paste it as frmCTSubform. Set the value of the RecordSource property of frmCTSubform to qryCrosstab.

3. Add a subform control (sbfCrosstab) to frmCrosstabQuery with frmCTSubform as the value of the subform control's SourceObject property.

4. Add a command button (cmdSave) with &Save as the value of the Caption property. This button is used to run a function, added later in the chapter, that saves the contents of the subform to an Excel worksheet.

The preceding steps were used to create frmCrosstabSubform, frmCTTemplate, and frmCTSubform, which are included in AB_EXAMP.MDB. As with the preceding examples, you can use tables attached from NWIND.MDB with AB_EXAMP.MDB or import the three forms into NWIND.MDB. The code described in the following sections is contained in the Create Subform From Crosstab module. If you are using the import method, you must import this module and the Create Worksheet From Subform module, which contains a required global variable declaration, from AB_EXAMP.MDB into NWIND.MDB to run the example application.

> **NOTE**
>
> The Create Worksheet From Subform module of AB_EXAMP.MDB includes declarations of two global variables, rgstrFields() and strSQLSource, that are required to compile the code Create Subform From Crosstab successfully. These variables are used with code in the Create Worksheet From Subform module and the code that is used to add crossfoot totals to subforms. Code is also included in the Create Worksheet From Subform module to create an additional totals column in the query and to use tables, rather than queries, as the RecordSource property of user-defined subforms. The Create Worksheet From Subform module and crossfooting

subform data is discussed later in this chapter. Code that does not relate specifically to creating a simple subform is not included in the listings that follow.

FIGURE 24.15.

The template for the replaceable subform, frmCTSubform.

The Declarations Section of the Create Subform From Query Module

The Declarations section of the Create Subform From Query module consists of statements to declare module-level variables of the **Variant** data type whose values are obtained from the combo boxes and text box on the frmCrosstabQuery form. Module-level scope is assigned to these variables to avoid the necessity of passing their values as arguments to the wGetComboValues() and wSetComboValues() functions that appear in listings that follow. Explicit declaration of these variables **As Variant** is not required because a variable declared without a data type is assigned the **Variant** data type by default. The **As Variant** data type assignment is added here for consistency in variable declaration.

```
'Purpose:  Create a new subform based on a query result.
'Uses:     Create Worksheet module to create an Excel worksheet

Option Compare Database   'Use database order for string
                          ➥comparisons
Option Explicit

'The following module-level declarations are specific to the form
➥used
'These variables preserve the values of the combo boxes on
➥frmCrosstab
Dim varDisplay As Variant
Dim varFromQuarter As Variant
Dim varToQuarter As Variant
Dim varFromMonth As Variant
Dim varToMonth As Variant
Dim varPeriod As Variant
Dim varCategory As Variant
Dim varProduct As Variant
Dim varAllProducts As Variant
Dim varEmployee As Variant
Dim varQueryName As Variant 'The query name from the SQL statement
```

The *wMakeSubForm*( ) function

The code of the wMakeSubForm() function is specific to the form and the query used to create the new subform. Thus `wMakeSubForm()` is intended to be included in the code of your application. The `wCreateSubForm()` function declares the variables that specify the source of the data for the subform, the name of the subform and the template on which the subform is based, the width of the description column, and other variables that are required to format controls that you create on the subform. This function calls two other form-specific functions, `wGetComboValues()` and `wSetComboValues()`, that preserve the values in the combo boxes of frmCrosstabQuery when this form is temporarily closed. The `wCreateSubForm()` function calls the general-purpose `csc_CreateSubform()` function that creates the new subform.

> **NOTE**
>
> As with frmCrosstabQuery and frmCrosstabGraph in the preceding examples, the `Form_Load` event of frmCrosstabSubform includes the line `strFormName = "strCrosstabSubform"` to synchronize the name of the form with the other functions used by frmCrosstabSubform.

Listing 24.12. Access Basic code for the `wMakeSubForm()` function.

```
Function wMakeSubForm () As Integer
    'Purpose:   Run query and create a new subform containing the
               ➥result
    'Returns:   True if successful, False on failure
    'Calls:     All functions in the Create Subform module
    'Requires: Global variables declared in Create Worksheet
    '          Create Worksheet module

    On Error GoTo NewSubFormError
    DoCmd Hourglass True

    Dim strSource As String        'Name of source table or query
                                   ➥for subform data
    Dim strTemplate As String      'Template for subform (minimizes
                                   ➥code)
    Dim strSubform As String       'Name for subform
    Dim wDescrCol As Integer       'Column number of description
                                   ➥column
    Dim wDescrWidth As Integer     'Width of description column in
                                   ➥twips
    Dim wCreateOK As Integer       'True if subform created without
                                   ➥error
    Dim strMsg As String           'Message box message
```

continues

Listing 24.12. continued

```
    strSource = "qryCrosstab"      'Name of base query
    strSQLSource = strSource       'Global in Create Worksheet
    strSubform = "frmCTSubform"    'Name of subform
    strTemplate = "frmCTTemplate"  'The template is REQUIRED
    wDescrCol = 1                  'Description is in first column
                                   ➥of query
    wDescrWidth = 1440             'One inch should be sufficient

    'Store the values of the combo boxes
    If wGetComboValues() = False Then
        strMsg = "Unable to obtain combo box values from form."
    End If

    'IMPORTANT: Comment the following line when debugging the code
    DoCmd Echo False
    DoCmd Close A_FORM, strFormName'Close the form but
    ➥leave it on display

    'Create the new subform

    wCreateOK = csc_wCreateSubForm(strTemplate, strSource,
    ➥strSubform, wDescrCol, wDescrWidth)

    DoCmd OpenForm strFormName
    DoCmd Echo True

    If wCreateOK Then
        If wSetComboValues() = 0 Then
            'Add an appropriate message box
        End If
    Else
        strMsg = "Error creating subform."
        GoTo NewSubFormError
    End If

    DoCmd Hourglass False
    wMakeSubForm = True
    Exit Function

NewSubFormError:
    DoCmd Echo True
    DoCmd Hourglass False
    If strMsg = "" Then
        MsgBox Error$, 16, "System Error"
    Else
        MsgBox strMsg, 16, "SQL Error"
    End If
    wMakeSubForm = False
    Exit Function
End Function
```

> **NOTE**
>
> You can run the `wMakeSubForm()` function by entering `? wMakeSubForm()` in the Immediate Window. After you have tested your code, add the line `wRetVal = wMakeSubForm()` before the first **Exit Function** statement in the `ctq_wRunQuery()` function of the Create Crosstab Query module. This statement runs `wMakeSubForm()` each time you click the Run Query button on `frmCrosstabQuery`.

The *wGetComboValues( )* and *wSetComboValues( )* Functions

The two functions, `wGetComboValues()` and `wSetComboValues()`, in Listing 24.13 and Listing 24.14, respectively, copy the data from and enter the data in the combo boxes and one text box on frmCrosstabQuery. You need to preserve the data when you close and then reopen the form.

Listing 24.13. Access Basic code for the `wGetComboValues()` function.

```
Function wGetComboValues () As Integer
    'Purpose:   Obtain the current values of the combo boxes
    'Called by: wMakeSubForm
    'Returns:   True if successful, False on failure

    Dim Temp As Form

    On Error GoTo GetValuesErr

    Set Temp = Forms(strFormName)

    varDisplay = Temp!cboDisplay
    varFromQuarter = Temp!cboFromQuarter
    varToQuarter = Temp!cboToQuarter
    varFromMonth = Temp!cboFromMonth
    varToMonth = Temp!cboToMonth
    varPeriod = Temp!grpPeriod
    varCategory = Temp!cboCategory
    varProduct = Temp!cboProduct
    varAllProducts = Temp!cboAllProducts
    varEmployee = Temp!cboEmployee
    varQueryName = Temp!txtQueryName

    wGetComboValues = True
    Exit Function
```

continues

Listing 24.13. continued

```
GetValuesErr:
    Exit Function
End Function
```

Listing 24.14. Access Basic code for the `wSetComboValue()` function.

```
Function wSetComboValues () As Integer
    'Purpose:    Set the prior values of the combo boxes
    'Called by:  wMakeSubForm
    'Returns:    True if successful, False on failure

    Dim Temp As Form

    On Error GoTo SetValuesErr

    Set Temp = Forms(strFormName)

    Temp!cboDisplay = varDisplay
    Temp!cboFromQuarter = varFromQuarter
    Temp!cboToQuarter = varToQuarter
    Temp!cboFromMonth = varFromMonth
    Temp!cboToMonth = varToMonth
    Temp!grpPeriod = varPeriod
    Temp!cboCategory = varCategory
    Temp!cboProduct = varProduct
    Temp!cboAllProducts = varAllProducts
    Temp!cboEmployee = varEmployee
    Temp!txtQueryName = varQueryName

    wSetComboValues = True
    Exit Function

SetValuesErr:
    Exit Function
End Function
```

The *csc_wCreateSubForm( )* Function

The `csc_wCreateSubForm()` function is a general-purpose function that creates a new subform with label and text-box control objects whose captions and contents are determined by the column properties of the query. This function, shown in Listing 24.15, and the two functions that `csc_wCreateSubform()` calls (`csc_wCreateLabel()` and `csc_wCreateText()`), are aliased with `csc_` so that these three functions can be included in a library. Members of Access 2.0's `Fields` collection of the **QueryDef** object supply the Name and Type property of each field to create the captions for the subform and format the values displayed in the subform' bound text boxes.

NOTE

Access 1.x required use of the **ListFields**() method to create a **Snapshot** object from a **Dynaset** object created from the **QueryDef** object. The **ListFields**() **Snapshot** contained field information. The **ListFields**() method is supported by Access 2.0 for backward compatibility only; using the Fields collection to obtain information about the fields of **QueryDef** objects now is the preferred method.

Listing 24.15. Access Basic code for the `wCreateSubForm()` function.

```
Function csc_wCreateSubForm() As Integer
    (strTemplate As String,
     strSource As String,
     strFormName As String,
     wDescrCol As Integer,
     wDescrWidth As Integer) As Integer

    'Purpose:    Creates a subform with a varying number of time
                 ➥periods
    '            Depending on the number of columns in a crosstab or
                 ➥similar query
    'Arguments: strTemplate = Name of template for form (determines
                 ➥dimensions)
    '            strSource = Name of source table or query
    '            strSubform = Name of subform
    '            wDescrCol = Number of description column (1 or 2, 2
                 ➥to delete the first column)
    '            wDescrWidth = Width of description column in twips
                 ➥(0 if no description column)
    'Returns:    True if successful, False on failure

    Dim wNumCols As Integer         'number of data columns (less
                                     ➥description)
    Dim wFormWidth As Integer       'width of template form, twips
    Dim wColWidth As Integer        'data column width, twips
    Dim wCtr As Integer             'general purpose counter
    Dim wRetVal As Integer          'general purpose return value for
                                     ➥functions
    Dim wColStart As Integer        'starting position of a column,
                                     ➥twips

    Dim strName As String           'Name of form created (Form1,
                                     ➥Form2, etc.)
```

continues

Listing 24.15. continued

```
Dim wSection As Integer        'Section number, 0 = Detail, 1 =
                               ➥Header
Dim wLeft As Integer           'X position of label or text box
Dim wWidth As Integer          'Increment to left for successive
                               ➥controls
Dim wTop As Integer            'Y position of label or text box
                               ➥(from top), twips
Dim wHeight As Integer         'Height of label or text box, twips
Dim strCaption As String       'Caption of label, bound field of
                               ➥text box
Dim strFormat As String        'Format string for values (not
                               ➥description)
Dim wTextWidth As Integer      'Width of label and text box (right
                               ➥formatted)

Dim dbCurrent As Database      'Current database
Dim qdfSource As QueryDef      'Underlying query for subform
Dim tdfSource As TableDef      'Definition of temporary table

Dim frmNewSubForm As Form      'New subform

DoCmd Hourglass True

On Error GoTo CreateError

'Create an array of the field names and field data types
Set dbCurrent = DBEngine(0)(0)
Set qdfSource = dbCurrent.OpenQueryDef(strSource)
wNumCols = qdfSource.Fields.Count
ReDim rgvarFields(wNumCols, 2)
For wCtr = 1 To wNumCols
    rgvarFields(wCtr, 0) = qdfSource.Fields(wCtr - 1).Name
    rgvarFields(wCtr, 1) = qdfSource.Fields(wCtr - 1).Type
Next wCtr

'Note: Include this line only if not done previously
'Turn off screen painting (only Save As dialog flashes)
'DoCmd Echo False

'Make sure the subform is closed before you start this procedure
DoCmd Close A_FORM, strSubform

'Create the new subform (Form1) based on strSource
Set frmNewSubForm = CreateForm("", strTemplate)
frmNewSubForm.RecordSource = strSource
strName = frmNewSubForm.FormName

'Get the width of the form, using alternate Forms syntax
'Note: The template form must be open to obtain the Width value
DoCmd OpenForm strTemplate, A_NORMAL, , , , A_HIDDEN
```

```
'Deduct the width of the vertical scrollbar from the form
wFormWidth = Forms(strTemplate).Width - 432
DoCmd Close A_FORM, strTemplate

wColStart = 144 'start 0.1" from left
wColWidth = (wFormWidth - wColStart - wDescrWidth) \ (wNumCols
➥- wDescrCol)

'Create labels and text boxes
wLeft = wColStart
For wCtr = 1 To wNumCols
    'Create array of field names
    If wCtr >= wDescrCol Then
        If wCtr = wDescrCol Then
            strFormat = ""
            wWidth = wDescrWidth
        Else
            'Format the columns without a decimal fraction
            If rgvarFields(wCtr, 1) = 5 Then
                'Data type is currency
                strFormat = "$#,###"
            Else
                'Date type is numeric (for a crosstab query)
                strFormat = "#,###"
            End If
            wWidth = wColWidth
        End If
        If wWidth > 0 Then
            'Provide standard values to label and text creation
            ➥functions
            'Note: These could be passed as arguments
            strCaption = rgvarFields(wCtr, 0)
            wTop = 36
            wHeight = 240
            wSection = 1
            wTextWidth = wWidth
            'Create a label
            wRetVal = csc_wCreateLabel(strName, wSection,
            ➥wLeft, wTop, wTextWidth, wHeight, strCaption,
            ➥strFormat)
            wSection = 0
            'Create a text box
            wRetVal = csc_wCreateText(strName, wSection, wLeft,
            ➥wTop, wTextWidth, wHeight, strCaption, strFormat)
            wLeft = wLeft + wWidth
        End If
    End If
Next wCtr

'Close open objects
dbCurrent.Close
```

continues

Listing 24.15. continued

```
'Note: The following block of 1.x code is not operable in Version
 ➡2.0,
'       regardless of the use of the A_MENU_VER1X or A_MENU_VER20
'       as the value of the Version argument of DoMenuItem
'DoCmd SetWarnings False
'SendKeys strFormName & "{Enter}", 0
'DoCmd DoMenuItem A_FORMBAR, A_FILE, A_SAVEFORMAS
'DoCmd Close A_FORM, strFormName
'DoCmd SetWarnings True

'Revised code for Version 2.0 substitutes for the above
'Delete frmCTSubform
DoCmd DeleteObject A_FORM, strSubform
DoEvents
'Save as default Form1
SendKeys "{Enter}", 0
'Close Form1
DoCmd Close A_FORM, "Form1"
DoEvents
'Rename Form1 to frmCTSubform (this is a more elegant method)
DoCmd Rename strSubform, A_FORM, "Form1"

'Turn on repaint, if it was set off in the above code
'DoCmd Echo True

DoCmd Hourglass False
csc_wCreateSubForm = True
Exit Function

CreateError:
    DoCmd Echo True
    DoCmd Hourglass False
    MsgBox Error$, 16, "Create Error"
    Exit Function
End Function
```

> **NOTE**
>
> The value of the `wTextWidth` variable can be used to more precisely deter-
> mine the width of the text by using the Windows API `GetTextMetrics()`
> and related functions. (See the code in WZFRMRPT.MDA that uses the
> `GetTextMetrics()` function.)

Figure 24.16 shows the crosstab query subform that displays the sales of Northwind
products for the period January 1, 1993 to December 31, 1993.

FIGURE 24.16.

The frmCrosstabQuery form with a replaceable subform.

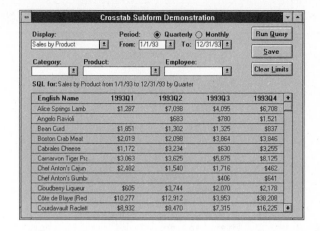

The csc_wCreateSubForm() function does not provide for niceties such as a wider subform and a horizontal scrollbar to accommodate more columns than the width of the subform control object can display. Implementing additional design features for the subform is discussed in sections that follow.

> **NOTE**
>
> You can create reports based on user-defined queries by creating a report template and modifying the code in csc_wCreateSubForm() to create a report rather than a subform. Substitute **CreateReport()** for **CreateForm()** to create a report based on the query.

The *csc_wCreateLabel( )* Function

The csc_wCreateLabel() function, shown in Listing 24.16, is a general-purpose function that you can use to create labels on either forms or reports. To create labels on reports, substitute **CreateReportControl()** for **CreateControl()**.

Listing 24.16. Access Basic code for the csc_wCreateLabel() function.

```
Function csc_wCreateLabel() As Integer
    (strName As String,
     wSection As Integer,
     wLeft As Integer,
     wTop As Integer,
     wWidth As Integer,
     wHeight As Integer,
```

continues

Listing 24.16. continued

```
    strCaption As String,
    strFormat As String) As Integer

'Purpose:   General purpose function to create labels for forms
➥or reports
'Arguments: strName = Name of form on which control is to be
➥created
'           wSection = Section number of form (0 = detail, 1 =
➥header)
'           wLeft = X-coordinate of left edge of control
'           wTop = Y-coordinate of top of control
'           wWidth = width of control
'           wHeight = height of control
'           Note: All dimensions are in twips
'           strCaption = label caption text
'           strFormat = format string if strCaption is numeric
'                       (aligns label with numeric text boxes)
'Returns:   True if successful, False on failure

Dim Temp As Control
Set Temp = CreateControl(strName, 100, wSection, "",
➥strCaption, wLeft, wTop, wWidth, wHeight)

'Remove the colon (AddColon is not available in Access Basic)
If Right$(Temp.Caption, 1) = ":" Then
    Temp.Caption = Left$(Temp.Caption, Len(Temp.Caption) - 1)
End If

Temp.Width = wWidth

'Align text right if the text box is numeric, left if not
If Len(strFormat) > 0 Then
    Temp.TextAlign = 3
Else
    Temp.TextAlign = 1
End If
csc_wCreateLabel = True
End Function
```

The *csc_wCreateText( )* Function

The csc_wCreateText() function is similar in structure to the csc_wCreateLabel()
function, as illustrated by Listing 24.17, but it requires that the value of the BackColor
property of the text box be set to that of the subform on which the text box is
located.

Listing 24.17. Access Basic code for the `csc_wCreateText()` function.

```
Function csc_wCreateText() As Integer
     (strName As String,
      wSection As Integer,
      wLeft As Integer,
      wTop As Integer,
      wWidth As Integer,
      wHeight As Integer,
      strBoundField As String,
      strFormat As String) As Integer

     'Purpose:   General purpose function to create labels for forms
     ➡or reports
     'Arguments: strName = Name of form on which control is to be
     ➡created
     '           wSection = Section number of form (0 = detail, 1 =
     ➡               header)
     '           wLeft = X-coordinate of left edge of control
     '           wTop = Y-coordinate of top of control
     '           wWidth = width of control
     '           wHeight = height of control
     '           Note: All dimensions are in twips
     '           strBoundField = field name to which text box is
     ➡               bound
     '           strFormat = format string if strCaption is numeric
     '                      (this format string changes depending on
     '                    ➡data type)
     'Returns:   True if successful, False on failure

     Dim Temp As Control
     Set Temp = CreateControl(strName, 109, wSection, "",
     ➡strBoundField, wLeft, wTop, wWidth, wHeight)

     'Set border style to clear and background color to form
     ➡back ground color
     Temp.BorderStyle = 0
     'Note: If your form background colors vary, get the background
     ➡color
     '      from the subform and substitute the variable for the
     '         ➡literal below
     Temp.BackColor = 12632256

     'Apply format to text box, if applicable
     If Len(strFormat) > 0 Then
         Temp.Format = strFormat
     End If

     csc_wCreateText = True
End Function
```

Crossfooting the Crosstab Values

One of the features that clients often request is the ability to crossfoot the result of their queries. Crossfooting is a term accountants use to describe a process wherein totals for each of the rows and columns of a worksheet are computed, and then the totals of the row and column totals are compared for equality. The worksheet is said to "crossfoot" if the row and column totals are equal.

Adding a column for row totals requires that you use a **Table** object, rather than a **QueryDef** object, as the data source for the subform. Thus, you need to add a make-table query to your code to create the table. The following code added to the wMakeSubForm() function, creates two tables, tblCrosstab1 and tblCrosstab2, that alternate as the underlying source of the data for the subform. Alternating (toggled) tables are used so that you do not have to close the form before replacing the table with the make-table query. Using alternating tables also offers the opportunity to demonstrate the syntax necessary to obtain the value of a property of a subform.

```
If strTotalsCol = "" And strTotalsRow = "" Then
    strSource = "qryCrosstab"      'Name of base query
Else
    'This code is required only for subforms with totals that
    ➥require tables
    'as their data source. This allows you to update the source
    ➥of the subform.

    'Change source of data alternately to two tables
    'Note the convoluted syntax to refer to a property of a
    ➥subform
    If Forms(strFormName)!sbfCrosstab.Form.RecordSource =
    ➥"tblCrosstab1" Then
        strSource = "tblCrosstab2"
    Else
        strSource = "tblCrosstab1"
    End If

    'Create a temporary Access make-table query definition
    ➥using qryCrosstab
    Dim strSQLMake As String
    Dim dbCurrent As Database
    Dim qdfTemp As QueryDef
    Set dbCurrent = DBEngine(0)(0)
    strSQLMake = "SELECT DISTINCTROW * INTO " & strSource & "
    ➥FROM qryCrosstab WITH OWNERACCESS OPTION;"
    On Error Resume Next
    dbCurrent.DeleteQueryDef ("qryTemp")
    On Error GoTo MakeSubFormError
    Set qdfTemp = dbCurrent.CreateQueryDef("qryTemp",
    ➥strSQLMake)
```

```
       'Execute the make-table query with system warnings off to
       ➥create the table
       DoCmd SetWarnings False
       DoCmd OpenQuery "qryTemp"
       DoCmd SetWarnings True

       'Close open objects
       qdfTemp.Close
    End If

    strSQLSource = strSource       'Global in Create Worksheet
```

The preceding code and that required to complete the crossfooting operation is included in the Create Subform From Crosstab module. The form designed to be used with this code is frmCrosstabRowTotals in AB_EXAMP.MDB. If you are using NWIND.MDB as your test database, import frmCrosstabRowTotals to NWIND.MDB

Creating a Totals Column

To create a column to accommodate row totals, you need to add a bogus field (a field to which the query returns no data) to your query with a name such as "Totals." This requires adding a field name, strTotalsCol, to the query. Fortunately, you can add as many bogus fields to your query as you want and Access will format the bogus fields with the same field data type as it uses for the fields with valid data. The following code in the ctq_strFixedHeads() function of the Create Crosstab Query module adds a totals column to the query:

```
    'The following code applies to subforms only
    'Add a totals column for crossfooting the subform
    If Len(strTotalsCol) > 0 Then
        strSQLIn = strSQLIn & Chr$(34) & strTotalsCol &
        ➥Chr$(34) & ", "
    End If
```

The following code in csc_wCreateSubform chooses between using a **QueryDef** or a **Table** object as the source recordset that provides the field names to use as column headings in the subform:

```
    'The following procedures used the ListFields method with Access 1.1
        If strTotalsCol = "" Then
            Set qdfSource = dbCurrent.OpenQueryDef(strSource)
            wNumCols = qdfSource.Fields.Count
            ReDim rgvarFields(wNumCols, 2)
            For wCtr = 1 To wNumCols
                rgvarFields(wCtr, 0) = qdfSource.Fields(wCtr - 1).Name
                rgvarFields(wCtr, 1) = qdfSource.Fields(wCtr - 1).Type
```

```
        Next wCtr
    Else
        'Note: This code is specific to subforms that include a totals
        ➡column
        Set tdfSource = dbCurrent.TableDefs(strSource)
        wNumCols = tdfSource.Fields.Count
        ReDim rgvarFields(wNumCols, 2)
        For wCtr = 1 To wNumCols
            rgvarFields(wCtr, 0) = tdfSource.Fields(wCtr - 1).Name
            rgvarFields(wCtr, 1) = tdfSource.Fields(wCtr - 1).Type
        Next wCtr
    End If
```

The csc_varSetRowTotals() function, shown in Listing 24.18, totals each of the data columns of the **Table** object that serves as the data source for the subform and computes the grand total for crossfoot testing. The **Variant** data type is used in all computations because you cannot predict whether the data in the table is of the **Currency**, **Double**, **Single**, **Long**, or **Integer** data type, nor is it desirable to declare five different variables to accommodate the different data types.

Listing 24.18. Code to create row totals for a subform.

```
Function csc_varSetRowTotals (strSource As String, wDescrCol As
➡Integer) As Variant
    'Purpose:    Total each of the rows of a crosstab query
    'Arguments: strSource = name of source table (or query)
    '           wDescrCol = column number for description
    'Returns:    Grand total of row totals (Variant)

    Dim varGrandTotal As Variant       'For crossfoot test, must be a
                                       ➡Variant
    Dim varRowTotal As Variant         'Totals for each row of data
    Dim wRowCtr As Integer             'Counts rows
    Dim wColCtr As Integer             'Counts columns

    Dim dbCurrent As Database          'Temporary objects
    Dim tblSource As Table
    Set dbCurrent = DBEngine(0)(0)
    Set tblSource = dbCurrent.OpenTable(strSource)

    wRowCtr = 1

    tblSource.MoveFirst
    'Process each row of the query
BeginTrans    'Use transaction processing to improve performance
    Do While Not tblSource.EOF
        'Total the columns that have values (skip the description
        ➡and totals fields)
        For wColCtr = (wDescrCol + 1) To (UBound(rgstrFields, 1) - 1)
            If Not IsNull(tblSource("[" & rgstrFields(wColCtr) &
```

```
➥"]")) Then
                'Do not attempt to add null values to numeric values
                varRowTotal = varRowTotal + tblSource("[" &
                ➥rgstrFields(wColCtr) & "]")
            End If
        Next

        'Update the totals column
        tblSource.Edit
        tblSource("[" & strTotalsCol & "]") = varRowTotal
        tblSource.Update

        'Increment the row
        varGrandTotal = varGrandTotal + varRowTotal
        tblSource.MoveNext
        wRowCtr = wRowCtr + 1

        'Reset the row total
        varRowTotal = 0

        'DoEvents       'For safety (comment out after testing)
    Loop
CommitTrans          'Commit the changes

    'Clean up
    tblSource.Close
    dbCurrent.Close

    csc_varSetRowTotals = varGrandTotal
End Function
```

To add the Totals column to the crosstab query, =ctq_wRunQuery("Totals","") is used as the value of the OnClick event of the Run Query button. The "Totals" argument supplies the name of the column added to the subform. Your crosstab subform with row totals appears as shown in Figure 24.17. Completing the crossfoot with column totals is the subject of the next section.

Totaling Subform Columns

You can choose from two methods of completing the crossfooting operation with column totals:

■ Column totals added as the last record of the table that acts as the source of data for the subform

■ Column totals displayed in the subform footer

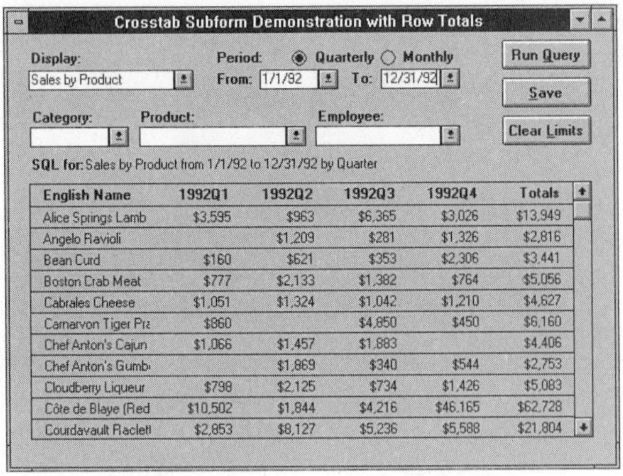
Crosstab Subform Demonstration with Row Totals
Display:
Sales by Product
Period:
Quarterly
Monthly
From: 1/1/92
To: 12/31/92
Run Query
Save
Category:
Product:
Employee:
Clear Limits
SQL for: Sales by Product from 1/1/92 to 12/31/92 by Quarter
English Name 1992Q1 1992Q2 1992Q3 1992Q4 Totals
Alice Springs Lamb $3,595 $963 $6,365 $3,026 $13,949
Angelo Ravioli $1,209 $281 $1,326 $2,816
Bean Curd $160 $621 $353 $2,306 $3,441
Boston Crab Meat $777 $2,133 $1,382 $764 $5,056
Cabrales Cheese $1,051 $1,324 $1,042 $1,210 $4,627
Carnarvon Tiger Pra $860 $4,850 $450 $6,160
Chef Anton's Cajun $1,066 $1,457 $1,883 $4,406
Chef Anton's Gumb $1,869 $340 $544 $2,753
Cloudberry Liqueur $798 $2,125 $734 $1,426 $5,083
Côte de Blaye (Red $10,502 $1,844 $4,216 $46,165 $62,728
Courdavault Raclett $2,853 $8,127 $5,236 $5,588 $21,804

FIGURE 24.17.
The crosstab query form with row totals added.

Adding column totals as a record has the advantage that both row and column totals appear when you transfer data from the subform table to another application. Placing column totals in the footer of a subform makes the totals visible at all times, regardless of the number of records in the table. You can apply attributes, such as bold, to the text boxes that display totals in subform footers. The example that follows is based on the subform footer approach.

You need to make several modifications to the code shown in the preceding examples to add the required label and unbound text boxes to the footer of the subform, and then update the values of the text boxes with the column totals. The modifications include the three additions to `csc_wCreateSubForm()` shown in the following listings. The first addition creates text boxes with a bold text attribute in the subform footer section:

```
'Note: The following code applies only to forms with column
➥totals
If Len(strTotalsRow) > 0 And wCtr > wDescrCol Then
    'Create text boxes in the form footer section (2)
    'The name of the control is the field name with a " Total"
    ➥suffix
    strControlName = strCaption & " Total"
    strCaption = ""        'The text box is not bound to a field
    wSection = 2           'The footer section
    fIsBold = True         'Add bold attribute
    wRetVal = csc_wCreateText(strName, wSection, wLeft, wTop,
    ➥wTextWidth, wHeight, strCaption, strFormat, strControlName,
    ➥fIsBold)
End If
```

You also need to alter the code of `csc_wCreateText()` to accept the `fIsBold` flag as an argument and to set the `FontWeight` property of the text box to 700 (bold) if `fIsBold` is true.

The second addition creates a label for the column totals in the subform footer:

```
'Note: The following code applies only to forms with column totals
If wCtr = wDescrCol Then
    If Len(strTotalsRow) > 0 Then
        'Set the depth (height) of the footer section equal to
        ➥the header
        Forms(strName).Section(2).Height =
        ➥Forms(strName).Section(1).Height

        'Add the label to the footer section (caption is
        ➥strTotalsRow)
        wSection = 2
        wRetVal = csc_wCreateLabel(strName, wSection,
        ➥wColStart, wTop, wTextWidth, wHeight, strTotalsRow,
        ➥strFormat)
    Else
        '"Disappear" the footer section
        Forms(strName).Section(2).Height = 0
    End If
End If
```

The preceding listing shows the syntax used to refer to properties of a specified section of a form, **Forms**(str*FormName*).**Section**(w*SectionNum*).*Property*.

The third addition tests whether the DefaultEditing property of the subform is set to Read-only (value = 3). You cannot set the values of text boxes on subforms with Read-only, so you need to set the value of the DefaultEditing property of the form to 2 (Allow Edits).

```
'This code is specific to subforms with column totals
If Len(strTotalsRow) > 0 Then
    'Test to see if editing is restricted
    fAllowEditing = Forms(strName).AllowEditing
    wDefaultEditing = Forms(strName).DefaultEditing
    If fAllowEditing = 0 Or wDefaultEditing = 3 Then
        'You need to turn on editing capability
        Forms(strName).AllowEditing = True
        Forms(strName).DefaultEditing = 2
    End If
End If
```

> **NOTE**
>
> The DefaultEditing property of the template on which you base the subform usually is set to Read-only for decision-support applications. If you fail to reset the Default Editing property of the subform that you create from the template, you receive a "Can't Set Value" message when your application attempts to set the values of the text boxes in the subform footer. You need not be overly concerned with changes that users can make to the

record source, because the table that acts as the record source for the subform is not linked to any other tables in the database.

You cannot set the values of the content of text boxes in design mode; you receive a "Can't Set Value" message if you attempt to do so. Thus, you need to set the values of the text boxes when the subform is in run mode. The code that reopens the frmCrosstabQuery form with the new subform is included in the wMakeSubForm() function. The call to the function that calculates the column totals, csc_varSetColTotals(), appears after the line that reopens the form:

```
DoCmd OpenForm "frmCrosstabQuery"
DoCmd Echo True

If Len(strTotalsRow) > 0 Then
    'Comment out this line if you try the DefaultValues
    ➥property to display totals
    varGrandTotal = csc_varSetColTotals(strSource, wDescrCol,
    ➥"")
End If
```

TIP

An alternate approach is to set the default values of the text boxes with values derived from csc_varSetColTotals() while the subform is in the design stage. This eliminates the necessity to reset the DefaultEditing property of the subform. Alternative code is included in csc_wCreateSubForm() for this method. Unfortunately, Access does not apply the Format property to default values, so this approach is applicable only to data for which you don't need special formatting.

The csc_varSetColTotals() function (see Listing 24.19) that totals each column is similar to csc_varSetRowTotal(), except that the **For...Next** and **Do While...Loop** structures are inverted in sequence. Following is a listing for the csc_varSetColTotals() function.

Listing 24.19. Access Basic code for the csc_VarSetColTotals() function.

```
Function csc_varSetColTotals (strSource As String, wDescrCol As Integer,
strName As String) As Variant
    'Purpose:   Total each of the data columns of a crosstab query
    'Arguments: strSource = name of source table (or query)
    '           wDescrCol = column number for description
    '           strName = name of form (if calculation is in design
             ➥mode)
```

```
'Returns:    Grand total of column totals (Variant)

Dim varGrandTotal As Variant    'For crossfoot test, must be a
                                ➥Variant
Dim varColTotal As Variant      'Totals for each column of data
Dim wColCtr As Integer          'Counts columns
Dim wCtrlCtr As Integer         'Counts controls on form
Dim varRetVal As Variant        'Return value for SysCmd()
Dim wSysCtr As Integer          'Counter for SysCmd()

Dim dbCurrent As Database       'Temporary objects
Dim tblSource As Table

Set dbCurrent = DBEngine(0)(0)
Set tblSource = dbCurrent.OpenTable(strSource)

varRetVal = SysCmd(1, "Totaling" & Str$(UBound(rgstrFields) -
➥wDescrCol - 1) & " columns.", (UBound(rgstrFields) - wDescrCol -
➥1))
wSysCtr = 1


'Process each column of the query
'Total the columns that have values (skip the description and
➥totals fields)
For wColCtr = (wDescrCol + 1) To (UBound(rgstrFields) - 1)
    'Go to the first record and total all of the values in the
    ➥column
    tblSource.MoveFirst
    Do While Not tblSource.EOF
        If Not IsNull(tblSource(rgstrFields(wColCtr))) Then
            'Don't add null values (Value + Null = Null)
            varColTotal = varColTotal + tblSource(
            ➥rgstrFields(wColCtr))
        End If
        tblSource.MoveNext
        'DoEvents    'For safety
    Loop

    'Alternative syntax for update in run mode or in design
    ➥mode
    If Len(strName) > 0 Then
        Forms(strName).Form(rgstrFields(wColCtr) & "
        ➥Total").DefaultValue = varColTotal
    Else
        Forms(strFormName)!sbfCrosstab.Form(rgstrFields(wColCtr)
        ➥& " Total") = varColTotal
    End If

    'Create the crosstab total
    varGrandTotal = varGrandTotal + varColTotal
    varColTotal = 0
```

continues

Listing 24.19. continued

```
        varRetVal = SysCmd(2, wSysCtr)
        wSysCtr = wSysCtr + 1
    Next

    'Enter the grand total in the totals column, if one exists
    If Len(strTotalsCol) > 0 Then
        If Len(strName) > 0 Then
            Forms(strName).Form(strTotalsCol & "
            ➡Total").DefaultValue = varGrandTotal
        Else
            Forms(strFormName)!sbfCrosstab.Form(strTotalsCol &
            ➡" Total") = varGrandTotal
        End If
    End If

    'Clean up
    tblSource.Close
    dbCurrent.Close

    csc_varSetColTotals = varGrandTotal
End Function
```

The code of Listing 22.19 uses the **SysCmd()** function to indicate the progress of the totaling operation. The code for other functions in the Create Subform from Crosstab module in AB_EXAMP.MDB uses **SysCmd()** to display progress. **SysCmd()** is useful for determining bottlenecks in your code. For example, you can observe the effect of using **BeginTrans...CommitTrans** by commenting out these two lines in the csc_varSetRowTotals() function, and then watch the progress bar slow to a crawl while Access individually rewrites each record, instead of rewriting the table as a whole with the transaction-processing method.

An example of a crossfooted subform appears in Figure 24.18. The column totals of the subform in Figure 24.18 are added to the subform in run mode so that the appropriate format is applied to the values.

Creating Worksheets from User-Defined Subform Data

The majority of the users of your Access applications are likely to employ spreadsheet applications in their everyday work. After creating a query, users may want to manipulate the data or try "what-ifs" on the query result displayed in the subform. Although OLE Automation is a more flexible method of creating Excel worksheets from Access 2.0 data, users of your applications may not own Excel 5.0. (Using OLE

Automation to create worksheets is one of the subjects of Chapter 17, "Charting Data with Microsoft Graph 5.0.")

FIGURE 24.18.

Row and column totals added to the Crosstab Query form.

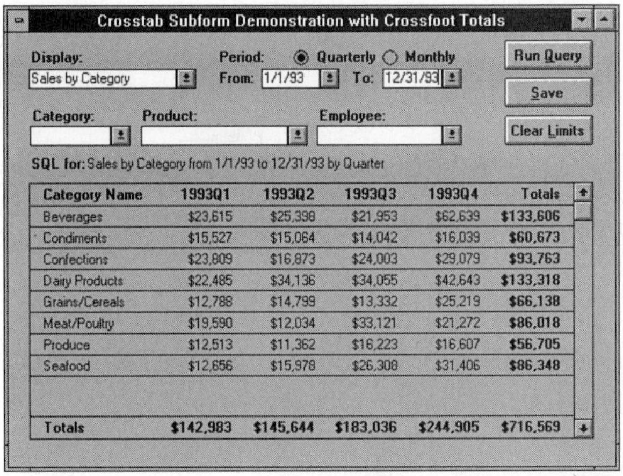

You can generate an Excel or Lotus 1-2-3 for Windows worksheet from the data contained in the subform by creating a temporary table from the user-defined **QueryDef** object and then using the TransferSpreadsheet action to create a worksheet file from the temporary table. Access 2.0 lets you export a spreadsheet file directly from the **QueryDef** object, but using a **Table** object provides the opportunity to add column totals to the exported file. You need to let the user choose the type of file for the spreadsheet application he or she employs, as well as to designate a filename under which to save the file. Thus, you need to provide a Save As common dialog box, shown in Figure 24.19, in addition to the code to create the table.

> **NOTE**
>
> You can modify the code in the listings that follow so that you do not need to re-create the table on which the subform is based when row or column totals are added to the subform. You can determine whether the subform is based on a **Table** or a **QueryDef** object by testing the value of the RecordSource property of the subform. The performance penalty for re-creating the table, however, is not substantial.

The code for the Create Worksheet from Subform module is included in the AB_EXAMP.MDB database on the accompanying diskette. Import the Create Worksheet from Subform module into NWIND.MDB to add the capability to save your subform data to an Excel or Lotus 1-2-3 worksheet file.

FIGURE 24.19.

Saving the content of a crosstab subform to a worksheet file.

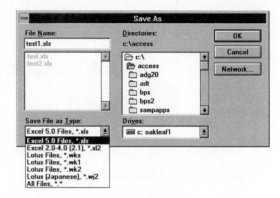

The Declarations Section of the Create Worksheet from Subform Module

The Declarations section of the Create Worksheet from Subform module is derived from the COMMDLGS.MDA library described in the section, "Converting the DIALOGS Visual Basic Application to an Access Basic Library," of Chapter 25, "Stretching the Limits of Access." In this case, only the function and constant declarations required to use the FileSaveAs dialog box are included in the Declarations section of the module.

Listing 24.20. The Declarations section of the Create Worksheet from Subform module.

```
'Purpose:  General purpose module to create worksheets from queries
'Requires: List of fields in array rgstrFields()
'          Name of source query in strSQLSource

Option Compare Database    'Use database order for string
                              ➥comparisons
Option Explicit

Global strSQLSource As String 'Source name for SQL operations (from
➥Create Subform)
Global rgstrFields() As String 'Array of field names for Excel
➥worksheet SQL

'Function prototype declaration for the CTL3D.DLL
'CTL3D.DLL provides a gray background for dialogs (comes with
➥Access)
Declare Function cws_GetModuleHandle Lib "Kernel"
     Alias "GetModuleHandle"
    (ByVal lpModuleName As String) As Integer
Declare Function cws_Ctl3dRegister Lib "CTL3D.DLL"
     Alias "Ctl3DRegister"
```

```
        (ByVal hInstance As Integer) As Integer
Declare Function cws_Ctl3dAutoSubClass Lib "CTL3D.DLL"
     Alias "Ctl3DAutoSubClass"
     (ByVal hInstance As Integer) As Integer
Declare Function cws_Ctl3dUnregister Lib "CTL3D.DLL"
     Alias "Ctl3DUnregister"
     (ByVal hInstance As Integer) As Integer

Dim hInstance As Integer

'File Open/Save structures and declarations

'Note the similarities between this type declaration and that for
'tagOPENFILENAME in the ANALYZER.MDA UI module

Type OPENFILENAME
     lStructSize As Long
     hwndOwner As Integer
     hInstance As Integer
     lpstrFilter As Long
     lpstrCustomFilter As Long
     nMaxCustFilter As Long
     nFilterIndex As Long
     lpstrFile As Long
     nMaxFile As Long
     lpstrFileTitle As Long
     nMaxFileTitle As Long
     lpstrInitialDir As Long
     lpstrTitle As Long
     dwFlags As Long
     nFileOffset As Integer
     nFileExtension As Integer
     lpstrDefExt As Long
     lCustData As Long
     lpfnHook As Long
     lpTemplateName As Long
End Type

Declare Function cws_GetOpenFileName Lib "COMMDLG.DLL"
     Alias "GetOpenFileName"
     (pOPENFILENAME As OPENFILENAME) As Integer

Declare Function cws_GetSaveFileName Lib "COMMDLG.DLL"
     Alias "GetSaveFileName"
     (pOPENFILENAME As OPENFILENAME) As Integer

Declare Function cws_GetFileTitle Lib "COMMDLG.DLL"
     Alias "GetFileTitle"
     (ByVal FName As String,
      ByVal Title As String,
      Size As Integer)
```

continues

Listing 24.20. continued

```
'Note: All constants are declared with module-level, not Global,
➥scope
'       Only the constants used in this module are declared
Const OFN_HIDEREADONLY = &H4
Const OFN_PATHMUSTEXIST = &H800

'Retrieves error value
Declare Function cws_CommDlgExtendedError Lib "COMMDLG.DLL"
        Alias "CommDlgExtendedError" () As Long

'GLOBAL MEMORY function declarations
'Note: These functions *must* be aliased because they are used by a
'       variety of Windows API function calls

Declare Function cws_GlobalAlloc Lib "Kernel"
        Alias "GlobalAlloc"
    (ByVal wdwFlags As Integer,
     ByVal dwBytes As Long) As Integer

Declare Function cws_GlobalFree Lib "Kernel"
        Alias "GlobalFree"
    (ByVal hMem As Integer) As Integer

Declare Function cws_GlobalLock Lib "Kernel"
        Alias "GlobalLock"
    (ByVal hMem As Integer) As Long

Declare Function cws_GlobalUnlock Lib "Kernel"
        Alias "GlobalUnlock"
    (ByVal hMem As Integer) As Integer

Const GMEM_MOVEABLE = &H2
Const GMEM_ZEROINIT = &H40
Const GHND = (GMEM_MOVEABLE Or GMEM_ZEROINIT)

Declare Sub cws_hmemcpy Lib "Kernel" Alias "hmemcpy"
     (lpDest As Any,
      lpSource As Any,
      ByVal dwBytes As Long)
```

The *cws_wCreateWorksheet( )* Function

The code for the `cws_wCreateWorksheet()` function uses a make-table query to create a temporary table, `tblWorksheet`, that serves as the source table for the worksheet file that results from execution of the `TransferSpreadsheet` action. Access has a limited number of worksheet export formats (Excel 2.1 to 4.0 and Excel 5.0 .XLS and Lotus 1-2-3 .WKS, .WK1, .WK2, and .WJ2), so you can define the filter used to choose the file type in cws_wCreateWorksheet(). This eliminates the need to include the filter-parsing procedure (ParseFilter) in your code.

> **NOTE**
>
> The Excel 5.0 .XLS (Workbook) format and Lotus 1-2-3 .WJ2 (Japanese version of Lotus 1-2-3) format are new spreadsheet formats added in Access 2.0.

Listing 24.23. Access Basic code for the cws_wCreateWorksheet() function.

```
Function cws_wCreateWorksheet () As Integer
    'Purpose: Create a table from the query, then export the table
    '         as an Excel worksheet to a designated file
    'Returns: True if successful, False on failure

    'Set up the required database objects
    Dim dbCurrent As Database
    Dim qdfExcel As QueryDef

    Dim strSQL As String            'The SQL string to create the
                                    ➥table
    Dim wCtr As Integer             'General-purpose counter
    Dim strFileSaveName As String   'The name of the saved
                                    ➥worksheet file
    Dim strFilter As String         'The filter from which to
                                    ➥choose the type of file
    Dim strDefaultExt As String     'The default extension for the
                                    ➥saved file
    Dim wResult As Integer          'Return value of function
    Dim wType As Integer            'Type of worksheet file (see
                                    ➥code that follows)

    'Create the worksheet filter string
    strFilter = "Excel 5.0 Files, *.xls" & Chr$(0) & "*.xls" & Chr$(0)
    strFilter = strFilter & "Excel 2.0-4.0 (2.1), *.xl2" & Chr$(0) &
    ➥"*.xls" & Chr$(0)

    strFilter = strFilter & "Lotus Files, *.wks" & Chr$(0) &
    ➥"*.wks" & Chr$(0)
    strFilter = strFilter & "Lotus Files, *.wk1" & Chr$(0) &
    ➥"*.wk1" & Chr$(0)
    strFilter = strFilter & "Lotus Files, *.wk2" & Chr$(0) &
    ➥"*.wk2" & Chr$(0)
    strFilter = strFilter & "Lotus (Japanese), *.wj2" & Chr$(0) &
    ➥"*.wk2" & Chr$(0)
    strFilter = strFilter & "All Files, *.*" & Chr$(0) & "*.*" &
```

continues

Listing 24.23. continued

```
➥Chr$(0)
    strFilter = strFilter + Chr$(0)      'strFilter is terminated by
                                         ➥double-null
    strDefaultExt = "XLS"

    DoCmd Hourglass True

    Set dbCurrent = DBEngine(0)(0)

    'Create the SQL statement for the make-table query
    'Note: Only values for one table are involved, so table name
    'identifiers are not required
    strSQL = "SELECT DISTINCTROW "
    For wCtr = 1 To UBound(rgstrFields)
        strSQL = strSQL & "[" & rgstrFields(wCtr) & "]"
        If wCtr <> UBound(rgstrFields) Then
            strSQL = strSQL & ","
        End If
        strSQL = strSQL & " "
    Next wCtr

    'Note: In Access SQL, the INTO clause must precede the FROM
    ➥clause
    strSQL = strSQL + "INTO tblWorkSheet FROM [" & strSQLSource &
    ➥"] WITH OWNERACCESS OPTION;"

    'Delete the QueryDef if it exists
    On Error Resume Next
    dbCurrent.DeleteQueryDef ("qryWorksheet")
    On Error GoTo 0

    'Create an Access make-table query definition using the SQL
    ➥string
    Set qdfExcel = dbCurrent.CreateQueryDef("qryWorksheet", strSQL)

    'Execute the make-table query with system warnings off
    DoCmd SetWarnings False
    DoCmd OpenQuery "qryWorksheet"
    DoCmd SetWarnings True

    'Call the Ctl3D function to make dialogs similar to Access
    hInstance = cws_GetModuleHandle("msaccess.exe")
    If hInstance > 0 Then
        wResult = cws_Ctl3dRegister(hInstance)
        wResult = cws_Ctl3dAutoSubClass(hInstance)
    End If

    DoCmd Hourglass False

    'Open the File Save As dialog
```

```
    strFileSaveName = cws_strFileSaveDlg(strFilter, strDefaultExt)

    'Turn off the Ctl3D function
    If hInstance > 0 Then
        wResult = cws_Ctl3dUnregister(hInstance)
    End If

    If Len(strFileSaveName) > 0 Then
        'Note: File is exported in Excel 2.1 format and is
        'converted by Excel to Excel 3.0 or 4.0 format
        'Note: Lotus .wk3 files are not supported, Lotus converts
        ➥them

        If InStr(strFileSaveName, ".xl2") > 0 Then
            wType = 0
        ElseIf InStr(strFileSaveName, ".wks") > 0 Then
            wType = 1
        ElseIf InStr(strFileSaveName, ".wk1") > 0 Then
            wType = 2
        ElseIf InStr(strFileSaveName, ".wk2") > 0 Then
            wType = 3
        ElseIf InStr(strFileSaveName, ".wkj") > 0 Then
            wType = 4
        Else
            wType = 5
        End If

        'Execute TransferSpreadsheet export with field names
        DoCmd TransferSpreadsheet A_EXPORT, wType, "tblWorkSheet",
        ➥strFileSaveName, True
    End If

    cws_wCreateWorksheet = True
    Exit Function

WorksheetError:
    DoCmd Hourglass False
    MsgBox Error$, 16, "Worksheet Creation Error"
    Exit Function
End Function
```

> **NOTE**
>
> If you choose the .XL2 extension for Excel 2.0-4.0, Access exports Excel worksheet files in Excel 2.1 BIFF format. When you open the worksheet in Excel 3.0 or 4.0 and then choose Save or Save As from Excel's File menu, you receive a message box asking whether you want to save the file in the format of the later version of Excel.

The *cws_strFileSaveDlg( )* Function

The cws_strFileSaveDlg() function is taken directly from the szFileSaveDlg() function of the Common Dialogs module of COMMDLGS.MDA. The cws_strFileSaveDlg() function returns the name of the file for the save operation, if the user chooses a valid filename.

Listing 24.24. Access Basic code for the cws_strFileSaveDlg() function.

```
Function cws_strFileSaveDlg (strFilter As String, strDefaultExt As
➥String) As String
    'Purpose:     Use the FileSave dialog to return a filename with a
                  ➥WFP
    'Accepts:     A filter string terminated in a double-null
    '             A default extension with the format *.ext
    'Returns:     Path and filename of the saved file, Null string on
                  ➥cancel
    'Uses:        Common Dialog File Save dialog

    'Note:        This procedure is similar to GetOpenFileName
    '             Normally used for FileSaveAs operations

    Dim S As OPENFILENAME
    Dim strFile As String
    Dim wSize As Integer
    Dim hMemHandle As Integer
    Dim lpAddress As Long
    Dim wOK As Integer
    Dim strFileName As String

    On Error GoTo FileSaveError:

    'Create a 128-byte buffer
    strFile = String$(128, 0)

    'Re-create a 128-byte buffer for strFile
    strFile = strDefaultExt & String$(128 - Len(strDefaultExt), 0)
    wSize = Len(strFile) + Len(strFilter)

    hMemHandle = cws_GlobalAlloc(GHND, wSize)

    If hMemHandle = 0 Then
        MsgBox "Unable to allocate memory", 16, "File Save Error"
        Exit Function
    End If

    lpAddress = cws_GlobalLock(hMemHandle)
```

```
    'Create local copy of Global memory block
    Call cws_hmemcpy(ByVal lpAddress, ByVal (strFile + strFilter),
    ➥wSize)

    S.1StructSize = Len(S)
    S.hwndOwner = Screen.ActiveForm.hWnd
    S.dwFlags = OFN_HIDEREADONLY Or OFN_PATHMUSTEXIST
    S.nFilterIndex = 1
    S.lpstrFile = lpAddress
    S.nMaxFile = Len(strFile)
    S.lpstrFilter = lpAddress + Len(strFile)

    'Open the FileSaveAs dialog with the structure as the argument
    If cws_GetSaveFileName(S) = 0 Then
        MsgBox "Operation canceled by user.", 16, "File Save
        ➥Dialog"
        Exit Function
    Else
        'Make a local copy of the filename specified in the dialog
        Call cws_hmemcpy(ByVal strFile, ByVal lpAddress,
        ➥Len(strFile))

        wOK = cws_GlobalUnlock(hMemHandle)    'Free the global
        ➥memory
        wOK = cws_GlobalFree(hMemHandle)
    End If

    'The filename is returned as a null-terminated string
    strFileName = Left$(strFile, InStr(strFile, Chr$(0)) - 1)

    cws_strFileSaveDlg = LCase$(strFileName)
    Exit Function

FileSaveError:
    MsgBox Error$, 16, "File Save Error"
    Exit Function
End Function
```

Figure 24.20 shows the TEST1.XLS workbook file (created in Figure 24.19) opened in Excel 5.0, after apply Auto-Fit column widths. The column totals do not appear because column totals are not included in a record of the table. It is a relatively simple process to append an additional record with the totals to the table, prior to exporting the table's content to the workbook file. However, it is equally simple to sum the columns in Excel.

FIGURE 24.20.

A worksheet created by the `cws_wCreate Worksheet()` *function opened in Excel 5.0.*

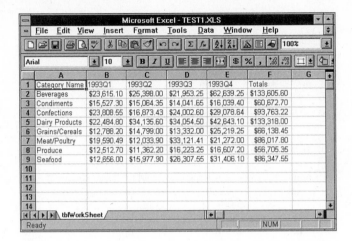

25

Stretching the Limits of Access

This chapter covers advanced topics in Access programming that are outside the development mainstream. The first part of the chapter discusses the use of Access 2.0 to add tables to a Microsoft SQL Server for Windows NT 4.2 database. You then use these tables with an online transaction processing (OLTP) application that demonstrates the capabilities of Access 2.0's new, built-in SQL pass-through feature. MSA_OLTP.MDB demonstrates that you can create a robust OLTP application with Access 2.0 that rivals or exceeds the transaction processing speed of OLTP applications created with Visual Basic 3.0, C++, or any other front-end generator application. Binary, random-access, and sequential file functions of Access Basic enable you to read from and create files with formats not supported by Access's import and export functions. Although OLE Object fields are designed specifically to store OLE objects, you can store anything you want in them with the **AppendChunk()** and **GetChunk()** methods. Each of these topics, plus suggestions for importing Visual Basic code to Access, are included in the topics of this chapter.

Using Access to Create SQL Server for Windows NT Tables

As an Access developer, you'll often be called upon to port an Access application to a client-server configuration. This is a straightforward process, especially if the application you are porting uses tables attached from a shared Access .MDB data file. The basic steps involved are as follows:

1. Create an ODBC data source for the test database. (Creating ODBC data sources is one of the subjects of Chapter 20, "Front-Ending Client-Server Databases.")

2. Export the data in the Access tables to a new test server database. Using Access 2.0's export feature ensures that the SQL data types in your server database will be compatible with your application.

3. Duplicate the indexes, default values, and validation (business) rules for each table using the features provided by the server RDBMS. Use a unique, clustered index for the primary key field(s) of each table, if your server RDBMS supports clustered indexes. (Use a reasonable fill-factor, such as 50 percent, to provide slack space for added pages in the clustered index to speed addition of new records to tables with clustered indexes.)

4. Create triggers, or the equivalent, required to enforce referential integrity in OLTP applications. Some client-server RDBMSs implement referential integrity enforcement using SQL-92's new referential integrity reserved

words; others use methods similar to those employed by Access 2.0's Relationships dialog box.

5. Write stored procedures, or the equivalent, to perform cascading updates and deletions, if your Access 2.0 application employs these features. Some server RDBMSs use SQL-92 CASCADE DELETE and CASCADE ON UPDATE reserved words to implement these features.

6. Decide which, if any, tables will remain as replicated local lookup tables in the application .MDB. Using local tables for static data minimizes network traffic and speeds lookup operations. Import the local tables to the application .MDB file.

7. Delete the existing attachments to the .MDB data file in the application .MDB and re-create the attachments from the test database. If the attached tables include the database owner prefix (usually dbo_ for SQL Server tables), rename the attachments to remove the prefix.

8. If your Access table or field names include spaces, symbols, or punctuation characters that are converted by the export process to underscores, you must change all such names in your application .MDB to conform to the server's naming convention.

9. Test your application with the attached server tables. It is especially important to set up more than one workstation with the modified application .MDB so that you can test server page-locking for multiuser OLTP applications.

10. To improve performance, especially with OLTP applications, you may want to modify your application to use Access 2.0's native SQL pass-through feature.

11. After completing the test program, shut down the existing application, create the production server database, and install the new application .MDB on each client workstation.

TIP

Unlike with Access, some table and field names in many client-server RDBMSs are case-sensitive. The default installation for Microsoft and Sybase SQL Server results in case-sensitive object names. If you need to rename tables or fields in your application .MDB, be sure to observe the case-sensitivity rules.

Microsoft SQL Server for Windows NT 4.2 (abbreviated SQLSNT in this book) includes a bulk copy program (BCP) that is designed for high-speed import of ASCII or ANSI text files in fixed-width or delimited formats. Using BCP, you can achieve table data import speeds of between 200 and 400 rows per second. BCP, however, requires that you define the table design and then create an import specification for the text data you plan to import. While these two steps are not especially difficult, they can be quite time-consuming when many tables are involved.

You can save a considerable amount of effort, at least in the test phase of a client-server port, by exporting the tables from your Access .MDB rather than using BCP. If your Access tables have more than 10,000 records, you may want to consider exporting a subset of the tables to create the table designs and to use for testing. (Exporting Access tables to a server database is not noted for its speed.) When you move to the production stage, you can delete the existing records and use BCP to import all of the records of each table.

> **TIP**
>
> When moving to a production environment and using BCP to import records to the server database, make sure you delete every index of every table in the database before you import the data. Indexes can slow the importation process greatly. You also may need to temporarily disable triggers and stored procedures that affect the import process. After the import process is completed and you have verified that the table data is intact, re-create the indexes and enable the triggers and stored procedures.

Exporting Northwind Traders Tables to SQL Server

The next section of this chapter uses server tables created from Access 2.0's NWIND.MDB sample database. Thus, this section shows you how to export to a client-server database the tables you need to use the demonstration OLTP application. Although this example uses SQLSNT as the back-end, the procedure for exporting tables to other client-server RDBMSs is quite similar. The primary differences between exporting data from Access 2.0 to modern client-server RDBMSs are the tools you use to add indexes, rules, and other server-specific methods to the server tables and the database. The following steps are required to create the new database, set up an ODBC data source for the new database, and export the Northwind Traders tables to the database. These steps are identical for the 32-bit versions of the SQL Server tools running under Windows NT and the 16-bit workstation version of these tools located on a WfWg 3.11 workstation.

1. Use SQLSNT's SQL Administrator to create a new database named "nwind" with a size of at least 1MB. If you don't have room for the database

in your master device, create a new device (.DAT file) to contain the nwind database. Grant public users of the database full permissions for all objects in the database. (See the *System Administrator's Guide* for SQLSNT for information on granting permissions for database objects.)

2. Choose **D**atabases from SQL Administrator's **M**anage menu, select the Database in the Manage Databases window, and choose **O**ptions from the submenu to display the Database Options dialog box. Select the Select Into/Bulkcopy Option and set its Value to True. Select the Trunc(ate) Log on Ch(ec)kp(oin)t Option and set its Value to True. (See Figure 25.1.) This step assures that you do not create a large transaction log when testing the OLTP application. Close the SQL Administrator.

FIGURE 25.1.

Setting the Truncate Log on Checkpoint option with the SQL Administrator application.

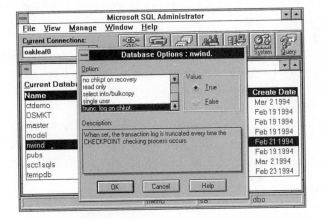

3. Create an SQL Server ODBC data source using the ODBC Administrator application with the Data Source Name = NWIND and Database Name = nwind, as shown in Figure 25.2. (See Chapter 20 for detailed instructions on creating ODBC data sources.) Close the ODBC Administrator (and the Control Panel if you are not using Windows NT). The following entries for your new data source are added to the [NWIND] section of ODBC.INI:

```
[NWIND]
Driver=D:\WINDOWS\SYSTEM\SQLSRVR.DLL
Description=Northwind Traders on SQL Server NT
Server=OAKLEAF0
Database=nwind
OemToAnsi=No
LastUser=sa
34Cancel=
Language=
```

FIGURE 25.2.

Creating the NWIND ODBC data source.

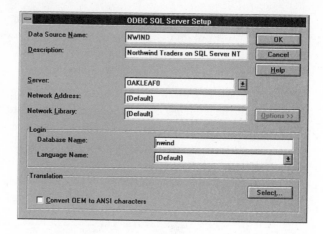

4. Launch Access and open NWIND.MDB. Choose **E**xport from the **F**ile menu to open the Export dialog box, and double-click the <SQL Database> item in the Destination Database list box (see Figure 25.3) to display the Select Microsoft Access Object dialog box.

FIGURE 25.3.

Choosing the ODBC driver manager for the data export process.

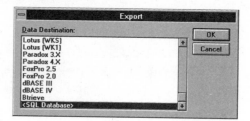

5. Double-click the Categories table of the Objects in NWIND list box (see Figure 25.4) to display the second version of the Export dialog box. (See Figure 25.5.) Click the OK button to accept the table name proposed by Access. (Access automatically substitutes underscore characters when spaces occur in table names.) The SQL Data Sources dialog box appears.

FIGURE 25.4.

Selecting the table to export in the Select Microsoft Access Object dialog box.

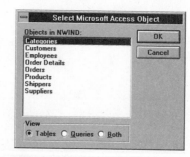

FIGURE 25.5.

Confirming the table name in the Export dialog box.

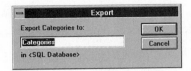

6. Double-click NWIND in the Select Data Source list box (see Figure 25.6) to display the SQL Server Login dialog box for the NWIND data source.

FIGURE 25.6.

Selecting the NWIND ODBC data source.

7. Enter your SQL Server Login ID and Password. Figure 25.7 shows the full SQL Server Login dialog box that appears when you click the Options button. The Database, Application Name, and Workstation ID text boxes are filled for you by the [NWIND] entry created in ODBC.INI and Access. (The initial, default login for SQL Server is "sa" with an empty password.)

FIGURE 25.7.

Logging into the nwind database.

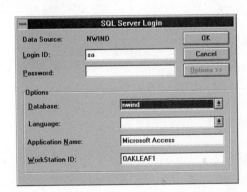

8. Click the OK button to export the table to the nwind database.

9. Repeat steps 5 through 8 for each of the tables in NWIND.MDB. The OLE Object fields of the Categories and Employees tables are not exported to SQL Server 4.2. (Future versions of Microsoft SQL Server for Windows NT are expected to accommodate the OLE Object data type of Access tables.)

To use SQL Object Manager to view the data in one or more of the tables to verify that the data was exported properly, follow these steps:

1. Launch SQL Object Manager from the SQL Server Tools program group and connect to the server.

2. Select nwind as the Current Database and click the Query button.

3. Type **SELECT * FROM tablename** in the Query window and click the Execute button. Make sure you type **tablename** in the correct case. A portion of the query result set for the Orders table appears in Figure 25.8. Note the substitution of underscore characters for spaces in the field names.

FIGURE 25.8.

Part of the query result set for the Orders table.

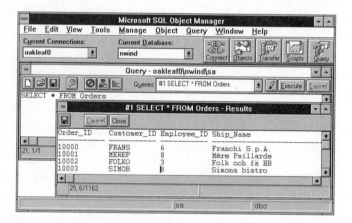

4. Close the two query windows and click the Objects button to display the Database Objects window. As with Access databases, SQL Server databases contain a variety of system tables whose names are prefixed with "sys." User tables appear in alphabetical order following the system tables. (See Figure 25.9.)

5. Double-click a user table entry to display the Manage Tables window. Figure 25.10 shows the Manage Tables window for the Orders table. You can verify that the SQL field data types for the fields of imported tables are correct in this window.

FIGURE 25.9.

Selecting a table in the Database Objects window.

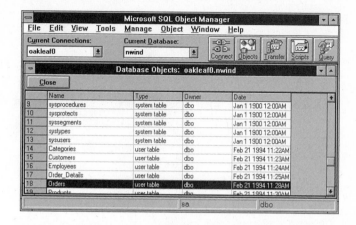

FIGURE 25.10.

Viewing the field properties of the Orders table in the Manage Tables window.

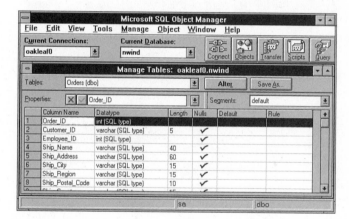

Adding Indexes to the Server Tables

You use the SQL Object Manager application to add indexes to each table. You also can use SQL Object Manager to designate primary and foreign key fields to enforce referential integrity. To add indexes to your SQL Server tables with SQL Object Manager, follow these steps:

1. Choose Indexes from SQL Object Manager's Manage menu to display the Manage Indexes window. Select the table to which you want to add indexes from the Tables drop-down list.

2. Click the New button to display the Specify New Index Name dialog box. Enter an identifier for your index (usually the field name, often preceded by i or idx), and click the OK button. (See Figure 25.11.)

FIGURE 25.11.

Adding a new index to a SQL Server table.

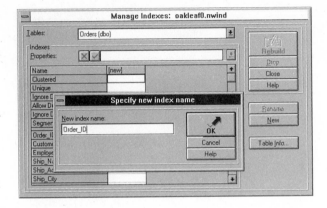

3. The Order_ID field of the Orders table is the primary key for the table. Therefore, you should create a unique, clustered index on this field. Click the Clustered and Unique cells of the Order_ID index column, and then click the Order_ID field. SQL Object Manager puts a 1 in the Order_ID column, indicating that Order_ID is the first field of the index and, in this case, the only field in the index. (See Figure 25.12.)

FIGURE 25.12.

Specifying a clustered, unique index on the Order_ID field.

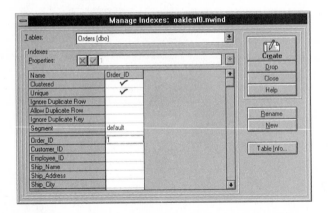

4. Click the Create button to display the Create New Index? dialog box shown in Figure 25.13. Order numbers are entered in sequence, so you don't need to provide slack space in the index for new entries. (Fill Factor = 0.) Click the Yes button to create the index. (You can tell that the index was created, because the Create button changes to the Rebuild button.)

FIGURE 25.13.

Creating the clustered, unique index on the primary key field of the Orders table.

5. To improve performance, you should add non-unique indexes on the Customer_ID and Order_Date fields. Repeat steps 3 and 4 for these two fields, naming the indexes Customer_ID and Order_Date. Don't check the Clustered or Unique cells for these indexes. You can specify only one clustered index on a table, and neither of these fields would allow a unique index. Specify a Fill Factor of 50 percent for these two indexes so that new records append more quickly. Your Manage Indexes window for the Orders Database appears as shown in Figure 25.14.

FIGURE 25.14.

The final index specification for the Orders table.

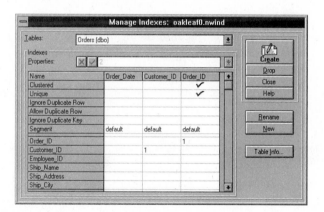

6. Repeat steps 2 through 5 for each of the other tables in your database. (Select the table to index in the Tables drop-down list.) Duplicate each of the indexes of the tables in NWIND.MDB in your server tables. In the case of the Order_Details table, the primary key fields are Order_ID and Product_ID, so these fields appear as field 1 and field 2 in the unique, clustered PrimaryKey index.

To establish the relations between tables with SQL Object manager, follow these optional steps:

1. Choose **K**eys from the **M**anage menu to display the Manage Keys window.

2. Select the table for which you want to designate the primary key field(s) in the Working Table/View drop-down list, and select the field(s) for the primary key in the Columns drop-down list. (See Figure 25.15.)

FIGURE 25.15.

Specifying primary key field(s) in the Manage Keys window.

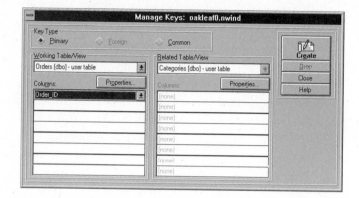

3. With the Primary option button selected in the Key Type group, click the Create button to establish the field(s) as the primary key.

4. Click the Foreign option button and select the related table in the Related Table/View drop-down list. If the primary key and foreign key field names are identical, the entry is made for you in the Columns list. (See Figure 25.16.)

FIGURE 25.16.

Specifying a foreign key field in a related table.

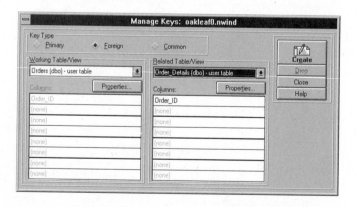

5. Repeat steps 2 through 4 to establish the primary key field(s) and related foreign keys for the remainder of the tables, except Employees and Shippers. Refer to Access 2.0's Relationships window and dialog box, if necessary, to determine the primary and foreign key fields for the relationships. You do

not establish relations for the Employees or Shippers tables, because the MSA_OLTP.MDB database uses local copies of these tables.

Attaching Server Tables and Renaming the Attachments

Attaching server tables from an SQL data source is almost as simple as attaching tables from an Access database. The attachments to the tables in the nwind server database are created with these steps:

1. Choose Attach Table from Access 2.0's File menu to display the Attach dialog box.
2. Double-click the <SQL Databases> item in the Data Source list box (see Figure 25.17) to open the SQL Data sources dialog box.

FIGURE 25.17.

The Attach dialog box that specifies the ODBC driver manager as the source of the attached tables.

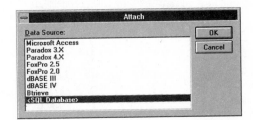

3. Double-click the NWIND item in the Select Data Source combo box (see Figure 25.18) to open the login dialog box. Enter your SQL Server Login ID and Password, and then click the OK button to display the Attach Tables dialog box.

FIGURE 25.18.

Selecting the SQL data source for the attached tables.

4. Select the table you want to attach in the Tables in <SQL Database> list box, and tick the Save Login ID and Password Locally check box to eliminate the necessity of re-entering your login ID and password each time your application uses one of the attached tables. (See Figure 25.19.) Click the Attach button to create the attachment.

FIGURE 25.19.

*Selecting the server
table to attach in
the Attach Tables
dialog box.*

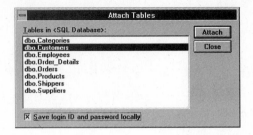

5. Repeat step 4 for each of the tables you want to attach to your Access application. MSA_OLTP.MDB uses tables attached from the Customers, Order_Details, Orders, and products tables. The Employees and Shippers tables are local replicated tables. (The tblOrder_Details table is a temporary local table.) When the process is completed, the Database window for MSA_OLTP.MDB appears as shown in Figure 25.20.

FIGURE 25.20.

*The Database
window after
attaching the four
tables required by
MSA_OLTP.MDB.*

6. To rename your attachments to conform to their original Access names, select the attachment and choose Rename from the File menu to display the Rename *tablename* dialog box. Delete the "dbo_" prefix from the attached tables and click the OK button. (See Figure 25.21.)

FIGURE 25.21.

*Renaming the
attached server
table to remove the
dbo_ prefix.*

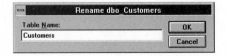

7. Repeat step 6 for each of the tables you attach. In the case of dbo_Order_Details, delete the "dbo_" prefix and replace the underscore between "Order" and "Details" with a space. This demonstrates that you can

retain references to table names that contain spaces in your application. (You cannot, however, retain references to Access field names with spaces, unless you alias all such field names in your queries.) The Database window with the renamed tables appears as shown in Figure 25.22.

FIGURE 25.22.

The renamed tables in the database window.

Importing Server Tables

It is a good policy to import initial copies of local tables from the server, rather than from the initial Access .MDB source, to ensure that field names and field data types expected by your Access application match those of the server tables. This is especially true when you plan to periodically replicate the local tables from the server database. You use the same process, except for the menu choice, to import tables to your Access application described in the preceding section to attach tables. The Employees and the Shippers tables are imported because the data in these tables changes infrequently.

> **WARNING**
>
> If the field names of the replicated table don't match the initial version supplied with your application, your application will experience runtime errors after the first replication process.

Speeding Client-Server Queries with SQL Pass-Through

New!

Chapter 20 provided a brief introduction to the use of Access 2.0's new SQL pass-through feature. This section expands on the subject of SQL pass-through, using a demonstration OLTP application to compare the speed of data retrieval and transaction processing using attached server tables versus SQL pass-through. The advantage of SQL pass-through is that your queries are not parsed and optimized by the Jet engine's query optimizer; this speeds transmission of the query to the sever. On the other hand, if the client workstations have sufficient memory, repetitive processing of similar queries may be faster with attached tables.

Although the Jet engine sends as much of the query directly to the server as Jet believes the server can handle, the optimization process requires a finite amount of time. The amount of traffic between the server and your application may increase significantly, compared to simply sending SQL statements to and receiving rows of data from the server. Updating server tables is handled by sending INSERT and UPDATE SQL statements to the server. Another advantage of SQL pass-through is that you don't need to attach the tables to your Access application to obtain or update data in the server database.

The MSA_OLTP.MDB database, included on the accompanying diskette, was developed for Microsoft Corporation and was demonstrated by Greg Nelson, a Microsoft Access product manager, at the Microsoft Tech*Ed '94 conference in New Orleans in the presentation called "Creating Scalable Client-Server Applications with Microsoft Access" (AC303). The application also was included as one of the Access 2.0 roll-out examples in the Microsoft DevCast live satellite uplink that originated from Tech*Ed '94.

MSA_OLTP.MDB is designed for live, online order entry from telephone calls placed by Northwind Traders' customers. Unlike most Access applications, the Northwind Traders Client-Server Order Entry application has a "plain vanilla" user interface. The design of the application is based on the following premises:

■ The application is required to find existing customer names by entering the first few letters of the company name or by entry of part or all of the assigned customer ID. When the specific customer is selected, all past orders for the customer must be displayed. Invoice line-item data for the order must be displayed on request.

■ When a customer calls to check on the status of an order, the application is required to find the order by entry of the complete sales order number, displaying the customer information, order data, and line-item details at once.

■ The application must provide the ability to add new customers and add new orders for new and existing customers.

■ The application must be easy for a variety of operators to use. Northwind Trader's order-entry operator has 20 years of IBM 032 keypunch experience and has used IBM 3270 and DOS character-based date entry front ends for the last 10 years. The order-entry operator will not use a mouse, so all features of the application must be accessible from Alt+*Key* combinations.

■ Operating speed, especially for obtaining customer information, is another critical requirement. Existing customer and order data must appear within a few seconds after entry of search criteria to prevent customers from becoming impatient while waiting for the order-entry operator to respond to their request.

■ Transaction-processing speed is another criterion of paramount importance, because Northwind Traders' business has improved and the firm now receives 200 to 250 orders per day. All sales employees in the main Redmond office, as well as those located in the London branch office, run the Order Entry application on their own computers. (The London branch is connected to Northwind Trader's WAN by a packet-switched satellite link.) Field sales people are equipped with monochrome-display notebook computers and access the database via 14,400-baud modems using NTAS's Remote Access Services.

The following sections describe the design of the Northwind Traders Client-Server Order Entry application and demonstrate the differences in the performance of the application using attached tables and SQL pass-through methods.

Exploring the Decision-Support Elements of the Application

The Order Entry application is designed to run in maximized window style on computers with 640×480-pixel displays, both monochrome and color. A white background is used to maximize display contrast for the salespersons using monochrome notebook computers. Figure 25.23 shows the sole form (frmOrderEntry) that constitutes the application. To maximize operating speed and provide for SQL pass-through methods, there are no bound controls on the form, with the exception of a subform (sbfOrder_Details) that is bound to a local temporary table (tblOrder_Details) for entering new order line items prior to updating the server tables.

The frmOrderEntry form borrows a number of tricks employed by Visual Basic programmers to improve performance, including the use of off-screen control objects that are invisible until needed and whose position is set by setting the value of the Top property of the control in the Form_Load event handler. Listing 25.1 shows the code that creates the ODBC connect string and positions the hidden objects. A few of the initially invisible off-screen objects appear in design mode in Figure 25.24. Placing these objects below one another in design mode eliminates superimposed objects, which are difficult to manage in design mode.

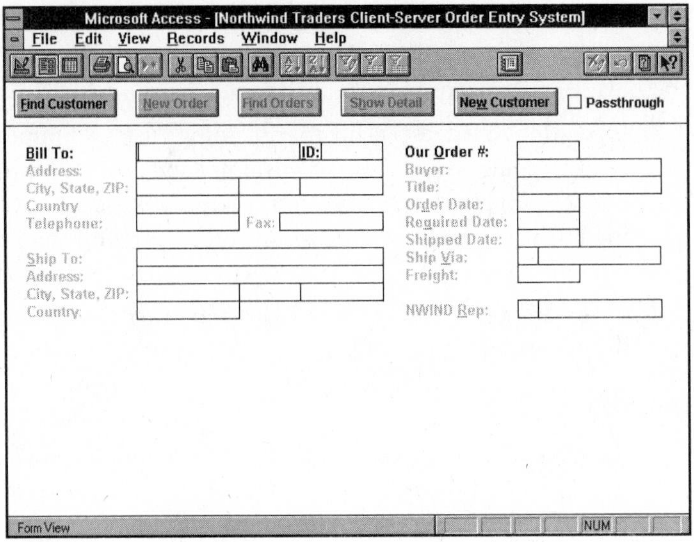

FIGURE 25.23.

The opening (and only) form of the Order Entry application.

Listing 25.1. The initialization code for the Order Entry application.

```
Sub Form_Load ()
    'ODBC connect string for SQL pass-through queries
    strConnect = "ODBC;DSN=NWIND;UID=" & strUserID & ";PWD=" &
    ➥strPassword & ";DATABASE=nwind"

    DoCmd Hourglass True

    Set wsCurrent = DBEngine(0)
    Set dbCurrent = DBEngine(0)(0)

    'Initialize for attached table operation
    fPassthru = False
    chkPassthru.Value = False
    Set rsCustomers = dbCurrent.OpenRecordset("Customers")
    Set rsOrders = dbCurrent.OpenRecordset("Orders")
    Set rsOrderDetails = dbCurrent.OpenRecordset("Order Details")

    'Clear the saved values in the text boxes
    Call ClearCustomerData
    Call ClearOrderData

    'Set the text box status for searches
    txtCompany_Name.Enabled = True
    txtCustomer_ID.Enabled = True
    txtOrder_ID.Enabled = True
```

```
'Eliminate Null problems
txtCompany_Name.Value = ""
txtCustomer_ID.Value = ""

'Relocate off-screen objects
lblOrderDetails.Top = 2 * 1440
lstOrderDetails.Top = 2.333 * 1440
cmdAddNewCustomer.Top = 2 * 1440
cmdCancelAddition.Top = 2 * 1440
cmdAddNewOrder.Top = 3.35 * 1440
cmdCancelNewOrder.Top = 3.35 * 1440
sbfOrderDetails.Top = 2 * 1440
txtGetID.Top = 3.45 * 1440
lblGetID.Top = 3.45 * 1440
txtWrap.Top = 3.45 * 1440
lblWrap.Top = 3.45 * 1440
txtCommit.Top = 3.45 * 1440
lblCommit.Top = 3.45 * 1440
lblSeconds.Top = 3.45 * 1440
txtGetOrder.Top = 3.45 * 1440
lblGetOrder.Top = 3.45 * 1440
txtGetDetails.Top = 3.45 * 1440
lblGetDetails.Top = 3.45 * 1440
lblGetSeconds.Top = 3.45 * 1440
DoEvents

    DoCmd Hourglass False
End Sub
```

FIGURE 25.24.

A design-mode view of a few of the auxiliary controls that become visible when needed.

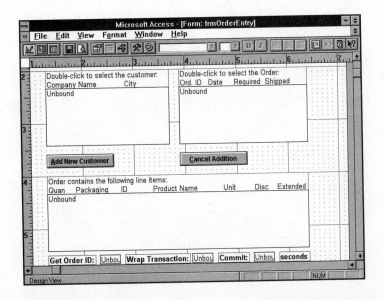

On opening the form, the user has the choice of finding information for an existing customer or entering data for a newly acquired customer. You can type the first few characters of the customer's company name in the **B**ill To text box, type part or all of the customer ID in the **ID** text box, or enter all five digits of an order number in the Our **O**rder number text box. Then press the Return key. If more than one customer meets the search criterion, each of the company names or IDs matching the criterion appears in a newly visible list box. If you double-click an entry in the list box, the customer data is transferred to the Bill To and related text boxes. If you select an entry in the list with the arrow keys and then press Enter, the orders placed by the customer appear in another list box, with the most recent appearing first. (See Figure 25.25.) (If you don't use the Enter key, you have to click the Find Orders button to display the current orders.) Text boxes are enabled only when the operator can enter data in the text box or the application has filled the text box with data.

FIGURE 25.25.

Displaying recent orders for a selected customer in list boxes.

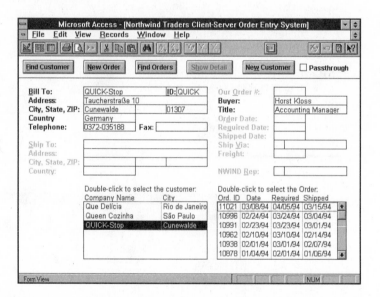

Listing 25.2 shows the code for the AfterUpdate event handler for the Bill To text box, txtCompany_Name, that performs the required case-insensitive search, using SQL pass-through or attached tables. The search is not performed when adding a new customer or if the Bill To text box is empty. Note that the % wildcard substitutes for the * wildcard and the UPPER() function substitutes for the UCase() function in LIKE operator expressions when you use SQL pass-through. Your SQL pass-through syntax must match the syntax used by the server, usually SQL-89 with minor variations.

Listing 25.2. Code to perform a case-insensitive search using SQL pass-through or attached tables.

```
Sub txtCompany_Name_AfterUpdate ()
    'Purpose: Search for Company Name values meeting criteria entered

    If fNewCustomer Then
        'Create a proposed Customer ID for the new customer based on the
        ➥company name
        txtCustomer_ID = UCase$(Left$(txtCompany_Name, 4))
        If InStr(txtCompany_Name, " ") > 0 Then
            txtCustomer_ID = txtCustomer_ID & UCase$(Mid$(txtCompany_Name,
            ➥InStr(txtCompany_Name, " ") + 1, 1))
        Else
            txtCustomer_ID = txtCustomer_ID & UCase$(Mid$(txtCompany_Name,
            ➥5, 1))
        End If
        Exit Sub
    Else
        If Len(txtCompany_Name.Value) = 0 Then
            Exit Sub
        End If
    End If


    Dim strSearch As String
    Dim strMsg As String
    strMsg = "No customers found beginning with " &
    ➥UCase$(txtCompany_Name)
    strMsg = strMsg & ". Re-enter customer name or click the New Customer
    ➥button."


    DoCmd Hourglass True

    'Search for the company name using SQL pass-through or attached
    ➥tables
    If fPassthru Then
        'Use SQL pass-through
        strSearch = "UPPER(Company_Name) Like '" & UCase(txtCompany_Name)
        ➥& "%'"
        Set qdfCustomers = dbCurrent.OpenQueryDef("qdfCustomers")
        qdfCustomers.Connect = strConnect
        qdfCustomers.SQL = "SELECT * FROM Customers WHERE " & strSearch
        qdfCustomers.ReturnsRecords = True
        Set rsCustomers = dbCurrent.OpenRecordset("qdfCustomers")
        If rsCustomers.RecordCount = 0 Then
            lstCustomers.Visible = False
            MsgBox strMsg, 48, "Order Entry (SQL Pass-Through)"
        Else
            rsCustomers.MoveLast
            If rsCustomers.RecordCount = 1 Then
                lstCustomers.Visible = False
```

continues

Listing 25.2. continued

```
            Call ClearOrderData
            Call LoadCustomerData
            cmdFindOrders.Enabled = True
            cmdNewOrder.Enabled = True
            DoCmd GoToControl "cmdFindOrders"
         Else
            'The row source is the pass-through QueryDef
            lstCustomers.RowSource = "qdfCustomers"
            DoCmd Requery "lstCustomers"
            DoEvents
            lstCustomers.Visible = True
            DoCmd GoToControl "lstCustomers"
         End If
      End If
   Else
      'Use attached tables
      strSearch = "UCase(Company_Name) Like '" & UCase(txtCompany_Name)
      ➡& "*'"
      rsCustomers.FindFirst strSearch
      If rsCustomers.NoMatch Then
         lstCustomers.Visible = False
         MsgBox strMsg, 48, "Order Entry (Attached)"
      Else
         'Repeated code here is for clarity
         rsCustomers.FindNext strSearch
         If rsCustomers.NoMatch Then
            lstCustomers.Visible = False
            rsCustomers.FindFirst strSearch
            Call ClearOrderData
            Call LoadCustomerData
            cmdFindOrders.Enabled = True
            cmdNewOrder.Enabled = True
            DoCmd GoToControl "cmdFindOrders"
         Else
            'The RowSource is a select query against the attached tables
            lstCustomers.RowSource = "SELECT Customer_ID, Company_Name,
            ➡City FROM Customers WHERE " & strSearch
            DoCmd Requery "lstCustomers"
            DoEvents
            lstCustomers.Visible = True
            DoCmd GoToControl "lstCustomers"
         End If
      End If
   End If

   DoCmd Hourglass False
End Sub
```

If you double-click an order in the list box, the Ship To and related entries appear. If you select an order in the list box and press Enter, the order line items (details) appear in a new list box. A list box, rather than a subform, is used to display the order details, because filling a list box with new data is faster than changing the RecordSource property of the subform and redisplaying the subform. Figure 25.26 shows the line item list box (lstOrder_Details) for a typical Northwind Traders order. Listing 25.3 shows the code that is used to fill the line item list box.

FIGURE 25.26.

Displaying sales order line items in a list box.

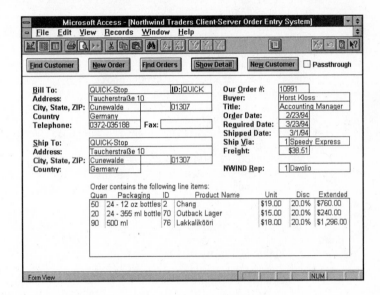

Listing 25.3. Code to display line items plus extended amounts in the lstOrder_Details list box.

```
Sub cmdShowDetail_Click ()
    'Purpose:  Fill the line items list box from the Order Details table

    Dim strSQL As String
    Dim sngTimer As Single

    If Not txtGetOrder.Visible Then
        Call HideTimerData
    End If

    lstCustomers.Visible = False
    lstOrders.Visible = False
    sngTimer = Timer
    If fPassthru Then
        'Use SQL Server-specific syntax
```

continues

Listing 25.3. continued

```
    strSQL = "SELECT Order_Details.Quantity,
    ➥Products.Quantity_Per_Unit, "
    strSQL = strSQL & "Order_Details.Product_ID,
    ➥Products.Product_Name, "
    strSQL = strSQL & "Order_Details.Unit_Price,
    ➥Order_Details.Discount "
    strSQL = strSQL & "FROM Order_Details, Products "
    strSQL = strSQL & "WHERE Order_Details.Product_ID =
    ➥Products.Product_ID "
    strSQL = strSQL & "AND Order_Details.Order_ID = " & txtOrder_ID

    'Prepare the pass-through query
    Set qdfOrderDetails = dbCurrent.OpenQueryDef("qdfOrderDetails")
    qdfOrderDetails.Connect = strConnect
    qdfOrderDetails.SQL = strSQL

    'Prepare the formatting nested query (see query below)
    strSQL = "SELECT Quantity, Quantity_Per_Unit, Product_ID,
    ➥Product_Name, "
    strSQL = strSQL & "Unit_Price, Format([Discount],""0.0%""), "
    strSQL = strSQL & "CCur(Unit_Price * (1-Discount) * Quantity)"
    strSQL = strSQL & "FROM qdfOrderDetails"

    'Execute both queries
    lstOrderDetails.RowSource = strSQL
  Else
    'Use Access SQL syntax to load the list box
    strSQL = "SELECT DISTINCTROW [Order Details].Quantity,
    ➥Products.Quantity_Per_Unit, "
    strSQL = strSQL & "[Order Details].Product_ID,
    ➥Products.Product_Name, "
    strSQL = strSQL & "[Order Details].Unit_Price,
    ➥Format([Discount],""0.0%"") AS Disc, "
    strSQL = strSQL & "CCur([Order Details].[Unit_Price]*(1
    ➥[Discount])*[Quantity]) AS Extended "
    strSQL = strSQL & "FROM [Order Details] INNER JOIN Products ON
    ➥[Order Details].Product_ID = Products.Product_ID "
    strSQL = strSQL & "WHERE [Order Details].Order_ID = " &
    ➥txtOrder_ID
    lstOrderDetails.RowSource = strSQL
  End If
  DoCmd Requery "lstOrderDetails"
  DoEvents
  lstOrderDetails.Visible = True
  If txtGetDetails.Visible Then
    txtGetDetails.Enabled = True
    txtGetDetails.Value = Timer - sngTimer
  End If
End Sub
```

Comparing the Performance with Attached Tables and SQL Pass-through

The search-by-order-number feature and the new-order-entry feature of the Order Entry application include text boxes that report the time required to complete a search for a new order and display the order data, as well as to add a new order to the server tables. The elapsed times your system reports may differ from those shown in the succeeding tables due to differing hardware, network traffic, the number of simultaneous users of SQLSNT, and the number of simultaneous users of the applications tables. The sections that follow provide a comparison between the decision-support and transaction-processing functions of the Order Entry application using attached server tables and SQL pass-through with a specific hardware configuration that is described in the next section.

The Computers Used to Test SQL Pass-through Performance

The client-server hardware configuration used to compare the performance of data retrieval and OLTP with MSA_OLTP.MDB is as follows:

■ The server computer (OAKLEAF0 in the OAKLEAF domain) has an ISA motherboard with an Intel 80486DX2-66 coprocessor, 32MB of RAM, 256KB of cache memory, and a VESA video local bus (VLB). A 1.2GB, 8-ms. SCSI-II fixed disk drive (Maxtor 1240S) is connected via an UltraStor 34F VLB SCSI-II adapter card. A Texcel DM-3024 double-speed CD-ROM drive and other devices also are attached to the UltraStor 34F. Dual-boot Windows NT Advanced Server 3.1 (NTAS) serves as the operating system and the FAT file system is employed. (There is no speed advantage to using the NT file system with NTAS 3.1.) Microsoft SQL Server for Windows NT 4.2 is installed in a 384MB D: partition of the fixed disk. A standard Intel EtherExpress 16 Ethernet card is used to connect the server to the network using thin Ethernet cabling. Both NetBEUI and TCP/IP protocols are supported, and NTAS's Remote Access Services (RAS) is implemented for test purposes. The NetBEUI protocol was used for the tests in this section.

■ The primary workstation (OAKLEAF1) is an ISA bus 80486DX2-66 computer with 16MB of RAM and a 300MB, 12-ms IDE fixed disk drive. This computer is configured with dual-boot Windows NT 3.1 and DOS 5.0. Under DOS, Windows for Workgroups 3.11 is the client operating environment, with both NetBEUI and TCP/IP protocol stacks installed. Windows NT and Access 2.0 are installed in the C: partition; WfWg 3.11 (plus all other Windows applications) are installed in the D: partition, which is compressed with Stac Electronic's Stacker 3.0. Stacker creates an E: partition, so the CD-ROM drive (Sony CDU-431) appears as drive F:. Server shares appear as drives G: and higher.

■ One of the secondary workstations (OAKLEAF2) is an ISA bus 80386DX-33 computer with 8MB of RAM and a 300MB fixed disk drive that is used primarily for musical composition and testing MIDI sequencing applications. This workstation also is used to test Access 2.0 and Visual Basic applications with the workstation configuration typically found in today's commercial environment. A special Access 2.0 application on this computer is used to emulate network traffic and multiuser access to the database. The application contains a loop that alternates data-retrieval operations and OLTP on the database under test.

■ The other secondary workstation (OAKLEAF3) is an ISA bus 808486DX2-66 with VLB and a 1.2GB, 8-ms SCSI-II fixed disk drive that is devoted primarily to testing "future versions of Windows," database replication, multimedia applications, and beta-stage software. This workstation is equipped with an ATI UltraPro VLB video adapter card with 2MB of RAM. OAKLEAF3 also runs NTAS in the OAKLEAF domain, SQLSNT, and WfWg 3.11. A duplicate of the special Access 2.0 application on OAKLEAF2 is used to generate additional network traffic and load the server RDBMS with more active connections.

The comparative performance data that follows was developed *without* the use of the Access application to generate additional network traffic and connections to SQLSNT. In all of the tests that follow, the initial entry is repeated to avoid including the time needed to establish a connection to the server database or to activate an inactive connection to it.

Testing the Performance of the Decision-Support Elements

There is a substantial difference in the attached-table and SQL pass-through performance of the search feature based on entry of single-letter criteria in the Bill To text box. The difference is sufficiently pronounced as to be readily observable. Although the Company_Name field of the Customers table is indexed, the Like `"letter*"` expression, when executed by the Jet database engine, is much slower that the equivalent LIKE `'letter%'` expression executed by SQLSNT. Table 25.1 shows the difference in the time required to display the lstCustomers list box for the four initial letters of the alphabet and the four last letters of the alphabet that display the lstCustomers list box. The difference between the elapsed times for the two sets of search criteria for the attached tables indicate that the Jet query parser is not using the Company_Name index but is performing a conventional unindexed **Find** operation on Customers table.

Table 25.1. A comparison of the elapsed time required to display the customers list box.

Search Entry	Find Customer, Attached, seconds	Find Customer, SQL Pass-through, seconds
a	2.531	1.383
b	1.809	1.539
c	2.910	1.699
d	3.020	1.430
s	6.531	1.869
t	6.480	1.762
v	6.211	2.309
w	6.539	1.758
Average	4.504	1.719

When you click the Find Customer button to clear the values in the customer and order data text boxes of the Order Entry application, you can search for a specific order number by pressing Alt+O (or tabbing to the Our Order # field) and entering a five-digit order number in the range of 10000 to 11077. When you enter an order number in this range in the txtOrder_ID field, the application executes the txtOrder_ID_AfterUpdate event handler, the code for which is shown in Listing 25.4.

Listing 25.4. Code to display customer and order data from a search by order number.

```
Sub txtOrder_ID_AfterUpdate ()
   If IsNull(txtCompany_Name) Then
      txtCompany_Name.Value = ""
   End If
   If IsNull(txtCustomer_ID) Then
      txtCustomer_ID.Value = ""
   End If

   If fNewOrder Or Len(txtCompany_Name) > 0 Or Len(txtCustomer_ID) > 0
   ➥Then
      Exit Sub
   End If

   Dim strOrderSearch As String
   Dim strCustSearch As String
   Dim strOrderMsg As String
   Dim strCustMsg As String
   Dim sngTimer As Single
```

continues

Listing 25.4. continued

```
'Test the entry
If txtOrder_ID < 10000 Then
    strOrderMsg = "Order numbers must be 10000 or higher."
    DoCmd GoToControl "txtOrder_ID"
    MsgBox strOrderMsg, 48, "Order Number Search"
    Exit Sub
End If

strOrderSearch = "Order_ID = " & txtOrder_ID
strOrderMsg = "Order number " & txtOrder_ID & " not found in Orders
➡table."

DoCmd Hourglass True

lblGetOrder.Visible = True
txtGetOrder.Visible = True
txtGetOrder.Value = ""
lblGetDetails.Visible = True
txtGetDetails.Visible = True
txtGetDetails.Value = ""
txtGetDetails.Enabled = False
lblGetSeconds.Visible = True

sngTimer = Timer
If fPassthru Then
    'Use SQL pass-through
    Set qdfOrders = dbCurrent.OpenQueryDef("qdfOrders")
    qdfOrders.Connect = strConnect
    qdfOrders.SQL = "SELECT * FROM Orders WHERE " & strOrderSearch
    qdfOrders.ReturnsRecords = True
    Set rsOrders = dbCurrent.OpenRecordset("qdfOrders")
    If rsOrders.RecordCount = 0 Then
        DoCmd GoToControl "txtOrder_ID"
        DoCmd Hourglass False
        MsgBox strOrderMsg, 48, "Order Number Search (SQL Pass
        ➡Through)"
    Else
        strCustSearch = "Customer_ID = '" & rsOrders!Customer_ID & "'"
        Set qdfCustomers = dbCurrent.OpenQueryDef("qdfCustomers")
        qdfCustomers.Connect = strConnect
        qdfCustomers.SQL = "SELECT * FROM Customers WHERE " &
        ➡strCustSearch
        qdfCustomers.ReturnsRecords = True
        Set rsCustomers = dbCurrent.OpenRecordset("qdfCustomers")
        If rsOrders.RecordCount = 0 Then
            DoCmd Hourglass False
            DoCmd GoToControl "txtOrder_ID"
            MsgBox strCustMsg, 48, "Order Number Search (SQL Pass
            ➡Through)"
        Else
```

```
                cmdFindOrders.Enabled = True
                cmdShowDetail.Enabled = True
                cmdNewOrder.Enabled = True
                DoCmd GoToControl "cmdShowDetail"
                rsOrders.MoveFirst
                lstOrders.Visible = False
                Call ClearCustomerData
                Call ClearOrderData
                Call LoadCustomerData
                Call LoadOrderData
                txtGetOrder.Value = Timer - sngTimer
            End If
        End If
    Else
        'Use attached tables
        rsOrders.FindFirst strOrderSearch
        If rsOrders.NoMatch Then
            DoCmd Hourglass False
            DoCmd GoToControl "txtOrder_ID"
            MsgBox strOrderMsg, 48, "Order Number Search (Attached)"
        Else
            'Repeated code here is for clarity
            strCustSearch = "Customer_ID = '" & rsOrders!Customer_ID & "'"
            strCustMsg = "Customer_ID " & rsCustomers!Customer_ID & " not
            ➥found in Customers table."
            rsCustomers.FindFirst strCustSearch
            If rsCustomers.NoMatch Then
                DoCmd Hourglass False
                DoCmd GoToControl "txtOrder_ID"
                MsgBox strCustMsg, 48, "Order Number Search (Attached)"
            Else
                cmdFindOrders.Enabled = True
                cmdShowDetail.Enabled = True
                cmdNewOrder.Enabled = True
                DoCmd GoToControl "cmdShowDetail"
                lstOrders.Visible = False
                Call ClearCustomerData
                Call ClearOrderData
                Call LoadCustomerData
                Call LoadOrderData
                txtGetOrder.Value = Timer - sngTimer
            End If
        End If
    End If
    DoCmd Hourglass False
End Sub
```

Figure 25.27 illustrates the text boxes that return the elapsed times for the search by Order_ID value. Click the Show Detail button to display the line items for the order. The comparative performance of the Order Entry application using attached tables and SQL pass-through is summarized for eight consecutive randomly selected order numbers in Table 25.2. In this case, the attached tables method is faster because the search is conducted on the primary key fields of both the Customers and Orders tables. The Jet engine uses the primary key indexes of the server tables and caches some of the rows of the attached tables. The two higher elapsed times in the first column of Table 25.2 are due to the need for Jet to fetch additional rows of data from the server tables.

FIGURE 25.27.

The result of entering a search by order ID and displaying the order's line item detail.

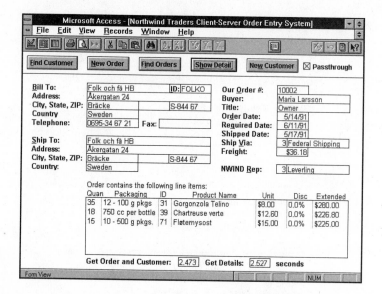

Table 25.2. A comparison of the elapsed time to display the customer and order data.

	Get Order and Customer, Attached	Get Details, Attached	Get Order and Customer, SQL Pass-through	Get Details, SQL Pass-through
Test 1	4.668	1.383	2.629	1.871
Test 2	0.770	1.539	2.191	1.871
Test 3	0.711	1.699	2.410	1.871
Test 4	0.770	1.430	2.629	4.281
Test 5	3.020	1.869	1.699	2.250
Test 6	0.723	1.762	2.301	2.418
Test 7	0.879	2.309	2.309	1.758
Test 8	0.719	1.758	2.473	2.527
Average	1.533	1.719	2.330	2.356

The comparative elapsed times of Tables 25.1 and Table 25.2 indicate that the choice between using attached tables and SQL pass-through can be determined by the most prevalent use of the application. It is probable that the number of customer name searches would be greater than the number of searches by order number, so SQL pass-through will provide better overall performance.

Testing the Online Transaction Processing Elements

Entering a new order for a customer is a two-step process: Find the record for the customer using a search from the Bill To or ID fields, and add the invoice line items in the subform that appears when you click the New Order button. Figure 25.28 illustrates the subform datasheet with the four line items that are used for comparative performance testing of the transaction that adds a new order for a customer.

FIGURE 25.28.

Entering a new order with four standard line items for an existing customer.

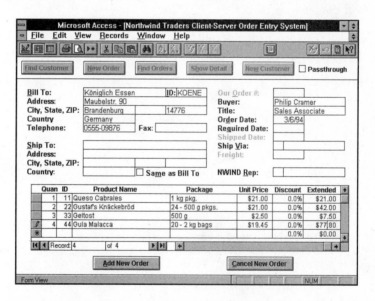

The code that is executed when you click the Add New Order button appears in Listing 25.5. The SQL pass-through version constructs a single Transact-SQL statement, starting with BEGIN TRAN and ending with COMMIT TRAN, and sends the entire statement to the server for execution. The attached-tables version uses conventional Access Basic **BeginTrans...AddNew...Update...CommitTrans** statements that act on the updatable **Recordset** objects created over the server's Orders and Order_Details tables.

Listing 25.5. Code to add a new order using SQL pass-through and attached tables.

```
Sub cmdAddNewOrder_Click ()
    'Purpose: Add a new order to the Orders and Order Details tables

    Dim rsLineItems As Recordset
    Dim strMsg As String
    Dim strSQL As String
    Dim lngOrder_ID As Long
    Dim sngStart As Single
    Dim sngGetID As Single
    Dim sngWrap As Single
    Dim sngCommit As Single

    On Error GoTo 0

    'Test the entries
    Call ResetLabelColors
    If Len(txtShip_Name) = 0 Then
        lblShip_Name.ForeColor = 255
        DoCmd GoToControl "txtShip_Name"
        Exit Sub
    End If
    If Len(txtShip_Address) = 0 Then
        lblShip_Address.ForeColor = 255
        DoCmd GoToControl "txtShip_Address"
        Exit Sub
    End If
    If Len(txtShip_City) = 0 Then
        lblShip_City.ForeColor = 255
        DoCmd GoToControl "txtShip_City"
        Exit Sub
    End If
    If Len(txtShip_Country) = 0 Then
        lblShip_Country.ForeColor = 255
        DoCmd GoToControl "txtShip_Country"
        Exit Sub
    End If
    If txtOrder_Date < Date Then
        lblOrder_Date.ForeColor = 255
        DoCmd GoToControl "txtOrder_Date"
        Exit Sub
    End If
    If txtRequired_Date <= txtOrder_Date Then
        lblRequired_Date.ForeColor = 255
        DoCmd GoToControl "txtRequired_Date"
        Exit Sub
    End If
    If Val(optShip_Via) < 1 Then
        lblShip_Via.ForeColor = 255
        DoCmd GoToControl "optShip_Via"
        Exit Sub
```

```
End If
If Val(cboEmployee_ID) = 0 Then
    lblEmployee_ID.ForeColor = 255
    DoCmd GoToControl "cboEmployee_ID"
    Exit Sub
End If

'Test for order line items
Set rsLineItems = dbCurrent.OpenRecordset("tblOrder_Details")
If rsLineItems.RecordCount = 0 Then
    strMsg = "No line items have been added. Please add an item or
    ➥cancel this order."
    Beep
    MsgBox strMsg, 48, "New Order Entry Error"
    Exit Sub
End If

DoCmd GoToControl "txtCompany_Name"
cmdAddNewOrder.Enabled = False
cmdCancelNewOrder.Enabled = False
DoCmd Hourglass True

sngStart = Timer

If fPassthru Then
    'Obtain the tentative order ID
    strSQL = "SELECT MAX(Order_ID) Last_Order FROM Orders"
    Set qdfOrderID = dbCurrent.OpenQueryDef("qdfOrderID")
    qdfOrderID.Connect = strConnect
    qdfOrderID.SQL = strSQL
    qdfOrderID.ReturnsRecords = True

    Set rsOrders = dbCurrent.OpenRecordset("qdfOrderID")
    lngOrder_ID = rsOrders.Last_Order + 1
    txtOrder_ID.Enabled = True
    txtOrder_ID.Value = lngOrder_ID
    sngGetID = Timer - sngStart
    sngStart = Timer

    'INSERT the order information (one _very_ long SQL statement)
    strSQL = "BEGIN TRAN INSERT Orders VALUES(" & txtOrder_ID & ", '"
    strSQL = strSQL & txtCustomer_ID & "', "
    strSQL = strSQL & cboEmployee_ID & ", '"
    strSQL = strSQL & txtShip_Name & "', '"
    strSQL = strSQL & txtShip_Address & "', '"
    strSQL = strSQL & txtShip_City & "', '"
    strSQL = strSQL & txtShip_Region & "', '"
    strSQL = strSQL & txtShip_Postal_Code & "', '"
    strSQL = strSQL & txtShip_Country & "', "
    strSQL = strSQL & optShip_Via & ", '"
    strSQL = strSQL & txtOrder_Date & "', '"
```

continues

Listing 25.5. continued

```
strSQL = strSQL & txtRequired_Date & "', "
strSQL = strSQL & "null, null) "

'INSERT the line item information for each record
rsLineItems.MoveFirst
Do Until rsLineItems.EOF
    strSQL = strSQL & "INSERT Order_Details VALUES(" & lngOrder_ID
    ➥& ", "
    strSQL = strSQL & rsLineItems!Product_ID & ", "
    strSQL = strSQL & rsLineItems!Unit_Price & ", "
    strSQL = strSQL & rsLineItems!Quantity & ", "
    strSQL = strSQL & rsLineItems!Discount & ") "
    rsLineItems.MoveNext
    If rsLineItems.EOF Then
        'Finish the transaction
        strSQL = strSQL & "COMMIT TRAN"
    End If
Loop
sngWrap = Timer - sngStart
sngStart = Timer

'Execute the SQL statement
Set qdfNewOrder = dbCurrent.OpenQueryDef("qdfNewOrder")
qdfNewOrder.Connect = strConnect
qdfNewOrder.SQL = strSQL
qdfNewOrder.ReturnsRecords = False
qdfNewOrder.Execute
sngCommit = Timer - sngStart

Else
    'Obtain a tentative order ID (performance hit here, traverses all
    ➥records)
    lngOrder_ID = DMax("Order_ID", "Orders") + 1
    txtOrder_ID.Enabled = True
    txtOrder_ID.Value = lngOrder_ID
    sngGetID = Timer - sngStart
    sngStart = Timer

    'Add order and detail items as a transaction
    On Error GoTo RollbackOrder
    wsCurrent.BeginTrans
        'Add the order to the Orders table
        rsOrders.AddNew
        rsOrders!Order_ID = lngOrder_ID
        rsOrders!Customer_ID = txtCustomer_ID
        rsOrders!Employee_ID = cboEmployee_ID
        rsOrders!Ship_Name = txtShip_Name
        rsOrders!Ship_Address = txtShip_Address
        rsOrders!Ship_City = txtShip_City
        rsOrders!Ship_Region = txtShip_Region
```

```
        rsOrders!Ship_Postal_Code = txtShip_Postal_Code
        rsOrders!Ship_Country = txtShip_Country
        rsOrders!Ship_Via = optShip_Via
        rsOrders!Order_Date = txtOrder_Date
        rsOrders!Required_Date = txtRequired_Date
        'Following fields are not updated for a new order
        'rsOrders!Shipped_Date = txtShipped_Date
        'rsOrders!Freight = txtFreight
        rsOrders.Update

        'Add the line item(s) to the Order Details table
        rsLineItems.MoveFirst
        Do Until rsLineItems.EOF
            rsOrderDetails.AddNew
            rsOrderDetails!Order_ID = lngOrder_ID
            rsOrderDetails!Product_ID = rsLineItems!Product_ID
            rsOrderDetails!Quantity = rsLineItems!Quantity
            rsOrderDetails!Unit_Price = rsLineItems!Unit_Price
            rsOrderDetails!Discount = rsLineItems!Discount
            rsOrderDetails.Update
            rsLineItems.MoveNext
        Loop
        sngWrap = Timer - sngStart
        sngStart = Timer
    wsCurrent.CommitTrans
        sngCommit = Timer - sngStart
End If

On Error GoTo 0

'Prevent further editing
Call LockOrderData

'Form and button housekeeping
sbfOrderDetails.Visible = False
cmdAddNewOrder.Visible = False
cmdCancelNewOrder.Visible = False
cmdAddNewOrder.Enabled = True
cmdCancelNewOrder.Enabled = True
cmdFindCust.Enabled = True
cmdNewOrder.Enabled = True
cmdFindOrders.Enabled = True
cmdNewCustomer.Enabled = True

'Display the order details in the listbox
Call cmdShowDetail_Click

'Display the transaction times
txtGetID.Value = sngGetID
txtWrap.Value = sngWrap
```

continues

Listing 25.5. continued

```
    txtCommit.Value = sngCommit
    Call ShowTimerData

    DoCmd Hourglass False
    fNewOrder = False
    Exit Sub

RollbackOrder:
    DoCmd Hourglass False
    MsgBox Error$, 48, "Unable to Add Order " & lngOrder_ID
    wsCurrent.Rollback
    cmdAddNewOrder.Enabled = True
    cmdCancelNewOrder.Enabled = True
    Exit Sub
End Sub
```

When you click the Add New Order button to add the order, the new order and its line items are verified in the lstOrder_Details list box, and the times required to obtain the new order number from the server, create (wrap) the transaction, and commit the transaction appear in the text boxes below the list box. (See Figure 25.29.) Table 25.3 lists the times required to perform the three operations. There is a substantial, but repeatable, inconsistency in creating the first two test transactions with attached tables that weights the transaction-time results in favor of SQL pass-through. However, when you add the time it takes to search for the company name to the transaction time, SQL pass-through clearly is the performance winner.

FIGURE 25.29.

Confirming the order and line items and reporting the transaction-processing time.

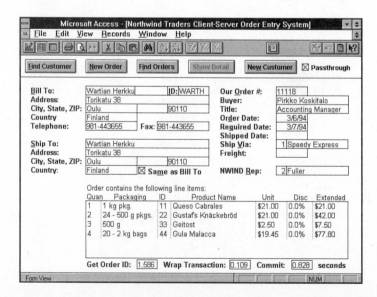

Table 25.3. Comparing the time required to execute transactions.

	Attached, seconds			SQL Pass-through, seconds		
Search	*Get ID*	*Wrap*	*Commit*	*Get ID*	*Wrap*	*Commit*
a	0.770	5.900	0.021	0.555	0.109	1.148
b	0.602	6.430	0.051	0.750	0.109	1.539
c	0.109	0.723	0.867	0.656	0.109	0.773
d	0.168	0.602	0.879	0.656	0.109	0.820
s	0.160	0.609	0.270	0.711	0.109	0.711
t	0.172	0.656	0.875	1.859	0.117	0.766
v	0.109	0.711	1.102	0.992	0.109	0.828
w	0.164	0.71	0.820	1.586	0.109	0.828
Average	0.282	2.043	0.611	0.971	0.110	0.927
Subtotal			2.936			2.008
Find Company			4.504			1.719
Total			6.440			3.727

> **NOTE**
>
> The time required to process the transaction is the most important of the three timing values discussed in this and the preceding section. If one user attempts to enter a transaction while another user's transaction is in the process of completion, both transactions will receive the same order number. The second user's transaction will encounter a primary key violation error on the Order_ID field. This causes the second user's transaction to be rolled back. If users are entering 240 transactions per day (30 transactions per hour), the probability of a consistency violation will be 2/120 (1.8 percent) for SQL pass-through and 3/120 (2.5 percent) for attached tables. This problem can be alleviated by using a stored procedure to create an empty order record with the new order number, and then performing an UPDATE operation on the empty record.

Reading and Writing Binary and Other Files with the Low-Level File Functions

Access Basic includes a complete set of reserved words used to create statements for reading data from and writing data to files other than the database, worksheet, and text files that Access supports directly. Access Basic's file input/output statements are referred to in this book as low-level file functions. If, for example, you find that Access's fixed-length file import feature does not work properly with certain types of computer-generated ASCII files, you probably need to use the low-level file functions and parse the resulting strings in order to place their contents correctly in the fields of your table. A substantial amount of code conversion is required if you need to read files in IBM's EBCDIC (extended-binary character data interchange code) format rather than standard ASCII or Window's ANSI.

The *Language Reference* manual that accompanies the Access Developer's Toolkit provides the syntax of the low-level file functions, but it is quite short on examples of use. Most Visual Basic programmers are familiar with the low-level file functions because these functions were the sole means of employing disk files with Visual Basic 1.0. There are, however, many instances when you may want to employ Access's low-level file operations. The most common use is to create Access tables from flat ASCII files created by mainframe and mini-computers that Access's text file import feature cannot format correctly. Another application is the use of OLE Object fields in Access databases to hold binary data of any type. If you are familiar with Visual Basic or Word Basic low-level file operations, you may want to skip the next section of this chapter.

Low-Level File Types in Object Basic

Access Basic provides the ability to read from and write to three different types of files: sequential, random access, and binary. The type of file is determined by the reserved words you choose for use with the **Open** statement that opens a specified low-level disk file. Most text files are sequential files; the records in sequential files are separated by newline pairs (the carriage-return, line-feed combination, CR/LF or `Chr$(13)` & `Chr$(10)`). You open a sequential file for reading with the **For Input** parameter and for writing with the **For Output** parameter. To add records to the end of a sequential file, you use the **For Append** parameter. Sequential format with fixed-length records is the most common type of file for use with PCs generated by mainframe computers. Sequential files, however, need not have fixed-length records. The general syntax of the **Open** statement is as follows:

```
Open strFileName [For {Random¦Binary¦Input¦Output¦Append }]
                 [Access {Read¦Write¦Read Write}]
                 [Lock {Shared¦Lock Read¦Lock Write¦
                 ➡}]
                  As [#] bFileHandle
                 [Len = wRecordLength]
```

If you omit all the optional arguments and use the simple statement **Open** str*FileName*
As 1, you open the specified file with the handle 1 for random-access with a default
record length of 128 bytes. Like the handles associated with Access databases and
tables, you use the file handle in all subsequent transactions, including closing the
file. If you use an optional parameter, you must choose one of the reserved words
(enclosed within French braces in the above example) or an integer as its value.

A more efficient method of storing data is the default mode of Access Basic's **Open**
statement, random access. When you **Open** a file with the **For Random** parameter, you
can read from or write to the file by using the **Get** or **Put** statements. Random-access
files have fixed-length records without newline pairs or other separators to identify
the end of one record and the beginning of another. Both xBase and Paradox files are
of the random-access type. You locate a record by specifying the length of a record
(**Len** = w*RecordLength*) when you open the file, and the number of the record in the
file, beginning with 1, as a parameter when you read from or write to the file with
Get and **Put**. You also can use the **Seek** statement to position the record pointer to
the record number where reading or writing is to commence. When you open a sequential file, the w*RecordLength* parameter of the **Open** statement specifies the size of
the buffer used temporarily to store data from the file. If you know the exact length
of a record, you can open sequential files as random-access files, provided that all
records are guaranteed to have the same length.

The most common practice in dealing with records in random-access files is to create a user-defined data type with fields that correspond to the fields of the record.
For example, if you have a file whose constant-length records consist of three characters, two integer, one long integer and a single-precision floating point field, your
type definition would be as follows:

```
Type RandFileRec
     strFixed1 As String * 20
     wInteger1 As Integer
     strFixed2 As String * 30
     wInteger2 As Integer
     strFixed3 As String * 10
     dwLongInteger1 As Long
     sngFloating1 As Single
End Type
```

The length of this record is 72 bytes—60 bytes of fixed-length strings, 4 bytes of integers, and 4 bytes each for the long integer and the floating-point value. You can verify the length of your user-defined type by declaring a variable with **Dim** *rfrFileRecord* **As** *RandFileRec* and then measuring its length with *wRecordLength* = **Len**(*rfrFileRecord*). You read values into the fields of *rfrFileRecord* with a **Get** **1**, *wRecordNumber*, *rfrFileRecord* statement. Substitute **Put** for **Get** in order to write the field values of *frfFileRecord* to the file.

Some types of files do not fall into either the sequential or random-access category. You **Open** this type of file **For** **Binary** and use the **Put** and **Get** statements; the record number parameter in this case specifies the position of a single byte in the file, beginning with 1 as the first byte. Here again, you can use the **Seek** statement to position the record pointer to a specific byte in the file. Basic's habit of specifying the first byte in the file as 1, rather than the now-more-accepted 0 (called the offset of the byte), is the source of many bugs when C programmers use the low-level Basic file functions. The number of bytes read from or written to a binary file is determined by the size of the buffer you create, in much the same manner as you create buffers for strings returned by Windows DLL functions.

Using Binary Mode in Place of Random Mode to Accommodate File Headers

Many random-access files include fixed- or variable-length headers at the beginning of the file. Headers provide information on the field names, field data types, the number of records, and other information about the file. This presents a dilemma, because it is very unlikely that the length of the records in the file is the same as the length of the header. Thus, you cannot **Open** the file **As** **Random** because you can't change the record length without reopening the file; reopening the file resets the record pointer to record 1.

Fortunately, you can employ user-defined data types as the content of buffers with files opened **As** **Binary**. It is up to you to position the byte pointer to the correct location with **Seek** statements that have *wRecordNumber* parameters calculated from header length and record number values before you read or write records from the file. The arithmetic is a bit challenging, but the programming is quite straightforward once you sit down and write the appropriate algorithm to calculate the file pointer position. Examples of calculating file pointer positions are given in the section that follows.

> **TIP**
>
> If you are using a file-editing application that displays the contents of the file in hexadecimal format, the byte numbers are shown as offsets. The first byte is at location 0 rather than location 1. Always add 1 to the offset to obtain the byte number for low-level binary file operations in Access Basic.

Storing Non-OLE Objects in OLE Object Fields

Microsoft Corporation intended the OLE Object Field data type of Access tables to be used solely to contain OLE objects created by OLE server applications. Suppliers of competitive Windows databases have decried Access's lack of a graphics field data type. In reality, OLE Object fields can contain any type of data you want to put into these fields. The problem is that Access has the capability to display or play only OLE objects, such as graphics or waveform audio files. As the number of installed copies of Access increases, you can expect independent software vendors (ISVs) to create DLLs that let you display graphic images directly from non-OLE data contained in BLOB files.

The following are some reasons for storing non-OLE data in Access tables:

- Your client-server database contains BLOB fields that store graphics or other data that was not created by an OLE server, and you want to be able to process this data in an access application.

- You want to store and process data for which OLE servers do not exist. An example is a table that stores binary system exclusive (SysEx) messages for use with MIDI (Musical Instrument Digital Interface) components.

- You want to archive graphic images stored in compressed formats and display the images with a third-party image-processing DLL.

The following example, contained in the BLOB.MDB database on the accompanying diskette, uses Access Basic's low-level binary file functions and the **AppendChunk()** and **GetChunk()** methods to store and retrieve binary data of any type in an OLE Object field. BLOB.MDB comes with four .PCX image files (25ADG26.PCX, 25ADG27.PCX, 25ADG28.PCX, and 25ADG29.PCX) that you can use with the **AppendBLOB()** function to test the code. These .PCX files contain four of the figures (Figure 25.26 through Figure 25.29) included in this chapter.

In addition to demonstrating the use of the **AppendChunk()** and **GetChunk()** methods, the code of BLOB.MDB shows how to use the low-level **Open**, **Get**, **Put**, **Kill**, and **Close** statements and the **LOF()** function. You use **AppendChunk()** and **GetChunk()** to handle data that exceeds the maximum length of strings in Access Basic (64KB -2 bytes). The error-handling procedures in the code examples are typical of those used in low-level file processing.

Examining BLOB.MDB

The BLOBs table of BLOB.MDB has four fields: BLOB Name, Data Size, BLOB Size, and BLOB. BLOB Name stores the filename that supplies the value to the BLOB field. BLOB size is required to set the number of chunks in the receiving array when you read the data from the BLOB field and write it to a binary file. The Data Size field is included so that you can verify that the size of the data in the BLOB field is the same as the size of the file that created the field's value.

The Declarations section of the BLOB Code module has only one line of code that needs explanation. wChunkSize must be declared as a constant, because the size of fixed-length strings cannot be established dynamically with a variable. A relatively small wChunkSize is used for this example; the .PCX files included with BLOB.MDB are relatively small. If you are dealing with large images, substitute 8192 or 16384 for the value of wChunkSize. Make sure that the value of wChunkSize is less than the size of your smallest graphic file.

```
Option Compare Database   'Use database order for string comparisons
Option Explicit           'Require declaration of variables

Const wChunkSize = 4096   'Use 16KB chunks for large bitmaps

Dim rgstrChunks()   As String * wChunkSize  'Size of chunk array
Dim strBlobFile     As String               'Name of blob file
Dim wNumChunks      As Integer              'Number of chunks in file
Dim wRemainder      As Integer              'Size of remainder
Dim dwDataSize      As Long                 'Current size of blob
                                            ➥data
Dim dwBlobSize      As Long                 'Size of blob in field
Dim strRemainder    As String               'Remainder of blob data
Dim dwCtr           As Long                 'General-purpose counter

Dim dbBlob          As Database             'BLOB database
Dim tblBlobs        As Table                'BLOBs table
```

Using the *AppendChunk( )* Method and Reading a Binary File

The AppendBLOB() function accepts the name of a file containing binary or any other kind of data as the value of its sole argument. You can enter any filename you want in the input box. When you **Open** a file **As Binary**, the **Open** statement creates a file handle for the filename you specify with 0 length. Thus, you first need to attempt to open the file **For Input** to determine whether the file you specified exists. If the file does not exist, an error occurs and the FileNotFound: error handler displays a message box. Once you open the binary file, the **LOF()** function reads the file header to determine the number of bytes it contains. The remaining code reads the file in wChunkSize increments, adds the chunks to an array, and then processes the array elements into the value of an OLE Object data cell with the **AppendChunk()** method.

Listing 25.6. Access basic code for the AppendBLOB() function.

```
Function AppendBLOB (strBlobFile As String) As Integer
    'Purpose: Get BLOB data from a bit map file for test
    'Accepts: Well-formed path and name of file
    'Uses:     Any type of file (25ADG26.PCX, 25ADG27.PCX,
    '              25ADG28.PCX and 25ADG29.PCX are provided for testing)
    'Returns: True if successful, False if not

    'Input box to confirm or change value of argument
    strBlobFile = InputBox("Enter the name of the file to append:",
    ➥"Append BLOB", strBlobFile)

    'Error handling for file not found
    On Error GoTo FileNotFound

    'Test to see if file exists by opening the file For Input
    Open strBlobFile For Input As #1

    'Reset error handler and close the test file
    On Error GoTo 0
    Close #1

    'Now open the file for binary read
    Open strBlobFile For Binary As #1

    'Determine the number of chunks in the array using integer
    ➥division
    dwDataSize = LOF(1)
    wNumChunks = (dwDataSize \ wChunkSize)

    'Get the remainder after the last chunk with Mod
    wRemainder = dwDataSize Mod wChunkSize
    ReDim rgstrChunks(wNumChunks - 1) As String * wChunkSize

    'Create the array from file data, wChunkSize at a time
    For dwCtr = 0 To wNumChunks - 1
        Get #1, , rgstrChunks(dwCtr)
    Next
```

continues

Listing 25.6. continued

```
'Get the remaining file data following the last chunk
If wRemainder > 0 Then
    'Create a buffer of length wRemainder
    strRemainder = String$(wRemainder, 0)
    Get #1, , strRemainder
End If

Close #1

'Declare the database object variables
Set dbBlob = DBEngine(0)(0)
Set tblBlobs = dbBlob.OpenTable("BLOBs")

'Append the array BLOB data to the OLE Object field
tblBlobs.AddNew
For dwCtr = 0 To wNumChunks - 1
    tblBlobs!BLOB.AppendChunk (rgstrChunks(dwCtr))
Next

'Append the remainder to the OLE Object field
If wRemainder > 0 Then
    tblBlobs!BLOB.AppendChunk (strRemainder)
End If

'Get the size of the data in the field
dwBlobSize = tblBlobs!BLOB.FieldSize()

'Store the data dwDataSize should equal dwBlobSize
tblBlobs![BLOB Name] = UCase$(strBlobFile)
tblBlobs![Data Size] = dwDataSize
tblBlobs![BLOB Size] = dwBlobSize
tblBlobs.Update

'Release array memory
ReDim rgstrChunks(0)

tblBlobs.Close
Exit Function

'Error handler
FileNotFound:
    MsgBox "File '" & UCase$(strBlobFile) & "' not found.", 16,
    ➥"Append Blob"
    Exit Function
End Function
```

> **NOTE**
>
> Do not use **Resume** in error handlers that do not enable you to fix the error that caused execution of the error handler. For example, if you substitute **Resume** for **Exit Function** in the FileNotFound: error handler in the preceding example, you end up in an infinite-loop trap. The message box appears, and then execution of the code resumes at the line that created the error. You cannot correct the error, nor can you stop execution with Ctrl+C, so your only escape is to exit Access and start over. If you substitute an input box to receive a new filename, you can safely substitute **Resume** for **Exit Function.**

If you inspect the table after running AppendBLOB(), you see that the value of the BLOB field is Long Binary Data. (Access 1.1 used the term "Invalid Object.") The description is correct, because the data cell does not contain a legitimate OLE object. The field does contain valid binary data, however. You can prove this by executing the WriteBLOB() function.

Writing the Data to a Binary File with the *GetChunk()* Method

The WriteBLOB() function performs the obverse of the AppendBLOB() function. WriteBLOB(), in the following example, is capable only of writing a binary file from the last record in the table. You can modify the code so that WriteBLOB() accepts a record number or a blob name argument. In this case, you need to substitute the appropriate code for the tblBlobs.**MoveLast** line of the example. The input box lets you change the file name from that of the value of the BLOB Name field, so you can compare the originating and newly written versions of the binary data. The code of WriteBLOB() is, in essence, a duplicate of AppendBLOB( ) with the **GetChunk()** method substituted for **AppendChunk().**

Listing 25.7. Access basic code for the WriteBLOB() function.

```
Function WriteBLOB ()
    'Purpose: Write the BLOB data from the field back to a file
    'Returns: Nil

    Set dbBlob = DBEngine(0)(0)
    Set tblBlobs = dbBlob.OpenTable("BLOBs")

    'Go to the last record and get the name and size of the BLOB
    tblBlobs.MoveLast
```

continues

Listing 25.7. continued

```
    strBlobFile = tblBlobs![BLOB Name]
    dwBlobSize = tblBlobs!BLOB.FieldSize()
    wNumChunks = dwBlobSize \ wChunkSize
    wRemainder = dwBlobSize Mod wChunkSize

    strBlobFile = InputBox("Enter the name of the file to save:",
    ➥"Save BLOB", strBlobFile)
    If strBlobFile = "" Then
        tblBlobs.Close
        Exit Function
    End If

    'Get rid of the existing file, if it exists, then open the file
    On Error Resume Next
    Kill strBlobFile
    On Error GoTo 0
    Open strBlobFile For Binary As #1

    'Write the data to a file, a chunk at a time, full chunks only
    'Here, dwDataSize is used as the file pointer
    For dwCtr = 0 To (wNumChunks - 1)
        dwDataSize = wChunkSize * dwCtr
        strRemainder = tblBlobs!BLOB.GetChunk(dwDataSize,
        ➥wChunkSize)
        Put #1, , strRemainder
    Next

    'Add the remainder, if any to the file
    dwCtr = wNumChunks
    If wRemainder > 0 Then
        dwDataSize = wChunkSize * dwCtr
        strRemainder = tblBlobs!BLOB.GetChunk(dwDataSize,
        ➥wRemainder)
        Put #1, , strRemainder
    End If

    'Close the binary file and the BLOBs table
    Close #1
    tblBlobs.Close
End Function
```

To run the preceding code with the example files, execute `?` `AppendBLOB("c:\access\adg20\25ADG26.PCX")` in the Immediate Window. Inspect the content of the table after you have appended one or two .PCX files. Once you have added the data to the file, execute `? WriteBLOB()` in the Immediate Window to create a file from the binary data in the table. You can verify the operation of these two functions by using Windows' Paintbrush application to view the original file and the version of the file created by `WriteBLOB()`.

Adapting Visual Basic Code for Use in Access

Access Basic and Visual Basic share a common ancestor, the Word Basic (formerly WordBASIC) macro language of Word for Windows. Visual Basic inherited the database-related data types of Access in version 2.0; Visual Basic 3.0 obtained full-fledged database front-end status through incorporation of the Jet database engine of Access version 1.1. Visual Basic syntax is the standard for the root application language for all future versions of mainstream Windows applications published by Microsoft; the language is called Object Basic in this book. Ultimately, all Microsoft productivity applications are likely to use the Visual Basic for Applications dialect of Object Basic.

The upshot of conversion to Visual Basic for Applications is that you will be able to import VBA code into Access Basic from any Windows application that uses VBA as its application programming language. You then modify the code to remove or adjust the extensions specific to the source applications. You can do this now with Visual Basic 1.0, 2.0, and 3.0 code. The Visual Basic_Win library of the Microsoft Basic on CompuServe (GO MSBASIC) forum contains a wealth of Visual Basic code. Following are the basic guidelines to converting Visual Basic to Access Basic code:

■ You need a copy of Visual Basic to be able to export the code to Access Basic modules. You do not need the Professional Edition of Visual Basic to export code that employs the custom controls supplied with the Professional Edition. You need Visual Basic 3.0 to export code that was created with version 3.0 or earlier. The only exception is Visual Basic code supplied in the form of ASCII files, an uncommon practice.

■ You can export code from Visual Basic to an ASCII file or via the Windows clipboard. Turn off syntax checking before you import the Visual Basic code by setting the value of the Syntax Checking method in the Module Design category of View Options.

■ The Declarations section of Visual Basic code modules, files with the extension .BAS, seldom requires substantial modification. Remove **Global** from declarations of constants and variables that you do not need to be global in scope. Alias Windows API function calls if you plan to use the imported code in an Access Basic library. You must alias any function calls that are employed by the Access Basic libraries you use regularly.

■ Code in Visual Basic code modules often contains references to Visual Basic forms and control objects. In Visual Basic 1.0 and 2.0, periods separate objects rather than bang symbols (!), as in `Screen.ActiveForm.Font` = `"Helvetica"`. Visual Basic does not require the `Forms!` identifier to classify objects, because forms are the foundation object of Visual Basic. (The syntax for `Screen.ActiveForm.Property` is the same in Visual Basic and Access Basic, however.) If you are creating a duplicate of a Visual Basic form in Access, importing the Visual Basic code into form modules makes the conversion process simpler.

■ Like Access 2.0's code behind forms feature, Visual Basic creates and names event-handling procedures for forms and control objects on forms automatically. Event handlers are subprocedures that use the naming convention `Sub Form_EventName` or `Sub ControlName_EventName`. The subprocedure code is stored in the file for the form (FormName.FRM) that contains the control object, rather than in a module file.

■ Visual Basic includes a `Print` method that lets you display text on an object, such as a form or picture box. There is no equivalent method in Access Basic. You need to find and change all Visual Basic `Print` instructions to code that places the text in an unbound text box.

The following sections demonstrate techniques for converting a Visual Basic application that shows how to use the Windows common dialog boxes to an Access library that lets you employ the common dialog boxes in a variety of applications.

Converting the DIALOGS Visual Basic Application to an Access Basic Library

Costas Kitsos, a consultant and developer in Southern California, created a Visual Basic application, DIALOGS, that demonstrates the use of the common dialog-box function calls contained in COMMDLGS.DLL, part of the Windows 3.1 API. The Professional Edition of Visual Basic includes a custom control, CMDIALOG.VBX, that eliminates the need for code to call the common dialog boxes in Visual Basic applications. Access, unfortunately, does not let you take advantage of Visual Basic common dialogs. Figure 25.30 shows DIALOGS displaying the File Open common dialog box.

You can download the original version of the application, DIAL0G.ZIP, from the Visual Basic_Win Library (5) of the MSBASIC Forum on CompuServe. The following sections describe the changes that are necessary to convert Mr. Kitsos's application to an Access Basic library.

FIGURE 25.30.

The Visual Basic DIALOGS application displaying the File Open common dialog box.

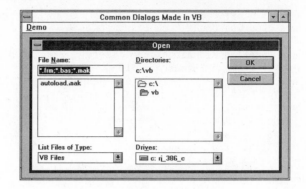

The Access library created from DIALOGS, COMMDLGS.MDA, is included on the accompanying diskette. You can attach COMMDLGS.MDA to your Access applications when you need to use one of the common dialog boxes. COMMDLGS.MDA includes a form, Test Common Dialogs, that you can use to activate each of the six common dialog boxes and display the data it returns in a text box. Figure 25.31 shows the Test Common Dialogs displaying data returned by the Fonts common dialog box (and an explanatory comment).

FIGURE 25.31.

The Test Common Dialogs form of COMMDLGS.MDA displaying the Font common dialog box.

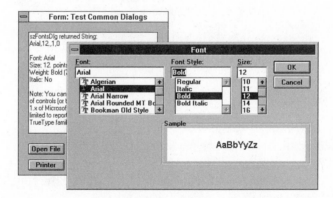

Changes to the Declarations Section of DIALOGS.BAS

The Declarations section of the Visual Basic global module, DIALOGS.BAS, can be used in the Declarations section of an Access Basic module without substantial modification. The principal changes are aliasing all Windows API function calls and changing variable and constant declarations scope from global to module level. For example, the global memory allocation functions appear in DIALOGS.BAS as follows:

```
Declare Function GlobalAlloc Lib "Kernel"
    (ByVal dwFlags As Integer,
```

```
    ByVal dwBytes As Long) As Integer
Declare Function GlobalFree Lib "Kernel"
    (ByVal hMem As Integer) As Integer
Declare Function GlobalLock Lib "Kernel"
    (ByVal hMem As Integer) As Long
Declare Function GlobalUnlock Lib "Kernel"
    (ByVal hMem As Integer) As Integer
Declare Sub hmemcpy Lib "Kernel"
    (lpDest As Any,
     lpSource As Any,
     ByVal dwBytes As Long)
```

All Windows API functions are aliased in COMMDLG.MDA with the prefix cd_, as in the following:

```
Declare Function cd_GlobalAlloc Lib "Kernel"
    Alias "GlobalAlloc"
    (ByVal dwFlags As Integer,
     ByVal dwBytes As Long) As Integer
Declare Function cd_GlobalFree Lib "Kernel"
    Alias "GlobalFree"
    (ByVal hMem As Integer) As Integer
Declare Function cd_GlobalLock Lib "Kernel"
    Alias "GlobalLock"
    (ByVal hMem As Integer) As Long
Declare Function cd_GlobalUnlock Lib "Kernel"
    Alias "GlobalUnlock"
    (ByVal hMem As Integer) As Integer
Declare Sub cd_hmemcpy Lib "Kernel"
    Alias "hmemcpy"
    (lpDest As Any,
     lpSource As Any,
     ByVal dwBytes As Long)
```

DIALOGS.BAS contains only a declarations section, so the preceding changes are all that are required to be made to the contents of this file.

Changing Visual Basic Event Handlers to Access Basic Functions

DIALOGS.FRM incorporates all the code that executes the functions declared in the Declarations section. With one exception, Form_**Load**(), all the subprocedures in DIALOGS.FRM are event handlers for the **Click** event of submenus of the Demo menu choice. The event that calls Form_**Load**() is the equivalent of the OnLoad event of forms in Access Basic. Table 25.4 lists the subprocedures in DIALOGS.FRM, the names of the functions created from the subprocedures in the Common Dialogs module of COMMDLGS.MDA, and the purpose of each function.

Table 25.4. Conversion of Visual Basic subprocedures to Access Basic functions.

VB Procedure	AB Function	Purpose
Form_Load()	OpenTestForm()	Initializes variables
mnu_Colors_Click()	strColorsDlg()	Opens Color Selection dialog
mnuExit_Click()	Not required	
mnuFonts_Click()	strFontsDlg()	Opens Fonts dialog
mnuFOpen_Click()	strFileOpenDlg()	Opens File Open dialog
mnuFSave_Click()	strFileSaveDlg()	Opens File Save dialog
mnuPDoc_Click()	strPrinterDlg()	Opens Print dialog
mnuPSetup_Click()	strSetupDlg()	Opens Printer Setup dialog

In each case, you need to change the first line of each subprocedure from **Sub** *SubName*() to **Function** *FunctionName*(). In addition, you want the Access Basic function to return the values from the functions to your Access application, and, in some cases, to supply argument values to the functions to serve as default values for the common dialog. Table 25.5 lists the functions, their return values, and the arguments required. The wShowForm argument (**True** to display the Test Common Dialogs form) is not shown in the Arguments column. Your application must parse CSV (comma-separated value) strings to obtain the individual items that these strings contain. The wIsForm argument of strFontsDlg() is discussed in a section that follows shortly.

Table 25.5. The return values and arguments of the functions in COMMDLGS.MDA.

Function	Returns	Arguments
strColorsDlg()	A string containing the RGB values of the color	An integer specifying RGB values (in &H a custom color number format, without &H)
strFontsDlg()	A CSV string with font	None (other than name and attributes wShowForm and wIsForm)
strFileOpenDlg()	A string with the path	Strings containing and file name, the filter list and a default extension
strFileSaveDlg()	Same as preceding	Same as preceding

continues

Table 25.5. continued

Function	Returns	Arguments
strPrinterDlg()	A CSV string	Integers for default containing MaxPage, values of MaxPage, FromPage, ToPage From Page, ToPage and Copies and Copies
strSetupDlg()	A CSV string	None containing the selected PrintDevice and Orientation

The function names shown in Table 25.3, together with literal argument values, are assigned to the OnClick event of the corresponding command buttons on the Test Common Dialogs form. Thus, you can call the function from your Access application when COMMDLGS.MDA is attached as a library. Alternately, you can open the Test Common Dialogs form manually and call the event-handling functions from the command buttons on the form when you open COMMDLGS.MDA as a database.

Changing Print Statements to Text Box Values

The lack of any capability to print directly to a form requires that you search for and replace all Visual Basic **Print** statements with code that sets the value of an Access Basic text box control. Thus, the following simple Visual Basic code block found at the end of the mnuColors_**Click()** procedure,

```
For i& = 0 To UBound(ClrArray)
    Print "Custom Color"; Str$(i&); ":", Hex$(ClrArray(i&))
Next
```

requires changes that reflect testing for the presence of a form and the code necessary to send the string to the text box, as follows:

```
If cd_IsLoaded(strTestForm) Then
    strDataStr = "strColorsDlg returned string: " & strDataStr &
    ➥strCrLf & strCrLf
    'Was a series of VB Print statements
    strDataStr = strDataStr & "Common Dialog Custom Colors" &
    ➥strCrLf & strCrLf
    For M = 0 To UBound(ClrArray)
        If Hex$(ClrArray(M)) <> "FFFFFF" Then
            'Don't print pure white, white is not a custom color
            strDataStr = strDataStr & Str$(M) & ": &H" &
            ➥Hex$(ClrArray(M)) & strCrLf
```

```
        End If
    Next
    Forms![Test Common Dialogs]![Dialog Data] = strDataStr
End If
```

In addition to the changes for the **Print** statement, it is a good practice to replace Visual Basic + string concatenation character with Access Basic's **&** symbol. Do not use the Replace All option, however, because Replace All changes the arithmetic plus sign, too.

Obtaining the Window Handle to the Presently Open Form or Report

As noted previously, similar syntax is employed by Visual Basic and Access Basic to identify the form with the focus. There is always an active form in Visual Basic, except under unusual circumstances, but often you may have a report, rather than a form, active in Access. Each of the structures for the common dialog-box functions declared with **Type** *DialogType*...**End Type** statement in the Declarations section includes a field, hwndOwner **As Integer**, that requires a window handle (the **hWnd** property) to the active MDI child window of your application. Each common dialog-box function includes a line, *Structure*.hwndOwner = **Screen.ActiveForm.hWnd**, that obtains the window handle of the form from which the function was called. If no form is active, as is the case when you call the function from a report, you receive a "No active form" runtime error message.

If you expect to use the common dialog boxes with both forms and reports, you have two alternatives for handling this problem:

- ■ Pass the value of the **hWnd** property of the form or report as an additional argument, whWnd, of the function.

- ■ Add an argument, wIsForm, that indicates whether the active window is a form (**True**) or a report (**False**).

The latter technique requires that you change the preceding line of code in each function that is to be used with both forms and reports to the following conditional structure:

```
If wIsForm Then
    Structure.hwndOwner = Screen.ActiveForm.hWnd
Else
    Structure.hwndOwner = Screen.ActiveReport.hWnd
End If
```

The advantage of this structure is that it enables you to test your library as it will be used with the application. Testing COMMDLGS.MDA for use as a library requires the special procedures described in the following section.

Testing COMMDLGS.MDA

Chapter 23, "Developing Access Libraries and Add-Ins," stressed the importance of testing libraries fully before you attach them to applications. You can test each function of COMMDLGS.MDA by opening the Test Common Dialogs form and clicking each command button. If you want to test how the functions of COMMDGLS.MDA behave when the database is attached as a library, you don't want to display the Test Common Dialogs form. In this case, you need to add Add-In submenu choices to the [Menu Add-Ins] section of your MSACC20.INI file for each function that you want to test. In addition, you need an active form or report to supply the value of its **hWnd** property to the library.

COMMDLGS.MDA includes two objects, Bogus Form and Bogus Report, that are used to supply an **hWnd** value for test purposes. If you add the conditional statement shown in the preceding section to the strFontsDlg() function, the following two [Menu Add-Ins] lines enable you to test the strFileOpenDlg() function after opening Bogus Form and the strFontsDlg() function with Bogus Report active:

```
&File Open==strFileOpenDlg("", "", False)
Fonts (&Report)==strFontsDlg (False, False)
```

Add additional lines to the [Menu Add-Ins] section of MSACC20.INI, using the values of the OnClick event of each button on the Test Common Dialogs form, to test the remaining functions in COMMDLGS.MDA.

> **NOTE**
>
> You cannot use a modeless pop-up form to perform the File Open dialog box test. A modeless pop-up form is deactivated when you make a menu selection. Try setting the PopUp property of Bogus Form to Yes and then choosing File Open from the Help menu. Bogus form loses the focus and you receive a "No form is active" error when the Access Basic interpreter reaches the statement that requires the **ActiveForm.hWnd** value.

Once you complete the tests of COMMDLGS.MDA as a database, attach COMMDLGS.MDA to Access by adding the line c:\access\adg20\commdlgs.mda=ro to your MSACCESS.INI file. Open any other database and use the Help menu choices to test operation of each function, with a form or report open as determined by the value you chose for wIsForm in your [Menu Add-Ins] entry.

Adding the Finishing
Touches to Your Application

P

VIII

26

Customizing Access Applications with Special Menus and Toolbars

The standard menu set of retail or runtime Access includes choices that are inappropriate for most Access database applications. This means that you need to create your own custom menu bar and add drop-down menu choices that are appropriate to your application. Today's users expect all mainstream Windows applications to have toolbars with graphic buttons that provide shortcuts to menu choices. This chapter describes how to create custom menus with Access 2.0's new `MenuBar` event and `AddMenu` macro actions, and how to create Access 2.0 custom toolbars to give your applications a professional look and feel. For most runtime applications, AutoExec, AutoKeys, custom menu, and custom toolbar macros constitute the entire set of application macros. This chapter describes how to write macros for custom menus and toolbars, and how to add custom menus to your applications and forms.

Creating Custom Menus

The majority of multiform Access database applications have a hierarchical structure. The form hierarchy usually is similar to the structure of menu-driven xBase or Paradox applications. In Windows applications, it is common to substitute command buttons for menu choices. If your application is sufficiently complex, you use a set of command buttons on a switchboard form to open a form in the second level of the hierarchy. The term "switchboard form," which appears to have originated with the Northwind Traders sample database, means a form whose sole purpose is to open other forms or exit the application. Once you open a second-level form from the switchboard, buttons on the second-level form create paths to open forms in the lower levels of the hierarchy.

The use of command buttons eliminates the necessity for the majority of the menu choices offered by either the retail or runtime version of Access. In many cases, your custom menu needs to include only two menu-bar entries, **File** and **Help**. The **File** menu includes only one drop-down menu choice, **Exit**. The primary **Help** menu choices are **Content** and **About**. The Help **Content** choice opens the main topic of your help file, and **About** leads to a form that displays copyright details and other information about the application. Access Basic code, command buttons, or other control objects on forms substitute for traditional menu choices, such as **File Open** and **File Print**, as well as menu choices such as **View Options** that are specific to Access.

The sections that follow provide details on how to create custom menus for your Access 2.0 applications and tips on how to avoid problems with custom menus, especially in applications destined for use under MSARN200.EXE.

Using Menu Macros

Initially, many users of Access are mystified by Microsoft's approach to creating custom menus with the AddMenu macro action. The usage of the AddMenu macro action is, to a great extent, dictated by the design of Access itself. All views of Access database objects appear in multiple document interface (MDI) child windows that, by definition, cannot have their own menus. Choices made in the menu bar of the parent window apply to the active MDI child window. The use of MDI child windows for Access forms dictates that each form must have its own custom menu set, if custom menus are used in your application.

You specify that a form is to have a custom menu by entering the name of a special menu-bar macro as the value of the MenuBar event of the form. The MenuBar event is new with Access 2.0, replacing the OnMenu event of Access 1.x. (Access 2.0 automatically converts the OnMenu event of Access 1.x applications to the MenuBar event.) The MenuBar event is triggered before the form opens, but only if the value of the MenuBar event is not **Null** (empty). If you specify a value for the MenuBar property of a form, Access removes all its default menu bars and choices from the parent window's menu, leaving the menu featureless except for the menu items you specify with your menu-bar macro.

> **NOTE**
>
> If you execute a macro that does not contain AddMenu actions from the MenuBar event of a form, the menu bar disappears completely. You can implement a menu-less application in this way. Windows without menus do not conform to the Common User Access (CUA) specification or the commonly accepted standards for the design of Windows applications. Under certain conditions, you cannot open the form if your menu-bar macro without AddMenu actions does not execute the CancelEvent action. See the section called "Controlling the Execution of Add Menu Macros," later in this chapter, for an explanation of this phenomenon.

You create a custom parent-window menu for a form by entering the name of a special menu macro as the value of the MenuBar event of the form. Menu macros are a special set of macros that have a predefined, hierarchical structure. The first level of the hierarchy, called a menu-bar macro, specifies the menu items that appear in the parent window's menu bar. Menu-bar macros can contain only AddMenu actions. The syntax for the actions of a menu-bar macro is as follows:

```
[MenuBarMacroName.]AddMenu MenuBarName, MenuMacroName[, StatusBarText]
```

> **NOTE**
>
> The syntax for the AddMenu action is shown as if the action comprised the parameters (arguments) of a **DoCmd** AddMenu action, but you cannot execute the AddMenu action from Access Basic. The preceding syntax example is used only for consistency with the Access Basic syntax examples in this book. MenuBarName, MenuMacroName, and StatusBarText are entries in the Action Arguments pane of the macro design window.

The MenuBarName parameter is the name that appears as the menu-bar choice. You can create a shortcut (accelerator) key for the menu choice by preceding the desired letter for the Alt+*Key* combination with an ampersand (&).

Adding the optional *MenuBarMacroName* in the Macro Name column of the macro design window lets you use macro groups to contain macros that provide the menu bars for several forms. Using a macro group to contain all your custom menu-bar macros minimizes the number of macros that appear in the Database window.

Figure 26.1 shows the macro design window for a mnuOrderReview menu-bar macro for the Order Review form of the Northwind Traders sample database. This menu-bar macro creates a menu with two choices, **F**ile and **E**dit.

You enter the name of the menu-bar macro as the value of the MenuBar property of your form. If you choose the macrogroup approach, enter *MacroGroupName.MenuBarMacroName* as the MenuBar event-handling macro.

The second level of the hierarchy consists of macros that define the menu choices of each of the menu-bar choices created by the menu-bar macro that you write. These macros are called menu macros. The syntax of a menu macro is as follows:

```
MenuMacroName, Action, ActionArguments[, StatusBarText]
```

You enter *ActionArguments* in the text boxes of the Action Arguments pane of the Macro Design window. You can add the optional StatusBarText element in the Status Bar Text cell. Providing status-bar text to explain the purpose of menu items adds a professional touch to your applications.

If you use Access Basic functions to implement macro actions, the approach recommended in this book, each of your menu macros contains the following single entry:

```
MenuMacroName, RunCode, FunctionName[, StatusBarText]
```

FIGURE 26.1.

The macro design window for the mnuOrderReview menu-bar macro.

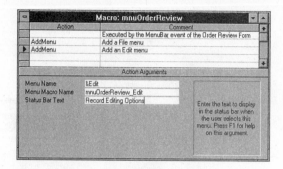

The section called "Standard Access Basic Functions for the DoMenuItem Action" that follows later in this chapter illustrates a standard structure for the *FunctionName* functions that execute menu commands.

> **NOTE**
>
> You cannot place menu macros in macrogroups because the *MenuMacroName* entry supplies the name of the menu choice in the drop-down menu. You can assign menu shortcut keys to drop-down menu choices by including an ampersand (&) at the appropriate location in *MenuMacroName*.

Figure 26.2 illustrates the mnuOrderReview_Edit menu macro that is executed by the second AddMenu action of the mnuOrderReview menu-bar macro of Figure 26.1. The **E**dit menu bar offers only one choice, **F**ind, which opens the Find dialog box to search for a record. Figure 26.3 shows the menu bar that results from adding mnuOrderDetails as the value of the MenuBar event of the Order Details form of NWIND.MDB, and then choosing **F**ind from the custom **E**dit menu.

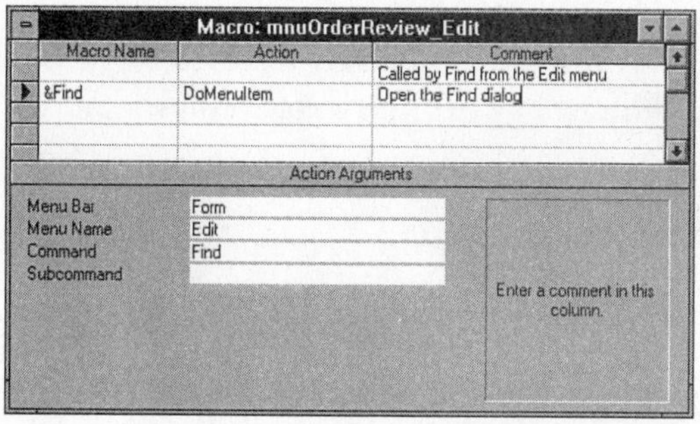

FIGURE 26.2.

The mnuOrderReview_Edit menu macro called by the mnuOrderReview menu-bar macro.

FIGURE 26.3.

The custom menu bar for the Order Review form and the result of choosing Find from the Edit menu.

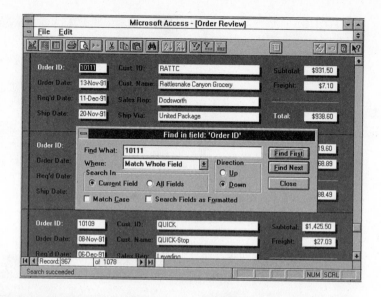

If you have a large number of forms in your application, an even larger number of menu macros may appear in the Database window. Make sure that you establish a uniform naming convention for menu macros before you begin creating custom menus. Consider using a naming convention such as mnu*FormName_MenuChoiceName*, in which "mnu" is an abbreviation for menu, *FormName* is the name of the form to which the menu-bar macro applies, and *MenuChoiceName* is the name of the menu bar choice, such as Edit. Substituting an underscore for a space eliminates the necessity for enclosing compound macro names within square brackets.

Alternatively, you can execute any retail Access menu command with the following entry, as illustrated by the menu macro shown previously in Figure 26.2:

```
MenuMacroName, DoMenuItem, MenuArguments[, StatusBarText]
```

You enter the *MenuArguments* for the menu choice in the Menu Arguments pane of the macro design window.

Executing Menu Choices of Retail and Runtime Access

You can execute any menu command of retail Access by applying the Access Basic **DoCmd** DoMenuItem method. All the menu commands of the retail version of Access, including those menu choices that are hidden from the user, are accessible when running your application under MSARN200.EXE by applying the **DoCmd** DoMenuItem method. (You also can use the DoMenuItem action to execute hidden menu choices in macros.) The syntax of the **DoCmd** DoMenuItem method is as follows:

```
DoCmd DoMenuItem irgwMenuType, irgwMenuBar, irgwMenuChoice[,
➥irgwSubMenuChoice]
```

The first argument, irgw*MenuType*, specifies the index to the enumeration of the types of Access windows. The remaining arguments of the **DoCmd** DoMenuItem method are indexes to the position of the menu item in a collection specific to the type of Access window; thus, the arguments are specified as the **Integer** index to an array with the irgw prefix. The values of the indexes start with 0 as the left menu-bar item (irgw*MenuBar*) or the top drop-down (irgw*MenuChoice*) and fly-out submenu choices (irgw*SubMenuChoice*), when submenus are available. Access intrinsic action constants, prefixed with A_, are available for the most common menu choices. Table 26.1 lists some of the intrinsic action constants for the four arguments of the **DoCmd** DoMenuItem method.

Access 2.0 now sports 77 action constants for menu operations, some of which are specific to Access 2.0. (Access 1.x had 67 action constants.) Action constants that apply to Access 2.0, such as A_DELETE_V2, carry a _V2 suffix. Choose Search from the

Help menu, type constants in the search text box, then double-click Macro Action Constants in the Topics list box to display an alphabetized list of Access 2.0's action constants. With Access 2.0, it is unlikely that you will need to define your own global action constants.

Table 26.1. The most common intrinsic constants for the arguments of the `DoMenuItem` action.

irgwMenuType	*irgwMenuBar*	*irgwMenuChoice*	*irgwSubMenuChoice*
A_FORMBAR	A_FILE	A_NEW	A_COPY
A_FORMDS	A_EDITMENU	A_SAVEFORM	A_PASTE
	A_RECORDSMENU	A_SAVEFORMAS	A_DELETE
		A_SAVERECORD	A_SELECTRECORD
		A_UNDO	A_SELECTALLRECORDS
		A_UNDOFIELD	A_OBJECT
		A_CUT	A_REFRESH

Several menu bars and menu choices have been revised in Access 2.0 to conform to standards established for the other applications that compose the Microsoft Office software suite. To maintain backward compatibility with Access 1.x applications, the menu-action constants of Access 2.0 reflect Access 1.x menu choices. The `DoMenuItem` macro action of Access 2.0 includes an additional argument, `intVersion`, that you can use to specify explicitly an Access 2.0, rather than an Access 1.x menu choice. The default value of the `intVersion` argument is `A_MENU_VER1X`. Use the intrinsic constant `A_MENU_VER20` as the value of the `intVersion` argument to specify an Access 2.0 menu choice as follows:

```
DoCmd DoMenuItem irgwMenuType, irgwMenuBar, irgwMenuChoice[,
➥irgwSubMenuChoice[, intVersion]]
```

> **TIP**
>
> To specify the values of arguments for which intrinsic action constants are not provided, open the Access window of the type of window you want, and then count the position of the desired menu bar from the menu bar at the extreme left (0). The count is the value of `irgwMenuBar`. Open the drop-down menu for the desired menu bar and count to the position of the menu choice you want, starting with the top menu choice (0).

Using the Menu Builder Add-In to Create Custom Menus

Visual Basic programmers are accustomed to using the Menu Design window to quickly create menus for Visual Basic forms. Andrew Miller, a member of Microsoft's quality-assurance staff for Access 1.x, created a library, FIRSTLIB.MDA, that included a custom menu builder modeled on Visual Basic's menu-design window. Miller's original custom menu builder has been incorporated in Access 2.0 as the Menu Builder add-in. You can invoke the Menu Builder add-in from the Add-Ins choice of the File menu or by clicking the ellipsis button that appears when you place the caret in the text box for the MenuBar event of the Other Properties window for a form. The latter method is the most common.

To create a custom menu for a form, in this example the Main Switchboard form of NWIND.MDB, follow these steps:

1. Open the form, then open the Other Properties window for the form and select the MenuBar property.

2. Click the ellipsis button to display the Menu Builder add-in's templates dialog. (See Figure 26.4.)

FIGURE 26.4.

Choosing a template from the Menu Builder add-in's opening templates dialog.

3. Unless you want to duplicate or modify a standard Access 2.0 menu, double-click the <Empty Menu Bar> item in the Template for New Menu Bar list box to open the Menu Builder add-in's menu-design dialog box. (See Figure 26.5.)

4. The Main Switchboard form has five buttons, shown in Figure 26.6. The OnClick event of each button calls the corresponding macro in the Main Switchboard Button macro group. (See Figure 26.7.)

FIGURE 26.5.

The menu-design dialog box of the Menu Builder add-in.

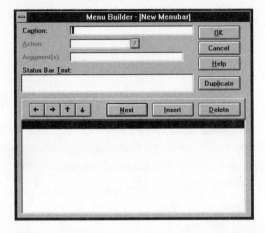

FIGURE 26.6.

The Main Switchboard form in run mode.

FIGURE 26.7.

The design of the Main Switchboard Buttons macro group.

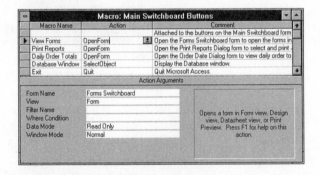

5. It is a common practice to duplicate the functions of command buttons, whether on forms or toolbars, with menu bars and menu choices. **F**ile, **V**iew, and **H**elp menu bars are appropriate for the Main Switchboard form. Type **&File** in the Caption text box, then add a description of the **F**ile menu choices in the Status Bar Text text box. The Action drop-down list and the Arguments() text box are disabled when you create menu bars or add menu

choices that lead to submenus. Click the Next button to add the menu bar to the menu list box at the bottom of the dialog box. Repeat the process for the View and Help menu bars. Figure 26.8 shows the entry for Help menu bar.

FIGURE 26.8.

Adding the entries for the menu-bar macros for the Main Switchboard form.

6. Select the View menu entry in the list box and click the Insert button to add a menu choice to the File menu bar. (The Insert button adds a blank menu bar, menu choice, or submenu choice above the selected menu item.) Type Print &Report in the Caption text box, then move the caret to the Status Bar Text box to add the entry for the menu choice to the list box.

7. Select the Print Report choice in the list box and click the right arrow button to demote the status of this entry from a menu bar to a menu choice. The Action drop-down list and Argument(s) text box now are enabled. You have macros for the menu choices, so select the RunMacro action from the three options offered: DoMenuItem, RunCode, and RunMacro. (See Figure 26.9.)

8. Type the name of the macro to run, [Main Switchboard Buttons].[Print Report], in the Arguments(s) text box, then type a description of the menu choice in the Status Bar Text text box. (See Figure 26.10.)

9. Repeat steps 6 and 7, but enter E&xit as the Caption and choose DoMenuItem from the Action drop-down list. The default entry for DoMenuItem, Form;File;New, appears in the Arguments text box. An ellipsis button appears at the right of the Arguments text box.

10. Click the ellipsis button to display the DoMenuItem Arguments dialog box. The Form;File menu and menu bar are appropriate for the Exit choice, so open the Command drop-down list and select Exit. (See Figure 26.11.)

FIGURE 26.9.

Choosing the
RunMacro action
for the menu choice.

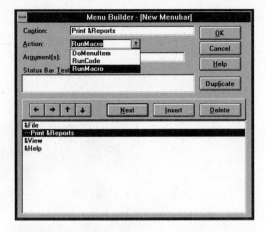

FIGURE 26.10.

Adding the
arguments for the
RunMacro action
and the status bar
text.

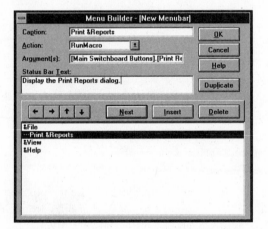

FIGURE 26.11.

Selecting the
command to execute
with the
DoMenuItem
action.

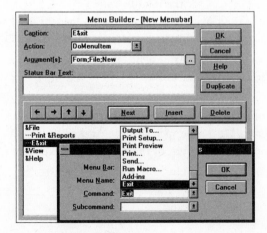

11. Add descriptive text for the status bar for the E**x**it menu choice.

12. Repeat steps 6 through 11 for the View and Help menus, adding the appropriate `RunMacro` actions and `DoMenuItem` choices. Figure 26.12 shows the complete menu structure for the Main Switchboard menu. You can add a separator bar to a menu by adding a menu with only a hyphen (-) as the caption.

FIGURE 26.12.

The menu structure of the Main Switchboard menu.

13. Click OK to save your new menu bar and menu macros with the name mnuMainSwitchboard.

14. Open the mnuMainSwitchboard_View macro group in design mode to display the work that the Menu Builder add-in did for you. (See Figure 26.13.) Each of the menu choices appears as an individual macro; the status bar text appears in the Comments section of each menu macro.

15. Open the Main Switchboard form in run mode to test your new menu. Figure 26.14 shows the View menu with the status bar text from the Comment cell of the mnuMainSwitchboard.[&Forms Switchboard] macro.

NOTE

The menu bar and menu macros created in the preceding example are included in the AB_EXAMP.MDB database on the accompanying diskette.

FIGURE 26.13.

The mnuMain-Switchboard_View macrogroup.

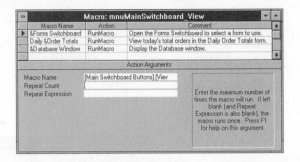

FIGURE 26.14.

The custom menu bar and View menu choices created by the mnuMainSwitchboard macros.

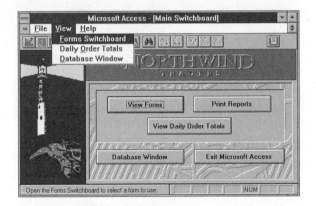

Standard Access Basic Functions for the *DoMenuItem* Action

For runtime applications, you should execute any `DoMenuItem` action that has even the slightest possibility of creating a "Command not available" error message with **DoCmd** `DoMenuItem` methods in your Access Basic module, rather than from the macro. The listing for a function that can execute any Access 2.0 `DoMenuItem` action follows:

```
Function wDoMenuItem(irgwMenuType As Integer,
                     irgwMenuBar As Integer,
                     irgwMenuChoice As Integer,
                     irgvSubMenuChoice As Variant,
                     irgvVersion As Variant) As Integer
    'Purpose:   Executes a DoMenuItem action with error trapping
    'Called by: Any macro that needs to execute a menu choice

    On Error GoTo DoMenuItem_Err
    If IsNull(irgvSubMenuChoice) Then
        If IsNull(irgvVersion) Then
            DoCmd DoMenuItem irgwMenuType, irgwMenuBar, irgwMenuChoice
```

```
        Else
            DoCmd DoMenuItem irgwMenuType, irgwMenuBar, irgwMenuChoice,
            ➥, irgvVersion
        End If
    Else
        If IsNull(irgvVersion) Then
            DoCmd DoMenuItem irgwMenuType, irgwMenuBar, irgwMenuChoice,
            ➥irgvSubMenuChoice
        Else
            DoCmd DoMenuItem irgwMenuType, irgwMenuBar, irgwMenuChoice,
            ➥irgvSubMenuChoice, irgvVersion
        End If
    End If
    wDoMenuItem = True
    Exit Function

DoMenuItem_Err:
    MsgBox "The menu command you chose is not available at this time.",
    ➥32, "Command Not Available"
    Exit Function
End Function
```

The optional submenu index, irgvSubMenuChoice, in this case is specified **As Variant** so that you can use the **Null** value to indicate that there is no submenu choice associated with the call to the wDoMenuItem() function. This makes the function almost universal; you can use this function with any menu item except those for which you need to make selections in dialog boxes automatically.

You call the wDoMenuItem() function by entering the function name and the arguments in the Function Name text box of the Action Arguments pane of the macro design window. As an example, type wDoMenuItem(0, 0, 4, Null, Null) to execute the Save Record choice (4) of the File menu bar (0) of the form window in run mode (0).

The following listing is a compilable prototype for creating functions that add entries to dialog boxes that appear as the result of executing a menu command that includes an ellipsis. You pass the keystrokes you need to complete the dialog entry as the value of the strKeyStrokes argument, if the value of this argument varies with a value on the form. Otherwise, you can declare the strKeyStrokes variable within the function.

```
Function wFunctionName(strKeyStrokes As String) As Integer
    'Purpose:    Executes a specified DoMenuItem action with
    ➥error_trapping
    '            Send required keystrokes to a dialog
    'Called by: MenuMacroName
```

```
Dim irgwMenuType As Integer
Dim irgwMenuBar As Integer
Dim irgwMenuChoice As Integer
Dim irgwSubMenuChoice As Integer
Dim irgwVersion As Integer

'The following variable is a module-level variable set by another
➥function
Dim wConditionPreventingExecution As Integer

'Set values of the variables here

On Error GoTo FunctionName_Err
If Not wConditionPreventingExecution Then
    SendKeys strKeyStrokes, 0    'Don't wait for execution
    'Remove comment in the next line if a sub-menu or Access 2.0
    ➥menu choice is_involved
    DoCmd DoMenuItem irgwMenuType, irgwMenuBar, irgwMenuChoice',
    ➥irgwSubMenuChoice, irgwVersion
    wFunctionName = True
End If
Exit Function

FunctionName_Err:
    MsgBox "The MenuCommandName menu command you chose is not _available
    ➥at this time.", 32, "Command Not Available"
    Exit Function
End Function
```

Controlling the Execution of *AddMenu* Macros

When you are designing applications that include custom menu bars, you may want to have all the menu choices available when you are testing the operation of a form or another database object, but return to the custom menu structure to emulate operation of the application by the user. Controlling which set of menus appears—Access's defaults or your custom version—is especially important when you use retail Access without a toolbar to emulate a runtime application that does not include a custom toolbar. Controlling sets of menu choices requires that you conditionally execute all the AddMenu actions of the menu-bar macro.

The logical approach to controlling which set of menus appears is to modify the macro to use the value of a user-defined function as a condition of execution of the AddMenu actions. If the function returns **True**, execute the AddMenu actions; if the function returns **False**, execute the CancelEvent action to cancel the MenuBar event. The problem is that the CancelEvent action does not cancel the MenuBar event; instead, CancelEvent cancels the OnOpen event, and thus the form will not open in run mode. To correct this problem, you need to reconstruct the original set of menus for the form window in run mode. The CustomMenu macro of the mcrMenuBarMacros macro group, shown in Figure 26.15, uses the value returned by the wUseCustomMenus() function to determine whether a simple, two-bar custom menu appears or Access's standard menu set is displayed.

FIGURE 26.15.

The mcrMenuBarMacros menu-bar macro selectively displays custom macros.

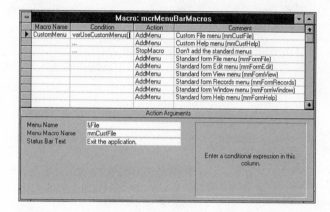

The varUseCustomMacros() function, whose listing follows, uses the **SysCmd**(6) function to test whether your application is running under MSARN200.EXE or under MSACCESS.EXE. Using the **SysCmd**(6) and **SysCmd**(7) functions is one of the subjects of Chapter 29, "Distributing Runtime Versions of Your Databases." The varUseCustomMacros() returns **True** for runtime Access applications.

```
Function varUseCustomMenus () As Integer
    'Purpose: Determine if MSARN200.EXE is in use
    'Returns: True for MSARN200.EXE, False for MSACCESS.EXE

    On Error GoTo IsRunTime_Err
    varUseCustomMenus = SysCmd(6)
    Exit Function

IsRunTime_Err:
    If Err = 5 Then   'Illegal function call
        varUseCustomMenus = False
    Else
        MsgBox "Error: " & Error$, 16, "Runtime Check Error"
    End If
    Exit Function
End Function
```

Each of the AddMenu actions requires its own menu macro. Fortunately, Microsoft included a set of standard menu macros in the Menu Builder add-in for each of the menu bar choices for the menus of the forms window in run mode. The Access menu macros of NWIND.MDB do not have consistent names, so they have been renamed to conform with the names used in mcrMenuBarMacros.CustomMenu. Figure 26.16 shows the File Menu Commands macro saved as the mmFormFile macro.

> **NOTE**
>
> There are six menu commands (New Query through New Form) in the mmFormFile menu macro that do not appear when you open the standard Access File menu. These menu choices take the place of the New menu choice of the normal Access File menu that opens a submenu to let you choose the new object to open (Table through Module). You cannot create submenus with the AddMenu action.

FIGURE 26.16.

The File Menu Commands macro of NWIND.MDB saved as mmFormFile.

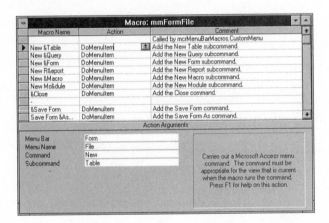

As noted previously, you can add separators to group menu choices by category by typing a hyphen (-) in the Macro Name column, as shown in Figure 26.16. Separators are particularly helpful when drop-down menus contain a large number of choices.

> **NOTE**
>
> If you use a menu-bar macro, such as mcrMenuBarMacros.CustomMenu, to execute standard Access menu choices under retail Access and custom menus under runtime Access, you do not need to use the wDoMenuItem() function for safety when executing standard Access menu choices. Standard Access menu choices added by the AddMenu action are enabled or disabled, as necessary by Access.

If you have runtime Access, you can test the behavior of the mcrMenuBarMacros.CustomMenu macro by following these steps:

1. Import the Custom Menus and Toolbars module, the mcrMenuBarMacros macrogroup, and each of the mmMenuMacros to NWIND.MDB.

2. Add a macro called mcrOpenCustForm to NWIND.MDB that has a single `OpenForm Customers` action. You need to open forms with macros or Access Basic functions in runtime Access.

3. Create a new program item with the name ADT NWIND and type `d:\access\msarn200.exe nwind.mdb /ini msaccess.ini /x mcrOpenCustForm` as the command line value.

4. Double-click the ADT NWIND icon to launch NWIND.MDB under runtime Access. The two custom menu bars, File and Help, appear, rather than the default menus of the form window of runtime Access.

The custom menu created by the mcrMenuBarMacros.CustomMenu macro appears when you run the application with MSARN200.EXE. The application title bar is created by an entry in the .INI file specified by the /ini parameter of the command line that launches MSARN200.EXE. See Chapter 29, "Distributing Runtime Versions of Your Databases," for details on how to use runtime Access.

When you open the Customers form under MSACCESS.EXE and click the File menu choice, the macro recreates the standard File menu of Access with the mcrMenuBarMacros.CustomMenu macro.

> **NOTE**
>
> The status bar text of the standard Access menu appears when your menu macro specifies a DoMenuItem action, regardless of the text you enter in the associated Comment cell.

Creating Custom Toolbars

Toolbars now are *de rigeur* for any database application to achieve a "professional appearance." Although Microsoft has been accused of exhibiting "toolbar dementia," there is little question that Microsoft-style toolbars are here to stay. There is, however, a lively and ongoing debate about how many toolbars an application should incorporate and the maximum number of tools that should appear on a single toolbar. Microsoft has established a pseudo-standard for many of the command and toggle buttons that appear on toolbars of applications in the Microsoft Office software suite. To the extent permitted by your Access 2.0 application, you should use the standard Microsoft designs whenever possible. Using familiar toolbar icons makes your database application easier to use.

You can customize the standard Access 2.0 toolbars to suit your own purposes as an Access developer. The changes you make to Access 2.0's built-in toolbars are stored in the MSysToolbars table of SYSTEM.MDA. The structure of the MSysToolbars table appears in Figure 26.17. One record is added to MSysToolbars for each modification you or other users of a shared SYSTEM.MDA file make to customize built-in Access toolbars. The details of the custom toolbars you add to your application's forms and reports are stored in the MSysToolbars system table in your application's .MDB file. The structure of the MSysToolbars table in your application's .MDB file is much simpler than that of the SYSTEM.MDA file. Figure 26.18 shows the single entry for the tlbFormsSwitchboard custom toolbar that you create later in this chapter. Although the toolbar design is stored in an OLE Object field (Grptbcd), the toolbar design currently is not an OLE Object. (You receive an error message that reads "The data in this field is not recognized as an OLE object" when you double-click the Grptbcd field in table Datasheet View.) It is likely that toolbars will be OLE 2.0 objects in future version of Access and other Microsoft productivity applications designed for Windows 4.0 (Chicago). The sections that follow describe how to build custom toolbars that execute macros.

FIGURE 26.17.

The design of the MSysToolbars table of SYSTEM.MDA.

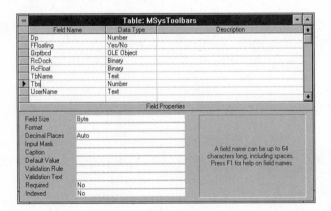

FIGURE 26.18.

*The entry in
MSysToolbars of
NWIND.MDB
for the
tlbFormsSwitchboard
custom toolbar.*

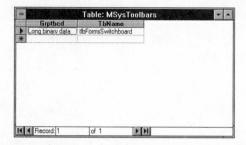

NOTE

Prior to creating a custom toolbar, you must create all of the macros that will be executed by the toolbar buttons. Like custom macros, most custom toolbars require macros to accomplish their objectives. (You don't need to create macros for buttons that simply open a form or report, or run a query.) You can use your custom menu (not menu bar) macros as the event handlers for toolbar buttons. If the application you are converting uses Access Basic functions or event-handling subprocedures, you'll need to create RunCode macros that execute these procedures. You also must change event-handling subprocedures contained in form modules to Access Basic functions, because the RunCode macro action is capable only of executing functions.

Adding a Custom Toolbar to NWIND.MDB

You can make effective use of custom toolbars to replace command buttons on forms. For example, a custom toolbar can substitute for a switchboard form that opens other forms. You can use a single toolbar for your entire application or add a custom toolbar for each form in your application. The following process creates a toolbar that takes the place of the Main Switchboard form:

1. Choose Toolbars from the **V**iew menu to display the Toolbars dialog box, then click the New button to create a new toolbar. The New Toolbar dialog box appears.

2. Enter a name for your new toolbar, such as tlbFormsSwitchboard, then click OK. (See Figure 26.19.) Your toolbar is added as the last item of the Toolbars list. (See Figure 26.20.)

FIGURE 26.19.

Creating a new custom toolbar.

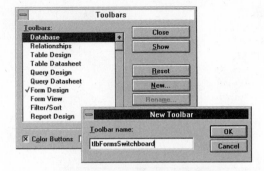

FIGURE 26.20.

The new custom toolbar added to the Toolbars list box.

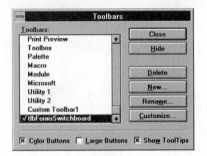

3. Select your new toolbar and click Customize to display the Categories and Objects list boxes. A small, empty floating toolbar appears. The buttons of your toolbar will execute the menu macros created earlier in this chapter, so select the All Macros category to display a list of the macros in NWIND.MDB in the Objects list box.

4. Click one of your mnuMainSwitchboard_*MenuBar.MenuChoice* macros and drag the selection to the floating toolbar. A button with a macro symbol appears in the toolbar. By default, Access adds "Run macro" and the macro name as the description of the button, which appears as a tooltip. (See Figure 26.21.)

   The sequence in which you select the macros is not important, because you can easily rearrange your toolbar buttons after you've created them.

5. Repeat step 4 for each of your Main Switchboard menu macros, with the exception of the Help **A**bout menu choice macro.

6. Place the mouse pointer on a toolbar button and click the right mouse button to display the shortcut menu with a single choice, Choose Button Face. (See Figure 26.22.) Click the right mouse button to display the Choose Button Face dialog box.

FIGURE 26.21.

Adding a toolbar button to the new custom toolbar.

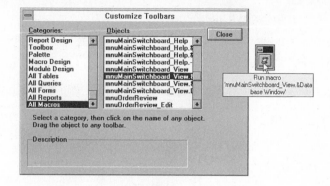

FIGURE 26.22.

Selecting a button to convert into a text button with a caption.

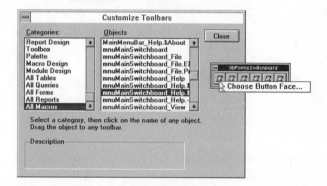

7. If you have relatively few toolbar buttons, using a caption is more effective than selecting one of the button designs offered in the Choose Button Face dialog box. Click the Text check box and enter the caption for the button. Replace the "Run macro..." text in the Description text box with the text to appear as a tooltip. (See Figure 26.23.)

FIGURE 26.23.

Adding a caption and changing the text of the tooltip for a toolbar button.

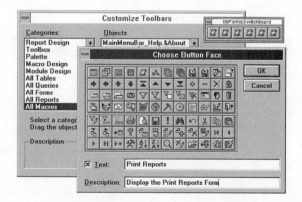

8. Repeat steps 6 and 7 for each of your toolbar buttons.

9. Drag the new toolbar to the top of Access's main window to dock the toolbar. Your new toolbar appears as shown in Figure 26.24.

FIGURE 26.24.

The new toolbar docked under the built-in Access toolbar.

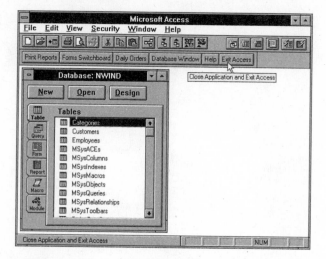

10. The new toolbar buttons appear by default with no intervening space. To add space between the buttons, place the mouse pointer on the toolbar and click the right mouse button to display the shortcut menu for the toolbar. Choose Customize from the shortcut menu to display the Customize Toolbars dialog box. Click and drag each button to the right to add a space between the buttons, as shown in Figure 26.25. (The space you add is fixed by Access; you cannot increase the distance between the buttons more than this fixed space.)

TIP

Although you can add what appears to be an accelerator key combination (Alt+*Letter*) to the caption of a toolbar button by preceding *Letter* with an ampersand (&), pressing Alt+*Letter* does not have the expected effect; nothing happens. You can emulate the effect of accelerator key combinations by creating an AutoKeys macro that assigns the Alt+*Letter* combinations to execute the macros corresponding to the underscored letter of the caption of your toolbar buttons.

FIGURE 26.25.

*Adding space
between the new
toolbar buttons.*

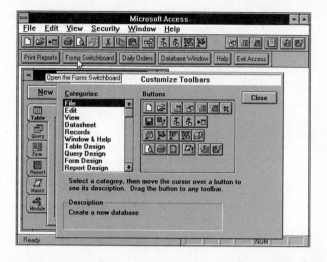

NOTE

You also can add buttons that open a table in Data sheet View, run a query and display the result set in Data sheet View, open a form, or open a report. Choose All Tables, All Queries, All Forms, or All Reports to display the list of objects and add a button to perform one of these functions. Unfortunately, there is no "All Modules" button to let you execute an Access Basic function directly from a toolbar button.

Controlling the Visibility and Alterability of Toolbars

Access 2.0 includes a new macro action, ShowToolbar, that you can use to control the visibility of your custom toolbars, as well as the built-in toolbars of Access 2.0. You can write macros that use the ShowToolbar action or add **DoCmd** ShowToolbar str*ToolbarName*, int*When* statements to your Access Basic code to determine when toolbars are visible. The value of str*ToolbarName* can be the name of your custom toolbar or any of the built-in Access toolbars. (The names of the built-in Access toolbars appear in the Categories list box of the Customize Toolbars dialog box; see preceding Figure 26.25.) You use the intrinsic constants A_TOOLBAR_YES and A_TOOLBAR_NO to show and hide toolbars, respectively. Use the A_TOOLBAR_WHERE_APPROP intrinsic constant to selectively display Access 2.0's built-in toolbars as Access itself displays them. You can experiment with the **DoCmd** ShowToolbar... statement in the Immediate Window. Figure 26.26 shows the effect of executing the **DoCmd** ShowToolbar

"Module", A_TOOLBAR_NO statement; the module design toolbar no longer appears in Access's parent window. Execute the **DoCmd** ShowToolbar "Module", A_TOOLBAR_WHERE_APROP statement to return to Access's normal toolbar behavior for modules.

FIGURE 26.26.

*Using **DoCmd** ShowToolbar statements to control the visibility of toolbars.*

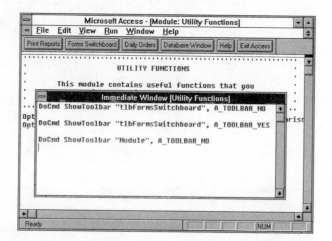

Use the Access Basic Application.SetOption "Built-In Toolbars Available", **False** statement to prevent Access 2.0's built-in toolbars from appearing at any time while your application is running. When you exit the application, make sure you execute the Application.SetOption "Built-In Toolbars Available", **True** statement to return Access to its normal operating mode.

It is unlikely that you want users to be able to modify your custom toolbar designs. To prevent the modification of custom or built-in toolbars, execute the Access Basic Application.SetOption "Can Customize Toolbars", **False** statement on opening your application. As mentioned in the preceding tip, you should return Access to its normal operating mode by executing the Application.SetOption "Can Customize Toolbars", **True** statement on exiting the application.

27

Documenting Your Access Applications

One of the principal benefits of using Access to develop database applications is the speed with which you can create database application prototypes and then turn the prototypes into production applications. This process is know as *Rapid Application Development* or RAD. When you release a production application, however, you'll usually need to document your application. As mentioned in the preceding introduction to this chapter, the scope and depth of the documentation depends on the standards established by your clients or your firm. Transaction processing applications usually require more comprehensive documentation than decision support products. Full documentation is especially necessary for transaction processing applications that are vital to client or employer finances. In many cases, a well-written help file, plus a brief description of how to install the application on the user's computer, is all that's required for decision support applications. Creating help files from application documentation is the subject of the next chapter, "Writing Help Files for Access Applications."

Documentation for database applications in general falls into the following three categories:

- ■ **Data dictionary.** A data dictionary is a document that describes the properties of each table in the database. Properties include the source of the table (if the table is attached), permissions to read and modify data contained in the table, and detailed information on the fields and indexes of the table. A description of the purpose of the table and each field of the table is a useful addition. Descriptions of constraints on field values, display formats, and other related properties complete a comprehensive data dictionary.

- ■ **Application documentation.** Documents the purpose and the design elements of the queries, forms, reports, macros, and Access Basic code that comprise the front end to the tables of the database(s) that underlie these objects. You need to record what control objects and Access Basic functions read and update values of particular fields in the table. The relationship between the events of control objects and the execution of code in Access Basic functions is also important, especially in large-scale applications.

- ■ **Version control documentation.** You need to know what version of each primary database object is currently included in each user's application. For major applications, version control requires a database that records each change made to an object, including Access Basic code, and a description of the change. Version control, with backups of the objects in the preceding version, is the only method of quickly recovering from an unexpected bug in a maintenance release of a production application.

If you created the database with a CASE tool, such as ServerWare, Inc.'s InfoModeler for Access described in Chapter 2, "Developing a Design Strategy for Access Applications," you need only polish the output of the data dictionary held in the CASE tool's repository. If you're creating Access database the traditional way, you need to create a data dictionary. Even if you attach all tables from a fully documented client-server database, you still need your own data dictionary to create comprehensive application documentation. This chapter discusses methods of creating data dictionaries for Access databases and obtaining the information that you need to document your applications.

Using the Database Documenter Add-In to Create Data Dictionaries

Access 2.0's Database Documenter add-in replaces the Database Analyzer library (ANALYZER.MDA) of Access 1.x. Database Documenter lets you print reports that describe any or all of the objects in your database. If you use Database Analyzer to document all of the objects in a complex database application, your report may be several hundred pages in length. Fortunately, data dictionaries traditionally consist only of information about the tables that comprise the database. Even documenting only table data, however, can generate a substantial number of pages; documenting the tables in NWIND.MDB, for example, requires 36 pages.

The following process creates an example data dictionary for NWIND.MDB using the Database Documenter:

1. Open NWIND.MDB, then choose Add-Ins from the File menu and Database Documenter from the submenu to display Database Documenter's opening dialog box.

2. The default object type is Tables, so click the Select All button to document all of the tables in NWIND.MDB. (See Figure 27.1.)

FIGURE 27.1.

Selecting all of the tables in NWIND.MDB for documentation.

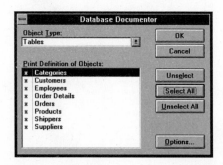

3. Click the options button to display the Print Table Definition dialog box. You can determine the amount of detail in the data dictionary by clearing check boxes or clicking option buttons. Permissions by User and Group is commonly not included in data dictionaries, although permissions by group may be useful for shared .MDB files. Figure 27.2 shows the options selected for this example.

FIGURE 27.2.

Setting options for printing a data dictionary.

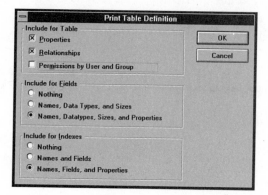

4. Click the OK button to create the reports for the eight tables. The status bar indicates the name of the table being processed. In a minute or two, depending on the speed of your computer, the report, in print preview mode, appears. (See Figure 27.3.)

FIGURE 27.3.

The first page of the data dictionary created by Database Documenter.

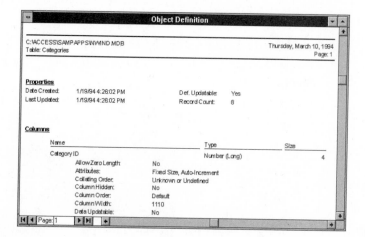

5. As mentioned earlier in this section, the data dictionary report is 36 pages in length. If you click the last page button, have a cup of coffee while Access formats each page of the report. (Formatting the 36 pages can take several minutes, depending on the speed of your computer and the amount of RAM installed.)

6. Click the Print button of the toolbar or choose **P**rint from the **F**ile menu. You can print all of the pages of the report, or a few selected pages. Figure 27.4 illustrates page 2 of the report that contains a graphic illustration of the relationships between the Categories and Products tables.

FIGURE 27.4.

Page 2 of the report printed from the data dictionary for NWIND.MDB.

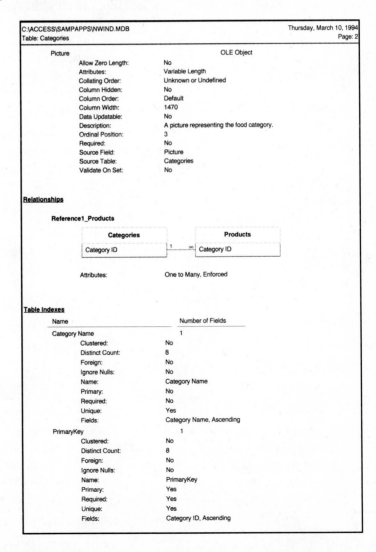

Printing the Database Documenter Report to a Text File

The version of Database Documenter shipped with Access 2.0 when this edition was written does not provide the ability to print the data dictionary to an Excel 5.0 worksheet to a rich-text format (.RTF) file that you can import into Microsoft Word or another Windows word processing application. You can, however, use the Generic/Text Only printer driver provided with Windows 3.1+ to print the report to an ASCII text file:

1. If you haven't installed the Generic/Text Only printer driver, launch Control Panel, open the Printers function, and click the Add button. Select Generic/Text Only in the List of Printers list box, then click the OK button. You need to have the distribution diskettes for Windows 3.1+ at hand, because this operation requests that you insert the distribution diskette that contains the TTY.DRV printer driver. Select the newly-installed driver in the Installed Printers list, then click the Connect button. Select FILE: in the Ports list box, then click OK. Close Control Panel after installing and connecting the new printer driver.

2. Choose P**r**int Setup from Access's **F**ile menu, Click the Specific Printer option button, then open the Specific Printer drop-down list, and select the Generic/Text Only printer. Set all of the margins for the report to 0.000 inches, then click OK. (See Figure 27.5.) Access reformats the print preview window using a fixed-pitch (10 cpi) font.

FIGURE 27.5.

Setting up the Generic/Text Only printer.

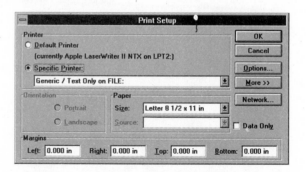

3. Click the Print button of the toolbar or choose **P**rint from the **F**ile menu. (You don't need to tick the Print to File check box of the Print dialog box when you specify FILE: as the destination for the print driver.) After a brief interval, the Print To File dialog box appears. Type the well-formed path and name of the text file in the Output File Name text box and click OK to create the file.

4. You can inspect the resulting file using Windows Write or another word processing application. (Most data dictionary files are too large for Notepad.) Figure 27.6 shows the first few lines of the file in Windows Write with the font changed from the default 10-point Arial to 10-point Courier (PostScript).

FIGURE 27.6.

The first few lines of the data dictionary file displayed in Windows Write.

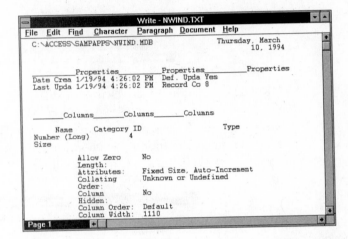

It is clear from Figure 27.6 that a substantial amount of reformatting is required before you can insert the content of the file into a word processing document or spreadsheet application. Some of the descriptor names, such as Allow Zero-Length Strings have been truncated. You can write a Word Basic macro to do much of the reformatting for you, but writing such a macro involves more time than writing an Access Basic application that creates a custom-formatted file suited to the application into which you want to import the file. A section that follows shortly explains how to create a file directly from the properties of the data access objects of your database application.

Documenting Queries

You may want to include definitions of selected **QueryDef** objects in your data dictionary, because many Access **QueryDef** objects are quite similar to views of data in conventional SQL databases. It is common to include views in data dictionaries, especially for client-server RDBMS applications. To document a **QueryDef** object, follow these steps:

1. Select Queries in the Object Type drop-down list, choose a typical query to document, and click the Options button to display the Print Query Definition dialog box. Figure 27.7 shows typical options to document a query.

FIGURE 27.7.

Setting options for documenting a **QueryDef** *object.*

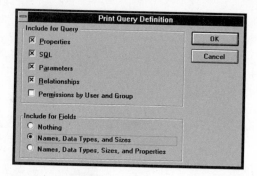

2. Click OK to close the Print Query Definition dialog box and click the OK button to document the selected **QueryDef** object. Most of the report appears as shown in Figure 27.8. In addition to properties and the SQL statement that defines the query, the options shown in Figure 27.7 also provide a list of the properties of the columns of the query result set.

FIGURE 27.8.

Part of the report for the Quarterly Orders by Product (Crosstab) query of NWIND.MDB.

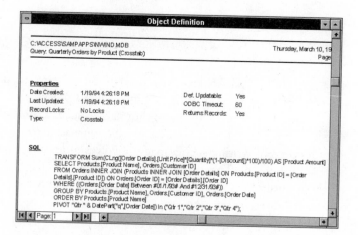

3. Click the Print button to print the report or use the method described in the preceding section to print the query definition created by Database Documenter to an ASCII .TXT file.

Writing Access Basic Code to Create Data Dictionaries

You can automate the preparation of data dictionaries for your applications with Access Basic's **List** methods. Preparing a comprehensive data dictionary for a large database can be a daunting project. A simple database, such as the Northwind Traders sample database that contains only eight tables, requires 120 lines of text just to list the tables, fields, and indexes in the database. Larger applications, such as MTX International's Accounting SDK, described in Chapter 11, "Examining an Access Accounting Application," requires more than 1,000 lines just to list its tables, fields, and indexes.

The sections that follow show you how to create an Access Basic application to create a custom data dictionary. The application, which contains only tables and a module, is provided on the accompanying diskette as DATADICT.MDB. Figure 27.9 illustrates a portion of a basic data dictionary created by DATADICT.MDB for the Northwind Traders sample database imported into an Excel 5.0 workbook. The data dictionary uses legal-style decimal headings to identify the table and its fields and indexes. Legal-style headings are easier to generate automatically than standard multilevel headings that include Roman numerals. The Access Basic code listings in the sections that follow use the TableDefs collection to create the data dictionary entries. (Access 1.x required that you use the **ListTables**, **ListFields**, and **ListIndexes** methods to create data dictionary entries.) Low-level file functions create the final tab-delimited text file that places the elements of the headings in individual cells of an Excel worksheet. You can copy and paste the cells from Excel into a Word for Windows table in your documentation or link the table to Word using OLE methods.

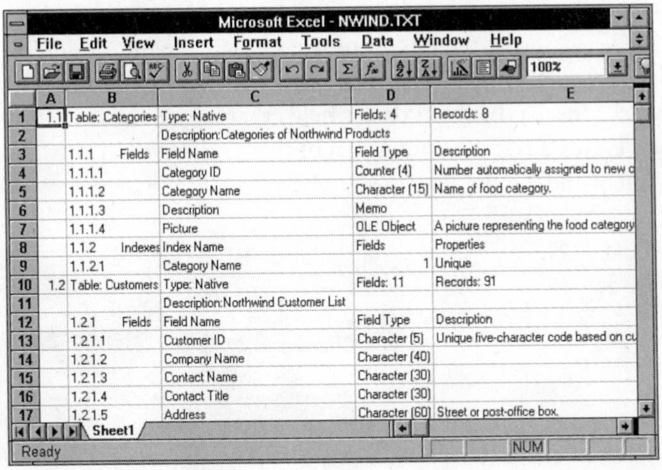

FIGURE 27.9.

Part of the formatted data dictionary for NWIND.MDB.

Tables for the Automated Data Dictionary

The data dictionary application has four tables, tblTables, tblFields, tblIndexes, and tblQueries. The first three tables hold the data used to create the data dictionary.

The tblQueries table is used to document queries, the subject of a section later in this chapter. The tblFields and tblIndexes tables have composite indexes on the field name and sequence of the fields or indexes, respectively. Indexing these two tables lets you use the **Seek** method to find the first field or index for a **Recordset** object of the **Table** type created over the table. Figure 27.10 displays most of the fields of the tblFields table. The structure of the tblTables and tblIndexes tables is similar. TableName is the foreign key field of tblFields and tblIndexes that links to the primary key field, Name, of tblTables.

FIGURE 27.10.

The tblFields table of the data dictionary application.

TableName	Seq	Name	FieldType	Description	Type
Categories	1	Category ID	Counter (4)	Number automatically assigned to new category.	4
Categories	2	Category Name	Character (15)	Name of food category.	10
Categories	3	Description	Memo		12
Categories	4	Picture	OLE Object	A picture representing the food category.	11
Customers	1	Customer ID	Character (5)	Unique five-character code based on customer name.	10
Customers	2	Company Name	Character (40)		10
Customers	3	Contact Name	Character (30)		10
Customers	4	Contact Title	Character (30)		10
Customers	5	Address	Character (60)	Street or post-office box.	10
Customers	6	City	Character (15)		10
Customers	7	Region	Character (15)	State or province.	10
Customers	8	Postal Code	Character (10)		10
Customers	9	Country	Character (15)		10
Customers	10	Phone	Character (24)	Phone number includes country code or area code.	10
Customers	11	Fax	Character (24)	Phone number includes country code or area code.	10
Employees	1	Employee ID	Counter (4)	Number automatically assigned to new employee.	4
Employees	2	Last Name	Character (20)		10
Employees	3	First Name	Character (10)		10
Employees	4	Title	Character (30)	Employee's title	10
Employees	5	Birth Date	Date/Time (8)		8

Record: 1   of 74

A query, qryTableDetails, is included in DATADICT.MDB so that you can validate the data dictionary before you use the text files that the application creates. Figure 27.11 shows the design of the query. The qryTableDetails query employs two left outer joins to link the tblIndexes table to the tblFields table. You need to use left outer joins so that records for fields that are not indexed appear in the query result set. Figure 27.12 illustrates part of the result set of the qryTableDetails query for the Northwind Traders sample database.

FIGURE 27.11.

The design of the validation query for the data dictionary application.

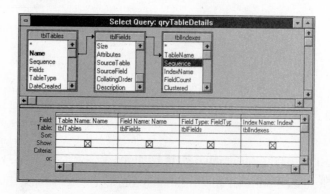

FIGURE 27.12.

Part of the query result set returned for a data dictionary of NWIND.MDB.

Table Name	Field Name	Field Type	Index Name	Description
Categories	Category ID	Counter (4)	Category Name	Number automatically assigned to new
Categories	Category Name	Character [15]	Category Name	Name of food category.
Categories	Description	Memo	Category Name	
Categories	Picture	OLE Object	Category Name	A picture representing the food catego
Customers	Customer ID	Character (5)	City	Unique five-character code based on c
Customers	Customer ID	Character (5)	PrimaryKey	Unique five-character code based on c
Customers	Company Name	Character (40)	City	
Customers	Company Name	Character (40)	PrimaryKey	
Customers	Contact Name	Character (30)	City	
Customers	Contact Name	Character (30)	PrimaryKey	
Customers	Contact Title	Character (30)	City	
Customers	Contact Title	Character (30)	PrimaryKey	
Customers	Address	Character (60)	City	Street or post-office box.
Customers	Address	Character (60)	PrimaryKey	Street or post-office box.
Customers	City	Character (15)	City	
Customers	City	Character (15)	PrimaryKey	
Customers	Region	Character (15)	City	State or province.
Customers	Region	Character (15)	PrimaryKey	State or province.

Record: 1 of 154

The Entry Point Function, *wCreateDataDict("DatabaseName")*

The DATADICT.MDB application is designed to be used as a stand-alone application or attached to Access as a library. The entry point function, wCreateDataDict(), accepts the path and file name of the database for which you want to create a data dictionary as its argument when you open DATADICT.MDB as a database. If you attach DATADICT.MDB as a library to Access, supply an empty string ("") for the value of strDBName. When you open DATADICT.MDB as a database, you initiate its operation by typing ? wCreateDataDict("d:\path\filename.mdb") in the Immediate window. To run wCreateDataDict() when you attach DATADICT.MDB as a library, add the line d:/path/datadict.mdb=rw to the [Libraries] section of MSACC20.INI, and the line Data D&ictionary==wCreateDataDict("") to MSACC20.INI's [Menu Add-Ins] section. Then choose the Data Dictionary entry of the Add-Ins submenu to create the data dictionary text files.

> **NOTE**
>
> The empty string argument of the D&ictionary==wCreateDataDict("") entry in the [Menu Add-Ins] section of MSACC20.INI is required. If you omit the empty string, you receive an error when you attempt to use the Data Dictionary application as a library.

The declarations section of the wCreateDataDict() function declares all database objects and two general-purpose variables at the module-level to eliminate the necessity of passing objects to procedures as parameters. The function determines whether the application is being run as a library; if it is, the function uses **DBEngine**(0)(0) to return a pointer to the source database and **CodeDB**() to specify the data dictionary tables in the library.

Transaction processing is used to delete all current records from each of the data dictionary tables so that you start with a clean slate. Once the tables have been cleared of prior entries, the code opens them again by name. The wCreateDataDict() function opens recordsets over each of the empty tables and opens a new **TableDef** object for each of the tables in sequence. The Fields and Indexes collections of each TableDef object are iterated by the AddTables and AddIndexes procedures. After the tables are filled, the CreateTextFile procedure generates a formatted text file from the table data. The AddQueries procedure adds records for **QueryDef** objects to tblQueries. The listing for the wCreateDataDict() function follows.

Listing 27.1. Access Basic code for the **wCreateDataDict()** function.

```
Function wCreateDataDict (strDBName As String) As Integer
    'Purpose:    Create a data dictionary for the strDBName database
    'Argument:   Path and file name of source database as a literal
    'Uses:       AddTable and AddQuery procedures
    'Note:       All database objects are module-level variables

    Dim wTableNum As Integer      'table number
    Dim wQueryNum As Integer      'query number

    If Len(strDBName) > 0 Then
        'Run as an application (no attached tables in source database)
        Set dbDataDict = DBEngine(0)(0)          'The data dictionary DB
        Set dbCurrent = OpenDatabase(strDBName)  'The source database
    Else
        'Run as a library
        Set dbDataDict = CodeDB()
        Set dbCurrent = DBEngine(0)(0)
        strDBName = dbCurrent.Name
    End If

    'Newline character (removed from SQL statement)
    strCrLF = Chr$(13) & Chr$(10)

    'Create an array of the names of the four tables created
    ReDim rgstrTableList(5)
    rgstrTableList(1) = "tblTables"
    rgstrTableList(2) = "tblQueries"
    rgstrTableList(3) = "tblFields"
    rgstrTableList(4) = "tblIndexes"

    'Delete the current entries in each of the tables
    vRetVal = SysCmd(1, "Deleting records of existing tables", 4)
    For wCtr = 1 To 4
        Set rstTemp = dbDataDict.OpenRecordset(rgstrTableList(wCtr), _
        ➡DB_OPEN_TABLE)
        If rstTemp.RecordCount > 0 Then
            rstTemp.MoveFirst
```

```
    BeginTrans
        Do While Not rstTemp.EOF
            rstTemp.Delete
            rstTemp.MoveNext
            'DoEvents    'Safety
        Loop
    CommitTrans
  End If
  rstTemp.Close
  vRetVal = SysCmd(2, wCtr)
Next wCtr

'Open the data dictionary tables
Set rstTables = dbDataDict.OpenRecordset(rgstrTableList(1),
➡DB_OPEN_TABLE)
Set rstQueries = dbDataDict.OpenRecordset(rgstrTableList(2),
➡DB_OPEN_TABLE)
Set rstFields = dbDataDict.OpenRecordset(rgstrTableList(3),
➡DB_OPEN_TABLE)
Set rstIndexes = dbDataDict.OpenRecordset(rgstrTableList(4),
➡DB_OPEN_TABLE)

vRetVal = SysCmd(1, "Creating Data Dictionary",
➡(dbCurrent.TableDefs.Count + dbCurrent.QueryDefs.Count))

wTableNum = 1
For wCtr = 1 To dbCurrent.TableDefs.Count
    Set tdfTable = dbCurrent.TableDefs(wCtr - 1)
    If InStr(tdfTable.Name, "MSys") = 0 Then
        'Add records for tables
        Call AddTables(wTableNum)
        wTableNum = wTableNum + 1
    End If
    vRetVal = SysCmd(2, wCtr)
    DoEvents    'Safety
Next wCtr
wTableNum = wTableNum - 1

For wCtr = 1 To dbCurrent.QueryDefs.Count
    Set qdfQuery = dbCurrent.QueryDefs(wCtr - 1)
    'Add records for queries
    Call AddQueries(wCtr)
    vRetVal = SysCmd(2, wCtr + wTableNum)
    DoEvents    'Safety
Next wCtr

'Create the tab-delimited text file for Excel or Word for Windows
Call CreateTextFile(strDBName)

'Create the query text file
Call CreateQueryText(strDBName)
```

continues

Listing 27.1. continued

```
'Close everything
rstTables.Close
rstQueries.Close
rstFields.Close
rstIndexes.Close

dbCurrent.Close
dbDataDict.Close

'Reset the status bar
vRetVal = SysCmd(5)
End Function
```

> **NOTE**
>
> The **ListTables()**, **ListFields()**, and **ListIndexes()** methods of Access 1.x
> also are available in Access 2.0 for backward compatibility. (The first edition
> of this book used the **List...()** methods to create the data dictionary.)
> Using **TableDef**, **Field**, and **Index** objects is the preferred method of obtain-
> ing data on tables in Access 2.0, because these objects contain property
> values that are not accessible from the now obsolescent **Snapshot** objects
> created by the **List...()** methods. There is no guarantee that future versions
> of Access will continue to support the **List...()** methods or the explicit
> **Snapshot** object that is required to use the **List...()** methods.

The *AddTables* Procedure

The AddTables procedure does most of the work of creating the records for the data
dictionary. AddTables first adds a record to tblTables and sets the field values of the
record from the property value of the tdfTable **TableDef** variable. It then creates a
Field object, fldField, whose properties contain the attributes of each field of the
table. The code then adds one record that contains data based on values of properties
in the **Field** object for each field of the table. The name of the table is added to
tblTables to provide the required foreign key field value. The GetFieldText procedure, the subject of the next section, returns a text description of the field data type.

Listing 27.2 illustrates the use of Access-defined properties of **Table** and **Field** objects. The Description property of **Table** and **Field** objects is defined by Access, but
is not a member of the default Properties collection of these objects. To obtain the

description of these objects, you must use the **CreateProperty**() method with the full syntax, obj*Name*.**CreateProperty**(str*PropertyName*, int*FieldDataType*, var*Value*). You then use the obj*Name*.Properties.**Append** method to add the Access-defined property to the Properties collection of the object.

Listing 27.2. Access Basic code for the AddTables procedure.

```
Sub AddTables (wTableNum As Integer)
    'Purpose:   Add records to the tables, fields and indexes tables
    'Called by: wCreateDataDict()
    'Calls:     AddIndexes (adds records for indexes, if present)

    Dim wSeq As Integer                'Field sequence counter

    'On Error GoTo Bail_Out

    'Add the Description Access-defined property to the Properties
    ➥collection
    On Error Resume Next
    Set prpDescription = tdfTable.CreateProperty("Description", DB_TEXT,
    ➥" ")
    tdfTable.Properties.Append prpDescription
    On Error GoTo 0

    'Add a record for the table
    rstTables.AddNew
    rstTables!Name = tdfTable.Name
    rstTables!Fields = tdfTable.Fields.Count
    rstTables!DateCreated = tdfTable.DateCreated
    rstTables!LastUpdated = tdfTable.LastUpdated
    rstTables!RecordCount = tdfTable.RecordCount
    rstTables!Attributes = tdfTable.Attributes
    rstTables!Connect = tdfTable.Connect
    rstTables!SourceTable = tdfTable.SourceTableName
    rstTables!Sequence = wTableNum
    rstTables!Description = tdfTable.Properties("Description")

    'Add text description of table type
    Select Case tdfTable.Attributes
        Case DB_ATTACHEDTABLE Or DB_ATTACHEXCLUSIVE Or DB_ATTACHSAVEPWD
            rstTables!TableType = "Attached"
        Case DB_ATTACHEDODBC
            rstTables!TableType = "ODBC"
        Case Else
            rstTables!TableType = "Native"
    End Select

    'Add a record for each field
    wSeq = 1
```

continues

Listing 27.2. continued

```
BeginTrans
    'Here, transaction processing is used for speed, not integrity
    For wSeq = 1 To tdfTable.Fields.Count
        Set fldField = tdfTable.Fields(wSeq - 1)

        'Add the Description Access-defined property to the Properties
        ➥collection
        On Error Resume Next
        Set prpDescription = fldField.CreateProperty("Description",
        ➥DB_TEXT, " ")
        fldField.Properties.Append prpDescription
        On Error GoTo 0

        rstFields.AddNew
        rstFields!TableName = tdfTable.Name
        rstFields!Name = fldField.Name
        rstFields!Type = fldField.Type
        rstFields!Size = fldField.Size
        rstFields!Attributes = fldField.Attributes
        rstFields!SourceTable = fldField.SourceTable
        rstFields!SourceField = fldField.SourceField
        rstFields!CollatingOrder = fldField.CollatingOrder
        rstFields!Sequence = wSeq
        rstFields!Description = fldField.Properties("Description")

        'Get English description of field data types
        Call GetFieldText
        rstFields.Update
    Next wSeq
CommitTrans

If tdfTable.Indexes.Count > 0 Then
    'If any fields are indexed, add the record(s)
    Call AddIndexes
End If

'Update the tables record
rstTables.Update

Exit Sub

Bail_Out:
    MsgBox "Error: " & Error$, 32, "Table Entry Error"
    'Update the tables record
    rstTables.Update
    Exit Sub
End Sub
```

Obtaining Text Descriptions of Field Data Types with the *GetFieldText* Procedure

The GetFieldText procedure translates the **Long** integer value contained in the Type field of tblFields to an English description of the data type using Access, not SQL, terminology. You could substitute SQL's "varchar" data-type descriptor for "Character," for example. Counter (auto-increment) fields are a special version of the **Long** integer type, so "Counter" replaces "Long" for such fields. The size of the field is added parenthetically to field data-type descriptors, except OLE Object and Memo fields, although it is only necessary for Character fields.

Listing 27.3. Access Basic code for the **GetFieldText** procedure.

```
Sub GetFieldText ()
    'Purpose:    Add English description of field data types
    'Called by: AddTables

    Select Case rstFields!Type
        Case DB_BOOLEAN
            rstFields!FieldType = "Yes/No"
        Case DB_BYTE
            rstFields!FieldType = "Byte"
        Case DB_INTEGER
            rstFields!FieldType = "Integer"
        Case DB_LONG
            rstFields!FieldType = "Long"
        Case DB_CURRENCY
            rstFields!FieldType = "Currency"
        Case DB_SINGLE
            rstFields!FieldType = "Single"
        Case DB_DOUBLE
            rstFields!FieldType = "Double"
        Case DB_DATE
            rstFields!FieldType = "Date/Time"
        Case DB_BINARY
            rstFields!FieldType = "Binary"
        Case DB_TEXT
            rstFields!FieldType = "Character"
        Case DB_OLE
            rstFields!FieldType = "OLE Object"
        Case DB_MEMO
            rstFields!FieldType = "Memo"
    End Select


    'Change Long to Counter, if a counter field
    If (ssFields!Attributes And DB_AUTOINCRFIELD) > 0 Then
        rstFields!FieldType = "Counter"
    End If
```

continues

Listing 27.3. continued

```
'Append the field size in parentheses
If Not (rstFields!Type = DB_OLE Or rstFields!Type = DB_MEMO
➡Or rstFields!Type = DB_BINARY) Then
    rstFields!FieldType = rstFields!FieldType &
    ➡" (" & LTrim$(Str$(fltField.Size)) & ")"
End If
End Sub
```

> **NOTE**
>
> Unlike Desktop RBDMSs that use fixed-length character fields, you cannot determine the size of the records of a table by adding up the lengths of the fields if one of the fields is a character field. If your tables have records, you can add code to the application that determines the average lengths of Text, Memo, and OLE Object fields and then adds the lengths of fixed-width fields, such as **Integer** or **Long**. The average is valid only if you have a substantial number of records that reflect real-world data.

Adding Records to Specify Indexed Fields

The AddIndexes procedure adds records to the tblIndexes table for the indexed fields of native Access tables. The value of the Name field of the idxIndex **Index** object is RelIndex, RelIndex1, and so forth, for indexes on individual fields that are included in a composite primary key index. To maintain consistency with Access Basic's naming convention for the **Index** objects of tables, the field name substitutes for RelIndex[#]. Reference (system) indexes are included in the Indexes collection of **TableDef** objects; reference indexes are created for query optimization purposes. Reference indexes are omitted from the data dictionary, because these indexes are created automatically by Access's query optimization "engine."

Listing 27.4. Access Basic code for the AddIndexes procedure.

```
Sub AddIndexes ()
    'Purpose:   Add records for indexed fields of native tables
    'Called by: AddTable procedure

    Dim wIdxCtr As Integer   'Index counter (for sequence)
    wIdxCtr = 1
```

```
        BeginTrans
            For wIdxCtr = 1 To tdfTable.Indexes.Count
                Set idxIndex = tdfTable.Indexes(wIdxCtr - 1)
                rstIndexes.AddNew
                rstIndexes!TableName = tdfTable.Name

                'Add the standard field values
                rstIndexes!FieldCount = idxIndex.Fields.Count
                rstIndexes!IndexName = idxIndex.Name
                rstIndexes!Sequence = wIdxCtr
                rstIndexes!Clustered = idxIndex.Clustered
                rstIndexes!Primary = idxIndex.Primary
                rstIndexes!Foreign = idxIndex.Foreign
                rstIndexes!Unique = idxIndex.Unique
                rstIndexes!Required = idxIndex.Required
                rstIndexes!IgnoreNulls = idxIndex.IgnoreNulls
                rstIndexes.Update
                wIdxCtr = wIdxCtr + 1
            Next wIdxCtr
        CommitTrans
End Sub
```

Creating the Data Dictionary's Text File

Chapter 25, "Stretching the Limits of Access," describes how to use the binary (low-level) file reserved words of Access Basic to create graphics files from non-OLE data stored in the OLE Object fields of Access tables. A more common use for the binary file features of Access is to create sequential text files. Sequential files are fixed-length or variable-length files in which each record is terminated by a newline pair (carriage return/line feed, `Chr$(13)` & `Chr$(10)`). The Setup Wizard of the Access Developer's Toolkit (ADT), described in Chapter 29, "Distributing Runtime Versions of Your Databases," uses sequential files to create the custom SETUP.IN_ file required to copy the proper files from the distribution diskettes for your application to the user's fixed-disk drive. The `CreateTextFile` procedures employs the sequential file commands to create a tab-delimited (`Chr$(9)`) text file that contains entries formatted for import by spreadsheet and word processing applications.

The `CreateTextFile` procedure uses the database file name with a .TXT extension. The code deletes an existing copy of the file, if it exists, because the **Open #** and **Write #** instructions append records to existing files. If the file does not exist, **Open #** creates a zero-length file on execution. Each time that you execute the **Write #** instruction, you add the value of its **String** argument to one new record of the file. **Write #** is the equivalent of the **AddNew** and **Update** methods with one intervening instruction to set the value of a field. You can add blank lines to the file with a **Write** #n, `""` line in your code.

Listing 27.5. Access Basic code for the `CreateTextFile` procedure.

```
Sub CreateTextFile (strTextFile As String)
  'Purpose:   Create a text data dictionary file
  'Argument:  Name of database file (used as text file name)
  'Called by: wCreateDataDict()

    Dim strWrite As String
    Dim strIndex As String

    'Create the file name (database.TXT) in the same directory
    strTextFile = Left$(strTextFile, InStr(strTextFile, ".")) & "txt"

    'Delete any prior version of this file
    On Error Resume Next
    Kill strTextFile
    On Error GoTo 0

    'Open the file for sequential (line-by-line) output
    Open strTextFile For Output As #1

    rstFields.Index = "Index1"
    rstIndexes.Index = "Index1"

    'Set progress indicator
    rstTables.MoveLast
    vRetVal = SysCmd(1, "Creating text file", rstTables.RecordCount)

    wCtr = 1
    'Create the records for each table using legal-style outlining
    rstTables.MoveFirst
    Do While Not rstTables.EOF
        'Create header entry for table
        strIndex = "1." & LTrim$(Str$(rstTables!Sequence))
        strWrite = strIndex & Chr$(9) & "Table: " & rstTables!Name
        strWrite = strWrite & Chr$(9) & "Type: " & rstTables!TableType

        If Not IsNull(rstTables!Fields) Then
            'Records from attached databases may not contain this entry
            strWrite = strWrite & Chr$(9) & "Fields:" &
            ➥Str$(rstTables!Fields)
        End If

        If (IsNull(rstTables!RecordCount) Or rstTables!RecordCount = -1)
        ➥Then
            strWrite = strWrite & Chr$(9)
        Else
            'Records from attached databases may not contain this entry
            strWrite = strWrite & Chr$(9) & "Records:" &
            ➥Str$(rstTables!RecordCount)
        End If
```

```
'Add source and connection data, if applicable
If Not IsNull(rstTables!SourceTable) Then
   'Only attached tables have a SourceTable entry
   If Len(rstTables!SourceTable) > 0 Then
      strWrite = strWrite & strCrLF & Chr$(9) & Chr$(9) & "Source:
      ➥" & rstTables!SourceTable
   End If
   If Not IsNull(rstTables!Connect) Then
      If Len(rstTables!Connect) > 0 Then
         strWrite = strWrite & Chr$(9) & "Connect: " &
         ➥rstTables!Connect
      End If
   End If
End If


'Add the description, if it exists
If Not IsNull(rstTables!Description) Then
   If Len(rstTables!Description) > 0 Then
      strWrite = strWrite & strCrLF & Chr$(9) & Chr$(9) &
      ➥"Description:" & rstTables!Description
   End If
End If


'Add the table record to the file
Print #1, strWrite


'Add the field data for the record
rstFields.Seek "=", rstTables!Name, 1
If Not rstFields.NoMatch Then
   'Add a header for the field values
   strWrite = Chr$(9) & strIndex & ".1        Fields" & Chr$(9) &
   ➥"Field Name" & Chr$(9) & "Field Type" & Chr$(9) &
   ➥"Description"
   Print #1, strWrite


   'Add the individual lines for each field
   Do While Not rstFields.EOF
      'This structure is required to inhibit "No Current Record"
      ➥errors
      If rstFields!TableName <> rstTables!Name Then
         Exit Do
      End If
      strWrite = Chr$(9) & strIndex & ".1." &
      ➥LTrim$(Str$(rstFields!Sequence))
      strWrite = strWrite & Chr$(9) & rstFields!Name & Chr$(9) &
      ➥rstFields!FieldType
      If rstFields!Name <> rstFields!SourceField Then
         strWrite = strWrite & Chr$(9) & "Source: " &
         ➥rstFields!SourceField
      End If
      If Not IsNull(rstFields!Description) Then
         strWrite = strWrite & Chr$(9) & rstFields!Description
```

continues

Listing 27.5. continued

```
            End If
            Print #1, strWrite
            rstFields.MoveNext
        Loop
    End If

    'Add the index data for the record
    rstIndexes.Seek "=", rstTables!Name, 1
    If Not rstIndexes.NoMatch Then
        'Add a header for the indexes
        strWrite = Chr$(9) & strIndex & ".2        Indexes" & Chr$(9) &
        ➥"Index Name"
        strWrite = strWrite & Chr$(9) & "Fields" & Chr$(9) &
        ➥"Properties"
        Print #1, strWrite

        'Add the entries for the indexes
        Do While Not rstIndexes.EOF
            If rstIndexes!TableName <> rstTables!Name Then
                Exit Do
            End If
            strWrite = Chr$(9) & strIndex & ".2." &
            ➥LTrim$(Str$(rstIndexes!Sequence))
            strWrite = strWrite & Chr$(9) & rstIndexes!IndexName
            strWrite = strWrite & Chr$(9) &
            ➥LTrim$(Str$(rstIndexes!FieldCount)) & Chr$(9)
            If rstIndexes!Clustered Then
                strWrite = strWrite & "Clustered, "
            End If
            If rstIndexes!Primary Then
                strWrite = strWrite & "Primary, "
            End If
            If rstIndexes!Foreign Then
                strWrite = strWrite & "Foreign, "
            End If
            If rstIndexes!Unique Then
                strWrite = strWrite & "Unique, "
            End If
            If rstIndexes!Required Then
                strWrite = strWrite & "Required, "
            End If
            If rstIndexes!IgnoreNulls Then
                strWrite = strWrite & "Ignore Nulls, "
            End If
            strWrite = Trim$(strWrite)
            If Right$(strWrite, 1) = "," Then
                strWrite = Left$(strWrite, Len(strWrite) - 1)
            End If
            Print #1, strWrite
            rstIndexes.MoveNext
```

```
        Loop
      End If
      rstTables.MoveNext
      vRetVal = SysCmd(2, wCtr)
      wCtr = wCtr + 1
   Loop

   'Close the text file
   Close #1
End Sub
```

Once you've created the text file of the data dictionary, you can import the file into Excel 5.0 or Word 6.0 and manipulate it as necessary. You can create a Word table quickly by importing the text file into Excel and then copying and pasting the cells to your data dictionary document. The next section shows a text file for the data dictionary of tables attached by the ODBC API imported into Word 6.0.

You can add additional information about the tables, such as who created the table, by opening the database contained in SYSTEM.MDA and matching the Id or ObjectId field values in MSysObjects with those in the MSysACEs table. Create a query to display ownership of objects by following these steps:

1. Set the value of the ShowSystemObjects property in the Option dialog box to Yes.

2. Choose Permissions from the Security menu and assign yourself read data or full permissions on the MSysACEs table.

3. Attach the MSysAccounts table of the SYSTEM.MDA library that is attached to Access. If Access does not allow you to attach the MSysAccounts table, you are not a member of the Admins group of the SYSTEM.MDA library attached to Access. Then attach the tblTables table from DATADICT.MDB after you've executed
   `wCreateDataDict("c:\access\sampapps\nwind.mdb")`.

4. The following query displays the ownership of the table objects in NWIND.MDB:

```
SELECT DISTINCT MSysObjects.Name AS Object, MSysAccounts.Name
AS Owner FROM ((MSysACEs INNER JOIN MSysAccounts ON
MSysACEs.SID = MSysAccounts.SID) INNER JOIN MSysObjects ON
MSysACEs.ObjectId = MSysObjects.Id) INNER JOIN tblTables ON
MSysObjects.Name = tblTables.Name WHERE
((([MSysAccounts].[Name]="Users" Or
[MSysAccounts].[Name]="Guests")=False));
```

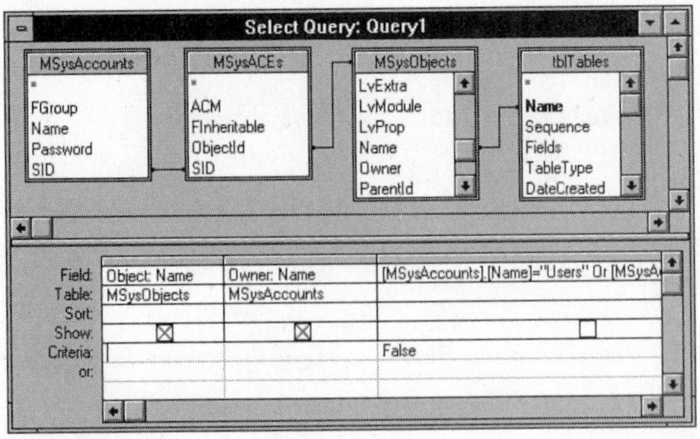

FIGURE 27.13.

The design of a query that returns the ownership of **Table** *objects.*

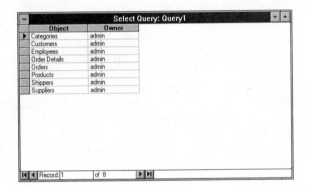

FIGURE 27.14.

The result set of the query of Figure 27.13.

If you have the necessary permissions, you create **Recordset** objects from MSysACEs and MSysAccounts. Use the **FindFirst** method to look up the security identification code (SID) of the owner in MSysACEs, and then find the Name value in MSysAccounts. Figure 27.13 shows the design of the query based on the preceding Access SQL statement, and Figure 27.14 displays the query result set from the NWIND.MDB sample database.

> **NOTE**
>
> The preceding method of determining the ownership of database objects is derived from SECURE.DOC, a Word for Windows 2.0 document file contributed to the MSACCESS forum of CompuServe by an anonymous author at Microsoft Corporation as SECURE.ZIP. SECURE.DOC explains many of the security features of Access more clearly and completely than the documentation that accompanies retail Access and the ADT. Although the version of SECURE.DOC available at the time this edition was written covers Access 1.x security, much of the material in SECURE.DOC also applies to Access 2.0.

You also can use the Containers and Documents collections to obtain ownership and related information for **Table**, **QueryDef** and other database objects stored in the current or a specified database. Listing 27.6 is a minor modification of the EnumerateDocuments() example function included in Access 2.0's on-line help file for the Containers and Documents collections. The ListDocuments() function prints the information for each **Container** object and the **Document** objects it contains in the Immediate Window.

Listing 27.6. Code for the ListDocuments() function.

```
Function ListDocuments () As Integer
    'Purpose:   List the Container and Document objects of the database
    'From:      Example code for the Containers and Documents collections
    '           in the on-line help file for Access 2.0
    'Revisions: Object names changed to comply with naming conventions

    Dim wspCurrent As WorkSpace
    Dim dbCurrent As Database
    Dim cntContainer As Container
    Dim docDocument As Document
    Dim intContainer As Integer
    Dim intDocument As Integer

    Set wspCurrent = DBEngine.Workspaces(0)
    Set dbCurrent = wspCurrent.Databases(0)

    For intDocument = 0 To dbCurrent.Containers.Count - 1
        Set cntContainer = dbCurrent.Containers(intDocument)
        Debug.Print ">> Container: "; cntContainer.Name;
        Debug.Print "  Owner: "; cntContainer.Owner
        Debug.Print "  UserName: "; cntContainer.UserName;
        Debug.Print "  Permissions: "; cntContainer.Permissions
        Debug.Print
        For intContainer = 0 To cntContainer.Documents.Count - 1
            Set docDocument = cntContainer.Documents(intContainer)
            Debug.Print " > Document: "; docDocument.Name;
            Debug.Print "  Owner: "; docDocument.Owner;
            Debug.Print "  Container: "; docDocument.Container
            Debug.Print "  UserName: "; docDocument.UserName;
            Debug.Print "  Permissions: "; docDocument.Permissions
            Debug.Print "  DateCreated: "; docDocument.DateCreated;
            Debug.Print "  LastUpdated: "; docDocument.LastUpdated
            Debug.Print
        Next intContainer

    Next intDocument
    ListDocuments = True
End Function
```

Figure 27.15 shows the result of executing the ListDocuments() function with DATADICT.MDB as the current database. The Immediate Window displays the properties of each **Container** object, followed by the list of properties for the **Document** objects in the container.

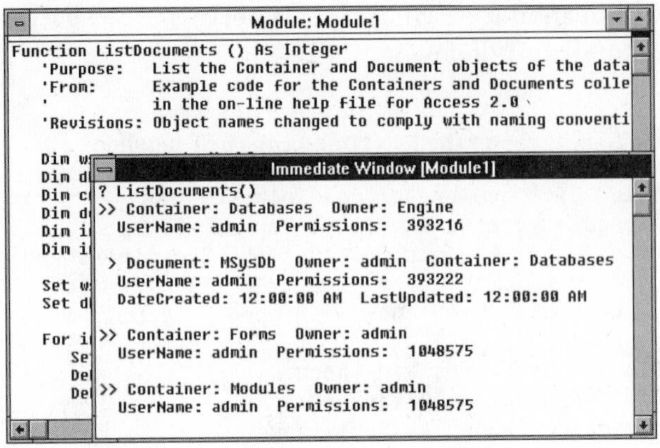

FIGURE 27.15.

The result of executing the ListDocuments() function.

Data Dictionaries for Tables Attached by the ODBC API

When you attach a table from a client-server or a desktop database with the ODBC API, the SourceTable and Connect properties of the attached **TableDef** objects are included in the data dictionary text file created by DATADICT.MDB. Figure 27.16 shows a table in Microsoft Word 6.0 that was created from MSA_OLTP.MDB, one of the examples in Chapter 25, "Stretching the Limits of Access." With the exception of the Employees and Shippers tables, the tables in MSA_OLTP.MDB are attached from a Microsoft SQL Server for Windows NT database created from selected tables contained in NWIND.MDB. Although Access converts the period separator of the *OwnerName.TableName* descriptor used by SQL Server to an underscore (*OwnerName_TableName*), the SourceTable property retains the original SQL Server table descriptor.

Documenting Queries

The wCreateDataDict() function also creates an alphabetic list of queries that includes the SQL statement which Access uses to create each query. Using the SQL statement to document queries saves a substantial amount of time compared with describing the query in tabular format. The wCreateDataDict() function calls the AddQueries procedure to create one record in the tblQueries table for each **QueryDef** object.

FIGURE 27.16.
The Word 6.0 table created from MSA_OLTP.MOB.

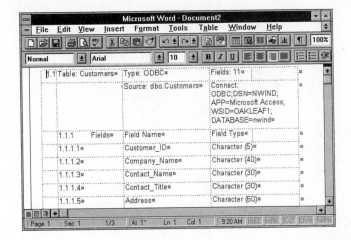

The procedure opens each **QueryDef** object that is included in the list and obtains the text of the SQL statement as the value of qdfTemp.**SQL**. You need to remove the null characters (ASCII 0, **Chr$(0)**) from the value returned by qdfTemp.**SQL**, and then remove the formatting that Access applies to the query in the form of newline pairs. Removing null characters is especially important when you print reports that contain Access SQL statements. Chapter 10, "Generating Meaningful Reports," includes a description of some of the problems that occur if your report's text box values include null characters.

The listing of the AddQueries procedure follows.

Listing 27.7. Access Basic code for the **AddQueries** procedure.

```
Sub AddQueries (wQueryNum As Integer)
    'Purpose:   Add records for queries to rstQueries
    '           SQL property is used to define the query
    'Argument:  Sequence number of query

    'Called by: wCreateDataDict() for TableType = DB_QUERYDEF

    Dim strTemp As String
    Dim wPos As Integer

    'Don't add the record if a QueryDef does not exist
    'On Error GoTo FatalQueryError

    'Only add queries that include FROM (others are system-related)
    rstQueries.AddNew
```

continues

Listing 27.7. continued

```
'Add the standard ListTables values
rstQueries!QueryName = qdfQuery.Name
rstQueries!Sequence = wQueryNum
rstQueries!DateCreated = qdfQuery.DateCreated
rstQueries!LastUpdated = qdfQuery.LastUpdated
rstQueries!Attributes = qdfQuery.Type

'Add a text description of the query type
Select Case qdfQuery.Type
    Case DB_QAPPEND
        rstQueries!QueryType = "Append"
    Case DB_QCROSSTAB
        rstQueries!QueryType = "Crosstab"
    Case DB_QDDL
        rstQueries!QueryType = "Data Definition"
    Case DB_QDELETE
        rstQueries!QueryType = "Delete"
    Case DB_QMAKETABLE
        rstQueries!QueryType = "Make Table"
    Case DB_QSQLPASSTHROUGH
        rstQueries!QueryType = "Delete"
    Case DB_QSETOPERATION
        rstQueries!QueryType = "Union"
    Case DB_QUPDATE
        rstQueries!QueryType = "Update"
    Case DB_SYSTEMOBJECT
        rstQueries!QueryType = "System"
    Case Else
        rstQueries!QueryType = "Select"
End Select

If InStr(qdfQuery.SQL, "PARAMETERS") > 0 Then
    rstQueries!QueryType = "Parameter " & rstQueries!QueryType
End If

'There are nulls in the SQL statements that cause BIG problems later
'Replace the with spaces. (Nulls cause problems in reports.)
strSQL = qdfQuery.SQL
Do While InStr(strSQL, Chr$(0)) > 0
    wPos = InStr(strSQL, Chr$(0))
    strSQL = Left$(strSQL, wPos - 1) & " " & Mid$(strSQL, wPos + 1)
    DoEvents    'Safety
Loop

'Remove newline pairs from SQL statement, substitute spaces
Do While InStr(strSQL, strCrLF) > 0
    wPos = InStr(strSQL, strCrLF)
    strSQL = Left$(strSQL, wPos - 1) & " " & Mid$(strSQL, wPos + 2)
    DoEvents    'Safety
Loop
```

```
    'Add the SQL statement
    rstQueries!SQLStatement = strSQL
    rstQueries.Update

    wQueryNum = wQueryNum + 1

    Exit Sub

FatalQueryError:
    MsgBox "Error: " & Error$, 16, "Query Error"
    Exit Sub
End Sub
```

The CreateQueryText procedure generates the text file, *DATABASE*.QRY, that includes one line of description of the query based on data in the tblQueries table, and
then adds the cleaned-up SQL statement. The CreateQueryText procedure is similar
in structure to the CreateTextFile procedure, except that CreateQueryText is considerably simpler.

Listing 27.8. Access Basic code for the **CreateQueryText** procedure.

```
Sub CreateQueryText (strTextFile As String)
    'Purpose:   Create a text query list with SQL statements
    'Argument:  Name of database file (used as query file name)
    'Called by: wCreateDataDict()

    Dim strWrite As String
    Dim strIndex As String

    'Create the query file name (database.QRY) in the same directory
    strTextFile = Left$(strTextFile, InStr(strTextFile, ".")) & "qry"

    'Delete any prior version of this file
    On Error Resume Next
    Kill strTextFile
    On Error GoTo 0

    'Open the file for sequential (line-by-line) output
    Open strTextFile For Output As #1

    'Set progress indicator
    rstQueries.MoveLast
    vRetVal = SysCmd(1, "Creating query file", rstQueries.RecordCount)

    wCtr = 1
    'Create the records for each table using legal-style outlining
    rstQueries.MoveFirst
    Do While Not rstQueries.EOF
```

continues

Listing 27.8. continued

```
    'Create header entry for table
    strIndex = "1." & LTrim$(Str$(rstQueries!Sequence))
    strWrite = strIndex & Chr$(9) & "Query: " & rstQueries!QueryName
    strWrite = strWrite & "  Type: " & rstQueries!QueryType
    strWrite = strWrite & "  Created: " & rstQueries!DateCreated

    'Add the query record to the file
    Print #1, strWrite

    'Add the SQL statement to the file
    strWrite = strIndex & ".1" & Chr$(9) & "SQL Statement: " & _
               ➥rstQueries!SQLStatement
    Print #1, strWrite

    'Skip a line
    Print #1, ""

    rstQueries.MoveNext
    vRetVal = SysCmd(2, wCtr)
    wCtr = wCtr + 1
Loop

'Close the text file
Close #1

End Sub
```

Figure 27.17 illustrates a Word 6.0 table created from the NWIND.QRY text file generated along with NWIND.TXT by executing wCreateDataDict ("c:\access\sampapps\nwind.mdb"). In some cases, there are two queries, one with the query name as it appears in the Database Window and a second query of the same name with the appended digits. Such a query is created in a two-step process to speed the return of query result sets, especially when you include SQL aggregate functions in your query.

TIP

You can use the Professional Edition of Visual Basic 3.0 to create a general-purpose data dictionary generator for all the database types supported by the Access database engine and the available ODBC drivers. Visual Basic provides the list methods (these methods are Object Basic reserved words), but the data on tables, fields, and indexes included in the collections for database objects make the program somewhat simpler. You can import the code of the Data Dictionary application directly into Visual Basic, and then make the necessary changes to comply with the rules of Visual Basic 3.0.

FIGURE 27.17.

The NWIND.QRY text file formatted as a Word for Windows table.

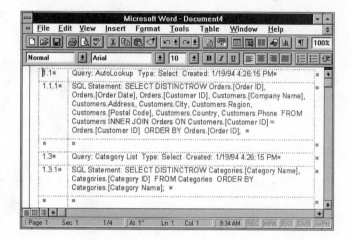

Using the DBStruct Application to Analyze Databases

The Access Developer's Toolkit (ADT) includes DBSTRUCT.MDB, an application created by Microsoft designed to analyze and report the properties of tables, queries, and relationships in Access 2.0 databases. You can use the two tables created by DBSTRUCT.MDB, ObjectInstances and PropertyInstances, with code similar to that contained in the `CreateText` subprocedure, described earlier in this chapter, to create a data dictionary.

TIP

Test the DBStruct application on a small database application before using it to analyze more complex databases with many TableDef and QueryDef objects. Running DBStruct on NWIND.MDB, as an example, creates a total of about 15,000 records in the two tables, and requires 10 minutes or more, depending on the speed of your computer and the amount of RAM available.

The following steps describe how to create the two DBStruct tables for the MSA_OLTP.MDB database on the accompanying diskette:

1. Open the DBSTRUCT.MDB application in your C:\ACCESS\ADT directory.

2. Open the DBStruct form and tick the Save Analysis Tables and Examine Queries on Exit check box. (See Figure 27.18.)

FIGURE 27.18.

The main form of the DBStruct application.

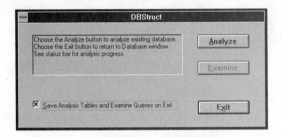

3. Click the Analyze button to display the FileOpen common dialog box, Open Database File, to select the .MDB file to analyze. (See Figure 27.19.) Click the OK button to proceed with the analysis.

FIGURE 27.19.

Selecting the database to analyze with DBStruct.

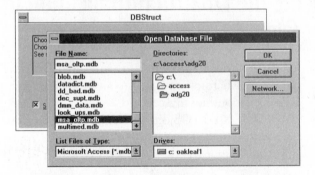

4. After a minute or two, DBStruct reports successful creation of the ObjectInstances and PropertyInstances tables. (See Figure 27.20.) Click the Examine button to display the Examine form.

5. Tick the check box for the class of object you want to examine, then choose the object name in the Name list box of the Object pane. Select the property in the Name List box of the Property pane whose value you want to inspect in the Value text box. (See Figure 27.21.)

FIGURE 27.20.

The DBStruct form reporting successful completion of the analysis.

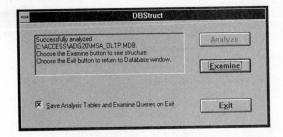

6. After you've inspected the properties in which you are interested, click the done button to close the Examine form. Open the ObjectInstances table to see a list of each **Table**, **QueryDef**, and **Document** object in the database. Figure 27.22 shows the ObjectInstances table in Datasheet View. Each object and property is identified by a sequential ID number. The value of the WholeID field for a property corresponds to the ID number of the object whose **Properties** collection of which the property is a member.

FIGURE 27.21.

Using the Examine form to determine the value of selected object properties.

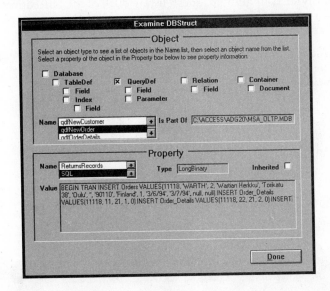

7. Open the PropertyInstances table to view the values of the properties corresponding to the ID value of the ObjectInstances table. (See Figure 27.23.)

FIGURE 27.22.
Part of the content of the ObjectInstances table for the MSA_OLTP.MDB application.

Table: ObjectInstances

ID	Type	Name	WholeID
1	Database	C:\ACCESS\ADG20\MSA_OLTP.MDB	1
2	Property	Name	1
3	Property	Connect	1
4	Property	Transactions	1
5	Property	Updatable	1
6	Property	CollatingOrder	1
7	Property	QueryTimeout	1
8	Property	Version	1
9	Property	Reserved	1
10	Property	AccessVersion	1
11	TableDef	Customers	1
12	Property	Name	11
13	Property	Updatable	11
14	Property	DateCreated	11
15	Property	LastUpdated	11
16	Property	Connect	11
17	Property	Attributes	11
18	Property	SourceTableName	11
19	Property	RecordCount	11
20	Property	ValidationRule	11

Record: 1 of 2473

The code contained in the AnalyzeExistingDB module of DBSTRUCT.MDB is a useful reference source for developers who are interested in creating custom data dictionary applications for Access 2.0 databases. The Declarations section of AnalyzeExistingDB includes a listing of all of the procedures in the module and the calls made by each procedure.

FIGURE 27.23.
Part of the content of the PropertyInstances table for the MSA_OLTP.MDB application.

Table: PropertyInstances

ID	DataType	StringValue
2	11	C:\ACCESS\ADG20\MSA_OLTP.MDB
3	11	
4	3	-1
5	3	0
6	3	256
7	4	60
8	11	2.0
9	3	-1
10	10	02.00
12	11	Customers
13	3	0
14	8	3/6/94 12:26:24 PM
15	8	3/6/94 12:38:00 PM
16	11	ODBC;DSN=NWIND;APP=Microsoft Access;WSID=OAKLEAF1;DATABASE=nw
17	4	536870912
18	11	dbo.Customers
19	4	-1
20	11	
21	11	
23	10	#NULL#

Record: 14 of 2316

NOTE

The ObjectInstances table does not conform to the rules of normalization of relational tables, because the table contains records for two entity types, names of database objects and properties of these objects. It is a relatively simple matter, however, to identify the record containing the name of the object by detecting a change in the value of the WhileID field of the ObjectInstances table.

Printing, Archiving, and Analyzing Access Basic Code

Like its Visual Basic cousin, Access can print your Access Basic code, but only with very limited (virtually no) formatting. Pinnacle Publishing, Inc.'s Code.Print Pro for Microsoft Access prints a fully formatted version of your code. (The version of Code.Print Pro for Access 2.0 was in the testing stage when this edition was written.) If you want to format your code for printing, and you don't have Code.Print Pro, you need to import the code into Microsoft Word, Windows Write, or, at the minimum, Windows Notepad to print the code with appropriate margins, page numbers, and other accoutrements that your clients expect. Microsoft Word is the best choice for printing code, because you can search for and replace varying numbers of leading spaces to styles that will properly wrap code that extends beyond the right margin. Make sure to use a fixed-pitch font, such as Courier or Courier New, for code listings; code printed in proportionally spaced fonts is harder to read.

You can use the Clipboard to cut and paste procedures into word processing applications in the sequence in which they logically should appear. Choose Save **T**ext from the **F**ile menu to save your Access Basic code in the form of a conventional DOS .TXT file. For maximum safety, archive your Access Basic code in the form of .TXT files on diskettes.

A variety of application structure analyzers are available for DOS database managers such as dBASE. Application structure analyzers create a map of the individual function and procedure calls within an application, as well as a concordance that indicates what function or procedure uses which variable. The event-driven structure of Windows applications makes creating structure analyzers for Access Basic more difficult. In addition to determining relationships between Access Basic functions and procedures, a structure analyzer for Access Basic needs to associate the event with the function that the event calls.

There were no commercial documentation and structure analysis applications for Access 2.0 available when this edition was written during early 1994. FMS, Inc., Vienna, VA, the publishers of the Total Access were in the process of completing Total Access 2.0 at the time the retail version of Access 2.0 was released. Total Access is a much more comprehensive and flexible documentation system for Access applications than the Database Documenter add-in. Other independent software vendors are likely to provide commercial applications to prepare text and graphic documentation of Access applications.

28

Writing Help Files for Access Applications

Users of Windows expect and deserve online, context-sensitive help for all their Windows applications. All but the simplest Access applications need a custom Windows help file that enables users to press F1 to obtain context-sensitive help for field entries, click a toolbar button to obtain help for the currently open form, or choose Contents from the Help menu to select a topic from the help system's opening window. No matter how much or how little written documentation you supply with your Access database application, few users of your application will take the time to read the documentation before beginning to use the application. This is especially true for decision-support applications that you design for supervisory and management personnel.

Your Access database applications should be sufficiently intuitive in their operation that all but the Windows neophyte can take full advantage of their features without employing online help. In reality, however, few Windows applications of any significance are fully comprehensible to the first-time user. Therefore, you need to create Windows help files to make sure that users employ all the features of your application and use the features in the way that you intended. If you develop a database application to a written specification, the contract undoubtedly stipulates that comprehensive printed documentation must accompany the production version of the application. Therefore, this chapter is oriented toward converting the text and graphics of your printed documentation to a help file for the application. Making documentation do "double-duty" as a help file saves time and expense.

This chapter is designed to supplement, not replace, the Help Compiler Guide included with the Access Developer's Toolkit (ADT). The previous chapter discusses documenting the objects in your Access application and preparing a data dictionary. This chapter also shows you how to use a commercial software product, WexTech Systems, Inc.'s Doc-To-Help, to convert your Word for Windows documentation files to a full-fledged, professional Windows help system.

Understanding How Access 2.0 and WinHelp Interact

The help file display features of Windows 3.1 are commonly referred to as the *WinHelp engine*. This term is derived from WINHELP.EXE, the Windows application in your \WINDOWS directory that implements the help system. Access 2.0 includes features that let you assign individual help windows to forms, and controls to create context-sensitive help. The interface between your Access application and your WinHelp .HLP file(s) is comprised of the following two basic elements:

■ The *APPNAME*.HLP file that you specify as the master WinHelp file for your application is the `HelpFile` entry of the `[Run-Time Options]` section of your *APPNAME*.INI file for runtime applications using MSARN200.EXE. Specifying a master WinHelp file is one of the subjects of the next chapter, "Distributing Runtime Versions of Your Databases." Most applications use a single help file, but you can specify different help files by assigning `filename.hlp` as the value of the `HelpFile` property of forms and reports when you want to change WinHelp files within an application. You also can specify a help file with Access Basic code, as described in the section titled "Calling the *WinHelp()* function with Access Basic Code."

■ The context ID number (**Long**) that corresponds to a help context string embedded in your WinHelp file. You add entries to the `[MAP]` section of your help project (.HPJ) file to assign context ID numbers to the help context strings. Context ID numbers are the key to creating context-sensitive help. You assign context ID numbers as the `HelpContextID` property of forms and controls. You also can set the current context ID value with a `[FormName]![ControlName].HelpContextID = lngContextID` statement.

The sections that follow describe how you create WinHelp files and how you assign context IDs to topics in order to create context-sensitive help.

NOTE

Making use of all of the features offered by the WinHelp engine is beyond the scope of this book. *Developing Online Help for Windows* (1993, Sams Publishing, ISBN 0-672-30230-6) is a detailed guide and reference for creating WinHelp systems. You can download a description and outline of *Developing Online Help for Windows* in .HLP format as BOOKHL.ZIP from Library 9, ElectronicPub/Multimedia, of the Windows Users Group Forum (GO WUGNET) on CompuServe. Microsoft's *Help Authoring Guide* also is available for downloading in .HLP format from the same forum as HAG.ZIP. The *Help Authoring Guide* also is included on the Microsoft Developer Network (MSDN) CD-ROMs. The MSDN CD-ROMs include the Microsoft Help Project Editor, WHPE.EXE (a Visual Basic 1.0 application), and help-authoring templates for Windows 3.0 and 3.1 WinHelp files.

Creating Rich Text Format Files for Help Systems

A WinHelp .HLP file is a compiled version of a word processing document file saved in Microsoft rich text format (.RTF). Rich text format is a page description language used to exchange formatted text between document processing applications. You use .RTF files, as an example, to transfer Word for Windows files to the Macintosh version of Word. Most Windows word processing applications are capable of saving documents as .RTF files. Rich text format is similar in concept to Adobe's PostScript page description language, but .RTF is not used to print documents. Figure 28.1 shows part of the .RTF version of this paragraph displayed in Notepad's window.

FIGURE 28.1.

Part of the .RTF version of a Word for Windows 2.0 document.

The .RTF files that you create include a header that describes the page format, fonts, and styles in use. PostScript files contain a header that serves a similar purpose. An escape character (\) precedes page and character formatting data in .RTF files, and French braces ({}) enclose groups of formatting data and text to which the formatting applies. Most of the header information in Word .RTF files is derived from the template (.DOT file) in use when you write the document. Only a small part of the .RTF file header appears in Figure 28.1; the first two words of the text are highlighted to identify the point where the paragraph starts.

Adding Instructions to the WinHelp Engine

Instructions to the WinHelp engine are embedded in the .RTF file in the form of footnotes designated by footnote symbols, such as $ and #, rather than conventional footnote numbers. Topic titles are designated by $ footnotes and the context strings that uniquely identify a topic to the WinHelp engine use the # symbol. A topic is a help window that is devoted to a single subject; topics are separated from one another in your word processing document by hard page breaks (usually created with the Ctrl+Enter key combination). Figure 28.2 shows part of a simple help topic from the HELPEX example included with the Help Authoring Guide on the Microsoft Developer's Network CD-ROM (MSDN CD 5).

FIGURE 28.2.

Part of the second topic of the HELPEX.RTF file used to create HELPEX.HLP.

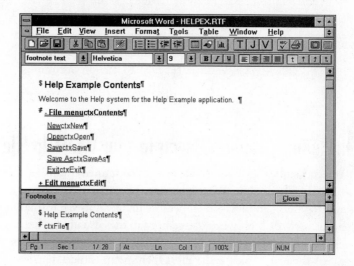

In Figure 28.2, `Help Example Contents` is the topic title and `ctxContents` is the help context string for the topic. *Hotspots* are individual words or blocks of text that are formatted with the double-underline or strike-through attribute and are followed by a help context string formatted as hidden text. When you click a hotspot, WinHelp jumps to the topic identified by the context string that follows the hotspot text. Figure 28.3 shows the first two help topic windows of HELPEX.HLP. Hotspots are green in help windows, so you should avoid the use of the green color attribute in your help text.

FIGURE 28.3.

The first two help topic windows of HELPEX.HLP.

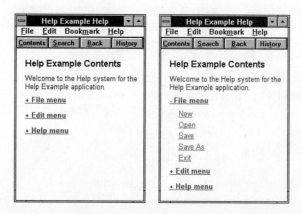

NOTE

The HELPEX.HLP file created from HELPEX.RTF uses an interesting technique to toggle expansion of the individual topics shown in the left help window of Figure 28.3. When you click the + File menu topic, the individual topics for the File menu appear as shown in the right help window of Figure 28.3. When you click the - File menu topic, the first topic window reappears. If you examine the context ID strings of the first two help topics of HELPEX.RTF, you can see how Microsoft accomplished the toggling trick.

Including Graphic Objects in Your WinHelp File

You can embed or link graphic objects contained in bitmap (.BMP) or vector image (.WMF) files in your WinHelp files. The easiest method of adding bitmapped images to your help files is to embed the image in .BMP format in your .DOC or .RTF file using Word. However, large bitmap files usually are handled more efficiently by linking the graphic file to the WinHelp file by reference to its filename. Figure 28.4 shows the help topic for the **File Open** menu choice. The icon (a bitmap image captured from Word 2.0's toolbar) is embedded in the .RTF document by choosing **Picture** from Word 2.0's **Insert** menu to display the Picture dialog and double-clicking cmdialog.bmp in the File Name list box. The {bmc cmdialog.bmp} entry below the line of text causes the CMDIALOG.BMP bitmap file to be inserted at the position of the { character.

NOTE

When you use bitmapped graphics, you may need to include a version of the bitmap file for each type of display resolution that might be employed by users of the help system. The Microsoft multiple-resolution bitmap compiler, MRBC.EXE, enables you to create a single bitmap file that supports CGA, EGA, VGA, SVGA, and 8514 resolutions. It is unlikely that any users of Access 2.0 database applications use CGA or EGA monitors, but MRBC.EXE is useful for providing scalable bitmaps for 640-by-480 (VGA) and 1,024-by-768 (8514, XGA, or UVGA) display resolutions. The vast majority of Windows database applications run on "plain vanilla" 16-color VGA systems. When you convert a .BMP file with MRBC.EXE, you substitute .MRB for the .BMP extension in references to the file. One of the advantages of using .WMF vector image files in help files is that the Windows metafiles are device-independent.

FIGURE 28.4.

A help topic with an embedded icon and a linked bitmap file.

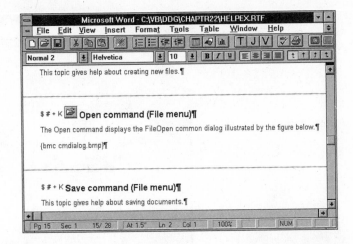

The term "link" is used in this chapter to differentiate between embedding a graphics file in the .RTF file and creating a reference to a separate graphics file with {bm? *filename.ext*} entries in your .RTF file. The ? placeholder determines whether the graphic is placed as a character (bmc), at the left margin (bml), or at the right margin (bmr). When you compile the help file with the WinHelp compiler, the graphic that you link is embedded in the .HLP file you create. (You do *not* need to supply the .BMP file along with your .HLP file.)

Figure 28.5 shows the Open command topic with the embedded icon bitmap and the bitmapped image of the Open dialog that is linked with the {bmc cmdialog.bmp} reference.

You can create hotspots in graphic images that you link to your WinHelp file by using the Hotspot Editor, SHED.EXE, which is included with the ADT. (You cannot add hotspots to bitmaps you embed in WinHelp .RTF files.) The Hotspot Editor creates a .SHG (system hypergraphic) file from .BMP, .DIB (device-independent bitmap), or .WMF files. To add hotspots to a .BMP, a .DIB, or a .WMF file, follow these steps:

1. Launch SHED.EXE and choose **O**pen from the Editor's **F**ile menu to display the File Open dialog box, which is not a Windows 3.1 common dialog box.

2. Select the directory and filename of the bitmap from the Directories and Files list boxes, and then click the OK button to close the File Open dialog box and display the image.

FIGURE 28.5.

*An embedded
bitmap of a toolbar
button and a linked
bitmap of a dialog
box in
HELPEX.HLP.*

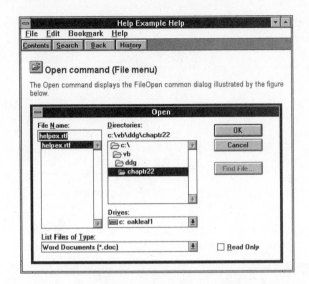

3. Position the mouse pointer at the upper-left corner of the area that you want to make active as a hotspot. Click the left mouse button and drag the enclosing rectangle to define the hotspot area. Then release the mouse button.

4. With the frame for your hotspot selected (with the eight sizing handles), choose **A**ttributes from the **E**dit window to display the Attributes dialog box. Enter the context string corresponding to the topic for the hotspot item in the Context String text box. Select Pop-up to create a pop-up window, or select Jump to jump to a new topic. Accept the default value, Visible, in the Attribute combo box and the Hotspot ID text box. You can manipulate the position of the enclosing rectangle by changing the entries in the text boxes within the Bounding Box frame. Figure 28.6 shows the typical entries that define the attributes of a hotspot.

5. Click the OK button to assign the attributes to the hotspot. Add additional hotspots as needed by repeating steps 3 and 4.

6. When you've completed the definitions of the hotspots you want, choose Save **A**s from the **F**ile menu and save your file with the same name as the original bitmap but with the .SHG extension, indicating that the bitmap file is now a hypergraphic file. Close SHED.EXE.

7. If you have referred to the bitmap in your .RTF file using the .BMP extension, change the file extension to .SHG. (You also need to change the reference in the [BITMAPS] section of the project file, the subject of the next section.)

FIGURE 28.6.

Defining the boundaries and attributes of a hotspot in a hypergraphic (.SHG) file.

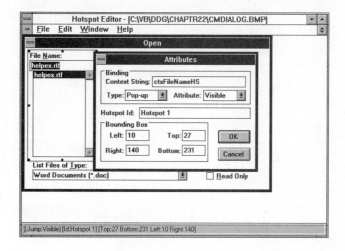

8. Add new topics to your WinHelp file for the pop-up or conventional help window(s) that appear when you click the hotspot(s). Each topic has a context string that corresponds to the context string you added during the editing process. Figure 28.7 shows two entries for the pop-up windows that open when you click hotspots on the bitmap of the FileOpen common dialog box.

FIGURE 28.7.

Pop-up help window topics for hotspots of the FileOpen common dialog topic.

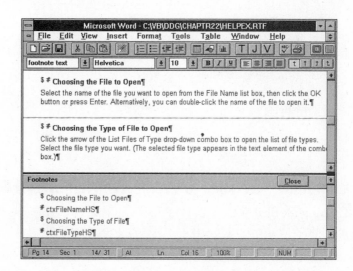

9. After you compile your WinHelp .RTF file to a .HLP file, clicking a hotspot displays the popup window whose context string corresponds to the context string you assigned as the hotspot's attribute. (Compiling .RTF to .HLP files

is the subject of the next section.) Figure 28.8 shows the pop-up window that appears when you click the area within the dashed lines surrounding the List Files of Type combo box. The dashed lines appear because Visible was selected as the attribute for the hotspot regions. (Normally you choose Invisible, so the dashed lines do not appear.)

FIGURE 28.8.

The pop-up window displayed when you click the List Files of Type hotspot.

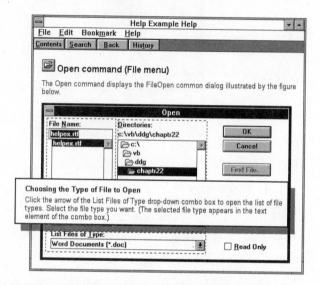

> **NOTE**
>
> One of the advantages of using SHED.EXE is that the Hotspot editor compresses the .BMP files. As an example, CMDIALOG.BMP requires 67,614 bytes of storage, while CMDIALOG.SHG occupies only 13,327 bytes.

Compiling .RTF Files to Create WinHelp .HLP Files

Creating the final WinHelp .HLP file from your .RTF file and any graphics that are referenced in the .RTF file is a three-step process, as follows:

1. Create a project file that provides information to the help compiler on the file(s) that constitute your help file and assigns help context ID values to the help context string.

2. Use HC31.EXE, the Windows 3.1 help compiler, to compile the .RTF and the other files you specify into the WinHelp .HLP file.

3. Test your .HLP file to make sure it conforms to your expectations.

The three sections that follow describe the preceding steps in detail.

Creating a Project File

Help project files, which usually are named *APPNAME*.HPJ, are similar in concept to Visual Basic 3.0 project files and to C and C++ make files. The content of the project file for the Help Example help file, HELPEX.HPJ, appears in Listing 28.1.

Listing 28.1. Sections and entries in the HELPEX.PRJ help project file.

```
; This help project requires hc 3.1
[OPTIONS]
errorlog = helpex.err
title = Help Example Help
contents = ctxContents
compress = 0
warning = 3
multikey = M

[FILES]
helpex.rtf

[BITMAPS]
cmdialog.shg

[ALIAS]
IDM_NEW = ctxNew
IDM_OPEN = ctxOpen
IDM_SAVE = ctxSave
IDM_SAVEAS = ctxSaveAs
IDM_PRINT = ctxPrint
IDM_EXIT = ctxExit
IDM_UNDO = ctxUndo
IDM_CUT = ctxCut
IDM_COPY = ctxCopy
IDM_PASTE = ctxPaste
IDM_CLEAR = ctxClear
IDM_ABOUT = ctxContents
IDM_HELP_CONTENTS = ctxContents
IDM_HELP_KEYBOARD = ctxKeys
IDM_HELP_MULTIKEY = ctxMultikeyCommand
IDM_HELP_SEARCH = ctxSearch
IDM_HELP_HELP = ctxContents
ERR_NOT_YET_IMPLEMENTED = ctxNYI
HELPID_FILE = ctxFile
HELPID_EDIT = ctxEdit
HELPID_HELP = ctxContents
HELPID_SYSTEM = ctxSystem
```

continues

Listing 28.1. continued

```
HELPID_EDIT_WINDOW = ctxEditWindow
HELPID_MAXIMIZE_ICON = ctxMinMax
HELPID_MINIMIZE_ICON = ctxMinMax
HELPID_TITLE_BAR = ctxTitle
HELPID_SIZING_BORDER = ctxSize
HELPID_SYSRESTORE = ctxSystem
HELPID_SYSMOVE = ctxSystem
HELPID_SYSSIZE = ctxSystem
HELPID_SYSMINIMIZE = ctxSystem
HELPID_SYSMAXIMIZE = ctxSystem
HELPID_SYSCLOSE = ctxSystem
HELPID_SYSSWITCH = ctxSystem
ABOUTBOX = ctxContents
EDITMULTIKEY = ctxMultikeyCommand

[MAP]
#define IDM_NEW 100
#define IDM_OPEN 101
#define IDM_SAVE 102
#define IDM_SAVEAS 103
#define IDM_PRINT 104
#define IDM_EXIT 105
#define IDM_UNDO 200
#define IDM_CUT 201
#define IDM_COPY 202
#define IDM_PASTE 203
#define IDM_CLEAR 204
#define IDM_ABOUT 300
#define IDM_HELP_CONTENTS 301
#define IDM_HELP_KEYBOARD 302
#define IDM_HELP_MULTIKEY 303
#define IDM_HELP_SEARCH 304
#define IDM_HELP_HELP 305
#define ERR_NOT_YET_IMPLEMENTED 1000
#define HELPID_FILE 400
#define HELPID_EDIT 401
#define HELPID_HELP 402
#define HELPID_SYSTEM 403
#define HELPID_EDIT_WINDOW 404
#define HELPID_MAXIMIZE_ICON 405
#define HELPID_MINIMIZE_ICON 406
#define HELPID_TITLE_BAR 408
#define HELPID_SIZING_BORDER 409
#define HELPID_SYSRESTORE 410
#define HELPID_SYSMOVE 411
#define HELPID_SYSSIZE 412
#define HELPID_SYSMINIMIZE 413
#define HELPID_SYSMAXIMIZE 414
#define HELPID_SYSCLOSE 415
```

```
#define HELPID_SYSSWITCH 416
#define ABOUTBOX 800
#define EDITMULTIKEY 801
```

Help project files are text files that are organized into sections and are similar in structure to Windows .INI files. Table 28.1 lists the most commonly used sections of a help project file, states whether the section is required in the file, and gives a brief description of the purpose of the section. Keywords for entries in the [Options] section also are described in Table 28.1.

Table 28.1. The sections of a help project (.HPJ) file.

Section of .HPJ File	Section Required?	Description
[OPTIONS]	No (but usually present)	Defines the options that control the WinHelp compilation process. Some of the more common option entries include the following:
[OPTIONS] Keywords	ROOT=*d:\path*	Defines the path to your help source files.
	CONTENTS= *ContextString*	Sets the context string for the index topic with the Windows 3.1 Help compiler, HC31.EXE.
	TITLE=*AppName Help*	Sets the title for the WinHelp file, which appears in the help window's title bar.
	ICON=*IconFile.ICO*	Sets the icon that is displayed when the help window is minimized.
	COMPRESS=0¦FALSE	Controls file compression. 0, or FALSE, means "do not compress files." 1, or TRUE, compresses the file.

continues

Table 28.1. continued

Section of .HPJ File	Section Required?	Description
		Compressing .HLP files saves disk space at the expense of speed in displaying Help windows (due to the time required to decompress the file). HC31.EXE supports varying degrees of compression.
	WARNING=3	Determines what errors are reported. 0 through 3 control the level of error reporting: 0 = no error reports; 1 = most severe warnings; 2 = intermediate warning level; and 3 = report all warnings.
	REPORT=1 ¦ ON	Determines whether progress reports of the compilation are provided. 1, or ON, = report progress of compile; 0, or OFF, = no report.
[FILES]	Yes	Specifies the help source files included in the compilation.
[BUILD]	No	Specifies topics to include in or exclude from the compiled file.
[BUILDTAGS]	No (Yes if [BUILD] specified)	Names valid build tags, enabling the selection of topics to be compiled within a file.
[CONFIG]	Only if DLL functions are called	Registers custom DLLs whose functions are called by WinHelp RegisterRoutine macros.

Section of .HPJ File	Section Required?	Description
[BITMAPS]	No	Specifies bitmap or .WMF files used in the compilation and not embedded in your WinHelp document. This section is not required if you used the ROOT= entry in the [OPTIONS] section to specify the path to the referenced bitmap files.
[MAP]	No	Associates context strings with context ID numbers. You need a map section to use the Context ID property of Access forms and control objects.
[ALIAS]	No	Allows you to assign more than one context string to a subject.
[WINDOWS]	No	Describes the main WinHelp window and any secondary window types in the help file.
[BAGGAGE]	No	Names any additional data files that are to be incorporated into the WinHelp file.

> **NOTE**
>
> The HELPEX.HPJ project file shown in Listing 28.1 uses the [ALIAS] section to assign symbolic constants that refer to help topics. The symbolic constants are assigned context ID values by #define statements in the [MAP] section. This is a relatively uncommon practice in simple help project files.

Using HC31.EXE to Compile Your WinHelp .RTF File

The Microsoft Help Compiler, HC31.EXE, is a DOS application that converts .RTF files to the format required by WinHelp .HLP files, incorporates graphics files, and creates the required look-up tables for help context strings and context IDs. Type **HC31 *PROJNAME*** and press Enter at the DOS prompt to create the *PROJNAME*.HLP file. If HC31.EXE is not in a directory on your DOS path, you need to specify the path, as in **C:\ACCESS\ADT\HC31 *PROJNAME***. (*PROJNAME* is the name of your project file. The file extension is not required if you use the .HPJ extension.)

To compile your application in a windowed DOS session, you need to create a program information file (.PIF) to run HC31.EXE. Assigning an icon to the .PIF file and launching the help compiler by double-clicking an icon is a quicker process than executing HC31.EXE from the DOS command line. Figure 28.9 shows the entries you need to make in PIF Editor's window to create HC31_MSA.PIF, which compiles HELPEX.HPJ.

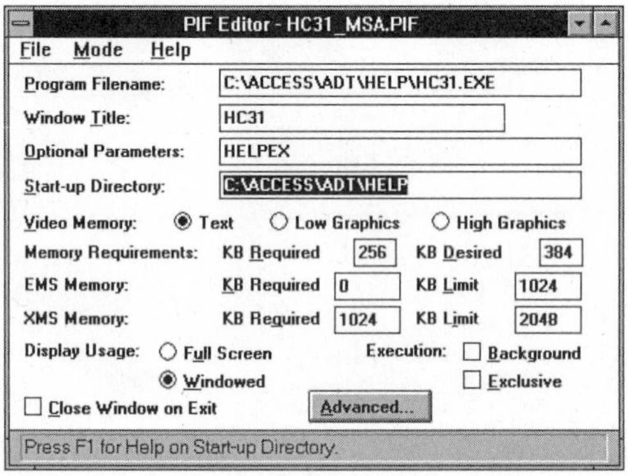

FIGURE 28.9.

Creating a program information file (.PIF) to compile HELPEX.HPJ.

After you create your .PIF file, choose New from Program Manager's File menu to add an icon to launch the .PIF file from an application group. Figure 28.10 shows the entries required to launch HC31_MSA.PIF by double-clicking the icon shown below the Shortcut Key label. The Swiss Army Knife icon is from MORICONS.DLL in the \WINDOWS directory.

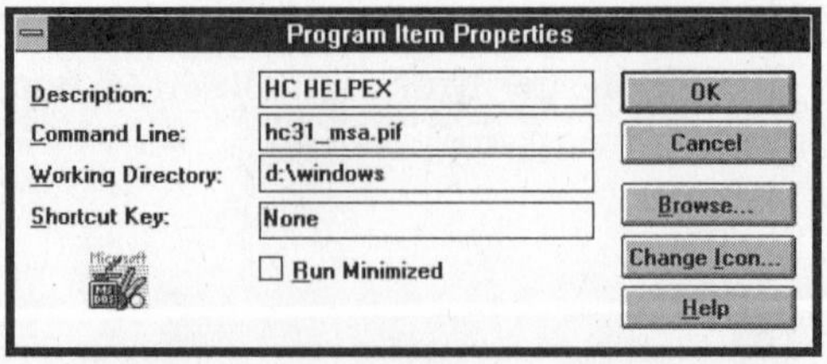

FIGURE 28.10.

Creating a Program Manager icon for HC31_MSA.PIF.

> **TIP**
>
> To associate the Swiss Army Knife icon with HC31_MSA.PIF, click the Change Icon button, click OK when the message box appears that advises you that no icons are associated with your .PIF file, click the Browse Icon, and double-click MORICONS.DLL from the File Name list box. Scroll the icon selections that appear in the Current Icon window until you find the icon you want, select that icon, and then click the OK button.

When you launch HC31.EXE with HC31_MSA.PIF, the DOS window appears as illustrated by Figure 28.11. The progress messages occur only if you add a `Report=1` entry to the `[OPTIONS]` section of your .HPJ file. If there are problems with your .RTF file or entries in your .HPJ file, you receive warnings or error messages from HC31.EXE. Error messages indicate a fatal flaw and cancel the compilation process; you get a compiled .HLP file when warnings appear. The meaning of error and warning messages is documented in Chapter 7, "Testing and Debugging Help Files," of the *Help Compiler Guide* included with the ADT. Unfortunately, little guidance is given for correcting the problem that led to the error or warning message.

> **TIP**
>
> Error message 5059, "Not enough memory to build Help file," is likely to occur if you have large bitmapped images embedded in your .RTF file. This message often appears even if you have 500K or so of DOS memory available. The only solution, in this case, is to save the bitmap(s) as .BMP file(s), add references to the bitmaps in your .RTF file, and specify the bitmap file(s) in the `[BITMAPS]` section of your .HPJ file.

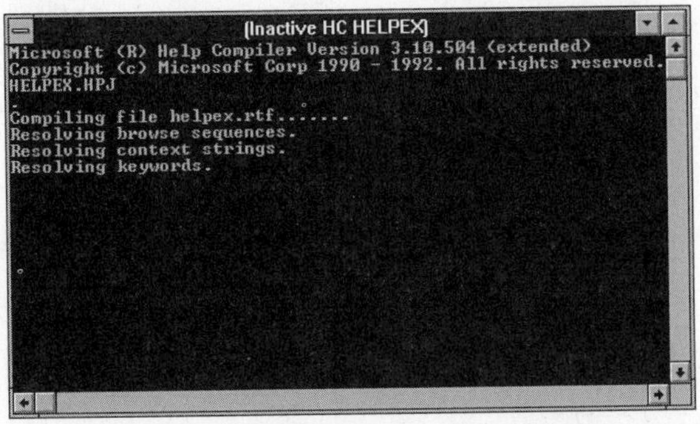

FIGURE 28.11.

Compiling HELPEX.HPJ in a DOS window.

```
                    (Inactive HC HELPEX)
Microsoft (R) Help Compiler Version 3.10.504 (extended)
Copyright (c) Microsoft Corp 1990 - 1992. All rights reserved.
HELPEX.HPJ

Compiling file helpex.rtf.......
Resolving browse sequences.
Resolving context strings.
Resolving keywords.
```

> **NOTE**
>
> Version 3.10.504 of HC31.EXE, which is supplied with the Access Developer's Toolkit, is a protected-mode application that requires the expanded memory provided by DPMI or VCPI servers. When you run HC31.EXE from Windows in enhanced or standard mode, the DPMI server provides the required expanded memory. If you run HC31.EXE from DOS (without Windows running), you need to provide 1MB to 2MB of expanded memory for HC31.EXE with EMM386, QEMM, or a similar DOS memory-manager application.

Creating Help Files from Your Application Manual

The process of manually creating help files for Access applications is thoroughly documented in Microsoft's *Help Compiler Guide*, which is also a component of the Professional Editions of Visual Basic 3.0 and FoxPro for Windows. Today, few help-file authors write help files in the manner described in the *Help Compiler Guide*. Third-party help-file authoring applications, such as Doc-To-Help by WexTech Systems, Inc. (New York, NY), and RoboHelp from Blue Sky Software (San Diego, CA), speed the organizing and writing of help files. This book proceeds on the assumption that most database developers possess the writing skills that are needed to prepare a better-than-adequate manual for the application. Those developers who are not authors by nature usually employ technical writers to prepare the required written documentation. Therefore, this chapter is oriented toward the design and use of text from the application manual as the basis for your application's help file(s). Almost without exception, Word for Windows is the preferred application for creating the rich text format (.RTF) files needed by the help compiler (HC31.EXE) that you use to create the final WinHelp (.HLP) file. All commercial help-file generation applications are based on Word 2+. More recent updates to these products use many of the new features offered by Word 6.

Using Doc-To-Help to Create Help Files for Access Applications

WexTech's Doc-To-Help 1.5 application is designed to convert application manuals to Windows 3.1 help files. Doc-To-Help consists of the following components:

- A collection of Word for Windows template (.DOT) files for producing manuals that will be copied to 8 1/2-by-11-inch or 7-by-9-inch paper, as well as a special template (D2H_HELP.DOT) that you use when you produce WinHelp files from the text of your manual. The templates make extensive use of Word Basic code to provide supplemental features, such as semi-automatic indexing.

- A DLL that is used to convert large bitmap files for incorporation into help files.

- Licensed copies of three versions of the Microsoft Help Compiler, HC.EXE (for Windows 3.0, now obsolete), HC31.EXE (for Windows 3.1 and Windows NT), and HCP.EXE, the protected-mode version of HC31.EXE, which allows you to compile larger help files than are possible with HC31.EXE.

- A set of tutorial and sample files from which many of the illustrations in this section are derived.

- A 200-page application manual created with Doc-To-Help.

Doc-To-Help has a preset collection of styles that are likely to meet your needs if your client or firm has not already established a set of graphic-design standards. You can alter these basic styles to suit others' requirements or your own taste in layout and typography.

Organizing Your Manual to Optimize Help File Conversion

One of the advantages that authors of application manuals have over authors of developers' guides for software is that the application itself provides the organizational framework for your work. The structure of your application's manual is dictated by the relationship between the forms that constitute the user interface of your application. Thus, a database application manual consists of the following major sections or topics:

- A table of contents (TOC), which lays the groundwork for the window that appears when you choose Contents from the Help menu. The level-one heading, called the supertitle, appears as the heading of the contents window.

- An overview of the application as a whole, including a brief description of the purpose of the application and the underlying database(s). The overview corresponds to the main switchboard form or the start-up form of your application. This window, or series of windows, appears when the user presses the F1 key or clicks the help button of a toolbar with the opening form displayed. The overview is a level-two heading.

■ Instructions on installing the application from the distribution diskettes. You don't include this topic in the help file, because the user can't read the help file until he or she completes the installation.

■ One chapter for each main form of your application. For example, an accounting package would have individual chapters for the General Ledger, Accounts Receivable, Accounts Payable, Payroll, Inventory, and Job Cost Accounting modules, each of which is likely to have its own main form. This help window appears when the user presses F1 or clicks the Help button when the control with the focus does not have a corresponding subtopic. Chapter headings are level 2 and appear in the Help Contents window.

■ Topics within each chapter that explain the next layer down in the hierarchy of forms. Using the Accounts Receivable module of the accounting system as the example, topics might include Invoice Creation, Printing Invoices, Receiving Payments, and Aging the Accounts Receivable. Topic names are highlighted in green with underscores, and usually are identified by larger, bold typefaces. Topics use level-three headings.

■ Subtopics within each chapter that explain how to enter data in text boxes and how to use any subsidiary forms that are at the next level of the hierarchy. You open subtopic help windows from the main topic (chapter) help windows or by pressing F1 when a control object is assigned a subtopic window. Subtopic names have the same format as topic names but use a font that is one or two points smaller than that used for topic names. Subtopic headings are level 4.

■ A glossary of potentially unfamiliar terms, or familiar terms that are used in an unusual context or have an uncommon meaning in the manual. Doc-To-Help converts glossary entries into pop-up windows that you open by clicking highlighted text with dashed underscores.

■ Index entries that create the entries that users see in the list box when they choose Search from the Help menu.

Figure 28.12 shows a sample Doc-To-Help document, D2HINTRO.DOC, in Word 2.0's Outline mode. This help document has four heading levels; thus, D2HINTRO.DOC typifies the structure of help files for Access applications. Writing your manual with one of Doc-To-Help's standard templates attached to it simplifies the help-file conversion process. Alternately, you can convert existing manuals to Doc-To-Help's format by importing the styles contained in the standard Doc-To-Help template. The graphics shown in D2HINTRO.DOC import directly into your help file.

Creating the Help File from the Source Document

Once you've completed and printed proof copies of your application manual, you convert the manual to a Microsoft rich text format (.RTF) file. Rich text format files are text files that include embedded page-, line-, and character-formatting instructions. Doc-To-Help adds several menu choices to Word for Windows' Tools and Format menus that display special-purpose dialog boxes in which you select options for converting your manual to the required .RTF file and compiling the .RTF file to a help file. Figure 28.13 shows the dialog boxes for the converting and compiling steps. When you click the OK button of the Reformat As Help File dialog box, Doc-To-Help creates a .RTF version of the Word .DOC file and then displays the Compile dialog box. When you click the OK button of the Compile dialog box, Doc-To-Help creates a help project file (.HPJ) and runs the help compiler to create the .HLP file.

FIGURE 28.12.

A Doc-To-Help manual shown in Word for Windows' Outline mode.

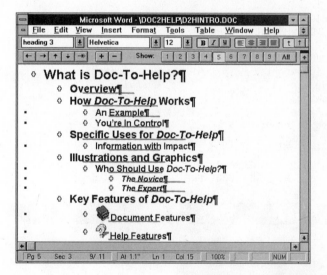

FIGURE 28.13.

The two Doc-To-Help dialog boxes that convert and compile the help document.

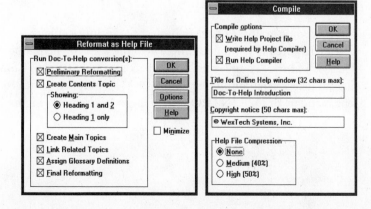

Help Project Files and the Compilation Process

The help project file (.HPJ) tells the compiler the names and locations of the .RTF and bitmap (.BMP) files to be included in the .HLP file. The structure of .HPJ files is similar to a Windows initialization file, such as MSACCESS.INI, and is related to the structure of the .MAK files used by Visual Basic and C compilers. Headings are enclosed in square brackets and are followed by related entries. A truncated version of the D2HINTRO.HPJ file that is automatically generated by Doc-To-Help and that creates D2HINTRO.HLP appears as follows:

```
[OPTIONS]
INDEX=HelpContents1
ROOT=C:\DOC2HELP
COMPRESS=FALSE
TITLE=Doc-To-Help Introduction

[FILES]
C:\DOC2HELP\D2HINTRO.RTF

[MAP]
HelpContents1            1    ; Help Contents
Overview.2               2    ; Overview
HowDoc.To.HelpWorks.3 3       ; How Doc-To-Help Works
AnExample.4              4    ; An Example
You.reInControl.5        5    ; You're In Control

[BITMAPS]
C:\DOC2HELP\HELP0003.BMP
C:\DOC2HELP\HELP0001.BMP
```

> **NOTE**
>
> Unless you specify otherwise, the names of the .RTF, .HPJ, and .HLP files are the same as the names of the source .DOC files. The extensions change to designate the type of file.

The preceding example of a help project file includes only those sections and entries that are required to compile a simple help file with five help topics and two bitmaps. The .HPJ files for complex .HLP files become quite lengthy. Compiling a large help file can take several minutes on an 80386DX computer. After compiling, the Contents window of D2HINTRO.HLP appears as shown in Figure 28.14.

FIGURE 28.14.

The Contents window of D2HINTRO.HLP.

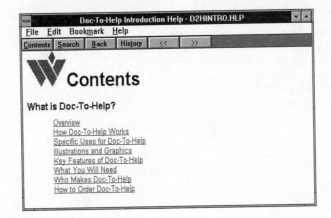

Including Graphic Images in Help Files

You can include large bitmap files, such as images captured from the forms of your application, in both your manual and the help file. The Hotspot Editor (SHED.EXE) included with the ADT lets you assign help context strings to control objects on your form. When the user clicks a control object, the window that explains the purpose of the control object appears. Figure 28.15 shows a pie chart created with Excel that appears when you click the Illustrations and Graphics topic in the Contents window of Figure 28.14.

FIGURE 28.15.

A bitmap illustration included in a help topic window.

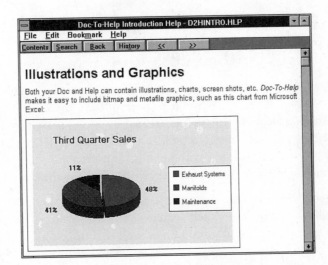

If you use SHED.EXE to assign help context strings to the Exhaust Systems, Manifold, and Maintenance sections of the pie chart, you can cause a jump to the window that deals with each of these subjects. Figure 28.16 shows the bitmap illustration from Figure 28.15 opened in SHED.EXE. You drag the mouse pointer to define a rectangular area that serves as the hotspot. Then you assign the help context string of the help topic to which you want to jump. When the user double-clicks the area defined as the hotspot, the Manifold's help topic appears.

FIGURE 28.16.

Adding a help context string to with the Hotspot editor.

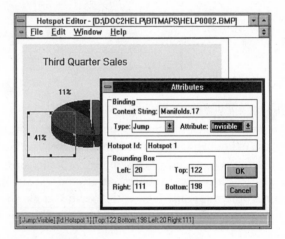

Assigning Help File and Context ID Numbers to Access Objects

Each topic window requires a help context string that the WinHelp engine (WINHELP.EXE) uses to create a jump from the Contents window to the topic window. Help context strings created by Doc-To-Help consist of the text of the headings of the chapters, topics, and subtopics (heading two through heading four) of your help document, with periods substituted for spaces and punctuation. Help context strings are footnotes that are identified by the pound (#) symbol.

If you want a specific help topic to appear when the user presses the F1 key, a feature called context-sensitive help, you need to assign a unique help context ID number to each of the topic and subtopic windows of your help file. You add help entries that contain the context string and the associated help context ID number as entries in the [MAP] section of your .HPJ file. Doc-To-Help automatically adds these entries to the [MAP] section for you.

After you make the final version of your help file, you enter the context ID number of the topic that corresponds to the form or control object in your application as the

HelpContextID property of the object. To test your help file with your application running under MSACCESS.EXE, you need to specify the directory and the filename of the help file as the HelpFile property of the object. (You don't need to include the path if the help file is located in your \ACCESS directory.) Figure 28.17 shows the values of the HelpFile and HelpContextID entries needed to display the Contents window of D2HINTRO.HLP when you press F1 with the Forms Switchboard form open.

> **NOTE**
>
> Control objects don't have a HelpFile property. The value of the HelpFile property of the form applies to all control objects on the form.

FIGURE 28.17.

Setting the values of the help properties of a form.

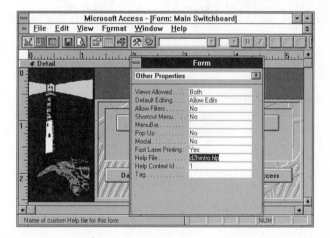

Unless you have more than one help file, you don't enter a value for the HelpFile property when you run your application under MSARN200.EXE. The help filename that you specify when you run the SetupWizard becomes the default help file for your application, replacing MSACCESS.HLP.

> **TIP**
>
> Make sure to remove any HelpFile property values that you added to forms and reports while developing your application under retail Access. If you accidentally specify a help filename or path that is not valid when the user installs your application, the user receives a "Cannot open help file" message after pressing F1.

> **NOTE**
>
> If you assign values to the `HelpContextID` property of control objects on your
> form, the help topic window corresponding to the `HelpContextID` value of
> the control object with the focus appears when the user presses the F1 key. If
> you assign a value to the `HelpContextID` property of the control object that
> receives the focus when you open the form (the first object in the tab order),
> F1 does not open the help topic window assigned to the form itself. If you
> want F1 to open a help topic window for the form, make sure that you
> assign the form's help topic `ContextID` value to the `ContextID` value of the
> first control object in the tab order.

Calling the *WinHelp()* Function with Access Basic Code

Designating the master help file for your project in *APPNAME*.INI and assigning
`HelpContextID` property values to form and control objects provides all the WinHelp
capabilities you need for most Access applications. However, if you use Access Basic
procedures that change how control objects behave, you may need to set the
`HelpContextID` values in Access Basic event-handling procedures.

To control the action of the WinHelp engine with Access Basic code, you call the
`WinHelp()` function when you need to change a help file name or context ID value.
The syntax of the `WinHelp()` function call, which is the sole help function contained
in the USER.EXE DLL, is as follows:

```
intHelpOK = WinHelp(hWnd, szHelpFile, wCommand, dwData)
```

In the preceding syntax, `intHelpOK` is an integer variable that is used to receive the
return value of the `WinHelp()` function. The arguments of the `WinHelp()` function
are explained in the following sections.

Declaring the *WinHelp()* Function Prototype

You declare the `WinHelp()` function in the Declarations section of a module with the
following statement:

```
Declare Function WinHelp Lib "User" (ByVal hWnd As Integer,
                                      ByVal szHelpFile As String,
                                      ByVal wCommand As Integer,
                                      dwData As Any) As Integer
```

The following list explains the statement's components:

- hWnd is a Windows handle (code number or integer) to the window that is active when the WinHelp() function is called with the F1 key. The hWnd property of a form or control provides this 16-bit handle.

- szHelpFile is the name of the WinHelp file, including the .HLP extension.

- wCommand is an integer value that specifies the action that the function is to perform. Table 28.2 lists and describes the intCommand constant values.

- dwData is a **Long** integer argument whose data type depends on the value of the wCommand argument you choose; thus, the dwData argument is declared as being of the **As Any** data type, and is not prefixed with the **ByVal** keyword.

Table 28.2. WinHelp wCommand Constant Values and Corresponding Actions.

wCommand Constant	Value	Description
HELP_CONTEXT	1	Causes a specific help topic, identified by a **Long** integer specified as the dwData argument, to be displayed.
HELP_QUIT	2	Notifies WinHelp that the specified help file is no longer in use and can be closed. The dwData argument is ignored.
HELP_INDEX	3	Displays the index of the specified WinHelp file, as designated by the author. The dwData argument is ignored.
HELP_HELPONHELP	4	Displays help for using the WinHelp application itself. The dwData argument is ignored.
HELP_SETINDEX	5	Sets the context number specified by the dwData argument, a long integer, as the current index for the specified WinHelp file.
HELP_KEY	257	Displays the first corresponding topic found in a search for the keyword specified by the dwData argument; in this case, a string variable.

continues

Table 28.2. continued

wCommand Constant	Value	Description
HELP_MULTIKEY	513	Displays help for a keyword found in an alternate keyword table. The dwData argument is a data structure (user-defined data type) containing the size of the string, the letter of the alternate table, and the keyword string.

Table 28.2 describes how the data type of the dwData argument changes with the value of wCommand. The dwData argument may be a **Long** integer, a **String** variable, or a user-defined data type. Therefore, dwData is declared **As Any** and is passed by reference, not by value. When you want dwData to be ignored by WinHelp( ), you should set dwData to **&H0** (null, rather than decimal 0) in your Access Basic WinHelp() function call.

The additions that you make to the Declarations section of your module to take advantage of all the features that WinHelp( ) offers appear in Listing 28.2.

Listing 28.2. Declarations needed to use the WinHelp() function.

```
'Declare WinHelp() function prototype
Declare Function WinHelp Lib "User" (ByVal hWnd As Integer, ByVal
➥szHelpFile As String, ByVal wCommand As Integer, dwData As Any) As
➥Integer

'Declare global constants for wCommand
Global Const HELP_CONTEXT = &H1        'Display a specified topic
Global Const HELP_QUIT = &H2           'Terminate WinHelp for application
Global Const HELP_INDEX = &H3          'Display the Help index
Global Const HELP_HELPONHELP = &H4     'Display Help on using Help
Global Const HELP_SETINDEX = &H5       'Set the current Help index
Global Const HELP_KEY = &H101          'Display a topic for keyword
Global Const HELP_MULTIKEY = &H201     'Use the alternate keyword table
Global Const KEY_F1 = &H70             'Key code for Help key

'Declare the multikey help user-defined variable type (structure)
Type MKH 'Multikey Help
    intSize As Integer                 'Size of record
    strKeylist As String * 1           'Code letter for keylist
    strKeyphrase As String * 100       'String length is arbitrary
End Type
```

```
'Declare global help variables
Global strHelpFile As String     'Name of Help file
Global intCommand As Integer     'Help command Constant
Global lngHelpCtx As Long        'Help context value when numeric
Global strHelpKey As String      'Help keyword for search when string
Global intHelpOK As Integer      'Return value from WinHelp()
```

You do not need to add the constants to the Declarations section of your module if you want to substitute the integer values shown in Table 28.2 as the intCommand argument when you use the WinHelp( ) function. You must, however, declare the MKH (multikey Help) structure in your global module, declare a record variable, and assign values to its fields in your code if you plan to use more than one help key in your application. It is a good programming practice to make the name of your help file a global variable.

Using the *WinHelp()* API Function in Your Access Basic Code

Change the name of your help file to strHelpFile and the default values to intCommand and lngHelpCtx in the Form_Load event handler of the start-up form. These variables are made global so that they retain the last value that is set to all modules contained in your application. You set lngHelpCtx to the value of the help context ID of the topic you want to display when the user requests help at a particular point in your code. Following is the code that appears in the Form_Load event handler:

```
'Assign initial values to help variables
strHelpFile = "TEST.HLP"
intCommand = HELP_CONTEXT
lngHelpCtx = &H1&
```

To display a help window with a minimum of typing, add two functions, FormHelp and ControlHelp, to a module. The code for the two functions is as follows:

```
Function FormHelp()
    'Purpose:  Display a help window for a form
    intHelpOK = WinHelp(Screen.ActiveForm.hWnd, strHelpFile, intCommand,
    ➥ByVal lngHelpCtx)
End Function

Function ControlHelp
    'Purpose:  Display a help window for a control
    intHelpOK = WinHelp(Screen.ActiveControl.hWnd, strHelpFile,
    ➥intCommand, ByVal lngHelpCtx)
End Function
```

> **NOTE**
>
> lngHelpCtx must be passed by value to dwData, but the function prototype declaration did not include **ByVal**, so you must include **ByVal** with the argument when you call the function. lngHelpCtx is set to **&H0&** when dwData is ignored by WinHelp().

If intCommand is set to the value of HELP_KEY for a keyword search, the syntax of the call to WinHelp( ) is as follows:

```
intCommand = HELP_KEY
strHelpKey = "Invoice"
intHelpOK = WinHelp(hWnd, strHelpFile, intCommand, ByVal lngHelpKey)
```

If you want to use the multikey command to select an entry in a multikey table, you need to create a variable of the MKH data type, mkhMultiKey, and assign values to each of its fields as shown in the following example:

```
Dim mkhMultiKey As MKH
mkhMultiKey.intSize = Len(mkhMultiKey)
mkhMultiKey.strKeyList = "A"
mkhMultiKey.strKeyphrase = "A Keyphrase in Keylist A"
```

Then call WinHelp() with the following code in your multikey help function, as follows:

```
intHelpOK = WinHelp(hWnd, szHelpFile, wCommand, mkhMultiKey)
```

29

Distributing Runtime Versions of Your Databases

The preceding 28 chapters of this book have discussed the techniques that Access developers need to employ to optimize applications for use with runtime Access, MSARN200.EXE. The principal added value of the Microsoft Access Developer's Toolkit (ADT) is your capability to distribute its MSARN200.EXE runtime executable file with your Access applications. In addition to MSARN200.EXE, the ADT provides the help compiler necessary to create .HLP files compatible with the Windows 3.1 WinHelp engine, a Setup Wizard to create sets of distribution diskettes for your applications, and documentation for the ADT itself, as well as the help compiler and the Access wizard functions described in Chapters 24 and 28. This chapter describes how to create distributable versions of your applications using the ADT. Even if you plan to install your own runtime applications locally, you need to know how to create the special .INI file needed to take full advantage of the features of runtime Access. This is the subject of the section, "Creating .INI Files for Runtime Applications," later in the chapter.

Examining the Content of the Access Developer's Toolkit

The Access Developer's Toolkit is a bargain at its $495 list price. You can distribute as many copies of your runtime Access database application as you want for a one-time license fee. There are no "per-seat" or other royalty charges payable to Microsoft Corporation for Access runtime applications. This is unlike many of the Windows database front-end applications, for which you pay a license fee for each user.

The ADT consists of 10 basic elements:

■ MSARN200.EXE, GRAPH.EXE, and a license to distribute copies of MSARN200.EXE and GRAPH5.EXE, the runtime version of Microsoft Graph 5.0. Files of which you can legally make copies by virtue of the license you acquire when you purchase the ADT are called distributable files, or distributables.

■ A license to copy specified files included with the retail version of Access necessary to run your Access database application. You can make one copy for each copy you make of your application.

■ A Setup Wizard to assist you in creating images of distribution diskettes for your applications and to write the basic STFSETUP.IN_ file that determines how and where the files on your distribution diskette are installed on the recipient's computer.

- The Microsoft Help Compiler, HC31.EXE, and the *Help Compiler Guide* that describes how to use HC31.EXE. HC31.EXE remains a DOS application.

- The Microsoft file-compression utility, COMPRESS.EXE, that enables you compress your database files and split the files, if necessary, to distribute the database across multiple diskettes. COMPRESS.EXE is a DOS application. The companion DOS decompression utility, DECOMP.EXE, is also supplied.

- The *Language Reference* for Access 2.0 and the *Advanced Topics* manual that covers material of particular interest to Access developers, including how to use the Setup Wizard.

- The Access 2.0 compatibility layer for Visual Basic 3.0 that includes a new MSAJT112.DLL and a replacement for VBDB300.DLL, the two files required to allow Visual Basic 3.0 to manipulate Access 2.0 .MDB files. MSAJT112.DLL and VBDB300.DLL are distributable.

- The ODBC driver for Access 2.0, ODBCJT16.DLL, that enables other members of the Microsoft Office software suite to use MSQuery with Access 2.0 .MDB files. ODBCJT16.DLL is distributable.

- The files required to use OLE Custom Controls with Access, three example OLE Custom Controls, and the Outline Control Wizard, WZOUTL.MDA. With the exception of OUTL1016.DLL and WZOUTL.MDA, the OLE Custom control files are distributable. Help files are provided for each OLE Custom Control.

- Example applications, including DBSTRUCT.MDB, a database structure analyzer, OUTLINE.MDB, which demonstrates use of the Outline OLE Custom Control, and tersely-documented versions of the Access wizards that accompany the retail version of Access 2.0.

NOTE

This chapter discusses only the first five members of the preceding list. ODBC drivers are discussed in Chapter 20, "Front-Ending Client-Server Databases," and OLE Custom Controls are the subject of Chapter 18, "Introducing OLE 2.0 Custom Controls." The DBSTRUCT.MDB application is described in Chapter 27, "Documenting Your Access Applications."

The underlying principle of the license that you acquire with the purchase of the ADT is that you can distribute copies only of those files that are necessary to run the application(s) on the distribution diskettes that include the copies. The license is similar to that granted to Visual Basic programmers to distribute VBRUN?00.DLL and most custom controls with their applications. Unlike VBRUN?00.DLL, however, do not expect to see standalone copies of MSARN200.EXE available for download from CompuServe, unless Microsoft chooses to post a public copy in the MSACCESS forum. ADT licensees cannot distribute MSARN200.EXE by itself.

> **WARNING**
>
> For the specific terms and conditions that apply to your distribution license from Microsoft, consult the license agreement that accompanies the ADT. Consult a lawyer if you question the applicability of provisions of the license to your particular circumstances. The preceding description of the ADT license agreement is based on information contained in the ADT documentation and from other sources, including representatives of Microsoft Corporation. This book does not purport to offer legal advice.

Creating .INI Files for Runtime Applications

Regardless of whether you distribute your runtime Access applications for installation by the client or purchaser or you install the application yourself, you need to create an initialization file, similar to MSACC20.INI, for the application. The minimal syntax of the command line for running applications with MSARN200.EXE is as follows:

```
MSARN200.EXE d:/path/Database.MDB /ini AppName.INI
```

The path to and the filename of the database to open when launching MSARN200.EXE is a required parameter; you receive a message that reads "Can't run application, missing command line arguments" if you don't specify the database name. /ini *AppName*.INI specifies the name of the initialization file (which is usually stored in the \WINDOWS directory) for your application. (You can specify that AppName.INI be located in your application's directory by an entry in your STFSETUP.IN_ setup information file.)

> **NOTE**
>
> If you omit the AppName.INI parameter and MSACC20.INI exists in the \WINDOWS directory of the target computer, MSARN200.EXE will use MSACC20.INI as the Access initialization file.

The simplest method of creating AppName.INI is to make a copy of the original version of Access 2.0's MSACC20.INI. Remove the sections of your *AppName*.INI file that are not necessary for your application. A bare-bones *AppName*.INI file for an application that does not import, export, or attach files other than Access database files consists of the following sections and entries:

```
[Microsoft Access]
Filter=Microsoft Access (*.mdb)¦*.mdb¦All Files (*.*)¦*.*¦
Extension=mdb
OneTablePerFile=No
IndexDialog=No
Maximized=1
CreateDbOnExport=No

[Options]
SystemDB=d:\app_dir\SYSTEM.MDA
UtilityDB=d:\app_dir\UTILITY.MDA
AllowCustomControls=1
AllowOLE1LinkFormat=0
DebugLibraries=True

[Clipboard Formats]
Microsoft Excel (*.xls)=soa200.dll,1,xls
Rich Text Format (*.rtf)=soa200.dll,2,rtf
MS-DOS Text (*.txt)=soa200.dll,3,txt

[Report Formats]
Microsoft Excel (*.xls)=xls,SOA_RptToBIFF,Biff3,Microsoft Excel (*.xls)
Rich Text Format (*.rtf)=rtf,SOA_RptToRTF,Rich Text Format,Rich Text
Format (*.rtf)
MS-DOS Text (*.txt)=txt,SOA_RptToAscii,1,MS-DOS Text (*.txt)

[Libraries]
;Add required libraries here

[Menu Add-Ins]

[Run-Time Options]
TitleBar=Windows 3.1 Multimedia Database
;Add other run-time options here
```

This .INI file disables the Import and Attach choices of runtime Access's File menu, but the Export choice remains enabled. If you attempt to export a table's data in a format other than Microsoft Access, you receive a message that reads "MSACC20.INI is missing or isn't the correct version. Import/Export isn't available."

MSARN200.EXE recognizes an additional topic, [Run-Time Options] in your AppName.INI file. The following entries are valid for the [Run-Time Options] section:

```
[Run-Time Options]
TitleBar=Name of Application
Icon=d:\path\IconFile.ICO
HelpFile=d:\path\HelpFile.HLP
```

The `Icon=` entry specifies the name and location of the icon file to use when you minimize your application. If you do not provide and specify your own .ICO file, your runtime application uses the standard icon of retail Access. Icon files are a special version of Windows' .BMP bitmap files and are 766 bytes long. There are a variety of utility applications that let you extract icons from the resource component of Windows .EXE and .DLL files and save the icons as .ICO files. Visual Basic includes a variety of icons, and you can use the IconWorks application to edit the sample icons or create new ones to suit your application.

The `HelpFile=` entry specifies the name of the default custom help file that appears when users press the F1 key, if a different help file is not specified as the HelpFile property of your forms or reports. The preceding chapter discusses the difference between default help files and those you specify as the value of the HelpFile property.

WARNING

The ACMSETUP.EXE application creates the SYSTEM.MDA file required to run MSARN200.EXE during the course of the installation process. If you install your application by copying the necessary files to a workstation's fixed disk or a file server, instead of installing the files from distribution diskette images created by the Setup Wizard, you need to install a new SYSTEM.MDA file manually. The problem with this approach is that the SYSTEM.MDA file is personalized with the company and user names that you entered when you installed your copy of retail Access, and an 11-digit serial number. Runtime Access does not display the Microsoft copyright notice when it opens, but you need to make sure that you remove all members of the Admins and Users groups, except the necessary single account that defaults to Admin. Also make sure to create a new Admins account with a name other than Admin, and password-protect the new Admins account to prevent others from gaining unwarranted permissions to your application's objects. The section at the end of this chapter, "Establishing Secure Distributed Applications," discusses security issues for applications that you distribute on diskettes.

Surveying Disk Space Requirement to Install and Run the ADT

You need a minimum of about 20MB of free disk space (plus the space required to store a copy of your distribution databases, libraries, and help files) to use the ADT to create distribution diskettes for your application. About 12MB of the space is required to install the files for the ADT itself and to hold the compressed versions of the distributable files in the *PATH*\DISK# directories that hold images of your distribution diskettes. (The Setup Wizard creates these directories for you.) Table 29.1 lists the typical disk space required by file type and directory location for 1.44MB diskettes. Add the size of the compressed versions of database(s), libraries, drivers for other types of databases, and help files to the 10MB total to determine the total amount of disk space that you need to create distribution diskettes for your application. The average compression ratio of your application files is likely to be about 2:1.

Table 29.1. Net fixed disk space requirement for installation and use of the ADT, less application files.

Type of Files	Location of Files	Size, in MB
ADT Files	\ACCESS\ADT	11.6
Diskete Images	\APPSETUP\DISK1	1.3
	\APPSETUP\DISK2	1.4
	\APPSETUP\DISK3	1.0
	\APPSETUP\DISK4	1.4
	\APPSETUP\DISK5	0.4
Total		17.1

> **NOTE**
>
> If you don't include the drivers for dBASE, FoxPro, Paradox, and Btrieve, and the ODBC distributable files, described in the section that follows, on your distribution diskettes, you save about 1.5MB in the space required to store your diskette images.

Distributing Microsoft and User-Created or Modified Files

The following sections list and describe the files that you can (or in certain cases might be able to) distribute with your Access applications. A list of files that you are explicitly prohibited from distributing appears following the lists of distributable files.

Distributable Runtime Access Files

The files listed in Table 29.2 and Table 29.3 with "Yes" in the "Req'd" column are required for MSARN200.EXE to open a database file. If any of the files listed in Table 29.2 are missing from your distribution diskettes, users cannot execute your Access database application. (An exception is the OLE 2.0 installation files that may have been installed by another application, such as Excel 5.0, that supports OLE 2.0 and OLE Automation.) The majority of the required files is compressed. All required files are added to the disk image directories for you by the Setup Wizard.

Table 29.2. Files installed on distribution diskette 1 (\PATH\DISK1).

File Name	Ext	Req'd?	Size	Purpose
SETUP	LST	Yes	652	List of files used by Setup
ADMIN	INF	Yes	4,292	List of files to be installed by Setup
MSAJU200	DL_	Yes	54,977	Jet database engine utilities
SETUP	INF	Yes	5,186	List of files to be installed by Setup
MSAFIN	DL_	Yes	13,560	Access 2.0 financial functions
SOA200	DL_	Yes	20,613	Export format library
MSAEXP20	DL_	Yes	45,899	Access 2.0 expression services library
MSJETERR	DL_	Yes	6,653	Jet error messages library
MSJETINT	DL_	Yes	10,365	Jet localization library
ODBCINST	DL_	No	46,569	ODBC Administrator for Control Panel
SETUP	EXE	Yes	39,856	Microsoft Setup executable
DECOMP	EXE	Yes	39,044	File decompression executable
ACMSETUP	HL_	Yes	13,007	Access Setup help
MSSETUP	DLL	Yes	191,376	Microsoft Setup library

File Name	Ext	Req'd?	Size	Purpose
MSCPYDIS	DL_	Yes	9,254	File copy library
_MSSETUP	EXE	Yes	14,103	Compressed Microsoft setup executable
MSACAHBB	DL_	Yes	67,189	Access 2.0 Setup bitmaps library
ACMSETUP	EX_	Yes	121,430	Access 2.0 Setup executable
SETUP	INI	Yes	149	Setup initialization file
SYSTEM	MD_	Yes	87,311	SYSTEM.MDA for application
BTRV200	DL_	No	62,125	Btrieve driver for Jet
GREN50	OL_	No	26,022	MSGraph5 localization file (English)
SCP	DL_	Yes	5,023	Standard Control Panel library
SDM	DL_	Yes	62,315	Standard dialog-box manager
WRKGADM	EX_	No	88,783	Workgroup Administrator executable
MSTOOLBR	DL_	Yes	5,818	Toolbar library
STDOLE	TL_	Yes	2,058	OLE 2.0 object registration
COMPOBJ	DL_	Yes	54,527	OLE 2.0 installation
OLE2CONV	DL_	Yes	32,201	OLE 2.0 installation
OLE2DISP	DL_	Yes	50,769	OLE 2.0 installation
OLE2PROX	DL_	Yes	22,307	OLE 2.0 installation
OLE2	RE_	Yes	3,710	OLE 2.0 installation
ODBC	DL_	No	26,712	ODBC 1.0 driver manager
ODBCINST	HL_	No	10,821	ODBCADM.EXE help file
DBNMP3	DL_	No	6,270	Named pipes library for SQL Server driver
DRVSSRVR	HL_	No	65,248	Help file for SQL Server driver
CTL3D	DL_	Yes	10,899	3-D dialogs and message boxes
CTL3DV2	DL_	Yes	11,194	New version of CTL3D.DLL
SETUP	STF	Yes	44,121	Additional information file for Access 2.0 Setup
Total, Disk 1			1,382,408	(Less application files)

In addition to the files shown in Table 29.2, your application's .INI and .ICO files are included on diskette 1, as well as your application's *AppName*.HLP file, if the compressed version of the .HLP file will fit on diskette 1. The remaining files are installed on diskettes 2 through 4 or 5, depending on the size of your application's .MDB file.

> **NOTE**
>
> The Access 1.1 ADK provided the files required to update Windows 3.0 to Windows 3.1, such as COMMDLG.DLL, OLECLI.DLL, and OLESVR.DLL. Access 2.0 requires that Windows 3.1+ be installed on the user's computer, so the upgrade files no longer are needed.

Table 29.3 lists the required and optional files on the remaining distribution diskettes, together with the diskette on which the files are located. The diskette numbers are based on use of 1.44MB diskettes and an .MDB file with a compressed size of approximately 500KB.

Table 29.3. Files installed on distribution diskettes 2 through 5 (\PATH\DISK#).

Disk	File Name	Ext	Req'd?	Size	Purpose
2	MSARN200	EX_	Yes	1,127,082	Access 2.0 runtime executable
2	DAO2016	DL_	Yes	198,538	Data Access Object support
2	UTILITY	MD_	Yes	100,075	UTILITY.MDA library
3	GRAPH5	EX_	No	951,462	Run-time version of MSGraph5
4	MSAJT200	DL_	Yes	553,649	Jet database engine library
4	MSAIN200	DL_	Yes	143,045	Access 2.0 international library
4	OLE2	DL_	Yes	169,656	Primary OLE 2.0 library
4	MSABC200	DL_	Yes	202,256	Access Basic library
4	XBS200	DL_	No	169,646	dBASE and FoxPro support for Jet
4	PDX200	DL_	No	133,853	Paradox 3.x and 4.x support for Jet

4	OLE2NLS	DL_	Yes	52,746	OLE 2.0 national language support library
5	STORAGE	DL_	Yes	81,328	OLE 2.0 installation
5	SQLSRVR	DL_	No	93,048	SQL Server ODBC driver
5	TYPELIB	DL_	Yes	86,967	OLE Automation installation
5	MSAOLE20	DL_	Yes	63,557	Access 2.0 OLE 2.0 library
5	GRINTL	DL_	No	62,180	MSGraph5 international library
	Total			4,189,088	(Less application files)

NOTE

If you create 1.2MB diskette image files, you can create 3 1/2- or 5 1/4-inch diskettes from the same subdirectories that contain your distribution diskette images. Specifying 1.2MB diskettes, however, may increase the number of 1.44MB diskettes by one, compared with the number of diskettes required if you specify 1.44MB.

Installing Microsoft and Other Third-Party Database Drivers

The Microsoft ODBC drivers for Access, dBASE, Excel, FoxPro, Paradox and text files that are included in the Microsoft ODBC Desktop Database Drivers kit or supplied with members of the Microsoft Office software suite are not distributable components. You need to acquire a distribution license from Microsoft Corp. to include any of the Desktop Database Drivers with your Access applications.

If your application needs to import, export, or attach tables of Btrieve databases, you need to include WBTRCALL.DLL with your application if your purchaser or client does not already have this file installed. WBTRCALL.DLL is not included with either the retail version of Access or the ADT. WBTRCALL.DLL is a component of Novell Inc.'s Windows Btrieve application. You need a license from Novell to distribute copies of WBTRCALL.DLL.

Third-party ODBC drivers, such as those supplied by Q+E Software, usually are provided on distribution diskettes with their own setup application. Licensing terms vary among publishers of third-party ODBC drivers, but a per-installation royalty is common. You need a license from the publisher of the ODBC driver to provide third-party ODBC drivers with your applications.

Using the *SysCmd(6)* and *SysCmd(7)* Functions in Your Code

You can determine whether your application is running under MSARN200.EXE or MSACCESS.EXE and the version (1.0 or 1.1) of the executable file with the values returned from or errors created by the **SysCmd**(6) and **SysCmd**(7) functions. (The **SysCmd**(1) through **SysCmd**(5) functions control the status bar display.) **SysCmd**(6) returns an integer flag that is **True** if the application is running under MSARN200.EXE and **False** if MSACCESS.EXE is in use. You can create a global variable, fRunTime, whose value you set in the applications initialization routine with the fIsRunTime() function, shown in the Listing 29.1 that follows. Listing 29.2 for the fIsAccess20() function returns **True** if retail Access 2.0 or MSARN200.EXE is in use. You need the error handling routines, because **SysCmd**(6) and **SysCmd**(7) return an "Illegal function call" message when executed under version 1.0 of retail Access.

Listing 29.1. The Access Basic code for the **fIsRunTime()** function.

```
Function fIsRunTime() As Integer
    'Purpose: Determine if MSARN200.EXE is in use
    'Returns: True for MSARN200.EXE, False for MSACCESS.EXE

    On Error GoTo IsRunTime_Err
    fIsRunTime = SysCmd(6)
    Exit Function

IsRunTime_Err:
    If Err = 5 Then  'Illegal function call
        fIsRunTime = False
    Else
        MsgBox "Error: " & Error$, 16, "Run-Time Check Error"
    End If
    Exit Function
End Function
```

Listing 29.2. The Access Basic code for the **fIsAccess11()** function.

```
Function fIsAccess20 () As Integer
    'Purpose: Determine if MSACCESS 1.1 or MSARN200.EXE is in use
    'Returns: True for MSARN200.EXE or MSACCESS.EXE version 1.1
```

```
'          False for MSACCESS.EXE version 1.0

    On Error GoTo IsAccess20Err
    If SysCmd(7) = "1.0" Then
        fIsAccess20 = True
    Else
        fIsAccess20 = False       'It's some other version
    End If
    Exit Function

IsAccess20_Err:
    If Err = 5 Then  'Illegal function call
        fIsAccess11 = False
    Else
        MsgBox "Error: " & Error$, 16, "Version Check Error"
    End If
    Exit Function
End Function
```

The code for both of these functions is included in the SysCmd(6) and SysCmd(7) module of the AB_EXAMP.MDB database on the accompanying diskette. An example of using the `fIsRunTime()` function to prevent execution of an AddMenu macro action when you open your runtime application under retail Access is included in Chapter 26, "Customizing Access Applications with Special Menus and Toolbars."

TIP

You might want to apply the DoCmd Quit method after the message box when the error appears, because an error other than "Illegal function call" should not occur.

Using the Setup Wizard to Create a Custom Setup Application

Microsoft Corporation uses a standard file setup application to install all its mainstream applications on the purchaser's fixed-disk drive. These setup applications consist of SETUP.EXE, which you run by typing *d*:\setup in the command-line text box of Program Manager's Run dialog box. In some cases, such as in the installation of retail Access, SETUP.EXE decompresses and runs another setup executable file, ACMSETUP.EXE. SETUP.EXE is accompanied by an initialization file,

SETUP.INI, that is not a readable text file. SETUP.EXE or ACMSETUP.EXE reads a script file, named SETUP.INF or SETUP.LST, that contains the instructions on how and where to copy the files on the distribution diskettes. Many of the setup .INF and .LST files resemble conventional initialization files, such as WIN.INI. The .INF script files can become very complex. As an example of the ultimate in complexity, the SETUP.INF script to install Windows for Workgroups from its eight distribution diskettes is about 60KB in size. The author of the WfWg SETUP.INF file calls it "this pig" in a comment line included in the file.

When you install the ADT, the setup application adds a program item, MS ADT Setup Wizard, to the ADT program group to launch retail Access and open the SETUPWIZ.MDB database located in the \ACCESS\ADT directory. The following sections describe the components you need to use the Setup Wizard to create the images of your distribution diskettes, how to use the Setup Wizard, and how to modify your STFSETUP.IN_ file to transfer special files that are not standard elements of Access applications.

The Components Needed to Create a Custom Setup Application

Before you create a custom setup application, you need to have prepared all of the files required for runtime applications. The most important file is AppName.INI, the private initialization file discussed earlier in this chapter. If your application requires a special icon or includes a help file, the *AppName*.ICO and *AppName*.HLP file must be available to the Setup Wizard. Finally, you must provide a SYSTEM.MDA file for the application. The SYSTEM.MDB file should be created specifically for distributing applications, and should not include the default, no-password admin user. Security issues with run-time applications are discussed later in this chapter.

> **TIP**
>
> You must create a separate copy of SYSTEM.MDA in a directory other than C:\ACCESS (or the directory from which you run MSACCESS.EXE). If you specify the same copy of SYSTEM.MDA that is attached to MSACCESS.EXE when you are running the Setup Wizard, you receive an erroneous message, "Can't find 'c:\access\system.mda'." The Setup Wizard found the SYSTEM.MDA file, but the Wizard cannot compress the file, because COMPRESS.EXE does not recognize SHARE.EXE (or VSHARE.386 for Windows for Workgroups 3.11), which allows sharing of the file for other purposes. At this point, you cannot use File Manager to create a new copy of the SYSTEM.MDA file, because File Manager exhibits

the same problem. (File Manager, however, displays the correct "file may be in use" error message.)

NOTE

The Access 1.1 Distribution Kit (ADK) required that you run SUFILES.EXE that created a compressed version of each of the files required to run Access 1.1 in the \ACCESS\ADK\SUFILES directory. Access 2.0's new Setup Wizard no longer requires creating compressed versions of the files prior to starting the distribution diskette image creation process. The Access 2.0 Setup Wizard compresses the required files that were expanded to your fixed disk drive when you installed Access 2.0. This contributes to slower operation of the Setup Wizard, but eliminates the need to store the compressed and uncompressed versions on your diskette. However, all of the required files listed in Table 29.2 and Table 29.3 must be accessible to the Setup Wizard before your start the diskette creation process.

Running the Setup Wizard

Access 2.0's Setup Wizard is a greatly-improved version of the original Setup Wizard supplied with the Access 1.1 Distribution Kit. More of the Wizard's functions are automated, and you can now add any number of files you want to your application directory, the \WINDOWS directory, or the \WINDOWS\SYSTEM directory. (If you needed to add more than a few files in addition to the standard files for a runtime application, you had to manually edit the STFSETUP.IN_ file created by the Access 1.1 ADK.)

The following steps demonstrate how to use the Setup Wizard to create distribution diskettes for an example Access 2.0 runtime application, NSC_ASK.MDB, that includes a private .INI file, NSC_ASK.INI, an icon file, NSC_ASK.ICO, and an uncompressed help file, NSC_ASK.HLP:

1. Launch the Setup Wizard by clicking the MS ADT Setup Wizard icon of the ADT program group, or launch the retail version of Access and then open \ACCESS\ADT\SETUPWIZ.MDB.

2. The opening dialog box of the Setup Wizard displays an empty list box of application-specific files to be included on the distribution diskettes. Click the Add File button to display the Add File dialog box, then click the ellipsis button adjacent to the File Name text box to open the Select File dialog box.

The List Files of Type drop-down list lets you specify that only database and library (.MDB/.MDA), help (.HLP), text (.TXT), or icon (.ICO) files appear in the File Name list box. (See Figure 29.1.)

FIGURE 29.1.

Adding your application's .MDB file to the default application directory.

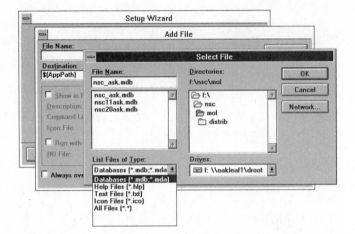

3. Select your application's .MDB file, then click OK to close the Select File dialog box and return to the Add File dialog box. The .MDB file you selected appears in the File Name text box. (See Figure 29.2.) The default directory for application files is the directory you or the user of your application specifies for installation of your application. The **$(AppPath)** entry in the Destination drop-down list is a placeholder for the default directory for your application on the user's computer. Alternative locations are **$(WinPath)** and **$(WinSysPath)**, which you can select by opening the Destination list. Add the program item description for the icon in your application program group in the Description text box. The Command Line text box is completed for you by the Wizard.

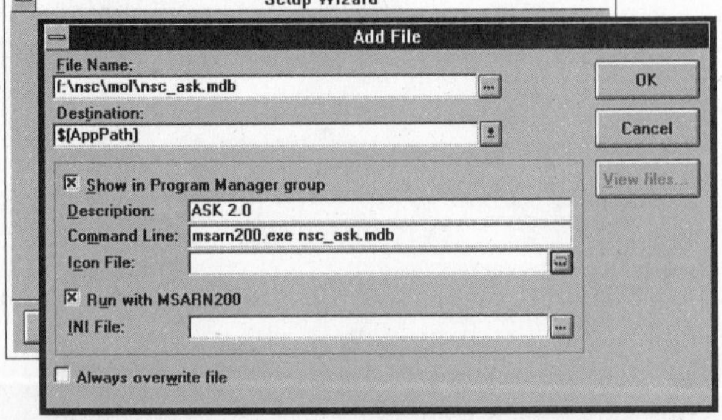

FIGURE 29.2.

Adding the program item description for your application.

4. Click the ellipsis button adjacent to the Icon File text box to open the Select Icon dialog box. Select the icon to represent your application in the program group that your setup application creates. (See Figure 29.3.) Click OK to return to Add File dialog box.

FIGURE 29.3.

Adding an icon file for the program item.

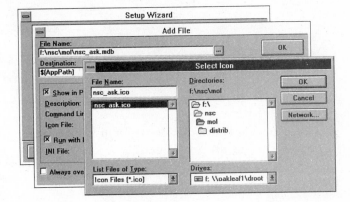

5. Click the ellipsis button adjacent to the INI File text box to open the Select Initialization File dialog box, then select your application's private .INI file. (See Figure 29.4.) Click OK to return to the Add File dialog box.

FIGURE 29.4.

Adding the application's private initialization file.

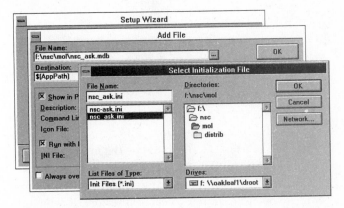

6. Your Add File dialog box appears as shown in Figure 29.5. The Wizard adds the entries for your icon file and initialization file to the Icon File and INI File text boxes, respectively. The Wizard also adds the **/ini appname.ini** entry in the Command Line Text box. Click the OK button of the Add File dialog box to add the files chosen to this point to your setup information files.

FIGURE 29.5.

The Add File dialog box with the application, icon, and initialization files specified.

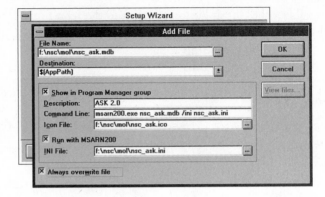

7. Click the Add File button of the Setup Wizard dialog box, then add your help file to the list. (See Figure 29.6.)

FIGURE 29.6.

Adding the help file for your application.

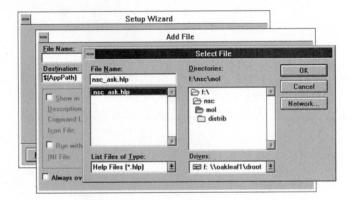

8. Repeat steps 6 and 7, but this time add your application SYSTEM.MDA file to the list. As mentioned in the preceding tip, make sure you don't specify the SYSTEM.MDA file in use by the instance of MSACCESS.EXE that is running SETUPWIZ.MDB. When you return to the Setup Wizard dialog box, the Files to Be Included list box contains all of the application files that are to be installed in the default directory. (See Figure 29.7.)

9. Click the Next button to display the Setup Wizard dialog box that lets you specify the optional Access and other components to be included on your distribution diskettes. This example was used to create the file lists of Table 29.2 and Table 29.3 for the worst-case installation of run-time Access 2.0. (See Figure 29.8.) Most Access applications require only a few of these options. You should, however, always specify the OLE 2.01 option, because the OLE 2.0 installation files included with Access 2.0 are likely to be updates to those installed by other Microsoft OLE 2.0-compliant

applications, such as Excel 5.0 and Word 6.0, released prior to Access 2.0. Select the option to install, then click the Install button. Click the Next button to display the next Setup Wizard dialog box.

FIGURE 29.7.
The Setup Wizard's dialog box with all application files added.

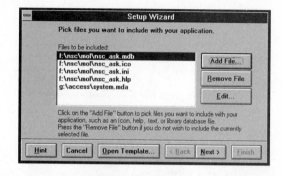

FIGURE 29.8.
Specifying the optional files to include on the distribution diskettes.

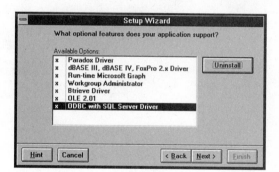

10. Type the name you want to appear in the title bar of the program group for your application in the Application Name text box. (The maximum length of this entry is 32 characters.) Type the well-formed path to the default installation directory in the Default Installation Directory. (See Figure 29.9.) Click the Next button to continue.

11. Type the well-formed path of the directory in which to create the DISK1...DISK# distribution images, or click the ellipsis button to display the Select Directory dialog box. (See Figure 29.10.) You can specify a directory on a network file server, if you wish. Click the option button to specify the diskette capacity (1.2MB or 1.44MB) or choose a network installation. The network installation creates a single installation directory on the network file server from which workstations can install your runtime application.

FIGURE 29.9.

Specifying the program group title and the default installation directory.

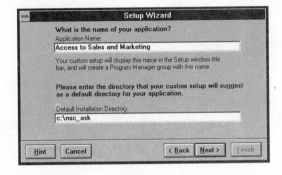

FIGURE 29.10.

Specifying the directory in which to create the diskette image subdirectories.

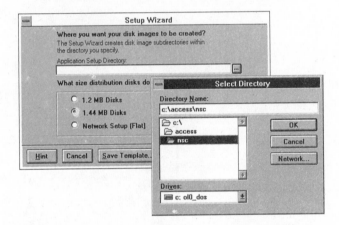

12. The Setup Wizard provides an option to create a template that you can use when you want to change or update the files of your distribution diskettes. Click the Save Template button to display the Save Template dialog box, and type the name of your application (without a file extension) in the Template Name text box. (See Figure 29.11.) Click OK to return to the Setup Wizard dialog box.

FIGURE 29.11.

Creating a template for your application's distribution diskettes.

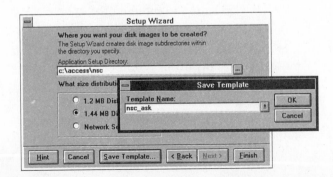

13. Click the Finish button to begin the file compression and diskette image-creation process. The message box of Figure 29.12 states, "This is a time-consuming process." Depending on the speed of your computer, this may be an understatement. Click the OK button to proceed.

FIGURE 29.12.

The message box that indicates that the Setup Wizard is about to create the diskette images.

14. A modal dialog box displays the progress of the disk image creation. (See Figure 29.13.) The first stage of the process creates all of the compressed files in the \DISK1 directory. After the Wizard compresses all of the files, she organizes the files into groups that take maximum advantage of the space available on each 1.44MB diskette, then moves the files that will not fit in the 1.44MB allocated to \DISK1 to the \DISK2...\DISK# directories.

FIGURE 29.13.

The progress monitor for the file compression process.

15. When the process finally completes, you receive the message box shown in Figure 29.14. On an Intel 80486DX2/66 computer with an 8-ms fixed disk drive, the process takes 20 minutes. Disk performance, and especially the degree of disk fragmentation, has the most noticeable effect on the time required to create the diskette images. The speed of your computer's CPU and available RAM have a lesser effect.

FIGURE 29.14.

The announcement that (finally) the diskette image subdirectories have been created.

Once the diskette image subdirectories are completed, you copy the content of each subdirectory to a blank, formatted diskette. It is not necessary to add a volume label to the diskettes; the correct diskette is detected by the setup application through a key file specified for each diskette.

Understanding the Setup Information Files Created by the Setup Wizard

All Microsoft applications released after about December 1993 use a common SETUP.EXE application with a standard set of setup information files that are customized for the application. The setup application created by the Setup Wizard conforms to these new standards, with the exception that no provision is made for uninstalling the application from setup files copied to a *APPDIR*\\SETUP directory. The following sections provide a brief description of the content of each of the four setup information files created by the Setup Wizard.

> **NOTE**
>
> The single setup information file, STFSETUP.INF, used by the runtime setup application of the Access 1.1 ADK was very simple compared with the four setup information files required by the Access 2.0 runtime setup application. It was a relatively simple process to create additional program items to run additional executable files from your application's program group by adding entries to STFSETUP.INF. This is no longer the case with the new setup application. There was no readily-available source of documentation of the entries required for the four setup information files when this edition was written. Manual editing of any of the entries in the setup information files involves a very high degree of risk.

SETUP.LST

The [Params] section of SETUP.LST specifies the title of the main setup window and messages that appear when the user starts the setup program, as well as the name of the temporary setup directory and the command line to execute the Access 2.0 setup application, ACMSETUP.EXE. The [Files] section specifies the compressed and expanded names of the files required to run the setup application.

Following is the content of the SETUP.LST file for the example application created by the Setup Wizard:

```
[Params]
        WndTitle    = Access to Sales and Marketing Setup
```

```
        WndMess     = Starting Access to Sales and Marketing Setup...
        TmpDirSize  = 900
        TmpDirName  = ~msstfgf.t
        CmdLine     = acmsetup /T setup.stf /S %s %s
        DrvModName  = acmsetup
        Require31   = This program requires Windows (R) 3.1 or higher.

[Files]
        setup.inf    = setup.inf
        setup.stf    = setup.stf
        acmsetup.hl_ = acmsetup.hlp
        mssetup.dll  = mssetup.dll
        mscpydis.dl_ = mscpydis.dll
        mssetup.exe  = _mssetup.exe
        msacahbb.dl_ = msacahbb.dll
        acmsetup.ex_ = acmsetup.exe
```

SETUP.INF and ADMIN.INF

The [Source Media Descriptions] section of SETUP.INF specifies the number of each diskette and the file used by SETUP.EXE to determine that the correct diskette has been inserted by the user. The remaining sections of SETUP.INF specify how the files are to be installed ([Default File Settings]), and the files required for Access 2.0 ([Program Files]) and the Jet Database Engine ([Jet SysFiles]). The [Files] and [Admin Files] sections specify files required during the setup process. The large decimal numbers, such as 412672 for "msain200", are the size of the expanded files. These numbers are used in the computation of required versus available disk space on the user's computer. The number immediately following the quoted name of the file is the diskette number on which the file is located.

```
[Source Media Descriptions]
        "1", "Disk 1", "SETUP.EXE", "."
        "2", "Disk 2", "MSARN200.EX_", "..\Disk2"
        "3", "Disk 3", "GRAPH5.EX_", "..\Disk3"
        "4", "Disk 4", "MSAJT200.DL_", "..\Disk4"
        "5", "Disk 5", "STORAGE.DL_", "..\Disk5"

[Default File Settings]
"STF_BACKUP" = ""
"STF_COPY" = "YES"
"STF_DATE" = ""
"STF_DECOMPRESS" = "YES"
"STF_OVERWRITE" = "OLDER"
"STF_READONLY" = ""
"STF_ROOT" = "YES"
"STF_SETTIME" = ""
"STF_TIME" = ""
"STF_VITAL" = ""
```

```
[Program Files]
"msain200" = 4,msain200.dll,,,,1994-03-
➡11,,1033,,,,,,,SHARED,412672,,,,2.0.0.5,
"msaju200" = 1,msaju200.dll,,,,1994-03-
➡11,,1033,,,,,,,SHARED,98304,,,,2.0.0.3,
"msarn200" = 2,msarn200.exe,,,,1994-03-
➡11,,1033,,,,,,,SHARED,1900544,,,,2.0.0.5,
"utility" = 2,utility.mda,,,,1994-03-11,,,,,,,,,SHARED,294912,,,,
"msafin" = 1,msafin.dll,,,,1994-03-
➡11,,1033,,,,,,,SHARED,26624,,,,2.0.0.5,
"msaole20" = 5,msaole20.dll,,,,1994-03-
➡11,,1033,,,,,,,SHARED,117248,,,,2.0.0.5,
"soa200" = 1,soa200.dll,,,,1994-03-
➡11,,1033,,,,,,,SHARED,35840,,,,2.0.0.1,

[Jet SysFiles]
"msajt200" = 4,msajt200.dll,,,,1994-03-
➡11,,1033,,,,,,,SHARED,993280,,,,2.0.0.3,
"msabc200" = 4,msabc200.dll,,,,1994-03-
➡11,,1033,,,,,,,SHARED,306176,,,,2.0.0.3,
"msaexp20" = 1,msaexp20.dll,,,,1994-03-
➡11,,1033,,,,,,,SHARED,82432,,,,2.0.0.4,
"dao2016" = 2,dao2016.dll,,,,1994-03-
➡11,,1033,,,,,,,SHARED,435712,,,,2.0.0.3,
"msjeterr" = 1,msjeterr.dll,,,,1994-03-
➡11,,1033,,,,,,,SHARED,10240,,,,2.0.0.3,
"msjetint" = 1,msjetint.dll,,,,1994-03-
➡11,,1033,,,,,,,SHARED,14848,,,,2.0.0.3,

[Files]
"bootstrp" = 1,setup.exe,,,,1994-03-
➡11,,1033,,,,,,,SHARED,39936,,,,2.50.0.126,
"stf" = 1,setup.stf,,,,1994-03-11,,,,,,,,,SHARED,44544,,,,,
"lst" = 1,setup.lst,,,,1994-03-11,,,,,,,,,SHARED,1024,,,,,

[Admin Files]
"decomp" = 1,decomp.exe,,,,1994-03-11,,,,,,,,,,,39424,SYSTEM,,,,
"help" = 1,acmsetup.hlp,,,,1994-03-11,,,,,,,,,,,19456,SYSTEM,,,,
"mssetup" = 1,mssetup.dll,,,,1994-03-
➡11,,1033,,,,,,,191488,SYSTEM,,,2.50.0.126,
"mscpydis" = 1,mscpydis.dll,,,,1994-03-
➡11,,1033,,,,,,,14848,SYSTEM,,,2.50.0.126,
"_mssetup" = 1,_mssetup.exe,,,,1994-03-11,,,,,,,,,,,14336,SYSTEM,,,,
"cahbb" = 1,msacahbb.dll,,,,1994-03-11,,,,,,,,,,,182784,SYSTEM,,,,
"EXE" = 1,acmsetup.exe,,,,1994-03-
➡11,,1033,ALWAYS,,,setup.exe,!ROOT,,,256000,SYSTEM,,,1.0.1.126,
"setupini" = 1,setup.ini,,,,1994-03-11,,,,,,,,,,,512,SYSTEM,,,,
"admin" = 1,admin.inf,,,,1994-03-
➡11,,,ALWAYS,,,setup.inf,!ROOT,,SHARED,10240,,,,,

[User Files]
"nsc_ask_mdb" = 3,nsc_ask.mdb,,,,1994-03-11,,,,,,,,,,,1212416,,,,
```

```
"nsc_ask_ico" = 1,nsc_ask.ico,,,,1994-03-11,,,,,,,,,,1024,,,,,
"nsc_ask_ini" = 1,nsc_ask.ini,,,,1994-03-11,,,,,,,,,,2560,,,,,
"nsc_ask_hlp" = 1,nsc_ask.hlp,,,,1994-03-11,,,,,,,,,,100352,,,,,
"system_mda" = 1,system.mda,,,,1994-03-11,,,,,,,,,,98304,,,,,
"wping_exe" = 1,wping.exe,,,,1994-03-11,,,,,,,,,,8192,,,,,

[Btrieve ISAM]
"DLL" = 1,BTRV200.DLL,,,,1994-03-
➡11,,1033,,,,,,,SHARED,111104,,,,2.0.0.3,

[dBASE ISAM]
"DLL" = 4,XBS200.DLL,,,,1994-03-11,,1033,,,,,,,SHARED,295936,,,,2.0.0.3,

[Paradox ISAM]
"DLL" = 4,PDX200.DLL,,,,1994-03-11,,1033,,,,,,,SHARED,231936,,,,2.0.0.3,

[Graph Files]
"msgraph" = 3,GRAPH5.EXE,,,,1994-03-
➡11,,1033,,,,,,,SHARED,1505280,,,,5.0.0.2530,
"en50" = 1,GREN50.OLB,,,,1994-03-
➡11,,1033,,,,,,,SHARED,57344,,,,5.0.1.2530,
"intl" = 5,GRINTL.DLL,,,,1994-03-
➡11,,1033,,,,,,,SHARED,123392,,,,5.0.1.2530,
"scp" = 1,SCP.DLL,,,,1994-03-11,,1033,,,,,,,SHARED,10240,,,,1.0.200.0,
"sdm" = 1,SDM.DLL,,,,1994-03-11,,1033,,,,,,,SHARED,102400,,,,3.0.0.2323,

[Workgroup Files]
"wrkgadm" = 1,WRKGADM.EXE,,,,1994-03-
➡11,,,,,,,,,SHARED,108544,,,,2.0.0.100,

[Ole2 Files]
"mstoolbr" = 1,MSTOOLBR.DLL,,,,1994-03-
➡11,,1033,,,,,,,9728,SYSTEM,,,1.0.0.4,
"stdole" = 1,STDOLE.TLB,,,,1994-03-11,,,,,,,,,SHARED,4608,,,,,
"compobj" = 1,COMPOBJ.DLL,,,,1994-03-
➡11,,1033,,,,,,,102400,SYSTEM,,,2.1.100.14,
"storage" = 5,STORAGE.DLL,,,,1994-03-
➡11,,,,,,,,,,157184,SYSTEM,,,2.1.100.15,
"typelib" = 5,TYPELIB.DLL,,,,1994-03-
➡11,,1033,,,,,,,153600,SYSTEM,,,2.1.100.34,
"ole2" = 4,OLE2.DLL,,,,1994-03-
➡11,,1033,,,,,,,313344,SYSTEM,,,2.1.100.14,
"ole2conv" = 1,OLE2CONV.DLL,,,,1994-03-
➡11,,1033,,,,,,,57344,SYSTEM,,,2.1.0.1,
"ole2disp" = 1,OLE2DISP.DLL,,,,1994-03-
➡11,,1033,,,,,,,98816,SYSTEM,,,2.1.100.34,
"ole2nls" = 4,OLE2NLS.DLL,,,,1994-03-
➡11,,1033,,,,,,,147456,SYSTEM,,,2.1.100.34,
"ole2prox" = 1,OLE2PROX.DLL,,,,1994-03-
➡11,,1033,,,,,,,55808,SYSTEM,,,2.1.100.14,
"ole2reg" = 1,OLE2.REG,,,,1994-03-11,,,,,,,,,SHARED,25088,,,,,
```

```
[ODBC Driver Manager]
"driver" = 1,ODBC.DLL,,,,1994-03-
➥11,,1033,,,,,,,,SHARED,53248,,,,1.5.11.10,
"installer" = 1,DBNMP3.DLL,,,,1994-03-
➥11,,1033,,,,,,,SHARED,10752,,,,1993.8.24.0,
"help" = 1,ODBCINST.HLP,,,,1994-03-11,,,,,,,,,SHARED,17920,,,,,
```

```
[SQL Server]
"network" = 1,DBNMP3.DLL,,,,1994-03-
➥11,,1033,,,,,,,,10752,SYSTEM,,,1993.8.24.0,
"help" = 1,DRVSSRVR.HLP,,,,1994-03-11,,,,,,,,,,88064,SYSTEM,,,,
"driver" = 5,SQLSRVR.DLL,,,,1994-03-
➥11,,1033,,,,,,,,156160,SYSTEM,,,1.2.32.31,
"setup" = 1,CTL3DV2.DLL,,,,1994-03-
➥11,,1033,,,,,,,,22016,SYSTEM,,,2.0.4.0,
```

```
[System Files]
"ctl3d" = 1,CTL3D.DLL,,,,1994-03-11,,1033,,,,,,,20992,SYSTEM,,,2.0.4.0,
"ctl3dv2" = 1,CTL3DV2.DLL,,,,1994-03-
➥11,,1033,,,,,,,,22016,SYSTEM,,,2.0.4.0,
```

ADMIN.INF is used for network installation from a single subdirectory and is almost identical to SETUP.INF. The primary difference is that there is only one entry in the [Source Media Descriptions] section, SETUP.EXE, and all of the diskette numbers are 1.

SETUP.STF

SETUP.STF is, by far, the most complex file created by the Setup Wizard. SETUP.STF provides most of the information required for the installation process. The SETUP.STF file for the example created by the Setup Wizard has 433 lines of text. An abbreviated listing of the content of SETUP.STF follows. (Lines deleted for brevity are indicated by ellipsis.) The first section of SETUP.STF specifies additional captions and titles during the installation process. The Installed By Us section comprises about 400 sequentially numbered lines that install the files, create the program group, add program items to the group, modify WIN.INI, and update the registration database, REG.DAT, with the entries required for OLE 2.01. The last section of SETUP.STF, Installing USER's Options, copies your application's files to the user's fixed disk. Installing the OLE 2.01 files and adding the required REG.DAT entries comprises more than half of the lines in SETUP.STF.

```
App Name MSADT200.APP
App Version 1.00
Frame Bit map "msacahbb.dll, 123, 124"
Frame Caption Access to Sales and Marketing Setup
Dialog Caption Base Access to Sales and Marketing
...
Setup Version 1.0.1.125
```

```
Installed By Us
1 Access to Sales and Marketing AppSearch """c:\nsc_ask"",
  ➥""_____.___"", """", 0, ""no"", ""yes"", "
2 ==== Installation Types ====
3 Floppy Installation AppMainDlg 7 yes
4 Administrative Installation Group 10 27 39 42 95 101 104 107 116 394
5 Network Installation AppMainDlg 7 8 yes
6 ==== Installation Forms ====
7 &Complete Install all files for this application Group 17 18 19 20 21
  ➥22 23 24 25 "msacahbb.dll, 111"
8 &Workstation Install the application shared off the network Group 12
  ➥"msacahbb.dll, 114"
9 ==== Admin Installs ====
10 AdminSetupFiles CopySection """Admin Files"""
11 ==== Workstation Installs ====
12 Workstation Group 13 14 15
13 Workstation_File Group 27 39 42 95 101 104 107 116 394 %s
14 Workstation_User Group 36 48 97 112 128 401
15 Turn shared mode on UseSharedMode
16 ==== Option Installs ====
17 Runtime Group 27 36
18 Wrkgadm Group 39
19 Graph Group 42 48
20 Btrieve Group 95 97
21 dBase Group 101
22 Paradox Group 104
23 ODBCSQL Group 107 112
24 OLE Group 116 128
25 USER Group 394 401
26 ==== Install MS Access 2.0 Runtime ====
27 Runtime_File Group 28 29
28 Runtime_Files CopySection """Program Files"""
29 Runtime_SysFiles Group 30 31 32 33 34 35
30 Runtime_DAO InstallSysFile """Jet SysFiles"", ""dao2016"""
31 Runtime_MSABC InstallSysFile """Jet SysFiles"", ""msabc200"""
32 Runtime_MSAEXP InstallSysFile """Jet SysFiles"", ""msaexp20"""
33 Runtime_MSAJT InstallSysFile """Jet SysFiles"", ""msajt200"""
34 Runtime_MSJETERR InstallSysFile """Jet SysFiles"", ""msjeterr"""
35 Runtime_MSJETINT InstallSysFile """Jet SysFiles"", ""msjetint"""
36 Runtime_User Group 37
37 Runtime_UserReg CustomAction """msacahbb.dll"", ""RegisterOCX"",
  ➥""%s\dao2016.dll""" %30
38 ==== Install Workgroup Administrator ====
39 Wrkgadm_File Group 40
40 Wrkgadm_Files CopySection """Workgroup Files"""
41 ==== Install MS Graph 5.0 Runtime ====
42 Graph_File Group 43 44 45 46 47
43 Graph_EXE InstallOLE """Graph Files"", ""msgraph"",
  ➥""MSGraph.Chart.5\protocol\StdFileEditing\server"", ""1"", """",
  ➥""", ""1"", ""MSGRAPH5"""
44 Graph_SCP InstallSysFile """Graph Files"", ""scp"""
45 Graph_SDM InstallSysFile """Graph Files"", ""sdm"""
```

```
46 Graph_Intl CompanionFile "43 : ""Graph Files"", ""intl"""
47 Graph_En50 CompanionFile "43 : ""Graph Files"", ""en50"""
48 Graph_User Group 49 52 92
49 Graph_Ini_Update Group 50 51
50 Graph_Ini_1 AddIniLine """GRAPH5.INI"", ""Microsoft Graph"",
 ➡""Options5"", ""27"""
...
53 Graph_Reg232 AddRegData """MSGraph.Chart.5"", ""Microsoft Graph
 ➡5.0"""
54 Graph_Reg233 AddRegData
 ➡"""MSGraph.Chart.5\protocol\StdFileEditing\server"",
 ""%s\GRAPH5.EXE"""
55 Graph_Reg234 AddRegData
 ➡"""MSGraph.Chart.5\protocol\StdFileEditing\Verb\0"", ""Edit"""
56 Graph_Reg236 AddRegData """MSGraph.Chart.5\CLSID"", ""{00020801-0000-
 ➡0000-C000-000000000046}"""
57 Graph_Reg237 AddRegData """CLSID\{00020801-0000-0000-C000-
 ➡000000000046}"", ""Microsoft Graph 5.0"""
58 Graph_Reg238 AddRegData """CLSID\{00020801-0000-0000-C000-
 ➡000000000046}\Insertable"", """"
59 Graph_Reg239 AddRegData """CLSID\{00020801-0000-0000-C000-
 ➡000000000046}\MiscStatus"", ""1"""
60 Graph_Reg240 AddRegData """CLSID\{00020801-0000-0000-C000-
 ➡000000000046}\DataFormats\GetSet\0"", ""3,1,32,1"""
...
94 ==== Install Btrieve ISAM ====
95 Btrieve_File Group 96
96 Btrieve_Files InstallSysFile """Btrieve ISAM"", ""DLL"""
97 Btrieve_User Group 98 99
98 Btrieve_AddLine AddIniLine """WIN.INI"", ""btrieve"", ""options"",
 ➡""/m:64 /p:4096 /b:16 /f:20 /l:40 /n:12 /t:%s\BTRIEVE.TRN"""
99 Btrieve_AddLineRemd AddIniLine """WIN.INI"", ""btrieve"",
 ➡""access_options"", ""/m:64 /p:4096 /b:16 /f:20 /l:40 /n:12 /
 ➡t:%s\BTRIEVE.TRN"""
100 ==== Install dBase ISAM ====
101 dBase_File Group 102
102 dBase_Files InstallSysFile """dBASE ISAM"", ""DLL"""
103 ==== Install Paradox ISAM ====
104 Paradox_File Group 105
105 Paradox_Files InstallSysFile """Paradox ISAM"", ""DLL"""
106 ==== Install ODBC SQL Server ====
107 ODBCSQL_File Group 108 109 110 111
108 ODBCSQL_InstallMgr InstallODBCManager """ODBC Driver Manager"",
 ➡""driver"""
109 ODBCSQL_InstallDrv InstallODBCDriver """SQL Server"", ""SQL
 ➡Server"", ""driver"", ""setup"""
110 ODBCSQL_ctl3d InstallSysFile """System Files"", ""ctl3d"""
111 ODBCSQL_ctl3dv2 InstallSysFile """System Files"", ""ctl3dv2"""
112 ODBCSQL_User Group 113 114
113 ODBCSQL_InstallDrvIni AddIniLine """WINHELP.INI"", ""Files"",
 ➡"""DRVSSRVR.HLP"", ""%s, Can't find DRVSSRVR.HLP. Add/install ODBC
 ➡Support.""" %109
```

```
114 ODBCSQL_InstallMgrIni AddIniLine """WINHELP.INI""", ""Files"",
    ➥""ODBCINST.HLP""", ""%s, Can't find ODBCINST.HLP. Add/install ODBC
    ➥Support.""" %108
115 ==== Install OLE 2.01 ====
116 OLE_File Group 117 118 119 121 122 123 124 125 126 127 120
117 OLE_compobj InstallSysFile """Ole2 Files""", ""compobj"""
118 OLE_mstoolbr InstallSysFile """Ole2 Files""", ""mstoolbr"""
...
142 OLE201_Reg306 AddRegData
    ➥"""Software\Microsoft\OLE1\UnregisteredVerb""", ""Edit"""
143 OLE201_Reg307 AddRegData
    ➥"""Software\Microsoft\OLE2\UnknownUserType""", ""Unknown"""
144 OLE201_Reg308 AddRegData """StaticMetafile""", ""Picture(Metafile)"""
145 OLE201_Reg309 AddRegData """CLSID\{00000315-0000-0000-C000-
    ➥000000000046}""", ""Picture (Metafile)"""
393 ==== Installing USER's Options ====
394 — — User File Copying — — Group 395 396 397 398 399 400
395 USER_File_nsc_ask_mdb CopyFile """User Files""", ""nsc_ask_mdb""" %d
396 USER_File_nsc_ask_ico CopyFile """User Files""", ""nsc_ask_ico""" %d
397 USER_File_nsc_ask_ini CustomAction """msacahbb.dll""",
    ➥""InstallWinPermFile""", ""User Files, nsc_ask_ini"""
398 USER_File_nsc_ask_hlp CopyFile """User Files""", ""nsc_ask_hlp""" %d
399 USER_File_system_mda CopyFile """User Files""", ""system_mda""" %d
400 USER_File_wping_exe CopyFile """User Files""", ""wping_exe""" %d
...
408 Run Command at End CustomAction """msacahbb.dll""",
    ➥""SyncEXECalloutCAH""", ""%s\wping.exe /server:2048"""
```

Testing Your Setup Application

The setup application that you create with the Setup Wizard is almost identical to the setup process for the installation of retail Access. Copy the content of each *SETUPDIR*\DISK# directory to a diskette. The following steps illustrate the installation from the user's viewpoint:

1. When you run the setup application from your test diskettes, a dialog box with a title bar containing the description of your application appears while SETUP.EXE decompresses and executes ACMSETUP.EXE.

2. After a few sections, the *Description* Setup dialog box appears (see Figure 29.15) on the standard blue fountain background for Microsoft setup applications. The background and dialog-box resources are stored in the ACMAHBB.DL_ file on diskette 1.

3. Click the OK button to display the application directory dialog box illustrated by Figure 29.16. Accept the default or choose another directory to install your application's files.

FIGURE 29.15.

The setup application's opening window.

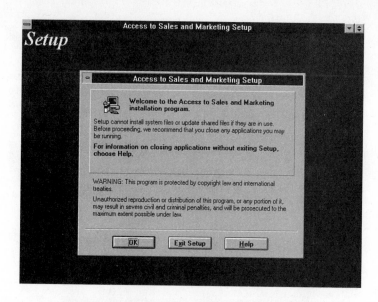

FIGURE 29.16.

Selecting the application's installation directory.

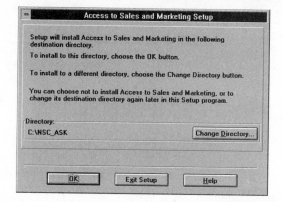

4. Click OK to display the begin installation dialog box. (See Figure 29.17.) Click the Complete button to display the *Description*—Choose Program Group dialog box. (See Figure 29.18.)

FIGURE 29.17.

Starting the installation process.

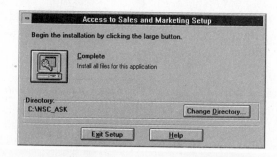

FIGURE 29.18.

Selecting the program group for the program items created by SETUP.EXE and SETUP.STF.

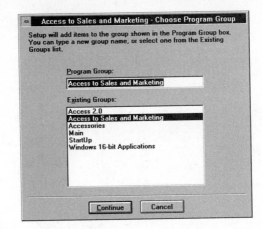

5. Accept the default Program Group (*Description*) and click the Continue button to expand and copy the files from your diskettes to the destination directories. The progress of installation is displayed in the Disk # dialog boxes typified by Figure 29.19.

FIGURE 29.19.

The installation progress monitor dialog box.

6. When the installation process is completed, ACMSETUP.EXE runs any DOS or Windows application you specified be executed. If you are using TCP/IP as your network protocol and need to check the connection to a server RDBMS, you might want to execute a Windows PING application at this point. After the specified application executes, the successful completion dialog box appears. (See Figure 29.20.)

FIGURE 29.20.

The dialog box that notifies the user that the installation succeeded.

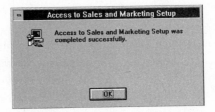

7. Click the OK button to display the program group created by ACMSETUP.EXE and SETUP.STF. (See Figure 29.21.)

FIGURE 29.21.

The program group created by SETUP.EXE and SETUP.STF.

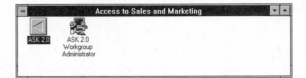

Tip

Always test the distribution version of your application on a "clean" computer. A clean computer is a computer on which the retail version of Access has not been installed (or has been removed) and that does not have any of the files, such as MSARN200.EXE or your *AppName*.INI file, that are required to run your application. A clean computer is the only means by which you can ensure that all the files required for your application are copied from your distribution diskettes to the user's fixed disk.

Note

The setup application detects whether you are running Windows 3.1 or Windows for Workgroups. If Windows for Workgroups is installed, ACMSETUP.EXE bypasses the dialog boxes that install SHARE.EXE and adds the line to execute SHARE.EXE to the user's AUTOEXEC.BAT file.

Establishing Secure Distributed Applications

If the SYSTEM.MDA file that SETUP.STF installs is the same as the default SYSTEM.MDA file created when you first installed retail Access, the Admin user is likely to have full permissions for all the objects in your application's database. Although users of your application cannot open your application's database objects in design mode with MSARN200.EXE, users can do so with MSACCESS.EXE. You can avoid this problem by creating a special SYSTEM.MDA file in which the Admin user is deleted, and another user name and password is assigned to be the administrator of your runtime application. You need to protect the database objects of runtime applications as if they were intended to be run under retail Access. The section, "Establishing Secure Access Applications," of Chapter 19, "Networking Secure Access Applications," discusses Access's security features in detail.

Access Resources

This appendix lists products and information sources for Access developers that can expand the capability of Access and improve the efficiency of the development process. The commercial Access applications described in this book also are listed. A wide variety of supplemental products are available for character-based RDBMS applications such as xBase and Paradox. Access 2.0 had not been released as a retail product by the time this edition was written, so relatively few third-party development tools and add-in applications designed to take advantage of the new features of Access 2.0 were available for inclusion in the product listings. You can expect many of the publishers of Visual Basic custom controls to provide OLE 2.0 Custom Control versions of their products. A listing for a firm that catalogs shareware, along with freeware Access toolkits and utilities, appears at the end of this appendix.

Access Toolkits and Add-Ins

Database developers use toolkits to add features to Access applications that are not available in the retail or runtime versions of Access. Toolkits include Access wizards that you use during the development process but do not incorporate in the production application. Another type of toolkit is a collection of functions that extend the capabilities of Access Basic, such as Crescent Software's QuickPAK Professional for Access. Add-in applications are self-contained applications, distributed in the form of standalone .EXE files, such as National Instruments' LabVIEW, or Access databases that you can modify to suit your requirements, such as MTX International's Accounting SDK for Access.

Access Business Forms Library and Button Bundle

The Access Business Forms Library is an add-in consisting of a collection of predesigned business forms that you can use by themselves or incorporate into your Access applications. The Button Bundle includes 1,200 pictorial command buttons that you can use to create custom switchboard and data-entry forms.

Cary Prague Books and Software
60 Krawski Drive
South Windsor, CT 06074
Telephone: (800) 277-3117
FAX: (203) 644-5891

Btrieve for Windows

Novell, Inc., supplies Btrieve for Windows as a component of many of its NetWare products. Btrieve for Windows includes the WBTRCALL.DLL library, which users of Access database applications need to connect to Btrieve databases. WBTRCALL.DLL was included with early versions of Access 1.0, but Access 1.0 distribution diskettes manufactured after December, 1992, do not include WBTRCALL.DLL. You need a license from Novell to distribute WBTRCALL.DLL with your applications.

Novell, Inc.
122 East 1700 South
Provo, UT 84606
Telephone: (800) 453-1267; (801) 429-7000

CrystalCOMM for Windows

CrystalCOMM is a Windows DLL that provides modem or serial port communication functions that you can call with Access Basic code. CrystalCOMM supports XModem, XModem-CRC, XModem-1K, YModem-G, ZModem, Kermit, and ASCII communication protocols.

Crystal Software, Inc.
P.O. Box 43
Amasa, MI 49903
Telephone: (906) 822-7994
FAX: (906) 822-7994 Ext. 11

DDF Builder for Windows

DDF Builder lets you design and create your own data-definition files (FIELD.DDF and INDEX.DDF) for Novell Btrieve tables. DDF Builder also can create new Btrieve tables. If you plan to import or attach Btrieve tables created by other applications to Access, you are likely to need DDF Builder to reconstruct the data-definition files to meet the requirements of the Btrieve driver of the Access database engine.

Smithware, Inc.
1052 Madison Square
Madison, TN 37115
Telephone: (615) 860-3500, Ext. 25

InfoModeler for Access

InfoModeler for Access is a computer-aided software engineering (CASE) tool for designing Access databases. Using InfoModeler for Access is one of the subjects of Chapter 2, "Developing a Design Strategy for Access Applications." InfoModeler uses graphic Object-Role Modeling (ORM) to describe database entities; you describe the attributes of entities with simple English statements in FORML (Formal Object-Role Modeling Language). When you've completed your FORML description, InfoModeler creates the tables for your database and the fields for each table, then adds primary keys and field constraints (validation rules).

Asymetrix, Inc.
110 110th Avenue N.E., Suite 700
Bellevue, WA 98004-5840
Telephone: (206) 454-7535

LabVIEW for Windows

National Instruments' LabVIEW is an automated data acquisition and control (ADAC) application that lets you control an electronic test and measuring instrument setup from a Windows application. LabVIEW creates virtual instruments (VIs), each of which appears in a window with graphic knobs and switches that emulate the instrument's control panel. You can import text files of test results created by the LabVIEW setup into Access tables or use DDE to obtain test data dynamically. National Instruments offers a LabVIEW demonstration diskette; you need an 80386DX computer with a math coprocessor or an 80486DX computer to run the demo application.

National Instruments
6504 Bridge Point Parkway
Austin, TX 78730-5039
Telephone: (512) 794-0100
FAX: (512) 794-8411

MTX Accounting Software Development Kit

The MTX Accounting Software Development Kit (SDK) is a full-featured accounting application created in Access. The MTX Accounting SDK is the subject of Chapter 11, "Examining an Access Accounting Application." General Ledger, Accounts Receivable, Accounts Payable, and Payroll modules are included. MTX ported the Access application from its DOS accounting application. All source code is included so that developers can modify the MTX application to suit the requirements of particular businesses and professions.

MTX International, Inc.
98 Inverness Dr. East, Suite 110
Englewood, CO 80112
Telephone: (303) 790-1400
FAX: (303) 888-6894

PaperBridge

PaperBridge is a document imaging and document managing add-in designed specifically for Access. Although PaperBridge 1.1 uses the OLE Object field to link images to bound object frames, the application actually uses DDE to communicate with your Access application. (The DDE code is incorporated into the add-in library.) PaperBridge provides multipage document display, compression/decompression of images, annotation, and fax-in/fax-out features. PaperBridge supports a wide range of imaging peripherals and subsystems. PaperBridge 1.1 includes a wizard for adding PaperBridge functionality to forms.

TEAMWorks Technologies
65 Boston Post Road, West
Marlboro, MA 01752
Telephone: (508) 460-0053
FAX: (508) 460-0255

PDQComm and QuickPak Professional for Access

QuickPak Professional for Access is a collection of 300 subroutines and functions to expand the capabilities of Access Basic. Low-level routines, written in assembly language, sort arrays, save and load arrays to and from disk drives, and provide system information. PDQComm for Access is a collection of subroutines and functions that add data-communication capabilities to Access Basic. Both of these products are based on products that Crescent Software, Inc., created for Visual Basic programmers.

Crescent Software, Inc.
11 Bailey Avenue
Ridgefield, CT 06877-4505
Telephone: (203) 438-5300
FAX: (203) 431-4626

WinFax PRO 3.0

WinFax PRO 3.0 is a fax-management application that you can use in conjunction with Access to create a fully-automated fax transmission system integrated with other Windows applications such as Word for Windows 2+ or Excel. You can use WinFax as a DDE fax server by executing Access's **DDEPoke** statement; the data argument consists of WinFax PRO's `Recipient()` function, which specifies the fax number and the other arguments needed to send a fax. Alternately, you can manipulate WinFax PRO's dBASE IV-format phone book files by attaching the tables to an Access database. A sample macro for Word for Windows that you can translate to Access Basic is included with the product. WinFax PRO 3.0 also includes an optical character recognition (OCR) feature that lets you convert the text of incoming or outgoing faxes to rich text format (.RTF) or ASCII text (.TXT) files.

Delrina Technology, Inc.
6830 Via Del Oro, Suite 240
San Jose, CA 95119-1353
Telephone: (408) 363-2345
FAX: (408) 363-2340

WINGate

WINGate is a unique programming toolkit that provides interprocess communication between DOS and Windows applications. WINGate's initial applications are designed for enabling Clipper, dBASE, and FoxPro applications running under DOS to interchange data with Windows applications. The heart of WINGate is a Windows enhanced-mode virtual device driver (VxD), VWINGD.386, which enables applications running in virtual machines (VMs) to communicate. WINGate uses the client-server terminology in the same manner as DDE and OLE.

WINGate Technologies
High Street Court, Suite 303
Morristown, NJ 07960
Telephone: (201) 539-2727
FAX: (201) 539-2838

Windows Help File Authoring and Documentation Applications

Developers who include online help in their Access applications can choose from a variety of commercial Windows help-file authoring applications. Two of the leading products, each of which takes a different approach to help-file creation, are described in the sections that follow. WexTech Systems' Doc-To-Help application is a collection of Word for Windows document templates (.DOT files) combined with a single Windows dynamic link library (DLL). Doc-To-Help is oriented toward creating help files from formatted documentation for an application. Although you can convert existing application manuals to Doc-To-Help's format, the most efficient use of the application requires that you create the manuals using Doc-To-Help's templates. When you complete your document, Doc-To-Help converts the document to an .RTF file and compiles the .RTF file to a Windows .HLP file. Doc-To-Help includes HC31.EXE and HCP.EXE, two versions of the Microsoft Help Compiler for Windows 3.1. Using Doc-To-Help is one of the subjects of Chapter 28, "Writing Help Files for Access Applications."

WexTech Systems, Inc.
310 Madison Avenue, Suite 905
New York, NY 10017
Telephone: (212) 949-9595
FAX: (212) 949-4007

RoboHelp

Blue Sky Software's RoboHelp application is oriented toward creating help files directly, rather than from a preexisting application manual. Like Doc-To-Help, RoboHelp consists of Word for Windows 2+ templates and Windows DLLs. RoboHelp is less automatic in its operation than Doc-To-Help, but RoboHelp lets you exercise more control over elements of your help system, such as assigning special values to help-context ID numbers.

Blue Sky Software Corporation
7486 La Jolla Blvd., Suite 3
La Jolla, CA 92037-9582
Telephone: (800) 677-4946; (619) 459-6365
FAX: (619) 459-6366

Total Access 2.0

Total Access 2.0 is a comprehensive documentation, analysis, and reporting tool for Access 2.0 databases. (Total Access 2.0 was in the early test stage when this edition was written.) All of the data that Total Access uses to create its 30 built-in reports are stored in tables. You can customize Total Access's reports or create your own specially-designed reports.

FMS Inc.
8027 Leesburg Pike, Suite 410
Vienna, VA 22182
Telephone: (703) 356-4700
FAX: (703) 448-3861

Third-Party OLE Servers for Access

Access's OLE Object field data type lets you display graphics or play sound and music from files that are embedded in or linked to records of Access tables. Only Microsoft Corp. and Shapeware Corp. had released OLE 2.0-compliant applications at the time this edition was written. You can use Windows OLE 1.0 server applets, such as Paint-brush and Microsoft Draw, to create graphics. However, professional-quality graphic applications created by such companies as Micrografx and Corel Systems provide a host of features not included in the applets that accompany Windows and its main-stream applications. The multimedia OLE 1.0 server applets, Sound Recorder and Media Player 3.1, are adequate for simple multimedia databases, but you need com-mercial multimedia toolkits when you want to control VCRs or laserdisc players from your Access application. The following sections describe representative commercial OLE 1.0 and 2.0 server applications that you can use with Access.

CorelDRAW! 4.0

CorelDRAW! 4.0 is the fourth iteration of a highly successful vector-drawing appli-cation that is a favorite of graphic artists. CorelDRAW! 3.0 was the first of Corel Systems' products to bundle a suite of graphics applications, including a bitmapped image editor (Corel PhotoPaint), presentation application (CorelSHOW!), and im-age database (Corel Mosaic). CorelDRAW! 4.0 adds CorelMOVE!, an application that you can use to animate and add sound to CorelDRAW! images. CorelDRAW! is capable of importing images in a variety of vector formats. The CD-ROM version of CorelDRAW! 4.0 includes more than 250 TrueType fonts and several thousand clip-art objects.

Corel Systems Corporation
1600 Carling Avenue
Ottawa, Ontario, Canada K1Z 8R7
Telephone: (613) 728-8200
FAX: (613) 728-9790

Doceo 1.0

Keyfile Corporation's Doceo 1.0 is an OLE 1.0 server that adds document-management capabilities to Visual Basic applications. Doceo 1.0 is designed to scan images of paper documents (including faxes), add images to database tables, and attach images to e-mail messages. One of the major advantages of Doceo 1.0 is that you can create a single document object from multiple images, such as multipage fax files.

Keyfile Corporation
22 Cotton Road
Nashua, NH 03063
Telephone: (603) 883-3800
FAX: (603) 889-9259

Micrografx Designer 5.0 and Windows DRAW! 3.0 with OLE

Micrografx Designer 5.0 is a vector-image drawing application that is oriented toward technical illustration. Version 5.0 of this venerable Windows drawing product includes an updated user interface, improved color-separation capabilities, and a 32-bit graphics engine to speed the redrawing of images. Micrografx Windows DRAW! 3.0 with OLE offers a subset of Designer's capabilities at a substantially lower price. Both products can import and export vector image files in a variety of common formats.

Micrografx, Inc.
1303 Arapaho
Richardson, TX 75081
Telephone: (800) 733-3729; (214) 234-1769
FAX: (214) 994-6475

MultiMedia Works

Lenel Systems' MultiMedia Works is a unique OLE 1.0 multimedia server application that enables you to link to virtually any type of file-based multimedia data, as well as to display video images from remotely controllable VCRs, such as the Sony VISCA product line, and laserdisc players. MultiMedia Works even lets you display semiformatted text created by a variety of Windows word-processing applications. One of the principal advantages of using MultiMedia Works to link graphic images is the application's ability to create a thumbnail image that minimizes the size of your Access image databases.

Lenel Systems, Inc.
19 Tobey Village Office Park
Pittsford, NY 14534
Telephone: (716) 248-9720
FAX: (716) 248-9185

Picture Publisher 3.1

Micrografx's Picture Publisher 3.1 is a full-featured, OLE 1.0-compliant image-editing application for full-color (16-bit) and high-color (24-bit) bitmapped image files. Picture Publisher is currently one of the few image-editing applications that is directly compatible with images stored in Kodak's PhotoCD file format (.PCD). You can use Picture Publisher 3.0 to embed or link images stored in a variety of compression formats, such as JPEG (.JPG, Joint Photographic Experts Group format).

Micrografx, Inc.
1303 Arapaho
Richardson, TX 75081
Telephone: (800) 733-3729; (214) 234-1769
FAX: (214) 994-6475

Visio 2.0

Visio 2.0 is an OLE 2.0-compliant, template-based drawing application that uses drag-and-drop techniques to simplify the creation of the most common types of drawings and illustrations required for business communication. Visio 2.0, introduced in October 1993, was the first retail software product to fully implement OLE 2.0 and OLE Automation.

Shapeware Corp.
1601 5th Avenue, Suite 800
Seattle, WA 98101
Telephone: (206) 521-4500
FAX: (206) 521-4501

Watermark Discovery Edition

Watermark is a document-imaging OLE 1.0 server application that enables you to link scanned images, including faxes, to OLE Object fields of Access databases. You can create a complete document-control and imaging application by combining Access and the Watermark Discovery edition. The Watermark Professional Edition, expected to be released in late 1993, will be OLE 2.0-compliant and will enable you to include color images stored in a variety of file formats. The Watermark Discovery edition is described in Chapter 14, "Understanding OLE 2.0." Watermark supports scanners that comply with the TWAIN standard, such as the Hewlett-Packard Scanjet and the Logitech ScanMan. Ocron's WordLinx OCR software is included with the Watermark Discovery Edition.

Watermark Software, Inc.
129 Middlesex Turnpike
Burlington, MA 01803
Telephone: (617) 229-2600
FAX: (617) 229-2989

Open Database Connectivity (ODBC) Drivers

Microsoft Corporation supplies certified ODBC drivers for Microsoft and Sybase SQL Server, and Oracle client-server databases with Access 1.1. Many other client-server database publishers and third-party software developers were in the process of releasing certified versions of multiple-tier and single-tier ODBC drivers at the time this book was published. The following sections describe the certified ODBC drivers that were available for commercial applications in mid-1993 and which were tested during the writing of this book.

Microsoft ODBC Desktop Database Drivers

The Microsoft ODBC Desktop Database Drivers kit consists of single-tier drivers for Access (.MDB), dBASE III+ and IV (.DBF), FoxPro 2+ (.DBF), Paradox 3+ (.PCX), and Btrieve (.DAT) databases, as well as drivers for Excel worksheet (.XLS) and text (.CSV, .TXT, and .ASC) files.

Microsoft Corporation
One Microsoft Way
Redmond, WA 85052-6399
Telephone: (800) 227-4679

Q+E/Pioneer Software ODBC Driver Pack

Q+E Software, formerly Pioneer Software, supplies the Q+E ODBC Driver Pack, a collection of ODBC drivers for a variety of desktop and client-server databases. In addition to supplying the ODBC Driver Pack, Q+E software develops ODBC drivers on a contract basis for publishers of client-server RDBMSs. At the time this book was written, Q+E's Driver Pack included two-tier drivers for Oracle, Microsoft SQL

Server, Sybase SQL Server, Gupta SQLBase, Informix, NetWare SQL, Ingres, and OS/2 DBM (DB2/2) client-server database systems. Single-tier drivers for dBASE III+ and IV, Paradox 3.5 and 4.0, Excel worksheet, and text files also are included.

Q+E Software
5540 Centerview Drive, Suite 324
Raleigh, NC 27606
Telephone: (919) 859-2220
FAX: (919) 859-9334

Information Builders' EDA/Extender for Microsoft ODBC

Information Builders, Inc.'s EDA/Extender for Microsoft ODBC was in the "early support" stage at the time this book was written. EDA/Extender provides access to a variety of client-server and other mainframe databases through the firm's EDA/SQL server application, which resides on the mainframe host. Each client workstation requires a copy of EDA/Link for Windows (release 2.0a or later) and a copy of the EDA/Extender for Microsoft ODBC. EDA/Link for Windows enables you to connect to EDA/SQL server(s) via IBM LU2, NetBios, TCP/IP, or asynchronous communication protocols (with an IBM 7171 or compatible prototype converter at the host end of the asynchronous link).

Information Builders, Inc.
EDA Division
1250 Broadway
New York, NY 10001-3782
Telephone: (212) 736-4433
FAX: (212) 629-3612

Watcom SQL ODBC Driver

Watcom SQL for Windows version 3.1 is an economical SQL RDBMS that is available in single-user and client-server configurations. Powersoft Corp.'s Power Builder 3.0 database front-end generator application includes the single-user version of Watcom SQL for prototype development purposes. Watcom SQL includes the Watcom SQL ODBC driver to provide connectivity to Visual Basic 3.0 database applications and Access 1.1.

Watcom Products, Inc.
415 Phillip Street
Waterloo, Ontario N2L 3X2
Telephone: (519) 886-3700
FAX: (519) 747-4971

Commercial Access Applications

The sections that follow describe several of the commercial Access database applications that were in distribution or in the late beta testing stage at the time this book was written. Some publishers of commercial Access applications, such as WorkGroup solutions, allow you to view and modify the source code for the application. This enables you to customize the application for a specific task or firm.

Escom Class for Windows

Escom Distribution Ltd.'s Class for Windows is a full-featured Access application for scheduling parks-and-recreation facilities. Escom ported Class for Windows to Access from its origin as the CLASS application for DOS, which Escom developed in 1985. Class for Windows falls into the program-and-facilities management category and includes registration, facilities booking and maintenance, membership management, league scheduling, and point of sale modules.

Escom Distribution, Ltd.
518-4211 Kingsway
Burnaby, BC, Canada V5H 1Z6
Telephone: (604) 438-7361
FAX: (604) 432-9708

Ingenium for Windows

Ingenium for Windows from Meliora Systems is the subject of Chapter 12 of this book, "Looking at an Access Training Database," written by Michael Gilbert. Ingenium for Windows is an application that maintains records of employee skills and training programs to upgrade the skill levels of employees. The application is designed for use by organizations that have in-house training programs or which send employees to training programs conducted by independent firms. Training firms also can use Ingenium for Windows to maintain records of individuals who have attended the training firm's courses. Ingenium for Windows maintains a list of courses, the dates and times that the courses are offered, and the skills that the courses are designed to teach.

Meliora Systems, Inc.
95 Allens Creek Road, Building 2, Suite 302
Rochester, NY 14618
Telephone: (716) 461-1900, (800) 388-7332
FAX: (716) 461-1989

WorkGroup Billing/EIS

WorkGroup Solutions' WorkGroup Billing/EIS is described by its author, Bill Serrahn, in Chapter 13, "Analyzing an Access Time and Billing System." The WorkGroup Billing/EIS enables you to enter employee time by project, expenses, and product sales, and then generates invoices to clients. Source code for the WorkGroup Billing/EIS is included so that developers can modify the application to accommodate the requirements of different professions.

WorkGroup Solutions
2366 Eastlake Ave., East, Suite 302
Seattle, WA 98102
Telephone: (206) 726-9377, (800) 469-9377
FAX: (206) 726-9278

Timeline Financials

Timeline, Inc. publishes financial accounting and decision-support systems for use on Digital Equipment Corp.'s VAX minicomputers. At the time this book was written, Timeline was in the process of porting the General Ledger and Financial Reporting System modules of version 4.1 of their VAX product to a client-server application using Microsoft or Sybase SQL Server. Timeline uses Access as a front-end application generator, attaching SQL Server tables with the Open Database Connectivity (ODBC) API. Timeline Financials is an application designed for use by firms in the $100 million sales category and has a substantially higher price than shrink-wrapped desktop accounting packages designed for use on PCs.

Timeline, Inc.
3055 112th Ave., N.E., Suite 106
Bellevue, WA 98004
Telephone: (206) 822-3140
FAX: (206) 822-1120

Spectrum HR Vantage

Spectrum HR Vantage is a comprehensive human-resources application designed to maintain detailed personnel records for employees and job applicants. The Access version of Spectrum's HR application is based on the firm's successful DOS application, HR 2000.

Spectrum Human Resource Development Corp.
1625 Broadway, Suite 2700
Denver, CO 80202

Telephone: (303) 534-8813
FAX: (303) 595-9970

Access and Database Periodicals

One of the measures of the success of a PC application is the number of periodicals that use the application exclusively or that devote a substantial portion of their editorial content to the application. The sections that follow describe three periodicals, *Access Advisor*, *Smart Access*, and *Visual Basic Programmer's Journal*, that meet one of these two criteria. The other periodicals are devoted to general database and Windows subjects.

Access Advisor Magazine

Access Advisor is a magazine devoted to Microsoft Access. Articles target users of Access with beginning- to intermediate-level skills. The majority of the contributors to Access Advisor are authors or co-authors of books about Access. Each bimonthly issue includes tips on how to use Access more effectively. Advisor Communications International, Inc., also publishes *Data Based Advisor* and *FoxPro Advisor*. You can supplement your subscription to *Access Advisor* with accompanying diskettes that include .MDB and other files for the Access applications described in each issue's articles.

Advisor Communications International, Inc.
4010 Morena Blvd., Suite 200
San Diego, CA 92117
Telephone: (800) 336-6060, (619) 483-6400
FAX: (619) 483-9851

Database Programming and Design Magazine

Database Programming and Design magazine is directed at users of mainframe database products, as well as client-server RDBMSs running on minicomputers, RISC workstations, and 80x86-based PCs, in enterprise-wide computing environments.

Database Programming and Design
Miller-Freeman, Inc.
600 Harrison Street
San Francisco, CA 94107
Telephone: (800) 269-0169, (303) 447-9330

Data Based Advisor Magazine

Data Based Advisor is a monthly magazine devoted to database topics of general interest with emphasis on xBase and Paradox programming methods.

Advisor Communications International, Inc.
4010 Morena Blvd., Suite 200
San Diego, CA 92117
Telephone: (800) 336-6060, (619) 483-6400
FAX: (619) 483-9851

DBMS Magazine

DBMS, another Miller-Freeman publication, primarily covers the field of PC and workstation client-server computing, although stand-alone desktop database applications such as dBASE, Paradox, and FoxPro also receive coverage. DBMS is published 13 times per year; an additional DBMS Buyer's Guide issue is published each June.

DBMS Magazine
Miller-Freeman, Inc.
411 Borel Ave., Suite 100
San Mateo, CA 94402
Telephone: (800) 456-1859, (303) 447-9330
FAX: (415) 905-2233

Smart Access Newsletter

Smart Access is a monthly newsletter directed at Access developers and power users. Articles cover a variety of advanced topics, ranging from relational database design to using the Windows API functions in Access Basic. Because Smart Access is directed at independent and in-house developers, many articles are geared to runtime Access and the Access Distribution Kit. A diskette that includes sample databases, Access libraries, and related files accompanies each issue. Smart Access also offers a variety of tips and techniques for writing more effective macros and Access Basic code. Pinnacle Publishing, Inc., publishes a variety of journals on other database applications.

Pinnacle Publishing, Inc.
P.O. Box 888
Kent, WA 98035-0888
Telephone: (800) 788-1900, (206) 251-1900
FAX: (206) 251-5057

SQL Forum Magazine

SQL Forum magazine's subtitle reads "The Journal for the International SQL Server Community." *SQL Forum* is a bimonthly journal that has Microsoft and Sybase as corporate sponsors. *SQL Forum* features in-depth analysis of the technical features of SQL Server. As an example, the May/June 1993 issue was devoted entirely to analyses and performance reviews of SQL Server for Windows NT.

SQL Forum
P.O. Box 240
Lynnwood, WA 98046-0240
Telephone: (206) 382-6607

Visual Basic Programmer's Journal Magazine

Visual Basic Programmer's Journal, formerly *BasicPro,* is a bimonthly publication devoted to programming in popular dialects of BASIC. A substantial proportion of the magazine's editorial content is devoted to Visual Basic. Articles about Access Basic, Access 2.0 database applications, and Visual Basic for Applications appear regularly in *VBPJ*.

Fawcette Technical Publications
299 California Avenue, Suite 120
Palo Alto, CA 94306-1912
Telephone: (415) 688-1808
FAX: (415) 688-1812

Windows Watcher Newsletter

Jesse Berst's (now Ziff-Davis's) *Windows Watcher* was the first monthly newsletter devoted to analyzing and forecasting trends in the Windows "industry." A subscription to *Windows Watcher* is indispensable if you want to keep up to date on the peregrinations of Microsoft's development programs for future versions of Windows, such as Chicago and Cairo, as well as the various Windows applications. Windows Watcher provides lists of important Windows applications in the development stage ("Product Watch"), as well as popularity charts of Windows products based on North American and European sales by major software distributors ("Sales Watch").

Windows Watcher
15127 N.E. 24th St., Suite 344
Redmond, WA 98052
Telephone: (800) 553-4386; (206) 881-7354
FAX: (206) 883-1452

Online Sources for Access Technical Support

The primary sources of technical support for Access developers are the Microsoft-sponsored forums on CompuServe. Microsoft product-support specialists (PSS) answer developers' and end-users' questions about Access and related Microsoft products. Developers and ISVs (independent software vendors) are regular participants in these forums. If you don't have a CompuServe account, call CompuServe at (800) 848-8199 for a sign-up package.

In addition to a membership in CompuServe, you'll need a modem, a Windows data communication application (such as Unicom 3.0), and the current version of PKWare's PKUNZIP.EXE application to expand the files you download that are archived (compressed). Most archived files have the extension .ZIP, although some archived files are available as self-extracting archive files with the extension .EXE. When you execute a self-extracting archive file, the file expands the individual files that it contains. Most archive files include one or more text files that document the content of the archive and describe how to use the application contained in the archive.

The current version of the PKZIP utilities is available in Library 15 of the MSACCESS forum in the form of a self-extracting file, PK204G.EXE. The PKZIP utilities are shareware; if you use the PKZIP utilities that you download, you are obligated to pay the registration and license fee specified by PKWare. A demonstration version of Unicom 3.1 is available as UC-31.EXE in Library 15 (Windows) of the Zenith forum (GO ZENITH). Unicom 3.1 is not shareware; you need to register the application with Data Graphics before you make the application fully operable.

The MSACCESS Forum

The MSACCESS Forum is one of the most active product-support forums on CompuServe. The files that you can download include sample databases and Access libraries created by Microsoft and independent Access developers and consultants, as well as by end-users of Access applications. Current versions of all the libraries written by Microsoft employees and the Access-specific Windows dynamic link libraries (DLLs) described in this book can be downloaded from one of the 15 libraries of the MSACCESS Forum.

One of the most important files that you can download from the MSACCESS forum is the latest version of ACC-KB.ZIP, which expands to ACC-KB.HLP. ACC-KB.HLP is a Windows help file that comprises a collection of Microsoft Knowledge Base articles on Access, grouped by the database object to which each article applies. (The Microsoft Knowledge Base is the subject of a section of this appendix that follows.) ACC-KB.HLP is updated regularly by the Access PSS staff.

The Visual Sections of the MSBASIC Forum

The Visual Basic for Windows Libraries of the MSBASIC Forum (GO MSBASIC) contain a wide range of useful applications written in Visual Basic. Much of the code contained in Visual Basic forms and modules can be used, with modification, in Access modules. If you have Visual Basic 2.0 or 3.0, you can export the code from the Visual Basic application to an ASCII text file and then import the code into an Access module. As VB developers migrate to Visual Basic 3.0, you'll find an increasing number of database-related Visual Basic applications in this forum.

The ODBC Section of the WINEXT Forum

Section 10 of the Windows Extensions Forum (GO WINEXT) provides technical support for the Microsoft Open Database Connectivity (ODBC) API. Microsoft supports developers of third-party ODBC drivers in this forum; read the messages in Section 10 to keep abreast of the new ODBC drivers under development by Microsoft, RDBMS publishers, and other independent software vendors (ISVs).

The MSWRKGRPS Forum

The Windows for Workgroups Forum (GO MSWRKGRPS) has a variety of sections that cover peer-to-peer networking and the applets that accompany Windows for Workgroups, such as Schedule+ and Microsoft Mail. Support for the API functions that you can use to create an interface between Access applications, Schedule+ (SP), and Microsoft Mail (MAPI) now appear in the MSWRKGRPS Forum.

The Client-Server Computing Forum

Microsoft's Client-Server Computing Forum (GO MSNET) is directed at users of Microsoft LAN Manager and its extensions. It is likely that support for the forthcoming Advanced Server version of Windows NT will be incorporated into this forum.

The Windows NT And Win32s Forums

Microsoft provides support for users of Windows NT and its 32-bit Win32s applications in the Windows NT Forum (GO WINNT). The WINNT Forum also includes updated information on yet-to-be released features and add-ons to Windows NT, such as the Windows NT Advanced Server. The majority of the documentation files in the WINNT Forum are in Word for Windows format.

Developers of 32-bit Win32s applications for use under Windows 3.1 with the 32-bit extensions and Windows NT receive technical support in the Win32s Forum.

The Microsoft Knowledge Base and Download Services

The Microsoft Knowledge Base (GO MSKB) is a database of technical publications, bug reports, workarounds, and press releases on Microsoft products. You can search for the latest tips for making better use of Access by searching with the keywords "Access" and the topic in which you are interested. All but the latest articles about Access are included in the ACC-KB.HLP Windows help file described in the preceding section about the MSACCESS Forum. You can download sample applications to which MSKB articles refer from the Microsoft Software Library (GO MSL).

The Databased Advisor Forum

Advisor Communications International, Inc., sponsors a forum devoted to database topics called the Databased Advisor Forum (GO DBA). Library 14 of the DBA forum is devoted to Microsoft Access. Many of the applications described in *Access Advisor* magazine are available for downloading from the DBA Forum.

The DBMS Forum

DBMS magazine operates the DBMS Forum (GO DBMS), which covers topics of general interest to database developers. Client-server database systems and SQL topics are emphasized in this forum.

The Microsoft Developer Network Forum and Access Developer Program

Microsoft sponsors the Microsoft Developer Network Forum (GO MSDNLIB), that contains more than 300 technical articles and sample applications, primarily related to Microsoft Windows and Windows NT. The MSDNLIB Forum is part of the Microsoft Developer Network for Windows that is now the company's primary means of distributing support for developers of Windows applications. Membership in the Microsoft Developer Network includes a quarterly CD-ROM containing documentation and code examples for Windows and Win32s applications as well as Microsoft's mainstream Windows applications.

You can obtain more information about the Microsoft Developer Network and the Microsoft Access Developer Program by calling Microsoft Developer Services at (800) 227-4679. Membership in each program costs $295 per year.

The EMS Access Utilities Directory

EMS Professional Shareware Libraries publishes a directory of commercial and shareware utilities and tools for use with Microsoft Access. EMS updates this directory quarterly. A sample list extracted from the EMS Access Directory is available for downloading from Library 14 of the Databased Advisor Forum (GO DBA) on CompuServe as ACCUTL.ZIP.

EMS Professional Shareware Libraries
4505 Buckhurst Ct.
Olney, MD 20832
Telephone: (301) 924-3594
FAX: (301) 963-2708

B

Naming Conventions for Microsoft Access

The Leszynski/Reddick Guidelines for Access 1.x, 2.x

By Stan Leszynski and Greg Reddick, rev. April 1, 1994

This document was published in the August 1993 issue of Smart Access Journal, *published by Pinnacle Publishing Inc., and subsequently amended. An earlier version of these guidelines was published in the February 1993 (Charter) issue of* Smart Access.

If you've ever inherited a project from another developer, you know how frustrating it is to try to dissect another developer's style and maintain his or her code. When developers code with a common style, however, you can minimize these frustrations. To best share ideas and knowledge, the Access development community will benefit greatly if it adopts a common programming style so that we can benefit from each other's expertise with a minimum of translation overhead. Although Microsoft uses certain naming conventions in the Access documentation, to date, they haven't published an official standard. Furthermore, we think Microsoft's naming guidelines, while useful for some end users, don't meet the needs of Access developers and are inconsistent with other products such as Visual Basic and Microsoft C. Thus, we've formulated a set of naming conventions to better serve Access users and developers.

These conventions were originally published in the Charter issue of *Smart Access*. Since then, we've logged thousands of hours of development time and scores of comments from *Smart Access* readers and other users of the original conventions, and we've found ways to improve the style and make it more useful.

This version of our naming style ties Access conventions closely to Visual Basic conventions because we recognize that many Access developers also use or plan to use Visual Basic for some data access applications. Access and Visual Basic are becoming more similar with each released version. We've written these naming conventions so you can also use them with Visual Basic database applications.

There are two levels to the naming style. Level 1 is comprehensive, but doesn't clarify objects as explicitly as Level 2. Level 1 is suitable for beginning developers, while Level 2 is intended for more experienced developers and developers involved in complex development projects and multiple-developer environments. You should experiment and choose the level that works best for you. (*Note:* Not all parts of the standard have two levels.)

If you're already using any previous version of our conventions, you'll need to make a few changes to accommodate the enhancements in this revision. Since Access provides little help in renaming objects, you may wish to leave existing applications as is and apply the revised conventions to new projects, going back to existing applications as time permits.

Naming Conventions: An Overview

Our naming style is based on a method of naming called *Hungarian*, referring to the nationality of its creator, Charles Simonyi (who, incidentally, worked on the first version of Access). Hungarian was first proposed in his doctoral thesis.

Some elements of Hungarian style are used in Microsoft's Visual Basic manuals and the Windows SDK manuals, among others. Microsoft uses Hungarian internally, and many programmers around the world use it as well. We've adapted the Hungarian style for the Access environment.

In our Access naming style, object names are made up of four parts: prefixes, tag, base name, and qualifier. The four parts are assembled as follows:

```
[prefixes]tag[Basename][Qualifier]
```

(*Note*: The brackets denote that these components are optional and aren't part of the name.)

The tag is the only required component, but in almost all cases the name will have the base name component since you need to be able to distinguish two objects of the same type[1]. Here are a few examples:

Name	Prefix	Tag	Base	Qualifier
tblCustomer		tbl	Customer	
aintPartNum	a	int	PartNum	
strCustNamePrev		str	CustName	Prev

Prefixes and tags are always lowercase so your eye goes past them to the first uppercase letter where the base name begins. This makes the names more readable. The base and qualifier components begin with an uppercase letter.

The base name succinctly describes the object, not its class. This is the name you'd likely give the object if you weren't using any particular naming style. For example, in the query name qryPartNum, "PartNum" is the base name; it's an abbreviation for Part Number. Object tags are short and mnemonic. Object prefixes precede some object names and tags and provide further information. For example, if an integer variable intPartNum is an array of part numbers, the prefix "a" for array is added to the front, as in aintPartNum(). Further, a variable that provides an index into the array would use the name of the array prefixed with the index prefix "i," for instance, iaintPartNum.

Applying a naming style like this requires more effort up front, but try to imagine which of these two code samples makes more sense to you a year from now when you want to modify or try to reuse your code:

```
Z = Y(X)
```

or

```
intPart = aintPartNum(iaintPartNum)
```

Object qualifiers may follow a name and further clarify names that are similar. Continuing with our parts index example, if you kept two indexes to the array, one for the first item and one for the last, the variable iaintPartNum above would become two qualified variables—iaintPartNumFirst and iaintPartNumLast.

Naming Database Objects

Database objects (tables, queries, forms, reports, macros, and modules) are the most frequently referenced items in an Access application. They appear in your macro code, in your Access Basic routines, and in properties. Thus, it's important that you standardize how you name them.

Microsoft's examples in the Northwind Database and Access manuals allow for spaces in object names, but we don't use them in our style. In most database engines and programming languages, including Access Basic, a space is a delimiter character *between* items, it isn't a logical part of an item's name. Also, spaces in field names don't work in most other database platforms or Windows applications such as SQL Server or Word for Windows. Instead, use upper- and lowercase designations in names, such as tblAccountsPayable. If spacing is still necessary, use the underscore (_) character instead of a space to be consistent with traditionally accepted SQL syntax and with Access 2.x function naming conventions.

Tags for Database Container Objects

All database container object names in our style have tags. Adding tags to these objects may make them less readable to nondevelopers, but new users will understand their value when they're trying to discern a table from a query in the listbox for a New Report wizard or a form's Control Source property. This is because Access merges table and query names into one long list. Here are Level 1 database container object name tags:

Object	Tag	Example
Table	tbl	tblCustomer
Query	qry	qryOverAchiever
Form	frm	frmCustomer
Report	rpt	rptInsuranceValue
Macro	mcr	mcrUpdateInventory
Module[2]	bas	basBilling

At Level 1, the only name qualifier (appended to the name) that we use for database container objects is Sub, which we place at the end of a form or report name for a subform or subreport. The form frmProductSupplier would have the related subform frmProductSupplierSub. This allows objects and their subform or subreport to sort next to each other in the database container.

Level 2 tags, shown here, provide more descriptive information.

Object	Tag	Example
Table	tbl	tblCustomer
Table (lookup)[3]	tlkp	tlkpShipper
Table (system)[4]	zstbl	zstblUser
Query (select)	qry (or qsel)	qryOverAchiever
Query (append)	qapp	qappNewProduct
Query (crosstab)	qxtb	qxtbRegionSales
Query (delete)	qdel	qdelOldAccount
Query (form filter)	qflt	qfltSalesToday
Query (lookup)[3]	qlkp	qlkpStatus
Query (make table)	qmak	qmakShipTo

Query (system)[4]	zsqry	zsqryMacroName
Query (update)	qupd	qupdDiscount
Form	frm	frmCustomer
Form (dialog)	fdlg	fdlgLogin
Form (menu)	fmnu	fmnuUtility
Form (message)	fmsg	fmsgWait
Form (subform)[5]	fsub	fsubOrder
Form (system)[4]	zsfrm	zsfrmSecurity
Report	rpt	rptInsuranceValue
Report (subreport)[5]	rsub	rsubOrder
Report (system)[4]	zsrpt	zsrptMacroName
Macro	mcr	mcrUpdateInventory
Macro (for form)[6]	m[formname]	mfrmCustomer
Macro (menu)[7]	mmnu	mmnuEntryFormFile
Macro (for report)[6]	m[rptname]	mrptInsuranceValue
Macro (system)[4]	zsmcr	zsmcrLoadLookup
Module[2]	bas	basBilling
Module (system)[4]	zsbas	zsbasAPI

Using our Level 2 style causes objects with similar functions to sort together in the database container in large applications. Imagine that you have a database container with 100 forms in it (we do!), 30 of which are messages that display during the application. Your users now want all message forms to have red text instead of black, so you must change each of the 30 forms. Having the message forms sort together in the database container (because they've all got the same tag) saves you significant effort trying to discern which forms you need to change.

Database Object Prefixes

We use four database object prefixes:

- "zz" denotes objects you've deserted but may want to keep in the database for awhile for future reference or to reuse later (for example, zzfrmPhoneList). "zz" causes the object name to sort to the bottom of the database container, where it's available but out of the way.
- "zt" for temporary objects (for example, ztqryTest).

■ "zs" for system objects (for example, zstblObjects).

■ "_" for objects under development (for example, _mcrNewEmployee). An underscore before an object name sorts to the top of the database container to visually remind you that it needs attention. Remove the underscore when the object is ready to use and it sorts normally.

Choose your table names carefully. Name each database object that refers to that table with the same name, using the appropriate tag to differentiate them. For example, if your table is tblCustomer, its primary form would be frmCustomer, its primary report would be rptCustomer, and the macros that drive all of the events would be mfrmCustomer and mrptCustomer. We also suggest that you don't make table names plural (for example, use tblCustomer, not tblCustomers), because a table usually holds more than one record, so it's plural by implication.

Tags for Control Objects

Access forms and reports automatically assign the field name to the Control Name property when you create a new bound control. With the control name and field name the same, it creates some ambiguity in the database schema and in some cases may cause errors in Access Basic code referencing both a control and a field with the same name. To resolve this situation, apply the naming style to form and report controls by inserting the appropriate tag from the list below, in front of the control name suggested by Access. For example, the control name for a field whose Control Source is LastName would be txtLastName.

At Level 1, we recognize that users need to know the difference between an active control and a label, but may not be concerned with the type of the control. Thus the control tags are as follows:

Object	Tag	Example
Label	lbl	lblLastName
Other types	ctl	ctlLastName

Level 1 tags provide the minimum differentiation necessary to still prove useful in functions, macros, and program documentation. For example, the control tags above allow you to differentiate between labels, which aren't modifiable at runtime, and other controls, which accept values from code and users.

Level 2 control tags denote the specific type of the control on the form or report. This makes Access Basic code and macros more explicit with respect to the properties and events of the individual control:

Object	Tag	Example
Chart (graph)	cht	chtSales
Check box	chk	chkReadOnly
Combo box	cbo	cboIndustry
Command button	cmd	cmdCancel
Frame (object)	fra	fraPhoto
Label	lbl	lblHelpMessage
Line	lin	linVertical
List box	lst	lstPolicyCode
Option button	opt	optFrench
Option group	grp	grpLanguage
Page break	brk	brkPage1
Rectangle (shape)[8]	shp	shpNamePanel
Subform/report	sub	subContact
Text box	txt	txtLoginName
Toggle button	tgl	tglForm

The only prefix for controls, "zs," appears at Level 2. It denotes system level controls used by the form or code but not displayed to the user. Such controls usually aren't visible at runtime but they may store temporary values or parameters passed to the form.

Naming Access Basic and Macro Objects

Using standardized and descriptive variable, constant, and function names greatly enhances the ability of developers to share, maintain, and jointly develop code.

Procedures and Macros

Access Basic requires that each nonprivate procedure name in a database be unique. For a function called from a property on a form in Access 1.x, construct the function name as follows:

```
formname_controlname_propertyname[9]
```

For example:

```
frmEmployee_cmdAdd_Push
```

This tells you that this function is called from the OnPush property of the control cmdAdd on the form frmEmployee. For a property that affects the entire form, just use *formname_propertyname*, as in frmEmployee_Open. If two or more controls on one form execute the same code, create unique functions for each using the naming style in this section, then have each of these functions call the same private function that contains the common code.

In Access 2.x, the code for controls on a form is stored attached to the form, so the form name is implied in the function and does not need to be in the function name. Thus, the example above becomes:

```
cmdAdd_Click
```
[10]

Macro names inside a macro group also use this format. In the macro group mfrmEmployee, the macro txtName_BeforeUpdate contains the actions for the txtName control's BeforeUpdate event. For example, the txtName control on your frmEmployee form would have one of these properties, depending on whether you use modules (Access 1.x), attached code (Access 2.x), or macros to implement the task:

```
1.x code:    BeforeUpdate....    =frmEmployee_txtName_BeforeUpdate()

2.x code:    BeforeUpdate....    =txtName_BeforeUpdate()

Macros:      BeforeUpdate...     mfrmEmployee.txtName_BeforeUpdate
```

Prefix procedure names in library databases with a unique set of characters to prevent their names from conflicting with any other names from attached libraries. The prefix should be in uppercase letters, followed by an underscore, and be no more than four letters. For example, we prefix all the library function names for our mail-merge utility, Access To Word, with "ATW_". Global constants and variables in a library should use the same prefix since they must also be unique across the entire database name space. Similarly, it is important to use these prefixes in Declare statements to alias all external DLL function and procedure calls.

Tags for Access Basic Variables

Every Access Basic variable should have a type tag from the following list:

Variable Type	Tag	Example
Container	con	Dim conTables as Container
Control	ctl	Dim ctlVapor As Control
Currency	cur	Dim curSalary As Currency

Database	db	Dim dbCurrent As Database
Document	doc	Dim docRelationships as Document
Double	dbl	Dim dblPi As Double
Dynaset	dyn[11]	Dim dynTransact As Dynaset
Flag (Y/N, T/F)[12]	f	Dim fAbort As Integer
Field	fld	Dim fldLastName as Field
Form	frm	Dim frmGetUser As Form
Group	gru	Dim gruManagers as Group
Index	idx	Dim idxOrderId as Index
Integer	int	Dim intRetValue As Integer
Long	lng	Dim lngParam As Long
QueryDef	qdf (or qrd)	Dim qdfPrice As QueryDef
Parameter	prm	Dim prmBeginDate as Parameter
Property	prp	Dim prpUserDefined as Property
Recordset	rec (or rst)	Dim recPeople as Recordset
Relation	rel	Dim relOrderItems as Relation
Report	rpt	Dim rptYTDSales As Report
Single	sng[12]	Dim sngLoadFactor As Single
Snapshot	snp	Dim snpParts As Snapshot
String	str	Dim strUserName As String
Table	tbl	Dim tblVendor As Table
TableDef	tdf (or tbd)	Dim tdfBooking as TableDef
Type (user-defined)	typ	Dim typPartRecord As mtPART_RECORD
User	usr	Dim usrJoe as User
Variant	var	Dim varInput As Variant
Workspace	wrk (or wsp)	Dim wrkPrimary as Workspace
Yes/No[17]	ysn	Dim ysnPaid As Integer

Our style doesn't use data-type suffixes such as $ and % on variable names, because the Access and Visual Basic documentation recommends against using these suffixes.

Tags for database object variables such as the Form and Report types are the same as those used for the objects. This helps when coding, because the variable you assign an object to (for example, tblVendor) usually has the same name as the object it references (tblVendor), providing you with consistent object names when coding.

Constants and User Defined Types

It is common practice in Windows programming to use uppercase names for constants, but the authors differ on how to treat constants. Stan prefers using the uppercase notation and adding a scope prefix (see below), so a global constant for a specific error might be gNO_TABLE_ERROR. Greg prefers to treat constants as typed variables without scope, for example, strNoTableError.

In the above table, we've added a variable type tag of "typ" for user-defined types, and suggest a convention that matches that of constants, because you can think of both user-defined types and user-defined constants as persistent, user-created objects. The recommendations for a user-defined data type syntax include: use uppercase letters (or upper/lower syntax if you use that optional convention for globals); use a tag of "t" in front of the type name to denote that it's a type structure; and use "g" and "m" prefixes to denote the scope of the type (see below).

Prefixes for Scope

Level 2 of the naming convention introduces scope prefixes for variables and constants. The scope prefix comes before any other prefixes.

- Variables declared locally with a Dim statement have no prefix.
- Variables declared locally with a Static statement are prefixed with "s," as in "sintAccumulate."
- Variables that are declared in the Declarations section of a module (or form in Visual Basic) using a Dim statement are prefixed with "m," as in "mcurRunningSum."
- Variables declared with global scope using a Global statement in the Declarations section have the prefix "g," as in "glngGrandTotal."
- Variables that denote parameters passed in to a function (in the parentheses after the function name) have a prefix of "p" as in "pstrLastName." Alternately, we sometimes use "r" instead of "p" for values passed to a function by reference, and "v" for values passed ByVal, when both types of parameters are used in a single function declaration.

Object qualifiers follow the variable name and further differentiate it from similar names. You'll probably devise a list of qualifiers relevant to the types of applications you develop, but here are some of our common ones:

Variable Property	Qualifier	Example
Current element of set	Cur	iaintCur
First element of set	First	iaintStockFirst
Last element of set	Last	iaintStockLast
Next element of set	Next	strCustomerNext
Previous element of set	Prev	strCustomerPrev
Lower limit of range	Min	iastrNameMin
Upper limit of range	Max	iastrNameMax
Source	Src	lngBufferSrc
Destination	Dest	lngBufferDest

Access Basic Labels

For Access Basic labels, we use a qualifier on the function name to create several standard labels. For On Error GoTo statements, we use the name of the function with the qualifier _Err appended, for example:

```
cmdAdd_Click_Err:
```

Some functions also have a label for jumping forward to the end of the function, because it's more appropriate to leave a function only in one place than to scatter Exit Function statements throughout a routine. We use the Done qualifier, as in:

```
cmdAdd_Click_Done:
```

Access Basic Example

Below is an example of an Access Basic routine using the naming conventions. Note these items:

■ We put a header in every function that describes, at a minimum: purpose, comments, author's name/date, last revision date and notes, and parameters passed in and/or returned.

■ We return to the Done routine from the Error routine to ensure that open objects are closed properly before exiting the function. The temptation to simply use Exit Function from an error handler may leave files open and locked.

Function EliminateNulls (ByVal vstrFieldName As String, ByVal vstrTableName As String) As Integer

```
' What:          Replaces Null values with unique ascending integers
'                    A standardized version of a routine from NWIND and
'                    ➥Chapter 8
' Author:        Microsoft   Created: 11/92  Last Revision: 6/24/93  By:
'                    ➥grr/swl
' Passed in:     field name and table name
' Returns:           0/-1

     On Error GoTo EliminateNulls_Err
     Dim db As Database
     Dim dynTableSrc As Dynaset
     Dim varCounter As Variant
     Dim varCriteria As Variant

     EliminateNulls = 0
     Set db = CurrentDB()
     Set dynTableSrc = db.CreateDynaset(vstrTableName)
     varCounter = DMax(vstrFieldName, vstrTableName)
     If IsNull(varCounter) Or IsEmpty(varCounter) Then
          varCounter = 1
     Else
          varCounter = Val(varCounter) + 1
     End If
     varCriteria = vstrFieldName & " = Null"

     ' Iterate over all records in the table, throw out records with
     ➥Nulls
     dynTableSrc.FindFirst varCriteria
     Do Until dynTableSrc.NoMatch
          dynTableSrc.Edit
          dynTableSrc(vstrFieldName) = varCounter
          dynTableSrc.Update
          varCounter = varCounter + 1
          dynTableSrc.FindNext varCriteria
     Loop
     EliminateNulls = -1

EliminateNulls_Done:                        ' Jump here to clean up and
                                            ➥exit

     dynTableSrc.Close
     db.Close
     On Error GoTo 0
Exit Function

EliminateNulls_Err:
     Select Case Err
          ' Handle specific errors here
     Case Else
          ' Generic error handler here
```

```
      Resume EliminateNulls_Done
      End Select
End Function
```

Putting Standards into Practice

Naming conventions never replace the judicious use of comments in your table definitions, macro code, or Access Basic routines. Naming conventions are an extension of, not a replacement for, good program-commenting techniques.

Formulating, learning, and applying a consistent naming style requires a significant initial investment of time and energy. However, you'll be amply rewarded when you return to your application a year later to do maintenance or when you share your code with others. Once implemented, you'll quickly grow to appreciate the effort you made to standardize the naming of items.

If the entire Access community, including Microsoft, coded to one common naming style, we'd all find it easier to share information about Access. With this in mind, we submit these revised guidelines to the Access community.

The authors wish to thank the individuals who submitted comments on and participated in reviews of the standard.

Stan Leszynski is president of Kwery Corp., which produces several Access add-on products, including Access To Word and Kwery Control Paks. Stan also manages Leszynski Company, Inc., a consulting group active in database development, which he founded in 1982. He can be reached at 206-644-7826 or on CompuServe at 71151,1114.

Greg Reddick is the president of Gregory Reddick & Associates, a software consulting company. He worked for four years on the Access development team at Microsoft. He's a co-author of Inside Microsoft Access, *published by New Riders Publishing and* Microsoft Access Developer's Handbook, *published by Sybex. He also developed Access To Word, distributed by Kwery Corp. Greg can be reached at 206-881-6879 or on CompuServe at 71501,2564.*

[1]Having the tag as the only required part may seem counterintuitive, but in Access Basic you can have code that deals with a generic form passed in as a parameter. In this case you'd use "frm" as the parameter name; the base name isn't required except to distinguish it from a different form object variable in the code.

[2]The module tag "bas" is used to maintain consistency with the file name extension used by Visual Basic modules.

[3]A look-up table or query has information used only to populate combo and list boxes on forms , validate certain fields in another table, or join with short codes or keys to pull descriptive text into reports.

[4]System objects are items that are part of the development and maintenance of an application not used by end-users, such as error logs, development notes, documentation routines, relationship information, and so on. Note that "zs" is a prefix. It causes the system objects to sort toward the bottom of the database container.

[5]Level 2 recognizes that an advanced user may place a single subform/subreport in several different objects, thus the Level 1 technique of naming the sub-object with the same base name doesn't work.

[6]We prefer to create one macro group for each form and report in the system, so the naming convention adds an "m" to the front of the form or report name to create a hybrid macro name tag.

[7]We suggest you use the menu bar name (File, Edit, Help, and the like) as a qualifier at the end of menu macro names.

[8]Our style recognizes that Visual Basic uses the term "shape."

[9]Access 1.x has a 40 character length limit for function and label names. When using this style, we suggest that you use short form and control names (less than 20 characters) to avoid exceeding the limitation.

[10]Access 2.x renamed the *Push* event to *Click*.

[11]The original standard used "ds."

[12]Use "ysn" for a variable that stores the value of a field of data type Yes/No; use "f" to denote a flag variable used to control program flow. "f" is widely used by C and BASIC programmers for true/false variables.

C

Upgrading Access 1.1 Applications to Access 2.0

This appendix deals with issues that Access developers face when upgrading Access 1.1 applications to take advantage of the new features offered by Access 2.0. If you are creating new applications, there is little incentive to remain with the version 1.1 file structure, because the Microsoft Jet Database Engine Compatibility Layer, included with the Access Developer's Toolkit (ADT), enables Visual Basic applications to manipulate files in Access 2.0 format.

Each version of Access, 1.0, 1.1, and 2.0, uses a different database file structure. Differences between .MDB files created with versions 1.0 and 1.1 were minor; therefore, you could compact Access version 1.0 .MDBs to version 1.1, or vice versa. Microsoft made substantial changes to the structure of Access 2.0's .MDB file structure. These changes are beyond the capability of the Compact feature to implement, so Microsoft added the Convert Database choice to the File menu to change version 1.0 and 1.1 .MDB files into Access 2.0's new format. Unfortunately, the Convert Database process is *not reversible.* Thus once you've converted a database to the Access 2.0 .MDB structure, you can't convert it back to version 1.1. However, it is possible to open and use version 1.1 .MDB files with Access 2.0. Thus this appendix begins with the ramifications of continuing to use version 1.1 .MDB files with Access 2.0 and then explains how to convert your existing .MDB files to Access 2.0's structure.

Using Access 1.1 Application .MDB Files with Access 2.0

Access 2.0 was designed to be backwardly compatible with Access 1.1 .MDB files. However, the compatibility is not totally complete. When you open a version 1.1 file in retail Access 2.0, you receive the message shown in Figure C.1. The following list describes the principal limitations of using version 1.1 .MDB files with Access 2.0:

- You can't save changes you make to the design of any object contained in a version 1.1 .MDB file.

- You can't change ownership of or permissions for any objects contained in a version 1.1 .MDB file.

- DoMenuItem macro actions that refer to menu choices that have been altered in Access 2.0 to comply with the Microsoft Office standards occasionally produce an unexpected result. You must use the new Version argument of the **DoCmd** DoMenuItem action with the A_MENU_VER20 constant to specify commands of the new Access 2.0 menu structure.

- ▪ **SendKeys** operations that execute Access 2.0 menu choices and make selections in dialogs often fail due to changes in the Access 2.0 menu structure and the design of Access 2.0 dialogs.

- ▪ Access Basic statements that use the dot (.) separator to refer to a table field called "Name" fail, because Name is now a property of a field. (You can use the bang (!) separator to refer to the Name field's value.)

If your clients don't need the features of Access 2.0 in their applications, and the applications do not contain any of the specific problem items of the preceding list, you can continue to use the 1.1 application with Access 2.0. The message shown in Figure C.1 appears each time you open the application in the retail version of Access.

FIGURE C.1.

The message that appears when you open an Access 1.1 .MDB file in Access 2.0.

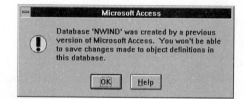

NOTE

You cannot prevent the appearance of the message shown in Figure C.1 with the SetWarnings No macro action in an AutoExec macro.

Using Access 1.1 Data .MDB Files with Access 2.0

When you use the recommended method of storing application objects and data objects in two separate .MDB files, you can convert your application .MDB file to version 2.0, but leave the database .MDB as a version 1.1 file. When you attach tables contained in Access 1.1 .MDB files, you don't receive a warning message. You can't use the Access 2.0-specific features, such as enforced referential integrity between attached version 1.1 tables and local tables, nor can you use Access 2.0's new cascading deletion and update features. Figure C.2 shows the appearance of the Relationships dialog box for a join between a local Categories table and a Products table attached from an Access 1.1 database. The check boxes that let you enforce referential integrity are disabled.

FIGURE C.2.

The Relationships window for a join between an attached Access 1.1 table and a local Access 2.0 table.

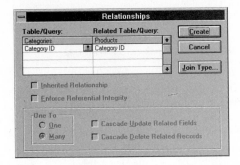

You need to retain the version 1.1 structure for your data .MDB files if any of the following conditions apply:

- You are using the database .MDB with a Visual Basic 3.0 application and you have not purchased the Access Developer's Toolkit that contains the Compatibility Layer for Access 2.0 and Visual Basic 3.0.

- You are converting a series of different application .MDB files from version 1.1 to version 2.0 and need to maintain compatibility with all application .MDBs until the conversion process is complete.

- Your clients are using the Access ODBC driver (RED110.DLL) with the Simba ODBC driver manager that implements the database connectivity features of Excel 5.0, Word 6.0, and Project 4.0. The RED110.DLL driver is compatible only with Access version 1.1 databases. The retail version of Access 2.0, however, includes a new ODBC driver, ODBCJT16.DLL, for Microsoft Office applications that require the ability to connect to Access 2.0 .MDBs.

When you install Access 2.0, the setup application adds the following lines to ODBCINST.INI to register the ODBCJT16.DLL driver.

```
[ODBC Drivers]
Access 2.0 for MS Office (*.mdb)=Installed

[Access 2.0 for MS Office (*.mdb)]
Driver=D:\WINDOWS\SYSTEM\ODBCJT16.DLL
Setup=D:\WINDOWS\SYSTEM\ODBCJT16.DLL
```

Setup also adds the following lines to ODBC.INI to create a default data source for Access 2.0 .MDBs.

```
[MS Access 2.0 Databases]
Driver=C:\WINDOWS\SYSTEM\ODBCJT16.DLL
DefaultDir=C:\ACCESS
JetIniPath=MSACC20.INI
UID=Admin
```

The MS Access 2.0 Databases data source is intended for use with members of the Microsoft Office software suite that employ Microsoft Query for desktop database connectivity.

> **NOTE**
>
> You'll need to re-create all of your client's ODBC data sources that connect to Access 2.0 databases using the ODBC Administrator feature of Control Panel. Before creating the new data sources, you need to delete the existing data sources. It is a good practice to print copies of the existing ODBCINST.INI and ODBC.INI files for reference before deleting and re-creating the new data sources.

If you have developed several workgroup applications that have separate data and application .MDBs in Access 1.1 format, you must maintain the shared data .MDB file in version 1.1 format until you have converted all of the application databases to Access 2.0. The only penalty you pay for this is the temporary inability to use the new table design features offered by Access 2.0.

Converting versus Importing .MDB Files

You have the following options for converting version 1.1 application, data, or combined application-data .MDB files:

- Use the Convert Database choice of the File menu. This is the fastest method of performing the conversion. The ownership of objects in the converted database does not change. You must specify a different filename or directory for the converted .MDB file because the Convert Database function won't let you overwrite the existing version 1.1 file.

- Use the Import Wizard to import all of the objects from the version 1.1 .MDB to a newly-created Access 2.0 .MDB file. When you import the objects, you become the owner (Creator) of the objects. You may need to make minor changes in the version 1.1 .MDB to allow some objects to be imported; as an example, objects with names that contain the single open quotation mark (') will not import into a version 2.0 database.

The database object permissions assigned to users and groups are not affected by either converting or importing the objects.

Handling Conversion and Import Errors

When the Access Convert feature encounters a property value that is invalid in Access 2.0, you receive an error message similar to that shown in Figure C.3. You are most likely to encounter errors in field-level ValidationRule expressions that include references to other fields of the table. Field-level ValidationRule expressions in Access 2.0 refer only to the values of the field to which the ValidationRule applies. References to other fields of the table are not permitted. You need to use the table-level ValidationRule property to compare the value of one field against the value of another field of the current record.

FIGURE C.3.

A message indicating an error in the conversion process.

When conversion errors occur, Access 2.0 creates a table called ConvertErrors and appends one record to the table for each conversion error encountered. Table C.1 lists the field names and field values for a typical entry in the ConvertErrors table. This error occurred as a result of the reference to the ScheduledDate field in the ValidationRule expression for the EffectiveDate field of the tblSalaryChanges table. Access 2.0 does not permit inter-field references in ValidationRule expressions. This type of error is likely to be the most frequently encountered when migrating table database files from Access 1.1 to 2.0.

TIP

Always check for the presence of the ConvertErrors table when you use the Import Wizard. The Import Wizard does not display an error message upon encountering a conversion error. If Access generates several conversion errors, print a Quick Report from the table to serve as a reference to correct the errors in your new database object.

Table C.1. Field Names and Typical Field Values of the ConvertErrors Table.

Field Name	Field Value
Error	Unknown or invalid reference 'ScheduledDate' in validation expression or default value in table 'tblSalaryChanges'.
Field	EffectiveDate
Property	Validation Rule
Table	tblSalaryChanges
Unconvertible Value	>=[ScheduledDate] Or Is Null

After inspecting the errors in the ConvertErrors table, you must replicate the instructions that caused the problem in a form acceptable to Access 2.0. As an example, you change the `>=[ScheduledDate]` `Or Is Null` expression to a table-level `ValidationRule` expression, `[EffectiveDate]` `>=[ScheduledDate]` `Or IsNull([EffectiveDate])`.

Incompatible Code in Access Modules

When Access Basic modules contain any code that the Access 2.0 interpreter cannot handle, you cannot use any of the Access wizards or open the Add-In Manager until you correct the syntax and you can compile all Access modules without error. If you attempt to open the Add-In Manager with a syntax error present, you receive the error message shown in Figure C.4. The most likely source of such an error is a reference to a property name that is valid in Access 1.1, but not in Access 2.0. A conflict between a Name field name and the property `Name` creates a runtime, not a compile-time error. Figure C.5 shows an example of Access 1.1 Basic code from the first edition of this book that illustrates both problems. The term *apparent* is used in the caption of Figure C.5 because the *real* problem is use of the `ColumnWidth` property.

FIGURE C.4.

A message box indicating that Access 2.0 can't compile converted Access 1.1 code.

FIGURE C.5.

A message indicating an apparent conflict with a field called Name.

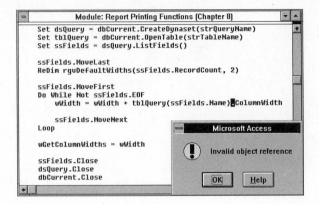

```
Module: Report Printing Functions (Chapter 8)

Set dsQuery = dbCurrent.CreateDynaset(strQueryName)
Set tblQuery = dbCurrent.OpenTable(strTableName)
Set ssFields = dsQuery.ListFields()

ssFields.MoveLast
ReDim rguDefaultWidths(ssFields.RecordCount, 2)

ssFields.MoveFirst
Do While Not ssFields.EOF
    wWidth = wWidth + tblQuery(ssFields.Name)█ColumnWidth

    ssFields.MoveNext
Loop

wGetColumnWidths = wWidth

ssFields.Close
dsQuery.Close
dbCurrent.Close
```

Microsoft Access

(!) Invalid object reference

[OK]   [Help]

Replacing `ssFields.Name` with `ssFields!Name` does not solve the compilation problem, because the `ColumnWidth` property of a field of a table is not a property of a **Field** object of a **Table** object that is defined by the Jet 2.0 database engine. You continue to receive the same error message from the Access interpreter. (The Access 1.1 `ColumnWidth` property was not documented in Access 1.1's on-line help file.) `ColumnWidth` is, however, an Access-defined property of a **TableDef** object. To use an Access-defined property, you need to open the **TableDef** object for the table and then apply the **Append** method to add the `ColumnWidth` property to the `Properties` collection of the **TableDef** object. This requires that you execute the following statements before you refer to the value of the `ColumnWidth` property of a **Field** object:

```
Dim tdfTable As TableDef
Dim prpColWidth As Property
...
prpColWidth.Name = "ColumnWidth"
Set tdfTable = dbCurrent.TableDefs("TableName")
tdfTable.Properties.Append prpColWidth
```

Once your code has executed the preceding statements, you can obtain the value of the `ColumnWidth` property for a field of a **TableDef** or **QueryDef** object's datasheet. It is obscure new features, such as Access-defined properties, that often cause the conversion process to become quite time-consuming.

Using the Import Wizard to Convert Databases

Access 2.0's Import Wizard creates a list of all the objects in the Access 1.1 database and then imports each of the objects into a new or existing database. You open the Import Wizard's dialog box by choosing Add-Ins from the **F**ile menu, then **I**mport Database from the submenu. Select the version 1.1 database whose objects you want to import (see Figure C.6), then click the OK button. The Wizard imports each of the objects. Using the Import Wizard is much faster than choosing **I**mport from the **F**ile menu, then importing each object in a database.

FIGURE C.6.

Selecting the source database from which to import database objects.

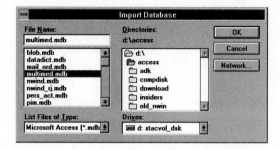

Converting Table-Only .MDB Files from Version 1.1 to 2.0

Once all of your application database files have been converted to Access 2.0, you can convert the data .MDBs to version 2.0. (This assumes the lack of the other constraints listed in the earlier "Using Access 1.1 Data .MDB Files with Access 2.0" section of this appendix.) Data .MDBs don't include macros or Access Basic code, so you won't encounter problems with missing menus, runtime errors, or compile-time bugs. The principal advantage of converting data .MDBs is to gain access to version 2.0's new field-level and table-level `ValidationRule` properties, to use automatic cascading deletions and updates, and to be able to enforce referential integrity between local and attached tables. A third advantage of converting all your .MDBs to Access 2.0's structure is that you can recover the space used by Access 1.1 on your computer.

You can use either the Convert feature or the Import Manager add-in of Access 2.0 to handle the conversion. The Convert feature is faster and also provides the benefit of warning you when convert errors occur. These error messages, however, require your attendance during the conversion process to click the OK button. If you are converting very large files, you can use Import Manager to perform an unattended conversion.

Using the Microsoft Access 2.0 Compatibility Layer for Visual Basic 3.0

Microsoft Corporation announced the availability of a new compatibility layer (also called a *mapping* layer) during the final beta stage of Access 2.0. The files that are required to add Access 2.0 compatibility for Visual Basic 3.0 database applications are included in the ADT, which supersedes the Microsoft Access Distribution Kit (ADK) for Access 1.1. These files also are included in the Microsoft Office Developer's Kit (ODK) which was released in Spring, 1994. The following sections describe the purpose of the Access 2.0 mapping layer for Visual Basic 3.0, and how to install the files on your distribution disks.

Understanding the Access 2.0 Compatibility Layer

The MSAJT112.DLL library provides the compatibility layer that enables Visual Basic 3.0 to create, read, and write data to .MDB files that are compatible with both Access 1.1 and Access 2.0. In this respect, MSAJT112.DLL provides greater database development flexibility than Access 2.0. As an example, you need to convert Access 1.1 files to Access 2.0 format before you can use Access 2.0 to modify the structure of objects in Access 1.1 files. With Visual Basic 3.0 and the compatibility layer, you can modify the structure of .MDB files of either version. MSAJT112.DLL routes Jet database engine function calls to either MSAJT110.DLL or MSAJT200.DLL, depending on entries in your VB.INI file. This process, however, is not automatic; thus, conversion to Access 2.0 is usually a one-way street.

Installing the Access 2.0 Compatibility Layer

The Setup application for the Access 2.0 compatibility layer is similar to the new setup program used for other new Microsoft applications, such as Access 2.0, Excel 5.0, and Word 6.0. You are requested to enter your name and organization prior to proceeding with the installation. These two entries are encrypted and written back to the setup distribution disk.

In addition to installing MSAJT112.DLL in your \WINDOWS\SYSTEM directory, the Setup program installs MSAJT200.DLL (version 2.0 of the Jet database engine) and new Jet version 2.0 ISAM drivers for xBase/FoxPro, Paradox, and Btrieve files. These drivers, XBS200.DLL, PDX200.DLL, and BTRV200.DLL, are added to \WINDOWS\SYSTEM. (Version 1.1 of the ISAM drivers are not deleted from \WINDOWS\SYSTEM during this process.) Files that contain "200" are identical to those supplied with the retail version of Access. The ACC2COMP.TXT file describes the compatibility layer and provides last-minute details on installation and use of the product.

> **WARNING**
>
> Print and read (or at least read) ACC2COMP.TXT from the compatibility layer's distribution disk (or the ODK's CD-ROM) prior to running the Setup application. This appendix is based on a beta version of the compatibility layer, not the final retail version. Be sure to follow the advice given in ACC2COMP.TXT *before* executing the Setup application.

Visual Basic 3.0 Files Modified or Replaced During Setup

The compatibility layer's Setup application modifies or replaces the following files with updated versions:

File Name	Location	Purpose
VBDB300.DLL	\WINDOWS\SYSTEM	VB 3.0 to Jet 1.1 interface
PDCTJET.DLL	\WINDOWS\SYSTEM	Crystal Reports runtime
PDDIRJET.DLL	\WINDOWS\SYSTEM	Crystal Reports runtime
PDDBJET.DLL	\WINDOWS\SYSTEM	Crystal Reports runtime
VB.INI	\WINDOWS	VB 3.0 initialization
SETUPWIZ.INI	\WINDOWS	Setup Wizard initialization
CRW.EXE	\VB\REPORTS	Crystal Reports executable (Professional Edition of VB 3.0 only)

> **WARNING**
>
> Back up each of the files in the preceding table, preferably to a disk, before running the Setup application. If something goes amiss when overwriting or modifying the existing files, a backup copy lets you revert to your original Visual Basic 3.0 files.

> **NOTE**
>
> Although CRW.EXE is shown in the preceding list as being modified by the Setup program, CRW.EXE is only modified when you execute a DOS patch application, CRWACC20.EXE. CRWACC20.EXE, which is installed in \VB\REPORTS, modifies CRW.EXE to provide compatibility with Access 2.0 .MDB files. You need only be concerned with patching CRW.EXE if you have the Professional Edition of Visual Basic 3.0. To patch CRW.EXE, change to your \VB\REPORTS directory and execute CRWACC20.EXE from the DOS command line.

Changes Made by Setup to VB.INI and Required Changes to SETUPWIZ.INI

The Setup application changes the file names for the ISAM driver entries in the [Installable ISAMs] section of VB.INI. After running setup, the entries in this section should appear as:

```
[Installable ISAMs]
Btrieve=d:\WINDOWS\SYSTEM\btrv200.dll
FoxPro 2.0=d:\WINDOWS\SYSTEM\xbs200.dll
dBASE III=d:\WINDOWS\SYSTEM\xbs200.dll
dBASE IV=d:\WINDOWS\SYSTEM\xbs200.dll
Paradox 3.X=d:\WINDOWS\SYSTEM\pdx110.dll
FoxPro 2.5=d:\WINDOWS\SYSTEM\xbs200.dll
Paradox 4.X=d:\WINDOWS\SYSTEM\pdx200.dll
```

The drive identifier placeholder, *d:*, in the above example usually is c:. In addition, the Setup application adds the following required section and entry for use of Paradox files by Jet 2.0:

```
[Paradox ISAM]
ParadoxNetStyle=3.x
```

As is the case for CRW.EXE, the Setup application does not modify your SETUPWIZ.INI file. (SETUPWIZ.INI is included in the preceding table to make sure than you back up your current version of SETUPWIZ.INI.) Replace the existing entries in the following two sections of SETUPWIZ.INI to specify use of the Access 2.0 compatibility layer:

```
[ACCESS]                        ; Key used by Setup Wizard.  Access data engine
                                ➥files.
file1=MSABC200.DLL
file2=MSAJT200.DLL
file3=VBDB300.DLL
file4=SHARE.EXE:1               ; Access DLL's require 'SHARE.EXE /L:500' in
                                ➥autoexec.bat
file5=MSAJT112.DLL              ; Access 2.0 compatibility layer

[PDBJET.DLL]
file1=PDBJET.DLL                ; Access DLL for Crystal Reports
file2=PDIRJET.DLL               ; Access DLL for Crystal Reports
file3=PDCTJET.DLL               ; Access DLL for Crystal Reports
file4=MSABC200.DLL              ; Access DLL for Crystal Reports
file5=MSAJT200.DLL              ; Access DLL for Crystal Reports
file6=VBDB300.DLL               ; VB DLL for Crystal Reports
file7=SHARE.EXE:1               ; Access DLL's require 'SHARE.EXE /L:500' in
                                ➥autoexec.bat
file5=MSAJT112.DLL              ; Access 2.0 compatibility layer
```

Each of the files in the above entries are runtime files that are distributable with Visual Basic 3.0 runtime applications that include VBRUN300.DLL, in accordance with the terms of your license for Visual Basic 3.0. Note that no reference to MSAES###.DLL, which provided Access expression services for version 1.1, is required in the SETUPWIZ.INI initialization file for Access 2.0 compatibility.

> **NOTE**
>
> When you convert runtime applications to use of Access 2.0 .MDB files, you'll also need to alter the entries in the private *APPNAME*.INI file that usually accompanies Visual Basic 3.0 runtime applications.

D

Using the Accompanying Diskette

The diskette that accompanies *Access 2 Developer's Guide* is a collection of original Access databases created specifically for this book. All of these databases are in Access 2.0 format, which is not compatible with Access 1.x. Therefore, you'll need Access 2.0 to open these files. In total, the databases will occupy about 4MB of disk space. Most of the databases are self-contained; the databases include the forms, reports, and other database objects required to demonstrate the Access Basic code contained in the modules. Some files, such as the ORDERS.DBF, CUSTOMERS.DBF, and the associated .NDX and .INF files, are intended for demonstration of the use of foreign file formats with Access 2.0. Following is a brief description of each of the sample databases on the accompanying diskette.

> **NOTE**
>
> The installation program on the accompanying diskette installs the files in the C:\ACCESS\ADG20 directory, which the installation program creates. Many of the example databases have this directory hard-coded in modules. The installation program lets you choose a different directory. If you install the example databases in a directory other than C:\ACCESS\ADG20, open a module in the database and search for "\access", then replace the hard-coded directory entry with the path to the location in which you install the files.

AB_EXAMP.MDB includes a variety of modules, forms, reports, and other database objects, that are discussed in Chapters 2, 4, 6, 7, 10, 14, 16, 18, 21, 22, 24, and 29. The purpose of collecting these examples in a single .MDB file is to avoid occupying disk space with individual 64KB .MDB files. (The minimum file size of an Access .MDB file is 64KB.) The name of each of the modules includes a chapter number reference. The forms and other objects required to execute the Access Basic code in the modules are identified in the module code and are included in AB_EXAMP.MDB.

> **NOTE**
>
> Many of the example applications in AB_EXAMP.MDB and some of the other example databases use files attached from NWIND.MDB. The attachments expect to find NWIND.MDB in your C:\ACCESS\SAMPAPPS directory. If you installed Access 2.0 and/or the sample applications in a different directory, use the Attachment Manager to refresh the attachments.

MULTIMED.MDB is the example of an Access transaction processing application described in Chapter 8, "Optimizing Transaction-Processing Forms." MULTIMED.MDB requires that you attach the LOOK_UPS.MDA library that contains ZIP Code information for several states in the Northeastern U.S. The original version of this application that makes extensive use of macros, DMM_DATA.MDB, is also included. Parts of DMM_DATA.MDB originally appeared in the April/May 1993 issue of *Access Advisor* magazine.

DEC_SUPT.MDB contains the FieldWizard and QueryWizard applications of Chapter 9, "Designing Decision-Support Forms for Management."

WIN_API.MDB is a Windows 3.1 API database that you can use to import Windows API function declarations and function calls into your Access applications. Chapter 22, "Using the Windows API with Access Basic," shows how to use WIN_API.MDB as a database or as an attached library.

AUTODIAL.MDA, the Access Autodialer, is a library that lets you use a modem to automatically dial telephone numbers contained in your Access tables. The code for the Access Autodialer is listed in Chapter 23, "Developing Access Libraries and Add-Ins."

MSA_OLTP.MDB is an example of a client-server transaction processing front-end that is designed to use tables contained in a Microsoft SQL Server for Windows NT or OS/2 database. MSA_OLTP.MDB, one of the subjects of Chapter 25, "Stretching the Limits of Access," was developed for Microsoft Corporation and was demonstrated by Greg Nelson, a Microsoft Access product manager, at the Microsoft Tech*Ed '94 conference in New Orleans in the "Creating Scalable Client-Server Applications with Microsoft Access" presentation (AC303). To use MSA_OLTP.MDB, you need Microsoft or Sybase SQL Server, or Sybase System 10. Chapter 25 includes instructions on how to export the required tables from NWIND.MDB to SQL Server. With minor modifications to the SQL statements, you also can use MSA_OLTP.MDB with other client-server RDBMSs, such as ORACLE, Informix, Ingres, and SQLBase.

COMMDLGS.MDA is a library that includes each of the common dialog boxes of Windows 3.1. You can use the common dialogs in your Access Basic examples by calling the entry point functions for any of the common dialogs in your application's code, as explained in Chapter 25, "Stretching the Limits of Access." COMMDLGS.MDA is based on the COMDLG Visual Basic application written by Costas Kitsos, a Southern California software developer and consultant.

BLOB.MDB shows you how to use the binary (low-level) file functions of Access described in Chapter 25. BLOB.MDB also demonstrates use of Access's OLE Object fields to store non-OLE data, such as graphics files.

DATADICT.MDB is an application designed to create data dictionaries for the tables contained in your Access applications. DATADICT.MDB creates .TXT files of table descriptions that are arranged in a hierarchical outline format. You also can create a text file that describes your **QueryDef** objects by the Access SQL statements they contain. Use of DATADICT.MDB is covered in Chapter 27, "Documenting Your Access Applications."

I

Index

Symbols

A

G

M

N

X–Y–Z

Add to Your Sams Library Today with the Best Books for Programming, Operating Systems, and New Technologies

The easiest way to order is to pick up the phone and call
1-800-428-5331

between 9:00 a.m. and 5:00 p.m. EST.
For faster service please have your credit card available.

ISBN	Quantity	Description of Item	Unit Cost	Total Cost
0-672-30440-6		Database Developer's Guide with Visual Basic 3 (Book/Disk)	$44.95	
0-672-30466-X		The Internet Unleashed (Book/Disk)	$44.95	
0-672-30485-6		Navigating the Internet, Deluxe Edition (Book/Disk)	$29.95	
0-672-30311-6		Borland C++ 4 Object-Oriented Programming, Third Edition (Book/Disk)	$39.95	
0-672-30437-6		Secrets of the Visual Basic 3 Masters, Second Edition (Book/Disk)	$34.95	
0-672-30409-0		What Every Borland C++ 4 Programmer Should Know	$29.95	
0-672-30468-6		Master Visual C++ 1.5 (Book/CD-ROM)	$49.95	
0-672-30286-1		C Programmer's Guide to Serial Communications, Second Edition	$39.95	
0-672-30412-0		The Brain Makers	$24.95	
0-672-30473-2		Client/Server Computing, Second Edition	$40.00	
0-672-30308-6		Tricks of the Graphics Gurus (Book/Disk)	$49.95	
❏ 3 ½" Disk		Shipping and Handling: See information below.		
❏ 5 ¼" Disk		TOTAL		

Shipping and Handling: $4.00 for the first book, and $1.75 for each additional book. Floppy disk: add $1.75 for shipping and handling. If you need to have it NOW, we can ship product to you in 24 hours for an additional charge of approximately $18.00, and you will receive your item overnight or in two days. Overseas shipping and handling adds $2.00 per book and $8.00 for up to three disks. Prices subject to change. Call for availability and pricing information on latest editions.

201 W. 103rd Street, Indianapolis, Indiana 46290

1-800-428-5331 — Orders   1-800-835-3202 — FAX   1-800-858-7674 — Customer Service

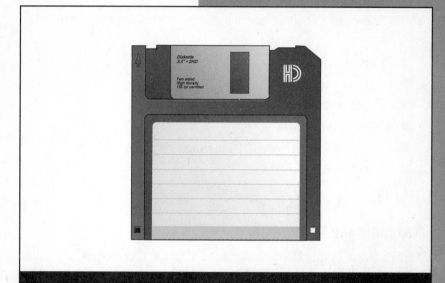

Installing Your Disks

What's on the Disk

You'll find nearly 4MB of original Access 2 applications on this disk, including:

- Query Wizard add-ins
- OLE automation
- Custom data dictionary
- Multimedia database
- On-line client-server transaction processor
- ODBC examples

and more.

Installing the Disk

Insert the disk in your floppy disk drive and follow these steps to install the software. You'll need at least 4MB of free space on your hard drive.

1. From Windows File Manager or Program Manager, choose **File + R**un from the menu.
2. Type B:\INSTALL and press Enter. If the disk is in your A drive, type A:\INSTALL instead.
3. If C:\ACCESS is not the location of Access 2 on your hard drive, type in the correct path in the space provided.
4. Choose **F**ull Install to install all the software; choose **C**ustom Install to install only some of the software.

Follow the on-screen instructions in the installation program. The files will be installed to a directory named C:\ACCESS\ADG20, unless you changed the default location of Access 2 during the install program.

When the installation is complete, the file ADG2.TXT will be displayed for you to read. This file contains information on the files that were installed.